FOOD AND DRUG LAW
STATUTORY SUPPLEMENT

REVISED 2014 EDITION

Compiled and Edited
by

PETER BARTON HUTT
Senior Counsel, Covington & Burling LLP, Washington, D.C.
Lecturer on Food and Drug Law, Harvard Law School

RICHARD A. MERRILL
Daniel Caplin Professor of Law Emeritus, University of Virginia

LEWIS A. GROSSMAN
Professor of Law
Washington College of Law, American University
Of Counsel, Covington & Burling LLP

FOUNDATION
PRESS

Mat #41712650

PREFACE

This Statutory Supplement contains, in full or partial text, the principal federal statutes that authorize and direct the regulatory activities of the U.S. Food and Drug Administration (FDA). The materials included are current as of October 17, 2014.

The most important law for FDA is the 1938 Federal Food, Drug, and Cosmetic Act (FD&C Act), which we have included in unabridged form. The original version of the FD&C Act was relatively brief, but it has since undergone repeated amendment, and the current version occupies more than four-fifths of the Supplement's pages. To help users navigate through the increasingly massive FD&C Act, we have included a detailed Table of Contents.

The most significant amendment to the FD&C Act since the publication of the 2013 edition of this Supplement is the Drug Quality and Security Act, Pub L. No. 113-54, 127 Stat. 587 (2013). Title I of this statute, called the "Compounding Quality Act," removes the provisions of FD&C Act 503A ("Pharmacy Compounding") that the United States Supreme Court deemed to violate the First Amendment in Thompson v. Western States Medical Center, 535 U.S. 357 (2002). In addition, the Compounding Quality Act adds a new section 503B, titled "Outsourcing Facilities," which establishes a voluntary system under which a compounder of an eligible drug can register as an "outsourcing facility" and thus be exempt from the FDA approval and adequate directions for use requirements. However, a registered outsourcing facility is subject to Current Good Manufacturing Practices (cGMP) requirements and inspections. Title II of the Drug Quality and Security Act, called the "Drug Supply Chain Security Act," amends the FD&C Act to mandate the implementation, over the next decade, of an electronic system to identify and trace certain prescription drugs throughout the domestic supply chain.

The Pandemic and All-Hazards Preparedness Reauthorization Act of 2013, Pub. L. No. 113-5, 127 Stat. 161 (2013), also made amendments to the FD&C Act that were not included in the prior edition of this Supplement.

In addition to the FD&C Act, we have included the full text of the 1906 Food and Drugs Act, which the 1938 Act replaced. We have inserted, in italics, all amendments made to the 1906 Act between its enactment and its revocation. Following the 1906 Act are various current federal statutes, including the Public Health Service Act; the Orphan Drug Act; the Medicare Prescription Drug, Improvement and Modernization Act; the Fair Packaging and Labeling Act; and the Federal Trade Commission Act. With the exception of the Fair Packaging and Labeling Act, which appears in full, we have included only those portions of these laws that are of particular relevance to FDA.

We have also included excerpts from the Federal Meat Inspection Act. Although this statute is administered primarily by the Food Safety and Inspection Service (FSIS) of the U.S. Department of Agriculture, not by FDA, it is a critical component of the legal framework for food safety in this country. Moreover, it presents a regulatory model that is, in important and interesting ways, different from the FD&C Act's approach. Because of space limitations, we have omitted the parallel food safety statutes administered by FSIS, namely, the Poultry Products Inspection Act, 21 U.S.C. §§ 451–71, and the Egg Products Inspection Act, 21 U.S.C. §§ 1031–56.

In this edition, we have also included, for the first time, excerpts from the Cigarette Labeling and Advertising Act of 1966. The Supplement contains some—but not all—of those provisions of this statute that FDA now administers pursuant to the Family Smoking Prevention and Tobacco Control Act, Pub. L. No. 111-31, 123 Stat. 1776 (2009). The FSPTCA similarly amended the Comprehensive Smokeless Tobacco Health Education Act of 1986 (15 U.S.C. 4401 *et seq.*), but we have not included those amendments in the Supplement.

Finally, we provide extensive excerpts from the Administrative Procedure Act (APA). With the exception of the APA, our Supplement does not reproduce any laws of general applicability, such as the National Environmental Policy Act (NEPA) or the Federal Advisory Committee Act (FACA). It should be noted, however, that several such general statutes have been codified as part of the APA and are included in this volume. Among the most important of these is the Freedom of Information Act.

We owe a special debt to Samantha Dietle, Charlotte McKiver, and Naomi Ahsan, students at the Washington College of Law at American University, who provided invaluable assistance on this edition of the Supplement.

PETER BARTON HUTT
RICHARD A. MERRILL
LEWIS A. GROSSMAN

TABLE OF CONTENTS

Page

PREFACE v

Federal Food, Drug, and Cosmetic Act 1

Chapter I—Short Title 1
Section 1 [21 U.S.C. 301]. 1
Chapter II—Definitions 1
Section 201 [21 U.S.C. 321]. 1
Chapter III—Prohibited Acts and Penalties 12
Section 301 [21 U.S.C. 331]. Prohibited Acts 12
Section 302 [21 U.S.C. 332]. Injunction Proceedings 18
Section 303 [21 U.S.C. 333]. Penalties 19
Section 304 [21 U.S.C. 334]. Seizure 28
Section 305 [21 U.S.C. 335]. Hearing Before Report of
   Criminal Violation 33
Section 306 [21 U.S.C. 335a]. Debarment, Temporary Denial of
   Approval, and Suspension 34
Section 307 [21 U.S.C. 335b]. Civil Penalties 44
Section 308 [21 U.S.C. 335c]. Authority to Withdraw Approval of
   Abbreviated Drug Applications 46
Section 309 [21 U.S.C. 336]. Report of Minor Violations 47
Section 310 [21 U.S.C. 337]. Proceedings in Name of United States;
   Provision as to Subpoenas 47
Section 311 [21 U.S.C. 337a]. Extraterritorial Jurisdiction 48
Chapter IV—Food 48
Section 401 [21 U.S.C. 341]. Definitions and Standards for Food 48
Section 402 [21 U.S.C. 342]. Adulterated Food 48
Section 403 [21 U.S.C. 343]. Misbranded Food 51
Section 403A [21 U.S.C. 343–1] 73
Section 403B [21 U.S.C. 343–2]. Dietary Supplement Labeling
   Exemptions 74
Section 403C [21 U.S.C. 343–3]. Disclosure 75
Section 404 [21 U.S.C. 344]. Emergency Permit Control 75
Section 405 [21 U.S.C. 345]. Regulations Making Exemptions 76
Section 406 [21 U.S.C. 346]. Tolerance for Poisonous or Deleterious
   Substances in Food; Regulations 76
Section 407 [21 U.S.C. 347]. Oleomargarine or Margarine 76
Section 408 [21 U.S.C. 346a]. Tolerances and Exemptions for
   Pesticide Chemical Residues 77

Page

Section 409 [21 U.S.C. 348]. Food Additives 102

Section 410 [21 U.S.C. 349]. Bottled Drinking Water
Standards 109

Section 411 [21 U.S.C. 350]. Vitamins and Minerals 110

Section 412 [21 U.S.C. 350a]. Requirements for Infant
Formulas 112

Section 413 [21 U.S.C. 350b]. New Dietary Ingredients 118

Section 414 [21 U.S.C. 350c]. Maintenance and Inspection
of Records 119

Section 415 [21 U.S.C. 350d]. Registration of Food Facilities.................... 120

Section 416 [21 U.S.C. 350e]. Sanitary Transportation
Practices 123

Section 417 [21 U.S.C. 350f]. Reportable Food Registry 125

Section 418 [21 U.S.C. 350g]. Hazard Analysis and
Risk–Based Preventive Controls.. 131

Section 419 [21 U.S.C. 350h]. Standards for Produce Safety..................... 138

Section 420 [21 U.S.C. 350i]. Protection Against Intentional
Adulteration 144

Section 421 [21 U.S.C. 350j]. Targeting of Inspection
Resources for Domestic Facilities, Foreign
Facilities, and Ports of Entry; Annual Report 145

Section 422 [21 U.S.C. 350k]. Laboratory Accreditation for
Analyses of Foods.. 148

Section 423 [21 U.S.C. 350l]. Mandatory Recall Authority 150

Chapter V—Drugs and Devices 154

  Subchapter A—Drugs and Devices 154

Section 501 [21 U.S.C. 351]. Adulterated Drugs and Devices................. 154

Section 502 [21 U.S.C. 352]. Misbranded Drugs and Devices 157

Section 503 [21 U.S.C. 353]. Exemptions and Consideration for
Certain Drugs, Devices, and Biological Products 163

Section 503A [21 U.S.C. 353a]. Pharmacy Compounding....................... 174

Section 503B [21 U.S.C. 353b]. Outsourcing Facilities........................... 177

Section 503C [21 U.S.C. 353c]. Preview of Television
Advertisements.. 184

Section 504 [21 U.S.C. 354]. Veterinary Feed Directive Drugs.............. 185

Section 505 [21 U.S.C. 355]. New Drugs.. 186

Section 505–1 [21 U.S.C. 355–1]. Risk Evaluation and
Mitigation Strategies 237

Section 505A [21 U.S.C. 355a]. Pediatric Studies of Drugs 251

Section 505B [21 U.S.C. 355c]. Research Into Pediatric Uses for
Drugs and Biological Products.. 261

Page

Section 505C [21 U.S.C. 355d]. Internal Committee for Review of Pediatric Plans, Assessments, Deferrals, Deferral Extensions, and Waivers 275

Section 505D [21 U.S.C. 355e]. Pharmaceutical Security 275

Section 505E [21 U.S.C. 355f]. Extension of Exclusivity Period for New Qualified Infectious Disease Products 276

Section 506 [21 U.S.C. 356]. Fast Track Products 279

Section 506A [21 U.S.C. 356a]. Manufacturing Changes 282

Section 506B [21 U.S.C. 356b]. Reports of Postmarketing Studies 284

Section 506C [21 U.S.C. 356c]. Discontinuance or Interruption in the Production of Life–Saving Drugs 286

Section 506C–1 [21 U.S.C. 356c–1]. Annual Reporting on Drug Shortages 289

Section 506D [21 U.S.C. 356d]. Coordination; Task Force and Strategic Plan 290

Section 506E [21 U.S.C. 356e]. Drug Shortage List 292

Section 506F [21 U.S.C. 356f]. Hospital Repackaging of Drugs in Shortage 293

Section 508 [21 U.S.C. 358]. Authority to Designate Official Names 294

Section 509 [21 U.S.C. 359]. Nonapplicability to Cosmetics 295

Section 510 [21 U.S.C. 360]. Registration of Producers of Drugs and Devices 295

Section 511 [21 U.S.C. 360a]. Clinical Trial Guidance for Antibiotic Drugs 306

Section 512 [21 U.S.C. 360b]. New Animal Drugs 306

Section 513 [21 U.S.C. 360c]. Classification of Devices Intended for Human Use 332

Section 514 [21 U.S.C. 360d]. Performance Standards 344

Section 515 [21 U.S.C. 360e]. Premarket Approval 349

Section 515A [21 U.S.C. 360e–1]. Pediatric Uses of Devices 362

Section 516 [21 U.S.C. 360f]. Banned Devices 363

Section 517 [21 U.S.C. 360g]. Judicial Review 364

Section 517A [21 U.S.C. 360g–1]. Agency Documentation and Review of Significant Decisions Regarding Devices 366

Section 518 [21 U.S.C. 360h]. Notification and Other Remedies 366

Section 518A [21 U.S.C. 360h–1]. Program to Improve to Device Recall System 370

Section 519 [21 U.S.C. 360i]. Records and Reports on Devices 371

Section 520 [21 U.S.C. 360j]. General Provisions Respecting Control of Devices Intended for Human Use 377

Page

Section 521 [21 U.S.C. 360k]. State and Local Requirements
Respecting Devices 394

Section 522 [21 U.S.C. 360l]. Postmarket Surveillance 395

Section 523 [21 U.S.C. 360m]. Accredited Persons 396

Section 524 [21 U.S.C. 360n]. Priority Review to Encourage
Treatments for Tropical Diseases 400

Section 524A [U.S.C. 360n–1]. Priority Review for Qualified
Infectious Disease Products.. 403

Subchapter B—Drugs for Rare Diseases or Conditions...................... 403

Section 525 [21 U.S.C. 360aa]. Recommendations for Investigations of
Drugs for Rare Diseases or Conditions 403

Section 526 [21 U.S.C. 360bb]. Designation of Drugs for Rare
Diseases or Conditions 403

Section 527 [21 U.S.C. 360cc]. Protection for Drugs for Rare
Diseases or Conditions 404

Section 528 [21 U.S.C. 360dd]. Open Protocols for Investigations or
Drugs for Rare Diseases or Conditions 405

Section 529 [21 U.S.C. 360ff]. Priority Review to Encourage
Treatments for Rare Pediatric Diseases... 405

Subchapter C—Electronic Product Radiation Control 411

Section 531 [21 U.S.C. 360hh]. Definitions 411

Section 532 [21 U.S.C. 360ii]. Electronic Product Radiation
Control Program 411

Section 533 [21 U.S.C. 360jj]. Studies by the Secretary 413

Section 534 [21 U.S.C. 360kk]. Performance Standards for
Electronic Products.. 414

Section 535 [21 U.S.C. 360ll]. Notification of Defects in, and
Repair or Replacement of, Electronic Products 417

Section 536 [21 U.S.C. 360mm]. Imports 419

Section 537 [21 U.S.C. 360nn]. Inspection, Records, And Reports 420

Section 538 [21 U.S.C. 360oo]. Prohibited Acts 422

Section 539 [21 U.S.C. 360pp]. Enforcement 423

Section 541 [21 U.S.C. 360rr]. Federal–State Cooperation 424

Section 542 [21 U.S.C. 360ss]. Effect on State Standards 424

Subchapter E—General Provisions Relating to Drugs and Devices... 424

Section 561 [21 U.S.C. 360bbb]. Expanded Access to Unapproved
Therapies and Diagnostics.. 424

Section 562 [21 U.S.C. 360bbb–1]. Dispute Resolution 426

Section 563 [21 U.S.C. 360bbb–2]. Classification of Products............... 427

Section 564 [21 U.S.C. 360bbb–3]. Authorization for Medical
Products for Use in Emergencies 427

TABLE OF CONTENTS

Page

Section 564A [21 U.S.C. 360bbb–3a]. Emergency Use of
Medical Products 435

Section 564B [21 U.S.C. 360bbb–3b]. Products Held for
Emergency Use 438

Section 565 [21 U.S.C. 360bbb–4]. Countermeasure Development,
Review, and Technical Assistance 438

Section 566 [21 U.S.C. 360bbb–5]. Critical Path Public–Private
Partnerships 444

Section 567 [21 U.S.C. 360bbb–6]. Risk Communication 446

Section 568 [21 U.S.C. 360bbb–7]. Notification 447

Section 569 [21 U.S.C. 360bbb–8]. Consultation With External
Experts on Rare Diseases, Targeted Therapies, and Genetic
Targeting of Treatments 447

Section 569A [21 U.S.C. 360bbb–8a]. Optimizing Global
Clinical Trials 449

Section 569B [21 U.S.C. 360bbb–8b]. Use of Clinical Investigation
Data From Outside the United States 450

Section 569C [21 U.S.C. 360bbb–8c]. Patient Participation in
Medical Product Discussion 450

**Subchapter F—New Animal Drugs for Minor Use and
Minor Species** 451

Section 571 [21 U.S.C. 360ccc]. Conditional Approval of New
Animal Drugs for Minor Use and Minor Species 451

Section 572 [21 U.S.C. 360ccc–1]. Index of Legally Marketed
Unapproved New Animal Drugs for Minor Species 455

Section 573 [21 U.S.C. 360ccc–2]. Designated New Animal Drugs for
Minor Use or Minor Species 461

Subchapter G—Medical Gases 462

Section 575 [21 U.S.C. 360ddd]. Definitions 462

Section 576 [21 U.S.C. 360ddd–1]. Regulation of Medical Gases 463

Section 577 [21 U.S.C. 360ddd–2]. Inapplicability of Drug Fees to
Designated Medical Gases 465

Subchapter H—Pharmaceutical Supply Chain Security 466

Section 581 [21 U.S.C. 360eee]. Definitions 466

Section 582 [21 U.S.C. 360eee–1]. Requirements 473

Section 583 [21 U.S.C. 360eee–2]. National Standards for Prescription
Drug Wholesale Distributors 500

Section 584 [21 U.S.C. 360eee–3]. National Standards for
Third-Party Logistics Providers 502

Section 585 [21 U.S.C. 360eee–4]. Uniform National Policy 505

Page

Chapter VI—Cosmetics 506

Section 601 [21 U.S.C. 361]. Adulterated Cosmetics..............................506

Section 602 [21 U.S.C. 362]. Misbranded Cosmetics 507

Section 603 [21 U.S.C. 363]. Regulations Making Exemptions 507

Chapter VII—General Authority 508

Subchapter A—General Administrative Provisions 508

Section 701 [21 U.S.C. 371]. Regulations and Hearings........................508

Section 702 [21 U.S.C. 372]. Examinations and Investigations..............511

Section 703 [21 U.S.C. 373]. Records..513

Section 704 [21 U.S.C. 374]. Factory Inspection 514

Section 705 [21 U.S.C. 375]. Publicity 523

Section 706 [21 U.S.C. 376]. Seafood Inspection 523

Section 707 [21 U.S.C. 378]. Advertising of Certain Foods 524

Section 708 [21 U.S.C. 379]. Confidential Information 526

Section 709 [21 U.S.C. 379a]. Presumption 528

Section 710 [21 U.S.C. 379b]. Consolidated Administrative and
Laboratory Facility 528

Section 711 [21 U.S.C. 379d]. Automation of Food and Drug
Administration..528

Section 712 [21 U.S.C. 379d–1]. Conflicts of Interest 528

Section 713 [21 U.S.C. 379d–2]. Policy on the Review and
Clearance of Scientific Articles Published By FDA Employees 531

Section 714 [21 U.S.C. 379d–3]. Streamlined Hiring Authority to
Support Activities Related to the Process for the Review of
Device Applications 532

Section 715 [21 U.S.C. 379d–4]. Reporting Requirements......................533

Subchapter B—Colors...534

Section 721 [21 U.S.C. 379e]. Listing and Certification of Color
Additives for Foods, Drugs, and Cosmetics..534

Subchapter C—Fees 540

Part 1—Freedom of Information Fees 540

Section 731 [21 U.S.C. 379f]. Recovery and Retention of Fees for
Freedom of Information Requests 540

Part 2—Fees Relating to Drugs 541

Section 735 [21 U.S.C. 379g]. Definitions 541

Section 736 [21 U.S.C. 379h]. Authority to Assess and
Use Drug Fees 543

Section 736B [21 U.S.C. 379h–2]. Reauthorization; Reporting
Requirements 553

Page

Part 3—Fees Relating to Devices 556

Section 737 [21 U.S.C. 379i]. Definitions 556

Section 738 [21 U.S.C. 379j]. Authority to Assess and Use
Device Fees 559

Section 738A [21 U.S.C. 379j–1]. Reauthorization; Reporting
Requirements 569

Part 4—Fees Relating to Animal Drugs 572

Section 739 [21 U.S.C. 379j–11]. Definitions 572

Section 740 [21 U.S.C. 379j–12]. Authority to Assess and
Use Animal Drug Fees 574

Section 740A [21 U.S.C. 379j–13]. Reauthorization; Reporting
Requirements 583

Part 5—Fees Relating to Generic New Animal Drugs 585

Section 741 [21 U.S.C. 379j–21]. Authority to Assess and
Use Generic New Animal Drug Fees 585

Section 742 [21 U.S.C. 379j–22]. Reauthorization; Reporting
Requirements 593

Part 6—Fees Related to Food 595

Section 743 [21 U.S.C. 379j–31]. Authority to Collect and
Use Fees 595

Part 7—Fees Relating to Generic Drugs 599

Section 744A [21 U.S.C. 379j–41]. Definitions 599

Section 744B [21 U.S.C. 379j–42]. Authority to Assess and
Use Human Generic Drug Fees 603

Section 744C [21 U.S.C. 379j–43]. Reauthorization; Reporting
Requirements 615

Part 8—Fees Relating to Biosimilar Biological Products 617

Section 744G [21 U.S.C. 379j–51]. Definitions 617

Section 744H [21 U.S.C. 379j–52]. Authority to Assess and
Use Biosimilar Biological Product Fees 621

Section 744I [21 U.S.C. 379j–53]. Reauthorization; Reporting
Requirements 629

Part 9—Fees Relating to Outsourcing Facilities 631

Section 744J [21 U.S.C. 379j–61]. Definitions 631

Section 744K [21 U.S.C. 379j–62]. Authority to Assess and
Use Outsourcing Facility Fees 631

Subchapter D—Information and Education 635

Section 745 [21 U.S.C. 379k]. Information System 635

Section 745A [21 U.S.C. 379k–1]. Electronic Format for
Submissions 635

Section 746 [21 U.S.C. 379l]. Education 636

Page

Subchapter E—Environmental Impact Review...................................636

Section 749 [21 U.S.C. 379o]. Environmental Impact 636

Subchapter F—National Uniformity for Nonprescription Drugs and Preemption for Labeling or Packaging of Cosmetics.....................636

Section 751 [21 U.S.C. 379r]. National Uniformity for Nonprescription Drugs 636

Section 752 [21 U.S.C. 379s]. Preemption for Labeling or Packaging of Cosmetics..638

Subchapter G—Safety Reports 639

Section 756 [21 U.S.C. 379v]. Safety Report Disclaimers 639

Subchapter H—Serious Adverse Event Reports...............................639

Section 760 [21 U.S.C. 379aa]. Serious Adverse Event Reporting for Nonprescription Drugs...639

Section 761 [21 U.S.C. 379aa–1]. Serious Adverse Event Reporting for Dietary Supplements 642

Subchapter I—Reagan–Udall Foundation for the Food and Drug Administration 645

Section 770 [21 U.S.C. 379dd]. Establishment and Functions of the Foundation 645

Section 771 [21 U.S.C. 379dd–1]. Location of Foundation 652

Section 772 [21 U.S.C. 379dd–2]. Activities of the Food and Drug Administration 653

Chapter VIII—Imports and Exports...653

Section 801 [21 U.S.C. 381]. Imports and Exports 653

Section 802 [21 U.S.C. 382]. Exports of Certain Unapproved Products..667

Section 803 [21 U.S.C. 383]. Office of International Relations 672

Section 804 [21 U.S.C. 384]. Importation of Prescription Drugs.............673

Section 805 [21 U.S.C. 384a]. Foreign Supplier Verification Program....679

Section 806 [21 U.S.C. 384b]. Voluntary Qualified Importer Program....681

Section 807 [21 U.S.C. 384c]. Inspection of Foreign Food Facilities......682

Section 808 [21 U.S.C. 384d]. Accreditation of Third–Party Auditors 683

Section 809 [21 U.S.C. 384e]. Recognition of Foreign Government Inspections...690

Chapter IX—Tobacco Products 691

Section 900 [21 U.S.C. 387]. Definitions 691

Section 901 [21 U.S.C. 387a]. FDA Authority Over Tobacco Products...694

Section 902 [21 U.S.C. 387b]. Adulterated Tobacco Products.................695

Section 903 [21 U.S.C. 387c]. Misbranded Tobacco Products.................696

Section 904 [21 U.S.C. 387d]. Submission of Health Information to the Secretary 698

Page

Section 905 [21 U.S.C. 387e]. Annual Registration 700

Section 906 [21 U.S.C. 387f]. General Provisions Respecting
Control of Tobacco Products 703

Section 907 [21 U.S.C. 387g]. Tobacco Product Standards 708

Section 908 [21 U.S.C. 387h]. Notification and Other Remedies 714

Section 909 [21 U.S.C. 387i]. Records and Reports on
Tobacco Products 715

Section 910 [21 U.S.C. 387j]. Application for Review of
Certain Tobacco Products 716

Section 911 [21 U.S.C. 387k]. Modified Risk Tobacco Products 722

Section 912 [21 U.S.C. 387l]. Judicial Review 730

Section 913 [21 U.S.C. 387m]. Equal Treatment of Retail Outlets 731

Section 914 [21 U.S.C. 387n]. Jurisdiction of and Coordination
With the Federal Trade Commission 731

Section 915 [21 U.S.C. 387o]. Regulation Requirement 732

Section 916 [21 U.S.C. 387p]. Preservation of State and
Local Authority 735

Section 917 [21 U.S.C. 387q]. Tobacco Products Scientific Advisory
Committee 736

Section 918 [21 U.S.C. 387r]. Drug Products Used to Treat Tobacco
Dependence 738

Section 919 [21 U.S.C. 387s]. User Fees 738

Section 920 [21 U.S.C. 387t]. Labeling, Recordkeeping, Records
Inspection 743

Chapter X—Miscellaneous 745

Section 1001 [21 U.S.C. 391]. Separability Clause 745

Section 1002 [21 U.S.C. 392]. Effective Date and Repeals 745

Section 1003 [21 U.S.C. 393]. Food and Drug Administration 746

Section 1003a [21 U.S.C. 393a]. Office of Pediatric Therapeutic 749

Section 1004 [21 U.S.C. 394]. Scientific Review Groups 750

Section 1005 [21 U.S.C. 395]. Loan Repayment Program 750

Section 1006 [21 U.S.C. 396]. Practice of Medicine 750

Section 1007 [21 U.S.C. 397]. Contracts for Expert Review 751

Section 1008 [21 U.S.C. 398]. Notices to States Regarding
Imported Food 752

Section 1009 [21 U.S.C. 399]. Grants to Enhance Food Safety 752

Section 1010 [21 U.S.C. 399a]. Office of the Chief Scientist 754

Section 1011 [21 U.S.C. 399b]. Office of Women's Health 755

Section 1011 [21 U.S.C. 399c]. Improving the Training of State,
Local, Territorial, and Tribal Food Safety Officials 756

Page

Section 1012 [21 U.S.C. 399d]. Employee Protections............................757

Section 1126 [21 U.S.C. 399e]. Nanotechnology....................................761

Section 1138 [21 U.S.C. 399f]. Ensuring Adequate Information
Regarding Pharmaceuticals for All Populations, Particularly
Underrepresented Subpopulations, Including Racial Subgroups.........762

Federal Food and Drugs Act of 1906..765

Section 1 [21 U.S.C. 1]. Manufacture of Adulterated Foods or Drugs........765

Section 2 [21 U.S.C. 2]. Interstate Commerce of Adulterated Goods..........765

Section 3 [21 U.S.C. 3]. Rules and Regulations...766

Section 4 [21 U.S.C. 11]. Chemical Examinations 766

Section 5 [21 U.S.C. 12]. Legal Proceedings...767

Section 6 [21 U.S.C. 7]. Definitions...767

Section 7 [21 U.S.C. 8]. Adulterations...767

Section 8 [21 U.S.C. 9 & 10]. Misbranding..768

Section 9 [21 U.S.C. 13]. Guaranty From Manufacturer 770

Section 10 [21 U.S.C. 14]. Seizure of Original Packages...........................770

Section 10A [21 U.S.C. 14a]. Sea Food Sold in Interstate Commerce........771

Section 11 [21 U.S.C. 15]. Examination of Imported Food and Drugs.......771

Section 12 [21 U.S.C. 5]. Definitions and Liabilities................................772

Section 13. Effective Date 772

Public Health Service Act..773

Section 351 [42 U.S.C. 262]. Regulation of Biological Products...............773

Section 361 [42 U.S.C. 264]. Regulations to Control Communicable
Diseases..788

Section 362 [42 U.S.C. 265]. Suspension of Entries and Imports from
Designated Places to Prevent Spread of Communicable Diseases..........789

Section 368 [42 U.S.C. 271]. Penalties for Violation of
Quarantine Laws 789

Section 5 of Orphan Drug Act...791

Section 5 [21 U.S.C. 360ee]. Grants and Contracts for Development of
Drugs for Rare Diseases and Conditions 791

**Medicare Prescription Drug, Improvement, and Modernization
Act of 2003**...793

Title XI—Access to Affordable Pharmaceuticals....................................793

Subtitle B—Federal Trade Commission Review................................793

Section 1111. Definitions..793

Section 1112. Notification of Agreements 793

Section 1113. Filing Deadlines 795

Page

Section 1114. Disclosure Exemption 795

Section 1115. Enforcement 795

Section 1116. Rulemaking 795

Section 1117. Savings Clause 796

Section 1118. Effective Date 796

Fair Packaging and Labeling Act 797

15 U.S.C. § 1451. Congressional Declaration of Policy 797

15 U.S.C. § 1452. Unfair and Deceptive Packaging and Labeling;
Scope of Prohibition 797

15 U.S.C. § 1453. Requirements of Labeling; Placement, Form, and
Contents of Statement of Quantity; Supplemental Statement of
Quantity..797

15 U.S.C. § 1454. Rules and Regulations 799

15 U.S.C. § 1455. Procedure for Promulgation of Regulations 801

15 U.S.C. § 1456. Enforcement...802

15 U.S.C. § 1458. Cooperation With State Authorities; Transmittal of
Regulations to States; Noninterference With Existing Programs 802

15 U.S.C. § 1459. Definitions 803

15 U.S.C. § 1460. Savings Provisions...804

15 U.S.C. § 1461. Effect Upon State Law 804

Federal Trade Commission Act 805

Section 5 [15 U.S.C. 45]. Unfair Methods of Competition Unlawful;
Prevention By Commission 805

Section 12 [15 U.S.C. 52]. Dissemination of False Advertisements............805

Section 13 [15 U.S.C. 53]. False Advertisements; Injunctions and
Restraining Orders 806

Section 14 [15 U.S.C. 54]. False Advertisements; Penalties......................807

Section 15 [15 U.S.C. 55]. Additional Definitions 808

Federal Meat Inspection Act 811

**Subchapter I—Inspection Requirements, Adulteration and
Misbranding** 811

21 U.S.C. § 601. Definitions 811

21 U.S.C. § 602. Congressional Statement of Findings 814

21 U.S.C. § 603. Examination of Animals Prior to Slaughter;
Use of Humane Methods 815

21 U.S.C. § 604. Post Mortem Examination of Carcasses and Marking or
Labeling; Destruction of Carcasses Condemned; Reinspection 815

21 U.S.C. § 605. Examination of Carcasses Brought Into Slaughtering or
Packing Establishments, and of Meat Food Products Issued From and
Returned Thereto; Conditions for Entry 816

Page

21 U.S.C. § 606. Inspection and Labeling of Meat Food Products 816

21 U.S.C. § 607. Labeling, Marking, and Container Requirements 817

21 U.S.C. § 608. Sanitary Inspection and Regulation of Slaughtering and
Packing Establishments; Rejection of Adulterated Meat or Meat Food
Products 819

21 U.S.C. § 609. Examination of Animals and Food Products Thereof,
Slaughtered and Prepared During Nighttime 819

21 U.S.C. § 610. Prohibited Acts 819

21 U.S.C. § 611. Devices, Marks, Labels and Certificates; Simulations 820

21 U.S.C. § 612. Notification 821

21 U.S.C. § 613. Plans and Reassessments 821

21 U.S.C. § 620. Imports 821

21 U.S.C. § 621. Inspectors to Make Examinations Provided for;
Appointment; Duties; Regulations 824

21 U.S.C. § 622. Bribery of or Gifts to Inspectors or Other Officers and
Acceptance of Gifts 824

Subchapter II—Meat Processors and Related Industries 825

21 U.S.C. § 641. Prohibition of Subchapter I Inspection of Articles
Not Intended for Use As Human Food; Denaturation or Other
Identification Prior to Distribution in Commerce; Inedible Articles 825

21 U.S.C. § 642. Recordkeeping Requirements 825

21 U.S.C. § 645. Federal Provisions Applicable to State or Territorial
Business Transactions of A Local Nature and Not Subject to
Local Authority 826

Subchapter III—Federal and State Cooperation 826

21 U.S.C. § 661. Federal and State Cooperation 826

Subchapter IV—Auxiliary Provisions 828

21 U.S.C. § 671. Inspection Services; Refusal or Withdrawal; Hearing;
Business Unfitness Based Upon Certain Convictions; Other Provisions
for Withdrawal of Services Unaffected; Responsible Connection With
Business; Finality of Secretary's Actions; Judicial Review; Record 828

21 U.S.C. § 672. Administrative Detention; Duration; Pending Judicial
Proceedings; Notification of Governmental Authorities; Release 828

21 U.S.C. § 673. Seizure and Condemnation 829

21 U.S.C. § 674. Federal Court Jurisdiction of Enforcement and
Injunction Proceedings and Other Kinds of Cases; Limitations of
Section 6079(E) of This Title 831

21 U.S.C. § 678. Non–Federal Jurisdiction of Federally Regulated Matters;
Prohibition of Additional or Different Requirements for Establishments
With Inspection Services and As to Marking, Labeling, Packaging, and
Ingredients; Recordkeeping and Related Requirements; Concurrent
Jurisdiction Over Distribution for Human Food Purposes of
Adulterated or Misbranded and Imported Articles; Other Matters 831

TABLE OF CONTENTS

Page

21 U.S.C. § 679. Application of Food, Drug, and Cosmetic Act 832

Cigarette Labeling and Advertising Act 833

   Section 4 [15 U.S.C. 1333]. Labeling. 833

Administrative Procedure Act and Related Statutes 837

   Chapter 5, Subchapter II — Administrative Procedure 837

   5 U.S.C. § 551. Definitions 837

   5 U.S.C. § 552. Public Information; Agency Rules, Opinions, Orders,
      Records, and Proceedings 838

   5 U.S.C. § 552b. Open Meetings 852

   5 U.S.C. § 553. Rule Making 858

   5 U.S.C. § 554. Adjudications 859

   5 U.S.C. § 555. Ancillary Matters 860

   5 U.S.C. § 556. Hearings; Presiding Employees; Powers and Duties;
      Burden of Proof; Evidence, Record As Basis of Decision 861

   5 U.S.C. § 557. Initial Decisions; Conclusiveness; Review by Agency;
      Submissions By Parties; Contents of Decisions; Record 863

   5 U.S.C. § 558. Imposition of Sanctions; Determination of Applications
      for Licenses; Suspension, Revocation, and Expiration of Licenses 865

   5 U.S.C. § 559. Effect on Other Laws; Effect of Subsequent Statute 865

   **Chapter 5, Subchapter III — Negotiated Rulemaking Procedure
      ("Negotiated Rulemaking Act")** 866

   5 U.S.C. § 561. Purpose 866

   5 U.S.C. § 562. Definitions 866

   5 U.S.C. § 563. Determination of Need for Negotiated Rulemaking
      Committee 867

   5 U.S.C. § 564. Publication of Notice; Applications for Membership on
      Committees 868

   5 U.S.C. § 565. Establishment of Committee 869

   5 U.S.C. § 566. Conduct of Committee Activity 869

   5 U.S.C. § 567. Termination of Committee 870

   5 U.S.C. § 568. Services, Facilities, and Payment of Committee
      Member Expenses 871

   5 U.S.C. § 569. Encouraging Negotiated Rulemaking 871

   5 U.S.C. § 570. Judicial Review 872

   **Chapter 5, Subchapter IV — Alternative Means of Dispute
      Resolution in the Administrative Process ("Alternative Dispute
      Resolution Act")** 872

   5 U.S.C. § 571. Definitions 872

   5 U.S.C. § 572. General Authority 873

   5 U.S.C. § 573. Neutrals 874

Page

5 U.S.C. § 574. Confidentiality 875
5 U.S.C. § 575. Authorization of Arbitration 877
5 U.S.C. § 576. Enforcement of Arbitration Agreements...........................877
5 U.S.C. § 578. Authority of the Arbitrator...877
5 U.S.C. § 579. Arbitration Proceedings 878
5 U.S.C. § 580. Arbitration Awards...879
5 U.S.C. § 581. Judicial Review 879
5 U.S.C. § 583. Support Services 879
Chapter 6—The Analysis of Regulatory Functions
    ("Regulatory Flexibility Act")..880
5 U.S.C. § 601. Definitions 880
5 U.S.C. § 602. Regulatory Agenda 881
5 U.S.C. § 603. Initial Regulatory Flexibility Analysis 881
5 U.S.C. § 604. Final Regulatory Flexibility Analysis...............................882
5 U.S.C. § 605. Avoidance of Duplicative or Unnecessary Analyses 883
5 U.S.C. § 606. Effect on Other Law 884
5 U.S.C. § 607. Preparation of Analyses 884
5 U.S.C. § 608. Procedure for Waiver or Delay of Completion...................884
5 U.S.C. § 609. Procedures for Gathering Comments 884
5 U.S.C. § 610. Periodic Review of Rules 886
5 U.S.C. § 611. Judicial Review...887
5 U.S.C. § 612. Reports and Intervention Rights 888
Chapter 7—Judicial Review..888
5 U.S.C. § 701. Application; Definitions..888
5 U.S.C. § 702. Right of Review...889
5 U.S.C. § 703. Form and Venue of Proceeding 889
5 U.S.C. § 704. Actions Reviewable 890
5 U.S.C. § 705. Relief Pending Review 890
5 U.S.C. § 706. Scope of Review..890

FOOD AND DRUG LAW
STATUTORY SUPPLEMENT
REVISED 2014 EDITION

FEDERAL FOOD, DRUG, AND COSMETIC ACT

21 U.S.C. §§ 301 *et seq*.

CHAPTER I—SHORT TITLE

SEC. 1 [21 U.S.C. 301].

This Act may be cited as the Federal Food, Drug, and Cosmetic Act.

CHAPTER II—DEFINITIONS[1]

SEC. 201 [21 U.S.C. 321].

For the purposes of this Act—

(a)(1) The term "State", except as used in the last sentence of section 702(a), means any State or Territory of the United States, the District of Columbia, and the Commonwealth of Puerto Rico.

(2) The term "Territory" means any Territory or possession of the United States, including the District of Columbia, and excluding the Commonwealth of Puerto Rico and the Canal Zone.

(b) The term "interstate commerce" means (1) commerce between any State or Territory and any place outside thereof, and (2) commerce within the District of Columbia or within any other Territory not organized with a legislative body.

(c) The term "Department" means the Department of Health and Human Services.

(d) The term "Secretary" means the Secretary of Health and Human Services.

(e) The term "person" includes individual, partnership, corporation, and association.

---

1. The following additional definitions applicable to this Act are provided for in other Acts:

Butter. The Act of March 4, 1923 (21 U.S.C. 321a), defines butter as "the food product usually known as butter, and which is made exclusively from milk or cream, or both, with or without common salt, and with or without additional coloring matter, and containing not less than 80 per centum by weight of milk fat, all tolerances having been allowed for."

Package. The Act of July 24, 1919 (21 U.S.C. 321b), states "The word 'package' shall include and shall be construed to include wrapped meats inclosed in papers or other materials as prepared by the manufacturers thereof for sale."

Nonfat Dry Milk, Milk. The Act of July 2, 1956 (21 U.S.C. 321c), defines nonfat dry milk as "the product resulting from the removal of fat and water from milk, and contains the lactose, milk proteins, and milk minerals in the same relative proportions as in the fresh milk from which made. It contains not over 5 per centum by weight of moisture. The fat content is not over $1\frac{1}{2}$ per centum by weight unless otherwise indicated. The term 'milk,' when used herein, means sweet milk of cows."

(f) The term "food" means (1) articles used for food or drink for man or other animals, (2) chewing gum, and (3) articles used for components of any such article.

(g)(1) The term "drug" means (A) articles recognized in the official United States Pharmacopeia, official Homeopathic Pharmacopeia of the United States, or official National Formulary, or any supplement to any of them; and (B) articles intended for use in the diagnosis, cure, mitigation, treatment, or prevention of disease in man or other animals; and (C) articles (other than food) intended to affect the structure or any function of the body of man or other animals; and (D) articles intended for use as a component of any articles specified in clause (A), (B), or (C). A food or dietary supplement for which a claim, subject to sections 403(r)(1)(B) and 403(r)(3) or sections 403(r)(1)(B) and 403(r)(5)(D), is made in accordance with the requirements of section 403(r) is not a drug solely because the label or the labeling contains such a claim. A food, dietary ingredient, or dietary supplement for which a truthful and not misleading statement is made in accordance with section 403(r)(6) is not a drug under clause (C) solely because the label or the labeling contains such a statement.

(2) The term "counterfeit drug" means a drug which, or the container or labeling of which, without authorization, bears the trademark, trade name, or other identifying mark, imprint, or device, or any likeness thereof, of a drug manufacturer, processor, packer, or distributor other than the person or persons who in fact manufactured, processed, packed, or distributed such drug and which thereby falsely purports or is represented to be the product of, or to have been packed or distributed by, such other drug manufacturer, processor, packer, or distributor.

(h) The term "device" (except when used in paragraph (n) of this section and in sections 301(i), 403(f), 502(c), and 602(c)) means an instrument, apparatus, implement, machine, contrivance, implant, in vitro reagent, or other similar or related article, including any component, part, or accessory, which is—

    (1) recognized in the official National Formulary, or the United States Pharmacopeia, or any supplement to them,

    (2) intended for use in the diagnosis of disease or other conditions, or in the cure, mitigation, treatment, or prevention of disease, in man or other animals, or

    (3) intended to affect the structure or any function of the body of man or other animals, and

which does not achieve its primary intended purposes through chemical action within or on the body of man or other animals and which is not dependent upon being metabolized for the achievement of its primary intended purposes.

(i) The term "cosmetic" means (1) articles intended to be rubbed, poured, sprinkled, or sprayed on, introduced into, or otherwise applied to the human body or any part thereof for cleansing, beautifying, promoting attractiveness, or altering the appearance, and (2) articles intended for use as a component of any such articles; except that such term shall not include soap.

(j) The term "official compendium" means the official United States Pharmacopeia, official Homeopathic Pharmacopeia of the United States, official National Formulary, or any supplement to any of them.

(k) The term "label" means a display of written, printed, or graphic matter upon the immediate container of any article; and a requirement made by or under authority of this Act that any word, statement, or other information appear on the label shall not be considered to be complied with unless such word, statement, or other information also appears on the outside container or wrapper, if any there be, of the retail package of such article, or is easily legible through the outside container or wrapper.

(*l*) The term "immediate container" does not include package liners.

(m) The term "labeling" means all labels and other written, printed, or graphic matter (1) upon any article or any of its containers or wrappers, or (2) accompanying such article.

(n) If an article is alleged to be misbranded because the labeling or advertising is misleading, then in determining whether the labeling or advertising is misleading there shall be taken into account (among other things) not only representations made or suggested by statement, word, design, device, or any combination thereof, but also the extent to which the labeling or advertising fails to reveal facts material in the light of such representations or material with respect to consequences which may result from the use of the article to which the labeling or advertising relates under the conditions of use prescribed in the labeling or advertising thereof or under such conditions of use as are customary or usual.

(*o*) The representation of a drug, in its labeling, as an antiseptic shall be considered to be a representation that it is a germicide, except in the case of a drug purporting to be, or represented as, an antiseptic for inhibitory use as a wet dressing, ointment, dusting powder, or such other use as involves prolonged contact with the body.

(p) The term "new drug" means—

(1) Any drug (except a new animal drug or an animal feed bearing or containing a new animal drug) the composition of which is such that such drug is not generally recognized, among experts qualified by scientific training and experience to evaluate the safety and effectiveness of drugs, as safe and effective for use under the conditions prescribed, recommended, or suggested in the labeling thereof, except that such a drug not so recognized shall not be deemed to be a "new drug" if at any time prior to the enactment of this Act it was subject to the Food and Drugs Act of June 30, 1906, as amended, and if at such time its labeling contained the same representations concerning the conditions of its use; or

(2) Any drug (except a new animal drug or an animal feed bearing or containing a new animal drug) the composition of which is such that such drug, as a result of investigations to determine its safety and effectiveness for use under such conditions, has become so recognized, but which has not, otherwise than in

3

such investigations, been used to a material extent or for a material time under such conditions.

(q)(1)(A) Except as provided in clause (B), the term "pesticide chemical" means any substance that is a pesticide within the meaning of the Federal Insecticide, Fungicide, and Rodenticide Act, including all active and inert ingredients of such pesticide. Notwithstanding any other provision of law, the term "pesticide" within such meaning includes ethylene oxide and propylene oxide when such substances are applied on food.

(B) In the case of the use, with respect to food, of a substance described in clause (A) to prevent, destroy, repel, or mitigate microorganisms (including bacteria, viruses, fungi, protozoa, algae, and slime), the following applies for purposes of clause (A):

(i) The definition in such clause for the term "pesticide chemical" does not include the substance if the substance is applied for such use on food, or the substance is included for such use in water that comes into contact with the food, in the preparing, packing, or holding of the food for commercial purposes. The substance is not excluded under this subclause from such definition if the substance is ethylene oxide or propylene oxide, and is applied for such use on food. The substance is not so excluded if the substance is applied for such use on a raw agricultural commodity, or the substance is included for such use in water that comes into contact with the commodity, as follows:

(I) The substance is applied in the field.

(II) The substance is applied at a treatment facility where raw agricultural commodities are the only food treated, and the treatment is in a manner that does not change the status of the food as a raw agricultural commodity (including treatment through washing, waxing, fumigating, and packing such commodities in such manner).

(III) The substance is applied during the transportation of such commodity between the field and such a treatment facility.

(ii) The definition in such clause for the term "pesticide chemical" does not include the substance if the substance is a food contact substance as defined in section 409(h)(6), and any of the following circumstances exist: The substance is included for such use in an object that has a food contact surface but is not intended to have an ongoing effect on any portion of the object; the substance is included for such use in an object that has a food contact surface and is intended to have an ongoing effect on a portion of the object but not on the food contact surface; or the substance is included for such use in or is applied for such use on food packaging (without regard to whether the substance is intended to have an ongoing effect on any portion of the packaging). The food contact substance is not excluded under this subclause from such definition if any of the following circumstances exist: The substance is applied for such use on a semipermanent

4

or permanent food contact surface (other than being applied on food packaging); or the substance is included for such use in an object that has a semipermanent or permanent food contact surface (other than being included in food packaging) and the substance is intended to have an ongoing effect on the food contact surface.

With respect to the definition of the term "pesticide" that is applicable to the Federal Insecticide, Fungicide, and Rodenticide Act, this clause does not exclude any substance from such definition.

(2) The term "pesticide chemical residue" means a residue in or on raw agricultural commodity or processed food of—

(A) a pesticide chemical; or

(B) any other added substance that is present on or in the commodity or food primarily as a result of the metabolism or other degradation of a pesticide chemical.

(3) Notwithstanding subparagraphs (1) and (2), the Administrator may by regulation except a substance from the definition of "pesticide chemical" or "pesticide chemical residue" if—

(A) its occurrence as a residue on or in a raw agricultural commodity or processed food is attributable primarily to natural causes or to human activities not involving the use of any substances for a pesticidal purpose in the production, storage, processing, or transportation of any raw agricultural commodity or processed food; and

(B) the Administrator, after consultation with the Secretary, determines that the substance more appropriately should be regulated under one or more provisions of this Act other than sections 402(a)(2)(B) and 408.

(r) The term "raw agricultural commodity" means any food in its raw or natural state, including all fruits that are washed, colored, or otherwise treated in their unpeeled natural form prior to marketing.

(s) The term "food additive" means any substance the intended use of which results or may reasonably be expected to result, directly or indirectly, in its becoming a component or otherwise affecting the characteristics of any food (including any substance intended for use in producing, manufacturing, packing, processing, preparing, treating, packaging, transporting, or holding food; and including any source of radiation intended for any such use), if such substance is not generally recognized, among experts qualified by scientific training and experience to evaluate its safety, as having been adequately shown through scientific procedures (or, in the case of a substance used in food prior to January 1, 1958, through either scientific procedures or experience based on common use in food) to be safe under the conditions of its intended use; except that such term does not include—

(1) a pesticide chemical residue in or on a raw agricultural commodity or processed food; or

(2) a pesticide chemical; or

(3) a color additive; or

(4) any substance used in accordance with a sanction or approval granted prior to the enactment of this paragraph pursuant to this Act, the Poultry Products Inspection Act (21 U.S.C. 451 and the following) or the Meat Inspection Act of March 4, 1907 (34 Stat. 1260), as amended and extended (21 U.S.C. 71 and the following);

(5) a new animal drug; or

(6) an ingredient described in paragraph (ff) in, or intended for use in, a dietary supplement.

(t)(1) The term "color additive" means a material which—

(A) is a dye, pigment, or other substance made by a process of synthesis or similar artifice, or extracted, isolated, or otherwise derived, with or without intermediate or final change of identity, from a vegetable, animal, mineral, or other source, and

(B) when added or applied to a food, drug, or cosmetic, or to the human body or any part thereof, is capable (alone or through reaction with other substance) of imparting color thereto;

except that such term does not include any material which the Secretary, by regulation, determines is used (or intended to be used) solely for a purpose or purposes other than coloring.

(2) The term "color" includes black, white, and intermediate grays.

(3) Nothing in subparagraph (1) of this paragraph shall be construed to apply to any pesticide chemical, soil or plant nutrient, or other agricultural chemical solely because of its effect in aiding, re other natural physiological processes of produce of the soil and thereby affecting its color, whether before or after harvest.

(u) The term "safe," as used in paragraph (s) of this section and in sections 409, 512, 571, and 721, has reference to the health of man or animal.

(v) The term "new animal drug" means any drug intended for use for animals other than man, including any drug intended for use in animal feed but not including such animal feed—

(1) the composition of which is such that such drug is not generally recognized, among experts qualified by scientific training and experience to evaluate the safety and effectiveness of animal drugs, as safe and effective for use under the conditions prescribed, recommended, or suggested in the labeling thereof; except that such a drug not so recognized shall not be deemed to be a "new animal drug" if at any time prior to June 25, 1938, it was subject to the Food and Drug

Act of June 30, 1906, as amended, and if at such time its labeling contained the same representations concerning the conditions of its use; or

(2) the composition of which is such that such drug, as a result of investigations to determine its safety and effectiveness for use under such conditions, has become so recognized but which has not, otherwise than in such investigations, been used to a material extent or for a material time under such conditions.

Provided that any drug intended for minor use or use in a minor species that is not the subject of a final regulation published by the Secretary through notice and comment rulemaking finding that the criteria of paragraphs (1) and (2) have not been met (or that the exception to the criterion in paragraph (1) has been met) is a new animal drug.

(w) The term "animal feed", as used in paragraph (w)[2] of this section, in section 512, and in provisions of this Act referring to such paragraph or section, means an article which is intended for use for food for animals other than man and which is intended for use as a substantial source of nutrients in the diet of the animal, and is not limited to a mixture intended to be the sole ration of the animal.

(x) The term "informal hearing" means a hearing which is not subject to section 554, 556, or 557 of title 5 of the United States Code and which provides for the following:

(1) The presiding officer in the hearing shall be designated by the Secretary from officers and employees of the Department who have not participated in any action of the Secretary which is the subject of the hearing and who are not directly responsible to an officer or employee of the Department who has participated in any such action.

(2) Each party to the hearing shall have the right at all times to be advised and accompanied by an attorney.

(3) Before the hearing, each party to the hearing shall be given reasonable notice of the matters to be considered at the hearing, including a comprehensive statement of the basis for the action taken or proposed by the Secretary which is the subject of the hearing and a general summary of the information which will be presented by the Secretary at the hearing in support of such action.

(4) At the hearing the parties to the hearing shall have the right to hear a full and complete statement of the action of the Secretary which is the subject of the hearing together with the information and reasons supporting such action, to conduct reasonable questioning, and to present any oral or written information relevant to such action.

(5) The presiding officer in such hearing shall prepare a written report of the hearing to which shall be attached all written material presented at the hearing. The participants in the hearing shall be given the opportunity to review and correct or supplement the presiding officer's report of the hearing.

2. So in law. Probably should be paragraph "(v)".

(6) The Secretary may require the hearing to be transcribed. A party to the hearing shall have the right to have the hearing transcribed at his expense. Any transcription of a hearing shall be included in the presiding officer's report of the hearing.

(y) The term "saccharin" includes calcium saccharin, sodium saccharin, and ammonium saccharin.

(z) The term "infant formula" means a food which purports to be or is represented for special dietary use solely as a food for infants by reason of its simulation of human milk or its suitability as a complete or partial substitute for human milk.

(aa) The term "abbreviated drug application" means an application submitted under section 505(j) for the approval of a drug that relies on the approved application of another drug with the same active ingredient to establish safety and efficacy, and—

(1) in the case of section 306, includes a supplement to such an application for a different or additional use of the drug but does not include a supplement to such an application for other than a different or additional use of the drug, and

(2) in the case of sections 307 and 308, includes any supplement to such an application.

(bb) The term "knowingly" or "knew" means that a person, with respect to information—

(1) has actual knowledge of the information, or

(2) acts in deliberate ignorance or reckless disregard of the truth or falsity of the information.

(cc) For purposes of section 306, the term "high managerial agent"—

(1) means—

(A) an officer or director of a corporation or an association,

(B) a partner of a partnership, or

(C) any employee or other agent of a corporation, association, or partnership, having duties such that the conduct of such officer, director, partner, employee, or agent may fairly be assumed to represent the policy of the corporation, association, or partnership, and

(2) includes persons having management responsibility for—

(A) submissions to the Food and Drug Administration regarding the development or approval of any drug product, any drug product, or

(B) production, quality assurance, or quality control of any drug product, or

(C) research and development of any drug product.

(dd) For purposes of sections 306 and 307, the term "drug product" means a drug subject to regulation under section 505, 512, or 802 of this Act or under section 351 of the Public Health Service Act.

(ee) The term "Commissioner" means the Commissioner of Food and Drugs.

(ff) The term "dietary supplement"—

(1) means a product (other than tobacco) intended to supplement the diet that bears or contains one or more of the following dietary ingredients:

(A) a vitamin;

(B) a mineral;

(C) an herb or other botanical;

(D) an amino acid;

(E) a dietary substance for use by man to supplement the diet by increasing the total dietary intake; or

(F) a concentrate, metabolite, constituent, extract, or combination of any ingredient described in clause (A), (B), (C), (D), or (E);

(2) means a product that—

(A)(i) is intended for ingestion in a form described in section 411(c)(1)(B)(i); or

(ii) complies with section 411(c)(1)(B)(ii);

(B) is not represented for use as a conventional food or as a sole item of a meal or the diet; and

(C) is labeled as a dietary supplement; and

(3) does—

(A) include an article that is approved as a new drug under section 505 or licensed as a biologic under section 351 of the Public Health Service Act (42 U.S.C. 262) and was, prior to such approval, certification, or license, marketed as a dietary supplement or as a food unless the Secretary has issued a regulation, after notice and comment, finding that the article, when used as or in a dietary supplement under the conditions of use and dosages set forth in the labeling for such dietary supplement, is unlawful under section 402(f); and

(B) not include—

(i) an article that is approved as a new drug under section 505, certified as an antibiotic under section 507,[3] or licensed as a biologic under section 351 of the Public Health Service Act (42 U.S.C. 262), or

_____

3. So in law. Section 507 was repealed by Pub. L. No. 105–115, § 125(b)(1), 111 Stat. 2296, 2325 (1997).

(ii) an article authorized for investigation as a new drug, antibiotic, or biological for which substantial clinical investigations have been instituted and for which the existence of such investigations has been made public,

which was not before such approval, certification, licensing, or authorization marketed as a dietary supplement or as a food unless the Secretary, in the Secretary's discretion, has issued a regulation, after notice and comment, finding that the article would be lawful under this Act.[4]

Except for purposes of sections 201(g) and 417, a dietary supplement shall be deemed to be a food within the meaning of this Act.

(gg) The term "processed food" means any food other than a raw agricultural commodity and includes any raw agricultural commodity that has been subject to processing, such as canning, cooking, freezing, dehydration, or milling.

(hh) The term "Administrator" means the Administrator of the United States Environmental Protection Agency.

(ii) The term "compounded positron emission tomography drug"—

(1) means a drug that—

(A) exhibits spontaneous disintegration of unstable nuclei by the emission of positrons and is used for the purpose of providing dual photon positron emission tomographic diagnostic images; and

(B) has been compounded by or on the order of a practitioner who is licensed by a State to compound or order compounding for a drug described in subparagraph (A), and is compounded in accordance with that State's law, for a patient or for research, teaching, or quality control; and

(2) includes any nonradioactive reagent, reagent kit, ingredient, nuclide generator, accelerator, target material, electronic synthesizer, or other apparatus or computer program to be used in the preparation of such a drug.

(jj) The term "antibiotic drug" means any drug (except drugs for use in animals other than humans) composed wholly or partly of any kind of penicillin, streptomycin, chlortetracycline, chloramphenicol, bacitracin, or any other drug intended for human use containing any quantity of any chemical substance which is produced by a micro-organism and which has the capacity to inhibit or destroy micro-organisms in dilute solution (including a chemically synthesized equivalent of any such substance) or any derivative thereof.

(kk) PRIORITY SUPPLEMENT.—The term "priority supplement" means a drug application referred to in section 101(4) of the Food and Drug Administration Modernization Act of 1997 (111 Stat. 2298).

(ll)(1) The term "single-use device" means a device that is intended for one use, or on a single patient during a single procedure.

4. So in law. Provision probably should be set
flush with subpar. (B).

(2)(A) The term "reprocessed", with respect to a single-use device, means an original device that has previously been used on a patient and has been subjected to additional processing and manufacturing for the purpose of an additional single use on a patient. The subsequent processing and manufacture of a reprocessed single-use device shall result in a device that is reprocessed within the meaning of this definition.

(B) A single-use device that meets the definition under clause (A) shall be considered a reprocessed device without regard to any description of the device used by the manufacturer of the device or other persons, including a description that uses the term "recycled" rather than the term "reprocessed".

(3) The term "original device" means a new, unused single-use device.

(mm)(1) The term "critical reprocessed single-use device" means a reprocessed single-use device that is intended to contact normally sterile tissue or body spaces during use.

(2) The term "semi-critical reprocessed single-use device" means a reprocessed single-use device that is intended to contact intact mucous membranes and not penetrate normally sterile areas of the body.

(nn) The term "major species" means cattle, horses, swine, chickens, turkeys, dogs, and cats, except that the Secretary may add species to this definition by regulation.

(oo) The term "minor species" means animals other than humans that are not major species.

(pp) The term "minor use" means the intended use of a drug in a major species for an indication that occurs infrequently and in only a small number of animals or in limited geographical areas and in only a small number of animals annually.

(qq) The term "major food allergen" means any of the following:

(1) Milk, egg, fish (e.g., bass, flounder, or cod), Crustacean shellfish (e.g., crab, lobster, or shrimp), tree nuts (e.g., almonds, pecans, or walnuts), wheat, peanuts, and soybeans.

(2) A food ingredient that contains protein derived from a food specified in paragraph (1), except the following:

(A) Any highly refined oil derived from a food specified in paragraph (1) and any ingredient derived from such highly refined oil.

(B) A food ingredient that is exempt under paragraph (6) or (7) of section 403(w).

(rr)(1) The term "tobacco product" means any product made or derived from tobacco that is intended for human consumption, including any component, part, or accessory of a tobacco product (except for raw materials other than tobacco used in manufacturing a component, part, or accessory of a tobacco product).

11

(2) The term "tobacco product" does not mean an article that is a drug under subsection (g)(1), a device under subsection (h), or a combination product described in section 503(g).

(3) The products described in paragraph (2) shall be subject to chapter V of this Act.

(4) A tobacco product shall not be marketed in combination with any other article or product regulated under this Act (including a drug, biologic, food, cosmetic, medical device, or a dietary supplement).

CHAPTER III—PROHIBITED ACTS AND PENALTIES

SEC. 301 [21 U.S.C. 331]. PROHIBITED ACTS

The following acts and the causing thereof are hereby prohibited:

(a) The introduction or delivery for introduction into interstate commerce of any food, drug, device, tobacco product, or cosmetic that is adulterated or misbranded.

(b) The adulteration or misbranding of any food, drug, device, tobacco product, or cosmetic in interstate commerce.

(c) The receipt in interstate commerce of any food, drug, device, tobacco product, or cosmetic that is adulterated or misbranded, and the delivery or proffered delivery thereof for pay or otherwise.

(d) The introduction or delivery for introduction into interstate commerce of any article in violation of section 404, 415, 505, or 564.

(e) The refusal to permit access to or copying of any record as required by section 412, 414, 417(j), 416, 504, 564, 703, 704(a), 760, or 761; or the failure to establish or maintain any record, or make any report, required under section 412, 414(b), 417(g), 416, 504, 505(i) or (k), 512(a)(4)(C), 512 (j), (l) or (m), 572(i), 515(f), 519, 564, 760, 761, 909, or 920 or the refusal to permit access to or verification or copying of any such required record; or the violation of any recordkeeping requirement under section 204 of the FDA Food Safety Modernization Act (except when such violation is committed by a farm).

(f) The refusal to permit entry or inspection as authorized by section 704.

(g) The manufacture within any Territory of any food, drug, device, tobacco product, or cosmetic that is adulterated or misbranded.

(h) The giving of a guaranty or undertaking referred to in section 303(c)(2) of this title, which guaranty or undertaking is false, except by a person who relied upon a guaranty or undertaking to the same effect signed by, and containing the name and address of, the person residing in the United States from whom he received in good faith the food, drug, device, tobacco product, or cosmetic; or the giving of a guaranty or undertaking referred to in section 303(c)(3) of this title, which guaranty or undertaking is false.

(i)(1) Forging, counterfeiting, simulating, or falsely representing, or without proper authority using any mark, stamp, tag, label, or other identification device authorized or required by regulations promulgated under the provisions of section 404, or 721.

(2) Making, selling, disposing of, or keeping in possession, control, or custody, or concealing any punch, die, plate, stone, or other thing designed to print, imprint, or reproduce the trademark, trade name, or other identifying mark, imprint, or device of another or any likeness of any of the foregoing upon any drug or container or labeling thereof so as to render such drug a counterfeit drug.

(3) The doing of any act which causes a drug to be a counterfeit drug, or the sale or dispensing, or the holding for sale or dispensing, of a counterfeit drug.

(j) The using by any person to his own advantage, or revealing, other than to the Secretary or officers or employees of the Department, or to the courts when relevant in any judicial proceeding under this Act, any information acquired under authority of section 404, 409, 412, 414, 505, 510, 512, 513, 514, 515, 516, 518, 519, 520, 571, 572, 573, 704, 708, 721, 904, 905, 906, 907, 908, 909, or 920(b) concerning any method or process which as a trade secret is entitled to protection, or the violating of section 408(i)(2) or any regulation issued under that section. This paragraph does not authorize the withholding of information from either House of Congress or from, to the extent of matter within its jurisdiction, any committee or subcommittee of such committee or any joint committee of Congress or any subcommittee of such joint committee.

(k) The alteration, mutilation, destruction, obliteration, or removal of the whole or any part of the labeling of, or the doing of any other act with respect to, a food, drug, device, tobacco product or cosmetic, if such act is done while such article is held for sale (whether or not the first sale) after shipment in interstate commerce and results in such article being adulterated or misbranded.

[(*l*) Repealed by Pub. L. No. 105–115, § 421, 111 Stat. 2296, 2380 (1997).]

(m) The sale or offering for sale of colored oleomargarine or colored margarine, or the possession or serving of colored oleomargarine or colored margarine in violation of section 407(b) or 407(c).

(n) The using, in labeling, advertising or other sales promotion of any reference to any report or analysis furnished in compliance with section 704.

(*o*) In the case of a prescription drug distributed or offered for sale in interstate commerce, the failure of the manufacturer, packer, or distributor thereof to maintain for transmittal, or to transmit, to any practitioner licensed by applicable State law to administer such drug who makes written request for information as to such drug, true and correct copies of all printed matter which is required to be included in any package in which that drug is distributed or sold, or such other printed matter as is approved by the Secretary. Nothing in this paragraph shall be construed to exempt any person from any labeling requirement imposed by or under other provisions of this Act.

(p) The failure to register in accordance with section 510 or 905, the failure to provide any information required by section 510(j), 510(k), 905(i), 905(j), or the failure to provide a notice required by section 510(j)(2) or 905(i)(3).

(q)(1) The failure or refusal—

(A) to comply with any requirement prescribed under section 518, 520(g), 903(b), 907, 908, or 915;

(B) to furnish any notification or other material or information required by or under section 519, 520(g), 904, 909, or 920; or

(C) to comply with a requirement under section 522 or 913.

(2) With respect to any device or tobacco product, the submission of any report that is required by or under this Act that is false or misleading in any material respect.

(r) The movement of a device or tobacco product in violation of an order under section 304(g) or the removal or alteration of any mark or label required by the order to identify the device or tobacco product as detained.

(s) The failure to provide the notice required by section 412(c) or 412(e), the failure to make the reports required by section 412(f)(1)(B), the failure to retain the records required by section 412(b)(4), or the failure to meet the requirements prescribed under section 412(f)(3).

(t) The importation of a drug in violation of section 801(d)(1), the sale, purchase, or trade of a drug or drug sample or the offer to sell, purchase, or trade a drug or drug sample in violation of section 503(c), the sale, purchase, or trade of a coupon, the offer to sell, purchase, or trade such a coupon, or the counterfeiting of such a coupon in violation of section 503(c)(2), the distribution of a drug sample in violation of section 503(d) or the failure to otherwise comply with the requirements of section 503(d), the distribution of drugs in violation of section 503(e), failure to comply with the requirements under section 582, the failure to comply with the requirements under section 584, as applicable, or the failure to otherwise comply with the requirements of section 503(e).

(u) The failure to comply with any requirements of the provisions of, or any regulations or orders of the Secretary, under section 512(a)(4)(A), 512(a)(4)(D), or 512(a)(5).

(v) The introduction or delivery for introduction into interstate commerce of a dietary supplement that is unsafe under section 413.

(w) The making of a knowingly false statement in any statement, certificate of analysis, record, or report required or requested under section 801(d)(3); the failure to submit a certificate of analysis as required under such section; the failure to maintain records or to submit records or reports as required by such section; the release into interstate commerce of any article or portion thereof imported into the United States under such section or any finished product made from such article or portion, except for export in accordance with section 801(e) or 802, or with section 351(h) of the Public Health Service Act; or the failure to so export or to destroy such an article or portions thereof, or such a finished product.

(x) The falsification of a declaration of conformity submitted under section 514(c) or the failure or refusal to provide data or information requested by the Secretary under paragraph (3) of such section.

(y) In the case of a drug, device, or food—

(1) the submission of a report or recommendation by a person accredited under section 523 that is false or misleading in any material respect;

(2) the disclosure by a person accredited under section 523 of confidential commercial information or any trade secret without the express written consent of the person who submitted such information or secret to such person; or

(3) the receipt by a person accredited under section 523 of a bribe in any form or the doing of any corrupt act by such person associated with a responsibility delegated to such person under this Act.

[(z) Terminated September 30, 2006, pursuant to Pub. L. No. 105–115, § 401(e), 111 Stat. 2296, 2364 (1997).]

(aa) The importation of a prescription drug in violation of section 804, the falsification of any record required to be maintained or provided to the Secretary under section, or any other violation of regulation under such section.

(bb) The transfer of an article of food in violation of an order under section 304(h), or the removal or alteration of any mark or label required by the order to identify the article as detained.

(cc) The importing or offering for import into the United States of an article of food by, with the assistance of, or at the direction of, a person debarred under section 306(b)(3).

(dd) The failure to register in accordance with section 415.

(ee) The importing or offering for import into the United States of an article of food in violation of the requirements under section 801(m).

(ff) The importing or offering for import into the United States of a drug or device with respect to which there is a failure to comply with a request of the Secretary to submit to the Secretary a statement under section 801(*o*).

(gg) The knowing failure to comply with paragraph (7)(E) of section 704(g); the knowing inclusion by a person accredited under paragraph (2) of such section of false information in an inspection report under paragraph (7)(A) of such section; or the knowing failure of such a person to include material facts in such a report.

(hh) The failure by a shipper, carrier by motor vehicle or rail vehicle, receiver, or any other person engaged in the transportation of food to comply with the sanitary transportation practices prescribed by the Secretary under section 416.

(ii) The falsification of a report of a serious adverse event submitted to a responsible person (as defined under section 760 or 761) or the falsification of a serious adverse event report (as defined under section 760 or 761) submitted to the Secretary.

(jj)(1) The failure to submit the certification required by section 402(j)(5)(B) of the Public Health Service Act, or knowingly submitting a false certification under such section.

(2) The failure to submit clinical trial information required under subsection (j) of section 402 of the Public Health Service Act.

(3) The submission of clinical trial information under subsection (j) of section 402 of the Public Health Service Act that is false or misleading in any particular under paragraph (5)(D) of such subsection (j).

(kk) The dissemination of a television advertisement without complying with section 503B.

(ll) The introduction or delivery for introduction into interstate commerce of any food to which has been added a drug approved under section 505, a biological product licensed under section 351 of the Public Health Service Act, or a drug or a biological product for which substantial clinical investigations have been instituted and for which the existence of such investigations has been made public, unless—

(1) such drug or such biological product was marketed in food before any approval of the drug under section 505, before licensure of the biological product under such section 351, and before any substantial clinical investigations involving the drug or the biological product have been instituted;

(2) the Secretary, in the Secretary's discretion, has issued a regulation, after notice and comment, approving the use of such drug or such biological product in the food;

(3) the use of the drug or the biological product in the food is to enhance the safety of the food to which the drug or the biological product is added or applied and not to have independent biological or therapeutic effects on humans, and the use is in conformity with—

(A) a regulation issued under section 409 prescribing conditions of safe use in food;

(B) a regulation listing or affirming conditions under which the use of the drug or the biological product in food is generally recognized as safe;

(C) the conditions of use identified in a notification to the Secretary of a claim of exemption from the premarket approval requirements for food additives based on the notifier's determination that the use of the drug or the biological product in food is generally recognized as safe, provided that the

Secretary has not questioned the general recognition of safety determination in a letter to the notifier;

(D) a food contact substance notification that is effective under section 409(h); or

(E) such drug or biological product had been marketed for smoking cessation prior to the date of the enactment of the Food and Drug Administration Amendments Act of 2007; or

(4) the drug is a new animal drug whose use is not unsafe under section 512.

(mm) The failure to submit a report or provide a notification required under section 417(d).

(nn) The falsification of a report or notification required under section 417(d).

(oo) The sale of tobacco products in violation of a no-tobacco-sale order issued under section 303(f).

(pp) The introduction or delivery for introduction into interstate commerce of a tobacco product in violation of section 911.

(qq)(1) Forging, counterfeiting, simulating, or falsely representing, or without proper authority using any mark, stamp (including tax stamp), tag, label, or other identification device upon any tobacco product or container or labeling thereof so as to render such tobacco product a counterfeit tobacco product.

(2) Making, selling, disposing of, or keeping in possession, control, or custody, or concealing any punch, die, plate, stone, or other item that is designed to print, imprint, or reproduce the trademark, trade name, or other identifying mark, imprint, or device of another or any likeness of any of the foregoing upon any tobacco product or container or labeling thereof so as to render such tobacco product a counterfeit tobacco product.

(3) The doing of any act that causes a tobacco product to be a counterfeit tobacco product, or the sale or dispensing, or the holding for sale or dispensing, of a counterfeit tobacco product.

(rr) The charitable distribution of tobacco products.

(ss) The failure of a manufacturer or distributor to notify the Attorney General and the Secretary of the Treasury of their knowledge of tobacco products used in illicit trade.

(tt) Making any express or implied statement or representation directed to consumers with respect to a tobacco product, in a label or labeling or through the media or advertising, that either conveys, or misleads or would mislead consumers into believing, that—

(1) the product is approved by the Food and Drug Administration;

(2) the Food and Drug Administration deems the product to be safe for use by consumers;

17

(3) the product is endorsed by the Food and Drug Administration for use by consumers; or

(4) the product is safe or less harmful by virtue of—

(A) its regulation or inspection by the Food and Drug Administration; or

(B) its compliance with regulatory requirements set by the Food and Drug Administration;

including any such statement or representation rendering the product misbranded under section 903.

(uu) The operation of a facility that manufactures, processes, packs, or holds food for sale in the United States if the owner, operator, or agent in charge of such facility is not in compliance with section 418.

(vv) The failure to comply with the requirements under section 419.

(ww) The failure to comply with section 420.

(xx) The refusal or failure to follow an order under section 423.

(yy) The knowing and willful failure to comply with the notification requirement under section 417(h).

(zz) The importation or offering for importation of a food if the importer (as defined in section 805) does not have in place a foreign supplier verification program in compliance with such section 805.

(aaa) The failure to register in accordance with section 801(s).

(bbb) The failure to notify the Secretary in violation of section 568.

(ccc)(1) The resale of a compounded drug that is labeled "not for resale" in accordance with section 503B.

(2) With respect to a drug to be compounded pursuant to section 503A or 503B, the intentional falsification of a prescription, as applicable.

(3) The failure to report drugs or adverse events by an entity that is registered in accordance with subsection (b) of section 503B.

SEC. 302 [21 U.S.C. 332]. INJUNCTION PROCEEDINGS

(a) The district courts of the United States and the United States courts of the Territories shall have jurisdiction, for cause shown[5] to restrain violations of section 301, except paragraphs (h), (i), and (j).

(b) In case of violation of an injunction or restraining order issued under this section, which also constitutes a violation of this Act, trial shall be by the court, or, upon demand of the accused, by a jury.

5. So in law. Section 507 was repealed by Pub. L. No. 105–115, § 125(b)(1), 111 Stat. 2296, 2325 (1997).

SEC. 303 [21 U.S.C. 333]. PENALTIES

(a)(1) Any person who violates a provision of section 301 shall be imprisoned for not more than one year or fined not more than $1,000, or both.

(2) Notwithstanding the provisions of paragraph (1) of this section, if any person commits such a violation after a conviction of him under this section has become final, or commits such a violation with the intent to defraud or mislead, such person shall be imprisoned for not more than three years or fined not more than $10,000 or both.

(b)(1) Notwithstanding subsection (a), any person who violates section 301(t) by—

(A) knowingly importing a drug in violation of section 801(d)(1),

(B) knowingly selling, purchasing, or trading a drug or drug sample or knowingly offering to sell, purchase, or trade a drug or drug sample, in violation of section 503(c)(1),

(C) knowingly selling, purchasing, or trading a coupon, knowingly offering to sell, purchase, or trade such a coupon, or knowingly counterfeiting such a coupon, in violation of section 503(c)(2), or

(D) knowingly distributing drugs in violation of section 503(e)(1),[6]

shall be imprisoned for not more than 10 years or fined not more than $250,000, or both.

(2) Any manufacturer or distributor who distributes drug samples by means other than the mail or common carrier whose representative, during the course of the representative's employment or association with that manufacturer or distributor, violated section 301(t) because of a violation of section 503(c)(1) or violated any State law prohibiting the sale, purchase, or trade of a drug sample subject to section 503(b) or the offer to sell, purchase, or trade such a drug sample shall, upon conviction of the representative for such violation, be subject to the following civil penalties:

(A) A civil penalty of not more than $50,000 for each of the first two such violations resulting in a conviction of any representative of the manufacturer or distributor in any 10–year period.

(B) A civil penalty of not more than $1,000,000 for each violation resulting in a conviction of any representative after the second conviction in any 10–year period.

For the purposes of this paragraph, multiple convictions of one or more persons arising out of the same event or transaction, or a related series of events or transactions, shall be considered as one violation.

6. Was "503(e)(2)(A)." According to Pub. L. No. 113–54, §207(b), 127 Stat. 640, amendment to "503(e)(1)" takes effect on January 1, 2015.

(3) Any manufacturer or distributor who violates section 301(t) because of a failure to make a report required by section 503(d)(3)(E) shall be subject to a civil penalty of not more than $100,000.

(4)(A) If a manufacturer or distributor or any representative of such manufacturer or distributor provides information leading to the institution of a criminal proceeding against, and conviction of, any representative of that manufacturer or distributor for a violation of section 301(t) because of a sale, purchase, or trade or offer to purchase, sell, or trade a drug sample in violation of section 503(c)(1) or for a violation of State law prohibiting the sale, purchase, or trade or offer to sell, purchase, or trade a drug sample, the conviction of such representative shall not be considered as a violation for purposes of paragraph (2).

(B) If, in an action brought under paragraph (2) against a manufacturer or distributor relating to the conviction of a representative of such manufacturer or distributor for the sale, purchase, or trade of a drug or the offer to sell, purchase, or trade a drug, it is shown, by clear and convincing evidence—

(i) that the manufacturer or distributor conducted, before the institution of a criminal proceeding against such representative for the violation which resulted in such conviction, an investigation of events or transactions which would have led to the reporting of information leading to the institution of a criminal proceeding against, and conviction of, such representative for such purchase, sale, or trade or offer to purchase, sell, or trade, or

(ii) that, except in the case of the conviction of a representative employed in a supervisory function, despite diligent implementation by the manufacturer or distributor of an independent audit and security system designed to detect such a violation, the manufacturer or distributor could not reasonably have been expected to have detected such violation,

the conviction of such representative shall not be considered as a conviction for purposes of paragraph (2).

(5) If a person provides information leading to the institution of a criminal proceeding against, and conviction of, a person for a violation of section 301(t) because of the sale, purchase, or trade of a drug sample or the offer to sell, purchase, or trade a drug sample in violation of section 503(c)(1), such person shall be entitled to one-half of the criminal fine imposed and collected for such violation but not more than $125,000.

(6) Notwithstanding subsection (a), any person who is a manufacturer or importer of a prescription drug under section 804(b) and knowingly fails to comply with a requirement of section 804(e) that is applicable to such manufacturer or importer, respectively, shall be imprisoned for not more than 10 years or fined not more than $250,000, or both.

(7) Notwithstanding subsection (a)(2), any person that knowingly and intentionally adulterates a drug such that the drug is adulterated under subsection (a)(1), (b),

(c), or (d) of section 501 and has a reasonable probability of causing serious adverse health consequences or death to humans or animals shall be imprisoned for not more than 20 years or fined not more than $1,000,000, or both.

(c) No person shall be subject to the penalties of subsection (a)(1) of this section, (1) for having received in interstate commerce any article and delivered it or proffered delivery of it, if such delivery or proffer was made in good faith, unless he refuses to furnish on request of an officer or employee duly designated by the Secretary the name and address of the person from whom he purchased or received such article and copies of all documents, if any there be, pertaining to the delivery of the article to him; or (2) for having violated section 301(a) or (d), if he establishes a guaranty or undertaking signed by, and containing the name and address of, the person residing in the United States from whom he received in good faith the article, to the effect, in case of an alleged violation of section 301(a), that such article is not adulterated or misbranded, within the meaning of this Act, designating this Act, or to the effect, in case of an alleged violation of section 301(d), that such article is not an article which may not, under the provisions of section 404 or 505, be introduced into interstate commerce; or (3) for having violated section 301(a), where the violation exists because the article is adulterated by reason of containing a color additive not from a batch certified in accordance with regulations promulgated by the Secretary under this Act, if such person establishes a guaranty or undertaking signed by, and containing the name and address of, the manufacturer of the color additive, to the effect that such color additive was from a batch certified in accordance with the applicable regulations promulgated by the Secretary under this Act; or (4) for having violated section 301 (b), (c), or (k) by failure to comply with section 502(f) in respect to an article received in interstate commerce to which neither section 503(a) nor section 503(b)(1) is applicable, if the delivery or proffered delivery was made in good faith and the labeling at the time thereof contained the same directions for use and warning statements as were contained in the labeling at the time of such receipt of such article; or (5) for having violated section 301(i)(2) if such person acted in good faith and had no reason to believe that use of the punch, die, plate, stone, or other thing involved would result in a drug being a counterfeit drug, or for having violated section 301(i)(3) if the person doing the act or causing it to be done acted in good faith and had no reason to believe that the drug was a counterfeit drug.

(d) No person shall be subject to the penalties of subsection (a)(1) of this section for a violation of section 301 involving misbranded food if the violation exists solely because the food is misbranded under section 403(a)(2) because of its advertising.

(e)(1) Except as provided in paragraph (2), whoever knowingly distributes, or possesses with intent to distribute, human growth hormone for any use in humans other than the treatment of a disease or other recognized medical condition, where such use has been authorized by the Secretary of Health and Human Services under section 505 and pursuant to the order of a physician, is guilty of an offense punishable by not more than 5 years in prison, such fines as are authorized by title 18, United States Code, or both.

(2) Whoever commits any offense set forth in paragraph (1) and such offense involves an individual under 18 years of age is punishable by not more than 10 years imprisonment, such fines as are authorized by title 18, United States Code, or both.

(3) Any conviction for a violation of paragraphs (1) and (2) of this subsection shall be considered a felony violation of the Controlled Substances Act for the purposes of forfeiture under section 413 of such Act.

(4) As used in this subsection the term "human growth hormone" means somatrem, somatropin, or an analogue of either of them.

(5) The Drug Enforcement Administration is authorized to investigate offenses punishable by this subsection.

(f)(1)(A) Except as provided in subparagraph (B), any person who violates a requirement of this Act which relates to devices shall be liable to the United States for a civil penalty in an amount not to exceed $15,000 for each such violation, and not to exceed $1,000,000 for all such violations adjudicated in a single proceeding. For purposes of the preceding sentence, a person accredited under paragraph (2) of section 704(g) who is substantially not in compliance with the standards of accreditation under such section, or who poses a threat to public health or fails to act in a manner that is consistent with the purposes of such section, shall be considered to have violated a requirement of this Act that relates to devices.

(B) Subparagraph (A) shall not apply—

(i) to any person who violates the requirements of section 519(a) or 520(f) unless such violation constitutes (I) a significant or knowing departure from such requirements, or (II) a risk to public health,

(ii) to any person who commits minor violations of section 519(e) or 519(g) (only with respect to correction reports) if such person demonstrates substantial compliance with such section, or

(iii) to violations of section 501(a)(2)(A) which involve one or more devices which are not defective.

(2)(A) Any person who introduces into interstate commerce or delivers for introduction into interstate commerce an article of food that is adulterated within the meaning of section 402(a)(2)(B) or any person who does not comply with a recall order under section 423 shall be subject to a civil money penalty of not more than $50,000 in the case of an individual and $250,000 in the case of any other person for such introduction or delivery, not to exceed $500,000 for all such violations adjudicated in a single proceeding.

(B) This paragraph shall not apply to any person who grew the article of food that is adulterated. If the Secretary assesses a civil penalty against any person under this paragraph, the Secretary may not use the criminal authorities under this section to sanction such person for the introduction or delivery for introduction into interstate commerce of the article of food that is adulterated. If the Secretary assesses a civil penalty against any person under this paragraph, the Secretary may not use the seizure authorities of section 304 or the injunction authorities of section 302 with respect to the article of food that is adulterated.

(C) In a hearing to assess a civil penalty under this paragraph, the presiding officer shall have the same authority with regard to compelling testimony or production of documents as a presiding officer has under section 408(g)(2)(B). The third sentence of paragraph (5)(A) shall not apply to any investigation under this paragraph.

(3)(A) Any person who violates section 301(jj) shall be subject to a civil monetary penalty of not more than $10,000 for all violations adjudicated in a single proceeding.

(B) If a violation of section 301(jj) is not corrected within the 30–day period following notification under section 402(j)(5)(C)(ii), the person shall, in addition to any penalty under subparagraph (A), be subject to a civil monetary penalty of not more than $10,000 for each day of the violation after such period until the violation is corrected.

(4)(A) Any responsible person (as such term is used in section 505–1) that violates a requirement of section 505(*o*), 505(p), or 505–1 shall be subject to a civil monetary penalty of—

(i) not more than $250,000 per violation, and not to exceed $1,000,000 for all such violations adjudicated in a single proceeding; or

(ii) in the case of a violation that continues after the Secretary provides written notice to the responsible person, the responsible person shall be subject to a civil monetary penalty of $250,000 for the first 30–day period (or any portion thereof) that the responsible person continues to be in violation, and such amount shall double for every 30–day period thereafter that the violation continues, not to exceed $1,000,000 for any 30–day period, and not to exceed $10,000,000 for all such violations adjudicated in a single proceeding.

(B) In determining the amount of a civil penalty under subparagraph (A)(ii), the Secretary shall take into consideration whether the responsible person is making efforts toward correcting the violation of the requirement of section 505(*o*), 505(p), or 505–1 for which the responsible person is subject to such civil penalty.

(5)(A) A civil penalty under paragraph (1), (2), (3), (4), or (9) shall be assessed, or a no-tobacco-sale order may be imposed, by the Secretary by an order made on the record after opportunity for a hearing provided in accordance with this subparagraph and section 554 of title 5, United States Code. Before issuing such an order, the Secretary shall give written notice to the person to be assessed a civil penalty, or upon whom a no-tobacco-sale order is to be imposed, under such order of the Secretary's proposal to issue such order and provide such person an opportunity for a hearing on the order. In the course of any investigation, the Secretary may issue subpoenas requiring the attendance and testimony of witnesses and the production of evidence that relates to the matter under investigation.

(B) In determining the amount of a civil penalty, or the period to be covered by a no-tobacco-sale order, the Secretary shall take into account the nature, circumstances, extent, and gravity of the violation or violations and, with respect to the violator, ability to pay, effect on ability to continue to do business, any history of prior such violations, the degree of culpability, and such other matters as justice may require. A no-tobacco-sale order permanently prohibiting an individual retail outlet from selling tobacco products shall include provisions that allow the outlet, after a specified period of time, to request that the Secretary compromise, modify, or terminate the order.

(C) The Secretary may compromise, modify, or remit, with or without conditions, any civil penalty which may be assessed under paragraph (1), (2), (3), (4), or (9). The amount of such penalty, when finally determined, or the amount agreed upon in compromise, may be deducted from any sums owing by the United States to the person charged.

(D) The Secretary may compromise, modify, or terminate, with or without conditions, any no-tobacco-sale order.

(6) Any person who requested, in accordance with paragraph (5)(A), a hearing respecting the assessment of a civil penalty or the imposition of a no-tobacco-sale order and who is aggrieved by an order assessing a civil penalty or the imposition of a no-tobacco-sale order may file a petition for judicial review of such order with the United States Court of Appeals for the District of Columbia Circuit or for any other circuit in which such person resides or transacts business. Such a petition may only be filed within the 60–day period beginning on the date the order making such assessment was issued, or on which the no-tobacco-sale order was imposed, as the case may be.

(7) If any person fails to pay an assessment of a civil penalty—

(A) after the order making the assessment becomes final, and if such person does not file a petition for judicial review of the order in accordance with paragraph (6), or

(B) after a court in an action brought under paragraph (6) has entered a final judgment in favor of the Secretary,

the Attorney General shall recover the amount assessed (plus interest at currently prevailing rates from the date of the expiration of the 60–day period referred to in paragraph (6) or the date of such final judgment, as the case may be) in an action brought in any appropriate district court of the United States. In such an action, the validity, amount, and appropriateness of such penalty shall not be subject to review.

(8)[7] If the Secretary finds that a person has committed repeated violations of restrictions promulgated under section 906(d) at a particular retail outlet then the Secretary may impose a no-tobacco-sale order on that person prohibiting the sale of tobacco products in that outlet. A no-tobacco-sale order may be imposed with a civil penalty under paragraph (1). Prior to the entry of a no-sale order under this paragraph, a person shall be entitled to a hearing pursuant to the procedures established through regulations of the Food and Drug Administration for assessing civil money penalties, including at a retailer's request a hearing by telephone, or at the nearest regional or field office of the Food and Drug Administration, or at a Federal, State, or county facility within 100 miles from the location of the retail outlet, if such a facility is available.

(9)[8] CIVIL MONETARY PENALTIES FOR VIOLATION OF TOBACCO PRODUCT REQUIREMENTS.—

(A) IN GENERAL.—Subject to subparagraph (B), any person who violates a requirement of this Act which relates to tobacco products shall be liable to the United States for a civil penalty in an amount not to exceed $15,000 for each such violation, and not to exceed $1,000,000 for all such violations adjudicated in a single proceeding.

(B) ENHANCED PENALTIES.—

(i) Any person who intentionally violates a requirement of section 902(5), 902(6), 904, 908(c), or 911(a), shall be subject to a civil monetary penalty of—

(I) not to exceed $250,000 per violation, and not to exceed $1,000,000 for all such violations adjudicated in a single proceeding; or

(II) in the case of a violation that continues after the Secretary provides written notice to such person, $250,000 for the first 30–day period (or any portion thereof) that the person continues to be in violation, and such amount shall double for every 30–day period thereafter that the violation continues, not to exceed $1,000,000 for any 30–day period, and not to exceed $10,000,000 for all such violations adjudicated in a single proceeding.

(ii) Any person who violates a requirement of section 911(g)(2)(C)(ii) or 911(i)(1), shall be subject to a civil monetary penalty of—

(I) not to exceed $250,000 per violation, and not to exceed $1,000,000 for all such violations adjudicated in a single proceeding; or

(II) in the case of a violation that continues after the Secretary provides written notice to such person, $250,000 for the first 30–day period

7. According to § 103(q)(3) of the Family Smoking Prevention and Tobacco Control Act, Pub. L. No. 111–31 Div. A, this paragraph takes effect upon the issuance of guidance described in § 103(q)(1) of that Act.

8. According to § 103(q)(3) of the Family Smoking Prevention and Tobacco Control Act, Pub. L. No. 111–31 Div. A, this paragraph takes effect upon the issuance of guidance described in § 103(q)(1) of that Act.

(or any portion thereof) that the person continues to be in violation, and such amount shall double for every 30–day period thereafter that the violation continues, not to exceed $1,000,000 for any 30–day period, and not to exceed $10,000,000 for all such violations adjudicated in a single proceeding.

(iii) In determining the amount of a civil penalty under clause (i)(II) or (ii)(II), the Secretary shall take into consideration whether the person is making efforts toward correcting the violation of the requirements of the section for which such person is subject to such civil penalty.

(g)(1) With respect to a person who is a holder of an approved application under section 505 for a drug subject to section 503(b) or under section 351 of the Public Health Service Act, any such person who disseminates or causes another party to disseminate a direct-to-consumer advertisement that is false or misleading shall be liable to the United States for a civil penalty in an amount not to exceed $250,000 for the first such violation in any 3–year period, and not to exceed $500,000 for each subsequent violation in any 3–year period. No other civil monetary penalties in this Act (including the civil penalty in section 303(f)(4)) shall apply to a violation regarding direct-to-consumer advertising. For purposes of this paragraph: (A) Repeated dissemination of the same or similar advertisement prior to the receipt of the written notice referred to in paragraph (2) for such advertisements shall be considered one violation. (B) On and after the date of the receipt of such a notice, all violations under this paragraph occurring in a single day shall be considered one violation. With respect to advertisements that appear in magazines or other publications that are published less frequently than daily, each issue date (whether weekly or monthly) shall be treated as a single day for the purpose of calculating the number of violations under this paragraph.

(2) A civil penalty under paragraph (1) shall be assessed by the Secretary by an order made on the record after providing written notice to the person to be assessed a civil penalty and an opportunity for a hearing in accordance with this paragraph and section 554 of title 5, United States Code. If upon receipt of the written notice, the person to be assessed a civil penalty objects and requests a hearing, then in the course of any investigation related to such hearing, the Secretary may issue subpoenas requiring the attendance and testimony of witnesses and the production of evidence that relates to the matter under investigation, including information pertaining to the factors described in paragraph (3).

(3) The Secretary, in determining the amount of the civil penalty under paragraph (1), shall take into account the nature, circumstances, extent, and gravity of the violation or violations, including the following factors:

(A) Whether the person submitted the advertisement or a similar advertisement for review under section 736A.

(B) Whether the person submitted the advertisement for review if required under section 503B.

(C) Whether, after submission of the advertisement as described in subparagraph (A) or (B), the person disseminated or caused another party to disseminate the advertisement before the end of the 45–day comment period.

(D) Whether the person incorporated any comments made by the Secretary with regard to the advertisement into the advertisement prior to its dissemination.

(E) Whether the person ceased distribution of the advertisement upon receipt of the written notice referred to in paragraph (2) for such advertisement.

(F) Whether the person had the advertisement reviewed by qualified medical, regulatory, and legal reviewers prior to its dissemination.

(G) Whether the violations were material.

(H) Whether the person who created the advertisement or caused the advertisement to be created acted in good faith.

(I) Whether the person who created the advertisement or caused the advertisement to be created has been assessed a civil penalty under this provision within the previous 1–year period.

(J) The scope and extent of any voluntary, subsequent remedial action by the person.

(K) Such other matters, as justice may require.

(4)(A) Subject to subparagraph (B), no person shall be required to pay a civil penalty under paragraph (1) if the person submitted the advertisement to the Secretary and disseminated or caused another party to disseminate such advertisement after incorporating each comment received from the Secretary.

(B) The Secretary may retract or modify any prior comments the Secretary has provided to an advertisement submitted to the Secretary based on new information or changed circumstances, so long as the Secretary provides written notice to the person of the new views of the Secretary on the advertisement and provides a reasonable time for modification or correction of the advertisement prior to seeking any civil penalty under paragraph (1).

(5) The Secretary may compromise, modify, or remit, with or without conditions, any civil penalty which may be assessed under paragraph (1). The amount of such penalty, when finally determined, or the amount charged upon in compromise, may be deducted from any sums owed by the United States to the person charged.

(6) Any person who requested, in accordance with paragraph (2), a hearing with respect to the assessment of a civil penalty and who is aggrieved by an order assessing a civil penalty, may file a petition for de novo judicial review of such order with the United States Court of Appeals for the District of Columbia Circuit or for any other circuit in which such person resides or transacts business. Such a petition may only be filed within the 60–day period beginning on the date the order making such assessments was issued.

(7) If any person fails to pay an assessment of a civil penalty under paragraph (1)—

> (A) after the order making the assessment becomes final, and if such person does not file a petition for judicial review of the order in accordance with paragraph (6), or

> (B) after a court in an action brought under paragraph (6) has entered a final judgment in favor of the Secretary,

the Attorney General of the United States shall recover the amount assessed (plus interest at currently prevailing rates from the date of the expiration of the 60–day period referred to in paragraph (6) or the date of such final judgment, as the case may be) in an action brought in any appropriate district court of the United States. In such an action, the validity, amount, and appropriateness of such penalty shall not be subject to review.

SEC. 304 [21 U.S.C. 334]. SEIZURE

(a)(1) Any article of food, drug, or cosmetic that is adulterated or misbranded when introduced into or while in interstate commerce or while held for sale (whether or not the first sale) after shipment in interstate commerce, or which may not, under the provisions of section 301(ll), 404, or 505, be introduced into interstate commerce, shall be liable to be proceeded against while in interstate commerce, or at any time thereafter, on libel of information and condemned in any district court of the United States or United States court of a Territory within the jurisdiction of which the article is found. No libel for condemnation shall be instituted under this Act, for any alleged misbranding if there is pending in any court a libel for condemnation proceeding under this Act based upon the same alleged misbranding, and not more than one such proceeding shall be instituted if no such proceeding is so pending, except that such limitations shall not apply (A) when such misbranding has been the basis of a prior judgment in favor of the United States, in a criminal, injunction, or libel for condemnation proceeding under this Act, or (B) when the Secretary has probable cause to believe from facts found, without hearing, by him or any officer or employee of the Department that the misbranded article is dangerous to health, or that the labeling of the misbranded article is fraudulent, or would be in a material respect misleading to the injury or damage of the purchaser or consumer. In any case where the number of libel for condemnation proceedings is limited as above provided the proceeding pending or instituted shall, on application of the claimant, seasonably made, be removed for trial to any district agreed upon by stipulation between the parties, or, in case of failure to so stipulate within a reasonable time, the claimant may apply to the court of the district in which the seizure has been made, and such court (after giving the United States attorney for such district reasonable notice and opportunity to be heard) shall by order, unless good cause to the contrary is shown, specify a district of reasonable proximity to the claimant's principal place of business, to which the case shall be removed for trial.

(2) The following shall be liable to be proceeded against at any time on libel of information and condemned in any district court of the United States or United States court of a Territory within the jurisdiction of which they are found: (A) Any drug that is a counterfeit drug, (B) Any container of a counterfeit drug, (C) Any punch, die, plate, stone, labeling, container, or other thing used or designed for use in making a counterfeit drug or drugs, (D) Any adulterated or misbranded device, and (E) Any adulterated or misbranded tobacco product.

(3)(A) Except as provided in subparagraph (B), no libel for condemnation may be instituted under paragraph (1) or (2) against any food which—

(i) is misbranded under section 403(a)(2) because of its advertising, and

(ii) is being held for sale to the ultimate consumer in an establishment other than an establishment owned or operated by a manufacturer, packer, or distributor of the food.

(B) A libel for condemnation may be instituted under paragraph (1) or (2) against a food described in subparagraph (A) if—

(i)(I) the food's advertising which resulted in the food being misbranded under section 403(a)(2) was disseminated in the establishment in which the food is being held for sale to the ultimate consumer,

(II) such advertising was disseminated by, or under the direction of, the owner or operator of such establishment, or

(III) all or part of the cost of such advertising was paid by such owner or operator; and

(ii) the owner or operator of such establishment used such advertising in the establishment to promote the sale of the food.

(b) The article, equipment, or other thing proceeded against shall be liable to seizure by process pursuant to the libel, and the procedure in cases under this section shall conform, as nearly as may be, to the procedure in admiralty; except that on demand of either party any issue of fact joined in any such case shall be tried by jury. When libel for condemnation proceedings under this section, involving the same claimant and the same issues of adulteration or misbranding, are pending in two or more jurisdictions, such pending proceedings, upon application of the claimant seasonably made to the court of one such jurisdiction, shall be consolidated for trial by order of such court, and tried in (1) any district selected by the claimant where one of such proceedings is pending; or (2) a district agreed upon by stipulation between the parties. If no order for consolidation is so made within a reasonable time, the claimant may apply to the court of one such jurisdiction and such court (after giving the United States attorney for such district reasonable notice and opportunity to be heard) shall by order, unless good cause to the contrary is shown, specify a district of reasonable proximity to the claimant's principal place of business, in which all such pending proceedings shall be consolidated for trial and tried. Such order of consolidation shall not apply so as to require the removal of any case the date for trial of which has been fixed. The court granting such order shall give prompt notification thereof to the other courts having jurisdiction of the cases covered thereby.

(c) The court at any time after seizure up to a reasonable time before trial shall by order allow any party to a condemnation proceeding, his attorney or agent, to obtain a representative sample of the article seized and a true copy of the analysis, if any, on which the proceeding is based and the identifying marks or numbers, if any, of the packages from which the samples analyzed were obtained.

(d)(1) Any food, drug, device, tobacco product, or cosmetic condemned under this section shall, after entry of the decree, be disposed of by destruction or sale as the court may, in accordance with the provisions of this section, direct and the proceeds thereof, if sold, less the legal costs and charges, shall be paid into the Treasury of the United States; but such article shall not be sold under such decree contrary to the provisions of this Act or the laws of the jurisdiction in which sold. After entry of the decree and upon the payment of the costs of such proceedings and the execution of a good and sufficient bond conditioned that such article shall not be sold or disposed of contrary to the provisions of this Act or the laws of any State or Territory in which sold, the court may by order direct that such article be delivered to the owner thereof to be destroyed or brought into compliance with the provisions of this Act, under the supervision of an officer or employee duly designated by the Secretary, and the expenses of such supervision shall be paid by the person obtaining release of the article under bond. If the article was imported into the United States and the person seeking its release establishes (A) that the adulteration, misbranding, or violation did not occur after the article was imported, and (B) that he had no cause for believing that it was adulterated, misbranded, or in violation before it was released from customs custody, the court may permit the article to be delivered to the owner for exportation in lieu of destruction upon a showing by the owner that all of the conditions of section 801(e) can and will be met. The provisions of this sentence shall not apply where condemnation is based upon violation of section 402(a)(1), (2), or (6), section 501(a)(3), section 502(j), or section 601(a) or (d). Where such exportation is made to the original foreign supplier, then subparagraphs (A) and (B) of section 801(e)(1) and the preceding sentence shall not be applicable; and in all cases of exportation the bond shall be conditioned that the article shall not be sold or disposed of until the applicable conditions of section 801(e) have been met. Any person seeking to export an imported article pursuant to any of the provisions of this subsection shall establish that the article was intended for export at the time the article entered commerce. Any article condemned by reason of its being an article which may not, under section 404 or 505, be introduced into interstate commerce, shall be disposed of by destruction.

(2) The provisions of paragraph (1) of this subsection shall, to the extent deemed appropriate by the court, apply to any equipment or other thing which is not otherwise within the scope of such paragraph and which is referred to in paragraph (2) of subsection (a).

(3) Whenever in any proceeding under this section, involving paragraph (2) of subsection (a), the condemnation of any equipment or thing (other than a drug) is decreed, the court shall allow the claim of any claimant, to the extent of such claimant's interest, for remission or mitigation of such forfeiture if such claimant proves to the satisfaction of the court (i) that he has not committed or caused to be committed any prohibited act referred to in such paragraph (2) and has no interest in any drug referred to therein, (ii) that he has an interest in such equipment or other thing as owner or lienor or otherwise, acquired by him in good faith, and (iii) that he at no time had any knowledge or reason to believe that such equipment or other thing was being or would be used in, or to facilitate, the violation of laws of the United States relating to counterfeit drugs.

(e) When a decree of condemnation is entered against the article, court costs and fees, and storage and other proper expenses, shall be awarded against the person, if any, intervening as claimant of the article.

(f) In the case of removal for trial of any case as provided by subsection (a) or (b)—

(1) The clerk of the court from which removal is made shall promptly transmit to the court in which the case is to be tried all records in the case necessary in order that such court may exercise jurisdiction.

(2) The court to which such case was removed shall have the powers and be subject to the duties, for purposes of such case, which the court from which removal was made would have had, or to which such court would have been subject, if such case had not been removed.

(g)(1) If during an inspection conducted under section 704 of a facility or a vehicle, a device, drug, or tobacco product which the officer or employee making the inspection has reason to believe is adulterated or misbranded is found in such facility or vehicle, such officer or employee may order the device, drug, or tobacco product detained (in accordance with regulations prescribed by the Secretary) for a reasonable period which may not exceed twenty days unless the Secretary determines that a period of detention greater than twenty days is required to institute an action under subsection (a) or section 302, in which case he may authorize a detention period of not to exceed thirty days. Regulations of the Secretary prescribed under this paragraph shall require that before a device, drug, or tobacco product may be ordered detained under this paragraph the Secretary or an officer or employee designated by the Secretary approve such order. A detention order under this paragraph may require the labeling or marking of a device, drug, or tobacco product during the period of its detention for the purpose of identifying the device, drug, or tobacco product as detained. Any person who would be entitled to claim a device, drug, or tobacco product if it were seized under subsection (a) may appeal to the Secretary a detention of such device, drug, or tobacco product under this paragraph. Within five days of the date an appeal of a detention is filed with the Secretary, the Secretary shall after affording opportunity for an informal hearing by order confirm the detention or revoke it.

31

(2)(A) Except as authorized by subparagraph (B), a device, drug, or tobacco product subject to a detention order issued under paragraph (1) shall not be moved by any person from the place at which it is ordered detained until—

(i) released by the Secretary, or

(ii) the expiration of the detention period applicable to such order,

whichever occurs first.

(B) A device or drug subject to a detention order under paragraph (1) may be moved—

(i) in accordance with regulations prescribed by the Secretary, and

(ii) if not in final form for shipment, at the discretion of the manufacturer of the device or drug for the purpose of completing the work required to put it in such form.

(h) ADMINISTRATIVE DETENTION OF FOODS.—

(1) DETENTION AUTHORITY.—

(A) IN GENERAL.—An officer or qualified employee of the Food and Drug Administration may order the detention, in accordance with this subsection, of any article of food that is found during an inspection, examination, or investigation under this Act conducted by such officer or qualified employee, if the officer or qualified employee has reason to believe that such article is adulterated or misbranded.

(B) SECRETARY'S APPROVAL.—An article of food may be ordered detained under subparagraph (A) only if the Secretary or an official designated by the Secretary approves the order. An official may not be so designated unless the official is the director of the district under this Act in which the article involved is located, or is an official senior to such director.

(2) PERIOD OF DETENTION.—An article of food may be detained under paragraph (1) for a reasonable period, not to exceed 20 days, unless a greater period, not to exceed 30 days, is necessary, to enable the Secretary to institute an action under subsection (a) or section 302. The Secretary shall by regulation provide for procedures for instituting such action on an expedited basis with respect to perishable foods.

(3) SECURITY OF DETAINED ARTICLE.—An order under paragraph (1) with respect to an article of food may require that such article be labeled or marked as detained, and shall require that the article be removed to a secure facility, as appropriate. An article subject to such an order shall not be transferred by any person from the place at which the article is ordered detained, or from the place to which the article is so removed, as the case may be, until released by the Secretary or until the expiration of the detention period applicable under such order, whichever occurs first. This subsection may not be construed as authorizing the delivery

of the article pursuant to the execution of a bond while the article is subject to the order, and section 801(b) does not authorize the delivery of the article pursuant to the execution of a bond while the article is subject to the order.

(4) APPEAL OF DETENTION ORDER.—

(A) IN GENERAL.—With respect to an article of food ordered detained under paragraph (1), any person who would be entitled to be a claimant for such article if the article were seized under subsection (a) may appeal the order to the Secretary. Within five days after such an appeal is filed, the Secretary, after providing opportunity for an informal hearing, shall confirm or terminate the order involved, and such confirmation by the Secretary shall be considered a final agency action for purposes of section 702 of title 5, United States Code. If during such five-day period the Secretary fails to provide such an opportunity, or to confirm or terminate such order, the order is deemed to be terminated.

(B) EFFECT OF INSTITUTING COURT ACTION.—The process under subparagraph (A) for the appeal of an order under paragraph (1) terminates if the Secretary institutes an action under subsection (a) or section 302 regarding the article of food involved.

(i) PROCEDURES FOR PROMULGATING REGULATIONS.—

(1) IN GENERAL.—In promulgating a regulation implementing this section, the Secretary shall—

(A) issue a notice of proposed rulemaking that includes the proposed regulation;

(B) provide a period of not less than 60 days for comments on the proposed regulation; and

(C) publish the final regulation not less than 30 days before the regulation's effective date.

(2) RESTRICTIONS.—Notwithstanding any other provision of Federal law, in implementing this section, the Secretary shall only promulgate regulations as described in paragraph (1).

SEC. 305 [21 U.S.C. 335]. HEARING BEFORE REPORT OF CRIMINAL VIOLATION

Before any violation of this Act is reported by the Secretary to any United States attorney for institution of a criminal proceeding, the person against whom such proceeding is contemplated shall be given appropriate notice and an opportunity to present his views, either orally or in writing, with regard to such contemplated proceeding.

SEC. 306 [21 U.S.C. 335a]. DEBARMENT, TEMPORARY DENIAL OF APPROVAL, AND SUSPENSION

(a) MANDATORY DEBARMENT; CERTAIN DRUG APPLICATIONS.—

(1) CORPORATIONS, PARTNERSHIPS, AND ASSOCIATIONS.—If the Secretary finds that a person other than an individual has been convicted, after the date of enactment of this section, of a felony under Federal law for conduct relating to the development or approval, including the process for development or approval, of any abbreviated drug application, the Secretary shall debar such person from submitting, or assisting in the submission of, any such application.

(2) INDIVIDUALS.—If the Secretary finds that an individual has been convicted of a felony under Federal law for conduct—

(A) relating to the development or approval, including the process for development or approval, of any drug product, or

(B) otherwise relating to the regulation of any drug product under this Act,

the Secretary shall debar such individual from providing services in any capacity to a person that has an approved or pending drug product application.

(b) PERMISSIVE DEBARMENT; CERTAIN DRUG APPLICATIONS; FOOD IMPORTS.—

(1) IN GENERAL.—The Secretary, on the Secretary's own initiative or in response to a petition, may, in accordance with paragraph (2), debar—

(A) a person other than an individual from submitting or assisting in the submission of any abbreviated drug application, or

(B) an individual from providing services in any capacity to a person that has an approved or pending drug product application, or

(C) a person from importing an article of food or offering such an article for import into the United States.

(2) PERSONS SUBJECT TO PERMISSIVE DEBARMENT; CERTAIN DRUG APPLICATIONS.— The following persons are subject to debarment under subparagraph (A) or (B) of paragraph (1):

(A) CORPORATIONS, PARTNERSHIPS, AND ASSOCIATIONS.—Any person other than an individual that the Secretary finds has been convicted—

(i) for conduct that—

(I) relates to the development or approval, including the process for the development or approval, of any abbreviated drug application; and

(II) is a felony under Federal law (if the person was convicted before the date of enactment of this section), a misdemeanor under Federal law, or a felony under State law, or

(ii) of a conspiracy to commit, or aiding or abetting, a criminal offense described in clause (i) or a felony described in subsection (a)(1), if the Secretary finds that the type of conduct which served as the basis for such conviction undermines the process for the regulation of drugs.

(B) INDIVIDUALS.—

(i) Any individual whom the Secretary finds has been convicted of—

(I) a misdemeanor under Federal law or a felony under State law for conduct relating to the development or approval, including the process for development or approval, of any drug product or otherwise relating to the regulation of drug products under this Act, or

(II) a conspiracy to commit, or aiding or abetting, such criminal offense or a felony described in subsection (a)(2),

if the Secretary finds that the type of conduct which served as the basis for such conviction undermines the process for the regulation of drugs.

(ii) Any individual whom the Secretary finds has been convicted of—

(I) a felony which is not described in subsection (a)(2) or clause (i) of this subparagraph and which involves bribery, payment of illegal gratuities, fraud, perjury, false statement, racketeering, blackmail, extortion, falsification or destruction of records, or interference with, obstruction of an investigation into, or prosecution of, any criminal offense, or

(II) a conspiracy to commit, or aiding or abetting, such felony,

if the Secretary finds, on the basis of the conviction of such individual and other information, that such individual has demonstrated a pattern of conduct sufficient to find that there is reason to believe that such individual may violate requirements under this Act relating to drug products.

(iii) Any individual whom the Secretary finds materially participated in acts that were the basis for a conviction for an offense described in subsection (a) or in clause (i) or (ii) for which a conviction was obtained, if the Secretary finds, on the basis of such participation and other information, that such individual has demonstrated a pattern of conduct sufficient to find that there is reason to believe that such individual may violate requirements under this Act relating to drug products.

(iv) Any high managerial agent whom the Secretary finds—

(I) worked for, or worked as a consultant for, the same person as another individual during the period in which such other individual took actions for which a felony conviction was obtained and which resulted in the debarment under subsection (a)(2), or clause (i), of such other individual,

(II) had actual knowledge of the actions described in subclause (I) of such other individual, or took action to avoid such actual knowledge, or failed to take action for the purpose of avoiding such actual knowledge,

(III) knew that the actions described in subclause (I) were violative of law, and

(IV) did not report such actions, or did not cause such actions to be reported, to an officer, employee, or agent of the Department or to an appropriate law enforcement officer, or failed to take other appropriate action that would have ensured that the process for the regulation of drugs was not undermined, within a reasonable time after such agent first knew of such actions,

if the Secretary finds that the type of conduct which served as the basis for such other individual's conviction undermines the process for the regulation of drugs.

(3) PERSONS SUBJECT TO PERMISSIVE DEBARMENT; FOOD IMPORTATION.—A person is subject to debarment under paragraph (1)(C) if—

(A) the person has been convicted of a felony for conduct relating to the importation into the United States of any food; or

(B) the person has engaged in a pattern of importing or offering for import adulterated food that presents a threat of serious adverse health consequences or death to humans or animals.

(4) STAY OF CERTAIN ORDERS.—An order of the Secretary under clause (iii) or (iv) of paragraph (2)(B) shall not take effect until 30 days after the order has been issued.

(c) DEBARMENT PERIODS AND CONSIDERATIONS.—

(1) EFFECT OF DEBARMENT.—The Secretary—

(A) shall not accept or review (other than in connection with an audit under this section) any abbreviated drug application submitted by or with the assistance of a person debarred under subsection (a)(1) or (b)(2)(A) during the period such person is debarred,

(B) shall, during the period of a debarment under subsection (a)(2) or (b) (2)(B), debar an individual from providing services in any capacity to a person that has an approved or pending drug product application and shall not accept or review (other than in connection with an audit under this section) an abbreviated drug application from such individual, and

(C) shall, if the Secretary makes the finding described in paragraph (6) or (7) of section 307(a), assess a civil penalty in accordance with section 307.

(2) DEBARMENT PERIODS.—

(A) IN GENERAL.—The Secretary shall debar a person under subsection (a) or (b) for the following periods:

(i) The period of debarment of a person (other than an individual) under subsection (a)(1) shall not be less than 1 year or more than 10 years, but if an act leading to a subsequent debarment under subsection (a) occurs within 10 years after such person has been debarred under subsection (a)(1), the period of debarment shall be permanent.

(ii) The debarment of an individual under subsection (a)(2) shall be permanent.

(iii) The period of debarment of any person under paragraph (2) or (3) of subsection (b) shall not be more than 5 years.

The Secretary may determine whether debarment periods shall run concurrently or consecutively in the case of a person debarred for multiple offenses.

(B) NOTIFICATION.—Upon a conviction for an offense described in subsection (a) or (b) or upon execution of an agreement with the United States to plead guilty to such an offense, the person involved may notify the Secretary that the person acquiesces to debarment and such person's debarment shall commence upon such notification.

(3) CONSIDERATIONS.—In determining the appropriateness and the period of a debarment of a person under subsection (b) and any period of debarment beyond the minimum specified in subparagraph (A)(i) of paragraph (2), the Secretary shall consider where applicable—

(A) the nature and seriousness of any offense involved,

(B) the nature and extent of management participation in any offense involved, whether corporate policies and practices encouraged the offense, including whether inadequate institutional controls contributed to the offense,

(C) the nature and extent of voluntary steps to mitigate the impact on the public of any offense involved, including the recall or the discontinuation of the distribution of suspect drugs, full cooperation with any investigations (including the extent of disclosure to appropriate authorities of all wrongdoing), the relinquishing of profits on drug approvals fraudulently obtained, and any other actions taken to substantially limit potential or actual adverse effects on the public health,

(D) whether the extent to which changes in ownership, management, or operations have corrected the causes of any offense involved and provide reasonable assurances that the offense will not occur in the future,

(E) whether the person to be debarred is able to present adequate evidence that current production of drugs subject to abbreviated drug applications and all pending abbreviated drug applications are free of fraud or material false statements, and

(F) prior convictions under this Act or under other Acts involving matters within the jurisdiction of the Food and Drug Administration.

(d) TERMINATION OF DEBARMENT.—

(1) APPLICATION.—Any person that is debarred under subsection (a) (other than a person permanently debarred) or any person that is debarred under subsection (b) of this section may apply to the Secretary for termination of the debarment under this subsection. Any information submitted to the Secretary under this paragraph does not constitute an amendment or supplement to pending or approved abbreviated drug applications.

(2) DEADLINE.—The Secretary shall grant or deny any application respecting a debarment which is submitted under paragraph (1) within 180 days of the date the application is submitted.

(3) ACTION BY THE SECRETARY.—

(A) CORPORATIONS.—

(i) CONVICTION REVERSAL.—If the conviction which served as the basis for the debarment of a person under subsection (a)(1) (b) or paragraph (2) (A) or (3) of subsection is reversed, the Secretary shall withdraw the order of debarment.

(ii) APPLICATION.—Upon application submitted under paragraph (1), the Secretary shall terminate the debarment of a person if the Secretary finds that—

(I) changes in ownership, management, or operations have fully corrected the causes of the offense involved and provide reasonable assurances that the offense will not occur in the future, and

(II) in applicable cases, sufficient audits, conducted by the Food and Drug Administration or by independent experts acceptable to the Food and Drug Administration, demonstrate that pending applications and the development of drugs being tested before the submission of an application are free of fraud or material false statements.

In the case of persons debarred under subsection (a)(1), such termination shall take effect no earlier than the expiration of one year from the date of the debarment.

(B) INDIVIDUALS.—

(i) CONVICTION REVERSAL.—If the conviction which served as the basis for the debarment of an individual under subsection (a)(2) or clause (i), (ii), (iii), or (iv) of subsection (b)(2)(B) or subsection (b)(3) is reversed, the Secretary shall withdraw the order of debarment.

(ii) APPLICATION.—Upon application submitted under paragraph (1), the Secretary shall terminate the debarment of an individual who has been debarred under subsection (b)(2)(B) or subsection (b)(3) if such termination serves the interests of justice and adequately protects the integrity of the drug approval process or the food importation process, as the case may be.

(4) SPECIAL TERMINATION.—

(A) APPLICATION.—Any person that is debarred under subsection (a)(1) (other than a person permanently debarred under subsection (c)(2)(A)(i)) or any individual who is debarred under subsection (a)(2) may apply to the Secretary for special termination of debarment under this subsection. Any information submitted to the Secretary under this subparagraph does not constitute an amendment or supplement to pending or approved abbreviated drug applications.

(B) CORPORATIONS.—Upon an application submitted under subparagraph (A), the Secretary may take the action described in subparagraph (D) if the Secretary, after an informal hearing, finds that—

(i) the person making the application under subparagraph (A) has demonstrated that the felony conviction which was the basis for such person's debarment involved the commission of an offense which was not authorized, requested, commanded, performed, or recklessly tolerated by the board of directors or by a high managerial agent acting on behalf of the person within the scope of the board's or agent's office or employment,

(ii) all individuals who were involved in the commission of the offense or who knew or should have known of the offense have been removed from employment involving the development or approval of any drug subject to sections[9] 505,

(iii) the person fully cooperated with all investigations and promptly disclosed all wrongdoing to the appropriate authorities, and

(iv) the person acted to mitigate any impact on the public of any offense involved, including the recall, or the discontinuation of the distribution, of any drug with respect to which the Secretary requested a recall or discontinuation of distribution due to concerns about the safety or efficacy of the drug.

(C) INDIVIDUALS.—Upon an application submitted under subparagraph (A), the Secretary may take the action described in subparagraph (D) if the Secretary, after an informal hearing, finds that such individual has provided substantial assistance in the investigations or prosecutions of offenses which are described in subsection (a) or (b) or which relate to any matter under the jurisdiction of the Food and Drug Administration.

(D) SECRETARIAL ACTION.—The action referred to in subparagraphs (B) and (C) is—

---

9. So in law. See Pub. L. No. 105–115, § 125(b) (2)(C), 111 Stat. 2296, 2325 (1997). Probably should be "section".

(i) in the case of a person other than an individual—

(I) terminating the debarment immediately, or

(II) limiting the period of debarment to less than one year, and

(ii) in the case of an individual, limiting the period of debarment to less than permanent but to no less than 1 year,

whichever best serves the interest of justice and protects the integrity of the drug approval process.

(e) PUBLICATION AND LIST OF DEBARRED PERSONS.—The Secretary shall publish in the Federal Register the name of any person debarred under subsection (a) or (b), the effective date of the debarment, and the period of the debarment. The Secretary shall also maintain and make available to the public a list, updated no less often than quarterly, of such persons, of the effective dates and minimum periods of such debarments, and of the termination of debarments.

(f) TEMPORARY DENIAL OF APPROVAL.—

(1) IN GENERAL.—The Secretary, on the Secretary's own initiative or in response to a petition, may, in accordance with paragraph (3), refuse by order, for the period prescribed by paragraph (2), to approve any abbreviated drug application submitted by any person—

(A) if such person is under an active Federal criminal investigation in connection with an action described in subparagraph (B),

(B) if the Secretary finds that such person—

(i) has bribed or attempted to bribe, has paid or attempted to pay an illegal gratuity, or has induced or attempted to induce another person to bribe or pay an illegal gratuity to any officer, employee, or agent of the Department of Health and Human Services or to any other Federal, State, or local official in connection with any abbreviated drug application, or has conspired to commit, or aided or abetted, such actions, or

(ii) has knowingly made or caused to be made a pattern or practice of false statements or misrepresentations with respect to material facts relating to any abbreviated drug application, or the production of any drug subject to an abbreviated drug application, to any officer, employee, or agent of the Department of Health and Human Services, or has conspired to commit, or aided or abetted, such actions, and

(C) if a significant question has been raised regarding—

(i) the integrity of the approval process with respect to such abbreviated drug application, or

(ii) the reliability of data in or concerning such person's abbreviated drug application.

Such an order may be modified or terminated at any time.

(2) APPLICABLE PERIOD.—

(A) IN GENERAL.—Except as provided in subparagraph (B), a denial of approval of an application of a person under paragraph (1) shall be in effect for a period determined by the Secretary but not to exceed 18 months beginning on the date the Secretary finds that the conditions described in subparagraphs (A), (B), and (C) of paragraph (1) exist. The Secretary shall terminate such denial—

(i) if the investigation with respect to which the finding was made does not result in a criminal charge against such person, if criminal charges have been brought and the charges have been dismissed, or if a judgment of acquittal has been entered, or

(ii) if the Secretary determines that such finding was in error.

(B) EXTENSION.—If, at the end of the period described in subparagraph (A), the Secretary determines that a person has been criminally charged for an action described in subparagraph (B) of paragraph (1), the Secretary may extend the period of denial of approval of an application for a period not to exceed 18 months. The Secretary shall terminate such extension if the charges have been dismissed, if a judgment of acquittal has been entered, or if the Secretary determines that the finding described in subparagraph (A) was in error.

(3) INFORMAL HEARING.—Within 10 days of the date an order is issued under paragraph (1), the Secretary shall provide such person with an opportunity for an informal hearing, to be held within such 10 days, on the decision of the Secretary to refuse approval of an abbreviated drug application. Within 60 days of the date on which such hearing is held, the Secretary shall notify the person given such hearing whether the Secretary's refusal of approval will be continued, terminated, or otherwise modified. Such notification shall be final agency action.

(g) SUSPENSION AUTHORITY.—

(1) IN GENERAL.—If—

(A) the Secretary finds—

(i) that a person has engaged in conduct described in subparagraph (B) of subsection (f)(1) in connection with 2 or more drugs under abbreviated drug applications, or

(ii) that a person has engaged in flagrant and repeated, material violations of good manufacturing practice or good laboratory practice in connection with the development, manufacturing, or distribution of one or more drugs approved under an abbreviated drug application during a 2–year period, and—

(I) such violations may undermine the safety and efficacy of such drugs, and

(II) the causes of such violations have not been corrected within a reasonable period of time following notice of such violations by the Secretary, and

(B) such person is under an active investigation by a Federal authority in connection with a civil or criminal action involving conduct described in subparagraph (A),

the Secretary shall issue an order suspending the distribution of all drugs the development or approval of which was related to such conduct described in subparagraph (A) or suspending the distribution of all drugs approved under abbreviated drug applications of such person if the Secretary finds that such conduct may have affected the development or approval of a significant number of drugs which the Secretary is unable to identify. The Secretary shall exclude a drug from such order if the Secretary determines that such conduct was not likely to have influenced the safety or efficacy of such drug.

(2) PUBLIC HEALTH WAIVER.—The Secretary shall, on the Secretary's own initiative or in response to a petition, waive the suspension under paragraph (1) (involving an action described in paragraph (1)(A)(i)) with respect to any drug if the Secretary finds that such waiver is necessary to protect the public health because sufficient quantities of the drug would not otherwise be available. The Secretary shall act on any petition seeking action under this paragraph within 180 days of the date the petition is submitted to the Secretary.

(h) TERMINATION OF SUSPENSION.—The Secretary shall withdraw an order of suspension of the distribution of a drug under subsection (g) if the person with respect to whom the order was issued demonstrates in a petition to the Secretary—

(1)(A) on the basis of an audit by the Food and Drug Administration or by experts acceptable to the Food and Drug Administration, or on the basis of other information, that the development, approval, manufacturing, and distribution of such drug is in substantial compliance with the applicable requirements of this Act, and

(B) changes in ownership, management, or operations—

(i) fully remedy the patterns or practices with respect to which the order was issued, and

(ii) provide reasonable assurances that such actions will not occur in the future, or

(2) the initial determination was in error.

The Secretary shall act on a submission of a petition under this subsection within 180 days of the date of its submission and the Secretary may consider the petition concurrently with the suspension proceeding. Any information submitted to the Secretary under this subsection does not constitute an amendment or supplement to a pending or approved abbreviated drug application.

(i) PROCEDURE.—The Secretary may not take any action under subsection (a), (b), (c), (d)(3), (g), or (h) with respect to any person unless the Secretary has issued an order for such action made on the record after opportunity for an agency hearing on disputed issues of material fact. In the course of any investigation or hearing under this subsection, the Secretary may administer oaths and affirmations, examine witnesses, receive evidence, and issue subpoenas requiring the attendance and testimony of witnesses and the production of evidence that relates to the matter under investigation.

(j) JUDICIAL REVIEW.—

(1) IN GENERAL.—Except as provided in paragraph (2), any person that is the subject of an adverse decision under subsection (a), (b), (c), (d), (f), (g), or (h) may obtain a review of such decision by the United States Court of Appeals for the District of Columbia or for the circuit in which the person resides, by filing in such court (within 60 days following the date the person is notified of the Secretary's decision) a petition requesting that the decision be modified or set aside.

(2) EXCEPTION.—Any person that is the subject of an adverse decision under clause (iii) or (iv) of subsection (b)(2)(B) may obtain a review of such decision by the United States District Court for the District of Columbia or a district court of the United States for the district in which the person resides, by filing in such court (within 30 days following the date the person is notified of the Secretary's decision) a complaint requesting that the decision be modified or set aside. In such an action, the court shall determine the matter de novo.

(k) CERTIFICATION.—Any application for approval of a drug product shall include—

(1) a certification that the applicant did not and will not use in any capacity the services of any person debarred under subsection (a) or (b), in connection with such application, and

(2) if such application is an abbreviated drug application, a list of all convictions, described in subsections (a) and (b) which occurred within the previous 5 years, of the applicant and affiliated persons responsible for the development or submission of such application.

(*l*) APPLICABILITY.—

(1) CONVICTION.—For purposes of this section, a person is considered to have been convicted of a criminal offense—

(A) when a judgment of conviction has been entered against the person by a Federal or State court, regardless of whether there is an appeal pending,

(B) when a plea of guilty or nolo contendere by the person has been accepted by a Federal or State court, or

(C) when the person has entered into participation in a first offender, deferred adjudication, or other similar arrangement or program where judgment of conviction has been withheld.

(2) EFFECTIVE DATES.—Subsection (a), subparagraph (A) of subsection (b)(2), and subsection (b)(3)(A) clauses (i) and (ii) of subsection (b)(2)(B) shall not apply to a conviction which occurred more than 5 years before the initiation of an agency action proposed to be taken under subsection (a) or (b). Clauses (iii) and (iv) of subsection (b)(2)(B), subsection (b)(3)(B) and subsections (f) and (g) shall not apply to an act or action which occurred more than 5 years before the initiation of an agency action proposed to be taken under subsection (b), (f), or (g). Clause (iv) of subsection (b)(2)(B) shall not apply to an action which occurred before June 1, 1992. Subsection (k) shall not apply to applications submitted to the Secretary before June 1, 1992.

(m) DEVICES; MANDATORY DEBARMENT REGARDING THIRD–PARTY INSPECTIONS AND REVIEWS.—

(1) IN GENERAL.—If the Secretary finds that a person has been convicted of a felony under section 301(gg), the Secretary shall debar such person from being accredited under section 523(b) or 704(g)(2) and from carrying out activities under an agreement described in section 803(b).

(2) DEBARMENT PERIOD.—The Secretary shall debar a person under paragraph (1) for the following periods:

(A) The period of debarment of a person (other than an individual) shall not be less than 1 year or more than 10 years, but if an act leading to a subsequent debarment under such paragraph occurs within 10 years after such person has been debarred under such paragraph, the period of debarment shall be permanent.

(B) The debarment of an individual shall be permanent.

(3) TERMINATION OF DEBARMENT; JUDICIAL REVIEW; OTHER MATTERS.—Subsections (c)(3), (d), (e), (i), (j), and (*l*)(1) apply with respect to a person (other than an individual) or an individual who is debarred under paragraph (1) to the same extent and in the same manner as such subsections apply with respect to a person who is debarred under subsection (a)(1), or an individual who is debarred under subsection (a)(2), respectively.

SEC. 307 [21 U.S.C. 335b]. CIVIL PENALTIES

(a) IN GENERAL.—Any person that the Secretary finds—

(1) knowingly made or caused to be made, to any officer, employee, or agent of the Department of Health and Human Services, a false statement or misrepresentation of a material fact in connection with an abbreviated drug application,

(2) bribed or attempted to bribe or paid or attempted to pay an illegal gratuity to any officer, employee, or agent of the Department of Health and Human Services in connection with an abbreviated drug application,

(3) destroyed, altered, removed, or secreted, or procured the destruction, alteration, removal, or secretion of, any material document or other material evidence which was the property of or in the possession of the Department of Health and Human Services for the purpose of interfering with that Department's discharge of its responsibilities in connection with an abbreviated drug application,

(4) knowingly failed to disclose, to an officer or employee of the Department of Health and Human Services, a material fact which such person had an obligation to disclose relating to any drug subject to an abbreviated drug application,

(5) knowingly obstructed an investigation of the Department of Health and Human Services into any drug subject to an abbreviated drug application,

(6) is a person that has an approved or pending drug product application and has knowingly—

(A) employed or retained as a consultant or contractor, or

(B) otherwise used in any capacity the services of, a person who was debarred under section 306, or

(7) is an individual debarred under section 306 and, during the period of debarment, provided services in any capacity to a person that had an approved or pending drug product application,

shall be liable to the United States for a civil penalty for each such violation in an amount not to exceed $250,000 in the case of an individual and $1,000,000 in the case of any other person.

(b) PROCEDURE.—

(1) IN GENERAL.—

(A) ACTION BY THE SECRETARY.—A civil penalty under subsection (a) shall be assessed by the Secretary on a person by an order made on the record after an opportunity for an agency hearing on disputed issues of material fact and the amount of the penalty. In the course of any investigation or hearing under this subparagraph, the Secretary may administer oaths and affirmations, examine witnesses, receive evidence, and issue subpoenas requiring the attendance and testimony of witnesses and the production of evidence that relates to the matter under investigation.

(B) ACTION BY THE ATTORNEY GENERAL.—In lieu of a proceeding under subparagraph (A), the Attorney General may, upon request of the Secretary, institute a civil action to recover a civil money penalty in the amount and for any of the acts set forth in subsection (a). Such an action may be instituted separately from or in connection with any other claim, civil or criminal, initiated by the Attorney General under this Act.

(2) AMOUNT.—In determining the amount of a civil penalty under paragraph (1), the Secretary or the court shall take into account the nature, circumstances, extent, and gravity of the act subject to penalty, the person's ability to pay, the effect on the person's ability to continue to do business, any history of prior, similar acts, and such other matters as justice may require.

(3) LIMITATION ON ACTIONS.—No action may be initiated under this section—

(A) with respect to any act described in subsection (a) that occurred before the date of the enactment of this section, or

(B) more than 6 years after the date when facts material to the act are known or reasonably should have been known by the Secretary but in no event more than 10 years after the date the act took place.

(c) JUDICIAL REVIEW.—Any person that is the subject of an adverse decision under subsection (b)(1)(A) may obtain a review of such decision by the United States Court of Appeals for the District of Columbia or for the circuit in which the person resides, by filing in such court (within 60 days following the date the person is notified of the Secretary's decision) a petition requesting that the decision be modified or set aside.

(d) RECOVERY OF PENALTIES.—The Attorney General may recover any civil penalty (plus interest at the currently prevailing rates from the date the penalty became final) assessed under subsection (b)(1)(A) in an action brought in the name of the United States. The amount of such penalty may be deducted, when the penalty has become final, from any sums then or later owing by the United States to the person against whom the penalty has been assessed. In an action brought under this subsection, the validity, amount, and appropriateness of the penalty shall not be subject to judicial review.

(e) INFORMANTS.—The Secretary may award to any individual (other than an officer or employee of the Federal Government or a person who materially participated in any conduct described in subsection (a)) who provides information leading to the imposition of a civil penalty under this section an amount not to exceed—

(1) $250,000, or

(2) one-half of the penalty so imposed and collected, whichever is less. The decision of the Secretary on such award shall not be reviewable.

SEC. 308 [21 U.S.C. 335c]. AUTHORITY TO WITHDRAW APPROVAL OF ABBREVIATED DRUG APPLICATIONS

(a) IN GENERAL.—The Secretary—

(1) shall withdraw approval of an abbreviated drug application if the Secretary finds that the approval was obtained, expedited, or otherwise facilitated through bribery, payment of an illegal gratuity, or fraud or material false statement, and

(2) may withdraw approval of an abbreviated drug application if the Secretary finds that the applicant has repeatedly demonstrated a lack of ability to produce

the drug for which the application was submitted in accordance with the formulations or manufacturing practice set forth in the abbreviated drug application and has introduced, or attempted to introduce, such adulterated or misbranded drug into commerce.

(b) PROCEDURE.—The Secretary may not take any action under subsection (a) with respect to any person unless the Secretary has issued an order for such action made on the record after opportunity for an agency hearing on disputed issues of material fact. In the course of any investigation or hearing under this subsection, the Secretary may administer oaths and affirmations, examine witnesses, receive evidence, and issue subpoenas requiring the attendance and testimony of witnesses and the production of evidence that relates to the matter under investigation.

(c) APPLICABILITY.—Subsection (a) shall apply with respect to offenses or acts regardless of when such offenses or acts occurred.

(d) JUDICIAL REVIEW.—Any person that is the subject of an adverse decision under subsection (a) may obtain a review of such decision by the United States Court of Appeals for the District of Columbia or for the circuit in which the person resides, by filing in such court (within 60 days following the date the person is notified of the Secretary's decision) a petition requesting that the decision be modified or set aside.

SEC. 309 [21 U.S.C. 336]. REPORT OF MINOR VIOLATIONS

Nothing in this Act shall be construed as requiring the Secretary to report for prosecution, or for the institution of libel or injunction proceedings, minor violations of this Act whenever he believes that the public interest will be adequately served by a suitable written notice or warning.

SEC. 310 [21 U.S.C. 337]. PROCEEDINGS IN NAME OF UNITED STATES; PROVISION AS TO SUBPOENAS

(a) Except as provided in subsection (b), all such proceedings for the enforcement, or to restrain violations, of this Act shall be by and in the name of the United States. Subpoenas for witnesses who are required to attend a court of the United States, in any district, may run into any other district in any proceeding under this section.

(b)(1) A State may bring in its own name and within its jurisdiction proceedings for the civil enforcement, or to restrain violations, of section 401, 403(b), 403(c), 403(d), 403(e), 403(f), 403(g), 403(h), 403(i), 403(k), 403(q), or 403(r) if the food that is the subject of the proceedings is located in the State.

(2) No proceeding may be commenced by a State under paragraph (1)—

(A) before 30 days after the State has given notice to the Secretary that the State intends to bring such proceeding,

(B) before 90 days after the State has given notice to the Secretary of such intent if the Secretary has, within such 30 days, commenced an informal or formal enforcement action pertaining to the food which would be the subject of such proceeding, or

(C) if the Secretary is diligently prosecuting a proceeding in court pertaining to such food, has settled such proceeding, or has settled the informal or formal enforcement action pertaining to such food.

In any court proceeding described in subparagraph (C), a State may intervene as a matter of right.

SEC. 311 [21 U.S.C. 337a]. EXTRATERRITORIAL JURISDICTION

There is extraterritorial jurisdiction over any violation of this Act relating to any article regulated under this Act if such article was intended for import into the United States or if any act in furtherance of the violation was committed in the United States.

CHAPTER IV—FOOD

SEC. 401 [21 U.S.C. 341]. DEFINITIONS AND STANDARDS FOR FOOD

Whenever in the judgment of the Secretary such action will promote honesty and fair dealing in the interest of consumers, he shall promulgate regulations fixing and establishing for any food, under its common or usual name so far as practicable, a reasonable definition and standard of identity, a reasonable standard of quality, or reasonable standards of fill of container. No definition and standard of identity and no standard of quality shall be established for fresh or dried fruits, fresh or dried vegetables, or butter, except that definitions and standards of identity may be established for avocados, cantaloupes, citrus fruits, and melons. In prescribing any standard of fill of container, the Secretary shall give due consideration to the natural shrinkage in storage and in transit of fresh natural food and to need for the necessary packing and protective material. In the prescribing of any standard of quality for any canned fruit or canned vegetable, consideration shall be given and due allowance made for the differing characteristics of the several varieties of such fruit or vegetable. In prescribing a definition and standard of identity for any food or class of food in which optional ingredients are permitted, the Secretary shall, for the purpose of promoting honesty and fair dealing in the interest of consumers, designate the optional ingredients which shall be named on the label. Any definition and standard of identity prescribed by the Secretary for avocados, cantaloupes, citrus fruits, or melons shall relate only to maturity and to the effects of freezing.

SEC. 402 [21 U.S.C. 342]. ADULTERATED FOOD

A food shall be deemed to be adulterated—

(a)(1) If it bears or contains any poisonous or deleterious substance which may render it injurious to health; but in case the substance is not an added substance such food shall not be considered adulterated under this clause if the quantity of such substance in such food does not ordinarily render it injurious to health;[10]

(2)(A) if it bears or contains any added poisonous or added deleterious substance (other than a substance that is a pesticide chemical residue in or on a raw agricultural commodity or processed food, a food additive, a color additive, or a new animal drug) that is unsafe within the meaning of section 406; or (B) if it bears or contains a pesticide chemical residue that is unsafe within the meaning of section 408(a); or (C) if it is or if it bears or contains (i) any food additive that is unsafe within the meaning of section 409; or (ii) a new animal drug (or conversion product thereof) that is unsafe within the meaning of section 512; or

(3) if it consists in whole or in part of any filthy, putrid, or decomposed substance, or if it is otherwise unfit for food; or

(4) if it has been prepared, packed, or held under insanitary conditions whereby it may have become contaminated with filth, or whereby it may have been rendered injurious to health; or

(5) if it is, in whole or in part, the product of a diseased animal or of an animal which has died otherwise than by slaughter; or

(6) if its container is composed, in whole or in part, of any poisonous or deleterious substance which may render the contents injurious to health; or

(7) if it has been intentionally subjected to radiation, unless the use of the radiation was in conformity with a regulation or exemption in effect pursuant to section 409.

(b)(1) If any valuable constituent has been in whole or in part omitted or abstracted therefrom; or (2) if any substance has been substituted wholly or in part therefore; or (3) if damage or inferiority has been concealed in any manner; or (4) if any substance has been added thereto or mixed or packed therewith so as to increase its bulk or weight, or reduce its quality or strength, or make it appear better or of greater value than it is.

(c) If it is, or it bears or contains, a color additive which is unsafe within the meaning of section 721(a).

(d) If it is confectionery, and—

(1) has partially or completely imbedded therein any nonnutritive object, except that this subparagraph shall not apply in the case of any nonnutritive object if, in the judgment of the Secretary as provided by regulations, such object is of practical functional value to the confectionery product and would not render the product injurious or hazardous to health;

---

10. So in law. See Pub. L. No. 103–80, § 3(i)   "or".
(1), 107 Stat. 773, 776 (1993). Probably should be

(2) bears or contains any alcohol other than alcohol not in excess of one-half of 1 per centum by volume derived solely from the use of flavoring extracts, except that this clause shall not apply to confectionery which is introduced or delivered for introduction into, or received or held for sale in, interstate commerce if the sale of such confectionery is permitted under the laws of the State in which such confectionery is intended to be offered for sale; or

(3) bears or contains any nonnutritive substance, except that this subparagraph shall not apply to a safe nonnutritive substance which is in or on confectionery by reason of its use for some practical functional purpose in the manufacture, packaging, or storage of such confectionery if the use of the substance does not promote deception of the consumer or otherwise result in adulteration or misbranding in violation of any provision of this Act, except that the Secretary may, for the purpose of avoiding or resolving uncertainty as to the application of this subparagraph, issue regulations allowing or prohibiting the use of particular nonnutritive substances.

(e) If it is oleomargarine or margarine or butter and any of the raw material used therein consisted in whole or in part of any filthy, putrid, or decomposed substance, or such oleomargarine or margarine or butter is otherwise unfit for food.

(f)(1) If it is a dietary supplement or contains a dietary ingredient that—

(A) presents a significant or unreasonable risk of illness or injury under—

(i) conditions of use recommended or suggested in labeling, or

(ii) if no conditions of use are suggested or recommended in the labeling, under ordinary conditions of use;

(B) is a new dietary ingredient for which there is inadequate information to provide reasonable assurance that such ingredient does not present a significant or unreasonable risk of illness or injury;

(C) the Secretary declares to pose an imminent hazard to public health or safety, except that the authority to make such declaration shall not be delegated and the Secretary shall promptly after such a declaration initiate a proceeding in accordance with sections 554 and 556 of title 5, United States Code, to affirm or withdraw the declaration; or

(D) is or contains a dietary ingredient that renders it adulterated under paragraph (a)(1) under the conditions of use recommended or suggested in the labeling of such dietary supplement.

In any proceeding under this subparagraph, the United States shall bear the burden of proof on each element to show that a dietary supplement is adulterated. The court shall decide any issue under this paragraph on a de novo basis.

(2) Before the Secretary may report to a United States attorney a violation of paragraph (1)(A) for a civil proceeding, the person against whom such proceeding would be initiated shall be given appropriate notice and the opportunity to present

views, orally and in writing, at least 10 days before such notice, with regard to such proceeding.

(g)(1) If it is a dietary supplement and it has been prepared, packed, or held under conditions that do not meet current good manufacturing practice regulations, including regulations requiring, when necessary, expiration date labeling, issued by the Secretary under subparagraph (2).

(2) The Secretary may by regulation prescribe good manufacturing practices for dietary supplements. Such regulations shall be modeled after current good manufacturing practice regulations for food and may not impose standards for which there is no current and generally available analytical methodology. No standard of current good manufacturing practice may be imposed unless such standard is included in a regulation promulgated after notice and opportunity for comment in accordance with chapter 5 of title 5, United States Code.

(h) If it is an article of food imported or offered for import into the United States and the article of food has previously been refused admission under section 801(a), unless the person reoffering the article affirmatively establishes, at the expense of the owner or consignee of the article, that the article complies with the applicable requirements of this Act, as determined by the Secretary.

(i) If it is transported or offered for transport by a shipper, carrier by motor vehicle or rail vehicle, receiver, or any other person engaged in the transportation of food under conditions that are not in compliance with regulations promulgated under section 416.

SEC. 403 [21 U.S.C. 343]. MISBRANDED FOOD

A food shall be deemed to be misbranded—

(a) If (1) its labeling is false or misleading in any particular, or (2) in the case of a food to which section 411 applies, its advertising is false or misleading in a material respect or its labeling is in violation of section 411(b)(2).

(b) If it is offered for sale under the name of another food.

(c) If it is an imitation of another food, unless its label bears, in type of uniform size and prominence, the word "imitation" and, immediately thereafter, the name of the food imitated.

(d) If its container is so made, formed, or filled as to be misleading.

(e) If in package form unless it bears a label containing (1) the name and place of business of the manufacturer, packer, or distributor; and (2) an accurate statement of the quantity of the contents in terms of weight, measure, or numerical count, except that under clause (2) of this paragraph reasonable variations shall be permitted, and exemptions as to small packages shall be established, by regulations prescribed by the Secretary.

(f) If any word, statement, or other information required by or under authority of this Act to appear on the label or labeling is not prominently placed thereon with such conspicuousness (as compared with other words, statements, designs, or devices, in the labeling) and in such terms as to render it likely to be read and understood by the ordinary individual under customary conditions of purchase and use.

(g) If it purports to be or is represented as a food for which a definition and standard of identity has been prescribed by regulations as provided by section 401, unless (1) it conforms to such definition and standard, and (2) its label bears the name of the food specified in the definition and standard, and, insofar as may be required by such regulations, the common names of optional ingredients (other than spices, flavoring, and coloring) present in such food.

(h) If it purports to be or is represented as—

(1) a food for which a standard of quality has been prescribed by regulations as provided by section 401, and its quality falls below such standard, unless its label bears, in such manner and form as such regulations specify, a statement that it falls below such standard; or

(2) a food for which a standard or standards of fill of container have been prescribed by regulations as provided by section 401, and it falls below the standard of fill of container applicable thereto, unless its label bears, in such manner and form as such regulations specify, a statement that it falls below such standard.

(3) a food that is pasteurized unless—

(A) such food has been subjected to a safe process or treatment that is prescribed as pasteurization for such food in a regulation promulgated under this Act; or

(B)(i) such food has been subjected to a safe process or treatment that—

(I) is reasonably certain to achieve destruction or elimination in the food of the most resistant microorganisms of public health significance that are likely to occur in the food;

(II) is at least as protective of the public health as a process or treatment described in subparagraph (A);

(III) is effective for a period that is at least as long as the shelf life of the food when stored under normal and moderate abuse conditions; and

(IV) is the subject of a notification to the Secretary, including effectiveness data regarding the process or treatment; and

(ii) at least 120 days have passed after the date of receipt of such notification by the Secretary without the Secretary making a determination that the process or treatment involved has not been shown to meet the requirements of subclauses (I) through (III) of clause (i).[11]

For purposes of paragraph (3), a determination by the Secretary that a process or treatment has not been shown to meet the requirements of subclauses (I) through (III) of subparagraph (B)(i) shall constitute final agency action under such subclauses.

(i) Unless its label bears (1) the common or usual name of the food, if any there be, and (2) in case it is fabricated from two or more ingredients, the common or usual name of each such ingredient and if the food purports to be a beverage containing vegetable or fruit juice, a statement with appropriate prominence on the information panel of the total percentage of such fruit or vegetable juice contained in the food; except that spices, flavorings, and colors not required to be certified under section 721(c)[12] unless sold as spices, flavorings, or such colors, may be designated as spices, flavorings, and colorings without naming each. To the extent that compliance with the requirements of clause (2) of this paragraph is impracticable, or results in deception or unfair competition, exemptions shall be established by regulations promulgated by the Secretary.

(j) If it purports to be or is represented for special dietary uses, unless its label bears such information concerning its vitamin, mineral, and other dietary properties as the Secretary determines to be, and by regulations prescribes as, necessary in order fully to inform purchasers as to its value for such uses.

(k) If it bears or contains any artificial flavoring, artificial coloring, or chemical preservative, unless it bears labeling stating that fact, except that to the extent that compliance with the requirements of this paragraph is impracticable, exemptions shall be established by regulations promulgated by the Secretary. The provisions of this paragraph and paragraphs (g) and (i) with respect to artificial coloring shall not apply in the case of butter, cheese, or ice cream. The provisions of this paragraph

11. References are so in law. See Pub. L. No. 107–171, § 10808(b)(3), 116 Stat. 134, 530 (2002). In order to be consistent with other cross-references within section 403 above, each reference in section 403(h)(3) to a paragraph, subparagraph, clause, or subclause should be a reference to a subparagraph, clause, subclause, or item, respectively. See, for example, cross-references in paragraph (q) (relating to nutrition information) and paragraph (r) (relating to nutrient levels and health claims).

Section 403 was enacted in 1938 and has organizational units and cross-references that are not in accordance with modern practice. In modern practice, "(a)" is a subsection, "(1)" is a paragraph, "(A)" is a subparagraph, "(i)" is a clause, "(I)" is a subclause, "(aa)" is an item, and "(AA)" is a subitem. The references in section 403(h)(3) follow this practice.

In modern practice, all of the section 403 text would be considered an undesignated subsection, and the list that begins after "A food shall be deemed to be misbranded—" would consist of paragraphs (1), (2), etc.

In section 403, however, the original authors of the 1938 Act used a list consisting of (a), (b), etc., and the authors referred to "(a)" as a paragraph, "(1)" as a subparagraph, "(A)" as a clause, and "(i)" as a subclause. (Express references to organizational units below the "(i)" level have been avoided.)

The original authors followed this approach in each section in this Act whose text was a list consisting of (a), (b), etc. Such sections include sections 201, 301, 402, 403, 501, 502, 601, and 602.

Some of these sections have numerous internal cross-references. Rather than conforming each of these to the modern practice, the usual approach in making amendments to these sections has been to follow the approach used by the original authors of the 1938 Act.

12. So in law. Probably should be followed by a comma.

with respect to chemical preservatives shall not apply to a pesticide chemical when used in or on a raw agricultural commodity which is the produce of the soil.

(*l*) If it is a raw agricultural commodity which is the produce of the soil, bearing or containing a pesticide chemical applied after harvest, unless the shipping container of such commodity bears labeling which declares the presence of such chemical in or on such commodity and the common or usual name and the function of such chemical, except that no such declaration shall be required while such commodity, having been removed from the shipping container, is being held or is played for sale at retail out of such container in accordance with the custom of the trade.

(m) If it is a color additive, unless its packaging and labeling are in conformity with such packaging and labeling requirements, applicable to such color additive, as may be contained in regulations issued under section 721.

(n) If its packaging or labeling is in violation of an applicable regulation issued pursuant to section 3 or 4 of the Poison Prevention Packaging Act of 1970.

[(*o*) Repealed by Pub. L. No. 106–554, app. A, § 517, 114 Stat. 2763, 2763A–73 (2000).]

[(p) Repealed by Pub. L. No. 104–124, § 1, 110 Stat. 882, 882 (1996).]

(q)(1) Except as provided in subparagraphs (3), (4), and (5), if it is a food intended for human consumption and is offered for sale, unless its label or labeling bears nutrition information that provides—

(A)(i) the serving size which is an amount customarily consumed and which is expressed in a common household measure that is appropriate to the food, or

(ii) if the use of the food is not typically expressed in a serving size, the common household unit of measure that expresses the serving size of the food,

(B) the number of servings or other units of measure per container,

(C) the total number of calories—

(i) derived from any source, and

(ii) derived from the total fat,

in each serving size or other unit of measure of the food,

(D) the amount of the following nutrients: Total fat, saturated fat, cholesterol, sodium, total carbohydrates, complex carbohydrates, sugars, dietary fiber, and total protein contained in each serving size or other unit of measure,

(E) any vitamin, mineral, or other nutrient required to be placed on the label and labeling of food under this Act before October 1, 1990, if the Secretary determines that such information will assist consumers in maintaining healthy dietary practices.

The Secretary may by regulation require any information required to be placed on the label or labeling by this subparagraph or subparagraph (2)(A) to be highlighted on the label or labeling by larger type, bold type, or contrasting color if the Secretary determines that such highlighting will assist consumers in maintaining healthy dietary practices.

(2)(A) If the Secretary determines that a nutrient other than a nutrient required by subparagraph (1)(C), (1)(D), or (1)(E) should be included in the label or labeling of food subject to subparagraph (1) for purposes of providing information regarding the nutritional value of such food that will assist consumers in maintaining healthy dietary practices, the Secretary may by regulation require that information relating to such additional nutrient be included in the label or labeling of such food.

(B) If the Secretary determines that the information relating to a nutrient required by subparagraph (1)(C), (1)(D), or (1)(E) or clause (A) of this subparagraph to be included in the label or labeling of food is not necessary to assist consumers in maintaining healthy dietary practices, the Secretary may by regulation remove information relating to such nutrient from such requirement.

(3) For food that is received in bulk containers at a retail establishment, the Secretary may, by regulation, provide that the nutrition information required by subparagraphs (1) and (2) be displayed at the location in the retail establishment at which the food is offered for sale.

(4)(A) The Secretary shall provide for furnishing the nutrition information required by subparagraphs (1) and (2) with respect to raw agricultural commodities and raw fish by issuing voluntary nutrition guidelines, as provided by clause (B) or by issuing regulations that are mandatory as provided by clause (D).

(B)(i) Upon the expiration of 12 months after the date of the enactment of the Nutrition Labeling and Education Act of 1990, the Secretary, after providing an opportunity for comment, shall issue guidelines for food retailers offering raw agricultural commodities or raw fish to provide nutrition information specified in subparagraphs (1) and (2). Such guidelines shall take into account the actions taken by food retailers during such 12–month period to provide to consumers nutrition information on raw agricultural commodities and raw fish. Such guidelines shall only apply—

(I) in the case of raw agricultural commodities, to the 20 varieties of vegetables most frequently consumed during a year and the 20 varieties of fruit most frequently consumed during a year, and

(II) to the 20 varieties of raw fish most frequently consumed during a year.

The vegetables, fruits, and raw fish to which such guidelines apply shall be determined by the Secretary by regulation and the Secretary may apply such guidelines regionally.

(ii) Upon the expiration of 12 months after the date of the enactment of the Nutrition Labeling and Education Act of 1990, the Secretary shall issue a final regulation defining the circumstances that constitute substantial compliance by food retailers with the guidelines issued under subclause (i). The regulation shall provide that there is not substantial compliance if a significant number of retailers have failed to comply with the guidelines. The size of the retailers and the portion of the market served by retailers in compliance with the guidelines shall be considered in determining whether the substantial-compliance standard has been met.

(C)(i) Upon the expiration of 30 months after the date of the enactment of the Nutrition Labeling and Education Act of 1990, the Secretary shall issue a report on actions taken by food retailers to provide consumers with nutrition information for raw agricultural commodities and raw fish under the guidelines issued under clause (A). Such report shall include a determination of whether there is substantial compliance with the guidelines.

(ii) If the Secretary finds that there is substantial compliance with the guidelines, the Secretary shall issue a report and make a determination of the type required in subclause (i) every two years.

(D)(i) If the Secretary determines that there is not substantial compliance with the guidelines issued under clause (A), the Secretary shall at the time such determination is made issue proposed regulations requiring that any person who offers raw agricultural commodities or raw fish to consumers provide, in a manner prescribed by regulations, the nutrition information required by subparagraphs (1) and (2). The Secretary shall issue final regulations imposing such requirements 6 months after issuing the proposed regulations. The final regulations shall become effective 6 months after the date of their promulgation.

(ii) Regulations issued under subclause (i) may require that the nutrition information required by subparagraphs (1) and (2) be provided for more than 20 varieties of vegetables, 20 varieties of fruit, and 20 varieties of fish most frequently consumed during a year if the Secretary finds that a larger number of such products are frequently consumed. Such regulations shall permit such information to be provided in a single location in each area in which raw agricultural commodities and raw fish are offered for sale. Such regulations may provide that information shall be expressed as an average or range per serving of the same type of raw agricultural commodity or raw fish. The Secretary shall develop and make available to the persons who offer such food to consumers the information required by subparagraphs (1) and (2).

(iii) Regulations issued under subclause (i) shall permit the required information to be provided in each area of an establishment in which raw agricultural commodities and raw fish are offered for sale. The regulations shall permit food retailers to display the required information by supplying copies of the information provided by the Secretary, by making the information available in brochure, notebook or leaflet form, or by posting a sign disclosing the information. Such regulations shall also permit presentation of the required information to be supplemented by a video, live demonstration, or other media which the Secretary approves.

(E) For purposes of this subparagraph, the term "fish" includes freshwater or marine fin fish, crustaceans, and mollusks, including shellfish, amphibians, and other forms of aquatic animal life.

(F) No person who offers raw agricultural commodities or raw fish to consumers may be prosecuted for minor violations of this subparagraph if there has been substantial compliance with the requirements of this paragraph.

(5)(A) Subparagraphs (1), (2), (3), and (4) shall not apply to food—

(i) except as provided in clause (H)(ii)(III), which is served in restaurants or other establishments in which food is served for immediate human consumption or which is sold for sale or use in such establishments,

(ii) except as provided in clause (H)(ii)(III), which is processed and prepared primarily in a retail establishment, which is ready for human consumption, which is of the type described in subclause (i), and which is offered for sale to consumers but not for immediate human consumption in such establishment and which is not offered for sale outside such establishment,

(iii) which is an infant formula subject to section 412,

(iv) which is a medical food as defined in section 5(b) of the Orphan Drug Act (21 U.S.C. 360ee(b)), or

(v) which is described in section 405(2).

(B) Subparagraphs (1) and (2) shall not apply to the label of a food if the Secretary determines by regulations that compliance with such subparagraphs is impracticable because the package of such food is too small to comply with the requirements of such subparagraphs and if the label of such food does not contain any nutrition information.

(C) If a food contains insignificant amounts, as determined by the Secretary, of all the nutrients required by subparagraphs (1) and (2) to be listed in the label or labeling of food, the requirements of such subparagraphs shall not apply to such food if the label, labeling, or advertising of such food does not make any claim with respect to the nutritional value of such food. If a food contains insignificant amounts, as determined by the Secretary, of more than one-half the nutrients required by subparagraphs (1) and (2) to be in the label or labeling of the food, the Secretary shall require the amounts of such nutrients to be stated in a simplified form prescribed by the Secretary.

(D) If a person offers food for sale and has annual gross sales made or business done in sales to consumers which is not more than $500,000 or has annual gross sales made or business done in sales of food to consumers which is not more than $50,000, the requirements of subparagraphs (1), (2), (3), and (4) shall not apply with respect to food sold by such person to consumers unless the label or labeling of food offered by such person provides nutrition information or makes a nutrition claim.

(E)(i) During the 12–month period for which an exemption from subparagraphs (1) and (2) is claimed pursuant to this subclause, the requirements of such subparagraphs shall not apply to any food product if—

(I) the labeling for such product does not provide nutrition information or make a claim subject to paragraph (r),

(II) the person who claims for such product an exemption from such subparagraphs employed fewer than an average of 100 full-time equivalent employees,

(III) such person provided the notice described in subclause (iii), and

(IV) in the case of a food product which was sold in the 12–month period preceding the period for which an exemption was claimed, fewer than 100,000 units of such product were sold in the United States during such preceding period, or in the case of a food product which was not sold in the 12–month period preceding the period for which such exemption is claimed, fewer than 100,000 units of such product are reasonably anticipated to be sold in the United States during the period for which such exemption is claimed.

(ii) During the 12–month period after the applicable date referred to in this sentence, the requirements of subparagraphs (1) and (2) shall not apply to any food product which was first introduced into interstate commerce before May 8, 1994, if the labeling for such product does not provide nutrition information or make a claim subject to paragraph (r), if such person provided the notice described in subclause (iii), and if—

(I) during the 12–month period preceding May 8, 1994, the person who claims for such product an exemption from such subparagraphs employed fewer than an average of 300 fulltime equivalent employees and fewer than 600,000 units of such product were sold in the United States,

(II) during the 12–month period preceding May 8, 1995, the person who claims for such product an exemption from such subparagraphs employed fewer than an average of 300 fulltime equivalent employees and fewer than 400,000 units of such product were sold in the United States, or

(III) during the 12–month period preceding May 8, 1996, the person who claims for such product an exemption from such subparagraphs employed fewer than an average of 200 full-time equivalent employees and fewer than 200,000 units of such product were sold in the United States.

(iii) The notice referred to in subclauses (i) and (ii) shall be given to the Secretary prior to the beginning of the period during which the exemption under subclause (i) or (ii) is to be in effect, shall state that the person claiming such exemption for a food product has complied with the applicable requirements of subclause (i) or (ii), and shall—

(I) state the average number of full-time equivalent employees such person employed during the 12 months preceding the date such person claims such exemption,

(II) state the approximate number of units the person claiming the exemption sold in the United States,

(III) if the exemption is claimed for a food product which was sold in the 12–month period preceding the period for which the exemption was claimed, state the approximate number of units of such product which were sold in the United States during such preceding period, and, if the exemption is claimed for a food product which was not sold in such preceding period, state the number of units of such product which such person reasonably anticipates will be sold in the United States during the period for which the exemption was claimed, and

(IV) contain such information as the Secretary may require to verify the information required by the preceding provisions of this subclause if the Secretary has questioned the validity of such information.

If a person is not an importer, has fewer than 10 full-time equivalent employees, and sells fewer than 10,000 units of any food product in any year, such person is not required to file a notice for such product under this subclause for such year.

(iv) In the case of a person who claimed an exemption under subclause (i) or (ii), if, during the period of such exemption, the number of full-time equivalent employees of such person exceeds the number in such subclause or if the number of food products sold in the United States exceeds the number in such subclause, such exemption shall extend to the expiration of 18 months after the date the number of full-time equivalent employees or food products sold exceeded the applicable number.

(v) For any food product first introduced into interstate commerce after May 8, 2002, the Secretary may by regulation lower the employee or units of food products requirement of subclause (i) if the Secretary determines that the cost of compliance with such lower requirement will not place an undue burden on persons subject to such lower requirement.

(vi) For purposes of subclauses (i), (ii), (iii), (iv), and (v)—

(I) the term "unit" means the packaging or, if there is no packaging, the form in which a food product is offered for sale to consumers,

(II) the term "food product" means food in any sized package which is manufactured by a single manufacturer or which bears the same brand name, which bears the same statement of identity, and which has similar preparation methods, and

(III) the term "person" in the case of a corporation includes all domestic and foreign affiliates of the corporation.

(F) A dietary supplement product (including a food to which section 411 applies) shall comply with the requirements of subparagraphs (1) and (2) in a manner which is appropriate for the product and which is specified in regulations of the Secretary which shall provide that—

(i) nutrition information shall first list those dietary ingredients that are present in the product in a significant amount and for which a recommendation for daily consumption has been established by the Secretary, except that a dietary ingredient shall not be required to be listed if it is not present in a significant amount, and shall list any other dietary ingredient present and identified as having no such recommendation;

(ii) the listing of dietary ingredients shall include the quantity of each such ingredient (or of a proprietary blend of such ingredients) per serving;

(iii) the listing of dietary ingredients may include the source of a dietary ingredient; and

(iv) the nutrition information shall immediately precede the ingredient information required under subclause (i), except that no ingredient identified pursuant to subclause (i) shall be required to be identified a second time.

(G) Subparagraphs (1), (2), (3), and (4) shall not apply to food which is sold by a food distributor if the food distributor principally sells food to restaurants or other establishments in which food is served for immediate human consumption and does not manufacture, process, or repackage the food it sells.

(H) Restaurants, Retail Food Establishments, And Vending Machines.—

(i) General requirements for restaurants and similar retail food establishments.—Except for food described in subclause (vii), in the case of food that is a standard menu item that is offered for sale in a restaurant or similar retail food establishment that is part of a chain with 20 or more locations doing business under the same name (regardless of the type of ownership of the locations) and offering for sale substantially the same menu items, the restaurant or similar retail food establishment shall disclose the information described in subclauses (ii) and (iii).

(ii) Information required to be disclosed by restaurants and retail food establishments.—Except as provided in subclause (vii), the restaurant or similar retail food establishment shall disclose in a clear and conspicuous manner—

(I)(aa) in a nutrient content disclosure statement adjacent to the name of the standard menu item, so as to be clearly associated with the standard menu item, on the menu listing the item for sale, the number of calories contained in the standard menu item, as usually prepared and offered for sale; and

(bb) a succinct statement concerning suggested daily caloric intake, as specified by the Secretary by regulation and posted prominently on the menu and designed to enable the public to understand, in the context of a total daily diet, the significance of the caloric information that is provided on the menu;

(II)(aa) in a nutrient content disclosure statement adjacent to the name of the standard menu item, so as to be clearly associated with the standard menu item, on the menu board, including a drive-through menu board, the number of calories contained in the standard menu item, as usually prepared and offered for sale; and

(bb) a succinct statement concerning suggested daily caloric intake, as specified by the Secretary by regulation and posted prominently on the menu board, designed to enable the public to understand, in the context of a total daily diet, the significance of the nutrition information that is provided on the menu board;

(III) in a written form, available on the premises of the restaurant or similar retail establishment and to the consumer upon request, the nutrition information required under clauses (C) and (D) of subparagraph (1); and

(IV) on the menu or menu board, a prominent, clear, and conspicuous statement regarding the availability of the information described in item (III).

(iii) SELF-SERVICE FOOD AND FOOD ON DISPLAY.—Except as provided in subclause (vii), in the case of food sold at a salad bar, buffet line, cafeteria line, or similar self-service facility, and for self-service beverages or food that is on display and that is visible to customers, a restaurant or similar retail food establishment shall place adjacent to each food offered a sign that lists calories per displayed food item or per serving.

(iv) REASONABLE BASIS.—For the purposes of this clause, a restaurant or similar retail food establishment shall have a reasonable basis for its nutrient content disclosures, including nutrient databases, cookbooks, laboratory analyses, and other reasonable means, as described in section 101.10 of title 21, Code of Federal Regulations (or any successor regulation) or in a related guidance of the Food and Drug Administration.

(v) MENU VARIABILITY AND COMBINATION MEALS.—The Secretary shall establish by regulation standards for determining and disclosing the nutrient content for standard menu items that come in different flavors, varieties, or combinations, but which are listed as a single menu item, such as soft drinks, ice cream, pizza, doughnuts, or children's combination meals, through means determined by the Secretary, including ranges, averages, or other methods.

(vi) ADDITIONAL INFORMATION.—If the Secretary determines that a nutrient, other than a nutrient required under subclause (ii)(III), should be disclosed for the purpose of providing information to assist consumers in maintaining healthy dietary practices, the Secretary may require, by regulation, disclosure of such nutrient in the written form required under subclause (ii)(III).

(vii) NONAPPLICABILITY TO CERTAIN FOOD.—

(I) IN GENERAL.—Subclauses (i) through (vi) do not apply to—

(aa) items that are not listed on a menu or menu board (such as condiments and other items placed on the table or counter for general use);

(bb) daily specials, temporary menu items appearing on the menu for less than 60 days per calendar year, or custom orders; or

(cc) such other food that is part of a customary market test appearing on the menu for less than 90 days, under terms and conditions established by the Secretary.

(II) WRITTEN FORMS.—Subparagraph (5)(C) shall apply to any regulations promulgated under subclauses (ii)(III) and (vi).

(viii) VENDING MACHINES.—

(I) IN GENERAL.—In the case of an article of food sold from a vending machine that—

(aa) does not permit a prospective purchaser to examine the Nutrition Facts Panel before purchasing the article or does not otherwise provide visible nutrition information at the point of purchase; and

(bb) is operated by a person who is engaged in the business of owning or operating 20 or more vending machines,

the vending machine operator shall provide a sign in close proximity to each article of food or the selection button that includes a clear and conspicuous statement disclosing the number of calories contained in the article.

(ix) VOLUNTARY PROVISION OF NUTRITION INFORMATION.—

(I) IN GENERAL.—An authorized official of any restaurant or similar retail food establishment or vending machine operator not subject to the requirements of this clause may elect to be subject to the requirements of such clause, by registering biannually the name and address of such restaurant or similar retail food establishment or vending machine operator with the Secretary, as specified by the Secretary by regulation.

(II) REGISTRATION.—Within 120 days of enactment of this clause, the Secretary shall publish a notice in the Federal Register specifying the terms and conditions for implementation of item (I), pending promulgation of regulations.

(III) RULE OF CONSTRUCTION.—Nothing in this subclause shall be construed to authorize the Secretary to require an application, review, or licensing process for any entity to register with the Secretary, as described in such item.

(x) REGULATIONS.—

(I) PROPOSED REGULATION.—Not later than 1 year after the date of enactment of this clause, the Secretary shall promulgate proposed regulations to carry out this clause.

(II) CONTENTS.—In promulgating regulations, the Secretary shall—

(aa) consider standardization of recipes and methods of preparation, reasonable variation in serving size and formulation of menu items, space on menus and menu boards, inadvertent human error, training of food service workers, variations in ingredients, and other factors, as the Secretary determines; and

(bb) specify the format and manner of the nutrient content disclosure requirements under this subclause.

(III) REPORTING.—The Secretary shall submit to the Committee on Health, Education, Labor, and Pensions of the Senate and the Committee on Energy and Commerce of the House of Representatives a quarterly report that describes the Secretary's progress toward promulgating final regulations under this subparagraph.

(xi) DEFINITION.—In this clause, the term "menu" or "menu board" means the primary writing of the restaurant or other similar retail food establishment from which a consumer makes an order selection.

(r)(1) Except as provided in clauses (A) through (C) of subparagraph (5), if it is a food intended for human consumption which is offered for sale and for which a claim is made in the label or labeling of the food which expressly or by implication—

(A) characterizes the level of any nutrient which is of the type required by paragraph (q)(1) or (q)(2) to be in the label or labeling of the food unless the claim is made in accordance with subparagraph (2), or

(B) characterizes the relationship of any nutrient which is of the type required by paragraph (q)(1) or (q)(2) to be in the label or labeling of the food to a disease or a health-related condition unless the claim is made in accordance with subparagraph (3) or (5)(D).

A statement of the type required by paragraph (q) that appears as part of the nutrition information required or permitted by such paragraph is not a claim which is subject to this paragraph and a claim subject to clause (A) is not subject to clause (B).

(2)(A) Except as provided in subparagraphs (4)(A)(ii) and (4)(A)(iii) and clauses (A) through (C) of subparagraph (5), a claim described in subparagraph (1)(A)—

(i) may be made only if the characterization of the level made in the claim uses terms which are defined in regulations of the Secretary,

(ii) may not state the absence of a nutrient unless—

(I) the nutrient is usually present in the food or in a food which substitutes for the food as defined by the Secretary by regulation, or

(II) the Secretary by regulation permits such a statement on the basis of a finding that such a statement would assist consumers in maintaining healthy dietary practices and the statement discloses that the nutrient is not usually present in the food,

(iii) may not be made with respect to the level of cholesterol in the food if the food contains, as determined by the Secretary by regulation, fat or saturated fat in an amount which increases to persons in the general population the risk of disease or a health related condition which is diet related unless—

(I) the Secretary finds by regulation that the level of cholesterol is substantially less than the level usually present in the food or in a food which substitutes for the food and which has a significant market share, or the Secretary by regulation permits a statement regarding the absence of cholesterol on the basis of a finding that cholesterol is not usually present in the food and that such a statement would assist consumers in maintaining healthy dietary practices and a requirement that the statement disclose that cholesterol is not usually present in the food, and

(II) the label or labeling of the food discloses the level of such fat or saturated fat in immediate proximity to such claim and with appropriate prominence which shall be no less than one-half the size of the claim with respect to the level of cholesterol,

(iv) may not be made with respect to the level of saturated fat in the food if the food contains cholesterol unless the label or labeling of the food discloses the level of cholesterol in the food in immediate proximity to such claim and with appropriate prominence which shall be no less than one-half the size of the claim with respect to the level of saturated fat,

(v) may not state that a food is high in dietary fiber unless the food is low in total fat as defined by the Secretary or the label or labeling discloses the level of total fat in the food in immediate proximity to such statement and with appropriate prominence which shall be no less than one-half the size of the claim with respect to the level of dietary fiber, and

(vi) may not be made if the Secretary by regulation prohibits the claim because the claim is misleading in light of the level of another nutrient in the food.

(B) If a claim described in subparagraph (1)(A) is made with respect to a nutrient in a food and the Secretary makes a determination that the food contains a nutrient at a level that increases to persons in the general population the risk of a disease or health related condition that is diet related, the label or labeling of such food shall contain, prominently and in immediate proximity to such claim, the following statement: "See nutrition information for _____ content." The blank shall identify the nutrient associated with the increased disease or health-related condition risk. In making the determination described in this clause, the Secretary shall take into account the significance of the food in the total daily diet.

(C) Subparagraph (2)(A) does not apply to a claim described in subparagraph (1)(A) and contained in the label or labeling of a food if such claim is contained in the brand name of such food and such brand name was in use on such food before October 25, 1989, unless the brand name contains a term defined by the Secretary under subparagraph (2)(A)(i). Such a claim is subject to paragraph (a).

(D) Subparagraph (2) does not apply to a claim described in subparagraph (1)(A) which uses the term "diet" and is contained in the label or labeling of a soft drink if (i) such claim is contained in the brand name of such soft drink, (ii) such brand name was in use on such soft drink before October 25, 1989, and (iii) the use of the term "diet" was in conformity with section 105.66 of title 21 of the Code of Federal Regulations. Such a claim is subject to paragraph (a).

(E) Subclauses (i) through (v) of subparagraph (2)(A) do not apply to a statement in the label or labeling of food which describes the percentage of vitamins and minerals in the food in relation to the amount of such vitamins and minerals recommended for daily consumption by the Secretary.

(F) Subclause (i) clause (A) does not apply to a statement in the labeling of a dietary supplement that characterizes the percentage level of a dietary ingredient for which the Secretary has not established a reference daily intake, daily recommended value, or other recommendation for daily consumption.

(G) A claim of the type described in subparagraph (1)(A) for a nutrient, for which the Secretary has not promulgated a regulation under clause (A)(i), shall be authorized and may be made with respect to a food if—

(i) a scientific body of the United States Government with official responsibility for public health protection or research directly relating to human nutrition (such as the National Institutes of Health or the Centers for Disease Control and Prevention) or the National Academy of Sciences or any of its subdivisions has published an authoritative statement, which is currently in effect, which identifies the nutrient level to which the claim refers;

(ii) a person has submitted to the Secretary, at least 120 days (during which the Secretary may notify any person who is making a claim as authorized by clause (C) that such person has not submitted all the information required by such clause) before the first introduction into interstate commerce of the food with a label containing the claim, (I) a notice of the claim, which shall include the exact words used in the claim and shall include a concise description of the basis upon which such person relied for determining that the requirements of subclause (i) have been satisfied, (II) a copy of the statement referred to in subclause (i) upon which such person relied in making the claim, and (III) a balanced representation of the scientific literature relating to the nutrient level to which the claim refers;

(iii) the claim and the food for which the claim is made are in compliance with clauses (A) and (B), and are otherwise in compliance with paragraph (a) and section 201(n); and

(iv) the claim is stated in a manner so that the claim is an accurate representation of the authoritative statement referred to in subclause (i) and so that the claim enables the public to comprehend the information provided in the claim and to understand the relative significance of such information in the context of a total daily diet.

For purposes of this clause, a statement shall be regarded as an authoritative statement of a scientific body described in subclause (i) only if the statement is published by the scientific body and shall not include a statement of an employee of the scientific body made in the individual capacity of the employee.

(H) A claim submitted under the requirements of clause (G) may be made until—

(i) such time as the Secretary issues a regulation—

(I) prohibiting or modifying the claim and the regulation has become effective, or

(II) finding that the requirements of clause (G) have not been met, including finding that the petitioner had not submitted all the information required by such clause; or

(ii) a district court of the United States in an enforcement proceeding under chapter III has determined that the requirements of clause (G) have not been met.

(3)(A) Except as provided in subparagraph (5), a claim described in subparagraph (1)(B) may only be made—

(i) if the claim meets the requirements of the regulations of the Secretary promulgated under clause (B), and

(ii) if the food for which the claim is made does not contain, as determined by the Secretary by regulation, any nutrient in an amount which increases to persons in the general population the risk of a disease or health-related condition which is diet related, taking into account the significance of the food in the total daily diet, except that the Secretary may by regulation permit such a claim based on a finding that such a claim would assist consumers in maintaining healthy dietary practices and based on a requirement that the label contain a disclosure of the type required by subparagraph (2)(B).

(B)(i) The Secretary shall promulgate regulations authorizing claims of the type described in subparagraph (1)(B) only if the Secretary determines, based on the totality of publicly available scientific evidence (including evidence from well-designed studies conducted in a manner which is consistent with generally recognized scientific procedures and principles), that there is significant scientific agreement, among experts qualified by scientific training and experience to evaluate such claims, that the claim is supported by such evidence.

(ii) A regulation described in subclause (i) shall describe—

(I) the relationship between a nutrient of the type required in the label or labeling of food by paragraph (q)(1) or (q)(2) and a disease or health-related condition, and

(II) the significance of each such nutrient in affecting such disease or health-related condition.

(iii) A regulation described in subclause (i) shall require such claim to be stated in a manner so that the claim is an accurate representation of the matters set out in subclause (ii) and so that the claim enables the public to comprehend the information provided in the claim and to understand the relative significance of such information in the context of a total daily diet.

(C) Notwithstanding the provisions of clauses (A)(i) and (B), a claim of the type described in subparagraph (1)(B) which is not authorized by the Secretary in a regulation promulgated in accordance with clause (B) shall be authorized and may be made with respect to a food if—

(i) a scientific body of the United States Government with official responsibility for public health protection or research directly relating to human nutrition (such as the National Institutes of Health or the Centers for Disease Control and Prevention) or the National Academy of Sciences or any of its subdivisions has published an authoritative statement, which is currently in effect, about the relationship between a nutrient and a disease or health-related condition to which the claim refers;

(ii) a person has submitted to the Secretary, at least 120 days (during which the Secretary may notify any person who is making a claim as authorized by clause (C) that such person has not submitted all the information required by such clause) before the first introduction into interstate commerce of the food with a label containing the claim, (I) a notice of the claim, which shall include the exact words used in the claim and shall include a concise description of the basis upon which such person relied for determining that the requirements of subclause (i) have been satisfied, (II) a copy of the statement referred to in subclause (i) upon which such person relied in making the claim, and (III) a balanced representation of the scientific literature relating to the relationship between a nutrient and a disease or health-related condition to which the claim refers;

(iii) the claim and the food for which the claim is made are in compliance with clause (A)(ii) and are otherwise in compliance with paragraph (a) and section 201(n); and

(iv) the claim is stated in a manner so that the claim is an accurate representation of the authoritative statement referred to in subclause (i) and so that the claim enables the public to comprehend the information provided in the claim and to understand the relative significance of such information in the context of a total daily diet.

For purposes of this clause, a statement shall be regarded as an authoritative statement of a scientific body described in subclause (i) only if the statement is published by the scientific body and shall not include a statement of an employee of the scientific body made in the individual capacity of the employee.

(D) A claim submitted under the requirements of clause (C) may be made until—

(i) such time as the Secretary issues a regulation under the standard in clause (B)(i)—

(I) prohibiting or modifying the claim and the regulation has become effective, or

(II) finding that the requirements of clause (C) have not been met, including finding that the petitioner has not submitted all the information required by such clause; or

(ii) a district court of the United States in an enforcement proceeding under chapter III has determined that the requirements of clause (C) have not been met.

(4)(A)(i) Any person may petition the Secretary to issue a regulation under subparagraph (2)(A)(i) or (3)(B) relating to a claim described in subparagraph (1)(A) or (1)(B). Not later than 100 days after the petition is received by the Secretary, the Secretary shall issue a final decision denying the petition or file the petition for further action by the Secretary. If the Secretary does not act within such 100 days, the petition shall be deemed to be denied unless an extension is mutually agreed upon by the Secretary and the petitioner. If the Secretary denies the petition or the petition is deemed to be denied, the petition shall not be made available to the public. If the Secretary files the petition, the Secretary shall deny the petition or issue a proposed regulation to take the action requested in the petition not later than 90 days after the date of such decision. If the Secretary does not act within such 90 days, the petition shall be deemed to be denied unless an extension is mutually agreed upon by the Secretary and the petitioner. If the Secretary issues a proposed regulation, the rulemaking shall be completed within 540 days of the date the petition is received by the Secretary. If the Secretary does not issue a regulation within such 540 days, the Secretary shall provide the Committee on Commerce of the House of Representatives and the Committee on Labor and Human Resources of the Senate the reasons action on the regulation did not occur within such 540 days.

(ii) Any person may petition the Secretary for permission to use in a claim described in subparagraph (1)(A) terms that are consistent with the terms defined by the Secretary under subparagraph (2)(A)(i). Within 90 days of the submission of such a petition, the Secretary shall issue a final decision denying the petition or granting such permission.

(iii) Any person may petition the Secretary for permission to use an implied claim described in subparagraph (1)(A) in a brand name. After publishing notice of an opportunity to comment on the petition in the Federal Register and making the petition available to the public, the Secretary shall grant the petition if the Secretary finds that such claim is not misleading and is consistent with terms defined by the Secretary under subparagraph (2)(A)(i). The Secretary shall grant or deny the petition within 100 days of the date it is submitted to the Secretary and the petition shall be considered granted if the Secretary does not act on it within such 100 days.

(B) A petition under clause (A)(i) respecting a claim described in subparagraph (1)(A) or (1)(B) shall include an explanation of the reasons why the claim meets the requirements of this paragraph and a summary of the scientific data which supports such reasons.

(C) If a petition for a regulation under subparagraph (3)(B) relies on a report from an authoritative scientific body of the United States, the Secretary shall consider such report and shall justify any decision rejecting the conclusions of such report.

(5)(A) This paragraph does not apply to infant formulas subject to section 412(h) and medical foods as defined in section 5(b) of the Orphan Drug Act.

(B) Subclauses (iii) through (v) of subparagraph (2)(A) and subparagraph (2)(B) do not apply to food which is served in restaurants or other establishments in which food is served for immediate human consumption or which is sold for sale or use in such establishments.

(C) A subparagraph (1)(A) claim made with respect to a food which claim is required by a standard of identity issued under section 401 shall not be subject to subparagraph (2)(A)(i) or (2)(B).

(D) A subparagraph (1)(B) claim made with respect to a dietary supplement of vitamins, minerals, herbs, or other similar nutritional substances shall not be subject to subparagraph (3) but shall be subject to a procedure and standard, respecting the validity of such claim, established by regulation of the Secretary.

(6) For purposes of paragraph (r)(1)(B), a statement for a dietary supplement may be made if—

(A) the statement claims a benefit related to a classical nutrient deficiency disease and discloses the prevalence of such disease in the United States, describes the role of a nutrient or dietary ingredient intended to affect the structure or function in humans, characterizes the documented mechanism by which a nutrient or dietary ingredient acts to maintain such structure or function, or describes general well-being from consumption of a nutrient or dietary ingredient,

(B) the manufacturer of the dietary supplement has substantiation that such statement is truthful and not misleading, and

(C) the statement contains, prominently displayed and in boldface type, the following: "This statement has not been evaluated by the Food and Drug Administration. This product is not intended to diagnose, treat, cure, or prevent any disease.".

A statement under this subparagraph may not claim to diagnose, mitigate, treat, cure, or prevent a specific disease or class of diseases. If the manufacturer of a dietary supplement proposes to make a statement described in the first sentence of this subparagraph in the labeling of the dietary supplement, the manufacturer shall notify the Secretary no later than 30 days after the first marketing of the dietary supplement with such statement that such a statement is being made.

(7) The Secretary may make proposed regulations issued under this paragraph effective upon publication pending consideration of public comment and publication of a final regulation if the Secretary determines that such action is necessary—

(A) to enable the Secretary to review and act promptly on petitions the Secretary determines provide for information necessary to—

(i) enable consumers to develop and maintain healthy dietary practices;

(ii) enable consumers to be informed promptly and effectively of important new knowledge regarding nutritional and health benefits of food; or

(iii) ensure that scientifically sound nutritional and health information is provided to consumers as soon as possible; or

(B) to enable the Secretary to act promptly to ban or modify a claim under this paragraph.

Such proposed regulations shall be deemed final agency action for purposes of judicial review.

(s) If—

(1) it is a dietary supplement; and

(2)(A) the label or labeling of the supplement fails to list—

(i) the name of each ingredient of the supplement that is described in section 201(ff); and

(ii)(I) the quantity of each such ingredient; or

(II) with respect to a proprietary blend of such ingredients, the total quantity of all ingredients in the blend;

(B) the label or labeling of the dietary supplement fails to identify the product by using the term "dietary supplement", which term may be modified with the name of such an ingredient;

(C) the supplement contains an ingredient described in section 201(ff)(1)(C), and the label or labeling of the supplement fails to identify any part of the plant from which the ingredient is derived;

(D) the supplement—

(i) is covered by the specifications of an official compendium;

(ii) is represented as conforming to the specifications of an official compendium; and

(iii) fails to so conform; or

(E) the supplement—

(i) is not covered by the specifications of an official compendium; and

(ii)(I) fails to have the identity and strength that the supplement is represented to have; or

(II) fails to meet the quality (including tablet or capsule disintegration), purity, or compositional specifications, based on validated assay or other appropriate methods, that the supplement is represented to meet.

A dietary supplement shall not be deemed misbranded solely because its label or labeling contains directions or conditions of use or warnings.

(t)[13] If it purports to be or is represented as catfish, unless it is fish classified within the family Ictaluridae.

(u)[14] If it purports to be or is represented as ginseng, unless it is an herb or herbal ingredient derived from a plant classified within the genus Panax.

(v) If—

(1) it fails to bear a label required by the Secretary under section 801(n)(1) (relating to food refused admission into the United States);

(2) the Secretary finds that the food presents a threat of serious adverse health consequences or death to humans or animals; and

(3) upon or after notifying the owner or consignee involved that the label is required under section 801, the Secretary informs the owner or consignee that the food presents such a threat.

(w)(1) If it is not a raw agricultural commodity and it is, or it contains an ingredient that bears or contains, a major food allergen, unless either—

(A) the word "Contains", followed by the name of the food source from which the major food allergen is derived, is printed immediately after or is adjacent to the list of ingredients (in a type size no smaller than the type size used in the list of ingredients) required under subsections (g) and (i); or

(B) the common or usual name of the major food allergen in the list of ingredients required under subsections (g) and (i) is followed in parentheses by the name of the food source from which the major food allergen is derived, except that the name of the food source is not required when—

(i) the common or usual name of the ingredient uses the name of the food source from which the major food allergen is derived; or

(ii) the name of the food source from which the major food allergen is derived appears elsewhere in the ingredient list, unless the name of the food source that appears elsewhere in the ingredient list appears as part of the name of a food ingredient that is not a major food allergen under section 201(qq) (2)(A) or (B).

---

13. Subsection (t) was added by Pub. L. No. 107–171, § 10806(a)(2), 116 Stat. 134, 526 (2002). Subsection (a)(1) of such section provides as follows:

(1) In general.—Notwithstanding any other provision of law, for purposes of the Federal Food, Drug, and Cosmetic Act (21 U.S.C. 301 et seq.)—

(A) the term "catfish" may only be considered to be a common or usual name (or part thereof) for fish classified within the family Ictaluridae; and

(B) only labeling or advertising for fish classified within that family may include the term "catfish".

14. Subsection (u) was added by Pub. L. No. 107–171, § 10806(b)(2), 116 Stat. 134, 527 (2002). Subsection (b)(1) of such section provides as follows:

(1) In general.—Notwithstanding any other provision of law, for purposes of the Federal Food, Drug, and Cosmetic Act (21 U.S.C. 301 et seq.)—

(A) the term "ginseng" may only be considered to be a common or usual name (or part thereof) for any herb or herbal ingredient derived from a plant classified within the genus Panax; and

(B) only labeling or advertising for herbs or herbal ingredients classified within that genus may include the term "ginseng".

(2) As used in this subsection, the term "name of the food source from which the major food allergen is derived" means the name described in section 201(qq)(1); provided that in the case of a tree nut, fish, or Crustacean shellfish, the term "name of the food source from which the major food allergen is derived" means the name of the specific type of nut or species of fish or Crustacean shellfish.

(3) The information required under this subsection may appear in labeling in lieu of appearing on the label only if the Secretary finds that such other labeling is sufficient to protect the public health. A finding by the Secretary under this paragraph (including any change in an earlier finding under this paragraph) is effective upon publication in the Federal Register as a notice.

(4) Notwithstanding subsection (g), (i), or (k), or any other law, a flavoring, coloring, or incidental additive that is, or that bears or contains, a major food allergen shall be subject to the labeling requirements of this subsection.

(5) The Secretary may by regulation modify the requirements of subparagraph (A) or (B) of paragraph (1), or eliminate either the requirement of subparagraph (A) or the requirements of subparagraph (B) of paragraph (1), if the Secretary determines that the modification or elimination of the requirement of subparagraph (A) or the requirements of subparagraph (B) is necessary to protect the public health.

(6)(A) Any person may petition the Secretary to exempt a food ingredient described in section 201(qq)(2) from the allergen labeling requirements of this subsection.

(B) The Secretary shall approve or deny such petition within 180 days of receipt of the petition or the petition shall be deemed denied, unless an extension of time is mutually agreed upon by the Secretary and the petitioner.

(C) The burden shall be on the petitioner to provide scientific evidence (including the analytical method used to produce the evidence) that demonstrates that such food ingredient, as derived by the method specified in the petition, does not cause an allergic response that poses a risk to human health.

(D) A determination regarding a petition under this paragraph shall constitute final agency action.

(E) The Secretary shall promptly post to a public site all petitions received under this paragraph within 14 days of receipt and the Secretary shall promptly post the Secretary's response to each.

(7)(A) A person need not file a petition under paragraph (6) to exempt a food ingredient described in section 201(qq)(2) from the allergen labeling requirements of this subsection, if the person files with the Secretary a notification containing—

(i) scientific evidence (including the analytical method used) that demonstrates that the food ingredient (as derived by the method specified in the notification, where applicable) does not contain allergenic protein; or

(ii) a determination by the Secretary that the ingredient does not cause an allergic response that poses a risk to human health under a premarket approval or notification program under section 409.

(B) The food ingredient may be introduced or delivered for introduction into interstate commerce as a food ingredient that is not a major food allergen 90 days after the date of receipt of the notification by the Secretary, unless the Secretary determines within the 90–day period that the notification does not meet the requirements of this paragraph, or there is insufficient scientific evidence to determine that the food ingredient does not contain allergenic protein or does not cause an allergenic response that poses a risk to human health.

(C) The Secretary shall promptly post to a public site all notifications received under this subparagraph within 14 days of receipt and promptly post any objections thereto by the Secretary.

(x) Notwithstanding subsection (g), (i), or (k), or any other law, a spice, flavoring, coloring, or incidental additive that is, or that bears or contains, a food allergen (other than a major food allergen), as determined by the Secretary by regulation, shall be disclosed in a manner specified by the Secretary by regulation.

(y) If it is a dietary supplement that is marketed in the United States, unless the label of such dietary supplement includes a domestic address or domestic phone number through which the responsible person (as described in section 761) may receive a report of a serious adverse event with such dietary supplement.

Sec. 403A[15] [21 U.S.C. 343–1].

(a) Except as provided in subsection (b), no State or political subdivision of a State may directly or indirectly establish under any authority or continue in effect as to any food in interstate commerce—

(1) any requirement for a food which is the subject of a standard of identity established under section 401 that is not identical to such standard of identity or that is not identical to the requirement of section 403(g), except that this paragraph does not apply to a standard of identity of a State or political subdivision of a State for maple syrup that is of the type required by sections 401 and 403(g),

(2) any requirement for the labeling of food of the type required by section 403(c), 403(e), or 403(i)(2) 403(i)(2), 403(w), or 403(x) that is not identical to the requirement of such section, except that this paragraph does not apply to a requirement of a State or political subdivision of a State that is of the type required by section 403(c) and that is applicable to maple syrup,

(3) any requirement for the labeling of food of the type required by section 403(b), 403(d), 403(f), 403(h), 403(i)(1), or 403(k) that is not identical to the requirement of such section, except that this paragraph does not apply to a re-

15. Section 403A was enacted without a section heading. See Pub. L. No. 101–535, § 6(a), 104 Stat. 2353, 2362 (1990).

quirement of a State or political subdivision of a State that is of the type required by section 403(h)(1) and that is applicable to maple syrup,

(4) any requirement for nutrition labeling of food that is not identical to the requirement of section 403(q), except that this paragraph does not apply to food that is offered for sale in a restaurant or similar retail food establishment that is not part of a chain with 20 or more locations doing business under the same name (regardless of the type of ownership of the locations) and offering for sale substantially the same menu items unless such restaurant or similar retail food establishment complies with the voluntary provision of nutrition information requirements under section 403(q)(5)(H)(ix), or

(5) any requirement respecting any claim of the type described in section 403(r)(1) made in the label or labeling of food that is not identical to the requirement of section 403(r), except a requirement respecting a claim made in the label or labeling of food which is exempt under section 403(r)(5)(B).

Paragraph (3) shall take effect in accordance with section 6(b) of the Nutrition Labeling and Education Act of 1990.

(b) Upon petition of a State or a political subdivision of a State, the Secretary may exempt from subsection (a), under such conditions as may be prescribed by regulation, any State or local requirement that—

(1) would not cause any food to be in violation of any applicable requirement under Federal law,

(2) would not unduly burden interstate commerce, and

(3) is designed to address a particular need for information which need is not met by the requirements of the sections referred to in subsection (a).

SEC. 403B [21 U.S.C. 343–2]. DIETARY SUPPLEMENT LABELING EXEMPTIONS

(a) IN GENERAL.—A publication, including an article, a chapter in a book, or an official abstract of a peer-reviewed scientific publication that appears in an article and was prepared by the author or the editors of the publication, which is reprinted in its entirety, shall not be defined as labeling when used in connection with the sale of a dietary supplement to consumers when it—

(1) is not false or misleading;

(2) does not promote a particular manufacturer or brand of a dietary supplement;

(3) is displayed or presented, or is displayed or presented with other such items on the same subject matter, so as to present a balanced view of the available scientific information on a dietary supplement;

(4) if displayed in an establishment, is physically separate from the dietary supplements; and

(5) does not have appended to it any information by sticker or any other method.

(b) Application.—Subsection (a) shall not apply to or restrict a retailer or wholesaler of dietary supplements in any way whatsoever in the sale of books or other publications as a part of the business of such retailer or wholesaler.

(c) Burden of Proof.—In any proceeding brought under subsection (a), the burden of proof shall be on the United States to establish that an article or other such matter is false or misleading.

Sec. 403C [21 U.S.C. 343–3]. Disclosure

(a) No provision of section 201(n), 403(a), or 409 shall be construed to require on the label or labeling of a food a separate radiation disclosure statement that is more prominent than the declaration of ingredients required by section 403(i)(2).

(b) In this section, the term "radiation disclosure statement" means a written statement that discloses that a food has been intentionally subject to radiation.

Sec. 404 [21 U.S.C. 344]. Emergency Permit Control

(a) Whenever the Secretary finds after investigation that the distribution in interstate commerce of any class of food may, by reason of contamination with micro-organisms during the manufacture, processing, or packing thereof in any locality, be injurious to health, and that such injurious nature cannot be adequately determined after such articles have entered interstate commerce, he then, and in such case only, shall promulgate regulations providing for the issuance, to manufacturers, processors, or packers of such class of food in such locality of permits to which shall be attached such conditions governing the manufacture, processing, or packaging of such class of food, for such temporary period of time, as may be necessary to protect the public health; and after the effective date of such regulations, and during such temporary period, no person shall introduce or deliver for introduction into interstate commerce any such food manufactured, processed, or packed by any such manufacturer, processor, or packer unless such manufacturer, processor, or packer holds a permit issued by the Secretary as provided by such regulations.

(b) The Secretary is authorized to suspend immediately upon notice any permit issued under authority of this section if it is found that any of the conditions of the permit have been violated. The holder of a permit so suspended shall be privileged at any time to apply for the reinstatement of such permit, and the Secretary shall, immediately after prompt hearing and an inspection of the establishment, reinstate such permit if it is found that adequate measures have been taken to comply with and maintain the conditions of the permit, as originally issued or as amended.

(c) Any officer or employee duly designated by the Secretary shall have access to any factory or establishment, the operator of which holds a permit from the Secretary, for the purpose of ascertaining whether or not the conditions of the permit are being complied with, and denial of access for such inspection shall be ground for suspension of the permit until such access is freely given by the operator.

SEC. 405 [21 U.S.C. 345]. REGULATIONS MAKING EXEMPTIONS

The Secretary shall promulgate regulations exempting from any labeling requirement of this Act (1) small open containers of fresh fruits and fresh vegetables and (2) food which is in accordance with the practice of the trade, to be processed, labeled, or repacked in substantial quantities at establishments other than those where originally processed or packed, or condition that such food is not adulterated or misbranded under the provisions of this Act upon removal from such processing, labeling, or repacking establishment. This section does not apply to the labeling requirements of sections 403(q) and 403(r).

SEC. 406 [21 U.S.C. 346]. TOLERANCE FOR POISONOUS OR DELETERIOUS SUBSTANCES IN FOOD; REGULATIONS

Any poisonous or deleterious substance added to any food, except where such substance is required in the production thereof or cannot be avoided by good manufacturing practice shall be deemed to be unsafe for purposes of the application of clause (2)(A) of section 402(a); but when such substance is so required or cannot be so avoided, the Secretary shall promulgate regulations limiting the quantity therein or thereon to such extent as he finds necessary for the protection of public health, and any quantity exceeding the limits so fixed shall also be deemed to be unsafe for purposes of the application of clause (2)(A) of section 402(a). While such a regulation is in effect limiting the quantity of any such substance in the case of any food, such food shall not, by reason of bearing or containing any added amount of such substance, be considered to be adulterated within the meaning of clause (1) of section 402(a). In determining the quantity of such added substance to be tolerated in or on different articles of food the Secretary shall take into account the extent to which the use of such substance is required or cannot be avoided in the production of each such article, and the other ways in which the consumer may be affected by the same or other poisonous or deleterious substances.

SEC. 407[16] [21 U.S.C. 347]. OLEOMARGARINE OR MARGARINE

(a) Colored oleomargarine or colored margarine which is sold in the same State or Territory in which it is produced shall be subject in the same manner and to the same extent to the provisions of this Act as if it had been introduced in interstate commerce.

---

16. Pub. L. No. 81–459, § 4, 64 Stat. 20, 21 (1950), amended section 15 of the Federal Trade Commission Act (15 U.S.C. 55) by adding the following subsection:
"(f) For the purposes of this section and section 407 of the Federal Food, Drug, and Cosmetic Act, as amended, the term 'oleomargarine' or 'margarine' includes—

"(1) all substances, mixtures, and compounds known as oleomargarine or margarine;
"(2) all substances, mixtures, and compounds which have a consistence [sic] similar to that of butter and which contain any edible oils or fats other than milk fat if made in imitation or semblance of butter."

(b) No person shall sell, or offer for sale, colored oleomargarine or colored margarine unless—

(1) such oleomargarine or margarine is packaged,

(2) the net weight of the contents of any package sold in a retail establishment is one pound or less,

(3) there appears on the label of the package (A) the word "oleomargarine" or "margarine" in type or lettering at least as large as any other type or lettering on such label, and (B) a full and accurate statement of all the ingredients contained in such oleomargarine, or margarine, and

(4) each part of the contents of the package is contained in a wrapper which bears the word "oleomargarine" or "margarine" in type or lettering not smaller than 20–point type.

The requirements of this subsection shall be in addition to and not in lieu of any of the other requirements of this Act.

(c) No person shall possess in a form ready for serving colored oleomargarine or colored margarine at a public eating place unless a notice that oleomargarine or margarine is served is displayed prominently and conspicuously in such place and in such manner as to render it likely to be read and understood by the ordinary individual being served in such eating place or is printed or is otherwise set forth on the menu in type or lettering not smaller than that normally used to designate the serving of other food items. No person shall serve colored oleomargarine or colored margarine at a public eating place, whether or not any charge is made therefore, unless (1) each separate serving bears or is accompanied by labeling identifying it as oleomargarine or margarine, or (2) each separate serving thereof is triangular in shape.

(d) Colored oleomargarine or colored margarine when served with meals at a public eating place shall at the time of such service be exempt from the labeling requirements of section 403 (except (a) and 403 (f))[17] if it complies with the requirements of subsection (b) of this section.

(e) For the purpose of this section colored oleomargarine or colored margarine is oleomargarine or margarine having a tint or shade containing more than one and six-tenths degrees of yellow, or of yellow and red collectively, but with an excess of yellow over red, measured in terms of Lovibond tintometer scale or its equivalent.

SEC. 408 [21 U.S.C. 346a]. TOLERANCES AND EXEMPTIONS FOR PESTICIDE CHEMICAL RESIDUES

(a) REQUIREMENT FOR TOLERANCE OR EXEMPTION.—

(1) GENERAL RULE.—Except as provided in paragraph (2) or (3), any pesticide chemical residue in or on a food shall be deemed unsafe for the purpose of section 402(a)(2)(B) unless—

17. So in law. Probably should be "(except paragraphs (a) and (f))".

(A) a tolerance for such pesticide chemical residue in or on such food is in effect under this section and the quantity of the residue is within the limits of the tolerance; or

(B) an exemption from the requirement of a tolerance is in effect under this section for the pesticide chemical residue.

For the purposes of this section, the term "food", when used as a noun without modification, shall mean a raw agricultural commodity or processed food.

(2) PROCESSED FOOD.—Notwithstanding paragraph (1)—

(A) if a tolerance is in effect under this section for a pesticide chemical residue in or on a raw agricultural commodity, a pesticide chemical residue that is present in or on a processed food because the food is made from that raw agricultural commodity shall not be considered unsafe within the meaning of section 402(a)(2)(B) despite the lack of a tolerance for the pesticide chemical residue in or on the processed food if the pesticide chemical has been used in or on the raw agricultural commodity in conformity with a tolerance under this section, such residue in or on the raw agricultural commodity has been removed to the extent possible in good manufacturing practice, and the concentration of the pesticide chemical residue in the processed food is not greater than the tolerance prescribed for the pesticide chemical residue in the raw agricultural commodity; or

(B) if an exemption for the requirement for a tolerance is in effect under this section for a pesticide chemical residue in or on a raw agricultural commodity, a pesticide chemical residue that is present in or on a processed food because the food is made from that raw agricultural commodity shall not be considered unsafe within the meaning of section 402(a)(2)(B).

(3) RESIDUES OF DEGRADATION PRODUCTS.—If a pesticide chemical residue is present in or on a food because it is a metabolite or other degradation product of a precursor substance that itself is a pesticide chemical or pesticide chemical residue, such a residue shall not be considered to be unsafe within the meaning of section 402(a)(2)(B) despite the lack of a tolerance or exemption from the need for a tolerance for such residue in or on such food if—

(A) the Administrator has not determined that the degradation product is likely to pose any potential health risk from dietary exposure that is of a different type than, or of a greater significance than, any risk posed by dietary exposure to the precursor substance;

(B) either—

(i) a tolerance is in effect under this section for residues of the precursor substance in or on the food, and the combined level of residues of the degradation product and the precursor substance in or on the food is at or below the stoichiometrically equivalent level that would be

78

permitted by the tolerance if the residue consisted only of the precursor substance rather than the degradation product; or

(ii) an exemption from the need for a tolerance is in effect under this section for residues of the precursor substance in or on the food; and

(C) the tolerance or exemption for residues of the precursor substance does not state that it applies only to particular named substances and does not state that it does not apply to residues of the degradation product.

(4) EFFECT OF TOLERANCE OR EXEMPTION.—While a tolerance or exemption from the requirement for a tolerance is in effect under this section for a pesticide chemical residue with respect to any food, the food shall not by reason of bearing or containing any amount of such a residue be considered to be adulterated within the meaning of section 402(a)(1).

(b) AUTHORITY AND STANDARD FOR TOLERANCE.—

(1) AUTHORITY.—The Administrator may issue regulations establishing, modifying, or revoking a tolerance for a pesticide chemical residue in or on a food—

(A) in response to a petition filed under subsection (d); or

(B) on the Administrator's own initiative under subsection (e).

As used in this section, the term "modify" shall not mean expanding the tolerance to cover additional foods.

(2) STANDARD.—

(A) GENERAL RULE.—

(i) STANDARD.—The Administrator may establish or leave in effect a tolerance for a pesticide chemical residue in or on a food only if the Administrator determines that the tolerance is safe. The Administrator shall modify or revoke a tolerance if the Administrator determines it is not safe.

(ii) DETERMINATION OF SAFETY.—As used in this section, the term "safe", with respect to a tolerance for a pesticide chemical residue, means that the Administrator has determined that there is a reasonable certainty that no harm will result from aggregate exposure to the pesticide chemical residue, including all anticipated dietary exposures and all other exposures for which there is reliable information.

(iii) RULE OF CONSTRUCTION.—With respect to a tolerance, a pesticide chemical residue meeting the standard under clause (i) is not an eligible pesticide chemical residue for purposes of subparagraph (B).

(B) TOLERANCES FOR ELIGIBLE PESTICIDE CHEMICAL RESIDUES.—

(i) DEFINITION.—As used in this subparagraph, the term "eligible pesticide chemical residue" means a pesticide chemical residue as to which—

(I) the Administrator is not able to identify a level of exposure to the residue at which the residue will not cause or contribute to a known or anticipated harm to human health (referred to in this section as a "non-threshold effect");

(II) the lifetime risk of experiencing the non-threshold effect is appropriately assessed by quantitative risk assessment; and

(III) with regard to any known or anticipated harm to human health for which the Administrator is able to identify a level at which the residue will not cause such harm (referred to in this section as a "threshold effect"), the Administrator determines that the level of aggregate exposure is safe.

(ii) DETERMINATION OF TOLERANCE.—Notwithstanding subparagraph (A)(i), a tolerance for an eligible pesticide chemical residue may be left in effect or modified under this subparagraph if—

(I) at least one of the conditions described in clause (iii) is met; and

(II) both of the conditions described in clause (iv) are met.

(iii) CONDITIONS REGARDING USE.—For purposes of clause (ii), the conditions described in this clause with respect to a tolerance for an eligible pesticide chemical residue are the following:

(I) Use of the pesticide chemical that produces the residue protects consumers from adverse effects on health that would pose a greater risk than the dietary risk from the residue.

(II) Use of the pesticide chemical that produces the residue is necessary to avoid a significant disruption in domestic production of an adequate, wholesome, and economical food supply.

(iv) CONDITIONS REGARDING RISK.—For purposes of clause (ii), the conditions described in this clause with respect to a tolerance for an eligible pesticide chemical residue are the following:

(I) The yearly risk associated with the nonthreshold effect from aggregate exposure to the residue does not exceed 10 times the yearly risk that would be allowed under subparagraph (A) for such effect.

(II) The tolerance is limited so as to ensure that the risk over a lifetime associated with the nonthreshold effect from aggregate exposure to the residue is not greater than twice the lifetime risk that would be allowed under subparagraph (A) for such effect.

(v) REVIEW.—Five years after the date on which the Administrator makes a determination to leave in effect or modify a tolerance under this subparagraph, and thereafter as the Administrator deems appropriate, the Administrator shall determine, after notice and opportunity for comment, whether it has been demonstrated to the Administrator that a condition described in clause (iii)(I) or clause (iii)(II) continues to exist with respect to the tolerance and that the yearly and lifetime risks from aggregate exposure to such residue continue to comply with the limits specified in clause (iv). If the Administrator determines by such date that such demonstration has not been made, the Administrator shall, not later than 180 days after the date of such determination, issue a regulation under subsection (e)(1) to modify or revoke the tolerance.

(vi) INFANTS AND CHILDREN.—Any tolerance under this subparagraph shall meet the requirements of subparagraph (C).

(C) EXPOSURE OF INFANTS AND CHILDREN.—In establishing, modifying, leaving in effect, or revoking a tolerance or exemption for a pesticide chemical residue, the Administrator—

(i) shall assess the risk of the pesticide chemical residue based on—

(I) available information about consumption patterns among infants and children that are likely to result in disproportionately high consumption of foods containing or bearing such residue among infants and children in comparison to the general population;

(II) available information concerning the special susceptibility of infants and children to the pesticide chemical residues, including neurological differences between infants and children and adults, and effects of in utero exposure to pesticide chemicals; and

(III) available information concerning the cumulative effects on infants and children of such residues and other substances that have a common mechanism of toxicity; and

(ii) shall—

(I) ensure that there is a reasonable certainty that no harm will result to infants and children from aggregate exposure to the pesticide chemical residue; and

(II) publish a specific determination regarding the safety of the pesticide chemical residue for infants and children.

The Secretary of Health and Human Services and the Secretary of Agriculture, in consultation with the Administrator, shall conduct surveys to document dietary exposure to pesticides among infants and children. In the case of threshold effects, for purposes of clause (ii)(I) an additional tenfold margin of safety for the pesticide chemical residue and other sources of exposure shall be applied for infants and children to take into account potential pre- and postnatal toxicity and completeness of the data with respect to exposure and toxicity to infants and children. Notwithstanding such requirement for an additional margin of safety, the Administrator may use a different margin of safety for the pesticide chemical residue only if, on the basis of reliable data, such margin will be safe for infants and children.

(D) FACTORS.—In establishing, modifying, leaving in effect, or revoking a tolerance or exemption for a pesticide chemical residue, the Administrator shall consider, among other relevant factors—

(i) the validity, completeness, and reliability of the available data from studies of the pesticide chemical and pesticide chemical residue;

(ii) the nature of any toxic effect shown to be caused by the pesticide chemical or pesticide chemical residue in such studies;

(iii) available information concerning the relationship of the results of such studies to human risk;

(iv) available information concerning the dietary consumption patterns of consumers (and major identifiable subgroups of consumers);

(v) available information concerning the cumulative effects of such residues and other substances that have a common mechanism of toxicity;

(vi) available information concerning the aggregate exposure levels of consumers (and major identifiable subgroups of consumers) to the pesticide chemical residue and to other related substances, including dietary exposure under the tolerance and all other tolerances in effect for the pesticide chemical residue, and exposure from other non-occupational sources;

(vii) available information concerning the variability of the sensitivities of major identifiable subgroups of consumers;

(viii) such information as the Administrator may require on whether the pesticide chemical may have an effect in humans that is similar to an effect produced by a naturally occurring estrogen or other endocrine effects; and

(ix) safety factors which in the opinion of experts qualified by scientific training and experience to evaluate the safety of food additives are generally recognized as appropriate for the use of animal experimentation data.

(E) DATA AND INFORMATION REGARDING ANTICIPATED AND ACTUAL RESIDUE LEVELS.—

(i) AUTHORITY.—In establishing, modifying, leaving in effect, or revoking a tolerance for a pesticide chemical residue, the Administrator may consider available data and information on the anticipated residue levels of the pesticide chemical in or on food and the actual residue levels of the pesticide chemical that have been measured in food, including residue data collected by the Food and Drug Administration.

(ii) REQUIREMENT.—If the Administrator relies on anticipated or actual residue levels in establishing, modifying, or leaving in effect a tolerance, the Administrator shall pursuant to subsection (f)(1) require that data be provided five years after the date on which the tolerance is established, modified, or left in effect, and thereafter as the Administrator deems appropriate, demonstrating that such residue levels are not above the levels so relied on. If such data are not so provided, or if the data do not demonstrate that the residue levels are not above the levels so relied on, the Administrator shall, not later than 180 days after the date on which the data were required to be provided, issue a regulation under subsection (e)(1), or an order under subsection (f)(2), as appropriate, to modify or revoke the tolerance.

(F) PERCENT OF FOOD ACTUALLY TREATED.—In establishing, modifying, leaving in effect, or revoking a tolerance for a pesticide chemical residue, the Administrator may, when assessing chronic dietary risk, consider available data and information on the percent of food actually treated with the pesticide chemical (including aggregate pesticide use data collected by the Department of Agriculture) only if the Administrator—

(i) finds that the data are reliable and provide a valid basis to show what percentage of the food derived from such crop is likely to contain such pesticide chemical residue;

(ii) finds that the exposure estimate does not understate exposure for any significant subpopulation group;

(iii) finds that, if data are available on pesticide use and consumption of food in a particular area, the population in such area is not dietarily exposed to residues above those estimated by the Administrator; and

(iv) provides for the periodic reevaluation of the estimate of anticipated dietary exposure.

(3) DETECTION METHODS.—

(A) GENERAL RULE.—A tolerance for a pesticide chemical residue in or on a food shall not be established or modified by the Administrator unless the Administrator determines, after consultation with the Secretary, that there is a practical method for detecting and measuring the levels of the pesticide chemical residue in or on the food.

(B) DETECTION LIMIT.—A tolerance for a pesticide chemical residue in or on a food shall not be established at or modified to a level lower than the limit of detection of the method for detecting and measuring the pesticide chemical residue specified by the Administrator under subparagraph (A).

(4) INTERNATIONAL STANDARDS.—In establishing a tolerance for a pesticide chemical residue in or on a food, the Administrator shall determine whether a maximum residue level for the pesticide chemical has been established by the Codex Alimentarius Commission. If a Codex maximum residue level has been established for the pesticide chemical and the Administrator does not propose to adopt the Codex level, the Administrator shall publish for public comment a notice explaining the reasons for departing from the Codex level.

(c) AUTHORITY AND STANDARD FOR EXEMPTIONS.—

(1) AUTHORITY.—The Administrator may issue a regulation establishing, modifying, or revoking an exemption from the requirement for a tolerance for a pesticide chemical residue in or on food—

(A) in response to a petition filed under subsection (d); or

(B) on the Administrator's initiative under subsection (e).

(2) STANDARD.—

(A) GENERAL RULE.—

(i) STANDARD.—The Administrator may establish or leave in effect an exemption from the requirement for a tolerance for a pesticide chemical residue in or on food only if the Administrator determines that the exemption is safe. The Administrator shall modify or revoke an exemption if the Administrator determines it is not safe.

(ii) DETERMINATION OF SAFETY.—The term "safe", with respect to an exemption for a pesticide chemical residue, means that the Administrator has determined that there is a reasonable certainty that no harm will result from aggregate exposure to the pesticide chemical residue, including all anticipated dietary exposures and all other exposures for which there is reliable information.

(B) FACTORS.—In making a determination under this paragraph, the Administrator shall take into account, among other relevant considerations, the considerations set forth in subparagraphs (C) and (D) of subsection (b)(2).

(3) LIMITATION.—An exemption from the requirement for a tolerance for a pesticide chemical residue in or on food shall not be established or modified by the Administrator unless the Administrator determines, after consultation with the Secretary—

(A) that there is a practical method for detecting and measuring the levels of such pesticide chemical residue in or on food; or

(B) that there is no need for such a method, and states the reasons for such determination in issuing the regulation establishing or modifying the exemption.

(d) PETITION FOR TOLERANCE OR EXEMPTION.—

(1) PETITIONS AND PETITIONERS.—Any person may file with the Administrator a petition proposing the issuance of a regulation—

(A) establishing, modifying, or revoking a tolerance for a pesticide chemical residue in or on a food; or

(B) establishing, modifying, or revoking an exemption from the requirement of a tolerance for such a residue.

(2) PETITION CONTENTS.—

(A) ESTABLISHMENT.—A petition under paragraph (1) to establish a tolerance or exemption for a pesticide chemical residue shall be supported by such data and information as are specified in regulations issued by the Administrator, including—

(i)(I) an informative summary of the petition and of the data, information, and arguments submitted or cited in support of the petition; and

(II) a statement that the petitioner agrees that such summary or any information it contains may be published as a part of the notice of filing of the petition to be published under this subsection and as part of a proposed or final regulation issued under this section;

(ii) the name, chemical identity, and composition of the pesticide chemical residue and of the pesticide chemical that produces the residue;

(iii) data showing the recommended amount, frequency, method, and time of application of that pesticide chemical;

(iv) full reports of tests and investigations made with respect to the safety of the pesticide chemical, including full information as to the methods and controls used in conducting those tests and investigations;

(v) full reports of tests and investigations made with respect to the nature and amount of the pesticide chemical residue that is likely to remain in or on the food, including a description of the analytical methods used;

(vi) a practical method for detecting and measuring the levels of the pesticide chemical residue in or on the food, or for exemptions, a statement why such a method is not needed;

(vii) a proposed tolerance for the pesticide chemical residue, if a tolerance is proposed;

(viii) if the petition relates to a tolerance for a processed food, reports of investigations conducted using the processing method(s) used to produce that food;

(ix) such information as the Administrator may require to make the determination under subsection (b)(2)(C);

(x) such information as the Administrator may require on whether the pesticide chemical may have an effect in humans that is similar to an effect produced by a naturally occurring estrogen or other endocrine effects;

(xi) information regarding exposure to the pesticide chemical residue due to any tolerance or exemption already granted for such residue;

(xii) practical methods for removing any amount of the residue that would exceed any proposed tolerance; and

(xiii) such other data and information as the Administrator requires by regulation to support the petition.

If information or data required by this subparagraph is available to the Administrator, the person submitting the petition may cite the availability of the information or data in lieu of submitting it. The Administrator may require a petition to be accompanied by samples of the pesticide chemical with respect to which the petition is filed.

(B) MODIFICATION OR REVOCATION.—The Administrator may by regulation establish the requirements for information and data to support a petition to modify or revoke a tolerance or to modify or revoke an exemption from the requirement for a tolerance.

(3) NOTICE.—A notice of the filing of a petition that the Administrator determines has met the requirements of paragraph (2) shall be published by the Administrator within 30 days after such determination. The notice shall announce the availability of a description of the analytical methods available to the Administrator for the detection and measurement of the pesticide chemical residue with respect to which the petition is filed or shall set forth the petitioner's statement of why such a method is not needed. The notice shall include the summary required by paragraph (2)(A)(i)(I).

(4) ACTIONS BY THE ADMINISTRATOR.—

(A) IN GENERAL.—The Administrator shall, after giving due consideration to a petition filed under paragraph (1) and any other information available to the Administrator—

(i) issue a final regulation (which may vary from that sought by the petition) establishing, modifying, or revoking a tolerance for the pesticide chemical residue or an exemption of the pesticide chemical residue from the requirement of a tolerance (which final regulation shall be issued without further notice and without further period for public comment);

(ii) issue a proposed regulation under subsection (e), and thereafter issue a final regulation under such subsection; or

(iii) issue an order denying the petition.

(B) PRIORITIES.—The Administrator shall give priority to petitions for the establishment or modification of a tolerance or exemption for a pesticide chemical residue that appears to pose a significantly lower risk to human health from dietary exposure than pesticide chemical residues that have tolerances in effect for the same or similar uses.

(C) EXPEDITED REVIEW OF CERTAIN PETITIONS.—

(i) DATE CERTAIN FOR REVIEW.—If a person files a complete petition with the Administrator proposing the issuance of a regulation establishing a tolerance or exemption for a pesticide chemical residue that presents a lower risk to human health than a pesticide chemical residue for which a tolerance has been left in effect or modified under subsection (b)(2)(B), the Administrator shall complete action on such petition under this paragraph within 1 year.

(ii) REQUIRED DETERMINATIONS.—If the Administrator issues a final regulation establishing a tolerance or exemption for a safer pesticide chemical residue under clause (i), the Administrator shall, not later than 180 days after the date on which the regulation is issued, determine whether a condition described in subclause (I) or (II) of subsection (b)(2)(B)(iii) continues to exist with respect to a tolerance that has been left in effect or modified under subsection (b)(2)(B). If such condition does not continue to exist, the Administrator shall, not later than 180 days after the date on which the determination under the preceding sentence is made, issue a regulation under subsection (e)(1) to modify or revoke the tolerance.

(e) ACTION ON ADMINISTRATOR'S OWN INITIATIVE.—

(1) GENERAL RULE.—The Administrator may issue a regulation—

(A) establishing, modifying, suspending under subsection (*l*)(3), or revoking a tolerance for a pesticide chemical or a pesticide chemical residue;

(B) establishing, modifying, suspending under subsection (*l*)(3), or revoking an exemption of a pesticide chemical residue from the requirement of a tolerance; or

(C) establishing general procedures and requirements to implement this section.

(2) NOTICE.—Before issuing a final regulation under paragraph (1), the Administrator shall issue a notice of proposed rulemaking and provide a period of not less than 60 days for public comment on the proposed regulation, except that a shorter period for comment may be provided if the Administrator for good cause finds that it would be in the public interest to do so and states the reasons for the finding in the notice of proposed rulemaking.

(f) SPECIAL DATA REQUIREMENTS.—

(1) REQUIRING SUBMISSION OF ADDITIONAL DATA.—If the Administrator determines that additional data or information are reasonably required to support the continuation of a tolerance or exemption that is in effect under this section for a pesticide chemical residue on a food, the Administrator shall—

(A) issue a notice requiring the person holding the pesticide registrations associated with such tolerance or exemption to submit the data or information under section 3(c)(2)(B) of the Federal Insecticide, Fungicide, and Rodenticide Act;

(B) issue a rule requiring that testing be conducted on a substance or mixture under section 4 of the Toxic Substances Control Act; or

(C) publish in the Federal Register, after first providing notice and an opportunity for comment of not less than 60 days' duration, an order—

(i) requiring the submission to the Administrator by one or more interested persons of a notice identifying the person or persons who will submit the required data and information;

(ii) describing the type of data and information required to be submitted to the Administrator and stating why the data and information could not be obtained under the authority of section 3(c)(2)(B) of the Federal Insecticide, Fungicide, and Rodenticide Act or section 4 of the Toxic Substances Control Act;

(iii) describing the reports of the Administrator required to be prepared during and after the collection of the data and information;

(iv) requiring the submission to the Administrator of the data, information, and reports referred to in clauses (ii) and (iii); and

(v) establishing dates by which the submissions described in clauses (i) and (iv) must be made.

The Administrator may under subparagraph (C) revise any such order to correct an error. The Administrator may under this paragraph require data or information pertaining to whether the pesticide chemical may have an effect in humans that is similar to an effect produced by a naturally occurring estrogen or other endocrine effects.

(2) NONCOMPLIANCE.—If a submission required by a notice issued in accordance with paragraph (1)(A), a rule issued under paragraph (1)(B), or an order issued under paragraph (1)(C) is not made by the time specified in such notice, rule, or order, the Administrator may by order published in the Federal Register modify or revoke the tolerance or exemption in question. In any review of such an order under subsection (g)(2), the only material issue shall be whether a submission required under paragraph (1) was not made by the time specified.

(g) EFFECTIVE DATE, OBJECTIONS, HEARINGS, AND ADMINISTRATIVE REVIEW.—

(1) EFFECTIVE DATE.—A regulation or order issued under subsection (d)(4), (e)(1), or (f)(2) shall take effect upon publication unless the regulation or order specifies otherwise. The Administrator may stay the effectiveness of the regulation or order if, after issuance of such regulation or order, objections are filed with respect to such regulation or order pursuant to paragraph (2).

(2) FURTHER PROCEEDINGS.—

(A) OBJECTIONS.—Within 60 days after a regulation or order is issued under subsection (d)(4), (e)(1)(A), (e)(1)(B), (f)(2), (n)(3), or (n)(5)(C), any person may file objections thereto with the Administrator, specifying with particularity the provisions of the regulation or order deemed objectionable and stating reasonable grounds therefor. If the regulation or order was issued in response to a petition under subsection (d)(1), a copy of each objection filed by a person other than the petitioner shall be served by the Administrator on the petitioner.

(B) HEARING.—An objection may include a request for a public evidentiary hearing upon the objection. The Administrator shall, upon the initiative of the Administrator or upon the request of an interested person and after due notice, hold a public evidentiary hearing if and to the extent the Administrator determines that such a public hearing is necessary to receive factual evidence relevant to material issues of fact raised by the objections. The presiding officer in such a hearing may authorize a party to obtain discovery from other persons and may upon a showing of good cause made by a party issue a subpoena to compel testimony or production of documents from any person. The presiding officer shall be governed by the Federal Rules of Civil Procedure in making any order for the protection of the witness or the content of documents produced and shall order the payment of reasonable fees and expenses as a condition to requiring testimony of the witness. On contest, such a subpoena may be enforced by a Federal district court.

(C) FINAL DECISION.—As soon as practicable after receiving the arguments of the parties, the Administrator shall issue an order stating the action taken upon each such objection and setting forth any revision to the regulation or prior order that the Administrator has found to be warranted. If a hearing was held under subparagraph (B), such order and any revision to the regulation or prior order shall, with respect to questions of fact at issue in the hearing, be based only on substantial evidence of record at such hearing, and shall set forth in detail the findings of facts and the conclusions of law or policy upon which the order or regulation is based.

(h) JUDICIAL REVIEW.—

(1) PETITION.—In a case of actual controversy as to the validity of any regulation issued under subsection (e)(1)(C), or any order issued under subsection (f)(1)(C) or (g)(2)(C), or any regulation that is the subject of such an order, any person who will be adversely affected by such order or regulation may obtain judicial review by filing in the United States Court of Appeals for the circuit wherein that person resides or has its principal place of business, or in the United States Court of Appeals for the District of Columbia Circuit, within 60 days after publication of such order or regulation, a petition praying that the order or regulation be set aside in whole or in part.

(2) RECORD AND JURISDICTION.—A copy of the petition under paragraph (1) shall be forthwith transmitted by the clerk of the court to the Administrator, or any officer designated by the Administrator for that purpose, and thereupon the Administrator shall file in the court the record of the proceedings on which the Administrator based the order or regulation, as provided in section 2112 of title 28, United States Code. Upon the filing of such a petition, the court shall have exclusive jurisdiction to affirm or set aside the order or regulation complained of in whole or in part. As to orders issued following a public evidentiary hearing, the findings of the Administrator with respect to questions of fact shall be sustained only if supported by substantial evidence when considered on the record as a whole.

(3) ADDITIONAL EVIDENCE.—If a party applies to the court for leave to adduce additional evidence and shows to the satisfaction of the court that the additional evidence is material and that there were reasonable grounds for the failure to adduce the evidence in the proceeding before the Administrator, the court may order that the additional evidence (and evidence in rebuttal thereof) shall be taken before the Administrator in the manner and upon the terms and conditions the court deems proper. The Administrator may modify prior findings as to the facts by reason of the additional evidence so taken and may modify the order or regulation accordingly. The Administrator shall file with the court any such modified finding, order, or regulation.

(4) FINAL JUDGMENT; SUPREME COURT REVIEW.—The judgment of the court affirming or setting aside, in whole or in part, any regulation or any order and

any regulation which is the subject of such an order shall be final, subject to review by the Supreme Court of the United States as provided in section 1254 of title 28 of the United States Code. The commencement of proceedings under this subsection shall not, unless specifically ordered by the court to the contrary, operate as a stay of a regulation or order.

(5) APPLICATION.—Any issue as to which review is or was obtainable under this subsection shall not be the subject of judicial review under any other provision of law.

(i) CONFIDENTIALITY AND USE OF DATA.—

(1) GENERAL RULE.—Data and information that are or have been submitted to the Administrator under this section or section 409 in support of a tolerance or an exemption from a tolerance shall be entitled to confidential treatment for reasons of business confidentiality and to exclusive use and data compensation to the same extent provided by sections 3 and 10 of the Federal Insecticide, Fungicide, and Rodenticide Act.

(2) EXCEPTIONS.—

(A) IN GENERAL.—Data and information that are entitled to confidential treatment under paragraph (1) may be disclosed, under such security requirements as the Administrator may provide by regulation, to—

(i) employees of the United States authorized by the Administrator to examine such data and information in the carrying out of their official duties under this Act or other Federal statutes intended to protect the public health; or

(ii) contractors with the United States authorized by the Administrator to examine such data and information in the carrying out of contracts under this Act or such statutes.

(B) CONGRESS.—This subsection does not authorize the withholding of data or information from either House of Congress or from, to the extent of matter within its jurisdiction, any committee or subcommittee of such committee or any joint committee of Congress or any subcommittee of such joint committee.

(3) SUMMARIES.—Notwithstanding any provision of this subsection or other law, the Administrator may publish the informative summary required by subsection (d)(2)(A)(i) and may, in issuing a proposed or final regulation or order under this section, publish an informative summary of the data relating to the regulation or order.

(j) STATUS OF PREVIOUSLY ISSUED REGULATIONS.—

(1) REGULATIONS UNDER SECTION 406.—Regulations affecting pesticide chemical residues in or on raw agricultural commodities promulgated, in accordance with section 701(e), under the authority of section 406(a) upon the

basis of public hearings instituted before January 1, 1953, shall be deemed to be regulations issued under this section and shall be subject to modification or revocation under subsections (d) and (e), and shall be subject to review under subsection (q).

(2) REGULATIONS UNDER SECTION 409.—Regulations that established tolerances for substances that are pesticide chemical residues in or on processed food, or that otherwise stated the conditions under which such pesticide chemicals could be safely used, and that were issued under section 409 on or before the date of the enactment of this paragraph, shall be deemed to be regulations issued under this section and shall be subject to modification or revocation under subsection (d) or (e), and shall be subject to review under subsection (q).

(3) REGULATIONS UNDER SECTION 408.—Regulations that established tolerances or exemptions under this section that were issued on or before the date of the enactment of this paragraph shall remain in effect unless modified or revoked under subsection (d) or (e), and shall be subject to review under subsection (q).

(4) CERTAIN SUBSTANCES.—With respect to a substance that is not included in the definition of the term "pesticide chemical" under section 201(q)(1) but was so included on the day before the date of the enactment of the Antimicrobial Regulation Technical Corrections Act of 1998, the following applies as of such date of enactment:

(A) Notwithstanding paragraph (2), any regulation applying to the use of the substance that was in effect on the day before such date, and was on such day deemed in such paragraph to have been issued under this section, shall be considered to have been issued under section 409.

(B) Notwithstanding paragraph (3), any regulation applying to the use of the substance that was in effect on such day and was issued under this section (including any such regulation issued before the date of the enactment of the Food Quality Protection Act of 1996) is deemed to have been issued under section 409.

(k) TRANSITIONAL PROVISION.—If, on the day before the date of the enactment of this subsection, a substance that is a pesticide chemical was, with respect to a particular pesticidal use of the substance and any resulting pesticide chemical residue in or on a particular food—

(1) regarded by the Administrator or the Secretary as generally recognized as safe for use within the meaning of the provisions of subsection (a) or section 201(s) as then in effect; or

(2) regarded by the Secretary as a substance described by section 201(s)(4);

such a pesticide chemical residue shall be regarded as exempt from the requirement for a tolerance, as of the date of enactment of this subsection. The Administrator shall by regulation indicate which substances are described by this subsection. Any exemption under this subsection may be modified or revoked as if it had been issued under subsection (c).

(*l*) HARMONIZATION WITH ACTION UNDER OTHER LAWS.—

(1) COORDINATION WITH FIFRA.—To the extent practicable and consistent with the review deadlines in subsection (q), in issuing a final rule under this subsection that suspends or revokes a tolerance or exemption for a pesticide chemical residue in or on food, the Administrator shall coordinate such action with any related necessary action under the Federal Insecticide, Fungicide, and Rodenticide Act.

(2) REVOCATION OF TOLERANCE OR EXEMPTION FOLLOWING CANCELLATION OF ASSOCIATED REGISTRATIONS.—If the Administrator, acting under the Federal Insecticide, Fungicide, and Rodenticide Act, cancels the registration of each pesticide that contains a particular pesticide chemical and that is labeled for use on a particular food, or requires that the registration of each such pesticide be modified to prohibit its use in connection with the production, storage, or transportation of such food, due in whole or in part to dietary risks to humans posed by residues of that pesticide chemical on that food, the Administrator shall revoke any tolerance or exemption that allows the presence of the pesticide chemical, or any pesticide chemical residue that results from its use, in or on that food. Subsection (e) shall apply to actions taken under this paragraph. A revocation under this paragraph shall become effective not later than 180 days after—

(A) the date by which each such cancellation of a registration has become effective; or

(B) the date on which the use of the canceled pesticide becomes unlawful under the terms of the cancellation, whichever is later.

(3) SUSPENSION OF TOLERANCE OR EXEMPTION FOLLOWING SUSPENSION OF ASSOCIATED REGISTRATIONS.—

(A) SUSPENSION.—If the Administrator, acting under the Federal Insecticide, Fungicide, and Rodenticide Act, suspends the use of each registered pesticide that contains a particular pesticide chemical and that is labeled for use on a particular food, due in whole or in part to dietary risks to humans posed by residues of that pesticide chemical on that food, the Administrator shall suspend any tolerance or exemption that allows the presence of the pesticide chemical, or any pesticide chemical residue that results from its use, in or on that food. Subsection (e) shall apply to actions taken under this paragraph. A suspension under this paragraph shall become effective not later than 60 days after the date by which each such suspension of use has become effective.

(B) EFFECT OF SUSPENSION.—The suspension of a tolerance or exemption under subparagraph (A) shall be effective as long as the use of each associated registration of a pesticide is suspended under the Federal Insecticide, Fungicide, and Rodenticide Act. While a suspension of a tolerance or exemption is effective the tolerance or exemption shall not be considered to be in effect. If the suspension of use of the pesticide under that Act is terminated, leaving the registration of the pesticide for such use in effect under that Act, the Administrator shall rescind any associated suspension of tolerance or exemption.

(4) TOLERANCES FOR UNAVOIDABLE RESIDUES.—In connection with action taken under paragraph (2) or (3), or with respect to pesticides whose registrations were suspended or canceled prior to the date of the enactment of this paragraph under the Federal Insecticide, Fungicide, and Rodenticide Act, if the Administrator determines that a residue of the canceled or suspended pesticide chemical will unavoidably persist in the environment and thereby be present in or on a food, the Administrator may establish a tolerance for the pesticide chemical residue. In establishing such a tolerance, the Administrator shall take into account both the factors set forth in subsection (b)(2) and the unavoidability of the residue. Subsection (e) shall apply to the establishment of such tolerance. The Administrator shall review any such tolerance periodically and modify it as necessary so that it allows no greater level of the pesticide chemical residue than is unavoidable.

(5) PESTICIDE RESIDUES RESULTING FROM LAWFUL APPLICATION OF PESTICIDE.—Notwithstanding any other provision of this Act, if a tolerance or exemption for a pesticide chemical residue in or on a food has been revoked, suspended, or modified under this section, an article of that food shall not be deemed unsafe solely because of the presence of such pesticide chemical residue in or on such food if it is shown to the satisfaction of the Secretary that—

(A) the residue is present as the result of an application or use of a pesticide at a time and in a manner that was lawful under the Federal Insecticide, Fungicide, and Rodenticide Act; and

(B) the residue does not exceed a level that was authorized at the time of that application or use to be present on the food under a tolerance, exemption, food additive regulation, or other sanction then in effect under this Act;

unless, in the case of any tolerance or exemption revoked, suspended, or modified under this subsection or subsection (d) or (e), the Administrator has issued a determination that consumption of the legally treated food during the period of its likely availability in commerce will pose an unreasonable dietary risk.

(6) TOLERANCE FOR USE OF PESTICIDES UNDER AN EMERGENCY EXEMPTION.—If the Administrator grants an exemption under section 18 of the Federal Insec-

ticide, Fungicide, and Rodenticide Act (7 U.S.C. 136p) for a pesticide chemical, the Administrator shall establish a tolerance or exemption from the requirement for a tolerance for the pesticide chemical residue. Such a tolerance or exemption from a tolerance shall have an expiration date. The Administrator may establish such a tolerance or exemption without providing notice or a period for comment on the tolerance or exemption. The Administrator shall promulgate regulations within 365 days after the date of the enactment of this paragraph governing the establishment of tolerances and exemptions under this paragraph. Such regulations shall be consistent with the safety standard under subsections (b)(2) and (c)(2) and with section 18 of the Federal Insecticide, Fungicide, and Rodenticide Act.

(m) FEES.—

(1) AMOUNT.—The Administrator shall by regulation require the payment of such fees as will in the aggregate, in the judgment of the Administrator, be sufficient over a reasonable term to provide, equip, and maintain an adequate service for the performance of the Administrator's functions under this section. Under the regulations, the performance of the Administrator's services or other functions under this section, including—

(A) the acceptance for filing of a petition submitted under subsection (d);

(B) establishing, modifying, leaving in effect, or revoking a tolerance or establishing, modifying, leaving in effect, or revoking an exemption from the requirement for a tolerance under this section;

(C) the acceptance for filing of objections under subsection (g); or

(D) the certification and filing in court of a transcript of the proceedings and the record under subsection (h); may be conditioned upon the payment of such fees. The regulations may further provide for waiver or refund of fees in whole or in part when in the judgment of the Administrator such a waiver or refund is equitable and not contrary to the purposes of this subsection.

(2) DEPOSIT.—All fees collected under paragraph (1) shall be deposited in the Reregistration and Expedited Processing Fund created by section 4(k) of the Federal Insecticide, Fungicide, and Rodenticide Act. Such fees shall be available to the Administrator, without fiscal year limitation, for the performance of the Administrator's services or functions as specified in paragraph (1).

(3) PROHIBITION.—During the period beginning on the effective date of the Pesticide Registration Improvement Renewal Act[18] and ending on September

---

18. Pub. L. No. 110–94, 121 Stat. 1000 (2007). Section 6 of such Public Law provides that "This Act and the amendments made by this Act take effect on October 1, 2007."

30, 2012, the Administrator shall not collect any tolerance fees under paragraph (1).

(n) NATIONAL UNIFORMITY OF TOLERANCES.—

(1) QUALIFYING PESTICIDE CHEMICAL RESIDUE.—For purposes of this subsection, the term "qualifying pesticide chemical residue" means a pesticide chemical residue resulting from the use, in production, processing, or storage of a food, of a pesticide chemical that is an active ingredient and that—

(A) was first approved for such use in a registration of a pesticide issued under section 3(c)(5) of the Federal Insecticide, Fungicide, and Rodenticide Act on or after April 25, 1985, on the basis of data determined by the Administrator to meet all applicable requirements for data prescribed by regulations in effect under that Act on April 25, 1985; or

(B) was approved for such use in a reregistration eligibility determination issued under section 4(g) of that Act on or after the date of enactment of this subsection.

(2) QUALIFYING FEDERAL DETERMINATION.—For purposes of this subsection, the term "qualifying Federal determination" means a tolerance or exemption from the requirement for a tolerance for a qualifying pesticide chemical residue that—

(A) is issued under this section after the date of the enactment of this subsection and determined by the Administrator to meet the standard under subsection (b)(2)(A) (in the case of a tolerance) or (c)(2) (in the case of an exemption); or

(B)(i) pursuant to subsection (j) is remaining in effect or is deemed to have been issued under this section, or is regarded under subsection (k) as exempt from the requirement for a tolerance; and

(ii) is determined by the Administrator to meet the standard under subsection (b)(2)(A) (in the case of a tolerance) or (c)(2) (in the case of an exemption).

(3) LIMITATION.—The Administrator may make the determination described in paragraph (2)(B)(ii) only by issuing a rule in accordance with the procedure set forth in subsection (d) or (e) and only if the Administrator issues a proposed rule and allows a period of not less than 30 days for comment on the proposed rule. Any such rule shall be reviewable in accordance with subsections (g) and (h).

(4) STATE AUTHORITY.—Except as provided in paragraphs (5), (6), and (8) no State or political subdivision may establish or enforce any regulatory limit on a qualifying pesticide chemical residue in or on any food if a qualifying Federal determination applies to the presence of such pesticide chemical

residue in or on such food, unless such State regulatory limit is identical to such qualifying Federal determination. A State or political subdivision shall be deemed to establish or enforce a regulatory limit on a pesticide chemical residue in or on a food if it purports to prohibit or penalize the production, processing, shipping, or other handling of a food because it contains a pesticide residue (in excess of a prescribed limit).

(5) PETITION PROCEDURE.—

(A) IN GENERAL.—Any State may petition the Administrator for authorization to establish in such State a regulatory limit on a qualifying pesticide chemical residue in or on any food that is not identical to the qualifying Federal determination applicable to such qualifying pesticide chemical residue.

(B) PETITION REQUIREMENTS.—Any petition under subparagraph (A) shall—

(i) satisfy any requirements prescribed, by rule, by the Administrator; and

(ii) be supported by scientific data about the pesticide chemical residue that is the subject of the petition or about chemically related pesticide chemical residues, data on the consumption within such State of food bearing the pesticide chemical residue, and data on exposure of humans within such State to the pesticide chemical residue.

(C) AUTHORIZATION.—The Administrator may, by order, grant the authorization described in subparagraph (A) if the Administrator determines that the proposed State regulatory limit—

(i) is justified by compelling local conditions; and

(ii) would not cause any food to be a violation of Federal law.

(D) TREATMENT.—In lieu of any action authorized under subparagraph (C), the Administrator may treat a petition under this paragraph as a petition under subsection (d) to modify or revoke a tolerance or an exemption. If the Administrator determines to treat a petition under this paragraph as a petition under subsection (d), the Administrator shall thereafter act on the petition pursuant to subsection (d).

(E) REVIEW.—Any order of the Administrator granting or denying the authorization described in subparagraph (A) shall be subject to review in the manner described in subsections (g) and (h).

(6) URGENT PETITION PROCEDURE.—Any State petition to the Administrator pursuant to paragraph (5) that demonstrates that consumption of a food containing such pesticide residue level during the period of the food's likely availability in the State will pose a significant public health threat from acute

exposure shall be considered an urgent petition. If an order by the Administrator to grant or deny the requested authorization in an urgent petition is not made within 30 days of receipt of the petition, the petitioning State may establish and enforce a temporary regulatory limit on a qualifying pesticide chemical residue in or on the food. The temporary regulatory limit shall be validated or terminated by the Administrator's final order on the petition.

(7) RESIDUES FROM LAWFUL APPLICATION.—No State or political subdivision may enforce any regulatory limit on the level of a pesticide chemical residue that may appear in or on any food if, at the time of the application of the pesticide that resulted in such residue, the sale of such food with such residue level was lawful under this section and under the law of such State, unless the State demonstrates that consumption of the food containing such pesticide residue level during the period of the food's likely availability in the State will pose an unreasonable dietary risk to the health of persons within such State.

(8) SAVINGS.—Nothing in this Act preempts the authority of any State or political subdivision to require that a food containing a pesticide chemical residue bear or be the subject of a warning or other statement relating to the presence of the pesticide chemical residue in or on such food.

(*o*) CONSUMER RIGHT TO KNOW.—Not later than 2 years after the date of the enactment of the Food Quality Protection Act of 1996, and annually thereafter, the Administrator shall, in consultation with the Secretary of Agriculture and the Secretary of Health and Human Services, publish in a format understandable to a lay person, and distribute to large retail grocers for public display (in a manner determined by the grocer), the following information, at a minimum:

(1) A discussion of the risks and benefits of pesticide chemical residues in or on food purchased by consumers.

(2) A listing of actions taken under subparagraph (B) of subsection (b)(2) that may result in pesticide chemical residues in or on food that present a yearly or lifetime risk above the risk allowed under subparagraph (A) of such subsection, and the food on which the pesticide chemicals producing the residues are used.

(3) Recommendations to consumers for reducing dietary exposure to pesticide chemical residues in a manner consistent with maintaining a healthy diet, including a list of food that may reasonably substitute for food listed under paragraph (2).

Nothing[19] in this subsection shall prevent retail grocers from providing additional information.

___

19. Indentation is so in law. Beginning of sentence probably should be moved to left.

(p) ESTROGENIC SUBSTANCES SCREENING PROGRAM.—

(1) DEVELOPMENT.—Not later than 2 years after the date of enactment of this section,[20] the Administrator shall in consultation with the Secretary of Health and Human Services develop a screening program, using appropriate validated test systems and other scientifically relevant information, to determine whether certain substances may have an effect in humans that is similar to an effect produced by a naturally occurring estrogen, or such other endocrine effect as the Administrator may designate.

(2) IMPLEMENTATION.—Not later than 3 years after the date of enactment of this section, after obtaining public comment and review of the screening program described in paragraph (1) by the scientific advisory panel established under section 25(d) of the Federal Insecticide, Fungicide, and Rodenticide Act or the science advisory board established by section 8 of the Environmental Research, Development, and Demonstration[21] Act of 1978 (42 U.S.C. 4365), the Administrator shall implement the program.

(3) SUBSTANCES.—In carrying out the screening program described in paragraph (1), the Administrator—

(A) shall provide for the testing of all pesticide chemicals; and

(B) may provide for the testing of any other substance that may have an effect that is cumulative to an effect of a pesticide chemical if the Administrator determines that a substantial population may be exposed to such substance.

(4) EXEMPTION.—Notwithstanding paragraph (3), the Administrator may, by order, exempt from the requirements of this section a biologic substance or other substance if the Administrator determines that the substance is anticipated not to produce any effect in humans similar to an effect produced by a naturally occurring estrogen.

(5) COLLECTION OF INFORMATION.—

(A) IN GENERAL.—The Administrator shall issue an order to a registrant of a substance for which testing is required under this subsection, or to a person who manufactures or imports a substance for which testing is required under this subsection, to conduct testing in accordance with the screening program described in paragraph (1), and submit information obtained from the testing to the Administrator, within a reasonable time period that the Administrator determines is sufficient for the generation of the information.

(B) PROCEDURES.—To the extent practicable the Administrator shall minimize duplicative testing of the same substance for the same endocrine

20. Provisions were added by Pub. L. No. 104–170, § 405, 110 Stat. 1489, 1532–34 (1996).

21. So in law. The word "Authorization" probably should appear after "Demonstration".

effect, develop, as appropriate, procedures for fair and equitable sharing of test costs, and develop, as necessary, procedures for handling of confidential business information.

(C) FAILURE OF REGISTRANTS TO SUBMIT INFORMATION.—

(i) SUSPENSION.—If a registrant of a substance referred to in paragraph (3)(A) fails to comply with an order under subparagraph (A) of this paragraph, the Administrator shall issue a notice of intent to suspend the sale or distribution of the substance by the registrant. Any suspension proposed under this paragraph shall become final at the end of the 30–day period beginning on the date that the registrant receives the notice of intent to suspend, unless during that period a person adversely affected by the notice requests a hearing or the Administrator determines that the registrant has complied fully with this paragraph.

(ii) HEARING.—If a person requests a hearing under clause (i), the hearing shall be conducted in accordance with section 554 of title 5, United States Code. The only matter for resolution at the hearing shall be whether the registrant has failed to comply with an order under subparagraph (A) of this paragraph. A decision by the Administrator after completion of a hearing shall be considered to be a final agency action.

(iii) TERMINATION OF SUSPENSIONS.—The Administrator shall terminate a suspension under this subparagraph issued with respect to a registrant if the Administrator determines that the registrant has complied fully with this paragraph.

(D) NONCOMPLIANCE BY OTHER PERSONS.—Any person (other than a registrant) who fails to comply with an order under subparagraph (A) shall be liable for the same penalties and sanctions as are provided under section 16 of the Toxic Substances Control Act (15 U.S.C. 2601 and following) in the case of a violation referred to in that section. Such penalties and sanctions shall be assessed and imposed in the same manner as provided in such section 16.

(6) AGENCY ACTION.—In the case of any substance that is found, as a result of testing and evaluation under this section, to have an endocrine effect on humans, the Administrator shall, as appropriate, take action under such statutory authority as is available to the Administrator, including consideration under other sections of this Act, as is necessary to ensure the protection of public health.

(7) REPORT TO CONGRESS.—Not later than 4 years after the date of enactment of this section, the Administrator shall prepare and submit to Congress a report containing—

(A) the findings of the Administrator resulting from the screening program described in paragraph (1);

(B) recommendations for further testing needed to evaluate the impact on human health of the substances tested under the screening program; and

(C) recommendations for any further actions (including any action described in paragraph (6)) that the Administrator determines are appropriate based on the findings.

(q) SCHEDULE FOR REVIEW.—

(1) IN GENERAL.—The Administrator shall review tolerances and exemptions for pesticide chemical residues in effect on the day before the date of the enactment of the Food Quality Protection Act of 1996, as expeditiously as practicable, assuring that—

(A) 33 percent of such tolerances and exemptions are reviewed within 3 years of the date of enactment of such Act;

(B) 66 percent of such tolerances and exemptions are reviewed within 6 years of the date of enactment of such Act; and

(C) 100 percent of such tolerances and exemptions are reviewed within 10 years of the date of enactment of such Act.

In conducting a review of a tolerance or exemption, the Administrator shall determine whether the tolerance or exemption meets the requirements of subsections[22] (b)(2) or (c)(2) and shall, by the deadline for the review of the tolerance or exemption, issue a regulation under subsection (d)(4) or (e)(1) to modify or revoke the tolerance or exemption if the tolerance or exemption does not meet such requirements.

(2) PRIORITIES.—In determining priorities for reviewing tolerances and exemptions under paragraph (1), the Administrator shall give priority to the review of the tolerances or exemptions that appear to pose the greatest risk to public health.

(3) PUBLICATION OF SCHEDULE.—Not later than 12 months after the date of the enactment of the Food Quality Protection Act of 1996, the Administrator shall publish a schedule for review of tolerances and exemptions established prior to the date of the enactment of the Food Quality Protection Act of 1996. The determination of priorities for the review of tolerances and exemptions pursuant to this subsection is not a rulemaking and shall not be subject to judicial review, except that failure to take final action pursuant to the schedule established by this paragraph shall be subject to judicial review.

(r) TEMPORARY TOLERANCE OR EXEMPTION.—The Administrator may, upon the request of any person who has obtained an experimental permit for a pesticide chemical under the Federal Insecticide, Fungicide, and Rodenticide Act or upon the Administrator's own initiative, establish a temporary tolerance or exemption

---

22. So in law. Probably should be "subsection".

for the pesticide chemical residue for the uses covered by the permit. Subsections (b)(2), (c)(2), (d), and (e) shall apply to actions taken under this subsection.

(s) SAVINGS CLAUSE.—Nothing in this section shall be construed to amend or modify the provisions of the Toxic Substances Control Act or the Federal Insecticide, Fungicide, and Rodenticide Act.

SEC. 409 [21 U.S.C. 348]. FOOD ADDITIVES

Unsafe Food Additives

(a) A food additive shall, with respect to any particular use or intended use of such additives, be deemed to be unsafe for the purposes of the application of clause (2)(C) of section 402(a), unless—

(1) it and its use or intended use conform to the terms of an exemption which is in effect pursuant to subsection (j) of this section;

(2) there is in effect, and it and its use or intended use are in conformity with, a regulation issued under this section prescribing the conditions under which such additive may be safely used; or

(3) in the case of a food additive as defined in this Act that is a food contact substance, there is—

(A) in effect, and such substance and the use of such substance are in conformity with, a regulation issued under this section prescribing the conditions under which such additive may be safely used; or

(B) a notification submitted under subsection (h) that is effective.

While such a regulation relating to a food additive, or such a notification under subsection (h)(1) relating to a food additive that is a food contact substance, is in effect, and has not been revoked pursuant to subsection (i), a food shall not, by reason of bearing or containing such a food additive in accordance with the regulation or notification, be considered adulterated under section 402(a)(1).

Petition To Establish Safety

(b)(1) Any person may, with respect to any intended use of a food additive, file with the Secretary a petition proposing the issuance of a regulation prescribing the conditions under which such additive may be safely used.

(2) Such petition shall, in addition to any explanatory or supporting data, contain—

(A) the name and all pertinent information concerning such food additive, including, where available, its chemical identity and composition;

(B) a statement of the conditions of the proposed use of such additive, including all directions, recommendations, and suggestions proposed for the use of such additive, and including specimens of its proposed labeling;

(C) all relevant data bearing on the physical or other technical effect such additive is intended to produce, and the quantity of such additive required to produce such effect;

(D) a description of practicable methods for determining the quantity of such additive in or on food, and any substance formed in or on food, because of its use; and

(E) full reports of investigations made with respect to the safety for use of such additive, including full information as to the methods and controls used in conducting such investigations.

(3) Upon request of the Secretary, the petitioner shall furnish (or, if the petitioner is not the manufacturer of such additive, the petitioner shall have the manufacturer of such additive furnish, without disclosure to the petitioner), a full description of the methods used in, and the facilities and controls used for, the production of such additive.

(4) Upon request of the Secretary, the petitioner shall furnish samples of the food additive involved, or articles used as components thereof, and of the food in or on which the additive is proposed to be used.

(5) Notice of the regulation proposed by the petitioner shall be published in general terms by the Secretary within thirty days after filing.

Action on the Petition

(c)(1) The Secretary shall—

(A) by order establish a regulation (whether or not in accord with that proposed by the petitioner) prescribing, with respect to one or more proposed uses of the food additive involved, the conditions under which such additive may be safely used (including, but not limited to, specifications as to the particular food or classes of food in or on which such additive may be used, the maximum quantity which may be used or permitted to remain in or on such food, the manner in which such additive may be added to or used in or on such food, and any directions or other labeling or packaging requirements for such additive deemed necessary by him to assure the safety of such use), and shall notify the petitioner of such order and the reasons for such action; or

(B) by order deny the petition, and shall notify the petitioner of such order and of the reasons for such action.

(2) The order required by paragraph (1) (A) or (B) of this subsection shall be issued within ninety days after the date of filing of the petition, except that the Secretary may (prior to such ninetieth day), by written notice to the petitioner, extend such ninety day period to such time (not more than one hundred and eighty days after the date of filing of the petition) as the Secretary deems necessary to enable him to study and investigate the petition.

(3) No such regulation shall issue if a fair evaluation of the data before the Secretary—

(A) fails to establish that the proposed use of the food additive, under the conditions of use to be specified in the regulation, will be safe: Provided, That no additive shall be deemed to be safe if it is found to induce cancer when ingested by man or animal, or if it is found, after tests which are appropriate for the evaluation of the safety of food additives, to induce cancer in man or animal, except that this proviso shall not apply with respect to the use of a substance as an ingredient of feed for animals which are raised for food production, if the Secretary finds (i) that, under the conditions of use and feeding specified in proposed labeling and reasonably certain to be followed in practice, such additive will not adversely affect the animals for which such feed is intended, and (ii) that no residue of the additive will be found (by methods of examination prescribed or approved by the Secretary by regulations, which regulations shall not be subject to subsections (f) and (g)) in any edible portion of such animal after slaughter or in any food yielded by or derived from the living animal; or

(B) shows that the proposed use of the additive would promote deception of the consumer in violation of this Act or would otherwise result in adulteration or in misbranding of food within the meaning of this Act.

(4) If, in the judgment of the Secretary, based upon a fair evaluation of the data before him, a tolerance limitation is required in order to assure that the proposed use of an additive will be safe, the Secretary—

(A) shall not fix such tolerance limitation at a level higher than he finds to be reasonably required to accomplish the physical or other technical effect for which such additive is intended; and

(B) shall not establish a regulation for such proposed use if he finds upon a fair evaluation of the data before him that such data do not establish that such use would accomplish the intended physical or other technical effect.

(5) In determining, for the purposes of this section, whether a proposed use of a food additive is safe, the Secretary shall consider among other relevant factors—

(A) the probable consumption of the additive and of any substance formed in or on food because of the use of the additive;

(B) the cumulative effect of such additive in the diet of man or animals, taking into account any chemically or pharmacologically related substance or substances in such diet; and

(C) safety factors which in the opinion of experts qualified by scientific training and experience to evaluate the safety of food additives are generally recognized as appropriate for the use of animal experimentation data.

Regulation Issued on Secretary's Initiative

(d) The Secretary may at any time, upon his own initiative, propose the issuance of a regulation prescribing, with respect to any particular use of a food additive, the conditions under which such additive may be safely used, and the reasons therefor. After the thirtieth day following publication of such a proposal, the Secretary may by order establish a regulation based upon the proposal.

Publication and Effective Date of Orders

(e) Any order, including any regulation established by such order, issued under subsection (c) or (d) of this section, shall be published and shall be effective upon publication, but the Secretary may stay such effectiveness if, after issuance of such order, a hearing is sought with respect to such order pursuant to subsection (f).

Objections and Public Hearing

(f)(1) Within thirty days after publication of an order made pursuant to subsection (c) or (d) of this section, any person adversely affected by such an order may file objections thereto with the Secretary, specifying with particularity the provisions of the order deemed objectionable, stating reasonable grounds therefor, and requesting a public hearing upon such objections. The Secretary shall, after due notice, as promptly as possible hold such public hearing for the purpose of receiving evidence relevant and material to the issues raised by such objections. As soon as practicable after completion of the hearing, the Secretary shall by order act upon such objections and make such order public.

(2) Such order shall be based upon a fair evaluation of the entire record at such hearing, and shall include a statement setting forth in detail the findings and conclusions upon which the order is based.

(3) The Secretary shall specify in the order the date on which it shall take effect, except that it shall not be made to take effect prior to the ninetieth day after its publication, unless the Secretary finds that emergency conditions exist necessitating an earlier effective date, in which event the Secretary shall specify in the order his findings as to such conditions.

Judicial Review

(g)(1) In a case of actual controversy as to the validity of any order issued under subsection (f), including any order thereunder with respect to amendment or repeal of a regulation issued under this section, any person who will be adversely affected by such order may obtain judicial review by filing in the United States Court of Appeals for the circuit wherein such person resides or has his principal place of business, or in the United States Court of Appeals for the District of Columbia Circuit, within sixty days after the entry of such order, a petition praying that the order be set aside in whole or in part.

(2) A copy of such petition shall be forthwith transmitted by the clerk of the court to the Secretary, or any officer designated by him for that purpose, and thereupon the Secretary shall file in the court the record of the proceedings on which he based his order, as provided in section 2112 of title 28, United States Code. Upon the filing of such petition the court shall have jurisdiction, which upon the filing of the record with it shall be exclusive, to affirm or set aside the order complained of in whole or in part. Until the filing of the record the Secretary may modify or set aside his order. The findings of the Secretary with respect to questions of fact shall be sustained if based upon a fair evaluation of the entire record at such hearing.

(3) The court, on such judicial review, shall not sustain the order of the Secretary if he failed to comply with any requirement imposed on him by subsection (f)(2) of this section.

(4) If application is made to the court for leave to adduce additional evidence, the court may order such additional evidence to be taken before the Secretary and to be adduced upon the hearing in such manner and upon such terms and conditions as to the court may seem proper, if such evidence is material and there were reasonable grounds for failure to adduce such evidence in the proceedings below. The Secretary may modify his findings as to the facts and order by reason of the additional evidence so taken, and shall file with the court such modified findings and order.

(5) The judgment of the court affirming or setting aside, in whole or in part, any order under this section shall be final, subject to review by the Supreme Court of the United States upon certiorari or certification as provided in section 1254 of title 28 of the United States Code. The commencement of proceedings under this section shall not, unless specifically ordered by the court to the contrary, operate as a stay of an order.

Notification Relating to a Food Contact Substance

(h)(1) Subject to such regulations as may be promulgated under paragraph (3), a manufacturer or supplier of a food contact substance may, at least 120 days prior to the introduction or delivery for introduction into interstate commerce of the food contact substance, notify the Secretary of the identity and intended use of the food contact substance, and of the determination of the manufacturer or supplier that the intended use of such food contact substance is safe under the standard described in subsection (c)(3)(A). The notification shall contain the information that forms the basis of the determination and all information required to be submitted by regulations promulgated by the Secretary.

(2)(A) A notification submitted under paragraph (1) shall become effective 120 days after the date of receipt by the Secretary and the food contact substance may be introduced or delivered for introduction into interstate commerce, unless the Secretary makes a determination within the 120–day period that, based on the data and information before the Secretary, such use of the food contact substance has not been shown to be safe under the standard described in subsection (c)(3)(A), and informs the manufacturer or supplier of such determination.

(B) A decision by the Secretary to object to a notification shall constitute final agency action subject to judicial review.

(C) In this paragraph, the term "food contact substance" means the substance that is the subject of a notification submitted under paragraph (1), and does not include a similar or identical substance manufactured or prepared by a person other than the manufacturer identified in the notification.

(3)(A) The process in this subsection shall be utilized for authorizing the marketing of a food contact substance except where the Secretary determines that submission and review of a petition under subsection (b) is necessary to provide adequate assurance of safety, or where the Secretary and any manufacturer or supplier agree that such manufacturer or supplier may submit a petition under subsection (b).

(B) The Secretary is authorized to promulgate regulations to identify the circumstances in which a petition shall be filed under subsection (b), and shall consider criteria such as the probable consumption of such food contact substance and potential toxicity of the food contact substance in determining the circumstances in which a petition shall be filed under subsection (b).

(4) The Secretary shall keep confidential any information provided in a notification under paragraph (1) for 120 days after receipt by the Secretary of the notification. After the expiration of such 120 days, the information shall be available to any interested party except for any matter in the notification that is a trade secret or confidential commercial information.

(5)(A)(i) Except as provided in clause (ii), the notification program established under this subsection shall not operate in any fiscal year unless—

(I) an appropriation equal to or exceeding the applicable amount under clause (iv) is made for such fiscal year for carrying out such program in such fiscal year; and

(II) the Secretary certifies that the amount appropriated for such fiscal year for the Center for Food Safety and Applied Nutrition of the Food and Drug Administration (exclusive of the appropriation referred to in subclause (I)) equals or exceeds the amount appropriated for the Center for fiscal year 1997, excluding any amount appropriated for new programs.

(ii) The Secretary shall, not later than April 1, 1999, begin accepting and reviewing notifications submitted under the notification program established under this subsection if—

(I) an appropriation equal to or exceeding the applicable amount under clause (iii) is made for the last six months of fiscal year 1999 for carrying out such program during such period; and

107

(II) the Secretary certifies that the amount appropriated for such period for the Center for Food Safety and Applied Nutrition of the Food and Drug Administration (exclusive of the appropriation referred to in subclause (I)) equals or exceeds an amount equivalent to one-half the amount appropriated for the Center for fiscal year 1997, excluding any amount appropriated for new programs.

(iii) For the last six months of fiscal year 1999, the applicable amount under this clause is $1,500,000, or the amount specified in the budget request of the President for the six-month period involved for carrying out the notification program in fiscal year 1999, whichever is less.

(iv) For fiscal year 2000 and subsequent fiscal years, the applicable amount under this clause is $3,000,000, or the amount specified in the budget request of the President for the fiscal year involved for carrying out the notification program under this subsection, whichever is less.

(B) For purposes of carrying out the notification program under this subsection, there are authorized to be appropriated such sums as may be necessary for each of the fiscal years 1999 through fiscal year 2003, except that such authorization of appropriations is not effective for a fiscal year for any amount that is less than the applicable amount under clause (iii) or (iv) of subparagraph (A), whichever is applicable.

(C) Not later than April 1 of fiscal year 1998 and February 1 of each subsequent fiscal year, the Secretary shall submit a report to the Committees on Appropriations of the House of Representatives and the Senate, the Committee on Commerce of the House of Representatives, and the Committee on Labor and Human Resources of the Senate that provides an estimate of the Secretary of the costs of carrying out the notification program established under this subsection for the next fiscal year.

(6) In this section, the term "food contact substance" means any substance intended for use as a component of materials used in manufacturing, packing, packaging, transporting, or holding food if such use is not intended to have any technical effect in such food.

Amendment or Repeal of Regulations

(i) The Secretary shall by regulation prescribe the procedure by which regulations under the foregoing provisions of this section may be amended or repealed, and such procedure shall conform to the procedure provided in this section for the promulgation of such regulations. The Secretary shall by regulation prescribe the procedure by which the Secretary may deem a notification under subsection (h) to no longer be effective.

Exemptions for Investigational Use

(j) Without regard to subsections (b) to (i), inclusive, of this section, the Secretary shall by regulation provide for exempting from the requirements of this section any food additive, and any food bearing or containing such additive, intended solely for investigational use by qualified experts when in his opinion such exemption is consistent with the public health.

Sec. 410 [21 U.S.C. 349]. BOTTLED DRINKING WATER STANDARDS

(a) Except as provided in subsection (b), whenever the Administrator of the Environmental Protection Agency prescribes interim or revised national primary drinking water regulations under section 1412 of the Public Health Service Act, the Secretary shall consult with the Administrator and within 180 days after the promulgation of such drinking water regulations either promulgate amendments to regulations under this chapter applicable to bottled drinking water or publish in the Federal Register his reasons for not making such amendments.

(b)(1) Not later than 180 days before the effective date of a national primary drinking water regulation promulgated by the Administrator of the Environmental Protection Agency for a contaminant under section 1412 of the Safe Drinking Water Act (42 U.S.C. 300g–1), the Secretary shall promulgate a standard of quality regulation under this subsection for that contaminant in bottled water or make a finding that such a regulation is not necessary to protect the public health because the contaminant is contained in water in public water systems (as defined under section 1401(4) of such Act (42 U.S.C. 300f(4))) but not in water used for bottled drinking water. The effective date for any such standard of quality regulation shall be the same as the effective date for such national primary drinking water regulation, except for any standard of quality of regulation promulgated by the Secretary before the date of enactment of the Safe Drinking Water Act Amendments of 1996 for which (as of such date of enactment) an effective date had not been established. In the case of a standard of quality regulation to which such exception applies, the Secretary shall promulgate monitoring requirements for the contaminants covered by the regulation not later than 2 years after such date of enactment.

(2) A regulation issued by the Secretary as provided in this subsection shall include any monitoring requirements that the Secretary determines appropriate for bottled water.

(3) A regulation issued by the Secretary as provided in this subsection shall require the following:

(A) In the case of contaminants for which a maximum contaminant level is established in a national primary drinking water regulation under section 1412 of the Safe Drinking Water Act (42 U.S.C. 300g–1), the regulation under this subsection shall establish a maximum contaminant level for the contaminant in bottled water which is no less stringent than the maximum contaminant level provided in the national primary drinking water regulation.

(B) In the case of contaminants for which a treatment technique is established in a national primary drinking water regulation under section 1412 of the Safe Drinking Water Act (42 U.S.C. 300g–1), the regulation under this subsection shall require that bottled water be subject to requirements no less protective of the public health than those applicable to water provided by public water systems using the treatment technique required by the national primary drinking water regulation.

(4)(A) If the Secretary does not promulgate a regulation under this subsection within the period described in paragraph (1), the national primary drinking water regulation referred to in paragraph (1) shall be considered, as of the date on which the Secretary is required to establish a regulation under paragraph (1), as the regulation applicable under this subsection to bottled water.

(B) In the case of a national primary drinking water regulation that pursuant to subparagraph (A) is considered to be a standard of quality regulation, the Secretary shall, not later than the applicable date referred to in such subparagraph, publish in the Federal Register a notice—

(i) specifying the contents of such regulation, including monitoring requirements; and

(ii) providing that for purposes of this paragraph the effective date for such regulation is the same as the effective date for the regulation for purposes of the Safe Drinking Water Act (or, if the exception under paragraph (1) applies to the regulation, that the effective date for the regulation is not later than 2 years and 180 days after the date of enactment of the Safe Drinking Water Act Amendments of 1996).

SEC. 411 [21 U.S.C. 350]. VITAMINS AND MINERALS

(a)(1) Except as provided in paragraph (2)—

(A) the Secretary may not establish, under section 201(n), 401, or 403, maximum limits on the potency of any synthetic or natural vitamin or mineral within a food to which this section applies;

(B) the Secretary may not classify any natural or synthetic vitamin or mineral (or combination thereof) as a drug solely because it exceeds the level of potency which the Secretary determines is nutritionally rational or useful;

(C) the Secretary may not limit, under section 201(n), 401, or 403, the combination or number of any synthetic or natural—

(i) vitamin,

(ii) mineral, or

(iii) other ingredient of food,

within a food to which this section applies.

(2) Paragraph (1) shall not apply in the case of a vitamin, mineral, other ingredient of food, or food, which is represented for use by individuals in the treatment or management of specific diseases or disorders, by children, or by pregnant or lactating

women. For purposes of this subparagraph,[23] the term "children" means individuals who are under the age of twelve years.

(b)(1) A food to which this section applies shall not be deemed under section 403 to be misbranded solely because its label bears, in accordance with section 403(i)(2), all the ingredients in the food or its advertising contains references to ingredients in the food which are not vitamins or minerals.

(2) The labeling for any food to which this section applies may not list its ingredients which are not dietary supplement ingredients described in section 201(ff) (i) except as a part of a list of all the ingredients of such food, and (ii) unless such ingredients are listed in accordance with applicable regulations under section 403. To the extent that compliance with clause (i) of this subparagraph is impracticable or results in deception or unfair competition, exemptions shall be established by regulations promulgated by the Secretary.

(c)(1) For purposes of this section, the term "food to which this section applies" means a food for humans which is a food for special dietary use—

(A) which is or contains any natural or synthetic vitamin or mineral, and

(B) which—

(i) is intended for ingestion in tablet, capsule, powder, softgel, gelcap, or liquid form, or

(ii) if not intended for ingestion in such a form, is not represented as conventional food and is not represented for use as a sole item of a meal or of the diet.

(2) For purposes of paragraph (1)(B)(i), a food shall be considered as intended for ingestion in liquid form only if it is formulated in a fluid carrier and it is intended for ingestion in daily quantities measured in drops or similar small units of measure.

(3) For purposes of paragraph (1) and of section 403 (j) insofar as that section is applicable to food to which this section applies, the term "special dietary use" as applied to food used by man means a particular use for which a food purports or is represented to be used, including but not limited to the following:

(A) Supplying a special dietary need that exists by reason of a physical, physiological, pathological, or other condition, including but not limited to the condition of disease, convalescence, pregnancy, lactation, infancy, allergic hypersensitivity to food, underweight, overweight, or the need to control the intake of sodium.

(B) Supplying a vitamin, mineral, or other ingredient for use by man to supplement his diet by increasing the total dietary intake.

(C) Supplying a special dietary need by reason of being a food for use as the sole item of the diet.

23. So in law. Probably should be "paragraph".

SEC. 412 [21 U.S.C. 350a]. REQUIREMENTS FOR INFANT FORMULAS

(a) An infant formula, including an infant formula powder, shall be deemed to be adulterated if—

(1) such infant formula does not provide nutrients as required by subsection (i),

(2) such infant formula does not meet the quality factor requirements prescribed by the Secretary under subsection (b)(1), or

(3) the processing of such infant formula is not in compliance with the good manufacturing practices and the quality control procedures prescribed by the Secretary under subsection (b)(2).

(b)(1) The Secretary shall by regulation establish requirements for quality factors for infant formulas to the extent possible consistent with current scientific knowledge, including quality factor requirements for the nutrients required by subsection (i).

(2)(A) The Secretary shall by regulation establish good manufacturing practices for infant formulas, including quality control procedures that the Secretary determines are necessary to assure that an infant formula provides nutrients in accordance with this subsection and subsection (i) and is manufactured in a manner designed to prevent adulteration of the infant formula.

(B) The good manufacturing practices and quality control procedures prescribed by the Secretary under subparagraph (A) shall include requirements for—

(i) the testing, in accordance with paragraph (3) and by the manufacturer of an infant formula or an agent of such manufacturer, of each batch of infant formula for each nutrient required by subsection (i) before the distribution of such batch,

(ii) regularly scheduled testing, by the manufacturer of an infant formula or an agent of such manufacturer, of samples of infant formulas during the shelf life of such formulas to ensure that such formulas are in compliance with this section,

(iii) in-process controls including, where necessary, testing required by good manufacturing practices designed to prevent adulteration of each batch of infant formula, and

(iv) the conduct by the manufacturer of an infant formula or an agent of such manufacturer of regularly scheduled audits to determine that such manufacturer has complied with the regulations prescribed under subparagraph (A).

In prescribing requirements for audits under clause (iv), the Secretary shall provide that such audits be conducted by appropriately trained individuals who do not have any direct responsibility for the manufacture or production of infant formula.

(3)(A) At the final product stage, each batch of infant formula shall be tested for vitamin A, vitamin B1, vitamin C, and vitamin E to ensure that such infant formula is in compliance with the requirements of this subsection and subsection (i) relating to such vitamins.

(B) Each nutrient premix used in the manufacture of an infant formula shall be tested for each relied upon nutrient required by subsection (i) which is contained in such premix to ensure that such premix is in compliance with its specifications or certifications by a premix supplier.

(C) During the manufacturing process or at the final product stage and before distribution of an infant formula, an infant formula shall be tested for all nutrients required to be included in such formula by subsection (i) for which testing has not been conducted pursuant to subparagraph (A) or (B). Testing under this subparagraph shall be conducted to—

(i) ensure that each batch of such infant formula is in compliance with the requirements of subsection (i) relating to such nutrients, and

(ii) confirm that nutrients contained in any nutrient premix used in such infant formula are present in each batch of such infant formula in the proper concentration.

(D) If the Secretary adds a nutrient to the list of nutrients in the table in subsection (i), the Secretary shall by regulation require that the manufacturer of an infant formula test each batch of such formula for such new nutrient in accordance with subparagraph (A), (B), or (C).

(E) For purposes of this paragraph, the term "final product stage" means the point in the manufacturing process, before distribution of an infant formula, at which an infant formula is homogenous and is not subject to further degradation.

(4)(A) The Secretary shall by regulation establish requirements respecting the retention of records. Such requirements shall provide for—

(i) the retention of all records necessary to demonstrate compliance with the good manufacturing practices and quality control procedures prescribed by the Secretary under paragraph (2), including records containing the results of all testing required under paragraph (2)(B),

(ii) the retention of all certifications or guarantees of analysis by premix suppliers,

(iii) the retention by a premix supplier of all records necessary to confirm the accuracy of all premix certifications and guarantees of analysis,

(iv) the retention of—

(I) all records pertaining to the microbiological quality and purity of raw materials used in infant formula powder and in finished infant formula, and

(II) all records pertaining to food packaging materials which show that such materials do not cause an infant formula to be adulterated within the meaning of section 402(a)(2)(C),

(v) the retention of all records of the results of regularly scheduled audits conducted pursuant to the requirements prescribed by the Secretary under paragraph (2)(B)(iv), and

(vi) the retention of all complaints and the maintenance of files with respect to, and the review of, complaints concerning infant formulas which may reveal the possible existence of a hazard to health.

(B)(i) Records required under subparagraph (A) with respect to an infant formula shall be retained for at least one year after the expiration of the shelf life of such infant formula. Except as provided in clause (ii), such records shall be made available to the Secretary for review and duplication upon request of the Secretary.

(ii) A manufacturer need only provide written assurances to the Secretary that the regularly scheduled audits required by paragraph (2)(B)(iv) are being conducted by the manufacturer, and need not make available to the Secretary the actual written reports of such audits.

(c)(1) No person shall introduce or deliver for introduction into interstate commerce any new infant formula unless—

(A) such person has, before introducing such new infant formula, or delivering such new infant formula for introduction, into interstate commerce, registered with the Secretary the name of such person, the place of business of such person, and all establishments at which such person intends to manufacture such new infant formula, and

(B) such person has at least 90 days before marketing such new infant formula, made the submission to the Secretary required by subsection (c)(1).

(2) For purposes of paragraph (1), the term "new infant formula" includes—

(A) an infant formula manufactured by a person which has not previously manufactured an infant formula, and

(B) an infant formula manufactured by a person which has previously manufactured infant formula and in which there is a major change, in processing or formulation, from a current or any previous formulation produced by such manufacturer.

For purposes of this paragraph, the term "major change" has the meaning given to such term in section 106.30(c)(2) of title 21, Code of Federal Regulations (as in effect on August 1, 1986), and guidelines issued thereunder.

(d)(1) A person shall, with respect to any infant formula subject to subsection (c), make a submission to the Secretary which shall include—

(A) the quantitative formulation of the infant formula,

(B) a description of any reformulation of the formula or change in processing of the infant formula,

(C) assurances that the infant formula will not be marketed unless it meets the requirements of subsections (b)(1) and (i), as demonstrated by the testing required under subsection (b)(3), and

(D) assurances that the processing of the infant formula complies with subsection (b)(2).

(2) After the first production of an infant formula subject to subsection (c), and before the introduction into interstate commerce of such formula, the manufacturer of such formula shall submit to the Secretary, in such form as may be prescribed by the Secretary, a written verification which summarizes test results and records demonstrating that such formula complies with the requirements of subsections (b)(1), (b)(2)(A), (b)(2)(B)(i), (b)(2)(B)(iii), (b)(3)(A), (b)(3)(C), and (i).

(3) If the manufacturer of an infant formula for commercial or charitable distribution for human consumption determines that a change in the formulation of the formula or a change in the processing of the formula may affect whether the formula is adulterated under subsection (a), the manufacturer shall, before the first processing of such formula, make the submission to the Secretary required by paragraph (1).

(e)(1) If the manufacturer of an infant formula has knowledge which reasonably supports the conclusion that an infant formula which has been processed by the manufacturer and which has left an establishment subject to the control of the manufacturer—

(A) may not provide the nutrients required by subsection (i), or

(B) may be otherwise adulterated or misbranded, the manufacturer shall promptly notify the Secretary of such knowledge. If the Secretary determines that the infant formula presents a risk to human health, the manufacturer shall immediately take all actions necessary to recall shipments of such infant formula from all wholesale and retail establishments, consistent with recall regulations and guidelines issued by the Secretary.

(2) For purposes of paragraph (1), the term "knowledge" as applied to a manufacturer means (A) the actual knowledge that the manufacturer had, or (B) the knowledge which a reasonable person would have had under like circumstances or which would have been obtained upon the exercise of due care.

(f)(1) If a recall of infant formula is begun by a manufacturer, the recall shall be carried out in accordance with such requirements as the Secretary shall prescribe under paragraph (2) and—

(A) the Secretary shall, not later than the 15th day after the beginning of such recall and at least once every 15 days thereafter until the recall is terminated, review the actions taken under the recall to determine whether the recall meets the requirements prescribed under paragraph (2), and

(B) the manufacturer shall, not later than the 14th day after the beginning of such recall and at least once every 14 days thereafter until the recall is terminated, report to the Secretary the actions taken to implement the recall.

(2) The Secretary shall by regulation prescribe the scope and extent of recalls of infant formulas necessary and appropriate for the degree of risks to human health presented by the formula subject to the recall.

(3) The Secretary shall by regulation require each manufacturer of an infant formula who begins a recall of such formula because of a risk to human health to request each retail establishment at which such formula is sold or available for sale to post at the point of purchase of such formula a notice of such recall at such establishment for such time that the Secretary determines necessary to inform the public of such recall.

(g)(1) Each manufacturer of an infant formula shall make and retain such records respecting the distribution of the infant formula through any establishment owned or operated by such manufacturer as may be necessary to effect and monitor recalls of the formula. Such records shall be retained for at least one year after the expiration of the shelf life of the infant formula.

(2) To the extent that the Secretary determines that records are not being made or maintained in accordance with paragraph (1), the Secretary may by regulation prescribe the records required to be made under paragraph (1) and requirements respecting the retention of such records under such paragraph. Such regulations shall take effect on such date as the Secretary prescribes but not sooner than the 180th day after the date such regulations are promulgated. Such regulations shall apply only with respect to distributions of infant formulas made after such effective date.

(h)(1) Any infant formula which is represented and labeled for use by an infant—

(A) who has an inborn error of metabolism or a low birth weight, or

(B) who otherwise has an unusual medical or dietary problem,

is exempt from the requirements of subsections (a), (b), and (c). The manufacturer of an infant formula exempt under this paragraph shall, in the case of the exempt formula, be required to provide the notice required by subsection (e)(1) only with respect to adulteration or misbranding described in subsection (e)(1)(B) and to comply with the regulations prescribed by the Secretary under paragraph (2).

(2) The Secretary may by regulation establish terms and conditions for the exemption of an infant formula from the requirements of subsections (a), (b), and (c). An exemption of an infant formula under paragraph (1) may be withdrawn by the Secretary if such formula is not in compliance with applicable terms and conditions prescribed under this paragraph.

(i)(1) An infant formula shall contain nutrients in accordance with the table set out in this subsection or, if revised by the Secretary under paragraph (2), as so revised.

(2) The Secretary may by regulation—

(A) revise the list of nutrients in the table in this subsection, and

(B) revise the required level for any nutrient required by the table.

NUTRIENTS

Nutrient	Minimum[1]	Maximum[1]
Protein (gm)	1.8[2]	4.5
Fat:		
gm.	3.3	6.0
percent cal.	30.0	54.0
Essential fatty acids (linoleate):		
percent cal	2.7	
mg	300.0	
Vitamins:		
A (IU)	250.0 (75μg)[3]	750.0 (225μg)[3]
D (IU)	40.0	100.0
K (μg)	4.0	
E (IU)	0.7 (with 0.7 IU/gm linoleic acid)	
C (ascorbic acid)		
(mg)	8.0	
B1(thiamine) (μg) . . .	40.0	
B2(riboflavin) (μg) . . .	60.0	
B6(pyridoxine) (μg) . .	35.0 (with 15 μg/gm of protein in formula)	
B12 (μg)	0.15	
Niacin (μg)	250.0	
Folic acid (μg)	4.0	
Pantothenic acid (μg) .	300.0	
Biotin (μg)	1.5[4]	
Choline (mg)	7.0[4]	
Inositol (mg)	4.0[4]	
Minerals:		
Calcium (mg)	50.0[5]	
Phosphorus (mg)	25.0[5]	
Magnesium (mg) .	6.0	
Iron (mg)	0.15	
Iodine (μg)	5.0	
Zinc (mg)	0.5	
Copper (μg)	60.0	
Manganese (μg)	5.0	
Sodium (mg)	20.0	60.0
Potassium (mg)	80.0	200.0
Chloride (mg)	55.0	150.0

1. Stated per 100 kilocalories.

2. The source of protein shall be at least nutritionally equivalent to casein.

3. Retinol equivalents.

4. Required to be included in this amount only in formulas which are not milk-based.

5. Calcium to phosphorus ratio must be no less than 1.1 nor more than 2.0.

SEC. 413 [21 U.S.C. 350b]. NEW DIETARY INGREDIENTS

(a) IN GENERAL.—A dietary supplement which contains a new dietary ingredient shall be deemed adulterated under section 402(f) unless it meets one of the following requirements:

(1) The dietary supplement contains only dietary ingredients which have been present in the food supply as an article used for food in a form in which the food has not been chemically altered.

(2) There is a history of use or other evidence of safety establishing that the dietary ingredient when used under the conditions recommended or suggested in the labeling of the dietary supplement will reasonably be expected to be safe and, at least 75 days before being introduced or delivered for introduction into interstate commerce, the manufacturer or distributor of the dietary ingredient or dietary supplement provides the Secretary with information, including any citation to published articles, which is the basis on which the manufacturer or distributor has concluded that a dietary supplement containing such dietary ingredient will reasonably be expected to be safe.

The Secretary shall keep confidential any information provided under paragraph (2) for 90 days following its receipt. After the expiration of such 90 days, the Secretary shall place such information on public display, except matters in the information which are trade secrets or otherwise confidential, commercial information.

(b) PETITION.—Any person may file with the Secretary a petition proposing the issuance of an order prescribing the conditions under which a new dietary ingredient under its intended conditions of use will reasonably be expected to be safe. The Secretary shall make a decision on such petition within 180 days of the date the petition is filed with the Secretary. For purposes of chapter 7 of title 5, United States Code, the decision of the Secretary shall be considered final agency action.

(c) NOTIFICATION.—

(1) IN GENERAL.—If the Secretary determines that the information in a new dietary ingredient notification submitted under this section for an article purported to be a new dietary ingredient is inadequate to establish that a dietary supplement containing such article will reasonably be expected to be safe because the article may be, or may contain, an anabolic steroid or an analogue of an anabolic steroid, the Secretary shall notify the Drug Enforcement Administration of such determination. Such notification by the Secretary shall include, at a minimum, the name of the dietary supplement or article, the name of the person or persons who marketed the product or made the submission of information regarding the article to the Secretary under this section, and any contact information for such person or persons that the Secretary has.

(2) DEFINITIONS.—For purposes of this subsection—

(A) the term "anabolic steroid" has the meaning given such term in section 102(41) of the Controlled Substances Act; and

(B) the term "analogue of an anabolic steroid" means a substance whose chemical structure is substantially similar to the chemical structure of an anabolic steroid.

(d) DEFINITION.—For purposes of this section, the term "new dietary ingredient" means a dietary ingredient that was not marketed in the United States before October 15, 1994 and does not include any dietary ingredient which was marketed in the United States before October 15, 1994.

SEC. 414 [21 U.S.C. 350c]. MAINTENANCE AND INSPECTION OF RECORDS

(a) RECORDS INSPECTION.—

(1) ADULTERATED FOOD.—If the Secretary has a reasonable belief that an article of food, and any other article of food that the Secretary reasonably believes is likely to be affected in a similar manner, is adulterated and presents a threat of serious adverse health consequences or death to humans or animals, each person (excluding farms and restaurants) who manufactures, processes, packs, distributes, receives, holds, or imports such article shall, at the request of an officer or employee duly designated by the Secretary, permit such officer or employee, upon presentation of appropriate credentials and a written notice to such person, at reasonable times and within reasonable limits and in a reasonable manner, to have access to and copy all records relating to such article, and to any other article of food that the Secretary reasonably believes is likely to be affected in a similar manner, that are needed to assist the Secretary in determining whether the food is adulterated and presents a threat of serious adverse health consequences or death to humans or animals.

(2) USE OF OR EXPOSURE TO FOOD OF CONCERN.—If the Secretary believes that there is a reasonable probability that the use of or exposure to an article of food, and any other article of food that the Secretary reasonably believes is likely to be affected in a similar manner, will cause serious adverse health consequences or death to humans or animals, each person (excluding farms and restaurants) who manufactures, processes, packs, distributes, receives, holds, or imports such article shall, at the request of an officer or employee duly designated by the Secretary, permit such officer or employee, upon presentation of appropriate credentials and a written notice to such person, at reasonable times and within reasonable limits and in a reasonable manner, to have access to and copy all records relating to such article and to any other article of food that the Secretary reasonably believes is likely to be affected in a similar manner, that are needed to assist the Secretary in determining whether there is a reasonable probability that the use of or exposure to the food will cause serious adverse health consequences or death to humans or animals.

(3) Application.—The requirement under paragraphs (1) and (2) applies to all records relating to the manufacture, processing, packing, distribution, receipt,

holding, or importation of such article maintained by or on behalf of such person in any format (including paper and electronic formats) and at any location.

(b) REGULATIONS CONCERNING RECORDKEEPING.—The Secretary, in consultation and coordination, as appropriate, with other Federal departments and agencies with responsibilities for regulating food safety, may by regulation establish requirements regarding the establishment and maintenance, for not longer than two years, of records by persons (excluding farms and restaurants) who manufacture, process, pack, transport, distribute, receive, hold, or import food, which records are needed by the Secretary for inspection to allow the Secretary to identify the immediate previous sources and the immediate subsequent recipients of food, including its packaging, in order to address credible threats of serious adverse health consequences or death to humans or animals. The Secretary shall take into account the size of a business in promulgating regulations under this section.

(c) PROTECTION OF SENSITIVE INFORMATION.—The Secretary shall take appropriate measures to ensure that there are in effect effective procedures to prevent the unauthorized disclosure of any trade secret or confidential information that is obtained by the Secretary pursuant to this section.

(d) LIMITATIONS.—This section shall not be construed—

(1) to limit the authority of the Secretary to inspect records or to require establishment and maintenance of records under any other provision of this Act;

(2) to authorize the Secretary to impose any requirements with respect to a food to the extent that it is within the exclusive jurisdiction of the Secretary of Agriculture pursuant to the Federal Meat Inspection Act (21 U.S.C. 601 et seq.), the Poultry Products Inspection Act (21 U.S.C. 451 et seq.), or the Egg Products Inspection Act (21 U.S.C. 1031 et seq.);

(3) to have any legal effect on section 552 of title 5, United States Code, or section 1905 of title 18, United States Code; or

(4) to extend to recipes for food, financial data, pricing data, personnel data, research data, or sales data (other than shipment data regarding sales).

SEC. 415 [21 U.S.C. 350d]. REGISTRATION OF FOOD FACILITIES

(a) REGISTRATION.—

(1) IN GENERAL.—The Secretary shall by regulation require that any facility engaged in manufacturing, processing, packing, or holding food for consumption in the United States be registered with the Secretary. To be registered—

(A) for a domestic facility, the owner, operator, or agent in charge of the facility shall submit a registration to the Secretary; and

(B) for a foreign facility, the owner, operator, or agent in charge of the facility shall submit a registration to the Secretary and shall include with the registration the name of the United States agent for the facility.

(2) REGISTRATION.—An entity (referred to in this section as the "registrant") shall submit a registration under paragraph (1) to the Secretary containing information necessary to notify the Secretary of the name and address of each facility at which, and all trade names under which, the registrant conducts business, the e-mail address for the contact person of the facility or, in the case of a foreign facility, the United States agent for the facility, and, when determined necessary by the Secretary through guidance, the general food category (as identified under section 170.3 of title 21, Code of Federal Regulations, or any other food categories as determined appropriate by the Secretary, including by guidance) of any food manufactured, processed, packed, or held at such facility. The registration shall contain an assurance that the Secretary will be permitted to inspect such facility at the times and in the manner permitted by this Act. The registrant shall notify the Secretary in a timely manner of changes to such information.

(3) BIENNIAL REGISTRATION RENEWAL.—During the period beginning on October 1 and ending on December 31 of each even-numbered year, a registrant that has submitted a registration under paragraph (1) shall submit to the Secretary a renewal registration containing the information described in paragraph (2). The Secretary shall provide for an abbreviated registration renewal process for any registrant that has not had any changes to such information since the registrant submitted the preceding registration or registration renewal for the facility involved.

(4) PROCEDURE.—Upon receipt of a completed registration described in paragraph (1), the Secretary shall notify the registrant of the receipt of such registration and assign a registration number to each registered facility.

(5) LIST.—The Secretary shall compile and maintain an up-to-date list of facilities that are registered under this section. Such list and any registration documents submitted pursuant to this subsection shall not be subject to disclosure under section 552 of title 5, United States Code. Information derived from such list or registration documents shall not be subject to disclosure under section 552 of title 5, United States Code, to the extent that it discloses the identity or location of a specific registered person.

(b) SUSPENSION OF REGISTRATION—

(1) IN GENERAL.—If the Secretary determines that food manufactured, processed, packed, received, or held by a facility registered under this section has a reasonable probability of causing serious adverse health consequences or death to humans or animals, the Secretary may by order suspend the registration of a facility—

(A) that created, caused, or was otherwise responsible for such reasonable probability; or

(B)(i) that knew of, or had reason to know of, such reasonable probability; and

(ii) packed, received, or held such food.

(2) HEARING ON SUSPENSION.—The Secretary shall provide the registrant subject to an order under paragraph (1) with an opportunity for an informal hearing, to be held as soon as possible but not later than 2 business days after the issuance of the order or such other time period, as agreed upon by the Secretary and the registrant, on the actions required for reinstatement of registration and why the registration that is subject to suspension should be reinstated. The Secretary shall reinstate a registration if the Secretary determines, based on evidence presented, that adequate grounds do not exist to continue the suspension of the registration.

(3) POST-HEARING CORRECTIVE ACTION PLAN; VACATION OF ORDER.—

(A) CORRECTIVE ACTION PLAN.—If, after providing opportunity for an informal hearing under paragraph (2), the Secretary determines that the suspension of registration remains necessary, the Secretary shall require the registrant to submit a corrective action plan to demonstrate how the registrant plans to correct the conditions found by the Secretary. The Secretary shall review such plan not later than 14 days after the submission of the corrective action plan or such other time period as determined by the Secretary.

(B) VACATING OF ORDER.—Upon a determination by the Secretary that adequate grounds do not exist to continue the suspension actions required by the order, or that such actions should be modified, the Secretary shall promptly vacate the order and reinstate the registration of the facility subject to the order or modify the order, as appropriate.

(4) EFFECT OF SUSPENSION.—If the registration of a facility is suspended under this subsection, no person shall import or export food into the United States from such facility, offer to import or export food into the United States from such facility, or otherwise introduce food from such facility into interstate or intrastate commerce in the United States.

(5) REGULATIONS.—

(A) IN GENERAL.—The Secretary shall promulgate regulations to implement this subsection. The Secretary may promulgate such regulations on an interim final basis.

(B) REGISTRATION REQUIREMENT.—The Secretary may require that registration under this section be submitted in an electronic format. Such requirement may not take effect before the date that is 5 years after the date of enactment of the FDA Food Safety Modernization Act.

(6) APPLICATION DATE.—Facilities shall be subject to the requirements of this subsection beginning on the earlier of—

(A) the date on which the Secretary issues regulations under paragraph (5); or

(B) 180 days after the date of enactment of the FDA Food Safety Modernization Act.

(7) No delegation.—The authority conferred by this subsection to issue an order to suspend a registration or vacate an order of suspension shall not be delegated to any officer or employee other than the Commissioner.

(c) Facility.—For purposes of this section:

(1) The term "facility" includes any factory, warehouse, or establishment (including a factory, warehouse, or establishment of an importer) that manufactures, processes, packs, or holds food. Such term does not include farms; restaurants; other retail food establishments; nonprofit food establishments in which food is prepared for or served directly to the consumer; or fishing vessels (except such vessels engaged in processing as defined in section 123.3(k) of title 21, Code of Federal Regulations).

(2) The term "domestic facility" means a facility located in any of the States or Territories.

(3)(A) The term "foreign facility" means a facility that manufacturers, processes, packs, or holds food, but only if food from such facility is exported to the United States without further processing or packaging outside the United States.

(B) A food may not be considered to have undergone further processing or packaging for purposes of subparagraph (A) solely on the basis that labeling was added or that any similar activity of a de minimis nature was carried out with respect to the food.

(d) Rule of Construction.—Nothing in this section shall be construed to authorize the Secretary to require an application, review, or licensing process for a facility to be registered, except with respect to the reinstatement of a registration that is suspended under subsection (b).

Sec. 416 [21 U.S.C. 350e]. SANITARY TRANSPORTATION PRACTICES

(a) Definitions.—In this section:

(1) Bulk vehicle.—The term "bulk vehicle" includes a tank truck, hopper truck, rail tank car, hopper car, cargo tank, portable tank, freight container, or hopper bin, and any other vehicle in which food is shipped in bulk, with the food coming into direct contact with the vehicle.

(2) Transportation.—The term "transportation" means any movement in commerce by motor vehicle or rail vehicle.

(b) Regulations.—The Secretary shall by regulation require shippers, carriers by motor vehicle or rail vehicle, receivers, and other persons engaged in the transportation of food to use sanitary transportation practices prescribed by the Secretary to ensure that food is not transported under conditions that may render the food adulterated.

(c) CONTENTS.—The regulations under subsection (b) shall—

(1) prescribe such practices as the Secretary determines to be appropriate relating to—

(A) sanitation;

(B) packaging, isolation, and other protective measures;

(C) limitations on the use of vehicles;

(D) information to be disclosed—

(i) to a carrier by a person arranging for the transport of food; and

(ii) to a manufacturer or other person that—

(I) arranges for the transportation of food by a carrier; or

(II) furnishes a tank vehicle or bulk vehicle for the transportation of food; and

(E) recordkeeping; and

(2) include—

(A) a list of nonfood products that the Secretary determines may, if shipped in a bulk vehicle, render adulterated food that is subsequently transported in the same vehicle; and

(B) a list of nonfood products that the Secretary determines may, if shipped in a motor vehicle or rail vehicle (other than a tank vehicle or bulk vehicle), render adulterated food that is simultaneously or subsequently transported in the same vehicle.

(d) WAIVERS.—

(1) IN GENERAL.—The Secretary may waive any requirement under this section, with respect to any class of persons, vehicles, food, or nonfood products, if the Secretary determines that the waiver—

(A) will not result in the transportation of food under conditions that would be unsafe for human or animal health; and

(B) will not be contrary to the public interest.

(2) PUBLICATION.—The Secretary shall publish in the Federal Register any waiver and the reasons for the waiver.

(e) PREEMPTION.—

(1) IN GENERAL.—A requirement of a State or political subdivision of a State that concerns the transportation of food is preempted if—

(A) complying with a requirement of the State or political subdivision and a requirement of this section, or a regulation prescribed under this section, is not possible; or

(B) the requirement of the State or political subdivision as applied or enforced is an obstacle to accomplishing and carrying out this section or a regulation prescribed under this section.

(2) APPLICABILITY.—This subsection applies to transportation that occurs on or after the effective date of the regulations promulgated under subsection (b).

(f) ASSISTANCE OF OTHER AGENCIES.—The Secretary of Transportation, the Secretary of Agriculture, the Administrator of the Environmental Protection Agency, and the heads of other Federal agencies, as appropriate, shall provide assistance on request, to the extent resources are available, to the Secretary for the purposes of carrying out this section.

SEC. 417[24] [21 U.S.C. 350f]. REPORTABLE FOOD REGISTRY

(a) DEFINITIONS.—In this section:

(1) RESPONSIBLE PARTY.—The term "responsible party", with respect to an article of food, means a person that submits the registration under section 415(a) for a food facility that is required to register under section 415(a), at which such article of food is manufactured, processed, packed, or held.

(2) REPORTABLE FOOD.—The term "reportable food" means an article of food (other than infant formula) for which there is a reasonable probability that the use of, or exposure to, such article of food will cause serious adverse health consequences or death to humans or animals.

(b) ESTABLISHMENT.—

(1) IN GENERAL.—Not later than 1 year after the date of the enactment of this section, the Secretary shall establish within the Food and Drug Administration a Reportable Food Registry to which instances of reportable food may be submitted by the Food and Drug Administration after receipt of reports under subsection (d), via an electronic portal, from—

(A) Federal, State, and local public health officials; or

(B) responsible parties.

(2) REVIEW BY SECRETARY.—The Secretary shall promptly review and assess the information submitted under paragraph (1) for the purposes of identifying reportable food, submitting entries to the Reportable Food Registry, acting under

---

24. Section 417 was added by Pub. L. No. 110–85, § 1005(b), 121 Stat. 823, 965–68, which was enacted September 27, 2007. Section 1005(e) of such Public Law provides as follows:

(e) Effective Date.—The requirements of section 417(d) of the Federal Food, Drug, and Cosmetic Act, as added by subsection (a), shall become effective 1 year after the date of the enactment of this Act.

The reference to "subsection (a)" is so in law. Probably should be "subsection (b)".

subsection (c), and exercising other existing food safety authorities under this Act to protect the public health.

(c) ISSUANCE OF AN ALERT BY THE SECRETARY.—

(1) IN GENERAL.—The Secretary shall issue, or cause to be issued, an alert or a notification with respect to a reportable food using information from the Reportable Food Registry as the Secretary deems necessary to protect the public health.

(2) EFFECT.—Paragraph (1) shall not affect the authority of the Secretary to issue an alert or a notification under any other provision of this Act.

(d) REPORTING AND NOTIFICATION.—

(1) IN GENERAL.—Except as provided in paragraph (2), as soon as practicable, but in no case later than 24 hours after a responsible party determines that an article of food is a reportable food, the responsible party shall—

(A) submit a report to the Food and Drug Administration through the electronic portal established under subsection (b) that includes the data elements described in subsection (e) (except the elements described in paragraphs (8), (9), and (10) of such subsection); and

(B) investigate the cause of the adulteration if the adulteration of the article of food may have originated with the responsible party.

(2) NO REPORT REQUIRED.—A responsible party is not required to submit a report under paragraph (1) if—

(A) the adulteration originated with the responsible party;

(B) the responsible party detected the adulteration prior to any transfer to another person of such article of food; and

(C) the responsible party—

(i) corrected such adulteration; or

(ii) destroyed or caused the destruction of such article of food.

(3) REPORTS BY PUBLIC HEALTH OFFICIALS.—A Federal, State, or local public health official may submit a report about a reportable food to the Food and Drug Administration through the electronic portal established under subsection (b) that includes the data elements described in subsection (e) that the official is able to provide.

(4) REPORT NUMBER.—The Secretary shall ensure that, upon submission of a report under paragraph (1) or (3), a unique number is issued through the electronic portal established under subsection (b) to the person submitting such report, by which the Secretary is able to link reports about the reportable food submitted and amended under this subsection and identify the supply chain for such reportable food.

(5) REVIEW.—The Secretary shall promptly review a report submitted under paragraph (1) or (3).

(6) RESPONSE TO REPORT SUBMITTED BY A RESPONSIBLE PARTY.—After consultation with the responsible party that submitted a report under paragraph (1), the Secretary may require such responsible party to perform, as soon as practicable, but in no case later than a time specified by the Secretary, 1 or more of the following:

(A) Amend the report submitted by the responsible party under paragraph (1) to include the data element described in subsection (e)(9).

(B) Provide a notification—

(i) to the immediate previous source of the article of food, if the Secretary deems necessary;

(ii) to the immediate subsequent recipient of the article of food, if the Secretary deems necessary; and

(iii) that includes—

(I) the data elements described in subsection (e) that the Secretary deems necessary;

(II) the actions described under paragraph (7) that the recipient of the notification shall perform, as required by the Secretary; and

(III) any other information that the Secretary may require.

(7) SUBSEQUENT REPORTS AND NOTIFICATIONS.—Except as provided in paragraph (8), the Secretary may require a responsible party to perform, as soon as practicable, but in no case later than a time specified by the Secretary, after the responsible party receives a notification under subparagraph (C) or paragraph (6)(B), 1 or more of the following:

(A) Submit a report to the Food and Drug Administration through the electronic portal established under subsection (b) that includes those data elements described in subsection (e) and other information that the Secretary deems necessary.

(B) Investigate the cause of the adulteration if the adulteration of the article of food may have originated with the responsible party.

(C) Provide a notification—

(i) to the immediate previous source of the article of food, if the Secretary deems necessary;

(ii) to the immediate subsequent recipient of the article of food, if the Secretary deems necessary; and

(iii) that includes—

(I) the data elements described in subsection (e) that the Secretary deems necessary;

(II) the actions described under this paragraph that the recipient of the notification shall perform, as required by the Secretary; and

(III) any other information that the Secretary may require.

(8) AMENDED REPORT.—If a responsible party receives a notification under paragraph (6)(B) or paragraph (7)(C) with respect to an article of food after the responsible party has submitted a report to the Food and Drug Administration under paragraph (1) with respect to such article of food—

(A) the responsible party is not required to submit an additional report or make a notification under paragraph (7); and

(B) the responsible party shall amend the report submitted by the responsible party under paragraph (1) to include the data elements described in paragraph (9), and, with respect to both such notification and such report, paragraph (11) of subsection (e).

(e) DATA ELEMENTS.—The data elements described in this subsection are the following:

(1) The registration numbers of the responsible party under section 415(a)(3).

(2) The date on which an article of food was determined to be a reportable food.

(3) A description of the article of food including the quantity or amount.

(4) The extent and nature of the adulteration.

(5) If the adulteration of the article of food may have originated with the responsible party, the results of the investigation required under paragraph (1)(B) or (7)(B) of subsection (d), as applicable and when known.

(6) The disposition of the article of food, when known.

(7) Product information typically found on packaging including product codes, use-by dates, and names of manufacturers, packers, or distributors sufficient to identify the article of food.

(8) Contact information for the responsible party.

(9) The contact information for parties directly linked in the supply chain and notified under paragraph (6)(B) or (7)(C) of subsection (d), as applicable.

(10) The information required by the Secretary to be included in a notification provided by the responsible party involved under paragraph (6)(B) or (7)(C) of subsection (d) or required in a report under subsection (d)(7)(A).

(11) The unique number described in subsection (d)(4).

(f) CRITICAL INFORMATION.—Except with respect to fruits and vegetables that are raw agricultural commodities, not more than 18 months after the date of enactment of the FDA Food Safety Modernization Act, the Secretary may require a responsible party to submit to the Secretary consumer-oriented information regarding a reportable food, which shall include—

(1) a description of the article of food as provided in subsection (e)(3);

(2) as provided in subsection (e)(7), affected product identification codes, such as UPC, SKU, or lot or batch numbers sufficient for the consumer to identify the article of food;

(3) contact information for the responsible party as provided in subsection (e)(8); and

(4) any other information the Secretary determines is necessary to enable a consumer to accurately identify whether such consumer is in possession of the reportable food.

(g) GROCERY STORE NOTIFICATION.—

(1) ACTION BY SECRETARY.—The Secretary shall—

(A) prepare the critical information described under subsection (f) for a reportable food as a standardized one-page summary;

(B) publish such one-page summary on the Internet website of the Food and Drug Administration in a format that can be easily printed by a grocery store for purposes of consumer notification.

(2) ACTION BY GROCERY STORE.—A notification described under paragraph (1)(B) shall include the date and time such summary was posted on the Internet website of the Food and Drug Administration.

(h) CONSUMER NOTIFICATION.—

(1) IN GENERAL.—If a grocery store sold a reportable food that is the subject of the posting and such establishment is part of chain of establishments with 15 or more physical locations, then such establishment shall, not later than 24 hours after a one page summary described in subsection (g) is published, prominently display such summary or the information from such summary via at least one of the methods identified under paragraph (2) and maintain the display for 14 days.

(2) LIST OF CONSPICUOUS LOCATIONS.—Not more than 1 year after the date of enactment of the FDA Food Safety Modernization Act, the Secretary shall develop and publish a list of acceptable conspicuous locations and manners, from which grocery stores shall select at least one, for providing the notification required in paragraph (1). Such list shall include—

(A) posting the notification at or near the register;

(B) providing the location of the reportable food;

(C) providing targeted recall information given to customers upon purchase of a food; and

(D) other such prominent and conspicuous locations and manners utilized by grocery stores as of the date of the enactment of the FDA Food Safety Modernization Act to provide notice of such recalls to consumers as considered appropriate by the Secretary.

(i) COORDINATION OF FEDERAL, STATE, AND LOCAL EFFORTS.—

(1) DEPARTMENT OF AGRICULTURE.—In implementing this section, the Secretary shall—

(A) share information and coordinate regulatory efforts with the Department of Agriculture; and

(B) if the Secretary receives a report submitted about a food within the jurisdiction of the Department of Agriculture, promptly provide such report to the Department of Agriculture.

(2) STATES AND LOCALITIES.—In implementing this section, the Secretary shall work with the State and local public health officials to share information and coordinate regulatory efforts, in order to—

(A) help to ensure coverage of the safety of the food supply chain, including those food establishments regulated by the States and localities that are not required to register under section 415; and

(B) reduce duplicative regulatory efforts.

(j) MAINTENANCE AND INSPECTION OF RECORDS.—The responsible party shall maintain records related to each report received, notification made, and report submitted to the Food and Drug Administration under this section for 2 years. A responsible party shall, at the request of the Secretary, permit inspection of such records as provided for section 414.

(k) REQUEST FOR INFORMATION.—Except as provided by section 415(a)(4), section 552 of title 5, United States Code, shall apply to any request for information regarding a record in the Reportable Food Registry.

(*l*) SAFETY REPORT.—A report or notification under subsection (d) shall be considered to be a safety report under section 756 and may be accompanied by a statement, which shall be part of any report released for public disclosure, that denies that the report or the notification constitutes an admission that the product involved caused or contributed to a death, serious injury, or serious illness.

(m) ADMISSION.—A report or notification under this section shall not be considered an admission that the article of food involved is adulterated or caused or contributed to a death, serious injury, or serious illness.

(n) HOMELAND SECURITY NOTIFICATION.—If, after receiving a report under subsection (d), the Secretary believes such food may have been deliberately adulterated, the Secretary shall immediately notify the Secretary of Homeland Security. The Secretary shall make relevant information from the Reportable Food Registry available to the Secretary of Homeland Security.

SEC. 418 [21 U.S.C. 350g]. HAZARD ANALYSIS AND RISK–BASED PREVENTIVE CONTROLS

(a) IN GENERAL.—The owner, operator, or agent in charge of a facility shall, in accordance with this section, evaluate the hazards that could affect food manufactured, processed, packed, or held by such facility, identify and implement preventive controls to significantly minimize or prevent the occurrence of such hazards and provide assurances that such food is not adulterated under section 402 or misbranded under section 403(w), monitor the performance of those controls, and maintain records of this monitoring as a matter of routine practice.

(b) HAZARD ANALYSIS.—The owner, operator, or agent in charge of a facility shall—

(1) identify and evaluate known or reasonably foreseeable hazards that may be associated with the facility, including—

(A) biological, chemical, physical, and radiological hazards, natural toxins, pesticides, drug residues, decomposition, parasites, allergens, and unapproved food and color additives; and

(B) hazards that occur naturally, or may be unintentionally introduced; and

(2) identify and evaluate hazards that may be intentionally introduced, including by acts of terrorism; and

(3) develop a written analysis of the hazards.

(c) PREVENTIVE CONTROLS.—The owner, operator, or agent in charge of a facility shall identify and implement preventive controls, including at critical control points, if any, to provide assurances that—

(1) hazards identified in the hazard analysis conducted under subsection (b)(1) will be significantly minimized or prevented;

(2) any hazards identified in the hazard analysis conducted under subsection (b)(2) will be significantly minimized or prevented and addressed, consistent with section 420, as applicable; and

(3) the food manufactured, processed, packed, or held by such facility will not be adulterated under section 402 or misbranded under section 403(w).

(d) MONITORING OF EFFECTIVENESS.—The owner, operator, or agent in charge of a facility shall monitor the effectiveness of the preventive controls implemented under subsection (c) to provide assurances that the outcomes described in subsection (c) shall be achieved.

(e) CORRECTIVE ACTIONS.—The owner, operator, or agent in charge of a facility shall establish procedures to ensure that, if the preventive controls implemented under subsection (c) are not properly implemented or are found to be ineffective—

(1) appropriate action is taken to reduce the likelihood of recurrence of the implementation failure;

(2) all affected food is evaluated for safety; and

(3) all affected food is prevented from entering into commerce if the owner, operator or agent in charge of such facility cannot ensure that the affected food is not adulterated under section 402 or misbranded under section 403(w).

(f) VERIFICATION.—The owner, operator, or agent in charge of a facility shall verify that—

(1) the preventive controls implemented under subsection (c) are adequate to control the hazards identified under subsection (b);

(2) the owner, operator, or agent is conducting monitoring in accordance with subsection (d);

(3) the owner, operator, or agent is making appropriate decisions about corrective actions taken under subsection (e);

(4) the preventive controls implemented under subsection (c) are effectively and significantly minimizing or preventing the occurrence of identified hazards, including through the use of environmental and product testing programs and other appropriate means; and

(5) there is documented, periodic reanalysis of the plan under subsection (i) to ensure that the plan is still relevant to the raw materials, conditions and processes in the facility, and new and emerging threats.

(g) RECORDKEEPING.—The owner, operator, or agent in charge of a facility shall maintain, for not less than 2 years, records documenting the monitoring of the preventive controls implemented under subsection (c), instances of nonconformance material to food safety, the results of testing and other appropriate means of verification under subsection (f)(4), instances when corrective actions were implemented, and the efficacy of preventive controls and corrective actions.

(h) WRITTEN PLAN AND DOCUMENTATION.—The owner, operator, or agent in charge of a facility shall prepare a written plan that documents and describes the procedures used by the facility to comply with the requirements of this section, including analyzing the hazards under subsection (b) and identifying the preventive controls adopted under subsection (c) to address those hazards. Such written plan, together with the documentation described in subsection (g), shall be made promptly available to a duly authorized representative of the Secretary upon oral or written request.

(i) REQUIREMENT TO REANALYZE.—The owner, operator, or agent in charge of a facility shall conduct a reanalysis under subsection (b) whenever a significant change is made in the activities conducted at a facility operated by such owner, operator, or agent if the change creates a reasonable potential for a new hazard or a significant increase in a previously identified hazard or not less frequently than once every 3 years, whichever is earlier. Such reanalysis shall be completed and additional preventive controls needed to address the hazard identified, if any, shall be implemented before the change in activities at the facility is operative. Such owner, operator, or agent shall revise the written plan required under subsection (h) if such a significant change is made or document the basis for the conclusion that no additional or revised preventive controls are needed. The Secretary may require a reanalysis under this section to respond to new hazards and developments in scientific understanding, including, as appropriate, results from the Department of Homeland Security biological, chemical, radiological, or other terrorism risk assessment.

(j) EXEMPTION FOR SEAFOOD, JUICE, AND LOW-ACID CANNED FOOD FACILITIES SUBJECT TO HACCP.—

(1) IN GENERAL.—This section shall not apply to a facility if the owner, operator, or agent in charge of such facility is required to comply with, and is in compliance with, 1 of the following standards and regulations with respect to such facility:

(A) The Seafood Hazard Analysis Critical Control Points Program of the Food and Drug Administration.

(B) The Juice Hazard Analysis Critical Control Points Program of the Food and Drug Administration.

(C) The Thermally Processed Low–Acid Foods Packaged in Hermetically Sealed Containers standards of the Food and Drug Administration (or any successor standards).

(2) APPLICABILITY.—The exemption under paragraph (1)(C) shall apply only with respect to microbiological hazards that are regulated under the standards for Thermally Processed Low–Acid Foods Packaged in Hermetically Sealed Containers under part 113 of chapter 21, Code of Federal Regulations (or any successor regulations).

(k) EXCEPTION FOR ACTIVITIES OF FACILITIES SUBJECT TO SECTION 419.—This section shall not apply to activities of a facility that are subject to section 419.

(*l*) MODIFIED REQUIREMENTS FOR QUALIFIED FACILITIES.—

(1) QUALIFIED FACILITIES.—

(A) IN GENERAL.—A facility is a qualified facility for purposes of this subsection if the facility meets the conditions under subparagraph (B) or (C).

(B) VERY SMALL BUSINESS.—A facility is a qualified facility under this subparagraph—

(i) if the facility, including any subsidiary or affiliate of the facility, is, collectively, a very small business (as defined in the regulations promulgated under subsection (n)); and

(ii) in the case where the facility is a subsidiary or affiliate of an entity, if such subsidiaries or affiliates, are, collectively, a very small business (as so defined).

133

(C) LIMITED ANNUAL MONETARY VALUE OF SALES.—

(i) IN GENERAL.—A facility is a qualified facility under this subparagraph if clause (ii) applies—

(I) to the facility, including any subsidiary or affiliate of the facility, collectively; and

(II) to the subsidiaries or affiliates, collectively, of any entity of which the facility is a subsidiary or affiliate.

(ii) AVERAGE ANNUAL MONETARY VALUE.—This clause applies if—

(I) during the 3–year period preceding the applicable calendar year, the average annual monetary value of the food manufactured, processed, packed, or held at such facility (or the collective average annual monetary value of such food at any subsidiary or affiliate, as described in clause (i)) that is sold directly to qualified end-users during such period exceeded the average annual monetary value of the food manufactured, processed, packed, or held at such facility (or the collective average annual monetary value of such food at any subsidiary or affiliate, as so described) sold by such facility (or collectively by any such subsidiary or affiliate) to all other purchasers during such period; and

(II) the average annual monetary value of all food sold by such facility (or the collective average annual monetary value of such food sold by any subsidiary or affiliate, as described in clause (i)) during such period was less than $500,000, adjusted for inflation.

(2) EXEMPTION.—A qualified facility—

(A) shall not be subject to the requirements under subsections (a) through (i) and subsection (n) in an applicable calendar year; and

(B) shall submit to the Secretary—

(i)(I) documentation that demonstrates that the owner, operator, or agent in charge of the facility has identified potential hazards associated with the food being produced, is implementing preventive controls to address the hazards, and is monitoring the preventive controls to ensure that such controls are effective; or

(II) documentation (which may include licenses, inspection reports, certificates, permits, credentials, certification by an appropriate agency (such as a State department of agriculture), or other evidence of oversight), as specified by the Secretary, that the facility is in compliance with State, local, county, or other applicable non-Federal food safety law; and

(ii) documentation, as specified by the Secretary in a guidance document issued not later than 1 year after the date of enactment of this section, that the facility is a qualified facility under paragraph (1)(B) or (1)(C).

(3) WITHDRAWAL; RULE OF CONSTRUCTION.—

(A) IN GENERAL.—In the event of an active investigation of a foodborne illness outbreak that is directly linked to a qualified facility subject to an exemption under this subsection, or if the Secretary determines that it is necessary to protect the public health and prevent or mitigate a foodborne illness outbreak based on conduct or conditions associated with a qualified facility that are material to the safety of the food manufactured, processed, packed, or held at such facility, the Secretary may withdraw the exemption provided to such facility under this subsection.

(B) RULE OF CONSTRUCTION.—Nothing in this subsection shall be construed to expand or limit the inspection authority of the Secretary.

(4) DEFINITIONS.—In this subsection:

(A) AFFILIATE.—The term "affiliate" means any facility that controls, is controlled by, or is under common control with another facility.

(B) QUALIFIED END-USER.—The term "qualified end-user", with respect to a food, means—

(i) the consumer of the food; or

(ii) a restaurant or retail food establishment (as those terms are defined by the Secretary for purposes of section 415) that—

(I) is located—

(aa) in the same State as the qualified facility that sold the food to such restaurant or establishment; or

(bb) not more than 275 miles from such facility; and

(II) is purchasing the food for sale directly to consumers at such restaurant or retail food establishment.

(C) CONSUMER.—For purposes of subparagraph (B), the term "consumer" does not include a business.

(D) SUBSIDIARY.—The term "subsidiary" means any company which is owned or controlled directly or indirectly by another company.

(5) STUDY.—

(A) IN GENERAL.—The Secretary, in consultation with the Secretary of Agriculture, shall conduct a study of the food processing sector regulated by the Secretary to determine—

(i) the distribution of food production by type and size of operation, including monetary value of food sold;

(ii) the proportion of food produced by each type and size of operation;

(iii) the number and types of food facilities co-located on farms, including the number and proportion by commodity and by manufacturing or processing activity;

(iv) the incidence of foodborne illness originating from each size and type of operation and the type of food facilities for which no reported or known hazard exists; and

(v) the effect on foodborne illness risk associated with commingling, processing, transporting, and storing food and raw agricultural commodities, including differences in risk based on the scale and duration of such activities.

(B) SIZE.—The results of the study conducted under subparagraph (A) shall include the information necessary to enable the Secretary to define the terms "small business" and "very small business", for purposes of promulgating the regulation under subsection (n). In defining such terms, the Secretary shall include consideration of harvestable acres, income, the number of employees, and the volume of food harvested.

(C) SUBMISSION OF REPORT.—Not later than 18 months after the date of enactment the FDA Food Safety Modernization Act, the Secretary shall submit to Congress a report that describes the results of the study conducted under subparagraph (A).

(6) NO PREEMPTION.—Nothing in this subsection preempts State, local, county, or other non-Federal law regarding the safe production of food. Compliance with this subsection shall not relieve any person from liability at common law or under State statutory law.

(7) NOTIFICATION TO CONSUMERS.—

(A) IN GENERAL.—A qualified facility that is exempt from the requirements under subsections (a) through (i) and subsection (n) and does not prepare documentation under paragraph (2)(B)(i)(I) shall—

(i) with respect to a food for which a food packaging label is required by the Secretary under any other provision of this Act, include prominently and conspicuously on such label the name and business address of the facility where the food was manufactured or processed; or

(ii) with respect to a food for which a food packaging label is not required by the Secretary under any other provisions of this Act, prominently and conspicuously display, at the point of purchase, the name and business address of the facility where the food was manufactured or processed, on a label, poster, sign, placard, or documents delivered contemporaneously with the food in the normal course of business, or, in the case of Internet sales, in an electronic notice.

(B) No ADDITIONAL LABEL.—Subparagraph (A) does not provide authority to the Secretary to require a label that is in addition to any label required under any other provision of this Act.

(m) AUTHORITY WITH RESPECT TO CERTAIN FACILITIES.—The Secretary may, by regulation, exempt or modify the requirements for compliance under this section with respect to facilities that are solely engaged in the production of food for animals other than man, the storage of raw agricultural commodities (other than fruits and vegetables) intended for further distribution or processing, or the storage of packaged foods that are not exposed to the environment.

(n) REGULATIONS.—

(1) IN GENERAL.—Not later than 18 months after the date of enactment of the FDA Food Safety Modernization Act, the Secretary shall promulgate regulations—

(A) to establish science-based minimum standards for conducting a hazard analysis, documenting hazards, implementing preventive controls, and documenting the implementation of the preventive controls under this section; and

(B) to define, for purposes of this section, the terms "small business" and "very small business", taking into consideration the study described in subsection (*l*)(5).

(2) COORDINATION.—In promulgating the regulations under paragraph (1)(A), with regard to hazards that may be intentionally introduced, including by acts of terrorism, the Secretary shall coordinate with the Secretary of Homeland Security, as appropriate.

(3) CONTENT.—The regulations promulgated under paragraph (1)(A) shall—

(A) provide sufficient flexibility to be practicable for all sizes and types of facilities, including small businesses such as a small food processing facility co-located on a farm;

(B) comply with chapter 35 of title 44, United States Code (commonly known as the "Paperwork Reduction Act"), with special attention to minimizing the burden (as defined in section 3502(2) of such Act) on the facility, and collection of information (as defined in section 3502(3) of such Act), associated with such regulations;

(C) acknowledge differences in risk and minimize, as appropriate, the number of separate standards that apply to separate foods; and

(D) not require a facility to hire a consultant or other third party to identify, implement, certify, or audit preventative controls, except in the case of negotiated enforcement resolutions that may require such a consultant or third party.

(4) RULE OF CONSTRUCTION.—Nothing in this subsection shall be construed to provide the Secretary with the authority to prescribe specific technologies, practices, or critical controls for an individual facility.

(5) REVIEW.—In promulgating the regulations under paragraph (1)(A), the Secretary shall review regulatory hazard analysis and preventive control programs in existence on the date of enactment of the FDA Food Safety Modernization Act, including the Grade "A" Pasteurized Milk Ordinance to ensure that such regulations are consistent, to the extent practicable, with applicable domestic and internationally-recognized standards in existence on such date.

(*o*) DEFINITIONS.—For purposes of this section:

(1) CRITICAL CONTROL POINT.—The term "critical control point" means a point, step, or procedure in a food process at which control can be applied and is essential to prevent or eliminate a food safety hazard or reduce such hazard to an acceptable level.

(2) FACILITY.—The term "facility" means a domestic facility or a foreign facility that is required to register under section 415.

(3) PREVENTIVE CONTROLS.—The term "preventive controls" means those risk-based, reasonably appropriate procedures, practices, and processes that a person knowledgeable about the safe manufacturing, processing, packing, or holding of food would employ to significantly minimize or prevent the hazards identified under the hazard analysis conducted under subsection (b) and that are consistent with the current scientific understanding of safe food manufacturing, processing, packing, or holding at the time of the analysis. Those procedures, practices, and processes may include the following:

(A) Sanitation procedures for food contact surfaces and utensils and food-contact surfaces of equipment.

(B) Supervisor, manager, and employee hygiene training.

(C) An environmental monitoring program to verify the effectiveness of pathogen controls in processes where a food is exposed to a potential contaminant in the environment.

(D) A food allergen control program.

(E) A recall plan.

(F) Current Good Manufacturing Practices (cGMPs) under part 110 of title 21, Code of Federal Regulations (or any successor regulations).

(G) Supplier verification activities that relate to the safety of food.

SEC. 419 [21 U.S.C. 350h]. STANDARDS FOR PRODUCE SAFETY

(a) PROPOSED RULEMAKING.—

(1) IN GENERAL.—

(A) RULEMAKING.—Not later than 1 year after the date of enactment of the FDA Food Safety Modernization Act, the Secretary, in coordination with the Secretary of Agriculture and representatives of State departments of agriculture (including with regard to the national organic program established under the Organic Foods Production Act of 1990), and in consultation with the Secretary of Homeland Security, shall publish a notice of proposed rulemaking to establish science-based minimum standards for the safe production and harvesting of those types of fruits and vegetables, including specific mixes or categories of fruits and vegetables, that are raw agricultural commodities for which the Secretary has determined that such standards minimize the risk of serious adverse health consequences or death.

(B) DETERMINATION BY SECRETARY.—With respect to small businesses and very small businesses (as such terms are defined in the regulation promulgated under subparagraph (A)) that produce and harvest those types of fruits and vegetables that are raw agricultural commodities that the Secretary has determined are low risk and do not present a risk of serious adverse health consequences or death, the Secretary may determine not to include production and harvesting of such fruits and vegetables in such rulemaking, or may modify the applicable requirements of regulations promulgated pursuant to this section.

(2) PUBLIC INPUT.—During the comment period on the notice of proposed rulemaking under paragraph (1), the Secretary shall conduct not less than 3 public meetings in diverse geographical areas of the United States to provide persons in different regions an opportunity to comment.

(3) CONTENT.—The proposed rulemaking under paragraph (1) shall—

(A) provide sufficient flexibility to be applicable to various types of entities engaged in the production and harvesting of fruits and vegetables that are raw agricultural commodities, including small businesses and entities that sell directly to consumers, and be appropriate to the scale and diversity of the production and harvesting of such commodities;

(B) include, with respect to growing, harvesting, sorting, packing, and storage operations, science-based minimum standards related to soil amendments, hygiene, packaging, temperature controls, animals in the growing area, and water;

(C) consider hazards that occur naturally, may be unintentionally introduced, or may be intentionally introduced, including by acts of terrorism;

(D) take into consideration, consistent with ensuring enforceable public health protection, conservation and environmental practice standards and policies established by Federal natural resource conservation, wildlife conservation, and environmental agencies;

(E) in the case of production that is certified organic, not include any requirements that conflict with or duplicate the requirements of the national organic program established under the Organic Foods Production Act of 1990, while providing the same level of public health protection as the requirements under guidance documents, including guidance documents regarding action levels, and regulations under the FDA Food Safety Modernization Act; and

(F) define, for purposes of this section, the terms "small business" and "very small business".

(4) PRIORITIZATION.—The Secretary shall prioritize the implementation of the regulations under this section for specific fruits and vegetables that are raw agricultural commodities based on known risks which may include a history and severity of foodborne illness outbreaks.

(b) FINAL REGULATION.—

(1) IN GENERAL.—Not later than 1 year after the close of the comment period for the proposed rulemaking under subsection (a), the Secretary shall adopt a final regulation to provide for minimum science-based standards for those types of fruits and vegetables, including specific mixes or categories of fruits or vegetables, that are raw agricultural commodities, based on known safety risks, which may include a history of foodborne illness outbreaks.

(2) FINAL REGULATION.—The final regulation shall—

(A) provide for coordination of education and enforcement activities by State and local officials, as designated by the Governors of the respective States or the appropriate elected State official as recognized by State statute; and

(B) include a description of the variance process under subsection (c) and the types of permissible variances the Secretary may grant.

(3) FLEXIBILITY FOR SMALL BUSINESSES.—Notwithstanding paragraph (1)—

(A) the regulations promulgated under this section shall apply to a small business (as defined in the regulation promulgated under subsection (a)(1)) after the date that is 1 year after the effective date of the final regulation under paragraph (1); and

(B) the regulations promulgated under this section shall apply to a very small business (as defined in the regulation promulgated under subsection (a)(1)) after the date that is 2 years after the effective date of the final regulation under paragraph (1).

(c) CRITERIA.—

(1) IN GENERAL.—The regulations adopted under subsection (b) shall—

(A) set forth those procedures, processes, and practices that the Secretary determines to minimize the risk of serious adverse health consequences or death, including procedures, processes, and practices that the Secretary determines to be reasonably necessary to prevent the introduction of known or reasonably foreseeable biological, chemical, and physical hazards, including hazards that occur naturally, may be unintentionally introduced, or may be intentionally introduced, including by acts of terrorism, into fruits and vegetables, including specific mixes or categories of fruits and vegetables, that are raw agricultural commodities and to provide reasonable assurances that the produce is not adulterated under section 402;

(B) provide sufficient flexibility to be practicable for all sizes and types of businesses, including small businesses such as a small food processing facility co-located on a farm;

(C) comply with chapter 35 of title 44, United States Code (commonly known as the "Paperwork Reduction Act"), with special attention to minimizing the burden (as defined in section 3502(2) of such Act) on the business, and collection of information (as defined in section 3502(3) of such Act), associated with such regulations;

(D) acknowledge differences in risk and minimize, as appropriate, the number of separate standards that apply to separate foods; and

(E) not require a business to hire a consultant or other third party to identify, implement, certify, compliance with these procedures, processes, and practices, except in the case of negotiated enforcement resolutions that may require such a consultant or third party; and

(F) permit States and foreign countries from which food is imported into the United States to request from the Secretary variances from the requirements of the regulations, subject to paragraph (2), where the State or foreign country determines that the variance is necessary in light of local growing conditions and that the procedures, processes, and practices to be followed under the variance are reasonably likely to ensure that the produce is not adulterated under section 402 and to provide the same level of public health protection as the requirements of the regulations adopted under subsection (b).

(2) VARIANCES.—

(A) REQUESTS FOR VARIANCES.—A State or foreign country from which food is imported into the United States may in writing request a variance from the Secretary. Such request shall describe the variance requested and present information demonstrating that the variance does not increase the likelihood that the food for which the variance is requested will be adulterated under section 402, and that the variance provides the same level of public health protection as the requirements of the regulations adopted under subsection (b). The Secretary shall review such requests in a reasonable timeframe.

(B) APPROVAL OF VARIANCES.—The Secretary may approve a variance in whole or in part, as appropriate, and may specify the scope of applicability of a variance to other similarly situated persons.

(C) DENIAL OF VARIANCES.—The Secretary may deny a variance request if the Secretary determines that such variance is not reasonably likely to ensure that the food is not adulterated under section 402 and is not reasonably likely to provide the same level of public health protection as the requirements of the regulation adopted under subsection (b). The Secretary shall notify the person requesting such variance of the reasons for the denial.

(D) MODIFICATION OR REVOCATION OF A VARIANCE.—The Secretary, after notice and an opportunity for a hearing, may modify or revoke a variance if the Secretary determines that such variance is not reasonably likely to ensure that the food is not adulterated under section 402 and is not reasonably likely to provide the same level of public health protection as the requirements of the regulations adopted under subsection (b).

(d) ENFORCEMENT.—The Secretary may coordinate with the Secretary of Agriculture and, as appropriate, shall contract and coordinate with the agency or department designated by the Governor of each State to perform activities to ensure compliance with this section.

(e) GUIDANCE.—

(1) IN GENERAL.—Not later than 1 year after the date of enactment of the FDA Food Safety Modernization Act, the Secretary shall publish, after consultation with the Secretary of Agriculture, representatives of State departments of agriculture, farmer representatives, and various types of entities engaged in the production and harvesting or importing of fruits and vegetables that are raw agricultural commodities, including small businesses, updated good agricultural practices and guidance for the safe production and harvesting of specific types of fresh produce under this section.

(2) PUBLIC MEETINGS.—The Secretary shall conduct not fewer than 3 public meetings in diverse geographical areas of the United States as part of an effort to conduct education and outreach regarding the guidance described in paragraph (1) for persons in different regions who are involved in the production and harvesting of fruits and vegetables that are raw agricultural commodities, including persons that sell directly to consumers and farmer representatives, and for importers of fruits and vegetables that are raw agricultural commodities.

(3) PAPERWORK REDUCTION.—The Secretary shall ensure that any updated guidance under this section will—

(A) provide sufficient flexibility to be practicable for all sizes and types of facilities, including small businesses such as a small food processing facility co-located on a farm; and

(B) acknowledge differences in risk and minimize, as appropriate, the number of separate standards that apply to separate foods.

(f) EXEMPTION FOR DIRECT FARM MARKETING.—

(1) IN GENERAL.—A farm shall be exempt from the requirements under this section in a calendar year if—

(A) during the previous 3–year period, the average annual monetary value of the food sold by such farm directly to qualified end-users during such period exceeded the average annual monetary value of the food sold by such farm to all other buyers during such period; and

(B) the average annual monetary value of all food sold during such period was less than $500,000, adjusted for inflation.

(2) NOTIFICATION TO CONSUMERS.—

(A) IN GENERAL.—A farm that is exempt from the requirements under this section shall—

(i) with respect to a food for which a food packaging label is required by the Secretary under any other provision of this Act, include prominently and conspicuously on such label the name and business address of the farm where the produce was grown; or

(ii) with respect to a food for which a food packaging label is not required by the Secretary under any other provision of this Act, prominently and conspicuously display, at the point of purchase, the name and business address of the farm where the produce was grown, on a label, poster, sign, placard, or documents delivered contemporaneously with the food in the normal course of business, or, in the case of Internet sales, in an electronic notice.

(B) NO ADDITIONAL LABEL.—Subparagraph (A) does not provide authority to the Secretary to require a label that is in addition to any label required under any other provision of this Act.

(3) WITHDRAWAL; RULE OF CONSTRUCTION.—

(A) IN GENERAL.—In the event of an active investigation of a foodborne illness outbreak that is directly linked to a farm subject to an exemption under this subsection, or if the Secretary determines that it is necessary to protect the public health and prevent or mitigate a foodborne illness outbreak based on conduct or conditions associated with a farm that are material to the safety of the food produced or harvested at such farm, the Secretary may withdraw the exemption provided to such farm under this subsection.

(B) RULE OF CONSTRUCTION.—Nothing in this subsection shall be construed to expand or limit the inspection authority of the Secretary.

(4) DEFINITIONS.—

(A) QUALIFIED END-USER.—In this subsection, the term "qualified end-user", with respect to a food means—

(i) the consumer of the food; or

(ii) a restaurant or retail food establishment (as those terms are defined by the Secretary for purposes of section 415) that is located—

(I) in the same State as the farm that produced the food; or

(II) not more than 275 miles from such farm.

(B) CONSUMER.—For purposes of subparagraph (A), the term "consumer" does not include a business.

(5) NO PREEMPTION.—Nothing in this subsection preempts State, local, county, or other non-Federal law regarding the safe production, harvesting, holding, transportation, and sale of fresh fruits and vegetables. Compliance with this subsection shall not relieve any person from liability at common law or under State statutory law.

(6) LIMITATION OF EFFECT.—Nothing in this subsection shall prevent the Secretary from exercising any authority granted in the other sections of this Act.

(g) CLARIFICATION.—This section shall not apply to produce that is produced by an individual for personal consumption.

(h) EXCEPTION FOR ACTIVITIES OF FACILITIES SUBJECT TO SECTION 418.—This section shall not apply to activities of a facility that are subject to section 418.

SEC. 420 [21 U.S.C. 350i]. PROTECTION AGAINST INTENTIONAL ADULTERATION

(a) DETERMINATIONS.—

(1) IN GENERAL.—The Secretary shall—

(A) conduct a vulnerability assessment of the food system, including by consideration of the Department of Homeland Security biological, chemical, radiological, or other terrorism risk assessments;

(B) consider the best available understanding of uncertainties, risks, costs, and benefits associated with guarding against intentional adulteration of food at vulnerable points; and

(C) determine the types of science-based mitigation strategies or measures that are necessary to protect against the intentional adulteration of food.

(2) LIMITED DISTRIBUTION.—In the interest of national security, the Secretary, in consultation with the Secretary of Homeland Security, may determine the time, manner, and form in which determinations made under paragraph (1) are made publicly available.

(b) REGULATIONS.—Not later than 18 months after the date of enactment of the FDA Food Safety Modernization Act, the Secretary, in coordination with the Secretary of Homeland Security and in consultation with the Secretary of Agriculture, shall promulgate regulations to protect against the intentional adulteration of food subject to this Act. Such regulations shall—

(1) specify how a person shall assess whether the person is required to implement mitigation strategies or measures intended to protect against the intentional adulteration of food; and

(2) specify appropriate science-based mitigation strategies or measures to prepare and protect the food supply chain at specific vulnerable points, as appropriate.

(c) APPLICABILITY.—Regulations promulgated under subsection (b) shall apply only to food for which there is a high risk of intentional contamination, as determined by the Secretary, in consultation with the Secretary of Homeland Security, under subsection (a), that could cause serious adverse health consequences or death to humans or animals and shall include those foods—

(1) for which the Secretary has identified clear vulnerabilities (including short shelf-life or susceptibility to intentional contamination at critical control points); and

(2) in bulk or batch form, prior to being packaged for the final consumer.

(d) EXCEPTION.—This section shall not apply to farms, except for those that produce milk.

(e) DEFINITION.—For purposes of this section, the term "farm" has the meaning given that term in section 1.227 of title 21, Code of Federal Regulations (or any successor regulation).

SEC. 421 [21 U.S.C. 350j]. TARGETING OF INSPECTION RESOURCES FOR DOMESTIC FACILITIES, FOREIGN FACILITIES, AND PORTS OF ENTRY; ANNUAL REPORT

(a) IDENTIFICATION AND INSPECTION OF FACILITIES.—

(1) IDENTIFICATION.—The Secretary shall identify high-risk facilities and shall allocate resources to inspect facilities according to the known safety risks of the facilities, which shall be based on the following factors:

(A) The known safety risks of the food manufactured, processed, packed, or held at the facility.

(B) The compliance history of a facility, including with regard to food recalls, outbreaks of foodborne illness, and violations of food safety standards.

(C) The rigor and effectiveness of the facility's hazard analysis and risk-based preventive controls.

(D) Whether the food manufactured, processed, packed, or held at the facility meets the criteria for priority under section 801(h)(1).

(E) Whether the food or the facility that manufactured, processed, packed, or held such food has received a certification as described in section 801(q) or 806, as appropriate.

(F) Any other criteria deemed necessary and appropriate by the Secretary for purposes of allocating inspection resources.

(2) INSPECTIONS.—

(A) IN GENERAL.—Beginning on the date of enactment of the FDA Food Safety Modernization Act, the Secretary shall increase the frequency of inspection of all facilities.

(B) DOMESTIC HIGH-RISK FACILITIES.—The Secretary shall increase the frequency of inspection of domestic facilities identified under paragraph (1) as high-risk facilities such that each such facility is inspected—

(i) not less often than once in the 5–year period following the date of enactment of the FDA Food Safety Modernization Act; and

(ii) not less often than once every 3 years thereafter.

(C) DOMESTIC NON-HIGH-RISK FACILITIES.—The Secretary shall ensure that each domestic facility that is not identified under paragraph (1) as a high-risk facility is inspected—

(i) not less often than once in the 7–year period following the date of enactment of the FDA Food Safety Modernization Act; and

(ii) not less often than once every 5 years thereafter.

(D) FOREIGN FACILITIES.—

(i) YEAR 1.—In the 1–year period following the date of enactment of the FDA Food Safety Modernization Act, the Secretary shall inspect not fewer than 600 foreign facilities.

(ii) SUBSEQUENT YEARS.—In each of the 5 years following the 1–year period described in clause (i), the Secretary shall inspect not fewer than twice the number of foreign facilities inspected by the Secretary during the previous year.

(E) RELIANCE ON FEDERAL, STATE, OR LOCAL INSPECTIONS.—In meeting the inspection requirements under this subsection for domestic facilities, the Secretary may rely on inspections conducted by other Federal, State, or local agencies under interagency agreement, contract, memoranda of understanding, or other obligation.

(b) IDENTIFICATION AND INSPECTION AT PORTS OF ENTRY.—The Secretary, in consultation with the Secretary of Homeland Security, shall allocate resources to inspect any article of food imported into the United States according to the known safety risks of the article of food, which shall be based on the following factors:

(1) The known safety risks of the food imported.

(2) The known safety risks of the countries or regions of origin and countries through which such article of food is transported.

(3) The compliance history of the importer, including with regard to food recalls, outbreaks of foodborne illness, and violations of food safety standards.

(4) The rigor and effectiveness of the activities conducted by the importer of such article of food to satisfy the requirements of the foreign supplier verification program under section 805.

(5) Whether the food importer participates in the voluntary qualified importer program under section 806.

(6) Whether the food meets the criteria for priority under section 801(h)(1).

(7) Whether the food or the facility that manufactured, processed, packed, or held such food received a certification as described in section 801(q) or 806.

(8) Any other criteria deemed necessary and appropriate by the Secretary for purposes of allocating inspection resources.

(c) INTERAGENCY AGREEMENTS WITH RESPECT TO SEAFOOD.—

(1) IN GENERAL.—The Secretary of Health and Human Services, the Secretary of Commerce, the Secretary of Homeland Security, the Chairman of the Federal Trade Commission, and the heads of other appropriate agencies may enter into such agreements as may be necessary or appropriate to improve seafood safety.

(2) SCOPE OF AGREEMENTS.—The agreements under paragraph (1) may include—

(A) cooperative arrangements for examining and testing seafood imports that leverage the resources, capabilities, and authorities of each party to the agreement;

(B) coordination of inspections of foreign facilities to increase the percentage of imported seafood and seafood facilities inspected;

(C) standardization of data on seafood names, inspection records, and laboratory testing to improve interagency coordination;

(D) coordination to detect and investigate violations under applicable Federal law;

(E) a process, including the use or modification of existing processes, by which officers and employees of the National Oceanic and Atmospheric Administration may be duly designated by the Secretary to carry out seafood examinations and investigations under section 801 of this Act or section 203 of the Food Allergen Labeling and Consumer Protection Act of 2004;

(F) the sharing of information concerning observed non-compliance with United States food requirements domestically and in foreign nations and new regulatory decisions and policies that may affect the safety of food imported into the United States;

(G) conducting joint training on subjects that affect and strengthen seafood inspection effectiveness by Federal authorities; and

(H) outreach on Federal efforts to enhance seafood safety and compliance with Federal food safety requirements.

(d) COORDINATION.—The Secretary shall improve coordination and cooperation with the Secretary of Agriculture and the Secretary of Homeland Security to target food inspection resources.

(e) FACILITY.—For purposes of this section, the term "facility" means a domestic facility or a foreign facility that is required to register under section 415.

SEC. 422 [21 U.S.C. 350k]. LABORATORY ACCREDITATION FOR ANALYSES OF FOODS

(a) RECOGNITION OF LABORATORY ACCREDITATION.—

(1) IN GENERAL.—Not later than 2 years after the date of enactment of the FDA Food Safety Modernization Act, the Secretary shall—

(A) establish a program for the testing of food by accredited laboratories;

(B) establish a publicly available registry of accreditation bodies recognized by the Secretary and laboratories accredited by a recognized accreditation body, including the name of, contact information for, and other information deemed appropriate by the Secretary about such bodies and laboratories; and

(C) require, as a condition of recognition or accreditation, as appropriate, that recognized accreditation bodies and accredited laboratories report to the Secretary any changes that would affect the recognition of such accreditation body or the accreditation of such laboratory.

(2) PROGRAM REQUIREMENTS.—The program established under paragraph (1)(A) shall provide for the recognition of laboratory accreditation bodies that meet criteria established by the Secretary for accreditation of laboratories, including independent private laboratories and laboratories run and operated by a Federal agency (including the Department of Commerce), State, or locality with a demonstrated capability to conduct 1 or more sampling and analytical testing methodologies for food.

(3) INCREASING THE NUMBER OF QUALIFIED LABORATORIES.—The Secretary shall work with the laboratory accreditation bodies recognized under paragraph (1), as appropriate, to increase the number of qualified laboratories that are eligible to perform testing under subparagraph (b) beyond the number so qualified on the date of enactment of the FDA Food Safety Modernization Act.

(4) LIMITED DISTRIBUTION.—In the interest of national security, the Secretary, in coordination with the Secretary of Homeland Security, may determine the time,

manner, and form in which the registry established under paragraph (1)(B) is made publicly available.

(5) FOREIGN LABORATORIES.—Accreditation bodies recognized by the Secretary under paragraph (1) may accredit laboratories that operate outside the United States, so long as such laboratories meet the accreditation standards applicable to domestic laboratories accredited under this section.

(6) MODEL LABORATORY STANDARDS.—The Secretary shall develop model standards that a laboratory shall meet to be accredited by a recognized accreditation body for a specified sampling or analytical testing methodology and included in the registry provided for under paragraph (1). In developing the model standards, the Secretary shall consult existing standards for guidance. The model standards shall include—

(A) methods to ensure that—

(i) appropriate sampling, analytical procedures (including rapid analytical procedures), and commercially available techniques are followed and reports of analyses are certified as true and accurate;

(ii) internal quality systems are established and maintained;

(iii) procedures exist to evaluate and respond promptly to complaints regarding analyses and other activities for which the laboratory is accredited; and

(iv) individuals who conduct the sampling and analyses are qualified by training and experience to do so; and

(B) any other criteria determined appropriate by the Secretary.

(7) REVIEW OF RECOGNITION.—To ensure compliance with the requirements of this section, the Secretary—

(A) shall periodically, and in no case less than once every 5 years, reevaluate accreditation bodies recognized under paragraph (1) and may accompany auditors from an accreditation body to assess whether the accreditation body meets the criteria for recognition; and

(B) shall promptly revoke the recognition of any accreditation body found not to be in compliance with the requirements of this section, specifying, as appropriate, any terms and conditions necessary for laboratories accredited by such body to continue to perform testing as described in this section.

(b) TESTING PROCEDURES.—

(1) IN GENERAL.—Not later than 30 months after the date of enactment of the FDA Food Safety Modernization Act, food testing shall be conducted by Federal laboratories or non-Federal laboratories that have been accredited for the appropriate sampling or analytical testing methodology or methodologies by a

recognized accreditation body on the registry established by the Secretary under subsection (a)(1)(B) whenever such testing is conducted—

(A) by or on behalf of an owner or consignee—

(i) in response to a specific testing requirement under this Act or implementing regulations, when applied to address an identified or suspected food safety problem; and

(ii) as required by the Secretary, as the Secretary deems appropriate, to address an identified or suspected food safety problem; or

(B) on behalf of an owner or consignee—

(i) in support of admission of an article of food under section 801(a); and

(ii) under an Import Alert that requires successful consecutive tests.

(2) RESULTS OF TESTING.—The results of any such testing shall be sent directly to the Food and Drug Administration, except the Secretary may by regulation exempt test results from such submission requirement if the Secretary determines that such results do not contribute to the protection of public health. Test results required to be submitted may be submitted to the Food and Drug Administration through electronic means.

(3) EXCEPTION.—The Secretary may waive requirements under this subsection if—

(A) a new methodology or methodologies have been developed and validated but a laboratory has not yet been accredited to perform such methodology or methodologies; and

(B) the use of such methodology or methodologies are necessary to prevent, control, or mitigate a food emergency or foodborne illness outbreak.

(c) REVIEW BY SECRETARY.—If food sampling and testing performed by a laboratory run and operated by a State or locality that is accredited by a recognized accreditation body on the registry established by the Secretary under subsection (a) result in a State recalling a food, the Secretary shall review the sampling and testing results for the purpose of determining the need for a national recall or other compliance and enforcement activities.

(d) NO LIMIT ON SECRETARIAL AUTHORITY.—Nothing in this section shall be construed to limit the ability of the Secretary to review and act upon information from food testing, including determining the sufficiency of such information and testing.

SEC. 423 [21 U.S.C. 350l]. MANDATORY RECALL AUTHORITY

(a) VOLUNTARY PROCEDURES.—If the Secretary determines, based on information gathered through the reportable food registry under section 417 or through any other means, that there is a reasonable probability that an article of food (other than infant formula) is adulterated under section 402 or misbranded under section 403(w) and the use of or exposure to such article will cause serious adverse health consequences or death to humans or animals, the Secretary shall provide the responsible party (as defined in section 417) with an opportunity to cease distribution and recall such article.

(b) PREHEARING ORDER TO CEASE DISTRIBUTION AND GIVE NOTICE.—

(1) IN GENERAL.—If the responsible party refuses to or does not voluntarily cease distribution or recall such article within the time and in the manner prescribed by the Secretary (if so prescribed), the Secretary may, by order require, as the Secretary deems necessary, such person to—

(A) immediately cease distribution of such article; and

(B) as applicable, immediately notify all persons—

(i) manufacturing, processing, packing, transporting, distributing, receiving, holding, or importing and selling such article; and

(ii) to which such article has been distributed, transported, or sold, to immediately cease distribution of such article.

(2) REQUIRED ADDITIONAL INFORMATION.—

(A) IN GENERAL.—If an article of food covered by a recall order issued under paragraph (1)(B) has been distributed to a warehouse-based third party logistics provider without providing such provider sufficient information to know or reasonably determine the precise identity of the article of food covered by a recall order that is in its possession, the notice provided by the responsible party subject to the order issued under paragraph (1)(B) shall include such information as is necessary for the warehouse-based third party logistics provider to identify the food.

(B) RULES OF CONSTRUCTION.—Nothing in this paragraph shall be construed—

(i) to exempt a warehouse-based third party logistics provider from the requirements of this Act, including the requirements in this section and section 414; or

(ii) to exempt a warehouse-based third party logistics provider from being the subject of a mandatory recall order.

(3) DETERMINATION TO LIMITED AREAS AFFECTED.—If the Secretary requires a responsible party to cease distribution under paragraph (1)(A) of an article of food identified in subsection (a), the Secretary may limit the size of the geographic area and the markets affected by such cessation if such limitation would not compromise the public health.

(c) HEARING ON ORDER.—The Secretary shall provide the responsible party subject to an order under subsection (b) with an opportunity for an informal hearing, to be held as soon as possible, but not later than 2 days after the issuance of the order, on the actions required by the order and on why the article that is the subject of the order should not be recalled.

(d) POST-HEARING RECALL ORDER AND MODIFICATION OF ORDER.—

(1) AMENDMENT OF ORDER.—If, after providing opportunity for an informal hearing under subsection (c), the Secretary determines that removal of the article from commerce is necessary, the Secretary shall, as appropriate—

(A) amend the order to require recall of such article or other appropriate action;

(B) specify a timetable in which the recall shall occur;

(C) require periodic reports to the Secretary describing the progress of the recall; and

(D) provide notice to consumers to whom such article was, or may have been, distributed.

(2) VACATING OF ORDER.—If, after such hearing, the Secretary determines that adequate grounds do not exist to continue the actions required by the order, or that such actions should be modified, the Secretary shall vacate the order or modify the order.

(e) RULE REGARDING ALCOHOLIC BEVERAGES.—The Secretary shall not initiate a mandatory recall or take any other action under this section with respect to any alcohol beverage until the Secretary has provided the Alcohol and Tobacco Tax and Trade Bureau with a reasonable opportunity to cease distribution and recall such article under the Alcohol and Tobacco Tax and Trade Bureau authority.

(f) COOPERATION AND CONSULTATION.—The Secretary shall work with State and local public health officials in carrying out this section, as appropriate.

(g) PUBLIC NOTIFICATION.—In conducting a recall under this section, the Secretary shall—

(1) ensure that a press release is published regarding the recall, as well as alerts and public notices, as appropriate, in order to provide notification—

(A) of the recall to consumers and retailers to whom such article was, or may have been, distributed; and

(B) that includes, at a minimum—

(i) the name of the article of food subject to the recall;

(ii) a description of the risk associated with such article; and

(iii) to the extent practicable, information for consumers about similar articles of food that are not affected by the recall;

(2) consult the policies of the Department of Agriculture regarding providing to the public a list of retail consignees receiving products involved in a Class I

recall and shall consider providing such a list to the public, as determined appropriate by the Secretary; and

(3) if available, publish on the Internet Web site of the Food and Drug Administration an image of the article that is the subject of the press release described in (1).

(h) NO DELEGATION.—The authority conferred by this section to order a recall or vacate a recall order shall not be delegated to any officer or employee other than the Commissioner.

(i) EFFECT.—Nothing in this section shall affect the authority of the Secretary to request or participate in a voluntary recall, or to issue an order to cease distribution or to recall under any other provision of this Act or under the Public Health Service Act.

(j) COORDINATED COMMUNICATION.—

(1) IN GENERAL.—To assist in carrying out the requirements of this subsection, the Secretary shall establish an incident command operation or a similar operation within the Department of Health and Human Services that will operate not later than 24 hours after the initiation of a mandatory recall or the recall of an article of food for which the use of, or exposure to, such article will cause serious adverse health consequences or death to humans or animals.

(2) REQUIREMENTS.—To reduce the potential for miscommunication during recalls or regarding investigations of a food borne illness outbreak associated with a food that is subject to a recall, each incident command operation or similar operation under paragraph (1) shall use regular staff and resources of the Department of Health and Human Services to—

(A) ensure timely and coordinated communication within the Department, including enhanced communication and coordination between different agencies and organizations within the Department;

(B) ensure timely and coordinated communication from the Department, including public statements, throughout the duration of the investigation and related foodborne illness outbreak;

(C) identify a single point of contact within the Department for public inquiries regarding any actions by the Secretary related to a recall;

(D) coordinate with Federal, State, local, and tribal authorities, as appropriate, that have responsibilities related to the recall of a food or a foodborne illness outbreak associated with a food that is subject to the recall, including notification of the Secretary of Agriculture and the Secretary of Education in the event such recalled food is a commodity intended for use in a child nutrition program (as identified in section 25(b) of the Richard B. Russell National School Lunch Act (42 U.S.C. 1769f(b))); and

(E) conclude operations at such time as the Secretary determines appropriate.

(3) MULTIPLE RECALLS.—The Secretary may establish multiple or concurrent incident command operations or similar operations in the event of multiple recalls or foodborne illness outbreaks necessitating such action by the Department of Health and Human Services.

CHAPTER V—DRUGS AND DEVICES

SUBCHAPTER A—DRUGS AND DEVICES

SEC. 501 [21 U.S.C. 351]. ADULTERATED DRUGS AND DEVICES

A drug or device shall be deemed to be adulterated—

(a)(1) If it consists in whole or in part of any filthy, putrid, or decomposed substance; or (2)(A) if it has been prepared, packed, or held under insanitary conditions whereby it may have been contaminated with filth, or whereby it may have been rendered injurious to health; or (B) if it is a drug and the methods used in, or the facilities or controls used for, its manufacture, processing, packing, or holding do not conform to or are not operated or administered in conformity with current good manufacturing practice to assure that such drug meets the requirements of this Act as to safety and has the identity and strength, and meets the quality and purity characteristics, which it purports or is represented to possess; or (C) if it is a compounded positron emission tomography drug and the methods used in, or the facilities and controls used for, its compounding, processing, packing, or holding do not conform to or are not operated or administered in conformity with the positron emission tomography compounding standards and the official monographs of the United States Pharmacopoeia to assure that such drug meets the requirements of this Act as to safety and has the identity and strength, and meets the quality and purity characteristics, that it purports or is represented to possess; or (3) if its container is composed, in whole or in part, of any poisonous or deleterious substance which may render the contents injurious to health; or (4) if (A) it bears or contains, for purposes of coloring only, a color additive which is unsafe within the meaning of section 721(a), or (B) it is a color additive the intended use of which in or on drugs or devices is for purposes of coloring only and is unsafe within the meaning of section 721(a); or (5) if it is a new animal drug which is unsafe within the meaning of section 512; or (6) if it is an animal feed bearing or containing a new animal drug, and such animal feed is unsafe within the meaning of section 512.

(b) If it purports to be or is represented as a drug the name of which is recognized in an official compendium, and its strength differs from, or its quality or purity falls below, the standards set forth in such compendium. Such determination as to strength, quality, or purity shall be made in accordance with the tests or methods of assay set forth in such compendium, except that whenever tests or methods of assay have not been prescribed in such compendium, or such tests or methods of assay as are prescribed are, in the judgment of the Secretary, insufficient for the making of such determination, the Secretary shall bring such fact to the attention of the appropriate body charged with the revision of such compendium, and if such body fails within a reasonable time to prescribe tests or methods of assay which, in the judgment of the Secretary, are sufficient for purposes of this paragraph, then the Secretary shall promulgate regulations prescribing appropriate tests or methods of assay in accordance with which such determination as to strength, quality, or purity shall be made. No drug defined in an official compendium shall be deemed to be adulterated under this paragraph because it differs from the standard of strength, quality, or purity therefor set forth in such compendium, if its difference in strength, quality, or purity from such standards is plainly stated on its label. Whenever a drug is recognized in both the United States Pharmacopeia and the Homeopathic Pharmacopeia of the United States it shall be subject to the requirements of the United States Pharmacopeia unless it is labeled and offered for sale as a homeopathic drug, in which case it shall be subject to the provisions of the Homeopathic Pharmacopeia of the United States and not to those of the United States Pharmacopeia.

(c) If it is not subject to the provisions of paragraph (b) of this section and its strength differs from, or its purity or quality falls below, that which it purports or is represented to possess.

(d) If it is a drug and any substance has been (1) mixed or packed therewith so as to reduce its quality or strength or (2) substituted wholly or in part therefor.

(e)(1) If it is, or purports to be or is represented as, a device which is subject to a performance standard established under section 514, unless such device is in all respects in conformity with such standard.

(2) If it is declared to be, purports to be, or is represented as, a device that is in conformity with any standard recognized under section 514(c) unless such device is in all respects in conformity with such standard.

(f)(1) If it is a class III device—

(A)(i) which is required by an order issued under subsection (b) of section 515 to have an approval under such section of an application for premarket approval and which is not exempt from section 515 under section 520(g), and

(ii)(I) for which an application for premarket approval or a notice of completion of a product development protocol was not filed with the Secretary within the ninety-day period beginning on the date of the issuance of such order, or

(II) for which such an application was filed and approval of the application has been denied, suspended, or withdrawn, or such a notice was filed and has been declared not completed or the approval of the device under the protocol has been withdrawn;

(B)(i) which was classified under section 513(f) into class III, which under section 515(a) is required to have in effect an approved application for premarket approval, and which is not exempt from section 515 under section 520(g), and

(ii) which has an application which has been suspended or is otherwise not in effect; or

(C) which was classified under section 520(*l*) into class III, which under such section is required to have in effect an approved application under section 515, and which has an application which has been suspended or is otherwise not in effect.

(2)(A) In the case of a device classified under section 513(f) into class III and intended solely for investigational use, paragraph (1)(B) shall not apply with respect to such device during the period ending on the ninetieth day after the date of the promulgation of the regulations prescribing the procedures and conditions required by section 520(g)(2).

(B) In the case of a device subject to an order issued under subsection (b) of section 515, paragraph (1) shall not apply with respect to such device during the period ending—

(i) on the last day of the thirtieth calendar month beginning after the month in which the classification of the device in class III became effective under section 513, or

(ii) on the ninetieth day after the date of the issuance of such order,

whichever occurs later.

(3) In the case of a device with respect to which a regulation was promulgated under section 515(b) prior to the date of enactment of the Food and Drug Administration Safety and Innovation Act,[25] a reference in this subsection to an order issued under section 515(b) shall be deemed to include such regulation.

(g) If it is a banned device.

(h) If it is a device and the methods used in, or the facilities or controls used for, its manufacture, packing, storage, or installation are not in conformity with applicable requirements under section 520(f)(1) or an applicable condition prescribed by an order under section 520(f)(2).

(i) If it is a device for which an exemption has been granted under section 520(g) for investigational use and the person who was granted such exemption or any investigator who uses such device under such exemption fails to comply with a requirement prescribed by or under such section.

(j) If it is a drug and it has been manufactured, processed, packed, or held in any factory, warehouse, or establishment and the owner, operator, or agent of such factory, warehouse, or establishment delays, denies, or limits an inspection, or refuses to permit entry or inspection.

For purposes of paragraph (a)(2)(B), the term "current good manufacturing practice" includes the implementation of oversight and controls over the manufacture of drugs

25. Pub. L. No. 112–144, 126 Stat. 993, which was enacted July 9, 2012.

to ensure quality, including managing the risk of and establishing the safety of raw materials, materials used in the manufacturing of drugs, and finished drug products.

SEC. 502 [21 U.S.C. 352]. MISBRANDED DRUGS AND DEVICES

A drug or device shall be deemed to be misbranded—

(a) If its labeling is false or misleading in any particular. Health care economic information provided to a formulary committee, or other similar entity, in the course of the committee or the entity carrying out its responsibilities for the selection of drugs for managed care or other similar organizations, shall not be considered to be false or misleading under this paragraph if the healthcare economic information directly relates to an indication approved under section 505 or under section 351(a) of the Public Health Service Act for such drug and is based on competent and reliable scientific evidence. The requirements set forth in section 505(a) or in section 351(a) of the Public Health Service Act shall not apply to health care economic information provided to such a committee or entity in accordance with this paragraph. Information that is relevant to the substantiation of the health care economic information presented pursuant to this paragraph shall be made available to the Secretary upon request. In this paragraph, the term "health care economic information" means any analysis that identifies, measures, or compares the economic consequences, including the costs of the represented health outcomes, of the use of a drug to the use of another drug, to another health care intervention, or to no intervention.

(b) If in a package form unless it bears a label containing (1) the name and place of business of the manufacturer, packer, or distributor; and (2) an accurate statement of the quantity of the contents in terms of weight, measure, or numerical count: Provided, That under clause (2) of this paragraph reasonable variations shall be permitted, and exemptions as to small packages shall be established, by regulations prescribed by the Secretary.

(c) If any word, statement, or other information required by or under authority of this Act to appear on the label or labeling is not prominently placed thereon with such conspicuousness (as compared with other words, statements, designs, or devices, in the labeling) and in such terms as to render it likely to be read and understood by the ordinary individual under customary conditions of purchase and use.

[(d) Repealed by Pub. L. No. 105–115, § 126(b), 111 Stat. 2296, 2327 (1997).]

(e)(1)(A) If it is a drug, unless its label bears, to the exclusion of any other non-proprietary name (except the applicable systematic chemical name or the chemical formula)—

(i) the established name (as defined in subparagraph (3)) of the drug, if there is such a name;

(ii) the established name and quantity or, if determined to be appropriate by the Secretary, the proportion of each active ingredient, including the quantity, kind, and proportion of any alcohol, and also including whether active or not the established name and quantity or if determined to be appropriate by the Secretary, the proportion of any bromides, ether, chloroform, acetanilide, acetophenetidin, amidopyrine, antipyrine, atropine, hyoscine, hyoscyamine, arsenic, digitalis, digitalis glucosides, mercury, ouabain, strophanthin, strychnine, thyroid, or any derivative or preparation of any such substances, contained therein, except that the requirement for stating the quantity of the active ingredients, other than the quantity of those specifically named in this subclause, shall not apply to nonprescription drugs not intended for human use; and

(iii) the established name of each inactive ingredient listed in alphabetical order on the outside container of the retail package and, if determined to be appropriate by the Secretary, on the immediate container, as prescribed in regulation promulgated by the Secretary, except that nothing in this subclause shall be deemed to require that any trade secret be divulged, and except that the requirements of this subclause with respect to alphabetical order shall apply only to nonprescription drugs that are not also cosmetics and that this subclause shall not apply to nonprescription drugs not intended for human use.

(B) For any prescription drug the established name of such drug or ingredient, as the case may be, on such label (and on any labeling on which a name for such drug or ingredient is used) shall be printed prominently and in type at least half as large as that used thereon for any proprietary name or designation for such drug or ingredient, except that to the extent that compliance with the requirements of subclause (ii) or (iii) of clause (A) or this clause is impracticable, exemptions shall be established by regulations promulgated by the Secretary.

(2) If it is a device and it has an established name, unless its label bears, to the exclusion of any other nonproprietary name, its established name (as defined in subparagraph (4)) prominently printed in type at least half as large as that used thereon for any proprietary name or designation for such device, except that to the extent compliance with the requirements of this subparagraph is impracticable, exemptions shall be established by regulations promulgated by the Secretary.

(3) As used in subparagraph (1), the term "established name", with respect to a drug or ingredient thereof, means (A) the applicable official name designated pursuant to section 508, or (B) if there is no such name and such drug, or such ingredient, is an article recognized in an official compendium, then the official title thereof in such compendium, or (C) if neither clause (A) nor clause (B) of this subparagraph applies, then the common or usual name, if any, of such drug or of such ingredient, except that where clause (B) of this subparagraph applies to an article recognized in the United States Pharmacopeia and in the Homeopathic Pharmacopeia under different official titles, the official title used in the United States Pharmacopeia shall apply unless it is labeled and offered for sale as a homeopathic drug, in which case the official title used in the Homeopathic Pharmacopeia shall apply.

(4) As used in subparagraph (2), the term "established name" with respect to a device means (A) the applicable official name of the device designated pursuant to

section 508, (B) if there is no such name and such device is an article recognized in an official compendium, then the official title thereof in such compendium, or (C) if neither clause (A) nor clause (B) of this subparagraph applies, then any common or usual name of such device.

(f) Unless its labeling bears (1) adequate directions for use; and (2) such adequate warnings against use in those pathological conditions or by children where its use may be dangerous to health, or against unsafe dosage or methods or duration of administration or application, in such manner and form, as are necessary for the protection of users, except that where any requirement of clause (1) of this paragraph, as applied to any drug or device, is not necessary for the protection of the public health, the Secretary shall promulgate regulations exempting such drug or device from such requirement. Required labeling for prescription devices intended for use in health care facilities or by a health care professional and required labeling for in vitro diagnostic devices intended for use by health care professionals or in blood establishments may be made available solely by electronic means, provided that the labeling complies with all applicable requirements of law, and that the manufacturer affords such users the opportunity to request the labeling in paper form, and after such request, promptly provides the requested information without additional cost.

(g) If it purports to be a drug the name of which is recognized in an official compendium, unless it is packaged and labeled as prescribed therein. The method of packing may be modified with the consent of the Secretary. Whenever a drug is recognized in both the United States Pharmacopeia and the Homeopathic Pharmacopeia of the United States, it shall be subject to the requirements of the United States Pharmacopeia with respect to packaging, and labeling unless it is labeled and offered for sale as a homeopathic drug, in which case it shall be subject to the provisions of the Homeopathic Pharmacopeia of the United States, and not to those of the United States Pharmacopeia, except that in the event of inconsistency between the requirements of this paragraph and those of paragraph (e) as to the name by which the drug or its ingredients shall be designated, the requirements of paragraph (e) shall prevail.

(h) If it has been found by the Secretary to be a drug liable to deterioration, unless it is packaged in such form and manner, and its label bears a statement of such precautions, as the Secretary shall by regulations require as necessary for the protection of the public health. No such regulation shall be established for any drug recognized in an official compendium until the Secretary shall have informed the appropriate body charged with the revision of such compendium of the need for such packaging or labeling requirements and such body shall have failed within a reasonable time to prescribe such requirements.

(i)(1) If it is a drug and its container is so made, formed, or filled as to be misleading; or (2) if it is an imitation of another drug; or (3) if it is offered for sale under the name of another drug.

(j) If it is dangerous to health when used in the dosage or manner; or with the frequency or duration prescribed, recommended, or suggested in the labeling thereof.

[(k) Repealed by Pub. L. No. 105–115, § 125(a)(2)(B), 111 Stat. 2296, 2325 (1997).]

[(*l*) Repealed by Pub. L. No. 105–115, § 125(b)(2)(D), 111 Stat. 2296, 2325 (1997).]

(m) If it is a color additive the intended use of which is for the purpose of coloring only, unless its packaging and labeling are in conformity with such packaging and labeling requirements applicable to such color additive, as may be contained in regulations issued under section 721.

(n) In the case of any prescription drug distributed or offered for sale in any State, unless the manufacturer, packer, or distributor thereof includes in all advertisements and other descriptive printed matter issued or caused to be issued by the manufacturer, packer, or distributor with respect to that drug a true statement of (1) the established name as defined in section 502(e), printed prominently and in type at least half as large as that used for any trade or brand name thereof, (2) the formula showing quantitatively each ingredient of such drug to the extent required for labels under section 502(e), and (3) such other information in brief summary relating to side effects, contraindications, and effectiveness as shall be required in regulations which shall be issued by the Secretary in accordance with section 701(a), and in the case of published direct-to-consumer advertisements the following statement printed in conspicuous text: "You are encouraged to report negative side effects of prescription drugs to the FDA. Visit www.fda.gov/medwatch, or call 1–800–FDA–1088.", except that (A) except in extraordinary circumstances, no regulation issued under this paragraph shall require prior approval by the Secretary of the content of any advertisement, and (B) no advertisement of a prescription drug, published after the effective date of regulations issued under this paragraph applicable to advertisements of prescription drugs, shall, with respect to the matters specified in this paragraph or covered by such regulations, be subject to the provisions of sections 12 through 17 of the Federal Trade Commission Act, as amended (15 U.S.C. 52–57). This paragraph (n) shall not be applicable to any printed matter which the Secretary determines to be labeling as defined in section 201(m) of this Act. Nothing in the Convention on Psychotropic Substances, signed at Vienna, Austria, on February 21, 1971, shall be construed to prevent drug price communications to consumers. In the case of an advertisement for a drug subject to section 503(b)(1) presented directly to consumers in television or radio format and stating the name of the drug and its conditions of use, the major statement relating to side effects and contraindications shall be presented in a clear, conspicuous, and neutral manner.

(*o*) If it was manufactured, prepared, propagated, compounded, or processed in an establishment not duly registered under section 510, if it is a drug and was imported or offered for import by a commercial importer of drugs not duly registered under section 801(s), if it was not included in a list required by section 510(j), if a notice or other information respecting it was not provided as required by such section or section 510(k), or if it does not bear such symbols from the uniform system for identification of devices prescribed under section 510(e) as the Secretary by regulation requires.

(p) If it is a drug and its packaging or labeling is in violation of an applicable regulation issued pursuant to section 3 or 4 of the Poison Prevention Packaging Act of 1970.

(q) In the case of any restricted device distributed or offered for sale in any State, if (1) its advertising is false or misleading in any particular, or (2) it is sold, distributed, or used in violation of regulations prescribed under section 520(e).

(r) In the case of any restricted device distributed or offered for sale in any State, unless the manufacturer, packer, or distributor thereof includes in all advertisements and other descriptive printed matter issued or caused to be issued by the manufacturer, packer, or distributor with respect to that device (1) a true statement of the device's established name as defined in section 502(e), printed prominently and in type at least half as large as that used for any trade or brand name thereof, and (2) a brief statement of the intended uses of the device and relevant warnings, precautions, side effects, and contraindications and, in the case of specific devices made subject to a finding by the Secretary after notice and opportunity for comment that such action is necessary to protect the public health, a full description of the components of such device or the formula showing quantitatively each ingredient of such device to the extent required in regulations which shall be issued by the Secretary after an opportunity for a hearing. Except in extraordinary circumstances, no regulation issued under this paragraph shall require prior approval by the Secretary of the content of any advertisement and no advertisement of a restricted device, published after the effective date of this paragraph shall, with respect to the matters specified in this paragraph or covered by regulations issued hereunder, be subject to the provisions of sections 12 through 15 of the Federal Trade Commission Act (15 U.S.C. 52–55). This paragraph shall not be applicable to any printed matter which the Secretary determines to be labeling as defined in section 201(m).

(s) If it is a device subject to a performance standard established under section 514, unless it bears such labeling as may be prescribed in such performance standard.

(t) If it is a device and there was a failure or refusal (1) to comply with any requirement prescribed under section 518 respecting the device, (2) to furnish any material or information required by or under section 519 respecting the device, or (3) to comply with a requirement under section 522.

(u)(1) Subject to paragraph (2), if it is a reprocessed single-use device, unless it, or an attachment thereto, prominently and conspicuously bears the name of the manufacturer of the reprocessed device, a generally recognized abbreviation of such name, or a unique and generally recognized symbol identifying such manufacturer.

(2) If the original device or an attachment thereto does not prominently and conspicuously bear the name of the manufacturer of the original device, a generally recognized abbreviation of such name, or a unique and generally recognized symbol

identifying such manufacturer, a reprocessed device may satisfy the requirements of paragraph (1) through the use of a detachable label on the packaging that identifies the manufacturer and is intended to be affixed to the medical record of a patient.

(v) If it is a reprocessed single-use device, unless all labeling of the device prominently and conspicuously bears the statement "Reprocessed device for single use. Reprocessed by ____." The name of the manufacturer of the reprocessed device shall be placed in the space identifying the person responsible for reprocessing.

(w) If it is a new animal drug—

(1) that is conditionally approved under section 571 and its labeling does not conform with the approved application or section 571(f), or that is not conditionally approved under section 571 and its label bears the statement set forth in section 571(f)(1)(A); or

(2) that is indexed under section 572 and its labeling does not conform with the index listing under section 572(e) or 572(h), or that has not been indexed under section 572 and its label bears the statement set forth in section 572(h).

(x) If it is a nonprescription drug (as defined in section 760) that is marketed in the United States, unless the label of such drug includes a domestic address or domestic phone number through which the responsible person (as described in section 760) may receive a report of a serious adverse event (as defined in section 760) with such drug.

(y) If it is a drug subject to an approved risk evaluation and mitigation strategy pursuant to section 505(p) and the responsible person (as such term is used in section 505–1) fails to comply with a requirement of such strategy provided for under subsection (d), (e), or (f) of section 505–1.

(z) If it is a drug, and the responsible person (as such term is used in section 505(*o*)) is in violation of a requirement established under paragraph (3) (relating to postmarket studies and clinical trials) or paragraph (4) (relating to labeling) of section 505(*o*) with respect to such drug.

(aa) If it is a drug, or an active pharmaceutical ingredient, and it was manufactured, prepared, propagated, compounded, or processed in a facility for which fees have not been paid as required by section 744A(a)(4) or for which identifying information required by section 744B(f) has not been submitted, or it contains an active pharmaceutical ingredient that was manufactured, prepared, propagated, compounded, or processed in such a facility.

(bb) If the advertising or promotion of a compounded drug is false or misleading in any particular.

(cc) If it is a drug and it fails to bear the product identifier as required by section 582.

SEC. 503 [21 U.S.C. 353]. EXEMPTIONS AND CONSIDERATION FOR CERTAIN DRUGS, DEVICES, AND BIOLOGICAL PRODUCTS

(a) The Secretary is hereby directed to promulgate regulations exempting from any labeling or packaging requirement of this Act drugs and devices which are, in accordance with the practice of the trade, to be processed, labeled, or repacked in substantial quantities at establishments other than those where originally processed or packed, on condition that such drugs and devices are not adulterated or misbranded, under the provisions of this Act upon removal from such processing, labeling, or repacking establishment.

(b)(1) A drug intended for use by man which—

(A) because of its toxicity or other potentiality for harmful effect, or the method of its use, or the collateral measures necessary to its use, is not safe for use except under the supervision of a practitioner licensed by law to administer such drug; or

(B) is limited by an approved application under section 505 to use under the professional supervision of a practitioner licensed by law to administer such drug;

shall be dispensed only (i) upon a written prescription of a practitioner licensed by law to administer such drug, or (ii) upon an oral prescription of such practitioner which is reduced promptly to writing and filed by the pharmacist, or (iii) by refilling any such written or oral prescription if such refilling is authorized by the prescriber either in the original prescription or by oral order which is reduced promptly to writing and filed by the pharmacist. The act of dispensing a drug contrary to the provisions of this paragraph shall be deemed to be an act which results in the drug being misbranded while held for sale.

(2) Any drug dispensed by filling or refilling a written or oral prescription of a practitioner licensed by law to administer such drug shall be exempt from the requirements of section 502, except paragraphs (a), (i) (2) and (3), (k), and (*l*), and the packaging requirements of paragraphs (g), (h), and (p), if the drug bears a label containing the name and address of the dispenser, the serial number and date of the prescription or of its filling, the name of the prescriber, and, if stated in the prescription, the name of the patient, and the directions for use and cautionary statements, if any, contained in such prescription. This exemption shall not apply to any drug dispensed in the course of the conduct of a business of dispensing drugs pursuant to diagnosis by mail, or to a drug dispensed in violation of paragraph (1) of this subsection.

(3) The Secretary may by regulation remove drugs subject to section 505 from the requirements of paragraph (1) of this subsection when such requirements are not necessary for the protection of the public health.

(4)(A) A drug that is subject to paragraph (1) shall be deemed to be misbranded if at any time prior to dispensing the label of the drug fails to bear, at a minimum, the symbol "Rx only".

(B) A drug to which paragraph (1) does not apply shall be deemed to be misbranded if at any time prior to dispensing the label of the drug bears the symbol described in subparagraph (A).

(5) Nothing in this subsection shall be construed to relieve any person from any requirement prescribed by or under authority of law with respect to drugs now included or which may hereafter be included within the classifications stated in section 3220 of the Internal Revenue Code (26 U.S.C. 3220), or to marihuana as defined in section 3238(b) of the Internal Revenue Code (26 U.S.C. 3238(b)).

(c)(1) No person may sell, purchase, or trade or offer to sell, purchase, or trade any drug sample. For purposes of this paragraph and subsection (d), the term "drug sample" means a unit of a drug, subject to subsection (b), which is not intended to be sold and is intended to promote the sale of the drug. Nothing in this paragraph shall subject an officer or executive of a drug manufacturer or distributor to criminal liability solely because of a sale, purchase, trade, or offer to sell, purchase, or trade in violation of this paragraph by other employees of the manufacturer or distributor.

(2) No person may sell, purchase, or trade, offer to sell, purchase, or trade, or counterfeit any coupon. For purposes of this paragraph, the term "coupon" means a form which may be redeemed, at no cost or at a reduced cost, for a drug which is prescribed in accordance with subsection (b).

(3)(A) No person may sell, purchase, or trade, or offer to sell, purchase, or trade, any drug—

(i) which is subject to subsection (b), and

(ii)(I) which was purchased by a public or private hospital or other health care entity, or

(II) which was donated or supplied at a reduced price to a charitable organization described in section 501(c)(3) of the Internal Revenue Code of 1954.

(B) Subparagraph (A) does not apply to—

(i) the purchase or other acquisition by a hospital or other health care entity which is a member of a group purchasing organization of a drug for its own use from the group purchasing organization or from other hospitals or health care entities which are members of such organization,

(ii) the sale, purchase, or trade of a drug or an offer to sell, purchase, or trade a drug by an organization described in subparagraph (A)(ii)(II) to a nonprofit affiliate of the organization to the extent otherwise permitted by law,

(iii) a sale, purchase, or trade of a drug or an offer to sell, purchase, or trade a drug among hospitals or other health care entities which are under common control,

(iv) a sale, purchase, or trade of a drug or an offer to sell, purchase, or trade a drug for emergency medical reasons, or

(v) a sale, purchase, or trade of a drug, an offer to sell, purchase, or trade a drug, or the dispensing of a drug pursuant to a prescription executed in accordance with subsection (b).

For purposes of this paragraph, the term "entity" does not include a wholesale distributor of drugs or a retail pharmacy licensed under State law and the term "emergency medical reasons" includes transfers of a drug between health care entities or from a health care entity to a retail pharmacy undertaken to alleviate temporary shortages of the drug arising from delays in or interruptions of regular distribution schedules.

(d)(1) Except as provided in paragraphs (2) and (3), no person may distribute any drug sample. For purposes of this subsection, the term "distribute" does not include the providing of a drug sample to a patient by a—

(A) practitioner licensed to prescribe such drug,

(B) health care professional acting at the direction and under the supervision of such a practitioner, or

(C) pharmacy of a hospital or of another health care entity that is acting at the direction of such a practitioner and that received such sample pursuant to paragraph (2) or (3).

(2)(A) The manufacturer or authorized distributor of record of a drug subject to subsection (b) may, in accordance with this paragraph, distribute drug samples by mail or common carrier to practitioners licensed to prescribe such drugs or, at the request of a licensed practitioner, to pharmacies of hospitals or other health care entities. Such a distribution of drug samples may only be made—

(i) in response to a written request for drug samples made on a form which meets the requirements of subparagraph (B), and

(ii) under a system which requires the recipient of the drug sample to execute a written receipt for the drug sample upon its delivery and the return of the receipt to the manufacturer or authorized distributor of record.

(B) A written request for a drug sample required by subparagraph (A)(i) shall contain—

(i) the name, address, professional designation, and signature of the practitioner making the request,

(ii) the identity of the drug sample requested and the quantity requested,

(iii) the name of the manufacturer of the drug sample requested, and

(iv) the date of the request.

(C) Each drug manufacturer or authorized distributor of record which makes distributions by mail or common carrier under this paragraph shall maintain, for a period of 3 years, the request forms submitted for such distributions and the receipts submitted for such distributions and shall maintain a record of distributions of drug samples which identifies the drugs distributed and the recipients of the distributions.

Forms, receipts, and records required to be maintained under this subparagraph shall be made available by the drug manufacturer or authorized distributor of record to Federal and State officials engaged in the regulation of drugs and in the enforcement of laws applicable to drugs.

(3) The manufacturer or authorized distributor of record of a drug subject to subsection (b) may, by means other than mail or common carrier, distribute drug samples only if the manufacturer or authorized distributor of record makes the distributions in accordance with subparagraph (A) and carries out the activities described in subparagraphs (B) through (F) as follows:

(A) Drug samples may only be distributed—

(i) to practitioners licensed to prescribe such drugs if they make a written request for the drug samples, or

(ii) at the written request of such a licensed practitioner, to pharmacies of hospitals or other health care entities.

A written request for drug samples shall be made on a form which contains the practitioner's name, address, and professional designation, the identity of the drug sample requested, the quantity of drug samples requested, the name of the manufacturer or authorized distributor of record of the drug sample, the date of the request and signature of the practitioner making the request.

(B) Drug manufacturers or authorized distributors of record shall store drug samples under conditions that will maintain their stability, integrity, and effectiveness and will assure that the drug samples will be free of contamination, deterioration, and adulteration.

(C) Drug manufacturers or authorized distributors of record shall conduct, at least annually, a complete and accurate inventory of all drug samples in the possession of representatives of the manufacturer or authorized distributor of record. Drug manufacturers or authorized distributors of record shall maintain lists of the names and address of each of their representatives who distribute drug samples and of the sites where drug samples are stored. Drug manufacturers or authorized distributors of record shall maintain records for at least 3 years of all drug samples distributed, destroyed, or returned to the manufacturer or authorized distributor of record, of all inventories maintained under this subparagraph, of all thefts or significant losses of drug samples, and of all requests made under subparagraph (A) for drug samples. Records and lists maintained under this subparagraph shall be made available by the drug manufacturer or authorized distributor of record to the Secretary upon request.

(D) Drug manufacturers or authorized distributors of record shall notify the Secretary of any significant loss of drug samples and any known theft of drug samples.

(E) Drug manufacturers or authorized distributors of record shall report to the Secretary any conviction of their representatives for violations of subsection (c)

(1) or a State law because of the sale, purchase, or trade of a drug sample or the offer to sell, purchase, or trade a drug sample.

(F) Drug manufacturers or authorized distributors of record shall provide to the Secretary the name and telephone number of the individual responsible for responding to a request for information respecting drug samples.

(4)[26] In this subsection, the term "authorized distributors of record" means those distributors with whom a manufacturer has established an ongoing relationship to distribute such manufacturer's products.

(e)[27] (1) Requirement.—Subject to section 583:

(A) IN GENERAL.—No person may engage in wholesale distribution of a drug subject to subsection (b)(1) in any State unless such person—

(i)(I) is licensed by the State from which the drug is distributed; or

(II) if the State from which the drug is distributed has not established a licensure requirement, is licensed by the Secretary; and

(ii) if the drug is distributed interstate, is licensed by the State into which the drug is distributed if the State into which the drug is distributed requires the licensure of a person that distributes drugs into the State.

(B) STANDARDS.—Each Federal and State license described in subparagraph (A) shall meet the standards, terms, and conditions established by the Secretary under section 583.

(2) REPORTING AND DATABASE.—

(A) REPORTING.—Beginning January 1, 2015, any person who owns or operates an establishment that engages in wholesale distribution shall—

(i) report to the Secretary, on an annual basis pursuant to a schedule determined by the Secretary—

(I) each State by which the person is licensed and the appropriate identification number of each such license; and

(II) the name, address, and contact information of each facility at which, and all trade names under which, the person conducts business; and

(ii) report to the Secretary within a reasonable period of time and in a reasonable manner, as determined by the Secretary, any significant disciplinary actions, such as the revocation or suspension of a wholesale distributor license, taken by a State or the Federal Government during the reporting period against the wholesale distributor.

---

26. Subsection (d)(4) was added by Pub. L. No. 113–54, and according to §204(c) of that law, this provision takes effect on January 1, 2015.

27. Subsection (e) was amended by Pub. L. No. 113–54, and according to §204(c) of that law, these amendments take effect on January 1, 2015.

(B) DATABASE.—Not later than January 1, 2015, the Secretary shall establish a database of authorized wholesale distributors. Such database shall—

(i) identify each authorized wholesale distributor by name, contact information, and each State where such wholesale distributor is appropriately licensed to engage in wholesale distribution;

(ii) be available to the public on the Internet Web site of the Food and Drug Administration; and

(iii) be regularly updated on a schedule determined by the Secretary.

(C) COORDINATION.—The Secretary shall establish a format and procedure for appropriate State officials to access the information provided pursuant to subparagraph (A) in a prompt and secure manner.

(D) CONFIDENTIALITY.—Nothing in this paragraph shall be construed as authorizing the Secretary to disclose any information that is a trade secret or confidential information subject to section 552(b)(4) of title 5, United States Code, or section 1905 of title 18, United States Code.

(3) COSTS.—

(A) AUTHORIZED FEES OF SECRETARY.—If a State does not establish a licensing program for persons engaged in the wholesale distribution of a drug subject to subsection (b), the Secretary shall license a person engaged in wholesale distribution located in such State and may collect a reasonable fee in such amount necessary to reimburse the Secretary for costs associated with establishing and administering the licensure program and conducting periodic inspections under this section. The Secretary shall adjust fee rates as needed on an annual basis to generate only the amount of revenue needed to perform this service. Fees authorized under this paragraph shall be collected and available for obligation only to the extent and in the amount provided in advance in appropriations Acts. Such fees are authorized to remain available until expended. Such sums as may be necessary may be transferred from the Food and Drug Administration salaries and expenses appropriation account without fiscal year limitation to such appropriation account for salaries and expenses with such fiscal year limitation.

(B) STATE LICENSING FEES.—Nothing in this Act shall prohibit States from collecting fees from wholesale distributors in connection with State licensing of such distributors.

(4) For the purposes of this subsection and subsection (d), the term 'wholesale distribution' means the distribution of a drug subject to subsection (b) to a person other than a consumer or patient, or receipt of a drug subject to subsection (b) by a person other than the consumer or patient, but does not include—

(A) intracompany distribution of any drug between members of an affiliate or within a manufacturer;

(B) the distribution of a drug, or an offer to distribute a drug among hospitals or other health care entities which are under common control;

(C) the distribution of a drug or an offer to distribute a drug for emergency medical reasons, including a public health emergency declaration pursuant to section 319 of the Public Health Service Act, except that, for purposes of this paragraph, a drug shortage not caused by a public health emergency shall not constitute an emergency medical reason;

(D) the dispensing of a drug pursuant to a prescription executed in accordance with subsection (b)(1);

(E) the distribution of minimal quantities of drug by a licensed retail pharmacy to a licensed practitioner for office use;

(F) the distribution of a drug or an offer to distribute a drug by a charitable organization to a nonprofit affiliate of the organization to the extent otherwise permitted by law;

(G) the purchase or other acquisition by a dispenser, hospital, or other health care entity of a drug for use by such dispenser, hospital, or other health care entity;

(H) the distribution of a drug by the manufacturer of such drug;

(I) the receipt or transfer of a drug by an authorized third-party logistics provider provided that such third-party logistics provider does not take ownership of the drug;

(J) a common carrier that transports a drug, provided that the common carrier does not take ownership of the drug;

(K) the distribution of a drug, or an offer to distribute a drug by an authorized repackager that has taken ownership or possession of the drug and repacks it in accordance with section 582(e);

(L) salable drug returns when conducted by a dispenser;

(M) the distribution of a collection of finished medical devices, which may include a product or biological product, assembled in kit form strictly for the convenience of the purchaser or user (referred to in this subparagraph as a 'medical convenience kit') if-

(i) the medical convenience kit is assembled in an establishment that is registered with the Food and Drug Administration as a device manufacturer in accordance with section 510(b)(2);

(ii) the medical convenience kit does not contain a controlled substance that appears in a schedule contained in the Comprehensive Drug Abuse Prevention and Control Act of 1970;

(iii) in the case of a medical convenience kit that includes a product, the person that manufacturers the kit—

(I) purchased such product directly from the pharmaceutical manufacturer or from a wholesale distributor that purchased the product directly from the pharmaceutical manufacturer; and

(II) does not alter the primary container or label of the product as purchased from the manufacturer or wholesale distributor; and

(iv) in the case of a medical convenience kit that includes a product, the product is—

(I) an intravenous solution intended for the replenishment of fluids and electrolytes;

(II) a product intended to maintain the equilibrium of water and minerals in the body;

(III) a product intended for irrigation or reconstitution;

(IV) an anesthetic;

(V) an anticoagulant;

(VI) a vasopressor; or

(VII) a sympathomimetic;

(N) the distribution of an intravenous drug that, by its formulation, is intended for the replenishment of fluids and electrolytes (such as sodium, chloride, and potassium) or calories (such as dextrose and amino acids);

(O) the distribution of an intravenous drug used to maintain the equilibrium of water and minerals in the body, such as dialysis solutions;

(P) the distribution of a drug that is intended for irrigation, or sterile water, whether intended for such purposes or for injection;

(Q) the distribution of medical gas, as defined in section 575;

(R) facilitating the distribution of a product by providing solely administrative services, including processing of orders and payments; or

(S) the transfer of a product by a hospital or other health care entity, or by a wholesale distributor or manufacturer operating at the direction of the hospital or other health care entity, to a repackager described in section 581(16)(B) and registered under section 510 for the purpose of repackaging the drug for use by that hospital, or other health care entity and other health care entities that are under common control, if ownership of the drug remains with the hospital or other health care entity at all times.

(5) THIRD-PARTY LOGISTICS PROVIDERS.—

Notwithstanding paragraphs (1) through (4), each entity that meets the definition of a third-party logistics provider under section 581(22) shall obtain a license as a third-party logistics provider as described in section 584(a) and is not required to obtain a license as a wholesale distributor if the entity never assumes an ownership interest in the product it handles.

(6) AFFILIATE.—

For purposes of this subsection, the term 'affiliate' means a business entity that has a relationship with a second business entity if, directly or indirectly—

(A) one business entity controls, or has the power to control, the other business entity; or

(B) a third party controls, or has the power to control, both of the business entities.

(f)(1)(A) A drug intended for use by animals other than man, other than a veterinary feed directive drug intended for use in animal feed or an animal feed bearing or containing a veterinary feed directive drug, which—

(i) because of its toxicity or other potentiality for harmful effect, or the method of its use, or the collateral measures necessary for its use, is not safe for animal use except under the professional supervision of a licensed veterinarian, or

(ii) is limited by an approved application under subsection (b) of section 512, a conditionally-approved application under section 571, or an index listing under section 572 to use under the professional supervision of a licensed veterinarian,

shall be dispensed only by or upon the lawful written or oral order of a licensed veterinarian in the course of the veterinarian's professional practice.

(B) For purposes of subparagraph (A), an order is lawful if the order—

(i) is a prescription or other order authorized by law,

(ii) is, if an oral order, promptly reduced to writing by the person lawfully filling the order, and filed by that person, and

(iii) is refilled only if authorized in the original order or in a subsequent oral order promptly reduced to writing by the person lawfully filling the order, and filed by that person.

(C) The act of dispensing a drug contrary to the provisions of this paragraph shall be deemed to be an act which results in the drug being misbranded while held for sale.

(2) Any drug when dispensed in accordance with paragraph (1) of this subsection—

(A) Shall be exempt from the requirements of section 502, except subsections (a), (g), (h), (i)(2), (i)(3), and (p) of such section, and

(B) shall be exempt from the packaging requirements of subsections (g), (h), and (p) of such section, if—

(i) when dispensed by a licensed veterinarian, the drug bears a label containing the name and address of the practitioner and any directions for use and cautionary statements specified by the practitioner, or

(ii) when dispensed by filling the lawful order of a licensed veterinarian, the drug bears a label containing the name and address of the dispenser, the serial number and date of the order or of its filing, the name of the licensed veterinarian, and the directions for use and cautionary statements, if any, contained in such order.

The preceding sentence shall not apply to any drug dispensed in the course of the conduct of a business of dispensing drugs pursuant to diagnosis by mail.

(3) The Secretary may by regulation exempt drugs for animals other than man subject to section 512, 571, or 572 from the requirements of paragraph (1) when such requirements are not necessary for the protection of the public health.

(4) A drug which is subject to paragraph (1) shall be deemed to be misbranded if at any time prior to dispensing its label fails to bear the statement "Caution: Federal law restricts this drug to use by or on the order of a licensed veterinarian.". A drug to which paragraph (1) does not apply shall be deemed to be misbranded if at any time prior to dispensing its label bears the statement specified in the preceding sentence.

(g)(1) The Secretary shall in accordance with this subsection assign an agency center to regulate products that constitute a combination of a drug, device, or biological product. The Secretary shall determine the primary mode of action of the combination product. If the Secretary determines that the primary mode of action is that of—

(A) a drug (other than a biological product), the agency center charged with premarket review of drugs shall have primary jurisdiction,

(B) a device, the agency center charged with premarket review of devices shall have primary jurisdiction, or

(C) a biological product, the agency center charged with premarket review of biological products shall have primary jurisdiction.

(2) Nothing in this subsection shall prevent the Secretary from using any agency resources of the Food and Drug Administration necessary to ensure adequate review of the safety, effectiveness, or substantial equivalence of an article.

(3) The Secretary shall promulgate regulations to implement market clearance procedures in accordance with paragraphs (1) and (2) not later than 1 year after the date of enactment of this subsection.[28]

---

28. The subsection was added by Pub. L. No. 101–629, § 16(a)(2), 104 Stat. 4511, 4526 (1990).

(4)(A) Not later than 60 days after the date of the enactment of this paragraph,[29] the Secretary shall establish within the Office of the Commissioner of Food and Drugs an office to ensure the prompt assignment of combination products to agency centers, the timely and effective premarket review of such products, and consistent and appropriate postmarket regulation of like products subject to the same statutory requirements to the extent permitted by law. Additionally, the office shall, in determining whether a product is to be designated a combination product, consult with the component within the Office of the Commissioner of Food and Drugs that is responsible for such determinations. Such office (referred to in this paragraph as the "Office") shall have appropriate scientific and medical expertise, and shall be headed by a director.

(B) In carrying out this subsection, the Office shall, for each combination product, promptly assign an agency center with primary jurisdiction in accordance with paragraph (1) for the premarket review of such product.

(C)(i) In carrying out this subsection, the Office shall ensure timely and effective premarket reviews by overseeing the timeliness of and coordinating reviews involving more than one agency center.

(ii) In order to ensure the timeliness of the premarket review of a combination product, the agency center with primary jurisdiction for the product, and the consulting agency center, shall be responsible to the Office with respect to the timeliness of the premarket review.

(D) In carrying out this subsection, the Office shall ensure the consistency and appropriateness of postmarket regulation of like products subject to the same statutory requirements to the extent permitted by law.

(E)(i) Any dispute regarding the timeliness of the premarket review of a combination product may be presented to the Office for resolution, unless the dispute is clearly premature.

(ii) During the review process, any dispute regarding the substance of the premarket review may be presented to the Commissioner of Food and Drugs after first being considered by the agency center with primary jurisdiction of the premarket review, under the scientific dispute resolution procedures for such center. The Commissioner of Food and Drugs shall consult with the Director of the Office in resolving the substantive dispute.

(F) The Secretary, acting through the Office, shall review each agreement, guidance, or practice of the Secretary that is specific to the assignment of combination products to agency centers and shall determine whether the agreement, guidance, or practice is consistent with the requirements of this subsection. In carrying out such review, the Secretary shall consult with stakeholders and the directors of the agency centers. After such consultation, the Secretary shall determine whether to continue in

---

29. Paragraph (4) was added by Pub. L. No. 107–250, § 204(3), 116 Stat. 1588, 1611–12 (2002).

effect, modify, revise, or eliminate such agreement, guidance, or practice, and shall publish in the Federal Register a notice of the availability of such modified or revised agreement, guidance or practice. Nothing in this paragraph shall be construed as preventing the Secretary from following each agreement, guidance, or practice until continued, modified, revised, or eliminated.

(G) Not later than one year after the date of the enactment of this paragraph and annually thereafter, the Secretary shall report to the appropriate committees of Congress on the activities and impact of the Office. The report shall include provisions—

(i) describing the numbers and types of combination products under review and the timeliness in days of such assignments, reviews, and dispute resolutions;

(ii) identifying the number of premarket reviews of such products that involved a consulting agency center; and

(iii) describing improvements in the consistency of postmarket regulation of combination products.

(H) Nothing in this paragraph shall be construed to limit the regulatory authority of any agency center.

(5) As used in this subsection:

(A) The term "agency center" means a center or alternative organizational component of the Food and Drug Administration.

(B) The term "biological product" has the meaning given the term in section 351(i) of the Public Health Service Act (42 U.S.C. 262(i)).

(C) The term "market clearance" includes—

(i) approval of an application under section 505, 507, 515, or 520(g),

(ii) a finding of substantial equivalence under this subchapter, and

(iii) approval of a biologics license application under subsection (a) of section 351 of the Public Health Service Act (42 U.S.C. 262).

SEC. 503A [21 U.S.C. 353a]. PHARMACY COMPOUNDING

(a) IN GENERAL.—Sections 501(a)(2)(B), 502(f)(1), and 505 shall not apply to a drug product if the drug product is compounded for an identified individual patient based on the receipt of a valid prescription order or a notation, approved by the prescribing practitioner, on the prescription order that a compounded product is necessary for the identified patient, if the drug product meets the requirements of this section, and if the compounding—

(1) is by—

(A) a licensed pharmacist in a State licensed pharmacy or a Federal facility, or

(B) a licensed physician,

on the prescription order for such individual patient made by a licensed physician or other licensed practitioner authorized by State law to prescribe drugs; or

(2)(A) is by a licensed pharmacist or licensed physician in limited quantities before the receipt of a valid prescription order for such individual patient; and

(B) is based on a history of the licensed pharmacist or licensed physician receiving valid prescription orders for the compounding of the drug product, which orders have been generated solely within an established relationship between—

(i) the licensed pharmacist or licensed physician; and

(ii)(I) such individual patient for whom the prescription order will be provided; or

(II) the physician or other licensed practitioner who will write such prescription order.

(b) COMPOUNDED DRUG.—

(1) LICENSED PHARMACIST AND LICENSED PHYSICIAN.—A drug product may be compounded under subsection (a) if the licensed pharmacist or licensed physician—

(A) compounds the drug product using bulk drug substances, as defined in regulations of the Secretary published at section 207.3(a)(4) of title 21 of the Code of Federal Regulations—

(i) that—

(I) comply with the standards of an applicable United States Pharmacopoeia or National Formulary monograph, if a monograph exists, and the United States Pharmacopoeia chapter on pharmacy compounding;

(II) if such a monograph does not exist, are drug substances that are components of drugs approved by the Secretary; or

(III) if such a monograph does not exist and the drug substance is not a component of a drug approved by the Secretary, that appear on a list developed by the Secretary through regulations issued by the Secretary under subsection (c);

(ii) that are manufactured by an establishment that is registered under section 510 (including a foreign establishment that is registered under section 510(i)); and

(iii) that are accompanied by valid certificates of analysis for each bulk drug substance;

(B) compounds the drug product using ingredients (other than bulk drug substances) that comply with the standards of an applicable United States

Pharmacopoeia or National Formulary monograph, if a monograph exists, and the United States Pharmacopoeia chapter on pharmacy compounding;

(C) does not compound a drug product that appears on a list published by the Secretary in the Federal Register of drug products that have been withdrawn or removed from the market because such drug products or components of such drug products have been found to be unsafe or not effective; and

(D) does not compound regularly or in inordinate amounts (as defined by the Secretary) any drug products that are essentially copies of a commercially available drug product.

(2) DEFINITION.—For purposes of paragraph (1)(D), the term "essentially a copy of a commercially available drug product" does not include a drug product in which there is a change, made for an identified individual patient, which produces for that patient a significant difference, as determined by the prescribing practitioner, between the compounded drug and the comparable commercially available drug product.

(3) DRUG PRODUCT.—A drug product may be compounded under subsection (a) only if—

(A) such drug product is not a drug product identified by the Secretary by regulation as a drug product that presents demonstrable difficulties for compounding that reasonably demonstrate an adverse effect on the safety or effectiveness of that drug product; and

(B) such drug product is compounded in a State—

(i) that has entered into a memorandum of understanding with the Secretary which addresses the distribution of inordinate amounts of compounded drug products interstate and provides for appropriate investigation by a State agency of complaints relating to compounded drug products distributed outside such State; or

(ii) that has not entered into the memorandum of understanding described in clause (i) and the licensed pharmacist, licensed pharmacy, or licensed physician distributes (or causes to be distributed) compounded drug products out of the State in which they are compounded in quantities that do not exceed 5 percent of the total prescription orders dispensed or distributed by such pharmacy or physician.

The Secretary shall, in consultation with the National Association of Boards of Pharmacy, develop a standard memorandum of understanding for use by the States in complying with subparagraph (B)(i).

(c) REGULATIONS.—

(1) IN GENERAL.—The Secretary shall issue regulations to implement this section. Before issuing regulations to implement subsections (b)(1)(A)(i)(III), (b)(1)(C), or (b)(3)(A), the Secretary shall convene and consult an advisory committee

on compounding unless the Secretary determines that the issuance of such regulations before consultation is necessary to protect the public health. The advisory committee shall include representatives from the National Association of Boards of Pharmacy, the United States Pharmacopoeia, pharmacy, physician, and consumer organizations, and other experts selected by the Secretary.

(2) LIMITING COMPOUNDING.—The Secretary, in consultation with the United States Pharmacopoeia Convention, Incorporated, shall promulgate regulations identifying drug substances that may be used in compounding under subsection (b)(1)(A)(i)(III) for which a monograph does not exist or which are not components of drug products approved by the Secretary. The Secretary shall include in the regulation the criteria for such substances, which shall include historical use, reports in peer reviewed medical literature, or other criteria the Secretary may identify.

(d) APPLICATION.—This section shall not apply to—

(1) compounded positron emission tomography drugs as defined in section 201(ii); or

(2) radiopharmaceuticals.

(e) DEFINITION.—As used in this section, the term "compounding" does not include mixing, reconstituting, or other such acts that are performed in accordance with directions contained in approved labeling provided by the product's manufacturer and other manufacturer directions consistent with that labeling.

SEC. 503B [21 U.S.C. 353b]. OUTSOURCING FACILITIES

(a) IN GENERAL.—Sections 502(f)(1), 505, and 582 shall not apply to a drug compounded by or under the direct supervision of a licensed pharmacist in a facility that elects to register as an outsourcing facility if each of the following conditions is met:

(1) REGISTRATION AND REPORTING.—The drug is compounded in an outsourcing facility that is in compliance with the requirements of subsection (b).

(2) BULK DRUG SUBSTANCES.—The drug is compounded in an outsourcing facility that does not compound using bulk drug substances (as defined in section 207.3(a)(4) of title 21, Code of Federal Regulations (or any successor regulation)), unless—

(A)(i) the bulk drug substance appears on a list established by the Secretary identifying bulk drug substances for which there is a clinical need, by—

(I) publishing a notice in the Federal Register proposing bulk drug substances to be included on the list, including the rationale for such proposal;

(II) providing a period of not less than 60 calendar days for comment on the notice; and

(III) publishing a notice in the Federal Register designating bulk drug substances for inclusion on the list; or

(ii) the drug compounded from such bulk drug substance appears on the drug shortage list in effect under section 506E at the time of compounding, distribution, and dispensing;

(B) if an applicable monograph exists under the United States Pharmacopeia, the National Formulary, or another compendium or pharmacopeia recognized by the Secretary for purposes of this paragraph, the bulk drug substances each comply with the monograph;

(C) the bulk drug substances are each manufactured by an establishment that is registered under section 510 (including a foreign establishment that is registered under section 510(i)); and

(D) the bulk drug substances are each accompanied by a valid certificate of analysis.

(3) INGREDIENTS (OTHER THAN BULK DRUG SUBSTANCES).—If any ingredients (other than bulk drug substances) are used in compounding the drug, such ingredients comply with the standards of the applicable United States Pharmacopeia or National Formulary monograph, if such monograph exists, or of another compendium or pharmacopeia recognized by the Secretary for purposes of this paragraph if any.

(4) DRUGS WITHDRAWN OR REMOVED BECAUSE UNSAFE OR NOT EFFECTIVE.—The drug does not appear on a list published by the Secretary of drugs that have been withdrawn or removed from the market because such drugs or components of such drugs have been found to be unsafe or not effective.

(5) ESSENTIALLY A COPY OF AN APPROVED DRUG.—The drug is not essentially a copy of one or more approved drugs.

(6) DRUGS PRESENTING DEMONSTRABLE DIFFICULTIES FOR COMPOUNDING.—The drug—

(A) is not identified (directly or as part of a category of drugs) on a list published by the Secretary, through the process described in subsection (c), of drugs or categories of drugs that present demonstrable difficulties for compounding that are reasonably likely to lead to an adverse effect on the safety or effectiveness of the drug or category of drugs, taking into account the risks and benefits to patients; or

(B) is compounded in accordance with all applicable conditions identified on the list described in subparagraph (A) as conditions that are necessary to prevent the drug or category of drugs from presenting the demonstrable difficulties described in subparagraph (A).

(7) ELEMENTS TO ASSURE SAFE USE.—In the case of a drug that is compounded from a drug that is the subject of a risk evaluation and mitigation strategy

approved with elements to assure safe use pursuant to section 505-1, or from a bulk drug substance that is a component of such drug, the outsourcing facility demonstrates to the Secretary prior to beginning compounding that such facility will utilize controls comparable to the controls applicable under the relevant risk evaluation and mitigation strategy.

(8) PROHIBITION ON WHOLESALING.—The drug will not be sold or transferred by an entity other than the outsourcing facility that compounded such drug. This paragraph does not prohibit administration of a drug in a health care setting or dispensing a drug pursuant to a prescription executed in accordance with section 503(b)(1).

(9) FEES.—The drug is compounded in an outsourcing facility that has paid all fees owed by such facility pursuant to section 744K.

(10) LABELING OF DRUGS.—

(A) LABEL.—The label of the drug includes—

(i) the statement "This is a compounded drug." or a reasonable comparable alternative statement (as specified by the Secretary) that prominently identifies the drug as a compounded drug;

(ii) the name, address, and phone number of the applicable outsourcing facility; and

(iii) with respect to the drug—

(I) the lot or batch number;

(II) the established name of the drug;

(III) the dosage form and strength;

(IV) the statement of quantity or volume, as appropriate;

(V) the date that the drug was compounded;

(VI) the expiration date;

(VII) storage and handling instructions;

(VIII) the National Drug Code number, if available;

(IX) the statement "Not for resale", and, if the drug is dispensed or distributed other than pursuant to a prescription for an individual identified patient, the statement "Office Use Only"; and

(X) subject to subparagraph (B)(i), a list of active and inactive ingredients, identified by established name and the quantity or proportion of each ingredient.

(B) CONTAINER.—The container from which the individual units of the drug are removed for dispensing or for administration (such as a plastic bag containing individual product syringes) shall include—

(i) the information described under subparagraph (A)(iii)(X), if there is not space on the label for such information;

(ii) the following information to facilitate adverse event reporting: www.fda.gov/medwatch and 1-800-FDA-1088 (or any successor Internet Web site or phone number); and

(iii) directions for use, including, as appropriate, dosage and administration.

(C) ADDITIONAL INFORMATION.—The label and labeling of the drug shall include any other information as determined necessary and specified in regulations promulgated by the Secretary.

(11) OUTSOURCING FACILITY REQUIREMENT.—The drug is compounded in an outsourcing facility in which the compounding of drugs occurs only in accordance with this section.

(b) REGISTRATION OF OUTSOURCING FACILITIES AND REPORTING OF DRUGS.—

(1) REGISTRATION OF OUTSOURCING FACILITIES.—

(A) ANNUAL REGISTRATION.—Upon electing and in order to become an outsourcing facility, and during the period beginning on October 1 and ending on December 31 of each year thereafter, a facility—

(i) shall register with the Secretary its name, place of business, and unique facility identifier (which shall conform to the requirements for the unique facility identifier established under section 510), and a point of contact email address; and

(ii) shall indicate whether the outsourcing facility intends to compound a drug that appears on the list in effect under section 506E during the subsequent calendar year.

(B) AVAILABILITY OF REGISTRATION FOR INSPECTION; LIST.—

(i) REGISTRATIONS.—The Secretary shall make available for inspection, to any person so requesting, any registration filed pursuant to this paragraph.

(ii) LIST.—The Secretary shall make available on the public Internet Web site of the Food and Drug Administration a list of the name of each facility registered under this subsection as an outsourcing facility, the State in which each such facility is located, whether the facility compounds from bulk drug substances, and whether any such compounding from bulk drug substances is for sterile or nonsterile drugs.

(2) DRUG REPORTING BY OUTSOURCING FACILITIES.—

(A) IN GENERAL.—Upon initially registering as an outsourcing facility, once during the month of June of each year, and once during the month of December of each year, each outsourcing facility that registers with the Secretary under paragraph (1) shall submit to the Secretary a report—

(i) identifying the drugs compounded by such outsourcing facility during the previous 6-month period; and

(ii) with respect to each drug identified under clause (i), providing the active ingredient, the source of such active ingredient, the National Drug Code number of the source drug or bulk active ingredient, if available, the strength of the active ingredient per unit, the dosage form and route of administration, the package description, the number of individual units produced, and the National Drug Code number of the final product, if assigned.

(B) FORM.—Each report under subparagraph (A) shall be prepared in such form and manner as the Secretary may prescribe by regulation or guidance.

(C) CONFIDENTIALITY.—Reports submitted under this paragraph shall be exempt from inspection under paragraph (1)(B)(i), unless the Secretary finds that such an exemption would be inconsistent with the protection of the public health.

(3) ELECTRONIC REGISTRATION AND REPORTING.—Registrations and drug reporting under this subsection (including the submission of updated information) shall be submitted to the Secretary by electronic means unless the Secretary grants a request for waiver of such requirement because use of electronic means is not reasonable for the person requesting waiver.

(4) RISK-BASED INSPECTION FREQUENCY.—

(A) IN GENERAL.—Outsourcing facilities—

(i) shall be subject to inspection pursuant to section 704; and

(ii) shall not be eligible for the exemption under section 704(a)(2)(A).

(B) RISK-BASED SCHEDULE.—The Secretary, acting through one or more officers or employees duly designated by the Secretary, shall inspect outsourcing facilities in accordance with a risk-based schedule established by the Secretary.

(C) RISK FACTORS.—In establishing the risk-based schedule, the Secretary shall inspect outsourcing facilities according to the known safety risks of such outsourcing facilities, which shall be based on the following factors:

(i) The compliance history of the outsourcing facility.

(ii) The record, history, and nature of recalls linked to the outsourcing facility.

(iii) The inherent risk of the drugs compounded at the outsourcing facility.

(iv) The inspection frequency and history of the outsourcing facility, including whether the outsourcing facility has been inspected pursuant to section 704 within the last 4 years.

(v) Whether the outsourcing facility has registered under this paragraph as an entity that intends to compound a drug that appears on the list in effect under section 506E.

(vi) Any other criteria deemed necessary and appropriate by the Secretary for purposes of allocating inspection resources.

(5) ADVERSE EVENT REPORTING.—Outsourcing facilities shall submit adverse event reports to the Secretary in accordance with the content and format requirements established through guidance or regulation under section 310.305 of title 21, Code of Federal Regulations (or any successor regulations).

(c) REGULATIONS.—

(1) IN GENERAL.—The Secretary shall implement the list described in subsection (a)(6) through regulations.

(2) ADVISORY COMMITTEE ON COMPOUNDING.—Before issuing regulations to implement subsection (a)(6), the Secretary shall convene and consult an advisory committee on compounding. The advisory committee shall include representatives from the National Association of Boards of Pharmacy, the United States Pharmacopeia, pharmacists with current experience and expertise in compounding, physicians with background and knowledge in compounding, and patient and public health advocacy organizations.

(3) INTERIM LIST.—

(A) IN GENERAL.—Before the effective date of the regulations finalized to implement subsection (a)(6), the Secretary may designate drugs, categories of drugs, or conditions as described such subsection by—

(i) publishing a notice of such substances, drugs, categories of drugs, or conditions proposed for designation, including the rationale for such designation, in the Federal Register;

(ii) providing a period of not less than 60 calendar days for comment on the notice; and

(iii) publishing a notice in the Federal Register designating such drugs, categories of drugs, or conditions.

(B) SUNSET OF NOTICE.—Any notice provided under subparagraph (A) shall not be effective after the earlier of—

(i) the date that is 5 years after the date of enactment of the Compounding Quality Act [enacted Nov. 27, 2013]; or

(ii) the effective date of the final regulations issued to implement subsection (a)(6).

(4) UPDATES.—The Secretary shall review, and update as necessary, the regulations containing the lists of drugs, categories of drugs, or conditions described in subsection (a)(6) regularly, but not less than once every 4 years. Nothing in the previous sentence prohibits submissions to the Secretary, before or during any 4-year period described in such sentence, requesting updates to such lists.

(d) DEFINITIONS.—In this section:

(1) The term "compounding" includes the combining, admixing, mixing, diluting, pooling, reconstituting, or otherwise altering of a drug or bulk drug substance to create a drug.

(2) The term "essentially a copy of an approved drug" means—

(A) a drug that is identical or nearly identical to an approved drug, or a marketed drug not subject to section 503(b) and not subject to approval in an application submitted under section 505, unless, in the case of an approved drug, the drug appears on the drug shortage list in effect under section 506E at the time of compounding, distribution, and dispensing; or

(B) a drug, a component of which is a bulk drug substance that is a component of an approved drug or a marketed drug that is not subject to section 503(b) and not subject to approval in an application submitted under section 505, unless there is a change that produces for an individual patient a clinical difference, as determined by the prescribing practitioner, between the compounded drug and the comparable approved drug.

(3) The term "approved drug" means a drug that is approved under section 505 and does not appear on the list described in subsection (a)(4) of drugs that have been withdrawn or removed from the market because such drugs or components of such drugs have been found to be unsafe or not effective.

(4)(A) The term "outsourcing facility" means a facility at one geographic location or address that—

(i) is engaged in the compounding of sterile drugs;

(ii) has elected to register as an outsourcing facility; and

(iii) complies with all of the requirements of this section.

(B) An outsourcing facility is not required to be a licensed pharmacy.

(C) An outsourcing facility may or may not obtain prescriptions for identified individual patients.

(5) The term "sterile drug" means a drug that is intended for parenteral administration, an ophthalmic or oral inhalation drug in aqueous format, or a drug that is required to be sterile under Federal or State law.".[30]

---

30. So in law. Should probably not include quotation mark and second period.

(d)[31] Obligation to pay fees.—Payment of the fee under section 744K, as described in subsection (a)(9), shall not relieve an outsourcing facility that is licensed as a pharmacy in any State that requires pharmacy licensing fees of its obligation to pay such State fees.

Sec. 503C [21 U.S.C. 353c]. Prereview of television advertisements

(a) In General.—The Secretary may require the submission of any television advertisement for a drug (including any script, story board, rough, or a completed video production of the television advertisement) to the Secretary for review under this section not later than 45 days before dissemination of the television advertisement.

(b) Review.—In conducting a review of a television advertisement under this section, the Secretary may make recommendations with respect to information included in the label of the drug—

(1) on changes that are—

(A) necessary to protect the consumer good and well-being; or

(B) consistent with prescribing information for the product under review; and

(2) if appropriate and if information exists, on statements for inclusion in the advertisement to address the specific efficacy of the drug as it relates to specific population groups, including elderly populations, children, and racial and ethnic minorities.

(c) No Authority to Require Changes.—Except as provided by subsection (e), this section does not authorize the Secretary to make or direct changes in any material submitted pursuant to subsection (a).

(d) Elderly Populations, Children, Racially and Ethnically Diverse Communities.—In formulating recommendations under subsection (b), the Secretary shall take into consideration the impact of the advertised drug on elderly populations, children, and racially and ethnically diverse communities.

(e) Specific Disclosures.—

(1) Serious risk; safety protocol.—In conducting a review of a television advertisement under this section, if the Secretary determines that the advertisement would be false or misleading without a specific disclosure about a serious risk listed in the labeling of the drug involved, the Secretary may require inclusion of such disclosure in the advertisement.

(2) Date of approval.—In conducting a review of a television advertisement under this section, the Secretary may require the advertisement to include, for

---

31. So in law. See Pub. L. No. 113–54, §102(a)(2), 127 Stat. 588, 593 (2013). Should be "(e)".

a period not to exceed 2 years from the date of the approval of the drug under section 505 or section 351 of the Public Health Service Act, a specific disclosure of such date of approval if the Secretary determines that the advertisement would otherwise be false or misleading.

(f) RULE OF CONSTRUCTION.—Nothing in this section may be construed as having any effect on requirements under section 502(n) or on the authority of the Secretary under section 314.550, 314.640, 601.45, or 601.94 of title 21, Code of Federal Regulations (or successor regulations).

SEC. 504 [21 U.S.C. 354]. VETERINARY FEED DIRECTIVE DRUGS

(a)(1) A drug intended for use in or on animal feed which is limited by an approved application filed pursuant to section 512(b), a conditionally-approved application filed pursuant to section 571, or an index listing pursuant to section 572 to use under the professional supervision of a licensed veterinarian is a veterinary feed directive drug. Any animal feed bearing or containing a veterinary feed directive drug shall be fed to animals only by or upon a lawful veterinary feed directive issued by a licensed veterinarian in the course of the veterinarian's professional practice. When labeled, distributed, held, and used in accordance with this section, a veterinary feed directive drug and any animal feed bearing or containing a veterinary feed directive drug shall be exempt from section 502(f).

(2) A veterinary feed directive is lawful if it—

(A) contains such information as the Secretary may by general regulation or by order require; and

(B) is in compliance with the conditions and indications for use of the drug set forth in the notice published pursuant to section 512(i), or the index listing pursuant to section 572(e).

(3)(A) Any persons involved in the distribution or use of animal feed bearing or containing a veterinary feed directive drug and the licensed veterinarian issuing the veterinary feed directive shall maintain a copy of the veterinary feed directive applicable to each such feed, except in the case of a person distributing such feed to another person for further distribution. Such person distributing the feed shall maintain a written acknowledgment from the person to whom the feed is shipped stating that that person shall not ship or move such feed to an animal production facility without a veterinary feed directive or ship such feed to another person for further distribution unless that person has provided the same written acknowledgment to its immediate supplier.

(B) Every person required under subparagraph (A) to maintain records, and every person in charge or custody thereof, shall, upon request of an officer or employee designated by the Secretary, permit such officer or employee at all reasonable times to have access to and copy and verify such records.

(C) Any person who distributes animal feed bearing or containing a veterinary feed directive drug shall upon first engaging in such distribution notify the Secretary of that person's name and place of business. The failure to provide such notification shall be deemed to be an act which results in the drug being misbranded.

(b) A veterinary feed directive drug and any feed bearing or containing a veterinary feed directive drug shall be deemed to be misbranded if their labeling fails to bear such cautionary statement and such other information as the Secretary may by general regulation or by order prescribe, or their advertising fails to conform to the conditions and indications for use published pursuant to section 512(i), or the index listing pursuant to section 572(e) or fails to contain the general cautionary statement prescribed by the Secretary.

(c) Neither a drug subject to this section, nor animal feed bearing or containing such a drug, shall be deemed to be a prescription article under any Federal or State law.

SEC. 505 [21 U.S.C. 355]. NEW DRUGS

(a) No person shall introduce or deliver for introduction into interstate commerce any new drug, unless an approval of an application filed pursuant to subsection (b) or (j) is effective with respect to such drug.

(b)(1) Any person may file with the Secretary an application with respect to any drug subject to the provisions of subsection (a). Such persons shall submit to the Secretary as a part of the application (A) full reports of investigations which have been made to show whether or not such drug is safe for use and whether such drug is effective in use; (B) a full list of the articles used as components of such drug; (C) a full statement of the composition of such drug; (D) a full description of the methods used in, and the facilities and controls used for, the manufacture, processing, and packing of such drug; (E) such samples of such drug and of the articles used as components thereof as the Secretary may require; (F) specimens of the labeling proposed to be used for such drug and (G) any assessments required under section 505B. The applicant shall file with the application the patent number and the expiration date of any patent which claims the drug for which the applicant submitted the application or which claims a method of using such drug and with respect to which a claim of patent infringement could reasonably be asserted if a person not licensed by the owner engaged in the manufacture use, or sale of the drug. If a application is filed under this subsection for a drug and a patent which claims such drug or a method of using such drug is issued after the filing date but before approval of the application, the applicant shall amend the application to include the information required by the preceding sentence. Upon approval of the application, the Secretary shall publish information submitted under the two preceding sentences. The Secretary shall, in consultation with the Director of the National Institutes of Health and with representatives of the drug manufacturing industry, review and develop guidance, as appropriate, on the inclusion of women and minorities in clinical trials required by clause (A).

(2) An application submitted under paragraph (1) for a drug for which the investigations described in clause (A) of such paragraph and relied upon by the applicant for approval of the application were not conducted by or for the applicant and for which the applicant has not obtained a right of reference or use from the person by or for whom the investigations were conducted shall also include—

(A) a certification, in the opinion of the applicant and to the best of his knowledge, with respect to each patent which claims the drug for which such investigations were conducted or which claims a use for such drug for which the applicant is seeking approval under this subsection and for which information is required to be filed under paragraph (1) or subsection (c)—

(i) that such patent information has not been filed,

(ii) that such patent has expired,

(iii) of the date on which such patent will expire, or

(iv) that such patent is invalid or will not be infringed by the manufacture, use, or sale of the new drug for which the application is submitted; and

(B) if with respect to the drug for which investigations described in paragraph (1)(A) were conducted information was filed under paragraph (1) or subsection (c) for a method of use patent which does not claim a use for which the applicant is seeking approval under this subsection, a statement that the method of use patent does not claim such a use.

(3) NOTICE OF OPINION THAT PATENT IS INVALID OR WILL NOT BE INFRINGED.—

(A) AGREEMENT TO GIVE NOTICE.—An applicant that makes a certification described in paragraph (2)(A)(iv) shall include in the application a statement that the applicant will give notice as required by this paragraph.

(B) TIMING OF NOTICE.—An applicant that makes a certification described in paragraph (2)(A)(iv) shall give notice as required under this paragraph—

(i) if the certification is in the application, not later than 20 days after the date of the postmark on the notice with which the Secretary informs the applicant that the application has been filed; or

(ii) if the certification is in an amendment or supplement to the application, at the time at which the applicant submits the amendment or supplement, regardless of whether the applicant has already given notice with respect to another such certification contained in the application or in an amendment or supplement to the application.

(C) RECIPIENTS OF NOTICE.—An applicant required under this paragraph to give notice shall give notice to—

(i) each owner of the patent that is the subject of the certification (or a representative of the owner designated to receive such a notice); and

(ii) the holder of the approved application under this subsection for the drug that is claimed by the patent or a use of which is claimed by the patent (or a representative of the holder designated to receive such a notice).

(D) CONTENTS OF NOTICE.—A notice required under this paragraph shall—

(i) state that an application that contains data from bioavailability or bioequivalence studies has been submitted under this subsection for the drug with respect to which the certification is made to obtain approval to engage in the commercial manufacture, use, or sale of the drug before the expiration of the patent referred to in the certification; and

(ii) include a detailed statement of the factual and legal basis of the opinion of the applicant that the patent is invalid or will not be infringed.

(4)(A) An applicant may not amend or supplement an application referred to in paragraph (2) to seek approval of a drug that is a different drug than the drug identified in the application as submitted to the Secretary.

(B) With respect to the drug for which such an application is submitted, nothing in this subsection or subsection (c)(3) prohibits an applicant from amending or supplementing the application to seek approval of a different strength.

(5)(A) The Secretary shall issue guidance for the individuals who review applications submitted under paragraph (1) or under section 351 of the Public Health Service Act, which shall relate to promptness in conducting the review, technical excellence, lack of bias and conflict of interest, and knowledge of regulatory and scientific standards, and which shall apply equally to all individuals who review such applications.

(B) The Secretary shall meet with a sponsor of an investigation or an applicant for approval for a drug under this subsection or section 351 of the Public Health Service Act if the sponsor or applicant makes a reasonable written request for a meeting for the purpose of reaching agreement on the design and size—

(i)(I) of clinical trials intended to form the primary basis of an effectiveness claim; or

(II) in the case where human efficacy studies are not ethical or feasible, of animal and any associated clinical trials which, in combination, are intended to form the primary basis of an effectiveness claim; or

(ii) with respect to an application for approval of a biological product under section 351(k) of the Public Health Service Act, of any necessary clinical study or studies.

The sponsor or applicant shall provide information necessary for discussion and agreement on the design and size of clinical trials. Minutes of any such meeting shall be prepared by the Secretary and made available to the sponsor or applicant upon request.

(C) Any agreement regarding the parameters of the design and size of clinical trials of a new drug under this paragraph that is reached between the Secretary and a sponsor or applicant shall be reduced to writing and made part of the administrative record by the Secretary. Such agreement shall not be changed after the testing begins, except—

(i) with the written agreement of the sponsor or applicant; or

(ii) pursuant to a decision, made in accordance with subparagraph (D) by the director of the reviewing division, that a substantial scientific issue essential to determining the safety or effectiveness of the drug has been identified after the testing has begun.

(D) A decision under subparagraph (C)(ii) by the director shall be in writing and the Secretary shall provide to the sponsor or applicant an opportunity for a meeting at which the director and the sponsor or applicant will be present and at which the director will document the scientific issue involved.

(E) The written decisions of the reviewing division shall be binding upon, and may not directly or indirectly be changed by, the field or compliance division personnel unless such field or compliance division personnel demonstrate to the reviewing division why such decision should be modified.

(F) No action by the reviewing division may be delayed because of the unavailability of information from or action by field personnel unless the reviewing division determines that a delay is necessary to assure the marketing of a safe and effective drug.

(G) For purposes of this paragraph, the reviewing division is the division responsible for the review of an application for approval of a drug under this subsection or section 351 of the Public Health Service Act (including all scientific and medical matters, chemistry, manufacturing, and controls).

(6) An application submitted under this subsection shall be accompanied by the certification required under section 402(j)(5)(B) of the Public Health Service Act. Such certification shall not be considered an element of such application.

(c)(1) Within one hundred and eighty days after the filing of an application under subsection (b), or such additional period as may be agreed upon by the Secretary and the applicant, the Secretary shall either—

(A) approve the application if he then finds that none of the grounds for denying approval specified in subsection (d) applies, or

(B) give the applicant notice of an opportunity for a hearing before the Secretary under subsection (d) on the question whether such application is approvable. If the applicant elects to accept the opportunity for hearing by written request within thirty days after such notice, such hearing shall commence not more than ninety days after the expiration of such thirty days unless the Secretary and the applicant otherwise agree. Any such hearing shall thereafter be conducted on an

189

expedited basis and the Secretary's order thereon shall be issued within ninety days after the date fixed by the Secretary for filing final briefs.

(2) If the patent information described in subsection (b) could not be filed with the submission of an application under subsection (b) because the application was filed before the patent information was required under subsection (b) or a patent was issued after the application was approved under such subsection, the holder of an approved application shall file with the Secretary, the patent number and the expiration date of any patent which claims the drug for which the application was submitted or which claims a method of using such drug and with respect to which a claim of patent infringement could reasonably be asserted if a person not licensed by the owner engaged in the manufacture, use, or sale of the drug. If the holder of an approved application could not file patent information under subsection (b) because it was not required at the time the application was approved, the holder shall file such information under this subsection not later than thirty days after the date of the enactment of this sentence,[32] and if the holder of an approved application could not file patent information under subsection (b) because no patent had been issued when an application was filed or approved, the holder shall file such information under this subsection not later than thirty days after the date the patent involved is issued. Upon the submission of patent information under this subsection, the Secretary shall publish it.

(3) The approval of an application filed under subsection (b) which contains a certification required by paragraph (2) of such subsection shall be made effective on the last applicable date determined by applying the following to each certification made under subsection (b)(2)(A):

(A) If the applicant only made a certification described in clause (i) or (ii) of subsection (b)(2)(A) or in both such clauses, the approval may be made effective immediately.

(B) If the applicant made a certification described in clause (iii) of subsection (b)(2)(A), the approval may be made effective on the date certified under clause (iii).

(C) If the applicant made a certification described in clause (iv) of subsection (b)(2)(A), the approval shall be made effective immediately unless, before the expiration of 45 days after the date on which the notice described in subsection (b)(3) is received, an action is brought for infringement of the patent that is the subject of the certification and for which information was submitted to the Secretary under paragraph (2) or subsection (b)(1) before the date on which the application (excluding an amendment or supplement to the application) was submitted. If such an action is brought before the expiration of such days, the approval may be made effective upon the expiration of the thirty-month period beginning on the date of the receipt of the notice provided under subsection (b)(3) or such shorter

---

32. The provision was added by Pub. L. No. 98–417, § 102(a)(2), 98 Stat. 1585, 1593 (1984).

or longer period as the court may order because either party to the action failed to reasonably cooperate in expediting the action, except that—

(i) if before the expiration of such period the district court decides that the patent is invalid or not infringed (including any substantive determination that there is no cause of action for patent infringement or invalidity), the approval shall be made effective on—

(I) the date on which the court enters judgment reflecting the decision; or

(II) the date of a settlement order or consent decree signed and entered by the court stating that the patent that is the subject of the certification is invalid or not infringed;

(ii) if before the expiration of such period the district court decides that the patent has been infringed—

(I) if the judgment of the district court is appealed, the approval shall be made effective on—

(aa) the date on which the court of appeals decides that the patent is invalid or not infringed (including any substantive determination that there is no cause of action for patent infringement or invalidity); or

(bb) the date of a settlement order or consent decree signed and entered by the court of appeals stating that the patent that is the subject of the certification is invalid or not infringed; or

(II) if the judgment of the district court is not appealed or is affirmed, the approval shall be made effective on the date specified by the district court in a court order under section 271(e)(4)(A) of title 35, United States Code;

(iii) if before the expiration of such period the court grants a preliminary injunction prohibiting the applicant from engaging in the commercial manufacture or sale of the drug until the court decides the issues of patent validity and infringement and if the court decides that such patent is invalid or not infringed, the approval shall be made effective as provided in clause (i); or

(iv) if before the expiration of such period the court grants a preliminary injunction prohibiting the applicant from engaging in the commercial manufacture or sale of the drug until the court decides the issues of patent validity and infringement and if the court decides that such patent has been infringed, the approval shall be made effective as provided in clause (ii).

In such an action, each of the parties shall reasonably cooperate in expediting the action.

(D) Civil action to obtain patent certainty.—

(i) Declaratory judgment absent infringement action.—

(I) In GENERAL.—No action may be brought under section 2201 of title 28, United States Code, by an applicant referred to in subsection (b)(2) for a declaratory judgment with respect to a patent which is the subject of the certification referred to in subparagraph (C) unless—

(aa) the 45–day period referred to in such subparagraph has expired;

(bb) neither the owner of such patent nor the holder of the approved application under subsection (b) for the drug that is claimed by the patent or a use of which is claimed by the patent brought a civil action against the applicant for infringement of the patent before the expiration of such period; and

(cc) in any case in which the notice provided under paragraph (2)(B)[33] relates to noninfringement, the notice was accompanied by a document described in subclause (III).

(II) FILING OF CIVIL ACTION.—If the conditions described in items (aa), (bb), and as applicable, (cc) of subclause (I) have been met, the applicant referred to in such subclause may, in accordance with section 2201 of title 28, United States Code, bring a civil action under such section against the owner or holder referred to in such subclause (but not against any owner or holder that has brought such a civil action against the applicant, unless that civil action was dismissed without prejudice) for a declaratory judgment that the patent is invalid or will not be infringed by the drug for which the applicant seeks approval, except that such civil action may be brought for a declaratory judgment that the patent will not be infringed only in a case in which the condition described in subclause (I)(cc) is applicable. A civil action referred to in this subclause shall be brought in the judicial district where the defendant has its principal place of business or a regular and established place of business.

(III) OFFER OF CONFIDENTIAL ACCESS TO APPLICATION.—For purposes of subclause (I)(cc), the document described in this subclause is a document providing an offer of confidential access to the application that is in the custody of the applicant referred to in subsection (b)(2) for the purpose of determining whether an action referred to in subparagraph (C) should be brought. The document providing the offer of confidential access shall contain such restrictions as to persons entitled to access, and on the use and disposition of any information accessed, as would apply had a protective order been entered for the purpose of protecting trade secrets and other confidential business information. A request for access to an application under an offer of confidential access shall be considered acceptance of the offer of confidential access with the restrictions as to persons entitled to access, and on the use and disposition of any information accessed, contained in the offer of confidential access, and those restrictions and other terms of the offer of confidential access shall be

33. So in law. See Pub. L. No. 108–173, § 1101(b)(2)(D), 117 Stat. 2066, 2454 (2003).   Probably should be "subsection (b)(3)".

considered terms of an enforceable contract. Any person provided an offer of confidential access shall review the application for the sole and limited purpose of evaluating possible infringement of the patent that is the subject of the certification under subsection (b)(2)(A)(iv) and for no other purpose, and may not disclose information of no relevance to any issue of patent infringement to any person other than a person provided an offer of confidential access. Further, the application may be redacted by the applicant to remove any information of no relevance to any issue of patent infringement.

(ii) COUNTERCLAIM TO INFRINGEMENT ACTION.—

(I) IN GENERAL.—If an owner of the patent or the holder of the approved application under subsection (b) for the drug that is claimed by the patent or a use of which is claimed by the patent brings a patent infringement action against the applicant, the applicant may assert a counterclaim seeking an order requiring the holder to correct or delete the patent information submitted by the holder under subsection (b) or this subsection on the ground that the patent does not claim either—

(aa) the drug for which the application was approved; or

(bb) an approved method of using the drug.

(II) NO INDEPENDENT CAUSE OF ACTION.—Subclause (I) does not authorize the assertion of a claim described in subclause (I) in any civil action or proceeding other than a counterclaim described in subclause (I).

(iii) NO DAMAGES.—An applicant shall not be entitled to damages in a civil action under clause (i) or a counterclaim under clause (ii).

(E)(i) If an application (other than an abbreviated new drug application) submitted under subsection (b) for a drug, no active ingredient (including any ester or salt of the active ingredient) of which has been approved in any other application under subsection (b), was approved during the period beginning January 1, 1982, and ending on the date of the enactment of this subsection, the Secretary may not make the approval of another application for a drug for which the investigations described in clause (A) of subsection (b)(1) and relied upon by the applicant for approval of the application were not conducted by or for the applicant and for which the applicant has not obtained a right of reference or use from the person by or for whom the investigations were conducted effective before the expiration of ten years from the date of the approval of the application previously approved under subsection (b).

(ii) If an application submitted under subsection (b) for a drug, no active ingredient (including any ester or salt of the active ingredient) of which has been approved in any other application under subsection (b), is approved after the date of the enactment of this clause, no application which refers to the drug for which the subsection (b) application was submitted and for which the investigations described in clause (A) of subsection (b)(1) and relied upon by the applicant for approval of the application were not conducted by or for the applicant and for which the applicant has not obtained a right of reference or use from the person by or for whom the investigations were conducted may be submitted under subsection (b) before the expiration of five years from the date of the approval of the application under subsection (b), except that such an application may be submitted under subsection (b) after the expiration of four years from the date of the approval of the subsection (b) application if it contains a certification of patent invalidity or noninfringement described in clause (iv) of subsection (b)(2)(A). The approval of such an application shall be made effective in accordance with this paragraph except that, if an action for patent infringement is commenced during the one-year period beginning forty-eight months after the date of the approval of the subsection (b) application, the thirty-month period referred to in subparagraph (C) shall be extended by such amount of time (if any) which is required for seven and one-half years to have elapsed from the date of approval of the subsection (b) application.

(iii) If an application submitted under subsection (b) for a drug, which includes an active ingredient (including any ester or salt of the active ingredient) that has been approved in another application approved under subsection (b), is approved after the date of the enactment of this clause and if such application contains reports of new clinical investigations (other than bioavailability studies) essential to the approval of the application and conducted or sponsored by the applicant, the Secretary may not make the approval of an application submitted under subsection (b) for the conditions of approval of such drug in the approved subsection (b) application effective before the expiration of three years from the date of the approval of the application under subsection (b) if the investigations described in clause (A) of subsection (b)(1) and relied upon by the applicant for approval of the application were not conducted by or for the applicant and if the applicant has not obtained a right of reference or use from the person by or for whom the investigations were conducted.

(iv) If a supplement to an application approved under subsection (b) is approved after the date of enactment of this clause and the supplement contains reports of new clinical investigations (other than bioavailabilty[34] studies) essential to the approval of the supplement and conducted or sponsored by the person submitting the supplement, the Secretary may not make the approval of an application submitted under subsection (b) for a change approved in the supplement effective before the expiration of three years from the date of the approval of the supplement under subsection (b) if the investigations described in clause (A) of subsection (b)(1) and relied upon by the applicant for approval of the application were not conducted by or for the applicant and if the applicant has not obtained a right of reference or use from the person by or for whom the investigations were conducted.

34. So in law. Probably should be "bioavailabil-ity".

(v) If an application (or supplement to an application) submitted under subsection (b) for a drug, which includes an active ingredient (including any ester or salt of the active ingredient) that has been approved in another application under subsection (b), was approved during the period beginning January 1, 1982, and ending on the date of the enactment of this clause, the Secretary may not make the approval of an application submitted under this subsection and for which the investigations described in clause (A) of subsection (b)(1) and relied upon by the applicant for approval of the application were not conducted by or for the applicant and for which the applicant has not obtained a right of reference or use from the person by or for whom the investigations were conducted and which refers to the drug for which the subsection (b) application was submitted effective before the expiration of two years from the date of enactment of this clause.

(4) A drug manufactured in a pilot or other small facility may be used to demonstrate the safety and effectiveness of the drug and to obtain approval for the drug prior to manufacture of the drug in a larger facility, unless the Secretary makes a determination that a full scale production facility is necessary to ensure the safety or effectiveness of the drug.

(d) If the Secretary finds, after due notice to the applicant in accordance with subsection (c) and giving him an opportunity for a hearing, in accordance with said subsection, that (1) the investigations, reports of which are required to be submitted to the Secretary pursuant to subsection (b), do not include adequate tests by all methods reasonably applicable to show whether or not such drug is safe for use under the conditions prescribed, recommended, or suggested in the proposed labeling thereof; (2) the results of such tests show that such drug is unsafe for use under such conditions or do not show that such drug is safe for use under such conditions; (3) the methods used in, and the facilities and controls used for, the manufacture, processing, and packing of such drug are inadequate to preserve its identity, strength, quality, and purity; (4) upon the basis of the information submitted to him as part of the application, or upon the basis of any other information before him with respect to such drug, he has insufficient information to determine whether such drug is safe for use under such conditions; or (5) evaluated on the basis of the information submitted to him as part of the application and any other information before him with respect to such drug, there is a lack of substantial evidence that the drug will have the effect it purports or is represented to have under the conditions of use prescribed, recommended, or suggested in the proposed labeling thereof; or (6) the application failed to contain the patent information prescribed by subsection (b); or (7) based on a fair evaluation of all material facts, such labeling is false or misleading in any particular; he shall issue an order refusing to approve the application. If, after such notice and opportunity for hearing, the Secretary finds that clauses (1) through (6) do not apply, he shall issue an order approving the application. As used in this subsection and subsection (e), the term "substantial evidence" means evidence consisting of adequate and well-controlled investigations, including clinical investigations, by experts qualified by scientific training and experience to evaluate the effectiveness of the drug involved, on the basis of which it could fairly and responsibly be concluded by such experts that the drug will have the effect it purports or is represented to have under the conditions of use prescribed, recommended, or suggested in the labeling or proposed labeling thereof. If the Secretary determines, based on relevant science, that data from one adequate and well-controlled clinical investigation and confirmatory evidence (obtained prior to or after such investigation) are sufficient to establish effectiveness, the Secretary may consider such data and evidence to constitute substantial evidence for purposes of the preceding sentence. The Secretary shall implement a structured risk-benefit assessment framework in the new drug approval process to facilitate the balanced consideration of benefits and risks, a consistent and systematic approach to the discussion and regulatory decisionmaking, and the communication of the benefits and risks of new drugs. Nothing in the preceding sentence shall alter the criteria for evaluating an application for premarket approval of a drug.

(e) The Secretary shall, after due notice and opportunity for hearing to the applicant, withdraw approval of an application with respect to any drug under this section if the Secretary finds (1) that clinical or other experience, tests, or other scientific data show that such drug is unsafe for use under the conditions of use upon the basis of which the application was approved; (2) that new evidence of clinical experience, not contained in such application or not available to the Secretary until after such application was approved, or tests by new methods, or tests by methods not deemed reasonably applicable when such application was approved, evaluated together with the evidence available to the Secretary when the application was approved, shows that such drug is not shown to be safe for use under the conditions of use upon the basis of which the application was approved; or (3) on the basis of new information before him with respect to such drug, evaluated together with the evidence available to him when the application was approved, that there is a lack of substantial evidence that the drug will have the effect it purports or is represented to have under the conditions of use prescribed, recommended, or suggested in the labeling thereof; or (4) the patent information prescribed by subsection (c) was not filed within thirty days after the receipt of written notice from the Secretary specifying the failure to file such information; or (5) that the application contains any untrue statement of a material fact: Provided, That if the Secretary (or in his absence the officer acting as Secretary) finds that there is an imminent hazard to the public health, he may suspend the approval of such application immediately, and give the applicant prompt notice of his action and afford the applicant the opportunity for an expedited hearing under this subsection; but the authority conferred by this proviso to suspend the approval of an application shall not be delegated. The Secretary may also, after due notice and opportunity for hearing to the applicant, withdraw the approval of an application submitted under subsection (b) or (j) with respect to any drug under this section if the Secretary finds (1) that the applicant has failed to establish a system for maintaining required records, or has repeatedly or deliberately failed to maintain such records or to make required reports, in accordance with a regulation or order under subsection (k) or to comply with the notice requirements of section 510(k)(2), or the applicant has refused to permit access to, or copying or verification of, such records as required by paragraph (2) of such subsection; or (2) that on the basis of new information before him, evaluated together with the evidence before him when the application was approved, the methods used in, or the facilities and controls used for, the manufacture, processing, and packing of such drug are inadequate to assure and preserve its identity, strength, quality, and purity and were not made adequate within a reasonable time after receipt of written notice from the Secretary specifying the matter complained of; or (3) that on the basis of new information before him, evaluated together with the evidence before him when the application was approved, the labeling of such drug, based on a fair evaluation of all material facts, is false or misleading in any particular and was not corrected within a reasonable time after receipt of written notice from the Secretary specifying the matter complained of. Any order under this subsection shall state the findings upon which it is based. The Secretary may withdraw the approval of an application submitted under this section, or suspend the approval of such an application, as provided under this subsection, without first ordering the applicant to submit an assessment of the approved risk evaluation and mitigation strategy for the drug under section 505–1(g)(2)(D).

(f) Whenever the Secretary finds that the facts so require, he shall revoke any previous order under subsection (d) or (e) refusing, withdrawing, or suspending approval of an application and shall approve such application or reinstate such approval, as may be appropriate.

(g) Orders of the Secretary issued under this section shall be served (1) in person by any officer or employee of the Department designated by the Secretary or (2) by mailing the order by registered mail or by certified mail addressed to the applicant or respondent at his last-known address in the records of the Secretary.

(h) An appeal may be taken by the applicant from an order of the Secretary refusing or withdrawing approval of an application under this section. Such appeal shall be taken by filing in the United States court of appeals for the circuit wherein such applicant resides or has his principal place of business, or in the United States Court of Appeals for the District of Columbia Circuit, within sixty days after the entry of such order, a written petition praying that the order of the Secretary be set aside. A copy of such petition shall be forthwith transmitted by the clerk of the court to the Secretary, or any officer designated by him for that purpose, and thereupon the Secretary shall certify and file in the court the record upon which the order complained of was entered, as provided in section 2112 of title 28, United States Code. Upon the filing of such petition such court shall have exclusive jurisdiction to affirm or set aside such order, except that until the filing of the record the Secretary may modify or set aside his order. No objection to the order of the Secretary shall be considered by the court unless such objection shall have been urged before the Secretary or unless there were reasonable grounds for failure so to do. The finding of the Secretary as to the facts, if supported by substantial evidence, shall be conclusive. If any person shall apply to the court for leave to adduce additional evidence, and shall show to the satisfaction of the court that such additional evidence is material and that there were reasonable grounds for failure to adduce such evidence in the proceeding before the Secretary, the court may order such additional evidence to be taken before the Secretary and to be adduced upon the hearing in such manner and upon such terms and conditions as to the court may seem proper. The Secretary may modify his findings as to the facts by reason of the additional evidence so taken, and he shall file with the court such modified findings which, if supported by substantial evidence, shall be conclusive, and his recommendation, if any, for the setting aside of the original order. The judgment of the court affirming or setting aside any such order of the Secretary shall be final, subject to review by the Supreme Court of the United States upon certiorari or certification as provided in section 1254 of title 28 of the United States Code. The commencement of proceedings under this subsection shall not, unless specifically ordered by the court to the contrary, operate as a stay of the Secretary's order.

(i)(1) The Secretary shall promulgate regulations for exempting from the operation of the foregoing subsections of this section drugs intended solely for investigational use by experts qualified by scientific training and experience to investigate the safety and effectiveness of drugs. Such regulations may, within the discretion of the Secretary, among other conditions relating to the protection of the public health, provide for conditioning such exemption upon—

(A) the submission to the Secretary, before any clinical testing of a new drug is undertaken, of reports, by the manufacturer or the sponsor of the investigation of such drug, or preclinical tests (including tests on animals) of such drug adequate to justify the proposed clinical testing;

(B) the manufacturer or the sponsor of the investigation of a new drug proposed to be distributed to investigators for clinical testing obtaining a signed agreement from each of such investigators that patients to whom the drug is administered will be under his personal supervision, or under the supervision of investigators responsible to him, and that he will not supply such drug to any other investigator, or to clinics, for administration to human beings;

(C) the establishment and maintenance of such records, and the making of such reports to the Secretary, by the manufacturer or the sponsor of the investigation of such drug, of data (including but not limited to analytical reports by investigators) obtained as the result of such investigational use of such drug, as the Secretary finds will enable him to evaluate the safety and effectiveness of such drug in the event of the filing of an application pursuant to subsection (b); and

(D) the submission to the Secretary by the manufacturer or the sponsor of the investigation of a new drug of a statement of intent regarding whether the manufacturer or sponsor has plans for assessing pediatric safety and efficacy.

(2) Subject to paragraph (3), a clinical investigation of a new drug may begin 30 days after the Secretary has received from the manufacturer or sponsor of the investigation a submission containing such information about the drug and the clinical investigation, including—

(A) information on design of the investigation and adequate reports of basic information, certified by the applicant to be accurate reports, necessary to assess the safety of the drug for use in clinical investigation; and

(B) adequate information on the chemistry and manufacturing of the drug, controls available for the drug, and primary data tabulations from animal or human studies.

(3)(A) At any time, the Secretary may prohibit the sponsor of an investigation from conducting the investigation (referred to in this paragraph as a "clinical hold") if the Secretary makes a determination described in subparagraph (B). The Secretary shall specify the basis for the clinical hold, including the specific information available to the Secretary which served as the basis for such clinical hold, and confirm such determination in writing.

(B) For purposes of subparagraph (A), a determination described in this subparagraph with respect to a clinical hold is that—

(i) the drug involved represents an unreasonable risk to the safety of the persons who are the subjects of the clinical investigation, taking into account the qualifications of the clinical investigators, information about the drug, the design of the clinical investigation, the condition for which the drug is to be investigated, and the health status of the subjects involved; or

(ii) the clinical hold should be issued for such other reasons as the Secretary may by regulation establish (including reasons established by regulation before the date of the enactment of the Food and Drug Administration Modernization Act of 1997).

(C) Any written request to the Secretary from the sponsor of an investigation that a clinical hold be removed shall receive a decision, in writing and specifying the reasons therefor, within 30 days after receipt of such request. Any such request shall include sufficient information to support the removal of such clinical hold.

(4) Regulations under paragraph (1) shall provide that such exemption shall be conditioned upon the manufacturer, or the sponsor of the investigation, requiring that experts using such drugs for investigational purposes certify to such manufacturer or sponsor that they will inform any human beings to whom such drugs, or any controls used in connection therewith, are being administered, or their representatives, that such drugs are being used for investigational purposes and will obtain the consent of such human beings or their representatives, except where it is not feasible or it is contrary to the best interests of such human beings. Nothing in this subsection shall be construed to require any clinical investigator to submit directly to the Secretary reports on the investigational use of drugs. The Secretary shall update such regulations to require inclusion in the informed consent documents and process a statement that clinical trial information for such clinical investigation has been or will be submitted for inclusion in the registry data bank pursuant to subsection (j) of section 402 of the Public Health Service Act.

(j)(1) Any person may file with the Secretary an abbreviated application for the approval of a new drug.

(2)(A) An abbreviated application for a new drug shall contain—

(i) information to show that the conditions of use prescribed, recommended, or suggested in the labeling proposed for the new drug have been previously approved for a drug listed under paragraph (7) (hereinafter in this subsection referred to as a "listed drug");

(ii)(I) if the listed drug referred to in clause (i) has only one active ingredient, information to show that the active ingredient of the new drug is the same as that of the listed drug;

(II) if the listed drug referred to in clause (i) has more than one active ingredient, information to show that the active ingredients of the new drug are the same as those of the listed drug, or

(III) if the listed drug referred to in clause (i) has more than one active ingredient and if one of the active ingredients of the new drug is different and the application is filed pursuant to the approval of a petition filed under subparagraph (C), information to show that the other active ingredients of the new drug are the same as the active ingredients of the listed drug, information to show that the different active ingredient is an active ingredient of a listed drug or of a drug which does not meet the requirements of section 201(p), and such other information respecting the different active ingredient with respect to which the petition was filed as the Secretary may require;

(iii) information to show that the route of administration, the dosage form, and the strength of the new drug are the same as those of the listed drug referred to in clause (i), or, if the route of administration, the dosage form, or the strength of the new drug is different and the application is filed pursuant to the approval of a petition filed under subparagraph (C), such information respecting the route of administration, dosage form, or strength with respect to which the petition was filed as the Secretary may require;

(iv) information to show that the new drug is bioequivalent to the listed drug referred to in clause (i), except that if the application is filed pursuant to the approval of a petition filed under subparagraph (C), information to show that the active ingredients of the new drug are of the same pharmacological or therapeutic class as those of the listed drug referred to in clause (i) and the new drug can be expected to have the same therapeutic effect as the listed drug when administered to patients for a condition of use referred to in clause (i);

(v) information to show that the labeling proposed for the new drug is the same as the labeling approved for the listed drug referred to in clause (i) except for changes required because of differences approved under a petition filed under subparagraph (C) or because the new drug and the listed drug are produced or distributed by different manufacturers;

(vi) the items specified in clauses (B) through (F) of subsection (b)(1);

(vii) a certification, the opinion of the applicant and to the best of his knowledge, with respect to each patent which claims the listed drug referred to in clause (i) or which claims a use for such listed drug for which the applicant is seeking approval under this subsection and for which information is required to be filed under subsection (b) or (c)—

(I) that such patent information has not been filed,

(II) that such patent has expired,

(III) of the date on which such patent will expire, or

(IV) that such patent is invalid or will not be infringed by the manufacture, use, or sale of the new drug for which the application is submitted; and

(viii) if with respect to the listed drug referred to in clause (i) information was filed under subsection (b) or (c) for a method of use patent which does not claim a use for which the applicant is seeking approval under this subsection, a statement that the method of use patent does not claim such a use.

The Secretary may not require that an abbreviated application contain information in addition to that required by clauses (i) through (viii).

(B) NOTICE OF OPINION THAT PATENT IS INVALID OR WILL NOT BE INFRINGED.—

(i) AGREEMENT TO GIVE NOTICE.—An applicant that makes a certification described in subparagraph (A)(vii)(IV) shall include in the application a statement that the applicant will give notice as required by this subparagraph.

(ii) TIMING OF NOTICE.—An applicant that makes a certification described in subparagraph (A)(vii)(IV) shall give notice as required under this subparagraph—

(I) if the certification is in the application, not later than 20 days after the date of the postmark on the notice with which the Secretary informs the applicant that the application has been filed; or

(II) if the certification is in an amendment or supplement to the application, at the time at which the applicant submits the amendment or supplement, regardless of whether the applicant has already given notice with respect to another such certification contained in the application or in an amendment or supplement to the application.

(iii) RECIPIENTS OF NOTICE.—An applicant required under this subparagraph to give notice shall give notice to—

(I) each owner of the patent that is the subject of the certification (or a representative of the owner designated to receive such a notice); and

(II) the holder of the approved application under subsection (b) for the drug that is claimed by the patent or a use of which is claimed by the patent (or a representative of the holder designated to receive such a notice).

(iv) CONTENTS OF NOTICE.— A notice required under this subparagraph shall—

(I) state that an application that contains data from bioavailability or bio-equivalence studies has been submitted under this subsection for the drug with respect to which the certification is made to obtain approval to engage in the commercial manufacture, use, or sale of the drug before the expiration of the patent referred to in the certification; and

(II) include a detailed statement of the factual and legal basis of the opinion of the applicant that the patent is invalid or will not be infringed.

(C) If a person wants to submit an abbreviated application for a new drug which has a different active ingredient or whose route of administration, dosage form, or strength differ from that of a listed drug, such person shall submit a petition to the Secretary seeking permission to file such an application. The Secretary shall approve or disapprove a petition submitted under this subparagraph within ninety days of the date the petition is submitted. The Secretary shall approve such a petition unless the Secretary finds—

(i) that investigations must be conducted to show the safety and effectiveness of the drug or of any of its active ingredients, the route of administration, the dosage form, or strength which differ from the listed drug; or

(ii) that any drug with a different active ingredient may not be adequately evaluated for approval as safe and effective on the basis of the information required to be submitted in an abbreviated application.

(D)(i) An applicant may not amend or supplement an application to seek approval of a drug referring to a different listed drug from the listed drug identified in the application as submitted to the Secretary.

(ii) With respect to the drug for which an application is submitted, nothing in this subsection prohibits an applicant from amending or supplementing the application to seek approval of a different strength.

(iii) Within 60 days after the date of the enactment of the Medicare Prescription Drug, Improvement, and Modernization Act of 2003, the Secretary shall issue guidance defining the term "listed drug" for purposes of this subparagraph.

(3)(A) The Secretary shall issue guidance for the individuals who review applications submitted under paragraph (1), which shall relate to promptness in conducting the review, technical excellence, lack of bias and conflict of interest, and knowledge of regulatory and scientific standards, and which shall apply equally to all individuals who review such applications.

(B) The Secretary shall meet with a sponsor of an investigation or an applicant for approval for a drug under this subsection if the sponsor or applicant makes a reasonable written request for a meeting for the purpose of reaching agreement on the design and size of bioavailability and bioequivalence studies needed for approval of such application. The sponsor or applicant shall provide information necessary for discussion and agreement on the design and size of such studies. Minutes of any such meeting shall be prepared by the Secretary and made available to the sponsor or applicant.

(C) Any agreement regarding the parameters of design and size of bioavailability and bioequivalence studies of a drug under this paragraph that is reached between the Secretary and a sponsor or applicant shall be reduced to writing and made part of the administrative record by the Secretary. Such agreement shall not be changed after the testing begins, except—

(i) with the written agreement of the sponsor or applicant; or

(ii) pursuant to a decision, made in accordance with subparagraph (D) by the director of the reviewing division, that a substantial scientific issue essential to determining the safety or effectiveness of the drug has been identified after the testing has begun.

(D) A decision under subparagraph (C)(ii) by the director shall be in writing and the Secretary shall provide to the sponsor or applicant an opportunity for a meeting at which the director and the sponsor or applicant will be present and at which the director will document the scientific issue involved.

(E) The written decisions of the reviewing division shall be binding upon, and may not directly or indirectly be changed by, the field or compliance office personnel unless such field or compliance office personnel demonstrate to the reviewing division why such decision should be modified.

(F) No action by the reviewing division may be delayed because of the unavailability of information from or action by field personnel unless the reviewing division determines that a delay is necessary to assure the marketing of a safe and effective drug.

(G) For purposes of this paragraph, the reviewing division is the division responsible for the review of an application for approval of a drug under this subsection (including scientific matters, chemistry, manufacturing, and controls).

(4) Subject to paragraph (5), the Secretary shall approve an application for a drug unless the Secretary finds—

(A) the methods used in, or the facilities and controls used for, the manufacture, processing, and packing of the drug are inadequate to assure and preserve its identity, strength, quality, and purity;

(B) information submitted with the application is insufficient to show that each of the proposed conditions of use have been previously approved for the listed drug referred to in the application;

(C)(i) if the listed drug has only one active ingredient, information submitted with the application is insufficient to show that the active ingredient is the same as that of the listed drug;

(ii) if the listed drug has more than one active ingredient, information submitted with the application is insufficient to show that the active ingredients are the same as the active ingredients of the listed drug, or

(iii) if the listed drug has more than one active ingredient and if the application is for a drug which has an active ingredient different from the listed drug, information submitted with the application is insufficient to show—

(I) that the other active ingredients are the same as the active ingredients of the listed drug, or

(II) that the different active ingredient is an active ingredient of a listed drug or a drug which does not meet the requirements of section 201(p),

or no petition to file an application for the drug with the different ingredient was approved under paragraph (2)(C);

(D)(i) if the application is for a drug whose route of administration, dosage form, or strength of the drug is the same as the route of administration, dosage form, or strength of the listed drug referred to in the application, information submitted in the application is insufficient to show that the route of administration, dosage form, or strength is the same as that of the listed drug, or

(ii) if the application is for a drug whose route of administration, dosage form, or strength of the drug is different from that of the listed drug referred to in the application, no petition to file an application for the drug with the different route of administration, dosage form, or strength was approved under paragraph (2)(C);

(E) if the application was filed pursuant to the approval of a petition under paragraph (2)(C), the application did not contain the information required by the Secretary respecting the active ingredient, route of administration, dosage form, or strength which is not the same;

(F) information submitted in the application is insufficient to show that the drug is bioequivalent to the listed drug referred to in the application or, if the application was filed pursuant to a petition approved under paragraph (2)(C) information submitted in the application is insufficient to show that the active ingredients of the new drug are of the same pharmacological or therapeutic class as those of the listed drug referred to in paragraph (2)(A)(i) and that the new drug can be expected to have the same therapeutic effect as the listed drug when administered to patients for a condition of use referred to in such paragraph;

(G) information submitted in the application is insufficient to show that the labeling proposed for the drug is the same as the labeling approved for the listed drug referred to in the application except for changes required because of differences approved under a petition filed under paragraph (2)(C) or because the drug and the listed drug are produced or distributed by different manufacturers;

(H) information submitted in the application or any other information available to the Secretary shows that (i) the inactive ingredients of the drug are unsafe for use under the conditions prescribed, recommended, or suggested in the labeling proposed for the drug, or (ii) the composition of the drug is unsafe under such conditions because of the type or quantity of inactive ingredients included or the manner in which the inactive ingredients are included;

(I) the approval under subsection (c) of the listed drug referred to in the application under this subsection has been withdrawn or suspended for grounds described in the first sentence of subsection (e), the Secretary has published a notice of opportunity for hearing to withdraw approval of the listed drug under subsection (c) for grounds described in the first sentence of subsection (e), the approval under this subsection of the listed drug referred to in the application under this subsection has been withdrawn or suspended under paragraph (6), or the Secretary has determined that the listed drug has been withdrawn from sale for safety or effectiveness reasons;

(J) the application does not meet any other requirement of paragraph (2)(A); or

(K) the application contains an untrue statement of material fact.

(5)(A) Within one hundred and eighty days of the initial receipt of an application under paragraph (2) or within such additional period as may be agreed upon by the Secretary and the applicant, the Secretary shall approve or disapprove the application.

(B) The approval of an application submitted under paragraph (2) shall be made effective on the last applicable date determined by applying the following to each certification made under paragraph (2)(A)(vii):

(i) If the applicant only made a certification described in subclause (I) or (II) of paragraph (2)(A)(vii) or in both such subclauses, the approval may be made effective immediately.

(ii) If the applicant made a certification described in subclause (III) of paragraph (2)(A)(vii), the approval may be made effective on the date certified under subclause (III).

(iii) If the applicant made a certification described in subclause (IV) of paragraph (2)(A)(vii), the approval shall be made effective immediately unless, before the expiration of 45 days after the date on which the notice described in paragraph (2)(B) is received, an action is brought for infringement of the patent that is the subject of the certification and for which information was submitted to the Secretary under subsection (b)(1) or (c)(2) before the date on which the application (excluding an amendment or supplement to the application), which the Secretary later determines to be substantially complete, was submitted. If such an action is brought before the expiration of such days, the approval shall be made effective upon the expiration of the thirty-month period beginning on the date of the receipt of the notice provided under paragraph (2)(B)(i) or such shorter or longer period as the court may order because either party to the action failed to reasonably cooperate in expediting the action, except that—

(I) if before the expiration of such period the district court decides that the patent is invalid or not infringed (including any substantive determination that there is no cause of action for patent infringement or invalidity), the approval shall be made effective on—

(aa) the date on which the court enters judgment reflecting the decision; or

(bb) the date of a settlement order or consent decree signed and entered by the court stating that the patent that is the subject of the certification is invalid or not infringed;

(II) if before the expiration of such period the district court decides that the patent has been infringed—

(aa) if the judgment of the district court is appealed, the approval shall be made effective on—

(AA) the date on which the court of appeals decides that the patent is invalid or not infringed (including any substantive determination that there is no cause of action for patent infringement or invalidity); or

(BB) the date of a settlement order or consent decree signed and entered by the court of appeals stating that the patent that is the subject of the certification is invalid or not infringed; or

(bb) if the judgment of the district court is not appealed or is affirmed, the approval shall be made effective on the date specified by the district court in a court order under section 271(e)(4)(A) of title 35, United States Code;

(III) if before the expiration of such period the court grants a preliminary injunction prohibiting the applicant from engaging in the commercial manufacture or sale of the drug until the court decides the issues of patent validity and infringement and if the court decides that such patent is invalid or not infringed, the approval shall be made effective as provided in subclause (I); or

(IV) if before the expiration of such period the court grants a preliminary injunction prohibiting the applicant from engaging in the commercial manufacture or sale of the drug until the court decides the issues of patent validity and infringement and if the court decides that such patent has been infringed, the approval shall be made effective as provided in subclause (II).

In such an action, each of the parties shall reasonably cooperate in expediting the action.

(iv) 180–DAY EXCLUSIVITY PERIOD.—

(I) Effectiveness of application.—Subject to subparagraph (D), if the application contains a certification described in paragraph (2)(A)(vii)(IV) and is for a drug for which a first applicant has submitted an application containing such a certification, the application shall be made effective on the date that is 180 days after the date of the first commercial marketing of the drug (including the commercial marketing of the listed drug) by any first applicant.

(II) Definitions.—In this paragraph:

(aa) 180–day exclusivity period.—The term "180–day exclusivity period" means the 180–day period ending on the day before the date on which an application submitted by an applicant other than a first applicant could become effective under this clause.

(bb) First applicant.—As used in this subsection, the term "first applicant" means an applicant that, on the first day on which a substantially complete application containing a certification described in paragraph (2) (A)(vii)(IV) is submitted for approval of a drug, submits a substantially complete application that contains and lawfully maintains a certification described in paragraph (2)(A)(vii)(IV) for the drug.

(cc) Substantially complete application.—As used in this subsection, the term "substantially complete application" means an application under this subsection that on its face is sufficiently complete to permit a substantive review and contains all the information required by paragraph (2)(A).

(dd) Tentative approval.—

(AA) In general.—The term "tentative approval" means notification to an applicant by the Secretary that an application under this subsection meets the requirements of paragraph (2)(A), but cannot receive effective approval because the application does not meet the requirements of this subparagraph, there is a period of exclusivity for the listed drug under subparagraph (F) or section 505A, or there is a 7–year period of exclusivity for the listed drug under section 527.

(BB) Limitation.—A drug that is granted tentative approval by the Secretary is not an approved drug and shall not have an effective approval until the Secretary issues an approval after any necessary additional review of the application.

(C) Civil action to obtain patent certainty.—

(i) Declaratory judgment absent infringement action.—

(I) In general.—No action may be brought under section 2201 of title 28, United States Code, by an applicant under paragraph (2) for a declaratory judgment with respect to a patent which is the subject of the certification referred to in subparagraph (B)(iii) unless—

(aa) the 45–day period referred to in such subparagraph has expired;

(bb) neither the owner of such patent nor the holder of the approved application under subsection (b) for the drug that is claimed by the patent or a use of which is claimed by the patent brought a civil action against the applicant for infringement of the patent before the expiration of such period; and

(cc) in any case in which the notice provided under paragraph (2)(B) relates to noninfringement, the notice was accompanied by a document described in subclause (III).

(II) FILING OF CIVIL ACTION.—If the conditions described in items (aa), (bb), and as applicable, (cc) of subclause (I) have been met, the applicant referred to in such subclause may, in accordance with section 2201 of title 28, United States Code, bring a civil action under such section against the owner or holder referred to in such subclause (but not against any owner or holder that has brought such a civil action against the applicant, unless that civil action was dismissed without prejudice) for a declaratory judgment that the patent is invalid or will not be infringed by the drug for which the applicant seeks approval, except that such civil action may be brought for a declaratory judgment that the patent will not be infringed only in a case in which the condition described in subclause (I)(cc) is applicable. A civil action referred to in this subclause shall be brought in the judicial district where the defendant has its principal place of business or a regular and established place of business.

(III) OFFER OF CONFIDENTIAL ACCESS TO APPLICATION.—For purposes of subclause (I)(cc), the document described in this subclause is a document providing an offer of confidential access to the application that is in the custody of the applicant under paragraph (2) for the purpose of determining whether an action referred to in subparagraph (B)(iii) should be brought. The document providing the offer of confidential access shall contain such restrictions as to persons entitled to access, and on the use and disposition of any information accessed, as would apply had a protective order been entered for the purpose of protecting trade secrets and other confidential business information. A request for access to an application under an offer of confidential access shall be considered acceptance of the offer of confidential access with the restrictions as to persons entitled to access, and on the use and disposition of any information accessed, contained in the offer of confidential access, and those restrictions and other terms of the offer of confidential access shall be considered terms of an enforceable contract. Any person provided an offer of confidential access shall review the application for the sole and limited purpose of evaluating possible infringement of the patent that is the subject of the certification under paragraph (2)(A)(vii)(IV) and for no other purpose, and may not disclose information of no relevance to any issue of patent infringement to any person other than a person provided an offer of confidential access. Further, the application may be redacted by the applicant to remove any information of no relevance to any issue of patent infringement.

(ii) COUNTERCLAIM TO INFRINGEMENT ACTION.—

(I) IN GENERAL.—If an owner of the patent or the holder of the approved application under subsection (b) for the drug that is claimed by the patent or a use of which is claimed by the patent brings a patent infringement action against the applicant, the applicant may assert a counterclaim seeking an order requiring the holder to correct or delete the patent information submitted by the holder under subsection (b) or (c) on the ground that the patent does not claim either—

(aa) the drug for which the application was approved; or

(bb) an approved method of using the drug.

(II) NO INDEPENDENT CAUSE OF ACTION.—Subclause (I) does not authorize the assertion of a claim described in subclause (I) in any civil action or proceeding other than a counterclaim described in subclause (I).

(iii) NO DAMAGES.—An applicant shall not be entitled to damages in a civil action under clause (i) or a counterclaim under clause (ii).

(D) FORFEITURE OF 180–DAY EXCLUSIVITY PERIOD.—

(i) DEFINITION OF FORFEITURE EVENT.—In this subparagraph, the term "forfeiture event", with respect to an application under this subsection, means the occurrence of any of the following:

(I) FAILURE TO MARKET.—The first applicant fails to market the drug by the later of—

(aa) the earlier of the date that is—

(AA) 75 days after the date on which the approval of the application of the first applicant is made effective under subparagraph (B)(iii); or

(BB) 30 months after the date of submission of the application of the first applicant; or

(bb) with respect to the first applicant or any other applicant (which other applicant has received tentative approval), the date that is 75 days after the date as of which, as to each of the patents with respect to which the first applicant submitted and lawfully maintained a certification qualifying the first applicant for the 180–day exclusivity period under subparagraph (B)(iv), at least 1 of the following has occurred:

(AA) In an infringement action brought against that applicant with respect to the patent or in a declaratory judgment action brought by that applicant with respect to the patent, a court enters a final decision from which no appeal (other than a petition to the Supreme Court for a writ of certiorari) has been or can be taken that the patent is invalid or not infringed.

(BB) In an infringement action or a declaratory judgment action described in subitem (AA), a court signs a settlement order or consent decree that enters a final judgment that includes a finding that the patent is invalid or not infringed.

(CC) The patent information submitted under subsection (b) or (c) is withdrawn by the holder of the application approved under subsection (b).

(II) WITHDRAWAL OF APPLICATION.—The first applicant withdraws the application or the Secretary considers the application to have been withdrawn as a result of a determination by the Secretary that the application does not meet the requirements for approval under paragraph (4).

(III) AMENDMENT OF CERTIFICATION.—The first applicant amends or withdraws the certification for all of the patents with respect to which that applicant submitted a certification qualifying the applicant for the 180–day exclusivity period.

(IV) FAILURE TO OBTAIN TENTATIVE APPROVAL.—The first applicant fails to obtain tentative approval of the application within 30 months after the date on which the application is filed, unless the failure is caused by a change in or a review of the requirements for approval of the application imposed after the date on which the application is filed.

(V) AGREEMENT WITH ANOTHER APPLICANT, THE LISTED DRUG APPLICATION HOLDER, OR A PATENT OWNER.—The first applicant enters into an agreement with another applicant under this subsection for the drug, the holder of the application for the listed drug, or an owner of the patent that is the subject of the certification under paragraph (2)(A)(vii)(IV), the Federal Trade Commission or the Attorney General files a complaint, and there is a final decision of the Federal Trade Commission or the court with regard to the complaint from which no appeal (other than a petition to the Supreme Court for a writ of certiorari) has been or can be taken that the agreement has violated the antitrust laws (as defined in section 1 of the Clayton Act (15 U.S.C. 12), except that the term includes section 5 of the Federal Trade Commission Act (15 U.S.C. 45) to the extent that that section applies to unfair methods of competition).

(VI) EXPIRATION OF ALL PATENTS.—All of the patents as to which the applicant submitted a certification qualifying it for the 180–day exclusivity period have expired.

(ii) FORFEITURE.—The 180–day exclusivity period described in subparagraph (B)(iv) shall be forfeited by a first applicant if a forfeiture event occurs with respect to that first applicant.

(iii) SUBSEQUENT APPLICANT.—If all first applicants forfeit the 180–day exclusivity period under clause (ii)—

(I) approval of any application containing a certification described in paragraph (2)(A)(vii)(IV) shall be made effective in accordance with subparagraph (B)(iii); and

(II) no applicant shall be eligible for a 180–day exclusivity period.

(E) If the Secretary decides to disapprove an application, the Secretary shall give the applicant notice of an opportunity for a hearing before the Secretary on the question of whether such application is approvable. If the applicant elects to accept the opportunity for hearing by written request within thirty days after such notice, such hearing shall commence not more than ninety days after the expiration of such thirty days unless the Secretary and the applicant otherwise agree. Any such hearing shall thereafter be conducted on an expedited basis and the Secretary's order thereon shall be issued within ninety days after the date fixed by the Secretary for filing final briefs.

(F)(i) If an application (other than an abbreviated new drug application) submitted under subsection (b) for a drug, no active ingredient (including any ester or salt of the active ingredient) of which has been approved in any other application under subsection (b), was approved during the period beginning January 1, 1982, and ending on the date of the enactment of this subsection, the Secretary may not make the approval of an application submitted under this subsection which refers to the drug for which the subsection (b) application was submitted effective before the expiration of ten years from the date of the approval of the application under subsection (b).

(ii) If an application submitted under subsection (b) for a drug, no active ingredient (including any ester or salt of the active ingredient) of which has been approved in any other application under subsection (b), is approved after the date of the enactment of this subsection, no application may be submitted under this subsection which refers to the drug for which the subsection (b) application was submitted before the expiration of five years from the date of the approval of the application under subsection (b), except that such an application may be submitted under this subsection after the expiration of four years from the date of the approval of the subsection (b) application if it contains a certification of patent invalidity or noninfringement described in subclause (IV) of paragraph (2)(A)(vii). The approval of such an application shall be made effective in accordance with subparagraph (B) except that, if an action for patent infringement is commenced during the one-year period beginning forty-eight months after the date of the approval of the subsection (b) application, the thirty-month period referred to in subparagraph (B)(iii) shall be extended by such amount of time (if any) which is required for seven and one-half years to have elapsed from the date of approval of the subsection (b) application.

(iii) If an application submitted under subsection (b) for a drug, which includes an active ingredient (including any ester or salt of the active ingredient) that has been approved in another application approved under subsection (b), is approved after the date of enactment of this subsection and if such application contains reports of new clinical investigations (other than bioavailability studies) essential to the approval of the application and conducted or sponsored by the applicant, the Secretary may not make the approval of an application submitted under this subsection for the conditions of approval of such drug in the subsection (b) application effective before the expiration of three years from the date of the approval of the application under subsection (b) for such drug.

(iv) If a supplement to an application approved under subsection (b) is approved after the date of enactment of this subsection and the supplement contains reports of new clinical investigations (other than bioavailability studies) essential to the approval of the supplement and conducted or sponsored by the person submitting the supplement, the Secretary may not make the approval of an application submitted under this subsection for a change approved in the supplement effective before the expiration of three years from the date of the approval of the supplement under subsection (b).

(v) If an application (or supplement to an application) submitted under subsection (b) for a drug, which includes an active ingredient (including any ester or salt of the active ingredient) that has been approved in another application under subsection (b), was approved during the period beginning January 1, 1982, and ending on the date of the enactment of this subsection, the Secretary may not make the approval of an application submitted under this subsection which refers to the drug for which the subsection (b) application was submitted or which refers to a change approved in a supplement to the subsection (b) application effective before the expiration of two years from the date of enactment of this subsection.

(6) If a drug approved under this subsection refers in its approved application to a drug the approval of which was withdrawn or suspended for grounds described in the first sentence of subsection (e) or was withdrawn or suspended under this paragraph or which, as determined by the Secretary, has been withdrawn from sale for safety or effectiveness reasons, the approval of the drug under this subsection shall be withdrawn or suspended—

(A) for the same period as the withdrawal or suspension under subsection (e) or this paragraph, or

(B) if the listed drug has been withdrawn from sale, for the period of withdrawal from sale or, if earlier, the period ending on the date the Secretary determines that the withdrawal from sale is not for safety or effectiveness reasons.

(7)(A)(i) Within sixty days of the date of the enactment of this subsection[35] the Secretary shall publish and make available to the public—

(I) a list in alphabetical order of the official and proprietary name of each drug which has been approved for safety and effectiveness under subsection (c) before the date of the enactment of this subsection;

(II) the date of approval if the drug is approved after 1981 and the number of the application which was approved; and

35. Subsection (j) was added by Pub. L. No. 98–417, § 101, 98 Stat. 1585, 1585–92 (1984).

212

(III) whether in vitro or in vivo bioequivalence studies, or both such studies, are required for applications filed under this subsection which will refer to the drug published.

(ii) Every thirty days after the publication of the first list under clause (i) the Secretary shall revise the list to include each drug which has been approved for safety and effectiveness under subsection (c) or approved under this subsection during the thirty day period.

(iii) When patent information submitted under subsection (b) or (c) respecting a drug included on the list is to be published by the Secretary, the Secretary shall, in revisions made under clause (ii), include such information for such drug.

(B) A drug approved for safety and effectiveness under subsection (c) or approved under this subsection shall, for purposes of this subsection, be considered to have been published under subparagraph (A) on the date of its approval or the date of enactment, whichever is later.

(C) If the approval of a drug was withdrawn or suspended for grounds described in the first sentence of subsection (e) or was withdrawn or suspended under paragraph (6) or if the Secretary determines that a drug has been withdrawn from sale for safety or effectiveness reasons, it may not be published in the list under subparagraph (A) or, if the withdrawal or suspension occurred after its publication in such list, it shall be immediately removed from such list—

(i) For the same period as the withdrawal or suspension under subsection (e) or paragraph (6), or

(ii) if the listed drug has been withdrawn from sale, for the period of withdrawal from sale or, if earlier, the period ending on the date the Secretary determines that the withdrawal from sale is not for safety or effectiveness reasons.

A notice of the removal shall be published in the Federal Register.

(8) For purposes of this subsection:

(A)(i) The term "bioavailability" means the rate and extent to which the active ingredient or therapeutic ingredient is absorbed from a drug and becomes available at the site of drug action.

(ii) For a drug that is not intended to be absorbed into the bloodstream, the Secretary may assess bioavailability by scientifically valid measurements intended to reflect the rate and extent to which the active ingredient or therapeutic ingredient becomes available at the site of drug action.

(B) A drug shall be considered to be bioequivalent to a listed drug if—

(i) the rate and extent of absorption of the drug do not show a significant difference from the rate and extent of absorption of the listed drug when administered at the same molar dose of the therapeutic ingredient under similar experimental conditions in either a single dose or multiple doses; or

(ii) the extent of absorption of the drug does not show a significant difference from the extent of absorption of the listed drug when administered at the same molar dose of the therapeutic ingredient under similar experimental conditions in either a single dose or multiple doses and the difference from the listed drug in the rate of absorption of the drug is intentional, is reflected in its proposed labeling, is not essential to the attainment of effective body drug concentrations on chronic use, and is considered medically insignificant for the drug.

(C) For a drug that is not intended to be absorbed into the bloodstream, the Secretary may establish alternative, scientifically valid methods to show bioequivalence if the alternative methods are expected to detect a significant difference between the drug and the listed drug in safety and therapeutic effect.

(9) The Secretary shall, with respect to each application submitted under this subsection, maintain a record of—

(A) the name of the applicant,

(B) the name of the drug covered by the application,

(C) the name of each person to whom the review of the chemistry of the application was assigned and the date of such assignment, and

(D) the name of each person to whom the bioequivalence review for such application was assigned and the date of such assignment.

The information the Secretary is required to maintain under this paragraph with respect to an application submitted under this subsection shall be made available to the public after the approval of such application.

(10)(A) If the proposed labeling of a drug that is the subject of an application under this subsection differs from the listed drug due to a labeling revision described under clause (i), the drug that is the subject of such application shall, notwithstanding any other provision of this Act, be eligible for approval and shall not be considered misbranded under section 502 if—

(i) the application is otherwise eligible for approval under this subsection but for expiration of patent, an exclusivity period, or of a delay in approval described in paragraph (5)(B)(iii), and a revision to the labeling of the listed drug has been approved by the Secretary within 60 days of such expiration;

(ii) the labeling revision described under clause (i) does not include a change to the "Warnings" section of the labeling;

(iii) the sponsor of the application under this subsection agrees to submit revised labeling of the drug that is the subject of such application not later than 60 days after the notification of any changes to such labeling required by the Secretary; and

(iv) such application otherwise meets the applicable requirements for approval under this subsection.

(B) If, after a labeling revision described in subparagraph (A)(i), the Secretary determines that the continued presence in interstate commerce of the labeling of the listed drug (as in effect before the revision described in subparagraph (A)(i)) adversely impacts the safe use of the drug, no application under this subsection shall be eligible for approval with such labeling.

(k)(1) In the case of any drug for which an approval of an application filed under subsection (b) or (j) is in effect, the applicant shall establish and maintain such records, and make such reports to the Secretary, of data relating to clinical experience and other data or information, received or otherwise obtained by such applicant with respect to such drug, as the Secretary may by general regulation, or by order with respect to such application, prescribe on the basis of a finding that such records and reports are necessary in order to enable the Secretary to determine, or facilitate a determination, whether there is or may be ground for invoking subsection (e) of this section. Regulations and orders issued under this subsection and under subsection (i) shall have due regard for the professional ethics of the medical profession and the interests of patients and shall provide, where the Secretary deems it to be appropriate, for the examination, upon request, by the persons to whom such regulations or orders are applicable, of similar information received or otherwise obtained by the Secretary.

(2) Every person required under this section to maintain records, and every person in charge or custody thereof, shall, upon request of an officer or employee designated by the Secretary, permit such officer or employee at all reasonable times to have access to and copy and verify such records.

(3) ACTIVE POSTMARKET RISK IDENTIFICATION.—

(A) DEFINITION.—In this paragraph, the term "data" refers to information with respect to a drug approved under this section or under section 351 of the Public Health Service Act, including claims data, patient survey data, standardized analytic files that allow for the pooling and analysis of data from disparate data environments, and any other data deemed appropriate by the Secretary.

(B) DEVELOPMENT OF POSTMARKET RISK IDENTIFICATION AND ANALYSIS METHODS.— The Secretary shall, not later than 2 years after the date of the enactment of the Food and Drug Administration Amendments Act of 2007, in collaboration with public, academic, and private entities—

(i) develop methods to obtain access to disparate data sources including the data sources specified in subparagraph (C);

(ii) develop validated methods for the establishment of a postmarket risk identification and analysis system to link and analyze safety data from multiple sources, with the goals of including, in aggregate—

(I) at least 25,000,000 patients by July 1, 2010; and

(II) at least 100,000,000 patients by July 1, 2012; and

(iii) convene a committee of experts, including individuals who are recognized in the field of protecting data privacy and security, to make recommendations to the Secretary on the development of tools and methods for the ethical and scientific uses for, and communication of, postmarketing data specified under subparagraph (C), including recommendations on the development of effective research methods for the study of drug safety questions.

(C) ESTABLISHMENT OF THE POSTMARKET RISK IDENTIFICATION AND ANALYSIS SYSTEM.—

(i) IN GENERAL.—The Secretary shall, not later than 1 year after the development of the risk identification and analysis methods under subparagraph (B), establish and maintain procedures—

(I) for risk identification and analysis based on electronic health data, in compliance with the regulations promulgated under section 264(c) of the Health Insurance Portability and Accountability Act of 1996, and in a manner that does not disclose individually identifiable health information in violation of paragraph (4)(B);

(II) for the reporting (in a standardized form) of data on all serious adverse drug experiences (as defined in section 505–1(b)) submitted to the Secretary under paragraph (1), and those adverse events submitted by patients, providers, and drug sponsors, when appropriate;

(III) to provide for active adverse event surveillance using the following data sources, as available:

(aa) Federal health-related electronic data (such as data from the Medicare program and the health systems of the Department of Veterans Affairs);

(bb) private sector health-related electronic data (such as pharmaceutical purchase data and health insurance claims data); and

(cc) other data as the Secretary deems necessary to create a robust system to identify adverse events and potential drug safety signals;

(IV) to identify certain trends and patterns with respect to data accessed by the system;

(V) to provide regular reports to the Secretary concerning adverse event trends, adverse event patterns, incidence and prevalence of adverse events, and other information the Secretary determines appropriate, which may include data on comparative national adverse event trends; and

(VI) to enable the program to export data in a form appropriate for further aggregation, statistical analysis, and reporting.

(ii) TIMELINESS OF REPORTING.—The procedures established under clause (i) shall ensure that such data are accessed, analyzed, and reported in a timely, routine, and systematic manner, taking into consideration the need for data completeness, coding, cleansing, and standardized analysis and transmission.

(iii) PRIVATE SECTOR RESOURCES.—To ensure the establishment of the active postmarket risk identification and analysis system under this subsection not later than 1 year after the development of the risk identification and analysis methods under subparagraph (B), as required under clause (i), the Secretary may, on a temporary or permanent basis, implement systems or products developed by private entities.

(iv) COMPLEMENTARY APPROACHES.—To the extent the active postmarket risk identification and analysis system under this subsection is not sufficient to gather data and information relevant to a priority drug safety question, the Secretary shall develop, support, and participate in complementary approaches to gather and analyze such data and information, including—

(I) approaches that are complementary with respect to assessing the safety of use of a drug in domestic populations not included, or underrepresented, in the trials used to approve the drug (such as older people, people with comorbidities, pregnant women, or children); and

(II) existing approaches such as the Vaccine Adverse Event Reporting System and the Vaccine Safety Datalink or successor databases.

(v) AUTHORITY FOR CONTRACTS.—The Secretary may enter into contracts with public and private entities to fulfill the requirements of this subparagraph.

(4) ADVANCED ANALYSIS OF DRUG SAFETY DATA.—

(A) PURPOSE.—The Secretary shall establish collaborations with public, academic, and private entities, which may include the Centers for Education and Research on Therapeutics under section 912 of the Public Health Service Act, to provide for advanced analysis of drug safety data described in paragraph (3)(C) and other information that is publicly available or is provided by the Secretary, in order to—

(i) improve the quality and efficiency of postmarket drug safety risk-benefit analysis;

(ii) provide the Secretary with routine access to outside expertise to study advanced drug safety questions; and

(iii) enhance the ability of the Secretary to make timely assessments based on drug safety data.

(B) PRIVACY.—Such analysis shall not disclose individually identifiable health information when presenting such drug safety signals and trends or when responding to inquiries regarding such drug safety signals and trends.

217

(C) Public process for priority questions.—At least biannually, the Secretary shall seek recommendations from the Drug Safety and Risk Management Advisory Committee (or any successor committee) and from other advisory committees, as appropriate, to the Food and Drug Administration on—

(i) priority drug safety questions; and

(ii) mechanisms for answering such questions, including through—

(I) active risk identification under paragraph (3); and

(II) when such risk identification is not sufficient, postapproval studies and clinical trials under subsection (*o*)(3).

(D) Procedures for the development of drug safety collaborations.—

(i) In general.—Not later than 180 days after the date of the establishment of the active postmarket risk identification and analysis system under this subsection, the Secretary shall establish and implement procedures under which the Secretary may routinely contract with one or more qualified entities to—

(I) classify, analyze, or aggregate data described in paragraph (3)(C) and information that is publicly available or is provided by the Secretary;

(II) allow for prompt investigation of priority drug safety questions, including—

(aa) unresolved safety questions for drugs or classes of drugs; and

(bb) for a newly-approved drugs, safety signals from clinical trials used to approve the drug and other preapproval trials; rare, serious drug side effects; and the safety of use in domestic populations not included, or underrepresented, in the trials used to approve the drug (such as older people, people with comorbidities, pregnant women, or children);

(III) perform advanced research and analysis on identified drug safety risks;

(IV) focus postapproval studies and clinical trials under subsection (*o*) (3) more effectively on cases for which reports under paragraph (1) and other safety signal detection is not sufficient to resolve whether there is an elevated risk of a serious adverse event associated with the use of a drug; and

(V) carry out other activities as the Secretary deems necessary to carry out the purposes of this paragraph.

(ii) Request for specific methodology.—The procedures described in clause (i) shall permit the Secretary to request that a specific methodology be used by the qualified entity. The qualified entity shall work with the Secretary to finalize the methodology to be used.

(E) USE OF ANALYSES.—The Secretary shall provide the analyses described in this paragraph, including the methods and results of such analyses, about a drug to the sponsor or sponsors of such drug.

(F) QUALIFIED ENTITIES.—

(i) IN GENERAL.—The Secretary shall enter into contracts with a sufficient number of qualified entities to develop and provide information to the Secretary in a timely manner.

(ii) QUALIFICATION.—The Secretary shall enter into a contract with an entity under clause (i) only if the Secretary determines that the entity has a significant presence in the United States and has one or more of the following qualifications:

(I) The research, statistical, epidemiologic, or clinical capability and expertise to conduct and complete the activities under this paragraph, including the capability and expertise to provide the Secretary de-identified data consistent with the requirements of this subsection.

(II) An information technology infrastructure in place to support electronic data and operational standards to provide security for such data.

(III) Experience with, and expertise on, the development of drug safety and effectiveness research using electronic population data.

(IV) An understanding of drug development or risk/benefit balancing in a clinical setting.

(V) Other expertise which the Secretary deems necessary to fulfill the activities under this paragraph.

(G) CONTRACT REQUIREMENTS.—Each contract with a qualified entity under subparagraph (F)(i) shall contain the following requirements:

(i) ENSURING PRIVACY.—The qualified entity shall ensure that the entity will not use data under this subsection in a manner that—

(I) violates the regulations promulgated under section 264(c) of the Health Insurance Portability and Accountability Act of 1996;

(II) violates sections 552 or 552a of title 5, United States Code, with regard to the privacy of individually-identifiable beneficiary health information; or

(III) discloses individually identifiable health information when presenting drug safety signals and trends or when responding to inquiries regarding drug safety signals and trends.

Nothing in this clause prohibits lawful disclosure for other purposes.

(ii) COMPONENT OF ANOTHER ORGANIZATION.—If a qualified entity is a component of another organization—

(I) the qualified entity shall establish appropriate security measures to maintain the confidentiality and privacy of such data; and

(II) the entity shall not make an unauthorized disclosure of such data to the other components of the organization in breach of such confidentiality and privacy requirement.

(iii) TERMINATION OR NONRENEWAL.—If a contract with a qualified entity under this subparagraph is terminated or not renewed, the following requirements shall apply:

(I) CONFIDENTIALITY AND PRIVACY PROTECTIONS.—The entity shall continue to comply with the confidentiality and privacy requirements under this paragraph with respect to all data disclosed to the entity.

(II) DISPOSITION OF DATA.—The entity shall return any data disclosed to such entity under this subsection to which it would not otherwise have access or, if returning the data is not practicable, destroy the data.

(H) COMPETITIVE PROCEDURES.—The Secretary shall use competitive procedures (as defined in section 4(5) of the Federal Procurement Policy Act) to enter into contracts under subparagraph (G).

(I) REVIEW OF CONTRACT IN THE EVENT OF A MERGER OR ACQUISITION.—The Secretary shall review the contract with a qualified entity under this paragraph in the event of a merger or acquisition of the entity in order to ensure that the requirements under this paragraph will continue to be met.

(J) COORDINATION.—In carrying out this paragraph, the Secretary shall provide for appropriate communications to the public, scientific, public health, and medical communities, and other key stakeholders, and to the extent practicable shall coordinate with the activities of private entities, professional associations, or other entities that may have sources of drug safety data.

(5) The Secretary shall—

(A) conduct regular, bi-weekly screening of the Adverse Event Reporting System database and post a quarterly report on the Adverse Event Reporting System Web site of any new safety information or potential signal of a serious risk identified by Adverse Event Reporting System within the last quarter;

(B) report to Congress not later than 2 year after the date of the enactment of the Food and Drug Administration Amendments Act of 2007 on procedures and processes of the Food and Drug Administration for addressing ongoing post market safety issues identified by the Office of Surveillance and Epidemiology and how recommendations of the Office of Surveillance and Epidemiology are handled within the agency; and

(C) on an annual basis, review the entire backlog of postmarket safety commitments to determine which commitments require revision or should be eliminated, report to the Congress on these determinations, and assign start dates and estimated completion dates for such commitments.

(*l*)(1) Safety and effectiveness data and information which has been submitted in an application under subsection (b) for a drug and which has not previously been disclosed to the public shall be made available to the public, upon request, unless extraordinary circumstances are shown—

(A) if no work is being or will be undertaken to have the application approved,

(B) if the Secretary has determined that the application is not approvable and all legal appeals have been exhausted,

(C) if approval of the application under subsection (c) is withdrawn and all legal appeals have been exhausted,

(D) if the Secretary has determined that such drug is not a new drug, or

(E) upon the effective date of the approval of the first application under subsection (j) which refers to such drug or upon the date upon which the approval of an application under subsection (j) which refers to such drug could be made effective if such an application had been submitted.

(2) ACTION PACKAGE FOR APPROVAL.—

(A) ACTION PACKAGE.—The Secretary shall publish the action package for approval of an application under subsection (b) or section 351 of the Public Health Service Act on the Internet Web site of the Food and Drug Administration—

(i) not later than 30 days after the date of approval of such application for a drug no active ingredient (including any ester or salt of the active ingredient) of which has been approved in any other application under this section or section 351 of the Public Health Service Act; and

(ii) not later than 30 days after the third request for such action package for approval received under section 552 of title 5, United States Code, for any other drug.

(B) IMMEDIATE PUBLICATION OF SUMMARY REVIEW.—Notwithstanding subparagraph (A), the Secretary shall publish, on the Internet Web site of the Food and Drug Administration, the materials described in subparagraph (C)(iv) not later than 48 hours after the date of approval of the drug, except where such materials require redaction by the Secretary.

(C) CONTENTS.—An action package for approval of an application under subparagraph (A) shall be dated and shall include the following:

(i) Documents generated by the Food and Drug Administration related to review of the application.

(ii) Documents pertaining to the format and content of the application generated during drug development.

(iii) Labeling submitted by the applicant.

(iv) A summary review that documents conclusions from all reviewing disciplines about the drug, noting any critical issues and disagreements with the applicant and within the review team and how they were resolved, recommendations for action, and an explanation of any nonconcurrence with review conclusions.

(v) The Division Director and Office Director's decision document which includes—

(I) a brief statement of concurrence with the summary review;

(II) a separate review or addendum to the review if disagreeing with the summary review; and

(III) a separate review or addendum to the review to add further analysis.

(vi) Identification by name of each officer or employee of the Food and Drug Administration who—

(I) participated in the decision to approve the application; and

(II) consents to have his or her name included in the package.

(D) REVIEW.—A scientific review of an application is considered the work of the reviewer and shall not be altered by management or the reviewer once final.

(E) CONFIDENTIAL INFORMATION.—This paragraph does not authorize the disclosure of any trade secret, confidential commercial or financial information, or other matter listed in section 552(b) of title 5, United States Code.

(m) For purposes of this section, the term "patent" means a patent issued by the United States Patent and Trademark Office.

(n)(1) For the purpose of providing expert scientific advice and recommendations to the Secretary regarding a clinical investigation of a drug or the approval for marketing of a drug under section 505 or section 351 of the Public Health Service Act, the Secretary shall establish panels of experts or use panels of experts established before the date of enactment of the Food and Drug Administration Modernization Act of 1997, or both.

(2) The Secretary may delegate the appointment and oversight authority granted under section 1004 to a director of a center or successor entity within the Food and Drug Administration.

(3) The Secretary shall make appointments to each panel established under paragraph (1) so that each panel shall consist of—

(A) members who are qualified by training and experience to evaluate the safety and effectiveness of the drugs to be referred to the panel and who, to the extent feasible, possess skill and experience in the development, manufacture, or utilization of such drugs;

(B) members with diverse expertise in such fields as clinical and administrative medicine, pharmacy, pharmacology, pharmacoeconomics, biological and physical sciences, and other related professions;

(C) a representative of consumer interests, and a representative of interests of the drug manufacturing industry not directly affected by the matter to be brought before the panel; and

(D) two or more members who are specialists or have other expertise in the particular disease or condition for which the drug under review is proposed to be indicated.

Scientific, trade, and consumer organizations shall be afforded an opportunity to nominate individuals for appointment to the panels. No individual who is in the regular full-time employ of the United States and engaged in the administration of this Act may be a voting member of any panel. The Secretary shall designate one of the members of each panel to serve as chairman thereof.

(4) The Secretary shall, as appropriate, provide education and training to each new panel member before such member participates in a panel's activities, including education regarding requirements under this Act and related regulations of the Secretary, and the administrative processes and procedures related to panel meetings.

(5) Panel members (other than officers or employees of the United States), while attending meetings or conferences of a panel or otherwise engaged in its business, shall be entitled to receive compensation for each day so engaged, including travel-time, at rates to be fixed by the Secretary, but not to exceed the daily equivalent of the rate in effect for positions classified above grade GS–15 of the General Schedule. While serving away from their homes or regular places of business, panel members may be allowed travel expenses (including per diem in lieu of subsistence) as authorized by section 5703 of title 5, United States Code, for persons in the Government service employed intermittently.

(6) The Secretary shall ensure that scientific advisory panels meet regularly and at appropriate intervals so that any matter to be reviewed by such a panel can be presented to the panel not more than 60 days after the matter is ready for such review. Meetings of the panel may be held using electronic communication to convene the meetings.

(7) Within 90 days after a scientific advisory panel makes recommendations on any matter under its review, the Food and Drug Administration official responsible for the matter shall review the conclusions and recommendations of the panel, and notify the affected persons of the final decision on the matter, or of the reasons that no such decision has been reached. Each such final decision shall be documented including the rationale for the decision.

(*o*) POSTMARKET STUDIES AND CLINICAL TRIALS; LABELING.—

(1) IN GENERAL.—A responsible person may not introduce or deliver for introduction into interstate commerce the new drug involved if the person is in violation of a requirement established under paragraph (3) or (4) with respect to the drug.

(2) DEFINITIONS.—For purposes of this subsection:

(A) RESPONSIBLE PERSON.—The term "responsible person" means a person who—

(i) has submitted to the Secretary a covered application that is pending; or

(ii) is the holder of an approved covered application.

(B) COVERED APPLICATION.—The term "covered application" means—

(i) an application under subsection (b) for a drug that is subject to section 503(b); and

(ii) an application under section 351 of the Public Health Service Act.

(C) NEW SAFETY INFORMATION; SERIOUS RISK.—The terms "new safety information", "serious risk", and "signal of a serious risk" have the meanings given such terms in section 505–1(b).

(3) STUDIES AND CLINICAL TRIALS.—

(A) IN GENERAL.—For any or all of the purposes specified in subparagraph (B), the Secretary may, subject to subparagraph (D), require a responsible person for a drug to conduct a postapproval study or studies of the drug, or a postapproval clinical trial or trials of the drug, on the basis of scientific data deemed appropriate by the Secretary, including information regarding chemically-related or pharmacologically-related drugs.

(B) PURPOSES OF STUDY OR CLINICAL TRIAL.—The purposes referred to in this subparagraph with respect to a postapproval study or postapproval clinical trial are the following:

(i) To assess a known serious risk related to the use of the drug involved.

(ii) To assess signals of serious risk related to the use of the drug.

(iii) To identify an unexpected serious risk when available data indicates the potential for a serious risk.

(C) ESTABLISHMENT OF REQUIREMENT AFTER APPROVAL OF COVERED APPLICATION.—The Secretary may require a postapproval study or studies or postapproval clinical trial or trials for a drug for which an approved covered application is in effect as of the date on which the Secretary seeks to establish such requirement only if the Secretary becomes aware of new safety information.

(D) DETERMINATION BY SECRETARY.—

(i) POSTAPPROVAL STUDIES.—The Secretary may not require the responsible person to conduct a study under this paragraph, unless the Secretary makes a determination that the reports under subsection (k)(1) and the active postmarket risk identification and analysis system as available under subsection (k)(3) will not be sufficient to meet the purposes set forth in subparagraph (B).

(ii) POSTAPPROVAL CLINICAL TRIALS.—The Secretary may not require the responsible person to conduct a clinical trial under this paragraph, unless the Secretary makes a determination that a postapproval study or studies will not be sufficient to meet the purposes set forth in subparagraph (B).

(E) NOTIFICATION; TIMETABLES; PERIODIC REPORTS.—

(i) NOTIFICATION.—The Secretary shall notify the responsible person regarding a requirement under this paragraph to conduct a postapproval study or clinical trial by the target dates for communication of feedback from the review team to the responsible person regarding proposed labeling and postmarketing study commitments as set forth in the letters described in section 101(c) of the Food and Drug Administration Amendments Act of 2007.

(ii) TIMETABLE; PERIODIC REPORTS.—For each study or clinical trial required to be conducted under this paragraph, the Secretary shall require that the responsible person submit a timetable for completion of the study or clinical trial. With respect to each study required to be conducted under this paragraph or otherwise undertaken by the responsible person to investigate a safety issue, the Secretary shall require the responsible person to periodically report to the Secretary on the status of such study including whether any difficulties in completing the study have been encountered. With respect to each clinical trial required to be conducted under this paragraph or otherwise undertaken by the responsible person to investigate a safety issue, the Secretary shall require the responsible person to periodically report to the Secretary on the status of such clinical trial including whether enrollment has begun, the number of participants enrolled, the expected completion date, whether any difficulties completing the clinical trial have been encountered, and registration information with respect to the requirements under section 402(j) of the Public Health Service Act. If the responsible person fails to comply with such timetable or violates any other requirement of this subparagraph, the responsible person shall be considered in violation of this subsection, unless the responsible person demonstrates good cause for such noncompliance or such other violation. The Secretary shall determine what constitutes good cause under the preceding sentence.

(F) DISPUTE RESOLUTION.—The responsible person may appeal a requirement to conduct a study or clinical trial under this paragraph using dispute resolution procedures established by the Secretary in regulation and guidance.

(4) SAFETY LABELING CHANGES REQUESTED BY SECRETARY.—

(A) NEW SAFETY INFORMATION.—If the Secretary becomes aware of new safety information that the Secretary believes should be included in the labeling of the drug, the Secretary shall promptly notify the responsible person or, if the same drug approved under section 505(b) is not currently marketed, the holder of an approved application under 505(j).

(B) RESPONSE TO NOTIFICATION.—Following notification pursuant to subparagraph (A), the responsible person or the holder of the approved application under section 505(j) shall within 30 days—

(i) submit a supplement proposing changes to the approved labeling to reflect the new safety information, including changes to boxed warnings, contraindications, warnings, precautions, or adverse reactions; or

(ii) notify the Secretary that the responsible person or the holder of the approved application under section 505(j) does not believe a labeling change is warranted and submit a statement detailing the reasons why such a change is not warranted.

(C) REVIEW.—Upon receipt of such supplement, the Secretary shall promptly review and act upon such supplement. If the Secretary disagrees with the proposed changes in the supplement or with the statement setting forth the reasons why no labeling change is necessary, the Secretary shall initiate discussions to reach agreement on whether the labeling for the drug should be modified to reflect the new safety information, and if so, the contents of such labeling changes.

(D) DISCUSSIONS.—Such discussions shall not extend for more than 30 days after the response to the notification under subparagraph (B), unless the Secretary determines an extension of such discussion period is warranted.

(E) ORDER.—Within 15 days of the conclusion of the discussions under subparagraph (D), the Secretary may issue an order directing the responsible person or the holder of the approved application under section 505(j) to make such a labeling change as the Secretary deems appropriate to address the new safety information. Within 15 days of such an order, the responsible person or the holder of the approved application under section 505(j) shall submit a supplement containing the labeling change.

(F) DISPUTE RESOLUTION.—Within 5 days of receiving an order under subparagraph (E), the responsible person or the holder of the approved application under section 505(j) may appeal using dispute resolution procedures established by the Secretary in regulation and guidance.

(G) VIOLATION.—If the responsible person or the holder of the approved application under section 505(j) has not submitted a supplement within 15 days of the date of such order under subparagraph (E), and there is no appeal or dispute resolution proceeding pending, the responsible person or holder shall be considered to be in violation of this subsection. If at the conclusion of any dispute resolution procedures the Secretary determines that a supplement must be submitted and such a supplement is not submitted within 15 days of the date of that determination, the responsible person or holder shall be in violation of this subsection.

(H) PUBLIC HEALTH THREAT.—Notwithstanding subparagraphs (A) through (F), if the Secretary concludes that such a labeling change is necessary to protect the public health, the Secretary may accelerate the timelines in such subparagraphs.

(I) RULE OF CONSTRUCTION.—This paragraph shall not be construed to affect the responsibility of the responsible person or the holder of the approved application under section 505(j) to maintain its label in accordance with existing requirements, including subpart B of part 201 and sections 314.70 and 601.12 of title 21, Code of Federal Regulations (or any successor regulations).

(5) NON-DELEGATION.—Determinations by the Secretary under this subsection for a drug shall be made by individuals at or above the level of individuals empowered to approve a drug (such as division directors within the Center for Drug Evaluation and Research).

(p) RISK EVALUATION AND MITIGATION STRATEGY.—

(1) IN GENERAL.—A person may not introduce or deliver for introduction into interstate commerce a new drug if—

(A)(i) the application for such drug is approved under subsection (b) or (j) and is subject to section 503(b); or

(ii) the application for such drug is approved under section 351 of the Public Health Service Act; and

(B) a risk evaluation and mitigation strategy is required under section 505–1 with respect to the drug and the person fails to maintain compliance with the requirements of the approved strategy or with other requirements under section 505–1, including requirements regarding assessments of approved strategies.

(2) CERTAIN POSTMARKET STUDIES.—The failure to conduct a postmarket study under section 506, subpart H of part 314, or subpart E of part 601 of title 21, Code of Federal Regulations (or any successor regulations), is deemed to be a violation of paragraph (1).

(q) PETITIONS AND CIVIL ACTIONS REGARDING APPROVAL OF CERTAIN APPLICATIONS.—

(1) IN GENERAL.—

(A) DETERMINATION.—The Secretary shall not delay approval of a pending application submitted under subsection (b)(2) or (j) of this section or section 351(k) of the Public Health Service Act because of any request to take any form of action relating to the application, either before or during consideration of the request, unless—

(i) the request is in writing and is a petition submitted to the Secretary pursuant to section 10.30 or 10.35 of title 21, Code of Federal Regulations (or any successor regulations); and

(ii) the Secretary determines, upon reviewing the petition, that a delay is necessary to protect the public health.

(B) NOTIFICATION.—If the Secretary determines under subparagraph (A) that a delay is necessary with respect to an application, the Secretary shall provide to the applicant, not later than 30 days after making such determination, the following information:

(i) Notification of the fact that a determination under subparagraph (A) has been made.

(ii) If applicable, any clarification or additional data that the applicant should submit to the docket on the petition to allow the Secretary to review the petition promptly.

(iii) A brief summary of the specific substantive issues raised in the petition which form the basis of the determination.

(C) FORMAT.—The information described in subparagraph (B) shall be conveyed via either, at the discretion of the Secretary—

(i) a document; or

(ii) a meeting with the applicant involved.

(D) PUBLIC DISCLOSURE.—Any information conveyed by the Secretary under subparagraph (C) shall be considered part of the application and shall be subject to the disclosure requirements applicable to information in such application.

(E) DENIAL BASED ON INTENT TO DELAY.—If the Secretary determines that a petition or a supplement to the petition was submitted with the primary purpose of delaying the approval of an application and the petition does not on its face raise valid scientific or regulatory issues, the Secretary may deny the petition at any point based on such determination. The Secretary may issue guidance to describe the factors that will be used to determine under this subparagraph whether a petition is submitted with the primary purpose of delaying the approval of an application.

(F) FINAL AGENCY ACTION.—The Secretary shall take final agency action on a petition not later than 150 days after the date on which the petition is submitted. The Secretary shall not extend such period for any reason, including—

(i) any determination made under subparagraph (A);

(ii) the submission of comments relating to the petition or supplemental information supplied by the petitioner; or

(iii) the consent of the petitioner.

(G) EXTENSION OF 30–MONTH PERIOD.—If the filing of an application resulted in first-applicant status under subsection (j)(5)(D)(i)(IV) and approval of the application was delayed because of a petition, the 30–month period under such subsection is deemed to be extended by a period of time equal to the period beginning on the date on which the Secretary received the petition and ending on the date of final agency action on the petition (inclusive of such beginning and ending dates), without regard to whether the Secretary grants, in whole or in part, or denies, in whole or in part, the petition.

(H) CERTIFICATION.—The Secretary shall not consider a petition for review unless the party submitting such petition does so in written form and the subject document is signed and contains the following certification: "I certify that, to my best knowledge and belief: (a) this petition includes all information and views upon which the petition relies; (b) this petition includes representative data and/or information known to the petitioner which are unfavorable to the petition; and (c) I have taken reasonable steps to ensure that any representative data and/or information which are unfavorable to the petition were disclosed to me. I further certify that the information upon which I have based the action requested herein first became known to the party on whose behalf this petition is submitted on or about the following date: _____. If I received or expect to receive payments, including cash and other forms of consideration, to file this information or its contents, I received or expect to receive those payments from the following persons or organizations: _____. I verify under penalty of perjury that the foregoing is true and correct as of the date of the submission of this petition.", with the date on which such information first became known to such party and the names of such persons or organizations inserted in the first and second blank space, respectively.

(I) VERIFICATION.—The Secretary shall not accept for review any supplemental information or comments on a petition unless the party submitting such information or comments does so in written form and the subject document is signed and contains the following verification: "I certify that, to my best knowledge and belief: (a) I have not intentionally delayed submission of this document or its contents; and (b) the information upon which I have based the action requested herein first became known to me on or about _____. If I received or expect to receive payments, including cash and other forms of consideration, to file this information or its contents, I received or expect to receive those payments from the following persons or organizations: _____. I verify under penalty of perjury that the foregoing is true and correct as of the date of the submission of this petition.", with the date on which such information first became known to the party and the names of such persons or organizations inserted in the first and second blank space, respectively.

(2) EXHAUSTION OF ADMINISTRATIVE REMEDIES.—

(A) FINAL AGENCY ACTION WITHIN 150 DAYS.—The Secretary shall be considered to have taken final agency action on a petition if—

(i) during the 150–day period referred to in paragraph (1)(F), the Secretary makes a final decision within the meaning of section 10.45(d) of title 21, Code of Federal Regulations (or any successor regulation); or

(ii) such period expires without the Secretary having made such a final decision.

(B) DISMISSAL OF CERTAIN CIVIL ACTIONS.—If a civil action is filed against the Secretary with respect to any issue raised in the petition before the Secretary has taken final agency action on the petition within the meaning of subparagraph (A), the court shall dismiss without prejudice the action for failure to exhaust administrative remedies.

(C) ADMINISTRATIVE RECORD.—For purposes of judicial review related to the approval of an application for which a petition under paragraph (1) was submitted, the administrative record regarding any issue raised by the petition shall include—

(i) the petition filed under paragraph (1) and any supplements and comments thereto;

(ii) the Secretary's response to such petition, if issued; and

(iii) other information, as designated by the Secretary, related to the Secretary's determinations regarding the issues raised in such petition, as long as the information was considered by the agency no later than the date of final agency action as defined under subparagraph (2)(A), and regardless of whether the Secretary responded to the petition at or before the approval of the application at issue in the petition.

(3) ANNUAL REPORT ON DELAYS IN APPROVALS PER PETITIONS.—The Secretary shall annually submit to the Congress a report that specifies—

(A) the number of applications that were approved during the preceding 12–month period;

(B) the number of such applications whose effective dates were delayed by petitions referred to in paragraph (1) during such period;

(C) the number of days by which such applications were so delayed; and

(D) the number of such petitions that were submitted during such period.

(4) EXCEPTIONS.—

(A) This subsection does not apply to—

(i) a petition that relates solely to the timing of the approval of an application pursuant to subsection (j)(5)(B)(iv); or

(ii) a petition that is made by the sponsor of an application and that seeks only to have the Secretary take or refrain from taking any form of action with respect to that application.

(B) Paragraph (2) does not apply to a petition addressing issues concerning an application submitted pursuant to section 351(k) of the Public Health Service Act.

(5) DEFINITIONS.—

(A) APPLICATION.—For purposes of this subsection, the term "application" means an application submitted under subsection (b)(2) or (j) of the Act or 351(k) of the Public Health Service Act.

(B) PETITION.—For purposes of this subsection, other than paragraph (1) (A)(i), the term "petition" means a request described in paragraph (1)(A)(i).

(r) POSTMARKET DRUG SAFETY INFORMATION FOR PATIENTS AND PROVIDERS.—

(1) ESTABLISHMENT.—Not later than 1 year after the date of the enactment of the Food and Drug Administration Amendments Act of 2007, the Secretary shall improve the transparency of information about drugs and allow patients and health care providers better access to information about drugs by developing and maintaining an Internet Web site that—

(A) provides links to drug safety information listed in paragraph (2) for prescription drugs that are approved under this section or licensed under section 351 of the Public Health Service Act; and

(B) improves communication of drug safety information to patients and providers.

(2) INTERNET WEB SITE.—The Secretary shall carry out paragraph (1) by—

(A) developing and maintaining an accessible, consolidated Internet Web site with easily searchable drug safety information, including the information found on United States Government Internet Web sites, such as the United States National Library of Medicine's Daily Med and Medline Plus Web sites, in addition to other such Web sites maintained by the Secretary;

(B) ensuring that the information provided on the Internet Web site is comprehensive and includes, when available and appropriate—

(i) patient labeling and patient packaging inserts;

(ii) a link to a list of each drug, whether approved under this section or licensed under such section 351, for which a Medication Guide, as provided for under part 208 of title 21, Code of Federal Regulations (or any successor regulations), is required;

(iii) a link to the registry and results data bank provided for under subsections (i) and (j) of section 402 of the Public Health Service Act;

(iv) the most recent safety information and alerts issued by the Food and Drug Administration for drugs approved by the Secretary under this section, such as product recalls, warning letters, and import alerts;

(v) publicly available information about implemented RiskMAPs and risk evaluation and mitigation strategies under subsection (*o*);

(vi) guidance documents and regulations related to drug safety; and

(vii) other material determined appropriate by the Secretary;

(C) providing access to summaries of the assessed and aggregated data collected from the active surveillance infrastructure under subsection (k)(3) to provide information of known and serious side-effects for drugs approved under this section or licensed under such section 351;

(D) preparing, by 18 months after approval of a drug or after use of the drug by 10,000 individuals, whichever is later, a summary analysis of the adverse drug reaction reports received for the drug, including identification of any new risks not previously identified, potential new risks, or known risks reported in unusual number;

(E) enabling patients, providers, and drug sponsors to submit adverse event reports through the Internet Web site;

(F) providing educational materials for patients and providers about the appropriate means of disposing of expired, damaged, or unusable medications; and

(G) supporting initiatives that the Secretary determines to be useful to fulfill the purposes of the Internet Web site.

(3) POSTING OF DRUG LABELING.—The Secretary shall post on the Internet Web site established under paragraph (1) the approved professional labeling and any required patient labeling of a drug approved under this section or licensed under such section 351 not later than 21 days after the date the drug is approved or licensed, including in a supplemental application with respect to a labeling change.

(4) PRIVATE SECTOR RESOURCES.—To ensure development of the Internet Web site by the date described in paragraph (1), the Secretary may, on a temporary or permanent basis, implement systems or products developed by private entities.

(5) AUTHORITY FOR CONTRACTS.—The Secretary may enter into contracts with public and private entities to fulfill the requirements of this subsection.

(6) REVIEW.—The Advisory Committee on Risk Communication under section 567 shall, on a regular basis, perform a comprehensive review and evaluation

of the types of risk communication information provided on the Internet Web site established under paragraph (1) and, through other means, shall identify, clarify, and define the purposes and types of information available to facilitate the efficient flow of information to patients and providers, and shall recommend ways for the Food and Drug Administration to work with outside entities to help facilitate the dispensing of risk communication information to patients and providers.

(s) REFERRAL TO ADVISORY COMMITTEE.—Prior to the approval of a drug no active ingredient (including any ester or salt of the active ingredient) of which has been approved in any other application under this section or section 351 of the Public Health Service Act, the Secretary shall—

(1) refer such drug to a Food and Drug Administration advisory committee for review at a meeting of such advisory committee; or

(2) if the Secretary does not refer such a drug to a Food and Drug Administration advisory committee prior to the approval of the drug, provide in the action letter on the application for the drug a summary of the reasons why the Secretary did not refer the drug to an advisory committee prior to approval.

(t) DATABASE FOR AUTHORIZED GENERIC DRUGS.—

(1) IN GENERAL.—

(A) PUBLICATION.—The Commissioner shall—

(i) not later than 9 months after the date of the enactment of the Food and Drug Administration Amendments Act of 2007, publish a complete list on the Internet Web site of the Food and Drug Administration of all authorized generic drugs (including drug trade name, brand company manufacturer, and the date the authorized generic drug entered the market); and

(ii) update the list quarterly to include each authorized generic drug included in an annual report submitted to the Secretary by the sponsor of a listed drug during the preceding 3–month period.

(B) NOTIFICATION.—The Commissioner shall notify relevant Federal agencies, including the Centers for Medicare & Medicaid Services and the Federal Trade Commission, when the Commissioner first publishes the information described in subparagraph (A) that the information has been published and that the information will be updated quarterly.

(2) INCLUSION.—The Commissioner shall include in the list described in paragraph (1) each authorized generic drug included in an annual report submitted to the Secretary by the sponsor of a listed drug after January 1, 1999.

(3) AUTHORIZED GENERIC DRUG.—In this section, the term "authorized generic drug" means a listed drug (as that term is used in subsection (j)) that—

(A) has been approved under subsection (c); and

(B) is marketed, sold, or distributed directly or indirectly to retail class of trade under a different labeling, packaging (other than repackaging as the listed drug in blister packs, unit doses, or similar packaging for use in institutions), product code, labeler code, trade name, or trade mark than the listed drug.

(u) Certain Drugs Containing Single Enantiomers.—

(1) In general.—For purposes of subsections (c)(3)(E)(ii) and (j)(5)(F)(ii), if an application is submitted under subsection (b) for a non-racemic drug containing as an active ingredient (including any ester or salt of the active ingredient) a single enantiomer that is contained in a racemic drug approved in another application under subsection (b), the applicant may, in the application for such non-racemic drug, elect to have the single enantiomer not be considered the same active ingredient as that contained in the approved racemic drug, if—

(A)(i) the single enantiomer has not been previously approved except in the approved racemic drug; and

(ii) the application submitted under subsection (b) for such non-racemic drug—

(I) includes full reports of new clinical investigations (other than bioavailability studies)—

(aa) necessary for the approval of the application under subsections (c) and (d); and

(bb) conducted or sponsored by the applicant; and

(II) does not rely on any clinical investigations that are part of an application submitted under subsection (b) for approval of the approved racemic drug; and

(B) the application submitted under subsection (b) for such non-racemic drug is not submitted for approval of a condition of use—

(i) in a therapeutic category in which the approved racemic drug has been approved; or

(ii) for which any other enantiomer of the racemic drug has been approved.

(2) Limitation.—

(A) No approval in certain therapeutic categories.—Until the date that is 10 years after the date of approval of a non-racemic drug described in paragraph (1) and with respect to which the applicant has made the election provided for by such paragraph, the Secretary shall not approve such non-racemic drug for any condition of use in the therapeutic category in which the racemic drug has been approved.

(B) LABELING.—If applicable, the labeling of a non-racemic drug described in paragraph (1) and with respect to which the applicant has made the election provided for by such paragraph shall include a statement that the non-racemic drug is not approved, and has not been shown to be safe and effective, for any condition of use of the racemic drug.

(3) DEFINITION.—

(A) IN GENERAL.—For purposes of this subsection, the term "therapeutic category" means a therapeutic category identified in the list developed by the United States Pharmacopeia pursuant to section 1860D–4(b)(3)(C)(ii) of the Social Security Act and as in effect on the date of the enactment of this subsection.

(B) PUBLICATION BY SECRETARY.—The Secretary shall publish the list described in subparagraph (A) and may amend such list by regulation.

(4) AVAILABILITY.—The election referred to in paragraph (1) may be made only in an application that is submitted to the Secretary after the date of the enactment of this subsection and before October 1, 2017.

(v) ANTIBIOTIC DRUGS SUBMITTED BEFORE NOVEMBER 21, 1997.—

(1) ANTIBIOTIC DRUGS APPROVED BEFORE NOVEMBER 21, 1997.—

(A) IN GENERAL.—Notwithstanding any provision of the Food and Drug Administration Modernization Act of 1997 or any other provision of law, a sponsor of a drug that is the subject of an application described in subparagraph (B)(i) shall be eligible for, with respect to the drug, the 3–year exclusivity period referred to under clauses (iii) and (iv) of subsection (c)(3)(E) and under clauses (iii) and (iv) of subsection (j)(5)(F), subject to the requirements of such clauses, as applicable.

(B) APPLICATION; ANTIBIOTIC DRUG DESCRIBED.—

(i) APPLICATION.—An application described in this clause is an application for marketing submitted under this section after the date of the enactment of this subsection in which the drug that is the subject of the application contains an antibiotic drug described in clause (ii).

(ii) ANTIBIOTIC DRUG.—An antibiotic drug described in this clause is an antibiotic drug that was the subject of an application approved by the Secretary under section 507 of this Act (as in effect before November 21, 1997).

(2) ANTIBIOTIC DRUGS SUBMITTED BEFORE NOVEMBER 21, 1997, BUT NOT APPROVED.—

(A) IN GENERAL.—Notwithstanding any provision of the Food and Drug Administration Modernization Act of 1997 or any other provision of law, a sponsor of a drug that is the subject of an application described in subparagraph (B)(i) may elect to be eligible for, with respect to the drug—

(i)(I) the 3–year exclusivity period referred to under clauses (iii) and (iv) of subsection (c)(3)(E) and under clauses (iii) and (iv) of subsection (j)(5)(F), subject to the requirements of such clauses, as applicable; and

(II) the 5–year exclusivity period referred to under clause (ii) of subsection (c)(3)(E) and under clause (ii) of subsection (j)(5)(F), subject to the requirements of such clauses, as applicable; or(ii) a patent term extension under section 156 of title 35, United States Code, subject to the requirements of such section.

(B) APPLICATION; ANTIBIOTIC DRUG DESCRIBED.—

(i) APPLICATION.—An application described in this clause is an application for marketing submitted under this section after the date of the enactment of this subsection in which the drug that is the subject of the application contains an antibiotic drug described in clause (ii).

(ii) ANTIBIOTIC DRUG.—An antibiotic drug described in this clause is an antibiotic drug that was the subject of 1 or more applications received by the Secretary under section 507 of this Act (as in effect before November 21, 1997), none of which was approved by the Secretary under such section.

(3) LIMITATIONS.—

(A) EXCLUSIVITIES AND EXTENSIONS.—Paragraphs (1)(A) and (2)(A) shall not be construed to entitle a drug that is the subject of an approved application described in subparagraphs (1)(B)(i) or (2)(B)(i), as applicable, to any market exclusivities or patent extensions other than those exclusivities or extensions described in paragraph (1)(A) or (2)(A).

(B) CONDITIONS OF USE.—Paragraphs (1)(A) and (2)(A)(i) shall not apply to any condition of use for which the drug referred to in subparagraph (1)(B)(i) or (2)(B)(i), as applicable, was approved before the date of the enactment of this subsection.

(4) APPLICATION OF CERTAIN PROVISIONS.—Notwithstanding section 125, or any other provision, of the Food and Drug Administration Modernization Act of 1997, or any other provision of law, and subject to the limitations in paragraphs (1), (2), and (3), the provisions of the Drug Price Competition and Patent Term Restoration Act of 1984 shall apply to any drug subject to paragraph (1) or any drug with respect to which an election is made under paragraph (2)(A).

(w) DEADLINE FOR DETERMINATION ON CERTAIN PETITIONS.—The Secretary shall issue a final, substantive determination on a petition submitted pursuant to subsection (b) of section 314.161 of title 21, Code of Federal Regulations (or any successor regulations), no later than 270 days after the date the petition is submitted.

SEC. 505–1 [21 U.S.C. 355–1]. RISK EVALUATION AND MITIGATION STRATEGIES

(a) SUBMISSION OF PROPOSED STRATEGY.—

(1) INITIAL APPROVAL.—If the Secretary, in consultation with the office responsible for reviewing the drug and the office responsible for postapproval safety with respect to the drug, determines that a risk evaluation and mitigation strategy is necessary to ensure that the benefits of the drug outweigh the risks of the drug, and informs the person who submits such application of such determination, then such person shall submit to the Secretary as part of such application a proposed risk evaluation and mitigation strategy. In making such a determination, the Secretary shall consider the following factors:

(A) The estimated size of the population likely to use the drug involved.

(B) The seriousness of the disease or condition that is to be treated with the drug.

(C) The expected benefit of the drug with respect to such disease or condition.

(D) The expected or actual duration of treatment with the drug.

(E) The seriousness of any known or potential adverse events that may be related to the drug and the background incidence of such events in the population likely to use the drug.

(F) Whether the drug is a new molecular entity.

(2) POSTAPPROVAL REQUIREMENT.—

(A) IN GENERAL.—If the Secretary has approved a covered application (including an application approved before the effective date of this section) and did not when approving the application require a risk evaluation and mitigation strategy under paragraph (1), the Secretary, in consultation with the offices described in paragraph (1), may subsequently require such a strategy for the drug involved (including when acting on a supplemental application seeking approval of a new indication for use of the drug) if the Secretary becomes aware of new safety information and makes a determination that such a strategy is necessary to ensure that the benefits of the drug outweigh the risks of the drug.

(B) SUBMISSION OF PROPOSED STRATEGY.—Not later than 120 days after the Secretary notifies the holder of an approved covered application that the Secretary has made a determination under subparagraph (A) with respect to the drug involved, or within such other reasonable time as the Secretary requires to protect the public health, the holder shall submit to the Secretary a proposed risk evaluation and mitigation strategy.

(3) ABBREVIATED NEW DRUG APPLICATIONS.—The applicability of this section to an application under section 505(j) is subject to subsection (i).

(4) NON-DELEGATION.—Determinations by the Secretary under this subsection for a drug shall be made by individuals at or above the level of individuals empowered to approve a drug (such as division directors within the Center for Drug Evaluation and Research).

(b) DEFINITIONS.—For purposes of this section:

(1) ADVERSE DRUG EXPERIENCE.—The term "adverse drug experience" means any adverse event associated with the use of a drug in humans, whether or not considered drug related, including—

(A) an adverse event occurring in the course of the use of the drug in professional practice;

(B) an adverse event occurring from an overdose of the drug, whether accidental or intentional;

(C) an adverse event occurring from abuse of the drug;

(D) an adverse event occurring from withdrawal of the drug; and

(E) any failure of expected pharmacological action of the drug.

(2) COVERED APPLICATION.—The term "covered application" means an application referred to in section 505(p)(1)(A).

(3) NEW SAFETY INFORMATION.—The term "new safety information", with respect to a drug, means information derived from a clinical trial, an adverse event report, a postapproval study (including a study under section 505(*o*)(3)), or peer-reviewed biomedical literature; data derived from the postmarket risk identification and analysis system under section 505(k); or other scientific data deemed appropriate by the Secretary about—

(A) a serious risk or an unexpected serious risk associated with use of the drug that the Secretary has become aware of (that may be based on a new analysis of existing information) since the drug was approved, since the risk evaluation and mitigation strategy was required, or since the last assessment of the approved risk evaluation and mitigation strategy for the drug; or

(B) the effectiveness of the approved risk evaluation and mitigation strategy for the drug obtained since the last assessment of such strategy.

(4) SERIOUS ADVERSE DRUG EXPERIENCE.—The term "serious adverse drug experience" is an adverse drug experience that—

(A) results in—

(i) death;

(ii) an adverse drug experience that places the patient at immediate risk of death from the adverse drug experience as it occurred (not including an adverse drug experience that might have caused death had it occurred in a more severe form);

(iii) inpatient hospitalization or prolongation of existing hospitalization;

(iv) a persistent or significant incapacity or substantial disruption of the ability to conduct normal life functions; or

(v) a congenital anomaly or birth defect; or

(B) based on appropriate medical judgment, may jeopardize the patient and may require a medical or surgical intervention to prevent an outcome described under subparagraph (A).

(5) SERIOUS RISK.—The term "serious risk" means a risk of a serious adverse drug experience.

(6) SIGNAL OF A SERIOUS RISK.—The term "signal of a serious risk" means information related to a serious adverse drug experience associated with use of a drug and derived from—

(A) a clinical trial;

(B) adverse event reports;

(C) a postapproval study, including a study under section 505(*o*)(3);

(D) peer-reviewed biomedical literature;

(E) data derived from the postmarket risk identification and analysis system under section 505(k)(4); or

(F) other scientific data deemed appropriate by the Secretary.

(7) RESPONSIBLE PERSON.—The term "responsible person" means the person submitting a covered application or the holder of the approved such application.

(8) UNEXPECTED SERIOUS RISK.—The term "unexpected serious risk" means a serious adverse drug experience that is not listed in the labeling of a drug, or that may be symptomatically and pathophysiologically related to an adverse drug experience identified in the labeling, but differs from such adverse drug experience because of greater severity, specificity, or prevalence.

(c) CONTENTS.—A proposed risk evaluation and mitigation strategy under subsection (a) shall—

(1) include the timetable required under subsection (d); and

(2) to the extent required by the Secretary, in consultation with the office responsible for reviewing the drug and the office responsible for postapproval safety with respect to the drug, include additional elements described in subsections (e) and (f).

(d) MINIMAL STRATEGY.—For purposes of subsection (c)(1), the risk evaluation and mitigation strategy for a drug shall require a timetable for submission of assessments of the strategy that—

(1) includes an assessment, by the date that is 18 months after the strategy is initially approved;

(2) includes an assessment by the date that is 3 years after the strategy is initially approved;

(3) includes an assessment in the seventh year after the strategy is so approved; and

(4) subject to paragraphs (1), (2), and (3)—

(A) is at a frequency specified in the strategy;

(B) is increased or reduced in frequency as necessary as provided for in subsection (g)(4)(A); and

(C) is eliminated after the 3–year period described in paragraph (1) if the Secretary determines that serious risks of the drug have been adequately identified and assessed and are being adequately managed.

(e) ADDITIONAL POTENTIAL ELEMENTS OF STRATEGY.—

(1) IN GENERAL.—The Secretary, in consultation with the offices described in subsection (c)(2), may under such subsection require that the risk evaluation and mitigation strategy for a drug include 1 or more of the additional elements described in this subsection if the Secretary makes the determination required with respect to each element involved.

(2) MEDICATION GUIDE; PATIENT PACKAGE INSERT.—The risk evaluation and mitigation strategy for a drug may require that, as applicable, the responsible person develop for distribution to each patient when the drug is dispensed—

(A) a Medication Guide, as provided for under part 208 of title 21, Code of Federal Regulations (or any successor regulations); and

(B) a patient package insert, if the Secretary determines that such insert may help mitigate a serious risk of the drug.

(3) COMMUNICATION PLAN.—The risk evaluation and mitigation strategy for a drug may require that the responsible person conduct a communication plan to health care providers, if, with respect to such drug, the Secretary determines that such plan may support implementation of an element of the strategy (including under this paragraph). Such plan may include—

(A) sending letters to health care providers;

(B) disseminating information about the elements of the risk evaluation and mitigation strategy to encourage implementation by health care providers of components that apply to such health care providers, or to explain certain safety protocols (such as medical monitoring by periodic laboratory tests); or

(C) disseminating information to health care providers through professional societies about any serious risks of the drug and any protocol to assure safe use.

(f) PROVIDING SAFE ACCESS FOR PATIENTS TO DRUGS WITH KNOWN SERIOUS RISKS THAT WOULD OTHERWISE BE UNAVAILABLE.—

(1) ALLOWING SAFE ACCESS TO DRUGS WITH KNOWN SERIOUS RISKS.—The Secretary, in consultation with the offices described in subsection (c)(2), may require that the risk evaluation and mitigation strategy for a drug include such elements as are necessary to assure safe use of the drug, because of its inherent toxicity or potential harmfulness, if the Secretary determines that—

(A) the drug, which has been shown to be effective, but is associated with a serious adverse drug experience, can be approved only if, or would be withdrawn unless, such elements are required as part of such strategy to mitigate a specific serious risk listed in the labeling of the drug; and

(B) for a drug initially approved without elements to assure safe use, other elements under subsections (c), (d), and (e) are not sufficient to mitigate such serious risk.

(2) ASSURING ACCESS AND MINIMIZING BURDEN.—Such elements to assure safe use under paragraph (1) shall—

(A) be commensurate with the specific serious risk listed in the labeling of the drug;

(B) within 30 days of the date on which any element under paragraph (1) is imposed, be posted publicly by the Secretary with an explanation of how such elements will mitigate the observed safety risk;

(C) considering such risk, not be unduly burdensome on patient access to the drug, considering in particular—

(i) patients with serious or life-threatening diseases or conditions; and

(ii) patients who have difficulty accessing health care (such as patients in rural or medically underserved areas); and

(D) to the extent practicable, so as to minimize the burden on the health care delivery system—

(i) conform with elements to assure safe use for other drugs with similar, serious risks; and

(ii) be designed to be compatible with established distribution, procurement, and dispensing systems for drugs.

(3) ELEMENTS TO ASSURE SAFE USE.—The elements to assure safe use under paragraph (1) shall include 1 or more goals to mitigate a specific serious risk listed in the labeling of the drug and, to mitigate such risk, may require that—

(A) health care providers who prescribe the drug have particular training or experience, or are specially certified (the opportunity to obtain such training or certification with respect to the drug shall be available to any willing provider from a frontier area in a widely available training or certification method (including an on-line course or via mail) as approved by the Secretary at reasonable cost to the provider);

(B) pharmacies, practitioners, or health care settings that dispense the drug are specially certified (the opportunity to obtain such certification shall be available to any willing provider from a frontier area);

(C) the drug be dispensed to patients only in certain health care settings, such as hospitals;

(D) the drug be dispensed to patients with evidence or other documentation of safe-use conditions, such as laboratory test results;

(E) each patient using the drug be subject to certain monitoring; or

(F) each patient using the drug be enrolled in a registry.

(4) IMPLEMENTATION SYSTEM.—The elements to assure safe use under paragraph (1) that are described in subparagraphs (B), (C), and (D) of paragraph (3) may include a system through which the applicant is able to take reasonable steps to—

(A) monitor and evaluate implementation of such elements by health care providers, pharmacists, and other parties in the health care system who are responsible for implementing such elements; and

(B) work to improve implementation of such elements by such persons.

(5) EVALUATION OF ELEMENTS TO ASSURE SAFE USE.—The Secretary, through the Drug Safety and Risk Management Advisory Committee (or successor committee) of the Food and Drug Administration, shall—

(A) seek input from patients, physicians, pharmacists, and other health care providers about how elements to assure safe use under this subsection for 1 or more drugs may be standardized so as not to be—

(i) unduly burdensome on patient access to the drug; and

(ii) to the extent practicable, minimize the burden on the health care delivery system;

(B) at least annually, evaluate, for 1 or more drugs, the elements to assure safe use of such drug to assess whether the elements—

(i) assure safe use of the drug;

(ii) are not unduly burdensome on patient access to the drug; and

(iii) to the extent practicable, minimize the burden on the health care delivery system; and

(C) considering such input and evaluations—

(i) issue or modify agency guidance about how to implement the requirements of this subsection; and

(ii) modify elements under this subsection for 1 or more drugs as appropriate.

(6) ADDITIONAL MECHANISMS TO ASSURE ACCESS.—The mechanisms under section 561 to provide for expanded access for patients with serious or life-threatening diseases or conditions may be used to provide access for patients with a serious or life-threatening disease or condition, the treatment of which is not an approved use for the drug, to a drug that is subject to elements to assure safe use under this subsection. The Secretary shall promulgate regulations for how a physician may provide the drug under the mechanisms of section 561.

(7) [Deleted]

(8) LIMITATION.—No holder of an approved covered application shall use any element to assure safe use required by the Secretary under this subsection to block or delay approval of an application under section 505(b)(2) or (j) or to prevent application of such element under subsection (i)(1)(B) to a drug that is the subject of an abbreviated new drug application.

(g) ASSESSMENT AND MODIFICATION OF APPROVED STRATEGY.—

(1) VOLUNTARY ASSESSMENTS.—After the approval of a risk evaluation and mitigation strategy under subsection (a), the responsible person involved may, subject to paragraph (2), submit to the Secretary an assessment of the approved strategy for the drug involved at any time.

(2) REQUIRED ASSESSMENTS.—A responsible person shall submit an assessment of the approved risk evaluation and mitigation strategy for a drug—

(A) when submitting a supplemental application for a new indication for use under section 505(b) or under section 351 of the Public Health Service Act, unless the drug is not subject to section 503(b) and the risk evaluation and mitigation strategy for the drug includes only the timetable under subsection (d);

(B) when required by the strategy, as provided for in such timetable under subsection (d);

(C) within a time period to be determined by the Secretary, if the Secretary, in consultation with the offices described in subsection (c)(2), determines an assessment is needed to evaluate whether the approved strategy should be modified to—

(i) ensure the benefits of the drug outweigh the risks of the drug; or

(ii) minimize the burden on the health care delivery system of complying with the strategy.

(3) REQUIREMENTS FOR ASSESSMENTS.—An assessment under paragraph (1) or (2) of an approved risk evaluation and mitigation strategy for a drug shall include, with respect to each goal included in the strategy, an assessment of the extent to which the approved strategy, including each element of the strategy, is meeting the goal or whether 1 or more such goals or such elements should be modified.

(4) MODIFICATION.—

(A) ON INITIATIVE OF RESPONSIBLE PERSON.—After the approval of a risk evaluation and mitigation strategy by the Secretary, the responsible person may, at any time, submit to the Secretary a proposal to modify the approved strategy. Such proposal may propose the addition, modification, or removal of any goal or element of the approved strategy and shall include an adequate rationale to support such proposed addition, modification, or removal of any goal or element of the strategy.

(B) ON INITIATIVE OF SECRETARY.—After the approval of a risk evaluation and mitigation strategy by the Secretary, the Secretary may, at any time, require a responsible person to submit a proposed modification to the strategy within 120 days or within such reasonable time as the Secretary specifies, if the Secretary, in consultation with the offices described in subsection (c)(2), determines that 1 or more goals or elements should be added, modified, or removed from the approved strategy to—

(i) ensure the benefits of the drug outweigh the risks of the drug; or

(ii) minimize the burden on the health care delivery system of complying with the strategy.

(h) REVIEW OF PROPOSED STRATEGIES; REVIEW OF ASSESSMENTS AND MODIFICATIONS OF APPROVED STRATEGIES.—

(1) IN GENERAL.—The Secretary, in consultation with the offices described in subsection (c)(2), shall promptly review each proposed risk evaluation and mitigation strategy for a drug submitted under subsection (a) and each assessment of and proposed modification to an approved risk evaluation and mitigation strategy for a drug submitted under subsection (g), and, if necessary, promptly initiate discussions with the responsible person about such proposed strategy, assessment, or modification.

(2) ACTION.—

(A) IN GENERAL.—

(i) TIMEFRAME.—Unless the dispute resolution process described under paragraph (3) or (4) applies, and, except as provided in clause (ii) or clause (iii) below, the Secretary, in consultation with the offices described in subsection (c)(2), shall review and act on the proposed risk evaluation and mitigation strategy for a drug or any proposed modification to any required strategy within 180 days of receipt of the proposed strategy or modification.

(ii) MINOR MODIFICATIONS.—The Secretary shall review and act on a proposed minor modification, as defined by the Secretary in guidance, within 60 days of receipt of such modification.

(iii) REMS MODIFICATION DUE TO SAFETY LABEL CHANGES.—Not later than 60 days after the Secretary receives a proposed modification to an approved risk evaluation and mitigation strategy to conform the strategy to approved safety label changes, including safety labeling changes initiated by the sponsor in accordance with FDA regulatory requirements, or to a safety label change that the Secretary has directed the holder of the application to make pursuant to section 505(*o*)(4), the Secretary shall review and act on such proposed modification to the approved strategy.

(iv) GUIDANCE.—The Secretary shall establish, through guidance, that responsible persons may implement certain modifications to an approved risk evaluation and mitigation strategy following notification to the Secretary.

(B) INACTION.—An approved risk evaluation and mitigation strategy shall remain in effect until the Secretary acts, if the Secretary fails to act as provided under subparagraph (A).

(C) PUBLIC AVAILABILITY.—Upon acting on a proposed risk evaluation and mitigation strategy or proposed modification to a risk evaluation and mitigation strategy under subparagraph (A), the Secretary shall make publicly available an action letter describing the actions taken by the Secretary under such subparagraph (A).

(3) DISPUTE RESOLUTION AT INITIAL APPROVAL.—If a proposed risk evaluation and mitigation strategy is submitted under subsection (a)(1) in an application for initial approval of a drug and there is a dispute about the strategy, the responsible person shall use the major dispute resolution procedures as set forth in the letters described in section 101(c) of the Food and Drug Administration Amendments Act of 2007.

(4) DISPUTE RESOLUTION IN ALL OTHER CASES.—

(A) REQUEST FOR REVIEW.—

(i) IN GENERAL.—The responsible person may, after the sponsor is required to make a submission under subsection (a)(2) or (g), request in writing that a dispute about the strategy be reviewed by the Drug Safety Oversight Board under subsection (j), except that the determination of the Secretary to require a risk evaluation and mitigation strategy is not subject to review under this paragraph. The preceding sentence does not prohibit review under this paragraph of the particular elements of such a strategy.

(ii) SCHEDULING.—Upon receipt of a request under clause (i), the Secretary shall schedule the dispute involved for review under subparagraph (B) and, not later than 5 business days of scheduling the dispute for review, shall publish by posting on the Internet or otherwise a notice that the dispute will be reviewed by the Drug Safety Oversight Board.

(B) SCHEDULING REVIEW.—If a responsible person requests review under subparagraph (A), the Secretary—

(i) shall schedule the dispute for review at 1 of the next 2 regular meetings of the Drug Safety Oversight Board, whichever meeting date is more practicable; or

(ii) may convene a special meeting of the Drug Safety Oversight Board to review the matter more promptly, including to meet an action deadline on an application (including a supplemental application).

(C) AGREEMENT AFTER DISCUSSION OR ADMINISTRATIVE APPEALS.—

(i) FURTHER DISCUSSION OR ADMINISTRATIVE APPEALS.—A request for review under subparagraph (A) shall not preclude further discussions to reach agreement on the risk evaluation and mitigation strategy, and such a request shall not preclude the use of administrative appeals within the Food and Drug Administration to reach agreement on the strategy, including appeals as described in the letters described in section 101(c) of the Food and Drug Administration Amendments Act of 2007 for procedural or scientific matters involving the review of human drug applications and supplemental applications that cannot be resolved at the divisional level. At the time a review has been scheduled under subparagraph (B) and notice of such review has been posted, the responsible person shall either withdraw the request under subparagraph (A) or terminate the use of such administrative appeals.

(ii) AGREEMENT TERMINATES DISPUTE RESOLUTION.—At any time before a decision and order is issued under subparagraph (G), the Secretary (in consultation with the offices described in subsection (c)(2)) and the responsible person may reach an agreement on the risk evaluation and mitigation strategy through further discussion or administrative appeals, terminating the dispute resolution process, and the Secretary shall issue an action letter or order, as appropriate, that describes the strategy.

(D) MEETING OF THE BOARD.—At a meeting of the Drug Safety Oversight Board described in subparagraph (B), the Board shall—

(i) hear from both parties via written or oral presentation; and

(ii) review the dispute.

(E) RECORD OF PROCEEDINGS.—The Secretary shall ensure that the proceedings of any such meeting are recorded, transcribed, and made public within

90 days of the meeting. The Secretary shall redact the transcript to protect any trade secrets and other information that is exempted from disclosure under section 552 of title 5, United States Code, or section 552a of title 5, United States Code.

(F) Recommendation of the board.—Not later than 5 days after any such meeting, the Drug Safety Oversight Board shall provide a written recommendation on resolving the dispute to the Secretary. Not later than 5 days after the Board provides such written recommendation to the Secretary, the Secretary shall make the recommendation available to the public.

(G) Action by the secretary.—

(i) Action letter.—With respect to a proposal or assessment referred to in paragraph (1), the Secretary shall issue an action letter that resolves the dispute not later than the later of—

(I) the action deadline for the action letter on the application; or

(II) 7 days after receiving the recommendation of the Drug Safety Oversight Board.

(ii) Order.—With respect to an assessment of an approved risk evaluation and mitigation strategy under subsection (g)(1) or under any of subparagraphs (B) through (D) of subsection (g)(2), the Secretary shall issue an order, which shall be made public, that resolves the dispute not later than 7 days after receiving the recommendation of the Drug Safety Oversight Board.

(H) Inaction.—An approved risk evaluation and mitigation strategy shall remain in effect until the Secretary acts, if the Secretary fails to act as provided for under subparagraph (G).

(I) Effect on action deadline.—With respect to a proposal or assessment referred to in paragraph (1), the Secretary shall be considered to have met the action deadline for the action letter on the application if the responsible person requests the dispute resolution process described in this paragraph and if the Secretary has complied with the timing requirements of scheduling review by the Drug Safety Oversight Board, providing a written recommendation, and issuing an action letter under subparagraphs (B), (F), and (G), respectively.

(J) Disqualification.—No individual who is an employee of the Food and Drug Administration and who reviews a drug or who participated in an administrative appeal under subparagraph (C)(i) with respect to such drug may serve on the Drug Safety Oversight Board at a meeting under subparagraph (D) to review a dispute about the risk evaluation and mitigation strategy for such drug.

(K) Additional expertise.—The Drug Safety Oversight Board may add members with relevant expertise from the Food and Drug Administration, including the Office of Pediatrics, the Office of Women's Health, or the Office of Rare Diseases, or from other Federal public health or health care agencies, for a meeting under subparagraph (D) of the Drug Safety Oversight Board.

(5) USE OF ADVISORY COMMITTEES.—The Secretary may convene a meeting of 1 or more advisory committees of the Food and Drug Administration to—

(A) review a concern about the safety of a drug or class of drugs, including before an assessment of the risk evaluation and mitigation strategy or strategies of such drug or drugs is required to be submitted under subparagraph (B) or (C) of subsection (g)(2);

(B) review the risk evaluation and mitigation strategy or strategies of a drug or group of drugs; or

(C) review a dispute under paragraph (3) or (4).

(6) PROCESS FOR ADDRESSING DRUG CLASS EFFECTS.—

(A) IN GENERAL.—When a concern about a serious risk of a drug may be related to the pharmacological class of the drug, the Secretary, in consultation with the offices described in subsection (c)(2), may defer assessments of the approved risk evaluation and mitigation strategies for such drugs until the Secretary has convened 1 or more public meetings to consider possible responses to such concern.

(B) NOTICE.—If the Secretary defers an assessment under subparagraph (A), the Secretary shall—

(i) give notice of the deferral to the holder of the approved covered application not later than 5 days after the deferral;

(ii) publish the deferral in the Federal Register; and

(iii) give notice to the public of any public meetings to be convened under subparagraph (A), including a description of the deferral.

(C) PUBLIC MEETINGS.—Such public meetings may include—

(i) 1 or more meetings of the responsible person for such drugs;

(ii) 1 or more meetings of 1 or more advisory committees of the Food and Drug Administration, as provided for under paragraph (6); or

(iii) 1 or more workshops of scientific experts and other stakeholders.

(D) ACTION.—After considering the discussions from any meetings under subparagraph (A), the Secretary may—

(i) announce in the Federal Register a planned regulatory action, including a modification to each risk evaluation and mitigation strategy, for drugs in the pharmacological class;

(ii) seek public comment about such action; and

(iii) after seeking such comment, issue an order addressing such regulatory action.

(7) INTERNATIONAL COORDINATION.—The Secretary, in consultation with the offices described in subsection (c)(2), may coordinate the timetable for submission of assessments under subsection (d), or a study or clinical trial under section 505(*o*)(3), with efforts to identify and assess the serious risks of such drug by the marketing authorities of other countries whose drug approval and risk management processes the Secretary deems comparable to the drug approval and risk management processes of the United States. If the Secretary takes action to coordinate such timetable, the Secretary shall give notice to the responsible person.

(8) EFFECT.—Use of the processes described in paragraphs (6) and (7) shall not be the sole source of delay of action on an application or a supplement to an application for a drug.

(i) ABBREVIATED NEW DRUG APPLICATIONS.—

(1) IN GENERAL.—A drug that is the subject of an abbreviated new drug application under section 505(j) is subject to only the following elements of the risk evaluation and mitigation strategy required under subsection (a) for the applicable listed drug:

(A) A Medication Guide or patient package insert, if required under subsection (e) for the applicable listed drug.

(B) Elements to assure safe use, if required under subsection (f) for the listed drug. A drug that is the subject of an abbreviated new drug application and the listed drug shall use a single, shared system under subsection (f). The Secretary may waive the requirement under the preceding sentence for a drug that is the subject of an abbreviated new drug application, and permit the applicant to use a different, comparable aspect of the elements to assure safe use, if the Secretary determines that—

(i) the burden of creating a single, shared system outweighs the benefit of a single, system, taking into consideration the impact on health care providers, patients, the applicant for the abbreviated new drug application, and the holder of the reference drug product; or

(ii) an aspect of the elements to assure safe use for the applicable listed drug is claimed by a patent that has not expired or is a method or process that, as a trade secret, is entitled to protection, and the applicant for the abbreviated new drug application certifies that it has sought a license for use of an aspect of the elements to assure safe use for the applicable listed drug and that it was unable to obtain a license.

A certification under clause (ii) shall include a description of the efforts made by the applicant for the abbreviated new drug application to obtain a license. In a case described in clause (ii), the Secretary may seek to negotiate a voluntary agreement with the owner of the patent, method, or process for a license under which the applicant for such abbreviated new drug application may use an aspect of the elements to assure safe use, if required under subsection (f) for the applicable listed drug, that is claimed by a patent that has not expired or is a method or process that as a trade secret is entitled to protection.

(2) ACTION BY SECRETARY.—For an applicable listed drug for which a drug is approved under section 505(j), the Secretary—

(A) shall undertake any communication plan to health care providers required under subsection (e)(3) for the applicable listed drug; and

(B) shall inform the responsible person for the drug that is so approved if the risk evaluation and mitigation strategy for the applicable listed drug is modified.

(j) DRUG SAFETY OVERSIGHT BOARD.—

(1) IN GENERAL.—There is established a Drug Safety Oversight Board.

(2) COMPOSITION; MEETINGS.—The Drug Safety Oversight Board shall—

(A) be composed of scientists and health care practitioners appointed by the Secretary, each of whom is an employee of the Federal Government;

(B) include representatives from offices throughout the Food and Drug Administration, including the offices responsible for postapproval safety of drugs;

(C) include at least 1 representative each from the National Institutes of Health and the Department of Health and Human Services (other than the Food and Drug Administration);

(D) include such representatives as the Secretary shall designate from other appropriate agencies that wish to provide representatives; and

(E) meet at least monthly to provide oversight and advice to the Secretary on the management of important drug safety issues.

(k) WAIVER IN PUBLIC HEALTH EMERGENCIES.—The Secretary may waive any requirement of this section with respect to a qualified countermeasure (as defined in section 319F–1(a)(2) of the Public Health Service Act) to which a requirement under this section has been applied, if the Secretary determines that such waiver is required to mitigate the effects of, or reduce the severity of, the circumstances under which—

(1) a determination described in subparagraph (A), (B), or (C) of section 564(b)(1) has been made by the Secretary of Homeland Security, the Secretary of Defense, or the Secretary, respectively; or

(2) the identification of a material threat described in subparagraph (D) of section 564(b)(1) has been made pursuant to section 319F–2 of the Public Health Service Act.

SEC. 505A [21 U.S.C. 355a]. PEDIATRIC STUDIES OF DRUGS

(a) DEFINITIONS.—As used in this section, the term "pediatric studies" or "studies" means at least one clinical investigation (that, at the Secretary's discretion, may include pharmacokinetic studies) in pediatric age groups (including neonates in appropriate cases) in which a drug is anticipated to be used, and, at the discretion of the Secretary, may include preclinical studies.

(b) MARKET EXCLUSIVITY FOR NEW DRUGS.—

(1) IN GENERAL.—Except as provided in paragraph (2), if, prior to approval of an application that is submitted under section 505(b)(1), the Secretary determines that information relating to the use of a new drug in the pediatric population may produce health benefits in that population, the Secretary makes a written request for pediatric studies (which shall include a timeframe for completing such studies), the applicant agrees to the request, such studies are completed using appropriate formulations for each age group for which the study is requested within any such timeframe, and the reports thereof are submitted and accepted in accordance with subsection (d)(3)—

(A)(i)(I) the period referred to in subsection (c)(3)(E)(ii) of section 505, and in subsection (j)(5)(F)(ii) of such section, is deemed to be five years and six months rather than five years, and the references in subsections (c)(3)(E)(ii) and (j)(5)(F)(ii) of such section to four years, to forty-eight months, and to seven and one-half years are deemed to be four and one-half years, fifty-four months, and eight years, respectively; or

(II) the period referred to in clauses (iii) and (iv) of subsection (c)(3)(E) of such section, and in clauses (iii) and (iv) of subsection (j)(5)(F) of such section, is deemed to be three years and six months rather than three years; and

(ii) if the drug is designated under section 526 for a rare disease or condition, the period referred to in section 527(a) is deemed to be seven years and six months rather than seven years; and

(B)(i) if the drug is the subject of—

(I) a listed patent for which a certification has been submitted under subsection (b)(2)(A)(ii) or (j)(2)(A)(vii)(II) of section 505 and for which pediatric studies were submitted prior to the expiration of the patent (including any patent extensions); or

(II) a listed patent for which a certification has been submitted under subsections (b)(2)(A)(iii) or (j)(2)(A)(vii)(III) of section 505,

the period during which an application may not be approved under section 505(c)(3) or section 505(j)(5)(B) shall be extended by a period of six months after the date the patent expires (including any patent extensions); or

(ii) if the drug is the subject of a listed patent for which a certification has been submitted under subsection (b)(2)(A)(iv) or (j)(2)(A)(vii)(IV) of section 505, and in the patent infringement litigation resulting from the certification the court determines that the patent is valid and would be infringed, the period during which an application may not be approved under section 505(c)(3) or section 505(j)(5)(B) shall be extended by a period of six months after the date the patent expires (including any patent extensions).

(2) EXCEPTION.—The Secretary shall not extend the period referred to in paragraph (1)(A) or (1)(B) if the determination made under subsection (d)(3) is made later than 9 months prior to the expiration of such period.

(c) MARKET EXCLUSIVITY FOR ALREADY-MARKETED DRUGS.—

(1) IN GENERAL.—Except as provided in paragraph (2), if the Secretary determines that information relating to the use of an approved drug in the pediatric population may produce health benefits in that population and makes a written request to the holder of an approved application under section 505(b)(1) for pediatric studies (which shall include a timeframe for completing such studies), the holder agrees to the request, such studies are completed using appropriate formulations for each age group for which the study is requested within any such timeframe, and the reports thereof are submitted and accepted in accordance with subsection (d)(3)—

(A)(i)(I) the period referred to in subsection (c)(3)(E)(ii) of section 505, and in subsection (j)(5)(F)(ii) of such section, is deemed to be five years and six months rather than five years, and the references in subsections (c)(3)(E)(ii) and (j)(5)(F)(ii) of such section to four years, to forty-eight months, and to seven and one-half years are deemed to be four and one-half years, fifty-four months, and eight years, respectively; or

(II) the period referred to in clauses (iii) and (iv) of subsection (c)(3)(D) of such section, and in clauses (iii) and (iv) of subsection (j)(5)(F) of such section, is deemed to be three years and six months rather than three years; and

(ii) if the drug is designated under section 526 for a rare disease or condition, the period referred to in section 527(a) is deemed to be seven years and six months rather than seven years; and

(B)(i) if the drug is the subject of—

(I) a listed patent for which a certification has been submitted under subsection (b)(2)(A)(ii) or (j)(2)(A)(vii)(II) of section 505 and for which pediatric studies were submitted prior to the expiration of the patent (including any patent extensions); or

(II) a listed patent for which a certification has been submitted under subsection (b)(2)(A)(iii) or (j)(2)(A)(vii)(III) of section 505, the period during which an application may not be approved under section 505(c)(3) or section 505(j)(5)(B)(ii) shall be extended by a period of six months after the date the patent expires (including any patent extensions); or

(ii) if the drug is the subject of a listed patent for which a certification has been submitted under subsection (b)(2)(A)(iv) or (j)(2)(A)(vii)(IV) of section 505, and in the patent infringement litigation resulting from the certification the court determines that the patent is valid and would be infringed, the period during which an application may not be approved under section 505(c)(3) or section 505(j)(5)(B) shall be extended by a period of six months after the date the patent expires (including any patent extensions).

(2) EXCEPTION.—The Secretary shall not extend the period referred to in paragraph (1)(A) or (1)(B) if the determination made under subsection (d)(3) is made later than 9 months prior to the expiration of such period.

(d) CONDUCT OF PEDIATRIC STUDIES.—

(1) REQUEST FOR STUDIES.—

(A) IN GENERAL.—The Secretary may, after consultation with the sponsor of an application for an investigational new drug under section 505(i), the sponsor of an application for a new drug under section 505(b)(1), or the holder of an approved application for a drug under section 505(b)(1), issue to the sponsor or holder a written request for the conduct of pediatric studies for such drug. In issuing such request, the Secretary shall take into account adequate representation of children of ethnic and racial minorities. Such request to conduct pediatric studies shall be in writing and shall include a timeframe for such studies and a request to the sponsor or holder to propose pediatric labeling resulting from such studies. If a request under this subparagraph does not request studies in neonates, such request shall include a statement describing the rationale for not requesting studies in neonates.

(B) SINGLE WRITTEN REQUEST.—A single written request—

(i) may relate to more than one use of a drug; and

(ii) may include uses that are both approved and unapproved.

(2) WRITTEN REQUEST FOR PEDIATRIC STUDIES.—

(A) REQUEST AND RESPONSE.—

(i) IN GENERAL.—If the Secretary makes a written request for pediatric studies (including neonates, as appropriate) under subsection (b) or (c), the applicant or holder, not later than 180 days after receiving the written request, shall respond to the Secretary as to the intention of the applicant or holder to act on the request by—

(I) indicating when the pediatric studies will be initiated, if the applicant or holder agrees to the request; or

(II) indicating that the applicant or holder does not agree to the request and stating the reasons for declining the request.

(ii) Disagree with request.—If, on or after the date of the enactment of the Best Pharmaceuticals for Children Act of 2007, the applicant or holder does not agree to the request on the grounds that it is not possible to develop the appropriate pediatric formulation, the applicant or holder shall submit to the Secretary the reasons such pediatric formulation cannot be developed.

(B) Adverse event reports.—An applicant or holder that, on or after the date of the enactment of the Best Pharmaceuticals for Children Act of 2007, agrees to the request for such studies shall provide the Secretary, at the same time as the submission of the reports of such studies, with all postmarket adverse event reports regarding the drug that is the subject of such studies and are available prior to submission of such reports.

(3) Meeting the studies requirement.—Not later than 180 days after the submission of the reports of the studies, the Secretary shall accept or reject such reports and so notify the sponsor or holder. The Secretary's only responsibility in accepting or rejecting the reports shall be to determine, within the 180–day period, whether the studies fairly respond to the written request, have been conducted in accordance with commonly accepted scientific principles and protocols, and have been reported in accordance with the requirements of the Secretary for filing.

(4) Effect of subsection.—Nothing in this subsection alters or amends section 301(j) of this Act or section 552 of title 5 or section 1905 of title 18, United States Code.

(5) Consultation.—With respect to a drug that is a qualified countermeasure (as defined in section 319F–1 of the Public Health Service Act), a security countermeasure (as defined in section 319F–2 of the Public Health Service Act), or a qualified pandemic or epidemic product (as defined in section 319F–3 of the Public Health Service Act), the Secretary shall solicit input from the Assistant Secretary for Preparedness and Response regarding the need for and, from the Director of the Biomedical Advanced Research and Development Authority regarding the conduct of, pediatric studies under this section.

(e) Notice of Determinations on Studies Requirement.—

(1) In general.—The Secretary shall publish a notice of any determination, made on or after the date of the enactment of the Best Pharmaceuticals for Children Act of 2007, that the requirements of subsection (d) have been met and that submissions and approvals under subsection (b)(2) or (j) of section 505 for a drug will be subject to the provisions of this section. Such notice shall be published not later than 30 days after the date of the Secretary's determination regarding

market exclusivity and shall include a copy of the written request made under subsection (b) or (c).

(2) IDENTIFICATION OF CERTAIN DRUGS.—The Secretary shall publish a notice identifying any drug for which, on or after the date of the enactment of the Best Pharmaceuticals for Children Act of 2007, a pediatric formulation was developed, studied, and found to be safe and effective in the pediatric population (or specified subpopulation) if the pediatric formulation for such drug is not introduced onto the market within one year after the date that the Secretary publishes the notice described in paragraph (1). Such notice identifying such drug shall be published not later than 30 days after the date of the expiration of such one year period.

(f) INTERNAL REVIEW OF WRITTEN REQUESTS AND PEDIATRIC STUDIES.—

(1) INTERNAL REVIEW.—The Secretary shall utilize the internal review committee established under section 505C to review all written requests issued on or after the date of the enactment of the Best Pharmaceuticals for Children Act of 2007, in accordance with paragraph (2).

(2) REVIEW OF WRITTEN REQUESTS.—The committee referred to in paragraph (1) shall review all written requests issued pursuant to this section prior to being issued.

(3) REVIEW OF PEDIATRIC STUDIES.—The committee referred to in paragraph (1) may review studies conducted pursuant to this section to make a recommendation to the Secretary whether to accept or reject such reports under subsection (d)(3).

(4) ACTIVITY BY COMMITTEE.—The committee referred to in paragraph (1) may operate using appropriate members of such committee and need not convene all members of the committee.

(5) DOCUMENTATION OF COMMITTEE ACTION.—For each drug, the committee referred to in paragraph (1) shall document, for each activity described in paragraph (2) or (3), which members of the committee participated in such activity.

(6) TRACKING PEDIATRIC STUDIES AND LABELING CHANGES.—The Secretary, in consultation with the committee referred to in paragraph (1), shall track and make available to the public, in an easily accessible manner, including through posting on the Web site of the Food and Drug Administration—

(A) the number of studies conducted under this section and under section 409I of the Public Health Service Act;

(B) the specific drugs and drug uses, including labeled and off-labeled indications, studied under such sections;

(C) the types of studies conducted under such sections, including trial design, the number of pediatric patients studied, and the number of centers and countries involved;

(D) the number of pediatric formulations developed and the number of pediatric formulations not developed and the reasons such formulations were not developed;

(E) the labeling changes made as a result of studies conducted under such sections;

(F) an annual summary of labeling changes made as a result of studies conducted under such sections for distribution pursuant to subsection (k)(2); and

(G) information regarding reports submitted on or after the date of the enactment of the Best Pharmaceuticals for Children Act of 2007.

(g) LIMITATIONS.—Notwithstanding subsection (c)(2), a drug to which the six-month period under subsection (b) or (c) has already been applied—

(1) may receive an additional six-month period under subsection (c)(1)(A)(i) (II) for a supplemental application if all other requirements under this section are satisfied, except that such drug may not receive any additional such period under subsection (c)(1)(B); and

(2) may not receive any additional such period under subsection (c)(1)(A)(ii).

(h) RELATIONSHIP TO PEDIATRIC RESEARCH REQUIREMENTS.—Exclusivity under this section shall only be granted for the completion of a study or studies that are the subject of a written request and for which reports are submitted and accepted in accordance with subsection (d)(3). Written requests under this section may consist of a study or studies required under section 505B.

(i) LABELING CHANGES.—

(1) PRIORITY STATUS FOR PEDIATRIC APPLICATIONS AND SUPPLEMENTS.—Any application or supplement to an application under section 505 proposing a labeling change as a result of any pediatric study conducted pursuant to this section—

(A) shall be considered to be a priority application or supplement; and

(B) shall be subject to the performance goals established by the Commissioner for priority drugs.

(2) DISPUTE RESOLUTION.—

(A) REQUEST FOR LABELING CHANGE AND FAILURE TO AGREE.—If, on or after the date of the enactment of the Best Pharmaceuticals for Children Act of 2007, the Commissioner determines that the sponsor and the Commissioner have been unable to reach agreement on appropriate changes to the labeling for the drug that is the subject of the application, not later than 180 days after the date of submission of the application—

(i) the Commissioner shall request that the sponsor of the application make any labeling change that the Commissioner determines to be appropriate; and

256

(ii) if the sponsor of the application does not agree within 30 days after the Commissioner's request to make a labeling change requested by the Commissioner, the Commissioner shall refer the matter to the Pediatric Advisory Committee.

(B) ACTION BY THE PEDIATRIC ADVISORY COMMITTEE.—Not later than 90 days after receiving a referral under subparagraph (A)(ii), the Pediatric Advisory Committee shall—

(i) review the pediatric study reports; and

(ii) make a recommendation to the Commissioner concerning appropriate labeling changes, if any.

(C) CONSIDERATION OF RECOMMENDATIONS.—The Commissioner shall consider the recommendations of the Pediatric Advisory Committee and, if appropriate, not later than 30 days after receiving the recommendation, make a request to the sponsor of the application to make any labeling change that the Commissioner determines to be appropriate.

(D) MISBRANDING.—If the sponsor of the application, within 30 days after receiving a request under subparagraph (C), does not agree to make a labeling change requested by the Commissioner, the Commissioner may deem the drug that is the subject of the application to be misbranded.

(E) NO EFFECT ON AUTHORITY.—Nothing in this subsection limits the authority of the United States to bring an enforcement action under this Act when a drug lacks appropriate pediatric labeling. Neither course of action (the Pediatric Advisory Committee process or an enforcement action referred to in the preceding sentence) shall preclude, delay, or serve as the basis to stay the other course of action.

(j) OTHER LABELING CHANGES.—If, on or after the date of the enactment of the Best Pharmaceuticals for Children Act of 2007, the Secretary determines that a pediatric study conducted under this section does or does not demonstrate that the drug that is the subject of the study is safe and effective, including whether such study results are inconclusive, in pediatric populations or subpopulations, the Secretary shall order the labeling of such product to include information about the results of the study and a statement of the Secretary's determination.

(k) DISSEMINATION OF PEDIATRIC INFORMATION.—

(1) IN GENERAL.—Not later than 210 days after the date of submission of a report on a pediatric study under this section, the Secretary shall make available to the public the medical, statistical, and clinical pharmacology reviews of pediatric studies conducted under subsection (b) or (c).

(2) DISSEMINATION OF INFORMATION REGARDING LABELING CHANGES.—Beginning on the date of the enactment of the Best Pharmaceuticals for Children Act of 2007, the Secretary shall include as a requirement of a written request that the

sponsors of the studies that result in labeling changes that are reflected in the annual summary developed pursuant to subsection (f)(6)(F) distribute, at least annually (or more frequently if the Secretary determines that it would be beneficial to the public health), such information to physicians and other health care providers.

(3) EFFECT OF SUBSECTION.—Nothing in this subsection alters or amends section 301(j) of this Act or section 552 of title 5 or section 1905 of title 18, United States Code.

(*l*) ADVERSE EVENT REPORTING.—

(1) REPORTING IN FIRST 18–MONTH PERIOD.—Beginning on the date of the enactment of the Best Pharmaceuticals for Children Act of 2007, during the 18–month period beginning on the date a labeling change is approved pursuant to subsection (i), the Secretary shall ensure that all adverse event reports that have been received for such drug (regardless of when such report was received) are referred to the Office of Pediatric Therapeutics established under section 6 of the Best Pharmaceuticals for Children Act (Public Law 107–109). In considering the reports, the Director of such Office shall provide for the review of the reports by the Pediatric Advisory Committee, including obtaining any recommendations of such Committee regarding whether the Secretary should take action under this Act in response to such reports.

(2) REPORTING IN SUBSEQUENT PERIODS.—Following the 18–month period described in paragraph (1), the Secretary shall, as appropriate, refer to the Office of Pediatric Therapeutics all pediatric adverse event reports for a drug for which a pediatric study was conducted under this section. In considering such reports, the Director of such Office may provide for the review of such reports by the Pediatric Advisory Committee, including obtaining any recommendation of such Committee regarding whether the Secretary should take action in response to such reports.

(3) PRESERVATION OF AUTHORITY.—Nothing in this subsection shall prohibit the Office of Pediatric Therapeutics from providing for the review of adverse event reports by the Pediatric Advisory Committee prior to the 18–month period referred to in paragraph (1), if such review is necessary to ensure safe use of a drug in a pediatric population.

(4) EFFECT.—The requirements of this subsection shall supplement, not supplant, other review of such adverse event reports by the Secretary.

(m) CLARIFICATION OF INTERACTION OF MARKET EXCLUSIVITY UNDER THIS SECTION AND MARKET EXCLUSIVITY AWARDED TO AN APPLICANT FOR APPROVAL OF A DRUG UNDER SECTION 505(j).—If a 180–day period under section 505(j)(5)(B)(iv) overlaps with a 6–month exclusivity period under this section, so that the applicant for approval of a drug under section 505(j) entitled to the 180–day period under that section loses a portion of the 180–day period to which the applicant is entitled for the drug, the 180–day period shall be extended from—

(1) the date on which the 180–day period would have expired by the number of days of the overlap, if the 180–day period would, but for the application of this subsection, expire after the 6–month exclusivity period; or

(2) the date on which the 6–month exclusivity period expires, by the number of days of the overlap if the 180–day period would, but for the application of this subsection, expire during the six-month exclusivity period.

(n) REFERRAL IF PEDIATRIC STUDIES NOT SUBMITTED.—

(1) IN GENERAL.—Beginning on the date of the enactment of the Best Pharmaceuticals for Children Act of 2007, if pediatric studies of a drug have not been submitted by the date specified in the written request issued or if the applicant or holder does not agree to the request under subsection (d) and if the Secretary, through the committee established under section 505C, determines that there is a continuing need for information relating to the use of the drug in the pediatric population (including neonates, as appropriate), the Secretary shall carry out the following:

(A) for a drug for which a listed patent has not expired, or for which a period of exclusivity eligible for extension under subsection (b)(1) or (c)(1) of this section or under subsection (m)(2) or (m)(3) of section 351 of the Public Health Service Act has not ended, make a determination regarding whether an assessment shall be required to be submitted under section 505B(b).

(B) for a drug that has no expired listed patents and for which no unexpired periods of exclusivity eligible for extension under subsection (b)(1) or (c)(1) of this section or under subsection (m)(2) or (m)(3) of section 351 of the Public Health Service Act apply, the Secretary shall refer the drug for inclusion on the list established under section 409I of the Public Health Service Act for the conduct of studies.

(C) for a drug that is a qualified countermeasure (as defined in section 319F–1 of the Public Health Service Act), a security countermeasure (as defined in section 319F–2 of the Public Health Service Act), or a qualified pandemic or epidemic product (as defined in section 319F–3 of such Act), in addition to any action with respect to such drug under subparagraph (A) or (B), the Secretary shall notify the Assistant Secretary for Preparedness and Response and the Director of the Biomedical Advanced Research and Development Authority of all pediatric studies in the written request issued by the Commissioner of Food and Drugs.

(2) PUBLIC NOTICE.—The Secretary shall give the public notice of a decision under paragraph (1)(A) not to require an assessment under section 505B and the basis for such decision.

(3) EFFECT OF SUBSECTION.—Nothing in this subsection alters or amends section 301(j) of this Act or section 552 of title 5 or section 1905 of title 18, United States Code.

(*o*) PROMPT APPROVAL OF DRUGS UNDER SECTION 505(J) WHEN PEDIATRIC INFORMATION IS ADDED TO LABELING.—

(1) GENERAL RULE.—A drug for which an application has been submitted or approved under section 505(j) shall not be considered ineligible for approval under that section or misbranded under section 502 on the basis that the labeling of the drug omits a pediatric indication or any other aspect of labeling pertaining to pediatric use when the omitted indication or other aspect is protected by patent or by exclusivity under clause (iii) or (iv) of section 505(j)(5)(F).

(2) LABELING.—Notwithstanding clauses (iii) and (iv) of section 505(j)(5) (F), the Secretary may require that the labeling of a drug approved under section 505(j) that omits a pediatric indication or other aspect of labeling as described in paragraph (1) include—

(A) a statement that, because of marketing exclusivity for a manufacturer—

(i) the drug is not labeled for pediatric use; or

(ii) in the case of a drug for which there is an additional pediatric use not referred to in paragraph (1), the drug is not labeled for the pediatric use under paragraph (1); and

(B) a statement of any appropriate pediatric contraindications, warnings, precautions, or other information that the Secretary considers necessary to assure safe use.

(3) PRESERVATION OF PEDIATRIC EXCLUSIVITY AND OTHER PROVISIONS.—This subsection does not affect—

(A) the availability or scope of exclusivity under this section;

(B) the availability or scope of exclusivity under section 505 for pediatric formulations;

(C) the question of the eligibility for approval of any application under section 505(j) that omits any other conditions of approval entitled to exclusivity under clause (iii) or (iv) of section 505(j)(5)(F); or

(D) except as expressly provided in paragraphs (1) and (2), the operation of section 505.

(p) INSTITUTE OF MEDICINE STUDY.—Not later than 3 years after the date of the enactment of the Best Pharmaceuticals for Children Act of 2007,[36] the Secretary shall enter into a contract with the Institute of Medicine to conduct a study and report to Congress regarding the written requests made and the studies conducted pursuant to this section. The Institute of Medicine may devise an appropriate mechanism to review a representative sample of requests made and studies conducted pursuant to this section in order to conduct such study. Such study shall—

36. Pub. L. No. 110–85, tit. V, 121 Stat. 823, 876–90, which was enacted September 27, 2007.

(1) review such representative written requests issued by the Secretary since 1997 under subsections (b) and (c);

(2) review and assess such representative pediatric studies conducted under subsections (b) and (c) since 1997 and labeling changes made as a result of such studies;

(3) review the use of extrapolation for pediatric subpopulations, the use of alternative endpoints for pediatric populations, neonatal assessment tools, and ethical issues in pediatric clinical trials;

(4) review and assess the number and importance of biological products for children that are being tested as a result of the amendments made by the Biologics Price Competition and Innovation Act of 2009 and the importance for children, health care providers, parents, and others of labeling changes made as a result of such testing;

(5) review and assess the number, importance, and prioritization of any biological products that are not being tested for pediatric use; and

(6) offer recommendations for ensuring pediatric testing of biological products, including consideration of any incentives, such as those provided under this section or section 351(m) of the Public Health Service Act.

SEC. 505B [21 U.S.C. 355c]. RESEARCH INTO PEDIATRIC USES FOR DRUGS AND BIOLOGICAL PRODUCTS

(a) NEW DRUGS AND BIOLOGICAL PRODUCTS.—

(1) IN GENERAL.—A person that submits, on or after the date of the enactment of the Pediatric Research Equity Act of 2007, an application (or supplement to an application) for a drug—

(A) under section 505 for a new active ingredient, new indication, new dosage form, new dosing regimen, or new route of administration, or

(B) under section 351 of the Public Health Service Act (42 U.S.C. 262) for a new active ingredient, new indication, new dosage form, new dosing regimen, or new route of administration,

shall submit with the application the assessments described in paragraph (2).

(2) ASSESSMENTS.—

(A) IN GENERAL.—The assessments referred to in paragraph (1) shall contain data, gathered using appropriate formulations for each age group for which the assessment is required, that are adequate—

(i) to assess the safety and effectiveness of the drug or the biological product for the claimed indications in all relevant pediatric subpopulations; and

(ii) to support dosing and administration for each pediatric subpopulation for which the drug or the biological product is safe and effective.

(B) SIMILAR COURSE OF DISEASE OR SIMILAR EFFECT OF DRUG OR BIOLOGICAL PRODUCT.—

(i) IN GENERAL.—If the course of the disease and the effects of the drug are sufficiently similar in adults and pediatric patients, the Secretary may conclude that pediatric effectiveness can be extrapolated from adequate and well-controlled studies in adults, usually supplemented with other information obtained in pediatric patients, such as pharmacokinetic studies.

(ii) EXTRAPOLATION BETWEEN AGE GROUPS.—A study may not be needed in each pediatric age group if data from one age group can be extrapolated to another age group.

(iii) INFORMATION ON EXTRAPOLATION.—A brief documentation of the scientific data supporting the conclusion under clauses (i) and (ii) shall be included in any pertinent reviews for the application under section 505 of this Act or section 351 of the Public Health Service Act (42 U.S.C. 262).

(3) DEFERRAL.—

(A) IN GENERAL.—On the initiative of the Secretary or at the request of the applicant, the Secretary may defer submission of some or all assessments required under paragraph (1) until a specified date after approval of the drug or issuance of the license for a biological product if—

(i) the Secretary finds that—

(I) the drug or biological product is ready for approval for use in adults before pediatric studies are complete;

(II) pediatric studies should be delayed until additional safety or effectiveness data have been collected; or

(III) there is another appropriate reason for deferral; and

(ii) the applicant submits to the Secretary—

(I) certification of the grounds for deferring the assessments;

(II)[37] a pediatric study plan as described in subsection (e);

(III) evidence that the studies are being conducted or will be conducted with due diligence and at the earliest possible time; and

(IV) a timeline for the completion of such studies.

---

37. Subsection (a)(3)(A)(ii)(II) was amended by Pub. L. No. 112–144, § 506(b)(1), and according to § 506(c) of that law, this provision becomes effective 180 calendar days after the July 9, 2012 date of enactment.

(B) Deferral extension.—

(i) In general.—On the initiative of the Secretary or at the request of the applicant, the Secretary may grant an extension of a deferral approved under subparagraph (A) for submission of some or all assessments required under paragraph (1) if—

(I) the Secretary determines that the conditions described in subclause (II) or (III) of subparagraph (A)(i) continue to be met; and

(II) the applicant submits a new timeline under subparagraph (A)(ii)(IV) and any significant updates to the information required under subparagraph (A)(ii).

(ii) Timing and information.—If the deferral extension under this subparagraph is requested by the applicant, the applicant shall submit the deferral extension request containing the information described in this subparagraph not less than 90 days prior to the date that the deferral would expire. The Secretary shall respond to such request not later than 45 days after the receipt of such letter. If the Secretary grants such an extension, the specified date shall be the extended date. The sponsor of the required assessment under paragraph (1) shall not be issued a letter described in subsection (d) unless the specified or extended date of submission for such required studies has passed or if the request for an extension is pending. For a deferral that has expired prior to the date of enactment of the Food and Drug Administration Safety and Innovation Act[38] or that will expire prior to 270 days after the date of enactment of such Act, a deferral extension shall be requested by an applicant not later than 180 days after the date of enactment of such Act. The Secretary shall respond to any such request as soon as practicable, but not later than 1 year after the date of enactment of such Act. Nothing in this clause shall prevent the Secretary from updating the status of a study or studies publicly if components of such study or studies are late or delayed.

(C) Annual review.—

(i) In general.—On an annual basis following the approval of a deferral under subparagraph (A), the applicant shall submit to the Secretary the following information:

(I) Information detailing the progress made in conducting pediatric studies.

(II) If no progress has been made in conducting such studies, evidence and documentation that such studies will be conducted with due diligence and at the earliest possible time.

38. Pub. L. No. 112–144, 126 Stat. 993, which was enacted July 9, 2012.

(III) Projected completion date for pediatric studies.

(IV) The reason or reasons why a deferral or deferral extension continues to be necessary.

(ii) PUBLIC AVAILABILITY.—Not later than 90 days after the submission to the Secretary of the information submitted through the annual review under clause (i), the Secretary shall make available to the public in an easily accessible manner, including through the Internet Web site of the Food and Drug Administration—

(I) such information;

(II) the name of the applicant for the product subject to the assessment;

(III) the date on which the product was approved; and

(IV) the date of each deferral or deferral extension under this paragraph for the product.

(4) WAIVERS.—

(A) FULL WAIVER.—On the initiative of the Secretary or at the request of an applicant, the Secretary shall grant a full waiver, as appropriate, of the requirement to submit assessments for a drug or biological product under this subsection if the applicant certifies and the Secretary finds that—

(i) necessary studies are impossible or highly impracticable (because, for example, the number of patients is so small or the patients are geographically dispersed);

(ii) there is evidence strongly suggesting that the drug or biological product would be ineffective or unsafe in all pediatric age groups; or

(iii) the drug or biological product—

(I) does not represent a meaningful therapeutic benefit over existing therapies for pediatric patients; and

(II) is not likely to be used in a substantial number of pediatric patients.

(B) PARTIAL WAIVER.—On the initiative of the Secretary or at the request of an applicant, the Secretary shall grant a partial waiver, as appropriate, of the requirement to submit assessments for a drug or biological product under this subsection with respect to a specific pediatric age group if the applicant certifies and the Secretary finds that—

(i) necessary studies are impossible or highly impracticable (because, for example, the number of patients in that age group is so small or patients in that age group are geographically dispersed);

(ii) there is evidence strongly suggesting that the drug or biological product would be ineffective or unsafe in that age group;

(iii) the drug or biological product—

(I) does not represent a meaningful therapeutic benefit over existing therapies for pediatric patients in that age group; and

(II) is not likely to be used by a substantial number of pediatric patients in that age group; or

(iv) the applicant can demonstrate that reasonable attempts to produce a pediatric formulation necessary for that age group have failed.

(C) PEDIATRIC FORMULATION NOT POSSIBLE.—If a partial waiver is granted on the ground that it is not possible to develop a pediatric formulation, the waiver shall cover only the pediatric groups requiring that formulation. An applicant seeking such a partial waiver shall submit to the Secretary documentation detailing why a pediatric formulation cannot be developed and, if the waiver is granted, the applicant's submission shall promptly be made available to the public in an easily accessible manner, including through posting on the Web site of the Food and Drug Administration.

(D) LABELING REQUIREMENT.—If the Secretary grants a full or partial waiver because there is evidence that a drug or biological product would be ineffective or unsafe in pediatric populations, the information shall be included in the labeling for the drug or biological product.

(b) MARKETED DRUGS AND BIOLOGICAL PRODUCTS.—

(1) IN GENERAL.—The Secretary may (by order in the form of a letter) require the sponsor or holder of an approved application for a drug under section 505 or the holder of a license for a biological product under section 351 of the Public Health Service Act to submit by a specified date the assessments described in subsection (a)(2), if the Secretary finds that—

(A)(i) the drug or biological product is used for a substantial number of pediatric patients for the labeled indications; and

(ii) adequate pediatric labeling could confer a benefit on pediatric patients;

(B) there is reason to believe that the drug or biological product would represent a meaningful therapeutic benefit over existing therapies for pediatric patients for 1 or more of the claimed indications; or

(C) the absence of adequate pediatric labeling could pose a risk to pediatric patients.

(2) WAIVERS.—

(A) FULL WAIVER.—At the request of an applicant, the Secretary shall grant a full waiver, as appropriate, of the requirement to submit assessments under this subsection if the applicant certifies and the Secretary finds that—

(i) necessary studies are impossible or highly impracticable (because, for example, the number of patients in that age group is so small or patients in that age group are geographically dispersed); or

(ii) there is evidence strongly suggesting that the drug or biological product would be ineffective or unsafe in all pediatric age groups.

(B) PARTIAL WAIVER.—At the request of an applicant, the Secretary shall grant a partial waiver, as appropriate, of the requirement to submit assessments under this subsection with respect to a specific pediatric age group if the applicant certifies and the Secretary finds that—

(i) necessary studies are impossible or highly impracticable (because, for example, the number of patients in that age group is so small or patients in that age group are geographically dispersed);

(ii) there is evidence strongly suggesting that the drug or biological product would be ineffective or unsafe in that age group;

(iii)(I) the drug or biological product—

(aa) does not represent a meaningful therapeutic benefit over existing therapies for pediatric patients in that age group; and

(bb) is not likely to be used in a substantial number of pediatric patients in that age group; and

(II) the absence of adequate labeling could not pose significant risks to pediatric patients; or

(iv) the applicant can demonstrate that reasonable attempts to produce a pediatric formulation necessary for that age group have failed.

(C) PEDIATRIC FORMULATION NOT POSSIBLE.—If a waiver is granted on the ground that it is not possible to develop a pediatric formulation, the waiver shall cover only the pediatric groups requiring that formulation. An applicant seeking either a full or partial waiver shall submit to the Secretary documentation detailing why a pediatric formulation cannot be developed and, if the waiver is granted, the applicant's submission shall promptly be made available to the public in an easily accessible manner, including through posting on the Web site of the Food and Drug Administration.

(D) LABELING REQUIREMENT.—If the Secretary grants a full or partial waiver because there is evidence that a drug or biological product would be ineffective or unsafe in pediatric populations, the information shall be included in the labeling for the drug or biological product.

(3) EFFECT OF SUBSECTION.—Nothing in this subsection alters or amends section 301(j) of this Act or section 552 of title 5 or section 1905 of title 18, United States Code.

(c) Meaningful Therapeutic Benefit.—For the purposes of paragraph (4)(A)(iii)(I) and (4)(B)(iii)(I) of subsection (a) and paragraphs (1)(B) and (2)(B)(iii)(I)(aa) of subsection (b), a drug or biological product shall be considered to represent a meaningful therapeutic benefit over existing therapies if the Secretary determines that—

(1) if approved, the drug or biological product could represent an improvement in the treatment, diagnosis, or prevention of a disease, compared with marketed products adequately labeled for that use in the relevant pediatric population; or

(2) the drug or biological product is in a class of products or for an indication for which there is a need for additional options.

(d) Submission of Assessments.—If a person fails to submit a required assessment described in subsection (a)(2), fails to meet the applicable requirements in subsection (a)(3), or fails to submit a request for approval of a pediatric formulation described in subsection (a) or (b), in accordance with applicable provisions of subsections (a) and (b), the following shall apply:

(1) Beginning 270 days after the date of enactment of the Food and Drug Administration Safety and Innovation Act,[39] the Secretary shall issue a non-compliance letter to such person informing them of such failure to submit or meet the requirements of the applicable subsection. Such letter shall require the person to respond in writing within 45 calendar days of issuance of such letter. Such response may include the person's request for a deferral extension if applicable. Such letter and the person's written response to such letter shall be made publicly available on the Internet Web site of the Food and Drug Administration 60 calendar days after issuance, with redactions for any trade secrets and confidential commercial information. If the Secretary determines that the letter was issued in error, the requirements of this paragraph shall not apply.

(2) The drug or biological product that is the subject of an assessment described in subsection (a)(2), applicable requirements in subsection (a)(3), or request for approval of a pediatric formulation, may be considered misbranded solely because of that failure and subject to relevant enforcement action (except that the drug or biological product shall not be subject to action under section 303), but such failure shall not be the basis for a proceeding—

(A) to withdraw approval for a drug under section 505(e); or

(B) to revoke the license for a biological product under section 351 of the Public Health Service Act.

39. Pub. L. No. 112–144, 126 Stat. 993, which was enacted July 9, 2012.

(e)[40] PEDIATRIC STUDY PLANS.—

(1) IN GENERAL.—An applicant subject to subsection (a) shall submit to the Secretary an initial pediatric study plan prior to the submission of the assessments described under subsection (a)(2).

(2) TIMING; CONTENT; MEETING.—

(A) TIMING.—An applicant shall submit the initial pediatric plan under paragraph (1)—

(i) before the date on which the applicant submits the assessments under subsection (a)(2); and

(ii) not later than—

(I) 60 calendar days after the date of the end-of-Phase 2 meeting (as such term is used in section 312.47 of title 21, Code of Federal Regulations, or successor regulations); or

(II) such other time as may be agreed upon between the Secretary and the applicant.

Nothing in this section shall preclude the Secretary from accepting the submission of an initial pediatric plan earlier than the date otherwise applicable under this subparagraph.

(B) CONTENT OF INITIAL PLAN.—The initial pediatric study plan shall include—

(i) an outline of the pediatric study or studies that the applicant plans to conduct (including, to the extent practicable study objectives and design, age groups, relevant endpoints, and statistical approach);

(ii) any request for a deferral, partial waiver, or waiver under this section, if applicable, along with any supporting information; and

(iii) other information specified in the regulations promulgated under paragraph (7).

(C) MEETING.—The Secretary—

(i) shall meet with the applicant to discuss the initial pediatric study plan as soon as practicable, but not later than 90 calendar days after the receipt of such plan under subparagraph (A);

---

40. Subsection (e) was amended by Pub. L. No. 112–144, § 506, 126 Stat. 993, 1043–44 (2012). Subsection (c) of such section provides as follows:

(c) Effective Date.—

(1) In general.—Subject to paragraph (2), the amendments made by this section shall take effect 180 calendar days after the [July 9, 2012] date of enactment of this Act, irrespective of whether the Secretary has promulgated final regulations to carry out such amendments.

(2) Rule of construction.—Paragraph (1) shall not be construed to affect the deadline for promulgation of proposed regulations under section 505(B)(e)(7) of the Federal Food, Drug, and Cosmetic Act, as added by subsection (a) of this section.

(ii) may determine that a written response to the initial pediatric study plan is sufficient to communicate comments on the initial pediatric study plan, and that no meeting is necessary; and

(iii) if the Secretary determines that no meeting is necessary, shall so notify the applicant and provide written comments of the Secretary as soon as practicable, but not later than 90 calendar days after the receipt of the initial pediatric study plan.

(3) AGREED INITIAL PEDIATRIC STUDY PLAN.—Not later than 90 calendar days following the meeting under paragraph (2)(C)(i) or the receipt of a written response from the Secretary under paragraph (2)(C)(iii), the applicant shall document agreement on the initial pediatric study plan in a submission to the Secretary marked "Agreed Initial Pediatric Study Plan", and the Secretary shall confirm such agreement to the applicant in writing not later than 30 calendar days of receipt of such agreed initial pediatric study plan.

(4) DEFERRAL AND WAIVER.—If the agreed initial pediatric study plan contains a request from the applicant for a deferral, partial waiver, or waiver under this section, the written confirmation under paragraph (3) shall include a recommendation from the Secretary as to whether such request meets the standards under paragraphs (3) or (4) of subsection (a).

(5) AMENDMENTS TO THE PLAN.—At the initiative of the Secretary or the applicant, the agreed initial pediatric study plan may be amended at any time. The requirements of paragraph (2)(C) shall apply to any such proposed amendment in the same manner and to the same extent as such requirements apply to an initial pediatric study plan under paragraph (1). The requirements of paragraphs (3) and (4) shall apply to any agreement resulting from such proposed amendment in the same manner and to the same extent as such requirements apply to an agreed initial pediatric study plan.

(6) INTERNAL COMMITTEE.—The Secretary shall consult the internal committee under section 505C on the review of the initial pediatric study plan, agreed initial pediatric plan, and any significant amendments to such plans.

(7) REQUIRED RULEMAKING.—Not later than 1 year after the date of enactment of the Food and Drug Administration Safety and Innovation Act,[41] the Secretary shall promulgate proposed regulations and issue guidance to implement the provisions of this subsection.

(f) REVIEW OF PEDIATRIC STUDY[42] PLANS, ASSESSMENTS, DEFERRALS, DEFERRAL EXTENSIONS, AND WAIVERS.—

---

41. Pub. L. No. 112–144, 126 Stat. 993, which was enacted July 9, 2012.

506(c) of that law, this provision becomes effective 180 days after the July 9, 2012 date of enactment.

42. The word "study" was added by Pub. L. No. 112–144, § 506(b)(2)(A), and according to §

(1) REVIEW.—Beginning not later than 30 days after the date of the enactment of the Pediatric Research Equity Act of 2007,[43] the Secretary shall utilize the internal committee established under section 505C to provide consultation to reviewing divisions on initial pediatric plans, agreed initial pediatric study plans,[44] and assessments prior to approval of an application or supplement for which a pediatric assessment is required under this section and all deferral, deferral extension, and waiver requests granted pursuant to this section.

(2) ACTIVITY BY COMMITTEE.—The committee referred to in paragraph (1) may operate using appropriate members of such committee and need not convene all members of the committee.

(3) DOCUMENTATION OF COMMITTEE ACTION.—For each drug or biological product, the committee referred to in paragraph (1) shall document, for each activity described in paragraph (4) or (5), which members of the committee participated in such activity.

(4) REVIEW OF INITIAL PEDIATRIC STUDY[45] PLANS, AGREED INITIAL PEDIATRIC STUDY PLANS, ASSESSMENTS, DEFERRALS, DEFERRAL EXTENSIONS, AND WAIVERS.—Consultation on initial pediatric study plans, agreed initial pediatric study plans,[46] and assessments by the committee referred to in paragraph (1) pursuant to this section shall occur prior to approval of an application or supplement for which a pediatric assessment is required under this section. The committee shall review all requests for deferrals, deferral extensions, and waivers from the requirement to submit a pediatric assessment granted under this section and shall provide recommendations as needed to reviewing divisions, including with respect to whether such a supplement, when submitted, shall be considered for priority review.

(5) RETROSPECTIVE REVIEW OF PEDIATRIC ASSESSMENTS, DEFERRALS, AND WAIVERS.—Not later than 1 year after the date of the enactment of the Pediatric Research Equity Act of 2007, the committee referred to in paragraph (1) shall conduct a retrospective review and analysis of a representative sample of assessments submitted and deferrals and waivers approved under this section since the enactment of the Pediatric Research Equity Act of 2003. Such review shall include an analysis of the quality and consistency of pediatric information in pediatric assessments and the appropriateness of waivers and deferrals granted. Based on such review, the Secretary shall issue recommendations to the review divisions for improvements

---

43. Pub. L. No. 110–85, tit. IV, 121 Stat. 823, 866–76, which was enacted September 27, 2007.

44. The words "initial pediatric study plans, agreed initial pediatric study plans" were added by Pub. L. No. 112–144, § 506(b)(2)(B), and according to § 506(c) of that law, this provision becomes effective 180 days after the July 9, 2012 date of enactment.

45. The word "study" was added by Pub. L. No. 112–144, § 506(b)(2)(C)(i), and according to § 506(c) of that law, this provision becomes effective 180 days after the July 9, 2012 date of enactment.

46. The words "initial pediatric study plans, agreed initial pediatric study plans" were added by Pub. L. No. 112–144, § 506(b)(2)(C)(ii), and according to § 506(c) of that law, this provision becomes effective 180 days after the July 9, 2012 date of enactment.

and initiate guidance to industry related to the scope of pediatric studies required under this section.

(6) TRACKING OF ASSESSMENTS AND LABELING CHANGES.—The Secretary, in consultation with the committee referred to in paragraph (1), shall track and make available to the public in an easily accessible manner, including through posting on the Web site of the Food and Drug Administration—

(A) the number of assessments conducted under this section;

(B) the specific drugs and biological products and their uses assessed under this section;

(C) the types of assessments conducted under this section, including trial design, the number of pediatric patients studied, and the number of centers and countries involved;

(D) aggregated on an annual basis—

(i) the total number of deferrals and deferral extensions requested and granted under this section and, if granted, the reasons for each such deferral or deferral extension;

(ii) the timeline for completion of the assessments;

(iii) the number of assessments completed and pending; and

(iv) the number of postmarket non-compliance letters issued pursuant to subsection (d), and the recipients of such letters;

(E) the number of waivers requested and granted under this section and, if granted, the reasons for the waivers;

(F) the number of pediatric formulations developed and the number of pediatric formulations not developed and the reasons any such formulation was not developed;

(G) the labeling changes made as a result of assessments conducted under this section;

(H) an annual summary of labeling changes made as a result of assessments conducted under this section for distribution pursuant to subsection (h)(2);

(I) an annual summary of information submitted pursuant to subsection (a)(3)(B); and

(J) the number of times the committee referred to in paragraph (1) made a recommendation to the Secretary under paragraph (4) regarding priority review, the number of times the Secretary followed or did not follow such a recommendation, and, if not followed, the reasons why such a recommendation was not followed.

(g) LABELING CHANGES.—

(1) DISPUTE RESOLUTION.—

(A) REQUEST FOR LABELING CHANGE AND FAILURE TO AGREE.—If, on or after the date of the enactment of the Pediatric Research Equity Act of 2007, the Commissioner determines that a sponsor and the Commissioner have been unable to reach agreement on appropriate changes to the labeling for the drug that is the subject of the application or supplement, not later than 180 days after the date of the submission of the application or supplement that receives a priority review or 330 days after the date of the submission of an application or supplement that receives a standard review—

(i) the Commissioner shall request that the sponsor of the application make any labeling change that the Commissioner determines to be appropriate; and

(ii) if the sponsor does not agree within 30 days after the Commissioner's request to make a labeling change requested by the Commissioner, the Commissioner shall refer the matter to the Pediatric Advisory Committee.

(B) ACTION BY THE PEDIATRIC ADVISORY COMMITTEE.—Not later than 90 days after receiving a referral under subparagraph (A)(ii), the Pediatric Advisory Committee shall—

(i) review the pediatric study reports; and

(ii) make a recommendation to the Commissioner concerning appropriate labeling changes, if any.

(C) CONSIDERATION OF RECOMMENDATIONS.—The Commissioner shall consider the recommendations of the Pediatric Advisory Committee and, if appropriate, not later than 30 days after receiving the recommendation, make a request to the sponsor of the application or supplement to make any labeling changes that the Commissioner determines to be appropriate.

(D) MISBRANDING.—If the sponsor of the application or supplement, within 30 days after receiving a request under subparagraph (C), does not agree to make a labeling change requested by the Commissioner, the Commissioner may deem the drug that is the subject of the application or supplement to be misbranded.

(E) NO EFFECT ON AUTHORITY.—Nothing in this subsection limits the authority of the United States to bring an enforcement action under this Act when a drug lacks appropriate pediatric labeling. Neither course of action (the Pediatric Advisory Committee process or an enforcement action referred to in the preceding sentence) shall preclude, delay, or serve as the basis to stay the other course of action.

(2) OTHER LABELING CHANGES.—If, on or after the date of the enactment of the Pediatric Research Equity Act of 2007, the Secretary makes a determination that

a pediatric assessment conducted under this section does or does not demonstrate that the drug that is the subject of such assessment is safe and effective in pediatric populations or subpopulations, including whether such assessment results are inconclusive, the Secretary shall order the labeling of such product to include information about the results of the assessment and a statement of the Secretary's determination.

(h) DISSEMINATION OF PEDIATRIC INFORMATION.—

(1) IN GENERAL.—Not later than 210 days after the date of submission of an application (or supplement to an application) that contains a pediatric assessment under this section, if the application (or supplement) receives a priority review, or not later than 330 days after the date of submission of an application (or supplement to an application) that contains a pediatric assessment under this section, if the application (or supplement) receives a standard review, the Secretary shall make available to the public in an easily accessible manner the medical, statistical, and clinical pharmacology reviews of such pediatric assessments, and shall post such assessments on the Web site of the Food and Drug Administration.

(2) DISSEMINATION OF INFORMATION REGARDING LABELING CHANGES.—Beginning on the date of the enactment of the Pediatric Research Equity Act of 2007, the Secretary shall require that the sponsors of the assessments that result in labeling changes that are reflected in the annual summary developed pursuant to subsection (f)(6)(H) distribute such information to physicians and other health care providers.

(3) EFFECT OF SUBSECTION.—Nothing in this subsection shall alter or amend section 301(j) of this Act or section 552 of title 5 or section 1905 of title 18, United States Code.

(i) ADVERSE EVENT REPORTING.—

(1) REPORTING IN FIRST 18–MONTH PERIOD.—Beginning on the date of the enactment of the Pediatric Research Equity Act of 2007, during the 18–month period beginning on the date a labeling change is made pursuant to subsection (g), the Secretary shall ensure that all adverse event reports that have been received for such drug (regardless of when such report was received) are referred to the Office of Pediatric Therapeutics. In considering such reports, the Director of such Office shall provide for the review of such reports by the Pediatric Advisory Committee, including obtaining any recommendations of such committee regarding whether the Secretary should take action under this Act in response to such reports.

(2) REPORTING IN SUBSEQUENT PERIODS.—Following the 18–month period described in paragraph (1), the Secretary shall, as appropriate, refer to the Office of Pediatric Therapeutics all pediatric adverse event reports for a drug for which a pediatric study was conducted under this section. In considering such reports, the Director of such Office may provide for the review of such reports by the Pediatric Advisory Committee, including obtaining any recommendation of such Committee regarding whether the Secretary should take action in response to such reports.

(3) PRESERVATION OF AUTHORITY.—Nothing in this subsection shall prohibit the Office of Pediatric Therapeutics from providing for the review of adverse event reports by the Pediatric Advisory Committee prior to the 18–month period referred to in paragraph (1), if such review is necessary to ensure safe use of a drug in a pediatric population.

(4) EFFECT.—The requirements of this subsection shall supplement, not supplant, other review of such adverse event reports by the Secretary.

(j) SCOPE OF AUTHORITY.—Nothing in this section provides to the Secretary any authority to require a pediatric assessment of any drug or biological product, or any assessment regarding other populations or uses of a drug or biological product, other than the pediatric assessments described in this section.

(k) ORPHAN DRUGS.—Unless the Secretary requires otherwise by regulation, this section does not apply to any drug for an indication for which orphan designation has been granted under section 526.

(*l*) INSTITUTE OF MEDICINE STUDY.—

(1) IN GENERAL.—Not later than three years after the date of the enactment of the Pediatric Research Equity Act of 2007, the Secretary shall contract with the Institute of Medicine to conduct a study and report to Congress regarding the pediatric studies conducted pursuant to this section or precursor regulations since 1997 and labeling changes made as a result of such studies.

(2) CONTENT OF STUDY.—The study under paragraph (1) shall review and assess the use of extrapolation for pediatric subpopulations, the use of alternative endpoints for pediatric populations, neonatal assessment tools, the number and type of pediatric adverse events, and ethical issues in pediatric clinical trials.

(3) REPRESENTATIVE SAMPLE.—The Institute of Medicine may devise an appropriate mechanism to review a representative sample of studies conducted pursuant to this section from each review division within the Center for Drug Evaluation and Research in order to make the requested assessment.

(m) NEW ACTIVE INGREDIENT.—

(1) NON-INTERCHANGEABLE BIOSIMILAR BIOLOGICAL PRODUCT.—A biological product that is biosimilar to a reference product under section 351 of the Public Health Service Act, and that the Secretary has not determined to meet the standards described in subsection (k)(4) of such section for interchangeability with the reference product, shall be considered to have a new active ingredient under this section.

(2) INTERCHANGEABLE BIOSIMILAR BIOLOGICAL PRODUCT.—A biological product that is interchangeable with a reference product under section 351 of the Public Health Service Act shall not be considered to have a new active ingredient under this section.

SEC. 505C [21 U.S.C. 355d]. INTERNAL COMMITTEE FOR REVIEW OF PEDIATRIC PLANS, ASSESSMENTS, DEFERRALS, DEFERRAL EXTENSIONS, AND WAIVERS

The Secretary shall establish an internal committee within the Food and Drug Administration to carry out the activities as described in sections 505A(f) and 505B(f). Such internal committee shall include employees of the Food and Drug Administration, with expertise in pediatrics (including representation from the Office of Pediatric Therapeutics), biopharmacology, statistics, chemistry, legal issues, pediatric ethics, neonatology, and the appropriate expertise pertaining to the pediatric product under review, such as expertise in child and adolescent psychiatry, and other individuals designated by the Secretary.

SEC. 505D [21 U.S.C. 355e]. PHARMACEUTICAL SECURITY

(a) IN GENERAL.—The Secretary shall develop standards and identify and validate effective technologies for the purpose of securing the drug supply chain against counterfeit, diverted, subpotent, substandard, adulterated, misbranded, or expired drugs.

(b) STANDARDS DEVELOPMENT.—

(1) IN GENERAL.—The Secretary shall, in consultation with the agencies specified in paragraph (4), manufacturers, distributors, pharmacies, and other supply chain stakeholders, prioritize and develop standards for the identification, validation, authentication, and tracking and tracing of prescription drugs.

(2) STANDARDIZED NUMERAL IDENTIFIER.—Not later than 30 months after the date of the enactment of the Food and Drug Administration Amendments Act of 2007,[47] the Secretary shall develop a standardized numerical identifier (which, to the extent practicable, shall be harmonized with international consensus standards for such an identifier) to be applied to a prescription drug at the point of manufacturing and repackaging (in which case the numerical identifier shall be linked to the numerical identifier applied at the point of manufacturing) at the package or pallet level, sufficient to facilitate the identification, validation, authentication, and tracking and tracing of the prescription drug.

(3) PROMISING TECHNOLOGIES.—The standards developed under this subsection shall address promising technologies, which may include—

(A) radio frequency identification technology;

(B) nanotechnology;

(C) encryption technologies; and

(D) other track-and-trace or authentication technologies.

---

47. Pub. L. No. 110–85, 121 Stat. 823, which was enacted September 27, 2007.

(4) INTERAGENCY COLLABORATION.—in carrying out this subsection, the Secretary shall consult with Federal health and security agencies, including—

(A) the Department of Justice;

(B) the Department of Homeland Security;

(C) the Department of Commerce; and

(D) other appropriate Federal and State agencies.

(c) INSPECTION AND ENFORCEMENT.—

(1) IN GENERAL.—The Secretary shall expand and enhance the resources and facilities of agency components of the Food and Drug Administration involved with regulatory and criminal enforcement of this Act to secure the drug supply chain against counterfeit, diverted, subpotent, substandard, adulterated, misbranded, or expired drugs including biological products and active pharmaceutical ingredients from domestic and foreign sources.

(2) ACTIVITIES.—The Secretary shall undertake enhanced and joint enforcement activities with other Federal and State agencies, and establish regional capacities for the validation of prescription drugs and the inspection of the prescription drug supply chain.

(d) DEFINITION.—In this section, the term "prescription drug" means a drug subject to section 503(b)(1).

SEC. 505E [21 U.S.C. 355f]. EXTENSION OF EXCLUSIVITY PERIOD FOR NEW QUALIFIED INFECTIOUS DISEASE PRODUCTS

(a) EXTENSION.—If the Secretary approves an application pursuant to section 505 for a drug that has been designated as a qualified infectious disease product under subsection (d), the 4– and 5–year periods described in subsections (c)(3)(E)(ii) and (j)(5)(F)(ii) of section 505, the 3–year periods described in clauses (iii) and (iv) of subsection (c)(3)(E) and clauses (iii) and (iv) of subsection (j)(5)(F) of section 505, or the 7–year period described in section 527, as applicable, shall be extended by 5 years.

(b) RELATION TO PEDIATRIC EXCLUSIVITY.—Any extension under subsection (a) of a period shall be in addition to any extension of the period under section 505A with respect to the drug.

(c) LIMITATIONS.—Subsection (a) does not apply to the approval of—

(1) a supplement to an application under section 505(b) for any qualified infectious disease product for which an extension described in subsection (a) is in effect or has expired;

(2) a subsequent application filed with respect to a product approved under section 505 for a change that results in a new indication, route of administration, dosing schedule, dosage form, delivery system, delivery device, or strength; or

(3) a product that does not meet the definition of a qualified infectious disease product under subsection (g) based upon its approved uses.

(d) DESIGNATION.—

(1) IN GENERAL.—The manufacturer or sponsor of a drug may request the Secretary to designate a drug as a qualified infectious disease product at any time before the submission of an application under section 505(b) for such drug. The Secretary shall, not later than 60 days after the submission of such a request, determine whether the drug is a qualified infectious disease product.

(2) LIMITATION.—Except as provided in paragraph (3), a designation under this subsection shall not be withdrawn for any reason, including modifications to the list of qualifying pathogens under subsection (f)(2)(C).

(3) REVOCATION OF DESIGNATION.—The Secretary may revoke a designation of a drug as a qualified infectious disease product if the Secretary finds that the request for such designation contained an untrue statement of material fact.

(e) REGULATIONS.—

(1) IN GENERAL.—Not later than 2 years after the date of enactment of the Food and Drug Administration Safety and Innovation Act, the Secretary shall adopt final regulations implementing this section, including developing the list of qualifying pathogens described in subsection (f).

(2) PROCEDURE.—In promulgating a regulation implementing this section, the Secretary shall—

(A) issue a notice of proposed rulemaking that includes the proposed regulation;

(B) provide a period of not less than 60 days for comments on the proposed regulation; and

(C) publish the final regulation not less than 30 days before the effective date of the regulation.

(3) RESTRICTIONS.—Notwithstanding any other provision of law, the Secretary shall promulgate regulations implementing this section only as described in paragraph (2), except that the Secretary may issue interim guidance for sponsors seeking designation under subsection (d) prior to the promulgation of such regulations.

(4) DESIGNATION PRIOR TO REGULATIONS.—The Secretary shall designate drugs as qualified infectious disease products under subsection (d) prior to the promulgation of regulations under this subsection, if such drugs meet the definition of a qualified infectious disease product described in subsection (g).

(f) QUALIFYING PATHOGEN.—

(1) DEFINITION.—In this section, the term "qualifying pathogen" means a pathogen identified and listed by the Secretary under paragraph (2) that has the potential to pose a serious threat to public health, such as—

(A) resistant gram positive pathogens, including methicillin-resistant Staphylococcus aureus, vancomycin-resistant Staphylococcus aureus, and vancomycin-resistant enterococcus;

(B) multi-drug resistant gram negative bacteria, including Acinetobacter, Klebsiella, Pseudomonas, and E. coli species;

(C) multi-drug resistant tuberculosis; and

(D) Clostridium difficile.

(2) LIST OF QUALIFYING PATHOGENS.—

(A) IN GENERAL.—The Secretary shall establish and maintain a list of qualifying pathogens, and shall make public the methodology for developing such list.

(B) CONSIDERATIONS.—In establishing and maintaining the list of pathogens described under this section, the Secretary shall—

(i) consider—

(I) the impact on the public health due to drug-resistant organisms in humans;

(II) the rate of growth of drug-resistant organisms in humans;

(III) the increase in resistance rates in humans; and

(IV) the morbidity and mortality in humans; and

(ii) consult with experts in infectious diseases and antibiotic resistance, including the Centers for Disease Control and Prevention, the Food and Drug Administration, medical professionals, and the clinical research community.

(C) REVIEW.—Every 5 years, or more often as needed, the Secretary shall review, provide modifications to, and publish the list of qualifying pathogens under subparagraph (A) and shall by regulation revise the list as necessary, in accordance with subsection (e).

(g) QUALIFIED INFECTIOUS DISEASE PRODUCT.—The term "qualified infectious disease product" means an antibacterial or antifungal drug for human use intended to treat serious or life-threatening infections, including those caused by—

(1) an antibacterial or antifungal resistant pathogen, including novel or emerging infectious pathogens; or

(2) qualifying pathogens listed by the Secretary under subsection (f).

Sec. 506 [21 U.S.C. 356]. Fast Track Products

(a) Designation of a Drug as a Breakthrough Therapy.—

(1) In general.—The Secretary shall, at the request of the sponsor of a drug, expedite the development and review of such drug if the drug is intended, alone or in combination with 1 or more other drugs, to treat a serious or life-threatening disease or condition and preliminary clinical evidence indicates that the drug may demonstrate substantial improvement over existing therapies on 1 or more clinically significant endpoints, such as substantial treatment effects observed early in clinical development. (In this section, such a drug is referred to as a "breakthrough therapy".)

(2) Request for designation.—The sponsor of a drug may request the Secretary to designate the drug as a break-through therapy. A request for the designation may be made concurrently with, or at any time after, the submission of an application for the investigation of the drug under section 505(i) or section 351(a)(3) of the Public Health Service Act.

(3) Designation.—

(A) In general.—Not later than 60 calendar days after the receipt of a request under paragraph (2), the Secretary shall determine whether the drug that is the subject of the request meets the criteria described in paragraph (1). If the Secretary finds that the drug meets the criteria, the Secretary shall designate the drug as a break-through therapy and shall take such actions as are appropriate to expedite the development and review of the application for approval of such drug.

(B) Actions.—The actions to expedite the development and review of an application under subparagraph (A) may include, as appropriate—

(i) holding meetings with the sponsor and the review team throughout the development of the drug;

(ii) providing timely advice to, and interactive communication with, the sponsor regarding the development of the drug to ensure that the development program to gather the nonclinical and clinical data necessary for approval is as efficient as practicable;

(iii) involving senior managers and experienced review staff, as appropriate, in a collaborative, cross-disciplinary review;

(iv) assigning a cross-disciplinary project lead for the Food and Drug Administration review team to facilitate an efficient review of the development program and to serve as a scientific liaison between the review team and the sponsor; and

(v) taking steps to ensure that the design of the clinical trials is as efficient as practicable, when scientifically appropriate, such as by minimizing the number of patients exposed to a potentially less efficacious treatment.

(b) DESIGNATION OF DRUG AS FAST TRACK PRODUCT.—

(1) IN GENERAL.—The Secretary shall, at the request of the sponsor of a new drug, facilitate the development and expedite the review of such drug if it is intended, whether alone or in combination with one or more other drugs, for the treatment of a serious or life-threatening disease or condition, and it demonstrates the potential to address unmet medical needs for such a disease or condition. (In this section, such a drug is referred to as a "fast track product".)

(2) REQUEST FOR DESIGNATION.—The sponsor of a new drug may request the Secretary to designate the drug as a fast track product. A request for the designation may be made concurrently with, or at any time after, submission of an application for the investigation of the drug under section 505(i) or section 351(a)(3) of the Public Health Service Act.

(3) DESIGNATION.—Within 60 calendar days after the receipt of a request under paragraph (2), the Secretary shall determine whether the drug that is the subject of the request meets the criteria described in paragraph (1). If the Secretary finds that the drug meets the criteria, the Secretary shall designate the drug as a fast track product and shall take such actions as are appropriate to expedite the development and review of the application for approval of such product.

(c) ACCELERATED APPROVAL OF A DRUG FOR A SERIOUS OR LIFE–THREATENING DISEASE OR CONDITION, INCLUDING A FAST TRACK PRODUCT.—

(1) IN GENERAL.—

(A) ACCELERATED APPROVAL.—The Secretary may approve an application for approval of a product for a serious or life-threatening disease or condition, including a fast track product, under section 505(c) or section 351(a) of the Public Health Service Act upon a determination that the product has an effect on a surrogate endpoint that is reasonably likely to predict clinical benefit, or on a clinical endpoint that can be measured earlier than irreversible morbidity or mortality, that is reasonably likely to predict an effect on irreversible morbidity or mortality or other clinical benefit, taking into account the severity, rarity, or prevalence of the condition and the availability or lack of alternative treatments. The approval described in the preceding sentence is referred to in this section as "accelerated approval".

(B) EVIDENCE.—The evidence to support that an end-point is reasonably likely to predict clinical benefit under subparagraph (A) may include epidemiological, pathophysiological, therapeutic, pharmacologic, or other evidence developed using biomarkers, for example, or other scientific methods or tools.

(2) LIMITATION.—Approval of a product under this subsection may be subject to 1 or both of the following requirements:

(A) That the sponsor conduct appropriate postapproval studies to verify and describe the predicted effect on irreversible morbidity or mortality or other clinical benefit.

(B) That the sponsor submit copies of all promotional materials related to the product during the preapproval review period and, following approval and for such period thereafter as the Secretary determines to be appropriate, at least 30 days prior to dissemination of the materials.

(3) EXPEDITED WITHDRAWAL OF APPROVAL.—The Secretary may withdraw approval of a product approved under accelerated approval using expedited procedures (as prescribed by the Secretary in regulations which shall include an opportunity for an informal hearing) if—

(A) the sponsor fails to conduct any required post-approval study of the drug with due diligence;

(B) a study required to verify and describe the predicted effect on irreversible morbidity or mortality or other clinical benefit of the product fails to verify and describe such effect or benefit;

(C) other evidence demonstrates that the product is not safe or effective under the conditions of use; or

(D) the sponsor disseminates false or misleading promotional materials with respect to the product.

(d) REVIEW OF INCOMPLETE APPLICATIONS FOR APPROVAL OF A FAST TRACK PRODUCT.—

(1) IN GENERAL.—If the Secretary determines, after preliminary evaluation of clinical data submitted by the sponsor, that a fast track product may be effective, the Secretary shall evaluate for filing, and may commence review of portions of, an application for the approval of the product before the sponsor submits a complete application. The Secretary shall commence such review only if the applicant—

(A) provides a schedule for submission of information necessary to make the application complete; and

(B) pays any fee that may be required under section 736.

(2) EXCEPTION.—Any time period for review of human drug applications that has been agreed to by the Secretary and that has been set forth in goals identified in letters of the Secretary (relating to the use of fees collected under section 736 to expedite the drug development process and the review of human drug applications) shall not apply to an application submitted under paragraph (1) until the date on which the application is complete.

(e) CONSTRUCTION.—

(1) PURPOSE.—The amendments made by the Food and Drug Administration Safety and Innovation Act to this section are intended to encourage the Secretary to utilize innovative and flexible approaches to the assessment of products under accelerated approval for treatments for patients with serious or life-threatening diseases or conditions and unmet medical needs.

(2) CONSTRUCTION.—Nothing in this section shall be construed to alter the standards of evidence under subsection (a) or (d) of section 505 (including the substantial evidence standard in section 505(d)) of this Act or under section 351(a) of the Public Health Service Act. Such sections and standards of evidence apply to the review and approval of products under this section, including whether a product is safe and effective. Nothing in this section alters the ability of the Secretary to rely on evidence that does not come from adequate and well-controlled investigations for the purpose of determining whether an endpoint is reasonably likely to predict clinical benefit as described in subsection (b)(1)(B).

(f) AWARENESS EFFORTS.—The Secretary shall—

(1) develop and disseminate to physicians, patient organizations, pharmaceutical and biotechnology companies, and other appropriate persons a description of the provisions of this section applicable to breakthrough therapies, accelerated approval, and fast track products; and

(2) establish a program to encourage the development of surrogate and clinical endpoints, including biomarkers, and other scientific methods and tools that can assist the Secretary in determining whether the evidence submitted in an application is reasonably likely to predict clinical benefit for serious or life-threatening conditions for which significant unmet medical needs exist.

SEC. 506A [21 U.S.C. 356a]. MANUFACTURING CHANGES

(a) IN GENERAL.—With respect to a drug for which there is in effect an approved application under section 505 or 512 or a license under section 351 of the Public Health Service Act, a change from the manufacturing process approved pursuant to such application or license may be made, and the drug as made with the change may be distributed, if—

(1) the holder of the approved application or license (referred to in this section as a "holder") has validated the effects of the change in accordance with subsection (b); and

(2)(A) in the case of a major manufacturing change, the holder has complied with the requirements of subsection (c); or

(B) in the case of a change that is not a major manufacturing change, the holder complies with the applicable requirements of subsection (d).

(b) VALIDATION OF EFFECTS OF CHANGES.—For purposes of subsection (a)(1), a drug made with a manufacturing change (whether a major manufacturing change or otherwise) may be distributed only if, before distribution of the drug as so made, the holder involved validates the effects of the change on the identity, strength, quality, purity, and potency of the drug as the identity, strength, quality, purity, and potency may relate to the safety or effectiveness of the drug.

(c) MAJOR MANUFACTURING CHANGES.—

(1) REQUIREMENT OF SUPPLEMENTAL APPLICATION.—For purposes of subsection (a)(2)(A), a drug made with a major manufacturing change may be distributed only if, before the distribution of the drug as so made, the holder involved submits to the Secretary a supplemental application for such change and the Secretary approves the application. The application shall contain such information as the Secretary determines to be appropriate, and shall include the information developed under subsection (b) by the holder in validating the effects of the change.

(2) CHANGES QUALIFYING AS MAJOR CHANGES.—For purposes of subsection (a)(2)(A), a major manufacturing change is a manufacturing change that is determined by the Secretary to have substantial potential to adversely affect the identity, strength, quality, purity, or potency of the drug as they may relate to the safety or effectiveness of a drug. Such a change includes a change that—

(A) is made in the qualitative or quantitative formulation of the drug involved or in the specifications in the approved application or license referred to in subsection (a) for the drug (unless exempted by the Secretary by regulation or guidance from the requirements of this subsection);

(B) is determined by the Secretary by regulation or guidance to require completion of an appropriate clinical study demonstrating equivalence of the drug to the drug as manufactured without the change; or

(C) is another type of change determined by the Secretary by regulation or guidance to have a substantial potential to adversely affect the safety or effectiveness of the drug.

(d) OTHER MANUFACTURING CHANGES.—

(1) IN GENERAL.—For purposes of subsection (a)(2)(B), the Secretary may regulate drugs made with manufacturing changes that are not major manufacturing changes as follows:

(A) The Secretary may in accordance with paragraph (2) authorize holders to distribute such drugs without submitting a supplemental application for such changes.

(B) The Secretary may in accordance with paragraph (3) require that, prior to the distribution of such drugs, holders submit to the Secretary supplemental applications for such changes.

(C) The Secretary may establish categories of such changes and designate categories to which subparagraph (A) applies and categories to which subparagraph (B) applies.

(2) CHANGES NOT REQUIRING SUPPLEMENTAL APPLICATION.—

(A) SUBMISSION OF REPORT.—A holder making a manufacturing change to which paragraph (1)(A) applies shall submit to the Secretary a report on the change, which shall contain such information as the Secretary determines to be appropriate, and which shall include the information developed under subsection (b) by the holder in validating the effects of the change. The report shall be submitted by such date as the Secretary may specify.

(B) AUTHORITY REGARDING ANNUAL REPORTS.—In the case of a holder that during a single year makes more than one manufacturing change to which paragraph (1)(A) applies, the Secretary may in carrying out subparagraph (A) authorize the holder to comply with such subparagraph by submitting a single report for the year that provides the information required in such subparagraph for all the changes made by the holder during the year.

(3) CHANGES REQUIRING SUPPLEMENTAL APPLICATION.—

(A) SUBMISSION OF SUPPLEMENTAL APPLICATION.—The supplemental application required under paragraph (1)(B) for a manufacturing change shall contain such information as the Secretary determines to be appropriate, which shall include the information developed under subsection (b) by the holder in validating the effects of the change.

(B) AUTHORITY FOR DISTRIBUTION.—In the case of a manufacturing change to which paragraph (1)(B) applies:

(i) The holder involved may commence distribution of the drug involved 30 days after the Secretary receives the supplemental application under such paragraph, unless the Secretary notifies the holder within such 30–day period that prior approval of the application is required before distribution may be commenced.

(ii) The Secretary may designate a category of such changes for the purpose of providing that, in the case of a change that is in such category, the holder involved may commence distribution of the drug involved upon the receipt by the Secretary of a supplemental application for the change.

(iii) If the Secretary disapproves the supplemental application, the Secretary may order the manufacturer to cease the distribution of the drugs that have been made with the manufacturing change.

SEC. 506B [21 U.S.C. 356b]. REPORTS OF POSTMARKETING STUDIES

(a) SUBMISSION.—

(1) IN GENERAL.—A sponsor of a drug that has entered into an agreement with the Secretary to conduct a postmarketing study of a drug shall submit to the Secretary, within 1 year after the approval of such drug and annually thereafter until the study is completed or terminated, a report of the progress of the study or the reasons for the failure of the sponsor to conduct the study. The report shall be submitted in such form as is prescribed by the Secretary in regulations issued by the Secretary.

(2) AGREEMENTS PRIOR TO EFFECTIVE DATE.—Any agreement entered into between the Secretary and a sponsor of a drug, prior to the date of enactment of the Food and Drug Administration Modernization Act of 1997, to conduct a postmarketing study of a drug shall be subject to the requirements of paragraph (1). An initial report for such an agreement shall be submitted within 6 months after the date of the issuance of the regulations under paragraph (1).

(b) CONSIDERATION OF INFORMATION AS PUBLIC INFORMATION.—Any information pertaining to a report described in subsection (a) shall be considered to be public information to the extent that the information is necessary—

(1) to identify the sponsor; and

(2) to establish the status of a study described in subsection (a) and the reasons, if any, for any failure to carry out the study.

(c) STATUS OF STUDIES AND REPORTS.—The Secretary shall annually develop and publish in the Federal Register a report that provides information on the status of the postmarketing studies—

(1) that sponsors have entered into agreements to conduct; and

(2) for which reports have been submitted under subsection (a)(1).

(d) DISCLOSURE.—If a sponsor fails to complete an agreed upon study required by this section by its original or otherwise negotiated deadline, the Secretary shall publish a statement on the Internet site of the Food and Drug Administration stating that the study was not completed and, if the reasons for such failure to complete the study were not satisfactory to the Secretary, a statement that such reasons were not satisfactory to the Secretary.

(e) NOTIFICATION.—With respect to studies of the type required under section 506(c)(2)(A) or under section 314.510 or 601.41 of title 21, Code of Federal Regulations, as each of such sections was in effect on the day before the effective date of this subsection,[48] the Secretary may require that a sponsor who, for reasons not satisfactory to the Secretary, fails to complete by its deadline a study under any of such sections of such type for a drug or biological product (including such a study conducted after such effective date) notify practitioners who prescribe such drug or biological product of the failure to complete such study and the questions of clinical benefit, and, where appropriate, questions of safety, that remain unanswered as a result of the failure to complete such study. Nothing in this subsection shall be construed as altering the requirements of the types of studies required under section 506(c)(2)(A) or under section 314.510 or 601.41 of title 21, Code of Federal Regulations, as so in effect, or as prohibiting the Secretary from modifying such sections of title 21 of such Code to provide for studies in addition to those of such type.

---

48. Subsection (e) was added by Pub. L. No. 107–188, § 506, 116 Stat. 594, 693 (2002). Section 506 was contained in subtitle A of title V of the Public Law, and section 508 of that subtitle provided that "The amendments made by this subtitle take effect October 1, 2002."

SEC. 506C [21 U.S.C. 356c]. DISCONTINUANCE OR INTERRUPTION IN THE PRODUCTION OF LIFE–SAVING DRUGS

(a) IN GENERAL.—A manufacturer of a drug—

(1) that is—

(A) life-supporting;

(B) life-sustaining; or

(C) intended for use in the prevention or treatment of a debilitating disease or condition, including any such drug used in emergency medical care or during surgery; and

(2) that is not a radio pharmaceutical drug product or any other product as designated by the Secretary, shall notify the Secretary, in accordance with subsection (b), of a permanent discontinuance in the manufacture of the drug or an interruption of the manufacture of the drug that is likely to lead to a meaningful disruption in the supply of that drug in the United States, and the reasons for such discontinuance or interruption.

(b) TIMING.—A notice required under subsection (a) shall be submitted to the Secretary—

(1) at least 6 months prior to the date of the discontinuance or interruption; or

(2) if compliance with paragraph (1) is not possible, as soon as practicable.

(c) DISTRIBUTION.—To the maximum extent practicable, the Secretary shall distribute, through such means as the Secretary deems appropriate, information on the discontinuation or interruption of the manufacture of the drugs described in subsection (a) to appropriate organizations, including physician, health provider, and patient organizations, as described in section 506E.

(d) CONFIDENTIALITY.—Nothing in this section shall be construed as authorizing the Secretary to disclose any information that is a trade secret or confidential information subject to section 552(b)(4) of title 5, United States Code, or section 1905 of title 18, United States Code.

(e) COORDINATION WITH ATTORNEY GENERAL.—Not later than 30 days after the receipt of a notification described in subsection (a), the Secretary shall—

(1) determine whether the notification pertains to a con-trolled substance subject to a production quota under section 306 of the Controlled Substances Act; and

(2) if necessary, as determined by the Secretary—

(A) notify the Attorney General that the Secretary has received such a notification;

(B) request that the Attorney General increase the aggregate and individual production quotas under section 306 of the Controlled Substances Act applicable to such controlled substance and any ingredient therein to a level the Secretary deems necessary to address a shortage of a controlled substance based on the best available market data; and

(C) if the Attorney General determines that the level requested is not necessary to address a shortage of a con-trolled substance, the Attorney General shall provide to the Secretary a written response detailing the basis for the Attorney General's determination. The Secretary shall make the written response provided under subparagraph (C) available to the public on the Internet Web site of the Food and Drug Administration.

(f) FAILURE TO MEET REQUIREMENTS.—If a person fails to submit information required under subsection (a) in accordance with subsection (b)—

(1) the Secretary shall issue a letter to such person informing such person of such failure;

(2) not later than 30 calendar days after the issuance of a letter under paragraph (1), the person who receives such letter shall submit to the Secretary a written response to such letter setting forth the basis for noncompliance and providing information required under subsection (a); and

(3) not later than 45 calendar days after the issuance of a letter under paragraph (1), the Secretary shall make such letter and any response to such letter under paragraph (2) available to the public on the Internet Web site of the Food and Drug Administration, with appropriate redactions made to protect information described in subsection (d), except that, if the Secretary determines that the letter under paragraph (1) was issued in error or, after review of such response, the person had a reasonable basis for not notifying as required under subsection (a), the requirements of this paragraph shall not apply.

(g) EXPEDITED INSPECTIONS AND REVIEWS.—If, based on notifications described in subsection (a) or any other relevant information, the Secretary concludes that there is, or is likely to be, a drug shortage of a drug described in subsection (a), the Secretary may—

(1) expedite the review of a supplement to a new drug application submitted under section 505(b), an abbreviated new drug application submitted under section 505(j), or a supplement to such an application submitted under section 505(j) that could help mitigate or prevent such shortage; or

(2) expedite an inspection or reinspection of an establishment that could help mitigate or prevent such drug shortage.

(h) DEFINITIONS.—For purposes of this section—

(1) the term "drug"—

(A) means a drug (as defined in section 201(g)) that is intended for human use and that is subject to section 503(b)(1); and

(B) does not include biological products (as defined in section 351 of the Public Health Service Act), unless otherwise provided by the Secretary in the regulations promulgated under subsection (i);

(2) the term "drug shortage" or "shortage", with respect to a drug, means a period of time when the demand or projected demand for the drug within the United States exceeds the supply of the drug; and

(3) the term "meaningful disruption"—

(A) means a change in production that is reasonably likely to lead to a reduction in the supply of a drug by a manufacturer that is more than negligible and affects the ability of the manufacturer to fill orders or meet expected demand for its product; and

(B) does not include interruptions in manufacturing due to matters such as routine maintenance or insignificant changes in manufacturing so long as the manufacturer expects to resume operations in a short period of time.

(i) REGULATIONS.—

(1) IN GENERAL.—Not later than 18 months after the date of enactment of the Food and Drug Administration Safety and Innovation Act, the Secretary shall adopt a final regulation implementing this section.

(2) CONTENTS.—Such regulation shall define, for purposes of this section, the terms "life-supporting", "life-sustaining", and "intended for use in the prevention or treatment of a debilitating disease or condition".

(3) INCLUSION OF BIOLOGICAL PRODUCTS.—

(A) IN GENERAL.—The Secretary may by regulation apply this section to biological products (as defined in section 351 of the Public Health Service Act), including plasma products derived from human plasma protein and their recombinant analogs, if the Secretary determines such inclusion would benefit the public health. Such regulation shall take into account any supply reporting programs and shall aim to reduce duplicative notification.

(B) RULE FOR VACCINES.—If the Secretary applies this section to vaccines pursuant to subparagraph (A), the Secretary shall—

(i) consider whether the notification requirement under subsection (a) may be satisfied by submitting a notification to the Centers for Disease Control and Prevention under the vaccine shortage notification program of such Centers; and

(ii) explain the determination made by the Secretary under clause (i) in the regulation.

(4) PROCEDURE.—In promulgating a regulation implementing this section, the Secretary shall—

 (A) issue a notice of proposed rulemaking that includes the proposed regulation;

 (B) provide a period of not less than 60 days for comments on the proposed regulation; and

 (C) publish the final regulation not less than 30 days before the regulation's effective date.

(5) RESTRICTIONS.—Notwithstanding any other provision of Federal law, in implementing this section, the Secretary shall only promulgate regulations as described in paragraph (4).

SEC. 506C–1 [21 U.S.C. 356c–1]. ANNUAL REPORTING ON DRUG SHORTAGES

(a) ANNUAL REPORTS TO CONGRESS.—Not later than the end of calendar year 2013, and not later than the end of each calendar year thereafter, the Secretary shall submit to the Committee on Energy and Commerce of the House of Representatives and the Committee on Health, Education, Labor, and Pensions of the Senate a report on drug shortages that—

(1) specifies the number of manufacturers that submitted a notification to the Secretary under section 506C(a) during such calendar year;

(2) describes the communication between the field investigators of the Food and Drug Administration and the staff of the Center for Drug Evaluation and Research's Office of Compliance and Drug Shortage Program, including the Food and Drug Administration's procedures for enabling and ensuring such communication;

(3)(A) lists the major actions taken by the Secretary to prevent or mitigate the drug shortages described in paragraph (7);

(B) in the list under subparagraph (A), includes—

 (i) the number of applications and supplements for which the Secretary expedited review under section 506C(g)(1) during such calendar year; and

 (ii) the number of establishment inspections or reinspections that the Secretary expedited under section 506C(g)(2) during such calendar year;

(4) describes the coordination between the Food and Drug Administration and the Drug Enforcement Administration on efforts to prevent or alleviate drug shortages;

(5) identifies the number of and describes the instances in which the Food and Drug Administration exercised regulatory flexibility and discretion to prevent or alleviate a drug shortage;

(6) lists the names of manufacturers that were issued letters under section 506C(f); and

(7) specifies the number of drug shortages occurring during such calendar year, as identified by the Secretary.

(b) TREND ANALYSIS.—The Secretary is authorized to retain a third party to conduct a study, if the Secretary believes such a study would help clarify the causes, trends, or solutions related to drug shortages.

(c) DEFINITION.—In this section, the term "drug shortage" or "shortage" has the meaning given such term in section 506C.

SEC. 506D [21 U.S.C. 356d]. COORDINATION; TASK FORCE AND STRATEGIC PLAN

(a) TASK FORCE AND STRATEGIC PLAN.—

(1) IN GENERAL.—

(A) TASK FORCE.—As soon as practicable after the date of enactment of the Food and Drug Administration Safety and Innovation Act, the Secretary shall establish a task force to develop and implement a strategic plan for enhancing the Secretary's response to preventing and mitigating drug shortages.

(B) STRATEGIC PLAN.—The strategic plan described in subparagraph (A) shall include—

(i) plans for enhanced interagency and intra-agency coordination, communication, and decisionmaking;

(ii) plans for ensuring that drug shortages are considered when the Secretary initiates a regulatory action that could precipitate a drug shortage or exacerbate an existing drug shortage;

(iii) plans for effective communication with outside stakeholders, including who the Secretary should alert about potential or actual drug shortages, how the communication should occur, and what types of information should be shared;

(iv) plans for considering the impact of drug shortages on research and clinical trials; and

(v) an examination of whether to establish a "qualified manufacturing partner program", as described in subparagraph (C).

(C) DESCRIPTION OF PROGRAM.—In conducting the examination of a "qualified manufacturing partner program" under subparagraph (B)(v), the Secretary—

(i) shall take into account that—

(I) a "qualified manufacturer", for purposes of such program, would need to have the capability and capacity to supply products determined or anticipated to be in shortage; and

(II) in examining the capability and capacity to supply products in shortage, the "qualified manufacturer" could have a site that manufactures a drug listed under section 506E or have the capacity to produce drugs in response to a shortage within a rapid timeframe; and

(ii) shall examine whether incentives are necessary to encourage the participation of "qualified manufacturers" in such a program.

(D) CONSULTATION.—In carrying out this paragraph, the task force shall ensure consultation with the appropriate offices within the Food and Drug Administration, including the Office of the Commissioner, the Center for Drug Evaluation and Research, the Office of Regulatory Affairs, and employees within the Department of Health and Human Services with expertise regarding drug shortages. The Secretary shall engage external stakeholders and experts as appropriate.

(2) TIMING.—Not later than 1 year after the date of enactment of the Food and Drug Administration Safety and Innovation Act, the task force shall—

(A) publish the strategic plan described in paragraph (1); and

(B) submit such plan to Congress.

(b) COMMUNICATION.—The Secretary shall ensure that, prior to any enforcement action or issuance of a warning letter that the Secretary determines could reasonably be anticipated to lead to a meaningful disruption in the supply in the United States of a drug described under section 506C(a), there is communication with the appropriate office of the Food and Drug Administration with expertise regarding drug shortages regarding whether the action or letter could cause, or exacerbate, a shortage of the drug.

(c) ACTION.—If the Secretary determines, after the communication described in subsection (b), that an enforcement action or a warning letter could reasonably cause or exacerbate a shortage of a drug described under section 506C(a), then the Secretary shall evaluate the risks associated with the impact of such shortage upon patients and those risks associated with the violation involved before taking such action or issuing such letter, unless there is imminent risk of serious adverse health consequences or death to humans.

(d) REPORTING BY OTHER ENTITIES.—The Secretary shall identify or establish a mechanism by which health care providers and other third-party organizations may report to the Secretary evidence of a drug shortage.

(e) REVIEW AND CONSTRUCTION.—No determination, finding, action, or omission of the Secretary under this section shall—

(1) be subject to judicial review; or

(2) be construed to establish a defense to an enforcement action by the Secretary.

(f) SUNSET.—Subsections (a), (b), (c), and (e) shall cease to be effective on the date that is 5 years after the date of enactment of the Food and Drug Administration Safety and Innovation Act.

SEC. 506E [21 U.S.C. 356e]. DRUG SHORTAGE LIST

(a) ESTABLISHMENT.—The Secretary shall maintain an up-to-date list of drugs that are determined by the Secretary to be in shortage in the United States.

(b) CONTENTS.—For each drug on such list, the Secretary shall include the following information:

(1) The name of the drug in shortage, including the National Drug Code number for such drug.

(2) The name of each manufacturer of such drug.

(3) The reason for the shortage, as determined by the Secretary, selecting from the following categories:

(A) Requirements related to complying with good manufacturing practices.

(B) Regulatory delay.

(C) Shortage of an active ingredient.

(D) Shortage of an inactive ingredient component.

(E) Discontinuation of the manufacture of the drug.

(F) Delay in shipping of the drug.

(G) Demand increase for the drug.

(4) The estimated duration of the shortage as determined by the Secretary.

(c) PUBLIC AVAILABILITY.—

(1) IN GENERAL.—Subject to paragraphs (2) and (3), the Secretary shall make the information in such list publicly available.

(2) TRADE SECRETS AND CONFIDENTIAL INFORMATION.—Nothing in this section alters or amends section 1905 of title 18, United States Code, or section 552(b)(4) of title 5 of such Code.

(3) PUBLIC HEALTH EXCEPTION.—The Secretary may choose not to make information collected under this section publicly available under paragraph (1) or section 506C(c) if the Secretary determines that disclosure of such information would adversely affect the public health (such as by increasing the possibility of hoarding or other disruption of the availability of drug products to patients).

Sec. 506F [21 U.S.C. 356f]. Hospital Repackaging of Drugs in Shortage

(a) Definitions.—In this section:

(1) Drug.—The term "drug" excludes any controlled sub stance (as such term is defined in section 102 of the Controlled Substances Act).

(2) Health system.—The term "health system" means a collection of hospitals that are owned and operated by the same entity and that share access to databases with drug order information for their patients.

(3) Repackage.—For the purposes of this section only, the term "repackage", with respect to a drug, means to divide the volume of a drug into smaller amounts in order to—

(A) extend the supply of a drug in response to the placement of the drug on a drug shortage list under section 506E; and

(B) facilitate access to the drug by hospitals within the same health system.

(b) Exclusion From Registration.—Notwithstanding any other provision of this Act, a hospital shall not be considered an establishment for which registration is required under section 510 solely because it repackages a drug and transfers it to another hospital within the same health system in accordance with the conditions in subsection (c)—

(1) during any period in which the drug is listed on the drug shortage list under section 506E; or

(2) during the 60–day period following any period described in paragraph (1).

(c) Conditions.—Subsection (b) shall only apply to a hospital, with respect to the repackaging of a drug for transfer to another hospital within the same health system, if the following conditions are met:

(1) Drug for intrasystem use only.—In no case may a drug that has been repackaged in accordance with this section be sold or otherwise distributed by the health system or a hospital within the system to an entity or individual that is not a hospital within such health system.

(2) Compliance with state rules.—Repackaging of a drug under this section shall be done in compliance with applicable State requirements of each State in which the drug is repackaged and received.

(d) Termination.—This section shall not apply on or after the date on which the Secretary issues final guidance that clarifies the policy of the Food and Drug Administration regarding hospital pharmacies repackaging and safely transferring repackaged drugs to other hospitals within the same health system during a drug shortage.

[Section 507 repealed by Pub. L. No. 105–115, § 125(b)(1), 111 Stat. 2296, 2325 (1997).]

SEC. 508 [21 U.S.C. 358]. AUTHORITY TO DESIGNATE OFFICIAL NAMES

(a) The Secretary may designate an official name for any drug or device if he determines that such action is necessary or desirable in the interest of usefulness and simplicity. Any official name designated under this section for any drug or device shall be the only official name of that drug or device used in any official compendium published after such name has been prescribed or for any other purpose of this Act. In no event, however, shall the Secretary establish an official name so as to infringe a valid trademark.

(b) Within a reasonable time after the effective date of this section, and at such other times as he may deem necessary, the Secretary shall cause a review to be made of the official names by which drugs are identified in the official United States Pharmacopeia, the official Homeopathic Pharmacopeia of the United States, and the official National Formulary, and all supplements thereto, and at such times as he may deem necessary shall cause a review to be made of the official names by which devices are identified in any official compendium (and all supplements thereto) to determine whether revision of any of those names is necessary or desirable in the interest of usefulness and simplicity.

(c) Whenever he determines after any such review that (1) any such official name is unduly complex or is not useful for any other reason, (2) two or more official names have been applied to a single drug or device, or to two or more drugs which are identical in chemical structure and pharmacological action and which are substantially identical in strength, quality, and purity, or to two or more devices which are substantially equivalent in design and purpose or (3) no official name has been applied to a medically useful drug or device, he shall transmit in writing to the compiler of each official compendium in which that drug or drugs or device are identified and recognized his request for the recommendation of a single official name for such drug or drugs or device which will have usefulness and simplicity. Whenever such a single official name has not been recommended within one hundred and eighty days after such request, or the Secretary determines that any name so recommended is not useful for any reason, he shall designate a single official name for such drug or drugs or device. Whenever he determines that the name so recommended is useful, he shall designate that name as the official name of such drug or drugs or device. Such designation shall be made as a regulation upon public notice and in accordance with the procedure set forth in section 553 of title 5, United States Code.

(d) After each such review, and at such other times as the Secretary may determine to be necessary or desirable, the Secretary shall cause to be compiled, published, and publicly distributed a list which shall list all revised official names of drugs or devices designated under this section and shall contain such descriptive and explanatory matter as the Secretary may determine to be required for the effective use of those names.

(e) Upon a request in writing by any compiler of any official compendium that the Secretary exercise the authority granted to him under section 508(a), he shall upon public notice and in accordance with the procedure set forth in section 553 of title 5, United States Code designate the official name of the drug or device for which the request is made.

Sec. 509 [21 U.S.C. 359]. NONAPPLICABILITY TO COSMETICS

This chapter, as amended by the Drug Amendments of 1962, shall not apply to any cosmetic unless such cosmetic is also a drug or device or component thereof.

Sec. 510 [21 U.S.C. 360]. REGISTRATION OF PRODUCERS OF DRUGS AND DEVICES

(a) As used in this section—

(1) the term "manufacture, preparation, propagation, compounding, or processing" shall include repackaging or otherwise changing the container, wrapper, or labeling of any drug package or device package in furtherance of the distribution of the drug or device from the original place of manufacture to the person who makes final delivery or sale to the ultimate consumer or user; and

(2) the term "name" shall include in the case of a partnership the name of each partner and, in the case of a corporation, the name of each corporate officer and director, and the State of incorporation.

(b)(1) During the period beginning on October 1 and ending on December 31 of each year, every person who owns or operates any establishment in any State engaged in the manufacture, preparation, propagation, compounding, or processing of a drug or drugs shall register with the Secretary the name of such person, places of business of such person, all such establishments, the unique facility identifier of each such establishment, and a point of contact e-mail address.

(2) During the period beginning on October 1 and ending on December 31 of each year, every person who owns or operates any establishment in any State engaged in the manufacture, preparation, propagation, compounding, or processing of a device or devices shall register with the Secretary his name, places of business, and all such establishments.

(3) The Secretary shall specify the unique facility identifier system that shall be used by registrants under paragraph (1). The requirement to include a unique facility identifier in a registration under paragraph (1) shall not apply until the date that the identifier system is specified by the Secretary under the preceding sentence.

(c) Every person upon first engaging in the manufacture, preparation, propagation, compounding, or processing of a drug or drugs or a device or devices in any establishment which he owns or operates in any State shall immediately register with the Secretary—

(1) with respect to drugs, the information described under subsection (b)(1); and

(2) with respect to devices, the information described under subsection (b)(2).

(d) Every person duly registered in accordance with the foregoing subsections of this section shall immediately register with the Secretary any additional establishment which he owns or operates in any State and in which he begins the manufacture, preparation, propagation, compounding, or processing of a drug or drugs or a device or devices.

(e) The Secretary may assign a registration number to any person or any establishment registered in accordance with this section. The Secretary may also assign a listing number to each drug or class of drugs listed under subsection (j). Any number assigned pursuant to the preceding sentence shall be the same as that assigned pursuant to the National Drug Code. The Secretary may by regulation prescribe a uniform system for the identification of devices intended for human use and may require that persons who are required to list such devices pursuant to subsection (j) shall list such devices in accordance with such system.

(f) The Secretary shall make available for inspection, to any person so requesting, any registration filed pursuant to this section; except that any list submitted pursuant to paragraph (3) of subsection (j) and the information accompanying any list or notice filed under paragraph (1) or (2) of that subsection shall be exempt from such inspection unless the Secretary finds that such an exemption would be inconsistent with protection of the public health.

(g) The foregoing subsections of this section shall not apply to—

(1) pharmacies which maintain establishments in conformance with any applicable local laws regulating the practice of pharmacy and medicine and which are regularly engaged in dispensing prescription drugs or devices, upon prescriptions of practitioners licensed to administer such drugs or devices to patients under the care of such practitioners in the course of their professional practice, and which do not manufacture, prepare, propagate, compound, or process drugs or devices for sale other than in the regular course of their business of dispensing or selling drugs or devices at retail;

(2) practitioners licensed by law to prescribe or administer drugs or devices and who manufacture, prepare, propagate, compound, or process drugs or devices solely for use in the course of their professional practice;

(3) persons who manufacture, prepare, propagate, compound, or process drugs or devices solely for use in research, teaching, or chemical analysis and not for sale;

(4) any distributor who acts as a wholesale distributor of devices, and who does not manufacture, repackage, process, or relabel a device; or

(5) such other classes of persons as the Secretary may by regulation exempt from the application of this section upon a finding that registration by such classes of persons in accordance with this section is not necessary for the protection of the public health.

In this subsection, the term "wholesale distributor" means any person (other than the manufacturer or the initial importer) who distributes a device from the original place of manufacture to the person who makes the final delivery or sale of the device to the ultimate consumer or user.

(h) INSPECTIONS.—

(1) IN GENERAL.—Every establishment that is required to be registered with the Secretary under this section shall be subject to inspection pursuant to section 704.

(2) BIENNIAL INSPECTIONS FOR DEVICES.—Every establishment described in paragraph (1), in any State, that is engaged in the manufacture, propagation, compounding, or processing of a device or devices classified in class II or III shall be so inspected by one or more officers or employees duly designated by the Secretary, or by persons accredited to conduct inspections under section 704(g), at least once in the 2–year period beginning with the date of registration of such establishment pursuant to this section and at least once in every successive 2–year period thereafter.

(3) RISK–BASED SCHEDULE FOR DRUGS.—The Secretary, acting through one or more officers or employees duly designated by the Secretary, shall inspect establishments described in paragraph (1) that are engaged in the manufacture, preparation, propagation, compounding, or processing of a drug or drugs (referred to in this subsection as "drug establishments") in accordance with a risk-based schedule established by the Secretary.

(4) RISK FACTORS.—In establishing the risk-based scheduled under paragraph (3), the Secretary shall inspect establishments according to the known safety risks of such establishments, which shall be based on the following factors:

(A) The compliance history of the establishment.

(B) The record, history, and nature of recalls linked to the establishment.

(C) The inherent risk of the drug manufactured, prepared, propagated, compounded, or processed at the establishment.

(D) The inspection frequency and history of the establishment, including whether the establishment has been inspected pursuant to section 704 within the last 4 years.

(E) Whether the establishment has been inspected by a foreign government or an agency of a foreign government recognized under section 809.

(F) Any other criteria deemed necessary and appropriate by the Secretary for purposes of allocating inspection resources.

(5) EFFECT OF STATUS.—In determining the risk associated with an establishment for purposes of establishing a risk-based schedule under paragraph (3), the Secretary shall not consider whether the drugs manufactured, prepared, propagated, compounded, or processed by such establishment are drugs described in section 503(b).

(6) ANNUAL REPORT ON INSPECTIONS OF ESTABLISHMENTS.—Beginning in 2014, not later than February 1 of each year, the Secretary shall make available on the Internet Web site of the Food and Drug Administration a report regarding—

(A)(i) the number of domestic and foreign establishments registered pursuant to this section in the previous fiscal year; and

(ii) the number of such domestic establishments and the number of such foreign establishments that the Secretary inspected in the previous fiscal year;

(B) with respect to establishments that manufacture, prepare, propagate, compound, or process an active ingredient of a drug, a finished drug product, or an excipient of a drug, the number of each such type of establishment; and

(C) the percentage of the budget of the Food and Drug Administration used to fund the inspections described under subparagraph (A).

(i) REGISTRATION OF FOREIGN ESTABLISHMENTS.—

(1) Every person who owns or operates any establishment within any foreign country engaged in the manufacture, preparation, propagation, compounding, or processing of a drug or device that is imported or offered for import into the United States shall, through electronic means in accordance with the criteria of the Secretary—

(A) upon first engaging in any such activity, immediately submit a registration to the Secretary that includes—

(i) with respect to drugs, the name and place of business of such person, all such establishments, the unique facility identifier of each such establishment, a point of contact e-mail address, the name of the United States agent of each such establishment, the name of each importer of such drug in the United States that is known to the establishment, and the name of each person who imports or offers for import such drug to the United States for purposes of importation; and

(ii) with respect to devices, the name and place of business of the establishment, the name of the United States agent for the establishment, the name of each importer of such device in the United States that is known to the establishment, and the name of each person who imports or offers for import such device to the United States for purposes of importation; and

(B) each establishment subject to the requirements of subparagraph (A) shall thereafter register with the Secretary during the period beginning on October 1 and ending on December 31 of each year.

(2) The establishment shall also provide the information required by subsection (j).

(3) The Secretary is authorized to enter into cooperative arrangements with officials of foreign countries to ensure that adequate and effective means are available for purposes of determining, from time to time, whether drugs or devices manufactured, prepared, propagated, compounded, or processed by an establishment described in paragraph (1), if imported or offered for import into the United States, shall be refused admission on any of the grounds set forth in section 801(a).

(4) The Secretary shall specify the unique facility identifier system that shall be used by registrants under paragraph (1) with respect to drugs. The requirement to include a unique facility identifier in a registration under paragraph (1) with respect to drugs shall not apply until the date that the identifier system is specified by the Secretary under the preceding sentence.

(j)(1) Every person who registers with the Secretary under subsection (b), (c), (d) or (i) shall, at the time of registration under any such subsection, file with the Secretary a list of all drugs and a list of all devices and a brief statement of the basis for believing that each device included in the list is a device rather than a drug (with each drug and device in each list listed by its established name (as defined in section 502(e)) and by any proprietary name) which are being manufactured, prepared, propagated, compounded, or processed by him for commercial distribution and which he has not included in any list of drugs or devices filed by him with the Secretary under this paragraph or paragraph (2) before such time of registration. Such list shall be prepared in such form and manner as the Secretary may prescribe and shall be accompanied by—

(A) in the case of a drug contained in the applicable list and subject to section 505 or 512, or a device intended for human use contained in the applicable list with respect to which a performance standard has been established under section 514 or which is subject to section 515, a reference to the authority for the marketing of such drug or device and a copy of all labeling for such drug or device;

(B) in the case of any other drug or device contained in an applicable list—

(i) which drug is subject to section 503(b)(1), or which device is a restricted device, a copy of all labeling for such drug or device, a representative sampling of advertisements for such drug or device, and, upon request made by the Secretary for good cause, a copy of all advertisements for a particular drug product or device, or

(ii) which drug is not subject to section 503(b)(1) or which device is not a restricted device, the label and package insert for such drug or device and a representative sampling of any other labeling for such drug or device;

(C) in the case of any drug contained in an applicable list which is described in subparagraph (B), a quantitative listing of its active ingredient or ingredients, except that with respect to a particular drug product the Secretary may require the submission of a quantitative listing of all ingredients if he finds that such submission is necessary to carry out the purposes of this Act;

(D) if the registrant filing a list has determined that a particular drug product or device contained in such list is not subject to section 505 or 512, or the particular device contained in such list is not subject to a performance standard established under section 514 or to section 515 or is not a restricted device, a brief statement of the basis upon which the registrant made such determination if the Secretary requests such a statement with respect to that particular drug product or device; and

(E) in the case of a drug contained in the applicable list, the name and place of business of each manufacturer of an excipient of the listed drug with which the person listing the drug conducts business, including all establishments used in the production of such excipient, the unique facility identifier of each such establishment, and a point of contact email address for each such excipient manufacturer.

(2) Each person who registers with the Secretary under this section shall report to the Secretary, with regard to drugs once during the month of June of each year and once during the month of December of each year, and with regard to devices once each year during the period beginning on October 1 and ending on December 31, the following information:

(A) A list of each drug or device introduced by the registrant for commercial distribution which has not been included in any list previously filed by him with the Secretary under this subparagraph or paragraph (1) of this subsection. A list under this subparagraph shall list a drug or device by its established name (as defined in section 502(e)) and by any proprietary name it may have and shall be accompanied by the other information required by paragraph (1).

(B) If since the date the registrant last made a report under this paragraph (or if he has not made a report under this paragraph, since the effective date of this subsection[49]) he has discontinued the manufacture, preparation, propagation, compounding, or processing for commercial distribution of a drug or device included in a list filed by him under subparagraph (A) or paragraph (1); notice of such discontinuance, the date of such discontinuance, and the identity (by established name (as defined in section 502(e)) and by any proprietary name) of such drug or device.

---

49. Subsection (j) was added by Pub. L. No. 92–387, § 3, 86 Stat. 559, 560–61 (1972).

(C) If since the date the registrant reported pursuant to subparagraph (B) a notice of discontinuance he has resumed the manufacture, preparation, propagation, compounding, or processing for commercial distribution of the drug or device with respect to which such notice of discontinuance was reported; notice of such resumption, the date of such resumption, the identity of such drug or device (by established name (as defined in section 502(e)) and by any proprietary name), and the other information required by paragraph (1), unless the registrant has previously reported such resumption to the Secretary pursuant to this subparagraph.

(D) Any material change in any information previously submitted pursuant to this paragraph or paragraph (1).

(3) The Secretary may also require each registrant under this section to submit a list of each drug product which (A) the registrant is manufacturing, preparing, propagating, compounding, or processing for commercial distribution, and (B) contains a particular ingredient. The Secretary may not require the submission of such a list unless he has made a finding that the submission of such a list is necessary to carry out the purposes of this Act.

(4) The Secretary shall require persons subject to this subsection to use, for purposes of this subsection, the unique facility identifier systems specified under subsections (b)(3) and (i)(4) with respect to drugs. Such requirement shall not apply until the date that the identifier system under subsection (b)(3) or (i)(4), as applicable, is specified by the Secretary.

(k) REPORT PRECEDING INTRODUCTION OF DEVICES INTO INTERSTATE COMMERCE.— Each person who is required to register under this section and who proposes to begin the introduction or delivery for introduction into interstate commerce for commercial distribution of a device intended for human use shall, at least ninety days before making such introduction or delivery, report to the Secretary or person who is accredited under section 523(a) (in such form and manner as the Secretary shall by regulation prescribe)—

(1) the class in which the device is classified under section 513 or if such person determines that the device is not classified under such section, a statement of that determination and the basis for such person's determination that the device is or is not so classified, and

(2) action taken by such person to comply with requirements under section 514 or 515 which are applicable to the device.

A notification submitted under this subsection that contains clinical trial data for an applicable device clinical trial (as defined in section 402(j)(1) of the Public Health Service Act) shall be accompanied by the certification required under section 402(j) (5)(B) of such Act. Such certification shall not be considered an element of such notification.

(*l*) A report under subsection (k) is not required for a device intended for human use that is exempted from the requirements of this subsection under subsection (m) or is within a type that has been classified into class I under section 513. The exception established in the preceding sentence does not apply to any class I device that is intended for a use which is of substantial importance in preventing impairment of human health, or to any class I device that presents a potential unreasonable risk of illness or injury.

(m)(1) Not later than 60 days after the date of enactment of the Food and Drug Administration Modernization Act of 1997, the Secretary shall publish in the Federal Register a list of each type of class II device that does not require a report under subsection (k) to provide reasonable assurance of safety and effectiveness. Each type of class II device identified by the Secretary as not requiring the report shall be exempt from the requirement to provide a report under subsection (k) as of the date of the publication of the list in the Federal Register. The Secretary shall publish such list on the Internet site of the Food and Drug Administration. The list so published shall be updated not later than 30 days after each revision of the list by the Secretary.

(2) Beginning on the date that is 1 day after the date of the publication of a list under this subsection, the Secretary may exempt a class II device from the requirement to submit a report under subsection (k), upon the Secretary's own initiative or a petition of an interested person, if the Secretary determines that such report is not necessary to assure the safety and effectiveness of the device. The Secretary shall publish in the Federal Register notice of the intent of the Secretary to exempt the device, or of the petition, and provide a 30–day period for public comment. Within 120 days after the issuance of the notice in the Federal Register, the Secretary shall publish an order in the Federal Register that sets forth the final determination of the Secretary regarding the exemption of the device that was the subject of the notice. If the Secretary fails to respond to a petition within 180 days of receiving it, the petition shall be deemed to be granted.

(n)(1) The Secretary shall review the report required in subsection (k) and make a determination under section 513(f)(1) not later than 90 days after receiving the report.

(2)(A) Not later than 18 months after the date of enactment of this paragraph, the Secretary shall submit to the Committee on Energy and Commerce of the House of Representatives and the Committee on Health, Education, Labor, and Pensions of the Senate a report regarding when a premarket notification under subsection (k) should be submitted for a modification or change to a legally marketed device. The report shall include the Secretary's interpretation of the following terms: "could significantly affect the safety or effectiveness of the device", "a significant change or modification in design, material, chemical composition, energy source, or manufacturing process", and "major change or modification in the intended use of the device". The report also shall discuss possible processes for industry to use to determine whether a new submission under subsection (k) is required and shall analyze how to leverage existing quality system requirements to reduce premarket burden, facilitate continual device improvement, and provide reasonable assurance of safety and effectiveness of modified devices. In developing such report, the Secretary shall consider the input of interested stakeholders.

(B) The Secretary shall withdraw the Food and Drug Administration draft guidance entitled "Guidance for Industry and FDA Staff—510(k) Device Modifications: Deciding When to Submit a 510(k) for a Change to an Existing Device", dated July 27, 2011, and shall not use this draft guidance as part of, or for the basis of, any premarket review or any compliance or enforcement decisions or actions. The Secretary shall not issue—

(i) any draft guidance or proposed regulation that addresses when to submit a premarket notification submission for changes and modifications made to a manufacturer's previously cleared device before the receipt by the Committee on Energy and Commerce of the House of Representatives and the Committee on Health, Education, Labor, and Pensions of the Senate of the report required in subparagraph (A); and

(ii) any final guidance or regulation on that topic for one year after date of receipt of such report by the Committee on Energy and Commerce of the House of Representatives and the Committee on Health, Education, Labor, and Pensions of the Senate.

(C) The Food and Drug Administration guidance entitled "Deciding When to Submit a 510(k) for a Change to an Existing Device", dated January 10, 1997, shall be in effect until the subsequent issuance of guidance or promulgation, if appropriate, of a regulation described in subparagraph (B), and the Secretary shall interpret such guidance in a manner that is consistent with the manner in which the Secretary has interpreted such guidance since 1997.

(*o*)(1) With respect to reprocessed single-use devices for which reports are required under subsection (k):

(A) The Secretary shall identify such devices or types of devices for which reports under such subsection must, in order to ensure that the device is substantially equivalent to a predicate device, include validation data, the types of which shall be specified by the Secretary, regarding cleaning and sterilization, and functional performance demonstrating that the single-use device will remain substantially equivalent to its predicate device after the maximum number of times the device is reprocessed as intended by the person submitting the premarket notification. Within six months after enactment of this subsection,[50] the Secretary shall publish in the Federal Register a list of the types so identified, and shall revise the list as appropriate. Reports under subsection (k) for devices or types of devices within a type included on the list are, upon publication of the list, required to include such validation data.

___

50. Subsection (*o*) was added by Pub. L. No. 107–250, § 302(b), 116 Stat. 1588, 1616–18 (2002).

(B) In the case of each report under subsection (k) that was submitted to the Secretary before the publication of the initial list under subparagraph (A), or any revision thereof, and was for a device or type of device included on such list, the person who submitted the report under subsection (k) shall submit validation data as described in subparagraph (A) to the Secretary not later than nine months after the publication of the list. During such nine-month period, the Secretary may not take any action under this Act against such device solely on the basis that the validation data for the device have not been submitted to the Secretary. After the submission of the validation data to the Secretary, the Secretary may not determine that the device is misbranded under section 502(*o*), or adulterated under section 501(f)(1)(B), or take action against the device under section 301(p) for failure to provide any information required by subsection (k) until (i) the review is terminated by withdrawal of the submission of the report under subsection (k); (ii) the Secretary finds the data to be acceptable and issues a letter; or (iii) the Secretary determines that the device is not substantially equivalent to a predicate device. Upon a determination that a device is not substantially equivalent to a predicate device, or if such submission is withdrawn, the device can no longer be legally marketed.

(C) In the case of a report under subsection (k) for a device identified under subparagraph (A) that is of a type for which the Secretary has not previously received a report under such subsection, the Secretary may, in advance of revising the list under subparagraph (A) to include such type, require that the report include the validation data specified in subparagraph (A).

(D) Section 502(*o*) applies with respect to the failure of a report under subsection (k) to include validation data required under subparagraph (A).

(2) With respect to critical or semi-critical reprocessed single-use devices that, under subsection (*l*) or (m), are exempt from the requirement of submitting reports under subsection (k):

(A) The Secretary shall identify such devices or types of devices for which such exemptions should be terminated in order to provide a reasonable assurance of the safety and effectiveness of the devices. The Secretary shall publish in the Federal Register a list of the devices or types of devices so identified, and shall revise the list as appropriate. The exemption for each device or type included on the list is terminated upon the publication of the list. For each report under subsection (k) submitted pursuant to this subparagraph the Secretary shall require the validation data described in paragraph (1)(A).

(B) For each device or type of device included on the list under subparagraph (A), a report under subsection (k) shall be submitted to the Secretary not later than 15 months after the publication of the initial list, or a revision of the list, whichever terminates the exemption for the device. During such 15–month period, the Secretary may not take any action under this Act against such device solely on the basis that such report has not been submitted to the Secretary. After the submission of the report to the Secretary the Secretary may not determine that the device is misbranded under section 502(*o*), or adulterated under section 501(f)(1)(B), or take action against the device under section 301(p) for failure to provide any information required by subsection (k) until (i) the review is terminated by withdrawal of the submission; (ii) the Secretary determines by order that the device is substantially equivalent to a predicate device; or (iii) the Secretary determines by order that the device is not substantially equivalent to a predicate device. Upon a determination that a device is not substantially equivalent to a predicate device, the device can no longer be legally marketed.

(C) In the case of semi-critical devices, the initial list under subparagraph (A) shall be published not later than 18 months after the effective date of this subsection. In the case of critical devices, the initial list under such subparagraph shall be published not later than six months after such effective date.

(D) Section 502(*o*) applies with respect to the failure to submit a report under subsection (k) that is required pursuant to subparagraph (A), including a failure of the report to include validation data required in such subparagraph.

(E) The termination under subparagraph (A) of an exemption under subsection (*l*) or (m) for a critical or semi-critical reprocessed single-use device does not terminate the exemption under subsection (*l*) or (m) for the original device.

(p) ELECTRONIC REGISTRATION AND LISTING—

(1) IN GENERAL.—Registrations and listings under this section (including the submission of updated information) shall be submitted to the Secretary by electronic means unless the Secretary grants a request for waiver of such requirement because use of electronic means is not reasonable for the person requesting such waiver.

(2) ELECTRONIC DATABASE.—Not later than 2 years after the Secretary specifies a unique facility identifier system under subsections (b) and (i), the Secretary shall maintain an electronic database, which shall not be subject to inspection under subsection (f), populated with the information submitted as described under paragraph (1) that—

(A) enables personnel of the Food and Drug Administration to search the database by any field of information submitted in a registration described under paragraph (1), or combination of such fields; and

(B) uses the unique facility identifier system to link with other relevant databases within the Food and Drug Administration, including the database for submission of information under section 801(r).

(3) RISK–BASED INFORMATION AND COORDINATION.—The Secretary shall ensure the accuracy and coordination of relevant Food and Drug Administration databases in order to identify and inform risk-based inspections under section 510(h).

Sec. 511 [21 U.S.C. 360a]. Clinical Trial Guidance for Antibiotic Drugs

(a) In General.—Not later than 1 year after the date of the enactment of this section,[51] the Secretary shall issue guidance for the conduct of clinical trials with respect to antibiotic drugs, including antimicrobials to treat acute bacterial sinusitis, acute bacterial otitis media, and acute bacterial exacerbation of chronic bronchitis. Such guidance shall indicate the appropriate models and valid surrogate markers.

(b) Review.—Not later than 5 years after the date of the enactment of this section, the Secretary shall review and update the guidance described under subsection (a) to reflect developments in scientific and medical information and technology.

Sec. 512 [21 U.S.C. 360b]. New Animal Drugs

(a)(1) A new animal drug shall, with respect to any particular use or intended use of such drug, be deemed unsafe for purposes of section 501(a)(5) and section 402(a)(2)(C)(ii) unless—

(A) there is in effect an approval of an application filed pursuant to subsection (b) with respect to such use or intended use of such drug, and such drug, its labeling, and such use conform to such approved application;

(B) there is in effect a conditional approval of an application filed pursuant to section 571 with respect to such use or intended use of such drug, and such drug, its labeling, and such use conform to such conditionally approved application; or

(C) there is in effect an index listing pursuant to section 572 with respect to such use or intended use of such drug in a minor species, and such drug, its labeling, and such use conform to such index listing.

A new animal drug shall also be deemed unsafe for such purposes in the event of removal from the establishment of a manufacturer, packer, or distributor of such drug for use in the manufacture of animal feed in any State unless at the time of such removal such manufacturer, packer, or distributor has an unrevoked written statement from the consignee of such drug, or notice from the Secretary, to the effect that, with respect to the use of such drug in animal feed, such consignee (i) holds a license issued under subsection (m) and has in its possession current approved labeling for such drug in animal feed; or (ii) will, if the consignee is not a user of the drug, ship such drug only to a holder of a license issued under subsection (m).

(2) An animal feed bearing or containing a new animal drug shall, with respect to any particular use or intended use of such animal feed be deemed unsafe for purposes of section 501(a)(6) unless—

(A) there is in effect—

---

51. Section 511 was added by Pub. L. No. 110–85, § 911, 121 Stat. 823, 951, which was enacted September 27, 2007.

(i) an approval of an application filed pursuant to subsection (b) with respect to such drug, as used in such animal feed, and such animal feed and its labeling, distribution, holding, and use conform to such approved application;

(ii) a conditional approval of an application filed pursuant to section 571 with respect to such drug, as used in such animal feed, and such animal feed and its labeling, distribution, holding, and use conform to such conditionally approved application; or

(iii) an index listing pursuant to section 572 with respect to such drug, as used in such animal feed, and such animal feed and its labeling, distribution, holding, and use conform to such index listing; and

(B) such animal feed is manufactured at a site for which there is in effect a license issued pursuant to subsection (m)(1) to manufacture such animal feed.

(3) A new animal drug or an animal feed bearing or containing a new animal drug shall not be deemed unsafe for the purposes of section 501(a)(5) or (6) if such article is for investigational use and conforms to the terms of an exemption in effect with respect thereto under section 512(j).

(4)(A) Except as provided in subparagraph (B), if an approval of an application filed under subsection (b) is in effect with respect to a particular use or intended use of a new animal drug, the drug shall not be deemed unsafe for the purposes of paragraph (1) and shall be exempt from the requirements of section 502(f) with respect to a different use or intended use of the drug, other than a use in or on animal feed, if such use or intended use—

(i) is by or on the lawful written or oral order of a licensed veterinarian within the context of a veterinarian-client-patient relationship, as defined by the Secretary; and

(ii) is in compliance with regulations promulgated by the Secretary that establish the conditions for such different use or intended use.

The regulations promulgated by the Secretary under clause (ii) may prohibit particular uses of an animal drug and shall not permit such different use of an animal drug if the labeling of another animal drug that contains the same active ingredient and which is in the same dosage form and concentration provides for such different use.

(B) If the Secretary finds that there is a reasonable probability that a use of an animal drug authorized under subparagraph (A) may present a risk to the public health, the Secretary may—

(i) establish a safe level for a residue of an animal drug when it is used for such different use authorized by subparagraph (A); and

(ii) require the development of a practical, analytical method for the detection of residues of such drug above the safe level established under clause (i).

The use of an animal drug that results in residues exceeding a safe level established under clause (i) shall be considered an unsafe use of such drug under paragraph (1). Safe levels may be established under clause (i) either by regulation or order.

(C) The Secretary may by general regulation provide access to the records of veterinarians to ascertain any use or intended use authorized under subparagraph (A) that the Secretary has determined may present a risk to the public health.

(D) If the Secretary finds, after affording an opportunity for public comment, that a use of an animal drug authorized under subparagraph (A) presents a risk to the public health or that an analytical method required under subparagraph (B) has not been developed and submitted to the Secretary, the Secretary may, by order, prohibit any such use.

(5) If the approval of an application filed under section 505 is in effect, the drug under such application shall not be deemed unsafe for purposes of paragraph (1) and shall be exempt from the requirements of section 502(f) with respect to a use or intended use of the drug in animals if such use or intended use—

(A) is by or on the lawful written or oral order of a licensed veterinarian within the context of a veterinarian-client-patient relationship, as defined by the Secretary; and

(B) is in compliance with regulations promulgated by the Secretary that establish the conditions for the use or intended use of the drug in animals.

(6) For purposes of section 402(a)(2)(D), a use or intended use of a new animal drug shall not be deemed unsafe under this section if the Secretary establishes a tolerance for such drug and any edible portion of any animal imported into the United States does not contain residues exceeding such tolerance. In establishing such tolerance, the Secretary shall rely on data sufficient to demonstrate that a proposed tolerance is safe based on similar food safety criteria used by the Secretary to establish tolerances for applications for new animal drugs filed under subsection (b)(1). The Secretary may consider and rely on data submitted by the drug manufacturer, including data submitted to appropriate regulatory authorities in any country where the new animal drug is lawfully used or data available from a relevant international organization, to the extent such data are not inconsistent with the criteria used by the Secretary to establish a tolerance for applications for new animal drugs filed under subsection (b)(1). For purposes of this paragraph, "relevant international organization" means the Codex Alimenterius Commission or other international organization deemed appropriate by the Secretary. The Secretary may, under procedures specified by regulation, revoke a tolerance established under this paragraph if information demonstrates that the use of the new animal drug under actual use conditions results in food being imported into the United States with residues exceeding the tolerance or if scientific evidence shows the tolerance to be unsafe.

(b)(1) Any person may file with the Secretary an application with respect to any intended use or uses of a new animal drug. Such person shall submit to the Secretary as a part of the application (A) full reports of investigations which have been made to show whether or not such drug is safe and effective for use; (B) a full list of the articles used as components of such drug; (C) a full statement of the composition of such drug; (D) a full description of the methods used in, and the facilities and controls used for, the manufacture, processing, and packing of such drug; (E) such samples of such drug and of the articles used as components thereof, of any animal feed for use in or on which such drug is intended, and of the edible portions or products (before or after slaughter) of animals to which such drug (directly or in or on animal feed) is intended to be administered, as the Secretary may require; (F) specimens of the labeling proposed to be used for such drug, or in case such drug is intended for use in animal feed, proposed labeling appropriate for such use, and specimens of the labeling for the drug to be manufactured, packed, or distributed by the applicant; (G) a description of practicable methods for determining the quantity, if any, of such drug in or on food, and any substance formed in or on food, because of its use; and (H) the proposed tolerance or withdrawal period or other use restrictions for such drug if any tolerance or withdrawal period or other use restrictions are required in order to assure that the proposed use of such drug will be safe. The applicant shall file with the application the patent number and the expiration date of any patent which claims the new animal drug for which the applicant filed the application or which claims a method of using such drug and with respect to which a claim of patent infringement could reasonably be asserted if a person not licensed by the owner engaged in the manufacture, use, or sale of the drug. If an application is filed under this subsection for a drug and a patent which claims such drug or a method of using such drug is issued after the filing date but before approval of the application, the applicant shall amend the application to include the information required by the preceding sentence. Upon approval of the application, the Secretary shall publish information submitted under the two preceding sentences.

(2) Any person may file with the Secretary an abbreviated application for the approval of a new animal drug. An abbreviated application shall contain the information required by subsection (n).

(3) Any person intending to file an application under paragraph (1), section 571, or a request for an investigational exemption under subsection (j) shall be entitled to one or more conferences prior to such submission to reach an agreement acceptable to the Secretary establishing a submission or an investigational requirement, which may include a requirement for a field investigation. A decision establishing a submission or an investigational requirement shall bind the Secretary and the applicant or requestor unless (A) the Secretary and the applicant or requestor mutually agree to modify the requirement, or (B) the Secretary by written order determines that a substantiated scientific requirement essential to the determination of safety or effectiveness of the animal drug involved has appeared after the conference. No later than 25 calendar days after each such conference, the Secretary shall provide a written order setting forth a scientific justification specific to the animal drug and intended uses under consideration if the agreement referred to in the first sentence requires

more than one field investigation as being essential to provide substantial evidence of effectiveness for the intended uses of the drug. Nothing in this paragraph shall be construed as compelling the Secretary to require a field investigation.

(c)(1) Within one hundred and eighty days after the filing of an application pursuant to subsection (b), or such additional period as may be agreed upon by the Secretary and the applicant, the Secretary shall either (A) issue an order approving the application if he then finds that none of the grounds for denying approval specified in subsection (d) applies, or (B) give the applicant notice of an opportunity for a hearing before the Secretary under subsection (d) on the question whether such application is approvable. If the applicant elects to accept the opportunity for a hearing by written request within thirty days after such notice, such hearing shall commence not more than ninety days after the expiration of such thirty days unless the Secretary and the applicant otherwise agree. Any such hearing shall thereafter be conducted on an expedited basis and the Secretary's order thereon shall be issued within ninety days after the date fixed by the Secretary for filing final briefs.

(2)(A) Subject to subparagraph (C), the Secretary shall approve an abbreviated application for a drug unless the Secretary finds—

(i) the methods used in, or the facilities and controls used for, the manufacture, processing, and packing of the drug are inadequate to assure and preserve its identity, strength, quality, and purity;

(ii) the conditions of use prescribed, recommended, or suggested in the proposed labeling are not reasonably certain to be followed in practice or, except as provided in subparagraph (B), information submitted with the application is insufficient to show that each of the proposed conditions of use or similar limitations (whether in the labeling or published pursuant to subsection (i)) have been previously approved for the approved new animal drug referred to in the application;

(iii) information submitted with the application is insufficient to show that the active ingredients are the same as those of the approved new animal drug referred to in the application;

(iv)(I) if the application is for a drug whose active ingredients, route of administration, dosage form, strength, or use with other animal drugs in animal feed is the same as the active ingredients, route of administration, dosage form, strength, or use with other animal drugs in animal feed of the approved new animal drug referred to in the application, information submitted in the application is insufficient to show that the active ingredients, route of administration, dosage form, strength, or use with other animal drugs in animal feed is the same as that of the approved new animal drug, or

(II) if the application is for a drug whose active ingredients, route of administration, dosage form, strength, or use with other animal drugs in animal feed is different from that of the approved new animal drug referred to in the application, no petition to file an application for the drug with the different active ingredients, route of administration, dosage form, strength, or use with other animal drugs in animal feed was approved under subsection (n)(3);

(v) if the application was filed pursuant to the approval of a petition under subsection (n)(3), the application did not contain the information required by the Secretary respecting the active ingredients, route of administration, dosage form, strength, or use with other animal drugs in animal feed which is not the same;

(vi) information submitted in the application is insufficient to show that the drug is bioequivalent to the approved new animal drug referred to in the application, or if the application is filed under a petition approved pursuant to subsection (n)(3), information submitted in the application is insufficient to show that the active ingredients of the new animal drug are of the same pharmacological or therapeutic class as the pharmacological or therapeutic class of the approved new animal drug and that the new animal drug can be expected to have the same therapeutic effect as the approved new animal drug when used in accordance with the labeling;

(vii) information submitted in the application is insufficient to show that the labeling proposed for the drug is the same as the labeling approved for the approved new animal drug referred to in the application except for changes required because of differences approved under a petition filed under subsection (n)(3), because of a different withdrawal period, or because the drug and the approved new animal drug are produced or distributed by different manufacturers;

(viii) information submitted in the application or any other information available to the Secretary shows that (I) the inactive ingredients of the drug are unsafe for use under the conditions prescribed, recommended, or suggested in the labeling proposed for the drug, (II) the composition of the drug is unsafe under such conditions because of the type or quantity of inactive ingredients included or the manner in which the inactive ingredients are included, or (III) in the case of a drug for food producing animals, the inactive ingredients of the drug or its composition may be unsafe with respect to human food safety;

(ix) the approval under subsection (b)(1) of the approved new animal drug referred to in the application filed under subsection (b)(2) has been withdrawn or suspended for grounds described in paragraph (1) of subsection (e), the Secretary has published a notice of a hearing to withdraw approval of the approved new animal drug for such grounds, the approval under this paragraph of the new animal drug for which the application under subsection (b)(2) was filed has been withdrawn or suspended under subparagraph (G) for such grounds, or the Secretary has determined that the approved new animal drug has been withdrawn from sale for safety or effectiveness reasons;

(x) the application does not meet any other requirement of subsection (n); or

(xi) the application contains an untrue statement of material fact.

(B) If the Secretary finds that a new animal drug for which an application is submitted under subsection (b)(2) is bioequivalent to the approved new animal drug referred to in such application and that residues of the new animal drug are consistent with the tolerances established for such approved new animal drug but at a withdrawal period which is different than the withdrawal period approved for such approved new animal drug, the Secretary may establish, on the basis of information submitted, such different withdrawal period as the withdrawal period for the new animal drug for purposes of the approval of such application for such drug.

(C) Within 180 days of the initial receipt of an application under subsection (b)(2) or within such additional period as may be agreed upon by the Secretary and the applicant, the Secretary shall approve or disapprove the application.

(D) The approval of an application filed under subsection (b)(2) shall be made effective on the last applicable date determined under the following:

(i) If the applicant only made a certification described in clause (i) or (ii) of subsection (n)(1)(G) or in both such clauses, the approval may be made effective immediately.

(ii) If the applicant made a certification described in clause (iii) of subsection (n)(1)(G), the approval may be made effective on the date certified under clause (iii).

(iii) If the applicant made a certification described in clause (iv) of subsection (n)(1)(G), the approval shall be made effective immediately unless an action is brought for infringement of a patent which is the subject of the certification before the expiration of 45 days from the date the notice provided under subsection (n)(2)(B)(i) is received. If such an action is brought before the expiration of such days, the approval shall be made effective upon the expiration of the 30 month period beginning on the date of the receipt of the notice provided under subsection (n)(2)(B) or such shorter or longer period as the court may order because either party to the action failed to reasonably cooperate in expediting the action, except that if before the expiration of such period—

(I) the court decides that such patent is invalid or not infringed, the approval shall be made effective on the date of the court decision,

(II) the court decides that such patent has been infringed, the approval shall be made effective on such date as the court orders under section 271(e)(4)(A) of title 35, United States Code, or

(III) the court grants a preliminary injunction prohibiting the applicant from engaging in the commercial manufacture or sale of the drug until the court decides the issues of patent validity and infringement and if the court decides that such patent is invalid or not infringed, the approval shall be made effective on the date of such court decision.

In such an action, each of the parties shall reasonably cooperate in expediting the action. Until the expiration of 45 days from the date the notice made under subsection (n)(2)(B) is received, no action may be brought under section 2201 of title 28, United States Code, for a declaratory judgment with respect to the patent. Any action brought under section 2201 shall be brought in the judicial district where the defendant has its principal place of business or a regular and established place of business.

(iv) If the application contains a certification described in clause (iv) of subsection (n)(1)(G) and is for a drug for which a previous application has been filed under this subsection containing such a certification, the application shall be made effective not earlier than 180 days after—

(I) the date the Secretary receives notice from the applicant under the previous application of the first commercial marketing of the drug under the previous application, or

(II) the date of a decision of a court in an action described in subclause (III)[52] holding the patent which is the subject of the certification to be invalid or not infringed,

whichever is earlier.

(E) If the Secretary decides to disapprove an application, the Secretary shall give the applicant notice of an opportunity for a hearing before the Secretary on the question of whether such application is approvable. If the applicant elects to accept the opportunity for hearing by written request within 30 days after such notice, such hearing shall commence not more than 90 days after the expiration of such 30 days unless the Secretary and the applicant otherwise agree. Any such hearing shall thereafter be conducted on an expedited basis and the Secretary's order thereon shall be issued within 90 days after the date fixed by the Secretary for filing final briefs.

(F)(i) If an application submitted under subsection (b)(1) for a drug, no active ingredient (including any ester or salt of the active ingredient) of which has been approved in any other application under subsection (b)(1), is approved after the date of the enactment of this paragraph, no application may be submitted under subsection (b)(2) which refers to the drug for which the subsection (b)(1) application was submitted before the expiration of 5 years from the date of the approval of the application under subsection (b)(1), except that such an application may be submitted under subsection (b)(2) after the expiration of 4 years from the date of the approval of the subsection (b)(1) application if it contains a certification of patent invalidity or noninfringement described in clause (iv) of subsection (n)(1)(G). The approval of such an application shall be made effective in accordance with subparagraph (B) except that, if an action for patent infringement is commenced during the one-year period beginning 48 months after the date of the approval of the subsection (b) application, the 30 month period referred to in subparagraph (D)(iii) shall be extended by such amount of time (if any) which is required for seven and one-half years to have elapsed from the date of approval of the subsection (b) application.

52. So in law. Probably should be "clause (iii) (III)".

(ii) If an application submitted under subsection (b)(1) for a drug, which includes an active ingredient (including any ester or salt of the active ingredient) that has been approved in another application approved under such subsection, is approved after the date of enactment of this paragraph and if such application contains substantial evidence of the effectiveness of the drug involved, any studies of animal safety, or, in the case of food producing animals, human food safety studies (other than bioequivalence studies or residue depletion studies, except residue depletion studies for minor uses or minor species) required for the approval of the application and conducted or sponsored by the applicant, the Secretary may not make the approval of an application submitted under subsection (b)(2) for the conditions of approval of such drug in the subsection (b)(1) application effective before the expiration of 3 years from the date of the approval of the application under subsection (b)(1) for such drug.

(iii) If a supplement to an application approved under subsection (b)(1) is approved after the date of enactment of this paragraph and the supplement contains substantial evidence of the effectiveness of the drug involved, any studies of animal safety, or, in the case of food producing animals, human food safety studies (other than bioequivalence studies or residue depletion studies, except residue depletion studies for minor uses or minor species)[53] required for the approval of the supplement and conducted or sponsored by the person submitting the supplement, the Secretary may not make the approval of an application submitted under subsection (b)(2) for a change approved in the supplement effective before the expiration of 3 years from the date of the approval of the supplement.

(iv) An applicant under subsection (b)(1) who comes within the provisions of clause (i) of this subparagraph as a result of an application which seeks approval for a use solely in non-food producing animals, may elect, within 10 days of receiving such approval, to waive clause (i) of this subparagraph, in which event the limitation on approval of applications submitted under subsection (b)(2) set forth in clause (ii) of this subparagraph shall be applicable to the subsection (b)(1) application.

(v) If an application (including any supplement to a new animal drug application) submitted under subsection (b)(1) for a new animal drug for a food-producing animal use, which includes an active ingredient (including any ester or salt of the active ingredient) which has been the subject of a waiver under clause (iv) is approved after the date of enactment of this paragraph, and if the application contains substantial evidence of the effectiveness of the drug involved, any studies of animal safety, or human food safety studies (other than bioequivalence studies or residue depletion studies, except residue depletion studies for minor uses or minor species) required for the new approval of the application and conducted or sponsored by the applicant, the Secretary may not make the approval of an application (including any supple-

---

53. The language within parentheses appears so as to reflect the probable intent of the Congress. Pub. L. No. 108–282, § 102(b)(2), 118 Stat. 891, 892 (2004), provides for amendments to the parenthetical language, and states that "Section 512(c) (2)(F) (ii), (iii), and (v) of the Federal Food, Drug, and Cosmetic Act is amended by". The probable intent of the Congress was to provide that "Clauses (ii), (iii), and (v) of section 512(c)(2)(F) of the Federal Food, Drug, and Cosmetic Act are each amended by".

ment to such application) submitted under subsection (b)(2) for the new conditions of approval of such drug in the subsection (b)(1) application effective before the expiration of five years from the date of approval of the application under subsection (b)(1) for such drug. The provisions of this paragraph shall apply only to the first approval for a food-producing animal use for the same applicant after the waiver under clause (iv).

(G) If an approved application submitted under subsection (b)(2) for a new animal drug refers to a drug the approval of which was withdrawn or suspended for grounds described in paragraph (1) or (2) of subsection (e) or was withdrawn or suspended under this subparagraph or which, as determined by the Secretary, has been withdrawn from sale for safety or effectiveness reasons, the approval of the drug under this paragraph shall be withdrawn or suspended—

(i) for the same period as the withdrawal or suspension under subsection (e) or this subparagraph, or

(ii) if the approved new animal drug has been withdrawn from sale, for the period of withdrawal from sale or, if earlier, the period ending on the date the Secretary determines that the withdrawal from sale is not for safety or effectiveness reasons.

(H) For purposes of this paragraph:

(i) The term "bioequivalence" means the rate and extent to which the active ingredient or therapeutic ingredient is absorbed from a new animal drug and becomes available at the site of drug action.

(ii) A new animal drug shall be considered to be bioequivalent to the approved new animal drug referred to in its application under subsection (n) if—

(I) the rate and extent of absorption of the drug do not show a significant difference from the rate and extent of absorption of the approved new animal drug referred to in the application when administered at the same dose of the active ingredient under similar experimental conditions in either a single dose or multiple doses;

(II) the extent of absorption of the drug does not show a significant difference from the extent of absorption of the approved new animal drug referred to in the application when administered at the same dose of the active ingredient under similar experimental conditions in either a single dose or multiple doses and the difference from the approved new animal drug in the rate of absorption of the drug is intentional, is reflected in its proposed labeling, is not essential to the attainment of effective drug concentrations in use, and is considered scientifically insignificant for the drug in attaining the intended purposes of its use and preserving human food safety; or

(III) in any case in which the Secretary determines that the measurement of the rate and extent of absorption or excretion of the new animal drug in biological fluids is inappropriate or impractical, an appropriate acute pharmacological effects test or other test of the new animal drug and, when deemed scientifically necessary, of the approved new animal drug referred to in the application in the species to be tested or in an appropriate animal model does not show a significant difference between the new animal drug and such approved new animal drug when administered at the same dose under similar experimental conditions.

If the approved new animal drug referred to in the application for a new animal drug under subsection (n) is approved for use in more than one animal species, the bioequivalency information described in subclauses (I), (II), and (III) shall be obtained for one species, or if the Secretary deems appropriate based on scientific principles, shall be obtained for more than one species. The Secretary may prescribe the dose to be used in determining bioequivalency under subclause (I), (II), or (III). To assure that the residues of the new animal drug will be consistent with the established tolerances for the approved new animal drug referred to in the application under subsection (b)(2) upon the expiration of the withdrawal period contained in the application for the new animal drug, the Secretary shall require bioequivalency data or residue depletion studies of the new animal drug or such other data or studies as the Secretary considers appropriate based on scientific principles. If the Secretary requires one or more residue studies under the preceding sentence, the Secretary may not require that the assay methodology used to determine the withdrawal period of the new animal drug be more rigorous than the methodology used to determine the withdrawal period for the approved new animal drug referred to in the application. If such studies are required and if the approved new animal drug, referred to in the application for the new animal drug for which such studies are required, is approved for use in more than one animal species, such studies shall be conducted for one species, or if the Secretary deems appropriate based on scientific principles, shall be conducted for more than one species.

(3) If the patent information described in subsection (b)(1) could not be filed with the submission of an application under subsection (b)(1) because the application was filed before the patent information was required under subsection (b)(1) or a patent was issued after the application was approved under such subsection, the holder of an approved application shall file with the Secretary the patent number and the expiration date of any patent which claims the new animal drug for which the application was filed or which claims a method of using such drug and with respect to which a claim of patent infringement could reasonably be asserted if a person not licensed by the owner engaged in the manufacture, use, or sale of the drug. If the holder of an approved application could not file patent information under subsection (b)(1) because it was not required at the time the application was approved, the holder shall file such information under this subsection not later than 30 days after the date of the enactment of this sentence,[54] and if the holder of an approved application could not

---

54. The sentence was added by Pub. L. No. 100–670, § 102(b)(1), 102 Stat. 3971, 3981 (1988).

file patent information under subsection (b)(1) because no patent had been issued when an application was filed or approved, the holder shall file such information under this subsection not later than 30 days after the date the patent involved is issued. Upon the submission of patent information under this subsection, the Secretary shall publish it.

(4) A drug manufactured in a pilot or other small facility may be used to demonstrate the safety and effectiveness of the drug and to obtain approval for the drug prior to manufacture of the drug in a larger facility, unless the Secretary makes a determination that a full scale production facility is necessary to ensure the safety or effectiveness of the drug.

(d)(1) If the Secretary finds, after due notice to the applicant in accordance with subsection (c) and giving him an opportunity for a hearing, in accordance with said subsection, that—

(A) the investigations, reports of which are required to be submitted to the Secretary pursuant to subsection (b), do not include adequate tests by all methods reasonably applicable to show whether or not such drug is safe for use under the conditions prescribed, recommended, or suggested in the proposed labeling thereof;

(B) the results of such tests show that such drug is unsafe for use under such conditions or do not show that such drug is safe for use under such conditions;

(C) the methods used in, and the facilities and controls used for, the manufacture, processing, and packing of such drug are inadequate to preserve its identity, strength, quality, and purity;

(D) upon the basis of the information submitted to him as part of the application, or upon the basis of any other information before him with respect to such drug, he has insufficient information to determine whether such drug is safe for use under such conditions;

(E) evaluated on the basis of the information submitted to him as part of the application and any other information before him with respect to such drug, there is a lack of substantial evidence that the drug will have the effect it purports or is represented to have under the conditions of use prescribed, recommended, or suggested in the proposed labeling thereof;

(F) upon the basis of information submitted to the Secretary as part of the application or any other information before the Secretary with respect to such drug, any use prescribed, recommended, or suggested in labeling proposed for such drug will result in a residue of such drug in excess of a tolerance found by the Secretary to be safe for such drug;

(G) the application failed to contain the patent information prescribed by subsection (b)(1);

(H) based on a fair evaluation of all material facts, such labeling is false or misleading in any particular; or

(I) such drug induces cancer when ingested by man or animal or, after tests which are appropriate for the evaluation of the safety of such drug, induces cancer in man or animal, except that the foregoing provisions of this subparagraph shall not apply with respect to such drug if the Secretary finds that, under the conditions of use specified in proposed labeling and reasonably certain to be followed in practice (i) such drug will not adversely affect the animals for which it is intended, and (ii) no residue of such drug will be found (by methods of examination prescribed or approved by the Secretary by regulations, which regulations shall not be subject to subsections (c), (d), and (h)), in any edible portion of such animals after slaughter or in any food yielded by or derived from the living animals;

he shall issue an order refusing to approve the application. If, after such notice and opportunity for hearing, the Secretary finds that subparagraphs (A) through (I) do not apply, he shall issue an order approving the application.

(2) In determining whether such drug is safe for use under the conditions prescribed, recommended, or suggested in the proposed labeling thereof, the Secretary shall consider, among other relevant factors, (A) the probable consumption of such drug and of any substance formed in or on food because of the use of such drug, (B) the cumulative effect on man or animal of such drug, taking into account any chemically or pharmacologically related substance, (C) safety factors which in the opinion of experts, qualified by scientific training and experience to evaluate the safety of such drugs, are appropriate for the use of animal experimentation data, and (D) whether the conditions of use prescribed, recommended, or suggested in the proposed labeling are reasonably certain to be followed in practice. Any order issued under this subsection refusing to approve an application shall state the findings upon which it is based.

(3) As used in this section, the term "substantial evidence" means evidence consisting of one or more adequate and well controlled investigations, such as —

(A) a study in a target species;

(B) a study in laboratory animals;

(C) any field investigation that may be required under this section and that meets the requirements of subsection (b)(3) if a presubmission conference is requested by the applicant;

(D) a bioequivalence study; or

(E) an in vitro study;

by experts qualified by scientific training and experience to evaluate the effectiveness of the drug involved, on the basis of which it could fairly and reasonably be concluded by such experts that the drug will have the effect it purports or is represented to have under the conditions of use prescribed, recommended, or suggested in the labeling or proposed labeling thereof.

(4) In a case in which an animal drug contains more than one active ingredient, or the labeling of the drug prescribes, recommends, or suggests use of the drug in combination with one or more other animal drugs, and the active ingredients or drugs intended for use in the combination have previously been separately approved pursuant to an application submitted under section 512(b)(1) for particular uses and conditions of use for which they are intended for use in the combination—

(A) the Secretary shall not issue an order under paragraph (1)(A), (1)(B), or (1)(D) refusing to approve the application for such combination on human food safety grounds unless the Secretary finds that the application fails to establish that—

(i) none of the active ingredients or drugs intended for use in the combination, respectively, at the longest withdrawal time of any of the active ingredients or drugs in the combination, respectively, exceeds its established tolerance; or

(ii) none of the active ingredients or drugs in the combination interferes with the methods of analysis for another of the active ingredients or drugs in the combination, respectively;

(B) the Secretary shall not issue an order under paragraph (1)(A), (1)(B), or (1)(D) refusing to approve the application for such combination on target animal safety grounds unless the Secretary finds that—

(i)(I) there is a substantiated scientific issue, specific to one or more of the active ingredients or animal drugs in the combination, that cannot adequately be evaluated based on information contained in the application for the combination (including any investigations, studies, or tests for which the applicant has a right of reference or use from the person by or for whom the investigations, studies, or tests were conducted); or

(II) there is a scientific issue raised by target animal observations contained in studies submitted to the Secretary as part of the application; and

(ii) based on the Secretary's evaluation of the information contained in the application with respect to the issues identified in clauses (i) (I) and (II), paragraph (1) (A), (B), or (D) apply;

(C) except in the case of a combination that contains a nontopical antibacterial ingredient or animal drug, the Secretary shall not issue an order under paragraph (1)(E) refusing to approve an application for a combination animal drug intended for use other than in animal feed or drinking water unless the Secretary finds that the application fails to demonstrate that—

(i) there is substantial evidence that any active ingredient or animal drug intended only for the same use as another active ingredient or animal drug in the combination makes a contribution to labeled effectiveness;

(ii) each active ingredient or animal drug intended for at least one use that is different from all other active ingredients or animal drugs used in the combination provides appropriate concurrent use for the intended target population; or

(iii) where based on scientific information the Secretary has reason to believe the active ingredients or animal drugs may be physically incompatible or have disparate dosing regimens, such active ingredients or animal drugs are physically compatible or do not have disparate dosing regimens; and

(D) the Secretary shall not issue an order under paragraph (1)(E) refusing to approve an application for a combination animal drug intended for use in animal feed or drinking water unless the Secretary finds that the application fails to demonstrate that—

(i) there is substantial evidence that any active ingredient or animal drug intended only for the same use as another active ingredient or animal drug in the combination makes a contribution to the labeled effectiveness;

(ii) each of the active ingredients or animal drugs intended for at least one use that is different from all other active ingredients or animal drugs used in the combination provides appropriate concurrent use for the intended target population;

(iii) where a combination contains more than one nontopical antibacterial ingredient or animal drug, there is substantial evidence that each of the nontopical antibacterial ingredients or animal drugs makes a contribution to the labeled effectiveness, except that for purposes of this clause, antibacterial ingredient or animal drug does not include the ionophore or arsenical classes of animal drugs; or

(iv) where based on scientific information the Secretary has reason to believe the active ingredients or animal drugs intended for use in drinking water may be physically incompatible, such active ingredients or animal drugs intended for use in drinking water are physically compatible.

(5) In reviewing an application that proposes a change to add an intended use for a minor use or a minor species to an approved new animal drug application, the Secretary shall reevaluate only the relevant information in the approved application to determine whether the application for the minor use or minor species can be approved. A decision to approve the application for the minor use or minor species is not, implicitly or explicitly, a reaffirmation of the approval of the original application.

(e)(1) The Secretary shall, after due notice and opportunity for hearing to the applicant, issue an order withdrawing approval of an application filed pursuant to subsection (b) with respect to any new animal drug if the Secretary finds—

(A) that experience or scientific data show that such drug is unsafe for use under the conditions of use upon the basis of which the application was approved or the condition of use authorized under subsection (a)(4)(A);

(B) that new evidence not contained in such application or not available to the Secretary until after such application was approved, or tests by new methods, or tests by methods not deemed reasonably applicable when such application was approved, evaluated together with the evidence available to the Secretary when the application was approved, shows that such drug is not shown to be safe for use under the conditions of use upon the basis of which the application was approved or that subparagraph (I) of paragraph (1) of subsection (d) applies to such drug;

(C) on the basis of new information before him with respect to such drug, evaluated together with the evidence available to him when the application was approved, that there is a lack of substantial evidence that such drug will have the effect it purports or is represented to have under the conditions of use prescribed, recommended, or suggested in the labeling thereof;

(D) the patent information prescribed by subsection (c)(3) was not filed within 30 days after the receipt of written notice from the Secretary specifying the failure to file such information;

(E) that the application contains any untrue statement of a material fact; or

(F) that the applicant has made any changes from the standpoint of safety or effectiveness beyond the variations provided for in the application unless he has supplemented the application by filing with the Secretary adequate information respecting all such changes and unless there is in effect an approval of the supplemental application. The supplemental application shall be treated in the same manner as the original application.

If the Secretary (or in his absence the officer acting as Secretary) finds that there is an imminent hazard to the health of man or of the animals for which such drug is intended, he may suspend the approval of such application immediately, and give the applicant prompt notice of his action and afford the applicant the opportunity for an expedited hearing under this subsection; but the authority conferred by this sentence to suspend the approval of an application shall not be delegated.

(2) The Secretary may also, after due notice and opportunity for hearing to the applicant, issue an order withdrawing the approval of an application with respect to any new animal drug under this section if the Secretary finds—

(A) that the applicant has failed to establish a system for maintaining required records, or has repeatedly or deliberately failed to maintain such records or to make required reports in accordance with a regulation or order under subsection (*l*), or the applicant has refused to permit access to, or copying or verification of, such records as required by paragraph (2) of such subsection;

(B) that on the basis of new information before him, evaluated together with the evidence before him when the application was approved, the methods used in, or the facilities and controls used for, the manufacture, processing, and packing of such drug are inadequate to assure and preserve its identity, strength, quality, and purity and were not made adequate within a reasonable time after receipt of written notice from the Secretary specifying the matter complained of; or

(C) that on the basis of new information before him, evaluated together with the evidence before him when the application was approved, the labeling of such drug, based on a fair evaluation of all material facts, is false or misleading in any particular and was not corrected within a reasonable time after receipt of written notice from the Secretary specifying the matter complained of.

(3) Any order under this subsection shall state the findings upon which it is based.

(f) Whenever the Secretary finds that the facts so require, he shall revoke any previous order under subsection (d), (e), or (m), or section 571 (c), (d), or (e) refusing, withdrawing, or suspending approval of an application and shall approve such application or reinstate such approval, as may be appropriate.

(g) Orders of the Secretary issued under this section, or section 571(other than orders issuing, amending, or repealing regulations) shall be served (1) in person by any officer or employee of the department designated by the Secretary or (2) by mailing the order by registered mail or by certified mail addressed to the applicant or respondent at his last known address in the records of the Secretary.

(h) An appeal may be taken by the applicant from an order of the Secretary refusing or withdrawing approval of an application filed under subsection (b) or (m) of this section. The provisions of subsection (h) of section 505 of this Act shall govern any such appeal.

(i) When a new animal drug application filed pursuant to subsection (b) or section 571 is approved, the Secretary shall by notice, which upon publication shall be effective as a regulation, publish in the Federal Register the name and address of the applicant and the conditions and indications of use of the new animal drug covered by such application, including any tolerance and withdrawal period or other use restrictions and, if such new animal drug is intended for use in animal feed, appropriate purposes and conditions of use (including special labeling requirements and any requirement that an animal feed bearing or containing the new animal drug be limited to use under the professional supervision of a licensed veterinarian) applicable to any animal feed for use in which such drug is approved, and such other information, upon the basis of which such application was approved, as the Secretary deems necessary to assure the safe and effective use of such drug. Upon withdrawal of approval of such new animal drug application or upon its suspension or upon failure to renew a conditional approval under section 571, the Secretary shall forthwith revoke or suspend, as the case may be, the regulation published pursuant to this subsection (i) insofar as it is based on the approval of such application.

(j) To the extent consistent with the public health, the Secretary shall promulgate regulations for exempting from the operation of this section new animal drugs, and animal feeds bearing or containing new animal drugs, intended solely for investigational use by experts qualified by scientific training and experience to investigate the safety and effectiveness of animal drugs. Such regulations may, in the discretion of the Secretary, among other conditions relating to the protection of the public health, provide for conditioning such exemption upon the establishment and maintenance of such records, and the making of such reports to the Secretary, by the manufacturer or the sponsor of the investigation of such article, of data (including but not limited to analytical reports by investigators) obtained as a result of such investigational use of such article, as the Secretary finds will enable him to evaluate the safety and effectiveness of such article in the event of the filing of an application pursuant to this section. Such regulations, among other things, shall set forth the conditions (if any) upon which animals treated with such articles, and any products of such animals (before or after slaughter), may be marketed for food use.

(k) While approval of an application for a new animal drug is effective, a food shall not, by reason of bearing or containing such drug or any substance formed in or on the food because of its use in accordance with such application (including the conditions and indications of use prescribed pursuant to subsection (i)), be considered adulterated within the meaning of clause (1) of section 402(a).

(*l*)(1) In the case of any new animal drug for which an approval of an application filed pursuant to subsection (b) or section 571 is in effect, the applicant shall establish and maintain such records, and make such reports to the Secretary, of data relating to experience, including experience with uses authorized under subsection (a)(4) (A), and other data or information, received or otherwise obtained by such applicant with respect to such drug, or with respect to animal feeds bearing or containing such drug, as the Secretary may by general regulation, or by order with respect to such application, prescribe on the basis of a finding that such records and reports are necessary in order to enable the Secretary to determine, or facilitate a determination, whether there is or may be ground for invoking subsection (e) or subsection (m)(4) of this section. Such regulation or order shall provide, where the Secretary deems it to be appropriate, for the examination, upon request, by the persons to whom such regulation or order is applicable, of similar information received or otherwise obtained by the Secretary.

(2) Every person required under this subsection to maintain records, and every person in charge or custody thereof, shall, upon request of an officer or employee designated by the Secretary, permit such officer or employee at all reasonable times to have access to and copy and verify such records.

(3)(A) In the case of each new animal drug described in paragraph (1) that contains an antimicrobial active ingredient, the sponsor of the drug shall submit an annual report to the Secretary on the amount of each antimicrobial active ingredient in the drug that is sold or distributed for use in food-producing animals, including information on any distributor-labeled product.

(B) Each report under this paragraph shall specify the amount of each antimicrobial active ingredient—

(i) by container size, strength, and dosage form;

(ii) by quantities distributed domestically and quantities exported; and

(iii) by dosage form, including, for each such dosage form, a listing of the target animals, indications, and production classes that are specified on the approved label of the product.

(C) Each report under this paragraph shall—

(i) be submitted not later than March 31 each year;

(ii) cover the period of the preceding calendar year; and

(iii) include separate information for each month of such calendar year.

(D) The Secretary may share information reported under this paragraph with the Antimicrobial Resistance Task Force established under section 319E of the Public Health Service Act.

(E) The Secretary shall make summaries of the information reported under this paragraph publicly available, except that—

(i) the summary data shall be reported by antimicrobial class, and no class with fewer than 3 distinct sponsors of approved applications shall be independently reported; and

(ii) the data shall be reported in a manner consistent with protecting both national security and confidential business information.

(m)(1) Any person may file with the Secretary an application for a license to manufacture animal feeds bearing or containing new animal drugs. Such person shall submit to the Secretary as part of the application (A) a full statement of the business name and address of the specific facility at which the manufacturing is to take place and the facility's registration number, (B) the name and signature of the responsible individual or individuals for that facility, (C) a certification that the animal feeds bearing or containing new animal drugs are manufactured and labeled in accordance with the applicable regulations published pursuant to subsection (i) or for indexed new animal drugs in accordance with the index listing published pursuant to section 572(e)(2) and the labeling requirements set forth in section 572(h), and (D) a certification that the methods used in, and the facilities and controls used for, manufacturing, processing, packaging, and holding such animal feeds are in conformity with current good manufacturing practice as described in section 501(a)(2)(B).

(2) Within 90 days after the filing of an application pursuant to paragraph (1), or such additional period as may be agreed upon by the Secretary and the applicant, the Secretary shall (A) issue an order approving the application if the Secretary then

finds that none of the grounds for denying approval specified in paragraph (3) applies, or (B) give the applicant notice of an opportunity for a hearing before the Secretary under paragraph (3) on the question whether such application is approvable. The procedure governing such a hearing shall be the procedure set forth in the last two sentences of subsection (c)(1).

(3) If the Secretary, after due notice to the applicant in accordance with paragraph (2) and giving the applicant an opportunity for a hearing in accordance with such paragraph, finds, on the basis of information submitted to the Secretary as part of the application, on the basis of a preapproval inspection, or on the basis of any other information before the Secretary—

(A) that the application is incomplete, false, or misleading in any particular;

(B) that the methods used in, and the facilities and controls used for, the manufacture, processing, and packing of such animal feed are inadequate to preserve the identity, strength, quality, and purity of the new animal drug therein; or

(C) that the facility manufactures animal feeds bearing or containing new animal drugs in a manner that does not accord with the specifications for manufacture or labels animal feeds bearing or containing new animal drugs in a manner that does not accord with the conditions or indications of use that are published pursuant to subsection (i) or an index listing pursuant to section 572(e),

the Secretary shall issue an order refusing to approve the application. If, after such notice and opportunity for hearing, the Secretary finds that subparagraphs (A) through (C) do not apply, the Secretary shall issue an order approving the application. An order under this subsection approving an application for a license to manufacture animal feeds bearing or containing new animal drugs shall permit a facility to manufacture only those animal feeds bearing or containing new animal drugs for which there are in effect regulations pursuant to subsection (i) or an index listing pursuant to section 572(e) relating to the use of such drugs in or on such animal feed.

(4)(A) The Secretary shall, after due notice and opportunity for hearing to the applicant, revoke a license to manufacture animal feeds bearing or containing new animal drugs under this subsection if the Secretary finds—

(i) that the application for such license contains any untrue statement of a material fact; or

(ii) that the applicant has made changes that would cause the application to contain any untrue statements of material fact or that would affect the safety or effectiveness of the animal feeds manufactured at the facility unless the applicant has supplemented the application by filing with the Secretary adequate information respecting all such changes and unless there is in effect an approval of the supplemental application.

If the Secretary (or in the Secretary's absence the officer acting as the Secretary) finds that there is an imminent hazard to the health of humans or of the animals for which such animal feed is intended, the Secretary may suspend the license immediately, and give the applicant prompt notice of the action and afford the applicant the opportunity for an expedited hearing under this subsection; but the authority conferred by this sentence shall not be delegated.

(B) The Secretary may also, after due notice and opportunity for hearing to the applicant, revoke a license to manufacture animal feed under this subsection if the Secretary finds—

(i) that the applicant has failed to establish a system for maintaining required records, or has repeatedly or deliberately failed to maintain such records or to make required reports in accordance with a regulation or order under paragraph (5)(A) of this subsection or section 504(a)(3)(A), or the applicant has refused to permit access to, or copying or verification of, such records as required by subparagraph (B) of such paragraph or section 504(a)(3)(B);

(ii) that on the basis of new information before the Secretary, evaluated together with the evidence before the Secretary when such license was issued, the methods used in, or the facilities and controls used for, the manufacture, processing, packing, and holding of such animal feed are inadequate to assure and preserve the identity, strength, quality, and purity of the new animal drug therein, and were not made adequate within a reasonable time after receipt of written notice from the Secretary, specifying the matter complained of;

(iii) that on the basis of new information before the Secretary, evaluated together with the evidence before the Secretary when such license was issued, the labeling of any animal feeds, based on a fair evaluation of all material facts, is false or misleading in any particular and was not corrected within a reasonable time after receipt of written notice from the Secretary specifying the matter complained of; or

(iv) that on the basis of new information before the Secretary, evaluated together with the evidence before the Secretary when such license was issued, the facility has manufactured, processed, packed, or held animal feed bearing or containing a new animal drug adulterated under section 501(a)(6) and the facility did not discontinue the manufacture, processing, packing, or holding of such animal feed within a reasonable time after receipt of written notice from the Secretary specifying the matter complained of.

(C) The Secretary may also revoke a license to manufacture animal feeds under this subsection if an applicant gives notice to the Secretary of intention to discontinue the manufacture of all animal feed covered under this subsection and waives an opportunity for a hearing on the matter.

(D) Any order under this paragraph shall state the findings upon which it is based.

(5) When a license to manufacture animal feeds bearing or containing new animal drugs has been issued—

(A) the applicant shall establish and maintain such records, and make such reports to the Secretary, or (at the option of the Secretary) to the appropriate person or persons holding an approved application filed under subsection (b), as the Secretary may by general regulation, or by order with respect to such application, prescribe on the basis of a finding that such records and reports are necessary in order to enable the Secretary to determine, or facilitate a determination, whether there is or may be ground for invoking subsection (e) or paragraph (4); and

(B) every person required under this subsection to maintain records, and every person in charge or custody thereof, shall, upon request of an officer or employee designated by the Secretary, permit such officer or employee at all reasonable times to have access to and copy and verify such records.

(6) To the extent consistent with the public health, the Secretary may promulgate regulations for exempting from the operation of this subsection facilities that manufacture, process, pack, or hold animal feeds bearing or containing new animal drugs.

(n)(1) An abbreviated application for a new animal drug shall contain—

(A)(i) except as provided in clause (ii), information to show that the conditions of use or similar limitations (whether in the labeling or published pursuant to subsection (i)) prescribed, recommended, or suggested in the labeling proposed for the new animal drug have been previously approved for a new animal drug listed under paragraph (4) (hereinafter in this subsection referred to as an "approved new animal drug"), and

(ii) information to show that the withdrawal period at which residues of the new animal drug will be consistent with the tolerances established for the approved new animal drug is the same as the withdrawal period previously established for the approved new animal drug or, if the withdrawal period is proposed to be different, information showing that the residues of the new animal drug at the proposed different withdrawal period will be consistent with the tolerances established for the approved new animal drug;

(B)(i) information to show that the active ingredients of the new animal drug are the same as those of the approved new animal drug, and

(ii) if the approved new animal drug has more than one active ingredient, and if one of the active ingredients of the new animal drug is different from one of the active ingredients of the approved new animal drug and the application is filed pursuant to the approval of a petition filed under paragraph (3)—

(I) information to show that the other active ingredients of the new animal drug are the same as the active ingredients of the approved new animal drug,

(II) information to show either that the different active ingredient is an active ingredient of another approved new animal drug or of an animal drug which does not meet the requirements of section 201(v), and

(III) such other information respecting the different active ingredients as the Secretary may require;

(C)(i) if the approved new animal drug is permitted to be used with one or more animal drugs in animal feed, information to show that the proposed uses of the new animal drug with other animal drugs in animal feed are the same as the uses of the approved new animal drug, and

(ii) if the approved new animal drug is permitted to be used with one or more other animal drugs in animal feed, and one of the other animal drugs proposed for use with the new animal drug in animal feed is different from one of the other animal drugs permitted to be used in animal feed with the approved new animal drug, and the application is filed pursuant to the approval of a petition filed under paragraph (3)—

(I) information to show either that the different animal drug proposed for use with the approved new animal drug in animal feed is an approved new animal drug permitted to be used in animal feed or does not meet the requirements of section 201(v) when used with another animal drug in animal feed,

(II) information to show that other animal drugs proposed for use with the new animal drug in animal feed are the same as the other animal drugs permitted to be used with the approved new animal drug, and

(III) such other information respecting the different animal drug or combination with respect to which the petition was filed as the Secretary may require,

(D) information to show that the route of administration, the dosage form, and the strength of the new animal drug are the same as those of the approved new animal drug or, if the route of administration, the dosage form, or the strength of the new animal drug is different and the application is filed pursuant to the approval of a petition filed under paragraph (3), such information respecting the route of administration, dosage form, or strength with respect to which the petition was filed as the Secretary may require;

(E) information to show that the new animal drug is bioequivalent to the approved new animal drug, except that if the application is filed pursuant to the approval of a petition filed under paragraph (3) for the purposes described in subparagraph (B) or (C), information to show that the active ingredients of the new animal drug are of the same pharmacological or therapeutic class as the pharmacological or therapeutic class of the approved new animal drug and that the new animal drug can be expected to have the same therapeutic effect as the approved new animal drug when used in accordance with the labeling;

(F) information to show that the labeling proposed for the new animal drug is the same as the labeling approved for the approved new animal drug except for changes required because of differences approved under a petition filed under paragraph (3), because of a different withdrawal period, or because the new animal drug and the approved new animal drug are produced or distributed by different manufacturers;

(G) the items specified in clauses (B) through (F) of subsection (b)(1);

(H) a certification, in the opinion of the applicant and to the best of his knowledge, with respect to each patent which claims the approved new animal drug or which claims a use for such approved new animal drug for which the applicant is seeking approval under this subsection and for which information is required to be filed under subsection (b)(1) or (c)(3)—

(i) that such patent information has not been filed,

(ii) that such patent has expired,

(iii) of the date on which such patent will expire, or

(iv) that such patent is invalid or will not be infringed by the manufacture, use, or sale of the new animal drug for which the application is filed; and

(I) if with respect to the approved new animal drug information was filed under subsection (b)(1) or (c)(3) for a method of use patent which does not claim a use for which the applicant is seeking approval of an application under subsection (c)(2), a statement that the method of use patent does not claim such a use.

The Secretary may not require that an abbreviated application contain information in addition to that required by subparagraphs (A) through (I).

(2)(A) An applicant who makes a certification described in paragraph (1)(G)(iv) shall include in the application a statement that the applicant will give the notice required by subparagraph (B) to—

(i) each owner of the patent which is the subject of the certification or the representative of such owner designated to receive such notice, and

(ii) the holder of the approved application under subsection (c)(1) for the drug which is claimed by the patent or a use of which is claimed by the patent or the representative of such holder designated to receive such notice.

(B) The notice referred to in subparagraph (A) shall state that an application, which contains data from bioequivalence studies, has been filed under this subsection for the drug with respect to which the certification is made to obtain approval to engage in the commercial manufacture, use, or sale of such drug before the expiration of the patent referred to in the certification. Such notice shall include a detailed statement of the factual and legal basis of the applicant's opinion that the patent is not valid or will not be infringed.

(C) If an application is amended to include a certification described in paragraph (1)(G)(iv), the notice required by subparagraph (B) shall be given when the amended application is filed.

(3) If a person wants to submit an abbreviated application for a new animal drug—

(A) whose active ingredients, route of administration, dosage form, or strength differ from that of an approved new animal drug, or

(B) whose use with other animal drugs in animal feed differs from that of an approved new animal drug,

such person shall submit a petition to the Secretary seeking permission to file such an application. The Secretary shall approve a petition for a new animal drug unless the Secretary finds that—

(C) investigations must be conducted to show the safety and effectiveness, in animals to be treated with the drug, of the active ingredients, route of administration, dosage form, strength, or use with other animal drugs in animal feed which differ from the approved new animal drug, or

(D) investigations must be conducted to show the safety for human consumption of any residues in food resulting from the proposed active ingredients, route of administration, dosage form, strength, or use with other animal drugs in animal feed for the new animal drug which is different from the active ingredients, route of administration, dosage form, strength, or use with other animal drugs in animal feed of the approved new animal drug.

The Secretary shall approve or disapprove a petition submitted under this paragraph within 90 days of the date the petition is submitted.

(4)(A)(i) Within 60 days of the date of the enactment of this subsection,[55] the Secretary shall publish and make available to the public a list in alphabetical order of the official and proprietary name of each new animal drug which has been approved for safety and effectiveness before the date of the enactment of this subsection.

(ii) Every 30 days after the publication of the first list under clause (i) the Secretary shall revise the list to include each new animal drug which has been approved for safety and effectiveness under subsection (c) during the 30 day period.

(iii) When patent information submitted under subsection (b)(1) or (c)(3) respecting a new animal drug included on the list is to be published by the Secretary, the Secretary shall, in revisions made under clause (ii), include such information for such drug.

(B) A new animal drug approved for safety and effectiveness before the date of the enactment of this subsection or approved for safety and effectiveness under subsection (c) shall, for purposes of this subsection, be considered to have been published under subparagraph (A) on the date of its approval or the date of enactment, whichever is later.

(C) If the approval of a new animal drug was withdrawn or suspended under subsection (c)(2)(G) or for grounds described in subsection (e) or if the Secretary determines that a drug has been withdrawn from sale for safety or effectiveness reasons, it may not be published in the list under subparagraph (A) or, if the withdrawal or suspension occurred after its publication in such list, it shall be immediately removed from such list—

55. Subsection (n) was added by Pub. L. No. 100–670, § 101, 102 Stat. 3971, 3971–75 (1988).

(i) for the same period as the withdrawal or suspension under subsection (c) (2)(G) or (e), or

(ii) if the listed drug has been withdrawn from sale, for the period of withdrawal from sale or, if earlier, the period ending on the date the Secretary determines that the withdrawal from sale is not for safety or effectiveness reasons.

A notice of the removal shall be published in the Federal Register.

(5) If an application contains the information required by clauses (A), (G), and (H) of subsection (b)(1) and such information—

(A) is relied on by the applicant for the approval of the application, and

(B) is not information derived either from investigations, studies, or tests conducted by or for the applicant or for which the applicant had obtained a right of reference or use from the person by or for whom the investigations, studies, or tests were conducted,

such application shall be considered to be an application filed under subsection (b) (2).

(*o*) For purposes of this section, the term "patent" means a patent issued by the United States Patent and Trademark Office.

(p)(1) Safety and effectiveness data and information which has been submitted in an application filed under subsection (b)(1) or section 571(a) for a drug and which has not previously been disclosed to the public shall be made available to the public, upon request, unless extraordinary circumstances are shown—

(A) if no work is being or will be undertaken to have the application approved,

(B) if the Secretary has determined that the application is not approvable and all legal appeals have been exhausted,

(C) if approval of the application under subsection (c) is withdrawn and all legal appeals have been exhausted,

(D) if the Secretary has determined that such drug is not a new drug, or

(E) upon the effective date of the approval of the first application filed under subsection (b)(2) which refers to such drug or upon the date upon which the approval of an application filed under subsection (b)(2) which refers to such drug could be made effective if such an application had been filed.

(2) Any request for data and information pursuant to paragraph (1) shall include a verified statement by the person making the request that any data or information received under such paragraph shall not be disclosed by such person to any other person—

(A) for the purpose of, or as part of a plan, scheme, or device for, obtaining the right to make, use, or market, or making, using, or marketing, outside the United States, the drug identified in the application filed under subsection (b)(1) or section 571(a), and

(B) without obtaining from any person to whom the data and information are disclosed an identical verified statement, a copy of which is to be provided by such person to the Secretary, which meets the requirements of this paragraph.

SEC. 513 [21 U.S.C. 360c]. CLASSIFICATION OF DEVICES INTENDED FOR HUMAN USE

Device Classes

(a)(1) There are established the following classes of devices intended for human use:

(A) CLASS I, GENERAL CONTROLS.—

(i) A device for which the controls authorized by or under section 501, 502, 510, 516, 518, 519, or 520 or any combination of such sections are sufficient to provide reasonable assurance of the safety and effectiveness of the device.

(ii) A device for which insufficient information exists to determine that the controls referred to in clause (i) are sufficient to provide reasonable assurance of the safety and effectiveness of the device or to establish special controls to provide such assurance, but because it—

(I) is not purported or represented to be for a use in supporting or sustaining human life or for a use which is of substantial importance in preventing impairment of human health, and

(II) does not present a potential unreasonable risk of illness or injury,

is to be regulated by the controls referred to in clause (i).

(B) CLASS II, SPECIAL CONTROLS.—A device which cannot be classified as a class I device because the general controls by themselves are insufficient to provide reasonable assurance of the safety and effectiveness of the device, and for which there is sufficient information to establish special controls to provide such assurance, including the promulgation of performance standards, postmarket surveillance, patient registries, development and dissemination of guidelines (including guidelines for the submission of clinical data in premarket notification submissions in accordance with section 510(k)), recommendations, and other appropriate actions as the Secretary deems necessary to provide such assurance. For a device that is purported or represented to be for a use in supporting or sustaining human life, the Secretary shall examine and identify the special controls, if any, that are necessary to provide adequate assurance of safety and effectiveness and describe how such controls provide such assurance.

(C) CLASS III, PREMARKET APPROVAL.—A device which because—

(i) it (I) cannot be classified as a class I device because insufficient information exists to determine that the application of general controls are sufficient to provide reasonable assurance of the safety and effectiveness of the device, and (II) cannot be classified as a class II device because insufficient information exists to determine that the special controls described in subparagraph (B) would provide reasonable assurance of its safety and effectiveness, and

(ii)(I) is purported or represented to be for a use in supporting or sustaining human life or for a use which is of substantial importance in preventing impairment of human health, or

(II) presents a potential unreasonable risk of illness or injury,

is to be subject, in accordance with section 515, to Premarket approval to provide reasonable assurance of its safety and effectiveness.

If there is not sufficient information to establish a performance standard for a device to provide reasonable assurance of its safety and effectiveness, the Secretary may conduct such activities as may be necessary to develop or obtain such information.

(2) For purposes of this section and sections 514 and 515, the safety and effectiveness of a device are to be determined—

(A) with respect to the persons for whose use the device is represented or intended,

(B) with respect to the conditions of use prescribed, recommended, or suggested in the labeling of the device, and

(C) weighing any probable benefit to health from the use of the device against any probable risk of injury or illness from such use.

(3)(A) Except as authorized by subparagraph (B), the effectiveness of a device is, for purposes of this section and sections 514 and 515, to be determined, in accordance with regulations promulgated by the Secretary, on the basis of well-controlled investigations, including 1 or more clinical investigations where appropriate, by experts qualified by training and experience to evaluate the effectiveness of the device, from which investigations it can fairly and responsibly be concluded by qualified experts that the device will have the effect it purports or is represented to have under the conditions of use prescribed, recommended, or suggested in the labeling of the device.

(B) If the Secretary determines that there exists valid scientific evidence (other than evidence derived from investigations described in subparagraph (A))—

(i) which is sufficient to determine the effectiveness of a device, and

(ii) from which it can fairly and responsibly be concluded by qualified experts that the device will have the effect it purports or is represented to have under the conditions of use prescribed, recommended, or suggested in the labeling of the device,

then, for purposes of this section and sections 514 and 515, the Secretary may authorize the effectiveness of the device to be determined on the basis of such evidence.

(C) In making a determination of a reasonable assurance of the effectiveness of a device for which an application under section 515 has been submitted, the Secretary shall consider whether the extent of data that otherwise would be required for approval of the application with respect to effectiveness can be reduced through reliance on postmarket controls.

(D)(i) The Secretary, upon the written request of any person intending to submit an application under section 515, shall meet with such person to determine the type of valid scientific evidence (within the meaning of subparagraphs (A) and (B)) that will be necessary to demonstrate for purposes of approval of an application the effectiveness of a device for the conditions of use proposed by such person. The written request shall include a detailed description of the device, a detailed description of the proposed conditions of use of the device, a proposed plan for determining whether there is a reasonable assurance of effectiveness, and, if available, information regarding the expected performance from the device. Within 30 days after such meeting, the Secretary shall specify in writing the type of valid scientific evidence that will provide a reasonable assurance that a device is effective under the conditions of use proposed by such person.

(ii) Any clinical data, including one or more well-controlled investigations, specified in writing by the Secretary for demonstrating a reasonable assurance of device effectiveness shall be specified as result of a determination by the Secretary that such data are necessary to establish device effectiveness. The Secretary shall consider, in consultation with the applicant, the least burdensome appropriate means of evaluating device effectiveness that would have a reasonable likelihood of resulting in approval.

(iii) For purposes of clause (ii), the term "necessary" means the minimum required information that would support a determination by the Secretary that an application provides reasonable assurance of the effectiveness of the device.

(iv) Nothing in this subparagraph shall alter the criteria for evaluating an application for premarket approval of a device.

(v) The determination of the Secretary with respect to the specification of valid scientific evidence under clauses (i) and (ii) shall be binding upon the Secretary, unless such determination by the Secretary could be contrary to the public health.

Classification; Classification Panels

(b)(1) For purposes of—

(A) determining which devices intended for human use should be subject to the requirements of general controls, performance standards, or premarket approval, and

(B) providing notice to the manufacturers and importers of such devices to enable them to prepare for the application of such requirements to devices manufactured or imported by them,

the Secretary shall classify all such devices (other than devices classified by subsection (f)) into the classes established by subsection (a). For the purpose of securing recommendations with respect to the classification of devices, the Secretary shall establish panels of experts or use panels of experts established before the date of the enactment of this section, or both. Section 14 of the Federal Advisory Committee Act shall not apply to the duration of a panel established under this paragraph.

(2) The Secretary shall appoint to each panel established under paragraph (1) persons who are qualified by training and experience to evaluate the safety and effectiveness of the devices to be referred to the panel and who, to the extent feasible, possess skill in the use of, or experience in the development, manufacture, or utilization of, such devices. The Secretary shall make appointments to each panel so that each panel shall consist of members with adequately diversified expertise in such fields as clinical and administrative medicine, engineering, biological and physical sciences, and other related professions. In addition, each panel shall include as nonvoting members a representative of consumer interests and a representative of interests of the device manufacturing industry. Scientific, trade, and consumer organizations shall be afforded an opportunity to nominate individuals for appointment to the panels. No individual who is in the regular full-time employ of the United States and engaged in the administration of this Act may be a member of any panel. The Secretary shall designate one of the members of each panel to serve as chairman thereof.

(3) Panel members (other than officers or employees of the United States), while attending meetings or conferences of a panel or otherwise engaged in its business, shall be entitled to receive compensation at rates to be fixed by the Secretary, but not at rates exceeding the daily equivalent of the rate in effect for grade GS–18 of the General Schedule,[56] for each day so engaged, including travel time; and while so serving away from their homes or regular places of business each member may be allowed travel expenses (including per diem in lieu of subsistence) as authorized by section 5703 of title 5, United States Code, for persons in the Government service employed intermittently.

(4) The Secretary shall furnish each panel with adequate clerical and other necessary assistance.

(5) Classification panels covering each type of device shall be scheduled to meet at such times as may be appropriate for the Secretary to meet applicable statutory deadlines.

(6)(A) Any person whose device is specifically the subject of review by a classification panel shall have—

(i) the same access to data and information submitted to a classification panel (except for data and information that are not available for public disclosure under section 552 of title 5, United States Code) as the Secretary;

(ii) the opportunity to submit, for review by a classification panel, information that is based on the data or information provided in the application submitted

---

56. The General Schedule under section 5332 of title 5, United States Code, no longer includes the grade GS–18. The grades are GS–1 through GS–15.

under section 515 by the person, which information shall be submitted to the Secretary for prompt transmittal to the classification panel; and

(iii) the same opportunity as the Secretary to participate in meetings of the panel.

(B) Any meetings of a classification panel shall provide adequate time for initial presentations and for response to any differing views by persons whose devices are specifically the subject of a classification panel review, and shall encourage free and open participation by all interested persons.

(7) After receiving from a classification panel the conclusions and recommendations of the panel on a matter that the panel has reviewed, the Secretary shall review the conclusions and recommendations, shall make a final decision on the matter in accordance with section 515(d)(2), and shall notify the affected persons of the decision in writing and, if the decision differs from the conclusions and recommendations of the panel, shall include the reasons for the difference.

(8) A classification panel under this subsection shall not be subject to the annual chartering and annual report requirements of the Federal Advisory Committee Act.

Classification Panel Organization and Operation

(c)(1) The Secretary shall organize the panels according to the various fields of clinical medicine and fundamental sciences in which devices intended for human use are used. The Secretary shall refer a device to be classified under this section to an appropriate panel established or authorized to be used under subsection (b) for its review and for its recommendation respecting the classification of the device. The Secretary shall by regulation prescribe the procedure to be followed by the panels in making their reviews and recommendations. In making their reviews of devices, the panels, to the maximum extent practicable, shall provide an opportunity for interested persons to submit data and views on the classification of the devices.

(2)(A) Upon completion of a panel's review of a device referred to it under paragraph (1), the panel shall, subject to subparagraphs (B) and (C), submit to the Secretary its recommendation for the classification of the device. Any such recommendation shall (i) contain (I) a summary of the reasons for the recommendation, (II) a summary of the data upon which the recommendation is based, and (III) an identification of the risks to health (if any) presented by the device with respect to which the recommendation is made, and (ii) to the extent practicable, include a recommendation for the assignment of a priority for the application of the requirements of section 514 or 515 to a device recommended to be classified in class II or class III.

(B) A recommendation of a panel for the classification of a device in class I shall include a recommendation as to whether the device should be exempted from the requirements of section 510, 519, or 520(f).

(C) In the case of a device which has been referred under paragraph (1) to a panel, and which—

(i) is intended to be implanted in the human body or is purported or represented to be for a use in supporting or sustaining human life, and

(ii)(I) has been introduced or delivered for introduction into interstate commerce for commercial distribution before the date of enactment of this section, or

(II) is within a type of device which was so introduced or delivered before such date and is substantially equivalent to another device within that type,

such panel shall recommend to the Secretary that the device be classified in class III unless the panel determines that classification of the device in such class is not necessary to provide reasonable assurance of its safety and effectiveness. If a panel does not recommend that such a device be classified in class III, it shall in its recommendation to the Secretary for the classification of the device set forth the reasons for not recommending classification of the device in such class.

(3) The panels shall submit to the Secretary within one year of the date funds are first appropriated for the implementation of this section their recommendations respecting all devices of a type introduced or delivered for introduction into interstate commerce for commercial distribution before the date of the enactment of this section.

Classification

(d)(1) Upon receipt of a recommendation from a panel respecting a device, the Secretary shall publish in the Federal Register the panel's recommendation and a proposed regulation classifying such device and shall provide interested persons an opportunity to submit comments on such recommendation and the proposed regulation. After reviewing such comments, the Secretary shall, subject to paragraph (2), by regulation classify such device.

(2)(A) A regulation under paragraph (1) classifying a device in class I shall prescribe which, if any, of the requirements of section 510, 519 or 520(f) shall not apply to the device. A regulation which makes a requirement of section 510, 519, or 520(f) inapplicable to a device shall be accompanied by a statement of the reasons of the Secretary for making such requirement inapplicable.

(B) A device described in subsection (c)(2)(C) shall be classified in class III unless the Secretary determines that classification of the device in such class is not necessary to provide reasonable assurance of its safety and effectiveness. A proposed regulation under paragraph (1) classifying such a device in a class other than class III shall be accompanied by a full statement of the reasons of the Secretary (and supporting documentation and data) for not classifying such device in such class and an identification of the risks to health (if any) presented by such device.

(3) In the case of devices classified in class II and devices classified under this subsection in class III and described in section 515(b)(1) the Secretary may establish priorities which, in his discretion, shall be used in applying sections 514 and 515, as appropriate, to such devices.

Classification Changes

(e)(1)(A)(i) Based on new information respecting a device, the Secretary may, upon the initiative of the Secretary or upon petition of an interested person, change the classification of such device, and revoke, on account of the change in classification, any regulation or requirement in effect under section 514 or 515 with respect to such device, by administrative order published in the Federal Register following publication of a proposed reclassification order in the Federal Register, a meeting of a device classification panel described in subsection (b), and consideration of comments to a public docket, notwithstanding subchapter II of chapter 5 of title 5, United States Code. The proposed reclassification order published in the Federal Register shall set forth the proposed reclassification, and a substantive summary of the valid scientific evidence concerning the proposed reclassification, including—

(I) the public health benefit of the use of the device, and the nature and, if known, incidence of the risk of the device;

(II) in the case of a reclassification from class II to class III, why general controls pursuant to subsection (a)(1)(A) and special controls pursuant to subsection (a)(1)(B) together are not sufficient to provide a reasonable assurance of safety and effectiveness for such device; and

(III) in the case of reclassification from class III to class II, why general controls pursuant to subsection (a)(1)(A) and special controls pursuant to subsection (a)(1)(B) together are sufficient to provide a reasonable assurance of safety and effectiveness for such device.

(ii) An order under this subsection changing the classification of a device from class III to class II may provide that such classification shall not take effect until the effective date of a performance standard established under section 514 for such device.

(B) Authority to issue such administrative order shall not be delegated below the Director of the Center for Devices and Radiological Health, acting in consultation with the Commissioner.

(2) By an order issued under paragraph (1), the Secretary may change the classification of a device from class III—

(A) to class II if the Secretary determines that special controls would provide reasonable assurance of the safety and effectiveness of the device and that general controls would not provide reasonable assurance of the safety and effectiveness of the device, or

(B) to class I if the Secretary determines that general controls would provide reasonable assurance of the safety and effectiveness of the device.

Initial Classification and Reclassification of Certain Devices

(f)(1) Any device intended for human use which was not introduced or delivered for introduction into interstate commerce for commercial distribution before the date of the enactment of this section is classified in class III unless—

(A) the device—

(i) is within a type of device (I) which was introduced or delivered for introduction into interstate commerce for commercial distribution before such date and which is to be classified pursuant to subsection (b), or (II) which was not so introduced or delivered before such date and has been classified in class I or II, and

(ii) is substantially equivalent to another device within such type;

(B) the Secretary in response to a petition submitted under paragraph (3) has classified such device in class I or II; or

(C) the device is classified pursuant to a request submitted under paragraph (2).

A device classified in class III under this paragraph shall be classified in that class until the effective date of an order of the Secretary under paragraph (2) or (3) classifying the device in class I or II.

(2)(A)(i) Any person who submits a report under section 510(k) for a type of device that has not been previously classified under this Act, and that is classified into class III under paragraph (1), may request, within 30 days after receiving written notice of such a classification, the Secretary to classify the device.

(ii) In lieu of submitting a report under section 510(k) and submitting a request for classification under clause (i) for a device, if a person determines there is no legally marketed device upon which to base a determination of substantial equivalence (as defined in subsection (i)), a person may submit a request under this clause for the Secretary to classify the device.

(iii) Upon receipt of a request under clause (i) or (ii), the Secretary shall classify the device subject to the request under the criteria set forth in subparagraphs (A) through (C) of subsection (a)(1) within 120 days.

(iv) Notwithstanding clause (iii), the Secretary may decline to undertake a classification request submitted under clause (ii) if the Secretary identifies a legally marketed device that could provide a reasonable basis for review of substantial equivalence under paragraph (1), or when the Secretary determines that the device submitted is not of low-moderate risk or that general controls would be inadequate to control the risks and special controls to mitigate the risks cannot be developed.

(v) The person submitting the request for classification under this subparagraph may recommend to the Secretary a classification for the device and shall, if recommending classification in class II, include in the request an initial draft proposal for applicable special controls, as described in subsection (a)(1)(B), that are necessary, in conjunction with general controls, to provide reasonable assurance of safety and effectiveness and a description of how the special controls provide such assurance. Any such request shall describe the device and provide detailed information and reasons for the recommended classification.

(B)(i) The Secretary shall by written order classify the device involved. Such classification shall be the initial classification of the device for purposes of paragraph (1) and any device classified under this paragraph shall be a predicate device for determining substantial equivalence under paragraph (1).

(ii) A device that remains in class III under this subparagraph shall be deemed to be adulterated within the meaning of section 501(f)(1)(B) until approved under section 515 or exempted from such approval under section 520(g).

(C) Within 30 days after the issuance of an order classifying a device under this paragraph, the Secretary shall publish a notice in the Federal Register announcing such classification.

(3)(A) The Secretary may initiate the reclassification of a device classified into class III under paragraph (1) of this subsection or the manufacturer or importer of a device classified under paragraph (1) may petition the Secretary (in such form and manner as he shall prescribe) for the issuance of an order classifying the device in class I or class II. Within thirty days of the filing of such a petition, the Secretary shall notify the petitioner of any deficiencies in the petition which prevent the Secretary from making a decision on the petition.

(B)(i) Upon determining that a petition does not contain any deficiency which prevents the Secretary from making a decision on the petition, the Secretary may for good cause shown refer the petition to an appropriate panel established or authorized to be used under subsection (b). A panel to which such a petition has been referred shall not later than ninety days after the referral of the petition make a recommendation to the Secretary respecting approval or denial of the petition. Any such recommendation shall contain (I) a summary of the reasons for the recommendation, (II) a summary of the data upon which the recommendation is based, and (III) an identification of the risks to health (if any) presented by the device with respect to which the petition was filed. In the case of a petition for a device which is intended to be implanted in the human body or which is purported or represented to be for a use in supporting or sustaining human life, the panel shall recommend that the petition be denied unless the panel determines that the classification in class III of the device is not necessary to provide reasonable assurance of its safety and effectiveness. If the panel recommends that such petition be approved, it shall in its recommendation to the Secretary set forth its reasons for such recommendation.

(ii) The requirements of paragraphs (1) and (2) of subsection (c) (relating to opportunities for submission of data and views and recommendations respecting priorities and exemptions from sections 510, 519, and 520(f)) shall apply with respect to consideration by panels of petitions submitted under subparagraph (A).

(C)(i) Within ninety days from the date the Secretary receives the recommendation of a panel respecting a petition (but not later than 210 days after the filing of such petition) the Secretary shall by order deny or approve the petition. If the Secretary approves the petition, the Secretary shall order the classification of the device into class I or class II in accordance with the criteria prescribed by subsection (a)(1)(A) or (a)(1)(B). In the case of a petition for a device which is intended to be implanted in the human body or which is purported or represented to be for a use in supporting or sustaining human life, the Secretary shall deny the petition unless the Secretary determines that the classification in class III of the device is not necessary to provide reasonable assurance of its safety and effectiveness. An order approving such petition shall be accompanied by a full statement of the reasons of the Secretary (and supporting documentation and data) for approving the petition and an identification of the risks to health (if any) presented by the device to which such order applies.

(ii) The requirements of paragraphs (1) and (2)(A) of subsection (d) (relating to publication of recommendations, opportunity for submission of comments, and exemption from sections 510, 519, and 520(f)) shall apply with respect to action by the Secretary on petitions submitted under subparagraph (A).

(4) If a manufacturer reports to the Secretary under section 510(k) that a device is substantially equivalent to another device—

(A) which the Secretary has classified as a class III device under subsection (b),

(B) which was introduced or delivered for introduction into interstate commerce for commercial distribution before December 1, 1990, and

(C) for which no final regulation requiring premarket approval has been promulgated under section 515(b),

the manufacturer shall certify to the Secretary that the manufacturer has conducted a reasonable search of all information known or otherwise available to the manufacturer respecting such other device and has included in the report under section 510(k) a summary of and a citation to all adverse safety and effectiveness data respecting such other device and respecting the device for which the section 510(k) report is being made and which has not been submitted to the Secretary under section 519. The Secretary may require the manufacturer to submit the adverse safety and effectiveness data described in the report.

(5) The Secretary may not withhold a determination of the initial classification of a device under paragraph (1) because of a failure to comply with any provision of this Act unrelated to a substantial equivalence decision, including a finding that the facility in which the device is manufactured is not in compliance with good manufacturing requirements as set forth in regulations of the Secretary under section 520(f) (other than a finding that there is a substantial likelihood that the failure to comply with such regulations will potentially present a serious risk to human health).

Information

(g) Within sixty days of the receipt of a written request of any person for information respecting the class in which a device has been classified or the requirements applicable to a device under this Act, the Secretary shall provide such person a written statement of the classification (if any) of such device and the requirements of this Act applicable to the device.

Definitions

(h) For purposes of this section and sections 501, 510, 514, 515, 516, 519, and 520 —

(1) a reference to "general controls" is a reference to the controls authorized by or under sections 501, 502, 510, 516, 518, 519, and 520,

(2) a reference to "class I," "class II," or "class III" is a reference to a class of medical devices described in subparagraph (A), (B), or (C) of subsection (a) (1), and

(3) a reference to a "panel under section 513" is a reference to a panel established or authorized to be used under this section.

Substantial Equivalence

(i)(1)(A) For purposes of determinations of substantial equivalence under subsection (f) and section 520(*l*), the term "substantially equivalent" or "substantial equivalence" means, with respect to a device being compared to a predicate device, that the device has the same intended use as the predicate device and that the Secretary by order has found that the device —

(i) has the same technological characteristics as the predicate device, or

(ii)(I) has different technological characteristics and the information submitted that the device is substantially equivalent to the predicate device contains information, including appropriate clinical or scientific data if deemed necessary by the Secretary or a person accredited under section 523, that demonstrates that the device is as safe and effective as a legally marketed device, and (II) does not raise different questions of safety and effectiveness than the predicate device.

(B) For purposes of subparagraph (A), the term "different technological characteristics" means, with respect to a device being compared to a predicate device, that there is a significant change in the materials, design, energy source, or other features of the device from those of the predicate device.

(C) To facilitate reviews of reports submitted to the Secretary under section 510(k), the Secretary shall consider the extent to which reliance on postmarket controls may expedite the classification of devices under subsection (f)(1) of this section.

(D)(i) Whenever the Secretary requests information to demonstrate that devices with differing technological characteristics are substantially equivalent, the Secretary shall only request information that is necessary to making substantial equivalence determinations. In making such request, the Secretary shall consider the least burdensome means of demonstrating substantial equivalence and request information accordingly.

(ii) For purposes of clause (i), the term "necessary" means the minimum required information that would support a determination of substantial equivalence between a new device and a predicate device.

(iii) Nothing in this subparagraph shall alter the standard for determining substantial equivalence between a new device and a predicate device.

(E)(i) Any determination by the Secretary of the intended use of a device shall be based upon the proposed labeling submitted in a report for the device under section 510(k). However, when determining that a device can be found substantially equivalent to a legally marketed device, the director of the organizational unit responsible for regulating devices (in this subparagraph referred to as the "Director") may require a statement in labeling that provides appropriate information regarding a use of the device not identified in the proposed labeling if, after providing an opportunity for consultation with the person who submitted such report, the Director determines and states in writing—

(I) that there is a reasonable likelihood that the device will be used for an intended use not identified in the proposed labeling for the device; and

(II) that such use could cause harm.

(ii) Such determination shall—

(I) be provided to the person who submitted the report within 10 days from the date of the notification of the Director's concerns regarding the proposed labeling;

(II) specify the limitations on the use of the device not included in the proposed labeling; and

(III) find the device substantially equivalent if the requirements of subparagraph (A) are met and if the labeling for such device conforms to the limitations specified in subclause (II).

(iii) The responsibilities of the Director under this subparagraph may not be delegated.

(F) Not later than 270 days after the date of the enactment of the Food and Drug Administration Modernization Act of 1997, the Secretary shall issue guidance specifying the general principles that the Secretary will consider in determining when a specific intended use of a device is not reasonably included within a general use of such device for purposes of a determination of substantial equivalence under subsection (f) or section 520(*l*).

(2) A device may not be found to be substantially equivalent to a predicate device that has been removed from the market at the initiative of the Secretary or that has been determined to be misbranded or adulterated by a judicial order.

(3)(A) As part of a submission under section 510(k) respecting a device, the person required to file a premarket notification under such section shall provide an adequate summary of any information respecting safety and effectiveness or state that such information will be made available upon request by any person.

(B) Any summary under subparagraph (A) respecting a device shall contain detailed information regarding data concerning adverse health effects and shall be made available to the public by the Secretary within 30 days of the issuance of a determination that such device is substantially equivalent to another device.

SEC. 514 [21 U.S.C. 360d]. PERFORMANCE STANDARDS

Provisions of Standards

(a)(1) The special controls required by section 513(a)(1)(B) shall include performance standards for a class II device if the Secretary determines that a performance standard is necessary to provide reasonable assurance of the safety and effectiveness of the device. A class III device may also be considered a class II device for purposes of establishing a standard for the device under subsection (b) if the device has been reclassified as a class II device under an administrative order under section 513(e) (or a regulation promulgated under such section prior to the date of enactment of the Food and Drug Administration Safety and Innovation Act[57]) but such order (or regulation) provides that the reclassification is not to take effect until the effective date of such a standard for the device.

(2) A performance standard established under subsection (b) for a device—

(A) shall include provisions to provide reasonable assurance of its safe and effective performance;

(B) shall, where necessary to provide reasonable assurance of its safe and effective performance, include—

(i) provisions respecting the construction, components, ingredients, and properties of the device and its compatibility with power systems and connections to such systems,

(ii) provisions for the testing (on a sample basis or, if necessary, on an individual basis) of the device or, if it is determined that no other more practicable means are available to the Secretary to assure the conformity of the device to the standard, provisions for the testing (on a sample basis or, if necessary, on an individual basis) by the Secretary or by another person at the direction of the Secretary,

(iii) provisions for the measurement of the performance characteristics of the device,

---

57. Pub. L. No. 112–144, 126 Stat. 993, which was enacted July 9, 2012.

(iv) provisions requiring that the results of each or of certain of the tests of the device required to be made under clause (ii) show that the device is in conformity with the portions of the standard for which the test or tests were required, and

(v) a provision requiring that the sale and distribution of the device be restricted but only to the extent that the sale and distribution of a device may be restricted under a regulation under section 520(e); and

(C) shall, where appropriate, require the use and prescribe the form and content of labeling for the proper installation, maintenance, operation, and use of the device.

(3) The Secretary shall provide for periodic evaluation of performance standards established under subsection (b) to determine if such standards should be changed to reflect new medical, scientific, or other technological data.

(4) In carrying out his duties under this subsection and subsection (b), the Secretary shall, to the maximum extent practicable—

(A) use personnel, facilities, and other technical support available in other Federal agencies,

(B) consult with other Federal agencies concerned with standard-setting and other nationally or internationally recognized standard-setting entities, and

(C) invite appropriate participation, through joint or other conferences, workshops, or other means, by informed persons representative of scientific, professional, industry, or consumer organizations who in his judgment can make a significant contribution.

Establishment of a Standard

(b)(1)(A) The Secretary shall publish in the Federal Register a notice of proposed rulemaking for the establishment, amendment, or revocation of any performance standard for a device.

(B) A notice of proposed rulemaking for the establishment or amendment of a performance standard for a device shall—

(i) set forth a finding with supporting justification that the performance standard is appropriate and necessary to provide reasonable assurance of the safety and effectiveness of the device,

(ii) set forth proposed findings with respect to the risk of illness or injury that the performance standard is intended to reduce or eliminate,

(iii) invite interested persons to submit to the Secretary, within 30 days of the publication of the notice, requests for changes in the classification of the device pursuant to section 513(e) based on new information relevant to the classification, and

(iv) invite interested persons to submit an existing performance standard for the device, including a draft or proposed performance standard, for consideration by the Secretary.

(C) A notice of proposed rulemaking for the revocation of a performance standard shall set forth a finding with supporting justification that the performance standard is no longer necessary to provide reasonable assurance of the safety and effectiveness of a device.

(D) The Secretary shall provide for a comment period of not less than 60 days.

(2) If, after publication of a notice in accordance with paragraph (1), the Secretary receives a request for a change in the classification of the device, the Secretary shall, within 60 days of the publication of the notice, after consultation with the appropriate panel under section 513, either deny the request or give notice of an intent to initiate such change under section 513(e).

(3)(A) After the expiration of the period for comment on a notice of proposed rulemaking published under paragraph (1) respecting a performance standard and after consideration of such comments and any report from an advisory committee under paragraph (5), the Secretary shall (i) promulgate a regulation establishing a performance standard and publish in the Federal Register findings on the matters referred to in paragraph (1), or (ii) publish a notice terminating the proceeding for the development of the standard together with the reasons for such termination. If a notice of termination is published, the Secretary shall (unless such notice is issued because the device is a banned device under section 516) initiate a proceeding under section 513(e) to reclassify the device subject to the proceeding terminated by such notice.

(B) A regulation establishing a performance standard shall set forth the date or dates upon which the standard shall take effect, but no such regulation may take effect before one year after the date of its publication unless (i) the Secretary determines that an earlier effective date is necessary for the protection of the public health and safety, or (ii) such standard has been established for a device which, effective upon the effective date of the standard, has been reclassified from class III to class II. Such date or dates shall be established so as to minimize, consistent with the public health and safety, economic loss to, and disruption or dislocation of, domestic and international trade.

(4)(A) The Secretary, upon his own initiative or upon petition of an interested person may by regulation, promulgated in accordance with the requirements of paragraphs (1), (2), and (3)(B) of this subsection, amend or revoke a performance standard.

(B) The Secretary may declare a proposed amendment of a performance standard to be effective on and after its publication in the Federal Register and until the effective date of any final action taken on such amendment if he determines that making it so effective is in the public interest. A proposed amendment of a performance standard made so effective under the preceding sentence may not prohibit, during the period in which it is so effective, the introduction or delivery for introduction into interstate commerce of a device which conforms to such standard without the change or changes provided by such proposed amendment.

(5)(A) The Secretary—

(i) may on his own initiative refer a proposed regulation for the establishment, amendment, or revocation of a performance standard, or

(ii) shall, upon the request of an interested person which demonstrates good cause for referral and which is made before the expiration of the period for submission of comments on such proposed regulation refer such proposed regulation,

to an advisory committee of experts, established pursuant to subparagraph (B) for a report and recommendation with respect to any matter involved in the proposed regulation which requires the exercise of scientific judgment. If a proposed regulation is referred under this subparagraph to an advisory committee, the Secretary shall provide the advisory committee with the data and information on which such proposed regulation is based. The advisory committee shall, within sixty days of the referral of a proposed regulation and after independent study of the data and information furnished to it by the Secretary and other data and information before it, submit to the Secretary a report and recommendation respecting such regulation, together with all underlying data and information and a statement of the reason or basis for the recommendation. A copy of such report and recommendation shall be made public by the Secretary.

(B) The Secretary shall establish advisory committees (which may not be panels under section 513) to receive referrals under subparagraph (A). The Secretary shall appoint as members of any such advisory committee persons qualified in the subject matter to be referred to the committee and of appropriately diversified professional background, except that the Secretary may not appoint to such a committee any individual who is in the regular full-time employ of the United States and engaged in the administration of this Act. Each such committee shall include as nonvoting members a representative of consumer interests and a representative of interests of the device manufacturing industry. Members of an advisory committee who are not officers or employees of the United States, while attending conferences or meetings of their committee or otherwise serving at the request of the Secretary, shall be entitled to receive compensation at rates to be fixed by the Secretary, which rates may not exceed the daily equivalent of the rate in effect for grade GS–18 of the General Schedule, for each day (including travel time) they are so engaged; and while so serving away from their homes or regular places of business each member may be allowed travel expenses, including per diem in lieu of subsistence, as authorized by section 5703 of title 5 of the United States Code for persons in the Government service employed intermittently. The Secretary shall designate one of the members of each advisory committee to serve as chairman thereof. The Secretary shall furnish each advisory committee with clerical and other assistance, and shall by regulation prescribe the procedures to be followed by each such committee in acting on referrals made under subparagraph (A).

Recognition of a Standard

(c)(1)(A) In addition to establishing a performance standard under this section, the Secretary shall, by publication in the Federal Register, recognize all or part of an appropriate standard established by a nationally or internationally recognized standard development organization for which a person may submit a declaration of conformity in order to meet a premarket submission requirement or other requirement under this Act to which such standard is applicable.

(B) If a person elects to use a standard recognized by the Secretary under subparagraph (A) to meet the requirements described in such subparagraph, the person shall provide a declaration of conformity to the Secretary that certifies that the device is in conformity with such standard. A person may elect to use data, or information, other than data required by a standard recognized under subparagraph (A) to meet any requirement regarding devices under this Act.

(2) The Secretary may withdraw such recognition of a standard through publication of a notice in the Federal Register if the Secretary determines that the standard is no longer appropriate for meeting a requirement regarding devices under this Act.

(3)(A) Subject to subparagraph (B), the Secretary shall accept a declaration of conformity that a device is in conformity with a standard recognized under paragraph (1) unless the Secretary finds—

(i) that the data or information submitted to support such declaration does not demonstrate that the device is in conformity with the standard identified in the declaration of conformity; or

(ii) that the standard identified in the declaration of conformity is not applicable to the particular device under review.

(B) The Secretary may request, at any time, the data or information relied on by the person to make a declaration of conformity with respect to a standard recognized under paragraph (1).

(C) A person making a declaration of conformity with respect to a standard recognized under paragraph (1) shall maintain the data and information demonstrating conformity of the device to the standard for a period of two years after the date of the classification or approval of the device by the Secretary or a period equal to the expected design life of the device, whichever is longer.

SEC. 515 [21 U.S.C. 360e]. PREMARKET APPROVAL

General Requirement

(a) A class III device—

(1) which is subject to a an[58] order issued under subsection (b) (or a regulation promulgated under such section prior to the date of enactment of the Food and Drug Administration Safety and Innovation Act[59]); or

(2) which is a class III device because of section 513(f), is required to have, unless exempt under section 520(g), an approval under this section of an application for premarket approval or, as applicable, an approval under subsection (c)(2) of a report seeking premarket approval.

Order To Require Premarket Approval

(b)(1) In the case of a class III device which—

(A) was introduced or delivered for introduction into interstate commerce for commercial distribution before the date of enactment of this section; or

(B) is (i) of a type so introduced or delivered, and (ii) is substantially equivalent to another device within that type;

the Secretary shall by administrative order following publication of a proposed order in the Federal Register, a meeting of a device classification panel described in section 513(b), and consideration of comments from all affected stakeholders, including patients, payors, and providers, notwithstanding subchapter II of chapter 5 of title 5, United States Code, require that such device have an approval under this section of an application for premarket approval. Authority to issue such administrative order shall not be delegated below the Director of the Center for Devices and Radiological Health, acting in consultation with the Commissioner.

(2) A proposed order required under paragraph (1) shall contain—

(A) the proposed order;

(B) proposed findings with respect to the degree of risk of illness or injury designed to be eliminated or reduced by requiring the device to have an approved application for Premarket approval and the benefit to the public from use of the device;

(C) opportunity for the submission of comments on the proposed order and the proposed findings; and

(D) opportunity to request a change in the classification of the device based on new information relevant to the classification of the device.

---

58. So in law. See Pub. L. No. 112–144, § 608(b)(1)(A), 126 Stat. 993, 1056–57 (2012). Probably should be "to an".

59. Pub. L. No. 112–144, 126 Stat. 993, which was enacted July 9, 2012.

(3) After the expiration of the period for comment on a proposed order and proposed findings published under paragraph (2) consideration of comments submitted on such proposed order and findings, and a meeting of a device classification panel described in section 513(b), the Secretary shall (A) issue an administrative order under paragraph (1) and publish in the Federal Register findings on the matters referred to in paragraph (2)(B), or (B) publish a notice terminating the proceeding for the issuance of the administrative order together with the reasons for such termination. If a notice of termination is published, the Secretary shall (unless such notice is issued because the device is a banned device under section 516) initiate a proceeding under section 513(e) to reclassify the device subject to the proceeding terminated by such notice.

Application for Premarket Approval

(c)(1) Any person may file with the Secretary an application for premarket approval for a class III device. Such an application for a device shall contain—

(A) full reports of all information, published or known to or which should reasonably be known to the applicant, concerning investigations which have been made to show whether or not such device is safe and effective;

(B) a full statement of the components, ingredients, and properties and of the principle or principles of operation, of such device;

(C) a full description of the methods used in, and the facilities and controls used for, the manufacture, processing, and, when relevant, packing and installation of, such device;

(D) an identifying reference to any performance standard under section 514 which would be applicable to any aspect of such device if it were a class II device, and either adequate information to show that such aspect of such device fully meets such performance standard or adequate information to justify any deviation from such standard;

(E) such samples of such device and of components thereof as the Secretary may reasonably require, except that where the submission of such samples is impracticable or unduly burdensome, the requirement of this subparagraph may be met by the submission of complete information concerning the location of one or more such devices readily available for examination and testing;

(F) specimens of the labeling proposed to be used for such device;

(G) the certification required under section 402(j)(5)(B) of the Public Health Service Act (which shall not be considered an element of such application); and

(H) such other information relevant to the subject matter of the application as the Secretary, with the concurrence of the appropriate panel under section 513, may require.

(2)(A) Any person may file with the Secretary a report seeking premarket approval for a class III device referred to in subsection (a) that is a reprocessed single-use device. Such a report shall contain the following:

(i) The device name, including both the trade or proprietary name and the common or usual name.

(ii) The establishment registration number of the owner or operator submitting the report.

(iii) Actions taken to comply with performance standards under section 514.

(iv) Proposed labels, labeling, and advertising sufficient to describe the device, its intended use, and directions for use.

(v) Full reports of all information, published or known to or which should be reasonably known to the applicant, concerning investigations which have been made to show whether or not the device is safe or effective.

(vi) A description of the device's components, ingredients, and properties.

(vii) A full description of the methods used in, and the facilities and controls used for, the reprocessing and packing of the device.

(viii) Such samples of the device that the Secretary may reasonably require.

(ix) A financial certification or disclosure statement or both, as required by part 54 of title 21, Code of Federal Regulations.

(x) A statement that the applicant believes to the best of the applicant's knowledge that all data and information submitted to the Secretary are truthful and accurate and that no material fact has been omitted in the report.

(xi) Any additional data and information, including information of the type required in paragraph (1) for an application under such paragraph, that the Secretary determines is necessary to determine whether there is reasonable assurance of safety and effectiveness for the reprocessed device.

(xii) Validation data described in section 510(o)(1)(A) that demonstrates that the reasonable assurance of the safety or effectiveness of the device will remain after the maximum number of times the device is reprocessed as intended by the person submitting such report.

(B) In the case of a class III device referred to in subsection (a) that is a reprocessed single-use device:

(i) Subparagraph (A) of this paragraph applies in lieu of paragraph (1).

(ii) Subject to clause (i), the provisions of this section apply to a report under subparagraph (A) to the same extent and in the same manner as such provisions apply to an application under paragraph (1).

(iii) Each reference in other sections of this Act to an application under this section, other than such a reference in section 737 or 738, shall be considered to be a reference to a report under subparagraph (A).

(iv) Each reference in other sections of this Act to a device for which an application under this section has been approved, or has been denied, suspended, or withdrawn, other than such a reference in section 737 or 738, shall be considered to be a reference to a device for which a report under subparagraph (A) has been approved, or has been denied, suspended, or withdrawn, respectively.

(3) Upon receipt of an application meeting the requirements set forth in paragraph (1), the Secretary—

(A) may on the Secretary's own initiative, or

(B) shall, upon the request of an applicant unless the Secretary finds that the information in the application which would be reviewed by a panel substantially duplicates information which has previously been reviewed by a panel appointed under section 513,

refer such application to the appropriate panel under section 513 for study and for submission (within such period as he may establish) of a report and recommendation respecting approval of the application, together with all underlying data and the reasons or basis for the recommendation.

(4)(A) Prior to the submission of an application under this subsection, the Secretary shall accept and review any portion of the application that the applicant and the Secretary agree is complete, ready, and appropriate for review, except that such requirement does not apply, and the Secretary has discretion whether to accept and review such portion, during any period in which, under section 738(h), the Secretary does not have the authority to collect fees under section 738(a).

(B) Each portion of a submission reviewed under subparagraph (A) and found acceptable by the Secretary shall not be further reviewed after receipt of an application that satisfies the requirements of paragraph (1), unless an issue of safety unless an issue of a significant safety or effectiveness provides the Secretary reason to review such accepted portion.

(C) Whenever the Secretary determines that a portion of a submission under subparagraph (A) is unacceptable, the Secretary shall, in writing, provide to the applicant a description of any deficiencies in such portion and identify the information that is required to correct these deficiencies, unless the applicant is no longer pursuing the application. Where appropriate, the Secretary shall ensure that such panel includes, or consults with, one or more pediatric experts.

Action on an Application for Premarket Approval

(d)(1)(A) As promptly as possible, but in no event later than one hundred and eighty days after the receipt of an application under subsection (c) (except as provided in section 520(*l*)(3)(D)(ii) or unless, in accordance with subparagraph (B)(i), an additional period as agreed upon by the Secretary and the applicant), the Secretary, after considering the report and recommendation submitted under paragraph (2) of such subsection, shall—

(i) issue an order approving the application if he finds that none of the grounds for denying approval specified in paragraph (2) of this subsection applies; or

(ii) deny approval of the application if he finds (and sets forth the basis for such finding as part of or accompanying such denial) that one or more grounds for denial specified in paragraph (2) of this subsection apply.

In making the determination whether to approve or deny the application, the Secretary shall rely on the conditions of use included in the proposed labeling as the basis for determining whether or not there is a reasonable assurance of safety and effectiveness, if the proposed labeling is neither false nor misleading. In determining whether or not such labeling is false or misleading, the Secretary shall fairly evaluate all material facts pertinent to the proposed labeling.

(B)(i) The Secretary may not enter into an agreement to extend the period in which to take action with respect to an application submitted for a device subject to a regulation promulgated under subsection (b) unless he finds that the continued availability of the device is necessary for the public health.

(ii) An order approving an application for a device may require as a condition to such approval that the sale and distribution of the device be restricted but only to the extent that the sale and distribution of a device may be restricted under a regulation under section 520(e).

(iii) The Secretary shall accept and review statistically valid and reliable data and any other information from investigations conducted under the authority of regulations required by section 520(g) to make a determination of whether there is a reasonable assurance of safety and effectiveness of a device subject to a pending application under this section if—

(I) the data or information is derived from investigations of an earlier version of the device, the device has been modified during or after the investigations (but prior to submission of an application under subsection (c)) and such a modification of the device does not constitute a significant change in the design or in the basic principles of operation of the device that would invalidate the data or information; or

(II) the data or information relates to a device approved under this section, is available for use under this Act, and is relevant to the design and intended use of the device for which the application is pending.

(2) The Secretary shall deny approval of an application for a device if, upon the basis of the information submitted to the Secretary as part of the application and any other information before him with respect to such device, the Secretary finds that—

(A) there is a lack of a showing of reasonable assurance that such device is safe under the conditions of use prescribed, recommended, or suggested in the proposed labeling thereof;

(B) there is a lack of a showing of reasonable assurance that the device is effective under the conditions of use prescribed, recommended, or suggested in the proposed labeling thereof;

(C) the methods used in, or the facilities or controls used for, the manufacture, processing, packing, or installation of such device do not conform to the requirements of section 520(f);

(D) based on a fair evaluation of all material facts, the proposed labeling is false or misleading in any particular; or

(E) such device is not shown to conform in all respects to a performance standard in effect under section 514 compliance with which is a condition to approval of the application and there is a lack of adequate information to justify the deviation from such standard.

Any denial of an application shall, insofar as the Secretary determines to be practicable, be accompanied by a statement informing the applicant of the measures required to place such application in approvable form (which measures may include further research by the applicant in accordance with one or more protocols prescribed by the Secretary).

(3)(A)(i) The Secretary shall, upon the written request of an applicant, meet with the applicant, not later than 100 days after the receipt of an application that has been filed as complete under subsection (c), to discuss the review status of the application.

(ii) The Secretary shall, in writing and prior to the meeting, provide to the applicant a description of any deficiencies in the application that, at that point, have been identified by the Secretary based on an interim review of the entire application and identify the information that is required to correct those deficiencies.

(iii) The Secretary shall notify the applicant promptly of—

(I) any additional deficiency identified in the application, or

(II) any additional information required to achieve completion of the review and final action on the application,

that was not described as a deficiency in the written description provided by the Secretary under clause (ii).

(B) The Secretary and the applicant may, by mutual consent, establish a different schedule for a meeting required under this paragraph.

(4) An applicant whose application has been denied approval may, by petition filed on or before the thirtieth day after the date upon which he receives notice of such denial, obtain review thereof in accordance with either paragraph (1) or (2) of subsection (g), and any interested person may obtain review, in accordance with

paragraph (1) or (2) of subsection (g), of an order of the Secretary approving an application.

(5) In order to provide for more effective treatment or diagnosis of life-threatening or irreversibly debilitating human diseases or conditions, the Secretary shall provide review priority for devices—

(A) representing breakthrough technologies,

(B) for which no approved alternatives exist,

(C) which offer significant advantages over existing approved alternatives, or

(D) the availability of which is in the best interest of the patients.

(6)(A)(i) A supplemental application shall be required for any change to a device subject to an approved application under this subsection that affects safety or effectiveness, unless such change is a modification in a manufacturing procedure or method of manufacturing and the holder of the approved application submits a written notice to the Secretary that describes in detail the change, summarizes the data or information supporting the change, and informs the Secretary that the change has been made under the requirements of section 520(f).

(ii) The holder of an approved application who submits a notice under clause (i) with respect to a manufacturing change of a device may distribute the device 30 days after the date on which the Secretary receives the notice, unless the Secretary within such 30–day period notifies the holder that the notice is not adequate and describes such further information or action that is required for acceptance of such change. If the Secretary notifies the holder that a supplemental application is required, the Secretary shall review the supplement within 135 days after the receipt of the supplement. The time used by the Secretary to review the notice of the manufacturing change shall be deducted from the 135–day review period if the notice meets appropriate content requirements for Premarket approval supplements.

(B)(i) Subject to clause (ii), in reviewing a supplement to an approved application, for an incremental change to the design of a device that affects safety or effectiveness, the Secretary shall approve such supplement if—

(I) nonclinical data demonstrate that the design modification creates the intended additional capacity, function, or performance of the device; and

(II) clinical data from the approved application and any supplement to the approved application provide a reasonable assurance of safety and effectiveness for the changed device.

(ii) The Secretary may require, when necessary, additional clinical data to evaluate the design modification of the device to provide a reasonable assurance of safety and effectiveness.

Withdrawal and Temporary Suspension of Approval of Application

(e)(1) The Secretary shall, upon obtaining, where appropriate, advice on scientific matters from a panel or panels under section 513, and after due notice and opportunity for informal hearing to the holder of an approved application for a device, issue an order withdrawing approval of the application if the Secretary finds—

(A) that such device is unsafe or ineffective under the conditions of use prescribed, recommended, or suggested in the labeling thereof;

(B) on the basis of new information before him with respect to such device, evaluated together with the evidence available to him when the application was approved, that there is a lack of a showing of reasonable assurance that the device is safe or effective under the conditions of use prescribed, recommended, or suggested in the labeling thereof;

(C) that the application contained or was accompanied by an untrue statement of a material fact;

(D) that the applicant (i) has failed to establish a system for maintaining records, or has repeatedly or deliberately failed to maintain records or to make reports, required by an applicable regulation under section 519(a), (ii) has refused to permit access to, or copying or verification of, such records as required by section 704, or (iii) has not complied with the requirements of section 510;

(E) on the basis of new information before him with respect to such device, evaluated together with the evidence before him when the application was approved, that the methods used in, or the facilities and controls used for, the manufacture, processing, packing, or installation of such device do not conform with the requirements of section 520(f) and were not brought into conformity with such requirements within a reasonable time after receipt of written notice from the Secretary of nonconformity;

(F) on the basis of new information before him, evaluated together with the evidence before him when the application was approved, that the labeling of such device, based on a fair evaluation of all material facts, is false or misleading in any particular and was not corrected within a reasonable time after receipt of written notice from the Secretary of such fact; or

(G) on the basis of new information before him, evaluated together with the evidence before him when the application was approved, that such device is not shown to conform in all respects to a performance standard which is in effect under section 514 compliance with which was a condition to approval of the application and that there is a lack of adequate information to justify the deviation from such standard.

(2) The holder of an application subject to an order issued under paragraph (1) withdrawing approval of the application may, by petition filed on or before the thirtieth day after the date upon which he receives notice of such withdrawal, obtain review thereof in accordance with either paragraph (1) or (2) of subsection (g).

(3) If, after providing an opportunity for an informal hearing, the Secretary determines there is reasonable probability that the continuation of distribution of a device under an approved application would cause serious, adverse health consequences or death, the Secretary shall by order temporarily suspend the approval of the application approved under this section. If the Secretary issues such an order, the Secretary shall proceed expeditiously under paragraph (1) to withdraw such application.

Product Development Protocol

(f)(1) In the case of a class III device which is required to have an approval of an application submitted under subsection (c), such device shall be considered as having such an approval if a notice of completion of testing conducted in accordance with a product development protocol approved under paragraph (4) has been declared completed under paragraph (6).

(2) Any person may submit to the Secretary a proposed product development protocol with respect to a device. Such a protocol shall be accompanied by data supporting it. If, within thirty days of the receipt of such a protocol, the Secretary determines that it appears to be appropriate to apply the requirements of this subsection to the device with respect to which the protocol is submitted, the Secretary—

(A) may, at the initiative of the Secretary, refer the proposed protocol to the appropriate panel under section 513 for its recommendation respecting approval of the protocol; or

(B) shall so refer such protocol upon the request of the submitter, unless the Secretary finds that the proposed protocol and accompanying data which would be reviewed by such panel substantially duplicate a product development protocol and accompanying data which have previously been reviewed by such a panel.

(3) A proposed product development protocol for a device may be approved only if—

(A) the Secretary determines that it is appropriate to apply the requirements of this subsection to the device in lieu of the requirement of approval of an application submitted under subsection (c); and

(B) the Secretary determines that the proposed protocol provides—

(i) a description of the device and the changes which may be made in the device,

(ii) a description of the preclinical trials (if any) of the device and a specification of (I) the results from such trials to be required before the commencement of clinical trials of the device, and (II) any permissible variations in preclinical trials and the results therefrom,

(iii) a description of the clinical trials (if any) of the device and a specification of (I) the results from such trials to be required before the filing of a notice of completion of the requirements of the protocol, and (II) any permissible variations in such trials and the results therefrom,

(iv) a description of the methods to be used in, and the facilities and controls to be used for, the manufacture, processing, and when relevant, packing and installation of the device,

(v) an identifying reference to any performance standard under section 514 to be applicable to any aspect of such device,

(vi) if appropriate, specimens of the labeling proposed to be used for such device,

(vii) such other information relevant to the subject matter of the protocol as the Secretary, with the concurrence of the appropriate panel or panels under section 513, may require, and

(viii) a requirement for submission of progress reports and, when completed, records of the trials conducted under the protocol which records are adequate to show compliance with the protocol.

(4) The Secretary shall approve or disapprove a proposed product development protocol submitted under paragraph (2) within one hundred and twenty days of its receipt unless an additional period is agreed upon by the Secretary and the person who submitted the protocol. Approval of a protocol or denial of approval of a protocol is final agency action subject to judicial review under chapter 7 of title 5, United States Code.

(5) At any time after a product development protocol for a device has been approved pursuant to paragraph (4), the person for whom the protocol was approved may submit a notice of completion—

(A) stating (i) his determination that the requirements of the protocol have been fulfilled and that, to the best of his knowledge, there is no reason bearing on safety or effectiveness why the notice of completion should not become effective, and (ii) the data and other information upon which such determination was made, and

(B) setting forth the results of the trials required by the protocol and all the information required by subsection (c)(1).

(6)(A) The Secretary may, after providing the person who has an approved protocol an opportunity for an informal hearing and at any time prior to receipt of notice of completion of such protocol, issue a final order to revoke such protocol if he finds that—

(i) such person has failed substantially to comply with the requirements of the protocol,

(ii) the results of the trials obtained under the protocol differ so substantially from the results required by the protocol that further trials cannot be justified, or

(iii) the results of the trials conducted under the protocol or available new information do not demonstrate that the device tested under the protocol does not present an unreasonable risk to health and safety.

(B) After the receipt of a notice of completion of an approved protocol the Secretary shall, within the ninety-day period beginning on the date such notice is received, by order either declare the protocol completed or declare it not completed. An order declaring a protocol not completed may take effect only after the Secretary has provided the person who has the protocol opportunity for an informal hearing on the order. Such an order may be issued only if the Secretary finds—

(i) such person has failed substantially to comply with the requirements of the protocol,

(ii) the results of the trials obtained under the protocol differ substantially from the results required by the protocol, or

(iii) there is a lack of a showing of reasonable assurance of the safety and effectiveness of the device under the conditions of use prescribed, recommended, or suggested in the proposed labeling thereof.

(C) A final order issued under subparagraph (A) or (B) shall be in writing and shall contain the reasons to support the conclusions thereof.

(7) At any time after a notice of completion has become effective, the Secretary may issue an order (after due notice and opportunity for an informal hearing to the person for whom the notice is effective) revoking the approval of a device provided by a notice of completion which has become effective as provided in subparagraph (B) if he finds that any of the grounds listed in subparagraphs (A) through (G) of subsection (e)(1) of this section apply. Each reference in such subparagraphs to an application shall be considered for purposes of this paragraph as a reference to a protocol and the notice of completion of such protocol, and each reference to the time when an application was approved shall be considered for purposes of this paragraph as a reference to the time when a notice of completion took effect.

(8) A person who has an approved protocol subject to an order issued under paragraph (6)(A) revoking such protocol, a person who has an approved protocol with respect to which an order under paragraph (6)(B) was issued declaring that the protocol had not been completed, or a person subject to an order issued under paragraph (7) revoking the approval of a device may, by petition filed on or before the thirtieth day after the date upon which he receives notice of such order, obtain review thereof in accordance with either paragraph (1) or (2) of subsection (g).

Review

(g)(1) Upon petition for review of—

(A) an order under subsection (d) approving or denying approval of an application or an order under subsection (e) withdrawing approval of an application, or

(B) an order under subsection (f)(6)(A) revoking an approved protocol, under subsection (f)(6)(B) declaring that an approved protocol has not been completed, or under subsection (f)(7) revoking the approval of a device,

the Secretary shall, unless he finds the petition to be without good cause or unless a petition for review of such order has been submitted under paragraph (2), hold a hearing, in accordance with section 554 of title 5 of the United States Code, on the order. The panel or panels which considered the application, protocol, or device subject to such order shall designate a member to appear and testify at any such hearing upon request of the Secretary, the petitioner, or the officer conducting the hearing, but this requirement does not preclude any other member of the panel or panels from appearing and testifying at any such hearing. Upon completion of such hearing and after considering the record established in such hearing, the Secretary shall issue an order either affirming the order subject to the hearing or reversing such order and, as appropriate, approving or denying approval of the application, reinstating the application's approval, approving the protocol, or placing in effect a notice of completion.

(2)(A) Upon petition for review of—

(i) an order under subsection (d) approving or denying approval of an application or an order under subsection (e) withdrawing approval of an application, or

(ii) an order under subsection (f)(6)(A) revoking an approved protocol, under subsection (f)(6)(B) declaring that an approved protocol has not been completed, or under subsection (f)(7) revoking the approval of a device,

the Secretary shall refer the application or protocol subject to the order and the basis for the order to an advisory committee of experts established pursuant to subparagraph (B) for a report and recommendation with respect to the order. The advisory committee shall, after independent study of the data and information furnished to it by the Secretary and other data and information before it, submit to the Secretary a report and recommendation, together with all underlying data and information and a statement of the reasons or basis for the recommendation. A copy of such report shall be promptly supplied by the Secretary to any person who petitioned for such referral to the advisory committee.

(B) The Secretary shall establish advisory committees (which may not be panels under section 513) to receive referrals under subparagraph (A). The Secretary shall appoint as members of any such advisory committee persons qualified in the subject matter to be referred to the committee and of appropriately diversified professional backgrounds, except that the Secretary may not appoint to such a committee any individual who is in the regular full-time employ of the United States and engaged in the administration of this Act. Members of an advisory committee (other than officers or employees of the United States), while attending conferences or meetings of their committee or otherwise serving at the request of the Secretary, shall be entitled to receive compensation at rates to be fixed by the Secretary which rates may not exceed the daily equivalent for grade GS–18 of the General Schedule for each day (including travel time) they are so engaged; and while so serving away from their homes or regular places of business each member may be allowed travel expenses, including per diem in lieu of subsistence, as authorized by section 5703 of title 5 of the United States Code for persons in the Government service employed intermittently. The Secretary shall designate the chairman of an advisory committee from its members. The Secretary shall furnish each advisory committee with clerical and other assistance, and shall by regulation prescribe the procedures to be followed by each such committee in acting on referrals made under subparagraph (A).

(C) The Secretary shall make public the report and recommendation made by an advisory committee with respect to an application and shall by order, stating the reasons therefor, either affirm the order referred to the advisory committee or reverse such order and, if appropriate, approve or deny approval of the application, reinstate the application's approval, approve the protocol, or place in effect a notice of completion.

Service of Orders

(h) Orders of the Secretary under this section shall be served (1) in person by any officer or employee of the department designated by the Secretary, or (2) by mailing the order by registered mail or certified mail addressed to the applicant at his last known address in the records of the Secretary.

Revision

(i)(1) Before December 1, 1995, the Secretary shall by order require manufacturers of devices, which were introduced or delivered for introduction into interstate commerce for commercial distribution before May 28, 1976, and which are subject to revision of classification under paragraph (2), to submit to the Secretary a summary of and citation to any information known or otherwise available to the manufacturer respecting such devices, including adverse safety or effectiveness information which has not been submitted under section 519. The Secretary may require the manufacturer to submit the adverse safety or effectiveness data for which a summary and citation were submitted, if such data are available to the manufacturer.

(2) After the issuance of an order under paragraph (1) but before the date that is 2 years after the date of enactment of the Food and Drug Administration Safety and Innovation Act,[60] the Secretary shall issue an administrative order following publication of a proposed order in the Federal Register, a meeting of a device classification panel described in section 513(b), and consideration of comments from all affected stakeholders, including patients, payors, and providers, notwithstanding subchapter II of chapter 5 of title 5, United States Code, for each device—

(A) which the Secretary has classified as a class III device, and

(B) for which no administrative order has been issued under subsection (b) (or no regulation has been promulgated under such subsection prior to the date of enactment of the Food and Drug Administration Safety and Innovation Act[61]),

60. Pub. L. No. 112–144, 126 Stat. 993, which was enacted July 9, 2012.

61. Pub. L. No. 112–144, 126 Stat. 993, which was enacted July 9, 2012.

revising the classification of the device so that the device is classified into class I or class II, unless the administrative order issued under this paragraph requires the device to remain in class III. In determining whether to revise the classification of a device or to require a device to remain in class III, the Secretary shall apply the criteria set forth in section 513(a).

(3) The Secretary shall, as promptly as is reasonably achievable, but not later than 12 months after the effective date of the order requiring a device to remain in class III, establish a schedule for the issuance of an administrative order under subsection (b) for each device which is subject to the order requiring the device to remain in class III.

SEC. 515A [21 U.S.C. 360e–1]. PEDIATRIC USES OF DEVICES

(a) NEW DEVICES.—

(1) IN GENERAL.—A person that submits to the Secretary an application under section 520(m), or an application (or supplement to an application) or a product development protocol under section 515, shall include in the application or protocol the information described in paragraph (2).

(2) REQUIRED INFORMATION.—The application or protocol described in paragraph (1) shall include, with respect to the device for which approval is sought and if readily available—

(A) a description of any pediatric subpopulations that suffer from the disease or condition that the device is intended to treat, diagnose, or cure; and

(B) the number of affected pediatric patients.

(3) ANNUAL REPORT.—Not later than 18 months after the date of the enactment of this section,[62] and annually thereafter, the Secretary shall submit to the Committee on Health, Education, Labor, and Pensions of the Senate and the Committee on Energy and Commerce of the House of Representatives a report that includes—

(A) the number of devices approved in the year preceding the year in which the report is submitted, for which there is a pediatric subpopulation that suffers from the disease or condition that the device is intended to treat, diagnose, or cure;

(B) the number of devices approved in the year preceding the year in which the report is submitted, labeled for use in pediatric patients;

(C) the number of pediatric devices approved in the year preceding the year in which the report is submitted, exempted from a fee pursuant to section 738(a)(2)(B)(v); and

---

62. Section 515A was added by Pub. L. No. 110–85, § 302, 121 Stat. 823, 859–60, which was enacted September 27, 2007.

(D) the review time for each device described in subparagraphs (A), (B), and (C).

(b) DETERMINATION OF PEDIATRIC EFFECTIVENESS BASED ON SIMILAR COURSE OF DISEASE OR CONDITION OR SIMILAR EFFECT OF DEVICE ON ADULTS—

(1) IN GENERAL.—If the course of the disease or condition and the effects of the device are sufficiently similar in adults and pediatric patients, the Secretary may conclude that adult data may be used to support a determination of a reasonable assurance of effectiveness in pediatric populations, as appropriate.

(2) EXTRAPOLATION BETWEEN SUBPOPULATIONS.—A study may not be needed in each pediatric subpopulation if data from one subpopulation can be extrapolated to another subpopulation.

(c) PEDIATRIC SUBPOPULATION.—For purposes of this section, the term "pediatric subpopulation" has the meaning given the term in section 520(m)(6)(E)(ii).

SEC. 516 [21 U.S.C. 360f]. BANNED DEVICES

General Rule

(a) Whenever the Secretary finds, on the basis of all available data and information, that—

(1) a device intended for human use presents substantial deception or an unreasonable and substantial risk of illness or injury; and

(2) in the case of substantial deception or an unreasonable and substantial risk of illness or injury which the Secretary determined could be corrected or eliminated by labeling or change in labeling and with respect to which the Secretary provided written notice to the manufacturer specifying the deception or risk of illness or injury, the labeling or change in labeling to correct the deception or eliminate or reduce such risk, and the period within which such labeling or change in labeling was to be done, such labeling or change in labeling was not done within such period;

he may initiate a proceeding to promulgate a regulation to make such device a banned device.

Special Effective Date

(b) The Secretary may declare a proposed regulation under subsection (a) to be effective upon its publication in the Federal Register and until the effective date of any final action taken respecting such regulation if (1) he determines, on the basis of all available data and information, that the deception or risk of illness or injury associated with the use of the device which is subject to the regulation presents an unreasonable, direct, and substantial danger to the health of individuals, and (2) before the date of the publication of such regulation, the Secretary notifies the manufacturer of such device that such regulation is to be made so effective. If the Secretary makes a proposed regulation so effective, he shall, as expeditiously as possible, give interested persons prompt notice of his action under this subsection, provide reasonable opportunity for an informal hearing on the proposed regulation, and either affirm, modify, or revoke such proposed regulation.

SEC. 517 [21 U.S.C. 360g]. JUDICIAL REVIEW

Application of Section

(a) Not later than thirty days after—

(1) the promulgation of a regulation under section 513 classifying a device in class I, an administrative order changing the classification of a device to class I, or an order under subsection (f)(2) of such section reclassifying a device or denying a petition for reclassification of a device,

(2) the promulgation of a regulation under section 514 establishing, amending, or revoking a performance standard for a device,

(3) the issuance of an order under section 514(b)(2) or 515 (b)(2)(B) denying a request for reclassification of a device,

(4) the promulgation of a regulation under paragraph (3) of section 515(b) requiring a device to have an approval of a premarket application, a regulation under paragraph (4) of that section amending or revoking a regulation under paragraph (3), or an order pursuant to section 515(g)(1) or 515(g)(2)(C),

(5) the promulgation of a regulation under section 516 (other than a proposed regulation made effective under subsection (b) of such section upon the regulation's publication) making a device a banned device,

(6) the issuance of an order under section 520(f)(2),

(7) an order under section 520(g)(4) disapproving an application for an exemption of a device for investigational use or an order under section 520(g)(5) withdrawing such an exemption for a device,

(8) an order pursuant to section 513(i), or

(9) a regulation under section 515(i)(2) or 520(*l*)(5)(B),

any person adversely affected by such regulation or order may file a petition with the United States Court of Appeals for the District of Columbia or for the circuit wherein such person resides or has his principal place of business for Judicial review of such regulation or order. A copy of the petition shall be transmitted by the clerk of the court to the Secretary or other officer designated by him for that purpose. The Secretary shall file in the court the record of the proceedings on which the Secretary based his regulation or order as provided in section 2112 of title 28, United States Code. For purposes of this section, the term "record" means all notices and other matter published in the Federal Register with respect to the regulation or order reviewed, all information submitted to the Secretary with respect to such regulation or order, proceedings of any panel or advisory committee with respect to such regulation or order, any hearing held with respect to such regulation or order, and any other information identified by the Secretary, in the administrative proceeding held with respect to such regulation or order, as being relevant to such regulation or order.

Additional Data, Views, and Arguments

(b) If the petitioner applies to the court for leave to adduce additional data, views, or arguments respecting the regulation or order being reviewed and shows to the satisfaction of the court that such additional data, views, or arguments are material and that there were reasonable grounds for the petitioner's failure to adduce such data, views, or arguments in the proceedings before the Secretary, the court may order the Secretary to provide additional opportunity for the oral presentation of data, views, or arguments and for written submissions. The Secretary may modify his findings, or make new findings by reason of the additional data, views, or arguments so taken and shall file with the court such modified or new findings, and his recommendation, if any, for the modification or setting aside of the regulation or order being reviewed, with the return of such additional data, views, or arguments.

Standard for Review

(c) Upon the filing of the petition under subsection (a) of this section for judicial review of a regulation or order, the court shall have jurisdiction to review the regulation or order in accordance with chapter 7 of title 5, United States Code, and to grant appropriate relief, including interim relief, as provided in such chapter. A regulation described in paragraph (2) or (5) of subsection (a) and an order issued after the review provided by section 515(g) shall not be affirmed if it is found to be unsupported by substantial evidence on the record taken as a whole.

Finality of Judgments

(d) The judgment of the court affirming or setting aside, in whole or in part, any regulation or order shall be final, subject to review by the Supreme Court of the United States upon certiorari or certification, as provided in section 1254 of title 28 of the United States Code.

Other Remedies

(e) The remedies provided for in this section shall be in addition to and not in lieu of any other remedies provided by law.

Statement of Reasons

(f) To facilitate judicial review under this section or under any other provision of law of a regulation or order issued under section 513, 514, 515, 516, 518, 519, 520, or 521 each such regulation or order shall contain a statement of the reasons for its issuance and the basis, in the record of the proceedings held in connection with its issuance, for its issuance.

Sec. 517A [21 U.S.C. 360g–1]. Agency Documentation and Review of Significant Decisions Regarding Devices

(a) Documentation of Rationale for Significant Decisions.—

(1) In general.—The Secretary shall provide a substantive summary of the scientific and regulatory rationale for any significant decision of the Center for Devices and Radiological Health regarding submission or review of a report under section 510(k), an application under section 515, or an application for an exemption under section 520(g), including documentation of significant controversies or differences of opinion and the resolution of such controversies or differences of opinion.

(2) Provision of documentation.—Upon request, the Secretary shall furnish such substantive summary to the person who is seeking to submit, or who has submitted, such report or application.

(b) Review of Significant Decisions.—

(1) Request for supervisory review of significant decision.—Any person may request a supervisory review of the significant decision described in subsection (a)(1). Such review may be conducted at the next supervisory level or higher above the individual who made the significant decision.

(2) Submission of request.—A person requesting a supervisory review under paragraph (1) shall submit such request to the Secretary not later than 30 days after such decision and shall indicate in the request whether such person seeks an in-person meeting or a teleconference review.

(3) Timeframe.—

(A) In general.—Except as provided in subparagraph (B), the Secretary shall schedule an in-person or teleconference review, if so requested, not later than 30 days after such request is made. The Secretary shall issue a decision to the person requesting a review under this subsection not later than 45 days after the request is made under paragraph (1), or, in the case of a person who requests an in-person meeting or teleconference, 30 days after such meeting or teleconference.

(B) Exception.—Subparagraph (A) shall not apply in cases that are referred to experts outside of the Food and Drug Administration.

Sec. 518 [21 U.S.C. 360h]. Notification and Other Remedies

Notification

(a) If the Secretary determines that—

(1) a device intended for human use which is introduced or delivered for introduction into interstate commerce for commercial distribution presents an unreasonable risk of substantial harm to the public health, and

(2) notification under this subsection is necessary to eliminate the unreasonable risk of such harm and no more practicable means is available under the provisions of this Act (other than this section) to eliminate such risk,

the Secretary may issue such order as may be necessary to assure that adequate notification is provided in an appropriate form, by the persons and means best suited under the circumstances involved, to all health professionals who prescribe or use the device and to any other person (including manufacturers, importers, distributors, retailers, and device users) who should properly receive such notification in order to eliminate such risk. An order under this subsection shall require that the individuals subject to the risk with respect to which the order is to be issued be included in the persons to be notified of the risk unless the Secretary determines that notice to such individuals would present a greater danger to the health of such individuals than no such notification. If the Secretary makes such a determination with respect to such individuals, the order shall require that the health professionals who prescribe or use the device provide for the notification of the individuals whom the health professionals treated with the device of the risk presented by the device and of any action which may be taken by or on behalf of such individuals to eliminate or reduce such risk. Before issuing an order under this subsection, the Secretary shall consult with the persons who are to give notice under the order.

Repair, Replacement, or Refund

(b)(1)(A) If, after affording opportunity for an informal hearing, the Secretary determines that—

(i) a device intended for human use which is introduced or delivered for introduction into interstate commerce for commercial distribution presents an unreasonable risk of substantial harm to the public health.

(ii) there are reasonable grounds to believe that the device was not properly designed or manufactured with reference to the state of the art as it existed at the time of its design or manufacture,

(iii) there are reasonable grounds to believe that the unreasonable risk was not caused by failure of a person other than a manufacturer, importer, distributor, or retailer of the device to exercise due care in the installation, maintenance, repair, or use of the device, and

(iv) the notification authorized by subsection (a) would not by itself be sufficient to eliminate the unreasonable risk and action described in paragraph (2) of this subsection is necessary to eliminate such risk,

the Secretary may order the manufacturer, importer, or any distributor of such device, or any combination of such persons, to submit to him within a reasonable time a plan for taking one or more of the actions described in paragraph (2). An order issued under the preceding sentence which is directed to more than one person shall specify which person may decide which action shall be taken under such plan and the person specified shall be the person who the Secretary determines bears the principal, ultimate financial responsibility for action taken under the plan unless the Secretary cannot determine who bears such responsibility or the Secretary determines that the protection of the public health requires that such decision be made by a person (including a device user or health professional) other than the person he determines bears such responsibility.

(B) The Secretary shall approve a plan submitted pursuant to an order issued under subparagraph (A) unless he determines (after affording opportunity for an informal hearing) that the action or actions to be taken under the plan or the manner in which such action or actions are to be taken under the plan will not assure that the unreasonable risk with respect to which such order was issued will be eliminated. If the Secretary disapproves a plan, he shall order a revised plan to be submitted to him within a reasonable time. If the Secretary determines (after affording opportunity for an informal hearing) that the revised plan is unsatisfactory or if no revised plan or no initial plan has been submitted to the Secretary within the prescribed time, the Secretary shall (i) prescribe a plan to be carried out by the person or persons to whom the order issued under subparagraph (A) was directed, or (ii) after affording an opportunity for an informal hearing, by order prescribe a plan to be carried out by a person who is a manufacturer, importer, distributor, or retailer of the device with respect to which the order was issued but to whom the order under subparagraph (A) was not directed.

(2) The actions which may be taken under a plan submitted under an order issued under paragraph (1) are as follows:

(A) To repair the device so that it does not present the unreasonable risk of substantial harm with respect to which the order under paragraph (1) was issued.

(B) To replace the device with a like or equivalent device which is in conformity with all applicable requirements of this Act.

(C) To refund the purchase price of the device (less a reasonable allowance for use if such device has been in the possession of the device user for one year or more —

(i) at the time of notification ordered under subsection (a), or

(ii) at the time the device user receives actual notice of the unreasonable risk with respect to which the order was issued under paragraph (1),

whichever first occurs).

(3) No charge shall be made to any person (other than a manufacturer, importer, distributor or retailer) for availing himself of any remedy, described in paragraph (2) and provided under an order issued under paragraph (1), and the person subject to the order shall reimburse each person (other than a manufacturer, importer, distributor,

or retailer) who is entitled to such a remedy for any reasonable and foreseeable expenses actually incurred by such person in availing himself of such remedy.

Reimbursement

(c) An order issued under subsection (b) with respect to a device may require any person who is a manufacturer, importer, distributor, or retailer of the device to reimburse any other person who is a manufacturer, importer, distributor, or retailer of such device for such other person's expenses actually incurred in connection with carrying out the order if the Secretary determines such reimbursement is required for the protection of the public health. Any such requirement shall not affect any rights or obligations under any contract to which the person receiving reimbursement or the person making such reimbursement is a party.

Effect on Other Liability

(d) Compliance with an order issued under this section shall not relieve any person from liability under Federal or State law. In awarding damages for economic loss in an action brought for the enforcement of any such liability, the value to the plaintiff in such action of any remedy provided him under such order shall be taken into account.

Recall Authority

(e)(1) If the Secretary finds that there is a reasonable probability that a device intended for human use would cause serious, adverse health consequences or death, the Secretary shall issue an order requiring the appropriate person (including the manufacturers, importers, distributors, or retailers of the device)—

(A) to immediately cease distribution of such device, and

(B) to immediately notify health professionals and device user facilities of the order and to instruct such professionals and facilities to cease use of such device.

The order shall provide the person subject to the order with an opportunity for an informal hearing, to be held not later than 10 days after the date of the issuance of the order, on the actions required by the order and on whether the order should be amended to require a recall of such device. If, after providing an opportunity for such a hearing, the Secretary determines that inadequate grounds exist to support the actions required by the order, the Secretary shall vacate the order.

(2)(A) If, after providing an opportunity for an informal hearing under paragraph (1), the Secretary determines that the order should be amended to include a recall of the device with respect to which the order was issued, the Secretary shall, except as provided in subparagraphs (B) and (C), amend the order to require a recall. The Secretary shall specify a timetable in which the device recall will occur and shall require periodic reports to the Secretary describing the progress of the recall.

(B) An amended order under subparagraph (A)—

(i) shall—

(I) not include recall of a device from individuals, and

(II) not include recall of a device from device user facilities if the Secretary determines that the risk of recalling such device from the facilities presents a greater health risk than the health risk of not recalling the device from use, and

(ii) shall provide for notice to individuals subject to the risks associated with the use of such device.

In providing the notice required by clause (ii), the Secretary may use the assistance of health professionals who prescribed or used such a device for individuals. If a significant number of such individuals cannot be identified, the Secretary shall notify such individuals pursuant to section 705(b).

(3) The remedy provided by this subsection shall be in addition to remedies provided by subsections (a), (b), and (c).

SEC. 518A [21 U.S.C. 360h–1]. PROGRAM TO IMPROVE THE DEVICE RECALL SYSTEM

(a) IN GENERAL.—The Secretary shall—

(1) establish a program to routinely and systematically assess information relating to device recalls and use such information to proactively identify strategies for mitigating health risks presented by defective or unsafe devices;

(2) clarify procedures for conducting device recall audit checks to improve the ability of investigators to perform those checks in a consistent manner;

(3) develop detailed criteria for assessing whether a person performing a device recall has performed an effective correction or action plan for the recall; and

(4) document the basis for each termination by the Food and Drug Administration of a device recall.

(b) ASSESSMENT CONTENT.—The program established under subsection (a)(1) shall, at a minimum, identify—

(1) trends in the number and types of device recalls;

(2) devices that are most frequently the subject of a recall; and

(3) underlying causes of device recalls.

(c) TERMINATION OF RECALLS.—The Secretary shall document the basis for the termination by the Food and Drug Administration of a device recall.

(d) DEFINITION.—In this section, the term "recall" means—

(1) the removal from the market of a device pursuant to an order of the Secretary under subsection (b) or (e) of section 518; or

(2) the correction or removal from the market of a device at the initiative of the manufacturer or importer of the device that is required to be reported to the Secretary under section 519(g).

Sec. 519 [21 U.S.C. 360i]. Records and Reports on Devices

General Rule

(a) Every person who is a manufacturer or importer of a device intended for human use shall establish and maintain such records, make such reports, and provide such information, as the Secretary may by regulation reasonably require to assure that such device is not adulterated or misbranded and to otherwise assure its safety and effectiveness. Regulations prescribed under the preceding sentence—

(1) shall require a device manufacturer or importer to report to the Secretary whenever the manufacturer or importer receives or otherwise becomes aware of information that reasonably suggests that one of its marketed devices—

(A) may have caused or contributed to a death or serious injury, or

(B) has malfunctioned and that such device or a similar device marketed by the manufacturer or importer would be likely to cause or contribute to a death or serious injury if the malfunction were to recur, which report under this subparagraph—

(i) shall be submitted in accordance with part 803 of title 21, Code of Federal Regulations (or successor regulations), unless the Secretary grants an exemption or variance from, or an alternative to, a requirement under such regulations pursuant to section 803.19 of such part, if the device involved is—

(I) a class III device;

(II) a class II device that is permanently implantable, is life supporting, or is life sustaining; or

(III) a type of device which the Secretary has, by notice published in the Federal Register or letter to the person who is the manufacturer or importer of the device, indicated should be subject to such part 803 in order to protect the public health;

(ii) shall, if the device is not subject to clause (i), be submitted in accordance with criteria established by the Secretary for reports made pursuant to this clause, which criteria shall require the reports to be in summary form and made on a quarterly basis; or

(iii) shall, if the device is imported into the United States and for which part 803 of title 21, Code of Federal Regulations (or successor regulations) requires an importer to submit a report to the manufacturer, be submitted by the importer to the manufacturer in accordance with part 803 of title 21, Code of Federal Regulations (or successor regulations);

(2) shall define the term "serious injury" to mean an injury that—

(A) is life threatening,

(B) results in permanent impairment of a body function or permanent damage to a body structure, or

(C) necessitates medical or surgical intervention to preclude permanent impairment of a body function or permanent damage to a body structure;

(3) shall require reporting of other significant adverse device experiences as determined by the Secretary to be necessary to be reported;

(4) shall not impose requirements unduly burdensome to a device manufacturer or importer taking into account his cost of complying with such requirements and the need for the protection of the public health and the implementation of this Act;

(5) which prescribe the procedure for making requests for reports or information shall require that each request made under such regulations for submission of a report or information to the Secretary state the reason or purpose for such request and identify to the fullest extent practicable such report or information;

(6) which require submission of a report or information to the Secretary shall state the reason or purpose for the submission of such report or information and identify to the fullest extent practicable such report or information;

(7) may not require that the identity of any patient be disclosed in records, reports, or information required under this subsection unless required for the medical welfare of an individual, to determine the safety or effectiveness of a device, or to verify a record, report, or information submitted under this Act; and

(8) may not require a manufacturer or importer of a class I device to—

(A) maintain for such a device records respecting information not in the possession of the manufacturer or importer, or

(B) to submit for such a device to the Secretary any report or information—

(i) not in the possession of the manufacturer or importer, or

(ii) on a periodic basis,

unless such report or information is necessary to determine if the device should be reclassified or if the device is adulterated or misbranded. and[63]

In prescribing such regulations, the Secretary shall have due regard for the professional ethics of the medical profession and the interests of patients. The prohibitions of paragraph (7) of this subsection continue to apply to records, reports, and information concerning any individual who has been a patient, irrespective of whether or when he ceases to be a patient. The Secretary shall by regulation require distributors

63. So in law. See Pub. L. No. 105–115, § 213(a)(1)(D)(ii), 111 Stat. 2296, 2347 (1997). That section struck former paragraph (9), and amended paragraph (8) "by striking the semicolon at the end and inserting a period", rather than by striking "; and"; and inserting a period.

to keep records and make such records available to the Secretary upon request. Paragraphs (4) and (8) apply to distributors to the same extent and in the same manner as such paragraphs apply to manufacturers and importers.

User Reports

(b)(1)(A) Whenever a device user facility receives or otherwise becomes aware of information that reasonably suggests that a device has or may have caused or contributed to the death of a patient of the facility, the facility shall, as soon as practicable but not later than 10 working days after becoming aware of the information, report the information to the Secretary and, if the identity of the manufacturer is known, to the manufacturer of the device. In the case of deaths, the Secretary may by regulation prescribe a shorter period for the reporting of such information.

(B) Whenever a device user facility receives or otherwise becomes aware of—

(i) information that reasonably suggests that a device has or may have caused or contributed to the serious illness of, or serious injury to, a patient of the facility, or

(ii) other significant adverse device experiences as determined by the Secretary by regulation to be necessary to be reported,

shall, as soon as practicable but not later than 10 working days after becoming aware of the information, report the information to the manufacturer of the device or to the Secretary if the identity of the manufacturer is not known.

(C) Each device user facility shall submit to the Secretary on an annual basis a summary of the reports made under subparagraphs (A) and (B). Such summary shall be submitted on January 1 of each year. The summary shall be in such form and contain such information from such reports as the Secretary may require and shall include—

(i) sufficient information to identify the facility which made the reports for which the summary is submitted,

(ii) in the case of any product which was the subject of a report, the product name, serial number, and model number,

(iii) the name and the address of the manufacturer of such device, and

(iv) a brief description of the event reported to the manufacturer.

(D) For purposes of subparagraphs (A), (B), and (C), a device user facility shall be treated as having received or otherwise become aware of information with respect to a device of that facility when medical personnel who are employed by or otherwise formally affiliated with the facility receive or otherwise become aware of information with respect to that device in the course of their duties.

(2) The Secretary may not disclose the identity of a device user facility which makes a report under paragraph (1) except in connection with—

(A) an action brought to enforce section 301(q), or

(B) a communication to a manufacturer of a device which is the subject of a report under paragraph (1).

This paragraph does not prohibit the Secretary from disclosing the identity of a device user facility making a report under paragraph (1) or any information in such a report to employees of the Department of Health and Human Services, to the Department of Justice, or to the duly authorized committees and subcommittees of the Congress.

(3) No report made under paragraph (1) by—

(A) a device user facility,

(B) an individual who is employed by or otherwise formally affiliated with such a facility, or

(C) a physician who is not required to make such a report,

shall be admissible into evidence or otherwise used in any civil action involving private parties unless the facility, individual, or physician who made the report had knowledge of the falsity of the information contained in the report.

(4) A report made under paragraph (1) does not affect any obligation of a manufacturer who receives the report to file a report as required under subsection (a).

(5) With respect to device user facilities:

(A) The Secretary shall by regulation plan and implement a program under which the Secretary limits user reporting under paragraphs (1) through (4) to a subset of user facilities that constitutes a representative profile of user reports for device deaths and serious illnesses or serious injuries.

(B) During the period of planning the program under subparagraph (A), paragraphs (1) through (4) continue to apply.

(C) During the period in which the Secretary is providing for a transition to the full implementation of the program, paragraphs (1) through (4) apply except to the extent that the Secretary determines otherwise.

(D) On and after the date on which the program is fully implemented, paragraphs (1) through (4) do not apply to a user facility unless the facility is included in the subset referred to in subparagraph (A).

(E) Not later than 2 years after the date of the enactment of the Food and Drug Administration Modernization Act of 1997, the Secretary shall submit to the Committee on Commerce of the House of Representatives, and to the Committee on Labor and Human Resources of the Senate, a report describing the plan developed by the Secretary under subparagraph (A) and the progress that has been made toward the implementation of the plan.

(6) For purposes of this subsection:

(A) The term "device user facility" means a hospital, ambulatory surgical facility, nursing home, or outpatient treatment facility which is not a physician's office. The Secretary may by regulation include an outpatient diagnostic facility which is not a physician's office in such term.

(B) The terms "serious illness" and "serious injury" mean illness or injury, respectively, that—

(i) is life threatening,

(ii) results in permanent impairment of a body function or permanent damage to a body structure, or

(iii) necessitates medical or surgical intervention to preclude permanent impairment of a body function or permanent damage to a body structure.

Persons Exempt

(c) Subsection (a) shall not apply to—

(1) any practitioner who is licensed by law to prescribe or administer devices intended for use in humans and who manufactures or imports devices solely for use in the course of his professional practice;

(2) any person who manufactures or imports devices intended for use in humans solely for such person's use in research or teaching and not for sale (including any person who uses a device under an exemption granted under section 520(g)); and

(3) any other class of persons as the Secretary may by regulation exempt from subsection (a) upon a finding that compliance with the requirements of such subsection by such class with respect to a device is not necessary to (A) assure that a device is not adulterated or misbranded or (B) otherwise to assure its safety and effectiveness.

[(d) Repealed by Pub. L. No. 105–115, § 213, 111 Stat. 2296, 2346 (1997).]

Device Tracking

(e)(1) The Secretary may by order require a manufacturer to adopt a method of tracking a class II or class III device—

(A) the failure of which would be reasonably likely to have serious adverse health consequences; or

(B) which is—

(i) intended to be implanted in the human body for more than one year, or

(ii) a life sustaining or life supporting device used outside a device user facility.

(2) Any patient receiving a device subject to tracking under paragraph (1) may refuse to release, or refuse permission to release, the patient's name, address, social security number, or other identifying information for the purpose of tracking.

Unique Device Identification System

(f) Not later than December 31, 2012, the Secretary shall issue proposed regulations establishing a unique device identification system for medical devices requiring the label of devices to bear a unique identifier, unless the Secretary requires an alternative placement or provides an exception for a particular device or type of device. The unique identifier shall adequately identify the device through distribution and use, and may include information on the lot or serial number. The Secretary shall finalize the proposed regulations not later than 6 months after the close of the comment period and shall implement the final regulations with respect to devices that are implantable, life-saving, and life sustaining not later than 2 years after the regulations are finalized, taking into account patient access to medical devices and therapies.

Reports of Removals and Corrections

(g)(1) Except as provided in paragraph (2), the Secretary shall by regulation require a manufacturer or importer of a device to report promptly to the Secretary any correction or removal of a device undertaken by such manufacturer or importer if the removal or correction was undertaken—

 (A) to reduce a risk to health posed by the device, or

 (B) to remedy a violation of this Act caused by the device which may present a risk to health.

A manufacturer or importer of a device who undertakes a correction or removal of a device which is not required to be reported under this paragraph shall keep a record of such correction or removal.

(2) No report of the corrective action or removal of a device may be required under paragraph (1) if a report of the corrective action or removal is required and has been submitted under subsection (a).

(3) For purposes of paragraphs (1) and (2), the terms "correction" and "removal" do not include routine servicing.

(h) INCLUSION OF DEVICES IN THE POSTMARKET RISK IDENTIFICATION AND ANALYSIS SYSTEM.—

 (1) IN GENERAL.—

  (A) APPLICATION TO DEVICES.—The Secretary shall amend the procedures established and maintained under clauses (i), (ii), (iii), and (v) of section 505(k)(3)(C) in order to expand the postmarket risk identification and analysis system established under such section to include and apply to devices.

(B) EXCEPTION.—Subclause (II) of clause (i) of section 505(k)(3)(C) shall not apply to devices.

(C) CLARIFICATION.—With respect to devices, the private sector health-related electronic data provided under section 505(k)(3)(C)(i)(III)(bb) may include medical device utilization data, health insurance claims data, and procedure and device registries.

(2) DATA.—In expanding the system as described in paragraph (1)(A), the Secretary shall use relevant data with respect to devices cleared under section 510(k) or approved under section 515, including claims data, patient survey data, and any other data deemed appropriate by the Secretary.

(3) STAKEHOLDER INPUT.—To help ensure effective implementation of the system as described in paragraph (1) with respect to devices, the Secretary shall engage outside stakeholders in development of the system, and gather information from outside stakeholders regarding the content of an effective sentinel program, through a public hearing, advisory committee meeting, maintenance of a public docket, or other similar public measures.

(4) VOLUNTARY SURVEYS.—Chapter 35 of title 44, United States Code, shall not apply to the collection of voluntary information from health care providers, such as voluntary surveys or questionnaires, initiated by the Secretary for purposes of postmarket risk identification, mitigation, and analysis for devices.

SEC. 520 [21 U.S.C. 360j]. GENERAL PROVISIONS RESPECTING CONTROL OF DEVICES INTENDED FOR HUMAN USE

General Rule

(a) Any requirement authorized by or under section 501, 502, 510, or 519 applicable to a device intended for human use shall apply to such device until the applicability of the requirement to the device has been changed by action taken under section 513, 514, or 515 or under subsection (g) of this section, and any requirement established by or under section 501, 502, 510, or 519 which is inconsistent with a requirement imposed on such device under section 514 or 515 or under subsection (g) of this section shall not apply to such device.

Custom Devices

(b)(1) IN GENERAL.—The requirements of sections 514 and 515 shall not apply to a device that—

(A) is created or modified in order to comply with the order of an individual physician or dentist (or any other specially qualified person designated under regulations promulgated by the Secretary after an opportunity for an oral hearing);

(B) in order to comply with an order described in subparagraph (A), necessarily deviates from an otherwise applicable performance standard under section 514 or requirement under section 515;

(C) is not generally available in the United States in finished form through labeling or advertising by the manufacturer, importer, or distributor for commercial distribution;

(D) is designed to treat a unique pathology or physiological condition that no other device is domestically available to treat;

(E)(i) is intended to meet the special needs of such physician or dentist (or other specially qualified person so designated) in the course of the professional practice of such physician or dentist (or other specially qualified person so designated); or

(ii) is intended for use by an individual patient named in such order of such physician or dentist (or other specially qualified person so designated);

(F) is assembled from components or manufactured and finished on a case-by-case basis to accommodate the unique needs of individuals described in clause (i) or (ii) of subparagraph (E); and

(G) may have common, standardized design characteristics, chemical and material compositions, and manufacturing processes as commercially distributed devices.

(2) LIMITATIONS.—Paragraph (1) shall apply to a device only if—

(A) such device is for the purpose of treating a sufficiently rare condition, such that conducting clinical investigations on such device would be impractical;

(B) production of such device under paragraph (1) is limited to no more than 5 units per year of a particular device type, provided that such replication otherwise complies with this section; and

(C) the manufacturer of such device notifies the Secretary on an annual basis, in a manner prescribed by the Secretary, of the manufacture of such device.

(3) GUIDANCE.—. Not later than 2 years after the date of enactment of this section, the Secretary shall issue final guidance on replication of multiple devices described in paragraph (2)(B).

Trade Secrets

(c) Any information reported to or otherwise obtained by the Secretary or his representative under section 513, 514, 515, 516, 518, 519, or 704 or under subsection (f) or (g) of this section which is exempt from disclosure pursuant to subsection (a) of section 552 of title 5, United States Code, by reason of subsection (b)(4) of such section shall be considered confidential and shall not be disclosed and may not be used by the Secretary as the basis for the reclassification of a device from class III to class II or class I or as the basis for the establishment or amendment of a performance standard under section 514 for a device reclassified from class III to class II, except (1) in accordance with subsection (h), and (2) that such information may be disclosed to other officers or employees concerned with carrying out this Act or when relevant in any proceeding under this Act (other than section 513 or 514 thereof).

Notices and Findings

(d) Each notice of proposed rulemaking under section 513, 514, 515, 516, 518, or 519, or under this section, any other notice which is published in the Federal Register with respect to any other action taken under any such section and which states the reasons for such action, and each publication of findings required to be made in connection with rulemaking under any such section shall set forth—

(1) the manner in which interested persons may examine data and other information on which the notice or findings is based, and

(2) the period within which interested persons may present their comments on the notice or findings (including the need therefor) orally or in writing, which period shall be at least sixty days but may not exceed ninety days unless the time is extended by the Secretary by a notice published in the Federal Register stating good cause therefor.

Restricted Devices

(e)(1) The Secretary may by regulation require that a device be restricted to sale, distribution, or use—

(A) only upon the written or oral authorization of a practitioner licensed by law to administer or use such device, or

(B) upon such other conditions as the Secretary may prescribe in such regulation,

if, because of its potentiality for harmful effect or the collateral measures necessary to its use, the Secretary determines that there cannot otherwise be reasonable assurance of its safety and effectiveness. No condition prescribed under subparagraph (B) may restrict the use of a device to persons with specific training or experience in its use or to persons for use in certain facilities unless the Secretary determines that such a restriction is required for the safe and effective use of the device. No such condition may exclude a person from using a device solely because the person does not have the training or experience to make him eligible for certification by a certifying board recognized by the American Board of Medical Specialties or has not been certified by such a Board. A device subject to a regulation under this subsection is a restricted device.

(2) The label of a restricted device shall bear such appropriate statements of the restrictions required by a regulation under paragraph (1) as the Secretary may in such regulation prescribe.

Good Manufacturing Practice Requirements

(f)(1)(A) The Secretary may, in accordance with subparagraph (B), prescribe regulations requiring that the methods used in, and the facilities and controls used for, the manufacture, pre-production design validation (including a process to assess the performance of a device but not including an evaluation of the safety or effectiveness of a device), packing, storage, and installation of a device conform to current good manufacturing practice, as prescribed in such regulations, to assure that the device will be safe and effective and otherwise in compliance with this Act.

(B) Before the Secretary may promulgate any regulation under subparagraph (A) he shall—

(i) afford the advisory committee established under paragraph (3) an opportunity to submit recommendations to him with respect to the regulation proposed to be promulgated;

(ii) afford opportunity for an oral hearing; and

(iii) ensure that such regulation conforms, to the extent practicable, with internationally recognized standards defining quality systems, or parts of the standards, for medical devices.

The Secretary shall provide the advisory committee a reasonable time to make its recommendation with respect to proposed regulations under subparagraph (A).

(2)(A) Any person subject to any requirement prescribed by regulations under paragraph (1) may petition the Secretary for an exemption or variance from such requirement. Such a petition shall be submitted to the Secretary in such form and manner as he shall prescribe and shall—

(i) in the case of a petition for an exemption from a requirement, set forth the basis for the petitioner's determination that compliance with the requirement is not required to assure that the device will be safe and effective and otherwise in compliance with this Act,

(ii) in the case of a petition for a variance from a requirement, set forth the methods proposed to be used in, and the facilities and controls proposed to be used for, the manufacture, packing, storage, and installation of the device in lieu of the methods, facilities, and controls prescribed by the requirement, and

(iii) contain such other information as the Secretary shall prescribe.

(B) The Secretary may refer to the advisory committee established under paragraph (3) any petition submitted under subparagraph (A). The advisory committee shall report its recommendations to the Secretary with respect to a petition referred to it within sixty days of the date of the petition's referral. Within sixty days after—

(i) the date the petition was submitted to the Secretary under subparagraph (A), or

(ii) if the petition was referred to an advisory committee, the expiration of the sixty-day period beginning on the date the petition was referred to the advisory committee,

whichever occurs later, the Secretary shall by order either deny the petition or approve it.

(C) The Secretary may approve—

(i) a petition for an exemption for a device from a requirement if he determines that compliance with such requirement is not required to assure that the device will be safe and effective and otherwise in compliance with this Act, and

(ii) a petition for a variance for a device from a requirement if he determines that the methods to be used in, and the facilities and controls to be used for, the manufacture, packing, storage, and installation of the device in lieu of the methods, controls, and facilities prescribed by the requirement are sufficient to assure that the device will be safe and effective and otherwise in compliance with this Act.

An order of the Secretary approving a petition for a variance shall prescribe such conditions respecting the methods used in, and the facilities and controls used for, the manufacture, packing, storage, and installation of the device to be granted the variance under the petition as may be necessary to assure that the device will be safe and effective and otherwise in compliance with this Act.

(D) After the issuance of an order under subparagraph (B) respecting a petition, the petitioner shall have an opportunity for an informal hearing on such order.

(3) The Secretary shall establish an advisory committee for the purpose of advising and making recommendations to him with respect to regulations proposed to be promulgated under paragraph (1)(A) and the approval or disapproval of petitions submitted under paragraph (2). The advisory committee shall be composed of nine members as follows:

(A) Three of the members shall be appointed from persons who are officers or employees of any State or local government or of the Federal Government.

(B) Two of the members shall be appointed from persons who are representative of interests of the device manufacturing industry; two of the members shall be appointed from persons who are representative of the interests of physicians and other health professionals; and two of the members shall be representative of the interests of the general public.

Members of the advisory committee who are not officers or employees of the United States, while attending conferences or meetings of the committee or otherwise engaged in its business, shall be entitled to receive compensation at rates to be fixed by the Secretary, which rates may not exceed the daily equivalent of the rate in effect for grade GS–18 of the General Schedule, for each day (including travel time) they are so engaged; and while so serving away from their homes or regular places of business each member may be allowed travel expenses, including per diem in lieu of subsistence, as authorized by section 5703 of title 5 of the United States Code for persons in the Government service employed intermittently. The Secretary shall designate one of the members of the advisory committee to serve as its chairman. The Secretary shall furnish the advisory committee with clerical and other assistance. Section 14 of the Federal Advisory Committee Act shall not apply with respect to the duration of the advisory committee established under this paragraph.

Exemption for Devices for Investigational Use

(g)(1) It is the purpose of this subsection to encourage to the extent consistent with the protection of the public health and safety and with ethical standards, the discovery and development of useful devices intended for human use and to that end to maintain optimum freedom for scientific investigators in their pursuit of that purpose.

(2)(A) The Secretary shall, within the one hundred and twenty day period beginning on the date of the enactment of this section,[64] by regulation prescribe procedures and conditions under which devices intended for human use may upon application be granted an exemption from the requirements of section 502, 510, 514, 515, 516, 519, or 721 or subsection (e) or (f) of this section or from any combination of such requirements to permit the investigational use of such devices by experts qualified by scientific training and experience to investigate the safety and effectiveness of such devices.

(B) The conditions prescribed pursuant to subparagraph (A) shall include the following:

(i) A requirement that an application be submitted to the Secretary before an exemption may be granted and that the application be submitted in such form and manner as the Secretary shall specify.

(ii) A requirement that the person applying for an exemption for a device assure the establishment and maintenance of such records, and the making of such reports to the Secretary of safety or effectiveness data obtained as a result of the investigational use of the device during the exemption, as the Secretary determines will enable him to assure compliance with such conditions, review the progress of the investigation, and evaluate the safety and effectiveness of the device.

(iii) Such other requirements as the Secretary may determine to be necessary for the protection of the public health and safety.

(C) Procedures and conditions prescribed pursuant to subparagraph (A) for an exemption may appropriately vary depending on (i) the scope and duration of clinical testing to be conducted under such exemption, (ii) the number of human subjects that are to be involved in such testing, (iii) the need to permit changes to be made

64. Section 520 was added by Pub. L. No. 94–295, § 2, 90 Stat. 539, 565–74 (1976).

in the device subject to the exemption during testing conducted in accordance with a clinical testing plan required under paragraph (3)(A), and (iv) whether the clinical testing of such device is for the purpose of developing data to obtain approval for the commercial distribution of such device.

(3) Procedures and conditions prescribed pursuant to paragraph (2)(A) shall require, as a condition to the exemption of any device to be the subject of testing involving human subjects, that the person applying for the exemption—

(A) submit a plan for any proposed clinical testing of the device and a report of prior investigations of the device (including, where appropriate, tests on animals) adequate to justify the proposed clinical testing—

(i) to the local institutional review committee which has been established in accordance with regulations of the Secretary to supervise clinical testing of devices in the facilities where the proposed clinical testing is to be conducted, or

(ii) to the Secretary, if—

(I) no such committee exists, or

(II) the Secretary finds that the process of review by such committee is inadequate (whether or not the plan for such testing has been approved by such committee),

For review for adequacy to justify the commencement of such testing; and, unless the plan and report are submitted to the Secretary, submit to the Secretary a summary of the plan and a report of prior investigations of the device (including, where appropriate, tests on animals);

(B) promptly notify the Secretary (under such circumstances and in such manner as the Secretary prescribes) of approval by a local institutional review committee of any clinical testing plan submitted to it in accordance with subparagraph (A);

(C) in the case of a device to be distributed to investigators for testing, obtain signed agreements from each of such investigators that any testing of the device involving human subjects will be under such investigator's supervision and in accordance with subparagraph (D) and submit such agreements to the Secretary; and

(D) assure that informed consent will be obtained from each human subject (or his representative) of proposed clinical testing involving such device, except where subject to such conditions as the Secretary may prescribe, the investigator conducting or supervising the proposed clinical testing of the device determines in writing that there exists a life threatening situation involving the human subject of such testing which necessitates the use of such device and it is not feasible to obtain informed consent from the subject and there is not sufficient time to obtain such consent from his representative.

The determination required by subparagraph (D) shall be concurred in by a licensed physician who is not involved in the testing of the human subject with respect to which such determination is made unless immediate use of the device is required to save the life of the human subject of such testing and there is not sufficient time to obtain such concurrence.

(4)(A) An application, submitted in accordance with the procedures prescribed by regulations under paragraph (2), for an exemption for a device (other than an exemption from section 516) shall be deemed approved on the thirtieth day after the submission of the application to the Secretary unless on or before such day the Secretary by order disapproves the application and notifies the applicant of the disapproval of the application.

(B) The Secretary may disapprove an application only if he finds that the investigation with respect to which the application is submitted does not conform to procedures and conditions prescribed under regulations under paragraph (2). Such a notification shall contain the order of disapproval and a complete statement of the reasons for the Secretary's disapproval of the application and afford the applicant opportunity for an informal hearing on the disapproval order.

(C) Consistent with paragraph (1), the Secretary shall not disapprove an application under this subsection because the Secretary determines that—

(i) the investigation may not support a substantial equivalence or de novo classification determination or approval of the device;

(ii) the investigation may not meet a requirement, including a data requirement, relating to the approval or clearance of a device; or

(iii) an additional or different investigation may be necessary to support clearance or approval of the device.

(5) The Secretary may by order withdraw an exemption granted under this subsection for a device if the Secretary determines that the conditions applicable to the device under this subsection for such exemption are not met. Such an order may be issued only after opportunity for an informal hearing, except that such an order may be issued before the provision of an opportunity for an informal hearing if the Secretary determines that the continuation of testing under the exemption with respect to which the order is to be issued will result in an unreasonable risk to the public health.

(6)(A) Not later than 1 year after the date of the enactment of the Food and Drug Administration Modernization Act of 1997, the Secretary shall by regulation establish, with respect to a device for which an exemption under this subsection is in effect, procedures and conditions that, without requiring an additional approval of an application for an exemption or the approval of a supplement to such an application, permit—

(i) developmental changes in the device (including manufacturing changes) that do not constitute a significant change in design or in basic principles of operation and that are made in response to information gathered during the course of an investigation; and

(ii) changes or modifications to clinical protocols that do not affect—

(I) the validity of data or information resulting from the completion of an approved protocol, or the relationship of likely patient risk to benefit relied upon to approve a protocol;

(II) the scientific soundness of an investigational plan submitted under paragraph (3)(A); or

(III) the rights, safety, or welfare of the human subjects involved in the investigation.

(B) Regulations under subparagraph (A) shall provide that a change or modification described in such subparagraph may be made if—

(i) the sponsor of the investigation determines, on the basis of credible information (as defined by the Secretary) that the applicable conditions under subparagraph (A) are met; and

(ii) the sponsor submits to the Secretary, not later than 5 days after making the change or modification, a notice of the change or modification.

(7)(A) In the case of a person intending to investigate the safety or effectiveness of a class III device or any implantable device, the Secretary shall ensure that the person has an opportunity, prior to submitting an application to the Secretary or to an institutional review committee, to submit to the Secretary, for review, an investigational plan (including a clinical protocol). If the applicant submits a written request for a meeting with the Secretary regarding such review, the Secretary shall, not later than 30 days after receiving the request, meet with the applicant for the purpose of reaching agreement regarding the investigational plan (including a clinical protocol). The written request shall include a detailed description of the device, a detailed description of the proposed conditions of use of the device, a proposed plan (including a clinical protocol) for determining whether there is a reasonable assurance of effectiveness, and, if available, information regarding the expected performance from the device.

(B) Any agreement regarding the parameters of an investigational plan (including a clinical protocol) that is reached between the Secretary and a sponsor or applicant shall be reduced to writing and made part of the administrative record by the Secretary. Any such agreement shall not be changed, except—

(i) with the written agreement of the sponsor or applicant; or

(ii) pursuant to a decision, made in accordance with subparagraph (C) by the director of the office in which the device involved is reviewed, that a substantial scientific issue essential to determining the safety or effectiveness of the device involved has been identified.

(C) A decision under subparagraph (B)(ii) by the director shall be in writing, and may be made only after the Secretary has provided to the sponsor or applicant an opportunity for a meeting at which the director and the sponsor or applicant are present and at which the director documents the scientific issue involved.

(8)(A) At any time, the Secretary may prohibit the sponsor of an investigation from conducting the investigation (referred to in this paragraph as a "clinical hold") if the Secretary makes a determination described in subparagraph (B). The Secretary shall specify the basis for the clinical hold, including the specific information available to the Secretary which served as the basis for such clinical hold, and confirm such determination in writing.

(B) For purposes of subparagraph (A), a determination described in this subparagraph with respect to a clinical hold is a determination that—

(i) the device involved represents an unreasonable risk to the safety of the persons who are the subjects of the clinical investigation, taking into account the qualifications of the clinical investigators, information about the device, the design of the clinical investigation, the condition for which the device is to be investigated, and the health status of the subjects involved; or

(ii) the clinical hold should be issued for such other reasons as the Secretary may by regulation establish.

(C) Any written request to the Secretary from the sponsor of an investigation that a clinical hold be removed shall receive a decision, in writing and specifying the reasons therefor, within 30 days after receipt of such request. Any such request shall include sufficient information to support the removal of such clinical hold.

Release of Safety and Effectiveness Information

(h)(1) The Secretary shall promulgate regulations under which a detailed summary of information respecting the safety and effectiveness of a device which information was submitted to the Secretary and which was the basis for—

(A) an order under section 515(d)(1)(A) approving an application for premarket approval for the device or denying approval of such an application or an order under section 515(e) withdrawing approval of such an application for the device,

(B) an order under section 515(f)(6)(A) revoking an approved protocol for the device, an order under section515(f)(6)(B) declaring a protocol for the device completed or not completed, or an order under section 515(f)(7) revoking the approval of the device, or

(C) an order approving an application under subsection (g) for an exemption for the device from section 516 or an order disapproving, or withdrawing approval of, an application for an exemption under such subsection for the device, shall be made available to the public upon issuance of the order. Summaries of information made available pursuant to this paragraph respecting a device shall include information respecting any adverse effects on health of the device.

(2) The Secretary shall promulgate regulations under which each advisory committee established under section 515(g)(2)(B) shall make available to the public a detailed summary of information respecting the safety and effectiveness of a device which information was submitted to the advisory committee and which was the basis for its recommendation to the Secretary made pursuant to section 515(g)(2)(A). A summary of information upon which such a recommendation is based shall be made available pursuant to this paragraph only after the issuance of the order with respect to which the recommendation was made and each summary shall include information respecting any adverse effect on health of the device subject to such order.

(3) Except as provided in paragraph (4), any information respecting a device which is made available pursuant to paragraph (1) or (2) of this subsection (A) may not be used to establish the safety or effectiveness of another device for purposes of this Act by any person other than the person who submitted the information so made available, and (B) shall be made available subject to subsection (c) of this section.

(4)(A) Any information contained in an application for Premarket approval filed with the Secretary pursuant to section 515(c) (including information from clinical and preclinical tests or studies that demonstrate the safety and effectiveness of a device, but excluding descriptions of methods of manufacture and product composition and other trade secrets) shall be available, 6 years after the application has been approved by the Secretary, for use by the Secretary in—

(i) approving another device;

(ii) determining whether a product development protocol has been completed, under section 515 for another device;

(iii) establishing a performance standard or special control under this Act; or

(iv) classifying or reclassifying another device under section 513 and subsection (*l*)(2).

(B) The publicly available detailed summaries of information respecting the safety and effectiveness of devices required by paragraph (1)(A) shall be available for use by the Secretary as the evidentiary basis for the agency actions described in subparagraph (A).

Proceedings of Advisory Panels and Committees

(i) Each panel under section 513 and each advisory committee established under section 514(b)(5)(B) or 515(g) or under subsection (f) of this section shall make and maintain a transcript of any proceeding of the panel or committee. Each such panel and committee shall delete from any transcript made pursuant to this subsection information which under subsection (c) of this section is to be considered confidential.

Traceability Requirements

(j) Except as provided in section 519(e), no regulation under this Act may impose on a type or class of device requirements for the traceability of such type or class of device unless such requirements are necessary to assure the protection of the public health.

Research and Development

(k) The Secretary may enter into contracts for research, testing, and demonstrations respecting devices and may obtain devices for research, testing, and demonstration purposes without regard to sections 3648 and 3709 of the Revised Statutes (31 U.S.C. 529, 41 U.S.C. 5).[65]

Transitional Provisions for Devices Considered as New Drugs

(*l*)(1) Any device intended for human use —

(A) for which on the date of enactment of the Medical Device Amendments of 1976 (hereinafter in this subsection referred to as the "enactment date") an approval of an application submitted under section 505(b) was in effect;

(B) for which such an application was filed on or before the enactment date and with respect to which application no order of approval or refusing to approve had been issued on such date under subsection (c) or (d) of such section;

(C) for which on the enactment date an exemption under subsection (i) of such section was in effect;

(D) which is within a type of device described in subparagraph (A), (B), or (C) and is substantially equivalent to another device within that type;

(E) which the Secretary in a notice published in the Federal Register before the enactment date has declared to be a new drug subject to section 505; or

(F) with respect to which on the enactment date an action is pending in a United States court under section 302, 303, or 304 for an alleged violation of a provision of section 301 which enforces a requirement of section 505 or for an alleged violation of section 505(a),

is classified in class III unless the Secretary in response to a petition submitted under paragraph (2) has classified such device in class I or II.

(2) The Secretary may initiate the reclassification of a device classified into class III under paragraph (1) of this subsection or the manufacturer or importer of a device classified under paragraph (1) may petition the Secretary (in such form and manner as he shall prescribe) for the issuance of an order classifying the device in class I or class II. Within thirty days of the filing of such a petition, the Secretary shall notify the petitioner of any deficiencies in the petition which prevent the Secretary from

---

65. Section 3648 of the Revised Statutes has been superseded by subsections (a) and (b) of section 3324 of title 31, United States Code. See Pub. L. No. 97–258, § 3, 96 Stat. 877, 1063–65 (1982).

making a decision on the petition. Except as provided in paragraph (3)(D)(ii), within one hundred and eighty days after the filing of a petition under this paragraph, the Secretary shall, after consultation with the appropriate panel under section 513, by order either deny the petition or order the classification, in accordance with the criteria prescribed by section 513(a)(1)(A) or 513(a)(1)(B), of the device in class I or class II.

(3)(A) In the case of a device which is described in paragraph (1)(A) and which is in class III—

(i) such device shall on the enactment date be considered a device with an approved application under section 515, and

(ii) the requirements applicable to such device before the enactment date under section 505 shall continue to apply to such device until changed by the Secretary as authorized by this Act.

(B) In the case of a device which is described in paragraph (1)(B) and which is in class III, an application for such device shall be considered as having been filed under section 515 on the enactment date. The period in which the Secretary shall act on such application in accordance with section 515(d)(1) shall be one hundred and eighty days from the enactment date (or such greater period as the Secretary and the applicant may agree upon after the Secretary has made the finding required by section 515(d)(1)(B)(i)) less the number of days in the period beginning on the date an application for such device was filed under section 505 and ending on the enactment date. After the expiration of such period such device is required, unless exempt under subsection (g), to have in effect an approved application under section 515.

(C) A device which is described in paragraph (1)(C) and which is in class III shall be considered a new drug until the expiration of the ninety-day period beginning on the date of the promulgation of regulations under subsection (g) of this section. After the expiration of such period such device is required, unless exempt under subsection (g), to have in effect an approved application under section 515.

(D)(i) Except as provided in clauses (ii) and (iii), a device which is described in subparagraph (D), (E), or (F) of paragraph (1) and which is in class III is required, unless exempt under subsection (g) of this section, to have on and after sixty days after the enactment date in effect an approved application under section 515.

(ii) If—

(I) a petition is filed under paragraph (2) for a device described in subparagraph (D), (E), or (F) of paragraph (1), or

(II) an application for premarket approval is filed under section 515 for such a device,

within the sixty-day period beginning on the enactment date (or within such greater period as the Secretary, after making the finding required under section 515(d)(1)(B), and the petitioner or applicant may agree upon), the Secretary shall act on such petition or application in accordance with paragraph (2) or section 515 except that the period within which the Secretary must act on the petition or application shall be within the one hundred and twenty-day period beginning on the date the petition or application is filed. If such a petition or application is filed within such sixty-day (or greater) period, clause (i) of this subparagraph shall not apply to such device before the expiration of such one hundred and twenty day period, or if such petition is denied or such application is denied approval, before the date of such denial, whichever occurs first.

(iii) In the case of a device which is described in subparagraph (E) of paragraph (1), which the Secretary in a notice published in the Federal Register after March 31, 1976, declared to be a new drug subject to section 505, and which is in class III—

(I) the device shall, after eighteen months after the enactment date, have in effect an approved application under section 515 unless exempt under subsection (g) of this section, and

(II) the Secretary may, during the period beginning one hundred and eighty days after the enactment date and ending eighteen months after such date, restrict the use of the device to investigational use by experts qualified by scientific training and experience to investigate the safety and effectiveness of such device, and to investigational use in accordance with the requirements applicable under regulations under subsection (g) of this section to investigational use of devices granted an exemption under such subsection.

If the requirements under subsection (g) of this section are made applicable to the investigational use of such a device, they shall be made applicable in such a manner that the device shall be made reasonably available to physicians meeting appropriate qualifications prescribed by the Secretary.

[(4) Repealed by Pub. L. No. 105–115, § 125(b)(2)(E), 111 Stat. 2296, 2325 (1997).]

(5)(A) Before December 1, 1991, the Secretary shall by order require manufacturers of devices described in paragraph (1), which are subject to revision of classification under subparagraph (B), to submit to the Secretary a summary of and citation to any information known or otherwise available to the manufacturers respecting the devices, including adverse safety or effectiveness information which has not been submitted under section 519. The Secretary may require a manufacturer to submit the adverse safety or effectiveness data for which a summary and citation were submitted, if such data are available to the manufacturer.

(B) Except as provided in subparagraph (C), after the issuance of an order under subparagraph (A) but before December 1, 1992, the Secretary shall publish a regulation in the Federal Register for each device which is classified in class III under paragraph (1) revising the classification of the device so that the device is classified into class I or class II, unless the regulation requires the device to remain in class III. In determining whether to revise the classification of a device or to require a device to remain in class III, the Secretary shall apply the criteria set forth in section 513(a). Before the publication of a regulation requiring a device to remain in class III or revising its classification, the Secretary shall publish a proposed regulation respecting the classification of a device under this subparagraph and provide an opportunity for the submission of comments on any such regulation. No regulation under this subparagraph requiring a device to remain in class III or revising its classification may take effect before the expiration of 90 days from the date of the publication in the Federal Register of the proposed regulation.

(C) The Secretary may by notice published in the Federal Register extend the period prescribed by subparagraph (B) for a device for an additional period not to exceed 1 year.

Humanitarian Device Exemption

(m)(1) To the extent consistent with the protection of the public health and safety and with ethical standards, it is the purpose of this subsection to encourage the discovery and use of devices intended to benefit patients in the treatment and diagnosis of diseases or conditions that affect fewer than 4,000 individuals in the United States.

(2) The Secretary may grant a request for an exemption from the effectiveness requirements of sections 514 and 515 for a device for which the Secretary finds that—

(A) the device is designed to treat or diagnose a disease or condition that affects fewer than 4,000 individuals in the United States,

(B) the device would not be available to a person with a disease or condition referred to in subparagraph (A) unless the Secretary grants such an exemption and there is no comparable device, other than under this exemption, available to treat or diagnose such disease or condition, and

(C) the device will not expose patients to an unreasonable or significant risk of illness or injury and the probable benefit to health from the use of the device outweighs the risk of injury or illness from its use, taking into account the probable risks and benefits of currently available device or alternative forms of treatment.

The request shall be in the form of an application submitted to the Secretary and such application shall include the certification required under section 402(j)(5)(B) of the Public Health Service Act (which shall not be considered an element of such application). Not later than 75 days after the date of the receipt of the application, the Secretary shall issue an order approving or denying the application.

(3) Except as provided in paragraph (6), no person granted an exemption under paragraph (2) with respect to a device may sell the device for an amount that exceeds the costs of research and development, fabrication, and distribution of the device.

(4) Devices granted an exemption under paragraph (2) may only be used—

(A) in facilities that have established, in accordance with regulations of the Secretary, a local institutional review committee to supervise clinical testing of devices in the facilities, and

(B) if, before the use of a device, an institutional review committee approves the use in the treatment or diagnosis of a disease or condition referred to in paragraph (2)(A), unless a physician determines in an emergency situation that approval from a local institutional review committee can not be obtained in time to prevent serious harm or death to a patient.

In a case described in subparagraph (B) in which a physician uses a device without an approval from an institutional review committee, the physician shall, after the use of the device, notify the chairperson of the local institutional review committee of such use. Such notification shall include the identification of the patient involved, the date on which the device was used, and the reason for the use.

(5) The Secretary may require a person granted an exemption under paragraph (2) to demonstrate continued compliance with the requirements of this subsection if the Secretary believes such demonstration to be necessary to protect the public health, if the Secretary has reason to believe that the requirements of paragraph (6) are no longer met, or if the Secretary has reason to believe that the criteria for the exemption are no longer met. If the person granted an exemption under paragraph (2) fails to demonstrate continued compliance with the requirements of this subsection, the Secretary may suspend or withdraw the exemption from the effectiveness requirements of sections 514 and 515 for a humanitarian device only after providing notice and an opportunity for an informal hearing.

(6)(A) Except as provided in subparagraph (D), the prohibition in paragraph (3) shall not apply with respect to a person granted an exemption under paragraph (2) if each of the following conditions apply:

(i) The device with respect to which the exemption is granted—

(I) is intended for the treatment or diagnosis of a disease or condition that occurs in pediatric patients or in a pediatric subpopulation, and such device is labeled for use in pediatric patients or in a pediatric subpopulation in which the disease or condition occurs; or

(II) is intended for the treatment or diagnosis of a disease or condition that does not occur in pediatric patients or that occurs in pediatric patients in such numbers that the development of the device for such patients is impossible, highly impracticable, or unsafe.

(ii) During any calendar year, the number of such devices distributed during that year under each exemption granted under this subsection does not exceed the annual distribution number for such device. In this paragraph, the term "annual distribution number" means the number of such devices reasonably needed to treat, diagnose, or cure a population of 4,000 individuals in the United States.

The Secretary shall determine the annual distribution number when the Secretary grants such exemption

(iii) Such person immediately notifies the Secretary if the number of such devices distributed during any calendar year exceeds the annual distribution number referred to in clause (ii).

(iv) The request for such exemption is submitted on or before October 1, 2017.

(B) The Secretary may inspect the records relating to the number of devices distributed during any calendar year of a person granted an exemption under paragraph (2) for which the prohibition in paragraph (3) does not apply.

(C) A person may petition the Secretary to modify the annual distribution number determined by the Secretary under subparagraph (A)(ii) with respect to a device if additional information arises, and the Secretary may modify such annual distribution number.

(D) If a person notifies the Secretary, or the Secretary determines through an inspection under subparagraph (B), that the number of devices distributed during any calendar year exceeds the annual distribution number, as required under subparagraph (A)(iii), and modified under subparagraph (C), if applicable, then the prohibition in paragraph (3) shall apply with respect to such person for such device for any sales of such device after such notification.

(E)(i) In this subsection, the term "pediatric patients" means patients who are 21 years of age or younger at the time of the diagnosis or treatment.

(ii) in this subsection, the term "pediatric subpopulation" means 1 of the following populations:

(I) Neonates.

(II) Infants.

(III) Children.

(IV) Adolescents.

(7) The Secretary shall refer any report of an adverse event regarding a device described in paragraph (6)(A)(i)(I) for which the prohibition under paragraph (3) does not apply pursuant to paragraph (6)(A) that the Secretary receives to the Office of Pediatric Therapeutics, established under section 6 of the Best Pharmaceuticals for Children Act (Public Law 107–109). In considering the report, the Director of the Office of Pediatric Therapeutics, in consultation with experts in the Center for Devices and Radiological Health, shall provide for periodic review of the report by the Pediatric Advisory Committee, including obtaining any recommendations of such committee regarding whether the Secretary should take action under this Act in response to the report.

(8) The Secretary, acting through the Office of Pediatric Therapeutics and the Center for Devices and Radiological Health, shall provide for an annual review by the Pediatric Advisory Committee of all devices described in paragraph (6)(A)(i)(I) to ensure that the exemption under paragraph (2) remains appropriate for the pediatric populations for which it is granted.

Regulation of Contact Lens as Devices

(n)(1) All contact lenses shall be deemed to be devices under section 201(h).

(2) Paragraph (1) shall not be construed as bearing on or being relevant to the question of whether any product other than a contact lens is a device as defined by section 201(h) or a drug as defined by section 201(g).

SEC. 521 [21 U.S.C. 360k]. STATE AND LOCAL REQUIREMENTS RESPECTING DEVICES

General Rule

(a) Except as provided in subsection (b), no State or political subdivision of a State may establish or continue in effect with respect to a device intended for human use any requirement—

(1) which is different from, or in addition to, any requirement applicable under this Act to the device, and

(2) which relates to the safety or effectiveness of the device or to any other matter included in a requirement applicable to the device under this Act.

Exempt Requirements

(b) Upon application of a State or a political subdivision thereof, the Secretary may, by regulation promulgated after notice and opportunity for an oral hearing, exempt from subsection (a), under such conditions as may be prescribed in such regulation, a requirement of such State or political subdivision applicable to a device intended for human use if—

(1) the requirement is more stringent than a requirement under this Act which would be applicable to the device if an exemption were not in effect under this subsection; or

(2) the requirement—

(A) is required by compelling local conditions, and

(B) compliance with the requirement would not cause the device to be in violation of any applicable requirement under this Act.

Sec. 522 [21 U.S.C. 360l]. Postmarket Surveillance

(a) Postmarket Surveillance.—

(1) In general.—

(A) Conduct.—The Secretary may by order, at the time of approval or clearance of a device or at any time thereafter, require a manufacturer to conduct postmarket surveillance for any device of the manufacturer that is a class II or class III device—

(i) the failure of which would be reasonably likely to have serious adverse health consequences;

(ii) that is expected to have significant use in pediatric populations; or

(iii) that is intended to be—

(I) implanted in the human body for more than 1 year; or

(II) a life-sustaining or life-supporting device used outside a device user facility.

(B) Condition.—The Secretary may order a postmarket surveillance under subparagraph (A) as a condition to approval or clearance of a device described in subparagraph (A)(ii).

(2) Rule of construction.—The provisions of paragraph (1) shall have no effect on authorities otherwise provided under the Act or regulations issued under this Act.

(b) Surveillance Approval.—

(1) In general.—Each manufacturer required to conduct a surveillance of a device shall, within 30 days of receiving an order from the Secretary prescribing that the manufacturer is required under this section to conduct such surveillance, submit, for the approval of the Secretary, a plan for the required surveillance. The Secretary, within 60 days of the receipt of such plan, shall determine if the person designated to conduct the surveillance has appropriate qualifications and experience to undertake such surveillance and if the plan will result in the collection of useful data that can reveal unforeseen adverse events or other information necessary to protect the public health. The manufacturer shall commence surveillance under this section not later than 15 months after the day on which the Secretary issues an order under this section. Except as provided in paragraph (2), the Secretary, in consultation with the manufacturer, may by order require a prospective surveillance period of up to 36 months. Except as provided in paragraph (2), any determination by the Secretary that a longer period is necessary shall be made by mutual agreement between the Secretary and the manufacturer or, if no agreement can be reached, after the completion of a dispute resolution process as described in section 562.

(2) LONGER SURVEILLANCE FOR PEDIATRIC DEVICES.—The Secretary may by order require a prospective surveillance period of more than 36 months with respect to a device that is expected to have significant use in pediatric populations if such period of more than 36 months is necessary in order to assess the impact of the device on growth and development, or the effects of growth, development, activity level, or other factors on the safety or efficacy of the device.

(c) DISPUTE RESOLUTION.—A manufacturer may request review under section 562 of any order or condition requiring postmarket surveillance under this section. During the pendency of such review, the device subject to such a postmarket surveillance order or condition shall not, because of noncompliance with such order or condition, be deemed in violation of section 301(q)(1)(C), adulterated under section 501(f)(1), misbranded under section 502(t)(3), or in violation of, as applicable, section 510(k) or section 515, unless deemed necessary to protect the public health.

SEC. 523 [21 U.S.C. 360m]. ACCREDITED PERSONS

(a) IN GENERAL.—

(1) REVIEW AND CLASSIFICATION OF DEVICES.—Not later than 1 year after the date of the enactment of the Food and Drug Administration Modernization Act of 1997, the Secretary shall, subject to paragraph (3), accredit persons for the purpose of reviewing reports submitted under section 510(k) and making recommendations to the Secretary regarding the initial classification of devices under section 513(f)(1).

(2) REQUIREMENTS REGARDING REVIEW.—

(A) IN GENERAL.—In making a recommendation to the Secretary under paragraph (1), an accredited person shall notify the Secretary in writing of the reasons for the recommendation.

(B) TIME PERIOD FOR REVIEW.—Not later than 30 days after the date on which the Secretary is notified under subparagraph (A) by an accredited person with respect to a recommendation of an initial classification of a device, the Secretary shall make a determination with respect to the initial classification.

(C) SPECIAL RULE.—The Secretary may change the initial classification under section 513(f)(1) that is recommended under paragraph (1) by an accredited person, and in such case shall provide to such person, and the person who submitted the report under section 510(k) for the device, a statement explaining in detail the reasons for the change.

(3) CERTAIN DEVICES.—

(A) IN GENERAL.—An accredited person may not be used to perform a review of—

(i) a class III device;

(ii) a class II device which is intended to be permanently implantable or life sustaining or life supporting; or

(iii) a class II device which requires clinical data in the report submitted under section 510(k) for the device, except that the number of class II devices to which the Secretary applies this clause for a year, less the number of such reports to which clauses (i) and (ii) apply, may not exceed 6 percent of the number that is equal to the total number of reports submitted to the Secretary under such section for such year less the number of such reports to which such clauses apply for such year.

(B) ADJUSTMENT.—In determining for a year the ratio described in subparagraph (A)(iii), the Secretary shall not include in the numerator class III devices that the Secretary reclassified into class II, and the Secretary shall include in the denominator class II devices for which reports under section 510(k) were not required to be submitted by reason of the operation of section 510(m).

(b) ACCREDITATION.—

(1) PROGRAMS.—The Secretary shall provide for such accreditation through programs administered by the Food and Drug Administration, other government agencies, or by other qualified non government organizations.

(2) ACCREDITATION.—

(A) IN GENERAL.—Not later than 180 days after the date of the enactment of the Food and Drug Administration Modernization Act of 1997, the Secretary shall establish and publish in the Federal Register criteria to accredit or deny accreditation to persons who request to perform the duties specified in subsection (a). The Secretary shall respond to a request for accreditation within 60 days of the receipt of the request. The accreditation of such person shall specify the particular activities under subsection (a) for which such person is accredited.

(B) WITHDRAWAL OF ACCREDITATION.—The Secretary may suspend or withdraw accreditation of any person accredited under this paragraph, after providing notice and an opportunity for an informal hearing, when such person is substantially not in compliance with the requirements of this section or poses a threat to public health or fails to act in a manner that is consistent with the purposes of this section.

(C) PERFORMANCE AUDITING.—To ensure that persons accredited under this section will continue to meet the standards of accreditation, the Secretary shall—

(i) make onsite visits on a periodic basis to each accredited person to audit the performance of such person; and

(ii) take such additional measures as the Secretary determines to be appropriate.

(D) ANNUAL REPORT.—The Secretary shall include in the annual report required under section 1003(g) the names of all accredited persons and the particular activities under subsection (a) for which each such person is accredited and the name of each accredited person whose accreditation has been withdrawn during the year.

(E) PERIODIC REACCREDITATION.—

(i) PERIOD.—Subject to suspension or withdrawal under subparagraph (B), any accreditation under this section shall be valid for a period of 3 years after its issuance.

(ii) RESPONSE TO REACCREDITATION REQUEST.—Upon the submission of a request by an accredited person for reaccreditation under this section, the Secretary shall approve or deny such request not later than 60 days after receipt of the request.

(iii) CRITERIA.—Not later than 120 days after the date of the enactment of this subparagraph, the Secretary shall establish and publish in the Federal Register criteria to reaccredit or deny reaccreditation to persons under this section. The reaccreditation of persons under this section shall specify the particular activities under subsection (a), and the devices, for which such persons are reaccredited.

(3) QUALIFICATIONS.—An accredited person shall, at a minimum, meet the following requirements:

(A) Such person may not be an employee of the Federal Government.

(B) Such person shall be an independent organization which is not owned or controlled by a manufacturer, supplier, or vendor of devices and which has no organizational, material, or financial affiliation with such a manufacturer, supplier, or vendor.

(C) Such person shall be a legally constituted entity permitted to conduct the activities for which it seeks accreditation.

(D) Such person shall not engage in the design, manufacture, promotion, or sale of devices.

(E) The operations of such person shall be in accordance with generally accepted professional and ethical business practices and shall agree in writing that as a minimum it will—

(i) certify that reported information accurately reflects data reviewed;

(ii) limit work to that for which competence and capacity are available;

(iii) treat information received, records, reports, and recommendations as proprietary information;

(iv) promptly respond and attempt to resolve complaints regarding its activities for which it is accredited; and

(v) protect against the use, in carrying out subsection (a) with respect to a device, of any officer or employee of the person who has a financial conflict of interest regarding the device, and annually make available to the public disclosures of the extent to which the person, and the officers and employees of the person, have maintained compliance with requirements under this clause relating to financial conflicts of interest.

(4) SELECTION OF ACCREDITED PERSONS.—The Secretary shall provide each person who chooses to use an accredited person to receive a section 510(k) report a panel of at least two or more accredited persons from which the regulated person may select one for a specific regulatory function.

(5) COMPENSATION OF ACCREDITED PERSONS.—Compensation for an accredited person shall be determined by agreement between the accredited person and the person who engages the services of the accredited person, and shall be paid by the person who engages such services.

(c) DURATION.—The authority provided by this section terminates October 1, 2017.

(d) REPORT.—Not later than January 10, 2007, the Secretary shall conduct a study based on the experience under the program under this section and submit to the Committee on Energy and Commerce of the House of Representatives, and the Committee on Health, Education, Labor, and Pensions of the Senate, a report describing the findings of the study. The objectives of the study shall include determining—

(1) the number of devices reviewed under this section;

(2) the number of devices reviewed under this section that were ultimately cleared by the Secretary;

(3) the number of devices reviewed under this section that were ultimately not cleared by the Secretary;

(4) the average time period for a review under this section (including the time it takes for the Secretary to review a recommendation of an accredited person under subsection (a) and determine the initial device classification);

(5) the average time period identified in paragraph (4) compared to the average time period for review of devices solely by the Secretary pursuant to section 510(k);

(6) if there is a difference in the average time period under paragraph (4) and the average time period under paragraph (5), the reasons for such difference;

(7) whether the quality of reviews under this section for devices for which no guidance has been issued is qualitatively inferior to reviews by the Secretary for devices for which no guidance has been issued;

(8) whether the quality of reviews under this section of devices for which no guidance has been issued is qualitatively inferior to reviews under this section of devices for which guidance has been issued;

(9) whether this section has in any way jeopardized or improved the public health;

(10) any impact of this section on resources available to the Secretary to review reports under section 510(k); and

(11) any suggestions for continuation, modification (including contraction or expansion of device eligibility), or termination of this section that the Secretary determines to be appropriate.

SEC. 524 [21 U.S.C. 360n]. PRIORITY REVIEW TO ENCOURAGE TREATMENTS FOR TROPICAL DISEASES

(a) DEFINITIONS.—In this section:

(1) PRIORITY REVIEW.—The term "priority review", with respect to a human drug application as defined in section 735(1), means review and action by the Secretary on such application not later than 6 months after receipt by the Secretary of such application, as described in the Manual of Policies and Procedures of the Food and Drug Administration and goals identified in the letters described in section 101(c) of the Food and Drug Administration Amendments Act of 2007.

(2) PRIORITY REVIEW VOUCHER.—The term "priority review voucher" means a voucher issued by the Secretary to the sponsor of a tropical disease product application that entitles the holder of such voucher to priority review of a single human drug application submitted under section 505(b)(1) or section 351 of the Public Health Service Act after the date of approval of the tropical disease product application.

(3) TROPICAL DISEASE.—The term "tropical disease" means any of the following:

    (A) Tuberculosis.

    (B) Malaria.

    (C) Blinding trachoma.

    (D) Buruli Ulcer.

    (E) Cholera.

    (F) Dengue/dengue haemorrhagic fever.

    (G) Dracunculiasis (guinea-worm disease).

    (H) Fascioliasis.

    (I) Human African trypanosomiasis.

    (J) Leishmaniasis.

(K) Leprosy.

(L) Lymphatic filariasis.

(M) Onchocerciasis.

(N) Schistosomiasis.

(O) Soil transmitted helmithiasis.

(P) Yaws.

(Q) Any other infectious disease for which there is no significant market in developed nations and that disproportionately affects poor and marginalized populations, designated by regulation by the Secretary.

(4) TROPICAL DISEASE PRODUCT APPLICATION.—The term "tropical disease product application" means an application that—

(A) is a human drug application as defined in section 735(1)—

(i) for prevention or treatment of a tropical disease; and

(ii) the Secretary deems eligible for priority review;

(B) is approved after the date of the enactment of the Food and Drug Administration Amendments Act of 2007, by the Secretary for use in the prevention, detection, or treatment of a tropical disease; and

(C) is for a human drug, no active ingredient (including any ester or salt of the active ingredient) of which has been approved in any other application under section 505(b)(1) or section 351 of the Public Health Service Act.

(b) PRIORITY REVIEW VOUCHER.—

(1) IN GENERAL.—The Secretary shall award a priority review voucher to the sponsor of a tropical disease product application upon approval by the Secretary of such tropical disease product application.

(2) TRANSFERABILITY.—The sponsor of a tropical disease product that receives a priority review voucher under this section may transfer (including by sale) the entitlement to such voucher to a sponsor of a human drug for which an application under section 505(b)(1) or section 351 of the Public Health Service Act will be submitted after the date of the approval of the tropical disease product application.

(3) LIMITATION.—

(A) NO AWARD FOR PRIOR APPROVED APPLICATION.—A sponsor of a tropical disease product may not receive a priority review voucher under this section if the tropical disease product application was submitted to the Secretary prior to the date of the enactment of this section.

(B) ONE-YEAR WAITING PERIOD.—The Secretary shall issue a priority review voucher to the sponsor of a tropical disease product no earlier than the date that is 1 year after the date of the enactment of the Food and Drug Administration Amendments Act of 2007.[66]

(4) NOTIFICATION.—The sponsor of a human drug application shall notify the Secretary not later than 365 days prior to submission of the human drug application that is the subject of a priority review voucher of an intent to submit the human drug application, including the date on which the sponsor intends to submit the application. Such notification shall be a legally binding commitment to pay for the user fee to be assessed in accordance with this section.

(c) PRIORITY REVIEW USER FEE.—

(1) IN GENERAL.—The Secretary shall establish a user fee program under which a sponsor of a human drug application that is the subject of a priority review voucher shall pay to the Secretary a fee determined under paragraph (2). Such fee shall be in addition to any fee required to be submitted by the sponsor under chapter VII.

(2) FEE AMOUNT.—The amount of the priority review user fee shall be determined each fiscal year by the Secretary and based on the average cost incurred by the agency in the review of a human drug application subject to priority review in the previous fiscal year.

(3) ANNUAL FEE SETTING.—The Secretary shall establish, before the beginning of each fiscal year beginning after September 30, 2007, for that fiscal year, the amount of the priority review user fee.

(4) PAYMENT.—

(A) IN GENERAL.—The priority review user fee required by this subsection shall be due upon the submission of a human drug application under section 505(b)(1) or section 351 of the Public Health Services Act for which the priority review voucher is used.

(B) COMPLETE APPLICATION.—An application described under subparagraph (A) for which the sponsor requests the use of a priority review voucher shall be considered incomplete if the fee required by this subsection and all other applicable user fees are not paid in accordance with the Secretary's procedures for paying such fees.

(C) NO WAIVERS, EXEMPTIONS, REDUCTIONS, OR REFUNDS.—The Secretary may not grant a waiver, exemption, reduction, or refund of any fees due and payable under this section.

(5) OFFSETTING COLLECTIONS.—Fees collected pursuant to this subsection for any fiscal year—

(A) shall be deposited and credited as offsetting collections to the account providing appropriations to the Food and Drug Administration; and

66. Pub. L. No. 110–85, 121 Stat. 823, which was enacted September 27, 2007.

(B) shall not be collected for any fiscal year except to the extent provided in advance in appropriation Acts.

SEC. 524A [U.S.C. 360n–1]. PRIORITY REVIEW FOR QUALIFIED INFECTIOUS DISEASE PRODUCTS

If the Secretary designates a drug under section 505E(d) as a qualified infectious disease product, then the Secretary shall give priority review to any application submitted for approval for such drug under section 505(b).

SUBCHAPTER B—DRUGS FOR RARE DISEASES OR CONDITIONS

SEC. 525 [21 U.S.C. 360aa]. RECOMMENDATIONS FOR INVESTIGATIONS OF DRUGS FOR RARE DISEASES OR CONDITIONS

(a) The sponsor of a drug for a disease or condition which is rare in the States may request the Secretary to provide written recommendations for the nonclinical and clinical investigations which must be conducted with the drug before—

(1) it may be approved for such disease or condition under section 505, or

(2) if the drug is a biological product, it may be licensed for such disease or condition under section 351 of the Public Health Service Act.

If the Secretary has reason to believe that a drug for which a request is made under this section is a drug for a disease or condition which is rare in the States, the Secretary shall provide the person making the request written recommendations for the nonclinical and clinical investigations which the Secretary believes, on the basis of information available to the Secretary at the time of the request under this section, would be necessary for approval of such drug for such disease or condition under section 505 or licensing of such drug for such disease or condition under section 351 of the Public Health Service Act.

(b) The Secretary shall by regulation promulgate procedures for the implementation of subsection (a).

SEC. 526 [21 U.S.C. 360bb]. DESIGNATION OF DRUGS FOR RARE DISEASES OR CONDITIONS

(a)(1) The manufacturer or the sponsor of a drug may request the Secretary to designate the drug as a drug for a rare disease or condition. A request for designation of a drug shall be made before the submission of an application under section 505(b) for the drug, or the submission of an application for licensing of the drug under section 351 of the Public Health Service Act. If the Secretary finds that a drug for which a request is submitted under this subsection is being or will be investigated for a rare disease or condition and—

(A) if an application for such drug is approved under section 505, or

(B) if a license for such drug is issued under section 351of the Public Health Service Act,

the approval, certification, or license would be for use for such disease or condition, the Secretary shall designate the drug as a drug for such disease or condition. A request for a designation of a drug under this subsection shall contain the consent of the applicant to notice being given by the Secretary under subsection (b) respecting the designation of the drug.

(2) For purposes of paragraph (1), the term "rare disease or condition" means any disease or condition which (A) affects less than 200,000 persons in the United States, or (B) affects more than 200,000 in the United States and for which there is no reasonable expectation that the cost of developing and making available in the United States a drug for such disease or condition will be recovered from sales in the United States of such drug. Determinations under the preceding sentence with respect to any drug shall be made on the basis of the facts and circumstances as of the date the request for designation of the drug under this subsection is made.

(b) A designation of a drug under subsection (a) shall be subject to the condition that—

(1) if an application was approved for the drug under section 505(b) or a license was issued for the drug under section 351 of the Public Health Service Act, the manufacturer of the drug will notify the Secretary of any discontinuance of the production of the drug at least one year before discontinuance, and

(2) if an application has not been approved for the drug under section 505(b) or a license has not been issued for the drug under section 351 of the Public Health Service Act and if preclinical investigations or investigations under section 505(i) are being conducted with the drug, the manufacturer or sponsor of the drug will notify the Secretary of any decision to discontinue active pursuit of approval of an application under section 505(b) or approval of a license under section 351 of the Public Health Service Act.

(c) Notice respecting the designation of a drug under subsection (a) shall be made available to the public.

(d) The Secretary shall by regulation promulgate procedures for the implementation of subsection (a).

SEC. 527 [21 U.S.C. 360cc]. PROTECTION FOR DRUGS FOR RARE DISEASES OR CONDITIONS

(a) Except as provided in subsection (b), if the Secretary—

(1) approves an application filed pursuant to section 505, or

(2) issues a license under section 351 of the Public Health Service Act

For a drug designated under section 526 for a rare disease or condition, the Secretary may not approve another application under section 505 or issue another license under section 351 of the Public Health Service Act for such drug for such disease or condition for a person who is not the holder of such approved application, of or of such license until the expiration of seven years from the date of the approval of the approved application, or the issuance of the license. Section 505(c)(2) does not apply to the refusal to approve an application under the preceding sentence.

(b) If an application filed pursuant to section 505 is approved for a drug designated under section 526 for a rare disease or condition or if a license is issued under section 351 of the Public Health Service Act for such a drug, the Secretary may, during the seven year period beginning on the date of the application approval or of the issuance of the license, approve another application under section 505 or issue a license under section 351 of the Public Health Service Act, for such drug for such disease or condition for a person who is not the holder of such approved application or of such license if—

(1) the Secretary finds, after providing the holder notice and opportunity for the submission of views, that in such period the holder of the approved application or of the license cannot assure the availability of sufficient quantities of the drug to meet the needs of persons with the disease or condition for which the drug was designated; or

(2) such holder provides the Secretary in writing the consent of such holder for the approval of other applications or the issuance of other licenses before the expiration of such seven year period.

SEC. 528 [21 U.S.C. 360dd]. OPEN PROTOCOLS FOR INVESTIGATIONS OF DRUGS FOR RARE DISEASES OR CONDITIONS

If a drug is designated under section 526 as a drug for a rare disease or condition and if notice of a claimed exemption under section 505(i) or regulations issued thereunder is filed for such drug, the Secretary shall encourage the sponsor of such drug to design protocols for clinical investigations of the drug which may be conducted under the exemption to permit the addition to the investigations of persons with the disease or condition who need the drug to treat the disease or condition and who cannot be satisfactorily treated by available alternative drugs.

SEC. 529 [21 U.S.C. 360ff]. PRIORITY REVIEW TO ENCOURAGE TREATMENTS FOR RARE PEDIATRIC DISEASES

(a) DEFINITIONS.—In this section:

(1) PRIORITY REVIEW.—The term "priority review", with respect to a human drug application as defined in section 735(1), means review and action by the Secretary on such application not later than 6 months after receipt by the Secretary of such application, as described in the Manual of Policies and Procedures of

the Food and Drug Administration and goals identified in the letters described in section 101(b) of the Prescription Drug User Fee Amendments of 2012.

(2) PRIORITY REVIEW VOUCHER.—The term "priority review voucher" means a voucher issued by the Secretary to the sponsor of a rare pediatric disease product application that entitles the holder of such voucher to priority review of a single human drug application submitted under section 505(b)(1) or section 351(a) of the Public Health Service Act after the date of approval of the rare pediatric disease product application.

(3) RARE PEDIATRIC DISEASE.—The term "rare pediatric disease" means a disease that meets each of the following criteria:

(A) The disease primarily affects individuals aged from birth to 18 years, including age groups often called neonates, infants, children, and adolescents.

(B) The disease is a rare disease or condition, within the meaning of section 526.

(4) RARE PEDIATRIC DISEASE PRODUCT APPLICATION.—The term "rare pediatric disease product application" means a human drug application, as defined in section 735(1), that—

(A) is for a drug or biological product—

(i) that is for the prevention or treatment of a rare pediatric disease; and

(ii) that contains no active ingredient (including any ester or salt of the active ingredient) that has been previously approved in any other application under section 505(b)(1), 505(b)(2), or 505(j) of this Act or section 351(a) or 351(k) of the Public Health Service Act;

(B) is submitted under section 505(b)(1) of this Act or section 351(a) of the Public Health Service Act;

(C) the Secretary deems eligible for priority review;

(D) that relies on clinical data derived from studies examining a pediatric population and dosages of the drug intended for that population;

(E) that does not seek approval for an adult indication in the original rare pediatric disease product application; and

(F) is approved after the date of the enactment of the Prescription Drug User Fee Amendments of 2012.

(b) PRIORITY REVIEW VOUCHER.—

(1) IN GENERAL.—The Secretary shall award a priority review voucher to the sponsor of a rare pediatric disease product application upon approval by the Secretary of such rare pediatric disease product application.

(2) TRANSFERABILITY.—

(A) IN GENERAL.—The sponsor of a rare pediatric disease product application that receives a priority review voucher under this section may transfer (including by sale) the entitlement to such voucher. There is no limit on the number of times a priority review voucher may be transferred before such voucher is used.

(B) NOTIFICATION OF TRANSFER.—Each person to whom a voucher is transferred shall notify the Secretary of such change in ownership of the voucher not later than 30 days after such transfer.

(3) LIMITATION.—A sponsor of a rare pediatric disease product application may not receive a priority review voucher under this section if the rare pediatric disease product application was submitted to the Secretary prior to the date that is 90 days after the date of enactment of the Prescription Drug User Fee Amendments of 2012.

(4) NOTIFICATION.—

(A) IN GENERAL.—The sponsor of a human drug application shall notify the Secretary not later than 90 days prior to submission of the human drug application that is the subject of a priority review voucher of an intent to submit the human drug application, including the date on which the sponsor intends to submit the application. Such notification shall be a legally binding commitment to pay for the user fee to be assessed in accordance with this section.

(B) TRANSFER AFTER NOTICE.—The sponsor of a human drug application that provides notification of the intent of such sponsor to use the voucher for the human drug application under subparagraph (A) may transfer the voucher after such notification is provided, if such sponsor has not yet submitted the human drug application described in the notification.

(5) TERMINATION OF AUTHORITY.—The Secretary may not award any priority review vouchers under paragraph (1) after the last day of the 1–year period that begins on the date that the Secretary awards the third rare pediatric disease priority voucher under this section.

(c) PRIORITY REVIEW USER FEE.—

(1) IN GENERAL.—The Secretary shall establish a user fee program under which a sponsor of a human drug application that is the subject of a priority review voucher shall pay to the Secretary a fee determined under paragraph (2). Such fee shall be in addition to any fee required to be submitted by the sponsor under chapter VII.

(2) FEE AMOUNT.—The amount of the priority review user fee shall be determined each fiscal year by the Secretary, based on the difference between—

(A) the average cost incurred by the Food and Drug Administration in the review of a human drug application subject to priority review in the previous fiscal year; and

(B) the average cost incurred by the Food and Drug Administration in the review of a human drug application that is not subject to priority review in the previous fiscal year.

(3) ANNUAL FEE SETTING.—The Secretary shall establish, before the beginning of each fiscal year beginning after September 30, 2012, the amount of the priority review user fee for that fiscal year.

(4) PAYMENT.—

(A) IN GENERAL.—The priority review user fee required by this subsection shall be due upon the notification by a sponsor of the intent of such sponsor to use the voucher, as specified in subsection (b)(4)(A). All other user fees associated with the human drug application shall be due as required by the Secretary or under applicable law.

(B) COMPLETE APPLICATION.—An application described under subparagraph (A) for which the sponsor requests the use of a priority review voucher shall be considered incomplete if the fee required by this subsection and all other applicable user fees are not paid in accordance with the Secretary's procedures for paying such fees.

(C) NO WAIVERS, EXEMPTIONS, REDUCTIONS, OR REFUNDS.—The Secretary may not grant a waiver, exemption, reduction, or refund of any fees due and payable under this section.

(5) OFFSETTING COLLECTIONS.—Fees collected pursuant to this subsection for any fiscal year—

(A) shall be deposited and credited as offsetting collections to the account providing appropriations to the Food and Drug Administration; and

(B) shall not be collected for any fiscal year except to the extent provided in advance in appropriations Acts.

(d) DESIGNATION PROCESS.—

(1) IN GENERAL.—Upon the request of the manufacturer or the sponsor of a new drug, the Secretary may designate—

(A) the new drug as a drug for a rare pediatric disease; and

(B) the application for the new drug as a rare pediatric disease product application.

(2) REQUEST FOR DESIGNATION.—The request for a designation under paragraph (1) shall be made at the same time a request for designation of orphan disease status under section 526 or fast-track designation under section 506 is made. Requesting designation under this subsection is not a pre-requisite to receiving a priority review voucher under this section.

(3) DETERMINATION BY SECRETARY.—Not later than 60 days after a request is submitted under paragraph (1), the Secretary shall determine whether—

(A) the disease or condition that is the subject of such request is a rare pediatric disease; and

(B) the application for the new drug is a rare pediatric disease product application.

(e) MARKETING OF RARE PEDIATRIC DISEASE PRODUCTS.—

(1) REVOCATION.—The Secretary may revoke any priority review voucher awarded under subsection (b) if the rare pediatric disease product for which such voucher was awarded is not marketed in the United States within the 365–day period beginning on the date of the approval of such drug under section 505 of this Act or section 351 of the Public Health Service Act.

(2) POSTAPPROVAL PRODUCTION REPORT.—The sponsor of an approved rare pediatric disease product shall submit a report to the Secretary not later than 5 years after the approval of the applicable rare pediatric disease product application. Such report shall provide the following information, with respect to each of the first 4 years after approval of such product:

(A) The estimated population in the United States suffering from the rare pediatric disease.

(B) The estimated demand in the United States for such rare pediatric disease product.

(C) The actual amount of such rare pediatric disease product distributed in the United States.

(f) NOTICE AND REPORT.—

(1) NOTICE OF ISSUANCE OF VOUCHER AND APPROVAL OF PRODUCTS UNDER VOUCHER.—The Secretary shall publish a notice in the Federal Register and on the Internet Web site of the Food and Drug Administration not later than 30 days after the occurrence of each of the following:

(A) The Secretary issues a priority review voucher under this section.

(B) The Secretary approves a drug pursuant to an application submitted under section 505(b) of this Act or section 351(a) of the Public Health Service Act for which the sponsor of the application used a priority review voucher under this section.

(2) NOTIFICATION.—If, after the last day of the 1–year period that begins on the date that the Secretary awards the third rare pediatric disease priority voucher under this section, a sponsor of an application submitted under section 505(b) of this Act or section 351(a) of the Public Health Service Act for a drug uses a priority review voucher under this section for such application, the Secretary shall submit to the Committee on Energy and Commerce of the House of Representatives and the Committee on Health, Education, Labor, and Pensions of the Senate a document—

(A) notifying such Committees of the use of such voucher; and

(B) identifying the drug for which such priority review voucher is used.

(g) ELIGIBILITY FOR OTHER PROGRAMS.—Nothing in this section precludes a sponsor who seeks a priority review voucher under this section from participating in any other incentive program, including under this Act.

(h) RELATION TO OTHER PROVISIONS.—The provisions of this section shall supplement, not supplant, any other provisions of this Act or the Public Health Service Act that encourage the development of drugs for tropical diseases and rare pediatric diseases.

(i) GAO STUDY AND REPORT.—

(1) STUDY.—

(A) IN GENERAL.—Beginning on the date that the Secretary awards the third rare pediatric disease priority voucher under this section, the Comptroller General of the United States shall conduct a study of the effectiveness of awarding rare pediatric disease priority vouchers under this section in the development of human drug products that treat or prevent such diseases.

(B) CONTENTS OF STUDY.—In conducting the study under subparagraph (A), the Comptroller General shall examine the following:

(i) The indications for which each rare disease product for which a priority review voucher was awarded was approved under section 505 or section 351 of the Public Health Service Act.

(ii) Whether, and to what extent, an unmet need related to the treatment or prevention of a rare pediatric disease was met through the approval of such a rare disease product.

(iii) The value of the priority review voucher if transferred.

(iv) Identification of each drug for which a priority review voucher was used.

(v) The length of the period of time between the date on which a priority review voucher was awarded and the date on which it was used.

(2) REPORT.—Not later than 1 year after the date under paragraph (1)(A), the Comptroller General shall submit to the Committee on Energy and Commerce of the House of Representatives and the Committee on Health, Education, Labor, and Pensions of the Senate, a report containing the results of the study under paragraph (1).

SUBCHAPTER C—ELECTRONIC PRODUCT RADIATION CONTROL

SEC. 531 [21 U.S.C. 360hh]. DEFINITIONS

As used in this subchapter—

(1) the term "electronic product radiation" means—

(A) any ionizing or non-ionizing electromagnetic or particulate radiation, or

(B) any sonic, infrasonic, or ultrasonic wave, which is emitted from an electronic product as the result of the operation of an electronic circuit in such product;

(2) the term "electronic product" means (A) any manufactured or assembled product which, when in operation, (i) contains or acts as part of an electronic circuit and (ii) emits (or in the absence of effective shielding or other controls would emit) electronic product radiation, or (B) any manufactured or assembled article which is intended for use as a component, part, or accessory of a product described in clause (A) and which when in operation emits (or in the absence of effective shielding or other controls would emit) such radiation;

(3) the term "manufacturer" means any person engaged in the business of manufacturing, assembling, or importing of electronic products;

(4) the term "commerce" means (A) commerce between any place in any State and any place outside thereof; and (B) commerce wholly within the District of Columbia; and

(5) the term "State" includes the District of Columbia, the Commonwealth of Puerto Rico, the Northern Mariana Islands, the Virgin Islands, Guam, and American Samoa.

SEC. 532 [21 U.S.C. 360ii]. ELECTRONIC PRODUCT RADIATION CONTROL PROGRAM

(a) The Secretary shall establish and carry out an electronic product radiation control program designed to protect the public health and safety from electronic product radiation. As a part of such program, he shall—

(1) pursuant to section 534, develop and administer performance standards for electronic products;

(2) plan, conduct, coordinate, and support research, development, training, and operational activities to minimize the emissions of and the exposure of people to, unnecessary electronic product radiation;

(3) maintain liaison with and receive information from other Federal and State departments and agencies with related interests, professional organizations, in-

411

dustry, industry and labor associations, and other organizations on present and future potential electronic product radiation;

(4) study and evaluate emissions of, and conditions of exposure to, electronic product radiation and intense magnetic fields;

(5) develop, test, and evaluate the effectiveness of procedures and techniques for minimizing exposure to electronic product radiation; and

(6) consult and maintain liaison with the Secretary of Commerce, the Secretary of Defense, the Secretary of Labor, the Atomic Energy Commission, and other appropriate Federal departments and agencies on (A) techniques, equipment, and programs for testing and evaluating electronic product radiation, and (B) the development of performance standards pursuant to section 534 to control such radiation emissions.

(b) In carrying out the purposes of subsection (a), the Secretary is authorized to—

(1)(A) collect and make available, through publications and other appropriate means, the results of, and other information concerning, research and studies relating to the nature and extent of the hazards and control of electronic product radiation; and (B) make such recommendations relating to such hazards and control as he considers appropriate;

(2) make grants to public and private agencies, organizations, and institutions, and to individuals for the purposes stated in paragraphs (2), (4), and (5) of subsection (a) of this section;

(3) contract with public or private agencies, institutions, and organizations, and with individuals, without regard to section 3324 of title 31, United States Code, and section 3709 of the Revised Statutes of the United States (41 U.S.C. 5); and

(4) procure (by negotiation or otherwise) electronic products for research and testing purposes, and sell or otherwise dispose of such products.

(c)(1) Each recipient of assistance under this subchapter pursuant to grants or contracts entered into under other than competitive bidding procedures shall keep such records as the Secretary shall prescribe, including records which fully disclose the amount and disposition by such recipient of the proceeds of such assistance, the total cost of the project or undertaking in connection with which such assistance is given or used, and the amount of that portion of the cost of the project or undertaking supplied by other sources, and such other records as will facilitate an effective audit.

(2) The Secretary and the Comptroller General of the United States, or any of their duly authorized representatives, shall have access for the purpose of audit and examination to any books, documents, papers, and records of the recipient that are pertinent to the grants or contracts entered into under this subchapter under other than competitive bidding procedures.

SEC. 533 [21 U.S.C. 360jj]. STUDIES BY THE SECRETARY

(a) The Secretary shall conduct the following studies, and shall make a report or reports of the results of such studies to the Congress on or before January 1, 1970, and from time to time thereafter as he may find necessary, together with such recommendations for legislation as he may deem appropriate:

(1) A study of present State and Federal control of health hazards from electronic product radiation and other types of ionizing radiation, which study shall include, but not be limited to—

(A) control of health hazards from radioactive materials other than materials regulated under the Atomic Energy Act of 1954;

(B) any gaps and inconsistencies in present controls;

(C) the need for controlling the sale of certain used electronic products, particularly antiquated X-ray equipment, without upgrading such products to meet the standards for new products or separate standards for used products;

(D) measures to assure consistent and effective control of the aforementioned health hazards;

(E) measures to strengthen radiological health programs of State governments; and

(F) the feasibility of authorizing the Secretary to enter into arrangements with individual States or groups of States to define their respective functions and responsibilities for the control of electronic product radiation and other ionizing radiation;

(2) A study to determine the necessity for the development of standards for the use of nonmedical electronic products for commercial and industrial purposes; and

(3) A study of the development of practicable procedures for the detection and measurement of electronic product radiation which may be emitted from electronic products manufactured or imported prior to the effective date of any applicable standard established pursuant to this subchapter.

(b) In carrying out these studies, the Secretary shall invite the participation of other Federal departments and agencies having related responsibilities and interests, State governments—particularly those of States which regulate radioactive materials under section 274 of the Atomic Energy Act of 1954, as amended, and interested professional, labor, and industrial organizations. Upon request from congressional committees interested in these studies, the Secretary shall keep these committees currently informed as to the progress of the studies and shall permit the committees to send observers to meetings of the study groups.

(c) The Secretary or his designee shall organize the studies and the participation of the invited participants as he deems best. Any dissent from the findings and recommendations of the Secretary shall be included in the report if so requested by the dissenter.

SEC. 534 [21 U.S.C. 360kk]. PERFORMANCE STANDARDS FOR ELECTRONIC PRODUCTS

(a)(1) The Secretary shall by regulation prescribe performance standards for electronic products to control the emission of electronic product radiation from such products if he determines that such standards are necessary for the protection of the public health and safety. Such standards may include provisions for the testing of such products and the measurement of their electronic product radiation emissions, may require the attachment of warning signs and labels, and may require the provision of instructions for the installation, operation, and use of such products. Such standards may be prescribed from time to time whenever such determinations are made, but the first of such standards shall be prescribed prior to January 1, 1970. In the development of such standards, the Secretary shall consult with Federal and State departments and agencies having related responsibilities or interests and with appropriate professional organizations and interested persons, including representatives of industries and labor organizations which would be affected by such standards, and shall give consideration to—

(A) the latest available scientific and medical data in the field of electronic product radiation;

(B) the standards currently recommended by (i) other Federal agencies having responsibilities relating to the control and measurement of electronic product radiation, and (ii) public or private groups having an expertise in the field of electronic product radiation;

(C) the reasonableness and technical feasibility of such standards as applied to a particular electronic product;

(D) the adaptability of such standards to the need for uniformity and reliability of testing and measuring procedures and equipment; and

(E) in the case of a component, or accessory described in paragraph (2)(B) of section 531, the performance of such article in the manufactured or assembled product for which it is designed.

(2) The Secretary may prescribe different and individual performance standards, to the extent appropriate and feasible, for different electronic products so as to recognize their different operating characteristics and uses.

(3) The performance standards prescribed under this section shall not apply to any electronic product which is intended solely for export if (A) such product and the outside of any shipping container used in the export of such product are labeled or tagged to show that such product is intended for export, and (B) such product meets

all the applicable requirements of the country to which such product is intended for export.

(4) The Secretary may by regulation amend or revoke any performance standard prescribed under this section.

(5) The Secretary may exempt from the provisions of this section any electronic product intended for use by departments or agencies of the United States provided such department or agency has prescribed procurement specifications governing emissions of electronic product radiation and provided further that such product is of a type used solely or predominantly by departments or agencies of the United States.

(b) The provisions of subchapter II of chapter 5 of title 5 of the United States Code (relating to the administrative procedure for rulemaking), and of chapter 7 of such title (relating to judicial review), shall apply with respect to any regulation prescribing, amending, or revoking any standard prescribed under this section.

(c) Each regulation prescribing, amending, or revoking a standard shall specify the date on which it shall take effect which, in the case of any regulation prescribing, or amending any standard, may not be sooner than one year or not later than two years after the date on which such regulation is issued, unless the Secretary finds, for good cause shown, that an earlier or later effective date is in the public interest and publishes in the Federal Register his reason for such finding, in which case such earlier or later date shall apply.

(d)(1) In a case of actual controversy as to the validity of any regulation issued under this section prescribing, amending, or revoking a performance standard, any person who will be adversely affected by such regulation when it is effective may at any time prior to the sixtieth day after such regulation is issued file a petition with the United States court of appeals for the circuit wherein such person resides or has his principal place of business, for a judicial review of such regulation. A copy of the petition shall be forthwith transmitted by the clerk of the court to the Secretary or other officer designated by him for that purpose. The Secretary thereupon shall file in the court the record of the proceedings on which the Secretary based the regulation, as provided in section 2112 of title 28 of the United States Code.

(2) If the petitioner applies to the court for leave to adduce additional evidence, and shows to the satisfaction of the court that such additional evidence is material and that there were reasonable grounds for the failure to adduce such evidence in the proceeding before the Secretary, the court may order such additional evidence (and evidence in rebuttal thereof) to be taken before the Secretary, and to be adduced upon the hearing, in such manner and upon such terms and conditions as to the court may seem proper. The Secretary may modify his findings, or make new findings, by reason of the additional evidence so taken, and he shall file such modified or new findings, and his recommendations, if any, for the modification or setting aside of his original regulation, with the return of such additional evidence.

(3) Upon the filing of the petition referred to in paragraph (1) of this subsection, the court shall have jurisdiction to review the regulation in accordance with chapter 7 of title 5 of the United States Code and to grant appropriate relief as provided in such chapter.

(4) The judgment of the court affirming or setting aside, in whole or in part, any such regulation of the Secretary shall be final, subject to review by the Supreme Court of the United States upon certiorari or certification as provided in section 1254 of title 28 of the United States Code.

(5) Any action instituted under this subsection shall survive, notwithstanding any change in the person occupying the office of Secretary or any vacancy in such office.

(6) The remedies provided for in this subsection shall be in addition to and not in substitution for any other remedies provided by law.

(e) A certified copy of the transcript of the record and administrative proceedings under this section shall be furnished by the Secretary to any interested party at his request, and payment of the costs thereof, and shall be admissible in any criminal, exclusion of imports, or other proceeding arising under or in respect of this subchapter, irrespective of whether proceedings with respect to the regulation have previously been initiated or become final under this section.

(f)(1)(A) The Secretary shall establish a Technical Electronic Product Radiation Safety Standards Committee (hereafter in this subchapter referred to as the "Committee") which he shall consult before prescribing any standard under this section. The Committee shall be appointed by the Secretary, after consultation with public and private agencies concerned with the technical aspect of electronic product radiation safety, and shall be composed of fifteen members each of whom shall be technically qualified by training and experience in one or more fields of science or engineering applicable to electronic product radiation safety, as follows:

(i) Five members shall be selected from governmental agencies, including State and Federal Governments;

(ii) Five members shall be selected from the affected industries after consultation with industry representatives; and

(iii) Five members shall be selected from the general public, of which at least one shall be a representative of organized labor.

(B) The Committee may propose electronic product radiation safety standards to the Secretary for his consideration. All proceedings of the Committee shall be recorded and the record of each such proceeding shall be available for public inspection.

(2) Payments to members of the Committee who are not officers or employees of the United States pursuant to subsection (c) of section 208 of the Public Health Service Act shall not render members of the Committee officers or employees of the United States for any purpose.

(g) The Secretary shall review and evaluate on a continuing basis testing programs carried out by industry to assure the adequacy of safeguards against hazardous electronic product radiation and to assure that electronic products comply with standards prescribed under this section.

(h) Every manufacturer of an electronic product to which is applicable a standard in effect under this section shall furnish to the distributor or dealer at the time of delivery of such product, in the form of a label or tag permanently affixed to such product or in such manner as approved by the Secretary, the certification that such product conforms to all applicable standards under this section. Such certification shall be based upon a test, in accordance with such standard, of the individual article to which it is attached or upon a testing program which is in accord with good manufacturing practice and which has not been disapproved by the Secretary (in such manner as he shall prescribe by regulation) on the grounds that it does not assure the adequacy of safeguards against hazardous electronic product radiation or that it does not assure that electronic products comply with the standards prescribed under this section.

SEC. 535 [21 U.S.C. 360ll]. NOTIFICATION OF DEFECTS IN, AND REPAIR OR REPLACEMENT OF, ELECTRONIC PRODUCTS

(a)(1) Every manufacturer of electronic products, who discovers that an electronic product produced, assembled, or imported by him has a defect which relates to the safety of use of such product by reason of the emission of electronic product radiation, or that an electronic product produced, assembled, or imported by him on or after the effective date of an applicable standard prescribed pursuant to section 534 fails to comply with such standard, shall immediately notify the Secretary of such defect or failure to comply if such product has left the place of manufacture and shall (except as authorized by paragraph (2)) with reasonable promptness furnish notification of such defect or failure to the persons (where known to the manufacturer) specified in subsection (b) of this section.

(2) If, in the opinion of such manufacturer, the defect or failure to comply is not such as to create a significant risk of injury, including genetic injury, to any person, he may, at the time of giving notice to the Secretary of such defect or failure to comply, apply to the Secretary for an exemption from the requirement of notice to the persons specified in subsection (b). If such application states reasonable grounds for such exemption, the Secretary shall afford such manufacturer an opportunity to present his views and evidence in support of the application, the burden of proof being on the manufacturer. If, after such presentation, the Secretary is satisfied that such defect or failure to comply is not such as to create a significant risk of injury, including genetic injury, to any person, he shall exempt such manufacturer from the requirement of notice to the persons specified in subsection (b) of this section and from the requirements of repair or replacement imposed by subsection (f) of this section.

(b) The notification (other than to the Secretary) required by paragraph (1) of subsection (a) of this section shall be accomplished—

    (1) by certified mail to the first purchaser of such product for purposes other than resale, and to any subsequent transferee of such product; and

    (2) by certified mail or other more expeditious means to the dealers or distributors of such manufacturer to whom such product was delivered.

(c) The notifications required by paragraph (1) of subsection (a) of this section shall contain a clear description of such defect or failure to comply with an applicable standard, an evaluation of the hazard reasonably related to such defect or failure to comply, and a statement of the measures to be taken to repair such defect. In the case of a notification to a person referred to in subsection (b) of this section, the notification shall also advise the person of his rights under subsection (f) of this section.

(d) Every manufacturer of electronic products shall furnish to the Secretary a true or representative copy of all notices, bulletins, and other communications to the dealers or distributors of such manufacturer or to purchasers (or subsequent transferees) of electronic products of such manufacturer regarding any such defect in such product or any such failure to comply with a standard applicable to such product. The Secretary shall disclose to the public so much of the information contained in such notice or other information obtained under section 537 as he deems will assist in carrying out the purposes of this subchapter, but he shall not disclose any information which contains or relates to a trade secret or other matter referred to in section 1905 of title 18 of the United States Code unless he determines that it is necessary to carry out the purposes of this subchapter.

(e) If through testing, inspection, investigation, or research carried out pursuant to this subchapter, or examination of reports submitted pursuant to section 537, or otherwise, the Secretary determines that any electronic product—

    (1) does not comply with an applicable standard prescribed pursuant to section 534; or

    (2) contains a defect which relates to the safety of use of such product by reason of the emission of electronic product radiation;

he shall immediately notify the manufacturer of such product of such defect or failure to comply. The notice shall contain the findings of the Secretary and shall include all information upon which the findings are based. The Secretary shall afford such manufacturer an opportunity to present his views and evidence in support thereof, to establish that there is no failure of compliance or that the alleged defect does not exist or does not relate to safety of use of the product by reason of the emission of such radiation hazard. If after such presentation by the manufacturer the Secretary determines that such product does not comply with an applicable standard prescribed pursuant to section 534, or that it contains a defect which relates to the safety of use of such product by reason of the emission of electronic product radiation, the Secretary shall direct the manufacturer to furnish the notification specified in subsection

(c) of this section to the persons specified in paragraphs (1) and (2) of subsection (b) of this section (where known to the manufacturer), unless the manufacturer has applied for an exemption from the requirement of such notification on the ground specified in paragraph (2) of subsection (a) and the Secretary is satisfied that such noncompliance or defect is not such as to create a significant risk of injury, including genetic injury, to any person.

(f) If any electronic product is found under subsection (a) or (e) to fail to comply with an applicable standard prescribed under this subchapter or to have a defect which relates to the safety of use of such product, and the notification specified in subsection (c) is required to be furnished on account of such failure or defect, the manufacturer of such product shall (1) without charge, bring such product into conformity with such standard or remedy such defect and provide reimbursement for any expenses for transportation of such product incurred in connection with having such product brought into conformity or having such defect remedied, (2) replace such product with a like or equivalent product which complies with each applicable standard prescribed under this subchapter and which has no defect relating to the safety of its use, or (3) make a refund of the cost of such product. The manufacturer shall take the action required by this subsection in such manner, and with respect to such persons, as the Secretary by regulations shall prescribe.

(g) This section shall not apply to any electronic product that was manufactured before the date of the enactment of this subchapter.

SEC. 536 [21 U.S.C. 360mm]. IMPORTS

(a) Any electronic product offered for importation into the United States which fails to comply with an applicable standard prescribed under this subchapter, or to which is not affixed a certification in the form of a label or tag in conformity with section 534(h) shall be refused admission into the United States. The Secretary of the Treasury shall deliver to the Secretary of Health and Human Services, upon the latter's request, samples of electronic products which are being imported or offered for import into the United States, giving notice thereof to the owner or consignee, who may have a hearing before the Secretary of Health and Human Services. If it appears from an examination of such samples or otherwise that any electronic product fails to comply with applicable standards prescribed pursuant to section 534, then, unless subsection (b) of this section applies and is complied with, (1) such electronic product shall be refused admission, and (2) the Secretary of the Treasury shall cause the destruction of such electronic product unless such article is exported, under regulations prescribed by the Secretary of the Treasury, within 90 days after the date of notice of refusal of admission or within such additional time as may be permitted by such regulations.

(b) If it appears to the Secretary of Health and Human Services that any electronic product refused admission pursuant to subsection (a) of this section can be brought into compliance with applicable standards prescribed pursuant to section 534, final determination as to admission of such electronic product may be deferred upon filing

419

of timely written application by the owner or consignee and the execution by him of a good and sufficient bond providing for the payment of such liquidated damages in the event of default as the Secretary of Health and Human Services may by regulation prescribe. If such application is filed and such bond is executed the Secretary of Health and Human Services may, in accordance with rules prescribed by him, permit the applicant to perform such operations with respect to such electronic product as may be specified in the notice of permission.

(c) All expenses (including travel, per diem or subsistence, and salaries of officers or employees of the United States) in connection with the destruction provided for in subsection (a) of this section and the supervision of operations provided for in subsection (b) of this section, and all expenses in connection with the storage, cartage, or labor with respect to any electronic product refused admission pursuant to subsection (a) of this section, shall be paid by the owner or consignee, and, in event of default, shall constitute a lien against any future importations made by such owner or consignee.

(d) It shall be the duty of every manufacturer offering an electronic product for importation into the United States to designate in writing an agent upon whom service of all administrative and judicial processes, notices, orders, decisions, and requirements may be made for and on behalf of said manufacturer, and to file such designation with the Secretary, which designation may from time to time be changed by like writing, similarly filed. Service of all administrative and judicial processes, notices, orders, decisions, and requirements may be made upon said manufacturer by service upon such designated agent at his office or usual place of residence with like effect as if made personally upon said manufacturer, and in default of such designation of such agent, service of process, notice, order, requirement, or decision in any proceeding before the Secretary or in any judicial proceeding for enforcement of this subchapter or any standards prescribed pursuant to this subchapter may be made by posting such process, notice, order, requirement, or decision in the Office of the Secretary or in a place designated by him by regulation.

SEC. 537 [21 U.S.C. 360nn]. INSPECTION, RECORDS, AND REPORTS

(a) If the Secretary finds for good cause that the methods, tests, or programs related to electronic product radiation safety in a particular factory, warehouse, or establishment in which electronic products are manufactured or held, may not be adequate or reliable, officers or employees duly designated by the Secretary, upon presenting appropriate credentials and a written notice to the owner, operator, or agent in charge, are thereafter authorized (1) to enter, at reasonable times, any area in such factory, warehouse, or establishment in which the manufacturer's tests (or testing programs) required by section 534(h) are carried out, and (2) to inspect, at reasonable times and within reasonable limits and in a reasonable manner, the facilities and procedures within such area which are related to electronic product radiation safety. Each such inspection shall be commenced and completed with reasonable promptness. In addition to other grounds upon which good cause may be found for purposes of this subsection, good cause will be considered to exist in any case where the manufacturer has introduced into commerce any electronic product which does not comply with an applicable standard prescribed under this subchapter and with respect to which no exemption from the notification requirements has been granted by the Secretary under section 535(a)(2) or 535(e).

(b) Every manufacturer of electronic products shall establish and maintain such records (including testing records), make such reports, and provide such information, as the Secretary may reasonably require to enable him to determine whether such manufacturer has acted or is acting in compliance with this subchapter and standards prescribed pursuant to this subchapter and shall, upon request of an officer or employee duly designated by the Secretary, permit such officer or employee to inspect appropriate books, papers, records, and documents relevant to determining whether such manufacturer has acted or is acting in compliance with standards prescribed pursuant to this subchapter.

(c) Every manufacturer of electronic products shall provide to the Secretary such performance data and other technical data related to safety as may be required to carry out the purposes of this subchapter. The Secretary is authorized to require the manufacturer to give such notification of such performance and technical data at the time of original purchase to the ultimate purchaser of the electronic product, as he determines necessary to carry out the purposes of this subchapter after consulting with the affected industry.

(d) Accident and investigation reports made under this subchapter by any officer, employee, or agent of the Secretary shall be available for use in any civil, criminal, or other judicial proceeding arising out of such accident. Any such officer, employee, or agent may be required to testify in such proceedings as to the fact developed in such investigations. Any such report shall be made available to the public in a manner which need not identify individuals. All reports on research projects, demonstration projects, and other related activities shall be public information.

(e) The Secretary or his representative shall not disclose any information reported to or otherwise obtained by him, pursuant to subsection (a) or (b) of this section, which concerns any information which contains or relates to a trade secret or other matter referred to in section 1905 of title 18 of the United States Code, except that such information may be disclosed to other officers or employees of the Department and of other agencies concerned with carrying out this subchapter or when relevant in any proceeding under this subchapter. Nothing in this section shall authorize the withholding of information by the Secretary, or by any officers or employees under his control, from the duly authorized committees of the Congress.

(f) The Secretary may by regulation (1) require dealers and distributors of electronic products, to which there are applicable standards prescribed under this subchapter and the retail prices of which is not less than $50, to furnish manufacturers of such products such information as may be necessary to identify and locate, for purposes of section 535, the first purchasers of such products for purposes other than resale, and (2) require manufacturers to preserve such information. Any regulation establishing a requirement pursuant to clause (1) of the preceding sentence shall (A) authorize such dealers and distributors to elect, in lieu of immediately furnishing such information to the manufacturer, to hold and preserve such information until advised by the manufacturer or Secretary that such information is needed by the manufacturer for purposes of section 535, and (B) provide that the dealer or distributor shall, upon making such election, give prompt notice of such election (together with information identifying the notifier and the product) to the manufacturer and shall, when advised by the manufacturer or Secretary, of the need therefor for the purposes of section 535, immediately furnish the manufacturer with the required information. If a dealer or distributor discontinues the dealing in or distribution of electronic products, he shall turn the information over to the manufacturer. Any manufacturer receiving information pursuant to this subsection concerning first purchasers of products for purposes other than resale shall treat it as confidential and may use it only if necessary for the purpose of notifying persons pursuant to section 535(a).

Sec. 538 [21 U.S.C. 360oo]. PROHIBITED ACTS

(a) It shall be unlawful—

(1) for any manufacturer to introduce, or to deliver for introduction, into commerce, or to import into the United States, any electronic product which does not comply with an applicable standard prescribed pursuant to section 534;

(2) for any person to fail to furnish any notification or other material or information required by section 535 or 537; or to fail to comply with the requirements of section 535(f);

(3) for any person to fail or to refuse to establish or maintain records required by this subchapter or to permit access by the Secretary or any of his duly authorized representatives to, or the copying of, such records, or to permit entry or inspection, as required by or pursuant to section 537;

(4) for any person to fail or to refuse to make any report required pursuant to section 537(b) or to furnish or preserve any information required pursuant to section 537(f); or

(5) for any person (A) to fail to issue a certification as required by section 534(h), or (B) to issue such a certification when such certification is not based upon a test or testing program meeting the requirements of section 534(h) or when the issuer, in the exercise of due care, would have reason to know that such certification is false or misleading in a material respect.

(b) The Secretary may exempt any electronic product, or class thereof, from all or part of subsection (a), upon such conditions as he may find necessary to protect the public health or welfare, for the purpose of research, investigations, studies, demonstrations, or training, or for reasons of national security.

SEC. 539 [21 U.S.C. 360pp]. ENFORCEMENT

(a) The district courts of the United States shall have jurisdiction, for cause shown, to restrain violations of section 538 and to restrain dealers and distributors of electronic products from selling or otherwise disposing of electronic products which do not conform to an applicable standard prescribed pursuant to section 534 except when such products are disposed of by returning them to the distributor or manufacturer from whom they were obtained. The district courts of the United States shall also have jurisdiction in accordance with section 1355 of title 28 of the United States Code to enforce the provisions of subsection (b) of this section.

(b)(1) Any person who violates section 538 shall be subject to a civil penalty of not more than $1,000. For purposes of this subsection, any such violation shall with respect to each electronic product involved, or with respect to each act or omission made unlawful by section 538, constitute a separate violation, except that the maximum civil penalty imposed on any person under this subsection for any related series of violations shall not exceed $300,000.

(2) Any such civil penalty may on application be remitted or mitigated by the Secretary. In determining the amount of such penalty, or whether it should be remitted or mitigated and in what amount, the appropriateness of such penalty to the size of the business of the person charged and the gravity of the violation shall be considered. The amount of such penalty, when finally determined, may be deducted from any sums owing by the United States to the person charged.

(c) Actions under subsections (a) and (b) of this section may be brought in the district court of the United States for the district wherein any act or omission or transaction constituting the violation occurred, or in such court for the district where the defendant is found or transacts business, and process in such cases may be served in any other district of which the defendant is an inhabitant or wherever the defendant may be found.

(d) Nothing in this subchapter shall be construed as requiring the Secretary to report for the institution of proceedings minor violations of this subchapter whenever he believes that the public interest will be adequately served by a suitable written notice or warning.

(e) Except as provided in the first sentence of section 542, compliance with this subchapter or any regulations issued thereunder shall not relieve any person from liability at common law or under statutory law.

(f) The remedies provided for in this subchapter shall be in addition to and not in substitution for any other remedies provided by law.

[Section 540 repealed by Pub. L. No. 105–362, § 601(a)(2)(A), 112 Stat. 3280, 3285 (1998).]

SEC. 541 [21 U.S.C. 360rr]. FEDERAL–STATE COOPERATION

The Secretary is authorized (1) to accept from State and local authorities engaged in activities related to health or safety or consumer protection, on a reimbursable basis or otherwise, any assistance in the administration and enforcement of this subchapter which he may request and which they may be able and willing to provide and, if so agreed, may pay in advance or otherwise for the reasonable cost of such assistance, and (2) he may, for the purpose of conducting examinations, investigations, and inspections, commission any officer or employee of any such authority as an officer of the Department.

SEC. 542 [21 U.S.C. 360ss]. EFFECT ON STATE STANDARDS

Whenever any standard prescribed pursuant to section 534 with respect to an aspect of performance of an electronic product is in effect, no State or political subdivision of a State shall have any authority either to establish, or to continue in effect, any standard which is applicable to the same aspect of performance of such product and which is not identical to the Federal standard. Nothing in this subchapter shall be construed to prevent the Federal Government or the government of any State or political subdivision thereof from establishing a requirement with respect to emission of radiation from electronic products procured for its own use if such requirement imposes a more restrictive standard than that required to comply with the otherwise applicable Federal standard.

[Sections 551–557 terminated September 30, 2006, pursuant to Pub. L. No. 105–115, § 401(e), 111 Stat. 2296, 2364 (1997).]

SUBCHAPTER E—GENERAL PROVISIONS RELATING TO DRUGS AND DEVICES

SEC. 561 [21 U.S.C. 360bbb]. EXPANDED ACCESS TO UNAPPROVED THERAPIES AND DIAGNOSTICS

(a) EMERGENCY SITUATIONS.—The Secretary may, under appropriate conditions determined by the Secretary, authorize the shipment of investigational drugs or investigational devices for the diagnosis, monitoring, or treatment of a serious disease or condition in emergency situations.

(b) INDIVIDUAL PATIENT ACCESS TO INVESTIGATIONAL PRODUCTS INTENDED FOR SERIOUS DISEASES.—Any person, acting through a physician licensed in accordance with State law, may request from a manufacturer or distributor, and any manufacturer or distributor may, after complying with the provisions of this subsection, provide to such physician an investigational drug or investigational device for the diagnosis, monitoring, or treatment of a serious disease or condition if—

(1) the licensed physician determines that the person has no comparable or satisfactory alternative therapy available to diagnose, monitor, or treat the disease or condition involved, and that the probable risk to the person from the investi-

gational drug or investigational device is not greater than the probable risk from the disease or condition;

(2) the Secretary determines that there is sufficient evidence of safety and effectiveness to support the use of the investigational drug or investigational device in the case described in paragraph (1);

(3) the Secretary determines that provision of the investigational drug or investigational device will not interfere with the initiation, conduct, or completion of clinical investigations to support marketing approval; and

(4) the sponsor, or clinical investigator, of the investigational drug or investigational device submits to the Secretary a clinical protocol consistent with the provisions of section 505(i) or 520(g), including any regulations promulgated under section 505(i) or 520(g), describing the use of the investigational drug or investigational device in a single patient or a small group of patients.

(c) TREATMENT INVESTIGATIONAL NEW DRUG APPLICATIONS AND TREATMENT INVESTIGATIONAL DEVICE EXEMPTIONS.—Upon submission by a sponsor or a physician of a protocol intended to provide widespread access to an investigational drug or investigational device for eligible patients (referred to in this subsection as an "expanded access protocol"), the Secretary shall permit such investigational drug or investigational device to be made available for expanded access under a treatment investigational new drug application or treatment investigational device exemption if the Secretary determines that—

(1) under the treatment investigational new drug application or treatment investigational device exemption, the investigational drug or investigational device is intended for use in the diagnosis, monitoring, or treatment of a serious or immediately life-threatening disease or condition;

(2) there is no comparable or satisfactory alternative therapy available to diagnose, monitor, or treat that stage of disease or condition in the population of patients to which the investigational drug or investigational device is intended to be administered;

(3)(A) the investigational drug or investigational device is under investigation in a controlled clinical trial for the use described in paragraph (1) under an investigational drug application in effect under section 505(i) or investigational device exemption in effect under section 520(g); or

(B) all clinical trials necessary for approval of that use of the investigational drug or investigational device have been completed;

(4) the sponsor of the controlled clinical trials is actively pursuing marketing approval of the investigational drug or investigational device for the use described in paragraph (1) with due diligence;

(5) in the case of an investigational drug or investigational device described in paragraph (3)(A), the provision of the investigational drug or investigational

device will not interfere with the enrollment of patients in ongoing clinical investigations under section 505(i) or 520(g);

(6) in the case of serious diseases, there is sufficient evidence of safety and effectiveness to support the use described in paragraph (1); and

(7) in the case of immediately life-threatening diseases, the available scientific evidence, taken as a whole, provides a reasonable basis to conclude that the investigational drug or investigational device may be effective for its intended use and would not expose patients to an unreasonable and significant risk of illness or injury.

A protocol submitted under this subsection shall be subject to the provisions of section 505(i) or 520(g), including regulations promulgated under section 505(i) or 520(g). The Secretary may inform national, State, and local medical associations and societies, voluntary health associations, and other appropriate persons about the availability of an investigational drug or investigational device under expanded access protocols submitted under this subsection. The information provided by the Secretary, in accordance with the preceding sentence, shall be the same type of information that is required by section 402(i)(3) of the Public Health Service Act.

(d) TERMINATION.—The Secretary may, at any time, with respect to a sponsor, physician, manufacturer, or distributor described in this section, terminate expanded access provided under this section for an investigational drug or investigational device if the requirements under this section are no longer met.

(e) DEFINITIONS.—In this section, the terms "investigational drug", "investigational device", "treatment investigational new drug application", and "treatment investigational device exemption" shall have the meanings given the terms in regulations prescribed by the Secretary.

SEC. 562 [21 U.S.C. 360bbb–1]. DISPUTE RESOLUTION

If, regarding an obligation concerning drugs or devices under this Act or section 351 of the Public Health Service Act, there is a scientific controversy between the Secretary and a person who is a sponsor, applicant, or manufacturer and no specific provision of the Act involved, including a regulation promulgated under such Act, provides a right of review of the matter in controversy, the Secretary shall, by regulation, establish a procedure under which such sponsor, applicant, or manufacturer may request a review of such controversy, including a review by an appropriate scientific advisory panel described in section 505(n) or an advisory committee described in section 515(g)(2)(B). Any such review shall take place in a timely manner. The Secretary shall promulgate such regulations within 1 year after the date of the enactment of the Food and Drug Administration Modernization Act of 1997.

SEC. 563 [21 U.S.C. 360bbb–2]. CLASSIFICATION OF PRODUCTS

(a) REQUEST.—A person who submits an application or submission (including a petition, notification, and any other similar form of request) under this Act for a product, may submit a request to the Secretary respecting the classification of the product as a drug, biological product, device, or a combination product subject to section 503(g) or respecting the component of the Food and Drug Administration that will regulate the product. In submitting the request, the person shall recommend a classification for the product, or a component to regulate the product, as appropriate.

(b) STATEMENT.—Not later than 60 days after the receipt of the request described in subsection (a), the Secretary shall determine the classification of the product under subsection (a), or the component of the Food and Drug Administration that will regulate the product, and shall provide to the person a written statement that identifies such classification or such component, and the reasons for such determination. The Secretary may not modify such statement except with the written consent of the person, or for public health reasons based on scientific evidence.

(c) INACTION OF SECRETARY.—If the Secretary does not provide the statement within the 60–day period described in subsection (b), the recommendation made by the person under subsection (a) shall be considered to be a final determination by the Secretary of such classification of the product, or the component of the Food and Drug Administration that will regulate the product, as applicable, and may not be modified by the Secretary except with the written consent of the person, or for public health reasons based on scientific evidence.

SEC. 564 [21 U.S.C. 360bbb–3]. AUTHORIZATION FOR MEDICAL PRODUCTS FOR USE IN EMERGENCIES

(a) IN GENERAL.—

(1) EMERGENCY USES.—Notwithstanding any provision of this Act and section 351 of the Public Health Service Act, and subject to the provisions of this section, the Secretary may authorize the introduction into interstate commerce, during the effective period of a declaration under subsection (b), of a drug, device, or biological product intended for use in an actual or potential emergency (referred to in this section as an "emergency use").

(2) APPROVAL STATUS OF PRODUCT.—An authorization under paragraph (1) may authorize an emergency use of a product that—

(A) is not approved, licensed, or cleared for commercial distribution under section 505, 510(k), or 515 of this Act or section 351 of the Public Health Service Act (referred to in this section as an "unapproved product"); or

(B) is approved, licensed, or cleared under such a provision, but which use is not under such provision an approved, licensed, or cleared use of the product (referred to in this section as an "unapproved use of an approved product").

(3) RELATION TO OTHER USES.—An emergency use authorized under paragraph (1) for a product is in addition to any other use that is authorized for the product under a section of this Act or the Public Health Service Act referred to in paragraph (2)(A).

(4) DEFINITIONS.—For purposes of this section:

(A) The term "biological product" has the meaning given such term in section 351 of the Public Health Service Act.

(B) The term "emergency use" has the meaning indicated for such term in paragraph (1).

(C) The term "product" means a drug, device, or biological product.

(D) The term "unapproved product" has the meaning indicated for such term in paragraph (2)(A).

(E) The term "unapproved use of an approved product" has the meaning indicated for such term in paragraph (2)(B).

(b) DECLARATION OF EMERGENCY OR THREAT JUSTIFYING EMERGENCY AUTHORIZED USE.—

(1) IN GENERAL.—The Secretary may make a declaration that the circumstances exist justifying the authorization under this subsection for a product on the basis of—

(A) a determination by the Secretary of Homeland Security that there is a domestic emergency, or a significant potential for a domestic emergency, involving a heightened risk of attack with a biological, chemical, radiological, or nuclear agent or agents;

(B) a determination by the Secretary of Defense that there is a military emergency, or a significant potential for a military emergency, involving a heightened risk to United States military forces of attack with a biological, chemical, radiological, or nuclear agent or agents;

(C) a determination by the Secretary that there is a public health emergency, or a significant potential for a public health emergency, that affects, or has a significant potential to affect, national security or the health and security of United States citizens living abroad, and that involves a biological, chemical, radiological, or nuclear agent or agents, or a disease or condition that may be attributable to such agent or agents; or

(D) the identification of a material threat pursuant to section 319F–2 of the Public Health Service Act sufficient to affect national security or the health and security of United States citizens living abroad.

(2) TERMINATION OF DECLARATION.—

(A) IN GENERAL.—A declaration under this subsection shall terminate upon the earlier of—

(i) a determination by the Secretary, in consultation with the Secretary of Defense, that the circumstances described in paragraph (1) have ceased to exist; or

(ii) a change in the approval status of the product such that the circumstances described in subsection (a)(2) have ceased to exist.

(B) DISPOSITION OF PRODUCT.—If an authorization under this section with respect to an unapproved product ceases to be effective as a result of a termination under subparagraph (A) of this paragraph, the Secretary shall consult with the manufacturer of such product with respect to the appropriate disposition of the product.

(3) ADVANCE NOTICE OF TERMINATION.—The Secretary shall provide advance notice that a declaration under this subsection will be terminated. The period of advance notice shall be a period reasonably determined to provide—

(A) in the case of an unapproved product, a sufficient period for disposition of the product, including the return of such product (except such quantities of product as are necessary to provide for continued use consistent with subsection (f)(2)) to the manufacturer (in the case of a manufacturer that chooses to have such product returned); and

(B) in the case of an unapproved use of an approved product, a sufficient period for the disposition of any labeling, or any information under subsection (e)(2)(B)(ii), as the case may be, that was provided with respect to the emergency use involved.

(4) PUBLICATION.—The Secretary shall promptly publish in the Federal Register each declaration, determination, and advance notice of termination under this subsection.

(5) EXPLANATION BY SECRETARY.—If an authorization under this section with respect to an unapproved product or an unapproved use of an approved product has been in effect for more than 1 year, the Secretary shall provide in writing to the sponsor of such product an explanation of the scientific, regulatory, or other obstacles to approval, licensure, or clearance of such product or use, including specific actions to be taken by the Secretary and the sponsor to overcome such obstacles.

(c) CRITERIA FOR ISSUANCE OF AUTHORIZATION.—The Secretary may issue an authorization under this section with respect to the emergency use of a product only if, after consultation with the Assistant Secretary for Preparedness and Response, the Director of the National Institutes of Health, and the Director of the Centers for Disease Control and Prevention (to the extent feasible and appropriate given the applicable circumstances described in subsection (b)(1)), the Secretary concludes—

(1) that an agent referred to in a declaration under subsection (b) can cause a serious or life-threatening disease or condition;

(2) that, based on the totality of scientific evidence available to the Secretary, including data from adequate and well-controlled clinical trials, if available, it is reasonable to believe that—

(A) the product may be effective in diagnosing, treating, or preventing—

(i) such disease or condition; or

(ii) a serious or life-threatening disease or condition caused by a product authorized under this section, approved or cleared under this Act, or licensed under section 351 of the Public Health Service Act, for diagnosing, treating, or preventing such a disease or condition caused by such an agent; and

(B) the known and potential benefits of the product, when used to diagnose, prevent, or treat such disease or condition, outweigh the known and potential risks of the product, taking into consideration the material threat posed by the agent or agents identified in a declaration under subsection (b)(1)(D), if applicable;

(3) that there is no adequate, approved, and available alternative to the product for diagnosing, preventing, or treating such disease or condition; and

(4) that such other criteria as the Secretary may by regulation prescribe are satisfied.

(d) Scope of Authorization.—An authorization of a product under this section shall state—

(1) each disease or condition that the product may be used to diagnose, prevent, or treat within the scope of the authorization;

(2) the Secretary's conclusions, made under subsection (c)(2)(B), that the known and potential benefits of the product, when used to diagnose, prevent, or treat such disease or condition, outweigh the known and potential risks of the product; and

(3) the Secretary's conclusions, made under subsection (c), concerning the safety and potential effectiveness of the product in diagnosing, preventing, or treating such diseases or conditions, including, to the extent practicable given the circumstances of the emergency, an assessment of the available scientific evidence.

(e) Conditions of Authorization.—

(1) Unapproved product.—

(A) Required conditions.—With respect to the emergency use of an unapproved product, the Secretary, to the extent practicable given the applicable circumstances described in subsection (b)(1), shall, for a person who carries out any activity for which the authorization is issued, establish such conditions on an authorization under this section as the Secretary finds necessary or appropriate to protect the public health, including the following:

(i) Appropriate conditions designed to ensure that health care professionals administering the product are informed—

(I) that the Secretary has authorized the emergency use of the product;

(II) of the significant known and potential benefits and risks of the emergency use of the product, and of the extent to which such benefits and risks are unknown; and

(III) of the alternatives to the product that are available, and of their benefits and risks.

(ii) Appropriate conditions designed to ensure that individuals to whom the product is administered are informed—

(I) that the Secretary has authorized the emergency use of the product;

(II) of the significant known and potential benefits and risks of such use, and of the extent to which such benefits and risks are unknown; and

(III) of the option to accept or refuse administration of the product, of the consequences, if any, of refusing administration of the product, and of the alternatives to the product that are available and of their benefits and risks.

(iii) Appropriate conditions for the monitoring and reporting of adverse events associated with the emergency use of the product.

(iv) For manufacturers of the product, appropriate conditions concerning recordkeeping and reporting, including records access by the Secretary, with respect to the emergency use of the product.

(B) AUTHORITY FOR ADDITIONAL CONDITIONS.—With respect to the emergency use of an unapproved product, the Secretary may, for a person who carries out any activity for which the authorization is issued, establish such conditions on an authorization under this section as the Secretary finds necessary or appropriate to protect the public health, including the following:

(i) Appropriate conditions on which entities may distribute the product with respect to the emergency use of the product (including limitation to distribution by government entities), and on how distribution is to be performed.

(ii) Appropriate conditions on who may administer the product with respect to the emergency use of the product, and on the categories of individuals to whom, and the circumstances under which, the product may be administered with respect to such use.

(iii) Appropriate conditions with respect to the collection and analysis of information concerning the safety and effectiveness of the product with respect to the use of such product during the period when the authorization is in effect and a reasonable time following such period.

(iv) For persons other than manufacturers of the product, appropriate conditions concerning recordkeeping and reporting, including records access by the Secretary, with respect to the emergency use of the product.

(2) UNAPPROVED USE.—With respect to the emergency use of a product that is an unapproved use of an approved product:

(A) For a person who carries out any activity for which the authorization is issued, the Secretary shall, to the extent practicable given the applicable circumstances described in (b)(1), establish conditions described in clauses (i) and (ii) of paragraph (1)(A), and may establish conditions described in clauses (iii) and (iv) of such paragraph or in paragraph (1)(B).

(B)(i) If the authorization under this section regarding the emergency use authorizes a change in the labeling of the product, but the manufacturer of the product chooses not to make such change, such authorization may not authorize distributors of the product or any other person to alter or obscure the labeling provided by the manufacturer, except as provided in section 564A with respect to authorized changes to the product expiration date.

(ii) In the circumstances described in clause (i), for a person who does not manufacture the product and who chooses to act under this clause, an authorization under this section regarding the emergency use shall, to the extent practicable given the circumstances of the emergency, authorize such person to provide appropriate information with respect to such product in addition to the labeling provided by the manufacturer, subject to compliance with clause (i). While the authorization under this section is effective, such additional information shall not be considered labeling for purposes of section 502.

(C) In establishing conditions under this paragraph with respect to the distribution and administration of the product for the unapproved use, the Secretary shall not impose conditions that would restrict distribution or administration of the product when distributed or administered for the approved use.

(3) GOOD MANUFACTURING PRACTICE; PRESCRIPTION.—With respect to the emergency use of a product for which an authorization under this section is issued (whether an unapproved product or an unapproved use of an approved product), the Secretary may waive or limit, to the extent appropriate given the applicable circumstances described in subsection (b)(1)—

(A) requirements regarding current good manufacturing practice otherwise applicable to the manufacture, processing, packing, or holding of products subject to regulation under this Act, including such requirements established under section 501 or 520(f)(1), and including relevant conditions prescribed with respect to the product by an order under section 520(f)(2);

(B) requirements established under section 503(b); and

(C) requirements established under section 520(e).

(4) ADVERTISING.—The Secretary may establish conditions on advertisements and other promotional descriptive printed matter that relate to the emergency use of a product for which an authorization under this section is issued (whether an unapproved product or an unapproved use of an approved product), including, as appropriate—

(A) with respect to drugs and biological products, requirements applicable to prescription drugs pursuant to section 502(n); or

(B) with respect to devices, requirements applicable to restricted devices pursuant to section 502(r).

(f) DURATION OF AUTHORIZATION.—

(1) IN GENERAL.—Except as provided in paragraph (2), an authorization under this section shall be effective until the earlier of the termination of the declaration under subsection (b) or a revocation under subsection (g).

(2) CONTINUED USE AFTER END OF EFFECTIVE PERIOD.—Notwithstanding the termination of the declaration under subsection (b) or a revocation under subsection (g), an authorization shall continue to be effective to provide for continued use of an unapproved product with respect to a patient to whom it was administered during the period described by paragraph (1), to the extent found necessary by such patient's attending physician.

(g) REVIEW AND REVOCATION OF AUTHORIZATION.—

(1) REVIEW.—The Secretary shall periodically review the circumstances and the appropriateness of an authorization under this section. As part of such review, the Secretary shall regularly review the progress made with respect to the approval, licensure, or clearance of—

(A) an unapproved product for which an authorization was issued under this section; or

(B) an unapproved use of an approved product for which an authorization was issued under this section.

(2) REVISION AND REVOCATION.—The Secretary may revise or revoke an authorization under this section if—

(A) the circumstances described under subsection (b)(1) no longer exist;

(B) the criteria under subsection (c) for issuance of such authorization are no longer met; or

(C) other circumstances make such revision or revocation appropriate to protect the public health or safety.

(h) PUBLICATION; CONFIDENTIAL INFORMATION.—

(1) PUBLICATION.—The Secretary shall promptly publish in the Federal Register a notice of each authorization, and each termination or revocation of an authorization under this section, and an explanation of the reasons therefore (which may include a summary of data or information that has been submitted to the Secretary in an application under section 505(i) or section 520(g), even if such summary may indirectly reveal the existence of such application). The Secretary shall make any revisions to an authorization under this section available on the Internet Web site of the Food and Drug Administration.

(2) CONFIDENTIAL INFORMATION.—Nothing in this section alters or amends section 1905 of title 18, United States Code, or section 552(b)(4) of title 5 of such Code.

(i) ACTIONS COMMITTED TO AGENCY DISCRETION.—Actions under the authority of this section by the Secretary or by the Secretary of Defense are committed to agency discretion.

(j) RULES OF CONSTRUCTION.—The following applies with respect to this section:

(1) Nothing in this section impairs the authority of the President as Commander in Chief of the Armed Forces of the United States under article II, section 2 of the United States Constitution.

(2) Nothing in this section impairs the authority of the Secretary of Defense with respect to the Department of Defense, including the armed forces, under other provisions of Federal law.

(3) Nothing in this section (including any exercise of authority by a manufacturer under subsection (e)(2)) impairs the authority of the United States to use or manage quantities of a product that are owned or controlled by the United States (including quantities in the stockpile maintained under section 319F–2 of the Public Health Service Act).

(4) Nothing in this section shall be construed as authorizing a delay in the review or other consideration by the Secretary of any application or submission pending before the Food and Drug Administration for a product for which an authorization under this section is issued.

(k) RELATION TO OTHER PROVISIONS.—If a product is the subject of an authorization under this section, the use of such product within the scope of the authorization shall not be considered to constitute a clinical investigation for purposes of section 505(i), section 520(g), or any other provision of this Act or section 351 of the Public Health Service Act.

(*l*) OPTION TO CARRY OUT AUTHORIZED ACTIVITIES.—Nothing in this section provides the Secretary any authority to require any person to carry out any activity that becomes lawful pursuant to an authorization under this section, and no person is required to inform the Secretary that the person will not be carrying out such activity, except that a manufacturer of a sole-source unapproved product authorized for emergency use shall report to the Secretary within a reasonable period of time after the issuance by the Secretary of such authorization if such manufacturer does not intend to carry out any activity under the authorization. This section only has legal effect on a person who carries out an activity for which an authorization under this section is issued. This section does not modify or affect activities carried out pursuant to other provisions of this Act or section 351 of the Public Health Service Act. Nothing in this subsection may be construed as restricting the Secretary from imposing conditions on persons who carry out any activity pursuant to an authorization under this section.

(m) CATEGORIZATION OF LABORATORY TESTS ASSOCIATED WITH DEVICES SUBJECT TO AUTHORIZATION.—

(1) IN GENERAL.—In issuing an authorization under this section with respect to a device, the Secretary may, subject to the provisions of this section, determine that a laboratory examination or procedure associated with such device shall be deemed, for purposes of section 353 of the Public Health Service Act, to be in a particular category of examinations and procedures (including the category described by subsection (d)(3) of such section) if, based on the totality of scientific evidence available to the Secretary—

(A) such categorization would be beneficial to protecting the public health; and

(B) the known and potential benefits of such categorization under the circumstances of the authorization outweigh the known and potential risks of the categorization.

(2) CONDITIONS OF DETERMINATION.—The Secretary may establish appropriate conditions on the performance of the examination or procedure pursuant to such determination.

(3) EFFECTIVE PERIOD.—A determination under this subsection shall be effective for purposes of section 353 of the Public Health Service Act notwithstanding any other provision of that section during the effective period of the relevant declaration under subsection (b).

SEC. 564A [21 U.S.C. 360bbb–3a]. EMERGENCY USE OF MEDICAL PRODUCTS

(a) DEFINITIONS.—In this section:

(1) ELIGIBLE PRODUCT.—The term "eligible product" means a product that—

(A) is approved or cleared under this chapter or licensed under section 351 of the Public Health Service Act;

(B)(i) is intended for use to prevent, diagnose, or treat a disease or condition involving a biological, chemical, radiological, or nuclear agent or agents; or

(ii) is intended for use to prevent, diagnose, or treat a serious or life-threatening disease or condition caused by a product described in clause (i); and

(C) is intended for use during the circumstances under which—

(i) a determination described in subparagraph (A), (B), or (C) of section 564(b)(1) has been made by the Secretary of Homeland Security, the Secretary of Defense, or the Secretary, respectively; or

(ii) the identification of a material threat described in subparagraph (D) of section 564(b)(1) has been made pursuant to section 319F–2 of the Public Health Service Act.

(2) PRODUCT.—The term "product" means a drug, device, or biological product.

(b) EXPIRATION DATING.—

(1) IN GENERAL.—The Secretary may extend the expiration date and authorize the introduction or delivery for introduction into interstate commerce of an eligible product after the expiration date provided by the manufacturer if—

(A) the expiration date extension is intended to support the United States[67] ability to protect—

(i) the public health; or

(ii) military preparedness and effectiveness; and

(B) the expiration date extension is supported by an appropriate scientific evaluation that is conducted or accepted by the Secretary.

(2) REQUIREMENTS AND CONDITIONS.—Any extension of an expiration date under paragraph (1) shall, as part of the extension, identify—

(A) each specific lot, batch, or other unit of the product for which extended expiration is authorized;

(B) the duration of the extension; and

(C) any other requirements or conditions as the Secretary may deem appropriate for the protection of the public health, which may include requirements for, or conditions on, product sampling, storage, packaging or repackaging, transport, labeling, notice to product recipients, recordkeeping, periodic testing or retesting, or product disposition.

(3) EFFECT.—Notwithstanding any other provision of this Act or the Public Health Service Act, an eligible product shall not be considered an unapproved

---

67. So in law. Probably should be "United States'".

product (as defined in section 564(a)(2)(A)) and shall not be deemed adulterated or misbranded under this Act because, with respect to such product, the Secretary has, under paragraph (1), extended the expiration date and authorized the introduction or delivery for introduction into interstate commerce of such product after the expiration date provided by the manufacturer.

(4) EXPIRATION DATE.—For purposes of this subsection, the term expiration date means the date established through appropriate stability testing required by the regulations issued by the Secretary to ensure that the product meets applicable standards of identity, strength, quality, and purity at the time of use.

(c) CURRENT GOOD MANUFACTURING PRACTICE.—

(1) IN GENERAL.—The Secretary may, when the circumstances of a domestic, military, or public health emergency or material threat described in subsection (a)(1)(C) so warrant, authorize, with respect to an eligible product, deviations from current good manufacturing practice requirements otherwise applicable to the manufacture, processing, packing, or holding of products subject to regulation under this Act, including requirements under section 501 or 520(f)(1) or applicable conditions prescribed with respect to the eligible product by an order under section 520(f)(2).

(2) EFFECT.—Notwithstanding any other provision of this Act or the Public Health Service Act, an eligible product shall not be considered an unapproved product (as defined in section 564(a)(2)(A)) and shall not be deemed adulterated or misbranded under this Act because, with respect to such product, the Secretary has authorized deviations from current good manufacturing practices under paragraph (1).

(d) EMERGENCY DISPENSING.—The requirements of sections 503(b) and 520(e) shall not apply to an eligible product, and the product shall not be considered an unapproved product (as defined in section 564(a)(2)(A)) and shall not be deemed adulterated or misbranded under this Act because it is dispensed without an individual prescription, if—

(1) the product is dispensed during the circumstances described in subsection (a)(1)(C); and

(2) such dispensing without an individual prescription occurs—

(A) as permitted under the law of the State in which the product is dispensed; or

(B) in accordance with an order issued by the Secretary, for the purposes and duration of the circumstances described in subsection (a)(1)(C).

(e) EMERGENCY USE INSTRUCTIONS.—

(1) IN GENERAL.—The Secretary, acting through an appropriate official within the Department of Health and Human Services, may create and issue emergency use instructions to inform health care providers or individuals to whom an eligi-

ble product is to be administered concerning such product's approved, licensed, or cleared conditions of use.

(2) EFFECT.—Notwithstanding any other provisions of this Act or the Public Health Service Act, a product shall not be considered an unapproved product and shall not be deemed adulterated or misbranded under this Act because of the issuance of emergency use instructions under paragraph (1) with respect to such product or the introduction or delivery for introduction of such product into interstate commerce accompanied by such instructions—

(A) during an emergency response to an actual emergency that is the basis for a determination described in subsection (a)(1)(C)(i); or

(B) by a government entity (including a Federal, State, local, or tribal government entity), or a person acting on behalf of such a government entity, in preparation for an emergency response.

SEC. 564B [21 U.S.C. 360bbb–3b]. PRODUCTS HELD FOR EMERGENCY USE

It is not a violation of any section of this Act or of the Public Health Service Act for a government entity (including a Federal, State, local, or tribal government entity), or a person acting on behalf of such a government entity, to introduce into interstate commerce a product (as defined in section 564(a)(4)) intended for emergency use, if that product—

(1) is intended to be held and not used; and

(2) is held and not used, unless and until that product—

(A) is approved, cleared, or licensed under section 505, 510(k), or 515 of this Act or section 351 of the Public Health Service Act;

(B) is authorized for investigational use under section 505 or 520 of this Act or section 351 of the Public Health Service Act; or

(C) is authorized for use under section 564.

SEC. 565 [21 U.S.C. 360bbb–4]. COUNTERMEASURE DEVELOPMENT, REVIEW, AND TECHNICAL ASSISTANCE

(a) DEFINITIONS.—In this section—

(1) the term "countermeasure" means a qualified countermeasure, a security countermeasure, and a qualified pandemic or epidemic product;

(2) the term "qualified countermeasure" has the meaning given such term in section 319F–1 of the Public Health Service Act;

(3) the term "security countermeasure" has the meaning given such term in section 319F–2 of such Act; and

(4) the term "qualified pandemic or epidemic product" means a product that meets the definition given such term in section 319F–3 of the Public Health Service Act and—

(A) that has been identified by the Department of Health and Human Services or the Department of Defense as receiving funding directly related to addressing chemical, biological, radiological, or nuclear threats, including pandemic influenza; or

(B) is included under this paragraph pursuant to a determination by the Secretary.

(b) GENERAL DUTIES.—In order to accelerate the development, stockpiling, approval, licensure, and clearance of qualified countermeasures, security countermeasures, and qualified pandemic or epidemic products, the Secretary, in consultation with the Assistant Secretary for Preparedness and Response, shall—

(1) ensure the appropriate involvement of Food and Drug Administration personnel in interagency activities related to countermeasure advanced research and development, consistent with sections 319F, 319F–1, 319F–2, 319F–3, 319L, and 2811 of the Public Health Service Act;

(2) ensure the appropriate involvement and consultation of Food and Drug Administration personnel in any flexible manufacturing activities carried out under section 319L of the Public Health Service Act, including with respect to meeting regulatory requirements set forth in this Act;

(3) promote countermeasure expertise within the Food and Drug Administration by—

(A) ensuring that Food and Drug Administration personnel involved in reviewing countermeasures for approval, licensure, or clearance are informed by the Assistant Secretary for Preparedness and Response on the material threat assessment conducted under section 319F–2 of the Public Health Service Act for the agent or agents for which the countermeasure under review is intended;

(B) training Food and Drug Administration personnel regarding review of countermeasures for approval, licensure, or clearance;

(C) holding public meetings at least twice annually to encourage the exchange of scientific ideas; and

(D) establishing protocols to ensure that countermeasure reviewers have sufficient training or experience with countermeasures;

(4) maintain teams, composed of Food and Drug Administration personnel with expertise on countermeasures, including specific countermeasures, populations with special clinical needs (including children and pregnant women that may use countermeasures, as applicable and appropriate), classes or groups of

countermeasures, or other countermeasure-related technologies and capabilities, that shall—

(A) consult with countermeasure experts, including countermeasure sponsors and applicants, to identify and help resolve scientific issues related to the approval, licensure, or clearance of countermeasures, through workshops or public meetings; and

(B) improve and advance the science relating to the development of new tools, standards, and approaches to assessing and evaluating countermeasures—

(i) in order to inform the process for countermeasure approval, clearance, and licensure; and

(ii) with respect to the development of countermeasures for populations with special clinical needs, including children and pregnant women, in order to meet the needs of such populations, as necessary and appropriate; and

(5) establish within the Food and Drug Administration a team of experts on manufacturing and regulatory activities (including compliance with current Good Manufacturing Practice) to provide both off-site and on-site technical assistance to the manufacturers of qualified countermeasures (as defined in section 319F-1 of the Public Health Service Act), security countermeasures (as defined in section 319F-2 of such Act), or vaccines, at the request of such a manufacturer and at the discretion of the Secretary, if the Secretary determines that a shortage or potential shortage may occur in the United States in the supply of such vaccines or countermeasures and that the provision of such assistance would be beneficial in helping alleviate or avert such shortage.

(c) FINAL GUIDANCE ON DEVELOPMENT OF ANIMAL MODELS.—

(1) IN GENERAL. Not later than 1 year after the date of the enactment of the Pandemic and All-Hazards Preparedness Reauthorization Act of 2013, the Secretary shall provide final guidance to industry regarding the development of animal models to support approval, clearance, or licensure of countermeasures referred to in subsection (a) when human efficacy studies are not ethical or feasible.

(2) AUTHORITY TO EXTEND DEADLINE.—The Secretary may extend the deadline for providing final guidance under paragraph (1) by not more than 6 months upon submission by the Secretary of a report on the status of such guidance to the Committee on Energy and Commerce of the House of Representatives and the Committee on Health, Education, Labor, and Pensions of the Senate.

(d) DEVELOPMENT AND ANIMAL MODELING PROCEDURES.—

(1) AVAILABILITY OF ANIMAL MODEL MEETINGS.—To facilitate the timely development of animal models and support the development, stockpiling, licensure, approval, and clearance of countermeasures, the Secretary shall, not later than

180 days after the enactment of this subsection, establish a procedure by which a sponsor or applicant that is developing a countermeasure for which human efficacy studies are not ethical or practicable, and that has an approved investigational new drug application or investigational device exemption, may request and receive—

(A) a meeting to discuss proposed animal model development activities; and

(B) a meeting prior to initiating pivotal animal studies.

(2) PEDIATRIC MODELS.—To facilitate the development and selection of animal models that could translate to pediatric studies, any meeting conducted under paragraph (1) shall include discussion of animal models for pediatric populations, as appropriate.

(e) REVIEW AND APPROVAL OF COUNTERMEASURES.—

(1) MATERIAL THREAT.—When evaluating an application or submission for approval, licensure, or clearance of a countermeasure, the Secretary shall take into account the material threat posed by the chemical, biological, radiological, or nuclear agent or agents identified under section 319F–2 of the Public Health Service Act for which the countermeasure under review is intended.

(2) REVIEW EXPERTISE.—When practicable and appropriate, teams of Food and Drug Administration personnel reviewing applications or submissions described under paragraph (1) shall include a reviewer with sufficient training or experience with countermeasures pursuant to the protocols established under subsection (b)(3)(D).

(f) REGULATORY MANAGEMENT PLAN.—

(1) DEFINITION.—In this subsection, the term "eligible countermeasure" means—

(A) a security countermeasure with respect to which the Secretary has entered into a procurement contract under section 319F–2(c) of the Public Health Service Act; or

(B) a countermeasure with respect to which the Biomedical Advanced Research and Development Authority has provided funding under section 319L of the Public Health Service Act for advanced research and development.

(2) REGULATORY MANAGEMENT PLAN PROCESS.—The Secretary, in consultation with the Assistant Secretary for Preparedness and Response and the Director of the Biomedical Advanced Research and Development Authority, shall establish a formal process for obtaining scientific feedback and interactions regarding the development and regulatory review of eligible countermeasures by facilitating the development of written regulatory management plans in accordance with this subsection.

(3) SUBMISSION OF REQUEST AND PROPOSED PLAN BY SPONSOR OR APPLICANT.—

(A) IN GENERAL.—A sponsor or applicant of an eligible countermeasure may initiate the process described under paragraph (2) upon submission of a written request to the Secretary. Such request shall include a proposed regulatory management plan.

(B) TIMING OF SUBMISSION.—A sponsor or applicant may submit a written request under subparagraph (A) after the eligible countermeasure has an investigational new drug or investigational device exemption in effect.

(C) RESPONSE BY SECRETARY.—The Secretary shall direct the Food and Drug Administration, upon submission of a written request by a sponsor or applicant under subparagraph (A), to work with the sponsor or applicant to agree on a regulatory management plan within a reasonable time not to exceed 90 days. If the Secretary determines that no plan can be agreed upon, the Secretary shall provide to the sponsor or applicant, in writing, the scientific or regulatory rationale why such agreement cannot be reached.

(4) PLAN.—The content of a regulatory management plan agreed to by the Secretary and a sponsor or applicant shall include—

(A) an agreement between the Secretary and the sponsor or applicant regarding developmental milestones that will trigger responses by the Secretary as described in subparagraph (B);

(B) performance targets and goals for timely and appropriate responses by the Secretary to the triggers described under subparagraph (A), including meetings between the Secretary and the sponsor or applicant, written feedback, decisions by the Secretary, and other activities carried out as part of the development and review process; and

(C) an agreement on how the plan shall be modified, if needed.

(5) MILESTONES AND PERFORMANCE TARGETS.—The developmental milestones described in paragraph (4)(A) and the performance targets and goals described in paragraph (4)(B) shall include—

(A) feedback from the Secretary regarding the data required to support the approval, clearance, or licensure of the eligible countermeasure involved;

(B) feedback from the Secretary regarding the data necessary to inform any authorization under section 564;

(C) feedback from the Secretary regarding the data necessary to support the positioning and delivery of the eligible countermeasure, including to the Strategic National Stockpile;

(D) feedback from the Secretary regarding the data necessary to support the submission of protocols for review under section 505(b)(5)(B);

(E) feedback from the Secretary regarding any gaps in scientific knowledge that will need resolution prior to approval, licensure, or clearance of the eligible countermeasure and plans for conducting the necessary scientific research;

(F) identification of the population for which the countermeasure sponsor or applicant seeks approval, licensure, or clearance and the population for which desired labeling would not be appropriate, if known; and

(G) as necessary and appropriate, and to the extent practicable, a plan for demonstrating safety and effectiveness in pediatric populations, and for developing pediatric dosing, formulation, and administration with respect to the eligible countermeasure, provided that such plan would not delay authorization under section 564, approval, licensure, or clearance for adults.

(6) PRIORITIZATION.—

(A) PLANS FOR SECURITY COUNTERMEASURES.—The Secretary shall establish regulatory management plans for all security countermeasures for which a request is submitted under paragraph (3)(A).

(B) PLANS FOR OTHER ELIGIBLE COUNTERMEASURES.—The Secretary shall determine whether resources are available to establish regulatory management plans for eligible countermeasures that are not security countermeasures. If resources are available to establish regulatory management plans for eligible countermeasures that are not security countermeasures, and if resources are not available to establish regulatory management plans for all eligible countermeasures for which requests have been submitted, the Director of the Biomedical Advanced Research and Development Authority, in consultation with the Commissioner, shall prioritize which eligible countermeasures may receive regulatory management plans.

(g) ANNUAL REPORT.—Not later than 180 days after the date of enactment of this subsection, and annually thereafter, the Secretary shall make publicly available on the Web site of the Food and Drug Administration a report that details the countermeasure development and review activities of the Food and Drug Administration, including—

(1) with respect to the development of new tools, standards, and approaches to assess and evaluate countermeasures—

(A) the identification of the priorities of the Food and Drug Administration and the progress made on such priorities; and

(B) the identification of scientific gaps that impede the development, approval, licensure, or clearance of countermeasures for populations with special clinical needs, including children and pregnant women, and the progress made on resolving these challenges;

(2) with respect to countermeasures for which a regulatory management plan has been agreed upon under subsection (f), the extent to which the performance targets and goals set forth in subsection (f)(4)(B) and the regulatory management plan have been met, including, for each such countermeasure—

(A) whether the regulatory management plan was completed within the required timeframe, and the length of time taken to complete such plan;

(B) whether the Secretary adhered to the timely and appropriate response times set forth in such plan; and

(C) explanations for any failure to meet such performance targets and goals;

(3) the number of regulatory teams established pursuant to subsection (b)(4), the number of products, classes of products, or technologies assigned to each such team, and the number of, type of, and any progress made as a result of consultations carried out under subsection (b)(4)(A);

(4) an estimate of resources obligated to countermeasure development and regulatory assessment, including—

(A) Center-specific objectives and accomplishments; and

(B) the number of full-time equivalent employees of the Food and Drug Administration who directly support the review of countermeasures;

(5) the number of countermeasure applications and submissions submitted, the number of countermeasures approved, licensed, or cleared, the status of remaining submitted applications and submissions, and the number of each type of authorization issued pursuant to section 564;

(6) the number of written requests for a regulatory management plan submitted under subsection (f)(3)(A), the number of regulatory management plans developed, and the number of such plans developed for security countermeasures; and

(7) the number, type, and frequency of meetings between the Food and Drug Administration and—

(A) sponsors of a countermeasure as defined in subsection (a); or

(B) another agency engaged in development or management of portfolios for such countermeasures, including the Centers for Disease Control and Prevention, the Biomedical Advanced Research and Development Authority, the National Institutes of Health, and the appropriate agencies of the Department of Defense.

SEC. 566 [21 U.S.C. 360bbb–5]. CRITICAL PATH PUBLIC– PRIVATE PARTNERSHIPS

(a) ESTABLISHMENT.—The Secretary, acting through the Commissioner of Food and Drugs, may enter into collaborative agreements, to be known as Critical Path Public–Private Partnerships, with one or more eligible entities to implement the Critical Path Initiative of the Food and Drug Administration by developing innovative, collaborative projects in research, education, and outreach for the purpose of fostering medical product innovation, enabling the acceleration of medical product development, manufacturing, and translational therapeutics, and enhancing medical product safety.

(b) ELIGIBLE ENTITY.—In this section, the term "eligible entity" means an entity that meets each of the following:

(1) The entity is—

(A) an institution of higher education (as such term is defined in section 101 of the Higher Education Act of 1965) or a consortium of such institutions; or

(B) an organization described in section 501(c)(3) of the Internal Revenue Code of 1986 and exempt from tax under section 501(a) of such Code.

(2) The entity has experienced personnel and clinical and other technical expertise in the biomedical sciences, which may include graduate training programs in areas relevant to priorities of the Critical Path Initiative.

(3) The entity demonstrates to the Secretary's satisfaction that the entity is capable of—

(A) developing and critically evaluating tools, methods, and processes—

(i) to increase efficiency, predictability, and productivity of medical product development; and

(ii) to more accurately identify the benefits and risks of new and existing medical products;

(B) establishing partnerships, consortia, and collaborations with health care practitioners and other providers of health care goods or services; pharmacists; pharmacy benefit managers and purchasers; health maintenance organizations and other managed health care organizations; health care insurers; government agencies; patients and consumers; manufacturers of prescription drugs, biological products, diagnostic technologies, and devices; and academic scientists; and

(C) securing funding for the projects of a Critical Path Public–Private Partnership from Federal and nonfederal governmental sources, foundations, and private individuals.

(c) FUNDING.—The Secretary may not enter into a collaborative agreement under subsection (a) unless the eligible entity involved provides an assurance that the entity will not accept funding for a Critical Path Public–Private Partnership project from any organization that manufactures or distributes products regulated by the Food and Drug Administration unless the entity provides assurances in its agreement with the Food and Drug Administration that the results of the Critical Path Public–Private Partnership project will not be influenced by any source of funding.

(d) ANNUAL REPORT.—Not later than 18 months after the date of the enactment of this section,[68] and annually thereafter, the Secretary, in collaboration with the parties to each Critical Path Public–Private Partnership, shall submit a report to the Committee on Health, Education, Labor, and Pensions of the Senate and the Committee on Energy and Commerce of the House of Representatives—

(1) reviewing the operations and activities of the Partnerships in the previous year; and

(2) addressing such other issues relating to this section as the Secretary determines to be appropriate.

(e) DEFINITION.—In this section, the term "medical product" includes a drug, a biological product as defined in section 351 of the Public Health Service Act, a device, and any combination of such products.

(f) AUTHORIZATION OF APPROPRIATIONS.—To carry out this section, there is authorized to be appropriated $6,000,000 for each of fiscal years 2013 through 2017.

SEC. 567 [21 U.S.C. 360bbb–6]. RISK COMMUNICATION

(a) ADVISORY COMMITTEE ON RISK COMMUNICATION.—

(1) IN GENERAL.—The Secretary shall establish an advisory committee to be known as the "Advisory Committee on Risk Communication" (referred to in this section as the "Committee").

(2) DUTIES OF COMMITTEE.—The Committee shall advise the Commissioner on methods to effectively communicate risks associated with the products regulated by the Food and Drug Administration.

(3) MEMBERS.—The Secretary shall ensure that the Committee is composed of experts on risk communication, experts on the risks described in subsection (b), and representatives of patient, consumer, and health professional organizations.

(4) PERMANENCE OF COMMITTEE.—Section 14 of the Federal Advisory Committee Act shall not apply to the Committee established under this subsection.

(b) PARTNERSHIPS FOR RISK COMMUNICATION.—

(1) IN GENERAL.—The Secretary shall partner with professional medical societies, medical schools, academic medical centers, and other stakeholders to develop robust and multi-faceted systems for communication to health care providers about emerging postmarket drug risks.

(2) PARTNERSHIPS.—The systems developed under paragraph (1) shall—

(A) account for the diversity among physicians in terms of practice, willingness to adopt technology, and medical specialty; and

___

68. Section 566 was added by Pub. L. No. 110–85, 121 Stat. 823, 898–900, which was enacted September 27, 2007.

(B) include the use of existing communication channels, including electronic communications, in place at the Food and Drug Administration.

SEC. 568 [21 U.S.C. 360bbb–7]. NOTIFICATION

(a) NOTIFICATION TO SECRETARY.—With respect to a drug, the Secretary may require notification to the Secretary by a regulated person if the regulated person knows—

(1) that the use of such drug in the United States may result in serious injury or death;

(2) of a significant loss or known theft of such drug intended for use in the United States; or

(3) that—

(A) such drug has been or is being counterfeited; and

(B)(i) the counterfeit product is in commerce in the United States or could be reasonably expected to be introduced into commerce in the United States; or

(ii) such drug has been or is being imported into the United States or may reasonably be expected to be offered for import into the United States.

(b) MANNER OF NOTIFICATION.—Notification under this section shall be made in such manner and by such means as the Secretary may specify by regulation or guidance.

(c) SAVINGS CLAUSE.—Nothing in this section shall be construed as limiting any other authority of the Secretary to require notifications related to a drug under any other provision of this Act or the Public Health Service Act.

(d) DEFINITION.—In this section, the term "regulated person" means—

(1) a person who is required to register under section 510 or 801(s);

(2) a wholesale distributor of a drug product; or

(3) any other person that distributes drugs except a person that distributes drugs exclusively for retail sale.

SEC. 569 [21 U.S.C. 360bbb–8]. CONSULTATION WITH EXTERNAL EXPERTS ON RARE DISEASES, TARGETED THERAPIES, AND GENETIC TARGETING OF TREATMENTS

(a) IN GENERAL.—For the purpose of promoting the efficiency of and informing the review by the Food and Drug Administration of new drugs and biological products for rare diseases and drugs and biological products that are genetically targeted, the following shall apply:

(1) CONSULTATION WITH STAKEHOLDERS.—Consistent with sections X.C and IX.E.4 of the PDUFA Reauthorization Performance Goals and Procedures Fiscal Years 2013 through 2017, as referenced in the letters described in section 101(b) of the Prescription Drug User Fee Amendments of 2012, the Secretary shall ensure that opportu-

nities exist, at a time the Secretary determines appropriate, for consultations with stakeholders on the topics described in subsection (b).

(2) CONSULTATION WITH EXTERNAL EXPERTS.—

(A) IN GENERAL.—The Secretary shall develop and maintain a list of external experts who, because of their special expertise, are qualified to provide advice on rare disease issues, including topics described in subsection (c). The Secretary may, when appropriate to address a specific regulatory question, consult such external experts on issues related to the review of new drugs and biological products for rare diseases and drugs and biological products that are genetically targeted, including the topics described in subsection (b), when such consultation is necessary because the Secretary lacks the specific scientific, medical, or technical expertise necessary for the performance of the Secretary's regulatory responsibilities and the necessary expertise can be provided by the external experts.

(B) EXTERNAL EXPERTS.—For purposes of subparagraph (A), external experts are individuals who possess scientific or medical training that the Secretary lacks with respect to one or more rare diseases.

(b) TOPICS FOR CONSULTATION.—Topics for consultation pursuant to this section may include—

(1) rare diseases;

(2) the severity of rare diseases;

(3) the unmet medical need associated with rare diseases;

(4) the willingness and ability of individuals with a rare disease to participate in clinical trials;

(5) an assessment of the benefits and risks of therapies to treat rare diseases;

(6) the general design of clinical trials for rare disease populations and subpopulations; and

(7) the demographics and the clinical description of patient populations.

(c) CLASSIFICATION AS SPECIAL GOVERNMENT EMPLOYEES.—The external experts who are consulted under this section may be considered special government employees, as defined under section 202 of title 18, United States Code.

(d) PROTECTION OF CONFIDENTIAL INFORMATION AND TRADE SECRETS.—

(1) RULE OF CONSTRUCTION.—Nothing in this section shall be construed to alter the protections offered by laws, regulations, and policies governing disclosure of confidential commercial or trade secret information, and any other information exempt from disclosure pursuant to section 552(b) of title 5, United States Code, as such provisions would be applied to consultation with individuals and organizations prior to the date of enactment of this section.

(2) Consent required for disclosure.—The Secretary shall not disclose confidential commercial or trade secret information to an expert consulted under this section without the written consent of the sponsor unless the expert is a special government employee (as defined under section 202 of title 18, United States Code) or the disclosure is otherwise authorized by law.

(e) Other Consultation.—Nothing in this section shall be construed to limit the ability of the Secretary to consult with individuals and organizations as authorized prior to the date of enactment of this section.

(f) No Right or Obligation.—

(1) No right to consultation.—Nothing in this section shall be construed to create a legal right for a consultation on any matter or require the Secretary to meet with any particular expert or stakeholder.

(2) No altering of goals.—Nothing in this section shall be construed to alter agreed upon goals and procedures identified in the letters described in section 101(b) of the Prescription Drug User Fee Amendments of 2012.

(3) No change to number of review cycles.—Nothing in this section is intended to increase the number of review cycles as in effect before the date of enactment of this section.

(g) No Delay in Product Review.—

(1) In general.—Prior to a consultation with an external expert, as described in this section, relating to an investigational new drug application under section 505(i), a new drug application under section 505(b), or a biologics license application under section 351 of the Public Health Service Act, the Director of the Center for Drug Evaluation and Research or the Director of the Center for Biologics Evaluation and Research (or appropriate Division Director), as appropriate, shall determine that—

(A) such consultation will—

(i) facilitate the Secretary's ability to complete the Secretary's review; and

(ii) address outstanding deficiencies in the application; or

(B) the sponsor authorized such consultation.

(2) Limitation.—The requirements of this subsection shall apply only in instances where the consultation is undertaken solely under the authority of this section. The requirements of this subsection shall not apply to any consultation initiated under any other authority.

Sec. 569A [21 U.S.C. 360bbb–8a]. OPTIMIZING GLOBAL CLINICAL TRIALS

(a) In General.—The Secretary shall—

(1) work with other regulatory authorities of similar standing, medical research companies, and international organizations to foster and encourage uniform, scien-

tifically driven clinical trial standards with respect to medical products around the world; and

(2) enhance the commitment to provide consistent parallel scientific advice to manufacturers seeking simultaneous global development of new medical products in order to—

(A) enhance medical product development;

(B) facilitate the use of foreign data; and

(C) minimize the need to conduct duplicative clinical studies, preclinical studies, or nonclinical studies.

(b) MEDICAL PRODUCT.—In this section, the term "medical product" means a drug, as defined in subsection (g) of section 201, a device, as defined in subsection (h) of such section, or a biological product, as defined in section 351(i) of the Public Health Service Act.

(c) SAVINGS CLAUSE.—Nothing in this section shall alter the criteria for evaluating the safety or effectiveness of a medical product under this Act.

SEC. 569B [21 U.S.C. 360bbb–8b]. USE OF CLINICAL INVESTIGATION DATA FROM OUTSIDE THE UNITED STATES

(a) IN GENERAL.—In determining whether to approve, license, or clear a drug or device pursuant to an application submitted under this chapter, the Secretary shall accept data from clinical investigations conducted outside of the United States, including the European Union, if the applicant demonstrates that such data are adequate under applicable standards to support approval, licensure, or clearance of the drug or device in the United States.

(b) NOTICE TO SPONSOR.—If the Secretary finds under sub-section (a) that the data from clinical investigations conducted outside the United States, including in the European Union, are inadequate for the purpose of making a determination on approval, clearance, or licensure of a drug or device pursuant to an application submitted under this chapter, the Secretary shall provide written notice to the sponsor of the application of such finding and include the rationale for such finding.

SEC. 569C [21 U.S.C. 360bbb–8c]. PATIENT PARTICIPATION IN MEDICAL PRODUCT DISCUSSION

(a) IN GENERAL.—The Secretary shall develop and implement strategies to solicit the views of patients during the medical product development process and consider the perspectives of patients during regulatory discussions, including by—

(1) fostering participation of a patient representative who may serve as a special government employee in appropriate agency meetings with medical product sponsors and investigators; and

(2) exploring means to provide for identification of patient representatives who do not have any, or have minimal, financial interests in the medical products industry.

(b) PROTECTION OF PROPRIETARY INFORMATION.—Nothing in this section shall be construed to alter the protections offered by laws, regulations, or policies governing disclosure of confidential commercial or trade secret information and any other information exempt from disclosure pursuant to section 552(b) of title 5, United States Code, as such laws, regulations, or policies would apply to consultation with individuals and organizations prior to the date of enactment of this section.

(c) OTHER CONSULTATION.—Nothing in this section shall be construed to limit the ability of the Secretary to consult with individuals and organizations as authorized prior to the date of enactment of this section.

(d) NO RIGHT OR OBLIGATION.—Nothing in this section shall be construed to create a legal right for a consultation on any matter or require the Secretary to meet with any particular expert or stakeholder. Nothing in this section shall be construed to alter agreed upon goals and procedures identified in the letters described in section 101(b) of the Prescription Drug User Fee Amendments of 2012. Nothing in this section is intended to increase the number of review cycles as in effect before the date of enactment of this section.

(e) FINANCIAL INTEREST.—In this section, the term "financial interest" means a financial interest under section 208(a) of title 18, United States Code.

SUBCHAPTER F—NEW ANIMAL DRUGS FOR MINOR USE AND MINOR SPECIES

SEC. 571 [21 U.S.C. 360ccc]. CONDITIONAL APPROVAL OF NEW ANIMAL DRUGS FOR MINOR USE AND MINOR SPECIES

(a)(1) Except as provided in paragraph (3) of this section, any person may file with the Secretary an application for conditional approval of a new animal drug intended for a minor use or a minor species. Such an application may not be a supplement to an application approved under section 512. Such application must comply in all respects with the provisions of section 512 of this Act except sections 512(a)(4), 512(b)(2), 512(c)(1), 512(c)(2), 512(c)(3), 512(d)(1), 512(e), 512(h), and 512(n) unless otherwise stated in this section, and any additional provisions of this section. New animal drugs are subject to application of the same safety standards that would be applied to such drugs under section 512(d) (including, for antimicrobial new animal drugs, with respect to antimicrobial resistance).

(2) The applicant shall submit to the Secretary as part of an application for the conditional approval of a new animal drug—

(A) all information necessary to meet the requirements of section 512(b)(1) except section 512(b)(1)(A);

(B) full reports of investigations which have been made to show whether or not such drug is safe under section 512(d) (including, for an antimicrobial new animal drug, with respect to antimicrobial resistance) and there is a reasonable expectation of effectiveness for use;

(C) data for establishing a conditional dose;

(D) projections of expected need and the justification for that expectation based on the best information available;

(E) information regarding the quantity of drug expected to be distributed on an annual basis to meet the expected need; and

(F) a commitment that the applicant will conduct additional investigations to meet the requirements for the full demonstration of effectiveness under section 512(d)(1)(E) within 5 years.

(3) A person may not file an application under paragraph (1) if—

(A) the application seeks conditional approval of a new animal drug that is contained in, or is a product of, a transgenic animal.

(B) the person has previously filed an application for conditional approval under paragraph (1) for the same drug in the same dosage form for the same intended use whether or not subsequently conditionally approved by the Secretary under subsection (b), or

(C) the person obtained the application, or data or other information contained therein, directly or indirectly from the person who filed for conditional approval under paragraph (1) for the same drug in the same dosage form for the same intended use whether or not subsequently conditionally approved by the Secretary under subsection (b).

(b) Within 180 days after the filing of an application pursuant to subsection (a), or such additional period as may be agreed upon by the Secretary and the applicant, the Secretary shall either—

(1) issue an order, effective for one year, conditionally approving the application if the Secretary finds that none of the grounds for denying conditional approval, specified in subsection (c) of this section applies and publish a Federal Register notice of the conditional approval, or

(2) give the applicant notice of an opportunity for an informal hearing on the question whether such application can be conditionally approved.

(c) If the Secretary finds, after giving the applicant notice and an opportunity for an informal hearing, that—

(1) any of the provisions of section 512(d)(1) (A) through (D) or (F) through (I) are applicable;

(2) the information submitted to the Secretary as part of the application and any other information before the Secretary with respect to such drug, is insuffi-

cient to show that there is a reasonable expectation that the drug will have the effect it purports or is represented to have under the conditions of use prescribed, recommended, or suggested in the proposed labeling thereof; or

(3) another person has received approval under section 512 for the same drug in the same dosage form for the same intended use, and that person is able to assure the availability of sufficient quantities of the drug to meet the needs for which the drug is intended;

the Secretary shall issue an order refusing to conditionally approve the application. If, after such notice and opportunity for an informal hearing, the Secretary finds that paragraphs (1) through (3) do not apply, the Secretary shall issue an order conditionally approving the application effective for one year and publish a Federal Register notice of the conditional approval. Any order issued under this subsection refusing to conditionally approve an application shall state the findings upon which it is based.

(d) A conditional approval under this section is effective for a 1–year period and is thereafter renewable by the Secretary annually for up to 4 additional 1–year terms. A conditional approval shall be in effect for no more than 5 years from the date of approval under subsection (b)(1) or (c) of this section unless extended as provided for in subsection (h) of this section. The following shall also apply:

(1) No later than 90 days from the end of the 1–year period for which the original or renewed conditional approval is effective, the applicant may submit a request to renew a conditional approval for an additional 1–year term.

(2) A conditional approval shall be deemed renewed at the end of the 1–year period, or at the end of a 90–day extension that the Secretary may, at the Secretary's discretion, grant by letter in order to complete review of the renewal request, unless the Secretary determines before the expiration of the 1–year period or the 90–day extension that—

(A) the applicant failed to submit a timely renewal request;

(B) the request fails to contain sufficient information to show that—

(i) the applicant is making sufficient progress toward meeting approval requirements under section 512(d)(1)(E), and is likely to be able to fulfill those requirements and obtain an approval under section 512 before the expiration of the 5–year maximum term of the conditional approval;

(ii) the quantity of the drug that has been distributed is consistent with the conditionally approved intended use and conditions of use, unless there is adequate explanation that ensures that the drug is only used for its intended purpose; or

(iii) the same drug in the same dosage form for the same intended use has not received approval under section 512, or if such a drug has been approved, that the holder of the approved application is unable to assure the availability of sufficient quantities of the drug to meet the needs for which the drug is intended; or

(C) any of the provisions of section 512(e)(1) (A) through (B) or (D) through (F) are applicable.

(3) If the Secretary determines before the end of the 1–year period or the 90–day extension, if granted, that a conditional approval should not be renewed, the Secretary shall issue an order refusing to renew the conditional approval, and such conditional approval shall be deemed withdrawn and no longer in effect. The Secretary shall thereafter provide an opportunity for an informal hearing to the applicant on the issue whether the conditional approval shall be reinstated.

(e)(1) The Secretary shall issue an order withdrawing conditional approval of an application filed pursuant to subsection (a) if the Secretary finds that another person has received approval under section 512 for the same drug in the same dosage form for the same intended use and that person is able to assure the availability of sufficient quantities of the drug to meet the needs for which the drug is intended.

(2) The Secretary shall, after due notice and opportunity for an informal hearing to the applicant, issue an order withdrawing conditional approval of an application filed pursuant to subsection (a) if the Secretary finds that—

(A) any of the provisions of section 512(e)(1) (A) through (B) or (D) through (F) are applicable; or

(B) on the basis of new information before the Secretary with respect to such drug, evaluated together with the evidence available to the Secretary when the application was conditionally approved, that there is not a reasonable expectation that such drug will have the effect it purports or is represented to have under the conditions of use prescribed, recommended, or suggested in the labeling thereof.

(3) The Secretary may also, after due notice and opportunity for an informal hearing to the applicant, issue an order withdrawing conditional approval of an application filed pursuant to subsection (a) if the Secretary finds that any of the provisions of section 512(e)(2) are applicable.

(f)(1) The label and labeling of a new animal drug with a conditional approval under this section shall—

(A) bear the statement, "conditionally approved by FDA pending a full demonstration of effectiveness under application number"; and

(B) contain such other information as prescribed by the Secretary.

(2) An intended use that is the subject of a conditional approval under this section shall not be included in the same product label with any intended use approved under section 512.

(g) A conditionally approved new animal drug application may not be amended or supplemented to add indications for use.

(h) 180 days prior to the termination date established under subsection (d) of this section, an applicant shall have submitted all the information necessary to support a complete new animal drug application in accordance with section 512(b)(1) or the conditional approval issued under this section is no longer in effect. Following review of this information, the Secretary shall either—

(1) issue an order approving the application under section 512(c) if the Secretary finds that none of the grounds for denying approval specified in section 512(d)(1) applies, or

(2) give the applicant an opportunity for a hearing before the Secretary under section 512(d) on the question whether such application can be approved.

Upon issuance of an order approving the application, product labeling and administrative records of approval shall be modified accordingly. If the Secretary has not issued an order under section 512(c) approving such application prior to the termination date established under subsection (d) of this section, the conditional approval issued under this section is no longer in effect unless the Secretary grants an extension of an additional 180–day period so that the Secretary can complete review of the application. The decision to grant an extension is committed to the discretion of the Secretary and not subject to judicial review.

(i) The decision of the Secretary under subsection (c), (d), or (e) of this section refusing or withdrawing conditional approval of an application shall constitute final agency action subject to judicial review.

(j) In this section and section 572, the term "transgenic animal" means an animal whose genome contains a nucleotide sequence that has been intentionally modified in vitro, and the progeny of such an animal; Provided that the term "transgenic animal" does not include an animal of which the nucleotide sequence of the genome has been modified solely by selective breeding.

SEC. 572 [21 U.S.C. 360ccc–1]. INDEX OF LEGALLY MARKETED UNAPPROVED NEW ANIMAL DRUGS FOR MINOR SPECIES

(a)(1) The Secretary shall establish an index limited to—

(A) new animal drugs intended for use in a minor species for which there is a reasonable certainty that the animal or edible products from the animal will not be consumed by humans or food-producing animals; and

(B) new animal drugs intended for use only in a hatchery, tank, pond, or other similar contained man-made structure in an early, non-food life stage of a food-producing minor species, where safety for humans is demonstrated in accordance with the standard of section 512(d) (including, for an antimicrobial new animal drug, with respect to antimicrobial resistance).

(2) The index shall not include a new animal drug that is contained in or a product of a transgenic animal.

(b) Any person intending to file a request under this section shall be entitled to one or more conferences to discuss the requirements for indexing a new animal drug.

(c)(1) Any person may submit a request to the Secretary for a determination whether a new animal drug may be eligible for inclusion in the index. Such a request shall include—

(A) information regarding the need for the new animal drug, the species for which the new animal drug is intended, the proposed intended use and conditions of use, and anticipated annual distribution;

(B) information to support the conclusion that the proposed use meets the conditions of subparagraph (A) or (B) of subsection (a)(1) of this section;

(C) information regarding the components and composition of the new animal drug;

(D) a description of the methods used in, and the facilities and controls used for, the manufacture, processing, and packing of such new animal drug;

(E) an environmental assessment that meets the requirements of the National Environmental Policy Act of 1969, as amended, and as defined in 21 CFR Part 25, as it appears on the date of enactment of this provision and amended thereafter or information to support a categorical exclusion from the requirement to prepare an environmental assessment;

(F) information sufficient to support the conclusion that the proposed use of the new animal drug is safe under section 512(d) with respect to individuals exposed to the new animal drug through its manufacture or use; and

(G) such other information as the Secretary may deem necessary to make this eligibility determination.

(2) Within 90 days after the submission of a request for a determination of eligibility for indexing based on subsection (a)(1)(A) of this section, or 180 days for a request submitted based on subsection (a)(1)(B) of this section, the Secretary shall grant or deny the request, and notify the person who requested such determination of the Secretary's decision. The Secretary shall grant the request if the Secretary finds that—

(A) the same drug in the same dosage form for the same intended use is not approved or conditionally approved;

(B) the proposed use of the drug meets the conditions of subparagraph (A) or (B) of subsection (a)(1), as appropriate;

(C) the person requesting the determination has established appropriate specifications for the manufacture and control of the new animal drug and has demonstrated an understanding of the requirements of current good manufacturing practices;

(D) the new animal drug will not significantly affect the human environment; and

(E) the new animal drug is safe with respect to individuals exposed to the new animal drug through its manufacture or use.

If the Secretary denies the request, the Secretary shall thereafter provide due notice and an opportunity for an informal conference. A decision of the Secretary to deny an eligibility request following an informal conference shall constitute final agency action subject to judicial review.

(d)(1) With respect to a new animal drug for which the Secretary has made a determination of eligibility under subsection (c), the person who made such a request may ask that the Secretary add the new animal drug to the index established under subsection (a). The request for addition to the index shall include—

(A) a copy of the Secretary's determination of eligibility issued under subsection (c);

(B) a written report that meets the requirements in subsection (d)(2) of this section;

(C) a proposed index entry;

(D) facsimile labeling;

(E) anticipated annual distribution of the new animal drug;

(F) a written commitment to manufacture the new animal drug and animal feeds bearing or containing such new animal drug according to current good manufacturing practices;

(G) a written commitment to label, distribute, and promote the new animal drug only in accordance with the index entry;

(H) upon specific request of the Secretary, information submitted to the expert panel described in paragraph (3); and

(I) any additional requirements that the Secretary may prescribe by general regulation or specific order.

(2) The report required in paragraph (1) shall—

(A) be authored by a qualified expert panel;

(B) include an evaluation of all available target animal safety and effectiveness information, including anecdotal information;

(C) state the expert panel's opinion regarding whether the benefits of using the new animal drug for the proposed use in a minor species outweigh its risks to the target animal, taking into account the harm being caused by the absence of an approved or conditionally approved new animal drug for the minor species in question;

(D) include information from which labeling can be written; and

(E) include a recommendation regarding whether the new animal drug should be limited to use under the professional supervision of a licensed veterinarian.

(3) A qualified expert panel, as used in this section, is a panel that—

(A) is composed of experts qualified by scientific training and experience to evaluate the target animal safety and effectiveness of the new animal drug under consideration;

(B) operates external to FDA; and

(C) is not subject to the Federal Advisory Committee Act, 5 U.S.C. App. 2.

The Secretary shall define the criteria for selection of a qualified expert panel and the procedures for the operation of the panel by regulation.

(4) Within 180 days after the receipt of a request for listing a new animal drug in the index, the Secretary shall grant or deny the request. The Secretary shall grant the request if the request for indexing continues to meet the eligibility criteria in subsection (a) and the Secretary finds, on the basis of the report of the qualified expert panel and other information available to the Secretary, that the benefits of using the new animal drug for the proposed use in a minor species outweigh its risks to the target animal, taking into account the harm caused by the absence of an approved or conditionally-approved new animal drug for the minor species in question. If the Secretary denies the request, the Secretary shall thereafter provide due notice and the opportunity for an informal conference. The decision of the Secretary following an informal conference shall constitute final agency action subject to judicial review.

(e)(1) The index established under subsection (a) shall include the following information for each listed drug—

(A) the name and address of the person who holds the index listing;

(B) the name of the drug and the intended use and conditions of use for which it is being indexed;

(C) product labeling; and

(D) conditions and any limitations that the Secretary deems necessary regarding use of the drug.

(2) The Secretary shall publish the index, and revise it periodically.

(3) The Secretary may establish by regulation a process for reporting changes in the conditions of manufacturing or labeling of indexed products.

(f)(1) If the Secretary finds, after due notice to the person who requested the index listing and an opportunity for an informal conference, that—

(A) the expert panel failed to meet the requirements as set forth by the Secretary by regulation;

(B) on the basis of new information before the Secretary, evaluated together with the evidence available to the Secretary when the new animal drug was listed in the index, the benefits of using the new animal drug for the indexed use do not outweigh its risks to the target animal;

(C) the conditions of subsection (c)(2) of this section are no longer satisfied;

(D) the manufacture of the new animal drug is not in accordance with current good manufacturing practices;

(E) the labeling, distribution, or promotion of the new animal drug is not in accordance with the index entry;

(F) the conditions and limitations of use associated with the index listing have not been followed; or

(G) the request for indexing contains any untrue statement of material fact,

the Secretary shall remove the new animal drug from the index. The decision of the Secretary following an informal conference shall constitute final agency action subject to judicial review.

(2) If the Secretary finds that there is a reasonable probability that the use of the drug would present a risk to the health of humans or other animals, the Secretary may—

(A) suspend the listing of such drug immediately;

(B) give the person listed in the index prompt notice of the Secretary's action; and

(C) afford that person the opportunity for an informal conference.

The decision of the Secretary following an informal conference shall constitute final agency action subject to judicial review.

(g) For purposes of indexing new animal drugs under this section, to the extent consistent with the public health, the Secretary shall promulgate regulations for exempting from the operation of section 512 minor species new animal drugs and animal feeds bearing or containing new animal drugs intended solely for investigational use by experts qualified by scientific training and experience to investigate the safety and effectiveness of minor species animal drugs. Such regulations may, at the discretion of the Secretary, among other conditions relating to the protection of the public health, provide for conditioning such exemption upon the establishment and maintenance of such records, and the making of such reports to the Secretary, by the manufacturer or the sponsor of the investigation of such article, of data (including but not limited to analytical reports by investigators) obtained as a result of such investigational use of such article, as the Secretary finds will enable the Secretary to evaluate the safety and effectiveness of such article in the event of the filing of a request for an index listing pursuant to this section.

(h) The labeling of a new animal drug that is the subject of an index listing shall state, prominently and conspicuously—

(1) "NOT APPROVED BY FDA.—Legally marketed as an FDA indexed product. Extra-label use is prohibited.";

(2) except in the case of new animal drugs indexed for use in an early life stage of a food-producing animal, "This product is not to be used in animals intended for use as food for humans or other animals."; and

(3) such other information as may be prescribed by the Secretary in the index listing.

(i)(1) In the case of any new animal drug for which an index listing pursuant to subsection (a) is in effect, the person who has an index listing shall establish and maintain such records, and make such reports to the Secretary, of data relating to experience, and other data or information, received or otherwise obtained by such person with respect to such drug, or with respect to animal feeds bearing or containing such drug, as the Secretary may by general regulation, or by order with respect to such listing, prescribe on the basis of a finding that such records and reports are necessary in order to enable the Secretary to determine, or facilitate a determination, whether there is or may be ground for invoking subsection (f). Such regulation or order shall provide, where the Secretary deems it to be appropriate, for the examination, upon request, by the persons to whom such regulation or order is applicable, of similar information received or otherwise obtained by the Secretary.

(2) Every person required under this subsection to maintain records, and every person in charge or custody thereof, shall, upon request of an officer or employee designated by the Secretary, permit such officer or employee at all reasonable times to have access to and copy and verify such records.

(j)(1) Safety and effectiveness data and information which has been submitted in support of a request for a new animal drug to be indexed under this section and which has not been previously disclosed to the public shall be made available to the public, upon request, unless extraordinary circumstances are shown—

(A) if no work is being or will be undertaken to have the drug indexed in accordance with the request,

(B) if the Secretary has determined that such drug cannot be indexed and all legal appeals have been exhausted,

(C) if the indexing of such drug is terminated and all legal appeals have been exhausted, or

(D) if the Secretary has determined that such drug is not a new animal drug.

(2) Any request for data and information pursuant to paragraph (1) shall include a verified statement by the person making the request that any data or information received under such paragraph shall not be disclosed by such person to any other person—

(A) for the purpose of, or as part of a plan, scheme, or device for, obtaining the right to make, use, or market, or making, using, or marketing, outside the United States, the drug identified in the request for indexing; and

(B) without obtaining from any person to whom the data and information are disclosed an identical verified statement, a copy of which is to be provided by such person to the Secretary, which meets the requirements of this paragraph.

SEC. 573 [21 U.S.C. 360ccc–2]. DESIGNATED NEW ANIMAL DRUGS FOR MINOR USE OR MINOR SPECIES

(a) DESIGNATION.—

(1) The manufacturer or the sponsor of a new animal drug for a minor use or use in a minor species may request that the Secretary declare that drug a "designated new animal drug". A request for designation of a new animal drug shall be made before the submission of an application under section 512(b) or section 571 for the new animal drug.

(2) The Secretary may declare a new animal drug a "designated new animal drug" if—

(A) it is intended for a minor use or use in a minor species; and

(B) the same drug in the same dosage form for the same intended use is not approved under section 512 or 571 or designated under this section at the time the request is made.

(3) Regarding the termination of a designation—

(A) the sponsor of a new animal drug shall notify the Secretary of any decision to discontinue active pursuit of approval under section 512 or 571 of an application for a designated new animal drug. The Secretary shall terminate the designation upon such notification;

(B) the Secretary may also terminate designation if the Secretary independently determines that the sponsor is not actively pursuing approval under section 512 or 571 with due diligence;

(C) the sponsor of an approved designated new animal drug shall notify the Secretary of any discontinuance of the manufacture of such new animal drug at least one year before discontinuance. The Secretary shall terminate the designation upon such notification; and

(D) the designation shall terminate upon the expiration of any applicable exclusivity period under subsection (c).

(4) Notice respecting the designation or termination of designation of a new animal drug shall be made available to the public.

(b) GRANTS AND CONTRACTS FOR DEVELOPMENT OF DESIGNATED NEW ANIMAL DRUGS.—

(1) The Secretary may make grants to and enter into contracts with public and private entities and individuals to assist in defraying the costs of qualified safety and effectiveness testing expenses and manufacturing expenses incurred in connection with the development of designated new animal drugs.

(2) For purposes of paragraph (1) of this section—

(A) The term "qualified safety and effectiveness testing" means testing—

(i) which occurs after the date such new animal drug is designated under this section and before the date on which an application with respect to such drug is submitted under section 512; and

(ii) which is carried out under an investigational exemption under section 512(j).

(B) The term "manufacturing expenses" means expenses incurred in developing processes and procedures associated with manufacture of the designated new animal drug which occur after the new animal drug is designated under this section and before the date on which an application with respect to such new animal drug is submitted under section 512 or 571.

(c) EXCLUSIVITY FOR DESIGNATED NEW ANIMAL DRUGS.—

(1) Except as provided in subsection (c)(2), if the Secretary approves or conditionally approves an application for a designated new animal drug, the Secretary may not approve or conditionally approve another application submitted for such new animal drug with the same intended use as the designated new animal drug for another applicant before the expiration of seven years from the date of approval or conditional approval of the application.

(2) If an application filed pursuant to section 512 or section 571 is approved for a designated new animal drug, the Secretary may, during the 7–year exclusivity period beginning on the date of the application approval or conditional approval, approve or conditionally approve another application under section 512 or section 571 for such drug for such minor use or minor species for another applicant if—

(A) the Secretary finds, after providing the holder of such an approved application notice and opportunity for the submission of views, that in the granted exclusivity period the holder of the approved application cannot assure the availability of sufficient quantities of the drug to meet the needs for which the drug was designated; or

(B) such holder provides written consent to the Secretary for the approval or conditional approval of other applications before the expiration of such exclusivity period.

SUBCHAPTER G—MEDICAL GASES

SEC. 575 [21 U.S.C. 360ddd]. DEFINITIONS

In this subchapter:

(1) The term "designated medical gas" means any of the following:

(A) Oxygen that meets the standards set forth in an official compendium.

(B) Nitrogen that meets the standards set forth in an official compendium.

(C) Nitrous oxide that meets the standards set forth in an official compendium.

(D) Carbon dioxide that meets the standards set forth in an official compendium.

(E) Helium that meets the standards set forth in an official compendium.

(F) Carbon monoxide that meets the standards set forth in an official compendium.

(G) Medical air that meets the standards set forth in an official compendium.

(H) Any other medical gas deemed appropriate by the Secretary, after taking into account any investigational new drug application or investigational new animal drug application for the same medical gas submitted in accordance with regulations applicable to such applications in title 21 of the Code of Federal Regulations, unless any period of exclusivity under section 505(c)(3)(E)(ii) or section 505(j)(5)(F)(ii), or the extension of any such period under section 505A, applicable to such medical gas has not expired.

(2) The term "medical gas" means a drug that—

(A) is manufactured or stored in a liquefied, nonliquefied, or cryogenic state; and

(B) is administered as a gas.

SEC. 576 [21 U.S.C. 360ddd–1]. REGULATION OF MEDICAL GASES

(a) CERTIFICATION OF DESIGNATED MEDICAL GASES.—

(1) SUBMISSION.—Beginning 180 days after the date of enactment of this section, any person may file with the Secretary a request for certification of a medical gas as a designated medical gas. Any such request shall contain the following information:

(A) A description of the medical gas.

(B) The name and address of the sponsor.

(C) The name and address of the facility or facilities where the medical gas is or will be manufactured.

(D) Any other information deemed appropriate by the Secretary to determine whether the medical gas is a designated medical gas.

(2) GRANT OF CERTIFICATION.—The certification requested under paragraph (1) is deemed to be granted unless, within 60 days of the filing of such request, the Secretary finds that—

(A) the medical gas subject to the certification is not a designated medical gas;

(B) the request does not contain the information required under paragraph (1) or otherwise lacks sufficient information to permit the Secretary to determine that the medical gas is a designated medical gas; or

(C) denying the request is necessary to protect the public health.

(3) EFFECT OF CERTIFICATION.—

(A) IN GENERAL.—

(i) APPROVED USES.—A designated medical gas for which a certification is granted under paragraph (2) is deemed, alone or in combination, as medically appropriate, with another designated medical gas or gases for which a certification or certifications have been granted, to have in effect an approved application under section 505 or 512, subject to all applicable postapproval requirements, for the following indications for use:

(I) In the case of oxygen, the treatment or prevention of hypoxemia or hypoxia.

(II) In the case of nitrogen, use in hypoxic challenge testing.

(III) In the case of nitrous oxide, analgesia.

(IV) In the case of carbon dioxide, use in extracorporeal membrane oxygenation therapy or respiratory stimulation.

(V) In the case of helium, the treatment of upper airway obstruction or increased airway resistance.

(VI) In the case of medical air, to reduce the risk of hyperoxia.

(VII) In the case of carbon monoxide, use in lung diffusion testing.

(VIII) Any other indication for use for a designated medical gas or combination of designated medical gases deemed appropriate by the Secretary, unless any period of exclusivity under clause (iii) or (iv) of section 505(c)(3)(E), clause (iii) or (iv) of section 505(j)(5)(F), or section 527, or the extension of any such period under section 505A, applicable to such indication for use for such gas or combination of gases has not expired.

(ii) LABELING.—The requirements of sections 503(b)(4) and 502(f) are deemed to have been met for a designated medical gas if the labeling on final use container for such medical gas bears—

(I) the information required by section 503(b)(4);

(II) a warning statement concerning the use of the medical gas as determined by the Secretary by regulation; and

(III) appropriate directions and warnings concerning storage and handling.

(B) INAPPLICABILITY OF EXCLUSIVITY PROVISIONS.—

(i) NO EXCLUSIVITY FOR A CERTIFIED MEDICAL GAS.—No designated medical gas deemed under subparagraph (A)(i) to have in effect an approved application is eligible for any period of exclusivity under section 505(c), 505(j), or 527, or the extension of any such period under section 505A, on the basis of such deemed approval.

(ii) Effect on certification.—No period of exclusivity under section 505(c), 505(j), or section 527, or the extension of any such period under section 505A, with respect to an application for a drug product shall prohibit, limit, or otherwise affect the submission, grant, or effect of a certification under this section, except as provided in subsection (a)(3)(A)(i)(VIII) and section 575(1)(H).

(4) Withdrawal, suspension, or revocation of approval.—

(A) Withdrawal, suspension of approval.—Nothing in this subchapter limits the Secretary's authority to with-draw or suspend approval of a drug product, including a designated medical gas deemed under this section to have in effect an approved application under section 505 or section 512 of this Act.

(B) Revocation of certification.—The Secretary may revoke the grant of a certification under paragraph (2) if the Secretary determines that the request for certification contains any material omission or falsification.

(b) Prescription Requirement.—

(1) In general.—A designated medical gas shall be subject to the requirements of section 503(b)(1) unless the Secretary exercises the authority provided in section 503(b)(3) to remove such medical gas from the requirements of section 503(b)(1), the gas is approved for use without a prescription pursuant to an application under section 505 or 512, or the use in question is authorized pursuant to another provision of this Act relating to use of medical products in emergencies.

(2) Oxygen.—

(A) No prescription required for certain uses.—Notwithstanding paragraph (1), oxygen may be provided without a prescription for the following uses:

(i) for use in the event of depressurization or other environmental oxygen deficiency.

(ii) for oxygen deficiency or for use in emergency resuscitation, when administered by properly trained personnel.

(B) Labeling.—For oxygen provided pursuant to subparagraph (A), the requirements of section 503(b)(4) shall be deemed to have been met if its labeling bears a warning that the oxygen can be used for emergency use only and for all other medical applications a prescription is required.

Sec. 577 [21 U.S.C. 360ddd–2]. INAPPLICABILITY OF DRUG FEES TO DESIGNATED MEDICAL GASES

A designated medical gas, alone or in combination with another designated gas or gases (as medically appropriate) deemed under section 576 to have in effect an approved application shall not be assessed fees under section 736(a) on the basis of such deemed approval.

SUBCHAPTER H—PHARMACEUTICAL SUPPLY CHAIN SECURITY

SEC. 581 [21 U.S.C. 360eee]. DEFINITIONS

In this subchapter:

(1) AFFILIATE.—The term "affiliate" means a business entity that has a relationship with a second business entity if, directly or indirectly—

(A) one business entity controls, or has the power to control, the other business entity; or

(B) a third party controls, or has the power to control, both of the business entities.

(2) AUTHORIZED.—The term "authorized" means—

(A) in the case of a manufacturer or repackager, having a valid registration in accordance with section 510;

(B) in the case of a wholesale distributor, having a valid license under State law or section 583, in accordance with section 582(a)(6), and complying with the licensure reporting requirements under section 503(e), as amended by the Drug Supply Chain Security Act;

(C) in the case of a third-party logistics provider, having a valid license under State law or section 584(a)(1), in accordance with section 582(a)(7), and complying with the licensure reporting requirements under section 584(b); and

(D) in the case of a dispenser, having a valid license under State law.

(3) DISPENSER.—The term "dispenser'—

(A) means a retail pharmacy, hospital pharmacy, a group of chain pharmacies under common ownership and control that do not act as a wholesale distributor, or any other person authorized by law to dispense or administer prescription drugs, and the affiliated warehouses or distribution centers of such entities under common ownership and control that do not act as a wholesale distributor; and

(B) does not include a person who dispenses only products to be used in animals in accordance with section 512(a)(5).

(4) DISPOSITION.—The term "disposition", with respect to a product within the possession or control of an entity, means the removal of such product from the pharmaceutical distribution supply chain, which may include disposal or return of the product for disposal or other appropriate handling and other actions, such as retaining a sample of the product for further additional physical examination or laboratory analysis of the product by a manufacturer or regulatory or law enforcement agency.

(5) DISTRIBUTE OR DISTRIBUTION.—The term "distribute" or "distribution" means the sale, purchase, trade, delivery, handling, storage, or receipt of a product, and does not include the dispensing of a product pursuant to a prescription executed in accordance with section 503(b)(1) or the dispensing of a product approved under section 512(b).

(6) EXCLUSIVE DISTRIBUTOR.—The term "exclusive distributor" means the wholesale distributor that directly purchased the product from the manufacturer and is the sole distributor of that manufacturer's product to a subsequent repackager, wholesale distributor, or dispenser.

(7) HOMOGENEOUS CASE.—The term "homogeneous case" means a sealed case containing only product that has a single National Drug Code number belonging to a single lot.

(8) ILLEGITIMATE PRODUCT.—The term "illegitimate product" means a product for which credible evidence shows that the product—

(A) is counterfeit, diverted, or stolen;

(B) is intentionally adulterated such that the product would result in serious adverse health consequences or death to humans;

(C) is the subject of a fraudulent transaction; or

(D) appears otherwise unfit for distribution such that the product would be reasonably likely to result in serious adverse health consequences or death to humans.

(9) LICENSED.—The term "licensed" means—

(A) in the case of a wholesale distributor, having a valid license in accordance with section 503(e) or section 582(a)(6), as applicable;

(B) in the case of a third-party logistics provider, having a valid license in accordance with section 584(a) or section 582(a)(7), as applicable; and

(C) in the case of a dispenser, having a valid license under State law.

(10) MANUFACTURER.—The term "manufacturer" means, with respect to a product—

(A) a person that holds an application approved under section 505 or a license issued under section 351 of the Public Health Service Act for such product, or if such product is not the subject of an approved application or license, the person who manufactured the product;

(B) a co-licensed partner of the person described in subparagraph (A) that obtains the product directly from a person described in this subparagraph or subparagraph (A) or (C); or

(C) an affiliate of a person described in subparagraph (A) or (B) that receives the product directly from a person described in this subparagraph or subparagraph (A) or (B).

(11) PACKAGE.—

(A) IN GENERAL.—The term "package" means the smallest individual saleable unit of product for distribution by a manufacturer or repackager that is intended by the manufacturer for ultimate sale to the dispenser of such product.

(B) INDIVIDUAL SALEABLE UNIT.—For purposes of this paragraph, an "individual saleable unit" is the smallest container of product introduced into commerce by the manufacturer or repackager that is intended by the manufacturer or repackager for individual sale to a dispenser.

(12) PRESCRIPTION DRUG.—The term "prescription drug" means a drug for human use subject to section 503(b)(1).

(13) PRODUCT.—The term "product" means a prescription drug in a finished dosage form for administration to a patient without substantial further manufacturing (such as capsules, tablets, and lyophilized products before reconstitution), but for purposes of section 582, does not include blood or blood components intended for transfusion, radioactive drugs or radioactive biological products (as defined in section 600.3(ee) of title 21, Code of Federal Regulations) that are regulated by the Nuclear Regulatory Commission or by a State pursuant to an agreement with such Commission under section 274 of the Atomic Energy Act of 1954 (42 U.S.C. 2021), imaging drugs, an intravenous product described in clause (xiv), (xv), or (xvi) of paragraph (24)(B), any medical gas (as defined in section 575), homeopathic drugs marketed in accordance with applicable guidance under this Act, or a drug compounded in compliance with section 503A or 503B.

(14) PRODUCT IDENTIFIER.—The term "product identifier" means a standardized graphic that includes, in both human-readable form and on a machine-readable data carrier that conforms to the standards developed by a widely recognized international standards development organization, the standardized numerical identifier, lot number, and expiration date of the product.

(15) QUARANTINE.—The term "quarantine" means the storage or identification of a product, to prevent distribution or transfer of the product, in a physically separate area clearly identified for such use or through other procedures.

(16) REPACKAGER.—The term "repackager" means a person who owns or operates an establishment that repacks and relabels a product or package for—

(A) further sale; or

(B) distribution without a further transaction.

(17) RETURN.—The term "return" means providing product to the authorized immediate trading partner from which such product was purchased or received, or to a returns processor or reverse logistics provider for handling of such product.

(18) RETURNS PROCESSOR OR REVERSE LOGISTICS PROVIDER.—The term "returns processor" or "reverse logistics provider" means a person who owns or operates

an establishment that dispositions or otherwise processes saleable or nonsaleable product received from an authorized trading partner such that the product may be processed for credit to the purchaser, manufacturer, or seller or disposed of for no further distribution.

(19) SPECIFIC PATIENT NEED.—The term "specific patient need" refers to the transfer of a product from one pharmacy to another to fill a prescription for an identified patient. Such term does not include the transfer of a product from one pharmacy to another for the purpose of increasing or replenishing stock in anticipation of a potential need.

(20) STANDARDIZED NUMERICAL IDENTIFIER.—The term "standardized numerical identifier" means a set of numbers or characters used to uniquely identify each package or homogenous case that is composed of the National Drug Code that corresponds to the specific product (including the particular package configuration) combined with a unique alphanumeric serial number of up to 20 characters.

(21) SUSPECT PRODUCT.—The term "suspect product" means a product for which there is reason to believe that such product—

(A) is potentially counterfeit, diverted, or stolen;

(B) is potentially intentionally adulterated such that the product would result in serious adverse health consequences or death to humans;

(C) is potentially the subject of a fraudulent transaction; or

(D) appears otherwise unfit for distribution such that the product would result in serious adverse health consequences or death to humans.

(22) THIRD-PARTY LOGISTICS PROVIDER.—The term "third-party logistics provider" means an entity that provides or coordinates warehousing, or other logistics services of a product in interstate commerce on behalf of a manufacturer, wholesale distributor, or dispenser of a product, but does not take ownership of the product, nor have responsibility to direct the sale or disposition of the product.

(23) TRADING PARTNER.—The term "trading partner" means—

(A) a manufacturer, repackager, wholesale distributor, or dispenser from whom a manufacturer, repackager, wholesale distributor, or dispenser accepts direct ownership of a product or to whom a manufacturer, repackager, wholesale distributor, or dispenser transfers direct ownership of a product; or

(B) a third-party logistics provider from whom a manufacturer, repackager, wholesale distributor, or dispenser accepts direct possession of a product or to whom a manufacturer, repackager, wholesale distributor, or dispenser transfers direct possession of a product.

(24) TRANSACTION.—

(A) IN GENERAL.—The term "transaction" means the transfer of product between persons in which a change of ownership occurs.

(B) EXEMPTIONS.—The term "transaction" does not include—

(i) intracompany distribution of any product between members of an affiliate or within a manufacturer;

(ii) the distribution of a product among hospitals or other health care entities that are under common control;

(iii) the distribution of a product for emergency medical reasons including a public health emergency declaration pursuant to section 319 of the Public Health Service Act, except that a drug shortage not caused by a public health emergency shall not constitute an emergency medical reason;

(iv) the dispensing of a product pursuant to a prescription executed in accordance with section 503(b)(1);

(v) the distribution of product samples by a manufacturer or a licensed wholesale distributor in accordance with section 503(d);

(vi) the distribution of blood or blood components intended for transfusion;

(vii) the distribution of minimal quantities of product by a licensed retail pharmacy to a licensed practitioner for office use;

(viii) the sale, purchase, or trade of a drug or an offer to sell, purchase, or trade a drug by a charitable organization described in section 501(c)(3) of the Internal Revenue Code of 1986 to a nonprofit affiliate of the organization to the extent otherwise permitted by law;

(ix) the distribution of a product pursuant to the sale or merger of a pharmacy or pharmacies or a wholesale distributor or wholesale distributors, except that any records required to be maintained for the product shall be transferred to the new owner of the pharmacy or pharmacies or wholesale distributor or wholesale distributors;

(x) the dispensing of a product approved under section 512(c);

(xi) products transferred to or from any facility that is licensed by the Nuclear Regulatory Commission or by a State pursuant to an agreement with such Commission under section 274 of the Atomic Energy Act of 1954 (42 U.S.C. 2021);

(xii) a combination product that is not subject to approval under section 505 or licensure under section 351 of the Public Health Service Act, and that is—

(I) a product comprised of a device and 1 or more other regulated components (such as a drug/device, biologic/device, or drug/device/biologic) that are physically, chemically, or otherwise combined or mixed and produced as a single entity;

(II) 2 or more separate products packaged together in a single package or as a unit and comprised of a drug and device or device and biological product; or

(III) 2 or more finished medical devices plus one or more drug or biological products that are packaged together in what is referred to as a "medical convenience kit" as described in clause (xiii);

(xiii) the distribution of a collection of finished medical devices, which may include a product or biological product, assembled in kit form strictly for the convenience of the purchaser or user (referred to in this clause as a "medical convenience kit") if—

(I) the medical convenience kit is assembled in an establishment that is registered with the Food and Drug Administration as a device manufacturer in accordance with section 510(b)(2);

(II) the medical convenience kit does not contain a controlled substance that appears in a schedule contained in the Comprehensive Drug Abuse Prevention and Control Act of 1970;

(III) in the case of a medical convenience kit that includes a product, the person that manufacturers the kit—

(aa) purchased such product directly from the pharmaceutical manufacturer or from a wholesale distributor that purchased the product directly from the pharmaceutical manufacturer; and

(bb) does not alter the primary container or label of the product as purchased from the manufacturer or wholesale distributor; and

(IV) in the case of a medical convenience kit that includes a product, the product is—

(aa) an intravenous solution intended for the replenishment of fluids and electrolytes;

(bb) a product intended to maintain the equilibrium of water and minerals in the body;

(cc) a product intended for irrigation or reconstitution;

(dd) an anesthetic;

(ee) an anticoagulant;

(ff) a vasopressor; or

(gg) a sympathomimetic;

(xiv) the distribution of an intravenous product that, by its formulation, is intended for the replenishment of fluids and electrolytes (such as sodium, chloride, and potassium) or calories (such as dextrose and amino acids);

471

(xv) the distribution of an intravenous product used to maintain the equilibrium of water and minerals in the body, such as dialysis solutions;

(xvi) the distribution of a product that is intended for irrigation, or sterile water, whether intended for such purposes or for injection;

(xvii) the distribution of a medical gas (as defined in section 575); or

(xviii) the distribution or sale of any licensed product under section 351 of the Public Health Service Act that meets the definition of a device under section 201(h).

(25) TRANSACTION HISTORY.—The term "transaction history" means a statement in paper or electronic form, including the transaction information for each prior transaction going back to the manufacturer of the product.

(26) TRANSACTION INFORMATION.—The term "transaction information" means—

(A) the proprietary or established name or names of the product;

(B) the strength and dosage form of the product;

(C) the National Drug Code number of the product;

(D) the container size;

(E) the number of containers;

(F) the lot number of the product;

(G) the date of the transaction;

(H) the date of the shipment, if more than 24 hours after the date of the transaction;

(I) the business name and address of the person from whom ownership is being transferred; and

(J) the business name and address of the person to whom ownership is being transferred.

(27) TRANSACTION STATEMENT.—The "transaction statement" is a statement, in paper or electronic form, that the entity transferring ownership in a transaction—

(A) is authorized as required under the Drug Supply Chain Security Act;

(B) received the product from a person that is authorized as required under the Drug Supply Chain Security Act;

(C) received transaction information and a transaction statement from the prior owner of the product, as required under section 582;

(D) did not knowingly ship a suspect or illegitimate product;

(E) had systems and processes in place to comply with verification requirements under section 582;

(F) did not knowingly provide false transaction information; and

(G) did not knowingly alter the transaction history.

(28) VERIFICATION OR VERIFY.—The term "verification" or "verify" means determining whether the product identifier affixed to, or imprinted upon, a package or homogeneous case corresponds to the standardized numerical identifier or lot number and expiration date assigned to the product by the manufacturer or the repackager, as applicable in accordance with section 582.

(29) WHOLESALE DISTRIBUTOR.—The term "wholesale distributor" means a person (other than a manufacturer, a manufacturer's co-licensed partner, a third-party logistics provider, or repackager) engaged in wholesale distribution (as defined in section 503(e)(4), as amended by the Drug Supply Chain Security Act).

SEC. 582 [21 U.S.C. 360eee–1]. REQUIREMENTS

(a) IN GENERAL.—

(1) OTHER ACTIVITIES.—Each manufacturer, repackager, wholesale distributor, and dispenser shall comply with the requirements set forth in this section with respect to the role of such manufacturer, repackager, wholesale distributor, or dispenser in a transaction involving product. If an entity meets the definition of more than one of the entities listed in the preceding sentence, such entity shall comply with all applicable requirements in this section, but shall not be required to duplicate requirements.

(2) INITIAL STANDARDS.—

(A) IN GENERAL.—The Secretary shall, in consultation with other appropriate Federal officials, manufacturers, repackagers, wholesale distributors, dispensers, and other pharmaceutical distribution supply chain stakeholders, issue a draft guidance document that establishes standards for the interoperable exchange of transaction information, transaction history, and transaction statements, in paper or electronic format, for compliance with this subsection and subsections (b), (c), (d), and (e). In establishing such standards, the Secretary shall consider the feasibility of establishing standardized documentation to be used by members of the pharmaceutical distribution supply chain to convey the transaction information, transaction history, and transaction statement to the subsequent purchaser of a product and to facilitate the exchange of lot level data. The standards established under this paragraph shall take into consideration the standards established under section 505D and shall comply with a form and format developed by a widely recognized international standards development organization.

(B) PUBLIC INPUT.—Prior to issuing the draft guidance under subparagraph (A), the Secretary shall gather comments and information from stakeholders and maintain such comments and information in a public docket for at least 60 days prior to issuing such guidance.

(C) PUBLICATION.—The Secretary shall publish the standards established under subparagraph (A) not later than 1 year after the date of enactment of the Drug Supply Chain Security Act [enacted Nov. 27, 2013].

(3) WAIVERS, EXCEPTIONS, AND EXEMPTIONS.—

(A) IN GENERAL.—Not later than 2 years after the date of enactment of the Drug Supply Chain Security Act [enacted Nov. 27, 2013], the Secretary shall, by guidance—

(i) establish a process by which an authorized manufacturer, repackager, wholesale distributor, or dispenser may request a waiver from any of the requirements set forth in this section, which the Secretary may grant if the Secretary determines that such requirements would result in an undue economic hardship or for emergency medical reasons, including a public health emergency declaration pursuant to section 319 of the Public Health Service Act;

(ii) establish a process by which the Secretary determines exceptions, and a process through which a manufacturer or repackager may request such an exception, to the requirements relating to product identifiers if a product is packaged in a container too small or otherwise unable to accommodate a label with sufficient space to bear the information required for compliance with this section; and

(iii) establish a process by which the Secretary may determine other products or transactions that shall be exempt from the requirements of this section.

(B) CONTENT.—The guidance issued under subparagraph (A) shall include a process for the biennial review and renewal of such waivers, exceptions, and exemptions, as applicable.

(C) PROCESS.—In issuing the guidance under this paragraph, the Secretary shall provide an effective date that is not later than 180 days prior to the date on which manufacturers are required to affix or imprint a product identifier to each package and homogenous case of product intended to be introduced in a transaction into commerce consistent with this section.

(4) SELF-EXECUTING REQUIREMENTS.—Except where otherwise specified, the requirements of this section may be enforced without further regulations or guidance from the Secretary.

(5) GRANDFATHERING PRODUCT.—

(A) PRODUCT IDENTIFIER.—Not later than 2 years after the date of enactment of the Drug Supply Chain Security Act [enacted Nov. 27, 2013], the Secretary shall finalize guidance specifying whether and under what circumstances product that is not labeled with a product identifier and that is in the pharmaceutical distribution supply chain at the time of the effective date of the requirements of this section shall be exempted from the requirements of this section.

(B) TRACING.—For a product that entered the pharmaceutical distribution supply chain prior to January 1, 2015—

(i) authorized trading partners shall be exempt from providing transaction information as required under subsections (b)(1)(A)(i), (c)(1)(A)(ii), (d)(1)(A)(ii), and (e)(1)(A)(ii);

(ii) transaction history required under this section shall begin with the owner of such product on such date; and

(iii) the owners of such product on such date shall be exempt from asserting receipt of transaction information and transaction statement from the prior owner as required under this section.

(6) WHOLESALE DISTRIBUTOR LICENSES.—Notwithstanding section 581(9)(A), until the effective date of the wholesale distributor licensing regulations under section 583, the term "licensed" or "authorized", as it relates to a wholesale distributor with respect to prescription drugs, shall mean a wholesale distributor with a valid license under State law.

(7) THIRD-PARTY LOGISTICS PROVIDER LICENSES.—Until the effective date of the third-party logistics provider licensing regulations under section 584, a third-party logistics provider shall be considered "licensed" under section 581(9)(B) unless the Secretary has made a finding that the third-party logistics provider does not utilize good handling and distribution practices and publishes notice thereof.

(8) LABEL CHANGES.—Changes made to package labels solely to incorporate the product identifier may be submitted to the Secretary in the annual report of an establishment, in accordance with section 314.70(d) of chapter 21, Code of Federal Regulations (or any successor regulation).

(9) PRODUCT IDENTIFIERS.—With respect to any requirement relating to product identifiers under this subchapter—

(A) unless the Secretary allows, through guidance, the use of other technologies for data instead of or in addition to the technologies described in clauses (i) and (ii), the applicable data—

(i) shall be included in a 2-dimensional data matrix barcode when affixed to, or imprinted upon, a package; and

(ii) shall be included in a linear or 2-dimensional data matrix barcode when affixed to, or imprinted upon, a homogeneous case; and

(B) verification of the product identifier may occur by using human-readable or machine-readable methods.

(b) MANUFACTURER REQUIREMENTS.—

(1) PRODUCT TRACING.—

(A) IN GENERAL.—Beginning not later than January 1, 2015, a manufacturer shall—

(i) prior to, or at the time of, each transaction in which such manufacturer transfers ownership of a product, provide the subsequent owner with transaction history, transaction information, and a transaction statement, in a single document in an paper or electronic format; and

(ii) capture the transaction information (including lot level information), transaction history, and transaction statement for each transaction and maintain such information, history, and statement for not less than 6 years after the date of the transaction.

(B) REQUESTS FOR INFORMATION.—Upon a request by the Secretary or other appropriate Federal or State official, in the event of a recall or for the purpose of investigating a suspect product or an illegitimate product, a manufacturer shall, not later than 1 business day, and not to exceed 48 hours, after receiving the request, or in other such reasonable time as determined by the Secretary, based on the circumstances of the request, provide the applicable transaction information, transaction history, and transaction statement for the product.

(C) ELECTRONIC FORMAT.—

(i) IN GENERAL.—Beginning not later than 4 years after the date of enactment of the Drug Supply Chain Security Act [enacted Nov. 27, 2013], except as provided under clause (ii), a manufacturer shall provide the transaction information, transaction history, and transaction statement required under subparagraph (A)(i) in electronic format.

(ii) EXCEPTION.—A manufacturer may continue to provide the transaction information, transaction history, and transaction statement required under subparagraph (A)(i) in a paper format to a licensed health care practitioner authorized to prescribe medication under State law or other licensed individual under the supervision or direction of such a practitioner who dispenses product in the usual course of professional practice.

(2) PRODUCT IDENTIFIER.—

(A) IN GENERAL.—Beginning not later than 4 years after the date of enactment of the Drug Supply Chain Security Act [enacted Nov. 27, 2013], a manufacturer shall affix or imprint a product identifier to each package and homogenous case of a product intended to be introduced in a transaction into commerce. Such manufacturer shall maintain the product identifier information for such product for not less than 6 years after the date of the transaction.

(B) EXCEPTION.—A package that is required to have a standardized numerical identifier is not required to have a unique device identifier.

(3) AUTHORIZED TRADING PARTNERS.—Beginning not later than January 1, 2015, the trading partners of a manufacturer may be only authorized trading partners.

(4) VERIFICATION.—Beginning not later than January 1, 2015, a manufacturer shall have systems in place to enable the manufacturer to comply with the following requirements:

(A) SUSPECT PRODUCT.—

(i) IN GENERAL.—Upon making a determination that a product in the possession or control of the manufacturer is a suspect product, or upon receiving a request for verification from the Secretary that has made a determination that a product within the possession or control of a manufacturer is a suspect product, a manufacturer shall—

(I) quarantine such product within the possession or control of the manufacturer from product intended for distribution until such product is cleared or dispositioned; and

(II) promptly conduct an investigation in coordination with trading partners, as applicable, to determine whether the product is an illegitimate product, which shall include validating any applicable transaction history and transaction information in the possession of the manufacturer and otherwise investigating to determine whether the product is an illegitimate product, and, beginning 4 years after the date of enactment of the Drug Supply Chain Security Act [enacted Nov. 27, 2013], verifying the product at the package level, including the standardized numerical identifier.

(ii) CLEARED PRODUCT.—If the manufacturer makes the determination that a suspect product is not an illegitimate product, the manufacturer shall promptly notify the Secretary, if applicable, of such determination and such product may be further distributed.

(iii) RECORDS.—A manufacturer shall keep records of the investigation of a suspect product for not less than 6 years after the conclusion of the investigation.

(B) ILLEGITIMATE PRODUCT.—

(i) IN GENERAL.—Upon determining that a product in the possession or control of a manufacturer is an illegitimate product, the manufacturer shall, in a manner consistent with the systems and processes of such manufacturer—

(I) quarantine such product within the possession or control of the manufacturer from product intended for distribution until such product is dispositioned;

(II) disposition the illegitimate product within the possession or control of the manufacturer;

(III) take reasonable and appropriate steps to assist a trading partner to disposition an illegitimate product not in the possession or control of the manufacturer; and

(IV) retain a sample of the product for further physical examination or laboratory analysis of the product by the manufacturer or Secretary (or other appropriate Federal or State official) upon request by the Secretary (or other appropriate Federal or State official), as necessary and appropriate.

(ii) MAKING A NOTIFICATION.—

(I) ILLEGITIMATE PRODUCT.—Upon determining that a product in the possession or control of the manufacturer is an illegitimate product, the manufacturer shall notify the Secretary and all immediate trading partners that the manufacturer has reason to believe may have received such illegitimate product of such determination not later than 24 hours after making such determination.

(II) HIGH RISK OF ILLEGITIMACY.—A manufacturer shall notify the Secretary and immediate trading partners that the manufacturer has reason to believe may have in the trading partner's possession a product manufactured by, or purported to be a product manufactured by, the manufacturer not later than 24 hours after determining or being notified by the Secretary or a trading partner that there is a high risk that such product is an illegitimate product. For purposes of this subclause, a "high risk" may include a specific high risk that could increase the likelihood that illegitimate product will enter the pharmaceutical distribution supply chain and other high risks as determined by the Secretary in guidance pursuant to subsection (h).

(iii) RESPONDING TO A NOTIFICATION.—Upon the receipt of a notification from the Secretary or a trading partner that a determination has been made that a product is an illegitimate product, a manufacturer shall identify all illegitimate product subject to such notification that is in the possession or control of the manufacturer, including any product that is subsequently received, and shall perform the activities described in subparagraph (A).

(iv) TERMINATING A NOTIFICATION.—Upon making a determination, in consultation with the Secretary, that a notification is no longer necessary, a manufacturer shall promptly notify immediate trading partners that the manufacturer notified pursuant to clause (ii) that such notification has been terminated.

(v) RECORDS.—A manufacturer shall keep records of the disposition of an illegitimate product for not less than 6 years after the conclusion of the disposition.

(C) REQUESTS FOR VERIFICATION.—Beginning 4 years after the date of enactment of the Drug Supply Chain Security Act [enacted Nov. 27, 2013], upon receiving a request for verification from an authorized repackager, wholesale distributor, or dispenser that is in possession or control of a product such person believes to be manufactured by such manufacturer, a manufacturer shall, not later than 24 hours after receiving the request for verification or in other such reasonable time as determined by the Secretary, based on the circumstances of the request, notify the person making the request whether the product identifier, including the standardized numerical identifier, that is the subject of the request corresponds to the product identifier affixed or imprinted by the manufacturer. If a manufacturer responding to a request for verification identifies a product identifier that does not correspond to that affixed or imprinted by the manufacturer, the manufacturer shall treat such product as suspect product and conduct an investigation as described in subparagraph (A). If the manufacturer has reason to believe the product is an illegitimate product, the manufacturer shall advise the person making the request of such belief at the time such manufacturer responds to the request for verification.

(D) ELECTRONIC DATABASE.—A manufacturer may satisfy the requirements of this paragraph by developing a secure electronic database or utilizing a secure electronic database developed or operated by another entity. The owner of such database shall establish the requirements and processes to respond to requests and may provide for data access to other members of the pharmaceutical distribution supply chain, as appropriate. The development and operation of such a database shall not relieve a manufacturer of the requirement under this paragraph to respond to a request for verification submitted by means other than a secure electronic database.

(E) SALEABLE RETURNED PRODUCT.—Beginning 4 years after the date of enactment of the Drug Supply Chain Security Act [enacted Nov. 27, 2013] (except as provided pursuant to subsection (a)(5)), upon receipt of a returned product that the manufacturer intends to further distribute, before further distributing such product, the manufacturer shall verify the product identifier, including the standardized numerical identifier, for each sealed homogeneous case of such product or, if such product is not in a sealed homogeneous case, verify the product identifier, including the standardized numerical identifier, on each package.

(F) NONSALEABLE RETURNED PRODUCT.—A manufacturer may return a nonsaleable product to the manufacturer or repackager, to the wholesale distributor from whom such product was purchased, or to a person acting on behalf of such a person, including a returns processor, without providing the information described in paragraph (1)(A)(i).

(c) WHOLESALE DISTRIBUTOR REQUIREMENTS.—

(1) PRODUCT TRACING.—

(A) In general.—Beginning not later than January 1, 2015, the following requirements shall apply to wholesale distributors:

(i) A wholesale distributor shall not accept ownership of a product unless the previous owner prior to, or at the time of, the transaction provides the transaction history, transaction information, and a transaction statement for the product, as applicable under this subparagraph.

(ii)(I)(aa) If the wholesale distributor purchased a product directly from the manufacturer, the exclusive distributor of the manufacturer, or a repackager that purchased directly from the manufacturer, then prior to, or at the time of, each transaction in which the wholesale distributor transfers ownership of a product, the wholesale distributor shall provide to the subsequent purchaser—

(AA) a transaction statement, which shall state that such wholesale distributor, or a member of the affiliate of such wholesale distributor, purchased the product directly from the manufacturer, exclusive distributor of the manufacturer, or repackager that purchased the product directly from the manufacturer; and

(BB) subject to subclause (II), the transaction history and transaction information.

(bb) The wholesale distributor shall provide the transaction history, transaction information, and transaction statement under item (aa)—

(AA) if provided to a dispenser, on a single document in a paper or electronic format; and

(BB) if provided to a wholesale distributor, through any combination of self-generated paper, electronic data, or manufacturer-provided information on the product package.

(II) For purposes of transactions described in subclause (I), transaction history and transaction information shall not be required to include the lot number of the product, the initial transaction date, or the initial shipment date from the manufacturer (as defined in subparagraphs (F), (G), and (H) of section 581(26)).

(iii) If the wholesale distributor did not purchase a product directly from the manufacturer, the exclusive distributor of the manufacturer, or a repackager that purchased directly from the manufacturer, as described in clause (ii), then prior to, or at the time of, each transaction or subsequent transaction, the wholesale distributor shall provide to the subsequent purchaser a transaction statement, transaction history, and transaction information, in a paper or electronic format that complies with the guidance document issued under subsection (a)(2).

(iv) For the purposes of clause (iii), the transaction history supplied shall begin only with the wholesale distributor described in clause (ii)(I), but the wholesale distributor described in clause (iii) shall inform the subsequent purchaser that such wholesale distributor received a direct purchase statement from a wholesale distributor described in clause (ii)(I).

(v) A wholesale distributor shall—

(I) capture the transaction information (including lot level information) consistent with the requirements of this section, transaction history, and transaction statement for each transaction described in clauses (i), (ii), and (iii) and maintain such information, history, and statement for not less than 6 years after the date of the transaction; and

(II) maintain the confidentiality of the transaction information (including any lot level information consistent with the requirements of this section), transaction history, and transaction statement for a product in a manner that prohibits disclosure to any person other than the Secretary or other appropriate Federal or State official, except to comply with clauses (ii) and (iii), and, as applicable, pursuant to an agreement under subparagraph (D).

(B) RETURNS.—

(i) SALEABLE RETURNS.—Notwithstanding subparagraph (A)(i), the following shall apply:

(I) REQUIREMENTS.—Until the date that is 6 years after the date of enactment of the Drug Supply Chain Security Act [enacted Nov. 27, 2013] (except as provided pursuant to subsection (a)(5)), a wholesale distributor may accept returned product from a dispenser or repackager pursuant to the terms and conditions of any agreement between the parties, and, notwithstanding subparagraph (A)(ii), may distribute such returned product without providing the transaction history. For transactions subsequent to the return, the transaction history of such product shall begin with the wholesale distributor that accepted the returned product, consistent with the requirements of this subsection.

(II) ENHANCED REQUIREMENTS.—Beginning 6 years after the date of enactment of the Drug Supply Chain Security Act [enacted Nov. 27, 2013] (except as provided pursuant to subsection (a)(5)), a wholesale distributor may accept returned product from a dispenser or repackager only if the wholesale distributor can associate returned product with the transaction information and transaction statement associated with that product. For all transactions after such date, the transaction history, as applicable, of such product shall begin with the wholesale distributor that accepted and verified the returned product. For purposes of this subparagraph, the transaction information and transaction history, as

481

applicable, need not include transaction dates if it is not reasonably practicable to obtain such dates.

(ii) NONSALEABLE RETURNS.—A wholesale distributor may return a non-saleable product to the manufacturer or repackager, to the wholesale distributor from whom such product was purchased, or to a person acting on behalf of such a person, including a returns processor, without providing the information required under subparagraph (A)(i).

(C) REQUESTS FOR INFORMATION.—Upon a request by the Secretary or other appropriate Federal or State official, in the event of a recall or for the purpose of investigating a suspect product or an illegitimate product, a wholesale distributor shall, not later than 1 business day, and not to exceed 48 hours, after receiving the request or in other such reasonable time as determined by the Secretary, based on the circumstances of the request, provide the applicable transaction information, transaction history, and transaction statement for the product.

(D) TRADING PARTNER AGREEMENTS.—Beginning 6 years after the date of enactment of the Drug Supply Chain Security Act [enacted Nov. 27, 2013], a wholesale distributor may disclose the transaction information, including lot level information, transaction history, or transaction statement of a product to the subsequent purchaser of the product, pursuant to a written agreement between such wholesale distributor and such subsequent purchaser. Nothing in this subparagraph shall be construed to limit the applicability of subparagraphs (A) through (C).

(2) PRODUCT IDENTIFIER.—Beginning 6 years after the date of enactment of the Drug Supply Chain Security Act [enacted Nov. 27, 2013], a wholesale distributor may engage in transactions involving a product only if such product is encoded with a product identifier (except as provided pursuant to subsection (a)(5)).

(3) AUTHORIZED TRADING PARTNERS.—Beginning not later than January 1, 2015, the trading partners of a wholesale distributor may be only authorized trading partners.

(4) VERIFICATION.—Beginning not later than January 1, 2015, a wholesale distributor shall have systems in place to enable the wholesale distributor to comply with the following requirements:

(A) SUSPECT PRODUCT.—

(i) IN GENERAL.—Upon making a determination that a product in the possession or control of a wholesale distributor is a suspect product, or upon receiving a request for verification from the Secretary that has made a determination that a product within the possession or control of a wholesale distributor is a suspect product, a wholesale distributor shall—

(I) quarantine such product within the possession or control of the wholesale distributor from product intended for distribution until such product is cleared or dispositioned; and

(II) promptly conduct an investigation in coordination with trading partners, as applicable, to determine whether the product is an illegitimate product, which shall include validating any applicable transaction history and transaction information in the possession of the wholesale distributor and otherwise investigating to determine whether the product is an illegitimate product, and, beginning 6 years after the date of enactment of the Drug Supply Chain Security Act [enacted Nov. 27, 2013] (except as provided pursuant to subsection (a)(5)), verifying the product at the package level, including the standardized numerical identifier.

(ii) CLEARED PRODUCT.—If the wholesale distributor determines that a suspect product is not an illegitimate product, the wholesale distributor shall promptly notify the Secretary, if applicable, of such determination and such product may be further distributed.

(iii) RECORDS.— A wholesale distributor shall keep records of the investigation of a suspect product for not less than 6 years after the conclusion of the investigation.

(B) ILLEGITIMATE PRODUCT.—

(i) IN GENERAL.—Upon determining, in coordination with the manufacturer, that a product in the possession or control of a wholesale distributor is an illegitimate product, the wholesale distributor shall, in a manner that is consistent with the systems and processes of such wholesale distributor—

(I) quarantine such product within the possession or control of the wholesale distributor from product intended for distribution until such product is dispositioned;

(II) disposition the illegitimate product within the possession or control of the wholesale distributor;

(III) take reasonable and appropriate steps to assist a trading partner to disposition an illegitimate product not in the possession or control of the wholesale distributor; and

(IV) retain a sample of the product for further physical examination or laboratory analysis of the product by the manufacturer or Secretary (or other appropriate Federal or State official) upon request by the manufacturer or Secretary (or other appropriate Federal or State official), as necessary and appropriate.

(ii) MAKING A NOTIFICATION.—Upon determining that a product in the possession or control of the wholesale distributor is an illegitimate product, the wholesale distributor shall notify the Secretary and all immediate trading partners that the wholesale distributor has reason to believe may have received such illegitimate product of such determination not later than 24 hours after making such determination.

(iii) RESPONDING TO A NOTIFICATION.—Upon the receipt of a notification from the Secretary or a trading partner that a determination has been made that a product is an illegitimate product, a wholesale distributor shall identify all illegitimate product subject to such notification that is in the possession or control of the wholesale distributor, including any product that is subsequently received, and shall perform the activities described in subparagraph (A).

(iv) TERMINATING A NOTIFICATION.—Upon making a determination, in consultation with the Secretary, that a notification is no longer necessary, a wholesale distributor shall promptly notify immediate trading partners that the wholesale distributor notified pursuant to clause (ii) that such notification has been terminated.

(v) RECORDS.—A wholesale distributor shall keep records of the disposition of an illegitimate product for not less than 6 years after the conclusion of the disposition.

(C) ELECTRONIC DATABASE.—A wholesale distributor may satisfy the requirements of this paragraph by developing a secure electronic database or utilizing a secure electronic database developed or operated by another entity. The owner of such database shall establish the requirements and processes to respond to requests and may provide for data access to other members of the pharmaceutical distribution supply chain, as appropriate. The development and operation of such a database shall not relieve a wholesale distributor of the requirement under this paragraph to respond to a verification request submitted by means other than a secure electronic database.

(D) VERIFICATION OF SALEABLE RETURNED PRODUCT.—Beginning 6 years after the date of enactment of the Drug Supply Chain Security Act [enacted Nov. 27, 2013], upon receipt of a returned product that the wholesale distributor intends to further distribute, before further distributing such product, the wholesale distributor shall verify the product identifier, including the standardized numerical identifier, for each sealed homogeneous case of such product or, if such product is not in a sealed homogeneous case, verify the product identifier, including the standardized numerical identifier, on each package.

(d) DISPENSER REQUIREMENTS.—

(1) PRODUCT TRACING.—

(A) IN GENERAL.—Beginning July 1, 2015, a dispenser—

(i) shall not accept ownership of a product, unless the previous owner prior to, or at the time of, the transaction, provides transaction history, transaction information, and a transaction statement;

(ii) prior to, or at the time of, each transaction in which the dispenser transfers ownership of a product (but not including dispensing to a patient or returns) shall provide the subsequent owner with transaction history, transaction information, and a transaction statement for the product, except that the requirements of this clause shall not apply to sales by a dispenser to another dispenser to fulfill a specific patient need; and

(iii) shall capture transaction information (including lot level information, if provided), transaction history, and transaction statements, as necessary to investigate a suspect product, and maintain such information, history, and statements for not less than 6 years after the transaction.

(B) AGREEMENTS WITH THIRD PARTIES.—A dispenser may enter into a written agreement with a third party, including an authorized wholesale distributor, under which the third party confidentially maintains the transaction information, transaction history, and transaction statements required to be maintained under this subsection on behalf of the dispenser. If a dispenser enters into such an agreement, the dispenser shall maintain a copy of the written agreement and shall not be relieved of the obligations of the dispenser under this subsection.

(C) RETURNS.—

(i) SALEABLE RETURNS.—A dispenser may return product to the trading partner from which the dispenser obtained the product without providing the information required under subparagraph (A).

(ii) NONSALEABLE RETURNS.—A dispenser may return a nonsaleable product to the manufacturer or repackager, to the wholesale distributor from whom such product was purchased, to a returns processor, or to a person acting on behalf of such a person without providing the information required under subparagraph (A).

(D) REQUESTS FOR INFORMATION.—Upon a request by the Secretary or other appropriate Federal or State official, in the event of a recall or for the purpose of investigating a suspect or an illegitimate product, a dispenser shall, not later than 2 business days after receiving the request or in another such reasonable time as determined by the Secretary, based on the circumstances of the request, provide the applicable transaction information, transaction statement, and transaction history which the dispenser received from the previous owner, which shall not include the lot number of the product, the initial transaction date, or the initial shipment date from the manufacturer unless such information was included in the transaction information, transaction statement, and transaction history provided by the manufacturer or wholesale distributor to the dispenser. The dispenser may respond to the request by providing the applicable information in either paper or electronic format. Until the date that is 4 years after the date of enactment of the Drug Supply Chain Security Act [enacted Nov. 27, 2013], the Secretary or other appropriate Federal or State official shall grant a dispenser additional time, as necessary, only with respect to a request to provide lot level information described in subparagraph (F) of section 581(26) that was provided to the dispenser in paper format, limit the request time period to the 6 months preceding the request or other relevant date, and, in the event of a recall, the Secretary, or other appropriate Federal or State official may request information only if such recall involves a serious adverse health consequence or death to humans.

(2) PRODUCT IDENTIFIER.—Beginning not later than 7 years after the date of enactment of the Drug Supply Chain Security Act [enacted Nov. 27, 2013], a dispenser may engage in transactions involving a product only if such product is encoded with a product identifier (except as provided pursuant to subsection (a)(5)).

(3) AUTHORIZED TRADING PARTNERS.—Beginning not later than January 1, 2015, the trading partners of a dispenser may be only authorized trading partners.

(4) VERIFICATION.—Beginning not later than January 1, 2015, a dispenser shall have systems in place to enable the dispenser to comply with the following requirements:

(A) SUSPECT PRODUCT.—

(i) IN GENERAL.—Upon making a determination that a product in the possession or control of the dispenser is a suspect product, or upon receiving a request for verification from the Secretary that has made a determination that a product within the possession or control of a dispenser is a suspect product, a dispenser shall—

(I) quarantine such product within the possession or control of the dispenser from product intended for distribution until such product is cleared or dispositioned; and

(II) promptly conduct an investigation in coordination with trading partners, as applicable, to determine whether the product is an illegitimate product.

(ii) INVESTIGATION.—An investigation conducted under clause (i)(II) shall include—

(I) beginning 7 years after the date of enactment of the Drug Supply Chain Security Act [enacted Nov. 27, 2013], verifying whether the lot number of a suspect product corresponds with the lot number for such product;

(II) beginning 7 years after the date of enactment of such Act [enacted Nov. 27, 2013], verifying that the product identifier, including the standardized numerical identifier, of at least 3 packages or 10 percent of such suspect product, whichever is greater, or all packages, if there are fewer than 3, corresponds with the product identifier for such product;

(III) validating any applicable transaction history and transaction information in the possession of the dispenser; and

(IV) otherwise investigating to determine whether the product is an illegitimate product.

(iii) CLEARED PRODUCT.—If the dispenser makes the determination that a suspect product is not an illegitimate product, the dispenser shall promptly notify the Secretary, if applicable, of such determination and such product may be further distributed or dispensed.

(iv) RECORDS.—A dispenser shall keep records of the investigation of a suspect product for not less than 6 years after the conclusion of the investigation.

(B) ILLEGITIMATE PRODUCT.—

(i) IN GENERAL.—Upon determining, in coordination with the manufacturer, that a product in the possession or control of a dispenser is an illegitimate product, the dispenser shall—

(I) disposition the illegitimate product within the possession or control of the dispenser;

(II) take reasonable and appropriate steps to assist a trading partner to disposition an illegitimate product not in the possession or control of the dispenser; and

(III) retain a sample of the product for further physical examination or laboratory analysis of the product by the manufacturer or Secretary (or other appropriate Federal or State official) upon request by the manufacturer or Secretary (or other appropriate Federal or State official), as necessary and appropriate.

(ii) MAKING A NOTIFICATION.—Upon determining that a product in the possession or control of the dispenser is an illegitimate product, the dispenser shall notify the Secretary and all immediate trading partners that the dispenser has reason to believe may have received such illegitimate product of such determination not later than 24 hours after making such determination.

(iii) RESPONDING TO A NOTIFICATION.—Upon the receipt of a notification from the Secretary or a trading partner that a determination has been made that a product is an illegitimate product, a dispenser shall identify all illegitimate product subject to such notification that is in the possession or control of the dispenser, including any product that is subsequently received, and shall perform the activities described in subparagraph (A).

(iv) TERMINATING A NOTIFICATION.—Upon making a determination, in consultation with the Secretary, that a notification is no longer necessary, a dispenser shall promptly notify immediate trading partners that the dispenser notified pursuant to clause (ii) that such notification has been terminated.

(v) RECORDS.—A dispenser shall keep records of the disposition of an illegitimate product for not less than 6 years after the conclusion of the disposition.

(C) ELECTRONIC DATABASE.—A dispenser may satisfy the requirements of this paragraph by developing a secure electronic database or utilizing a secure electronic database developed or operated by another entity.

(5) EXCEPTION.—Notwithstanding any other provision of law, the requirements under paragraphs (1) and (4) shall not apply to licensed health care practitioners authorized to prescribe or administer medication under State law or other licensed individuals under the supervision or direction of such practitioners who dispense or administer product in the usual course of professional practice.

(e) REPACKAGER REQUIREMENTS.—

(1) PRODUCT TRACING.—

(A) IN GENERAL.—Beginning not later than January 1, 2015, a repackager described in section 581(16)(A) shall—

(i) not accept ownership of a product unless the previous owner, prior to, or at the time of, the transaction, provides transaction history, transaction information, and a transaction statement for the product;

(ii) prior to, or at the time of, each transaction in which the repackager transfers ownership of a product, provide the subsequent owner with transaction history, transaction information, and a transaction statement for the product; and

(iii) capture the transaction information (including lot level information), transaction history, and transaction statement for each transaction described in clauses (i) and (ii) and maintain such information, history, and statement for not less than 6 years after the transaction.

(B) RETURNS.—

(i) NONSALEABLE PRODUCT.—A repackager described in section 581(16)(A) may return a nonsaleable product to the manufacturer or repackager, or to the wholesale distributor from whom such product was purchased, or to a person acting on behalf of such a person, including a returns processor, without providing the information required under subparagraph (A)(ii).

(ii) SALEABLE OR NONSALEABLE PRODUCT.—A repackager described in section 581(16)(B) may return a saleable or nonsaleable product to the manufacturer, repackager, or to the wholesale distributor from whom such product was received without providing the information required under subparagraph (A)(ii) on behalf of the hospital or other health care entity that took ownership of such product pursuant to the terms and conditions of any agreement between such repackager and the entity that owns the product.

(C) REQUESTS FOR INFORMATION.—Upon a request by the Secretary or other appropriate Federal or State official, in the event of a recall or for the purpose of investigating a suspect product or an illegitimate product, a repackager described in section 581(16)(A) shall, not later than 1 business day, and not to exceed 48 hours, after receiving the request or in other such reasonable time as determined by the Secretary, provide the applicable transaction information, transaction history, and transaction statement for the product.

(2) PRODUCT IDENTIFIER.—

(A) IN GENERAL.—Beginning not later than 5 years after the date of enactment of the Drug Supply Chain Security Act [enacted Nov. 27, 2013], a repackager described in section 581(16)(A)—

(i) shall affix or imprint a product identifier to each package and homogenous case of product intended to be introduced in a transaction in commerce;

(ii) shall maintain the product identifier information for such product for not less than 6 years after the date of the transaction;

(iii) may engage in transactions involving a product only if such product is encoded with a product identifier (except as provided pursuant to subsection (a)(5)); and

(iv) shall maintain records for not less than 6 years to allow the repackager to associate the product identifier the repackager affixes or imprints with the product identifier assigned by the original manufacturer of the product.

(B) EXCEPTION.—A package that is required to have a standardized numerical identifier is not required to have a unique device identifier.

(3) AUTHORIZED TRADING PARTNERS.—Beginning January 1, 2015, the trading partners of a repackager described in section 581(16) may be only authorized trading partners.

(4) VERIFICATION.—Beginning not later than January 1, 2015, a repackager described in section 581(16)(A) shall have systems in place to enable the repackager to comply with the following requirements:

(A) SUSPECT PRODUCT.—

(i) IN GENERAL.—Upon making a determination that a product in the possession or control of the repackager is a suspect product, or upon receiving a request for verification from the Secretary that has made a determination that a product within the possession or control of a repackager is a suspect product, a repackager shall—

(I) quarantine such product within the possession or control of the repackager from product intended for distribution until such product is cleared or dispositioned; and

(II) promptly conduct an investigation in coordination with trading partners, as applicable, to determine whether the product is an illegitimate product, which shall include validating any applicable transaction history and transaction information in the possession of the repackager and otherwise investigating to determine whether the product is an illegitimate product, and, beginning 5 years after the date of enactment of the Drug Supply Chain Security Act [enacted Nov. 27, 2013] (except as provided pursuant to subsection (a)(5)), verifying the product at the package level, including the standardized numerical identifier.

(ii) CLEARED PRODUCT.—If the repackager makes the determination that a suspect product is not an illegitimate product, the repackager shall promptly notify the Secretary, if applicable, of such determination and such product may be further distributed.

(iii) RECORDS.—A repackager shall keep records of the investigation of a suspect product for not less than 6 years after the conclusion of the investigation.

(B) ILLEGITIMATE PRODUCT.—

(i) IN GENERAL.—Upon determining, in coordination with the manufacturer, that a product in the possession or control of a repackager is an illegitimate product, the repackager shall, in a manner that is consistent with the systems and processes of such repackager—

(I) quarantine such product within the possession or control of the repackager from product intended for distribution until such product is dispositioned;

(II) disposition the illegitimate product within the possession or control of the repackager;

(III) take reasonable and appropriate steps to assist a trading partner to disposition an illegitimate product not in the possession or control of the repackager; and

(IV) retain a sample of the product for further physical examination or laboratory analysis of the product by the manufacturer or Secretary (or other appropriate Federal or State official) upon request by the manufacturer or Secretary (or other appropriate Federal or State official), as necessary and appropriate.

(ii) Making a notification.—Upon determining that a product in the possession or control of the repackager is an illegitimate product, the repackager shall notify the Secretary and all immediate trading partners that the repackager has reason to believe may have received the illegitimate product of such determination not later than 24 hours after making such determination.

(iii) Responding to a notification.—Upon the receipt of a notification from the Secretary or a trading partner, a repackager shall identify all illegitimate product subject to such notification that is in the possession or control of the repackager, including any product that is subsequently received, and shall perform the activities described in subparagraph (A).

(iv) Terminating a notification.—Upon making a determination, in consultation with the Secretary, that a notification is no longer necessary, a repackager shall promptly notify immediate trading partners that the repackager notified pursuant to clause (ii) that such notification has been terminated.

(v) Records.—A repackager shall keep records of the disposition of an illegitimate product for not less than 6 years after the conclusion of the disposition.

(C) Requests for verification.—Beginning 5 years after the date of enactment of the Drug Supply Chain Security Act [enacted Nov. 27, 2013], upon receiving a request for verification from an authorized manufacturer, wholesale distributor, or dispenser that is in possession or control of a product they believe to be repackaged by such repackager, a repackager shall, not later than 24 hours after receiving the verification request or in other such reasonable time as determined by the Secretary, based on the circumstances of the request, notify the person making the request whether the product identifier, including the standardized numerical identifier, that is the subject of the request corresponds to the product identifier affixed or imprinted by the repackager. If a repackager responding to a verification request identifies a product identifier that does not correspond to that affixed or imprinted by the repackager, the repackager shall treat such product as suspect product and conduct an investigation as described in subparagraph (A). If the repackager has reason to believe the product is an illegitimate product, the repackager shall advise the person making the request of such belief at the time such repackager responds to the verification request.

(D) Electronic database.—A repackager may satisfy the requirements of paragraph (4) by developing a secure electronic database or utilizing a secure electronic database developed or operated by another entity. The owner of such database shall establish the requirements and processes to respond to requests and may provide for data access to other members of the pharmaceutical distribution supply chain, as appropriate. The development and operation of such a database shall not relieve a repackager of the requirement under subparagraph (C) to respond to a verification request submitted by means other than a secure electronic database.

(E) VERIFICATION OF SALEABLE RETURNED PRODUCT.—Beginning 5 years after the date of enactment of the Drug Supply Chain Security Act [enacted Nov. 27, 2013], upon receipt of a returned product that the repackager intends to further distribute, before further distributing such product, the repackager shall verify the product identifier for each sealed homogeneous case of such product or, if such product is not in a sealed homogeneous case, verify the product identifier on each package.

(f) DROP SHIPMENTS.—

(1) IN GENERAL.—A wholesale distributor that does not physically handle or store product shall be exempt from the provisions of this section, except the notification requirements under clauses (ii), (iii), and (iv) of subsection (c)(4)(B), provided that the manufacturer, repackager, or other wholesale distributor that distributes the product to the dispenser by means of a drop shipment for such wholesale distributor includes on the transaction information and transaction history to the dispenser the contact information of such wholesale distributor and provides the transaction information, transaction history, and transaction statement directly to the dispenser.

(2) CLARIFICATION.—For purposes of this subsection, providing administrative services, including processing of orders and payments, shall not by itself, be construed as being involved in the handling, distribution, or storage of a product.

(g) ENHANCED DRUG DISTRIBUTION SECURITY.—

(1) IN GENERAL.—On the date that is 10 years after the date of enactment of the Drug Supply Chain Security Act [enacted Nov. 27, 2013], the following interoperable, electronic tracing of product at the package level requirements shall go into effect:

(A) The transaction information and the transaction statements as required under this section shall be exchanged in a secure, interoperable, electronic manner in accordance with the standards established under the guidance issued pursuant to paragraphs (3) and (4) of subsection (h), including any revision of such guidance issued in accordance with paragraph (5) of such subsection.

(B) The transaction information required under this section shall include the product identifier at the package level for each package included in the transaction.

(C) Systems and processes for verification of product at the package level, including the standardized numerical identifier, shall be required in accordance with the standards established under the guidance issued pursuant to subsection (a)(2) and the guidances issued pursuant to paragraphs (2), (3), and (4) of subsection (h), including any revision of such guidances issued in accordance with paragraph (5) of such subsection, which may include the use of aggregation and inference as necessary.

(D) The systems and processes necessary to promptly respond with the transaction information and transaction statement for a product upon a request by the Secretary (or other appropriate Federal or State official) in the event of a recall or for the purposes of investigating a suspect product or an illegitimate product shall be required.

(E) The systems and processes necessary to promptly facilitate gathering the information necessary to produce the transaction information for each transaction going back to the manufacturer, as applicable, shall be required—

(i) in the event of a request by the Secretary (or other appropriate Federal or State official), on account of a recall or for the purposes of investigating a suspect product or an illegitimate product; or

(ii) in the event of a request by an authorized trading partner, in a secure manner that ensures the protection of confidential commercial information and trade secrets, for purposes of investigating a suspect product or assisting the Secretary (or other appropriate Federal or State official) with a request described in clause (i).

(F) Each person accepting a saleable return shall have systems and processes in place to allow acceptance of such product and may accept saleable returns only if such person can associate the saleable return product with the transaction information and transaction statement associated with that product.

(2) COMPLIANCE.—

(A) INFORMATION MAINTENANCE AGREEMENT.—A dispenser may enter into a written agreement with a third party, including an authorized wholesale distributor, under which the third party shall confidentially maintain any information and statements required to be maintained under this section. If a dispenser enters into such an agreement, the dispenser shall maintain a copy of the written agreement and shall not be relieved of the obligations of the dispenser under this subsection.

(B) ALTERNATIVE METHODS.—The Secretary, taking into consideration the assessment conducted under paragraph (3), shall provide for alternative methods of compliance with any of the requirements set forth in paragraph (1), including—

(i) establishing timelines for compliance by small businesses (including small business dispensers with 25 or fewer full-time employees) with such requirements, in order to ensure that such requirements do not impose undue economic hardship for small businesses, including small business dispensers for whom the criteria set forth in the assessment under paragraph (3) is not met, if the Secretary determines that such requirements under paragraph (1) would result in undue economic hardship; and

(ii) establishing a process by which a dispenser may request a waiver from any of the requirements set forth in paragraph (1) if the Secretary determines that such requirements would result in an undue economic hardship, which shall include a process for the biennial review and renewal of any such waiver.

(3) ASSESSMENT.—

(A) IN GENERAL.—Not later than the date that is 18 months after the Secretary issues the final guidance required under subsection (h), the Secretary shall enter into a contract with a private, independent consulting firm with expertise to conduct a technology and software assessment that looks at the feasibility of dispensers with 25 or fewer full-time employees conducting interoperable, electronic tracing of products at the package level. Such assessment shall be completed not later than 8 1/2 years after the date of enactment of the Drug Supply Chain Security Act [enacted Nov. 27, 2013].

(B) CONDITION.—As a condition of the award of the contract under subparagraph (A), the private, independent consulting firm shall agree to consult with dispensers with 25 or fewer full-time employees when conducting the assessment under such subparagraph.

(C) CONTENT.—The assessment under subparagraph (A) shall assess whether—

(i) the necessary software and hardware is readily accessible to such dispensers;

(ii) the necessary software and hardware is prohibitively expensive to obtain, install, and maintain for such dispensers; and

(iii) the necessary hardware and software can be integrated into business practices, such as interoperability with wholesale distributors, for such dispensers.

(D) PUBLICATION.—The Secretary shall—

(i) publish the statement of work for the assessment under subparagraph (A) for public comment prior to beginning the assessment;

(ii) publish the final assessment for public comment not later than 30 calendar days after receiving such assessment; and

(iii) hold a public meeting not later than 180 calendar days after receiving the final assessment at which public stakeholders may present their views on the assessment.

(4) PROCEDURE.—Notwithstanding section 553 of title 5, United States Code, the Secretary, in promulgating any regulation pursuant to this section, shall—

(A) provide appropriate flexibility by—

(i) not requiring the adoption of specific business systems for the maintenance and transmission of data;

(ii) prescribing alternative methods of compliance for any of the requirements set forth in paragraph (1) or set forth in regulations implementing such requirements, including—

(I) timelines for small businesses to comply with the requirements set forth in the regulations in order to ensure that such requirements do not impose undue economic hardship for small businesses (including small business dispensers for whom the criteria set forth in the assessment under paragraph (3) is not met), if the Secretary determines that such requirements would result in undue economic hardship; and

(II) the establishment of a process by which a dispenser may request a waiver from any of the requirements set forth in such regulations if the Secretary determines that such requirements would result in an undue economic hardship; and

(iii) taking into consideration—

(I) the results of pilot projects, including pilot projects pursuant to this section and private sector pilot projects, including those involving the use of aggregation and inference;

(II) the public meetings held and related guidance documents issued under this section;

(III) the public health benefits of any additional regulations in comparison to the cost of compliance with such requirements, including on entities of varying sizes and capabilities;

(IV) the diversity of the pharmaceutical distribution supply chain by providing appropriate flexibility for each sector, including both large and small businesses; and

(V) the assessment pursuant to paragraph (3) with respect to small business dispensers, including related public comment and the public meeting, and requirements under this section;

(B) issue a notice of proposed rulemaking that includes a copy of the proposed regulation;

(C) provide a period of not less than 60 days for comments on the proposed regulation; and

(D) publish in the Federal Register the final regulation not less than 2 years prior to the effective date of the regulation.

(h) GUIDANCE DOCUMENTS.—

(1) IN GENERAL.—For the purposes of facilitating the successful and efficient adoption of secure, interoperable product tracing at the package level in order to enhance drug distribution security and further protect the public health, the Secretary shall issue the guidance documents as provided for in this subsection.

(2) SUSPECT AND ILLEGITIMATE PRODUCT.—

(A) IN GENERAL.—Not later than 180 days after the date of enactment of the Drug Supply Chain Security Act [enacted Nov. 27, 2013], the Secretary shall issue a guidance document to aid trading partners in the identification of a suspect product and notification termination. Such guidance document shall—

(i) identify specific scenarios that could significantly increase the risk of a suspect product entering the pharmaceutical distribution supply chain;

(ii) provide recommendation on how trading partners may identify such product and make a determination on whether the product is a suspect product as soon as practicable; and

(iii) set forth the process by which manufacturers, repackagers, wholesale distributors, and dispensers shall terminate notifications in consultation with the Secretary regarding illegitimate product pursuant to subsections (b)(4)(B), (c)(4)(B), (d)(4)(B), and (e)(4)(B).

(B) Revised guidance. If the Secretary revises the guidance issued under subparagraph (A), the Secretary shall follow the procedure set forth in paragraph (5).

(3) UNIT LEVEL TRACING.—

(A) IN GENERAL.—In order to enhance drug distribution security at the package level, not later than 18 months after conducting a public meeting on the system attributes necessary to enable secure tracing of product at the package level, including allowing for the use of verification, inference, and aggregation, as necessary, the Secretary shall issue a final guidance document that outlines and makes recommendations with respect to the system attributes necessary to enable secure tracing at the package level as required under the requirements established under subsection (g). Such guidance document shall—

(i) define the circumstances under which the sectors within the pharmaceutical distribution supply chain may, in the most efficient manner practicable, infer the contents of a case, pallet, tote, or other aggregate

496

of individual packages or containers of product, from a product identifier associated with the case, pallet, tote, or other aggregate, without opening each case, pallet, tote, or other aggregate or otherwise individually scanning each package;

(ii) identify methods and processes to enhance secure tracing of product at the package level, such as secure processes to facilitate the use of inference, enhanced verification activities, the use of aggregation and inference, processes that utilize the product identifiers to enhance tracing of product at the package level, including the standardized numerical identifier, or package security features; and

(iii) ensure the protection of confidential commercial information and trade secrets.

(B) PROCEDURE.—In issuing the guidance under subparagraph (A), and in revising such guidance, if applicable, the Secretary shall follow the procedure set forth in paragraph (5).

(4) STANDARDS FOR INTEROPERABLE DATA EXCHANGE.—

(A) IN GENERAL.—In order to enhance secure tracing of a product at the package level, the Secretary, not later than 18 months after conducting a public meeting on the interoperable standards necessary to enhance the security of the pharmaceutical distribution supply chain, shall update the guidance issued pursuant to subsection (a)(2), as necessary and appropriate, and finalize such guidance document so that the guidance document—

(i) identifies and makes recommendations with respect to the standards necessary for adoption in order to support the secure, interoperable electronic data exchange among the pharmaceutical distribution supply chain that comply with a form and format developed by a widely recognized international standards development organization;

(ii) takes into consideration standards established pursuant to subsection (a)(2) and section 505D;

(iii) facilitates the creation of a uniform process or methodology for product tracing; and

(iv) ensures the protection of confidential commercial information and trade secrets.

(B) PROCEDURE.—In issuing the guidance under subparagraph (A), and in revising such guidance, if applicable, the Secretary shall follow the procedure set forth in paragraph (5).

(5) PROCEDURE.—In issuing or revising any guidance issued pursuant to this subsection or subsection (g), except the initial guidance issued under paragraph (2)(A), the Secretary shall—

(A) publish a notice in the Federal Register for a period not less than 30 days announcing that the draft or revised draft guidance is available;

(B) post the draft guidance document on the Internet Web site of the Food and Drug Administration and make such draft guidance document available in hard copy;

(C) provide an opportunity for comment and review and take into consideration any comments received;

(D) revise the draft guidance, as appropriate;

(E) publish a notice in the Federal Register for a period not less than 30 days announcing that the final guidance or final revised guidance is available;

(F) post the final guidance document on the Internet Web site of the Food and Drug Administration and make such final guidance document available in hard copy; and

(G) provide for an effective date of not earlier than 1 year after such guidance becomes final.

(i) PUBLIC MEETINGS.—

(1) IN GENERAL.—The Secretary shall hold not less than 5 public meetings to enhance the safety and security of the pharmaceutical distribution supply chain and provide for comment. The Secretary may hold the first such public meeting not earlier than 1 year after the date of enactment of the Drug Supply Chain Security Act [enacted Nov. 27, 2013]. In carrying out the public meetings described in this paragraph, the Secretary shall—

(A) prioritize topics necessary to inform the issuance of the guidance described in paragraphs (3) and (4) of subsection (h); and

(B) take all measures reasonable and practicable to ensure the protection of confidential commercial information and trade secrets.

(2) CONTENT.—Each of the following topics shall be addressed in at least one of the public meetings described in paragraph (1):

(A) An assessment of the steps taken under subsections (b) through (e) to build capacity for a unit-level system, including the impact of the requirements of such subsections on—

(i) the ability of the health care system collectively to maintain patient access to medicines;

(ii) the scalability of such requirements, including as it relates to product lines; and

(iii) the capability of different sectors and subsectors, including both large and small businesses, to affix and utilize the product identifier.

(B) The system attributes necessary to support the requirements set forth under subsection (g), including the standards necessary for adoption in order to support the secure, interoperable electronic data exchange among sectors within the pharmaceutical distribution supply chain.

(C) Best practices in each of the different sectors within the pharmaceutical distribution supply chain to implement the requirements of this section.

(D) The costs and benefits of the implementation of this section, including the impact on each pharmaceutical distribution supply chain sector and on public health.

(E) Whether electronic tracing requirements, including tracing of product at the package level, are feasible, cost effective, and needed to protect the public health.

(F) The systems and processes needed to utilize the product identifiers to enhance tracing of product at the package level, including allowing for verification, aggregation, and inference, as necessary.

(G) The technical capabilities and legal authorities, if any, needed to establish an interoperable, electronic system that provides for tracing of product at the package level.

(H) The impact that such additional requirements would have on patient safety, the drug supply, cost and regulatory burden, and timely patient access to prescription drugs.

(I) Other topics, as determined appropriate by the Secretary.

(j) PILOT PROJECTS.—

(1) IN GENERAL.—The Secretary shall establish 1 or more pilot projects, in coordination with authorized manufacturers, repackagers, wholesale distributors, and dispensers, to explore and evaluate methods to enhance the safety and security of the pharmaceutical distribution supply chain. Such projects shall build upon efforts, in existence as of the date of enactment of the Drug Supply Chain Security Act [enacted Nov. 27, 2013], to enhance the safety and security of the pharmaceutical distribution supply chain, take into consideration any pilot projects conducted prior to such date of enactment, including any pilot projects that use aggregation and inference, and inform the draft and final guidance under paragraphs (3) and (4) of subsection (h).

(2) CONTENT.—

(A) IN GENERAL.—The Secretary shall ensure that the pilot projects under paragraph (1) reflect the diversity of the pharmaceutical distribution supply chain and that the pilot projects, when taken as a whole, include participants representative of every sector, including both large and small businesses.

(B) PROJECT DESIGN.—The pilot projects under paragraph (1) shall be designed to—

(i) utilize the product identifier for tracing of a product, which may include verification of the product identifier of a product, including the use of aggregation and inference;

(ii) improve the technical capabilities of each sector and subsector to comply with systems and processes needed to utilize the product identifiers to enhance tracing of a product;

(iii) identify system attributes that are necessary to implement the requirements established under this section; and

(iv) complete other activities as determined by the Secretary.

(k) SUNSET.—The following requirements shall have no force or effect beginning on the date that is 10 years after the date of enactment of the Drug Supply Chain Security Act [enacted Nov. 27, 2013]:

(1) The provision and receipt of transaction history under this section.

(2) The requirements set forth for returns under subsections (b)(4)(E), (c)(1)(B)(i), (d)(1)(C)(i), and (e)(4)(E).

(3) The requirements set forth under subparagraphs (A)(v)(II) and (D) of subsection (c)(1), as applied to lot level information only.

(*l*) RULE OF CONSTRUCTION.—The requirements set forth in subsections (g)(4), (i), and (j) shall not be construed as a condition, prohibition, or precedent for precluding or delaying the provisions becoming effective pursuant to subsection (g).

(m) REQUESTS FOR INFORMATION.—On the date that is 10 years after the date of enactment of the Drug Supply Chain Security Act [enacted Nov. 27, 2013], the timeline for responses to requests for information from the Secretary, or other appropriate Federal or State official, as applicable, under subsections (b)(1)(B), (c)(1)(C), and (e)(1)(C) shall be not later than 24 hours after receiving the request from the Secretary or other appropriate Federal or State official, as applicable, or in such other reasonable time as determined by the Secretary based on the circumstances of the request.

SEC. 583 [21 U.S.C. 360eee–2]. NATIONAL STANDARDS FOR PRESCRIPTION DRUG WHOLESALE DISTRIBUTORS[69]

(a) IN GENERAL.—The Secretary shall, not later than 2 years after the date of enactment of the Drug Supply Chain Security Act [enacted Nov. 27, 2013], establish by regulation standards for the licensing of persons under section 503(e)(1) (as amended by the Drug Supply Chain Security Act), including the revocation, reissuance, and renewal of such license.

---

69. Section 583 was added by Pub. L. No. 113–54, and according to § 204(c) of that law, this section takes effect on January 1, 2015.

(b) CONTENT.—For the purpose of ensuring uniformity with respect to standards set forth in this section, the standards established under subsection (a) shall apply to all State and Federal licenses described under section 503(e)(1) (as amended by the Drug Supply Chain Security Act) and shall include standards for the following:

(1) The storage and handling of prescription drugs, including facility requirements.

(2) The establishment and maintenance of records of the distributions of such drugs.

(3) The furnishing of a bond or other equivalent means of security, as follows:

(A)(i) For the issuance or renewal of a wholesale distributor license, an applicant that is not a government owned and operated wholesale distributor shall submit a surety bond of $ 100,000 or other equivalent means of security acceptable to the State.

(ii) For purposes of clause (i), the State or other applicable authority may accept a surety bond in the amount of $ 25,000 if the annual gross receipts of the previous tax year for the wholesaler is $ 10,000,000 or less.

(B) If a wholesale distributor can provide evidence that it possesses the required bond in a State, the requirement for a bond in another State shall be waived.

(4) Mandatory background checks and fingerprinting of facility managers or designated representatives.

(5) The establishment and implementation of qualifications for key personnel.

(6) The mandatory physical inspection of any facility to be used in wholesale distribution within a reasonable time frame from the initial application of the facility and to be conducted by the licensing authority or by the State, consistent with subsection (c).

(7) In accordance with subsection (d), the prohibition of certain persons from receiving or maintaining licensure for wholesale distribution.

(c) INSPECTIONS.—To satisfy the inspection requirement under subsection (b)(6), the Federal or State licensing authority may conduct the inspection or may accept an inspection by the State in which the facility is located, or by a third-party accreditation or inspection service approved by the Secretary or the State licensing such wholesale distributor.

(d) PROHIBITED PERSONS.—The standards established under subsection (a) shall include requirements to prohibit a person from receiving or maintaining licensure for wholesale distribution if the person—

(1) has been convicted of any felony for conduct relating to wholesale distribution, any felony violation of subsection (i) or (k) of section 301, or any felony

violation of section 1365 of title 18, United States Code, relating to product tampering; or

(2) has engaged in a pattern of violating the requirements of this section, or State requirements for licensure, that presents a threat of serious adverse health consequences or death to humans.

(e) REQUIREMENTS.—The Secretary, in promulgating any regulation pursuant to this section, shall, notwithstanding section 553 of title 5, United States Code—

(1) issue a notice of proposed rulemaking that includes a copy of the proposed regulation;

(2) provide a period of not less than 60 days for comments on the proposed regulation; and

(3) provide that the final regulation take effect on the date that is 2 years after the date such final regulation is published.

SEC. 584 [21 U.S.C. 360eee–3]. NATIONAL STANDARDS FOR THIRD-PARTY LOGISTICS PROVIDERS

(a) REQUIREMENTS.—No third-party logistics provider in any State may conduct activities in any State unless each facility of such third-party logistics provider—

(1)(A) is licensed by the State from which the drug is distributed by the third-party logistics provider, in accordance with the regulations promulgated under subsection (d); or

(B) if the State from which the drug distributed by the third-party logistics provider has not established a licensure requirement, is licensed by the Secretary, in accordance with the regulations promulgated under subsection (d); and

(2) if the drug is distributed interstate, is licensed by the State into which the drug is distributed by the third-party logistics provider if such State licenses third-party logistics providers that distribute drugs into the State and the third-party logistics provider is not licensed by the Secretary as described in paragraph (1)(B).

(b) REPORTING.—Beginning 1 year after the date of enactment of the Drug Supply Chain Security Act [enacted Nov. 27, 2013], a facility of a third-party logistics provider shall report to the Secretary, on an annual basis pursuant to a schedule determined by the Secretary—

(1) the State by which the facility is licensed and the appropriate identification number of such license; and

(2) the name and address of the facility and all trade names under which such facility conducts business.

(c) COSTS.—

(1) AUTHORIZED FEES OF SECRETARY.—If a State does not establish a licensing program for a third-party logistics provider, the Secretary shall license the third-party logistics provider located in such State and may collect a reasonable fee in such amount necessary to reimburse the Secretary for costs associated with establishing and administering the licensure program and conducting periodic inspections under this section. The Secretary shall adjust fee rates as needed on an annual basis to generate only the amount of revenue needed to perform this service. Fees authorized under this paragraph shall be collected and available for obligation only to the extent and in the amount provided in advance in appropriations Acts. Such fees are authorized to remain available until expended. Such sums as may be necessary may be transferred from the Food and Drug Administration salaries and expenses appropriation account without fiscal year limitation to such appropriation account for salaries and expenses with such fiscal year limitation.

(2) STATE LICENSING FEES.—

(A) STATE ESTABLISHED PROGRAM.—Nothing in this Act shall prohibit a State that has established a program to license a third-party logistics provider from collecting fees from a third-party logistics provider for such a license.

(B) NO STATE ESTABLISHED PROGRAM.—A State that does not establish a program to license a third-party logistics provider in accordance with this section shall be prohibited from collecting a State licensing fee from a third-party logistics provider.

(d) REGULATIONS.—

(1) IN GENERAL.—Not later than 2 years after the date of enactment of the Drug Supply Chain Security Act [enacted Nov. 27, 2013], the Secretary shall issue regulations regarding the standards for licensing under subsection (a), including the revocation and reissuance of such license, to third-party logistics providers under this section.

(2) CONTENT.—Such regulations shall—

(A) establish a process by which a third-party accreditation program approved by the Secretary shall, upon request by a third-party logistics provider, issue a license to each third-party logistics provider that meets the requirements set forth in this section;

(B) establish a process by which the Secretary shall issue a license to each third-party logistics provider that meets the requirements set forth in this section if the Secretary is not able to approve a third-party accreditation program because no such program meets the Secretary's requirements necessary for approval of such a third-party accreditation program;

(C) require that the entity complies with storage practices, as determined by the Secretary for such facility, including—

(i) maintaining access to warehouse space of suitable size to facilitate safe operations, including a suitable area to quarantine suspect product;

(ii) maintaining adequate security; and

(iii) having written policies and procedures to—

(I) address receipt, security, storage, inventory, shipment, and distribution of a product;

(II) identify, record, and report confirmed losses or thefts in the United States;

(III) correct errors and inaccuracies in inventories;

(IV) provide support for manufacturer recalls;

(V) prepare for, protect against, and address any reasonably foreseeable crisis that affects security or operation at the facility, such as a strike, fire, or flood;

(VI) ensure that any expired product is segregated from other products and returned to the manufacturer or repackager or destroyed;

(VII) maintain the capability to trace the receipt and outbound distribution of a product, and supplies and records of inventory; and

(VIII) quarantine or destroy a suspect product if directed to do so by the respective manufacturer, wholesale distributor, dispenser, or an authorized government agency;

(D) provide for periodic inspection by the licensing authority, as determined by the Secretary, of such facility warehouse space to ensure compliance with this section;

(E) prohibit a facility from having as a manager or designated representative anyone convicted of any felony violation of subsection (i) or (k) of section 301 or any violation of section 1365 of title 18, United States Code relating to product tampering;

(F) provide for mandatory background checks of a facility manager or a designated representative of such manager;

(G) require a third-party logistics provider to provide the applicable licensing authority, upon a request by such authority, a list of all product manufacturers, wholesale distributors, and dispensers for whom the third-party logistics provider provides services at such facility; and

(H) include procedures under which any third-party logistics provider license—

(i) expires on the date that is 3 years after issuance of the license; and

(ii) may be renewed for additional 3-year periods.

(3) Procedure.—In promulgating the regulations under this subsection, the Secretary shall, notwithstanding section 553 of title 5, United States Code—

(A) issue a notice of proposed rulemaking that includes a copy of the proposed regulation;

(B) provide a period of not less than 60 days for comments on the proposed regulation; and

(C) provide that the final regulation takes effect upon the expiration of 1 year after the date that such final regulation is issued.

(e) Validity.—A license issued under this section shall remain valid as long as such third-party logistics provider remains licensed consistent with this section. If the Secretary finds that the third-party accreditation program demonstrates that all applicable requirements for licensure under this section are met, the Secretary shall issue a license under this section to a third-party logistics provider receiving accreditation, pursuant to subsection (d)(2)(A).

Sec. 585 [21 U.S.C. 360eee–4]. Uniform National Policy

(a) Product Tracing and Other Requirements.—Beginning on the date of enactment of the Drug Supply Chain Security Act [enacted Nov. 27, 2013], no State or political subdivision of a State may establish or continue in effect any requirements for tracing products through the distribution system (including any requirements with respect to statements of distribution history, transaction history, transaction information, or transaction statement of a product as such product changes ownership in the supply chain, or verification, investigation, disposition, notification, or recordkeeping relating to such systems, including paper or electronic pedigree systems or for tracking and tracing drugs throughout the distribution system) which are inconsistent with, more stringent than, or in addition to, any requirements applicable under section 503(e) (as amended by such Act) or this subchapter (or regulations issued thereunder), or which are inconsistent with—

(1) any waiver, exception, or exemption pursuant to section 581 or 582; or

(2) any restrictions specified in section 582.

(b) Wholesale Distributor and Third-Party Logistics Provider Standards.—

(1) In general.—Beginning on the date of enactment of the Drug Supply Chain Security Act [enacted Nov. 27, 2013], no State or political subdivision of a State may establish or continue any standards, requirements, or regulations with respect to wholesale prescription drug distributor or third-party logistics provider licensure that are inconsistent with, less stringent than, directly related to, or covered by the standards and requirements applicable under section 503(e) (as amended by such Act), in the case of a wholesale distributor, or section 584, in the case of a third-party logistics provider.

(2) STATE REGULATION OF THIRD-PARTY LOGISTICS PROVIDERS.—No State shall regulate third-party logistics providers as wholesale distributors.

(3) ADMINISTRATION FEES.—Notwithstanding paragraph (1), a State may administer fee collections for effectuating the wholesale drug distributor and third-party logistics provider licensure requirements under sections 503(e) (as amended by the Drug Supply Chain Security Act), 583, and 584.

(4) ENFORCEMENT, SUSPENSION, AND REVOCATION.—Notwithstanding paragraph (1), a State—

(A) may take administrative action, including fines, to enforce a requirement promulgated by the State in accordance with section 503(e) (as amended by the Drug Supply Chain Security Act) or this subchapter;

(B) may provide for the suspension or revocation of licenses issued by the State for violations of the laws of such State;

(C) upon conviction of violations of Federal, State, or local drug laws or regulations, may provide for fines, imprisonment, or civil penalties; and

(D) may regulate activities of licensed entities in a manner that is consistent with product tracing requirements under section 582.

(c) EXCEPTION.—Nothing in this section shall be construed to preempt State requirements related to the distribution of prescription drugs if such requirements are not related to product tracing as described in subsection (a) or wholesale distributor and third-party logistics provider licensure as described in subsection (b) applicable under section 503(e) (as amended by the Drug Supply Chain Security Act) or this subchapter (or regulations issued thereunder).

CHAPTER VI—COSMETICS

SEC. 601 [21 U.S.C. 361]. ADULTERATED COSMETICS

A cosmetic shall be deemed to be adulterated—

(a) If it bears or contains any poisonous or deleterious substance which may render it injurious to users under the conditions of use prescribed in the labeling thereof, or, under such conditions of use as are customary or usual, except that this provision shall not apply to coal-tar hair dye, the label of which bears the following legend conspicuously displayed thereon: "Caution—This product contains ingredients which may cause skin irritation on certain individuals and a preliminary test according to accompanying directions should first be made. This product must not be used for dyeing the eyelashes or eyebrows; to do so may cause blindness.", and the labeling of which bears adequate directions for such preliminary testing. For the purposes of this paragraph and paragraph (e) the term "hair dye" shall not include eyelash dyes or eyebrow dyes.

(b) If it consists in whole or in part of any filthy, putrid, or decomposed substance.

(c) If it has been prepared, packed, or held under insanitary conditions whereby it may have become contaminated with filth, or whereby it may have been rendered injurious to health.

(d) If its container is composed, in whole or in part, of any poisonous or deleterious substance which may render the contents injurious to health.

(e) If it is not a hair dye and it is, or it bears or contains, a color additive which is unsafe within the meaning of section 721(a).

SEC. 602 [21 U.S.C. 362]. MISBRANDED COSMETICS

A cosmetic shall be deemed to be misbranded—

(a) If its labeling is false or misleading in any particular.

(b) If in package form unless it bears a label containing (1) the name and place of business of the manufacturer, packer, or distributor; and (2) an accurate statement of the quantity of the contents in terms of weight, measure, or numerical count: Provided, That under clause (2) of this paragraph reasonable variations shall be permitted, and exemptions as to small packages shall be established, by regulations prescribed by the Secretary.

(c) If any word, statement, or other information required by or under authority of this Act to appear on the label or labeling is not prominently placed thereon with such conspicuousness (as compared with other words, statements, designs, or devices in the labeling) and in such terms as to render it likely to be read and understood by the ordinary individual under customary conditions of purchase and use.

(d) If its container is so made, formed, or filled as to be misleading.

(e) If it is a color additive, unless its packaging and labeling are in conformity with such packaging and labeling requirements, applicable to such color additive, as may be contained in regulations issued under section 721. This paragraph shall not apply to packages of color additives which, with respect to their use for cosmetics, are marketed and intended for use only in or on hair dyes (as defined in the last sentence of section 601(a)).

(f) If its packaging or labeling is in violation of an applicable regulation issued pursuant to section 3 or 4 of the Poison Prevention Packaging Act of 1970.

SEC. 603 [21 U.S.C. 363]. REGULATIONS MAKING EXEMPTIONS

The Secretary shall promulgate regulations exempting from any labeling requirement of this Act cosmetics which are, in accordance with the practice of the trade, to be processed, labeled, or repacked in substantial quantities at establishments other than those where originally processed or packed, on condition that such cosmetics are not adulterated or misbranded under the provisions of this Act upon removal from such processing, labeling, or repacking establishment.

CHAPTER VII—GENERAL AUTHORITY

SUBCHAPTER A—GENERAL ADMINISTRATIVE PROVISIONS

SEC. 701 [21 U.S.C. 371]. REGULATIONS AND HEARINGS

(a) The authority to promulgate regulations for the efficient enforcement of this Act, except as otherwise provided in this section, is hereby vested in the Secretary.

(b) The Secretary of the Treasury and the Secretary of Health and Human Services shall jointly prescribe regulations for the efficient enforcement of the provisions of section 801, except as otherwise provided therein. Such regulations shall be promulgated in such manner and take effect at such time, after due notice, as the Secretary of Health and Human Services shall determine.

(c) Hearings authorized or required by this Act shall be conducted by the Secretary or such officer or employee as he may designate for the purpose.

(d) The definitions and standards of identity promulgated in accordance with the provisions of this Act shall be effective for the purposes of the enforcement of this Act, notwithstanding such definitions and standards as may be contained in other laws of the United States and regulations promulgated thereunder.

(e)(1) Any action for the issuance, amendment, or repeal of any regulation under section 403(j), 404(a), 406, 501(b), or 502 (d) or (h) of this Act, and any action for the amendment or repeal of any definition and standard of identity under section 401 of this Act for any dairy product (including products regulated under parts 131, 133 and 135 of title 21, Code of Federal Regulations) or maple sirup (regulated under section 168.140 of title 21, Code of Federal Regulations)[70] shall be begun by a proposal made (A) by the Secretary on his own initiative, or (B) by petition of any interested persons, showing reasonable grounds therefor, filed with the Secretary. The Secretary shall publish such proposal and shall afford all interested persons an opportunity to present their views thereon, orally or in writing. As soon as practicable thereafter, the Secretary shall by order act upon such proposal and shall make such order public. Except as provided in paragraph (2), the order shall become effective at such time as may be specified therein, but not prior to the day following the last day on which objections may be filed under such paragraph.

(2) On or before the thirtieth day after the date on which an order entered under paragraph (1) is made public, any person who will be adversely affected by such order if placed in effect may file objections thereto with the Secretary, specifying with particularity the provisions of the order deemed objectionable, stating the grounds

---

70. The probable intent of the Congress is that the reference to maple sirup be struck. Pub. L. No. 103–396, § 3(b), 108 Stat. 4153, 4155 (1994) attempted to amend subsection (e)(1) by striking "or maple syrup (regulated under section 168.140 of ti-tle 21, Code of Federal Regulations).". The amendment cannot be executed because the amendatory instructions referred to "maple syrup" rather than "maple sirup".

therefor, and requesting a public hearing upon such objections. Until final action upon such objections is taken by the Secretary under paragraph (3), the filing of such objections shall operate to stay the effectiveness of those provisions of the order to which the objections are made. As soon as practicable after the time for filing objections has expired the Secretary shall publish a notice in the Federal Register specifying those parts of the order which have been stayed by the filing of objections and, if no objections have been filed, stating that fact.

(3) As soon as practicable after such request for a public hearing, the Secretary, after due notice, shall hold such a public hearing for the purpose of receiving evidence relevant and material to the issues raised by such objections. At the hearing, any interested person may be heard in person or by representative. As soon as practicable after completion of the hearing, the Secretary shall by order act upon such objections and make such order public. Such order shall be based only on substantial evidence of record at such hearing and shall set forth, as part of the order, detailed findings of fact on which the order is based. The Secretary shall specify in the order the date on which it shall take effect, except that it shall not be made to take effect prior to the ninetieth day after its publication unless the Secretary finds that emergency conditions exist necessitating an earlier effective date, in which event the Secretary shall specify in the order his findings as to such conditions.

(f)(1) In a case of actual controversy as to the validity of any order under subsection (e), any person who will be adversely affected by such order if placed in effect may at any time prior to the ninetieth day after such order is issued file a petition with the Circuit Court of Appeals of the United States for the circuit wherein such person resides or has his principal place of business, for a judicial review of such order. A copy of the petition shall be forthwith transmitted by the clerk of the court to the Secretary or other officer designated by him for that purpose. The Secretary thereupon shall file in the court the record of the proceedings on which the Secretary based his order, as provided in section 2112 of title 28, United States Code.

(2) If the petitioner applies to the court for leave to adduce additional evidence, and shows to the satisfaction of the court that such additional evidence is material and that there were reasonable grounds for the failure to adduce such evidence in the proceeding before the Secretary the court may order such additional evidence (and evidence in rebuttal thereof) to be taken before the Secretary, and to be adduced upon the hearing, in such manner and upon such terms and conditions as to the court may seem proper. The Secretary may modify his findings as to the facts, or make new findings, by reason of the additional evidence, so taken, and he shall file such modified or new findings, and his recommendation, if any, for the modification or setting aside of his original order, with the return of such additional evidence.

(3) Upon the filing of the petition referred to in paragraph (1) of this subsection, the court shall have jurisdiction to affirm the order, or to set it aside in whole or in part, temporarily or permanently. If the order of the Secretary refuses to issue, amend, or repeal a regulation and such order is not in accordance with law the court shall by its judgment order the Secretary to take action with respect to such regula-

tion, in accordance with law. The findings of the Secretary as to the facts, if supported by substantial evidence, shall be conclusive.

(4) The judgment of the court affirming or setting aside, in whole or in part, any such order of the Secretary shall be final, subject to review by the Supreme Court of the United States upon certiorari or certification as provided in section 1254 of title 28, United States Code.

(5) Any action instituted under this subsection shall survive notwithstanding any change in the person occupying the office of Secretary or any vacancy in such office.

(6) The remedies provided for in this subsection shall be in addition to and not in substitution for any other remedies provided by law.

(g) A certified copy of the transcript of the record and proceedings under subsection (e) shall be furnished by the Secretary to any interested party at his request, and payment of the costs thereof, and shall be admissible in any criminal libel for condemnation, exclusion of imports, or other proceeding arising under or in respect of this Act, irrespective of whether proceedings with respect to the order have previously been instituted or become final under subsection (f).

(h)(1)(A) The Secretary shall develop guidance documents with public participation and ensure that information identifying the existence of such documents and the documents themselves are made available to the public both in written form and, as feasible, through electronic means. Such documents shall not create or confer any rights for or on any person, although they present the views of the Secretary on matters under the jurisdiction of the Food and Drug Administration.

(B) Although guidance documents shall not be binding on the Secretary, the Secretary shall ensure that employees of the Food and Drug Administration do not deviate from such guidances without appropriate justification and supervisory concurrence. The Secretary shall provide training to employees in how to develop and use guidance documents and shall monitor the development and issuance of such documents.

(C)(i) For guidance documents that set forth initial interpretations of a statute or regulation, changes in interpretation or policy that are of more than a minor nature, complex scientific issues, or highly controversial issues, the Secretary shall ensure public participation prior to implementation of guidance documents, unless the Secretary determines that such prior public participation is not feasible or appropriate. In such cases, the Secretary shall provide for public comment upon implementation and take such comment into account.

(ii) With respect to devices, if a notice to industry guidance letter, a notice to industry advisory letter, or any similar notice sets forth initial interpretations of a regulation or policy or sets forth changes in interpretation or policy, such notice shall be treated as a guidance document for purposes of this subparagraph.

(D) For guidance documents that set forth existing practices or minor changes in policy, the Secretary shall provide for public comment upon implementation.

(2) In developing guidance documents, the Secretary shall ensure uniform nomenclature for such documents and uniform internal procedures for approval of such documents. The Secretary shall ensure that guidance documents and revisions of such documents are properly dated and indicate the nonbinding nature of the documents. The Secretary shall periodically review all guidance documents and, where appropriate, revise such documents.

(3) The Secretary, acting through the Commissioner, shall maintain electronically and update and publish periodically in the Federal Register a list of guidance documents. All such documents shall be made available to the public.

(4) The Secretary shall ensure that an effective appeals mechanism is in place to address complaints that the Food and Drug Administration is not developing and using guidance documents in accordance with this subsection.

(5) Not later than July 1, 2000, the Secretary after evaluating the effectiveness of the Good Guidance Practices document, published in the Federal Register at 62 Fed. Reg. 8961, shall promulgate a regulation consistent with this subsection specifying the policies and procedures of the Food and Drug Administration for the development, issuance, and use of guidance documents.

SEC. 702 [21 U.S.C. 372]. EXAMINATIONS AND INVESTIGATIONS

(a)(1)(A) The Secretary is authorized to conduct examinations and investigations for the purposes of this Act through officers and employees of the Department or through any health, food, or drug officer or employee of any State, Territory, or political subdivision thereof, duly commissioned by the Secretary as an officer of the Department.

(B)(i) For a tobacco product, to the extent feasible, the Secretary shall contract with the States in accordance with this paragraph to carry out inspections of retailers within that State in connection with the enforcement of this Act.

(ii) The Secretary shall not enter into any contract under clause (i) with the government of any of the several States to exercise enforcement authority under this Act on Indian country without the express written consent of the Indian tribe involved.

(2)(A) In addition to the authority established in paragraph (1), the Secretary, pursuant to a memorandum of understanding between the Secretary and the head of another Federal department or agency, is authorized to conduct examinations and investigations for the purposes of this Act through the officers and employees of such other department or agency, subject to subparagraph (B). Such a memorandum shall include provisions to ensure adequate training of such officers and employees to conduct the examinations and investigations. The memorandum of understanding shall contain provisions regarding reimbursement. Such provisions may, at the sole discretion of the head of the other department or agency, require reimbursement, in whole or in part, from the Secretary for the examinations or investigations performed under this section by the officers or employees of the other department or agency.

(B) A memorandum of understanding under subparagraph (A) between the Secretary and another Federal department or agency is effective only in the case of examinations or inspections at facilities or other locations that are jointly regulated by the Secretary and such department or agency.

(C) For any fiscal year in which the Secretary and the head of another Federal department or agency carries out one or more examinations or inspections under a memorandum of understanding under subparagraph (A), the Secretary and the head of such department or agency shall with respect to their respective departments or agencies submit to the committees of jurisdiction (authorizing and appropriating) in the House of Representatives and the Senate a report that provides, for such year—

(i) the number of officers or employees that carried out one or more programs, projects, or activities under such memorandum;

(ii) the number of additional articles that were inspected or examined as a result of such memorandum; and

(iii) the number of additional examinations or investigations that were carried out pursuant to such memorandum.

(3) In the case of food packed in the Commonwealth of Puerto Rico or a Territory the Secretary shall attempt to make inspection of such food at the first point of entry within the United States, when in his opinion and with due regard to the enforcement of all the provisions of this Act, the facilities at his disposal will permit of such inspection.

(4) For the purposes of this subsection the term "United States" means the States and the District of Columbia.

(b) Where a sample of a food, drug, or cosmetic is collected for analysis under this Act the Secretary shall, upon request, provide a part of such official sample for examination or analysis by any person named on the label of the article, or the owner thereof, or his attorney or agent; except that the Secretary is authorized, by regulations, to make such reasonable exceptions from, and impose such reasonable terms and conditions relating to, the operation of this subsection as he finds necessary for the proper administration of the provisions of this Act.

(c) For purposes of enforcement of this Act, records of any department or independent establishment in the executive branch of the Government shall be open to inspection by any official of the Department duly authorized by the Secretary to make such inspection.

(d) The Secretary is authorized and directed, upon request from the Under Secretary of Commerce for Intellectual Property and Director of the United States Patent and Trademark Office, to furnish full and complete information with respect to such questions relating to drugs as the Director may submit concerning any patent application. The Secretary is further authorized, upon receipt of any such request, to conduct or cause to be conducted, such research as may be required.

(e) Any officer or employee of the Department designated by the Secretary to conduct examinations, investigations, or inspections under this Act relating to counterfeit drugs may, when so authorized by the Secretary—

(1) carry firearms;

(2) execute and serve search warrants and arrest warrants;

(3) execute seizure by process issued pursuant to libel under section 304;

(4) make arrests without warrant for offenses under this Act with respect to such drugs if the offense is committed in his presence or, in the case of a felony, if he has probable cause to believe that the person so arrested has committed, or is committing, such offense; and

(5) make, prior to the institution of libel proceedings under section 304(a)(2), seizures of drugs or containers or of equipment, punches, dies, plates, stones, labeling, or other things, if they are, or he has reasonable grounds to believe that they are, subject to seizure and condemnation under such section 304(a)(2). In the event of seizure pursuant to this paragraph (5), libel proceedings under section 304(a)(2) shall be instituted promptly and the property seized be placed under the jurisdiction of the court.

Sec. 703 [21 U.S.C. 373]. Records

(a) In General.—For the purpose of enforcing the provisions of this Act, carriers engaged in interstate commerce, and persons receiving food, drugs, devices, tobacco products, or cosmetics in interstate commerce or holding such articles so received, shall, upon the request of an officer or employee duly designated by the Secretary, permit such officer or employee, at reasonable times, to have access to and to copy all records showing the movement in interstate commerce of any food, drug, device, tobacco product, or cosmetic, or the holding thereof during or after such movement, and the quantity, shipper, and consignee thereof; and it shall be unlawful for any such carrier or person to fail to permit such access to and copying of any such record so requested when such request is accompanied by a statement in writing specifying the nature or kind of food, drug, device, tobacco product, or cosmetic to which such request relates, except that evidence obtained under this section, or any evidence which is directly or indirectly derived from such evidence, shall not be used in a criminal prosecution of the person from whom obtained, and except that carriers shall not be subject to the other provisions of this Act by reason of their receipt, carriage, holding, or delivery of food, drugs, devices, tobacco products, or cosmetics in the usual course of business as carriers, except as provided in subsection (b).

(b) Food Transportation Records.—A shipper, carrier by motor vehicle or rail vehicle, receiver, or other person subject to section 416 shall, on request of an officer or employee designated by the Secretary, permit the officer or employee, at reasonable times, to have access to and to copy all records that the Secretary requires to be kept under section 416(c)(1)(E).

Sec. 704 [21 U.S.C. 374]. Factory Inspection

(a)(1) For purposes of enforcement of this Act, officers or employees duly designated by the Secretary, upon presenting appropriate credentials and a written notice to the owner, operator, or agent in charge, are authorized (A) to enter, at reasonable times, any factory, warehouse, or establishment in which food, drugs, devices, tobacco products, or cosmetics are manufactured, processed, packed, or held, for introduction into interstate commerce or after such introduction, or to enter any vehicle, being used to transport or hold such food, drugs, devices, tobacco products, or cosmetics in interstate commerce; and (B) to inspect, at reasonable times and within reasonable limits and in a reasonable manner, such factory, warehouse, establishment, or vehicle and all pertinent equipment, finished and unfinished materials, containers, and labeling therein. In the case of any person (excluding farms and restaurants) who manufactures, processes, packs, transports, distributes, holds, or imports foods, the inspection shall extend to all records and other information described in section 414, when the standard for records inspection under paragraph (1) or (2) of section 414(a) applies, subject to the limitations established in section 414(d). In the case of any factory, warehouse, establishment, or consulting laboratory in which prescription drugs, nonprescription drugs intended for human use, restricted devices, or tobacco products are manufactured, processed, packed, or held, inspection shall extend to all things therein (including records, files, papers, processes, controls, and facilities) bearing on whether prescription drugs, nonprescription drugs intended for human use, restricted devices, or tobacco products which are adulterated or misbranded within the meaning of this Act, or which may not be manufactured, introduced into interstate commerce, or sold, or offered for sale by reason of any provision of this Act, have been or are being manufactured, processed, packed, transported, or held in any such place, or otherwise bearing on violation of this Act. No inspection authorized by the preceding sentence or by paragraph (3) shall extend to financial data, sales data other than shipment data, pricing data, personnel data (other than data as to qualifications of technical and professional personnel performing functions subject to this Act), and research data (other than data relating to new drugs, antibiotic drugs, devices, and tobacco products and subject to reporting and inspection under regulations lawfully issued pursuant to section 505 (i) or (k), section 519, section 520(g), or chapter IX and data relating to other drugs, devices, or tobacco products which in the case of a new drug would be subject to reporting or inspection under lawful regulations issued pursuant to section 505(j)). A separate notice shall be given for each such inspection, but a notice shall not be required for each entry made during the period covered by the inspection. Each such inspection shall be commenced and completed with reasonable promptness.

(2) The provisions of the third sentence of paragraph (1) shall not apply to—

(A) pharmacies which maintain establishments in conformance with any applicable local laws regulating the practice of pharmacy and medicine and which are regularly engaged in dispensing prescription drugs or devices, upon prescriptions of practitioners licensed to administer such drugs or devices to patients under the care of such practitioners in the course of their professional practice, and which do not, either through a subsidiary or otherwise, manufacture, prepare, propagate, compound, or process drugs or devices for sale other than in the regular course of their business of dispensing or selling drugs or devices at retail;

(B) practitioners licensed by law to prescribe or administer drugs, or prescribe or use devices, as the case may be, and who manufacture, prepare, propagate, compound, or process drugs, or manufacture or process devices solely for use in the course of their professional practice;

(C) persons who manufacture, prepare, propagate, compound, or process drugs, or manufacture or process devices solely for use in research, teaching, or chemical analysis and not for sale;

(D) such other classes of persons as the Secretary may by regulation exempt from the application of this section upon a finding that inspection as applied to such classes of persons in accordance with this section is not necessary for the protection of the public health.

(3) An officer or employee making an inspection under paragraph (1) for purposes of enforcing the requirements of section 412 applicable to infant formulas shall be permitted, at all reasonable times, to have access to and to copy and verify any records—

(A) bearing on whether the infant formula manufactured or held in the facility inspected meets the requirements of section 412, or

(B) required to be maintained under section 412.

(4)(A) Any records or other information that the Secretary may inspect under this section from a person that owns or operates an establishment that is engaged in the manufacture, preparation, propagation, compounding, or processing of a drug shall, upon the request of the Secretary, be provided to the Secretary by such person, in advance of or in lieu of an inspection, within a reasonable timeframe, within reasonable limits, and in a reasonable manner, and in either electronic or physical form, at the expense of such person. The Secretary's request shall include a sufficient description of the records requested.

(B) Upon receipt of the records requested under subparagraph (A), the Secretary shall provide to the person confirmation of receipt.

(C) Nothing in this paragraph supplants the authority of the Secretary to conduct inspections otherwise permitted under this Act in order to ensure compliance with this Act.

(b) Upon completion of any such inspection of a factory, warehouse, consulting laboratory, or other establishment, and prior to leaving the premises, the officer or employee making the inspection shall give to the owner, operator, or agent in charge a report in writing setting forth any conditions or practices observed by him which, in his judgment, indicate that any food, drug, device, tobacco product, or cosmetic

515

in such establishment (1) consists in whole or in part of any filthy, putrid, or decomposed substance, or (2) has been prepared, packed, or held under insanitary conditions whereby it may have become contaminated with filth, or whereby it may have been rendered injurious to health. A copy of such report shall be sent promptly to the Secretary.

(c) If the officer or employee making any such inspection of a factory, warehouse, or other establishment has obtained any sample in the course of the inspection, upon completion of the inspection and prior to leaving the premises he shall give to the owner, operator, or agent in charge a receipt describing the samples obtained.

(d) Whenever in the course of any such inspection of a factory or other establishment where food is manufactured, processed, or packed, the officer or employee making the inspection obtains a sample of any such food, and an analysis is made of such sample for the purpose of ascertaining whether such food consists in whole or in part of any filthy, putrid, or decomposed substance, or is otherwise unfit for food, a copy of the results of such analysis shall be furnished promptly to the owner, operator, or agent in charge.

(e) Every person required under section 519 or 520(g) to maintain records and every person who is in charge or custody of such records shall, upon request of an officer or employee designated by the Secretary, permit such officer or employee at all reasonable times to have access to, and to copy and verify, such records.

(f)(1) An accredited person described in paragraph (3) shall maintain records documenting the training qualifications of the person and the employees of the person, the procedures used by the person for handling confidential information, the compensation arrangements made by the person, and the procedures used by the person to identify and avoid conflicts of interest. Upon the request of an officer or employee designated by the Secretary, the person shall permit the officer or employee, at all reasonable times, to have access to, to copy, and to verify, the records.

(2) Within 15 days after the receipt of a written request from the Secretary an accredited person described in paragraph (3) for copies of records described in paragraph (1), the person shall produce the copies of the records at the place designated by the Secretary.

(3) For purposes of paragraphs (1) and (2), an accredited person described in this paragraph is a person who—

(A) is accredited under subsection (g); or

(B) is accredited under section 523.

(g)(1) The Secretary shall, subject to the provisions of this subsection, accredit persons for the purpose of conducting inspections of establishments that manufacture, prepare, propagate, compound, or process class II or class III devices, which inspections are required under section 510(h) or are inspections of such establishments required to register pursuant to section 510(i).

516

(2) The Secretary shall publish in the Federal Register criteria to accredit or deny accreditation to persons who request to perform the duties specified in paragraph (1). Thereafter, the Secretary shall inform those requesting accreditation, within 60 days after the receipt of such request, whether the request for accreditation is adequate for review, and the Secretary shall promptly act on the request for accreditation. Any resulting accreditation shall state that such person is accredited to conduct inspections at device establishments identified in paragraph (1). The accreditation of such person shall specify the particular activities under this subsection for which such person is accredited.

(3) An accredited person shall, at a minimum, meet the following requirements:

(A) Such person may not be an employee of the Federal Government.

(B) Such person shall be an independent organization which is not owned or controlled by a manufacturer, supplier, or vendor of articles regulated under this Act and which has no organizational, material, or financial affiliation (including a consultative affiliation) with such a manufacturer, supplier, or vendor.

(C) Such person shall be a legally constituted entity permitted to conduct the activities for which it seeks accreditation.

(D) Such person shall not engage in the design, manufacture, promotion, or sale of articles regulated under this Act.

(E) The operations of such person shall be in accordance with generally accepted professional and ethical business practices, and such person shall agree in writing that at a minimum the person will—

(i) certify that reported information accurately reflects data reviewed, inspection observations made, other matters that relate to or may influence compliance with this Act, and recommendations made during an inspection or at an inspection's closing meeting;

(ii) limit work to that for which competence and capacity are available;

(iii) treat information received, records, reports, and recommendations as confidential commercial or financial information or trade secret information, except such information may be made available to the Secretary;

(iv) promptly respond and attempt to resolve complaints regarding its activities for which it is accredited; and

(v) protect against the use, in carrying out paragraph (1), of any officer or employee of the accredited person who has a financial conflict of interest regarding any product regulated under this Act, and annually make available to the public disclosures of the extent to which the accredited person, and the officers and employees of the person, have maintained compliance with requirements under this clause relating to financial conflicts of interest.

(F) Such person shall notify the Secretary of any withdrawal, suspension, restriction, or expiration of certificate of conformance with the quality systems standard referred to in paragraph (7) for any device establishment that such person inspects under this subsection not later than 30 days after such withdrawal, suspension, restriction, or expiration.

(G) Such person may conduct audits to establish conformance with the quality systems standard referred to in paragraph (7).

(4) The Secretary shall publish on the Internet site of the Food and Drug Administration a list of persons who are accredited under paragraph (2). Such list shall be updated to ensure that the identity of each accredited person, and the particular activities for which the person is accredited, is known to the public. The updating of such list shall be no later than one month after the accreditation of a person under this subsection or the suspension or withdrawal of accreditation, or the modification of the particular activities for which the person is accredited.

(5)(A) To ensure that persons accredited under this subsection continue to meet the standards of accreditation, the Secretary shall (i) audit the performance of such persons on a periodic basis through the review of inspection reports and inspections by persons designated by the Secretary to evaluate the compliance status of a device establishment and the performance of accredited persons, and (ii) take such additional measures as the Secretary determines to be appropriate.

(B) The Secretary may withdraw accreditation of any person accredited under paragraph (2), after providing notice and an opportunity for an informal hearing, when such person is substantially not in compliance with the standards of accreditation, poses a threat to public health, fails to act in a manner that is consistent with the purposes of this subsection, or where the Secretary determines that there is a financial conflict of interest in the relationship between the accredited person and the owner or operator of a device establishment that the accredited person has inspected under this subsection. The Secretary may suspend the accreditation of such person during the pendency of the process under the preceding sentence.

(6)(A) Subject to subparagraphs (B) and (C), a device establishment is eligible for inspection by persons accredited under paragraph (2) if the following conditions are met:

(i) The Secretary classified the results of the most recent inspection of the establishment as "no action indicated" or "voluntary action indicated".

(ii) With respect to inspections of the establishment to be conducted by an accredited person, the owner or operator of the establishment submits to the Secretary a notice that—

(I) provides the date of the last inspection of the establishment by the Secretary and the classification of that inspection;

(II) states the intention of the owner or operator to use an accredited person to conduct inspections of the establishment;

(III) identifies the particular accredited person the owner or operator intends to select to conduct such inspections; and

(IV) includes a certification that, with respect to the devices that are manufactured, prepared, propagated, compounded, or processed in the establishment—

(aa) at least 1 of such devices is marketed in the United States; and

(bb) at least 1 of such devices is marketed, or is intended to be marketed, in 1 or more foreign countries, 1 of which countries certifies, accredits, or otherwise recognizes the person accredited under paragraph (2) and identified under subclause (III) as a person authorized to conduct inspections of device establishments.

(B)(i) Except with respect to the requirement of subparagraph (A)(i), a device establishment is deemed to have clearance to participate in the program and to use the accredited person identified in the notice under subparagraph (A)(ii) for inspections of the establishment unless the Secretary, not later than 30 days after receiving such notice, issues a response that—

(I) denies clearance to participate as provided under subparagraph (C); or

(II) makes a request under clause (ii).

(ii) The Secretary may request from the owner or operator of a device establishment in response to the notice under subparagraph (A)(ii) with respect to the establishment, or from the particular accredited person identified in such notice—

(I) compliance data for the establishment in accordance with clause (iii)(I); or

(II) information concerning the relationship between the owner or operator of the establishment and the accredited person identified in such notice in accordance with clause (iii)(II).

The owner or operator of the establishment, or such accredited person, as the case may be, shall respond to such a request not later than 60 days after receiving such request.

(iii)(I) The compliance data to be submitted by the owner or operator of a device establishment in response to a request under clause (ii)(I) are data describing whether the quality controls of the establishment have been sufficient for ensuring consistent compliance with current good manufacturing practice within the meaning of section 501(h) and with other applicable provisions of this Act. Such data shall include complete reports of inspectional findings regarding good manufacturing practice or other quality control audits that, during the preceding 2–year period, were conducted at the establishment by persons other than the owner or operator of the establishment, together with all other compliance data the Secretary deems necessary. Data under the preceding sentence shall demonstrate to the Secretary whether the establishment has facilitated consistent compliance by promptly correcting any compliance problems identified in such inspections.

(II) A request to an accredited person under clause (ii)(II) may not seek any information that is not required to be maintained by such person in records under subsection (f)(1).

(iv) A device establishment is deemed to have clearance to participate in the program and to use the accredited person identified in the notice under subparagraph (A)(ii) for inspections of the establishment unless the Secretary, not later than 60 days after receiving the information requested under clause (ii), issues a response that denies clearance to participate as provided under subparagraph (C).

(C)(i) The Secretary may deny clearance to a device establishment if the Secretary has evidence that the certification under subparagraph (A)(ii)(IV) is untrue and the Secretary provides to the owner or operator of the establishment a statement summarizing such evidence.

(ii) The Secretary may deny clearance to a device establishment if the Secretary determines that the establishment has failed to demonstrate consistent compliance for purposes of subparagraph (B)(iii)(I) and the Secretary provides to the owner or operator of the establishment a statement of the reasons for such determination.

(iii)(I) The Secretary may reject the selection of the accredited person identified in the notice under subparagraph (A)(ii) if the Secretary provides to the owner or operator of the establishment a statement of the reasons for such rejection. Reasons for the rejection may include that the establishment or the accredited person, as the case may be, has failed to fully respond to the request, or that the Secretary has concerns regarding the relationship between the establishment and such accredited person.

(II) If the Secretary rejects the selection of an accredited person by the owner or operator of a device establishment, the owner or operator may make an additional selection of an accredited person by submitting to the Secretary a notice that identifies the additional selection. Clauses (i) and (ii) of subparagraph (B), and subclause (I) of this clause, apply to the selection of an accredited person through a notice under the preceding sentence in the same manner and to the same extent as such provisions apply to a selection of an accredited person through a notice under subparagraph (A)(ii).

(iv) In the case of a device establishment that is denied clearance under clause (i) or (ii) or with respect to which the selection of the accredited person is rejected under clause (iii), the Secretary shall designate a person to review the statement of reasons, or statement summarizing such evidence, as the case may be, of the Secretary under such clause if, during the 30–day period beginning on the date on which the owner or operator of the establishment receives such statement, the owner or operator requests the review. The review shall commence not later than 30 days after the owner or operator requests the review, unless the Secretary and the owner or operator otherwise agree.

(7)(A) Persons accredited under paragraph (2) to conduct inspections shall record in writing their inspection observations and shall present the observations to the device establishment's designated representative and describe each observation. Additionally, such accredited person shall prepare an inspection report in a form and manner designated by the Secretary to conduct inspections, taking into consideration the goals of international harmonization of quality systems standards. Any official classification of the inspection shall be determined by the Secretary.

(B) At a minimum, an inspection report under subparagraph (A) shall identify the persons responsible for good manufacturing practice compliance at the inspected device establishment, the dates of the inspection, the scope of the inspection, and shall describe in detail each observation identified by the accredited person, identify other matters that relate to or may influence compliance with this Act, and describe any recommendations during the inspection or at the inspection's closing meeting.

(C) An inspection report under subparagraph (A) shall be sent to the Secretary and to the designated representative of the inspected device establishment at the same time, but under no circumstances later than three weeks after the last day of the inspection. The report to the Secretary shall be accompanied by all written inspection observations previously provided to the designated representative of the establishment.

(D) Any statement or representation made by an employee or agent of a device establishment to a person accredited under paragraph (2) to conduct inspections shall be subject to section 1001 of title 18, United States Code.

(E) If at any time during an inspection by an accredited person the accredited person discovers a condition that could cause or contribute to an unreasonable risk to the public health, the accredited person shall immediately notify the Secretary of the identification of the device establishment subject to inspection and such condition.

(F) For the purpose of setting risk-based inspectional priorities, the Secretary shall accept voluntary submissions of reports of audits assessing conformance with appropriate quality systems standards set by the International Organization for Standardization (ISO) and identified by the Secretary in public notice. If the owner or operator of an establishment elects to submit audit reports under this subparagraph, the owner or operator shall submit all such audit reports with respect to the establishment during the preceding 2–year periods.

(8) Compensation for an accredited person shall be determined by agreement between the accredited person and the person who engages the services of the accredited person, and shall be paid by the person who engages such services.

(9) Nothing in this subsection affects the authority of the Secretary to inspect any device establishment pursuant to this Act.

(10)(A) For fiscal year 2005 and each subsequent fiscal year, no device establishment may be inspected during the fiscal year involved by a person accredited under paragraph (2) if—

(i) of the amounts appropriated for salaries and expenses of the Food and Drug Administration for the preceding fiscal year (referred to in this subparagraph as the "first prior fiscal year"), the amount obligated by the Secretary for inspections of device establishments by the Secretary was less than the adjusted base amount applicable to such first prior fiscal year; and

(ii) of the amounts appropriated for salaries and expenses of the Food and Drug Administration for the fiscal year preceding the first prior fiscal year (referred to in this subparagraph as the "second prior fiscal year"), the amount obligated by the Secretary for inspections of device establishments by the Secretary was less than the adjusted base amount applicable to such second prior fiscal year.

(B)(i) Subject to clause (ii), the Comptroller General of the United States shall determine the amount that was obligated by the Secretary for fiscal year 2002 for compliance activities of the Food and Drug Administration with respect to devices (referred to in this subparagraph as the "compliance budget"), and of such amount, the amount that was obligated for inspections by the Secretary of device establishments (referred to in this subparagraph as the "inspection budget").

(ii) For purposes of determinations under clause (i), the Comptroller General shall not include in the compliance budget or the inspection budget any amounts obligated for inspections of device establishments conducted as part of the process of reviewing applications under section 515.

(iii) Not later than March 31, 2003, the Comptroller General shall complete the determinations required in this subparagraph and submit to the Secretary and the Congress a report describing the findings made through such determinations.

(C) For purposes of this paragraph:

(i) The term "base amount" means the inspection budget determined under subparagraph (B) for fiscal year 2002.

(ii) The term "adjusted base amount", in the case of applicability to fiscal year 2003, means an amount equal to the base amount increased by 5 percent.

(iii) The term "adjusted base amount", with respect to applicability to fiscal year 2004 or any subsequent fiscal year, means the adjusted base amount applicable to the preceding year increased by 5 percent.

(11) The authority provided by this subsection terminates on October 1, 2017.

(12) No later than four years after the enactment of this subsection[71] the Comptroller General shall report to the Committee on Energy and Commerce of the House of Representatives and the Committee on Health, Education, Labor and Pensions of the Senate—

(A) the number of inspections conducted by accredited persons pursuant to this subsection and the number of inspections conducted by Federal employees

71. Subsection (g) was added by Pub. L. No. 107–250, § 201(a), 116 Stat. 1588, 1602–09 (2002).

pursuant to section 510(h) and of device establishments required to register under section 510(i);

(B) the number of persons who sought accreditation under this subsection, as well as the number of persons who were accredited under this subsection;

(C) the reasons why persons who sought accreditation, but were denied accreditation, were denied;

(D) the number of audits conducted by the Secretary of accredited persons, the quality of inspections conducted by accredited persons, whether accredited persons are meeting their obligations under this Act, and whether the number of audits conducted is sufficient to permit these assessments;

(E) whether this subsection is achieving the goal of ensuring more information about device establishment compliance is being presented to the Secretary, and whether that information is of a quality consistent with information obtained by the Secretary pursuant to inspections conducted by Federal employees;

(F) whether this subsection is advancing efforts to allow device establishments to rely upon third-party inspections for purposes of compliance with the laws of foreign governments; and

(G) whether the Congress should continue, modify, or terminate the program under this subsection.

(13) The Secretary shall include in the annual report required under section 1003(g) the names of all accredited persons and the particular activities under this subsection for which each such person is accredited and the name of each accredited person whose accreditation has been withdrawn during the year.

(14) Notwithstanding any provision of this subsection, this subsection does not have any legal effect on any agreement described in section 803(b) between the Secretary and a foreign country.

SEC. 705 [21 U.S.C. 375]. PUBLICITY

(a) The Secretary shall cause to be published from time to time reports summarizing all judgments, decrees, and court orders which have been rendered under this Act, including the nature of the charge and the disposition thereof.

(b) The Secretary may also cause to be disseminated information regarding food, drugs, devices, tobacco products, or cosmetics in situations involving, in the opinion of the Secretary, imminent danger to health, or gross deception of the consumer. Nothing in this section shall be construed to prohibit the Secretary from collecting, reporting, and illustrating the results of the investigations of the Department.

SEC. 706 [21 U.S.C. 376]. SEAFOOD INSPECTION

The Secretary, upon application of any packer of any seafood for shipment or sale within the jurisdiction of this Act, may, at his discretion, designate inspectors to examine and inspect such food and the production, packing, and labeling thereof. If on such examination and inspection compliance is found with the provisions of this Act and regulations promulgated thereunder, the applicant shall be authorized or required to mark the food as provided by regulation to show such compliance. Services under this section shall be rendered only upon payment by the applicant of fees fixed by regulation in such amounts as may be necessary to provide, equip, and maintain an adequate and efficient inspection service. Receipts from such fees shall be covered into the Treasury and shall be available to the Secretary for expenditures incurred in carrying out the purposes of this section, including expenditures for salaries of additional inspectors when necessary to supplement the number of inspectors for whose salaries Congress has appropriated. The Secretary is hereby authorized to promulgate regulations governing the sanitary and other conditions under which the service herein provided shall be granted and maintained and for otherwise carrying out the purposes of this section. Any person who forges, counterfeits, simulates, or falsely represents, or without proper authority uses any mark, stamp, tag, label, or other identification devices authorized or required by the provisions of this section or regulations thereunder, shall be guilty of a misdemeanor, and shall on conviction thereof be subject to imprisonment for not more than one year or a fine of not less than $1,000 nor more than $5,000 or both such imprisonment and fine.

SEC. 707 [21 U.S.C. 378]. ADVERTISING OF CERTAIN FOODS

(a)(1) Except as provided in subsection (c), before the Secretary may initiate any action under chapter III—

(A) with respect to any food which the Secretary determines is misbranded under section 403(a)(2) because of its advertising, or

(B) with respect to a food's advertising which the Secretary determines causes the food to be so misbranded,

the Secretary shall, in accordance with paragraph (2), notify in writing the Federal Trade Commission of the action the Secretary proposes to take respecting such food or advertising.

(2) The notice required by paragraph (1) shall—

(A) contain (i) a description of the action the Secretary proposes to take and of the advertising which the Secretary has determined causes a food to be misbranded, (ii) a statement of the reasons for the Secretary's determination that such advertising has caused such food to be misbranded, and

(B) be accompanied by the records, documents, and other written materials which the Secretary determines supports his determination that such food is misbranded because of such advertising.

(b)(1) If the Secretary notifies the Federal Trade Commission under subsection (a) of action proposed to be taken under chapter III with respect to a food or food advertising and the Commission notifies the Secretary in writing, within the 30–day period beginning on the date of the receipt of such notice, that—

(A) it has initiated under the Federal Trade Commission Act an investigation of such advertising to determine if it is prohibited by such Act or any order or rule under such Act,

(B) it has commenced (or intends to commence) a civil action under section 5, 13, or 19 with respect to such advertising or the Attorney General has commenced (or intends to commence) a civil action under section 5 with respect to such advertising,

(C) it has issued and served (or intends to issue and serve) a complaint under section 5(b) of such Act respecting such advertising, or

(D) pursuant to section 16(b) of such Act it has made a certification to the Attorney General respecting such advertising,

the Secretary may not, except as provided by paragraph (2), initiate the action described in the Secretary's notice to the Federal Trade Commission.

(2) If, before the expiration of the 60–day period beginning on the date the Secretary receives a notice described in paragraph (1) from the Federal Trade Commission in response to a notice of the Secretary under subsection (a)—

(A) the Commission or the Attorney General does not commence a civil action described in subparagraph (B) of paragraph (1) of this subsection respecting the advertising described in the Secretary's notice,

(B) the Commission does not issue and serve a complaint described in subparagraph (C) of such paragraph respecting such advertising, or

(C) the Commission does not (as described in subparagraph (D) of such paragraph) make a certification to the Attorney General respecting such advertising, or, if the Commission does make such a certification to the Attorney General respecting such advertising, the Attorney General, before the expiration of such period, does not cause appropriate criminal proceedings to be brought against such advertising,

the Secretary may, after the expiration of such period, initiate the action described in the notice to the Commission pursuant to subsection (a). The Commission shall promptly notify the Secretary of the commencement by the Commission of such a civil action, the issuance and service by it of such a complaint, or the causing by the Attorney General of criminal proceedings to be brought against such advertising.

(c) The requirements of subsections (a) and (b) do not apply with respect to action under chapter III with respect to any food or food advertising if the Secretary determines that such action is required to eliminate an imminent hazard to health.

(d) For the purpose of avoiding unnecessary duplication, the Secretary shall coordinate any action taken under chapter III because of advertising which the Secretary determines causes a food to be misbranded with any action of the Federal Trade Commission under the Federal Trade Commission Act with respect to such advertising.

SEC. 708 [21 U.S.C. 379]. CONFIDENTIAL INFORMATION

(a) CONTRACTORS.—The Secretary may provide any information which is exempt from disclosure pursuant to subsection (a) of section 552 of title 5, United States Code, by reason of subsection (b)(4) of such section to a person other than an officer or employee of the Department if the Secretary determines such other person requires the information in connection with an activity which is undertaken under contract with the Secretary, which relates to the administration of this Act, and with respect to which the Secretary (or an officer or employee of the Department) is not prohibited from using such information. The Secretary shall require as a condition to the provision of information under this section that the person receiving it take such security precautions respecting the information as the Secretary may by regulation prescribe.

(b) ABILITY TO RECEIVE AND PROTECT CONFIDENTIAL INFORMATION OBTAINED FROM FOREIGN GOVERNMENTS.—

(1) IN GENERAL.—The Secretary shall not be required to disclose under section 552 of title 5, United States Code (commonly referred to as the "Freedom of Information Act"), or any other provision of law, any information relating to drugs obtained from a foreign government agency, if—

(A) the information concerns the inspection of a facility, is part of an investigation, alerts the United States to the potential need for an investigation, or concerns a drug that has a reasonable probability of causing serious adverse health consequences or death to humans or animals;

(B) the information is provided or made available to the United States Government voluntarily on the condition that it not be released to the public; and

(C) the information is covered by, and subject to, a written agreement between the Secretary and the foreign government.

(2) TIME LIMITATIONS.—The written agreement described in paragraph (1)(C) shall specify the time period for which paragraph (1) shall apply to the voluntarily disclosed information. Paragraph (1) shall not apply with respect to such information after the date specified in such agreement, but all other applicable legal protections, including the provisions of section 552 of title 5, United States Code, and section 319L(e)(1) of the Public Health Service Act, as applicable, shall continue to apply to such information. If no date is specified in the written agreement, paragraph (1) shall not apply with respect to such information for a period of more than 36 months.

(3) DISCLOSURES NOT AFFECTED.—Nothing in this section authorizes any official to withhold, or to authorize the with-holding of, information from Congress or

information required to be disclosed pursuant to an order of a court of the United States.

(4) RELATION TO OTHER LAW.—For purposes of section 552 of title 5, United States Code, this subsection shall be considered a statute described in subsection (b)(3)(B) of such section 552.

(c) AUTHORITY TO ENTER INTO MEMORANDA OF UNDERSTANDING FOR PURPOSES OF INFORMATION EXCHANGE.—The Secretary may enter into written agreements to provide information referenced in section 301(j) to foreign governments subject to the following criteria:

(1) CERTIFICATION.—The Secretary may enter into a written agreement to provide information under this subsection to a foreign government only if the Secretary has certified such government as having the authority and demonstrated ability to protect trade secret information from disclosure. Responsibility for this certification shall not be delegated to any officer or employee other than the Commissioner of Food and Drugs.

(2) WRITTEN AGREEMENT.—The written agreement to provide information to the foreign government under this sub-section shall include a commitment by the foreign government to protect information exchanged under this subsection from disclosure unless and until the sponsor gives written permission for disclosure or the Secretary makes a declaration of a public health emergency pursuant to section 319 of the Public Health Service Act that is relevant to the information.

(3) INFORMATION EXCHANGE.—The Secretary may provide to a foreign government that has been certified under paragraph (1) and that has executed a written agreement under paragraph (2) information referenced in section 301(j) in only the following circumstances:

(A) Information concerning the inspection of a facility may be provided to a foreign government if—

(i) the Secretary reasonably believes, or the written agreement described in paragraph (2) establishes, that the government has authority to otherwise obtain such information; and

(ii) the written agreement executed under paragraph (2) limits the recipient's use of the information to the recipient's civil regulatory purposes.

(B) Information not described in subparagraph (A) may be provided as part of an investigation, or to alert the foreign government to the potential need for an investigation, if the Secretary has reasonable grounds to believe that a drug has a reasonable probability of causing serious adverse health consequences or death to humans or animals.

(4) EFFECT OF SUBSECTION.—Nothing in this subsection affects the ability of the Secretary to enter into any written agreement authorized by other provisions of law to share confidential information.

Sec. 709 [21 U.S.C. 379a]. PRESUMPTION

In any action to enforce the requirements of this Act respecting a device, food, drug, tobacco product, or cosmetic the connection with interstate commerce required for jurisdiction in such action shall be presumed to exist.

Sec. 710 [21 U.S.C. 379b]. CONSOLIDATED ADMINISTRATIVE AND LABORATORY FACILITY

(a) AUTHORITY.—The Secretary, in consultation with the Administrator of the General Services Administration, shall enter into contracts for the design, construction, and operation of a consolidated Food and Drug Administration administrative and laboratory facility.

(b) AWARDING OF CONTRACT.—The Secretary shall solicit contract proposals under subsection (a) from interested parties. In awarding contracts under such subsection, the Secretary shall review such proposals and give priority to those alternatives that are the most cost effective for the Federal Government and that allow for the use of donated land, federally owned property, or lease-purchase arrangements. A contract under this subsection shall not be entered into unless such contract results in a net cost savings to the Federal Government over the duration of the contract, as compared to the Government purchase price including borrowing by the Secretary of the Treasury.

(c) DONATIONS.—In carrying out this section, the Secretary shall have the power, in connection with real property, buildings, and facilities, to accept on behalf of the Food and Drug Administration gifts or donations of services or property, real or personal, as the Secretary determines to be necessary.

(d) AUTHORIZATION OF APPROPRIATIONS.—There are authorized to be appropriated to carry out this section $100,000,000 for fiscal year 1991, and such sums as may be necessary for each of the subsequent fiscal years, to remain available until expended.

Sec. 711 [21 U.S.C. 379d]. AUTOMATION OF FOOD AND DRUG ADMINISTRATION

(a) IN GENERAL.—The Secretary, acting through the Commissioner of Food and Drugs, shall automate appropriate activities of the Food and Drug Administration to ensure timely review of activities regulated under this Act.

(b) AUTHORIZATION OF APPROPRIATIONS.—There are authorized to be appropriated each fiscal year such sums as are necessary to carry out this section.

Sec. 712 [21 U.S.C. 379d–1]. CONFLICTS OF INTEREST

(a) DEFINITIONS.—For purposes of this section:

(1) ADVISORY COMMITTEE.—The term "advisory committee" means an advisory committee under the Federal Advisory Committee Act that provides advice or recommendations to the Secretary regarding activities of the Food and Drug Administration.

(2) FINANCIAL INTEREST.—The term "financial interest" means a financial interest under section 208(a) of title 18, United States Code.

(b) RECRUITMENT FOR ADVISORY COMMITTEES.—

(1) IN GENERAL.—The Secretary shall—

(A) develop and implement strategies on effective out-reach to potential members of advisory committees at universities, colleges, other academic research centers, professional and medical societies, and patient and consumer groups;

(B) seek input from professional medical and scientific societies to determine the most effective informational and recruitment activities;

(C) at least every 180 days, request referrals for potential members of advisory committees from a variety of stakeholders, including—

(i) product developers, patient groups, and disease advocacy organizations; and

(ii) relevant—

(I) professional societies;

(II) medical societies;

(III) academic organizations; and

(IV) governmental organizations; and

(D) in carrying out subparagraphs (A) and (B), take into account the levels of activity (including the numbers of annual meetings) and the numbers of vacancies of the advisory committees.

(2) RECRUITMENT ACTIVITIES.—The recruitment activities under paragraph (1) may include—

(A) advertising the process for becoming an advisory committee member at medical and scientific society conferences;

(B) making widely available, including by using existing electronic communications channels, the contact information for the Food and Drug Administration point of contact regarding advisory committee nominations; and

(C) developing a method through which an entity receiving funding from the National Institutes of Health, the Agency for Healthcare Research and Quality, the Centers for Disease Control and Prevention, or the Veterans Health Administration can identify a person whom the Food and Drug Administration can contact regarding the nomination of individuals to serve on advisory committees.

(3) EXPERTISE.—In carrying out this subsection, the Secretary shall seek to ensure that the Secretary has access to the most current expert advice.

(c) DISCLOSURE OF DETERMINATIONS AND CERTIFICATIONS.—Notwithstanding section 107(a)(2) of the Ethics in Government Act of 1978, the following shall apply:

(1) 15 OR MORE DAYS IN ADVANCE.—As soon as practicable, but (except as provided in paragraph (2)) not later than 15 days prior to a meeting of an advisory committee to which a written determination as referred to in section 208(b)(1) of title 18, United States Code, or a written certification as referred to in section 208(b)(3) of such title, applies, the Secretary shall disclose (other than information exempted from disclosure under section 552 or section 552a of title 5, United States Code (popularly known as the Freedom of Information Act and the Privacy Act of 1974, respectively)) on the Internet Web site of the Food and Drug Administration—

(A) the type, nature, and magnitude of the financial interests of the advisory committee member to which such determination or certification applies; and

(B) the reasons of the Secretary for such determination or certification, including, as appropriate, the public health interest in having the expertise of the member with respect to the particular matter before the advisory committee.

(2) LESS THAN 30 DAYS IN ADVANCE.—In the case of a financial interest that becomes known to the Secretary less than 30 days prior to a meeting of an advisory committee to which a written determination as referred to in section 208(b)(1) of title 18, United States Code, or a written certification as referred to in section 208(b)(3) of such title applies, the Secretary shall disclose (other than information exempted from disclosure under section 552 or 552a of title 5, United States Code) on the Internet Web site of the Food and Drug Administration, the information described in subparagraphs (A) and (B) of paragraph (1) as soon as practicable after the Secretary makes such determination or certification, but in no case later than the date of such meeting.

(d) PUBLIC RECORD.—The Secretary shall ensure that the public record and transcript of each meeting of an advisory committee includes the disclosure required under subsection (c) (other than information exempted from disclosure under section 552 of title 5, United States Code, and section 552a of title 5, United States Code).

(e) ANNUAL REPORT.—

(1) IN GENERAL.—Not later than February 1 of each year, the Secretary shall submit to the Committee on Appropriations and the Committee on Health, Education, Labor, and Pensions of the Senate, and the Committee on Appropriations and the Committee on Energy and Commerce of the House of Representatives, a report that describes—

(A) with respect to the fiscal year that ended on September 30 of the previous year, the number of persons nominated for participation at meetings for each advisory committee, the number of persons so nominated, and willing to serve, the number of vacancies on each advisory committee, and the number of persons contacted for service as members on each advisory committee meeting for each advisory committee who did not participate because of the potential for such participation to constitute a disqualifying financial interest under section 208 of title 18, United States Code;

(B) with respect to such year, the number of persons contacted for services as members for each advisory committee meeting for each advisory committee who did not participate because of reasons other than the potential for such participation to constitute a disqualifying financial interest under section 208 of title 18, United States Code;

(C) with respect to such year, the number of members attending meetings for each advisory committee; and

(D) with respect to such year, the aggregate number of disclosures required under subsection (d) and the percentage of individuals to whom such disclosures did not apply who served on such committee.

(2) PUBLIC AVAILABILITY.—Not later than 30 days after submitting any report under paragraph (1) to the committees specified in such paragraph, the Secretary shall make each such report available to the public.

(f) PERIODIC REVIEW OF GUIDANCE.—Not less than once every 5 years, the Secretary shall—

(1) review guidance of the Food and Drug Administration with respect to advisory committees regarding disclosure of conflicts of interest and the application of section 208 of title 18, United States Code; and

(2) update such guidance as necessary to ensure that the Food and Drug Administration receives appropriate access to needed scientific expertise, with due consideration of the requirements of such section 208.

(g) GUIDANCE ON REPORTED DISCLOSED FINANCIAL INTEREST OR INVOLVEMENT.—The Secretary shall issue guidance that describes how the Secretary reviews the financial interests and involvement of advisory committee members that are disclosed under subsection (c) but that the Secretary determines not to meet the definition of a disqualifying interest under section 208 of title 18, United States Code for the purposes of participating in a particular matter.

SEC. 713 [21 U.S.C. 379d–2]. POLICY ON THE REVIEW AND CLEARANCE OF SCIENTIFIC ARTICLES PUBLISHED BY FDA EMPLOYEES

(a) DEFINITION.—In this section, the term "article" means a paper, poster, abstract, book, book chapter, or other published writing.

(b) POLICIES.—The Secretary, through the Commissioner of Food and Drugs, shall establish and make publicly available clear written policies to implement this section and govern the timely submission, review, clearance, and disclaimer requirements for articles.

(c) TIMING OF SUBMISSION FOR REVIEW.—If an officer or employee, including a Staff Fellow and a contractor who performs staff work, of the Food and Drug Administration is directed by the policies established under subsection (b) to submit an article to the supervisor of such officer or employee, or to some other official of the Food and Drug Administration, for review and clearance before such officer or employee may seek to publish or present such an article at a conference, such officer or employee shall submit such article for such review and clearance not less than 30 days before submitting the article for publication or presentation.

(d) TIMING FOR REVIEW AND CLEARANCE.—The supervisor or other reviewing official shall review such article and provide written clearance, or written clearance on the condition of specified changes being made, to such officer or employee not later than 30 days after such officer or employee submitted such article for review.

(e) NON–TIMELY REVIEW.—If, 31 days after such submission under subsection (c), the supervisor or other reviewing official has not cleared or has not reviewed such article and provided written clearance, such officer or employee may consider such article not to have been cleared and may submit the article for publication or presentation with an appropriate disclaimer as specified in the policies established under subsection (b).

(f) EFFECT.—Nothing in this section shall be construed as affecting any restrictions on such publication or presentation provided by other provisions of law.

SEC. 714 [21 U.S.C. 379d–3]. STREAMLINED HIRING AUTHORITY TO SUPPORT ACTIVITIES RELATED TO THE PROCESS FOR THE REVIEW OF DEVICE APPLICATIONS

(a) IN GENERAL.—In addition to any other personnel authorities under other provisions of law, the Secretary may, without regard to the provisions of title 5, United States Code, governing appointments in the competitive service, appoint employees to positions in the Food and Drug Administration to perform, administer, or support activities described in subsection (b), if the Secretary determines that such appointments are needed to achieve the objectives specified in subsection (c).

(b) ACTIVITIES DESCRIBED.—The activities described in this subsection are—

(1) activities under this Act related to the process for the review of device applications (as defined in section 737(8)); and

(2) activities under this Act related to human generic drug activities (as defined in section 744A).

(c) OBJECTIVES SPECIFIED.—The objectives specified in this subsection are—

(1) with respect to the activities under subsection (b)(1), the goals referred to in section 738A(a)(1); and

(2) with respect to the activities under subsection (b)(2), the goals referred to in section 744C(a).

(d) INTERNAL CONTROLS.—The Secretary shall institute appropriate internal controls for appointments under this section.

(e) SUNSET.—The authority to appoint employees under this section shall terminate on the date that is 3 years after the date of enactment of this section.

SEC. 715 [21 U.S.C. 379d–4]. REPORTING REQUIREMENTS

(a) GENERIC DRUGS.—Beginning with fiscal year 2013 and ending after fiscal year 2017, not later than 120 days after the end of each fiscal year for which fees are collected under part 7 of subchapter C, the Secretary shall prepare and submit to the Committee on Health, Education, Labor, and Pensions of the Senate and the Committee on Energy and Commerce of the House of Representatives a report concerning, for all applications for approval of a generic drug under section 505(j), amendments to such applications, and prior approval supplements with respect to such applications filed in the previous fiscal year—

(1) the number of such applications that met the goals identified for purposes of part 7 of subchapter C, in the letters from the Secretary of Health and Human Services to the Chairman of the Committee on Health, Education, Labor, and Pensions of the Senate and the Chairman of the Committee on Energy and Commerce of the House of Representatives, as set forth in the Congressional Record;

(2) the average total time to decision by the Secretary for applications for approval of a generic drug under section 505(j), amendments to such applications, and prior approval supplements with respect to such applications filed in the previous fiscal year, including the number of calendar days spent during the review by the Food and Drug Administration and the number of calendar days spent by the sponsor responding to a complete response letter;

(3) the total number of applications under section 505(j), amendments to such applications, and prior approval supplements with respect to such applications that were pending with the Secretary for more than 10 months on the date of enactment of the Food and Drug Administration Safety and Innovation Act;[72] and

(4) the number of applications described in paragraph (3) on which the Food and Drug Administration took final regulatory action in the previous fiscal year.

(b) BIOSIMILAR BIOLOGICAL PRODUCTS.—

(1) IN GENERAL.—Beginning with fiscal year 2014, not later than 120 days after the end of each fiscal year for which fees are collected under part 8 of subchapter C, the Secretary shall prepare and submit to the Committee on Health, Education, Labor, and Pensions of the Senate and the Committee on Energy and Commerce of the House of Representatives a report concerning—

---

72. Pub. L. No. 112–144, 126 Stat. 993, which was enacted July 9, 2012.

(A) the number of applications for approval filed under section 351(k) of the Public Health Service Act; and

(B) the percentage of applications described in subparagraph (A) that were approved by the Secretary.

(2) ADDITIONAL INFORMATION.—As part of the performance report described in paragraph (1), the Secretary shall include an explanation of how the Food and Drug Administration is managing the biological product review program to ensure that the user fees collected under part 2 are not used to review an application under section 351(k) of the Public Health Service Act.

SUBCHAPTER B—COLORS

SEC. 721 [21 U.S.C. 379e]. LISTING AND CERTIFICATION OF COLOR ADDITIVES FOR FOODS, DRUGS, AND COSMETICS

When Color Additives Deemed Unsafe

(a) A color additive shall, with respect to any particular use (for which it is being used or intended to be used or is represented as suitable) in or on food or drugs or devices or cosmetics be deemed unsafe for the purposes of the application of section 402(c), section 501(a)(4), or section 601(e), as the case may be unless—

(1)(A) there is in effect, and such additive and such use are in conformity with, a regulation issued under subsection (b) of this section listing such additive for such use, including any provision of such regulation prescribing the conditions under which such additive may be safely used, and (B) such additive either (i) is from a batch certified, in accordance with regulations issued pursuant to subsection (c), for such use, or (ii) has, with respect to such use, been exempted by the Secretary from the requirement of certification; or

(2) such additive and such use thereof conform to the terms of an exemption which is in effect pursuant to subsection (f) of this section.

While there are in effect regulations under subsections (b) and (c) of this section relating to a color additive or an exemption pursuant to subsection (f) with respect to such additive, an article shall not, by reason of bearing or containing such additive in all respects in accordance with such regulations or such exemption, be considered adulterated within the meaning of clause (1) of section 402(a) if such article is a food, or within the meaning of section 601(a) if such article is a cosmetic other than a hair dye (as defined in the last sentence of section 601(a)). A color additive for use in or on a device shall be subject to this section only if the color additive comes in direct contact with the body of man or other animals for a significant period of time. The Secretary may by regulation designate the uses of color additives in or on devices which are subject to this section.

Listing of Colors

(b)(1) The Secretary shall, by regulation, provide for separately listing color additives for use in or on food, color additives for use in or on drugs or devices, and color additives for use in or on cosmetics, if and to the extent that such additives are suitable and safe for any such use when employed in accordance with such regulations.

(2)(A) Such regulations may list any color additive for use generally in or on food, or in or on drugs or devices, or in or on cosmetics, if the Secretary finds that such additive is suitable and may safely be employed for such general use.

(B) If the data before the Secretary do not establish that the additive satisfies the requirements for listing such additive on the applicable list pursuant to subparagraph (A) of this paragraph, or if the proposal is for listing such additive for a more limited use or uses, such regulations may list such additive only for any more limited use or uses for which it is suitable and may safely be employed.

(3) Such regulations shall, to the extent deemed necessary by the Secretary to assure the safety of the use or uses for which a particular color additive is listed, prescribe the conditions under which such additive may be safely employed for such use or uses (including, but not limited to, specifications, hereafter in this section referred to as tolerance limitations, as to the maximum quantity or quantities which may be used or permitted to remain in or on the article or articles in or on which it is used; specifications as to the manner in which such additive may be added to or used in or on such article or articles; and directions or other labeling or packaging requirements for such additive).

(4) The Secretary shall not list a color additive under this section for a proposed use unless the data before him establish that such use, under the conditions of use specified in the regulations, will be safe: Provided, however, That a color additive shall be deemed to be suitable and safe for the purpose of listing under this subsection for use generally in or on food, while there is in effect a published finding of the Secretary declaring such substance exempt from the term "food additive" because of its being generally recognized by qualified experts as safe for its intended use, as provided in section 201(s).

(5)(A) In determining, for the purposes of this section, whether a proposed use of a color additive is safe, the Secretary shall consider, among other relevant factors—

(i) the probable consumption of, or other relevant exposure from, the additive and of any substance formed in or on food, drugs or devices, or cosmetics because of the use of the additive;

(ii) the cumulative effect, if any, of such additive in the diet of man or animals, taking into account the same or any chemically or pharmacologically related substance or substances in such diet;

(iii) safety factors which, in the opinion of experts qualified by scientific training and experience to evaluate the safety of color additives for the use or uses for which the additive is proposed to be listed, are generally recognized as appropriate for the use of animal experimentation data; and

(iv) the availability of any needed practicable methods of analysis for determining the identity and quantity of (I) the pure dye and all intermediates and other impurities contained in such color additive, (II) such additive in or on any article of food, drug or devices, or cosmetic, and (III) any substance formed in or on such article because of the use of such additive.

(B) A color additive (i) shall be deemed unsafe, and shall not be listed, for any use which will or may result in ingestion of all or part of such additive, if the additive is found by the Secretary to induce cancer when ingested by man or animal, or if it is found by the Secretary, after tests which are appropriate for the evaluation of the safety of additives for use in food, to induce cancer in man or animal, and (ii) shall be deemed unsafe, and shall not be listed, for any use which will not result in ingestion of any part of such additive, if, after tests which are appropriate for the evaluation of the safety of additives for such use, or after other relevant exposure of man or animal to such additive, it is found by the Secretary to induce cancer in man or animal: Provided, That clause (i) of this subparagraph (B) shall not apply with respect to the use of a color additive as an ingredient of feed for animals which are raised for food production, if the Secretary finds that, under the conditions of use and feeding specified in proposed labeling and reasonably certain to be followed in practice, such additive will not adversely affect the animals for which such feed is intended, and that no residue of the additive will be found (by methods of examination prescribed or approved by the Secretary by regulations, which regulations shall not be subject to subsection (d)) in any edible portion of such animals after slaughter or in any food yielded by or derived from the living animal.

(C)(i) In any proceeding for the issuance, amendment, or repeal of a regulation listing a color additive, whether commenced by a proposal of the Secretary on his own initiative or by a proposal contained in a petition, the petitioner, or any other person who will be adversely affected by such proposal or by the Secretary's order issued in accordance with paragraph (1) of section 701(e) if placed in effect, may request, within the time specified in this subparagraph, that the petition or order thereon, or the Secretary's proposal, be referred to an advisory committee for a report and recommendations with respect to any matter arising under subparagraph (B) of this paragraph, which is involved in such proposal or order and which requires the exercise of scientific judgment. Upon such request, or if the Secretary within such time deems such a referral necessary, the Secretary shall forthwith appoint an advisory committee under subparagraph (D) of this paragraph and shall refer to it, together with all the data before him, such matter arising under subparagraph (B) for study thereof and for a report and recommendations on such matter. A person who has filed a petition or who has requested the referral of a matter to an advisory committee pursuant to this subparagraph (C), as well as representatives of the Department, shall have the right to consult with such advisory committee in connection with the matter referred to it. The request for referral under this subparagraph, or the Secretary's referral on his own initiative, may be made at any time before, or within thirty days after, publication of an order of the Secretary acting upon the petition or proposal.

(ii) Within sixty days after the date of such referral, or within an additional thirty days if the committee deems such additional time necessary, the committee shall, after independent study of the data furnished to it by the Secretary and other data before it, certify to the Secretary a report and recommendations, together with all underlying data and a statement of the reasons or basis for the recommendations. A copy of the foregoing shall be promptly supplied by the Secretary to any person who has filed a petition, or who has requested such referral to the advisory committee. Within thirty days after such certification, and after giving due consideration to all data then before him, including such report, recommendation, underlying data, and statement, and to any prior order issued by him in connection with such matter, the Secretary shall by order confirm or modify any order therefore issued or, if no such prior order has been issued, shall by order act upon the petition or other proposal.

(iii) Where—

(I) by reason of subparagraph (B) of this paragraph, the Secretary has initiated a proposal to remove from listing a color additive previously listed pursuant to this section; and

(II) a request has been made for referral of such proposal to an advisory committee;

the Secretary may not act by order on such proposal until the advisory committee has made a report and recommendations to him under clause (ii) of this subparagraph and he has considered such recommendations, unless the Secretary finds that emergency conditions exist necessitating the issuance of an order notwithstanding this clause.

(D) The advisory committee referred to in subparagraph (C) of this paragraph shall be composed of experts selected by the National Academy of Sciences, qualified in the subject matter referred to the committee and of adequately diversified professional background, except that in the event of the inability or refusal of the National Academy of Sciences to act, the Secretary shall select the members of the committee. The size of the committee shall be determined by the Secretary. Members of any advisory committee established under this Act, while attending conferences or meetings of their committees or otherwise serving at the request of the Secretary, shall be entitled to receive compensation at rates to be fixed by the Secretary but at rates not exceeding the daily equivalent of the rate specified at the time of such service for grade GS–18 of the General Schedule, including travel time; and while away from their homes or regular places of business they may be allowed travel expenses, including per diem in lieu of subsistence, as authorized by section 5703 of title 5 of the United States Code for persons in the Government service employed intermittently. The members shall not be subject to any other provisions of law regarding the appointment and compensation of employees of the United States. The Secretary shall furnish the committee with adequate clerical and other assistance, and shall by rules and regulations prescribe the procedure to be followed by the committee.

(6) The Secretary shall not list a color additive under this subsection for a proposed use if the data before him show that such proposed use would promote deception of the consumer in violation of this Act or would otherwise result in misbranding or adulteration within the meaning of this Act.

(7) If, in the judgment of the Secretary, a tolerance limitation is required in order to assure that a proposed use of a color additive will be safe, the Secretary—

(A) shall not list the additive for such use if he finds that the data before him do not establish that such additive, if used within a safe tolerance limitation, would achieve the intended physical or other technical effect; and

(B) shall not fix such tolerance limitation at a level higher than he finds to be reasonably required to accomplish the intended physical or other technical effect.

(8) If, having regard to the aggregate quantity of color additive likely to be consumed in the diet or to be applied to the human body, the Secretary finds that the data before him fail to show that it would be safe and otherwise permissible to list a color additive (or pharmacologically related color additives) of all uses proposed therefor and at the levels of concentration proposed, the Secretary shall, in determining for which use or uses such additive (or such related additives) shall be or remain listed, or how the aggregate allowable safe tolerance for such additive or additives shall be allocated by him among the uses under consideration, take into account, among other relevant factors (and subject to the paramount criterion of safety), (A) the relative marketability of the articles involved as affected by the proposed uses of the color additive (or of such related additives) in or on such articles, and the relative dependence of the industries concerned on such uses; (B) the relative aggregate amounts of such color additive which he estimates would be consumed in the diet or applied to the human body by reason of the various uses and levels of concentration proposed; and (C) the availability, if any, of other color additives suitable and safe for one or more of the uses proposed.

Certification of Colors

(c) The Secretary shall further, by regulation, provide (1) for the certification, with safe diluents or without diluents, of batches of color additives listed pursuant to subsection (b) and conforming to the requirements for such additives established by regulations under such subsection and this subsection, and (2) for exemption from the requirement of certification in the case of any such additive, or any listing or use thereof, for which he finds such requirement not to be necessary in the interest of the protection of the public health: Provided, That, with respect to any use in or on food for which a listed color additive is deemed to be safe by reason of the proviso to paragraph (4) of subsection (b), the requirement of certification shall be deemed not to be necessary in the interest of public health protection.

Procedure for Issuance, Amendment, or Repeal of Regulations

(d) The provisions of section 701 (e), (f), and (g) of this Act shall, subject to the provisions of subparagraph (C) of subsection (b)(5) of this section, apply to and in all respects govern proceedings for the issuance, amendment, or repeal of regulations under subsection (b) or (c) of this section (including judicial review of the Secretary's action in such proceedings) and the admissibility of transcripts of the record of such proceedings in other proceedings, except that—

(1) if the proceeding is commenced by the filing of a petition, notice of the proposal made by the petition shall be published in general terms by the Secretary within thirty days after such filing, and the Secretary's order (required by paragraph (1) of section 701(e)) acting upon such proposal shall, in the absence of prior referral (or request for referral) to an advisory committee, be issued within ninety days after the date of such filing, except that the Secretary may (prior to such ninetieth day) by written notice to the petitioner, extend such ninety-day period to such time (not more than one hundred and eighty days after the date of filing of the petition) as the Secretary deems necessary to enable him to study and investigate the petition;

(2) any report, recommendations, underlying data, and reasons certified to the Secretary by an advisory committee appointed pursuant to subparagraph (D) of subsection (b)(5) of this section, shall be made a part of the record of any hearing if relevant and material, subject to the provisions of section 7(c) of the Administrative Procedure Act (5 U.S.C., sec. 1006(c)).[73] The advisory committee shall designate a member to appear and testify at any such hearing with respect to the report and recommendations of such committee upon request of the Secretary, the petitioner, or the officer conducting the hearing, but this shall not preclude any other member of the advisory committee from appearing and testifying at such hearing;

(3) the Secretary's order after public hearing (acting upon objections filed to an order made prior to hearings) shall be subject to the requirements of section 409(f)(2); and

(4) the scope of judicial review of such order shall be in accordance with the fourth sentence of paragraph (2), and with the provisions of paragraph (3), of section 409(g).

Fees

(e) The admitting to listing and certification of color additives, in accordance with regulations prescribed under this Act, shall be performed only upon payment of such fees, which shall be specified in such regulations, as may be necessary to provide, maintain, and equip an adequate service for such purposes.

Exemptions

(f) The Secretary shall by regulations (issued without regard to subsection (d)) provide for exempting from the requirements of this section any color additive or

---

73. Section 7(c) of the Administrative Procedure Act has been superseded by section 556(d) of title 5, United States Code. See Pub. L. No. 89–554, § 8, 80 Stat. 378, 653 (1966).

any specific type of use thereof, and any article of food, drug or device, or cosmetic bearing or containing such additive, intended solely for investigational use by qualified experts when in his opinion such exemption is consistent with the public health.

NOTE.—Section 201 of the Labor–Federal Security Appropriation Act, 1944 (21 U.S.C. 377), provides that the Secretary in carrying into effect this Act "is authorized to cooperate with associations and scientific societies in the revision of the United States Pharmacopeia and in the development of methods of analysis and mechanical and physical tests necessary to carry out the work of the Food and Drug Administration."

SUBCHAPTER C—FEES

PART 1—FREEDOM OF INFORMATION FEES

SEC. 731 [21 U.S.C. 379f]. RECOVERY AND RETENTION OF FEES FOR FREEDOM OF INFORMATION REQUESTS

(a) IN GENERAL.—The Secretary, acting through the Commissioner of Food and Drugs, may—

(1) set and charge fees, in accordance with section 552(a)(4)(A) of title 5, United States Code, to recover all reasonable costs incurred in processing requests made under section 552 of title 5, United States Code, for records obtained or created under this Act or any other Federal law for which responsibility for administration has been delegated to the Commissioner by the Secretary;

(2) retain all fees charged for such requests; and

(3) establish an accounting system and procedures to control receipts and expenditures of fees received under this section.

(b) USE OF FEES.—The Secretary and the Commissioner of Food and Drugs shall not use fees received under this section for any purpose other than funding the processing of requests described in subsection (a)(1). Such fees shall not be used to reduce the amount of funds made to carry out other provisions of this Act.

(c) WAIVER OF FEES.—Nothing in this section shall supersede the right of a requester to obtain a waiver of fees pursuant to section 552(a)(4)(A) of title 5, United States Code.

PART 2—FEES RELATING TO DRUGS[74]

SEC. 735 [21 U.S.C. 379g]. DEFINITIONS

For purposes of this part:

(1) The term "human drug application" means an application for—

(A) approval of a new drug submitted under section 505(b), or

(B) licensure of a biological product under subsection (a) of section 351 of the Public Health Service Act.

Such term does not include a supplement to such an application, does not include an application with respect to whole blood or a blood component for transfusion, does not include an application with respect to a bovine blood product for topical application licensed before September 1, 1992, an allergenic extract product, or an in vitro diagnostic biologic product licensed under section 351 of the Public Health Service Act, does not include an application with respect to a large volume parenteral drug product approved before September 1, 1992, does not include an application for a licensure of a biological product for further manufacturing use only, and does not include an application or supplement submitted by a State or Federal Government entity for a drug that is not distributed commercially. Such term does include an application for licensure, as described in subparagraph (B), of a large volume biological product intended for single dose injection for intravenous use or infusion.

(2) The term "supplement" means a request to the Secretary to approve a change in a human drug application which has been approved.

(3) The term "prescription drug product" means a specific strength or potency of a drug in final dosage form—

(A) for which a human drug application has been approved,

(B) which may be dispensed only under prescription pursuant to section 503(b), and

(C) which is on the list of products described in section 505(j)(7)(A) (not including the discontinued section of such list) or is on a list created and maintained by the Secretary of products approved under human drug applications under section 351 of the Public Health Service Act (not including the discontinued section of such list).

Such term does not include whole blood or a blood component for transfusion, does not include a bovine blood product for topical application licensed before September 1, 1992, an allergenic extract product, or an in vitro diagnostic biologic product

---

74. Part 2 was amended by Pub. L. No. 112–144, tit. I, 126 Stat. 993, 996–1001 (2012). Sections 105(a) and (b) of that title provides as follows:

SEC. 105. SUNSET DATES.

(a) Authorization.—Sections 735 and 736 of the Federal Food, Drug, and Cosmetic Act (21 U.S.C.

379g; 379h) shall cease to be effective October 1, 2017.

(b) Reporting Requirements.—Section 736B of the Federal Food, Drug, and Cosmetic Act (21 U.S.C. 379h–2) shall cease to be effective January 31, 2018.

licensed under section 351 of the Public Health Service Act. Such term does not include a biological product that is licensed for further manufacturing use only, and does not include a drug that is not distributed commercially and is the subject of an application or supplement submitted by a State or Federal Government entity. Such term does include a large volume biological product intended for single dose injection for intravenous use or infusion.

(4) The term "final dosage form" means, with respect to a prescription drug product, a finished dosage form which is approved for administration to a patient without substantial further manufacturing (such as capsules, tablets, or lyophilized products before reconstitution).

(5) The term "prescription drug establishment" means a foreign or domestic place of business which is at one general physical location consisting of one or more buildings all of which are within five miles of each other and at which one or more prescription drug products are manufactured in final dosage form. For purposes of this paragraph, the term "manufactured" does not include packaging.

(6) The term "process for the review of human drug applications" means the following activities of the Secretary with respect to the review of human drug applications and supplements:

(A) The activities necessary for the review of human drug applications and supplements.

(B) The issuance of action letters which approve human drug applications or which set forth in detail the specific deficiencies in such applications and, where appropriate, the actions necessary to place such applications in condition for approval.

(C) The inspection of prescription drug establishments and other facilities undertaken as part of the Secretary's review of pending human drug applications and supplements.

(D) Activities necessary for the review of applications for licensure of establishments subject to section 351 of the Public Health Service Act and for the release of lots of biologics under such section.

(E) Monitoring of research conducted in connection with the review of human drug applications.

(F) Postmarket safety activities with respect to drugs approved under human drug applications or supplements, including the following activities:

(i) Collecting, developing, and reviewing safety information on approved drugs, including adverse event reports.

(ii) Developing and using improved adverse-event data-collection systems, including information technology systems.

(iii) Developing and using improved analytical tools to assess potential safety problems, including access to external data bases.

542

(iv) Implementing and enforcing section 505(*o*) (relating to postapproval studies and clinical trials and labeling changes) and section 505(p) (relating to risk evaluation and mitigation strategies).

(v) Carrying out section 505(k)(5) (relating to adverse event reports and postmarket safety activities).

(7) The term "costs of resources allocated for the process for the review of human drug applications" means the expenses in connection with the process for the review of human drug applications for—

(A) officers and employees of the Food and Drug Administration, contractors of the Food and Drug Administration, advisory committees, and costs related to such officers, employees, and committees and to contracts with such contractors,

(B) management of information, and the acquisition, maintenance, and repair of computer resources,

(C) leasing, maintenance, renovation, and repair of facilities and acquisition, maintenance, and repair of fixtures, furniture, scientific equipment, and other necessary materials and supplies, and

(D) collecting fees under section 736 and accounting for resources allocated for the review of human drug applications and supplements.

(8) The term "adjustment factor" applicable to a fiscal year is the Consumer Price Index for all urban consumers (all items; United States city average) for October of the preceding fiscal year divided by such Index for October 1996.

(9) The term "person" includes an affiliate thereof.

(10) The term "active", with respect to a commercial investigational new drug application, means such an application to which information was submitted during the relevant period.

(11) The term "affiliate" means a business entity that has a relationship with a second business entity if, directly or indirectly—

(A) one business entity controls, or has the power to control, the other business entity; or

(B) a third party controls, or has power to control, both of the business entities.

SEC. 736 [21 U.S.C. 379h]. AUTHORITY TO ASSESS AND USE DRUG FEES

(a) TYPES OF FEES.—Beginning in fiscal year 2013, the Secretary shall assess and collect fees in accordance with this section as follows:

(1) HUMAN DRUG APPLICATION AND SUPPLEMENT FEE.—

(A) IN GENERAL.—Each person that submits, on or after September 1, 1992, a human drug application or a supplement shall be subject to a fee as follows:

(i) A fee established under subsection (c)(4) for a human drug application for which clinical data (other than bioavailability or bioequivalence studies) with respect to safety or effectiveness are required for approval.

(ii) A fee established under subsection (c)(4) for a human drug application for which clinical data with respect to safety or effectiveness are not required or a supplement for which clinical data (other than bioavailability or bioequivalence studies) with respect to safety or effectiveness are required. Such fee shall be half of the amount of the fee established under clause (i).

(B) PAYMENT.—The fee required by subparagraph (A) shall be due upon submission of the application or supplement.

(C) EXCEPTION FOR PREVIOUSLY FILED APPLICATION OR SUPPLEMENT.—If a human drug application or supplement was submitted by a person that paid the fee for such application or supplement, was accepted for filing, and was not approved or was withdrawn (without a waiver), the submission of a human drug application or a supplement for the same product by the same person (or the person's licensee, assignee, or successor) shall not be subject to a fee under subparagraph (A).

(D) REFUND OF FEE IF APPLICATION REFUSED FOR FILING OR WITHDRAWN BEFORE FILING.—The Secretary shall refund 75 percent of the fee paid under subparagraph (B) for any application or supplement which is refused for filing or withdrawn without a waiver before filing.

(E) FEES FOR APPLICATIONS PREVIOUSLY REFUSED FOR FILING OR WITHDRAWN BEFORE FILING.—A human drug application or supplement that was submitted but was refused for filing, or was withdrawn before being accepted or refused for filing, shall be subject to the full fee under subparagraph (A) upon being resubmitted or filed over protest, unless the fee is waived or reduced under subsection (d).

(F) EXCEPTION FOR DESIGNATED ORPHAN DRUG OR INDICATION.—A human drug application for a prescription drug product that has been designated as a drug for a rare disease or condition pursuant to section 526 shall not be subject to a fee under subparagraph (A), unless the human drug application includes an indication for other than a rare disease or condition. A supplement proposing to include a new indication for a rare disease or condition in a human drug application shall not be subject to a fee under subparagraph (A), if the drug has been designated pursuant to section 526 as a drug for a rare disease or condition with regard to the indication proposed in such supplement.

(G) REFUND OF FEE IF APPLICATION WITHDRAWN.—If an application or supplement is withdrawn after the application or supplement was filed, the Secretary may refund the fee or a portion of the fee if no substantial work was performed on the application or supplement after the application or supplement was filed.

The Secretary shall have the sole discretion to refund a fee or a portion of the fee under this subparagraph. A determination by the Secretary concerning a refund under this paragraph shall not be reviewable.

(2) PRESCRIPTION DRUG ESTABLISHMENT FEE.—

(A) IN GENERAL.—Except as provided in subparagraphs (B) and (C), each person that—

(i) is named as the applicant in a human drug application; and

(ii) after September 1, 1992, had pending before the Secretary a human drug application or supplement,

shall be assessed an annual fee established under subsection (c)(4) for each prescription drug establishment listed in its approved human drug application as an establishment that manufactures the prescription drug product named in the application. The annual establishment fee shall be assessed in each fiscal year in which the prescription drug product named in the application is assessed a fee under paragraph (3) unless the prescription drug establishment listed in the application does not engage in the manufacture of the prescription drug product during the fiscal year. The establishment fee shall be due on the later of the first business day on or after October 1 of each fiscal year or the first business day after the enactment of an appropriations Act providing for the collection and obligation of fees for such fiscal year under this section. Each such establishment shall be assessed only one fee per establishment, notwithstanding the number of prescription drug products manufactured at the establishment. In the event an establishment is listed in a human drug application by more than one applicant, the establishment fee for the fiscal year shall be divided equally and assessed among the applicants whose prescription drug products are manufactured by the establishment during the fiscal year and assessed product fees under paragraph (3).

(B) EXCEPTION.—If, during the fiscal year, an applicant initiates or causes to be initiated the manufacture of a prescription drug product at an establishment listed in its human drug application—

(i) that did not manufacture the product in the previous fiscal year; and

(ii) for which the full establishment fee has been assessed in the fiscal year at a time before manufacture of the prescription drug product was begun;

the applicant will not be assessed a share of the establishment fee for the fiscal year in which the manufacture of the product began.

(C) SPECIAL RULES FOR POSITRON EMISSION TOMOGRAPHY DRUGS.—

(i) IN GENERAL.—Except as provided in clause (ii), each person who is named as the applicant in an approved human drug application for a positron emission tomography drug shall be subject under subparagraph

(A) to one-sixth of an annual establishment fee with respect to each such establishment identified in the application as producing positron emission tomography drugs under the approved application.

(ii) EXCEPTION FROM ANNUAL ESTABLISHMENT FEE.—Each person who is named as the applicant in an application described in clause (i) shall not be assessed an annual establishment fee for a fiscal year if the person certifies to the Secretary, at a time specified by the Secretary and using procedures specified by the Secretary, that—

(I) the person is a not-for-profit medical center that has only 1 establishment for the production of positron emission tomography drugs; and

(II) at least 95 percent of the total number of doses of each positron emission tomography drug produced by such establishment during such fiscal year will be used within the medical center.

(iii) DEFINITION.—For purposes of this subparagraph, the term "positron emission tomography drug" has the meaning given to the term "compounded positron emission tomography drug" in section 201(ii), except that paragraph (1)(B) of such section shall not apply.

(3) PRESCRIPTION DRUG PRODUCT FEE.—

(A) IN GENERAL.—Except as provided in subparagraph (B), each person who is named as the applicant in a human drug application, and who, after September 1, 1992, had pending before the Secretary a human drug application or supplement, shall pay for each such prescription drug product the annual fee established under subsection (c)(4). Such fee shall be due on the later of the first business day on or after October 1 of each fiscal year or the first business day after the enactment of an appropriations Act providing for the collection and obligation of fees for such fiscal year under this section. Such fee shall be paid only once for each product for a fiscal year in which the fee is payable.

(B) EXCEPTION.—A prescription drug product shall not be assessed a fee under subparagraph (A) if such product is—

(i) identified on the list compiled under section 505(j)(7) with a potency described in terms of per 100 mL;

(ii) the same product as another product that—

(I) was approved under an application filed under section 505(b) or 505(j); and

(II) is not in the list of discontinued products compiled under section 505(j)(7);

(iii) the same product as another product that was approved under an abbreviated application filed under section 507[75] (as in effect on the day before the date of enactment of the Food and Drug Administration Modernization Act of 1997); or

(iv) the same product as another product that was approved under an abbreviated new drug application pursuant to regulations in effect prior to the implementation of the Drug Price Competition and Patent Term Restoration Act of 1984.

(b) FEE REVENUE AMOUNTS.—

(1) IN GENERAL.—For each of the fiscal years 2013 through 2017, fees under subsection (a) shall, except as provided in subsections (c), (d), (f), and (g), be established to generate a total revenue amount under such subsection that is equal to the sum of—

(A) $693,099,000; and

(B) the dollar amount equal to the inflation adjustment for fiscal year 2013 (as determined under paragraph (3)(A)); and

(C) the dollar amount equal to the workload adjustment for fiscal year 2013 (as determined under paragraph (3)(B)).

(2) TYPES OF FEES.—Of the total revenue amount determined for a fiscal year under paragraph (1)—

(A) one-third shall be derived from fees under subsection (a)(1) (relating to human drug applications and supplements);

(B) one-third shall be derived from fees under subsection (a)(2) (relating to prescription drug establishments); and

(C) one-third shall be derived from fees under subsection (a)(3) (relating to prescription drug products).

(3) FISCAL YEAR 2013 INFLATION AND WORKLOAD ADJUSTMENTS.—For purposes of paragraph (1), the dollar amount of the inflation and workload adjustments for fiscal year 2013 shall be determined as follows:

(A) INFLATION ADJUSTMENT.—The inflation adjustment for fiscal year 2013 shall be the sum of—

(i) $652,709,000 multiplied by the result of an inflation adjustment calculation determined using the methodology described in subsection (c)(1)(B); and

(ii) $652,709,000 multiplied by the result of an inflation adjustment calculation determined using the methodology described in subsection (c)(1)(C).

75. Section 507 was repealed by Pub. L. No. 105–115, § 125(b)(1), 111 Stat. 2296, 2325 (1997).

(B) WORKLOAD ADJUSTMENT.—Subject to subparagraph (C), the workload adjustment for fiscal 2013 shall be—

(i) $652,709,000 plus the amount of the inflation adjustment calculated under subparagraph (A); multiplied by

(ii) the amount (if any) by which a percentage workload adjustment for fiscal year 2013, as determined using the methodology described in subsection (c)(2)(A), would exceed the percentage workload adjustment (as so determined) for fiscal year 2012, if both such adjustment percentages were calculated using the 5–year base period consisting of fiscal years 2003 through 2007.

(C) LIMITATION.—Under no circumstances shall the adjustment under subparagraph (B) result in fee revenues for fiscal year 2013 that are less than the sum of the amount under paragraph (1)(A) and the amount under paragraph (1)(B).

(c) ADJUSTMENTS.—

(1) INFLATION ADJUSTMENT.—For fiscal year 2014 and subsequent fiscal years, the revenues established in subsection (b) shall be adjusted by the Secretary by notice, published in the Federal Register, for a fiscal year by the amount equal to the sum of—

(A) one;

(B) the average annual percent change in the cost, per full-time equivalent position of the Food and Drug Administration, of all personnel compensation and benefits paid with respect to such positions for the first 3 years of the preceding 4 fiscal years, multiplied by the proportion of personnel compensation and benefits costs to total costs of the process for the review of human drug applications (as defined in section 735(6)) for the first 3 years of the preceding 4 fiscal years, and

(C) the average annual percent change that occurred in the Consumer Price Index for urban customers (Washington–Baltimore, DC–MD–VA–WV; Not Seasonally Adjusted; All items; Annual Index) for the first 3 years of the preceding 4 years of available data multiplied by the proportion of all costs other than personnel compensation and benefits costs to total costs of the process for the review of human drug applications (as defined in section 735(6)) for the first 3 years of the preceding 4 fiscal years.

The adjustment made each fiscal year under this paragraph shall be added on a compounded basis to the sum of all adjustments made each fiscal year after fiscal year 2013 under this paragraph.

(2) WORKLOAD ADJUSTMENT.—For fiscal year 2014 and subsequent fiscal years, after the fee revenues established in subsection (b) are adjusted for a fiscal year for inflation in accordance with paragraph (1), the fee revenues shall be adjusted further for such fiscal year to reflect changes in the workload of the Secretary

for the process for the review of human drug applications. With respect to such adjustment:

(A) The adjustment shall be determined by the Secretary based on a weighted average of the change in the total number of human drug applications (adjusted for changes in review activities, as described in the notice that the Secretary is required to publish in the Federal Register under this subparagraph), efficacy supplements, and manufacturing supplements submitted to the Secretary, and the change in the total number of active commercial investigational new drug applications (adjusted for changes in review activities, as so described) during the most recent 12–month period for which data on such submissions is available. The Secretary shall publish in the Federal Register the fee revenues and fees resulting from the adjustment and the supporting methodologies.

(B) Under no circumstances shall the adjustment result in fee revenues for a fiscal year that are less than the sum of the amount under subsection (b)(1)(A) and the amount under subsection (b)(1)(B), as adjusted for inflation under paragraph (1).

(C) The Secretary shall contract with an independent accounting or consulting firm to periodically review the adequacy of the adjustment and publish the results of those reviews. The first review shall be conducted and published by the end of fiscal year 2013 (to examine the performance of the adjustment since fiscal year 2009), and the second review shall be conducted and published by the end of fiscal year 2015 (to examine the continued performance of the adjustment). The reports shall evaluate whether the adjustment reasonably represents actual changes in workload volume and complexity and present options to discontinue, retain, or modify any elements of the adjustment. The reports shall be published for public comment. After review of the reports and receipt of public comments, the Secretary shall, if warranted, adopt appropriate changes to the methodology. If the Secretary adopts changes to the methodology based on the first report, the changes shall be effective for the first fiscal year for which fees are set after the Secretary adopts such changes and each subsequent fiscal year.

(3) FINAL YEAR ADJUSTMENT.—For fiscal year 2017, the Secretary may, in addition to adjustments under this paragraph and paragraphs (1) and (2), further increase the fee revenues and fees established in subsection (b) if such an adjustment is necessary to provide for not more than 3 months of operating reserves of carryover user fees for the process for the review of human drug applications for the first 3 months of fiscal year 2018. If such an adjustment is necessary, the rationale for the amount of the increase shall be contained in the annual notice establishing fee revenues and fees for fiscal year 2017. If the Secretary has carryover balances for such process in excess of 3 months of such operating reserves, the adjustment under this paragraph shall not be made.

(4) Annual fee setting.—The Secretary shall, not later than 60 days before the start of each fiscal year that begins after September 30, 2012, establish, for the next fiscal year, application, product, and establishment fees under subsection (a), based on the revenue amounts established under subsection (b) and the adjustments provided under this subsection.

(5) Limit.—The total amount of fees charged, as adjusted under this subsection, for a fiscal year may not exceed the total costs for such fiscal year for the resources allocated for the process for the review of human drug applications.

(d) Fee Waiver or Reduction.—

(1) In general.—The Secretary shall grant to a person who is named as the applicant in a human drug application a waiver from or a reduction of one or more fees assessed to that person under subsection (a) where the Secretary finds that—

(A) such waiver or reduction is necessary to protect the public health,

(B) the assessment of the fee would present a significant barrier to innovation because of limited resources available to such person or other circumstances,

(C) the fees to be paid by such person will exceed the anticipated present and future costs incurred by the Secretary in conducting the process for the review of human drug applications for such person, or

(D) the applicant involved is a small business submitting its first human drug application to the Secretary for review.

(2) Considerations.—In determining whether to grant a waiver or reduction of a fee under paragraph (1), the Secretary shall consider only the circumstances and assets of the applicant involved and any affiliate of the applicant.

(3) Use of standard costs.—In making the finding in paragraph (1)(C), the Secretary may use standard costs.

(4) Rules relating to small businesses.—

(A) Definition.—In paragraph (1)(D), the term "small business" means an entity that has fewer than 500 employees, including employees of affiliates, and that does not have a drug product that has been approved under a human drug application and introduced or delivered for introduction into interstate commerce.

(B) Waiver of application fee.—The Secretary shall waive under paragraph (1)(D) the application fee for the first human drug application that a small business or its affiliate submits to the Secretary for review. After a small business or its affiliate is granted such a waiver, the small business or its affiliate shall pay—

(i) application fees for all subsequent human drug applications submitted to the Secretary for review in the same manner as an entity that does not qualify as a small business; and

(ii) all supplement fees for all supplements to human drug applications submitted to the Secretary for review in the same manner as an entity that does not qualify as a small business.

(e) EFFECT OF FAILURE TO PAY FEES.—A human drug application or supplement submitted by a person subject to fees under subsection (a) shall be considered incomplete and shall not be accepted for filing by the Secretary until all fees owed by such person have been paid.

(f) LIMITATIONS.—

(1) IN GENERAL.—Fees under subsection (a) shall be refunded for a fiscal year beginning after fiscal year 1997 unless appropriations for salaries and expenses of the Food and Drug Administration for such fiscal year (excluding the amount of fees appropriated for such fiscal year) are equal to or greater than the amount of appropriations for the salaries and expenses of the Food and Drug Administration for the fiscal year 1997 (excluding the amount of fees appropriated for such fiscal year) multiplied by the adjustment factor applicable to the fiscal year involved.

(2) AUTHORITY.—If the Secretary does not assess fees under subsection (a) during any portion of a fiscal year because of paragraph (1) and if at a later date in such fiscal year the Secretary may assess such fees, the Secretary may assess and collect such fees, without any modification in the rate, for human drug applications and supplements, prescription drug establishments, and prescription drug products at any time in such fiscal year notwithstanding the provisions of subsection (a) relating to the date fees are to be paid.

(g) CREDITING AND AVAILABILITY OF FEES.—

(1) IN GENERAL.—Subject to paragraph (2)(C), fees authorized under subsection (a) shall be collected and available for obligation only to the extent and in the amount provided in advance in appropriations Acts. Such fees are authorized to remain available until expended. Such sums as may be necessary may be transferred from the Food and Drug Administration salaries and expenses appropriation account without fiscal year limitation to such appropriation account for salaries and expenses with such fiscal year limitation. The sums transferred shall be available solely for the process for the review of human drug applications.

(2) COLLECTIONS AND APPROPRIATION ACTS.—

(A) IN GENERAL.—The fees authorized by this section—

(i) subject to subparagraph (C), shall be collected and available in each fiscal year in an amount not to exceed the amount specified in appropriation Acts, or otherwise made available for obligation, for such fiscal year, and

(ii) shall be available to defray increases in the costs of the resources allocated for the process for the review of human drug applications (including increases in such costs for an additional number of full-time equivalent positions in the Department of Health and Human Services to be engaged in such process) over such costs, excluding costs paid from fees collected under this section, for fiscal year 1997 multiplied by the adjustment factor.

(B) COMPLIANCE.—The Secretary shall be considered to have met the requirements of subparagraph (A)(ii) in any fiscal year if the costs funded by appropriations and allocated for the process for the review of human drug applications—

(i) are not more than 3 percent below the level specified in subparagraph (A)(ii); or

(ii)(I) are more than 3 percent below the level specified in subparagraph (A)(ii), and fees assessed for the fiscal year following the subsequent fiscal year are decreased by the amount in excess of 3 percent by which such costs fell below the level specified in such subparagraph; and

(II) such costs are not more than 5 percent below the level specified in such subparagraph.

(C) PROVISION FOR EARLY PAYMENTS.—Payment of fees authorized under this section for a fiscal year, prior to the due date for such fees, may be accepted by the Secretary in accordance with authority provided in advance in a prior year appropriations Act.

(3) AUTHORIZATION OF APPROPRIATIONS.—For each of the fiscal years 2013 through 2017, there is authorized to be appropriated for fees under this section an amount equal to the total revenue amount determined under subsection (b) for the fiscal year, as adjusted or otherwise affected under subsection (c) and paragraph (4) of this subsection.

(4) OFFSET.—If the sum of the cumulative amount of fees collected under this section for the fiscal years 2013 through 2015 and the amount of fees estimated to be collected under this section for fiscal year 2016 exceeds the cumulative amount appropriated under paragraph (3) for the fiscal years 2013 through 2016, the excess shall be credited to the appropriation account of the Food and Drug Administration as provided in paragraph (1), and shall be subtracted from the amount of fees that would otherwise be authorized to be collected under this section pursuant to appropriation Acts for fiscal year 2017.

(h) COLLECTION OF UNPAID FEES.—In any case where the Secretary does not receive payment of a fee assessed under subsection (a) within 30 days after it is due, such fee shall be treated as a claim of the United States Government subject to subchapter II of chapter 37 of title 31, United States Code.

(i) WRITTEN REQUESTS FOR WAIVERS, REDUCTIONS, AND REFUNDS.—To qualify for consideration for a waiver or reduction under subsection (d), or for a refund of any fee collected in accordance with subsection (a), a person shall submit to the Secretary a written request for such waiver, reduction, or refund not later than 180 days after such fee is due.

(j) CONSTRUCTION.—This section may not be construed to require that the number of full-time equivalent positions in the Department of Health and Human Services, for officers, employers, and advisory committees not engaged in the process of the review of human drug applications, be reduced to offset the number of officers, employees, and advisory committees so engaged.

(k) ORPHAN DRUGS.—

(1) EXEMPTION.—A drug designated under section 526 for a rare disease or condition and approved under section 505 or under section 351 of the Public Health Service Act shall be exempt from product and establishment fees under this section, if the drug meets all of the following conditions:

(A) The drug meets the public health requirements contained in this Act as such requirements are applied to requests for waivers for product and establishment fees.

(B) The drug is owned or licensed and is marketed by a company that had less than $50,000,000 in gross worldwide revenue during the previous year.

(2) EVIDENCE OF QUALIFICATION.—An exemption under paragraph (1) applies with respect to a drug only if the applicant involved submits a certification that its gross annual revenues did not exceed $50,000,000 for the preceding 12 months before the exemption was requested.

[Section 736A terminated October 1, 2012, pursuant to Pub. L. No. 110–85, § 106(a), 121 Stat. 823, 842 (2007).]

SEC. 736B [21 U.S.C. 379h–2]. REAUTHORIZATION;
REPORTING REQUIREMENTS

(a) PERFORMANCE REPORT.—

(1) IN GENERAL.—Beginning with fiscal year 2013, not later than 120 days after the end of each fiscal year for which fees are collected under this part, the Secretary shall prepare and submit to the Committee on Energy and Commerce of the House of Representatives and the Committee on Health, Education, Labor, and Pensions of the Senate a report concerning—

(A) the progress of the Food and Drug Administration in achieving the goals identified in the letters described in section 101(b) of the Prescription Drug User Fee Amendments of 2012 during such fiscal year and the future plans of the Food and Drug Administration for meeting the goals, including the status of the independent assessment described in such letters; and

(B) the progress of the Center for Drug Evaluation and Research and the Center for Biologics Evaluation and Research in achieving the goals, and future plans for meeting the goals, including, for each review division—

> (i) the number of original standard new drug applications and biologics license applications filed per fiscal year for each review division;

> (ii) the number of original priority new drug applications and biologics license applications filed per fiscal year for each review division;

> (iii) the number of standard efficacy supplements filed per fiscal year for each review division;

> (iv) the number of priority efficacy supplements filed per fiscal year for each review division;

> (v) the number of applications filed for review under accelerated approval per fiscal year for each review division;

> (vi) the number of applications filed for review as fast track products per fiscal year for each review division;

> (vii) the number of applications filed for orphan-designated products per fiscal year for each review division; and

> (viii) the number of breakthrough designations for a fiscal year for each review division.

(2) INCLUSION.—The report under this subsection for a fiscal year shall include information on all previous cohorts for which the Secretary has not given a complete response on all human drug applications and supplements in the cohort.

(b) FISCAL REPORT.—Beginning with fiscal year 2013, not later than 120 days after the end of each fiscal year for which fees are collected under this part, the Secretary shall prepare and submit to the Committee on Energy and Commerce of the House of Representatives and the Committee on Health, Education, Labor, and Pensions of the Senate a report on the implementation of the authority for such fees during such fiscal year and the use, by the Food and Drug Administration, of the fees collected for such fiscal year.

(c) PUBLIC AVAILABILITY.—The Secretary shall make the reports required under subsections (a) and (b) available to the public on the Internet Web site of the Food and Drug Administration.

(d) REAUTHORIZATION.—

(1) CONSULTATION.—In developing recommendations to present to the Congress with respect to the goals, and plans for meeting the goals, for the process for the review of human drug applications for the first 5 fiscal years after fiscal year 2017, and for the reauthorization of this part for such fiscal years, the Secretary shall consult with—

(A) the Committee on Energy and Commerce of the House of Representatives;

(B) the Committee on Health, Education, Labor, and Pensions of the Senate;

(C) scientific and academic experts;

(D) health care professionals;

(E) representatives of patient and consumer advocacy groups; and

(F) the regulated industry.

(2) PRIOR PUBLIC INPUT.—Prior to beginning negotiations with the regulated industry on the reauthorization of this part, the Secretary shall—

(A) publish a notice in the Federal Register requesting public input on the reauthorization;

(B) hold a public meeting at which the public may present its views on the reauthorization, including specific suggestions for changes to the goals referred to in subsection (a);

(C) provide a period of 30 days after the public meeting to obtain written comments from the public suggesting changes to this part; and

(D) publish the comments on the Food and Drug Administration's Internet Web site.

(3) PERIODIC CONSULTATION.—Not less frequently than once every month during negotiations with the regulated industry, the Secretary shall hold discussions with representatives of patient and consumer advocacy groups to continue discussions of their views on the reauthorization and their suggestions for changes to this part as expressed under paragraph (2).

(4) PUBLIC REVIEW OF RECOMMENDATIONS.—After negotiations with the regulated industry, the Secretary shall—

(A) present the recommendations developed under paragraph (1) to the Congressional committees specified in such paragraph;

(B) publish such recommendations in the Federal Register;

(C) provide for a period of 30 days for the public to provide written comments on such recommendations;

(D) hold a meeting at which the public may present its views on such recommendations; and

(E) after consideration of such public views and comments, revise such recommendations as necessary.

(5) TRANSMITTAL OF RECOMMENDATIONS.—Not later than January 15, 2017, the Secretary shall transmit to the Congress the revised recommendations under para-

graph (4), a summary of the views and comments received under such paragraph, and any changes made to the recommendations in response to such views and comments.

(6) MINUTES OF NEGOTIATION MEETINGS.—

(A) PUBLIC AVAILABILITY.—Before presenting the recommendations developed under paragraphs (1) through (5) to the Congress, the Secretary shall make publicly available, on the public Web site of the Food and Drug Administration, minutes of all negotiation meetings conducted under this subsection between the Food and Drug Administration and the regulated industry.

(B) CONTENT.—The minutes described under subparagraph (A) shall summarize any substantive proposal made by any party to the negotiations as well as significant controversies or differences of opinion during the negotiations and their resolution.

PART 3—FEES RELATING TO DEVICES[76]

SEC. 737 [21 U.S.C. 379i]. DEFINITIONS

For purposes of this part:

(1) The term "premarket application" means—

(A) an application for approval of a device submitted under section 515(c) or section 351 of the Public Health Service Act; or

(B) a product development protocol described in section 515(f).

Such term does not include a supplement, a premarket report, or a premarket notification submission.

(2) The term "premarket report" means a report submitted under section 515(c)(2).

(3) The term "premarket notification submission" means a report submitted under section 510(k).

(4)(A) The term "supplement", with respect to a panel-track supplement, a 180–day supplement, a real-time supplement, or an efficacy supplement, means a request to the Secretary to approve a change in a device for which—

(i) an application or report has been approved under section 515(d), or an application has been approved under section 351 of the Public Health Service Act; or

(ii) a notice of completion has become effective under section 515(f).

---

76. Part 3 was amended by Pub. L. No. 112–144, tit. II, 126 Stat. 993, 1002–07 (2012). Section 207(a) of that title provides as follows:

SEC. 207. SUNSET CLAUSE.

(a) In General..—Sections 737 and 738 of the Federal Food, Drug, and Cosmetic Act (21 U.S.C. 739i; 739j) shall cease to be effective October 1, 2017. Section 738A (21 U.S.C. 739j–1) of the Federal Food, Drug, and Cosmetic Act (regarding reauthorization and reporting requirements) shall cease to be effective January 31, 2018.

(B) The term "panel-track supplement" means a supplement to an approved premarket application or premarket report under section 515 that requests a significant change in design or performance of the device, or a new indication for use of the device, and for which substantial clinical data are necessary to provide a reasonable assurance of safety and effectiveness.

(C) The term "180–day supplement" means a supplement to an approved premarket application or premarket report under section 515 that is not a panel-track supplement and requests a significant change in components, materials, design, specification, software, color additives, or labeling.

(D) The term "real-time supplement" means a supplement to an approved premarket application or premarket report under section 515 that requests a minor change to the device, such as a minor change to the design of the device, software, sterilization, or labeling, and for which the applicant has requested and the agency has granted a meeting or similar forum to jointly review and determine the status of the supplement.

(E) The term "efficacy supplement" means a supplement to an approved premarket application under section 351 of the Public Health Service Act that requires substantive clinical data.

(5) The term "30–day notice" means a notice under section 515(d)(6) that is limited to a request to make modifications to manufacturing procedures or methods of manufacture affecting the safety and effectiveness of the device.

(6) The term "request for classification information" means a request made under section 513(g) for information respecting the class in which a device has been classified or the requirements applicable to a device.

(7) The term "annual fee", for periodic reporting concerning a class III device, means the annual fee associated with periodic reports required by a premarket application approval order.

(8) The term "process for the review of device applications" means the following activities of the Secretary with respect to the review of premarket applications, premarket reports, supplements, and premarket notification submissions:

(A) The activities necessary for the review of premarket applications, premarket reports, supplements, and premarket notification submissions.

(B) The issuance of action letters that allow the marketing of devices or which set forth in detail the specific deficiencies in such applications, reports, supplements, or submissions and, where appropriate, the actions necessary to place them in condition for approval.

(C) The inspection of manufacturing establishments and other facilities undertaken as part of the Secretary's review of pending premarket applications, premarket reports, and supplements.

(D) Monitoring of research conducted in connection with the review of such applications, reports, supplements, and submissions.

(E) Review of device applications subject to section 351 of the Public Health Service Act for an investigational new drug application under section 505(i) or for an investigational device exemption under section 520(g) and activities conducted in anticipation of the submission of such applications under section 505(i) or 520(g).

(F) The development of guidance, policy documents, or regulations to improve the process for the review of premarket applications, premarket reports, supplements, and premarket notification submissions.

(G) The development of voluntary test methods, consensus standards, or mandatory performance standards under section 514 in connection with the review of such applications, reports, supplements, or submissions and related activities.

(H) The provision of technical assistance to device manufacturers in connection with the submission of such applications, reports, supplements, or submissions.

(I) Any activity undertaken under section 513 or 515(i) in connection with the initial classification or reclassification of a device or under section 515(b) in connection with any requirement for approval of a device.

(J) Evaluation of postmarket studies required as a condition of an approval of a premarket application or premarket report under section 515 or a premarket application under section 351 of the Public Health Service Act.

(K) Compiling, developing, and reviewing information on relevant devices to identify safety and effectiveness issues for devices subject to premarket applications, premarket reports, supplements, or premarket notification submissions.

(9) The term "costs of resources allocated for the process for the review of device applications" means the expenses in connection with the process for the review of device applications for—

(A) officers and employees of the Food and Drug Administration, contractors of the Food and Drug Administration, advisory committees, and costs related to such officers, employees, and committees and to contracts with such contractors;

(B) management of information, and the acquisition, maintenance, and repair of computer resources;

(C) leasing, maintenance, renovation, and repair of facilities and acquisition, maintenance, and repair of fixtures, furniture, scientific equipment, and other necessary materials and supplies; and

(D) collecting fees and accounting for resources allocated for the review of premarket applications, premarket reports, supplements, and submissions.

(10) The term "adjustment factor" applicable to a fiscal year is the Consumer Price Index for all urban consumers (all items; United States city average) for October of the preceding fiscal year divided by such Index for October 2011.

(11) The term "person" includes an affiliate thereof.

(12) The term "affiliate" means a business entity that has a relationship with a second business entity (whether domestic or international) if, directly or indirectly—

(A) one business entity controls, or has the power to control, the other business entity; or

(B) a third party controls, or has power to control, both of the business entities.

(13) The term "establishment subject to a registration fee" means an establishment that is registered (or is required to register) with the Secretary under section 510 because such establishment is engaged in the manufacture, preparation, propagation, compounding, or processing of a device.

SEC. 738 [21 U.S.C. 379j]. AUTHORITY TO ASSESS AND USE DEVICE FEES

(a) TYPES OF FEES.—

(1) IN GENERAL.—Beginning in fiscal year 2013, the Secretary shall assess and collect fees in accordance with this section.

(2) PREMARKET APPLICATION, PREMARKET REPORT, SUPPLEMENT, AND SUBMISSION FEE, AND ANNUAL FEE FOR PERIODIC REPORTING CONCERNING A CLASS III DEVICE—

(A) IN GENERAL.—Except as provided in subparagraph (B) and subsections (d), (e), and (f), each person who submits any of the following, on or after October 1, 2012, shall be subject to a fee established under subsection (c) for the fiscal year involved in accordance with the following:

(i) A premarket application.

(ii) For a premarket report, a fee equal to the fee that applies under clause (i).

(iii) For a panel track supplement, a fee equal to 75 percent of the fee that applies under clause (i).

(iv) For a 180–day supplement, a fee equal to 15 percent of the fee that applies under clause (i).

(v) For a real-time supplement, a fee equal to 7 percent of the fee that applies under clause (i).

(vi) For a 30–day notice, a fee equal to 1.6 percent of the fee that applies under clause (i).

(vii) For an efficacy supplement, a fee equal to the fee that applies under clause (i).

(viii) For a premarket notification submission, a fee equal to 2 percent of the fee that applies under clause (i).

(ix) For a request for classification information, a fee equal to 1.35 percent of the fee that applies under clause (i).

(x) For periodic reporting concerning a class III device, an annual fee equal to 3.5 percent of the fee that applies under clause (i).

(B) EXCEPTIONS.—

(i) HUMANITARIAN DEVICE EXEMPTION.—An application under section 520(m) is not subject to any fee under subparagraph (A).

(ii) FURTHER MANUFACTURING USE.—No fee shall be required under subparagraph (A) for the submission of a premarket application under section 351 of the Public Health Service Act for a product licensed for further manufacturing use only.

(iii) STATE OR FEDERAL GOVERNMENT SPONSORS.—No fee shall be required under subparagraph (A) for a premarket application, premarket report, supplement, or premarket notification submission submitted by a State or Federal Government entity unless the device involved is to be distributed commercially.

(iv) PREMARKET NOTIFICATIONS BY THIRD PARTIES.—No fee shall be required under subparagraph (A) for a premarket notification submission reviewed by an accredited person pursuant to section 523.

(v) PEDIATRIC CONDITIONS OF USE.—

(I) IN GENERAL.—No fee shall be required under subparagraph (A) for a premarket application, premarket report, or premarket notification submission if the proposed conditions of use for the device involved are solely for a pediatric population. No fee shall be required under such subparagraph for a supplement if the sole purpose of the supplement is to propose conditions of use for a pediatric population.

(II) SUBSEQUENT PROPOSAL OF ADULT CONDITIONS OF USE.—In the case of a person who submits a premarket application or premarket report for which, under subclause (I), a fee under subparagraph (A) is not required, any supplement to such application that proposes conditions of use for any adult population is subject to the fee that applies under such subparagraph for a premarket application.

(C) PAYMENT.—The fee required by subparagraph (A) shall be due upon submission of the premarket application, premarket report, supplement, premarket notification submission, 30–day notice, request for classification information, or periodic reporting concerning a class III device. Applicants submitting portions of applications pursuant to section 515(c)(4) shall pay such fees upon submission of the first portion of such applications.

(D) REFUNDS.—

    (i) APPLICATION REFUSED FOR FILING.—The Secretary shall refund 75 percent of the fee paid under subparagraph (A) for any application or supplement that is refused for filing.

    (ii) APPLICATION WITHDRAWN BEFORE FILING.—The Secretary shall refund 75 percent of the fee paid under subparagraph (A) for any application or supplement that is withdrawn prior to the filing decision of the Secretary.

    (iii) APPLICATION WITHDRAWN BEFORE FIRST ACTION.—After receipt of a request for a refund of the fee paid under subparagraph (A) for a premarket application, premarket report, or supplement that is withdrawn after filing but before a first action, the Secretary may return some or all of the fee. The amount of refund, if any, shall be based on the level of effort already expended on the review of such application, report, or supplement.

    (iv) MODULAR APPLICATIONS WITHDRAWN BEFORE FIRST ACTION.—The Secretary shall refund 75 percent of the application fee paid for an application submitted under section 515(c)(4) that is withdrawn before a second portion is submitted and before a first action on the first portion.

    (v) LATER WITHDRAWN MODULAR APPLICATIONS.—If an application submitted under section 515(c)(4) is withdrawn after a second or subsequent portion is submitted but before any first action, the Secretary may return a portion of the fee. The amount of refund, if any, shall be based on the level of effort already expended on the review of the portions submitted.

    (vi) SOLE DISCRETION TO REFUND.—The Secretary shall have sole discretion to refund a fee or portion of the fee under clause (iii) or (v). A determination by the Secretary concerning a refund under clause (iii) or (v) shall not be reviewable.

(3) ANNUAL ESTABLISHMENT REGISTRATION FEE.—

(A) IN GENERAL.—Except as provided in subparagraph (B) and subsection (f), each establishment subject to a registration fee shall be subject to a fee for each initial or annual registration under section 510 beginning with its registration for fiscal year 2008.

(B) EXCEPTION.—No fee shall be required under subparagraph (A) for an establishment operated by a State or Federal governmental entity or an Indian tribe (as defined in the Indian Self Determination and Educational Assistance Act), unless a device manufactured by the establishment is to be distributed commercially.

(C) PAYMENT.—The fee required under subparagraph (A) shall be due once each fiscal year, upon the later of—

    (i) the initial or annual registration (as applicable) of the establishment under section 510; or

(ii) the first business day after the date of enactment of an appropriations Act providing for the collection and obligation of fees for such year under this section.

(b) FEE AMOUNTS.—

(1) IN GENERAL.—Subject to subsections (c), (d), (e), (f), and (i), for each of fiscal years 2013 through 2017, fees under subsection (a) shall be derived from the base fee amounts specified in paragraph (2), to generate the total revenue amounts specified in paragraph (3).

(2) BASE FEE AMOUNTS SPECIFIED.—For purposes of paragraph (1), the base fee amounts specified in this paragraph are as follows:

Fee Type	Fiscal Year 2013	Fiscal Year 2014	Fiscal Year 2015	Fiscal Year 2016	Fiscal Year 2017
Premarket Application	$248,000	$252,960	$258,019	$263,180	$268,443
Establishment Registration	$2,575	$3,200	$3,750	$3,872	$3,872

(3) TOTAL REVENUE AMOUNTS SPECIFIED.—For purposes of paragraph (1), the total revenue amounts specified in this paragraph are as follows:

(A) $97,722,301 for fiscal year 2013

(B) $112,580,497 for fiscal year 2014

(C) $125,767,107 for fiscal year 2015

(D) $129,339,949 for fiscal year 2016

(E) $130,184,348 for fiscal year 2017

(c) ANNUAL FEE SETTING; ADJUSTMENTS.—

(1) IN GENERAL.—The Secretary shall, 60 days before the start of each fiscal year after September 30, 2012, establish fees under subsection (a), based on amounts specified under subsection (b) and the adjustments provided under this subsection, and publish such fees, and the rationale for any adjustments to such fees, in the Federal Register.

(2) INFLATION ADJUSTMENTS.—

(A) ADJUSTMENT TO TOTAL REVENUE AMOUNTS.—For fiscal year 2014 and each subsequent fiscal year, the Secretary shall adjust the total revenue amount specified in subsection (b)(3) for such fiscal year by multiplying such amount by the applicable inflation adjustment under subparagraph (B) for such year.

(B) APPLICABLE INFLATION ADJUSTMENT TO TOTAL REVENUE AMOUNTS.—The applicable inflation adjustment for a fiscal year is—

(i) for fiscal year 2014, the base inflation adjustment under subparagraph (C) for such fiscal year; and

(ii) for fiscal year 2015 and each subsequent fiscal year, the product of—

(I) the base inflation adjustment under subparagraph (C) for such fiscal year; and

(II) the product of the base inflation adjustment under subparagraph (C) for each of the fiscal years preceding such fiscal year, beginning with fiscal year 2014.

(C) BASE INFLATION ADJUSTMENT TO TOTAL REVENUE AMOUNTS.—

(i) IN GENERAL.—Subject to further adjustment under clause (ii), the base inflation adjustment for a fiscal year is the sum of one plus—

(I) the average annual percent change in the cost, per full-time equivalent position of the Food and Drug Administration, of all personnel compensation and benefits paid with respect to such positions for the first 3 years of the preceding 4 fiscal years, multiplied by 0.60; and

(II) the average annual percent change that occurred in the Consumer Price Index for urban consumers (Washington–Baltimore, DC–MD–VA–WV; Not Seasonally Adjusted; All items; Annual Index) for the first 3 years of the preceding 4 years of available data multiplied by 0.40.

(ii) LIMITATIONS.—For purposes of subparagraph (B), if the base inflation adjustment for a fiscal year under clause (i)—

(I) is less than 1, such adjustment shall be considered to be equal to 1; or

(II) is greater than 1.04, such adjustment shall be considered to be equal to 1.04.

(D) ADJUSTMENT TO BASE FEE AMOUNTS.—For each of fiscal years 2014 through 2017, the base fee amounts specified in subsection (b)(2) shall be adjusted as needed, on a uniform proportionate basis, to generate the total revenue amounts under subsection (b)(3), as adjusted for inflation under subparagraph (A).

(3) VOLUME-BASED ADJUSTMENTS TO ESTABLISHMENT REGISTRATION BASE FEES.—For each of fiscal years 2014 through 2017, after the base fee amounts specified in subsection (b)(2) are adjusted under paragraph (2)(D), the base establishment registration fee amounts specified in such subsection shall be further adjusted, as the Secretary estimates is necessary in order for total fee collections for such fiscal year to generate the total revenue amounts, as adjusted under paragraph (2).

(4) LIMIT.—The total amount of fees charged, as adjusted under this subsection, for a fiscal year may not exceed the total costs for such fiscal year for the resources allocated for the process for the review of device applications.

(5) SUPPLEMENT.—

(A) IN GENERAL.—The Secretary may use unobligated carryover balances from fees collected in previous fiscal years to ensure that sufficient fee revenues are available in that fiscal year, so long as the Secretary maintains unobligated carryover balances of not less than 1 month of operating reserves for the first month of the next fiscal year.

(B) NOTICE TO CONGRESS.—Not later than 14 days before the Secretary anticipates the use of funds described in subparagraph (A), the Secretary shall provide notice to the Committee on Health, Education, Labor, and Pensions and the Committee on Appropriations of the Senate and the Committee on Energy and Commerce and the Committee on Appropriations of the House of Representatives.

(d) SMALL BUSINESSES; FEE WAIVER AND FEE REDUCTION REGARDING PREMARKET APPROVAL FEES.—

(1) IN GENERAL.—The Secretary shall grant a waiver of the fee required under subsection (a) for one premarket application, or one premarket report, where the Secretary finds that the applicant involved is a small business submitting its first premarket application to the Secretary, or its first premarket report, respectively, for review. For the purposes of this paragraph, the term "small business" means an entity that reported $30,000,000 or less of gross receipts or sales in its most recent Federal income tax return for a taxable year, including such returns of all of its affiliates. In addition, for subsequent premarket applications, premarket reports, and supplements where the Secretary finds that the applicant involved is a small business, the fees specified in clauses (i) through (v) and clauses (vii), (ix), and (x) of subsection (a)(2)(A) may be paid at a reduced rate in accordance with paragraph (2)(C).

(2) RULES RELATING TO PREMARKET APPROVAL FEES.—

(A) DEFINITION.—For purposes of this paragraph, the term "small business" means an entity that reported $100,000,000 or less of gross receipts or sales in its most recent Federal income tax return for a taxable year, including such returns of all of its affiliates.

(B) EVIDENCE OF QUALIFICATION.—

(i) IN GENERAL.—An applicant shall pay the higher fees established by the Secretary each year unless the applicant submits evidence that it qualifies for a waiver of the fee or the lower fee rate.

(ii) FIRMS SUBMITTING TAX RETURNS TO THE UNITED STATES INTERNAL REVENUE SERVICE.—The applicant shall support its claim that it meets the definition under subparagraph (A) by submission of a copy of its most recent Federal income tax return for a taxable year, and a copy of such returns of its affiliates, which show an amount of gross sales or receipts that is less than the maximum established in subparagraph (A). The applicant, and each of such affiliates, shall certify that the information provided is a true and accurate copy of the actual tax forms they submitted to the Internal Revenue Service. If no tax forms are submitted for any affiliate, the applicant shall certify that the applicant has no affiliates.

(iii) FIRMS NOT SUBMITTING TAX RETURNS TO THE UNITED STATES INTERNAL REVENUE SERVICE.—In the case of an applicant that has not previously submitted a Federal income tax return, the applicant and each of its affiliates shall demonstrate that it meets the definition under subparagraph (A) by submission of a signed certification, in such form as the Secretary may direct through a notice published in the Federal Register, that the applicant or affiliate meets the criteria for a small business and a certification, in English, from the national taxing authority of the country in which the applicant or, if applicable, affiliate is headquartered. The certification from such taxing authority shall bear the official seal of such taxing authority and shall provide the applicant's or affiliate's gross receipts or sales for the most recent year in both the local currency of such country and in United States dollars, the exchange rate used in converting such local currency to dollars, and the dates during which these receipts or sales were collected. The applicant shall also submit a statement signed by the head of the applicant's firm or by its chief financial officer that the applicant has submitted certifications for all of its affiliates, or that the applicant has no affiliates.

(C) REDUCED FEES.—Where the Secretary finds that the applicant involved meets the definition under subparagraph (A), the fees established under subsection (c)(1) may be paid at a reduced rate of—

(i) 25 percent of the fee established under such subsection for a premarket application, a premarket report, a supplement, or periodic reporting concerning a class III device; and

(ii) 50 percent of the fee established under such subsection for a 30–day notice or a request for classification information.

(D) REQUEST FOR FEE WAIVER OR REDUCTION.—An applicant seeking a fee waiver or reduction under this subsection shall submit supporting information to the Secretary at least 60 days before the fee is required pursuant to subsection (a). The decision of the Secretary regarding whether an entity qualifies for such a waiver or reduction is not reviewable.

(e) SMALL BUSINESSES; FEE REDUCTION REGARDING PREMARKET NOTIFICATION SUBMISSIONS.—

(1) IN GENERAL.—For fiscal year 2008 and each subsequent fiscal year, where the Secretary finds that the applicant involved is a small business, the fee specified in subsection (a)(2)(A)(viii) may be paid at a reduced rate in accordance with paragraph (2)(C).

(2) RULES RELATING TO PREMARKET NOTIFICATION SUBMISSIONS.—

(A) DEFINITION.—For purposes of this subsection, the term "small business" means an entity that reported $100,000,000 or less of gross receipts or sales in its most recent Federal income tax return for a taxable year, including such returns of all of its affiliates.

(B) EVIDENCE OF QUALIFICATION.—

(i) IN GENERAL.—An applicant shall pay the higher fees established by the Secretary each year unless the applicant submits evidence that it qualifies for the lower fee rate.

(ii) FIRMS SUBMITTING TAX RETURNS TO THE UNITED STATES INTERNAL REVENUE SERVICE.—The applicant shall support its claim that it meets the definition under subparagraph (A) by submission of a copy of its most recent Federal income tax return for a taxable year, and a copy of such returns of its affiliates, which show an amount of gross sales or receipts that is less than the maximum established in subparagraph (A). The applicant, and each of such affiliates, shall certify that the information provided is a true and accurate copy of the actual tax forms they submitted to the Internal Revenue Service. If no tax forms are submitted for any affiliate, the applicant shall certify that the applicant has no affiliates.

(iii) FIRMS NOT SUBMITTING TAX RETURNS TO THE UNITED STATES INTERNAL REVENUE SERVICE.—In the case of an applicant that has not previously submitted a Federal income tax return, the applicant and each of its affiliates shall demonstrate that it meets the definition under subparagraph (A) by submission of a signed certification, in such form as the Secretary may direct through a notice published in the Federal Register, that the applicant or affiliate meets the criteria for a small business and a certification, in English, from the national taxing authority of the country in which the applicant or, if applicable, affiliate is headquartered. The certification from such taxing authority shall bear the official seal of such taxing authority and shall provide the applicant's or affiliate's gross receipts or sales for the most recent year in both the local currency of such country and in United States dollars, the exchange rate used in converting such local currency to dollars, and the dates during which these receipts or sales were collected. The applicant shall also submit a statement signed by the head of the applicant's firm or by its chief financial officer that the applicant has submitted certifications for all of its affiliates, or that the applicant has no affiliates.

(C) REDUCED FEES.—For fiscal year 2008 and each subsequent fiscal year, where the Secretary finds that the applicant involved meets the definition under subparagraph (A), the fee for a premarket notification submission may be paid at 50 percent of the fee that applies under subsection (a)(2)(A)(viii), and as established under subsection (c)(1).

(D) REQUEST FOR REDUCTION.—An applicant seeking a fee reduction under this subsection shall submit supporting information to the Secretary at least 60 days before the fee is required pursuant to subsection (a). The decision of the Secretary regarding whether an entity qualifies for such a reduction is not reviewable.

(f) FEE WAIVER OR REDUCTION.—

(1) IN GENERAL.—The Secretary may, at the Secretary's sole discretion, grant a waiver or reduction of fees under subsection (a)(2) or (a)(3) if the Secretary finds that such waiver or reduction is in the interest of public health.

(2) LIMITATION.—The sum of all fee waivers or reductions granted by the Secretary in any fiscal year under paragraph (1) shall not exceed 2 percent of the total fee revenue amounts established for such year under subsection (c).

(3) DURATION.—The authority provided by this subsection terminates October 1, 2017.

(g) EFFECT OF FAILURE TO PAY FEES.—

(1) NO ACCEPTANCE OF SUBMISSIONS.—A premarket application, premarket report, supplement, premarket notification submission, 30–day notice, request for classification information, or periodic reporting concerning a class III device submitted by a person subject to fees under subsections (a)(2) and (a)(3) shall be considered incomplete and shall not be accepted by the Secretary until all fees owed by such person have been paid.

(2) NO REGISTRATION.—Registration information submitted under section 510 by an establishment subject to a registration fee shall be considered incomplete and shall not be accepted by the Secretary until the registration fee under subsection (a)(3) owed for the establishment has been paid. Until the fee is paid and the registration is complete, the establishment is deemed to have failed to register in accordance with section 510.

(h) CONDITIONS.—

(1) PERFORMANCE GOALS; TERMINATION OF PROGRAM.—With respect to the amount that, under the salaries and expenses account of the Food and Drug Administration, is appropriated for a fiscal year for devices and radiological products, fees may not be assessed under subsection (a) for the fiscal year, and the Secretary is not expected to meet any performance goals identified for the fiscal year, if—

(A) the amount so appropriated for the fiscal year, excluding the amount of fees appropriated for the fiscal year, is more than 1 percent less than $280,587,000 multiplied by the adjustment factor applicable to such fiscal year; or

(B) fees were not assessed under subsection (a) for the previous fiscal year.

(2) AUTHORITY.—If the Secretary does not assess fees under subsection (a) during any portion of a fiscal year because of paragraph (1) and if at a later date

in such fiscal year the Secretary may assess such fees, the Secretary may assess and collect such fees, without any modification in the rate for premarket applications, supplements, premarket reports, premarket notification submissions, 30–day notices, requests for classification information, periodic reporting concerning a class III device, and establishment registrations at any time in such fiscal year, notwithstanding the provisions of subsection (a) relating to the date fees are to be paid.

(i) CREDITING AND AVAILABILITY OF FEES.—

(1) IN GENERAL.—Subject to paragraph (2)(C), fees authorized under subsection (a) shall be collected and available for obligation only to the extent and in the amount provided in advance in appropriation Acts. Such fees are authorized to be appropriated to remain available until expended. Such sums as may be necessary may be transferred from the Food and Drug Administration salaries and expenses appropriation account without fiscal year limitation to such appropriation account for salaries and expenses with such fiscal year limitation. The sums transferred shall be available solely for the process for the review of device applications.

(2) COLLECTIONS AND APPROPRIATION ACTS.—

(A) IN GENERAL.—The fees authorized by this section—

(i) subject to subparagraph (C), shall be collected and available in each fiscal year in an amount not to exceed the amount specified in appropriation Acts, or otherwise made available for obligation, for such fiscal year, and

(ii) shall only be available to defray increases in the costs of the resources allocated for the process for the review of device applications (including increases in such costs for an additional number of full-time equivalent positions in the Department of Health and Human Services to be engaged in such process) over such costs, excluding costs paid from fees collected under this section, for fiscal year 2009 multiplied by the adjustment factor.

(B) COMPLIANCE.—

(i) IN GENERAL.—The Secretary shall be considered to have met the requirements of subparagraph (A)(ii) in any fiscal year if the costs funded by appropriations and allocated for the process for the review of device applications—

(I) are not more than 3 percent below the level specified in subparagraph (A)(ii); or

(II)(aa) are more than 3 percent below the level specified in subparagraph (A)(ii), and fees assessed for a subsequent fiscal year are decreased by the amount in excess of 3 percent by which such costs fell below the level specified in such subparagraph; and (bb) such costs are not more than 5 percent below the level specified in such subparagraph.

(ii) MORE THAN 5 PERCENT.—To the extent such costs are more than 5 percent below the specified level in subparagraph (A)(ii), fees may not collected under this section for that fiscal year.

(C) PROVISION FOR EARLY PAYMENTS.—Payment of fees authorized under this section for a fiscal year, prior to the due date for such fees, may be accepted by the Secretary in accordance with authority provided in advance in a prior year appropriations Act.

(3) AUTHORIZATION OF APPROPRIATIONS.—For each of the fiscal years 2013 through 2017, there is authorized to be appropriated for fees under this section an amount equal to the total revenue amount specified under subsection (b)(3) for the fiscal year, as adjusted under subsection (c) and, for fiscal year 2017 only, as further adjusted under paragraph (4).

(4) OFFSET.—If the cumulative amount of fees collected during fiscal years 2013, 2014, and 2015, added to the amount estimated to be collected for fiscal year 2016, which estimate shall be based upon the amount of fees received by the Secretary through June 30, 2016, exceeds the cumulative amount appropriated pursuant to paragraph (3) for these four fiscal years, the excess shall be credited to the appropriation account of the Food and Drug Administration as provided in paragraph (1), and shall be subtracted from the amount of fees that would otherwise be authorized to be collected under this section pursuant to appropriation Acts for fiscal year 2017.

(j) COLLECTION OF UNPAID FEES.—In any case where the Secretary does not receive payment of a fee assessed under subsection (a) within 30 days after it is due, such fee shall be treated as a claim of the United States Government subject to subchapter II of chapter 37 of title 31, United States Code.

(k) WRITTEN REQUESTS FOR REFUNDS.—To qualify for consideration for a refund under subsection (a)(2)(D), a person shall submit to the Secretary a written request for such refund not later than 180 days after such fee is due.

(*l*) CONSTRUCTION.—This section may not be construed to require that the number of full-time equivalent positions in the Department of Health and Human Services, for officers, employees, and advisory committees not engaged in the process of the review of device applications, be reduced to offset the number of officers, employees, and advisory committees so engaged.

SEC. 738A [21 U.S.C. 379j–1]. REAUTHORIZATION; REPORTING REQUIREMENTS

(a) REPORTS.—

(1) PERFORMANCE REPORT.—

(A) In general.—Beginning with fiscal year 2013, for each fiscal year for which fees are collected under this part, the Secretary shall prepare and submit to the Committee on Health, Education, Labor, and Pensions of the Senate and the Committee on Energy and Commerce of the House of Representatives annual reports concerning the progress of the Food and Drug Administration in achieving the goals identified in the letters described in section 201(b) of the Medical Device User Fee Amendments of 2012 during such fiscal year and the future plans of the Food and Drug Administration for meeting the goals.

(B) Publication.—With regard to information to be reported by the Food and Drug Administration to industry on a quarterly and annual basis pursuant to the letters described in section 201(b) of the Medical Device User Fee Amendments Act of 2012, the Secretary shall make such information publicly available on the Internet Web site of the Food and Drug Administration not later than 60 days after the end of each quarter or 120 days after the end of each fiscal year, respectively, to which such information applies. This information shall include the status of the independent assessment identified in the letters described in such section 201(b).

(C) Updates.—The Secretary shall include in each report under subparagraph (A) information on all previous cohorts for which the Secretary has not given a complete response on all device premarket applications and reports, supplements, and premarket notifications in the cohort.

(2) Fiscal report.—For fiscal years 2013 through 2017, not later than 120 days after the end of each fiscal year during which fees are collected under this part, the Secretary shall prepare and submit to the Committee on Health, Education, Labor, and Pensions of the Senate and the Committee on Energy and Commerce of the House of Representatives, a report on the implementation of the authority for such fees during such fiscal year and the use, by the Food and Drug Administration, of the fees collected during such fiscal year for which the report is made.

(3) Public availability.—The Secretary shall make the reports required under paragraphs (1) and (2) available to the public on the Internet Web site of the Food and Drug Administration.

(b) Reauthorization.—

(1) Consultation.—In developing recommendations to present to Congress with respect to the goals, and plans for meeting the goals, for the process for the review of device applications for the first 5 fiscal years after fiscal year 2017, and for the reauthorization of this part for such fiscal years, the Secretary shall consult with—

(A) the Committee on Energy and Commerce of the House of Representatives;

(B) the Committee on Health, Education, Labor, and Pensions of the Senate;

(C) scientific and academic experts;

(D) health care professionals;

(E) representatives of patient and consumer advocacy groups; and

(F) the regulated industry.

(2) PRIOR PUBLIC INPUT.—Prior to beginning negotiations with the regulated industry on the reauthorization of this part, the Secretary shall—

(A) publish a notice in the Federal Register requesting public input on the reauthorization;

(B) hold a public meeting at which the public may present its views on the reauthorization, including specific suggestions for changes to the goals referred to in subsection (a)(1);

(C) provide a period of 30 days after the public meeting to obtain written comments from the public suggesting changes to this part; and

(D) publish the comments on the Food and Drug Administration's Internet Web site.

(3) PERIODIC CONSULTATION.—Not less frequently than once every month during negotiations with the regulated industry, the Secretary shall hold discussions with representatives of patient and consumer advocacy groups to continue discussions of their views on the reauthorization and their suggestions for changes to this part as expressed under paragraph (2).

(4) PUBLIC REVIEW OF RECOMMENDATIONS.—After negotiations with the regulated industry, the Secretary shall—

(A) present the recommendations developed under paragraph (1) to the Congressional committees specified in such paragraph;

(B) publish such recommendations in the Federal Register;

(C) provide for a period of 30 days for the public to provide written comments on such recommendations;

(D) hold a meeting at which the public may present its views on such recommendations; and

(E) after consideration of such public views and comments, revise such recommendations as necessary.

(5) TRANSMITTAL OF RECOMMENDATIONS.—Not later than January 15, 2017, the Secretary shall transmit to Congress the revised recommendations under paragraph (4), a summary of the views and comments received under such paragraph, and any changes made to the recommendations in response to such views and comments.

(6) MINUTES OF NEGOTIATION MEETINGS.—

(A) PUBLIC AVAILABILITY.—Before presenting the recommendations developed under paragraphs (1) through (5) to the Congress, the Secretary shall make publicly available, on the public Web site of the Food and Drug Administration, minutes of all negotiation meetings conducted under this subsection between the Food and Drug Administration and the regulated industry.

(B) CONTENT.—The minutes described under subparagraph (A) shall summarize any substantive proposal made by any party to the negotiations as well as significant controversies or differences of opinion during the negotiations and their resolution.

PART 4—FEES RELATING TO ANIMAL DRUGS[77]

SEC. 739 [21 U.S.C. 379j–11]. DEFINITIONS

For purposes of this part:

(1) The term "animal drug application" means an application for approval of any new animal drug submitted under section 512(b)(1). Such term does not include either a new animal drug application submitted under section 512(b)(2) or a supplemental animal drug application.

(2) The term "supplemental animal drug application" means—

(A) a request to the Secretary to approve a change in an animal drug application which has been approved; or

(B) a request to the Secretary to approve a change to an application approved under section 512(c)(2) for which data with respect to safety or effectiveness are required.

(3) The term "animal drug product" means each specific strength or potency of a particular active ingredient or ingredients in final dosage form marketed by a particular manufacturer or distributor, which is uniquely identified by the labeler code and product code portions of the national drug code, and for which an animal drug application or a supplemental animal drug application has been approved.

(4) The term "animal drug establishment" means a foreign or domestic place of business which is at one general physical location consisting of one or more buildings all of which are within 5 miles of each other, at which one or more animal drug products are manufactured in final dosage form.

(5) The term "investigational animal drug submission" means—

---

77. Part 4 was amended and reauthorized by the Animal Drug and Animal Generic Drug User Fee Reauthorization Act of 2013, Pub. L. No. 113–14 (June 14, 2013). Section 107 of such Public Law provides as follows:

SUNSET DATES.

(a) Authorization.—Section 740 of the Federal Food, Drug, and Cosmetic Act (21 U.S.C. 379j–12) shall cease to be effective October 1, 2018.

(b) Reporting Requirements.—Section 740A of the Federal Food, Drug, and Cosmetic Act (21 U.S.C. 379j–13) shall cease to be effective January 31, 2019.

(A) the filing of a claim for an investigational exemption under section 512(j) for a new animal drug intended to be the subject of an animal drug application or a supplemental animal drug application, or

(B) the submission of information for the purpose of enabling the Secretary to evaluate the safety or effectiveness of an animal drug application or supplemental animal drug application in the event of their filing.

(6) The term "animal drug sponsor" means either an applicant named in an animal drug application that has not been withdrawn by the applicant and for which approval has not been withdrawn by the Secretary, or a person who has submitted an investigational animal drug submission that has not been terminated or otherwise rendered inactive by the Secretary.

(7) The term "final dosage form" means, with respect to an animal drug product, a finished dosage form which is approved for administration to an animal without substantial further manufacturing. Such term includes animal drug products intended for mixing in animal feeds.

(8) The term "process for the review of animal drug applications" means the following activities of the Secretary with respect to the review of animal drug applications, supplemental animal drug applications, and investigational animal drug submissions:

(A) The activities necessary for the review of animal drug applications, supplemental animal drug applications, and investigational animal drug submissions.

(B) The issuance of action letters which approve animal drug applications or supplemental animal drug applications or which set forth in detail the specific deficiencies in animal drug applications, supplemental animal drug applications, or investigational animal drug submissions and, where appropriate, the actions necessary to place such applications, supplements or submissions in condition for approval.

(C) The inspection of animal drug establishments and other facilities undertaken as part of the Secretary's review of pending animal drug applications, supplemental animal drug applications, and investigational animal drug submissions.

(D) Monitoring of research conducted in connection with the review of animal drug applications, supplemental animal drug applications, and investigational animal drug submissions.

(E) The development of regulations and policy related to the review of animal drug applications, supplemental animal drug applications, and investigational animal drug submissions.

(F) Development of standards for products subject to review.

(G) Meetings between the agency and the animal drug sponsor.

(H) Review of advertising and labeling prior to approval of an animal drug application or supplemental animal drug application, but not after such application has been approved.

(9) The term "costs of resources allocated for the process for the review of animal drug applications" means the expenses incurred in connection with the process for the review of animal drug applications for—

(A) officers and employees of the Food and Drug Administration, contractors of the Food and Drug Administration, advisory committees consulted with respect to the review of specific animal drug applications, supplemental animal drug applications, or investigational animal drug submissions, and costs related to such officers, employees, committees, and contractors, including costs for travel, education, and recruitment and other personnel activities,

(B) management of information, and the acquisition, maintenance, and repair of computer resources,

(C) leasing, maintenance, renovation, and repair of facilities and acquisition, maintenance, and repair of fixtures, furniture, scientific equipment, and other necessary materials and supplies, and

(D) collecting fees under section 740 and accounting for resources allocated for the review of animal drug applications, supplemental animal drug applications, and investigational animal drug submissions.

(10) The term "adjustment factor" applicable to a fiscal year refers to the formula set forth in section 735(8) with the base or comparator month being October 2002.

(11) The term "person" includes an affiliate thereof.

(12) The term "affiliate" refers to the definition set forth in section 735(11).

SEC. 740 [21 U.S.C. 379j–12]. AUTHORITY TO ASSESS AND USE ANIMAL DRUG FEES

(a) TYPES OF FEES.—Beginning in fiscal year 2004, the Secretary shall assess and collect fees in accordance with this section as follows:

(1) ANIMAL DRUG APPLICATION AND SUPPLEMENT FEE.—

(A) IN GENERAL.—Each person that submits, on or after September 1, 2003, an animal drug application or a supplemental animal drug application shall be subject to a fee as follows:

(i) A fee established in subsection (c) for an animal drug application, except an animal drug application subject to the criteria set forth in section 512(d)(4); and

(ii) A fee established in subsection (c), in an amount that is equal to 50 percent of the amount of the fee under clause (i), for—

(I) a supplemental animal drug application for which safety or effectiveness data are required; and

(II) an animal drug application subject to the criteria set forth in section 512(d)(4).

(B) PAYMENT.—The fee required by subparagraph (A) shall be due upon submission of the animal drug application or supplemental animal drug application.

(C) EXCEPTION FOR PREVIOUSLY FILED APPLICATION OR SUPPLEMENT.—If an animal drug application or a supplemental animal drug application was submitted by a person that paid the fee for such application or supplement, was accepted for filing, and was not approved or was withdrawn (without a waiver or refund), the submission of an animal drug application or a supplemental animal drug application for the same product by the same person (or the person's licensee, assignee, or successor) shall not be subject to a fee under subparagraph (A).

(D) REFUND OF FEE IF APPLICATION REFUSED FOR FILING.—The Secretary shall refund 75 percent of the fee paid under subparagraph (B) for any animal drug application or supplemental animal drug application which is refused for filing.

(E) REFUND OF FEE IF APPLICATION WITHDRAWN.—If an animal drug application or a supplemental animal drug application is withdrawn after the application or supplement was filed, the Secretary may refund the fee or portion of the fee paid under subparagraph (B) if no substantial work was performed on the application or supplement after the application or supplement was filed. The Secretary shall have the sole discretion to refund the fee under this paragraph. A determination by the Secretary concerning a refund under this paragraph shall not be reviewable.

(2) ANIMAL DRUG PRODUCT FEE.

(A) IN GENERAL.—Each person—

(i) who is named as the applicant in an animal drug application or supplemental animal drug application for an animal drug product which has been submitted for listing under section 510, and

(ii) who, after September 1, 2003, had pending before the Secretary an animal drug application or supplemental animal drug application;

shall pay for each such animal drug product the annual fee established in subsection (c).

(B) PAYMENT; FEE DUE DATE.—Such fee shall be payable for the fiscal year in which the animal drug product is first submitted for listing under section 510, or is submitted for relisting under section 510 if the animal drug product has been withdrawn from listing and relisted. After such fee is paid for that fiscal year, such fee shall be due each subsequent fiscal year that the product remains listed, upon the later of—

(i) the first business day after the date of enactment of an appropriations Act providing for the collection and obligation of fees for such fiscal year under this section; or

(ii) January 31 of each year.

(C) LIMITATION.—Such fee shall be paid only once for each animal drug product for a fiscal year in which a fee is payable.

(3) ANIMAL DRUG ESTABLISHMENT FEE.—

(A) IN GENERAL.—Each person—

(i) who owns or operates, directly or through an affiliate, an animal drug establishment, and

(ii) who is named as the applicant in an animal drug application or supplemental animal drug application for an animal drug product which has been submitted for listing under section 510, and

(iii) who, after September 1, 2003, had pending before the Secretary an animal drug application or supplemental animal drug application,

shall be assessed an annual fee established in subsection (b) for each animal drug establishment listed in its approved animal drug application as an establishment that manufactures the animal drug product named in the application.

(B) PAYMENT, FEE DUE DATE.—The annual establishment fee shall be assessed in each fiscal year in which the animal drug product named in the application is assessed a fee under paragraph (2) unless the animal drug establishment listed in the application does not engage in the manufacture of the animal drug product during the fiscal year. The fee under this paragraph for a fiscal year shall be due upon the later of—

(i) the first business day after the date of enactment of an appropriations Act providing for the collection and obligation of fees for such fiscal year under this section; or

(ii) January 31 of each year.

(C) LIMITATION.—

(i) IN GENERAL. An establishment shall be assessed only one fee per fiscal year under this section, subject to clause (ii)

(ii) CERTAIN MANUFACTURERS.—If a single establishment manufactures both animal drug products and prescription drug products, as defined in section 735(3), such establishment shall be assessed both the animal drug establishment fee and the prescription drug establishment fee, as set forth in section 736(a)(2), within a single fiscal year.

(4) Animal drug sponsor fee.—

(A) In general.—Each person—

(i) who meets the definition of an animal drug sponsor within a fiscal year; and

(ii) who, after September 1, 2003, had pending before the Secretary an animal drug application, a supplemental animal drug application, or an investigational animal drug submission,

shall be assessed an annual sponsor fee as established under subsection (c).

(B) Payment; fee due date.—The fee under this paragraph for a fiscal year shall be due upon the later of—

(i) the first business day after the date of enactment of an appropriations Act providing for the collection and obligation of fees for such fiscal year under this section; or

(ii) January 31 of each year.

(C) Limitation.—Each animal drug sponsor shall pay only one such fee each fiscal year.

(b) Fee Revenue Amounts.—

(1) In general.—Subject to subsections (c), (d), (f), and (g)—

(A) for fiscal year 2014, the fees required under sub-section (a) shall be established to generate a total revenue amount of $23,600,000; and

(B) for each of fiscal years 2015 through 2018, the fees required under subsection (a) shall be established to generate a total revenue amount of $21,600,000.

(2) Types of fees.—Of the total revenue amount determined for a fiscal year under paragraph (1)—

(A) 20 percent shall be derived from fees under sub-section (a)(1) (relating to animal drug applications and supplements);

(B) 27 percent shall be derived from fees under subsection (a)(2) (relating to animal drug products);

(C) 26 percent shall be derived from fees under sub-section (a)(3) (relating to animal drug establishments); and

(D) 27 percent shall be derived from fees under sub-section (a)(4) (relating to animal drug sponsors).

(c) Annual Fee Setting; Adjustments.—

(1) Annual fee setting.—The Secretary shall establish, 60 days before the start of each fiscal year beginning after September 30, 2003, for that fiscal year, animal drug application fees, supplemental animal drug application fees, animal

drug sponsor fees, animal drug establishment fees, and animal drug product fees based on the revenue amounts established under subsection (b) and the adjustments provided under this subsection.

(2) INFLATION ADJUSTMENT.—For fiscal year 2015 and subsequent fiscal years, the revenue amounts established in subsection (b) shall be adjusted by the Secretary by notice, published in the Federal Register, for a fiscal year, by an amount equal to the sum of—

(A) one;

(B) the average annual percent change in the cost, per full-time equivalent position of the Food and Drug Administration, of all personnel compensation and benefits paid with respect to such positions for the first 3 of the preceding 4 fiscal years for which data are available, multiplied by the average proportion of personnel compensation and benefits costs to total Food and Drug Administration costs for the first 3 years of the preceding 4 fiscal years for which data are available; and

(C) the average annual percent change that occurred in the Consumer Price Index for urban consumers (Washington-Baltimore, DC-MD-VA-WV; not seasonally adjusted; all items less food and energy; annual index) for the first 3 years of the preceding 4 years for which data are available multiplied by the average proportion of all costs other than personnel compensation and benefits costs to total Food and Drug Administration costs for the first 3 years of the preceding 4 fiscal years for which data are available.

The adjustment made each fiscal year under this paragraph shall be added on a compounded basis to the sum of all adjustments made each fiscal year after fiscal year 2014 under this paragraph.

(3) WORKLOAD ADJUSTMENT.—For fiscal year 2015 and subsequent fiscal years, after the revenue amounts established in subsection (b) are adjusted for inflation in accordance with paragraph (2), the revenue amounts shall be further adjusted for such fiscal year to reflect changes in the workload of the Secretary for the process for the review of animal drug applications. With respect to such adjustment—

(A) Such adjustment shall be determined by the Secretary based on a weighted average of the change in the total number of animal drug applications, supplemental animal drug applications for which data with respect to safety or effectiveness are required, manufacturing supplemental animal drug applications, investigational animal drug study submissions, and investigational animal drug protocol submissions submitted to the Secretary;

(B) the Secretary shall publish in the Federal Register the fees resulting from this adjustment and the supporting methodologies; and

(C) under no circumstances shall such adjustment result in fee revenues for a fiscal year that are less than the fee revenues for that fiscal year established in subsection (b) as adjusted for inflation under paragraph (2).

(4) FINAL YEAR ADJUSTMENT.—For fiscal year 2018, the Secretary may, in addition to other adjustments under this subsection, further increase the fees under this section, if such an adjustment is necessary, to provide for up to 3 months of operating reserves of carryover fees for the process of fiscal year 2019. If the Food and Drug Administration has carryover balances for the process for the review of animal drug applications in excess of 3 months of such operating reserves, then this adjustment will not be made. If this adjustment is necessary, then the rationale for the amount of the increase shall be contained in the annual notice setting fees for fiscal year 2018.

(5) LIMIT.—The total amount of fees charged, as adjusted under this subsection, for a fiscal year may not exceed the total costs for such fiscal year for the resources allocated for the process for the review of animal drug applications.

(d) FEE WAIVER OR REDUCTION.—

(1) IN GENERAL.—The Secretary shall grant a waiver from or a reduction of one or more fees assessed under subsection (a) where the Secretary finds that—

(A) the assessment of the fee would present a significant barrier to innovation because of limited resources available to such person or other circumstances,

(B) the fees to be paid by such person will exceed the anticipated present and future costs incurred by the Secretary in conducting the process for the review of animal drug applications for such person,

(C) the animal drug application or supplemental animal drug application is intended solely to provide for use of the animal drug in—

(i) a Type B medicated feed (as defined in section 558.3(b)(3) of title 21, Code of Federal Regulations (or any successor regulation)) intended for use in the manufacture of Type C free-choice medicated feeds, or

(ii) a Type C free-choice medicated feed (as defined in section 558.3(b)(4) of title 21, Code of Federal Regulations (or any successor regulation)),

(D) the animal drug application or supplemental animal drug application is intended solely to provide for a minor use or minor species indication, or

(E) the sponsor involved is a small business submitting its first animal drug application to the Secretary for review.

(2) USE OF STANDARD COSTS.—In making the finding in paragraph (1)(B), the Secretary may use standard costs.

(3) RULES FOR SMALL BUSINESSES.—

(A) DEFINITION.—In paragraph (1)(E), the term "small business" means an entity that has fewer than 500 employees, including employees of affiliates.

(B) WAIVER OF APPLICATION FEE.—The Secretary shall waive under paragraph (1)(E) the application fee for the first animal drug application that a small business or its affiliate submits to the Secretary for review. After a small business or its affiliate is granted such a waiver, the small business or its affiliate shall pay application fees for all subsequent animal drug applications and supplemental animal drug applications for which safety or effectiveness data are required in the same manner as an entity that does not qualify as a small business.

(C) CERTIFICATION.—The Secretary shall require any person who applies for a waiver under paragraph (1)(E) to certify their qualification for the waiver. The Secretary shall periodically publish in the Federal Register a list of persons making such certifications.

(e) EFFECT OF FAILURE TO PAY FEES.—An animal drug application or supplemental animal drug application submitted by a person subject to fees under subsection (a) shall be considered incomplete and shall not be accepted for filing by the Secretary until all fees owed by such person have been paid. An investigational animal drug submission under section 739(5)(B) that is submitted by a person subject to fees under subsection (a) shall be considered incomplete and shall not be accepted for review by the Secretary until all fees owed by such person have been paid. The Secretary may discontinue review of any animal drug application, supplemental animal drug application or investigational animal drug submission from a person if such person has not submitted for payment all fees owed under this section by 30 days after the date upon which they are due.

(f) ASSESSMENT OF FEES.—

(1) LIMITATION.—Fees may not be assessed under subsection (a) for a fiscal year beginning after fiscal year 2003 unless appropriations for salaries and expenses of the Food and Drug Administration for such fiscal year (excluding the amount of fees appropriated for such fiscal year) are equal to or greater than the amount of appropriations for the salaries and expenses of the Food and Drug Administration for the fiscal year 2003 (excluding the amount of fees appropriated for such fiscal year) multiplied by the adjustment factor applicable to the fiscal year involved.

(2) AUTHORITY.—If the Secretary does not assess fees under subsection (a) during any portion of a fiscal year because of paragraph (1) and if at a later date in such fiscal year the Secretary may assess such fees, the Secretary may assess and collect such fees, without any modification in the rate, for animal drug applications, supplemental animal drug applications, investigational animal drug submissions, animal drug sponsors, animal drug establishments and animal drug products at any time in such fiscal year notwithstanding the provisions of subsection (a) relating to the date fees are to be paid.

(g) CREDITING AND AVAILABILITY OF FEES.—

(1) IN GENERAL.—Subject to paragraph (2)(C), fees authorized under subsection (a) shall be collected and available for obligation only to the extent and in the amount provided in advance in appropriations Acts. Such fees are authorized to be appropriated to remain available until expended. Such sums as may be necessary may be transferred from the Food and Drug Administration salaries and expenses appropriation account without fiscal year limitation to such appropriation account for salary and expenses with such fiscal year limitation. The sums transferred shall be available solely for the process for the review of animal drug applications.

(2) COLLECTIONS AND APPROPRIATION ACTS.—

(A) IN GENERAL.—The fees authorized by this section—

(i) subject to paragraph (C), shall be collected and available in each fiscal year in an amount not to exceed the amount specified in appropriation Acts, or otherwise made available for obligation for such fiscal year, and

(ii) shall be available to defray increases in the costs of the resources allocated for the process for the review of animal drug applications (including increases in such costs for an additional number of full-time equivalent positions in the Department of Health and Human Services to be engaged in such process) over such costs, excluding costs paid from fees collected under this section, for fiscal year 2003 multiplied by the adjustment factor.

(B) COMPLIANCE.—The Secretary shall be considered to have met the requirements of subparagraph (A)(ii) in any fiscal year if the costs funded by appropriations and allocated for the process for the review of animal drug applications—

(i) are not more than 3 percent below the level specified in subparagraph (A)(ii); or

(ii)(I) are more than 3 percent below the level specified in subparagraph (A)(ii), and fees assessed for the fiscal year following the subsequent fiscal year are decreased by the amount in excess of 3 percent by which such costs fell below the level specified in subparagraph (A)(ii); and

(II) such costs are not more than 5 percent below the level specified in subparagraph (A)(ii).

(C) PROVISION FOR EARLY PAYMENTS.—Payment of fees authorized under this section for a fiscal year, prior to the due date for such fees, may be accepted by the Secretary in advance in a prior year appropriations Act.

(3) AUTHORIZATION OF APPROPRIATIONS.—For each of the fiscal years 2014 through 2018, there is authorized to be appropriated for fees under this section an amount equal to the total revenue amount determined under subsection (b) for the fiscal year, as adjusted or otherwise affected under subsection (c) and paragraph (4).

(4) Offset of overcollections; recovery of collection shortfalls.

(A) Offset of overcollections.—If the sum of the cumulative amount of fees collected under this section for fiscal years 2014 through 2016 and the amount of fees estimated to be collected under this section for fiscal year 2017 (including any increased fee collections attributable to subparagraph (B)), exceeds the cumulative amount appropriated pursuant to paragraph (3) for the fiscal years 2014 through 2017, the excess amount shall be credited to the appropriation account of the Food and Drug Administration as provided in paragraph (1), and shall be subtracted from the amount of fees that would otherwise be authorized to be collected under this section pursuant to appropriation Acts for fiscal year 2018.

(B) Recovery of collection shortfalls.—

(i) Fiscal year 2016.—For fiscal year 2016, the amount of fees otherwise authorized to be collected under this section shall be increased by the amount, if any, by which the amount collected under this section and appropriated for fiscal year 2014 falls below the amount of fees authorized for fiscal year 2014 under paragraph (3).

(ii) Fiscal year 2017.—For fiscal year 2017, the amount of fees otherwise authorized to be collected under this section shall be increased by the amount, if any, by which the amount collected under this section and appropriated for fiscal year 2015 falls below the amount of fees authorized for fiscal year 2015 under paragraph (3).

(iii) Fiscal year 2018.—For fiscal year 2018, the amount of fees otherwise authorized to be collected under this section (including any reduction in the authorized amount under subparagraph (A)), shall be increased by the cumulative amount, if any, by which the amount collected under this section and appropriated for fiscal years 2016 and 2017 (including estimated collections for fiscal year 2017) falls below the cumulative amount of fees authorized under paragraph (3) for fiscal years 2016 and 2017.

(h) Collection of Unpaid Fees.—In any case where the Secretary does not receive payment of a fee assessed under subsection (a) within 30 days after it is due, such fee shall be treated as a claim of the United States Government subject to subchapter II of chapter 37 of title 31, United States Code.

(i) Written Requests for Waivers, Reductions, and Refunds.—To qualify for consideration for a waiver or reduction under subsection (d), or for a refund of any fee collected in accordance with subsection (a), a person shall submit to the Secretary a written request for such waiver, reduction, or refund not later than 180 days after such fee is due.

(j) Construction.—This section may not be construed to require that the number of full-time equivalent positions in the Department of Health and Human Services, for officers, employees, and advisory committees not engaged in the process of the review of animal drug applications, be reduced to offset the number of officers, employees, and advisory committees so engaged.

(k) ABBREVIATED NEW ANIMAL DRUG APPLICATIONS.—The Secretary shall—

(1) to the extent practicable, segregate the review of abbreviated new animal drug applications from the process for the review of animal drug applications; and

(2) adopt other administrative procedures to ensure that review times of abbreviated new animal drug applications do not increase from their current level due to activities under the user fee program.

SEC. 740A [21 U.S.C. 379j–13]. REAUTHORIZATION; REPORTING REQUIREMENTS

(a) PERFORMANCE REPORT.—Beginning with fiscal year 2014, not later than 120 days after the end of each fiscal year during which fees are collected under this part, the Secretary shall prepare and submit to the Committee on Health, Education, Labor, and Pensions of the Senate and the Committee on Energy and Commerce of the House of Representatives a report concerning the progress of the Food and Drug Administration in achieving the goals identified in the letters described in section 101(b) of the Animal Drug User Fee Amendments of 2013 toward expediting the animal drug development process and the review of the new and supplemental animal drug applications and investigational animal drug submissions during such fiscal year, the future plans of the Food and Drug Administration for meeting the goals, the review times for abbreviated new animal drug applications, and the administrative procedures adopted by the Food and Drug Administration to ensure that review times for abbreviated new animal drug applications are not increased from their current level due to activities under the user fee program.

(b) FISCAL REPORT.—Beginning with fiscal year 2014, not later than 120 days after the end of each fiscal year during which fees are collected under this part, the Secretary shall prepare and submit to the Committee on Health, Education, Labor, and Pensions of the Senate and the Committee on Energy and Commerce of the House of Representatives a report on the implementation of the authority for such fees during such fiscal year and the use, by the Food and Drug Administration, of the fees collected during such fiscal year for which the report is made.

(c) PUBLIC AVAILABILITY.—The Secretary shall make the reports required under subsections (a) and (b) available to the public on the Internet Web site of the Food and Drug Administration.

(d) REAUTHORIZATION.—

(1) CONSULTATION.—In developing recommendations to present to the Congress with respect to the goals, and plans for meeting the goals, for the process for the review of animal drug applications for the first 5 fiscal years after fiscal year 2018, and for the reauthorization of this part for such fiscal years, the Secretary shall consult with—

(A) the Committee on Health, Education, Labor, and Pensions of the Senate;

(B) the Committee on Energy and Commerce of the House of Representatives;

(C) scientific and academic experts;

(D) veterinary professionals;

(E) representatives of patient and consumer advocacy groups; and

(F) the regulated industry.

(2) PRIOR PUBLIC INPUT.—Prior to beginning negotiations with the regulated industry on the reauthorization of this part, the Secretary shall—

(A) publish a notice in the Federal Register requesting public input on the reauthorization;

(B) hold a public meeting at which the public may present its views on the reauthorization, including specific suggestions for changes to the goals referred to in subsection (a);

(C) provide a period of 30 days after the public meeting to obtain written comments from the public suggesting changes to this part; and

(D) publish the comments on the Food and Drug Administration's Internet Web site.

(3) PERIODIC CONSULTATION.—Not less frequently than once every 4 months during negotiations with the regulated industry, the Secretary shall hold discussions with representatives of veterinary, patient, and consumer advocacy groups to continue discussions of their views on the reauthorization and their suggestions for changes to this part as expressed under paragraph (2).

(4) PUBLIC REVIEW OF RECOMMENDATIONS.—After negotiations with the regulated industry, the Secretary shall—

(A) present the recommendations developed under paragraph (1) to the Congressional committees specified in such paragraph;

(B) publish such recommendations in the Federal Register;

(C) provide for a period of 30 days for the public to provide written comments on such recommendations;

(D) hold a meeting at which the public may present its views on such recommendations; and

(E) after consideration of such public views and comments, revise such recommendations as necessary.

(5) TRANSMITTAL OF RECOMMENDATIONS.—Not later than January 15, 2018, the Secretary shall transmit to the Congress the revised recommendations under para-

graph (4), a summary of the views and comments received under such paragraph, and any changes made to the recommendations in response to such views and comments.

(6) MINUTES OF NEGOTIATION MEETINGS.—

(A) PUBLIC AVAILABILITY.—Before presenting the recommendations developed under paragraphs (1) through (5) to the Congress, the Secretary shall make publicly available, on the Internet Web site of the Food and Drug Administration, minutes of all negotiation meetings conducted under this subsection between the Food and Drug Administration and the regulated industry.

(B) CONTENT.—The minutes described under subparagraph (A) shall summarize any substantive proposal made by any party to the negotiations as well as significant controversies or differences of opinion during the negotiations and their resolution.

PART 5—FEES RELATING TO GENERIC NEW ANIMAL DRUGS[78]

SEC. 741 [21 U.S.C. 379j–21]. AUTHORITY TO ASSESS AND USE GENERIC NEW ANIMAL DRUG FEES

(a) TYPES OF FEES.—Beginning with respect to fiscal year 2009, the Secretary shall assess and collect fees in accordance with this section as follows:

(1) ABBREVIATED APPLICATION FEE.—

(A) IN GENERAL.—Each person that submits, on or after July 1, 2008, an abbreviated application for a generic new animal drug shall be subject to a fee as established in subsection (c) for such an application.

(B) PAYMENT.—The fee required by subparagraph (A) shall be due upon submission of the abbreviated application.

(C) EXCEPTIONS.—

(i) PREVIOUSLY FILED APPLICATION.—If an abbreviated application was submitted by a person that paid the fee for such application, was accepted for filing, and was not approved or was withdrawn (without a waiver or refund), the submission of an abbreviated application for the same product by the same person (or the person's licensee, assignee, or successor) shall not be subject to a fee under subparagraph (A).

78. Part 5 was reauthorized by the Animal Drug and Animal Generic Drug User Fee Reauthorization Act of 2013, Pub. L. No. 113-14 (June 14, 2013). Section 206 of such Public Law provides as follows:

SUNSET DATES.

(a) Authorization.—Section 741 of the Federal Food, Drug, and Cosmetic Act (21 U.S.C. 379j–21) shall cease to be effective October 1, 2018.

(b) Reporting Requirements.—Section 742 of the Federal Food, Drug, and Cosmetic Act (21 U.S.C. 379j–22) shall cease to be effective January 31, 2019.

(ii) CERTAIN ABBREVIATED APPLICATIONS INVOLVING COMBINATION ANIMAL DRUGS.—An abbreviated application which is subject to the criteria in section 512(d)(4) and submitted on or after October 1, 2013 shall be subject to a fee equal to 50 percent of the amount of the abbreviated application fee established in subsection (c).

(D) REFUND OF FEE IF APPLICATION REFUSED FOR FILING.—The Secretary shall refund 75 percent of the fee paid under subparagraph (B) for any abbreviated application which is refused for filing.

(E) REFUND OF FEE IF APPLICATION WITHDRAWN.—If an abbreviated application is withdrawn after the application was filed, the Secretary may refund the fee or portion of the fee paid under subparagraph (B) if no substantial work was performed on the application after the application was filed. The Secretary shall have the sole discretion to refund the fee under this subparagraph. A determination by the Secretary concerning a refund under this subparagraph shall not be reviewable.

(2) GENERIC NEW ANIMAL DRUG PRODUCT FEE.—

(A) IN GENERAL.—Each person—

(i) who is named as the applicant in an abbreviated application or supplemental abbreviated application for a generic new animal drug product which has been submitted for listing under section 510; and

(ii) who, after September 1, 2008, had pending before the Secretary an abbreviated application or supplemental abbreviated application,

shall pay for each such generic new animal drug product the annual fee established in subsection (c).

(B) PAYMENT; FEE DUE DATE.—Such fee shall be payable for the fiscal year in which the generic new animal drug product is first submitted for listing under section 510, or is submitted for relisting under section 510 if the generic new animal drug product has been withdrawn from listing and relisted. After such fee is paid for that fiscal year, such fee shall be due each subsequent fiscal year that the product remains listed, upon the later of—

(i) the first business day after the date of enactment of an appropriations Act providing for the collection and obligation of fees for such fiscal year under this section; or

(ii) January 31 of each year.

(C) LIMITATION.—Such fee shall be paid only once for each generic new animal drug product for a fiscal year in which the fee is payable.

(3) GENERIC NEW ANIMAL DRUG SPONSOR FEE.—

(A) IN GENERAL.—Each person—

(i) who meets the definition of a generic new animal drug sponsor within a fiscal year, and

(ii) who, after September 1, 2008, had pending before the Secretary an abbreviated application, a supplemental abbreviated application, or an investigational submission,

shall be assessed an annual fee established under subsection (c).

(B) PAYMENT; FEE DUE DATE.—Such fee shall be due each fiscal year upon the later of—

(i) the first business day after the date of enactment of an appropriations Act providing for the collection and such obligation of fees for such fiscal year under this section; or

(ii) January 31 of each year.

(C) AMOUNT OF FEE.—Each generic new animal drug sponsor shall pay only 1 such fee each fiscal year, as follows:

(i) 100 percent of the amount of the generic new animal drug sponsor fee published for that fiscal year under subsection (c) for an applicant with more than 6 approved abbreviated applications.

(ii) 75 percent of the amount of the generic new animal drug sponsor fee published for that fiscal year under subsection (c) for an applicant with more than 1 and fewer than 7 approved abbreviated applications.

(iii) 50 percent of the amount of the generic new animal drug sponsor fee published for that fiscal year under subsection (c) for an applicant with 1 or fewer approved abbreviated applications.

(b) FEE AMOUNTS.—Subject to subsections (c), (d), (f), and (g), the fees required under subsection (a) shall be established to generate fee revenue amounts as follows:

(1) TOTAL FEE REVENUES FOR APPLICATION FEES.—The total fee revenues to be collected in abbreviated application fees under subsection (a)(1) shall be $1,832,000 for fiscal year 2014, $1,736,000 for fiscal year 2015, $1,857,000 for fiscal year 2016, $1,934,000 for fiscal year 2017, and $2,117,000 for fiscal year 2018.

(2) TOTAL FEE REVENUES FOR PRODUCT FEES.—The total fee revenues to be collected in generic new animal drug product fees under subsection (a)(2) shall be $2,748,000 for fiscal year 2014, $2,604,000 for fiscal year 2015, $2,786,000 for fiscal year 2016, $2,976,000 for fiscal year 2017, and $3,175,000 for fiscal year 2018.

(3) TOTAL FEE REVENUES FOR SPONSOR FEES.—The total fee revenues to be collected in generic new animal drug sponsor fees under subsection (a)(3) shall be $2,748,000 for fiscal year 2014, $2,604,000 for fiscal year 2015, $2,786,000 for fiscal year 2016, $2,967,000 for fiscal year 2017, and $3,175,000 for fiscal year 2018.

(c) ANNUAL FEE SETTING; ADJUSTMENTS.—

(1) ANNUAL FEE SETTING.—The Secretary shall establish, 60 days before the start of each fiscal year beginning after September 30, 2008, for that fiscal year, abbreviated application fees, generic new animal drug sponsor fees, and generic new animal drug product fees, based on the revenue amounts established under subsection (b) and the adjustments provided under this subsection.

(2) WORKLOAD ADJUSTMENT.—The fee revenues shall be adjusted each fiscal year after fiscal year 2014 to reflect changes in review workload. With respect to such adjustment:

(A) This adjustment shall be determined by the Secretary based on a weighted average of the change in the total number of abbreviated applications for generic new animal drugs, manufacturing supplemental abbreviated applications for generic new animal drugs, investigational generic new animal drug study submissions, and investigational generic new animal drug protocol submissions submitted to the Secretary. The Secretary shall publish in the Federal Register the fees resulting from this adjustment and the supporting methodologies.

(B) Under no circumstances shall this workload adjustment result in fee revenues for a fiscal year that are less than the fee revenues for that fiscal year established in subsection (b).

(3) FINAL YEAR ADJUSTMENT.—For fiscal year 2018, the Secretary may, in addition to other adjustments under this subsection, further increase the fees to provide for up to 3 months of operating reserves of carryover user fees for the process for the review of abbreviated applications for generic new animal drugs for the first 3 months of fiscal year 2019. If the Food and Drug Administration has carryover balances for the process for the review of abbreviated applications for generic new animal drugs in excess of 3 months of such operating reserves, then this adjustment shall not be made. If this adjustment is necessary, then the rationale for the amount of the increase shall be contained in the annual notice setting fees for fiscal year 2018.

(4) LIMIT.—The total amount of fees charged, as adjusted under this subsection, for a fiscal year may not exceed the total costs for such fiscal year for the resources allocated for the process for the review of abbreviated applications for generic new animal drugs.

(d) FEE WAIVER OR REDUCTION.—The Secretary shall grant a waiver from or a reduction of 1 or more fees assessed under subsection (a) where the Secretary finds that the generic new animal drug is intended solely to provide for a minor use or minor species indication.

(e) EFFECT OF FAILURE TO PAY FEES.—An abbreviated application for a generic new animal drug submitted by a person subject to fees under subsection (a) shall be considered incomplete and shall not be accepted for filing by the Secretary until all fees owed by such person have been paid. An investigational submission for a generic new animal drug that is submitted by a person subject to fees under subsection (a) shall be considered incomplete and shall not be accepted for review by the Secretary until all fees owed by such person have been paid. The Secretary may discontinue review of any abbreviated application for a generic new animal drug, supplemental abbreviated application for a generic new animal drug, or investigational submission for a generic new animal drug from a person if such person has not submitted for payment all fees owed under this section by 30 days after the date upon which they are due.

(f) ASSESSMENT OF FEES.—

(1) LIMITATION.—Fees may not be assessed under subsection (a) for a fiscal year beginning after fiscal year 2008 unless appropriations for salaries and expenses of the Food and Drug Administration for such fiscal year (excluding the amount of fees appropriated for such fiscal year) are equal to or greater than the amount of appropriations for the salaries and expenses of the Food and Drug Administration for the fiscal year 2003 (excluding the amount of fees appropriated for such fiscal year) multiplied by the adjustment factor applicable to the fiscal year involved.

(2) AUTHORITY.—If the Secretary does not assess fees under subsection (a) during any portion of a fiscal year because of paragraph (1) and if at a later date in such fiscal year the Secretary may assess such fees, the Secretary may assess and collect such fees, without any modification in the rate, for abbreviated applications, generic new animal drug sponsors, and generic new animal drug products at any time in such fiscal year notwithstanding the provisions of subsection (a) relating to the date fees are to be paid.

(g) CREDITING AND AVAILABILITY OF FEES.—

(1) IN GENERAL.—Subject to paragraph (2)(C), fees authorized under subsection (a) shall be collected and available for obligation only to the extent and in the amount provided in advance in appropriations Acts. Such fees are authorized to be appropriated to remain available until expended. Such sums as may be necessary may be transferred from the Food and Drug Administration salaries and expenses appropriation account without fiscal year limitation to such appropriation account for salary and expenses with such fiscal year limitation. The sums transferred shall be available solely for the process for the review of abbreviated applications for generic new animal drugs.

(2) COLLECTIONS AND APPROPRIATION ACTS.—

(A) IN GENERAL.—The fees authorized by this section—

(i) subject to subparagraph (C), shall be collected and available in each fiscal year in an amount not to exceed the amount specified in appropriation Acts, or otherwise made available for obligation for such fiscal year; and

(ii) shall be available to defray increases in the costs of the resources allocated for the process for the review of abbreviated applications for generic new animal drugs (including increases in such costs for an additional number of full-time equivalent positions in the Department of Health and Human Services to be engaged in such process) over such costs, excluding costs paid from fees collected under this section, for fiscal year 2008 multiplied by the adjustment factor.

(B) COMPLIANCE.—The Secretary shall be considered to have met the requirements of subparagraph (A)(ii) in any fiscal year if the costs funded by appropriations and allocated for the process for the review of abbreviated applications for generic new animal drugs—

(i) are not more than 3 percent below the level specified in subparagraph (A)(ii); or

(ii)(I) are more than 3 percent below the level specified in subparagraph (A)(ii), and fees assessed for the fiscal year following the subsequent fiscal year are decreased by the amount in excess of 3 percent by which such costs fell below the level specified in subparagraph (A)(ii); and

(II) such costs are not more than 5 percent below the level specified in subparagraph (A)(ii).

(C) PROVISION FOR EARLY PAYMENTS.—Payment of fees authorized under this section for a fiscal year, prior to the due date for such fees, may be accepted by the Secretary in accordance with the authority provided in advance in a prior year appropriations Act.

(3) AUTHORIZATION OF APPROPRIATIONS.—There are authorized to be appropriated for fees under this section—

(A) $7,328,000 for fiscal year 2014;

(B) $6,994,000 for fiscal year 2015;

(C) $7,429,000 for fiscal year 2016;

(D) $7,936,000 for fiscal year 2017; and

(E) $8,467,000 for fiscal year 2018;

as adjusted to reflect adjustments in the total fee revenues made under this section and changes in the total amounts collected by abbreviated application fees, generic new animal drug sponsor fees, and generic new animal drug product fees.

(4) OFFSET.—If the sum of the cumulative amount of fees collected under this section for the fiscal years 2014 through 2016 and the amount of fees estimated to be collected under this section for fiscal year 2017 exceeds the cumulative amount appropriated under paragraph (3) for the fiscal years 2014 through 2017, the excess amount shall be credited to the appropriation account of the Food and Drug Administration as provided in paragraph (1), and shall be subtracted from

the amount of fees that would otherwise be authorized to be collected under this section pursuant to appropriation Acts for fiscal year 2018.

(h) COLLECTION OF UNPAID FEES.—In any case where the Secretary does not receive payment of a fee assessed under subsection (a) within 30 days after it is due, such fee shall be treated as a claim of the United States Government subject to subchapter II of chapter 37 of title 31, United States Code.

(i) WRITTEN REQUESTS FOR WAIVERS, REDUCTIONS, AND REFUNDS.—To qualify for consideration for a waiver or reduction under subsection (d), or for a refund of any fee collected in accordance with subsection (a), a person shall submit to the Secretary a written request for such waiver, reduction, or refund not later than 180 days after such fee is due.

(j) CONSTRUCTION.—This section may not be construed to require that the number of full-time equivalent positions in the Department of Health and Human Services, for officers, employees, and advisory committees not engaged in the process of the review of abbreviated applications for generic new animal drugs, be reduced to offset the number of officers, employees, and advisory committees so engaged.

(k) DEFINITIONS.—In this section and section 742:

(1) ABBREVIATED APPLICATION FOR A GENERIC NEW ANIMAL DRUG.—The terms "abbreviated application for a generic new animal drug" and "abbreviated application" mean an abbreviated application for the approval of any generic new animal drug submitted under section 512(b)(2). Such term does not include a supplemental abbreviated application for a generic new animal drug.

(2) ADJUSTMENT FACTOR.—The term "adjustment factor" applicable to a fiscal year is the Consumer Price Index for all urban consumers (all items; United States city average) for October of the preceding fiscal year divided by—

(A) for purposes of subsection (f)(1), such Index for October 2002; and

(B) for purposes of subsection (g)(2)(A)(ii), such Index for October 2007.

(3) COSTS OF RESOURCES ALLOCATED FOR THE PROCESS FOR THE REVIEW OF ABBREVIATED APPLICATIONS FOR GENERIC NEW ANIMAL DRUGS.—The term "costs of resources allocated for the process for the review of abbreviated applications for generic new animal drugs" means the expenses incurred in connection with the process for the review of abbreviated applications for generic new animal drugs for—

(A) officers and employees of the Food and Drug Administration, contractors of the Food and Drug Administration, advisory committees consulted with respect to the review of specific abbreviated applications, supplemental abbreviated applications, or investigational submissions, and costs related to such officers, employees, committees, and contractors, including costs for travel, education, and recruitment and other personnel activities;

(B) management of information, and the acquisition, maintenance, and repair of computer resources;

591

(C) leasing, maintenance, renovation, and repair of facilities and acquisition, maintenance, and repair of fixtures, furniture, scientific equipment, and other necessary materials and supplies; and

(D) collecting fees under this section and accounting for resources allocated for the review of abbreviated applications, supplemental abbreviated applications, and investigational submissions.

(4) FINAL DOSAGE FORM.—The term "final dosage form" means, with respect to a generic new animal drug product, a finished dosage form which is approved for administration to an animal without substantial further manufacturing. Such term includes generic new animal drug products intended for mixing in animal feeds.

(5) GENERIC NEW ANIMAL DRUG.—The term "generic new animal drug" means a new animal drug that is the subject of an abbreviated application.

(6) GENERIC NEW ANIMAL DRUG PRODUCT.—The term "generic new animal drug product" means each specific strength or potency of a particular active ingredient or ingredients in final dosage form marketed by a particular manufacturer or distributor, which is uniquely identified by the labeler code and product code portions of the national drug code, and for which an abbreviated application for a generic new animal drug or a supplemental abbreviated application has been approved.

(7) GENERIC NEW ANIMAL DRUG SPONSOR.—The term "generic new animal drug sponsor" means either an applicant named in an abbreviated application for a generic new animal drug that has not been withdrawn by the applicant and for which approval has not been withdrawn by the Secretary, or a person who has submitted an investigational submission for a generic new animal drug that has not been terminated or otherwise rendered inactive by the Secretary.

(8) INVESTIGATIONAL SUBMISSION FOR A GENERIC NEW ANIMAL DRUG.—The terms "investigational submission for a generic new animal drug" and "investigational submission" mean—

(A) the filing of a claim for an investigational exemption under section 512(j) for a generic new animal drug intended to be the subject of an abbreviated application or a supplemental abbreviated application; or

(B) the submission of information for the purpose of enabling the Secretary to evaluate the safety or effectiveness of a generic new animal drug in the event of the filing of an abbreviated application or supplemental abbreviated application for such drug.

(9) PERSON.—The term "person" includes an affiliate thereof (as such term is defined in section 735(11)).

(10) PROCESS FOR THE REVIEW OF ABBREVIATED APPLICATIONS FOR GENERIC NEW ANIMAL DRUGS.—The term "process for the review of abbreviated applications for generic new animal drugs" means the following activities of the Secretary

with respect to the review of abbreviated applications, supplemental abbreviated applications, and investigational submissions:

(A) The activities necessary for the review of abbreviated applications, supplemental abbreviated applications, and investigational submissions.

(B) The issuance of action letters which approve abbreviated applications or supplemental abbreviated applications or which set forth in detail the specific deficiencies in abbreviated applications, supplemental abbreviated applications, or investigational submissions and, where appropriate, the actions necessary to place such applications, supplemental applications, or submissions in condition for approval.

(C) The inspection of generic new animal drug establishments and other facilities undertaken as part of the Secretary's review of pending abbreviated applications, supplemental abbreviated applications, and investigational submissions.

(D) Monitoring of research conducted in connection with the review of abbreviated applications, supplemental abbreviated applications, and investigational submissions.

(E) The development of regulations and policy related to the review of abbreviated applications, supplemental abbreviated applications, and investigational submissions.

(F) Development of standards for products subject to review.

(G) Meetings between the agency and the generic new animal drug sponsor.

(H) Review of advertising and labeling prior to approval of an abbreviated application or supplemental abbreviated application, but not after such application has been approved.

(11) SUPPLEMENTAL ABBREVIATED APPLICATION FOR GENERIC NEW ANIMAL DRUG.— The terms "supplemental abbreviated application for a generic new animal drug" and "supplemental abbreviated application" mean a request to the Secretary to approve a change in an approved abbreviated application.

SEC. 742 [21 U.S.C. 379j–22]. REAUTHORIZATION; REPORTING REQUIREMENTS

(a) PERFORMANCE REPORTS.—Beginning with fiscal year 2014, not later than 120 days after the end of each fiscal year during which fees are collected under this part, the Secretary shall prepare and submit to the Committee on Health, Education, Labor, and Pensions of the Senate, and the Committee on Energy and Commerce of the House of Representatives a report concerning the progress of the Food and Drug Administration in achieving the goals identified in the letters described in section 201(b) of the Animal Generic Drug User Fee Act of 2013 toward expediting the generic new animal drug development process and the review of abbreviated applications for generic new animal drugs, supplemental abbreviated applications for generic new animal drugs, and investigational submissions for generic new animal drugs during such fiscal year.

(b) FISCAL REPORT.—Beginning with fiscal year 2014, not later than 120 days after the end of each fiscal year during which fees are collected under this part, the Secretary shall prepare and submit to Committee on Health, Education, Labor, and Pensions of the Senate and the Committee on Energy and Commerce of the House of Representatives a report on the implementation of the authority for such fees during such fiscal year and the use, by the Food and Drug Administration, of the fees collected during such fiscal year for which the report is made.

(c) PUBLIC AVAILABILITY.—The Secretary shall make the reports required under subsections (a) and (b) available to the public on the Internet Web site of the Food and Drug Administration.

(d) REAUTHORIZATION.—

(1) CONSULTATION.—In developing recommendations to present to Congress with respect to the goals, and plans for meeting the goals, for the process for the review of abbreviated applications for generic new animal drugs for the first 5 fiscal years after fiscal year 2018, and for the reauthorization of this part for such fiscal years, the Secretary shall consult with—

(A) the Committee on Energy and Commerce of the House of Representatives;

(B) the Committee on Health, Education, Labor, and Pensions of the Senate;

(C) scientific and academic experts;

(D) veterinary professionals;

(E) representatives of patient and consumer advocacy groups; and

(F) the regulated industry.

(2) PRIOR PUBLIC INPUT.—Prior to beginning negotiations with the regulated industry on the reauthorization of this part, the Secretary shall—

(A) publish a notice in the Federal Register requesting public input on the reauthorization;

(B) hold a public meeting at which the public may present its views on the reauthorization, including specific suggestions for changes to the goals referred to in subsection (a);

(C) provide a period of 30 days after the public meeting to obtain written comments from the public suggesting changes to this part; and

(D) publish the comments on the Food and Drug Administration's Internet Web site.

(3) PERIODIC CONSULTATION.—Not less frequently than once every 4 months during negotiations with the regulated industry, the Secretary shall hold discus-

sions with representatives of veterinary, patient, and consumer advocacy groups to continue discussions of their views on the reauthorization and their suggestions for changes to this part as expressed under paragraph (2).

(4) PUBLIC REVIEW OF RECOMMENDATIONS.—After negotiations with the regulated industry, the Secretary shall—

(A) present the recommendations developed under paragraph (1) to the congressional committees specified in such paragraph;

(B) publish such recommendations in the Federal Register;

(C) provide for a period of 30 days for the public to provide written comments on such recommendations;

(D) hold a meeting at which the public may present its views on such recommendations; and

(E) after consideration of such public views and comments, revise such recommendations as necessary.

(5) TRANSMITTAL OF RECOMMENDATIONS.—Not later than January 15, 2018, the Secretary shall transmit to Congress the revised recommendations under paragraph (4), a summary of the views and comments received under such paragraph, and any changes made to the recommendations in response to such views and comments.

(6) MINUTES OF NEGOTIATION MEETINGS.—

(A) PUBLIC AVAILABILITY.—Before presenting the recommendations developed under paragraphs (1) through (5) to Congress, the Secretary shall make publicly available, on the Internet Web site of the Food and Drug Administration, minutes of all negotiation meetings conducted under this subsection between the Food and Drug Administration and the regulated industry.

(B) CONTENT.—The minutes described under subparagraph (A) shall summarize any substantive proposal made by any party to the negotiations as well as significant controversies or differences of opinion during the negotiations and their resolution.

PART 6—FEES RELATED TO FOOD

SEC. 743 [21 U.S.C. 379j–31]. AUTHORITY TO COLLECT AND USE FEES

(a) IN GENERAL.—

(1) PURPOSE AND AUTHORITY.—For fiscal year 2010 and each subsequent fiscal year, the Secretary shall, in accordance with this section, assess and collect fees from—

(A) the responsible party for each domestic facility (as defined in section 415(b)) and the United States agent for each foreign facility subject to a reinspection in such fiscal year, to cover reinspection-related costs for such year;

(B) the responsible party for a domestic facility (as defined in section 415(b)) and an importer who does not comply with a recall order under section 423 or under section 412(f) in such fiscal year, to cover food recall activities associated with such order performed by the Secretary, including technical assistance, follow-up effectiveness checks, and public notifications, for such year;

(C) each importer participating in the voluntary qualified importer program under section 806 in such year, to cover the administrative costs of such program for such year; and

(D) each importer subject to a reinspection in such fiscal year, to cover reinspection-related costs for such year.

(2) DEFINITIONS.—For purposes of this section—

(A) the term "reinspection" means—

(i) with respect to domestic facilities (as defined in section 415(b)), 1 or more inspections conducted under section 704 subsequent to an inspection conducted under such provision which identified noncompliance materially related to a food safety requirement of this Act, specifically to determine whether compliance has been achieved to the Secretary's satisfaction; and

(ii) with respect to importers, 1 or more examinations conducted under section 801 subsequent to an examination conducted under such provision which identified noncompliance materially related to a food safety requirement of this Act, specifically to determine whether compliance has been achieved to the Secretary's satisfaction;

(B) the term "reinspection-related costs" means all expenses, including administrative expenses, incurred in connection with—

(i) arranging, conducting, and evaluating the results of reinspections; and

(ii) assessing and collecting reinspection fees under this section; and

(C) the term "responsible party" has the meaning given such term in section 417(a)(1).

(b) ESTABLISHMENT OF FEES.—

(1) IN GENERAL.—Subject to subsections (c) and (d), the Secretary shall establish the fees to be collected under this section for each fiscal year specified in subsection (a)(1), based on the methodology described under paragraph (2), and shall publish such fees in a Federal Register notice not later than 60 days before the start of each such year.

(2) FEE METHODOLOGY.—

(A) FEES.—Fees amounts established for collection—

(i) under subparagraph (A) of subsection (a)(1) for a fiscal year shall be based on the Secretary's estimate of 100 percent of the costs of the reinspection-related activities (including by type or level of reinspection activity, as the Secretary determines applicable) described in such subparagraph (A) for such year;

(ii) under subparagraph (B) of subsection (a)(1) for a fiscal year shall be based on the Secretary's estimate of 100 percent of the costs of the activities described in such subparagraph (B) for such year;

(iii) under subparagraph (C) of subsection (a)(1) for a fiscal year shall be based on the Secretary's estimate of 100 percent of the costs of the activities described in such subparagraph (C) for such year; and

(iv) under subparagraph (D) of subsection (a)(1) for a fiscal year shall be based on the Secretary's estimate of 100 percent of the costs of the activities described in such subparagraph (D) for such year.

(B) OTHER CONSIDERATIONS.—

(i) VOLUNTARY QUALIFIED IMPORTER PROGRAM.—

(I) [Not enacted]

(II) RECOUPMENT.—In establishing the fee amounts under subparagraph (A)(iii) for the first 5 fiscal years after the date of enactment of this section, the Secretary shall include in such fee a reasonable surcharge that provides a recoupment of the costs expended by the Secretary to establish and implement the first year of the program under section 806.

(ii) CREDITING OF FEES.—In establishing the fee amounts under subparagraph (A) for a fiscal year, the Secretary shall provide for the crediting of fees from the previous year to the next year if the Secretary overestimated the amount of fees needed to carry out such activities, and consider the need to account for any adjustment of fees and such other factors as the Secretary determines appropriate.

(iii) PUBLISHED GUIDELINES.—Not later than 180 days after the date of enactment of the FDA Food Safety Modernization Act, the Secretary shall publish in the Federal Register a proposed set of guidelines in consideration of the burden of fee amounts on small business. Such consideration may include reduced fee amounts for small businesses. The Secretary shall provide for a period of public comment on such guidelines. The Secretary shall adjust the fee schedule for small businesses subject to such fees only through notice and comment rulemaking.

(3) USE OF FEES.—The Secretary shall make all of the fees collected pursuant to clause (i), (ii), (iii), and (iv) of paragraph (2)(A) available solely to pay for the costs referred to in such clause (i), (ii), (iii), and (iv) of paragraph (2)(A), respectively.

597

(c) LIMITATIONS.—

(1) IN GENERAL.—Fees under subsection (a) shall be refunded for a fiscal year beginning after fiscal year 2010 unless the amount of the total appropriations for food safety activities at the Food and Drug Administration for such fiscal year (excluding the amount of fees appropriated for such fiscal year) is equal to or greater than the amount of appropriations for food safety activities at the Food and Drug Administration for fiscal year 2009 (excluding the amount of fees appropriated for such fiscal year), multiplied by the adjustment factor under paragraph (3).

(2) AUTHORITY.—If—

(A) the Secretary does not assess fees under subsection (a) for a portion of a fiscal year because paragraph (1) applies; and

(B) at a later date in such fiscal year, such paragraph (1) ceases to apply,

the Secretary may assess and collect such fees under subsection (a), without any modification to the rate of such fees, notwithstanding the provisions of subsection (a) relating to the date fees are to be paid.

(3) ADJUSTMENT FACTOR.—

(A) IN GENERAL.—The adjustment factor described in paragraph (1) shall be the total percentage change that occurred in the Consumer Price Index for all urban consumers (all items; United States city average) for the 12–month period ending June 30 preceding the fiscal year, but in no case shall such adjustment factor be negative.

(B) COMPOUNDED BASIS.—The adjustment under subparagraph (A) made each fiscal year shall be added on a compounded basis to the sum of all adjustments made each fiscal year after fiscal year 2009.

(4) LIMITATION ON AMOUNT OF CERTAIN FEES.—

(A) IN GENERAL.—Notwithstanding any other provision of this section and subject to subparagraph (B), the Secretary may not collect fees in a fiscal year such that the amount collected—

(i) under subparagraph (B) of subsection (a)(1) exceeds $20,000,000; and

(ii) under subparagraphs (A) and (D) of subsection (a)(1) exceeds $25,000,000 combined.

(B) EXCEPTION.—If a domestic facility (as defined in section 415(b)) or an importer becomes subject to a fee described in subparagraph (A), (B), or (D) of subsection (a)(1) after the maximum amount of fees has been collected by the Secretary under subparagraph (A), the Secretary may collect a fee from such facility or importer.

(d) CREDITING AND AVAILABILITY OF FEES.—Fees authorized under subsection (a) shall be collected and available for obligation only to the extent and in the amount provided in appropriations Acts. Such fees are authorized to remain available until expended. Such sums as may be necessary may be transferred from the Food and Drug Administration salaries and expenses account without fiscal year limitation to such appropriation account for salaries and expenses with such fiscal year limitation. The sums transferred shall be available solely for the purpose of paying the operating expenses of the Food and Drug Administration employees and contractors performing activities associated with these food safety fees.

(e) COLLECTION OF FEES.—

(1) IN GENERAL.—The Secretary shall specify in the Federal Register notice described in subsection (b)(1) the time and manner in which fees assessed under this section shall be collected.

(2) COLLECTION OF UNPAID FEES.—In any case where the Secretary does not receive payment of a fee assessed under this section within 30 days after it is due, such fee shall be treated as a claim of the United States Government subject to provisions of subchapter II of chapter 37 of title 31, United States Code.

(f) ANNUAL REPORT TO CONGRESS.—Not later than 120 days after each fiscal year for which fees are assessed under this section, the Secretary shall submit a report to the Committee on Health, Education, Labor, and Pensions of the Senate and the Committee on Energy and Commerce of the House of Representatives, to include a description of fees assessed and collected for each such year and a summary description of the entities paying such fees and the types of business in which such entities engage.

(g) AUTHORIZATION OF APPROPRIATIONS.—For fiscal year 2010 and each fiscal year thereafter, there is authorized to be appropriated for fees under this section an amount equal to the total revenue amount determined under subsection (b) for the fiscal year, as adjusted or otherwise affected under the other provisions of this section.

PART 7—FEES RELATING TO GENERIC DRUGS[79]

SEC. 744A [21 U.S.C. 379j–41]. DEFINITIONS

For purposes of this part:

(1) The term "abbreviated new drug application"—

(A) means an application submitted under section 505(j), an abbreviated application submitted under section 507 (as in effect on the day before the date of

---

[79]. Part 7 was added by Pub. L. No. 112–144, tit. III, 126 Stat. 993, 1008–24 (2012). Section 304 of that title provides as follows:

SEC. 304. SUNSET DATES.

(a) Authorization.—Sections 744A and 744B of the Federal Food, Drug, and Cosmetic Act, as added by section 302 of this Act, shall cease to be effective October 1, 2017.

(b) Reporting Requirements.—Section 744C of the Federal Food, Drug, and Cosmetic Act, as added by section 303 of this Act, shall cease to be effective January 31, 2018.

enactment of the Food and Drug Administration Modernization Act of 1997), or an abbreviated new drug application submitted pursuant to regulations in effect prior to the implementation of the Drug Price Competition and Patent Term Restoration Act of 1984; and

(B) does not include an application for a positron emission tomography drug.

(2) The term "active pharmaceutical ingredient" means—

(A) a substance, or a mixture when the substance is unstable or cannot be transported on its own, intended—

(i) to be used as a component of a drug; and

(ii) to furnish pharmacological activity or other direct effect in the diagnosis, cure, mitigation, treatment, or prevention of disease, or to affect the structure or any function of the human body; or

(B) a substance intended for final crystallization, purification, or salt formation, or any combination of those activities, to become a substance or mixture described in subparagraph (A).

(3) The term "adjustment factor" means a factor applicable to a fiscal year that is the Consumer Price Index for all urban consumers (all items; United States city average) for October of the preceding fiscal year divided by such Index for October 2011.

(4) The term "affiliate" means a business entity that has a relationship with a second business entity if, directly or indirectly—

(A) one business entity controls, or has the power to control, the other business entity; or

(B) a third party controls, or has power to control, both of the business entities.

(5)(A) The term "facility"—

(i) means a business or other entity—

(I) under one management, either direct or indirect; and

(II) at one geographic location or address engaged in manufacturing or processing an active pharmaceutical ingredient or a finished dosage form; and

(ii) does not include a business or other entity whose only manufacturing or processing activities are one or more of the following: repackaging, relabeling, or testing.

(B) For purposes of subparagraph (A), separate buildings within close proximity are considered to be at one geographic location or address if the activities in them are—

(i) closely related to the same business enterprise;

(ii) under the supervision of the same local management; and

(iii) capable of being inspected by the Food and Drug Administration during a single inspection.

(C) If a business or other entity would meet the definition of a facility under this paragraph but for being under multiple management, the business or other entity is deemed to constitute multiple facilities, one per management entity, for purposes of this paragraph.

(6) The term "finished dosage form" means—

(A) a drug product in the form in which it will be administered to a patient, such as a tablet, capsule, solution, or topical application;

(B) a drug product in a form in which reconstitution is necessary prior to administration to a patient, such as oral suspensions or lyophilized powders; or

(C) any combination of an active pharmaceutical ingredient with another component of a drug product for purposes of production of a drug product described in subparagraph (A) or (B).

(7) The term "generic drug submission" means an abbreviated new drug application, an amendment to an abbreviated new drug application, or a prior approval supplement to an abbreviated new drug application.

(8) The term "human generic drug activities" means the following activities of the Secretary associated with generic drugs and inspection of facilities associated with generic drugs:

(A) The activities necessary for the review of generic drug submissions, including review of drug master files referenced in such submissions.

(B) The issuance of—

(i) approval letters which approve abbreviated new drug applications or supplements to such applications; or

(ii) complete response letters which set forth in detail the specific deficiencies in such applications and, where appropriate, the actions necessary to place such applications in condition for approval.

(C) The issuance of letters related to Type II active pharmaceutical drug master files which—

(i) set forth in detail the specific deficiencies in such submissions, and where appropriate, the actions necessary to resolve those deficiencies; or

(ii) document that no deficiencies need to be addressed.

(D) Inspections related to generic drugs.

(E) Monitoring of research conducted in connection with the review of generic drug submissions and drug master files.

(F) Postmarket safety activities with respect to drugs approved under abbreviated new drug applications or supplements, including the following activities:

(i) Collecting, developing, and reviewing safety information on approved drugs, including adverse event reports.

(ii) Developing and using improved adverse-event data-collection systems, including information technology systems.

(iii) Developing and using improved analytical tools to assess potential safety problems, including access to external data bases.

(iv) Implementing and enforcing section 505(*o*) (relating to postapproval studies and clinical trials and labeling changes) and section 505(p) (relating to risk evaluation and mitigation strategies) insofar as those activities relate to abbreviated new drug applications.

(v) Carrying out section 505(k)(5) (relating to adverse-event reports and postmarket safety activities).

(G) Regulatory science activities related to generic drugs.

(9) The term "positron emission tomography drug" has the meaning given to the term "compounded positron emission tomography drug" in section 201(ii), except that paragraph (1)(B) of such section shall not apply.

(10) The term "prior approval supplement" means a request to the Secretary to approve a change in the drug substance, drug product, production process, quality controls, equipment, or facilities covered by an approved abbreviated new drug application when that change has a substantial potential to have an adverse effect on the identity, strength, quality, purity, or potency of the drug product as these factors may relate to the safety or effectiveness of the drug product.

(11) The term "resources allocated for human generic drug activities" means the expenses for—

(A) officers and employees of the Food and Drug Administration, contractors of the Food and Drug Administration, advisory committees, and costs related to such officers and employees and to contracts with such contractors;

(B) management of information, and the acquisition, maintenance, and repair of computer resources;

(C) leasing, maintenance, renovation, and repair of facilities and acquisition, maintenance, and repair of fixtures, furniture, scientific equipment, and other necessary materials and supplies; and

(D) collecting fees under subsection (a) and accounting for resources allocated for the review of abbreviated new drug applications and supplements and inspection related to generic drugs.

(12) The term "Type II active pharmaceutical ingredient drug master file" means a submission of information to the Secretary by a person that intends to authorize the Food and Drug Administration to reference the information to support approval of a

generic drug submission without the submitter having to disclose the information to the generic drug submission applicant.

Sec. 744B [21 U.S.C. 379j–42]. Authority to Assess and Use Human Generic Drug Fees

(a) Types of Fees.—Beginning in fiscal year 2013, the Secretary shall assess and collect fees in accordance with this section as follows:

(1) One-time backlog fee for abbreviated new drug applications pending on October 1, 2012.—

(A) In general.—Each person that owns an abbreviated new drug application that is pending on October 1, 2012, and that has not received a tentative approval prior to that date, shall be subject to a fee for each such application, as calculated under subparagraph (B).

(B) Method of fee amount calculation.—The amount of each one-time backlog fee shall be calculated by dividing $50,000,000 by the total number of abbreviated new drug applications pending on October 1, 2012, that have not received a tentative approval as of that date.

(C) Notice.—Not later than October 31, 2012, the Secretary shall publish in the Federal Register a notice announcing the amount of the fee required by subparagraph (A).

(D) Fee due date.—The fee required by subparagraph (A) shall be due no later than 30 calendar days after the date of the publication of the notice specified in subparagraph (C).

(2) Drug master file fee.—

(A) In general.—Each person that owns a Type II active pharmaceutical ingredient drug master file that is referenced on or after October 1, 2012, in a generic drug submission by any initial letter of authorization shall be subject to a drug master file fee.

(B) One-time payment.—If a person has paid a drug master file fee for a Type II active pharmaceutical ingredient drug master file, the person shall not be required to pay a subsequent drug master file fee when that Type II active pharmaceutical ingredient drug master file is subsequently referenced in generic drug submissions.

(C) Notice.—

(i) Fiscal year 2013.—Not later than October 31, 2012, the Secretary shall publish in the Federal Register a notice announcing the amount of the drug master file fee for fiscal year 2013.

(ii) Fiscal year 2014 through 2017.—Not later than 60 days before the start of each of fiscal years 2014 through 2017, the Secretary shall publish in the Federal Register the amount of the drug master file fee established by this paragraph for such fiscal year.

(D) AVAILABILITY FOR REFERENCE.—

(i) IN GENERAL.—Subject to subsection (g)(2)(C), for a generic drug submission to reference a Type II active pharmaceutical ingredient drug master file, the drug master file must be deemed available for reference by the Secretary.

(ii) CONDITIONS.—A drug master file shall be deemed available for reference by the Secretary if—

(I) the person that owns a Type II active pharmaceutical ingredient drug master file has paid the fee required under subparagraph (A) within 20 calendar days after the applicable due date under subparagraph (E); and

(II) the drug master file has not failed an initial completeness assessment by the Secretary, in accordance with criteria to be published by the Secretary.

(iii) LIST.—The Secretary shall make publicly available on the Internet Web site of the Food and Drug Administration a list of the drug master file numbers that correspond to drug master files that have successfully undergone an initial completeness assessment, in accordance with criteria to be published by the Secretary, and are available for reference.

(E) FEE DUE DATE.—

(i) IN GENERAL.—Subject to clause (ii), a drug master file fee shall be due no later than the date on which the first generic drug submission is submitted that references the associated Type II active pharmaceutical ingredient drug master file.

(ii) LIMITATION.—No fee shall be due under subparagraph (A) for a fiscal year until the later of—

(I) 30 calendar days after publication of the notice provided for in clause (i) or (ii) of subparagraph (C), as applicable; or

(II) 30 calendar days after the date of enactment of an appropriations Act providing for the collection and obligation of fees under this section.

(3) ABBREVIATED NEW DRUG APPLICATION AND PRIOR APPROVAL SUPPLEMENT FILING FEE.—

(A) IN GENERAL.—Each applicant that submits, on or after October 1, 2012, an abbreviated new drug application or a prior approval supplement to an abbreviated new drug application shall be subject to a fee for each such submission in the amount established under subsection (d).

(B) NOTICE.—

(i) FISCAL YEAR 2013.—Not later than October 31, 2012, the Secretary shall publish in the Federal Register a notice announcing the amount of the fees under subparagraph (A) for fiscal year 2013.

(ii) FISCAL YEARS 2014 THROUGH 2017.—Not later than 60 days before the start of each of fiscal years 2014 through 2017, the Secretary shall publish in the Federal Register the amount of the fees under subparagraph (A) for such fiscal year.

(C) FEE DUE DATE.—

(i) IN GENERAL.—Except as provided in clause (ii), the fees required by subparagraphs (A) and (F) shall be due no later than the date of submission of the abbreviated new drug application or prior approval supplement for which such fee applies.

(ii) SPECIAL RULE FOR 2013.—For fiscal year 2013, such fees shall be due on the later of—

(I) the date on which the fee is due under clause (i);

(II) 30 calendar days after publication of the notice referred to in subparagraph (B)(i); or

(III) if an appropriations Act is not enacted providing for the collection and obligation of fees under this section by the date of submission of the application or prior approval supplement for which the fees under subparagraphs (A) and (F) apply, 30 calendar days after the date that such an appropriations Act is enacted.

(D) REFUND OF FEE IF ABBREVIATED NEW DRUG APPLICATION IS NOT CONSIDERED TO HAVE BEEN RECEIVED.—The Secretary shall refund 75 percent of the fee paid under subparagraph (A) for any abbreviated new drug application or prior approval supplement to an abbreviated new drug application that the Secretary considers not to have been received within the meaning of section 505(j)(5)(A) for a cause other than failure to pay fees.

(E) FEE FOR AN APPLICATION THE SECRETARY CONSIDERS NOT TO HAVE BEEN RECEIVED, OR THAT HAS BEEN WITHDRAWN.—An abbreviated new drug application or prior approval supplement that was submitted on or after October 1, 2012, and that the Secretary considers not to have been received, or that has been withdrawn, shall, upon resubmission of the application or a subsequent new submission following the applicant's withdrawal of the application, be subject to a full fee under subparagraph (A).

(F) ADDITIONAL FEE FOR ACTIVE PHARMACEUTICAL INGREDIENT INFORMATION NOT INCLUDED BY REFERENCE TO TYPE II ACTIVE PHARMACEUTICAL INGREDIENT DRUG MASTER FILE.—An applicant that submits a generic drug submission on or after

October 1, 2012, shall pay a fee, in the amount determined under subsection (d)(3), in addition to the fee required under subparagraph (A), if—

(i) such submission contains information concerning the manufacture of an active pharmaceutical ingredient at a facility by means other than reference by a letter of authorization to a Type II active pharmaceutical drug master file; and

(ii) a fee in the amount equal to the drug master file fee established in paragraph (2) has not been previously paid with respect to such information.

(4) GENERIC DRUG FACILITY FEE AND ACTIVE PHARMACEUTICAL INGREDIENT FACILITY FEE.—

(A) IN GENERAL.—Facilities identified, or intended to be identified, in at least one generic drug submission that is pending or approved to produce a finished dosage form of a human generic drug or an active pharmaceutical ingredient contained in a human generic drug shall be subject to fees as follows:

(i) GENERIC DRUG FACILITY.—Each person that owns a facility which is identified or intended to be identified in at least one generic drug submission that is pending or approved to produce one or more finished dosage forms of a human generic drug shall be assessed an annual fee for each such facility.

(ii) ACTIVE PHARMACEUTICAL INGREDIENT FACILITY.—Each person that owns a facility which produces, or which is pending review to produce, one or more active pharmaceutical ingredients identified, or intended to be identified, in at least one generic drug submission that is pending or approved or in a Type II active pharmaceutical ingredient drug master file referenced in such a generic drug submission, shall be assessed an annual fee for each such facility.

(iii) FACILITIES PRODUCING BOTH ACTIVE PHARMACEUTICAL INGREDIENTS AND FINISHED DOSAGE FORMS.—Each person that owns a facility identified, or intended to be identified, in at least one generic drug submission that is pending or approved to produce both one or more finished dosage forms subject to clause (i) and one or more active pharmaceutical ingredients subject to clause (ii) shall be subject to fees under both such clauses for that facility.

(B) AMOUNT.—The amount of fees established under subparagraph (A) shall be established under subsection (d).

(C) NOTICE.—

(i) FISCAL YEAR 2013.—For fiscal year 2013, the Secretary shall publish in the Federal Register a notice announcing the amount of the fees provided for in subparagraph (A) within the timeframe specified in subsection (d)(1)(B).

(ii) Fiscal years 2014 through 2017.—Within the timeframe specified in subsection (d)(2), the Secretary shall publish in the Federal Register the amount of the fees under subparagraph (A) for such fiscal year.

(D) Fee due date.—

(i) Fiscal year 2013.—For fiscal year 2013, the fees under subparagraph (A) shall be due on the later of—

(I) not later than 45 days after the publication of the notice under subparagraph (B); or

(II) if an appropriations Act is not enacted providing for the collection and obligation of fees under this section by the date of the publication of such notice, 30 days after the date that such an appropriations Act is enacted.

(ii) Fiscal years 2014 through 2017.—For each of fiscal years 2014 through 2017, the fees under subparagraph (A) for such fiscal year shall be due on the later of—

(I) the first business day on or after October 1 of each such year; or

(II) the first business day after the enactment of an appropriations Act providing for the collection and obligation of fees under this section for such year.

(5) Date of submission.—For purposes of this Act, a generic drug submission or Type II pharmaceutical master file is deemed to be "submitted" to the Food and Drug Administration—

(A) if it is submitted via a Food and Drug Administration electronic gateway, on the day when transmission to that electronic gateway is completed, except that a submission or master file that arrives on a weekend, Federal holiday, or day when the Food and Drug Administration office that will review that submission is not otherwise open for business shall be deemed to be submitted on the next day when that office is open for business; or

(B) if it is submitted in physical media form, on the day it arrives at the appropriate designated document room of the Food and Drug Administration.

(b) Fee Revenue Amounts.—

(1) In general.—

(A) Fiscal year 2013.—For fiscal year 2013, fees under subsection (a) shall be established to generate a total estimated revenue amount under such subsection of $299,000,000. Of that amount—

(i) $50,000,000 shall be generated by the one-time backlog fee for generic drug applications pending on October 1, 2012, established in subsection (a)(1); and

(ii) $249,000,000 shall be generated by the fees under paragraphs (2) through (4) of subsection (a).

(B) FISCAL YEARS 2014 THROUGH 2017.—For each of the fiscal years 2014 through 2017, fees under paragraphs (2) through (4) of subsection (a) shall be established to generate a total estimated revenue amount under such subsection that is equal to $299,000,000, as adjusted pursuant to subsection (c).

(2) TYPES OF FEES.—In establishing fees under paragraph (1) to generate the revenue amounts specified in paragraph (1)(A)(ii) for fiscal year 2013 and paragraph (1)(B) for each of fiscal years 2014 through 2017, such fees shall be derived from the fees under paragraphs (2) through (4) of subsection (a) as follows:

(A) Six percent shall be derived from fees under subsection (a)(2) (relating to drug master files).

(B) Twenty-four percent shall be derived from fees under subsection (a)(3) (relating to abbreviated new drug applications and supplements). The amount of a fee for a prior approval supplement shall be half the amount of the fee for an abbreviated new drug application.

(C) Fifty-six percent shall be derived from fees under subsection (a)(4) (A)(i) (relating to generic drug facilities). The amount of the fee for a facility located outside the United States and its territories and possessions shall be not less than $15,000 and not more than $30,000 higher than the amount of the fee for a facility located in the United States and its territories and possessions, as determined by the Secretary on the basis of data concerning the difference in cost between inspections of facilities located in the United States, including its territories and possessions, and those located outside of the United States and its territories and possessions.

(D) Fourteen percent shall be derived from fees under subsection (a)(4)(A) (ii) (relating to active pharmaceutical ingredient facilities). The amount of the fee for a facility located outside the United States and its territories and possessions shall be not less than $15,000 and not more than $30,000 higher than the amount of the fee for a facility located in the United States, including its territories and possessions, as determined by the Secretary on the basis of data concerning the difference in cost between inspections of facilities located in the United States and its territories and possessions and those located outside of the United States and its territories and possessions.

(c) ADJUSTMENTS.—

(1) INFLATION ADJUSTMENT.—For fiscal year 2014 and subsequent fiscal years, the revenues established in subsection (b) shall be adjusted by the Secretary by notice, published in the Federal Register, for a fiscal year, by an amount equal to the sum of—

(A) one;

(B) the average annual percent change in the cost, per full-time equivalent position of the Food and Drug Administration, of all personnel compensation and benefits paid with respect to such positions for the first 3 years of the preceding 4 fiscal years multiplied by the proportion of personnel compensation and benefits costs to total costs of human generic drug activities for the first 3 years of the preceding 4 fiscal years; and

(C) the average annual percent change that occurred in the Consumer Price Index for urban consumers (Washington–Baltimore, DC–MD–VA–WV; Not Seasonally Adjusted; All items; Annual Index) for the first 3 years of the preceding 4 years of available data multiplied by the proportion of all costs other than personnel compensation and benefits costs to total costs of human generic drug activities for the first 3 years of the preceding 4 fiscal years.

The adjustment made each fiscal year under this subsection shall be added on a compounded basis to the sum of all adjustments made each fiscal year after fiscal year 2013 under this subsection.

(2) FINAL YEAR ADJUSTMENT.—For fiscal year 2017, the Secretary may, in addition to adjustments under paragraph (1), further increase the fee revenues and fees established in subsection (b) if such an adjustment is necessary to provide for not more than 3 months of operating reserves of carryover user fees for human generic drug activities for the first 3 months of fiscal year 2018. Such fees may only be used in fiscal year 2018. If such an adjustment is necessary, the rationale for the amount of the increase shall be contained in the annual notice establishing fee revenues and fees for fiscal year 2017. If the Secretary has carryover balances for such activities in excess of 3 months of such operating reserves, the adjustment under this subparagraph shall not be made.

(d) ANNUAL FEE SETTING.—

(1) FISCAL YEAR 2013.—For fiscal year 2013—

(A) the Secretary shall establish, by October 31, 2012, the one-time generic drug backlog fee for generic drug applications pending on October 1, 2012, the drug master file fee, the abbreviated new drug application fee, and the prior approval supplement fee under subsection (a), based on the revenue amounts established under subsection (b); and

(B) the Secretary shall establish, not later than 45 days after the date to comply with the requirement for identification of facilities in subsection (f)(2), the generic drug facility fee and active pharmaceutical ingredient facility fee under subsection (a) based on the revenue amounts established under subsection (b).

(2) FISCAL YEARS 2014 THROUGH 2017.—Not more than 60 days before the first day of each of fiscal years 2014 through 2017, the Secretary shall establish the drug master file fee, the abbreviated new drug application fee, the prior approval supplement fee, the generic drug facility fee, and the active pharmaceutical ingre-

dient facility fee under subsection (a) for such fiscal year, based on the revenue amounts established under subsection (b) and the adjustments provided under subsection (c).

(3) FEE FOR ACTIVE PHARMACEUTICAL INGREDIENT INFORMATION NOT INCLUDED BY REFERENCE TO TYPE II ACTIVE PHARMACEUTICAL INGREDIENT DRUG MASTER FILE.—In establishing the fees under paragraphs (1) and (2), the amount of the fee under subsection (a)(3)(F) shall be determined by multiplying—

(A) the sum of—

(i) the total number of such active pharmaceutical ingredients in such submission; and

(ii) for each such ingredient that is manufactured at more than one such facility, the total number of such additional facilities; and

(B) the amount equal to the drug master file fee established in subsection (a)(2) for such submission.

(e) LIMIT.—The total amount of fees charged, as adjusted under subsection (c), for a fiscal year may not exceed the total costs for such fiscal year for the resources allocated for human generic drug activities.

(f) IDENTIFICATION OF FACILITIES.—

(1) PUBLICATION OF NOTICE; DEADLINE FOR COMPLIANCE.—Not later than October 1, 2012, the Secretary shall publish in the Federal Register a notice requiring each person that owns a facility described in subsection (a)(4)(A), or a site or organization required to be identified by paragraph (4), to submit to the Secretary information on the identity of each such facility, site, or organization. The notice required by this paragraph shall specify the type of information to be submitted and the means and format for submission of such information.

(2) REQUIRED SUBMISSION OF FACILITY IDENTIFICATION.—Each person that owns a facility described in subsection (a)(4)(A) or a site or organization required to be identified by paragraph (4) shall submit to the Secretary the information required under this subsection each year. Such information shall—

(A) for fiscal year 2013, be submitted not later than 60 days after the publication of the notice under paragraph (1); and

(B) for each subsequent fiscal year, be submitted, updated, or reconfirmed on or before June 1 of the previous year.

(3) CONTENTS OF NOTICE.—At a minimum, the submission required by paragraph (2) shall include for each such facility—

(A) identification of a facility identified or intended to be identified in an approved or pending generic drug submission;

(B) whether the facility manufactures active pharmaceutical ingredients or finished dosage forms, or both;

610

(C) whether or not the facility is located within the United States and its territories and possessions;

(D) whether the facility manufactures positron emission tomography drugs solely, or in addition to other drugs; and

(E) whether the facility manufactures drugs that are not generic drugs.

(4) CERTAIN SITES AND ORGANIZATIONS.—

(A) IN GENERAL.—Any person that owns or operates a site or organization described in subparagraph (B) shall submit to the Secretary information concerning the ownership, name, and address of the site or organization.

(B) SITES AND ORGANIZATIONS.—A site or organization is described in this subparagraph if it is identified in a generic drug submission and is—

(i) a site in which a bioanalytical study is conducted;

(ii) a clinical research organization;

(iii) a contract analytical testing site; or

(iv) a contract repackager site.

(C) NOTICE.—The Secretary may, by notice published in the Federal Register, specify the means and format for submission of the information under subparagraph (A) and may specify, as necessary for purposes of this section, any additional information to be submitted.

(D) INSPECTION AUTHORITY.—The Secretary's inspection authority under section 704(a)(1) shall extend to all such sites and organizations.

(g) EFFECT OF FAILURE TO PAY FEES.—

(1) GENERIC DRUG BACKLOG FEE.—Failure to pay the fee under subsection (a)(1) shall result in the Secretary placing the person that owns the abbreviated new drug application subject to that fee on a publicly available arrears list, such that no new abbreviated new drug applications or supplement submitted on or after October 1, 2012, from that person, or any affiliate of that person, will be received within the meaning of section 505(j)(5)(A) until such outstanding fee is paid.

(2) DRUG MASTER FILE FEE.—

(A) Failure to pay the fee under subsection (a)(2) within 20 calendar days after the applicable due date under subparagraph (E) of such subsection (as described in subsection (a)(2)(D)(ii)(I)) shall result in the Type II active pharmaceutical ingredient drug master file not being deemed available for reference.

(B)(i) Any generic drug submission submitted on or after October 1, 2012, that references, by a letter of authorization, a Type II active pharmaceutical ingredient drug master file that has not been deemed available for reference shall not be received within the meaning of section 505(j)(5)(A) unless the condition specified in clause (ii) is met.

(ii) The condition specified in this clause is that the fee established under subsection (a)(2) has been paid within 20 calendar days of the Secretary providing the notification to the sponsor of the abbreviated new drug application or supplement of the failure of the owner of the Type II active pharmaceutical ingredient drug master file to pay the drug master file fee as specified in subparagraph (C).

(C)(i) If an abbreviated new drug application or supplement to an abbreviated new drug application references a Type II active pharmaceutical ingredient drug master file for which a fee under subsection (a)(2)(A) has not been paid by the applicable date under subsection (a)(2)(E), the Secretary shall notify the sponsor of the abbreviated new drug application or supplement of the failure of the owner of the Type II active pharmaceutical ingredient drug master file to pay the applicable fee.

(ii) If such fee is not paid within 20 calendar days of the Secretary providing the notification, the abbreviated new drug application or supplement to an abbreviated new drug application shall not be received within the meaning of 505(j)(5)(A).

(3) ABBREVIATED NEW DRUG APPLICATION FEE AND PRIOR APPROVAL SUPPLEMENT FEE.—Failure to pay a fee under subparagraph (A) or (F) of subsection (a)(3) within 20 calendar days of the applicable due date under subparagraph (C) of such subsection shall result in the abbreviated new drug application or the prior approval supplement to an abbreviated new drug application not being received within the meaning of section 505(j)(5)(A) until such outstanding fee is paid.

(4) GENERIC DRUG FACILITY FEE AND ACTIVE PHARMACEUTICAL INGREDIENT FACILITY FEE.—

(A) IN GENERAL.—Failure to pay the fee under subsection (a)(4) within 20 calendar days of the due date as specified in subparagraph (D) of such subsection shall result in the following:

(i) The Secretary shall place the facility on a publicly available arrears list, such that no new abbreviated new drug application or supplement submitted on or after October 1, 2012, from the person that is responsible for paying such fee, or any affiliate of that person, will be received within the meaning of section 505(j)(5)(A).

(ii) Any new generic drug submission submitted on or after October 1, 2012, that references such a facility shall not be received, within the meaning of section 505(j)(5)(A) if the outstanding facility fee is not paid within 20 calendar days of the Secretary providing the notification to the sponsor of the failure of the owner of the facility to pay the facility fee under subsection (a)(4)(C).

(iii) All drugs or active pharmaceutical ingredients manufactured in such a facility or containing an ingredient manufactured in such a facility shall be deemed misbranded under section 502(aa).

(B) APPLICATION OF PENALTIES.—The penalties under this paragraph shall apply until the fee established by subsection (a)(4) is paid or the facility is removed from all generic drug submissions that refer to the facility.

(C) NONRECEIVAL FOR NONPAYMENT.—

(i) NOTICE.—If an abbreviated new drug application or supplement to an abbreviated new drug application submitted on or after October 1, 2012, references a facility for which a facility fee has not been paid by the applicable date under subsection (a)(4)(C), the Secretary shall notify the sponsor of the generic drug submission of the failure of the owner of the facility to pay the facility fee.

(ii) NONRECEIVAL.—If the facility fee is not paid within 20 calendar days of the Secretary providing the notification under clause (i), the abbreviated new drug application or supplement to an abbreviated new drug application shall not be received within the meaning of section 505(j)(5)(A).

(h) LIMITATIONS.—

(1) IN GENERAL.—Fees under subsection (a) shall be refunded for a fiscal year beginning after fiscal year 2012, unless appropriations for salaries and expenses of the Food and Drug Administration for such fiscal year (excluding the amount of fees appropriated for such fiscal year) are equal to or greater than the amount of appropriations for the salaries and expenses of the Food and Drug Administration for fiscal year 2009 (excluding the amount of fees appropriated for such fiscal year) multiplied by the adjustment factor (as defined in section 744A) applicable to the fiscal year involved.

(2) AUTHORITY.—If the Secretary does not assess fees under subsection (a) during any portion of a fiscal year and if at a later date in such fiscal year the Secretary may assess such fees, the Secretary may assess and collect such fees, without any modification in the rate, for Type II active pharmaceutical ingredient drug master files, abbreviated new drug applications and prior approval supplements, and generic drug facilities and active pharmaceutical ingredient facilities at any time in such fiscal year notwithstanding the provisions of subsection (a) relating to the date fees are to be paid.

(i) CREDITING AND AVAILABILITY OF FEES.—

(1) IN GENERAL.—Fees authorized under subsection (a) shall be collected and available for obligation only to the extent and in the amount provided in advance in appropriations Acts, subject to paragraph (2). Such fees are authorized to remain available until expended. Such sums as may be necessary may be transferred from the Food and Drug Administration salaries and expenses appropriation account without fiscal year limitation to such appropriation account for salaries and

expenses with such fiscal year limitation. The sums transferred shall be available solely for human generic drug activities.

(2) COLLECTIONS AND APPROPRIATION ACTS.—

(A) IN GENERAL.—The fees authorized by this section—

(i) subject to subparagraphs (C) and (D), shall be collected and available in each fiscal year in an amount not to exceed the amount specified in appropriation Acts, or otherwise made available for obligation for such fiscal year; and

(ii) shall be available for a fiscal year beginning after fiscal year 2012 to defray the costs of human generic drug activities (including such costs for an additional number of full-time equivalent positions in the Department of Health and Human Services to be engaged in such activities), only if the Secretary allocates for such purpose an amount for such fiscal year (excluding amounts from fees collected under this section) no less than $97,000,000 multiplied by the adjustment factor defined in section 744A(3) applicable to the fiscal year involved.

(B) COMPLIANCE.—The Secretary shall be considered to have met the requirements of subparagraph (A)(ii) in any fiscal year if the costs funded by appropriations and allocated for human generic activities are not more than 10 percent below the level specified in such subparagraph.

(C) FEE COLLECTION DURING FIRST PROGRAM YEAR.—Until the date of enactment of an Act making appropriations through September 30, 2013 for the salaries and expenses account of the Food and Drug Administration, fees authorized by this section for fiscal year 2013, may be collected and shall be credited to such account and remain available until expended.

(D) PROVISION FOR EARLY PAYMENTS IN SUBSEQUENT YEARS.—Payment of fees authorized under this section for a fiscal year (after fiscal year 2013), prior to the due date for such fees, may be accepted by the Secretary in accordance with authority provided in advance in a prior year appropriations Act.

(3) AUTHORIZATION OF APPROPRIATIONS.—For each of the fiscal years 2013 through 2017, there is authorized to be appropriated for fees under this section an amount equivalent to the total revenue amount determined under subsection (b) for the fiscal year, as adjusted under subsection (c), if applicable, or as otherwise affected under paragraph (2) of this subsection.

(j) COLLECTION OF UNPAID FEES.—In any case where the Secretary does not receive payment of a fee assessed under subsection (a) within 30 calendar days after it is due, such fee shall be treated as a claim of the United States Government subject to subchapter II of chapter 37 of title 31, United States Code.

(k) CONSTRUCTION.—This section may not be construed to require that the number of full-time equivalent positions in the Department of Health and Human Services, for officers, employees, and advisory committees not engaged in human generic drug activities, be reduced to offset the number of officers, employees, and advisory committees so engaged.

(*l*) POSITRON EMISSION TOMOGRAPHY DRUGS.—

(1) EXEMPTION FROM FEES.—Submission of an application for a positron emission tomography drug or active pharmaceutical ingredient for a positron emission tomography drug shall not require the payment of any fee under this section. Facilities that solely produce positron emission tomography drugs shall not be required to pay a facility fee as established in subsection (a)(4).

(2) IDENTIFICATION REQUIREMENT.—Facilities that produce positron emission tomography drugs or active pharmaceutical ingredients of such drugs are required to be identified pursuant to subsection (f).

(m) DISPUTES CONCERNING FEES.—To qualify for the return of a fee claimed to have been paid in error under this section, a person shall submit to the Secretary a written request justifying such return within 180 calendar days after such fee was paid.

(n) SUBSTANTIALLY COMPLETE APPLICATIONS.—An abbreviated new drug application that is not considered to be received within the meaning of section 505(j)(5)(A) because of failure to pay an applicable fee under this provision within the time period specified in subsection (g) shall be deemed not to have been "substantially complete" on the date of its submission within the meaning of section 505(j)(5)(B)(iv)(II)(cc). An abbreviated new drug application that is not substantially complete on the date of its submission solely because of failure to pay an applicable fee under the preceding sentence shall be deemed substantially complete and received within the meaning of section 505(j)(5)(A) as of the date such applicable fee is received.

SEC. 744C [21 U.S.C. 379j–43]. REAUTHORIZATION; REPORTING REQUIREMENTS

(a) PERFORMANCE REPORT.—Beginning with fiscal year 2013, not later than 120 days after the end of each fiscal year for which fees are collected under this part, the Secretary shall prepare and submit to the Committee on Energy and Commerce of the House of Representatives and the Committee on Health, Education, Labor, and Pensions of the Senate a report concerning the progress of the Food and Drug Administration in achieving the goals identified in the letters described in section 301(b) of the Generic Drug User Fee Amendments of 2012 during such fiscal year and the future plans of the Food and Drug Administration for meeting the goals.

(b) FISCAL REPORT.—Beginning with fiscal year 2013, not later than 120 days after the end of each fiscal year for which fees are collected under this part, the Secretary shall prepare and submit to the Committee on Energy and Commerce of the House of Representatives and the Committee on Health, Education, Labor, and Pensions of the Senate a report on the implementation of the authority for such fees during such fiscal year and the use, by the Food and Drug Administration, of the fees collected for such fiscal year.

(c) PUBLIC AVAILABILITY.—The Secretary shall make the reports required under subsections (a) and (b) available to the public on the Internet Web site of the Food and Drug Administration.

(d) REAUTHORIZATION.—

(1) CONSULTATION.—In developing recommendations to present to the Congress with respect to the goals, and plans for meeting the goals, for human generic drug activities for the first 5 fiscal years after fiscal year 2017, and for the reauthorization of this part for such fiscal years, the Secretary shall consult with—

(A) the Committee on Energy and Commerce of the House of Representatives;

(B) the Committee on Health, Education, Labor, and Pensions of the Senate;

(C) scientific and academic experts;

(D) health care professionals;

(E) representatives of patient and consumer advocacy groups; and

(F) the generic drug industry.

(2) PRIOR PUBLIC INPUT.—Prior to beginning negotiations with the generic drug industry on the reauthorization of this part, the Secretary shall—

(A) publish a notice in the Federal Register requesting public input on the reauthorization;

(B) hold a public meeting at which the public may present its views on the reauthorization, including specific suggestions for changes to the goals referred to in subsection (a);

(C) provide a period of 30 days after the public meeting to obtain written comments from the public suggesting changes to this part; and

(D) publish the comments on the Food and Drug Administration's Internet Web site.

(3) PERIODIC CONSULTATION.—Not less frequently than once every month during negotiations with the generic drug industry, the Secretary shall hold discussions with representatives of patient and consumer advocacy groups to continue discussions of their views on the reauthorization and their suggestions for changes to this part as expressed under paragraph (2).

(4) PUBLIC REVIEW OF RECOMMENDATIONS.—After negotiations with the generic drug industry, the Secretary shall—

(A) present the recommendations developed under paragraph (1) to the congressional committees specified in such paragraph;

(B) publish such recommendations in the Federal Register;

(C) provide for a period of 30 days for the public to provide written comments on such recommendations;

(D) hold a meeting at which the public may present its views on such recommendations; and

(E) after consideration of such public views and comments, revise such recommendations as necessary.

(5) TRANSMITTAL OF RECOMMENDATIONS.—Not later than January 15, 2017, the Secretary shall transmit to the Congress the revised recommendations under paragraph (4), a summary of the views and comments received under such paragraph, and any changes made to the recommendations in response to such views and comments.

(6) MINUTES OF NEGOTIATION MEETINGS.—

(A) PUBLIC AVAILABILITY.—Before presenting the recommendations developed under paragraphs (1) through (5) to the Congress, the Secretary shall make publicly available, on the Internet Web site of the Food and Drug Administration, minutes of all negotiation meetings conducted under this subsection between the Food and Drug Administration and the generic drug industry.

(B) CONTENT.—The minutes described under subparagraph (A) shall summarize any substantive proposal made by any party to the negotiations as well as significant controversies or differences of opinion during the negotiations and their resolution.

PART 8—FEES RELATING TO BIOSIMILAR BIOLOGICAL PRODUCTS[80]

SEC. 744G [21 U.S.C. 379j–51]. DEFINITIONS

For purposes of this part:

(1) The term "adjustment factor" applicable to a fiscal year that is the Consumer Price Index for all urban consumers (Washington–Baltimore, DC–MD–VA–WV; Not Seasonally Adjusted; All items) of the preceding fiscal year divided by such Index for September 2011.

(2) The term "affiliate" means a business entity that has a relationship with a second business entity if, directly or indirectly—

---

80. Part 8 was added by Pub. L. No. 112–144, tit. IV, 126 Stat. 993, 1026–38 (2012). Section 404 of that title provides as follows:

SEC. 404. SUNSET DATES.

(a) Authorization.—Sections 744G and 744H of the Federal Food, Drug, and Cosmetic Act, as added by section 402 of this Act, shall cease to be effective October 1, 2017.

(b) Reporting Requirements.—Section 744I of the Federal Food, Drug, and Cosmetic Act, as added by section 403 of this Act, shall cease to be effective January 31, 2018.

(A) one business entity controls, or has the power to control, the other business entity; or

(B) a third party controls, or has power to control, both of the business entities.

(3) The term "biosimilar biological product" means a product for which a biosimilar biological product application has been approved.

(4)(A) Subject to subparagraph (B), the term "biosimilar biological product application" means an application for licensure of a biological product under section 351(k) of the Public Health Service Act.

(B) Such term does not include —

(i) a supplement to such an application;

(ii) an application filed under section 351(k) of the Public Health Service Act that cites as the reference product a bovine blood product for topical application licensed before September 1, 1992, or a large volume parenteral drug product approved before such date;

(iii) an application filed under section 351(k) of the Public Health Service Act with respect to —

(I) whole blood or a blood component for transfusion;

(II) an allergenic extract product;

(III) an in vitro diagnostic biological product; or

(IV) a biological product for further manufacturing use only; or

(iv) an application for licensure under section 351(k) of the Public Health Service Act that is submitted by a State or Federal Government entity for a product that is not distributed commercially.

(5) The term "biosimilar biological product development meeting" means any meeting, other than a biosimilar initial advisory meeting, regarding the content of a development program, including a proposed design for, or data from, a study intended to support a biosimilar biological product application.

(6) The term "biosimilar biological product development program" means the program under this part for expediting the process for the review of submissions in connection with biosimilar biological product development.

(7)(A) The term "biosimilar biological product establishment" means a foreign or domestic place of business —

(i) that is at one general physical location consisting of one or more buildings, all of which are within 5 miles of each other; and

(ii) at which one or more biosimilar biological products are manufactured in final dosage form.

(B) For purposes of subparagraph (A)(ii), the term "manufactured" does not include packaging.

(8) The term "biosimilar initial advisory meeting"—

(A) means a meeting, if requested, that is limited to—

(i) a general discussion regarding whether licensure under section 351(k) of the Public Health Service Act may be feasible for a particular product; and

(ii) if so, general advice on the expected content of the development program; and

(B) does not include any meeting that involves substantive review of summary data or full study reports.

(9) The term "costs of resources allocated for the process for the review of biosimilar biological product applications" means the expenses in connection with the process for the review of biosimilar biological product applications for—

(A) officers and employees of the Food and Drug Administration, contractors of the Food and Drug Administration, advisory committees, and costs related to such officers employees and committees and to contracts with such contractors;

(B) management of information, and the acquisition, maintenance, and repair of computer resources;

(C) leasing, maintenance, renovation, and repair of facilities and acquisition, maintenance, and repair of fixtures, furniture, scientific equipment, and other necessary materials and supplies; and

(D) collecting fees under section 744H and accounting for resources allocated for the review of submissions in connection with biosimilar biological product development, biosimilar biological product applications, and supplements.

(10) The term "final dosage form" means, with respect to a biosimilar biological product, a finished dosage form which is approved for administration to a patient without substantial further manufacturing (such as lyophilized products before reconstitution).

(11) The term "financial hold"—

(A) means an order issued by the Secretary to prohibit the sponsor of a clinical investigation from continuing the investigation if the Secretary determines that the investigation is intended to support a biosimilar biological product application and the sponsor has failed to pay any fee for the product required under subparagraph (A), (B), or (D) of section 744H(a)(1); and

(B) does not mean that any of the bases for a "clinical hold" under section 505(i)(3) have been determined by the Secretary to exist concerning the investigation.

(12) The term "person" includes an affiliate of such person.

(13) The term "process for the review of biosimilar biological product applications" means the following activities of the Secretary with respect to the review of submissions in connection with biosimilar biological product development, biosimilar biological product applications, and supplements:

(A) The activities necessary for the review of submissions in connection with biosimilar biological product development, biosimilar biological product applications, and supplements.

(B) Actions related to submissions in connection with biosimilar biological product development, the issuance of action letters which approve biosimilar biological product applications or which set forth in detail the specific deficiencies in such applications, and where appropriate, the actions necessary to place such applications in condition for approval.

(C) The inspection of biosimilar biological product establishments and other facilities undertaken as part of the Secretary's review of pending biosimilar biological product applications and supplements.

(D) Activities necessary for the release of lots of biosimilar biological products under section 351(k) of the Public Health Service Act.

(E) Monitoring of research conducted in connection with the review of biosimilar biological product applications.

(F) Postmarket safety activities with respect to biologics approved under biosimilar biological product applications or supplements, including the following activities:

(i) Collecting, developing, and reviewing safety information on biosimilar biological products, including adverse-event reports.

(ii) Developing and using improved adverse-event data-collection systems, including information technology systems.

(iii) Developing and using improved analytical tools to assess potential safety problems, including access to external data bases.

(iv) Implementing and enforcing section 505(*o*) (relating to postapproval studies and clinical trials and labeling changes) and section 505(p) (relating to risk evaluation and mitigation strategies).

(v) Carrying out section 505(k)(5) (relating to adverse-event reports and postmarket safety activities).

(14) The term "supplement" means a request to the Secretary to approve a change in a biosimilar biological product application which has been approved, including a supplement requesting that the Secretary determine that the biosimilar biological product meets the standards for interchangeability described in section 351(k)(4) of the Public Health Service Act.

SEC. 744H [21 U.S.C. 379j–52]. AUTHORITY TO ASSESS AND USE BIOSIMILAR BIOLOGICAL PRODUCT FEES

(a) TYPES OF FEES.—Beginning in fiscal year 2013, the Secretary shall assess and collect fees in accordance with this section as follows:

(1) BIOSIMILAR DEVELOPMENT PROGRAM FEES.—

(A) INITIAL BIOSIMILAR BIOLOGICAL PRODUCT DEVELOPMENT FEE.—

(i) IN GENERAL.—Each person that submits to the Secretary a meeting request described under clause (ii) or a clinical protocol for an investigational new drug protocol described under clause (iii) shall pay for the product named in the meeting request or the investigational new drug application the initial biosimilar biological product development fee established under subsection (b)(1)(A).

(ii) MEETING REQUEST.—The meeting request described in this clause is a request for a biosimilar biological product development meeting for a product.

(iii) CLINICAL PROTOCOL FOR IND.—A clinical protocol for an investigational new drug protocol described in this clause is a clinical protocol consistent with the provisions of section 505(i), including any regulations promulgated under section 505(i), (referred to in this section as "investigational new drug application") describing an investigation that the Secretary determines is intended to support a biosimilar biological product application for a product.

(iv) DUE DATE.—The initial biosimilar biological product development fee shall be due by the earlier of the following:

(I) Not later than 5 days after the Secretary grants a request for a biosimilar biological product development meeting.

(II) The date of submission of an investigational new drug application describing an investigation that the Secretary determines is intended to support a biosimilar biological product application.

(v) TRANSITION RULE.—Each person that has submitted an investigational new drug application prior to the date of enactment of the Biosimilars User Fee Act of 2012 shall pay the initial biosimilar biological product development fee by the earlier of the following:

(I) Not later than 60 days after the date of the enactment of the Biosimilars User Fee Act of 2012, if the Secretary determines that the investigational new drug application describes an investigation that is intended to support a biosimilar biological product application.

(II) Not later than 5 days after the Secretary grants a request for a biosimilar biological product development meeting.

(B) Annual biosimilar biological product development fee.—

(i) In general.—A person that pays an initial biosimilar biological product development fee for a product shall pay for such product, beginning in the fiscal year following the fiscal year in which the initial biosimilar biological product development fee was paid, an annual fee established under subsection (b)(1)(B) for biosimilar biological product development (referred to in this section as "annual biosimilar biological product development fee").

(ii) Due date.—The annual biosimilar biological product development program fee for each fiscal year will be due on the later of—

(I) the first business day on or after October 1 of each such year; or

(II) the first business day after the enactment of an appropriations Act providing for the collection and obligation of fees for such year under this section.

(iii) Exception.—The annual biosimilar development program fee for each fiscal year will be due on the date specified in clause (ii), unless the person has—

(I) submitted a marketing application for the biological product that was accepted for filing; or

(II) discontinued participation in the biosimilar biological product development program for the product under subparagraph (C).

(C) Discontinuation of fee obligation.—A person may discontinue participation in the biosimilar biological product development program for a product effective October 1 of a fiscal year by, not later than August 1 of the preceding fiscal year—

(i) if no investigational new drug application concerning the product has been submitted, submitting to the Secretary a written declaration that the person has no present intention of further developing the product as a biosimilar biological product; or

(ii) if an investigational new drug application concerning the product has been submitted, withdrawing the investigational new drug application in accordance with part 312 of title 21, Code of Federal Regulations (or any successor regulations).

(D) Reactivation fee.—

(i) In general.—A person that has discontinued participation in the biosimilar biological product development program for a product under subparagraph (C) shall pay a fee (referred to in this section as "reactivation fee") by the earlier of the following:

(I) Not later than 5 days after the Secretary grants a request for a biosimilar biological product development meeting for the product (after the date on which such participation was discontinued).

(II) Upon the date of submission (after the date on which such participation was discontinued) of an investigational new drug application describing an investigation that the Secretary determines is intended to support a biosimilar biological product application for that product.

(ii) APPLICATION OF ANNUAL FEE.—A person that pays a reactivation fee for a product shall pay for such product, beginning in the next fiscal year, the annual biosimilar biological product development fee under subparagraph (B).

(E) EFFECT OF FAILURE TO PAY BIOSIMILAR DEVELOPMENT PROGRAM FEES.—

(i) NO BIOSIMILAR BIOLOGICAL PRODUCT DEVELOPMENT MEETINGS.—If a person has failed to pay an initial or annual biosimilar biological product development fee as required under subparagraph (A) or (B), or a reactivation fee as required under subparagraph (D), the Secretary shall not provide a biosimilar biological product development meeting relating to the product for which fees are owed.

(ii) NO RECEIPT OF INVESTIGATIONAL NEW DRUG APPLICATIONS.—Except in extraordinary circumstances, the Secretary shall not consider an investigational new drug application to have been received under section 505(i)(2) if—

(I) the Secretary determines that the investigation is intended to support a biosimilar biological product application; and

(II) the sponsor has failed to pay an initial or annual biosimilar biological product development fee for the product as required under subparagraph (A) or (B), or a reactivation fee as required under subparagraph (D).

(iii) FINANCIAL HOLD.—Notwithstanding section 505(i)(2), except in extraordinary circumstances, the Secretary shall prohibit the sponsor of a clinical investigation from continuing the investigation if—

(I) the Secretary determines that the investigation is intended to support a biosimilar biological product application; and

(II) the sponsor has failed to pay an initial or annual biosimilar biological product development fee for the product as required under subparagraph (A) or (B), or a reactivation fee for the product as required under subparagraph (D).

(iv) NO ACCEPTANCE OF BIOSIMILAR BIOLOGICAL PRODUCT APPLICATIONS OR SUPPLEMENTS.—If a person has failed to pay an initial or annual biosimilar biological product development fee as required under subparagraph (A) or

(B), or a reactivation fee as required under subparagraph (D), any biosimilar biological product application or supplement submitted by that person shall be considered incomplete and shall not be accepted for filing by the Secretary until all such fees owed by such person have been paid.

(F) Limits regarding biosimilar development program fees.—

(i) No refunds.—The Secretary shall not refund any initial or annual biosimilar biological product development fee paid under subparagraph (A) or (B), or any reactivation fee paid under subparagraph (D).

(ii) No waivers, exemptions, or reductions.—The Secretary shall not grant a waiver, exemption, or reduction of any initial or annual biosimilar biological product development fee due or payable under subparagraph (A) or (B), or any reactivation fee due or payable under subparagraph (D).

(2) Biosimilar biological product application and supplement fee.—

(A) In general.—Each person that submits, on or after October 1, 2012, a biosimilar biological product application or a supplement shall be subject to the following fees:

(i) A fee for a biosimilar biological product application that is equal to—

(I) the amount of the fee established under subsection (b)(1)(D) for a biosimilar biological product application for which clinical data (other than comparative bioavailability studies) with respect to safety or effectiveness are required for approval; minus

(II) the cumulative amount of fees paid, if any, under subparagraphs (A), (B), and (D) of paragraph (1) for the product that is the subject of the application.

(ii) A fee for a biosimilar biological product application for which clinical data (other than comparative bioavailability studies) with respect to safety or effectiveness are not required, that is equal to—

(I) half of the amount of the fee established under subsection (b)(1) (D) for a biosimilar biological product application; minus

(II) the cumulative amount of fees paid, if any, under subparagraphs (A), (B), and (D) of paragraph (1) for that product.

(iii) A fee for a supplement for which clinical data (other than comparative bioavailability studies) with respect to safety or effectiveness are required, that is equal to half of the amount of the fee established under subsection (b)(1)(D) for a biosimilar biological product application.

(B) Reduction in fees.—Notwithstanding section 404 of the Biosimilars User Fee Act of 2012, any person who pays a fee under subparagraph (A), (B), or (D) of paragraph (1) for a product before October 1, 2017, but submits a biosimilar biological product application for that product after such date, shall be entitled to the reduction of any biosimilar biological product application fees that may be assessed at the time when such biosimilar biological product application is submitted, by the cumulative amount of fees paid under subparagraphs (A), (B), and (D) of paragraph (1) for that product.

(C) PAYMENT DUE DATE.—Any fee required by subparagraph (A) shall be due upon submission of the application or supplement for which such fee applies.

(D) EXCEPTION FOR PREVIOUSLY FILED APPLICATION OR SUPPLEMENT.—If a biosimilar biological product application or supplement was submitted by a person that paid the fee for such application or supplement, was accepted for filing, and was not approved or was withdrawn (without a waiver), the submission of a biosimilar biological product application or a supplement for the same product by the same person (or the person's licensee, assignee, or successor) shall not be subject to a fee under subparagraph (A).

(E) REFUND OF APPLICATION FEE IF APPLICATION REFUSED FOR FILING OR WITHDRAWN BEFORE FILING.—The Secretary shall refund 75 percent of the fee paid under this paragraph for any application or supplement which is refused for filing or withdrawn without a waiver before filing.

(F) FEES FOR APPLICATIONS PREVIOUSLY REFUSED FOR FILING OR WITHDRAWN BEFORE FILING.—A biosimilar biological product application or supplement that was submitted but was refused for filing, or was withdrawn before being accepted or refused for filing, shall be subject to the full fee under subparagraph (A) upon being resubmitted or filed over protest, unless the fee is waived under subsection (c).

(3) BIOSIMILAR BIOLOGICAL PRODUCT ESTABLISHMENT FEE.—

(A) IN GENERAL.—Except as provided in subparagraph (E), each person that is named as the applicant in a biosimilar biological product application shall be assessed an annual fee established under subsection (b)(1)(E) for each biosimilar biological product establishment that is listed in the approved biosimilar biological product application as an establishment that manufactures the biosimilar biological product named in such application.

(B) ASSESSMENT IN FISCAL YEARS.—The establishment fee shall be assessed in each fiscal year for which the biosimilar biological product named in the application is assessed a fee under paragraph (4) unless the biosimilar biological product establishment listed in the application does not engage in the manufacture of the biosimilar biological product during such fiscal year.

(C) DUE DATE.—The establishment fee for a fiscal year shall be due on the later of—

(i) the first business day on or after October 1 of such fiscal year; or

(ii) the first business day after the enactment of an appropriations Act providing for the collection and obligation of fees for such fiscal year under this section.

(D) APPLICATION TO ESTABLISHMENT.—

(i) Each biosimilar biological product establishment shall be assessed only one fee per biosimilar biological product establishment, notwithstanding the number of biosimilar biological products manufactured at the establishment, subject to clause (ii).

(ii) In the event an establishment is listed in a biosimilar biological product application by more than one applicant, the establishment fee for the fiscal year shall be divided equally and assessed among the applicants whose biosimilar biological products are manufactured by the establishment during the fiscal year and assessed biosimilar biological product fees under paragraph (4).

(E) EXCEPTION FOR NEW PRODUCTS.—If, during the fiscal year, an applicant initiates or causes to be initiated the manufacture of a biosimilar biological product at an establishment listed in its biosimilar biological product application—

(i) that did not manufacture the biosimilar biological product in the previous fiscal year; and

(ii) for which the full biosimilar biological product establishment fee has been assessed in the fiscal year at a time before manufacture of the biosimilar biological product was begun,

the applicant shall not be assessed a share of the biosimilar biological product establishment fee for the fiscal year in which the manufacture of the product began.

(4) BIOSIMILAR BIOLOGICAL PRODUCT FEE.—

(A) IN GENERAL.—Each person who is named as the applicant in a biosimilar biological product application shall pay for each such biosimilar biological product the annual fee established under subsection (b)(1)(F).

(B) DUE DATE.—The biosimilar biological product fee for a fiscal year shall be due on the later of—

(i) the first business day on or after October 1 of each such year; or

(ii) the first business day after the enactment of an appropriations Act providing for the collection and obligation of fees for such year under this section.

(C) ONE FEE PER PRODUCT PER YEAR.—The biosimilar biological product fee shall be paid only once for each product for each fiscal year.

(b) FEE **S**ETTING AND **A**MOUNTS.—

(1) I**N** GENERAL.—Subject to paragraph (2), the Secretary shall, 60 days before the start of each fiscal year that begins after September 30, 2012, establish, for the next fiscal year, the fees under subsection (a). Except as provided in subsection (c), such fees shall be in the following amounts:

(A) I**NITIAL BIOSIMILAR BIOLOGICAL PRODUCT DEVELOPMENT FEE.**—The initial biosimilar biological product development fee under subsection (a)(1)(A) for a fiscal year shall be equal to 10 percent of the amount established under section 736(c)(4) for a human drug application described in section 736(a)(1)(A)(i) for that fiscal year.

(B) A**NNUAL BIOSIMILAR BIOLOGICAL PRODUCT DEVELOPMENT FEE.**—The annual biosimilar biological product development fee under subsection (a)(1)(B) for a fiscal year shall be equal to 10 percent of the amount established under section 736(c)(4) for a human drug application described in section 736(a)(1)(A)(i) for that fiscal year.

(C) R**EACTIVATION FEE.**—The reactivation fee under subsection (a)(1)(D) for a fiscal year shall be equal to 20 percent of the amount of the fee established under section 736(c)(4) for a human drug application described in section 736(a)(1)(A)(i) for that fiscal year.

(D) B**IOSIMILAR BIOLOGICAL PRODUCT APPLICATION FEE.**—The biosimilar biological product application fee under subsection (a)(2) for a fiscal year shall be equal to the amount established under section 736(c)(4) for a human drug application described in section 736(a)(1)(A)(i) for that fiscal year.

(E) B**IOSIMILAR BIOLOGICAL PRODUCT ESTABLISHMENT FEE.**—The biosimilar biological product establishment fee under subsection (a)(3) for a fiscal year shall be equal to the amount established under section 736(c)(4) for a prescription drug establishment for that fiscal year.

(F) B**IOSIMILAR BIOLOGICAL PRODUCT FEE.**—The biosimilar biological product fee under subsection (a)(4) for a fiscal year shall be equal to the amount established under section 736(c)(4) for a prescription drug product for that fiscal year.

(2) L**IMIT.**—The total amount of fees charged for a fiscal year under this section may not exceed the total amount for such fiscal year of the costs of resources allocated for the process for the review of biosimilar biological product applications.

(c) APPLICATION **F**EE **W**AIVER FOR **S**MALL **B**USINESS.—

(1) W**AIVER OF APPLICATION FEE.**—The Secretary shall grant to a person who is named in a biosimilar biological product application a waiver from the application fee assessed to that person under subsection (a)(2)(A) for the first biosimilar biological product application that a small business or its affiliate submits to the

Secretary for review. After a small business or its affiliate is granted such a waiver, the small business or its affiliate shall pay—

(A) application fees for all subsequent biosimilar biological product applications submitted to the Secretary for review in the same manner as an entity that is not a small business; and

(B) all supplement fees for all supplements to biosimilar biological product applications submitted to the Secretary for review in the same manner as an entity that is not a small business.

(2) CONSIDERATIONS.—In determining whether to grant a waiver of a fee under paragraph (1), the Secretary shall consider only the circumstances and assets of the applicant involved and any affiliate of the applicant.

(3) SMALL BUSINESS DEFINED.—In this subsection, the term "small business" means an entity that has fewer than 500 employees, including employees of affiliates, and does not have a drug product that has been approved under a human drug application (as defined in section 735) or a biosimilar biological product application (as defined in section 744G(4)) and introduced or delivered for introduction into interstate commerce.

(d) EFFECT OF FAILURE TO PAY FEES.—A biosimilar biological product application or supplement submitted by a person subject to fees under subsection (a) shall be considered incomplete and shall not be accepted for filing by the Secretary until all fees owed by such person have been paid.

(e) CREDITING AND AVAILABILITY OF FEES.—

(1) IN GENERAL.—Subject to paragraph (2), fees authorized under subsection (a) shall be collected and available for obligation only to the extent and in the amount provided in advance in appropriations Acts. Such fees are authorized to remain available until expended. Such sums as may be necessary may be transferred from the Food and Drug Administration salaries and expenses appropriation account without fiscal year limitation to such appropriation account for salaries and expenses with such fiscal year limitation. The sums transferred shall be available solely for the process for the review of biosimilar biological product applications.

(2) COLLECTIONS AND APPROPRIATION ACTS.—

(A) IN GENERAL.—Subject to subparagraphs (C) and (D), the fees authorized by this section shall be collected and available in each fiscal year in an amount not to exceed the amount specified in appropriation Acts, or otherwise made available for obligation for such fiscal year.

(B) USE OF FEES AND LIMITATION.—The fees authorized by this section shall be available for a fiscal year beginning after fiscal year 2012 to defray the costs of the process for the review of biosimilar biological product applications (including such costs for an additional number of full-time equivalent positions in the Department of Health and Human Services to be engaged in such process), only if the Secretary allocates for such purpose an amount for such fiscal year (excluding amounts from fees collected under this section) no less than $20,000,000, multiplied by the adjustment factor applicable to the fiscal year involved.

(C) Fee collection during first program year.—Until the date of enactment of an Act making appropriations through September 30, 2013, for the salaries and expenses account of the Food and Drug Administration, fees authorized by this section for fiscal year 2013 may be collected and shall be credited to such account and remain available until expended.

(D) Provision for early payments in subsequent years.—Payment of fees authorized under this section for a fiscal year (after fiscal year 2013), prior to the due date for such fees, may be accepted by the Secretary in accordance with authority provided in advance in a prior year appropriations Act.

(3) Authorization of appropriations.—For each of fiscal years 2013 through 2017, there is authorized to be appropriated for fees under this section an amount equivalent to the total amount of fees assessed for such fiscal year under this section.

(f) Collection of Unpaid Fees.—In any case where the Secretary does not receive payment of a fee assessed under subsection (a) within 30 days after it is due, such fee shall be treated as a claim of the United States Government subject to subchapter II of chapter 37 of title 31, United States Code.

(g) Written Requests for Waivers and Refunds.—To qualify for consideration for a waiver under subsection (c), or for a refund of any fee collected in accordance with subsection (a)(2)(A), a person shall submit to the Secretary a written request for such waiver or refund not later than 180 days after such fee is due.

(h) Construction.—This section may not be construed to require that the number of full-time equivalent positions in the Department of Health and Human Services, for officers, employers, and advisory committees not engaged in the process of the review of biosimilar biological product applications, be reduced to offset the number of officers, employees, and advisory committees so engaged.

Sec. 744I [21 U.S.C. 379j–53]. Reauthorization; Reporting Requirements

(a) Performance Report.—Beginning with fiscal year 2013, not later than 120 days after the end of each fiscal year for which fees are collected under this part, the Secretary shall prepare and submit to the Committee on Energy and Commerce of the House of Representatives and the Committee on Health, Education, Labor, and Pensions of the Senate a report concerning the progress of the Food and Drug Administration in achieving the goals identified in the letters described in section 401(b) of the Biosimilar User Fee Act of 2012 during such fiscal year and the future plans of the Food and Drug Administration for meeting such goals. The report for a fiscal year shall include information on all previous cohorts for which the Secretary has not given a complete response on all biosimilar biological product applications and supplements in the cohort.

(b) FISCAL REPORT.—Not later than 120 days after the end of fiscal year 2013 and each subsequent fiscal year for which fees are collected under this part, the Secretary shall prepare and submit to the Committee on Energy and Commerce of the House of Representatives and the Committee on Health, Education, Labor, and Pensions of the Senate a report on the implementation of the authority for such fees during such fiscal year and the use, by the Food and Drug Administration, of the fees collected for such fiscal year.

(c) PUBLIC AVAILABILITY.—The Secretary shall make the reports required under subsections (a) and (b) available to the public on the Internet Web site of the Food and Drug Administration.

(d) STUDY.—

(1) IN GENERAL.—The Secretary shall contract with an independent accounting or consulting firm to study the workload volume and full costs associated with the process for the review of biosimilar biological product applications.

(2) INTERIM RESULTS.—Not later than June 1, 2015, the Secretary shall publish, for public comment, interim results of the study described under paragraph (1).

(3) FINAL RESULTS.—Not later than September 30, 2016, the Secretary shall publish, for public comment, the final results of the study described under paragraph (1).

(e) REAUTHORIZATION.—

(1) CONSULTATION.—In developing recommendations to present to the Congress with respect to the goals described in subsection (a), and plans for meeting the goals, for the process for the review of biosimilar biological product applications for the first 5 fiscal years after fiscal year 2017, and for the reauthorization of this part for such fiscal years, the Secretary shall consult with—

(A) the Committee on Energy and Commerce of the House of Representatives;

(B) the Committee on Health, Education, Labor, and Pensions of the Senate;

(C) scientific and academic experts;

(D) health care professionals;

(E) representatives of patient and consumer advocacy groups; and

(F) the regulated industry.

(2) PUBLIC REVIEW OF RECOMMENDATIONS.—After negotiations with the regulated industry, the Secretary shall—

(A) present the recommendations developed under paragraph (1) to the congressional committees specified in such paragraph;

(B) publish such recommendations in the Federal Register;

(C) provide for a period of 30 days for the public to provide written comments on such recommendations;

(D) hold a meeting at which the public may present its views on such recommendations; and

(E) after consideration of such public views and comments, revise such recommendations as necessary.

(3) TRANSMITTAL OF RECOMMENDATIONS.—Not later than January 15, 2017, the Secretary shall transmit to the Congress the revised recommendations under paragraph (2), a summary of the views and comments received under such paragraph, and any changes made to the recommendations in response to such views and comments.

PART 9—FEES RELATING TO OUTSOURCING FACILITIES

SEC. 744J [21 U.S.C. 379j–61]. DEFINITIONS

In this part:

(1) The term "affiliate" has the meaning given such term in section 735(11).

(2) The term "gross annual sales" means the total worldwide gross annual sales, in United States dollars, for an outsourcing facility, including the sales of all the affiliates of the outsourcing facility.

(3) The term "outsourcing facility" has the meaning given to such term in section 503B(d)(4).

(4) The term "reinspection" means, with respect to an outsourcing facility, 1 or more inspections conducted under section 704 subsequent to an inspection conducted under such provision which identified noncompliance materially related to an applicable requirement of this Act, specifically to determine whether compliance has been achieved to the Secretary's satisfaction.

SEC. 744K [21 U.S.C. 379j–62]. AUTHORITY TO ASSESS AND USE OUTSOURCING FACILITY FEES

(a) ESTABLISHMENT AND REINSPECTION FEES.—

(1) IN GENERAL.—For fiscal year 2015 and each subsequent fiscal year, the Secretary shall, in accordance with this subsection, assess and collect—

(A) an annual establishment fee from each outsourcing facility; and

(B) a reinspection fee from each outsourcing facility subject to a reinspection in such fiscal year.

(2) MULTIPLE REINSPECTIONS.—An outsourcing facility subject to multiple reinspections in a fiscal year shall be subject to a reinspection fee for each reinspection.

(b) ESTABLISHMENT AND REINSPECTION FEE SETTING.—The Secretary shall—

(1) establish the amount of the establishment fee and reinspection fee to be collected under this section for each fiscal year based on the methodology described in subsection (c); and

(2) publish such fee amounts in a Federal Register notice not later than 60 calendar days before the start of each such year.

(c) AMOUNT OF ESTABLISHMENT FEE AND REINSPECTION FEE.—

(1) IN GENERAL.—For each outsourcing facility in a fiscal year—

(A) except as provided in paragraph (4), the amount of the annual establishment fee under subsection (b) shall be equal to the sum of—

(i) $ 15,000, multiplied by the inflation adjustment factor described in paragraph (2); plus

(ii) the small business adjustment factor described in paragraph (3); and

(B) the amount of any reinspection fee (if applicable) under subsection (b) shall be equal to $ 15,000, multiplied by the inflation adjustment factor described in paragraph (2).

(2) INFLATION ADJUSTMENT FACTOR.—

(A) IN GENERAL.—For fiscal year 2015 and subsequent fiscal years, the fee amounts established in paragraph (1) shall be adjusted by the Secretary by notice, published in the Federal Register, for a fiscal year by the amount equal to the sum of—

(i) 1;

(ii) the average annual percent change in the cost, per full-time equivalent position of the Food and Drug Administration, of all personnel compensation and benefits paid with respect to such positions for the first 3 years of the preceding 4 fiscal years, multiplied by the proportion of personnel compensation and benefits costs to total costs of an average full-time equivalent position of the Food and Drug Administration for the first 3 years of the preceding 4 fiscal years; plus

(iii) the average annual percent change that occurred in the Consumer Price Index for urban consumers (U.S. City Average; Not Seasonally Adjusted; All items; Annual Index) for the first 3 years of the preceding 4 years of available data multiplied by the proportion of all costs other than personnel compensation and benefits costs to total costs of an average full-time equivalent position of the Food and Drug Administration for the first 3 years of the preceding 4 fiscal years.

(B) Compounded basis.—The adjustment made each fiscal year under subparagraph (A) shall be added on a compounded basis to the sum of all adjustments made each fiscal year after fiscal year 2014 under subparagraph (A).

(3) Small business adjustment factor.—The small business adjustment factor described in this paragraph shall be an amount established by the Secretary for each fiscal year based on the Secretary's estimate of—

(A) the number of small businesses that will pay a reduced establishment fee for such fiscal year; and

(B) the adjustment to the establishment fee necessary to achieve total fees equaling the total fees that the Secretary would have collected if no entity qualified for the small business exception in paragraph (4).

(4) Exception for small businesses.—

(A) In general.—In the case of an outsourcing facility with gross annual sales of $ 1,000,000 or less in the 12 months ending April 1 of the fiscal year immediately preceding the fiscal year in which the fees under this section are assessed, the amount of the establishment fee under subsection (b) for a fiscal year shall be equal to 1/3 of the amount calculated under paragraph (1)(A)(i) for such fiscal year.

(B) Application.—To qualify for the exception under this paragraph, a small business shall submit to the Secretary a written request for such exception, in a format specified by the Secretary in guidance, certifying its gross annual sales for the 12 months ending April 1 of the fiscal year immediately preceding the fiscal year in which fees under this subsection are assessed. Any such application shall be submitted to the Secretary not later than April 30 of such immediately preceding fiscal year.

(5) Crediting of fees.—In establishing the small business adjustment factor under paragraph (3) for a fiscal year, the Secretary shall—

(A) provide for the crediting of fees from the previous year to the next year if the Secretary overestimated the amount of the small business adjustment factor for such previous fiscal year; and

(B) consider the need to account for any adjustment of fees and such other factors as the Secretary determines appropriate.

(d) Use of Fees.—The Secretary shall make all of the fees collected pursuant to subparagraphs (A) and (B) of subsection (a)(1) available solely to pay for the costs of oversight of outsourcing facilities.

(e) Supplement Not Supplant.—Funds received by the Secretary pursuant to this section shall be used to supplement and not supplant any other Federal funds available to carry out the activities described in this section.

(f) Crediting and Availability of Fees.—Fees authorized under this section shall be collected and available for obligation only to the extent and in the amount provided in advance in appropriations Acts. Such fees are authorized to remain available until expended. Such sums as may be necessary may be transferred from the Food and Drug Administration salaries and expenses appropriation account without fiscal year limitation to such appropriation account for salaries and expenses with such fiscal year limitation. The sums transferred shall be available solely for the purpose of paying the costs of oversight of outsourcing facilities.

(g) COLLECTION OF FEES.—

(1) ESTABLISHMENT FEE.—An outsourcing facility shall remit the establishment fee due under this section in a fiscal year when submitting a registration pursuant to section 503B(b) for such fiscal year.

(2) REINSPECTION FEE.—The Secretary shall specify in the Federal Register notice described in subsection (b)(2) the manner in which reinspection fees assessed under this section shall be collected and the timeline for payment of such fees. Such a fee shall be collected after the Secretary has conducted a reinspection of the outsourcing facility involved.

(3) EFFECT OF FAILURE TO PAY FEES.—

(A) REGISTRATION.—An outsourcing facility shall not be considered registered under section 503B(b) in a fiscal year until the date that the outsourcing facility remits the establishment fee under this subsection for such fiscal year.

(B) MISBRANDING.—All drugs manufactured, prepared, propagated, compounded, or processed by an outsourcing facility for which any establishment fee or reinspection fee has not been paid, as required by this section, shall be deemed misbranded under section 502 until the fees owed for such outsourcing facility under this section have been paid.

(4) COLLECTION OF UNPAID FEES.—In any case where the Secretary does not receive payment of a fee assessed under this section within 30 calendar days after it is due, such fee shall be treated as a claim of the United States Government subject to provisions of subchapter II of chapter 37 of title 31, United States Code.

(h) ANNUAL REPORT TO CONGRESS.—Not later than 120 calendar days after each fiscal year in which fees are assessed and collected under this section, the Secretary shall submit a report to the Committee on Health, Education, Labor, and Pensions of the Senate and the Committee on Energy and Commerce of the House of Representatives, to include a description of fees assessed and collected for such year, a summary description of entities paying the fees, a description of the hiring and placement of new staff, a description of the use of fee resources to support inspecting outsourcing facilities, and the number of inspections and reinspections of such facilities performed each year.

(i) AUTHORIZATION OF APPROPRIATIONS.—For fiscal year 2014 and each subsequent fiscal year, there is authorized to be appropriated for fees under this section an amount equivalent to the total amount of fees assessed for such fiscal year under this section.

SUBCHAPTER D—INFORMATION AND EDUCATION

SEC. 745 [21 U.S.C. 379k]. INFORMATION SYSTEM

The Secretary shall establish and maintain an information system to track the status and progress of each application or submission (including a petition, notification, or other similar form of request) submitted to the Food and Drug Administration requesting agency action.

SEC. 745A [21 U.S.C. 379k–1]. ELECTRONIC FORMAT FOR SUBMISSIONS

(a) DRUGS AND BIOLOGICS.—

(1) IN GENERAL.—Beginning no earlier than 24 months after the issuance of a final guidance issued after public notice and opportunity for comment, submissions under subsection (b), (i), or (j) of section 505 of this Act or subsection (a) or (k) of section 351 of the Public Health Service Act shall be submitted in such electronic format as specified by the Secretary in such guidance.

(2) GUIDANCE CONTENTS.—In the guidance under paragraph (1), the Secretary may—

(A) provide a timetable for establishment by the Secretary of further standards for electronic submission as required by such paragraph; and

(B) set forth criteria for waivers of and exemptions from the requirements of this subsection.

(3) EXCEPTION.—This subsection shall not apply to submissions described in section 561.

(b) DEVICES.—

(1) IN GENERAL.—Beginning after the issuance of final guidance implementing this paragraph, presubmissions and submissions for devices under section 510(k), 513(f)(2)(A), 515(c), 515(d), 515(f), 520(g), 520(m), or 564 of this Act or section 351 of the Public Health Service Act, and any supplements to such presubmissions or submissions, shall include an electronic copy of such presubmissions or submissions.

(2) GUIDANCE CONTENTS.—In the guidance under paragraph (1), the Secretary may—

(A) provide standards for the electronic copy required under such paragraph; and

(B) set forth criteria for waivers of and exemptions from the requirements of this subsection.

Sec. 746 [21 U.S.C. 379l]. EDUCATION

(a) In General.—The Secretary shall conduct training and education programs for the employees of the Food and Drug Administration relating to the regulatory responsibilities and policies established by this Act, including programs for—

(1) scientific training;

(2) training to improve the skill of officers and employees authorized to conduct inspections under section 704;

(3) training to achieve product specialization in such inspections; and

(4) training in administrative process and procedure and integrity issues.

(b) Intramural Fellowships and Other Training Programs.—The Secretary, acting through the Commissioner, may, through fellowships and other training programs, conduct and support intramural research training for predoctoral and postdoctoral scientists and physicians. Any such fellowships and training programs under this section or under section 770(d)(2)(A)(ix) may include provision by such scientists and physicians of services on a voluntary and uncompensated basis, as the Secretary determines appropriate. Such scientists and physicians shall be subject to all legal and ethical requirements otherwise applicable to officers or employees of the Department of Health and Human Services.

SUBCHAPTER E—ENVIRONMENTAL IMPACT REVIEW

Sec. 749 [21 U.S.C. 379o]. ENVIRONMENTAL IMPACT

Notwithstanding any other provision of law, an environmental impact statement prepared in accordance with the regulations published in part 25 of title 21, Code of Federal Regulations (as in effect on August 31, 1997) in connection with an action carried out under (or a recommendation or report relating to) this Act, shall be considered to meet the requirements for a detailed statement under section 102(2)(C) of the National Environmental Policy Act of 1969 (42 U.S.C. 4332(2)(C)).

SUBCHAPTER F—NATIONAL UNIFORMITY FOR NONPRESCRIPTION DRUGS AND PREEMPTION FOR LABELING OR PACKAGING OF COSMETICS

Sec. 751 [21 U.S.C. 379r]. NATIONAL UNIFORMITY FOR NONPRESCRIPTION DRUGS

(a) In General.—Except as provided in subsection (b), (c)(1), (d), (e), or (f), no State or political subdivision of a State may establish or continue in effect any requirement—

(1) that relates to the regulation of a drug that is not subject to the requirements of section 503(b)(1) or 503(f)(1)(A); and

(2) that is different from or in addition to, or that is otherwise not identical with, a requirement under this Act, the Poison Prevention Packaging Act of 1970 (15 U.S.C. 1471 et seq.), or the Fair Packaging and Labeling Act (15 U.S.C. 1451 et seq.).

(b) EXEMPTION.—

(1) IN GENERAL.—Upon application of a State or political subdivision thereof, the Secretary may by regulation, after notice and opportunity for written and oral presentation of views, exempt from subsection (a), under such conditions as may be prescribed in such regulation, a State or political subdivision requirement that—

(A) protects an important public interest that would otherwise be unprotected, including the health and safety of children;

(B) would not cause any drug to be in violation of any applicable requirement or prohibition under Federal law; and

(C) would not unduly burden interstate commerce.

(2) TIMELY ACTION.—The Secretary shall make a decision on the exemption of a State or political subdivision requirement under paragraph (1) not later than 120 days after receiving the application of the State or political subdivision under paragraph(1).

(c) SCOPE.—

(1) IN GENERAL.—This section shall not apply to—

(A) any State or political subdivision requirement that relates to the practice of pharmacy; or

(B) any State or political subdivision requirement that a drug be dispensed only upon the prescription of a practitioner licensed by law to administer such drug.

(2) SAFETY OR EFFECTIVENESS.—For purposes of subsection (a), a requirement that relates to the regulation of a drug shall be deemed to include any requirement relating to public information or any other form of public communication relating to a warning of any kind for a drug.

(d) EXCEPTIONS.—

(1) IN GENERAL.—In the case of a drug described in subsection (a)(1) that is not the subject of an application approved under section 505 or section 507 (as in effect on the day before the date of enactment of the Food and Drug Administration Modernization Act of 1997) or a final regulation promulgated by the Secretary establishing conditions under which the drug is generally recognized as safe and effective and not misbranded, subsection (a) shall apply only with respect to a requirement of a State or political subdivision of a State that relates

to the same subject as, but is different from or in addition to, or that is otherwise not identical with—

> (A) a regulation in effect with respect to the drug pursuant to a statute described in subsection (a)(2); or

> (B) any other requirement in effect with respect to the drug pursuant to an amendment to such a statute made on or after the date of enactment of the Food and Drug Administration Modernization Act of 1997.

> (2) STATE INITIATIVES.—This section shall not apply to a State requirement adopted by a State public initiative or referendum enacted prior to September 1, 1997.

(e) NO EFFECT ON PRODUCT LIABILITY LAW.—Nothing in this section shall be construed to modify or otherwise affect any action or the liability of any person under the product liability law of any State.

(f) STATE ENFORCEMENT AUTHORITY.—Nothing in this section shall prevent a State or political subdivision thereof from enforcing, under any relevant civil or other enforcement authority, a requirement that is identical to a requirement of this Act.

SEC. 752 [21 U.S.C. 379s]. PREEMPTION FOR LABELING OR PACKAGING OF COSMETICS

(a) IN GENERAL.—Except as provided in subsection (b), (d), or (e), no State or political subdivision of a State may establish or continue in effect any requirement for labeling or packaging of a cosmetic that is different from or in addition to, or that is otherwise not identical with, a requirement specifically applicable to a particular cosmetic or class of cosmetics under this Act, the Poison Prevention Packaging Act of 1970 (15 U.S.C. 1471 et seq.), or the Fair Packaging and Labeling Act (15 U.S.C. 1451 et seq.).

(b) EXEMPTION.—Upon application of a State or political subdivision thereof, the Secretary may by regulation, after notice and opportunity for written and oral presentation of views, exempt from subsection (a), under such conditions as may be prescribed in such regulation, a State or political subdivision requirement for labeling or packaging that—

> (1) protects an important public interest that would otherwise be unprotected;

> (2) would not cause a cosmetic to be in violation of any applicable requirement or prohibition under Federal law; and

> (3) would not unduly burden interstate commerce.

(c) SCOPE.—For purposes of subsection (a), a reference to a State requirement that relates to the packaging or labeling of a cosmetic means any specific requirement relating to the same aspect of such cosmetic as a requirement specifically applicable to that particular cosmetic or class of cosmetics under this Act for packaging or labeling, including any State requirement relating to public information or any other form of public communication.

(d) No Effect on Product Liability Law.—Nothing in this section shall be construed to modify or otherwise affect any action or the liability of any person under the product liability law of any State.

(e) State Initiative.—This section shall not apply to a State requirement adopted by a State public initiative or referendum enacted prior to September 1, 1997.

SUBCHAPTER G—SAFETY REPORTS

Sec. 756 [21 U.S.C. 379v]. Safety Report Disclaimers

With respect to any entity that submits or is required to submit a safety report or other information in connection with the safety of a product (including a product that is a food, drug, device, dietary supplement, or cosmetic) under this Act (and any release by the Secretary of that report or information), such report or information shall not be construed to reflect necessarily a conclusion by the entity or the Secretary that the report or information constitutes an admission that the product involved malfunctioned, caused or contributed to an adverse experience, or otherwise caused or contributed to a death, serious injury, or serious illness. Such an entity need not admit, and may deny, that the report or information submitted by the entity constitutes an admission that the product involved malfunctioned, caused or contributed to an adverse experience, or caused or contributed to a death, serious injury, or serious illness.

SUBCHAPTER H—SERIOUS ADVERSE EVENT REPORTS

Sec. 760 [21 U.S.C. 379aa]. Serious Adverse Event
REPORTING FOR NONPRESCRIPTION DRUGS

(a) Definitions.—In this section:

(1) Adverse event.—The term "adverse event" means any health-related event associated with the use of a nonprescription drug that is adverse, including—

(A) an event occurring from an overdose of the drug, whether accidental or intentional;

(B) an event occurring from abuse of the drug;

(C) an event occurring from withdrawal from the drug; and

(D) any failure of expected pharmacological action of the drug.

(2) Nonprescription drug.—The term "nonprescription drug" means a drug that is—

(A) not subject to section 503(b); and

(B) not subject to approval in an application submitted under section 505.

(3) SERIOUS ADVERSE EVENT.—The term "serious adverse event" is an adverse event that—

(A) results in—

(i) death;

(ii) a life-threatening experience;

(iii) inpatient hospitalization;

(iv) a persistent or significant disability or incapacity; or

(v) a congenital anomaly or birth defect; or

(B) requires, based on reasonable medical judgment, a medical or surgical intervention to prevent an outcome described under subparagraph (A).

(4) SERIOUS ADVERSE EVENT REPORT.—The term "serious adverse event report" means a report that is required to be submitted to the Secretary under subsection (b).

(b) REPORTING REQUIREMENT.—

(1) IN GENERAL.—The manufacturer, packer, or distributor whose name (pursuant to section 502(b)(1)) appears on the label of a nonprescription drug marketed in the United States (referred to in this section as the "responsible person") shall submit to the Secretary any report received of a serious adverse event associated with such drug when used in the United States, accompanied by a copy of the label on or within the retail package of such drug.

(2) RETAILER.—A retailer whose name appears on the label described in paragraph (1) as a distributor may, by agreement, authorize the manufacturer or packer of the nonprescription drug to submit the required reports for such drugs to the Secretary so long as the retailer directs to the manufacturer or packer all adverse events associated with such drug that are reported to the retailer through the address or telephone number described in section 502(x).

(c) SUBMISSION OF REPORTS.—

(1) TIMING OF REPORTS.—The responsible person shall submit to the Secretary a serious adverse event report no later than 15 business days after the report is received through the address or phone number described in section 502(x).

(2) NEW MEDICAL INFORMATION.—The responsible person shall submit to the Secretary any new medical information, related to a submitted serious adverse event report that is received by the responsible person within 1 year of the initial report, no later than 15 business days after the new information is received by the responsible person.

(3) CONSOLIDATION OF REPORTS.—The Secretary shall develop systems to ensure that duplicate reports of, and new medical information related to, a serious adverse event shall be consolidated into a single report.

(4) EXEMPTION.—The Secretary, after providing notice and an opportunity for comment from interested parties, may establish an exemption to the requirements under paragraphs (1) and (2) if the Secretary determines that such exemption would have no adverse effect on public health.

(d) CONTENTS OF REPORTS.—Each serious adverse event report under this section shall be submitted to the Secretary using the MedWatch form, which may be modified by the Secretary for nonprescription drugs, and may be accompanied by additional information.

(e) MAINTENANCE AND INSPECTION OF RECORDS.—

(1) MAINTENANCE.—The responsible person shall maintain records related to each report of an adverse event received by the responsible person for a period of 6 years.

(2) RECORDS INSPECTION.—

(A) IN GENERAL.—The responsible person shall permit an authorized person to have access to records required to be maintained under this section, during an inspection pursuant to section 704.

(B) AUTHORIZED PERSON.—For purposes of this paragraph, the term "authorized person" means an officer or employee of the Department of Health and Human Services who has—

(i) appropriate credentials, as determined by the Secretary; and

(ii) been duly designated by the Secretary to have access to the records required under this section.

(f) PROTECTED INFORMATION.—A serious adverse event report submitted to the Secretary under this section, including any new medical information submitted under subsection (c)(2), or an adverse event report voluntarily submitted to the Secretary shall be considered to be—

(1) a safety report under section 756 and may be accompanied by a statement, which shall be a part of any report that is released for public disclosure, that denies that the report or the records constitute an admission that the product involved caused or contributed to the adverse event; and

(2) a record about an individual under section 552a of title 5, United States Code (commonly referred to as the "Privacy Act of 1974") and a medical or similar file the disclosure of which would constitute a violation of section 552 of such title 5 (commonly referred to as the "Freedom of Information Act"), and shall not be publicly disclosed unless all personally identifiable information is redacted.

(g) RULE OF CONSTRUCTION.—The submission of any adverse event report in compliance with this section shall not be construed as an admission that the nonprescription drug involved caused or contributed to the adverse event.

(h) PREEMPTION.—

(1) IN GENERAL.—No State or local government shall establish or continue in effect any law, regulation, order, or other requirement, related to a mandatory system for adverse event reports for nonprescription drugs, that is different from, in addition to, or otherwise not identical to, this section.

(2) EFFECT OF SECTION.—

(A) IN GENERAL.—Nothing in this section shall affect the authority of the Secretary to provide adverse event reports and information to any health, food, or drug officer or employee of any State, territory, or political subdivision of a State or territory, under a memorandum of understanding between the Secretary and such State, territory, or political subdivision.

(B) PERSONALLY-IDENTIFIABLE INFORMATION.—Notwithstanding any other provision of law, personally-identifiable information in adverse event reports provided by the Secretary to any health, food, or drug officer or employee of any State, territory, or political subdivision of a State or territory, shall not—

(i) be made publicly available pursuant to any State or other law requiring disclosure of information or records; or

(ii) otherwise be disclosed or distributed to any party without the written consent of the Secretary and the person submitting such information to the Secretary.

(C) USE OF SAFETY REPORTS.—Nothing in this section shall permit a State, territory, or political subdivision of a State or territory, to use any safety report received from the Secretary in a manner inconsistent with subsection (g) or section 756.

(i) AUTHORIZATION OF APPROPRIATIONS.—There are authorized to be appropriated to carry out this section such sums as may be necessary.

SEC. 761 [21 U.S.C. 379aa–1]. SERIOUS ADVERSE EVENT REPORTING FOR DIETARY SUPPLEMENTS

(a) DEFINITIONS.—In this section:

(1) ADVERSE EVENT.—The term "adverse event" means any health-related event associated with the use of a dietary supplement that is adverse.

(2) SERIOUS ADVERSE EVENT.—The term "serious adverse event" is an adverse event that—

(A) results in—

(i) death;

(ii) a life-threatening experience;

(iii) inpatient hospitalization;

(iv) a persistent or significant disability or incapacity; or

(v) a congenital anomaly or birth defect; or

(B) requires, based on reasonable medical judgment, a medical or surgical intervention to prevent an outcome described under subparagraph (A).

(3) SERIOUS ADVERSE EVENT REPORT.—The term "serious adverse event report" means a report that is required to be submitted to the Secretary under subsection (b).

(b) REPORTING REQUIREMENT.—

(1) IN GENERAL.—The manufacturer, packer, or distributor of a dietary supplement whose name (pursuant to section 403(e)(1)) appears on the label of a dietary supplement marketed in the United States (referred to in this section as the "responsible person") shall submit to the Secretary any report received of a serious adverse event associated with such dietary supplement when used in the United States, accompanied by a copy of the label on or within the retail packaging of such dietary supplement.

(2) RETAILER.—A retailer whose name appears on the label described in paragraph (1) as a distributor may, by agreement, authorize the manufacturer or packer of the dietary supplement to submit the required reports for such dietary supplements to the Secretary so long as the retailer directs to the manufacturer or packer all adverse events associated with such dietary supplement that are reported to the retailer through the address or telephone number described in section 403(y).

(c) SUBMISSION OF REPORTS.—

(1) TIMING OF REPORTS.—The responsible person shall submit to the Secretary a serious adverse event report no later than 15 business days after the report is received through the address or phone number described in section 403(y).

(2) NEW MEDICAL INFORMATION.—The responsible person shall submit to the Secretary any new medical information, related to a submitted serious adverse event report that is received by the responsible person within 1 year of the initial report, no later than 15 business days after the new information is received by the responsible person.

(3) CONSOLIDATION OF REPORTS.—The Secretary shall develop systems to ensure that duplicate reports of, and new medical information related to, a serious adverse event shall be consolidated into a single report.

(4) EXEMPTION.—The Secretary, after providing notice and an opportunity for comment from interested parties, may establish an exemption to the requirements under paragraphs (1) and (2) if the Secretary determines that such exemption would have no adverse effect on public health.

(d) CONTENTS OF REPORTS.—Each serious adverse event report under this section shall be submitted to the Secretary using the MedWatch form, which may be modified by the Secretary for dietary supplements, and may be accompanied by additional information.

(e) MAINTENANCE AND INSPECTION OF RECORDS.—

(1) MAINTENANCE.—The responsible person shall maintain records related to each report of an adverse event received by the responsible person for a period of 6 years.

(2) RECORDS INSPECTION.—

(A) IN GENERAL.—The responsible person shall permit an authorized person to have access to records required to be maintained under this section during an inspection pursuant to section 704.

(B) AUTHORIZED PERSON.—For purposes of this paragraph, the term "authorized person" means an officer or employee of the Department of Health and Human Services, who has—

(i) appropriate credentials, as determined by the Secretary; and

(ii) been duly designated by the Secretary to have access to the records required under this section.

(f) PROTECTED INFORMATION.—A serious adverse event report submitted to the Secretary under this section, including any new medical information submitted under subsection (c)(2), or an adverse event report voluntarily submitted to the Secretary shall be considered to be—

(1) a safety report under section 756 and may be accompanied by a statement, which shall be a part of any report that is released for public disclosure, that denies that the report or the records constitute an admission that the product involved caused or contributed to the adverse event; and

(2) a record about an individual under section 552a of title 5, United States Code (commonly referred to as the "Privacy Act of 1974") and a medical or similar file the disclosure of which would constitute a violation of section 552 of such title 5 (commonly referred to as the "Freedom of Information Act"), and shall not be publicly disclosed unless all personally identifiable information is redacted.

(g) RULE OF CONSTRUCTION.—The submission of any adverse event report in compliance with this section shall not be construed as an admission that the dietary supplement involved caused or contributed to the adverse event.

(h) PREEMPTION.—

(1) IN GENERAL.—No State or local government shall establish or continue in effect any law, regulation, order, or other requirement, related to a mandatory system for adverse event reports for dietary supplements, that is different from, in addition to, or otherwise not identical to, this section.

(2) EFFECT OF SECTION.—

(A) IN GENERAL.—Nothing in this section shall affect the authority of the Secretary to provide adverse event reports and information to any health, food, or drug officer or employee of any State, territory, or political subdivision of a State or territory, under a memorandum of understanding between the Secretary and such State, territory, or political subdivision.

(B) PERSONALLY-IDENTIFIABLE INFORMATION.—Notwithstanding any other provision of law, personally-identifiable information in adverse event reports provided by the Secretary to any health, food, or drug officer or employee of any State, territory, or political subdivision of a State or territory, shall not—

(i) be made publicly available pursuant to any State or other law requiring disclosure of information or records; or

(ii) otherwise be disclosed or distributed to any party without the written consent of the Secretary and the person submitting such information to the Secretary.

(C) USE OF SAFETY REPORTS.—Nothing in this section shall permit a State, territory, or political subdivision of a State or territory, to use any safety report received from the Secretary in a manner inconsistent with subsection (g) or section 756.

(i) AUTHORIZATION OF APPROPRIATIONS.—There are authorized to be appropriated to carry out this section such sums as may be necessary.

SUBCHAPTER I—REAGAN–UDALL FOUNDATION FOR THE FOOD AND DRUG ADMINISTRATION

SEC. 770 [21 U.S.C. 379dd]. ESTABLISHMENT AND FUNCTIONS OF THE FOUNDATION

(a) IN GENERAL.—A nonprofit corporation to be known as the Reagan–Udall Foundation for the Food and Drug Administration (referred to in this subchapter as the "Foundation") shall be established in accordance with this section. The Foundation shall be headed by an Executive Director, appointed by the members of the Board of Directors under subsection (e). The Foundation shall not be an agency or instrumentality of the United States Government.

(b) PURPOSE OF FOUNDATION.—The purpose of the Foundation is to advance the mission of the Food and Drug Administration to modernize medical, veterinary, food, food ingredient, and cosmetic product development, accelerate innovation, and enhance product safety.

(c) DUTIES OF THE FOUNDATION.—The Foundation shall—

(1) taking into consideration the Critical Path reports and priorities published by the Food and Drug Administration, identify unmet needs in the development, manufacture, and evaluation of the safety and effectiveness, including postapproval, of devices, including diagnostics, biologics, and drugs, and the safety of

food, food ingredients, and cosmetics, and including the incorporation of more sensitive and predictive tools and devices to measure safety;

(2) establish goals and priorities in order to meet the unmet needs identified in paragraph (1);

(3) in consultation with the Secretary, identify existing and proposed Federal intramural and extramural research and development programs relating to the goals and priorities established under paragraph (2), coordinate Foundation activities with such programs, and minimize Foundation duplication of existing efforts;

(4) award grants to, or enter into contracts, memoranda of understanding, or cooperative agreements with, scientists and entities, which may include the Food and Drug Administration, university consortia, public-private partnerships, institutions of higher education, entities described in section 501(c)(3) of the Internal Revenue Code (and exempt from tax under section 501(a) of such Code), and industry, to efficiently and effectively advance the goals and priorities established under paragraph (2);

(5) recruit meeting participants and hold or sponsor (in whole or in part) meetings as appropriate to further the goals and priorities established under paragraph (2);

(6) release and publish information and data and, to the extent practicable, license, distribute, and release material, reagents, and techniques to maximize, promote, and coordinate the availability of such material, reagents, and techniques for use by the Food and Drug Administration, nonprofit organizations, and academic and industrial researchers to further the goals and priorities established under paragraph (2);

(7) ensure that—

(A) action is taken as necessary to obtain patents for inventions developed by the Foundation or with funds from the Foundation;

(B) action is taken as necessary to enable the licensing of inventions developed by the Foundation or with funds from the Foundation; and

(C) executed licenses, memoranda of understanding, material transfer agreements, contracts, and other such instruments, promote, to the maximum extent practicable, the broadest conversion to commercial and noncommercial applications of licensed and patented inventions of the Foundation to further the goals and priorities established under paragraph (2);

(8) provide objective clinical and scientific information to the Food and Drug Administration and, upon request, to other Federal agencies to assist in agency determinations of how to ensure that regulatory policy accommodates scientific advances and meets the agency's public health mission;

(9) conduct annual assessments of the unmet needs identified in paragraph (1); and

(10) carry out such other activities consistent with the purposes of the Foundation as the Board determines appropriate.

(d) BOARD OF DIRECTORS.—

(1) ESTABLISHMENT.—

(A) IN GENERAL.—The Foundation shall have a Board of Directors (referred to in this subchapter as the "Board"), which shall be composed of ex officio and appointed members in accordance with this subsection. All appointed members of the Board shall be voting members.

(B) EX OFFICIO MEMBERS.—The ex officio members of the Board shall be the following individuals or their designees:

(i) The Commissioner.

(ii) The Director of the National Institutes of Health.

(iii) The Director of the Centers for Disease Control and Prevention.

(iv) The Director of the Agency for Healthcare Research and Quality.

(C) APPOINTED MEMBERS.—

(i) IN GENERAL.—The ex officio members of the Board under subparagraph (B) shall, by majority vote, appoint to the Board 14 individuals, of which 9 shall be from a list of candidates to be provided by the National Academy of Sciences and 5 shall be from lists of candidates provided by patient and consumer advocacy groups, professional scientific and medical societies, and industry trade organizations. Of such appointed members—

(I) 4 shall be representatives of the general pharmaceutical, device, food, cosmetic, and biotechnology industries;

(II) 3 shall be representatives of academic research organizations;

(III) 2 shall be representatives of patient or consumer advocacy organizations;

(IV) 1 shall be a representative of health care providers; and

(V) 4 shall be at-large members with expertise or experience relevant to the purpose of the Foundation.

(ii) REQUIREMENTS.—

(I) EXPERTISE.—The ex officio members shall ensure the Board membership includes individuals with expertise in areas including the sciences of developing, manufacturing, and evaluating the safety and effectiveness of devices, including diagnostics, biologics, and drugs, and the safety of food, food ingredients, and cosmetics.

(II) FEDERAL EMPLOYEES.—No employee of the Federal Government shall be appointed as a member of the Board under this subparagraph or under paragraph (3)(B).

(D) INITIAL MEETING.—

(i) IN GENERAL.—Not later than 30 days after the date of the enactment of this subchapter,[81] the Secretary shall convene a meeting of the ex officio members of the Board to—

(I) incorporate the Foundation; and

(II) appoint the members of the Board in accordance with subparagraph (C).

(ii) SERVICE OF EX OFFICIO MEMBERS.—Upon the appointment of the members of the Board under clause (i)(II)—

(I) the terms of service of the Director of the Centers for Disease Control and Prevention and of the Director of the Agency for Healthcare Research and Quality as ex officio members of the Board shall terminate; and

(II) the Commissioner and the Director of the National Institutes of Health shall continue to serve as ex officio members of the Board, but shall be nonvoting members.

(iii) CHAIR.—The ex officio members of the Board under subparagraph (B) shall designate an appointed member of the Board to serve as the Chair of the Board.

(2) DUTIES OF BOARD.—The Board shall—

(A) establish bylaws for the Foundation that—

(i) are published in the Federal Register and available for public comment;

(ii) establish policies for the selection of the officers, employees, agents, and contractors of the Foundation;

(iii) establish policies, including ethical standards, for the acceptance, solicitation, and disposition of donations and grants to the Foundation and for the disposition of the assets of the Foundation, including appropriate limits on the ability of donors to designate, by stipulation or restriction, the use or recipient of donated funds;

(iv) establish policies that would subject all employees, fellows, and trainees of the Foundation to the conflict of interest standards under section 208 of title 18, United States Code;

---

81. Subchapter I was added by Pub. L. No. 110–85, § 601, 121 Stat. 823, 890–97, which was enacted September 27, 2007.

(v) establish licensing, distribution, and publication policies that support the widest and least restrictive use by the public of information and inventions developed by the Foundation or with Foundation funds to carry out the duties described in paragraphs (6) and (7) of subsection (c), and may include charging cost-based fees for published material produced by the Foundation;

(vi) specify principles for the review of proposals and awarding of grants and contracts that include peer review and that are consistent with those of the Foundation for the National Institutes of Health, to the extent determined practicable and appropriate by the Board;

(vii) specify a cap on administrative expenses for recipients of a grant, contract, or cooperative agreement from the Foundation;

(viii) establish policies for the execution of memoranda of understanding and cooperative agreements between the Foundation and other entities, including the Food and Drug Administration;

(ix) establish policies for funding training fellowships, whether at the Foundation, academic or scientific institutions, or the Food and Drug Administration, for scientists, doctors, and other professionals who are not employees of regulated industry, to foster greater understanding of and expertise in new scientific tools, diagnostics, manufacturing techniques, and potential barriers to translating basic research into clinical and regulatory practice;

(x) specify a process for annual Board review of the operations of the Foundation; and

(xi) establish specific duties of the Executive Director;

(B) prioritize and provide overall direction to the activities of the Foundation;

(C) evaluate the performance of the Executive Director; and

(D) carry out any other necessary activities regarding the functioning of the Foundation.

(3) TERMS AND VACANCIES.—

(A) TERM.—The term of office of each member of the Board appointed under paragraph (1)(C) shall be 4 years, except that the terms of offices for the initial appointed members of the Board shall expire on a staggered basis as determined by the ex officio members.

(B) VACANCY.—Any vacancy in the membership of the Board—

(i) shall not affect the power of the remaining members to execute the duties of the Board; and

(ii) shall be filled by appointment by the appointed members described in paragraph (1)(C) by majority vote.

(C) PARTIAL TERM.—If a member of the Board does not serve the full term applicable under subparagraph (A), the individual appointed under subparagraph (B) to fill the resulting vacancy shall be appointed for the remainder of the term of the predecessor of the individual.

(D) SERVING PAST TERM.—A member of the Board may continue to serve after the expiration of the term of the member until a successor is appointed.

(4) COMPENSATION.—Members of the Board may not receive compensation for service on the Board. Such members may be reimbursed for travel, subsistence, and other necessary expenses incurred in carrying out the duties of the Board, as set forth in the bylaws issued by the Board.

(e) INCORPORATION.—The ex officio members of the Board shall serve as incorporators and shall take whatever actions necessary to incorporate the Foundation.

(f) NONPROFIT STATUS.—In carrying out subsection (b), the Board shall establish such policies and bylaws under subsection (d), and the Executive Director shall carry out such activities under subsection (g), as may be necessary to ensure that the Foundation maintains status as an organization that—

(1) is described in subsection (c)(3) of section 501 of the Internal Revenue Code of 1986; and

(2) is, under subsection (a) of such section, exempt from taxation.

(g) EXECUTIVE DIRECTOR.—

(1) IN GENERAL.—The Board shall appoint an Executive Director who shall serve at the pleasure of the Board. The Executive Director shall be responsible for the day-to-day operations of the Foundation and shall have such specific duties and responsibilities as the Board shall prescribe.

(2) COMPENSATION.—The compensation of the Executive Director shall be fixed by the Board but shall not be greater than the compensation of the Commissioner.

(h) ADMINISTRATIVE POWERS.—In carrying out this subchapter, the Board, acting through the Executive Director, may—

(1) adopt, alter, and use a corporate seal, which shall be judicially noticed;

(2) hire, promote, compensate, and discharge 1 or more officers, employees, and agents, as may be necessary, and define their duties;

(3) prescribe the manner in which—

(A) real or personal property of the Foundation is acquired, held, and transferred;

(B) general operations of the Foundation are to be conducted; and

(C) the privileges granted to the Board by law are exercised and enjoyed;

(4) with the consent of the applicable executive department or independent agency, use the information, services, and facilities of such department or agencies in carrying out this section;

(5) enter into contracts with public and private organizations for the writing, editing, printing, and publishing of books and other material;

(6) hold, administer, invest, and spend any gift, devise, or bequest of real or personal property made to the Foundation under subsection (i);

(7) enter into such other contracts, leases, cooperative agreements, and other transactions as the Board considers appropriate to conduct the activities of the Foundation;

(8) modify or consent to the modification of any contract or agreement to which it is a party or in which it has an interest under this subchapter;

(9) take such action as may be necessary to obtain patents and licenses for devices and procedures developed by the Foundation and its employees;

(10) sue and be sued in its corporate name, and complain and defend in courts of competent jurisdiction;

(11) appoint other groups of advisors as may be determined necessary to carry out the functions of the Foundation; and

(12) exercise other powers as set forth in this section, and such other incidental powers as are necessary to carry out its powers, duties, and functions in accordance with this subchapter.

(i) ACCEPTANCE OF FUNDS FROM OTHER SOURCES.—The Executive Director may solicit and accept on behalf of the Foundation, any funds, gifts, grants, devises, or bequests of real or personal property made to the Foundation, including from private entities, for the purposes of carrying out the duties of the Foundation.

(j) SERVICE OF FEDERAL EMPLOYEES.—Federal Government employees may serve on committees advisory to the Foundation and otherwise cooperate with and assist the Foundation in carrying out its functions, so long as such employees do not direct or control Foundation activities.

(k) DETAIL OF GOVERNMENT EMPLOYEES; FELLOWSHIPS.—

(1) DETAIL FROM FEDERAL AGENCIES.—Federal Government employees may be detailed from Federal agencies with or without reimbursement to those agencies to the Foundation at any time, and such detail shall be without interruption or loss of civil service status or privilege. Each such employee shall abide by the statutory, regulatory, ethical, and procedural standards applicable to the employees of the agency from which such employee is detailed and those of the Foundation.

(2) VOLUNTARY SERVICE; ACCEPTANCE OF FEDERAL EMPLOYEES.—

(A) FOUNDATION.—The Executive Director of the Foundation may accept the services of employees detailed from Federal agencies with or without reimbursement to those agencies.

(B) FOOD AND DRUG ADMINISTRATION.—The Commissioner may accept the uncompensated services of Foundation fellows or trainees. Such services shall be considered to be undertaking an activity under contract with the Secretary as described in section 708.

(*l*) ANNUAL REPORTS.—

(1) REPORTS TO FOUNDATION.—Any recipient of a grant, contract, fellowship, memorandum of understanding, or cooperative agreement from the Foundation under this section shall submit to the Foundation a report on an annual basis for the duration of such grant, contract, fellowship, memorandum of understanding, or cooperative agreement, that describes the activities carried out under such grant, contract, fellowship, memorandum of understanding, or cooperative agreement.

(2) REPORT TO CONGRESS AND THE FDA.—Beginning with fiscal year 2009, the Executive Director shall submit to Congress and the Commissioner an annual report that—

(A) describes the activities of the Foundation and the progress of the Foundation in furthering the goals and priorities established under subsection (c)(2), including the practical impact of the Foundation on regulated product development;

(B) provides a specific accounting of the source and use of all funds used by the Foundation to carry out such activities; and

(C) provides information on how the results of Foundation activities could be incorporated into the regulatory and product review activities of the Food and Drug Administration.

(m) SEPARATION OF FUNDS.—The Executive Director shall ensure that the funds received from the Treasury are held in separate accounts from funds received from entities under subsection (i).

(n) FUNDING.—From amounts appropriated to the Food and Drug Administration for each fiscal year, the Commissioner shall transfer not less than $500,000 and not more than $1,250,000, to the Foundation to carry out subsections (a), (b), and (d) through (m).

SEC. 771 [21 U.S.C. 379dd–1]. LOCATION OF FOUNDATION

The Foundation shall, if practicable, be located not more than 20 miles from the District of Columbia.

SEC. 772 [21 U.S.C. 379dd–2]. ACTIVITIES OF THE FOOD AND DRUG ADMINISTRATION

(a) IN GENERAL.—The Commissioner shall receive and assess the report submitted to the Commissioner by the Executive Director of the Foundation under section 770(*l*)(2).

(b) REPORT TO CONGRESS.—Beginning with fiscal year 2009, the Commissioner shall submit to Congress an annual report summarizing the incorporation of the information provided by the Foundation in the report described under section 770(*l*)(2) and by other recipients of grants, contracts, memoranda of understanding, or cooperative agreements into regulatory and product review activities of the Food and Drug Administration.

(c) EXTRAMURAL GRANTS.—The provisions of this subchapter and section 566 shall have no effect on any grant, contract, memorandum of understanding, or cooperative agreement between the Food and Drug Administration and any other entity entered into before, on, or after the date of the enactment of this subchapter.

CHAPTER VIII—IMPORTS AND EXPORTS

SEC. 801 [21 U.S.C. 381]. IMPORTS AND EXPORTS

(a) The Secretary of the Treasury shall deliver to the Secretary of Health and Human Services, upon his request, samples of food, drugs, devices, tobacco products, and cosmetics which are being imported or offered for import into the United States, giving notice thereof to the owner or consignee, who may appear before the Secretary of Health and Human Services and have the right to introduce testimony. The Secretary of Health and Human Services shall furnish to the Secretary of the Treasury a list of establishments registered pursuant to subsection (i) of section 510 or section 905(h) and shall request that if any drugs, devices, or tobacco products manufactured, prepared, propagated, compounded, or processed in an establishment not so registered are imported or offered for import into the United States, samples of such drugs, devices, or tobacco products be delivered to the Secretary of Health and Human Services, with notice of such delivery to the owner or consignee, who may appear before the Secretary of Health and Human Services and have the right to introduce testimony. If it appears from the examination of such samples or otherwise that (1) such article has been manufactured, processed, or packed under insanitary conditions or, in the case of a device, the methods used in, or the facilities or controls used for, the manufacture, packing, storage, or installation of the device do not conform to the requirements of section 520(f), or (2) such article is forbidden or restricted in sale in the country in which it was produced or from which it was exported, or (3) such article is adulterated, misbranded, or in violation of section 505 or the importer (as defined in section 805) is in violation of such section 805,[82] or prohibited from introduction or delivery for introduction into interstate commerce under section 301(ll), or (4) the recordkeeping requirements under section 204 of the FDA Food Safety Modernization Act (other than the requirements under subsection (f) of such

653

section) have not been complied with regarding such article, then such article shall be refused admission, except as provided in subsection (b) of this section. With respect to an article of food, if importation of such food is subject to, but not compliant with, the requirement under subsection (q) that such food be accompanied by a certification or other assurance that the food meets applicable requirements of this Act, then such article shall be refused admission. If such article is subject to a requirement under section 760 or 761 and if the Secretary has credible evidence or information indicating that the responsible person (as defined in such section 760 or 761) has not complied with a requirement of such section 760 or 761 with respect to any such article, or has not allowed access to records described in such section 760 or 761, then such article shall be refused admission, except as provided in subsection (b) of this section. The Secretary of the Treasury shall cause the destruction of any such article refused admission unless such article is exported, under regulations prescribed by the Secretary of the Treasury, within ninety days of the date of notice of such refusal or within such additional time as may be permitted pursuant to such regulations, except that the Secretary of Health and Human Services may destroy, without the opportunity for export, any drug refused admission under this section, if such drug is valued at an amount that is $2,500 or less (or such higher amount as the Secretary of the Treasury may set by regulation pursuant to section 498(a)(1) of the Tariff Act of 1930 (19 U.S.C. 1498(a)(1))[83] and was not brought into compliance as described under subsection (b). The Secretary of Health and Human Services shall issue regulations providing for notice and an opportunity to appear before the Secretary of Health and Human Services and introduce testimony, as described in the first sentence of this subsection, on destruction of a drug under the sixth sentence of this subsection. The regulations shall provide that prior to destruction, appropriate due process is available to the owner or consignee seeking to challenge the decision to destroy the drug. Where the Secretary of Health and Human Services provides notice and an opportunity to appear and introduce testimony on the destruction of a drug, the Secretary of Health and Human Services shall store and, as applicable, dispose of the drug after the issuance of the notice, except that the owner and consignee shall remain liable for costs pursuant to subsection (c). Such process may be combined with the notice and opportunity to appear before the Secretary and introduce testimony, as described in the first sentence of this subsection, as long as appropriate notice is provided to the owner or consignee. Clause (2) of the third sentence of this paragraph shall not be construed to prohibit the admission of narcotic drugs the importation of which is permitted under the Controlled Substances Import and Export Act.

(b) Pending decision as to the admission of an article being imported or offered for import, the Secretary of the Treasury may authorize delivery of such article to the owner or consignee upon the execution by him of a good and sufficient bond

---

82. The words "or the importer (as defined in section 805) is in violation of such section 805" were added by Pub. L. No. 111–353, § 301(c), and according to § 301(d) of that law, this provision becomes effective Jan. 4, 2013, two years after enactment.

83. So in law. See Pub. L. No. 112–144, § 708(a), 126 Stat. 993, 1068 (2012). Probably should be ")))".

providing for the payment of such liquidated damages in the event of default as may be required pursuant to regulations of the Secretary of the Treasury. If it appears to the Secretary of Health and Human Services that (1) an article included within the provisions of clause (3) of subsection (a) of this section can, by relabeling or other action, be brought into compliance with the Act or rendered other than a food, drug, device, or cosmetic, or (2) with respect to an article described in subsection (a) relating to the requirements of sections 760 or 761, the responsible person (as defined in section 760 or 761) can take action that would assure that the responsible person is in compliance with section 760 or 761, as the case may be, final determination as to admission of such article may be deferred and, upon filing of timely written application by the owner or consignee and the execution by him of a bond as provided in the preceding provisions of this subsection, the Secretary may, in accordance with regulations, authorize the applicant, or, with respect to clause (2), the responsible person, to perform such relabeling or other action specified in such authorization (including destruction or export of rejected articles or portions thereof, as may be specified in the Secretary's authorization). All such relabeling or other action pursuant to such authorization shall in accordance with regulations be under the supervision of an officer or employee of the Department of Health and Human Services designated by the Secretary, or an officer or employee of the Department of the Treasury designated by the Secretary of the Treasury.

(c) All expenses (including travel, per diem or subsistence, and salaries of officers or employees of the United States) in connection with the destruction provided for in subsection (a) of this section and the supervision of the relabeling or other action authorized under the provisions of subsection (b) of this section, the amount of such expenses to be determined in accordance with regulations, and all expenses in connection with the storage, cartage, or labor with respect to any article refused admission under subsection (a) of this section, shall be paid by the owner or consignee and, in default of such payment, shall constitute a lien against any future importations made by such owner or consignee.

(d)(1) Except as provided in paragraph (2) and section 804, no drug subject to section 503(b) or composed wholly or partly of insulin which is manufactured in a State and exported may be imported into the United States unless the drug is imported by the manufacturer of the drug.

(2) The Secretary may authorize the importation of a drug the importation of which is prohibited by paragraph (1) if the drug is required for emergency medical care.

(3)(A) Subject to subparagraph (B), no component of a drug, no component part or accessory of a device, or other article of device requiring further processing, which is ready or suitable for use for health-related purposes, and no article of a food additive, color additive, or dietary supplement, including a product in bulk form, shall be excluded from importation into the United States under subsection (a) if each of the following conditions is met:

(i) The importer of such article of a drug or device or importer of such article of a food additive, color additive, or dietary supplement submits to the Secretary, at the time of initial importation, a statement in accordance with the following:

(I) Such statement provides that such article is intended to be further processed by the initial owner or consignee, or incorporated by the initial owner or consignee, into a drug, biological product, device, food, food additive, color additive, or dietary supplement that will be exported by the initial owner or consignee from the United States in accordance with subsection (e) of section 802, or with section 351(h) of the Public Health Service Act.

(II) The statement identifies the manufacturer of such article and each processor, packer, distributor, or other entity that had possession of the article in the chain of possession of the article from the manufacturer to such importer of the article.

(III) The statement is accompanied by such certificates of analysis as are necessary to identify such article, unless the article is a device or is an article described in paragraph (4).

(ii) At the time of initial importation and before the delivery of such article to the importer or the initial owner or consignee, such owner or consignee executes a good and sufficient bond providing for the payment of such liquidated damages in the event of default as may be required pursuant to regulations of the Secretary of the Treasury.

(iii) Such article is used and exported by the initial owner or consignee in accordance with the intent described under clause (i)(I), except for any portions of the article that are destroyed.

(iv) The initial owner or consignee maintains records on the use or destruction of such article or portions thereof, as the case may be, and submits to the Secretary any such records requested by the Secretary.

(v) Upon request of the Secretary, the initial owner or consignee submits a report that provides an accounting of the exportation or destruction of such article or portions thereof, and the manner in which such owner or consignee complied with the requirements of this subparagraph.

(B) Notwithstanding subparagraph (A), the Secretary may refuse admission to an article that otherwise would be imported into the United States under such subparagraph if the Secretary determines that there is credible evidence or information indicating that such article is not intended to be further processed by the initial owner or consignee, or incorporated by the initial owner or consignee, into a drug, biological product, device, food, food additive, color additive, or dietary supplement that will be exported by the initial owner or consignee from the United States in accordance with subsection (e) or section 802, or with section 351(h) of the Public Health Service Act.

(C) This section may not be construed as affecting the responsibility of the Secretary to ensure that articles imported into the United States under authority of subparagraph (A) meet each of the conditions established in such subparagraph for importation.

(4) The importation into the United States of blood, blood components, source plasma, or source leukocytes or of a component, accessory, or part thereof is not permitted pursuant to paragraph (3) unless the importation complies with section 351(a) of the Public Health Service Act or the Secretary permits the importation under appropriate circumstances and conditions, as determined by the Secretary. The importation of tissue or a component or part of tissue is not permitted pursuant to paragraph (3) unless the importation complies with section 361 of the Public Health Service Act.

(e)(1) A food, drug, device, tobacco product, or cosmetic intended for export shall not be deemed to be adulterated or misbranded under this Act, and a tobacco product intended for export shall not be deemed to be in violation of section 906(e), 907, 911, or 920(a), if it—

(A) accords to the specifications of the foreign purchaser,

(B) is not in conflict with the laws of the country to which it is intended for export,

(C) is labeled on the outside of the shipping package that it is intended for export, and

(D) is not sold or offered for sale in domestic commerce.

(2) Paragraph (1) does not apply to any device—

(A) which does not comply with an applicable requirement of section 514 or 515,

(B) which under section 520(g) is exempt from either such section, or

(C) which is a banned device under section 516,

unless, in addition to the requirements of paragraph (1), either (i) the Secretary has determined that the exportation of the device is not contrary to public health and safety and has the approval of the country to which it is intended for export or (ii) the device is eligible for export under section 802.

(3) A new animal drug that requires approval under section 512 shall not be exported pursuant to paragraph (1) if such drug has been banned in the United States.

(4)(A) Any person who exports a food, drug, animal drug, or device may request that the Secretary—

(i) certify in writing that the exported food, drug, animal drug, or device meets the requirements of paragraph (1) or section 802; or

(ii) certify in writing that the food, drug, animal drug, or device being export-ed meets the applicable requirements of this Act upon a showing that the food, drug or device meets the applicable requirements of this Act.

The Secretary shall issue such a certification within 20 days of the receipt of a request for such certification.

(B) If the Secretary issues a written export certification within the 20 days pre-scribed by subparagraph (A), a fee for such certification may be charged but shall not exceed $175 for each certification. Fees collected for a fiscal year pursuant to this subparagraph shall be credited to the appropriation account for salaries and expens-es of the Food and Drug Administration and shall be available in accordance with appropriations Acts until expended without fiscal year limitation. Such fees shall be collected in each fiscal year in an amount equal to the amount specified in appropri-ations Acts for such fiscal year and shall only be collected and available for the costs of the Food and Drug Administration.

(C) For purposes of this paragraph, a certification by the Secretary shall be made on such basis, and in such form (including a publicly available listing) as the Secre-tary determines appropriate.

(D) With regard to fees pursuant to subparagraph (B) in connection with written export certifications for food:

(i) Such fees shall be collected and available solely for the costs of the Food and Drug Administration associated with issuing such certifications.

(ii) Such fees may not be retained in an amount that exceeds such costs for the respective fiscal year.

(f)(1) If a drug (other than insulin, an antibiotic drug, an animal drug, or a drug exported under section 802) being exported in accordance with subsection (e) is being exported to a country that has different or additional labeling requirements or conditions for use and such country requires the drug to be labeled in accordance with those requirements or uses, such drug may be labeled in accordance with such requirements and conditions for use in the country to which such drug is being ex-ported if it also is labeled in accordance with the requirements of this Act.

(2) If, pursuant to paragraph (1), the labeling of an exported drug includes con-ditions for use that have not been approved under this Act, the labeling must state that such conditions for use have not been approved under this Act. A drug exported under section 802 is exempt from this section.

(g)(1) With respect to a prescription drug being imported or offered for import into the United States, the Secretary, in the case of an individual who is not in the business of such importations, may not send a warning notice to the individual unless the following conditions are met:

(A) The notice specifies, as applicable to the importation of the drug, that the Secretary has made a determination that—

(i) importation is in violation of section 801(a) because the drug is or appears to be adulterated, misbranded, or in violation of section 505;

(ii) importation is in violation of section 801(a) because the drug is or appears to be forbidden or restricted in sale in the country in which it was produced or from which it was exported;

(iii) importation is or appears to be in violation of section 801(d)(1); or

(iv) importation otherwise is or appears to be in violation of Federal law.

(B) The notice does not specify any provision described in subparagraph (A) that is not applicable to the importation of the drug.

(C) The notice states the reasons underlying such determination by the Secretary, including a brief application to the principal facts involved of the provision of law described in subparagraph (A) that is the basis of the determination by the Secretary.

(2) For purposes of this section, the term "warning notice", with respect to the importation of a drug, means a communication from the Secretary (written or otherwise) notifying a person, or clearly suggesting to the person, that importing the drug for personal use is, or appears to be, a violation of this Act.

(h)(1) The Secretary shall give high priority to increasing the number of inspections under this section for the purpose of enabling the Secretary to inspect food offered for import at ports of entry into the United States, with the greatest priority given to inspections to detect the intentional adulteration of food.

(2) The Secretary shall give high priority to making necessary improvements to the information management systems of the Food and Drug Administration that contain information related to foods imported or offered for import into the United States for purposes of improving the ability of the Secretary to allocate resources, detect the intentional adulteration of food, and facilitate the importation of food that is in compliance with this Act.

(3) The Secretary shall improve linkages with other regulatory agencies of the Federal Government that share responsibility for food safety, and shall with respect to such safety improve linkages with the States and Indian tribes (as defined in section 4(e) of the Indian Self–Determination and Education Assistance Act (25 U.S.C. 450b(e))).

(i)(1) For use in inspections of food under this section, the Secretary shall provide for research on the development of tests and sampling methodologies—

(A) whose purpose is to test food in order to rapidly detect the adulteration of the food, with the greatest priority given to detect the intentional adulteration of food; and

(B) whose results offer significant improvements over the available technology in terms of accuracy, timing, or costs.

(2) In providing for research under paragraph (1), the Secretary shall give priority to conducting research on the development of tests that are suitable for inspections of food at ports of entry into the United States.

(3) In providing for research under paragraph (1), the Secretary shall as appropriate coordinate with the Director of the Centers for Disease Control and Prevention, the Director of the National Institutes of Health, the Administrator of the Environmental Protection Agency, and the Secretary of Agriculture.

(4) The Secretary shall annually submit to the Committee on Energy and Commerce of the House of Representatives, and the Committee on Health, Education, Labor, and Pensions of the Senate, a report describing the progress made in research under paragraph (1), including progress regarding paragraph (2).

(j)(1) If an officer or qualified employee of the Food and Drug Administration has credible evidence or information indicating that an article of food presents a threat of serious adverse health consequences or death to humans or animals, and such officer or qualified employee is unable to inspect, examine, or investigate such article upon the article being offered for import at a port of entry into the United States, the officer or qualified employee shall request the Secretary of Treasury to hold the food at the port of entry for a reasonable period of time, not to exceed 24 hours, for the purpose of enabling the Secretary to inspect, examine, or investigate the article as appropriate.

(2) The Secretary shall request the Secretary of Treasury to remove an article held pursuant to paragraph (1) to a secure facility, as appropriate. During the period of time that such article is so held, the article shall not be transferred by any person from the port of entry into the United States for the article, or from the secure facility to which the article has been removed, as the case may be. Subsection (b) does not authorize the delivery of the article pursuant to the execution of a bond while the article is so held.

(3) An officer or qualified employee of the Food and Drug Administration may make a request under paragraph (1) only if the Secretary or an official designated by the Secretary approves the request. An official may not be so designated unless the official is the director of the district under this Act in which the article involved is located, or is an official senior to such director.

(4) With respect to an article of food for which a request under paragraph (1) is made, the Secretary, promptly after the request is made, shall notify the State in which the port of entry involved is located that the request has been made, and as applicable, that such article is being held under this subsection.

(k)(1) If an article of food is being imported or offered for import into the United States, and the importer, owner, or consignee of the article is a person who has been debarred under section 306(b)(3), such article shall be held at the port of entry for the article, and may not be delivered to such person. Subsection (b) does not authorize the delivery of the article pursuant to the execution of a bond while the article is so held. The article shall be removed to a secure facility, as appropriate. During the period of time that such article is so held, the article shall not be transferred by any person from the port of entry into the United States for the article, or from the secure facility to which the article has been removed, as the case may be.

(2) An article of food held under paragraph (1) may be delivered to a person who is not a debarred person under section 306(b)(3) if such person affirmatively establishes, at the expense of the person, that the article complies with the requirements of this Act, as determined by the Secretary.

(*l*)(1)[84] If an article of food is being imported or offered for import into the United States, and such article is from a foreign facility for which a registration has not been submitted to the Secretary under section 415 (or for which a registration has been suspended under such section), such article shall be held at the port of entry for the article, and may not be delivered to the importer, owner, or consignee of the article, until the foreign facility is so registered. Subsection (b) does not authorize the delivery of the article pursuant to the execution of a bond while the article is so held. The article shall be removed to a secure facility, as appropriate. During the period of time that such article is so held, the article shall not be transferred by any person from the port of entry into the United States for the article, or from the secure facility to which the article has been removed, as the case may be.

(m)(1) In the case of an article of food that is being imported or offered for import into the United States, the Secretary, after consultation with the Secretary of the Treasury, shall by regulation require, for the purpose of enabling such article to be inspected at ports of entry into the United States, the submission to the Secretary of a notice providing the identity of each of the following: The article; the manufacturer and shipper of the article; if known within the specified period of time that notice is required to be provided, the grower of the article; the country from which the article originates; the country from which the article is shipped; any country to which the article has been refused entry;[85] and the anticipated port of entry for the article. An article of food imported or offered for import without submission of such notice in accordance with the requirements under this paragraph shall be refused admission into the United States. Nothing in this section may be construed as a limitation on the port of entry for an article of food.

(2)(A) Regulations under paragraph (1) shall require that a notice under such paragraph be provided by a specified period of time in advance of the time of the importation of the article of food involved or the offering of the food for import, which period shall be no less than the minimum amount of time necessary for the Secretary to receive, review, and appropriately respond to such notification, but may not exceed five days. In determining the specified period of time required under this

---

84. So in law. There is no paragraph (2). See Pub. L. No. 107–188, § 305(c), 116 Stat. 594, 668 (2002).

85. The words "any country to which the article has been refused entry" were added by Pub. L. No. 111–353, § 304(a), and according to § 304(c) of that law, this provision becomes effective 180 days after the Jan. 4, 2011 date of enactment.

subparagraph, the Secretary may consider, but is not limited to consideration of, the effect on commerce of such period of time, the locations of the various ports of entry into the United States, the various modes of transportation, the types of food imported into the United States, and any other such consideration. Nothing in the preceding sentence may be construed as a limitation on the obligation of the Secretary to receive, review, and appropriately respond to any notice under paragraph (1).

(B)(i) If an article of food is being imported or offered for import into the United States and a notice under paragraph (1) is not provided in advance in accordance with the requirements under paragraph (1), such article shall be held at the port of entry for the article, and may not be delivered to the importer, owner, or consignee of the article, until such notice is submitted to the Secretary, and the Secretary examines the notice and determines that the notice is in accordance with the requirements under paragraph (1). Subsection (b) does not authorize the delivery of the article pursuant to the execution of a bond while the article is so held. The article shall be removed to a secure facility, as appropriate. During the period of time that such article is so held, the article shall not be transferred by any person from the port of entry into the United States for the article, or from the secure facility to which the article has been removed, as the case may be.

(ii) In carrying out clause (i) with respect to an article of food, the Secretary shall determine whether there is in the possession of the Secretary any credible evidence or information indicating that such article presents a threat of serious adverse health consequences or death to humans or animals.

(3)(A) This subsection may not be construed as limiting the authority of the Secretary to obtain information under any other provision of this Act.

(B) This subsection may not be construed as authorizing the Secretary to impose any requirements with respect to a food to the extent that it is within the exclusive jurisdiction of the Secretary of Agriculture pursuant to the Federal Meat Inspection Act (21 U.S.C. 601 et seq.), the Poultry Products Inspection Act (21 U.S.C. 451 et seq.), or the Egg Products Inspection Act (21 U.S.C. 1031 et seq.).

(n)(1) If a food has been refused admission under subsection (a), other than such a food that is required to be destroyed, the Secretary may require the owner or consignee of the food to affix to the container of the food a label that clearly and conspicuously bears the statement: "UNITED STATES: REFUSED ENTRY".

(2) All expenses in connection with affixing a label under paragraph (1) shall be paid by the owner or consignee of the food involved, and in default of such payment, shall constitute a lien against future importations made by such owner or consignee.

(3) A requirement under paragraph (1) remains in effect until the Secretary determines that the food involved has been brought into compliance with this Act.

(*o*) If an article that is a device is being imported or offered for import into the United States, and the importer, owner, or consignee of such article does not, at the time of offering the article for import, submit to the Secretary a statement that identifies the registration under section 510(i) of each establishment that with respect to such article is required under such section to register with the Secretary, the article may be refused admission. If the article is refused admission for failure to submit such a statement, the article shall be held at the port of entry for the article, and may not be delivered to the importer, owner, or consignee of the article, until such a statement is submitted to the Secretary. Subsection (b) does not authorize the delivery of the article pursuant to the execution of a bond while the article is so held. The article shall be removed to a secure facility, as appropriate. During the period of time that such article is so held, the article shall not be transferred by any person from the port of entry into the United States for the article, or from the secure facility to which the article has been removed, as the case may be.

(p)(1) Not later than 36 months after the date of enactment of the Family Smoking Prevention and Tobacco Control Act, and annually thereafter, the Secretary shall submit to the Committee on Health, Education, Labor, and Pensions of the Senate and the Committee on Energy and Commerce of the House of Representatives, a report regarding—

(A) the nature, extent, and destination of United States tobacco product exports that do not conform to tobacco product standards established pursuant to this Act;

(B) the public health implications of such exports, including any evidence of a negative public health impact; and

(C) recommendations or assessments of policy alternatives available to Congress and the executive branch to reduce any negative public health impact caused by such exports.

(2) The Secretary is authorized to establish appropriate information disclosure requirements to carry out this subsection.

(q) CERTIFICATIONS CONCERNING IMPORTED FOODS.—

(1) IN GENERAL.—The Secretary may require, as a condition of granting admission to an article of food imported or offered for import into the United States, that an entity described in paragraph (3) provide a certification, or such other assurances as the Secretary determines appropriate, that the article of food complies with applicable requirements of this Act. Such certification or assurances may be provided in the form of shipment-specific certificates, a listing of certified facilities that manufacture, process, pack, or hold such food, or in such other form as the Secretary may specify.

(2) FACTORS TO BE CONSIDERED IN REQUIRING CERTIFICATION.—The Secretary shall base the determination that an article of food is required to have a certification described in paragraph (1) on the risk of the food, including—

(A) known safety risks associated with the food;

(B) known food safety risks associated with the country, territory, or region of origin of the food;

(C) a finding by the Secretary, supported by scientific, risk-based evidence, that—

(i) the food safety programs, systems, and standards in the country, territory, or region of origin of the food are inadequate to ensure that the article of food is as safe as a similar article of food that is manufactured, processed, packed, or held in the United States in accordance with the requirements of this Act; and

(ii) the certification would assist the Secretary in determining whether to refuse or admit the article of food under subsection (a); and

(D) information submitted to the Secretary in accordance with the process established in paragraph (7).

(3) CERTIFYING ENTITIES.—For purposes of paragraph (1), entities that shall provide the certification or assurances described in such paragraph are—

(A) an agency or a representative of the government of the country from which the article of food at issue originated, as designated by the Secretary; or

(B) such other persons or entities accredited pursuant to section 808 to provide such certification or assurance.

(4) RENEWAL AND REFUSAL OF CERTIFICATIONS.—The Secretary may—

(A) require that any certification or other assurance provided by an entity specified in paragraph (2) be renewed by such entity at such times as the Secretary determines appropriate; and

(B) refuse to accept any certification or assurance if the Secretary determines that such certification or assurance is not valid or reliable.

(5) ELECTRONIC SUBMISSION.—The Secretary shall provide for the electronic submission of certifications under this subsection.

(6) FALSE STATEMENTS.—Any statement or representation made by an entity described in paragraph (2) to the Secretary shall be subject to section 1001 of title 18, United States Code.

(7) ASSESSMENT OF FOOD SAFETY PROGRAMS, SYSTEMS, AND STANDARDS.—If the Secretary determines that the food safety programs, systems, and standards in a foreign region, country, or territory are inadequate to ensure that an article of food is as safe as a similar article of food that is manufactured, processed, packed, or held in the United States in accordance with the requirements of this Act, the Secretary shall, to the extent practicable, identify such inadequacies and establish a process by which the foreign region, country, or territory may inform the Secretary of improvements made to such food safety program, system, or standard and demonstrate that those controls are adequate to ensure that an article of food is as

safe as a similar article of food that is manufactured, processed, packed, or held in the United States in accordance with the requirements of this Act.

(r)(1) The Secretary may require, pursuant to the regulations promulgated under paragraph (4)(A), as a condition of granting admission to a drug imported or offered for import into the United States, that the importer electronically submit information demonstrating that the drug complies with applicable requirements of this Act.

(2) The information described under paragraph (1) may include—

(A) information demonstrating the regulatory status of the drug, such as the new drug application, abbreviated new drug application, or investigational new drug or drug master file number;

(B) facility information, such as proof of registration and the unique facility identifier;

(C) indication of compliance with current good manufacturing practice, testing results, certifications relating to satisfactory inspections, and compliance with the country of export regulations; and

(D) any other information deemed necessary and appropriate by the Secretary to assess compliance of the article being offered for import.

(3) Information requirements referred to in paragraph (2)(C) may, at the discretion of the Secretary, be satisfied—

(A) through representation by a foreign government, if an inspection is conducted by a foreign government using standards and practices as determined appropriate by the Secretary;

(B) through representation by a foreign government or an agency of a foreign government recognized under section 809; or

(C) other appropriate documentation or evidence as described by the Secretary.

(4)(A) Not later than 18 months after the date of enactment of the Food and Drug Administration Safety and Innovation Act, the Secretary shall adopt final regulations implementing this sub-section. Such requirements shall be appropriate for the type of import, such as whether the drug is for import into the United States for use in preclinical research or in a clinical investigation under an investigational new drug exemption under 505(i).

(B) In promulgating the regulations under subparagraph (A), the Secretary—

(i) may, as appropriate, take into account differences among importers and types of imports, and, based on the level of risk posed by the imported drug, provide for expedited clearance for those importers that volunteer to participate in partnership programs for highly compliant companies and pass a review of internal controls, including sourcing of foreign manufacturing inputs, and plant inspections; and

(ii) shall—

(I) issue a notice of proposed rulemaking that includes the proposed regulation;

(II) provide a period of not less than 60 days for comments on the proposed regulation; and

(III) publish the final regulation not less than 30 days before the effective date of the regulation.

(C) Notwithstanding any other provision of law, the Secretary shall promulgate regulations implementing this subsection only as described in subparagraph (B).

(s) REGISTRATION OF COMMERCIAL IMPORTERS.—

(1) REGISTRATION.—The Secretary shall require a commercial importer of drugs—

(A) to be registered with the Secretary in a form and manner specified by the Secretary; and

(B) subject to paragraph (4), to submit, at the time of registration, a unique identifier for the principal place of business for which the importer is required to register under this subsection.

(2) REGULATIONS.—

(A) IN GENERAL.—The Secretary, in consultation with the Secretary of Homeland Security acting through U.S Customs and Border Protection, shall promulgate regulations to establish good importer practices that specify the measures an importer shall take to ensure imported drugs are in compliance with the requirements of this Act and the Public Health Service Act.

(B) PROCEDURE.—In promulgating a regulation under subparagraph (A), the Secretary shall—

(i) issue a notice of proposed rulemaking that includes the proposed regulation;

(ii) provide a period of not less than 60 days for comments on the proposed regulation; and

(iii) publish the final regulation not less than 30 days before the regulation's effective date.

(C) RESTRICTIONS.—Notwithstanding any other provision of Federal law, in implementing this subsection, the Secretary shall only promulgate regulations as described in subparagraph (B).

(3) DISCONTINUANCE OF REGISTRATION.—The Secretary shall discontinue the registration of any commercial importer of drugs that fails to comply with the regulations promulgated under this subsection.

(4) Unique facility identifier.—The Secretary shall specify the unique facility identifier system that shall be used by registrants under paragraph (1). The requirement to include a unique facility identifier in a registration under paragraph (1) shall not apply until the date that the identifier system is specified by the Secretary under the preceding sentence.

(5) Exemptions.—The Secretary, by notice in the Federal Register, may establish exemptions from the requirements of this subsection.

Sec. 802 [21 U.S.C. 382]. EXPORTS OF CERTAIN UNAPPROVED PRODUCTS

(a) A drug or device—

(1) which, in the case of a drug—

(A)(i) requires approval by the Secretary under section 505 before such drug may be introduced or delivered for introduction into interstate commerce; or

(ii) requires licensing by the Secretary under section 351 of the Public Health Service Act or by the Secretary of Agriculture under the Act of March 4, 1913 (known as the Virus–Serum Toxin Act) before it may be introduced or delivered for introduction into interstate commerce;

(B) does not have such approval or license; and

(C) is not exempt from such sections or Act; and

(2) which, in the case of a device—

(A) does not comply with an applicable requirement under section 514 or 515;

(B) under section 520(g) is exempt from either such section; or

(C) is a banned device under section 516, is adulterated, misbranded, and in violation of such sections or Act unless the export of the drug or device is, except as provided in subsection (f), authorized under subsection (b), (c), (d), or (e) or section 801(e)(2). If[86] a drug or device described in paragraphs (1) and (2) may be exported under subsection (b) and if an application for such drug or device under section 505 or 515 or section 351 of the Public Health Service Act was disapproved, the Secretary shall notify the appropriate public health official of the country to which such drug will be exported of such disapproval.

(b)(1)(A) A drug or device described in subsection (a) may be exported to any country, if the drug or device complies with the laws of that country and has valid marketing authorization by the appropriate authority—

86. Placement of sentence is so in law. See Pub. L. No. 104–134, tit. II, § 2102(d)(1), 110 Stat. 1321, 1321–315 (1996). Sentence probably should appear after and below subparagraph (C), with the same indentation as the section designation.

(i) in Australia, Canada, Israel, Japan, New Zealand, Switzerland, or South Africa; or

(ii) in the European Union or a country in the European Economic Area (the countries in the European Union and the European Free Trade Association) if the drug or device is marketed in that country or the drug or device is authorized for general marketing in the European Economic Area.

(B) The Secretary may designate an additional country to be included in the list of countries described in clauses (i) and (ii) of subparagraph (A) if all of the following requirements are met in such country:

(i) Statutory or regulatory requirements which require the review of drugs and devices for safety and effectiveness by an entity of the government of such country and which authorize the approval of only those drugs and devices which have been determined to be safe and effective by experts employed by or acting on behalf of such entity and qualified by scientific training and experience to evaluate the safety and effectiveness of drugs and devices on the basis of adequate and well-controlled investigations, including clinical investigations, conducted by experts qualified by scientific training and experience to evaluate the safety and effectiveness of drugs and devices.

(ii) Statutory or regulatory requirements that the methods used in, and the facilities and controls used for—

(I) the manufacture, processing, and packing of drugs in the country are adequate to preserve their identity, quality, purity, and strength; and

(II) the manufacture, preproduction design validation, packing, storage, and installation of a device are adequate to assure that the device will be safe and effective.

(iii) Statutory or regulatory requirements for the reporting of adverse reactions to drugs and devices and procedures to withdraw approval and remove drugs and devices found not to be safe or effective.

(iv) Statutory or regulatory requirements that the labeling and promotion of drugs and devices must be in accordance with the approval of the drug or device.

(v) The valid marketing authorization system in such country or countries is equivalent to the systems in the countries described in clauses (i) and (ii) of subparagraph (A).

The Secretary shall not delegate the authority granted under this subparagraph.

(C) An appropriate country official, manufacturer, or exporter may request the Secretary to take action under subparagraph (B) to designate an additional country or countries to be added to the list of countries described in clauses (i) and (ii) of subparagraph (A) by submitting documentation to the Secretary in support of such designation. Any person other than a country requesting such designation shall include, along with the request, a letter from the country indicating the desire of such country to be designated.

(2) A drug described in subsection (a) may be directly exported to a country which is not listed in clause (i) or (ii) of paragraph (1)(A) if—

(A) the drug complies with the laws of that country and has valid marketing authorization by the responsible authority in that country; and

(B) the Secretary determines that all of the following requirements are met in that country:

(i) Statutory or regulatory requirements which require the review of drugs for safety and effectiveness by an entity of the government of such country and which authorize the approval of only those drugs which have been determined to be safe and effective by experts employed by or acting on behalf of such entity and qualified by scientific training and experience to evaluate the safety and effectiveness of drugs on the basis of adequate and well-controlled investigations, including clinical investigations, conducted by experts qualified by scientific training and experience to evaluate the safety and effectiveness of drugs.

(ii) Statutory or regulatory requirements that the methods used in, and the facilities and controls used for the manufacture, processing, and packing of drugs in the country are adequate to preserve their identity, quality, purity, and strength.

(iii) Statutory or regulatory requirements for the reporting of adverse reactions to drugs and procedures to withdraw approval and remove drugs found not to be safe or effective.

(iv) Statutory or regulatory requirements that the labeling and promotion of drugs must be in accordance with the approval of the drug.

(3) The exporter of a drug described in subsection (a) which would not meet the conditions for approval under this Act or conditions for approval of a country described in clause (i) or (ii) of paragraph (1)(A) may petition the Secretary for authorization to export such drug to a country which is not described in clause (i) or (ii) of paragraph (1)(A) or which is not described in paragraph (2). The Secretary shall permit such export if—

(A) the person exporting the drug—

(i) certifies that the drug would not meet the conditions for approval under this Act or the conditions for approval of a country described in clause (i) or (ii) of paragraph (1)(A); and

(ii) provides the Secretary with credible scientific evidence, acceptable to the Secretary, that the drug would be safe and effective under the conditions of use in the country to which it is being exported; and

(B) the appropriate health authority in the country to which the drug is being exported—

(i) requests approval of the export of the drug to such country;

(ii) certifies that the health authority understands that the drug is not approved under this Act or in a country described in clause (i) or (ii) of paragraph (1)(A); and

(iii) concurs that the scientific evidence provided pursuant to subparagraph (A) is credible scientific evidence that the drug would be reasonably safe and effective in such country.

The Secretary shall take action on a request for export of a drug under this paragraph within 60 days of receiving such request.

(c) A drug or device intended for investigational use in any country described in clause (i) or (ii) of subsection (b)(1)(A) may be exported in accordance with the laws of that country and shall be exempt from regulation under section 505(i) or 520(g).

(d) A drug or device intended for formulation, filling, packaging, labeling, or further processing in anticipation of market authorization in any country described in clause (i) or (ii) of subsection (b)(1)(A) may be exported for use in accordance with the laws of that country.

(e)(1) A drug or device which is used in the diagnosis, prevention, or treatment of a tropical disease or another disease not of significant prevalence in the United States and which does not otherwise qualify for export under this section shall, upon approval of an application, be permitted to be exported if the Secretary finds that the drug or device will not expose patients in such country to an unreasonable risk of illness or injury and the probable benefit to health from the use of the drug or device (under conditions of use prescribed, recommended, or suggested in the labeling or proposed labeling of the drug or device) outweighs the risk of injury or illness from its use, taking into account the probable risks and benefits of currently available drug or device treatment.

(2) The holder of an approved application for the export of a drug or device under this subsection shall report to the Secretary—

(A) the receipt of any credible information indicating that the drug or device is being or may have been exported from a country for which the Secretary made a finding under paragraph (1)(A) to a country for which the Secretary cannot make such a finding; and

(B) the receipt of any information indicating adverse reactions to such drug.

(3)(A) If the Secretary determines that—

(i) a drug or device for which an application is approved under paragraph (1) does not continue to meet the requirements of such paragraph; or

(ii) the holder of an approved application under paragraph (1) has not made the report required by paragraph (2),

the Secretary may, after providing the holder of the application an opportunity for an informal hearing, withdraw the approved application.

(B) If the Secretary determines that the holder of an approved application under paragraph (1) or an importer is exporting a drug or device from the United States to an importer and such importer is exporting the drug or device to a country for which the Secretary cannot make a finding under paragraph (1) and such export presents an imminent hazard, the Secretary shall immediately prohibit the export of the drug or device to such importer, provide the person exporting the drug or device from the United States prompt notice of the prohibition, and afford such person an opportunity for an expedited hearing.

(f) A drug or device may not be exported under this section—

(1) if the drug or device is not manufactured, processed, packaged, and held in substantial conformity with current good manufacturing practice requirements or does not meet international standards as certified by an international standards organization recognized by the Secretary;

(2) if the drug or device is adulterated under clause (1), (2)(A), or (3) of section 501(a) or subsection (c) or (d) of section 501;

(3) if the requirements of subparagraphs (A) through (D) of section 801(e)(1) have not been met;

(4)(A) if the drug or device is the subject of a notice by the Secretary or the Secretary of Agriculture of a determination that the probability of reimportation of the exported drug or device would present an imminent hazard to the public health and safety of the United States and the only means of limiting the hazard is to prohibit the export of the drug or device; or

(B) if the drug or device presents an imminent hazard to the public health of the country to which the drug or device would be exported;

(5) if the labeling of the drug or device is not—

(A) in accordance with the requirements and conditions for use in—

(i) the country in which the drug or device received valid marketing authorization under subsection (b); and

(ii) the country to which the drug or device would be exported; and

(B) in the language and units of measurement of the country to which the drug or device would be exported or in the language designated by such country; or

(6) if the drug or device is not promoted in accordance with the labeling requirements set forth in paragraph (5).

In making a finding under paragraph (4)(B), (5), or (6) the Secretary shall consult with the appropriate public health official in the affected country.

(g) The exporter of a drug or device exported under subsection (b)(1) shall provide a simple notification to the Secretary identifying the drug or device when the exporter first begins to export such drug or device to any country listed in clause (i) or (ii) of subsection (b)(1)(A). When an exporter of a drug or device first begins to export a drug or device to a country which is not listed in clause (i) or (ii) of subsection (b)(1)(A),[87] the exporter shall provide a simple notification to the Secretary identifying the drug or device and the country to which such drug or device is being exported. Any exporter of a drug or device shall maintain records of all drugs or devices exported and the countries to which they were exported.

(h) For purposes of this section—

(1) a reference to the Secretary shall in the case of a biological product which is required to be licensed under the Act of March 4, 1913 (37 Stat. 832–833) (commonly known as the Virus–Serum Toxin Act) be considered to be a reference to the Secretary of Agriculture, and

(2) the term "drug" includes drugs for human use as well as biologicals under section 351 of the Public Health Service Act or the Act of March 4, 1913 (37 Stat. 832–833) (commonly known as the Virus–Serum Toxin Act).

(i) Insulin and antibiotic drugs may be exported without regard to the requirements in this section if the insulin and antibiotic drugs meet the requirements of section 801(e)(1).

SEC. 803 [21 U.S.C. 383]. OFFICE OF INTERNATIONAL RELATIONS

(a) There is established in the Department of Health and Human Services an Office of International Relations.

(b) In carrying out the functions of the office under subsection (a), the Secretary may enter into agreements with foreign countries to facilitate commerce in devices between the United States and such countries consistent with the requirements of this Act. In such agreements, the Secretary shall encourage the mutual recognition of—

(1) good manufacturing practice regulations promulgated under section 520(f), and

(2) other regulations and testing protocols as the Secretary determines to be appropriate.

(c)(1) The Secretary shall support the Office of the United States Trade Representative, in consultation with the Secretary of Commerce, in meetings with representatives of other countries to discuss methods and approaches to reduce the burden

---

87. So in law. See Pub. L. No. 104–134, tit. II, § 2102(d)(1), 110 Stat. 1321, 1321–315 (1996).   Probably should have a beginning parentheses before "A".

of regulation and harmonize regulatory requirements if the Secretary determines that such harmonization continues consumer protections consistent with the purposes of this Act.

(2) The Secretary shall support the Office of the United States Trade Representative, in consultation with the Secretary of Commerce, in efforts to move toward the acceptance of mutual recognition agreements relating to the regulation of drugs, biological products, devices, foods, food additives, and color additives, and the regulation of good manufacturing practices, between the European Union and the United States.

(3)(A) The Secretary shall regularly participate in meetings with representatives of other foreign governments to discuss and reach agreement on methods and approaches to harmonize regulatory requirements.

(B) In carrying out subparagraph (A), the Secretary may participate in appropriate fora, including the International Medical Device Regulators Forum, and may—

(i) provide guidance to such fora on strategies, policies, directions, membership, and other activities of a forum as appropriate;

(ii) to the extent appropriate, solicit, review, and consider comments from industry, academia, health care professionals, and patient groups regarding the activities of such fora; and

(iii) to the extent appropriate, inform the public of the Secretary's activities within such fora, and share with the public any documentation relating to a forum's strategies, policies, and other activities of such fora.

(4) With respect to devices, the Secretary may, when appropriate, enter into arrangements with nations regarding methods and approaches to harmonizing regulatory requirements for activities, including inspections and common international labeling symbols.

(5) Paragraphs (1) through (4) shall not apply with respect to products defined in section 201(ff).

SEC. 804 [21 U.S.C. 384]. IMPORTATION OF PRESCRIPTION DRUGS

(a) DEFINITIONS.—In this section:

(1) IMPORTER.—The term "importer" means a pharmacist or wholesaler.

(2) PHARMACIST.—The term "pharmacist" means a person licensed by a State to practice pharmacy, including the dispensing and selling of prescription drugs.

(3) PRESCRIPTION DRUG.—The term "prescription drug" means a drug subject to section 503(b), other than—

(A) a controlled substance (as defined in section 102 of the Controlled Substances Act (21 U.S.C. 802));

(B) a biological product (as defined in section 351 of the Public Health Service Act (42 U.S.C. 262));

(C) an infused drug (including a peritoneal dialysis solution);

(D) an intravenously injected drug;

(E) a drug that is inhaled during surgery; or

(F) a drug which is a parenteral drug, the importation of which pursuant to subsection (b) is determined by the Secretary to pose a threat to the public health, in which case section 801(d)(1) shall continue to apply.

(4) QUALIFYING LABORATORY.—The term "qualifying laboratory" means a laboratory in the United States that has been approved by the Secretary for the purposes of this section.

(5) WHOLESALER.—

(A) IN GENERAL.—The term "wholesaler" means a person licensed as a wholesaler or distributor of prescription drugs in the United States under section 503(e)(2)(A).

(B) EXCLUSION.—The term "wholesaler" does not include a person authorized to import drugs under section 801(d)(1).

(b) REGULATIONS.—The Secretary, after consultation with the United States Trade Representative and the Commissioner of Customs, shall promulgate regulations permitting pharmacists and wholesalers to import prescription drugs from Canada into the United States.

(c) LIMITATION.—The regulations under subsection (b) shall—

(1) require that safeguards be in place to ensure that each prescription drug imported under the regulations complies with section 505 (including with respect to being safe and effective for the intended use of the prescription drug), with sections 501 and 502, and with other applicable requirements of this Act;

(2) require that an importer of a prescription drug under the regulations comply with subsections (d)(1) and (e); and

(3) contain any additional provisions determined by the Secretary to be appropriate as a safeguard to protect the public health or as a means to facilitate the importation of prescription drugs.

(d) INFORMATION AND RECORDS.—

(1) IN GENERAL.—The regulations under subsection (b) shall require an importer of a prescription drug under subsection (b) to submit to the Secretary the following information and documentation:

(A) The name and quantity of the active ingredient of the prescription drug.

(B) A description of the dosage form of the prescription drug.

(C) The date on which the prescription drug is shipped.

(D) The quantity of the prescription drug that is shipped.

(E) The point of origin and destination of the prescription drug.

(F) The price paid by the importer for the prescription drug.

(G) Documentation from the foreign seller specifying—

(i) the original source of the prescription drug; and

(ii) the quantity of each lot of the prescription drug originally received by the seller from that source.

(H) The lot or control number assigned to the prescription drug by the manufacturer of the prescription drug.

(I) The name, address, telephone number, and professional license number (if any) of the importer.

(J)(i) In the case of a prescription drug that is shipped directly from the first foreign recipient of the prescription drug from the manufacturer:

(I) Documentation demonstrating that the prescription drug was received by the recipient from the manufacturer and subsequently shipped by the first foreign recipient to the importer.

(II) Documentation of the quantity of each lot of the prescription drug received by the first foreign recipient demonstrating that the quantity being imported into the United States is not more than the quantity that was received by the first foreign recipient.

(III)(aa) In the case of an initial imported shipment, documentation demonstrating that each batch of the prescription drug in the shipment was statistically sampled and tested for authenticity and degradation.

(bb) In the case of any subsequent shipment, documentation demonstrating that a statistically valid sample of the shipment was tested for authenticity and degradation.

(ii) In the case of a prescription drug that is not shipped directly from the first foreign recipient of the prescription drug from the manufacturer, documentation demonstrating that each batch in each shipment offered for importation into the United States was statistically sampled and tested for authenticity and degradation.

(K) Certification from the importer or manufacturer of the prescription drug that the prescription drug—

(i) is approved for marketing in the United States and is not adulterated or misbranded; and

(ii) meets all labeling requirements under this Act.

675

(L) Laboratory records, including complete data derived from all tests necessary to ensure that the prescription drug is in compliance with established specifications and standards.

(M) Documentation demonstrating that the testing required by subparagraphs (J) and (L) was conducted at a qualifying laboratory.

(N) Any other information that the Secretary determines is necessary to ensure the protection of the public health.

(2) MAINTENANCE BY THE SECRETARY.—The Secretary shall maintain information and documentation submitted under paragraph (1) for such period of time as the Secretary determines to be necessary.

(e) TESTING.—The regulations under subsection (b) shall require—

(1) that testing described in subparagraphs (J) and (L) of subsection (d)(1) be conducted by the importer or by the manufacturer of the prescription drug at a qualified laboratory;

(2) if the tests are conducted by the importer—

(A) that information needed to—

(i) authenticate the prescription drug being tested; and

(ii) confirm that the labeling of the prescription drug complies with labeling requirements under this Act;

be supplied by the manufacturer of the prescription drug to the pharmacist or wholesaler; and

(B) that the information supplied under subparagraph (A) be kept in strict confidence and used only for purposes of testing or otherwise complying with this Act; and

(3) may include such additional provisions as the Secretary determines to be appropriate to provide for the protection of trade secrets and commercial or financial information that is privileged or confidential.

(f) REGISTRATION OF FOREIGN SELLERS.—Any establishment within Canada engaged in the distribution of a prescription drug that is imported or offered for importation into the United States shall register with the Secretary the name and place of business of the establishment and the name of the United States agent for the establishment.

(g) SUSPENSION OF IMPORTATION.—The Secretary shall require that importations of a specific prescription drug or importations by a specific importer under subsection (b) be immediately suspended on discovery of a pattern of importation of that specific prescription drug or by that specific importer of drugs that are counterfeit or in violation of any requirement under this section, until an investigation is completed and the Secretary determines that the public is adequately protected from counterfeit and violative prescription drugs being imported under subsection (b).

(h) APPROVED LABELING.—The manufacturer of a prescription drug shall provide an importer written authorization for the importer to use, at no cost, the approved labeling for the prescription drug.

(i) CHARITABLE CONTRIBUTIONS.—Notwithstanding any other provision of this section, section 801(d)(1) continues to apply to a prescription drug that is donated or otherwise supplied at no charge by the manufacturer of the drug to a charitable or humanitarian organization (including the United Nations and affiliates) or to a government of a foreign country.

(j) WAIVER AUTHORITY FOR IMPORTATION BY INDIVIDUALS.—

(1) DECLARATIONS.—Congress declares that in the enforcement against individuals of the prohibition of importation of prescription drugs and devices, the Secretary should—

(A) focus enforcement on cases in which the importation by an individual poses a significant threat to public health; and

(B) exercise discretion to permit individuals to make such importations in circumstances in which—

(i) the importation is clearly for personal use; and

(ii) the prescription drug or device imported does not appear to present an unreasonable risk to the individual.

(2) WAIVER AUTHORITY.—

(A) IN GENERAL.—The Secretary may grant to individuals, by regulation or on a case-by-case basis, a waiver of the prohibition of importation of a prescription drug or device or class of prescription drugs or devices, under such conditions as the Secretary determines to be appropriate.

(B) GUIDANCE ON CASE-BY-CASE WAIVERS.—The Secretary shall publish, and update as necessary, guidance that accurately describes circumstances in which the Secretary will consistently grant waivers on a case-by-case basis under subparagraph (A), so that individuals may know with the greatest practicable degree of certainty whether a particular importation for personal use will be permitted.

(3) DRUGS IMPORTED FROM CANADA.—In particular, the Secretary shall by regulation grant individuals a waiver to permit individuals to import into the United States a prescription drug that—

(A) is imported from a licensed pharmacy for personal use by an individual, not for resale, in quantities that do not exceed a 90–day supply;

(B) is accompanied by a copy of a valid prescription;

(C) is imported from Canada, from a seller registered with the Secretary;

(D) is a prescription drug approved by the Secretary under chapter V;

(E) is in the form of a final finished dosage that was manufactured in an establishment registered under section 510; and

(F) is imported under such other conditions as the Secretary determines to be necessary to ensure public safety.

(k) CONSTRUCTION.—Nothing in this section limits the authority of the Secretary relating to the importation of prescription drugs, other than with respect to section 801(d)(1) as provided in this section.

(*l*) EFFECTIVENESS OF SECTION.—

(1) COMMENCEMENT OF PROGRAM.—This section shall become effective only if the Secretary certifies to the Congress that the implementation of this section will—

(A) pose no additional risk to the public's health and safety; and

(B) result in a significant reduction in the cost of covered products to the American consumer.

(2) TERMINATION OF PROGRAM.—

(A) IN GENERAL.—If, after the date that is 1 year after the effective date of the regulations under subsection (b) and before the date that is 18 months after the effective date, the Secretary submits to Congress a certification that, in the opinion of the Secretary, based on substantial evidence obtained after the effective date, the benefits of implementation of this section do not outweigh any detriment of implementation of this section, this section shall cease to be effective as of the date that is 30 days after the date on which the Secretary submits the certification.

(B) PROCEDURE.—The Secretary shall not submit a certification under subparagraph (A) unless, after a hearing on the record under sections 556 and 557 of title 5, United States Code, the Secretary—

(i)(I) determines that it is more likely than not that implementation of this section would result in an increase in the risk to the public health and safety;

(II) identifies specifically, in qualitative and quantitative terms, the nature of the increased risk;

(III) identifies specifically the causes of the increased risk; and

(IV)(aa) considers whether any measures can be taken to avoid, reduce, or mitigate the increased risk; and

(bb) if the Secretary determines that any measures described in item (aa) would require additional statutory authority, submits to Congress a report describing the legislation that would be required;

(ii) identifies specifically, in qualitative and quantitative terms, the benefits that would result from implementation of this section (including the benefit of reductions in the cost of covered products to consumers in the United States, allowing consumers to procure needed medication that consumers might not otherwise be able to procure without foregoing other necessities of life); and

(iii)(I) compares in specific terms the detriment identified under clause (i) with the benefits identified under clause (ii); and

(II) determines that the benefits do not outweigh the detriment.

(m) AUTHORIZATION OF APPROPRIATIONS.—There are authorized to be appropriated such sums as are necessary to carry out this section.

SEC. 805 [21 U.S.C. 384a]. FOREIGN SUPPLIER VERIFICATION PROGRAM[88]

(a) IN GENERAL.—

(1) VERIFICATION REQUIREMENT.—Except as provided under subsections (e) and (f), each importer shall perform risk-based foreign supplier verification activities for the purpose of verifying that the food imported by the importer or agent of an importer is—

(A) produced in compliance with the requirements of section 418 or section 419, as appropriate; and

(B) is not adulterated under section 402 or misbranded under section 403(w).

(2) IMPORTER DEFINED.—For purposes of this section, the term "importer" means, with respect to an article of food—

(A) the United States owner or consignee of the article of food at the time of entry of such article into the United States; or

(B) in the case when there is no United States owner or consignee as described in subparagraph (A), the United States agent or representative of a foreign owner or consignee of the article of food at the time of entry of such article into the United States.

(b) GUIDANCE.—Not later than 1 year after the date of enactment of the FDA Food Safety Modernization Act, the Secretary shall issue guidance to assist importers in developing foreign supplier verification programs.

(c) REGULATIONS.—

(1) IN GENERAL.—Not later than 1 year after the date of enactment of the FDA Food Safety Modernization Act, the Secretary shall promulgate regulations to

---

88. Section 805 was added by Pub. L. No. 111–353, § 301(c), and according to § 301(d) of that law, this section becomes effective Jan. 4, 2013, two years after enactment.

provide for the content of the foreign supplier verification program established under subsection (a).

(2) REQUIREMENTS.—The regulations promulgated under paragraph (1)—

(A) shall require that the foreign supplier verification program of each importer be adequate to provide assurances that each foreign supplier to the importer produces the imported food in compliance with—

(i) processes and procedures, including reasonably appropriate risk-based preventive controls, that provide the same level of public health protection as those required under section 418 or section 419 (taking into consideration variances granted under section 419), as appropriate; and

(ii) section 402 and section 403(w).

(B) shall include such other requirements as the Secretary deems necessary and appropriate to verify that food imported into the United States is as safe as food produced and sold within the United States.

(3) CONSIDERATIONS.—In promulgating regulations under this subsection, the Secretary shall, as appropriate, take into account differences among importers and types of imported foods, including based on the level of risk posed by the imported food.

(4) ACTIVITIES.—Verification activities under a foreign supplier verification program under this section may include monitoring records for shipments, lot-by-lot certification of compliance, annual on-site inspections, checking the hazard analysis and risk-based preventive control plan of the foreign supplier, and periodically testing and sampling shipments.

(d) RECORD MAINTENANCE AND ACCESS.—Records of an importer related to a foreign supplier verification program shall be maintained for a period of not less than 2 years and shall be made available promptly to a duly authorized representative of the Secretary upon request.

(e) EXEMPTION OF SEAFOOD, JUICE, AND LOW-ACID CANNED FOOD FACILITIES IN COMPLIANCE WITH HACCP.—This section shall not apply to a facility if the owner, operator, or agent in charge of such facility is required to comply with, and is in compliance with, 1 of the following standards and regulations with respect to such facility:

(1) The Seafood Hazard Analysis Critical Control Points Program of the Food and Drug Administration.

(2) The Juice Hazard Analysis Critical Control Points Program of the Food and Drug Administration.

(3) The Thermally Processed Low–Acid Foods Packaged in Hermetically Sealed Containers standards of the Food and Drug Administration (or any successor standards).

The exemption under paragraph (3) shall apply only with respect to microbiological hazards that are regulated under the standards for Thermally Processed Low–Acid Foods Packaged in Hermetically Sealed Containers under part 113 of chapter 21, Code of Federal Regulations (or any successor regulations).

(f) ADDITIONAL EXEMPTIONS.—The Secretary, by notice published in the Federal Register, shall establish an exemption from the requirements of this section for articles of food imported in small quantities for research and evaluation purposes or for personal consumption, provided that such foods are not intended for retail sale and are not sold or distributed to the public.

(g) PUBLICATION OF LIST OF PARTICIPANTS.—The Secretary shall publish and maintain on the Internet Web site of the Food and Drug Administration a current list that includes the name of, location of, and other information deemed necessary by the Secretary about, importers participating under this section.

SEC. 806 [21 U.S.C. 384b]. VOLUNTARY QUALIFIED IMPORTER PROGRAM

(a) IN GENERAL.—Beginning not later than 18 months after the date of enactment of the FDA Food Safety Modernization Act, the Secretary shall—

(1) establish a program, in consultation with the Secretary of Homeland Security—

(A) to provide for the expedited review and importation of food offered for importation by importers who have voluntarily agreed to participate in such program; and

(B) consistent with section 808, establish a process for the issuance of a facility certification to accompany food offered for importation by importers who have voluntarily agreed to participate in such program; and

(2) issue a guidance document related to participation in, revocation of such participation in, reinstatement in, and compliance with, such program.

(b) VOLUNTARY PARTICIPATION.—An importer may request the Secretary to provide for the expedited review and importation of designated foods in accordance with the program established by the Secretary under subsection (a).

(c) NOTICE OF INTENT TO PARTICIPATE.—An importer that intends to participate in the program under this section in a fiscal year shall submit a notice and application to the Secretary of such intent at the time and in a manner established by the Secretary.

(d) ELIGIBILITY.—Eligibility shall be limited to an importer offering food for importation from a facility that has a certification described in subsection (a). In reviewing the applications and making determinations on such applications, the Secretary shall consider the risk of the food to be imported based on factors, such as the following:

(1) The known safety risks of the food to be imported.

(2) The compliance history of foreign suppliers used by the importer, as appropriate.

(3) The capability of the regulatory system of the country of export to ensure compliance with United States food safety standards for a designated food.

(4) The compliance of the importer with the requirements of section 805.

(5) The recordkeeping, testing, inspections and audits of facilities, traceability of articles of food, temperature controls, and sourcing practices of the importer.

(6) The potential risk for intentional adulteration of the food.

(7) Any other factor that the Secretary determines appropriate.

(e) REVIEW AND REVOCATION.—Any importer qualified by the Secretary in accordance with the eligibility criteria set forth in this section shall be reevaluated not less often than once every 3 years and the Secretary shall promptly revoke the qualified importer status of any importer found not to be in compliance with such criteria.

(f) FALSE STATEMENTS.—Any statement or representation made by an importer to the Secretary shall be subject to section 1001 of title 18, United States Code.

(g) DEFINITION.—For purposes of this section, the term "importer" means the person that brings food, or causes food to be brought, from a foreign country into the customs territory of the United States.

SEC. 807 [21 U.S.C. 384c]. INSPECTION OF FOREIGN FOOD FACILITIES

(a) INSPECTION.—The Secretary—

(1) may enter into arrangements and agreements with foreign governments to facilitate the inspection of foreign facilities registered under section 415; and

(2) shall direct resources to inspections of foreign facilities, suppliers, and food types, especially such facilities, suppliers, and food types that present a high risk (as identified by the Secretary), to help ensure the safety and security of the food supply of the United States.

(b) EFFECT OF INABILITY TO INSPECT.—Notwithstanding any other provision of law, food shall be refused admission into the United States if it is from a foreign factory, warehouse, or other establishment of which the owner, operator, or agent in charge, or the government of the foreign country, refuses to permit entry of United States inspectors or other individuals duly designated by the Secretary, upon request, to inspect such factory, warehouse, or other establishment. For purposes of this subsection, such an owner, operator, or agent in charge shall be considered to have refused an inspection if such owner, operator, or agent in charge does not permit an inspection of a factory, warehouse, or other establishment during the 24–hour period after such request is submitted, or after such other time period, as agreed upon by the Secretary and the foreign factory, warehouse, or other establishment.

SEC. 808 [21 U.S.C. 384d]. ACCREDITATION OF THIRD–PARTY AUDITORS

(a) DEFINITIONS.—In this section:

(1) AUDIT AGENT.—The term "audit agent" means an individual who is an employee or agent of an accredited third-party auditor and, although not individually accredited, is qualified to conduct food safety audits on behalf of an accredited third-party auditor.

(2) ACCREDITATION BODY.—The term "accreditation body" means an authority that performs accreditation of third-party auditors.

(3) THIRD-PARTY AUDITOR.—The term "third-party auditor" means a foreign government, agency of a foreign government, foreign cooperative, or any other third party, as the Secretary determines appropriate in accordance with the model standards described in subsection (b)(2), that is eligible to be considered for accreditation to conduct food safety audits to certify that eligible entities meet the applicable requirements of this section. A third-party auditor may be a single individual. A third-party auditor may employ or use audit agents to help conduct consultative and regulatory audits.

(4) ACCREDITED THIRD-PARTY AUDITOR.—The term "accredited third-party auditor" means a third-party auditor accredited by an accreditation body to conduct audits of eligible entities to certify that such eligible entities meet the applicable requirements of this section. An accredited third-party auditor may be an individual who conducts food safety audits to certify that eligible entities meet the applicable requirements of this section.

(5) CONSULTATIVE AUDIT.—The term "consultative audit" means an audit of an eligible entity—

(A) to determine whether such entity is in compliance with the provisions of this Act and with applicable industry standards and practices; and

(B) the results of which are for internal purposes only.

(6) ELIGIBLE ENTITY.—The term "eligible entity" means a foreign entity, including a foreign facility registered under section 415, in the food import supply chain that chooses to be audited by an accredited third-party auditor or the audit agent of such accredited third-party auditor.

(7) REGULATORY AUDIT.—The term "regulatory audit" means an audit of an eligible entity—

(A) to determine whether such entity is in compliance with the provisions of this Act; and

(B) the results of which determine—

(i) whether an article of food manufactured, processed, packed, or held by such entity is eligible to receive a food certification under section 801(q); or

(ii) whether a facility is eligible to receive a facility certification under section 806(a) for purposes of participating in the program under section 806.

(b) ACCREDITATION SYSTEM.—

(1) ACCREDITATION BODIES.—

(A) RECOGNITION OF ACCREDITATION BODIES.—

(i) IN GENERAL.—Not later than 2 years after the date of enactment of the FDA Food Safety Modernization Act, the Secretary shall establish a system for the recognition of accreditation bodies that accredit third-party auditors to certify that eligible entities meet the applicable requirements of this section.

(ii) DIRECT ACCREDITATION.—If, by the date that is 2 years after the date of establishment of the system described in clause (i), the Secretary has not identified and recognized an accreditation body to meet the requirements of this section, the Secretary may directly accredit third-party auditors.

(B) NOTIFICATION.—Each accreditation body recognized by the Secretary shall submit to the Secretary a list of all accredited third-party auditors accredited by such body and the audit agents of such auditors.

(C) REVOCATION OF RECOGNITION AS AN ACCREDITATION BODY.—The Secretary shall promptly revoke the recognition of any accreditation body found not to be in compliance with the requirements of this section.

(D) REINSTATEMENT.—The Secretary shall establish procedures to reinstate recognition of an accreditation body if the Secretary determines, based on evidence presented by such accreditation body, that revocation was inappropriate or that the body meets the requirements for recognition under this section.

(2) MODEL ACCREDITATION STANDARDS.—Not later than 18 months after the date of enactment of the FDA Food Safety Modernization Act, the Secretary shall develop model standards, including requirements for regulatory audit reports, and each recognized accreditation body shall ensure that third-party auditors and audit agents of such auditors meet such standards in order to qualify such third-party auditors as accredited third-party auditors under this section. In developing the model standards, the Secretary shall look to standards in place on the date of the enactment of this section for guidance, to avoid unnecessary duplication of efforts and costs.

(c) THIRD-PARTY AUDITORS.—

(1) REQUIREMENTS FOR ACCREDITATION AS A THIRD-PARTY AUDITOR.—

(A) FOREIGN GOVERNMENTS.—Prior to accrediting a foreign government or an agency of a foreign government as an accredited third-party auditor, the accreditation body (or, in the case of direct accreditation under subsection (b)(1)(A)(ii), the Secretary) shall perform such reviews and audits of food safety programs, systems, and standards of the government or agency of the government as the Secretary deems necessary, including requirements under the model standards developed under subsection (b)(2), to determine that the foreign government or agency of the foreign government is capable of adequately ensuring that eligible entities or foods certified by such government or agency meet the requirements of this Act with respect to food manufactured, processed, packed, or held for import into the United States.

(B) FOREIGN COOPERATIVES AND OTHER THIRD PARTIES.—Prior to accrediting a foreign cooperative that aggregates the products of growers or processors, or any other third party to be an accredited third-party auditor, the accreditation body (or, in the case of direct accreditation under subsection (b)(1)(A)(ii), the Secretary) shall perform such reviews and audits of the training and qualifications of audit agents used by that cooperative or party and conduct such reviews of internal systems and such other investigation of the cooperative or party as the Secretary deems necessary, including requirements under the model standards developed under subsection (b)(2), to determine that each eligible entity certified by the cooperative or party has systems and standards in use to ensure that such entity or food meets the requirements of this Act.

(2) REQUIREMENTS TO ISSUE CERTIFICATION OF ELIGIBLE ENTITIES OR FOODS.—

(A) IN GENERAL.—An accreditation body (or, in the case of direct accreditation under subsection (b)(1)(A)(ii), the Secretary) may not accredit a third-party auditor unless such third-party auditor agrees to issue a written and, as appropriate, electronic food certification, described in section 801(q), or facility certification under section 806(a), as appropriate, to accompany each food shipment for import into the United States from an eligible entity, subject to requirements set forth by the Secretary. Such written or electronic certification may be included with other documentation regarding such food shipment. The Secretary shall consider certifications under section 801(q) and participation in the voluntary qualified importer program described in section 806 when targeting inspection resources under section 421.

(B) PURPOSE OF CERTIFICATION.—The Secretary shall use certification provided by accredited third-party auditors to—

(i) determine, in conjunction with any other assurances the Secretary may require under section 801(q), whether a food satisfies the requirements of such section; and

(ii) determine whether a facility is eligible to be a facility from which food may be offered for import under the voluntary qualified importer program under section 806.

(C) REQUIREMENTS FOR ISSUING CERTIFICATION.—

(i) IN GENERAL.—An accredited third-party auditor shall issue a food certification under section 801(q) or a facility certification described under subparagraph (B) only after conducting a regulatory audit and such other activities that may be necessary to establish compliance with the requirements of such sections.

(ii) PROVISION OF CERTIFICATION.—Only an accredited third-party auditor or the Secretary may provide a facility certification under section 806(a). Only those parties described in 801(q)(3) or the Secretary may provide a food certification under 301(g).

(3) AUDIT REPORT SUBMISSION REQUIREMENTS.—

(A) REQUIREMENTS IN GENERAL.—As a condition of accreditation, not later than 45 days after conducting an audit, an accredited third-party auditor or audit agent of such auditor shall prepare, and, in the case of a regulatory audit, submit, the audit report for each audit conducted, in a form and manner designated by the Secretary, which shall include—

(i) the identity of the persons at the audited eligible entity responsible for compliance with food safety requirements;

(ii) the dates of the audit;

(iii) the scope of the audit; and

(iv) any other information required by the Secretary that relates to or may influence an assessment of compliance with this Act.

(B) RECORDS.—Following any accreditation of a third-party auditor, the Secretary may, at any time, require the accredited third-party auditor to submit to the Secretary an onsite audit report and such other reports or documents required as part of the audit process, for any eligible entity certified by the third-party auditor or audit agent of such auditor. Such report may include documentation that the eligible entity is in compliance with any applicable registration requirements.

(C) LIMITATION.—The requirement under subparagraph (B) shall not include any report or other documents resulting from a consultative audit by the accredited third-party auditor, except that the Secretary may access the results of a consultative audit in accordance with section 414.

(4) REQUIREMENTS OF ACCREDITED THIRD-PARTY AUDITORS AND AUDIT AGENTS OF SUCH AUDITORS.—

(A) RISKS TO PUBLIC HEALTH.—If, at any time during an audit, an accredited third-party auditor or audit agent of such auditor discovers a condition that could cause or contribute to a serious risk to the public health, such auditor shall immediately notify the Secretary of—

(i) the identification of the eligible entity subject to the audit; and

(ii) such condition.

(B) TYPES OF AUDITS.—An accredited third-party auditor or audit agent of such auditor may perform consultative and regulatory audits of eligible entities.

(C) LIMITATIONS.—

(i) IN GENERAL.—An accredited third party auditor may not perform a regulatory audit of an eligible entity if such agent has performed a consultative audit or a regulatory audit of such eligible entity during the previous 13–month period.

(ii) WAIVER.—The Secretary may waive the application of clause (i) if the Secretary determines that there is insufficient access to accredited third-party auditors in a country or region.

(5) CONFLICTS OF INTEREST.—

(A) THIRD-PARTY AUDITORS.—An accredited third-party auditor shall—

(i) not be owned, managed, or controlled by any person that owns or operates an eligible entity to be certified by such auditor;

(ii) in carrying out audits of eligible entities under this section, have procedures to ensure against the use of any officer or employee of such auditor that has a financial conflict of interest regarding an eligible entity to be certified by such auditor; and

(iii) annually make available to the Secretary disclosures of the extent to which such auditor and the officers and employees of such auditor have maintained compliance with clauses (i) and (ii) relating to financial conflicts of interest.

(B) AUDIT AGENTS.—An audit agent shall—

(i) not own or operate an eligible entity to be audited by such agent;

(ii) in carrying out audits of eligible entities under this section, have procedures to ensure that such agent does not have a financial conflict of interest regarding an eligible entity to be audited by such agent; and

(iii) annually make available to the Secretary disclosures of the extent to which such agent has maintained compliance with clauses (i) and (ii) relating to financial conflicts of interest.

(C) REGULATIONS.—The Secretary shall promulgate regulations not later than 18 months after the date of enactment of the FDA Food Safety Modernization Act to implement this section and to ensure that there are protections against conflicts of interest between an accredited third-party auditor and the eligible entity to be certified by such auditor or audited by such audit agent. Such regulations shall include—

    (i) requiring that audits performed under this section be unannounced;

    (ii) a structure to decrease the potential for conflicts of interest, including timing and public disclosure, for fees paid by eligible entities to accredited third-party auditors; and

    (iii) appropriate limits on financial affiliations between an accredited third-party auditor or audit agents of such auditor and any person that owns or operates an eligible entity to be certified by such auditor, as described in subparagraphs (A) and (B).

(6) WITHDRAWAL OF ACCREDITATION.—

    (A) IN GENERAL.—The Secretary shall withdraw accreditation from an accredited third-party auditor—

    (i) if food certified under section 801(q) or from a facility certified under paragraph (2)(B) by such third-party auditor is linked to an outbreak of foodborne illness that has a reasonable probability of causing serious adverse health consequences or death in humans or animals;

    (ii) following an evaluation and finding by the Secretary that the third-party auditor no longer meets the requirements for accreditation; or

    (iii) following a refusal to allow United States officials to conduct such audits and investigations as may be necessary to ensure continued compliance with the requirements set forth in this section.

    (B) ADDITIONAL BASIS FOR WITHDRAWAL OF ACCREDITATION.—The Secretary may withdraw accreditation from an accredited third-party auditor in the case that such third-party auditor is accredited by an accreditation body for which recognition as an accreditation body under subsection (b)(1)(C) is revoked, if the Secretary determines that there is good cause for the withdrawal.

    (C) EXCEPTION.—The Secretary may waive the application of subparagraph (A)(i) if the Secretary—

    (i) conducts an investigation of the material facts related to the outbreak of human or animal illness; and

    (ii) reviews the steps or actions taken by the third party auditor to justify the certification and determines that the accredited third-party auditor satisfied the requirements under section 801(q) of certifying the food, or the requirements under paragraph (2)(B) of certifying the entity.

(7) REACCREDITATION.—The Secretary shall establish procedures to reinstate the accreditation of a third-party auditor for which accreditation has been withdrawn under paragraph (6)—

(A) if the Secretary determines, based on evidence presented, that the third-party auditor satisfies the requirements of this section and adequate grounds for revocation no longer exist; and

(B) in the case of a third-party auditor accredited by an accreditation body for which recognition as an accreditation body under subsection (b)(1)(C) is revoked—

(i) if the third-party auditor becomes accredited not later than 1 year after revocation of accreditation under paragraph (6)(A), through direct accreditation under subsection (b)(1)(A)(ii) or by an accreditation body in good standing; or

(ii) under such conditions as the Secretary may require for a third-party auditor under paragraph (6)(B).

(8) Neutralizing costs.—The Secretary shall establish by regulation a reimbursement (user fee) program, similar to the method described in section 203(h) of the Agriculture Marketing Act of 1946, by which the Secretary assesses fees and requires accredited third-party auditors and audit agents to reimburse the Food and Drug Administration for the work performed to establish and administer the accreditation system under this section. The Secretary shall make operating this program revenue-neutral and shall not generate surplus revenue from such a reimbursement mechanism. Fees authorized under this paragraph shall be collected and available for obligation only to the extent and in the amount provided in advance in appropriation Acts. Such fees are authorized to remain available until expended.

(d) Recertification of Eligible Entities.—An eligible entity shall apply for annual recertification by an accredited third-party auditor if such entity—

(1) intends to participate in voluntary qualified importer program under section 806; or

(2) is required to provide to the Secretary a certification under section 801(q) for any food from such entity.

(e) False Statements.—Any statement or representation made—

(1) by an employee or agent of an eligible entity to an accredited third-party auditor or audit agent; or

(2) by an accredited third-party auditor to the Secretary,

shall be subject to section 1001 of title 18, United States Code.

(f) Monitoring.—To ensure compliance with the requirements of this section, the Secretary shall—

(1) periodically, or at least once every 4 years, reevaluate the accreditation bodies described in subsection (b)(1);

(2) periodically, or at least once every 4 years, evaluate the performance of each accredited third-party auditor, through the review of regulatory audit reports by such auditors, the compliance history as available of eligible entities certified by such auditors, and any other measures deemed necessary by the Secretary;

(3) at any time, conduct an onsite audit of any eligible entity certified by an accredited third-party auditor, with or without the auditor present; and

(4) take any other measures deemed necessary by the Secretary.

(g) PUBLICLY AVAILABLE REGISTRY.—The Secretary shall establish a publicly available registry of accreditation bodies and of accredited third-party auditors, including the name of, contact information for, and other information deemed necessary by the Secretary about such bodies and auditors.

(h) LIMITATIONS.—

(1) NO EFFECT OF SECTION 704 INSPECTIONS.—The audits performed under this section shall not be considered inspections under section 704.

(2) NO EFFECT ON INSPECTION AUTHORITY.—Nothing in this section affects the authority of the Secretary to inspect any eligible entity pursuant to this Act.

SEC. 809 [21 U.S.C. 384e]. RECOGNITION OF FOREIGN GOVERNMENT INSPECTIONS

(a) INSPECTION.—The Secretary—

(1) may enter into arrangements and agreements with a foreign government or an agency of a foreign government to recognize the inspection of foreign establishments registered under section 510(i) in order to facilitate risk-based inspections in accordance with the schedule established in section 510(h)(3);

(2) may enter into arrangements and agreements with a foreign government or an agency of a foreign government under this section only with a foreign government or an agency of a foreign government that the Secretary has determined as having the capability of conduction inspections that meet the applicable requirements of this Act; and

(3) shall perform such reviews and audits of drug safety programs, systems, and standards of a foreign government or agency for the foreign government as the Secretary deems necessary to determine that the foreign government or agency of the foreign government is capable of conducting inspections that meet the applicable requirements of this Act.

(b) RESULTS OF INSPECTION.—The results of inspections per-formed by a foreign government or an agency of a foreign government under this section may be used as—

(1) evidence of compliance with section 501(a)(2)(B) or section 801(r); and

(2) for any other purposes as determined appropriate by the Secretary.

CHAPTER IX—TOBACCO PRODUCTS

SEC. 900 [21 U.S.C. 387]. DEFINITIONS

In this chapter:

(1) ADDITIVE.—The term "additive" means any substance the intended use of which results or may reasonably be expected to result, directly or indirectly, in its becoming a component or otherwise affecting the characteristic of any tobacco product (including any substances intended for use as a flavoring or coloring or in producing, manufacturing, packing, processing, preparing, treating, packaging, transporting, or holding), except that such term does not include tobacco or a pesticide chemical residue in or on raw tobacco or a pesticide chemical.

(2) BRAND.—The term "brand" means a variety of tobacco product distinguished by the tobacco used, tar content, nicotine content, flavoring used, size, filtration, packaging, logo, registered trademark, brand name, identifiable pattern of colors, or any combination of such attributes.

(3) CIGARETTE.—The term "cigarette"—

(A) means a product that—

(i) is a tobacco product; and

(ii) meets the definition of the term "cigarette" in section 3(1) of the Federal Cigarette Labeling and Advertising Act; and

(B) includes tobacco, in any form, that is functional in the product, which, because of its appearance, the type of tobacco used in the filler, or its packaging and labeling, is likely to be offered to, or purchased by, consumers as a cigarette or as roll-your-own tobacco.

(4) CIGARETTE TOBACCO.—The term "cigarette tobacco" means any product that consists of loose tobacco that is intended for use by consumers in a cigarette. Unless otherwise stated, the requirements applicable to cigarettes under this chapter shall also apply to cigarette tobacco.

(5) COMMERCE.—The term "commerce" has the meaning given that term by section 3(2) of the Federal Cigarette Labeling and Advertising Act.

(6) COUNTERFEIT TOBACCO PRODUCT.—The term "counterfeit tobacco product" means a tobacco product (or the container or labeling of such a product) that, without authorization, bears the trademark, trade name, or other identifying mark, imprint, or device, or any likeness thereof, of a tobacco product listed in a registration under section 905(i)(1).

(7) DISTRIBUTOR.—The term "distributor" as regards a tobacco product means any person who furthers the distribution of a tobacco product, whether domestic or imported, at any point from the original place of manufacture to the per-

son who sells or distributes the product to individuals for personal consumption. Common carriers are not considered distributors for purposes of this chapter.

(8) ILLICIT TRADE.—The term "illicit trade" means any practice or conduct prohibited by law which relates to production, shipment, receipt, possession, distribution, sale, or purchase of tobacco products including any practice or conduct intended to facilitate such activity.

(9) INDIAN COUNTRY.—The term "Indian country" has the meaning given such term in section 1151 of title 18, United States Code.

(10) INDIAN TRIBE.—The term "Indian tribe" has the meaning given such term in section 4(e) of the Indian Self–Determination and Education Assistance Act.

(11) LITTLE CIGAR.—The term "little cigar" means a product that—

(A) is a tobacco product; and

(B) meets the definition of the term "little cigar" in section 3(7) of the Federal Cigarette Labeling and Advertising Act.

(12) NICOTINE.—The term "nicotine" means the chemical substance named 3–(1–Methyl–2–pyrrolidinyl) pyridine or $C[10]H[14]N[2]$, including any salt or complex of nicotine.

(13) PACKAGE.—The term "package" means a pack, box, carton, or container of any kind or, if no other container, any wrapping (including cellophane), in which a tobacco product is offered for sale, sold, or otherwise distributed to consumers.

(14) RETAILER.—The term "retailer" means any person, government, or entity who sells tobacco products to individuals for personal consumption, or who operates a facility where self-service displays of tobacco products are permitted.

(15) ROLL-YOUR-OWN TOBACCO.—The term "roll-your-own tobacco" means any tobacco product which, because of its appearance, type, packaging, or labeling, is suitable for use and likely to be offered to, or purchased by, consumers as tobacco for making cigarettes.

(16) SMALL TOBACCO PRODUCT MANUFACTURER.—The term "small tobacco product manufacturer" means a tobacco product manufacturer that employs fewer than 350 employees. For purposes of determining the number of employees of a manufacturer under the preceding sentence, the employees of a manufacturer are deemed to include the employees of each entity that controls, is controlled by, or is under common control with such manufacturer.

(17) SMOKE CONSTITUENT.—The term "smoke constituent" means any chemical or chemical compound in mainstream or sidestream tobacco smoke that either transfers from any component of the cigarette to the smoke or that is formed by the combustion or heating of tobacco, additives, or other component of the tobacco product.

(18) SMOKELESS TOBACCO.—The term "smokeless tobacco" means any tobacco product that consists of cut, ground, powdered, or leaf tobacco and that is intended to be placed in the oral or nasal cavity.

(19) STATE; TERRITORY.—The terms "State" and "Territory" shall have the meanings given to such terms in section 201

(20) TOBACCO PRODUCT MANUFACTURER.—The term "tobacco product manufacturer" means any person, including any repacker or relabeler, who—

(A) manufactures, fabricates, assembles, processes, or labels a tobacco product; or

(B) imports a finished tobacco product for sale or distribution in the United States.

(21) TOBACCO WAREHOUSE.—

(A) Subject to subparagraphs (B) and (C), the term "tobacco warehouse" includes any person—

(i) who—

(I) removes foreign material from tobacco leaf through nothing other than a mechanical process;

(II) humidifies tobacco leaf with nothing other than potable water in the form of steam or mist; or

(III) de-stems, dries, and packs tobacco leaf for storage and shipment;

(ii) who performs no other actions with respect to tobacco leaf; and

(iii) who provides to any manufacturer to whom the person sells tobacco all information related to the person's actions described in clause (i) that is necessary for compliance with this Act.

(B) The term "tobacco warehouse" excludes any person who—

(i) reconstitutes tobacco leaf;

(ii) is a manufacturer, distributor, or retailer of a tobacco product; or

(iii) applies any chemical, additive, or substance to the tobacco leaf other than potable water in the form of steam or mist.

(C) The definition of the term "tobacco warehouse" in subparagraph (A) shall not apply to the extent to which the Secretary determines, through rulemaking, that regulation under this chapter of the actions described in such subparagraph is appropriate for the protection of the public health.

(22) UNITED STATES.—The term "United States" means the 50 States of the United States of America and the District of Columbia, the Commonwealth of Puerto Rico, Guam, the Virgin Islands, American Samoa, Wake Island, Midway

Islands, Kingman Reef, Johnston Atoll, the Northern Mariana Islands, and any other trust territory or possession of the United States.

SEC. 901 [21 U.S.C. 387a]. FDA AUTHORITY OVER TOBACCO PRODUCTS

(a) IN GENERAL.—Tobacco products, including modified risk tobacco products for which an order has been issued in accordance with section 911, shall be regulated by the Secretary under this chapter and shall not be subject to the provisions of chapter V.

(b) APPLICABILITY.—This chapter shall apply to all cigarettes, cigarette tobacco, roll-your-own tobacco, and smokeless tobacco and to any other tobacco products that the Secretary by regulation deems to be subject to this chapter.

(c) SCOPE.—

(1) IN GENERAL.—Nothing in this chapter, or any policy issued or regulation promulgated thereunder, or in sections 101(a), 102, or 103 of title I, title II, or title III of the Family Smoking Prevention and Tobacco Control Act, shall be construed to affect, expand, or limit the Secretary's authority over (including the authority to determine whether products may be regulated), or the regulation of, products under this Act that are not tobacco products under chapter V or any other chapter.

(2) LIMITATION ON AUTHORITY.—

(A) IN GENERAL.—The provisions of this chapter shall not apply to tobacco leaf that is not in the possession of a manufacturer of tobacco products, or to the producers of tobacco leaf, including tobacco growers, tobacco warehouses, and tobacco grower cooperatives, nor shall any employee of the Food and Drug Administration have any authority to enter onto a farm owned by a producer of tobacco leaf without the written consent of such producer.

(B) EXCEPTION.—Notwithstanding subparagraph (A), if a producer of tobacco leaf is also a tobacco product manufacturer or controlled by a tobacco product manufacturer, the producer shall be subject to this chapter in the producer's capacity as a manufacturer. The exception in this subparagraph shall not apply to a producer of tobacco leaf who grows tobacco under a contract with a tobacco product manufacturer and who is not otherwise engaged in the manufacturing process.

(C) RULE OF CONSTRUCTION.—Nothing in this chapter shall be construed to grant the Secretary authority to promulgate regulations on any matter that involves the production of tobacco leaf or a producer thereof, other than activities by a manufacturer affecting production.

(d) RULEMAKING PROCEDURES.—Each rulemaking under this chapter shall be in accordance with chapter 5 of title 5, United States Code. This subsection shall not be construed to affect the rulemaking provisions of section 102(a) of the Family Smoking Prevention and Tobacco Control Act.

(e) CENTER FOR TOBACCO PRODUCTS.—Not later than 90 days after the date of enactment of the Family Smoking Prevention and Tobacco Control Act, the Secretary shall establish within the Food and Drug Administration the Center for Tobacco Products, which shall report to the Commissioner of Food and Drugs in the same manner as the other agency centers within the Food and Drug Administration. The Center shall be responsible for the implementation of this chapter and related matters assigned by the Commissioner.

(f) OFFICE TO ASSIST SMALL TOBACCO PRODUCT MANUFACTURERS.—The Secretary shall establish within the Food and Drug Administration an identifiable office to provide technical and other nonfinancial assistance to small tobacco product manufacturers to assist them in complying with the requirements of this Act.

(g) CONSULTATION PRIOR TO RULEMAKING.—Prior to promulgating rules under this chapter, the Secretary shall endeavor to consult with other Federal agencies as appropriate.

SEC. 902 [21 U.S.C. 387b]. ADULTERATED TOBACCO PRODUCTS

A tobacco product shall be deemed to be adulterated if—

(1) it consists in whole or in part of any filthy, putrid, or decomposed substance, or is otherwise contaminated by any added poisonous or added deleterious substance that may render the product injurious to health;

(2) it has been prepared, packed, or held under insanitary conditions whereby it may have been contaminated with filth, or whereby it may have been rendered injurious to health;

(3) its package is composed, in whole or in part, of any poisonous or deleterious substance which may render the contents injurious to health;

(4) the manufacturer or importer of the tobacco product fails to pay a user fee assessed to such manufacturer or importer pursuant to section 919 by the date specified in section 919 or by the 30th day after final agency action on a resolution of any dispute as to the amount of such fee;

(5) it is, or purports to be or is represented as, a tobacco product which is subject to a tobacco product standard established under section 907 unless such tobacco product is in all respects in conformity with such standard;

(6)(A) it is required by section 910(a) to have premarket review and does not have an order in effect under section 910(c)(1)(A)(i); or

(B) it is in violation of an order under section 910(c)(1)(A);

(7) the methods used in, or the facilities or controls used for, its manufacture, packing, or storage are not in conformity with applicable requirements under

section 906(e)(1) or an applicable condition prescribed by an order under section 906(e)(2); or

(8) it is in violation of section 911.

Sec. 903 [21 U.S.C. 387c]. Misbranded Tobacco Products

(a) In General.—A tobacco product shall be deemed to be misbranded—

(1) if its labeling is false or misleading in any particular;

(2) if in package form unless it bears a label containing—

(A) the name and place of business of the tobacco product manufacturer, packer, or distributor;

(B) an accurate statement of the quantity of the contents in terms of weight, measure, or numerical count;

(C) an accurate statement of the percentage of the tobacco used in the product that is domestically grown tobacco and the percentage that is foreign grown tobacco; and

(D) the statement required under section 920(a), except that under subparagraph (B) reasonable variations shall be permitted, and exemptions as to small packages shall be established, by regulations prescribed by the Secretary;

(3) if any word, statement, or other information required by or under authority of this chapter to appear on the label or labeling is not prominently placed thereon with such conspicuousness (as compared with other words, statements, or designs in the labeling) and in such terms as to render it likely to be read and understood by the ordinary individual under customary conditions of purchase and use;

(4) if it has an established name, unless its label bears, to the exclusion of any other nonproprietary name, its established name prominently printed in type as required by the Secretary by regulation;

(5) if the Secretary has issued regulations requiring that its labeling bear adequate directions for use, or adequate warnings against use by children, that are necessary for the protection of users unless its labeling conforms in all respects to such regulations;

(6) if it was manufactured, prepared, propagated, compounded, or processed in an establishment not duly registered under section 905(b), 905(c), 905(d), or 905(h), if it was not included in a list required by section 905(i), if a notice or other information respecting it was not provided as required by such section or section 905(j), or if it does not bear such symbols from the uniform system for identification of tobacco products prescribed under section 905(e) as the Secretary by regulation requires;

(7) if, in the case of any tobacco product distributed or offered for sale in any State—

(A) its advertising is false or misleading in any particular; or

(B) it is sold or distributed in violation of regulations prescribed under section 906(d);

(8) unless, in the case of any tobacco product distributed or offered for sale in any State, the manufacturer, packer, or distributor thereof includes in all advertisements and other descriptive printed matter issued or caused to be issued by the manufacturer, packer, or distributor with respect to that tobacco product—

(A) a true statement of the tobacco product's established name as described in paragraph (4), printed prominently; and

(B) a brief statement of—

(i) the uses of the tobacco product and relevant warnings, precautions, side effects, and contraindications; and

(ii) in the case of specific tobacco products made subject to a finding by the Secretary after notice and opportunity for comment that such action is appropriate to protect the public health, a full description of the components of such tobacco product or the formula showing quantitatively each ingredient of such tobacco product to the extent required in regulations which shall be issued by the Secretary after an opportunity for a hearing;

(9) if it is a tobacco product subject to a tobacco product standard established under section 907, unless it bears such labeling as may be prescribed in such tobacco product standard; or

(10) if there was a failure or refusal—

(A) to comply with any requirement prescribed under section 904 or 908; or

(B) to furnish any material or information required under section 909.

(b) PRIOR APPROVAL OF LABEL STATEMENTS.—The Secretary may, by regulation, require prior approval of statements made on the label of a tobacco product to ensure that such statements do not violate the misbranding provisions of subsection (a) and that such statements comply with other provisions of the Family Smoking Prevention and Tobacco Control Act (including the amendments made by such Act). No regulation issued under this subsection may require prior approval by the Secretary of the content of any advertisement, except for modified risk tobacco products as provided in section 911. No advertisement of a tobacco product published after the date of enactment of the Family Smoking Prevention and Tobacco Control Act shall, with respect to the language of label statements as prescribed under section 4 of the Federal Cigarette Labeling and Advertising Act and section 3 of the Comprehensive Smokeless Tobacco Health Education Act of 1986 or the regulations issued under such sections, be subject to the provisions of sections 12 through 15 of the Federal Trade Commission Act.

SEC. 904 [21 U.S.C. 387d]. SUBMISSION OF HEALTH INFORMATION TO THE SECRETARY

(a) REQUIREMENT.—Each tobacco product manufacturer or importer, or agents thereof, shall submit to the Secretary the following information:

(1) Not later than 6 months after the date of enactment of the Family Smoking Prevention and Tobacco Control Act, a listing of all ingredients, including tobacco, substances, compounds, and additives that are, as of such date, added by the manufacturer to the tobacco, paper, filter, or other part of each tobacco product by brand and by quantity in each brand and subbrand.

(2) A description of the content, delivery, and form of nicotine in each tobacco product measured in milligrams of nicotine in accordance with regulations promulgated by the Secretary in accordance with section 4(e) of the Federal Cigarette Labeling and Advertising Act.

(3) Beginning 3 years after the date of enactment of the Family Smoking Prevention and Tobacco Control Act, a listing of all constituents, including smoke constituents as applicable, identified by the Secretary as harmful or potentially harmful to health in each tobacco product, and as applicable in the smoke of each tobacco product, by brand and by quantity in each brand and subbrand. Effective beginning 3 years after such date of enactment, the manufacturer, importer, or agent shall comply with regulations promulgated under section 915 in reporting information under this paragraph, where applicable.

(4) Beginning 6 months after the date of enactment of the Family Smoking Prevention and Tobacco Control Act, all documents developed after such date of enactment that relate to health, toxicological, behavioral, or physiologic effects of current or future tobacco products, their constituents (including smoke constituents), ingredients, components, and additives.

(b) DATA SUBMISSION.—At the request of the Secretary, each tobacco product manufacturer or importer of tobacco products, or agents thereof, shall submit the following:

(1) Any or all documents (including underlying scientific information) relating to research activities, and research findings, conducted, supported, or possessed by the manufacturer (or agents thereof) on the health, toxicological, behavioral, or physiologic effects of tobacco products and their constituents (including smoke constituents), ingredients, components, and additives.

(2) Any or all documents (including underlying scientific information) relating to research activities, and research findings, conducted, supported, or possessed by the manufacturer (or agents thereof) that relate to the issue of whether a reduction in risk to health from tobacco products can occur upon the employment of technology available or known to the manufacturer.

(3) Any or all documents (including underlying scientific or financial information) relating to marketing research involving the use of tobacco products or marketing practices and the effectiveness of such practices used by tobacco manufacturers and distributors.

An importer of a tobacco product not manufactured in the United States shall supply the information required of a tobacco product manufacturer under this subsection.

(c) TIME FOR SUBMISSION.—

(1) IN GENERAL.—At least 90 days prior to the delivery for introduction into interstate commerce of a tobacco product not on the market on the date of enactment of the Family Smoking Prevention and Tobacco Control Act, the manufacturer of such product shall provide the information required under subsection (a).

(2) DISCLOSURE OF ADDITIVE.—If at any time a tobacco product manufacturer adds to its tobacco products a new tobacco additive or increases the quantity of an existing tobacco additive, the manufacturer shall, except as provided in paragraph (3), at least 90 days prior to such action so advise the Secretary in writing.

(3) DISCLOSURE OF OTHER ACTIONS.—If at any time a tobacco product manufacturer eliminates or decreases an existing additive, or adds or increases an additive that has by regulation been designated by the Secretary as an additive that is not a human or animal carcinogen, or otherwise harmful to health under intended conditions of use, the manufacturer shall within 60 days of such action so advise the Secretary in writing.

(d) DATA LIST.—

(1) IN GENERAL.—Not later than 3 years after the date of enactment of the Family Smoking Prevention and Tobacco Control Act, and annually thereafter, the Secretary shall publish in a format that is understandable and not misleading to a lay person, and place on public display (in a manner determined by the Secretary) the list established under subsection (e).

(2) CONSUMER RESEARCH.—The Secretary shall conduct periodic consumer research to ensure that the list published under paragraph (1) is not misleading to lay persons. Not later than 5 years after the date of enactment of the Family Smoking Prevention and Tobacco Control Act, the Secretary shall submit to the appropriate committees of Congress a report on the results of such research, together with recommendations on whether such publication should be continued or modified.

(e) DATA COLLECTION.—Not later than 24 months after the date of enactment of the Family Smoking Prevention and Tobacco Control Act, the Secretary shall establish, and periodically revise as appropriate, a list of harmful and potentially harmful constituents, including smoke constituents, to health in each tobacco product by brand and by quantity in each brand and subbrand. The Secretary shall publish a public notice requesting the submission by interested persons of scientific and other information concerning the harmful and potentially harmful constituents in tobacco products and tobacco smoke.

Sec. 905 [21 U.S.C. 387e]. Annual Registration

(a) Definitions.—In this section:

(1) Manufacture, preparation, compounding, or processing.—The term "manufacture, preparation, compounding, or processing" shall include repackaging or otherwise changing the container, wrapper, or labeling of any tobacco product package in furtherance of the distribution of the tobacco product from the original place of manufacture to the person who makes final delivery or sale to the ultimate consumer or user.

(2) Name.—The term "name" shall include in the case of a partnership the name of each partner and, in the case of a corporation, the name of each corporate officer and director, and the State of incorporation.

(b) Registration by Owners and Operators.—On or before December 31 of each year, every person who owns or operates any establishment in any State engaged in the manufacture, preparation, compounding, or processing of a tobacco product or tobacco products shall register with the Secretary the name, places of business, and all such establishments of that person. If enactment of the Family Smoking Prevention and Tobacco Control Act occurs in the second half of the calendar year, the Secretary shall designate a date no later than 6 months into the subsequent calendar year by which registration pursuant to this subsection shall occur.

(c) Registration by New Owners and Operators.—Every person upon first engaging in the manufacture, preparation, compounding, or processing of a tobacco product or tobacco products in any establishment owned or operated in any State by that person shall immediately register with the Secretary that person's name, place of business, and such establishment.

(d) Registration of Added Establishments.—Every person required to register under subsection (b) or (c) shall immediately register with the Secretary any additional establishment which that person owns or operates in any State and in which that person begins the manufacture, preparation, compounding, or processing of a tobacco product or tobacco products.

(e) Uniform Product Identification System.—The Secretary may by regulation prescribe a uniform system for the identification of tobacco products and may require that persons who are required to list such tobacco products under subsection (i) shall list such tobacco products in accordance with such system.

(f) Public Access to Registration Information.—The Secretary shall make available for inspection, to any person so requesting, any registration filed under this section.

(g) Biennial Inspection of Registered Establishments.—Every establishment registered with the Secretary under this section shall be subject to inspection under section 704 or subsection (h), and every such establishment engaged in the manufacture, compounding, or processing of a tobacco product or tobacco products shall be so inspected by 1 or more officers or employees duly designated by the Secretary at least once in the 2–year period beginning with the date of registration of such establishment under this section and at least once in every successive 2–year period thereafter.

(h) REGISTRATION BY FOREIGN ESTABLISHMENTS.—Any establishment within any foreign country engaged in the manufacture, preparation, compounding, or processing of a tobacco product or tobacco products, shall register under this section under regulations promulgated by the Secretary. Such regulations shall require such establishment to provide the information required by subsection (i) and shall include provisions for registration of any such establishment upon condition that adequate and effective means are available, by arrangement with the government of such foreign country or otherwise, to enable the Secretary to determine from time to time whether tobacco products manufactured, prepared, compounded, or processed in such establishment, if imported or offered for import into the United States, shall be refused admission on any of the grounds set forth in section 801(a).

(i) REGISTRATION INFORMATION.—

(1) PRODUCT LIST.—Every person who registers with the Secretary under subsection (b), (c), (d), or (h) shall, at the time of registration under any such subsection, file with the Secretary a list of all tobacco products which are being manufactured, prepared, compounded, or processed by that person for commercial distribution and which have not been included in any list of tobacco products filed by that person with the Secretary under this paragraph or paragraph (2) before such time of registration. Such list shall be prepared in such form and manner as the Secretary may prescribe and shall be accompanied by—

(A) in the case of a tobacco product contained in the applicable list with respect to which a tobacco product standard has been established under section 907 or which is subject to section 910, a reference to the authority for the marketing of such tobacco product and a copy of all labeling for such tobacco product;

(B) in the case of any other tobacco product contained in an applicable list, a copy of all consumer information and other labeling for such tobacco product, a representative sampling of advertisements for such tobacco product, and, upon request made by the Secretary for good cause, a copy of all advertisements for a particular tobacco product; and

(C) if the registrant filing a list has determined that a tobacco product contained in such list is not subject to a tobacco product standard established under section 907, a brief statement of the basis upon which the registrant made such determination if the Secretary requests such a statement with respect to that particular tobacco product.

(2) CONSULTATION WITH RESPECT TO FORMS.—The Secretary shall consult with the Secretary of the Treasury in developing the forms to be used for registration under this section to minimize the burden on those persons required to register with both the Secretary and the Tax and Trade Bureau of the Department of the Treasury.

(3) BIANNUAL REPORT OF ANY CHANGE IN PRODUCT LIST.— Each person who registers with the Secretary under this section shall report to the Secretary once during the month of June of each year and once during the month of December of each year the following:

(A) A list of each tobacco product introduced by the registrant for commercial distribution which has not been included in any list previously filed by that person with the Secretary under this subparagraph or paragraph (1). A list under this subparagraph shall list a tobacco product by its established name and shall be accompanied by the other information required by paragraph (1).

(B) If since the date the registrant last made a report under this paragraph that person has discontinued the manufacture, preparation, compounding, or processing for commercial distribution of a tobacco product included in a list filed under subparagraph (A) or paragraph (1), notice of such discontinuance, the date of such discontinuance, and the identity of its established name.

(C) If since the date the registrant reported under subparagraph (B) a notice of discontinuance that person has resumed the manufacture, preparation, compounding, or processing for commercial distribution of the tobacco product with respect to which such notice of discontinuance was reported, notice of such resumption, the date of such resumption, the identity of such tobacco product by established name, and other information required by paragraph (1), unless the registrant has previously reported such resumption to the Secretary under this subparagraph.

(D) Any material change in any information previously submitted under this paragraph or paragraph (1).

(j) REPORT PRECEDING INTRODUCTION OF CERTAIN SUBSTANTIALLY EQUIVALENT PRODUCTS INTO INTERSTATE COMMERCE.—

(1) IN GENERAL.—Each person who is required to register under this section and who proposes to begin the introduction or delivery for introduction into interstate commerce for commercial distribution of a tobacco product intended for human use that was not commercially marketed (other than for test marketing) in the United States as of February 15, 2007, shall, at least 90 days prior to making such introduction or delivery, report to the Secretary (in such form and manner as the Secretary shall prescribe)—

(A) the basis for such person's determination that—

(i) the tobacco product is substantially equivalent, within the meaning of section 910, to a tobacco product commercially marketed (other than for test marketing) in the United States as of February 15, 2007, or to a tobacco product that the Secretary has previously determined, pursuant to subsection (a)(3) of section 910, is substantially equivalent and that is in compliance with the requirements of this Act; or

(ii) the tobacco product is modified within the meaning of paragraph (3), the modifications are to a product that is commercially marketed and in compliance with the requirements of this Act, and all of the modifications are covered by exemptions granted by the Secretary pursuant to paragraph (3); and

(B) action taken by such person to comply with the requirements under section 907 that are applicable to the tobacco product.

(2) APPLICATION TO CERTAIN POST-FEBRUARY 15, 2007.—A report under this subsection for a tobacco product that was first introduced or delivered for introduction into interstate commerce for commercial distribution in the United States after February 15, 2007, and prior to the date that is 21 months after the date of enactment of the Family Smoking Prevention and Tobacco Control Act shall be submitted to the Secretary not later than 21 months after such date of enactment.

(3) EXEMPTIONS.—

(A) IN GENERAL.—The Secretary may exempt from the requirements of this subsection relating to the demonstration that a tobacco product is substantially equivalent within the meaning of section 910, tobacco products that are modified by adding or deleting a tobacco additive, or increasing or decreasing the quantity of an existing tobacco additive, if the Secretary determines that—

(i) such modification would be a minor modification of a tobacco product that can be sold under this Act;

(ii) a report under this subsection is not necessary to ensure that permitting the tobacco product to be marketed would be appropriate for protection of the public health; and

(iii) an exemption is otherwise appropriate.

(B) REGULATIONS.—Not later than 15 months after the date of enactment of the Family Smoking Prevention and Tobacco Control Act, the Secretary shall issue regulations to implement this paragraph.

SEC. 906 [21 U.S.C. 387f]. GENERAL PROVISIONS RESPECTING CONTROL OF TOBACCO PRODUCTS

(a) IN GENERAL.—Any requirement established by or under section 902, 903, 905, or 909 applicable to a tobacco product shall apply to such tobacco product until the applicability of the requirement to the tobacco product has been changed by action taken under section 907, section 910, section 911, or subsection (d) of this section, and any requirement established by or under section 902, 903, 905, or 909 which is inconsistent with a requirement imposed on such tobacco product under section 907, section 910, section 911, or subsection (d) of this section shall not apply to such tobacco product.

(b) INFORMATION ON PUBLIC ACCESS AND COMMENT.—Each notice of proposed rulemaking or other notification under section 907, 908, 909, 910, or 911 or under this section, any other notice which is published in the Federal Register with respect to any other action taken under any such section and which states the reasons for such action, and each publication of findings required to be made in connection with rulemaking under any such section shall set forth—

(1) the manner in which interested persons may examine data and other information on which the notice or findings is based; and

(2) the period within which interested persons may present their comments on the notice or findings (including the need therefore) orally or in writing, which period shall be at least 60 days but may not exceed 90 days unless the time is extended by the Secretary by a notice published in the Federal Register stating good cause therefore.

(c) LIMITED CONFIDENTIALITY OF INFORMATION.—Any information reported to or otherwise obtained by the Secretary or the Secretary's representative under section 903, 904, 907, 908, 909, 910, 911, or 704, or under subsection (e) or (f) of this section, which is exempt from disclosure under subsection (a) of section 552 of title 5, United States Code, by reason of subsection (b)(4) of that section shall be considered confidential and shall not be disclosed, except that the information may be disclosed to other officers or employees concerned with carrying out this chapter, or when relevant in any proceeding under this chapter.

(d) RESTRICTIONS.—

(1) IN GENERAL.—The Secretary may by regulation require restrictions on the sale and distribution of a tobacco product, including restrictions on the access to, and the advertising and promotion of, the tobacco product, if the Secretary determines that such regulation would be appropriate for the protection of the public health. The Secretary may by regulation impose restrictions on the advertising and promotion of a tobacco product consistent with and to full extent permitted by the first amendment to the Constitution. The finding as to whether such regulation would be appropriate for the protection of the public health shall be determined with respect to the risks and benefits to the population as a whole, including users and nonusers of the tobacco product, and taking into account—

(A) the increased or decreased likelihood that existing users of tobacco products will stop using such products; and

(B) the increased or decreased likelihood that those who do not use tobacco products will start using such products.

No such regulation may require that the sale or distribution of a tobacco product be limited to the written or oral authorization of a practitioner licensed by law to prescribe medical products.

(2) LABEL STATEMENTS.—The label of a tobacco product shall bear such appropriate statements of the restrictions required by a regulation under subsection (a) as the Secretary may in such regulation prescribe.

(3) LIMITATIONS.—

(A) IN GENERAL.—No restrictions under paragraph (1) may—

(i) prohibit the sale of any tobacco product in face-to-face transactions by a specific category of retail outlets; or

(ii) establish a minimum age of sale of tobacco products to any person older than 18 years of age.

(B) MATCHBOOKS.—For purposes of any regulations issued by the Secretary, matchbooks of conventional size containing not more than 20 paper matches, and which are customarily given away for free with the purchase of tobacco products, shall be considered as adult-written publications which shall be permitted to contain advertising. Notwithstanding the preceding sentence, if the Secretary finds that such treatment of matchbooks is not appropriate for the protection of the public health, the Secretary may determine by regulation that matchbooks shall not be considered adult-written publications.

(4) REMOTE SALES.—

(A) IN GENERAL.—The Secretary shall—

(i) within 18 months after the date of enactment of the Family Smoking Prevention and Tobacco Control Act, promulgate regulations regarding the sale and distribution of tobacco products that occur through means other than a direct, face-to-face exchange between a retailer and a consumer in order to prevent the sale and distribution of tobacco products to individuals who have not attained the minimum age established by applicable law for the purchase of such products, including requirements for age verification; and

(ii) within 2 years after such date of enactment, issue regulations to address the promotion and marketing of tobacco products that are sold or distributed through means other than a direct, face-to-face exchange between a retailer and a consumer in order to protect individuals who have not attained the minimum age established by applicable law for the purchase of such products.

(B) RELATION TO OTHER AUTHORITY.—Nothing in this paragraph limits the authority of the Secretary to take additional actions under the other paragraphs of this subsection.

(e) GOOD MANUFACTURING PRACTICE REQUIREMENTS.—

(1) METHODS, FACILITIES, AND CONTROLS TO CONFORM.—

(A) IN GENERAL.—In applying manufacturing restrictions to tobacco, the Secretary shall, in accordance with subparagraph (B), prescribe regulations (which may differ based on the type of tobacco product involved) requiring that the methods used in, and the facilities and controls used for, the manufacture, preproduction design validation (including a process to assess the performance of a tobacco product), packing, and storage of a tobacco product conform to current good manufacturing practice, or hazard analysis and critical control point methodology, as prescribed in such regulations to assure that the public health is protected and that the tobacco product is in compliance with this chapter. Such regulations may provide for the testing of raw tobacco for pesticide chemical residues regardless of whether a tolerance for such chemical residues has been established.

(B) REQUIREMENTS.—The Secretary shall—

(i) before promulgating any regulation under subparagraph (A), afford the Tobacco Products Scientific Advisory Committee an opportunity to submit recommendations with respect to the regulation proposed to be promulgated;

(ii) before promulgating any regulation under subparagraph (A), afford opportunity for an oral hearing;

(iii) provide the Tobacco Products Scientific Advisory Committee a reasonable time to make its recommendation with respect to proposed regulations under subparagraph (A);

(iv) in establishing the effective date of a regulation promulgated under this subsection, take into account the differences in the manner in which the different types of tobacco products have historically been produced, the financial resources of the different tobacco product manufacturers, and the state of their existing manufacturing facilities, and shall provide for a reasonable period of time for such manufacturers to conform to good manufacturing practices; and

(v) not require any small tobacco product manufacturer to comply with a regulation under subparagraph (A) for at least 4 years following the effective date established by the Secretary for such regulation.

(2) EXEMPTIONS; VARIANCES.—

(A) PETITION.—Any person subject to any requirement prescribed under paragraph (1) may petition the Secretary for a permanent or temporary exemption or variance from such requirement. Such a petition shall be submitted to the Secretary in such form and manner as the Secretary shall prescribe and shall—

(i) in the case of a petition for an exemption from a requirement, set forth the basis for the petitioner's determination that compliance with the requirement is not required to assure that the tobacco product will be in compliance with this chapter;

(ii) in the case of a petition for a variance from a requirement, set forth the methods proposed to be used in, and the facilities and controls proposed to be used for, the manufacture, packing, and storage of the tobacco product in lieu of the methods, facilities, and controls prescribed by the requirement; and

(iii) contain such other information as the Secretary shall prescribe.

(B) REFERRAL TO THE TOBACCO PRODUCTS SCIENTIFIC ADVISORY COMMITTEE.— The Secretary may refer to the Tobacco Products Scientific Advisory Committee any petition submitted under subparagraph (A). The Tobacco Products Scientific Advisory Committee shall report its recommendations to the Secretary with respect to a petition referred to it within 60 days after the date of the petition's referral. Within 60 days after—

(i) the date the petition was submitted to the Secretary under subparagraph (A); or

(ii) the day after the petition was referred to the Tobacco Products Scientific Advisory Committee, whichever occurs later, the Secretary shall by order either deny the petition or approve it.

(C) APPROVAL.—The Secretary may approve—

(i) a petition for an exemption for a tobacco product from a requirement if the Secretary determines that compliance with such requirement is not required to assure that the tobacco product will be in compliance with this chapter; and

(ii) a petition for a variance for a tobacco product from a requirement if the Secretary determines that the methods to be used in, and the facilities and controls to be used for, the manufacture, packing, and storage of the tobacco product in lieu of the methods, facilities, and controls prescribed by the requirement are sufficient to assure that the tobacco product will be in compliance with this chapter.

(D) CONDITIONS.—An order of the Secretary approving a petition for a variance shall prescribe such conditions respecting the methods used in, and the facilities and controls used for, the manufacture, packing, and storage of the tobacco product to be granted the variance under the petition as may be necessary to assure that the tobacco product will be in compliance with this chapter.

(E) Hearing.—After the issuance of an order under subparagraph (B) respecting a petition, the petitioner shall have an opportunity for an informal hearing on such order.

(3) Compliance.—Compliance with requirements under this subsection shall not be required before the end of the 3–year period following the date of enactment of the Family Smoking Prevention and Tobacco Control Act.

(f) Research and Development.—The Secretary may enter into contracts for research, testing, and demonstrations respecting tobacco products and may obtain tobacco products for research, testing, and demonstration purposes.

Sec. 907 [21 U.S.C. 387g]. TOBACCO PRODUCT STANDARDS

(a) In General.—

(1) Special rules.—

(A) Special rule for cigarettes.—Beginning 3 months after the date of enactment of the Family Smoking Prevention and Tobacco Control Act, a cigarette or any of its component parts (including the tobacco, filter, or paper) shall not contain, as a constituent (including a smoke constituent) or additive, an artificial or natural flavor (other than tobacco or menthol) or an herb or spice, including strawberry, grape, orange, clove, cinnamon, pineapple, vanilla, coconut, licorice, cocoa, chocolate, cherry, or coffee, that is a characterizing flavor of the tobacco product or tobacco smoke. Nothing in this subparagraph shall be construed to limit the Secretary's authority to take action under this section or other sections of this Act applicable to menthol or any artificial or natural flavor, herb, or spice not specified in this subparagraph.

(B) Additional special rule.—Beginning 2 years after the date of enactment of the Family Smoking Prevention and Tobacco Control Act, a tobacco product manufacturer shall not use tobacco, including foreign grown tobacco, that contains a pesticide chemical residue that is at a level greater than is specified by any tolerance applicable under Federal law to domestically grown tobacco.

(2) Revision of tobacco product standards.—The Secretary may revise the tobacco product standards in paragraph (1) in accordance with subsection (c).

(3) Tobacco product standards.—

(A) In general.—The Secretary may adopt tobacco product standards in addition to those in paragraph (1) if the Secretary finds that a tobacco product standard is appropriate for the protection of the public health.

(B) Determinations.—

(i) Considerations.—In making a finding described in subparagraph (A), the Secretary shall consider scientific evidence concerning—

(I) the risks and benefits to the population as a whole, including users and nonusers of tobacco products, of the proposed standard;

(II) the increased or decreased likelihood that existing users of tobacco products will stop using such products; and

(III) the increased or decreased likelihood that those who do not use tobacco products will start using such products.

(ii) ADDITIONAL CONSIDERATIONS.—In the event that the Secretary makes a determination, set forth in a proposed tobacco product standard in a proposed rule, that it is appropriate for the protection of public health to require the reduction or elimination of an additive, constituent (including a smoke constituent), or other component of a tobacco product because the Secretary has found that the additive, constituent, or other component is or may be harmful, any party objecting to the proposed standard on the ground that the proposed standard will not reduce or eliminate the risk of illness or injury may provide for the Secretary's consideration scientific evidence that demonstrates that the proposed standard will not reduce or eliminate the risk of illness or injury.

(4) CONTENT OF TOBACCO PRODUCT STANDARDS.—A tobacco product standard established under this section for a tobacco product—

(A) shall include provisions that are appropriate for the protection of the public health, including provisions, where appropriate—

(i) for nicotine yields of the product;

(ii) for the reduction or elimination of other constituents, including smoke constituents, or harmful components of the product; or

(iii) relating to any other requirement under subparagraph (B);

(B) shall, where appropriate for the protection of the public health, include—

(i) provisions respecting the construction, components, ingredients, additives, constituents, including smoke constituents, and properties of the tobacco product;

(ii) provisions for the testing (on a sample basis or, if necessary, on an individual basis) of the tobacco product;

(iii) provisions for the measurement of the tobacco product characteristics of the tobacco product;

(iv) provisions requiring that the results of each or of certain of the tests of the tobacco product required to be made under clause (ii) show that the tobacco product is in conformity with the portions of the standard for which the test or tests were required; and

(v) a provision requiring that the sale and distribution of the tobacco product be restricted but only to the extent that the sale and distribution of a tobacco product may be restricted under a regulation under section 906(d);

(C) shall, where appropriate, require the use and prescribe the form and content of labeling for the proper use of the tobacco product; and

(D) shall require tobacco products containing foreign-grown tobacco to meet the same standards applicable to tobacco products containing domestically grown tobacco.

(5) PERIODIC REEVALUATION OF TOBACCO PRODUCT STANDARDS.—The Secretary shall provide for periodic evaluation of tobacco product standards established under this section to determine whether such standards should be changed to reflect new medical, scientific, or other technological data. The Secretary may provide for testing under paragraph (4)(B) by any person.

(6) INVOLVEMENT OF THE OTHER AGENCIES; INFORMED PERSONS.—In carrying out duties under this section, the Secretary shall endeavor to—

(A) use personnel, facilities, and other technical support available in other Federal agencies;

(B) consult with other Federal agencies concerned with standard setting and other nationally or internationally recognized standard-setting entities; and

(C) invite appropriate participation, through joint or other conferences, workshops, or other means, by informed persons representative of scientific, professional, industry, agricultural, or consumer organizations who in the Secretary's judgment can make a significant contribution.

(b) CONSIDERATION BY SECRETARY.—

(1) TECHNICAL ACHIEVABILITY.—The Secretary shall consider information submitted in connection with a proposed standard regarding the technical achievability of compliance with such standard.

(2) OTHER CONSIDERATIONS.—The Secretary shall consider all other information submitted in connection with a proposed standard, including information concerning the countervailing effects of the tobacco product standard on the health of adolescent tobacco users, adult tobacco users, or nontobacco users, such as the creation of a significant demand for contraband or other tobacco products that do not meet the requirements of this chapter and the significance of such demand.

(c) PROPOSED STANDARDS.—

(1) IN GENERAL.—The Secretary shall publish in the Federal Register a notice of proposed rulemaking for the establishment, amendment, or revocation of any tobacco product standard.

(2) REQUIREMENTS OF NOTICE.—A notice of proposed rulemaking for the establishment or amendment of a tobacco product standard for a tobacco product shall—

(A) set forth a finding with supporting justification that the tobacco product standard is appropriate for the protection of the public health;

(B) invite interested persons to submit a draft or proposed tobacco product standard for consideration by the Secretary;

(C) invite interested persons to submit comments on structuring the standard so that it does not advantage foreign-grown tobacco over domestically grown tobacco; and

(D) invite the Secretary of Agriculture to provide any information or analysis which the Secretary of Agriculture believes is relevant to the proposed tobacco product standard.

(3) FINDING.—A notice of proposed rulemaking for the revocation of a tobacco product standard shall set forth a finding with supporting justification that the tobacco product standard is no longer appropriate for the protection of the public health.

(4) COMMENT.—The Secretary shall provide for a comment period of not less than 60 days.

(d) PROMULGATION.—

(1) IN GENERAL.—After the expiration of the period for comment on a notice of proposed rulemaking published under subsection (c) respecting a tobacco product standard and after consideration of comments submitted under subsections (b) and (c) and any report from the Tobacco Products Scientific Advisory Committee, the Secretary shall—

(A) if the Secretary determines that the standard would be appropriate for the protection of the public health, promulgate a regulation establishing a tobacco product standard and publish in the Federal Register findings on the matters referred to in subsection (c); or

(B) publish a notice terminating the proceeding for the development of the standard together with the reasons for such termination.

(2) EFFECTIVE DATE.—A regulation establishing a tobacco product standard shall set forth the date or dates upon which the standard shall take effect, but no such regulation may take effect before 1 year after the date of its publication unless the Secretary determines that an earlier effective date is necessary for the protection of the public health. Such date or dates shall be established so as to minimize, consistent with the public health, economic loss to, and disruption or dislocation of, domestic and international trade. In establishing such effective date or dates, the Secretary shall consider information submitted in connection with a proposed product standard by interested parties, including manufacturers

711

and tobacco growers, regarding the technical achievability of compliance with the standard, and including information concerning the existence of patents that make it impossible to comply in the timeframe envisioned in the proposed standard. If the Secretary determines, based on the Secretary's evaluation of submitted comments, that a product standard can be met only by manufacturers requiring substantial changes to the methods of farming the domestically grown tobacco used by the manufacturer, the effective date of that product standard shall be not less than 2 years after the date of publication of the final regulation establishing the standard.

(3) LIMITATION ON POWER GRANTED TO THE FOOD AND DRUG ADMINISTRATION.— Because of the importance of a decision of the Secretary to issue a regulation—

(A) banning all cigarettes, all smokeless tobacco products, all little cigars, all cigars other than little cigars, all pipe tobacco, or all roll-your-own tobacco products; or

(B) requiring the reduction of nicotine yields of a tobacco product to zero, the Secretary is prohibited from taking such actions under this Act.

(4) AMENDMENT; REVOCATION.—

(A) AUTHORITY.—The Secretary, upon the Secretary's own initiative or upon petition of an interested person, may by a regulation, promulgated in accordance with the requirements of subsection (c) and paragraph (2), amend or revoke a tobacco product standard.

(B) EFFECTIVE DATE.—The Secretary may declare a proposed amendment of a tobacco product standard to be effective on and after its publication in the Federal Register and until the effective date of any final action taken on such amendment if the Secretary determines that making it so effective is in the public interest.

(5) REFERRAL TO ADVISORY COMMITTEE.—

(A) IN GENERAL.—The Secretary may refer a proposed regulation for the establishment, amendment, or revocation of a tobacco product standard to the Tobacco Products Scientific Advisory Committee for a report and recommendation with respect to any matter involved in the proposed regulation which requires the exercise of scientific judgment.

(B) INITIATION OF REFERRAL.—The Secretary may make a referral under this paragraph—

(i) on the Secretary's own initiative; or (ii) upon the request of an interested person that—

(I) demonstrates good cause for the referral; and

(II) is made before the expiration of the period for submission of comments on the proposed regulation.

(C) Provision of data.—If a proposed regulation is referred under this paragraph to the Tobacco Products Scientific Advisory Committee, the Secretary shall provide the Advisory Committee with the data and information on which such proposed regulation is based.

(D) Report and recommendation.—The Tobacco Products Scientific Advisory Committee shall, within 60 days after the referral of a proposed regulation under this paragraph and after independent study of the data and information furnished to it by the Secretary and other data and information before it, submit to the Secretary a report and recommendation respecting such regulation, together with all underlying data and information and a statement of the reason or basis for the recommendation.

(E) Public availability.—The Secretary shall make a copy of each report and recommendation under subparagraph (D) publicly available.

(e) Menthol Cigarettes.—

(1) Referral; considerations.—Immediately upon the establishment of the Tobacco Products Scientific Advisory Committee under section 917(a), the Secretary shall refer to the Committee for report and recommendation, under section 917(c)(4), the issue of the impact of the use of menthol in cigarettes on the public health, including such use among children, African–Americans, Hispanics, and other racial and ethnic minorities. In its review, the Tobacco Products Scientific Advisory Committee shall address the considerations listed in subsections (a)(3)(B)(i) and (b).

(2) Report and recommendation.—Not later than 1 year after its establishment, the Tobacco Product Scientific Advisory Committee shall submit to the Secretary the report and recommendations required pursuant to paragraph (1).

(3) Rule of construction.—Nothing in this subsection shall be construed to limit the Secretary's authority to take action under this section or other sections of this Act applicable to menthol.

(f) Dissolvable Tobacco Products.—

(1) Referral; considerations.—The Secretary shall refer to the Tobacco Products Scientific Advisory Committee for report and recommendation, under section 917(c)(4), the issue of the nature and impact of the use of dissolvable tobacco products on the public health, including such use among children. In its review, the Tobacco Products Scientific Advisory Committee shall address the considerations listed in subsection (a)(3)(B)(i).

(2) Report and recommendation.—Not later than 2 years after its establishment, the Tobacco Product Scientific Advisory Committee shall submit to the Secretary the report and recommendations required pursuant to paragraph (1).

(3) RULE OF CONSTRUCTION.—Nothing in this subsection shall be construed to limit the Secretary's authority to take action under this section or other sections of this Act at any time applicable to any dissolvable tobacco product.

SEC. 908 [21 U.S.C. 387h]. NOTIFICATION AND OTHER REMEDIES

(a) NOTIFICATION.—If the Secretary determines that—

(1) a tobacco product which is introduced or delivered for introduction into interstate commerce for commercial distribution presents an unreasonable risk of substantial harm to the public health; and

(2) notification under this subsection is necessary to eliminate the unreasonable risk of such harm and no more practicable means is available under the provisions of this chapter (other than this section) to eliminate such risk,

the Secretary may issue such order as may be necessary to assure that adequate notification is provided in an appropriate form, by the persons and means best suited under the circumstances involved, to all persons who should properly receive such notification in order to eliminate such risk. The Secretary may order notification by any appropriate means, including public service announcements. Before issuing an order under this subsection, the Secretary shall consult with the persons who are to give notice under the order.

(b) NO EXEMPTION FROM OTHER LIABILITY.—Compliance with an order issued under this section shall not relieve any person from liability under Federal or State law. In awarding damages for economic loss in an action brought for the enforcement of any such liability, the value to the plaintiff in such action of any remedy provided under such order shall be taken into account.

(c) RECALL AUTHORITY.—

(1) IN GENERAL.—If the Secretary finds that there is a reasonable probability that a tobacco product contains a manufacturing or other defect not ordinarily contained in tobacco products on the market that would cause serious, adverse health consequences or death, the Secretary shall issue an order requiring the appropriate person (including the manufacturers, importers, distributors, or retailers of the tobacco product) to immediately cease distribution of such tobacco product. The order shall provide the person subject to the order with an opportunity for an informal hearing, to be held not later than 10 days after the date of the issuance of the order, on the actions required by the order and on whether the order should be amended to require a recall of such tobacco product. If, after providing an opportunity for such a hearing, the Secretary determines that inadequate grounds exist to support the actions required by the order, the Secretary shall vacate the order.

(2) AMENDMENT OF ORDER TO REQUIRE RECALL.—

(A) IN GENERAL.—If, after providing an opportunity for an informal hearing under paragraph (1), the Secretary determines that the order should be amended to include a recall of the tobacco product with respect to which the order was issued, the Secretary shall, except as provided in subparagraph (B), amend the order to require a recall. The Secretary shall specify a timetable in which the tobacco product recall will occur and shall require periodic reports to the Secretary describing the progress of the recall.

(B) NOTICE.—An amended order under subparagraph (A)—

(i) shall not include recall of a tobacco product from individuals; and

(ii) shall provide for notice to persons subject to the risks associated with the use of such tobacco product.

In providing the notice required by clause (ii), the Secretary may use the assistance of retailers and other persons who distributed such tobacco product. If a significant number of such persons cannot be identified, the Secretary shall notify such persons under section 705(b).

(3) REMEDY NOT EXCLUSIVE.—The remedy provided by this subsection shall be in addition to remedies provided by subsection (a).

SEC. 909 [21 U.S.C. 387i]. RECORDS AND REPORTS ON TOBACCO PRODUCTS

(a) IN GENERAL.—Every person who is a tobacco product manufacturer or importer of a tobacco product shall establish and maintain such records, make such reports, and provide such information, as the Secretary may by regulation reasonably require to assure that such tobacco product is not adulterated or misbranded and to otherwise protect public health. Regulations prescribed under the preceding sentence—

(1) may require a tobacco product manufacturer or importer to report to the Secretary whenever the manufacturer or importer receives or otherwise becomes aware of information that reasonably suggests that one of its marketed tobacco products may have caused or contributed to a serious unexpected adverse experience associated with the use of the product or any significant increase in the frequency of a serious, expected adverse product experience;

(2) shall require reporting of other significant adverse tobacco product experiences as determined by the Secretary to be necessary to be reported;

(3) shall not impose requirements unduly burdensome to a tobacco product manufacturer or importer, taking into account the cost of complying with such requirements and the need for the protection of the public health and the implementation of this chapter;

(4) when prescribing the procedure for making requests for reports or information, shall require that each request made under such regulations for submission

of a report or information to the Secretary state the reason or purpose for such request and identify to the fullest extent practicable such report or information;

(5) when requiring submission of a report or information to the Secretary, shall state the reason or purpose for the submission of such report or information and identify to the fullest extent practicable such report or information; and

(6) may not require that the identity of any patient or user be disclosed in records, reports, or information required under this subsection unless required for the medical welfare of an individual, to determine risks to public health of a tobacco product, or to verify a record, report, or information submitted under this chapter.

In prescribing regulations under this subsection, the Secretary shall have due regard for the professional ethics of the medical profession and the interests of patients. The prohibitions of paragraph (6) continue to apply to records, reports, and information concerning any individual who has been a patient, irrespective of whether or when he ceases to be a patient.

(b) Reports of Removals and Corrections.—

(1) In general.—Except as provided in paragraph (2), the Secretary shall by regulation require a tobacco product manufacturer or importer of a tobacco product to report promptly to the Secretary any corrective action taken or removal from the market of a tobacco product undertaken by such manufacturer or importer if the removal or correction was undertaken—

(A) to reduce a risk to health posed by the tobacco product; or

(B) to remedy a violation of this chapter caused by the tobacco product which may present a risk to health.

A tobacco product manufacturer or importer of a tobacco product who undertakes a corrective action or removal from the market of a tobacco product which is not required to be reported under this subsection shall keep a record of such correction or removal.

(2) Exception.—No report of the corrective action or removal of a tobacco product may be required under paragraph (1) if a report of the corrective action or removal is required and has been submitted under subsection (a).

Sec. 910 [21 U.S.C. 387j]. APPLICATION FOR REVIEW OF CERTAIN TOBACCO PRODUCTS

(a) In General.—

(1) New tobacco product defined.—For purposes of this section the term "new tobacco product" means—

(A) any tobacco product (including those products in test markets) that was not commercially marketed in the United States as of February 15, 2007; or

(B) any modification (including a change in design, any component, any part, or any constituent, including a smoke constituent, or in the content, delivery or form of nicotine, or any other additive or ingredient) of a tobacco product where the modified product was commercially marketed in the United States after February 15, 2007.

(2) PREMARKET REVIEW REQUIRED.—

(A) NEW PRODUCTS.—An order under subsection (c)(1)(A)(i) for a new tobacco product is required unless—

(i) the manufacturer has submitted a report under section 905(j); and the Secretary has issued an order that the tobacco product—

(I) is substantially equivalent to a tobacco product commercially marketed (other than for test marketing) in the United States as of February 15, 2007; and

(II) is in compliance with the requirements of this Act; or

(ii) the tobacco product is exempt from the requirements of section 905(j) pursuant to a regulation issued under section 905(j)(3).

(B) APPLICATION TO CERTAIN POST-FEBRUARY 15, 2007 PRODUCTS.—Subparagraph (A) shall not apply to a tobacco product—

(i) that was first introduced or delivered for introduction into interstate commerce for commercial distribution in the United States after February 15, 2007, and prior to the date that is 21 months after the date of enactment of the Family Smoking Prevention and Tobacco Control Act; and

(ii) for which a report was submitted under section 905(j) within such 21–month period,

except that subparagraph (A) shall apply to the tobacco product if the Secretary issues an order that the tobacco product is not substantially equivalent.

(3) SUBSTANTIALLY EQUIVALENT DEFINED.—

(A) IN GENERAL.—In this section and section 905(j), the term "substantially equivalent" or "substantial equivalence" means, with respect to the tobacco product being compared to the predicate tobacco product, that the Secretary by order has found that the tobacco product—

(i) has the same characteristics as the predicate tobacco product; or

(ii) has different characteristics and the information submitted contains information, including clinical data if deemed necessary by the Secretary, that demonstrates that it is not appropriate to regulate the product under this section because the product does not raise different questions of public health.

(B) CHARACTERISTICS.—In subparagraph (A), the term "characteristics" means the materials, ingredients, design, composition, heating source, or other features of a tobacco product.

(C) LIMITATION.—A tobacco product may not be found to be substantially equivalent to a predicate tobacco product that has been removed from the market at the initiative of the Secretary or that has been determined by a judicial order to be misbranded or adulterated.

(4) HEALTH INFORMATION.—

(A) SUMMARY.—As part of a submission under section 905(j) respecting a tobacco product, the person required to file a premarket notification under such section shall provide an adequate summary of any health information related to the tobacco product or state that such information will be made available upon request by any person.

(B) REQUIRED INFORMATION.—Any summary under subparagraph (A) respecting a tobacco product shall contain detailed information regarding data concerning adverse health effects and shall be made available to the public by the Secretary within 30 days of the issuance of a determination that such tobacco product is substantially equivalent to another tobacco product.

(b) APPLICATION.—

(1) CONTENTS.—An application under this section shall contain—

(A) full reports of all information, published or known to, or which should reasonably be known to, the applicant, concerning investigations which have been made to show the health risks of such tobacco product and whether such tobacco product presents less risk than other tobacco products;

(B) a full statement of the components, ingredients, additives, and properties, and of the principle or principles of operation, of such tobacco product;

(C) a full description of the methods used in, and the facilities and controls used for, the manufacture, processing, and, when relevant, packing and installation of, such tobacco product;

(D) an identifying reference to any tobacco product standard under section 907 which would be applicable to any aspect of such tobacco product, and either adequate information to show that such aspect of such tobacco product fully meets such tobacco product standard or adequate information to justify any deviation from such standard;

(E) such samples of such tobacco product and of components thereof as the Secretary may reasonably require;

(F) specimens of the labeling proposed to be used for such tobacco product; and

(G) such other information relevant to the subject matter of the application as the Secretary may require.

(2) REFERRAL TO TOBACCO PRODUCTS SCIENTIFIC ADVISORY COMMITTEE.—Upon receipt of an application meeting the requirements set forth in paragraph (1), the Secretary—

(A) may, on the Secretary's own initiative; or

(B) may, upon the request of an applicant, refer such application to the Tobacco Products Scientific Advisory Committee for reference and for submission (within such period as the Secretary may establish) of a report and recommendation respecting the application, together with all underlying data and the reasons or basis for the recommendation.

(c) ACTION ON APPLICATION.—

(1) DEADLINE.—

(A) IN GENERAL.—As promptly as possible, but in no event later than 180 days after the receipt of an application under subsection (b), the Secretary, after considering the report and recommendation submitted under subsection (b)(2), shall—

(i) issue an order that the new product may be introduced or delivered for introduction into interstate commerce if the Secretary finds that none of the grounds specified in paragraph (2) of this subsection applies; or

(ii) issue an order that the new product may not be introduced or delivered for introduction into interstate commerce if the Secretary finds (and sets forth the basis for such finding as part of or accompanying such denial) that 1 or more grounds for denial specified in paragraph (2) of this subsection apply.

(B) RESTRICTIONS ON SALE AND DISTRIBUTION.—An order under subparagraph (A)(i) may require that the sale and distribution of the tobacco product be restricted but only to the extent that the sale and distribution of a tobacco product may be restricted under a regulation under section 906(d).

(2) DENIAL OF APPLICATION.—The Secretary shall deny an application submitted under subsection (b) if, upon the basis of the information submitted to the Secretary as part of the application and any other information before the Secretary with respect to such tobacco product, the Secretary finds that—

(A) there is a lack of a showing that permitting such tobacco product to be marketed would be appropriate for the protection of the public health;

(B) the methods used in, or the facilities or controls used for, the manufacture, processing, or packing of such tobacco product do not conform to the requirements of section 906(e);

(C) based on a fair evaluation of all material facts, the proposed labeling is false or misleading in any particular; or

(D) such tobacco product is not shown to conform in all respects to a tobacco product standard in effect under section 907, and there is a lack of adequate information to justify the deviation from such standard.

(3) DENIAL INFORMATION.—Any denial of an application shall, insofar as the Secretary determines to be practicable, be accompanied by a statement informing the applicant of the measures required to remove such application from deniable form (which measures may include further research by the applicant in accordance with 1 or more protocols prescribed by the Secretary).

(4) BASIS FOR FINDING.—For purposes of this section, the finding as to whether the marketing of a tobacco product for which an application has been submitted is appropriate for the protection of the public health shall be determined with respect to the risks and benefits to the population as a whole, including users and nonusers of the tobacco product, and taking into account—

(A) the increased or decreased likelihood that existing users of tobacco products will stop using such products; and

(B) the increased or decreased likelihood that those who do not use tobacco products will start using such products.

(5) BASIS FOR ACTION.—

(A) INVESTIGATIONS.—For purposes of paragraph (2)(A), whether permitting a tobacco product to be marketed would be appropriate for the protection of the public health shall, when appropriate, be determined on the basis of well-controlled investigations, which may include 1 or more clinical investigations by experts qualified by training and experience to evaluate the tobacco product.

(B) OTHER EVIDENCE.—If the Secretary determines that there exists valid scientific evidence (other than evidence derived from investigations described in subparagraph (A)) which is sufficient to evaluate the tobacco product, the Secretary may authorize that the determination for purposes of paragraph (2) (A) be made on the basis of such evidence.

(d) WITHDRAWAL AND TEMPORARY SUSPENSION.—

(1) IN GENERAL.—The Secretary shall, upon obtaining, where appropriate, advice on scientific matters from the Tobacco Products Scientific Advisory Committee, and after due notice and opportunity for informal hearing for a tobacco product for which an order was issued under subsection (c)(1)(A)(i), issue an order withdrawing the order if the Secretary finds—

(A) that the continued marketing of such tobacco product no longer is appropriate for the protection of the public health;

(B) that the application contained or was accompanied by an untrue statement of a material fact;

(C) that the applicant—

(i) has failed to establish a system for maintaining records, or has repeatedly or deliberately failed to maintain records or to make reports, required by an applicable regulation under section 909;

(ii) has refused to permit access to, or copying or verification of, such records as required by section 704; or

(iii) has not complied with the requirements of section 905;

(D) on the basis of new information before the Secretary with respect to such tobacco product, evaluated together with the evidence before the Secretary when the application was reviewed, that the methods used in, or the facilities and controls used for, the manufacture, processing, packing, or installation of such tobacco product do not conform with the requirements of section 906(e) and were not brought into conformity with such requirements within a reasonable time after receipt of written notice from the Secretary of nonconformity;

(E) on the basis of new information before the Secretary, evaluated together with the evidence before the Secretary when the application was reviewed, that the labeling of such tobacco product, based on a fair evaluation of all material facts, is false or misleading in any particular and was not corrected within a reasonable time after receipt of written notice from the Secretary of such fact; or

(F) on the basis of new information before the Secretary, evaluated together with the evidence before the Secretary when such order was issued, that such tobacco product is not shown to conform in all respects to a tobacco product standard which is in effect under section 907, compliance with which was a condition to the issuance of an order relating to the application, and that there is a lack of adequate information to justify the deviation from such standard.

(2) APPEAL.—The holder of an application subject to an order issued under paragraph (1) withdrawing an order issued pursuant to subsection (c)(1)(A)(i) may, by petition filed on or before the 30th day after the date upon which such holder receives notice of such withdrawal, obtain review thereof in accordance with section 912.

(3) TEMPORARY SUSPENSION.—If, after providing an opportunity for an informal hearing, the Secretary determines there is reasonable probability that the continuation of distribution of a tobacco product under an order would cause serious, adverse health consequences or death, that is greater than ordinarily caused by tobacco products on the market, the Secretary shall by order temporarily suspend the authority of the manufacturer to market the product. If the Secretary issues

such an order, the Secretary shall proceed expeditiously under paragraph (1) to withdraw such application.

(e) SERVICE OF ORDER.—An order issued by the Secretary under this section shall be served—

(1) in person by any officer or employee of the department designated by the Secretary; or

(2) by mailing the order by registered mail or certified mail addressed to the applicant at the applicant's last known address in the records of the Secretary.

(f) RECORDS.—

(1) ADDITIONAL INFORMATION.—In the case of any tobacco product for which an order issued pursuant to subsection (c)(1)(A)(i) for an application filed under subsection (b) is in effect, the applicant shall establish and maintain such records, and make such reports to the Secretary, as the Secretary may by regulation, or by order with respect to such application, prescribe on the basis of a finding that such records and reports are necessary in order to enable the Secretary to determine, or facilitate a determination of, whether there is or may be grounds for withdrawing or temporarily suspending such order.

(2) ACCESS TO RECORDS.—Each person required under this section to maintain records, and each person in charge of custody thereof, shall, upon request of an officer or employee designated by the Secretary, permit such officer or employee at all reasonable times to have access to and copy and verify such records.

(g) INVESTIGATIONAL TOBACCO PRODUCT EXEMPTION FOR INVESTIGATIONAL USE.—The Secretary may exempt tobacco products intended for investigational use from the provisions of this chapter under such conditions as the Secretary may by regulation prescribe.

SEC. 911 [21 U.S.C. 387k]. MODIFIED RISK TOBACCO PRODUCTS

(a) IN GENERAL.—No person may introduce or deliver for introduction into interstate commerce any modified risk tobacco product unless an order issued pursuant to subsection (g) is effective with respect to such product.

(b) DEFINITIONS.—In this section:

(1) MODIFIED RISK TOBACCO PRODUCT.—The term "modified risk tobacco product" means any tobacco product that is sold or distributed for use to reduce harm or the risk of tobacco-related disease associated with commercially marketed tobacco products.

(2) SOLD OR DISTRIBUTED.—

(A) IN GENERAL.—With respect to a tobacco product, the term "sold or distributed for use to reduce harm or the risk of tobacco-related disease associated with commercially marketed tobacco products" means a tobacco product—

(i) the label, labeling, or advertising of which represents explicitly or implicitly that—

(I) the tobacco product presents a lower risk of tobacco-related disease or is less harmful than one or more other commercially marketed tobacco products;

(II) the tobacco product or its smoke contains a reduced level of a substance or presents a reduced exposure to a substance; or

(III) the tobacco product or its smoke does not contain or is free of a substance;

(ii) the label, labeling, or advertising of which uses the descriptors "light", "mild", or "low" or similar descriptors; or

(iii) the tobacco product manufacturer of which has taken any action directed to consumers through the media or otherwise, other than by means of the tobacco product's label, labeling, or advertising, after the date of enactment of the Family Smoking Prevention and Tobacco Control Act, respecting the product that would be reasonably expected to result in consumers believing that the tobacco product or its smoke may present a lower risk of disease or is less harmful than one or more commercially marketed tobacco products, or presents a reduced exposure to, or does not contain or is free of, a substance or substances.

(B) LIMITATION.—No tobacco product shall be considered to be "sold or distributed for use to reduce harm or the risk of tobacco-related disease associated with commercially marketed tobacco products", except as described in subparagraph (A).

(C) SMOKELESS TOBACCO PRODUCT.—No smokeless tobacco product shall be considered to be "sold or distributed for use to reduce harm or the risk of tobacco-related disease associated with commercially marketed tobacco products" solely because its label, labeling, or advertising uses the following phrases to describe such product and its use: "smokeless tobacco", "smokeless tobacco product", "not consumed by smoking", "does not produce smoke", "smokefree", "smoke-free", "without smoke", "no smoke", or "not smoke".

(3) EFFECTIVE DATE.—The provisions of paragraph (2)(A)(ii) shall take effect 12 months after the date of enactment of the Family Smoking Prevention and Tobacco Control Act for those products whose label, labeling, or advertising contains the terms described in such paragraph on such date of enactment. The effective date shall be with respect to the date of manufacture, provided that, in any case, beginning 30 days after such effective date, a manufacturer shall not introduce into the domestic commerce of the United States any product, irrespective of the date of manufacture, that is not in conformance with paragraph (2)(A)(ii).

(c) TOBACCO DEPENDENCE PRODUCTS.—A product that is intended to be used for the treatment of tobacco dependence, including smoking cessation, is not a modified risk tobacco product under this section if it has been approved as a drug or device by the Food and Drug Administration and is subject to the requirements of chapter V.

(d) FILING.—Any person may file with the Secretary an application for a modified risk tobacco product. Such application shall include—

(1) a description of the proposed product and any proposed advertising and labeling;

(2) the conditions for using the product;

(3) the formulation of the product;

(4) sample product labels and labeling;

(5) all documents (including underlying scientific information) relating to research findings conducted, supported, or possessed by the tobacco product manufacturer relating to the effect of the product on tobacco-related diseases and health-related conditions, including information both favorable and unfavorable to the ability of the product to reduce risk or exposure and relating to human health;

(6) data and information on how consumers actually use the tobacco product; and

(7) such other information as the Secretary may require.

(e) PUBLIC AVAILABILITY.—The Secretary shall make the application described in subsection (d) publicly available (except matters in the application which are trade secrets or otherwise confidential, commercial information) and shall request comments by interested persons on the information contained in the application and on the label, labeling, and advertising accompanying such application.

(f) ADVISORY COMMITTEE.—

(1) IN GENERAL.—The Secretary shall refer to the Tobacco Products Scientific Advisory Committee any application submitted under this section.

(2) RECOMMENDATIONS.—Not later than 60 days after the date an application is referred to the Tobacco Products Scientific Advisory Committee under paragraph (1), the Advisory Committee shall report its recommendations on the application to the Secretary.

(g) MARKETING.—

(1) MODIFIED RISK PRODUCTS.—Except as provided in paragraph (2), the Secretary shall, with respect to an application submitted under this section, issue an order that a modified risk product may be commercially marketed only if the Secretary determines that the applicant has demonstrated that such product, as it is actually used by consumers, will—

(A) significantly reduce harm and the risk of tobacco-related disease to individual tobacco users; and

(B) benefit the health of the population as a whole taking into account both users of tobacco products and persons who do not currently use tobacco products.

(2) SPECIAL RULE FOR CERTAIN PRODUCTS.—

(A) IN GENERAL.—The Secretary may issue an order that a tobacco product may be introduced or delivered for introduction into interstate commerce, pursuant to an application under this section, with respect to a tobacco product that may not be commercially marketed under paragraph (1) if the Secretary makes the findings required under this paragraph and determines that the applicant has demonstrated that—

(i) such order would be appropriate to promote the public health;

(ii) any aspect of the label, labeling, and advertising for such product that would cause the tobacco product to be a modified risk tobacco product under subsection (b) is limited to an explicit or implicit representation that such tobacco product or its smoke does not contain or is free of a substance or contains a reduced level of a substance, or presents a reduced exposure to a substance in tobacco smoke;

(iii) scientific evidence is not available and, using the best available scientific methods, cannot be made available without conducting long-term epidemiological studies for an application to meet the standards set forth in paragraph (1); and

(iv) the scientific evidence that is available without conducting long-term epidemiological studies demonstrates that a measurable and substantial reduction in morbidity or mortality among individual tobacco users is reasonably likely in subsequent studies.

(B) ADDITIONAL FINDINGS REQUIRED.—To issue an order under subparagraph (A) the Secretary must also find that the applicant has demonstrated that—

(i) the magnitude of the overall reductions in exposure to the substance or substances which are the subject of the application is substantial, such substance or substances are harmful, and the product as actually used exposes consumers to the specified reduced level of the substance or substances;

(ii) the product as actually used by consumers will not expose them to higher levels of other harmful substances compared to the similar types of tobacco products then on the market unless such increases are minimal and the reasonably likely overall impact of use of the product remains a substantial and measurable reduction in overall morbidity and mortality among individual tobacco users;

(iii) testing of actual consumer perception shows that, as the applicant proposes to label and market the product, consumers will not be misled into believing that the product—

(I) is or has been demonstrated to be less harmful; or

(II) presents or has been demonstrated to present less of a risk of disease than 1 or more other commercially marketed tobacco products; and

(iv) issuance of an order with respect to the application is expected to benefit the health of the population as a whole taking into account both users of tobacco products and persons who do not currently use tobacco products.

(C) Conditions of Marketing.—

(i) In General.—Applications subject to an order under this paragraph shall be limited to a term of not more than 5 years, but may be renewed upon a finding by the Secretary that the requirements of this paragraph continue to be satisfied based on the filing of a new application.

(ii) Agreements by Applicant.—An order under this paragraph shall be conditioned on the applicant's agreement to conduct postmarket surveillance and studies and to submit to the Secretary the results of such surveillance and studies to determine the impact of the order on consumer perception, behavior, and health and to enable the Secretary to review the accuracy of the determinations upon which the order was based in accordance with a protocol approved by the Secretary.

(iii) Annual Submission.—The results of such postmarket surveillance and studies described in clause (ii) shall be submitted annually.

(3) Basis.—The determinations under paragraphs (1) and (2) shall be based on—

(A) the scientific evidence submitted by the applicant; and

(B) scientific evidence and other information that is made available to the Secretary.

(4) Benefit to Health of Individuals and of Population as a Whole.—In making the determinations under paragraphs (1) and (2), the Secretary shall take into account—

(A) the relative health risks to individuals of the tobacco product that is the subject of the application;

(B) the increased or decreased likelihood that existing users of tobacco products who would otherwise stop using such products will switch to the tobacco product that is the subject of the application;

(C) the increased or decreased likelihood that persons who do not use tobacco products will start using the tobacco product that is the subject of the application;

(D) the risks and benefits to persons from the use of the tobacco product that is the subject of the application as compared to the use of products for smoking cessation approved under chapter V to treat nicotine dependence; and

(E) comments, data, and information submitted by interested persons.

(h) ADDITIONAL CONDITIONS FOR MARKETING.—

(1) MODIFIED RISK PRODUCTS.—The Secretary shall require for the marketing of a product under this section that any advertising or labeling concerning modified risk products enable the public to comprehend the information concerning modified risk and to understand the relative significance of such information in the context of total health and in relation to all of the diseases and health-related conditions associated with the use of tobacco products.

(2) COMPARATIVE CLAIMS.—

(A) IN GENERAL.—The Secretary may require for the marketing of a product under this subsection that a claim comparing a tobacco product to 1 or more other commercially marketed tobacco products shall compare the tobacco product to a commercially marketed tobacco product that is representative of that type of tobacco product on the market (for example the average value of the top 3 brands of an established regular tobacco product).

(B) QUANTITATIVE COMPARISONS.—The Secretary may also require, for purposes of subparagraph (A), that the percent (or fraction) of change and identity of the reference tobacco product and a quantitative comparison of the amount of the substance claimed to be reduced shall be stated in immediate proximity to the most prominent claim.

(3) LABEL DISCLOSURE.—

(A) IN GENERAL.—The Secretary may require the disclosure on the label of other substances in the tobacco product, or substances that may be produced by the consumption of that tobacco product, that may affect a disease or health-related condition or may increase the risk of other diseases or health-related conditions associated with the use of tobacco products.

(B) CONDITIONS OF USE.—If the conditions of use of the tobacco product may affect the risk of the product to human health, the Secretary may require the labeling of conditions of use.

(4) TIME.—An order issued under subsection (g)(1) shall be effective for a specified period of time.

(5) ADVERTISING.—The Secretary may require, with respect to a product for which an applicant obtained an order under subsection (g)(1), that the product comply with requirements relating to advertising and promotion of the tobacco product.

(i) POSTMARKET SURVEILLANCE AND STUDIES.—

(1) IN GENERAL.—The Secretary shall require, with respect to a product for which an applicant obtained an order under subsection (g)(1), that the applicant conduct postmarket surveillance and studies for such a tobacco product to determine the impact of the order issuance on consumer perception, behavior, and health, to enable the Secretary to review the accuracy of the determinations upon which the order was based, and to provide information that the Secretary determines is otherwise necessary regarding the use or health risks involving the tobacco product. The results of postmarket surveillance and studies shall be submitted to the Secretary on an annual basis.

(2) SURVEILLANCE PROTOCOL.—Each applicant required to conduct a surveillance of a tobacco product under paragraph (1) shall, within 30 days after receiving notice that the applicant is required to conduct such surveillance, submit, for the approval of the Secretary, a protocol for the required surveillance. The Secretary, within 60 days of the receipt of such protocol, shall determine if the principal investigator proposed to be used in the surveillance has sufficient qualifications and experience to conduct such surveillance and if such protocol will result in collection of the data or other information designated by the Secretary as necessary to protect the public health.

(j) WITHDRAWAL OF AUTHORIZATION.—The Secretary, after an opportunity for an informal hearing, shall withdraw an order under subsection (g) if the Secretary determines that—

(1) the applicant, based on new information, can no longer make the demonstrations required under subsection (g), or the Secretary can no longer make the determinations required under subsection (g);

(2) the application failed to include material information or included any untrue statement of material fact;

(3) any explicit or implicit representation that the product reduces risk or exposure is no longer valid, including if—

(A) a tobacco product standard is established pursuant to section 907;

(B) an action is taken that affects the risks presented by other commercially marketed tobacco products that were compared to the product that is the subject of the application; or

(C) any postmarket surveillance or studies reveal that the order is no longer consistent with the protection of the public health;

(4) the applicant failed to conduct or submit the postmarket surveillance and studies required under subsection (g)(2)(C)(ii) or subsection (i); or

(5) the applicant failed to meet a condition imposed under subsection (h).

(k) CHAPTER IV OR V.—A product for which the Secretary has issued an order pursuant to subsection (g) shall not be subject to chapter IV or V.

(*l*) IMPLEMENTING REGULATIONS OR GUIDANCE.—

(1) SCIENTIFIC EVIDENCE.—Not later than 2 years after the date of enactment of the Family Smoking Prevention and Tobacco Control Act, the Secretary shall issue regulations or guidance (or any combination thereof) on the scientific evidence required for assessment and ongoing review of modified risk tobacco products. Such regulations or guidance shall—

(A) to the extent that adequate scientific evidence exists, establish minimum standards for scientific studies needed prior to issuing an order under subsection (g) to show that a substantial reduction in morbidity or mortality among individual tobacco users occurs for products described in subsection (g)(1) or is reasonably likely for products described in subsection (g)(2);

(B) include validated biomarkers, intermediate clinical endpoints, and other feasible outcome measures, as appropriate;

(C) establish minimum standards for postmarket studies, that shall include regular and long-term assessments of health outcomes and mortality, intermediate clinical endpoints, consumer perception of harm reduction, and the impact on quitting behavior and new use of tobacco products, as appropriate;

(D) establish minimum standards for required postmarket surveillance, including ongoing assessments of consumer perception;

(E) require that data from the required studies and surveillance be made available to the Secretary prior to the decision on renewal of a modified risk tobacco product; and

(F) establish a reasonable timetable for the Secretary to review an application under this section.

(2) CONSULTATION.—The regulations or guidance issued under paragraph (1) shall be developed in consultation with the Institute of Medicine, and with the input of other appropriate scientific and medical experts, on the design and conduct of such studies and surveillance.

(3) REVISION.—The regulations or guidance under paragraph (1) shall be revised on a regular basis as new scientific information becomes available.

(4) NEW TOBACCO PRODUCTS.—Not later than 2 years after the date of enactment of the Family Smoking Prevention and Tobacco Control Act, the Secretary shall issue a regulation or guidance that permits the filing of a single application

for any tobacco product that is a new tobacco product under section 910 and which the applicant seeks to commercially market under this section.

(m) DISTRIBUTORS.—Except as provided in this section, no distributor may take any action, after the date of enactment of the Family Smoking Prevention and Tobacco Control Act, with respect to a tobacco product that would reasonably be expected to result in consumers believing that the tobacco product or its smoke may present a lower risk of disease or is less harmful than one or more commercially marketed tobacco products, or presents a reduced exposure to, or does not contain or is free of, a substance or substances.

SEC. 912 [21 U.S.C. 387l]. JUDICIAL REVIEW

(a) RIGHT TO REVIEW.—

(1) IN GENERAL.—Not later than 30 days after—

(A) the promulgation of a regulation under section 907 establishing, amending, or revoking a tobacco product standard; or

(B) a denial of an application under section 910(c), any person adversely affected by such regulation or denial may file a petition for judicial review of such regulation or denial with the United States Court of Appeals for the District of Columbia or for the circuit in which such person resides or has their principal place of business.

(2) REQUIREMENTS.—

(A) COPY OF PETITION.—A copy of the petition filed under paragraph (1) shall be transmitted by the clerk of the court involved to the Secretary.

(B) RECORD OF PROCEEDINGS.—On receipt of a petition under subparagraph (A), the Secretary shall file in the court in which such petition was filed—

(i) the record of the proceedings on which the regulation or order was based; and

(ii) a statement of the reasons for the issuance of such a regulation or order.

(C) DEFINITION OF RECORD.—In this section, the term "record" means—

(i) all notices and other matter published in the Federal Register with respect to the regulation or order reviewed;

(ii) all information submitted to the Secretary with respect to such regulation or order;

(iii) proceedings of any panel or advisory committee with respect to such regulation or order;

(iv) any hearing held with respect to such regulation or order; and

(v) any other information identified by the Secretary, in the administrative proceeding held with respect to such regulation or order, as being relevant to such regulation or order.

(b) STANDARD OF REVIEW.—Upon the filing of the petition under subsection (a) for judicial review of a regulation or order, the court shall have jurisdiction to review the regulation or order in accordance with chapter 7 of title 5, United States Code, and to grant appropriate relief, including interim relief, as provided for in such chapter. A regulation or denial described in subsection (a) shall be reviewed in accordance with section 706(2)(A) of title 5, United States Code.

(c) FINALITY OF JUDGMENT.—The judgment of the court affirming or setting aside, in whole or in part, any regulation or order shall be final, subject to review by the Supreme Court of the United States upon certiorari or certification, as provided in section 1254 of title 28, United States Code.

(d) OTHER REMEDIES.—The remedies provided for in this section shall be in addition to, and not in lieu of, any other remedies provided by law.

(e) REGULATIONS AND ORDERS MUST RECITE BASIS IN RECORD.—To facilitate judicial review, a regulation or order issued under section 906, 907, 908, 909, 910, or 916 shall contain a statement of the reasons for the issuance of such regulation or order in the record of the proceedings held in connection with its issuance.

SEC. 913 [21 U.S.C. 387m]. EQUAL TREATMENT OF RETAIL OUTLETS

The Secretary shall issue regulations to require that retail establishments for which the predominant business is the sale of tobacco products comply with any advertising restrictions applicable to retail establishments accessible to individuals under the age of 18.

SEC. 914 [21 U.S.C. 387n]. JURISDICTION OF AND COORDINATION WITH THE FEDERAL TRADE COMMISSION

(a) JURISDICTION.—

(1) IN GENERAL.—Except where expressly provided in this chapter, nothing in this chapter shall be construed as limiting or diminishing the authority of the Federal Trade Commission to enforce the laws under its jurisdiction with respect to the advertising, sale, or distribution of tobacco products.

(2) ENFORCEMENT.—Any advertising that violates this chapter or a provision of the regulations referred to in section 102 of the Family Smoking Prevention and Tobacco Control Act, is an unfair or deceptive act or practice under section 5(a) of the Federal Trade Commission Act and shall be considered a violation of a rule promulgated under section 18 of that Act.

(b) Coordination.—With respect to the requirements of section 4 of the Federal Cigarette Labeling and Advertising Act and section 3 of the Comprehensive Smokeless Tobacco Health Education Act of 1986—

(1) the Chairman of the Federal Trade Commission shall coordinate with the Secretary concerning the enforcement of such Act as such enforcement relates to unfair or deceptive acts or practices in the advertising of cigarettes or smokeless tobacco; and

(2) the Secretary shall consult with the Chairman of such Commission in revising the label statements and requirements under such sections.

Sec. 915 [21 U.S.C. 387o]. REGULATION REQUIREMENT

(a) Testing, Reporting, and Disclosure.—Not later than 36 months after the date of enactment of the Family Smoking Prevention and Tobacco Control Act, the Secretary shall promulgate regulations under this Act that meet the requirements of subsection (b).

(b) Contents of Rules.—The regulations promulgated under subsection (a)—

(1) shall require testing and reporting of tobacco product constituents, ingredients, and additives, including smoke constituents, by brand and subbrand that the Secretary determines should be tested to protect the public health, provided that, for purposes of the testing requirements of this paragraph, tobacco products manufactured and sold by a single tobacco product manufacturer that are identical in all respects except the labels, packaging design, logo, trade dress, trademark, brand name, or any combination thereof, shall be considered as a single brand; and

(2) may require that tobacco product manufacturers, packagers, or importers make disclosures relating to the results of the testing of tar and nicotine through labels or advertising or other appropriate means, and make disclosures regarding the results of the testing of other constituents, including smoke constituents, ingredients, or additives, that the Secretary determines should be disclosed to the public to protect the public health and will not mislead consumers about the risk of tobacco-related disease.

(c) Authority.—The Secretary shall have the authority under this chapter to conduct or to require the testing, reporting, or disclosure of tobacco product constituents, including smoke constituents.

(d) Small Tobacco Product Manufacturers.—

(1) First compliance date.—The initial regulations promulgated under subsection (a) shall not impose requirements on small tobacco product manufacturers before the later of—

(A) the end of the 2–year period following the final promulgation of such regulations; and

(B) the initial date set by the Secretary for compliance with such regulations by manufacturers that are not small tobacco product manufacturers.

(2) TESTING AND REPORTING INITIAL COMPLIANCE PERIOD.—

(A) 4–YEAR PERIOD.—The initial regulations promulgated under subsection (a) shall give each small tobacco product manufacturer a 4–year period over which to conduct testing and reporting for all of its tobacco products. Subject to paragraph (1), the end of the first year of such 4–year period shall coincide with the initial date of compliance under this section set by the Secretary with respect to manufacturers that are not small tobacco product manufacturers or the end of the 2–year period following the final promulgation of such regulations, as described in paragraph (1)(A). A small tobacco product manufacturer shall be required—

(i) to conduct such testing and reporting for 25 percent of its tobacco products during each year of such 4–year period; and

(ii) to conduct such testing and reporting for its largest-selling tobacco products (as determined by the Secretary) before its other tobacco products, or in such other order of priority as determined by the Secretary.

(B) CASE-BY-CASE DELAY.—Notwithstanding subparagraph (A), the Secretary may, on a case-by-case basis, delay the date by which an individual small tobacco product manufacturer must conduct testing and reporting for its tobacco products under this section based upon a showing of undue hardship to such manufacturer. Notwithstanding the preceding sentence, the Secretary shall not extend the deadline for a small tobacco product manufacturer to conduct testing and reporting for all of its tobacco products beyond a total of 5 years after the initial date of compliance under this section set by the Secretary with respect to manufacturers that are not small tobacco product manufacturers.

(3) SUBSEQUENT AND ADDITIONAL TESTING AND REPORTING.—The regulations promulgated under subsection (a) shall provide that, with respect to any subsequent or additional testing and reporting of tobacco products required under this section, such testing and reporting by a small tobacco product manufacturer shall be conducted in accordance with the timeframes described in paragraph (2)(A), except that, in the case of a new product, or if there has been a modification described in section 910(a)(1)(B) of any product of a small tobacco product manufacturer since the last testing and reporting required under this section, the Secretary shall require that any subsequent or additional testing and reporting be conducted in accordance with the same timeframe applicable to manufacturers that are not small tobacco product manufacturers.

(4) JOINT LABORATORY TESTING SERVICES.—The Secretary shall allow any 2 or more small tobacco product manufacturers to join together to purchase laboratory

testing services required by this section on a group basis in order to ensure that such manufacturers receive access to, and fair pricing of, such testing services.

(e) EXTENSIONS FOR LIMITED LABORATORY CAPACITY.—

(1) IN GENERAL.—The regulations promulgated under subsection (a) shall provide that a small tobacco product manufacturer shall not be considered to be in violation of this section before the deadline applicable under paragraphs (3) and (4), if—

(A) the tobacco products of such manufacturer are in compliance with all other requirements of this chapter; and

(B) the conditions described in paragraph (2) are met.

(2) CONDITIONS.—Notwithstanding the requirements of this section, the Secretary may delay the date by which a small tobacco product manufacturer must be in compliance with the testing and reporting required by this section until such time as the testing is reported if, not later than 90 days before the deadline for reporting in accordance with this section, a small tobacco product manufacturer provides evidence to the Secretary demonstrating that—

(A) the manufacturer has submitted the required products for testing to a laboratory and has done so sufficiently in advance of the deadline to create a reasonable expectation of completion by the deadline;

(B) the products currently are awaiting testing by the laboratory; and

(C) neither that laboratory nor any other laboratory is able to complete testing by the deadline at customary, nonexpedited testing fees.

(3) EXTENSION.—The Secretary, taking into account the laboratory testing capacity that is available to tobacco product manufacturers, shall review and verify the evidence submitted by a small tobacco product manufacturer in accordance with paragraph (2). If the Secretary finds that the conditions described in such paragraph are met, the Secretary shall notify the small tobacco product manufacturer that the manufacturer shall not be considered to be in violation of the testing and reporting requirements of this section until the testing is reported or until 1 year after the reporting deadline has passed, whichever occurs sooner. If, however, the Secretary has not made a finding before the reporting deadline, the manufacturer shall not be considered to be in violation of such requirements until the Secretary finds that the conditions described in paragraph (2) have not been met, or until 1 year after the reporting deadline, whichever occurs sooner.

(4) ADDITIONAL EXTENSION.—In addition to the time that may be provided under paragraph (3), the Secretary may provide further extensions of time, in increments of no more than 1 year, for required testing and reporting to occur if the Secretary determines, based on evidence properly and timely submitted by a small tobacco product manufacturer in accordance with paragraph (2), that a lack

of available laboratory capacity prevents the manufacturer from completing the required testing during the period described in paragraph (3).

(f) RULE OF CONSTRUCTION.—Nothing in subsection (d) or (e) shall be construed to authorize the extension of any deadline, or to otherwise affect any timeframe, under any provision of this Act or the Family Smoking Prevention and Tobacco Control Act other than this section.

SEC. 916 [21 U.S.C. 387p]. PRESERVATION OF STATE AND LOCAL AUTHORITY

(a) IN GENERAL.—

(1) PRESERVATION.—Except as provided in paragraph (2)(A), nothing in this chapter, or rules promulgated under this chapter, shall be construed to limit the authority of a Federal agency (including the Armed Forces), a State or political subdivision of a State, or the government of an Indian tribe to enact, adopt, promulgate, and enforce any law, rule, regulation, or other measure with respect to tobacco products that is in addition to, or more stringent than, requirements established under this chapter, including a law, rule, regulation, or other measure relating to or prohibiting the sale, distribution, possession, exposure to, access to, advertising and promotion of, or use of tobacco products by individuals of any age, information reporting to the State, or measures relating to fire safety standards for tobacco products. No provision of this chapter shall limit or otherwise affect any State, tribal, or local taxation of tobacco products.

(2) PREEMPTION OF CERTAIN STATE AND LOCAL REQUIREMENTS.—

(A) IN GENERAL.—No State or political subdivision of a State may establish or continue in effect with respect to a tobacco product any requirement which is different from, or in addition to, any requirement under the provisions of this chapter relating to tobacco product standards, premarket review, adulteration, misbranding, labeling, registration, good manufacturing standards, or modified risk tobacco products.

(B) EXCEPTION.—Subparagraph (A) does not apply to requirements relating to the sale, distribution, possession, information reporting to the State, exposure to, access to, the advertising and promotion of, or use of, tobacco products by individuals of any age, or relating to fire safety standards for tobacco products. Information disclosed to a State under subparagraph (A) that is exempt from disclosure under section 552(b)(4) of title 5, United States Code, shall be treated as a trade secret and confidential information by the State.

(b) RULE OF CONSTRUCTION REGARDING PRODUCT LIABILITY.—No provision of this chapter relating to a tobacco product shall be construed to modify or otherwise affect any action or the liability of any person under the product liability law of any State.

Sec. 917 [21 U.S.C. 387q]. Tobacco Products Scientific Advisory Committee

(a) Establishment.—Not later than 6 months after the date of enactment of the Family Smoking Prevention and Tobacco Control Act, the Secretary shall establish a 12–member advisory committee, to be known as the Tobacco Products Scientific Advisory Committee (in this section referred to as the "Advisory Committee").

(b) Membership.—

(1) In general.—

(A) Members.—The Secretary shall appoint as members of the Tobacco Products Scientific Advisory Committee individuals who are technically qualified by training and experience in medicine, medical ethics, science, or technology involving the manufacture, evaluation, or use of tobacco products, who are of appropriately diversified professional backgrounds. The committee shall be composed of—

(i) 7 individuals who are physicians, dentists, scientists, or health care professionals practicing in the area of oncology, pulmonology, cardiology, toxicology, pharmacology, addiction, or any other relevant specialty;

(ii) 1 individual who is an officer or employee of a State or local government or of the Federal Government;

(iii) 1 individual as a representative of the general public;

(iv) 1 individual as a representative of the interests of the tobacco manufacturing industry;

(v) 1 individual as a representative of the interests of the small business tobacco manufacturing industry, which position may be filled on a rotating, sequential basis by representatives of different small business tobacco manufacturers based on areas of expertise relevant to the topics being considered by the Advisory Committee; and

(vi) 1 individual as a representative of the interests of the tobacco growers.

(B) Nonvoting members.—The members of the committee appointed under clauses (iv), (v), and (vi) of subparagraph (A) shall serve as consultants to those described in clauses (i) through (iii) of subparagraph (A) and shall be nonvoting representatives.

(C) Conflicts of interest.—No members of the committee, other than members appointed pursuant to clauses (iv), (v), and (vi) of subparagraph (A) shall, during the member's tenure on the committee or for the 18–month period prior to becoming such a member, receive any salary, grants, or other payments or support from any business that manufactures, distributes, markets, or sells cigarettes or other tobacco products.

(2) LIMITATION.—The Secretary may not appoint to the Advisory Committee any individual who is in the regular full-time employ of the Food and Drug Administration or any agency responsible for the enforcement of this Act. The Secretary may appoint Federal officials as ex officio members.

(3) CHAIRPERSON.—The Secretary shall designate 1 of the members appointed under clauses (i), (ii), and (iii) of paragraph (1)(A) to serve as chairperson.

(c) DUTIES.—The Tobacco Products Scientific Advisory Committee shall provide advice, information, and recommendations to the Secretary—

(1) as provided in this chapter;

(2) on the effects of the alteration of the nicotine yields from tobacco products;

(3) on whether there is a threshold level below which nicotine yields do not produce dependence on the tobacco product involved; and

(4) on its review of other safety, dependence, or health issues relating to tobacco products as requested by the Secretary.

(d) COMPENSATION; SUPPORT; FACA.—

(1) COMPENSATION AND TRAVEL.—Members of the Advisory Committee who are not officers or employees of the United States, while attending conferences or meetings of the committee or otherwise engaged in its business, shall be entitled to receive compensation at rates to be fixed by the Secretary, which may not exceed the daily equivalent of the rate in effect under the Senior Executive Schedule under section 5382 of title 5, United States Code, for each day (including travel time) they are so engaged; and while so serving away from their homes or regular places of business each member may be allowed travel expenses, including per diem in lieu of subsistence, as authorized by section 5703 of title 5, United States Code, for persons in the Government service employed intermittently.

(2) ADMINISTRATIVE SUPPORT.—The Secretary shall furnish the Advisory Committee clerical and other assistance.

(3) NONAPPLICATION OF FACA.—Section 14 of the Federal Advisory Committee Act does not apply to the Advisory Committee.

(e) PROCEEDINGS OF ADVISORY PANELS AND COMMITTEES.—The Advisory Committee shall make and maintain a transcript of any proceeding of the panel or committee. Each such panel and committee shall delete from any transcript made under this subsection information which is exempt from disclosure under section 552(b) of title 5, United States Code.

SEC. 918 [21 U.S.C. 387r]. DRUG PRODUCTS USED TO TREAT TOBACCO DEPENDENCE

(a) IN GENERAL.—The Secretary shall—

(1) at the request of the applicant, consider designating products for smoking cessation, including nicotine replacement products as fast track research and approval products within the meaning of section 506;

(2) consider approving the extended use of nicotine replacement products (such as nicotine patches, nicotine gum, and nicotine lozenges) for the treatment of tobacco dependence; and

(3) review and consider the evidence for additional indications for nicotine replacement products, such as for craving relief or relapse prevention.

(b) REPORT ON INNOVATIVE PRODUCTS.—

(1) IN GENERAL.—Not later than 3 years after the date of enactment of the Family Smoking Prevention and Tobacco Control Act, the Secretary, after consultation with recognized scientific, medical, and public health experts (including both Federal agencies and nongovernmental entities, the Institute of Medicine of the National Academy of Sciences, and the Society for Research on Nicotine and Tobacco), shall submit to the Congress a report that examines how best to regulate, promote, and encourage the development of innovative products and treatments (including nicotine-based and non-nicotine-based products and treatments) to better achieve, in a manner that best protects and promotes the public health—

(A) total abstinence from tobacco use;

(B) reductions in consumption of tobacco; and

(C) reductions in the harm associated with continued tobacco use.

(2) RECOMMENDATIONS.—The report under paragraph (1) shall include the recommendations of the Secretary on how the Food and Drug Administration should coordinate and facilitate the exchange of information on such innovative products and treatments among relevant offices and centers within the Administration and within the National Institutes of Health, the Centers for Disease Control and Prevention, and other relevant agencies.

SEC. 919 [21 U.S.C. 387s]. USER FEES

(a) ESTABLISHMENT OF QUARTERLY FEE.—Beginning on the date of enactment of the Family Smoking Prevention and Tobacco Control Act, the Secretary shall in accordance with this section assess user fees on, and collect such fees from, each manufacturer and importer of tobacco products subject to this chapter. The fees shall be assessed and collected with respect to each quarter of each fiscal year, and the total amount assessed and collected for a fiscal year shall be the amount specified in subsection (b)(1) for such year, subject to subsection (c).

(b) ASSESSMENT OF USER FEE.—

(1) AMOUNT OF ASSESSMENT.—The total amount of user fees authorized to be assessed and collected under subsection (a) for a fiscal year is the following, as applicable to the fiscal year involved:

(A) For fiscal year 2009, $85,000,000 (subject to subsection (e)).

(B) For fiscal year 2010, $235,000,000.

(C) For fiscal year 2011, $450,000,000.

(D) For fiscal year 2012, $477,000,000.

(E) For fiscal year 2013, $505,000,000.

(F) For fiscal year 2014, $534,000,000.

(G) For fiscal year 2015, $566,000,000.

(H) For fiscal year 2016, $599,000,000.

(I) For fiscal year 2017, $635,000,000.

(J) For fiscal year 2018, $672,000,000.

(K) For fiscal year 2019 and each subsequent fiscal year, $712,000,000.

(2) ALLOCATIONS OF ASSESSMENT BY CLASS OF TOBACCO PRODUCTS.—

(A) IN GENERAL.—The total user fees assessed and collected under subsection (a) each fiscal year with respect to each class of tobacco products shall be an amount that is equal to the applicable percentage of each class for the fiscal year multiplied by the amount specified in paragraph (1) for the fiscal year.

(B) APPLICABLE PERCENTAGE

(i) IN GENERAL.—For purposes of subparagraph (A), the applicable percentage for a fiscal year for each of the following classes of tobacco products shall be determined in accordance with clause (ii):

(I) Cigarettes.

(II) Cigars, including small cigars and cigars other than small cigars.

(III) Snuff.

(IV) Chewing tobacco.

(V) Pipe tobacco.

(VI) Roll-your-own tobacco.

(ii) ALLOCATIONS.—The applicable percentage of each class of tobacco product described in clause (i) for a fiscal year shall be the percentage determined under section 625(c) of Public Law 108–357 for each such class of product for such fiscal year.

(iii) REQUIREMENT OF REGULATIONS.—Notwithstanding clause (ii), no user fees shall be assessed on a class of tobacco products unless such class of tobacco products is listed in section 901(b) or is deemed by the Secretary in a regulation under section 901(b) to be subject to this chapter.

(iv) REALLOCATIONS.—In the case of a class of tobacco products that is not listed in section 901(b) or deemed by the Secretary in a regulation under section 901(b) to be subject to this chapter, the amount of user fees that would otherwise be assessed to such class of tobacco products shall be reallocated to the classes of tobacco products that are subject to this chapter in the same manner and based on the same relative percentages otherwise determined under clause (ii).

(3) DETERMINATION OF USER FEE BY COMPANY.—

(A) IN GENERAL.—The total user fee to be paid by each manufacturer or importer of a particular class of tobacco products shall be determined for each quarter by multiplying—

(i) such manufacturer's or importer's percentage share as determined under paragraph (4); by

(ii) the portion of the user fee amount for the current quarter to be assessed on all manufacturers and importers of such class of tobacco products as determined under paragraph (2).

(B) NO FEE IN EXCESS OF PERCENTAGE SHARE.—No manufacturer or importer of tobacco products shall be required to pay a user fee in excess of the percentage share of such manufacturer or importer.

(4) ALLOCATION OF ASSESSMENT WITHIN EACH CLASS OF TOBACCO PRODUCT.—The percentage share of each manufacturer or importer of a particular class of tobacco products of the total user fee to be paid by all manufacturers or importers of that class of tobacco products shall be the percentage determined for purposes of allocations under subsections (e) through (h) of section 625 of Public Law 108–357.

(5) ALLOCATION FOR CIGARS.—Notwithstanding paragraph (4), if a user fee assessment is imposed on cigars, the percentage share of each manufacturer or importer of cigars shall be based on the excise taxes paid by such manufacturer or importer during the prior fiscal year.

(6) TIMING OF ASSESSMENT.—The Secretary shall notify each manufacturer and importer of tobacco products subject to this section of the amount of the quarterly assessment imposed on such manufacturer or importer under this subsection for each quarter of each fiscal year. Such notifications shall occur not later than 30 days prior to the end of the quarter for which such assessment is made, and payments of all assessments shall be made by the last day of the quarter involved.

(7) MEMORANDUM OF UNDERSTANDING.—

(A) IN GENERAL.—The Secretary shall request the appropriate Federal agency to enter into a memorandum of understanding that provides for the regular and timely transfer from the head of such agency to the Secretary of the information described in paragraphs (2)(B)(ii) and (4) and all necessary information regarding all tobacco product manufacturers and importers required to pay user fees. The Secretary shall maintain all disclosure restrictions established by the head of such agency regarding the information provided under the memorandum of understanding.

(B) ASSURANCES.—Beginning not later than fiscal year 2015, and for each subsequent fiscal year, the Secretary shall ensure that the Food and Drug Administration is able to determine the applicable percentages described in paragraph (2) and the percentage shares described in paragraph (4). The Secretary may carry out this subparagraph by entering into a contract with the head of the Federal agency referred to in subparagraph (A) to continue to provide the necessary information.

(c) CREDITING AND AVAILABILITY OF FEES.—

(1) IN GENERAL.—Fees authorized under subsection (a) shall be collected and available for obligation only to the extent and in the amount provided in advance in appropriations Acts, subject to paragraph (2)(D). Such fees are authorized to remain available until expended. Such sums as may be necessary may be transferred from the Food and Drug Administration salaries and expenses appropriation account without fiscal year limitation to such appropriation account for salaries and expenses with such fiscal year limitation.

(2) AVAILABILITY.—

(A) IN GENERAL.—Fees appropriated under paragraph (3) are available only for the purpose of paying the costs of the activities of the Food and Drug Administration related to the regulation of tobacco products under this chapter and the Family Smoking Prevention and Tobacco Control Act (referred to in this subsection as "tobacco regulation activities"), except that such fees may be used for the reimbursement specified in subparagraph (C).

(B) PROHIBITION AGAINST USE OF OTHER FUNDS.—

(i) IN GENERAL.—Except as provided in clause (ii), fees collected under subsection (a) are the only funds authorized to be made available for tobacco regulation activities.

(ii) STARTUP COSTS.—Clause (i) does not apply until October 1, 2009. Until such date, any amounts available to the Food and Drug Administration (excluding user fees) shall be available and allocated as needed to pay the costs of tobacco regulation activities.

(C) REIMBURSEMENT OF START-UP AMOUNTS.—

(i) IN GENERAL.—Any amounts allocated for the start-up period pursuant to subparagraph (B)(ii) shall be reimbursed through any appropriated fees collected under subsection (a), in such manner as the Secretary determines appropriate to ensure that such allocation results in no net change in the total amount of funds otherwise available, for the period from October 1, 2008, through September 30, 2010, for Food and Drug Administration programs and activities (other than tobacco regulation activities) for such period.

(ii) TREATMENT OF REIMBURSED AMOUNTS.—Amounts reimbursed under clause (i) shall be available for the programs and activities for which funds allocated for the start-up period were available, prior to such allocation, until September 30, 2010, notwithstanding any otherwise applicable limits on amounts for such programs or activities for a fiscal year.

(D) FEE COLLECTED DURING START-UP PERIOD.—Notwithstanding the first sentence of paragraph (1), fees under subsection (a) may be collected through September 30, 2009 under subparagraph (B)(ii) and shall be available for obligation and remain available until expended. Such offsetting collections shall be credited to the salaries and expenses account of the Food and Drug Administration.

(E) OBLIGATION OF START-UP COSTS IN ANTICIPATION OF AVAILABLE FEE COLLECTIONS.—Notwithstanding any other provision of law, following the enactment of an appropriation for fees under this section for fiscal year 2010, or any portion thereof, obligations for costs of tobacco regulation activities during the start-up period may be incurred in anticipation of the receipt of offsetting fee collections through procedures specified in section 1534 of title 31, United States Code.

(3) AUTHORIZATION OF APPROPRIATIONS.—For fiscal year 2009 and each subsequent fiscal year, there is authorized to be appropriated for fees under this section an amount equal to the amount specified in subsection (b)(1) for the fiscal year.

(d) COLLECTION OF UNPAID FEES.—In any case where the Secretary does not receive payment of a fee assessed under subsection (a) within 30 days after it is due, such fee shall be treated as a claim of the United States Government subject to subchapter II of chapter 37 of title 31, United States Code.

(e) APPLICABILITY TO FISCAL YEAR 2009.—If the date of enactment of the Family Smoking Prevention and Tobacco Control Act occurs during fiscal year 2009, the following applies, subject to subsection (c):

(1) The Secretary shall determine the fees that would apply for a single quarter of such fiscal year according to the application of subsection (b) to the amount specified in paragraph (1)(A) of such subsection (referred to in this subsection as the "quarterly fee amounts").

(2) For the quarter in which such date of enactment occurs, the amount of fees assessed shall be a pro rata amount, determined according to the number of days remaining in the quarter (including such date of enactment) and according to the daily equivalent of the quarterly fee amounts. Fees assessed under the preceding sentence shall not be collected until the next quarter.

(3) For the quarter following the quarter to which paragraph (2) applies, the full quarterly fee amounts shall be assessed and collected, in addition to collection of the pro rata fees assessed under paragraph (2).

SEC. 920 [21 U.S.C. 387t]. LABELING, RECORDKEEPING, RECORDS INSPECTION

(a) ORIGIN LABELING.—

(1) REQUIREMENT.—Beginning 1 year after the date of enactment of the Family Smoking Prevention and Tobacco Control Act, the label, packaging, and shipping containers of tobacco products other than cigarettes for introduction or delivery for introduction into interstate commerce in the United States shall bear the statement "sale only allowed in the United States". Beginning 15 months after the issuance of the regulations required by section 4(d) of the Federal Cigarette Labeling and Advertising Act (15 U.S.C. 1333), as amended by section 201 of Family Smoking Prevention and Tobacco Control Act, the label, packaging, and shipping containers of cigarettes for introduction or delivery for introduction into interstate commerce in the United States shall bear the statement "Sale only allowed in the United States".

(2) EFFECTIVE DATE.—The effective date specified in paragraph (1) shall be with respect to the date of manufacture, provided that, in any case, beginning 30 days after such effective date, a manufacturer shall not introduce into the domestic commerce of the United States any product, irrespective of the date of manufacture, that is not in conformance with such paragraph.

(b) REGULATIONS CONCERNING RECORDKEEPING FOR TRACKING AND TRACING.—

(1) IN GENERAL.—The Secretary shall promulgate regulations regarding the establishment and maintenance of records by any person who manufactures, processes, transports, distributes, receives, packages, holds, exports, or imports tobacco products.

(2) INSPECTION.—In promulgating the regulations described in paragraph (1), the Secretary shall consider which records are needed for inspection to monitor the movement of tobacco products from the point of manufacture through distribution to retail outlets to assist in investigating potential illicit trade, smuggling, or counterfeiting of tobacco products.

(3) CODES.—The Secretary may require codes on the labels of tobacco products or other designs or devices for the purpose of tracking or tracing the tobacco product through the distribution system.

(4) SIZE OF BUSINESS.—The Secretary shall take into account the size of a business in promulgating regulations under this section.

(5) RECORDKEEPING BY RETAILERS.—The Secretary shall not require any retailer to maintain records relating to individual purchasers of tobacco products for personal consumption.

(c) RECORDS INSPECTION.—If the Secretary has a reasonable belief that a tobacco product is part of an illicit trade or smuggling or is a counterfeit product, each person who manufactures, processes, transports, distributes, receives, holds, packages, exports, or imports tobacco products shall, at the request of an officer or employee duly designated by the Secretary, permit such officer or employee, at reasonable times and within reasonable limits and in a reasonable manner, upon the presentation of appropriate credentials and a written notice to such person, to have access to and copy all records (including financial records) relating to such article that are needed to assist the Secretary in investigating potential illicit trade, smuggling, or counterfeiting of tobacco products. The Secretary shall not authorize an officer or employee of the government of any of the several States to exercise authority under the preceding sentence on Indian country without the express written consent of the Indian tribe involved.

(d) KNOWLEDGE OF ILLEGAL TRANSACTION.—

(1) NOTIFICATION.—If the manufacturer or distributor of a tobacco product has knowledge which reasonably supports the conclusion that a tobacco product manufactured or distributed by such manufacturer or distributor that has left the control of such person may be or has been—

(A) imported, exported, distributed, or offered for sale in interstate commerce by a person without paying duties or taxes required by law; or

(B) imported, exported, distributed, or diverted for possible illicit marketing, the manufacturer or distributor shall promptly notify the Attorney General and the Secretary of the Treasury of such knowledge.

(2) KNOWLEDGE DEFINED.—For purposes of this subsection, the term "knowledge" as applied to a manufacturer or distributor means—

(A) the actual knowledge that the manufacturer or distributor had; or

(B) the knowledge which a reasonable person would have had under like circumstances or which would have been obtained upon the exercise of due care.

(e) CONSULTATION.—In carrying out this section, the Secretary shall consult with the Attorney General of the United States and the Secretary of the Treasury, as appropriate.

CHAPTER X—MISCELLANEOUS

SEC. 1001 [21 U.S.C. 391]. SEPARABILITY CLAUSE

If any provision of this Act is declared unconstitutional, or the applicability there-of to any person or circumstances is held invalid, the constitutionality of the remainder of the Act and the applicability thereof to other persons and circumstances shall not be affected thereby.

SEC. 1002 [21 U.S.C. 392]. EFFECTIVE DATE AND REPEALS

(a) This Act shall take effect twelve months after the date of its enactment. The Federal Food and Drug Act of June 30, 1906, as amended (U.S.C., 1934 ed., title 21, secs.1–15), shall remain in force until such effective date, and except as otherwise provided in this subsection, is hereby repealed effective upon such date: Provided, That the provisions of section 701 shall become effective on the enactment of this Act, and thereafter the Secretary [of Agriculture] is authorized hereby to (1) conduct hearings and to promulgate regulations which shall become effective on or after the effective date of this Act as the Secretary [of Agriculture] shall direct, and (2) designate prior to the effective date of this Act food having common or usual names and exempt such food from the requirements of clause (2) of section 403(i) for a reasonable time to permit the formulation, promulgation, and effective application of definitions and standards of identity therefor as provided by section 401: Provided further, That sections 502(j), 505, and 601(a), and all other provisions of this Act to the extent that they may relate to the enforcement of such sections, shall take effect on the date of the enactment of this Act, except that in the case of a cosmetic to which the proviso of section 601(a) relates, such cosmetic shall not, prior to the ninetieth day after such date of enactment, be deemed adulterated by reason of the failure of its label to bear the legend prescribed in such proviso: Provided further, That the Act of March 4, 1923 (U.S.C., 1945 ed., title 21, sec. 321a; 32 Stat. 1500, ch. 268), defining butter and providing a standard therefor; the Act of July 24, 1919 (U.S.C., 1946 ed., title 21, sec. 321b; 41 Stat. 271, ch. 26), defining wrapped meats as in package form; and the amendment to the Food and Drug Act, section 10A, approved August 27, 1935 (U.S.C., 1946 ed., title 21, sec. 372a [49 Stat. 871, ch. 739]), shall remain in force and effect and be applicable to the provisions of this Act.

(b) Meats and meat food products shall be exempt from the provisions of this Act to the extent of the application or the extension thereto of the Meat Inspection Act, approved March 4, 1907, as amended (U.S.C., 1946 ed., title 21, secs. 71–96; 34 Stat. 1260 et seq.).

(c) Nothing contained in this Act shall be construed as in any way affecting, modifying, repealing, or superseding the provisions of section 351 of Public Health Service Act (relating to viruses, serums, toxins, and analogous products applicable to man); the virus, serum, toxin, and analogous products provisions, applicable to domestic animals, of the Act of Congress approved March 4, 1913 (37 Stat. 832–833); the Filled Cheese Act of June 6, 1896 (U.S.C., 1946 ed., title 26, ch. 17, secs.

2350–2362); the Filled Milk Act of March 4, 1923 (U.S.C. 1946 ed., title 21, ch. 3, secs. 61–64); or the Import Milk Act of February 15, 1927 (U.S.C., 1946 ed., title 21, ch. 4, secs. 141–149).

Sec. 1003 [21 U.S.C. 393]. FOOD AND DRUG ADMINISTRATION

(a) IN GENERAL.—There is established in the Department of Health and Human Services the Food and Drug Administration (hereinafter in this section referred to as the "Administration").

(b) MISSION.—The Administration shall—

(1) promote the public health by promptly and efficiently reviewing clinical research and taking appropriate action on the marketing of regulated products in a timely manner;

(2) with respect to such products, protect the public health by ensuring that—

(A) foods are safe, wholesome, sanitary, and properly labeled;

(B) human and veterinary drugs are safe and effective;

(C) there is reasonable assurance of the safety and effectiveness of devices intended for human use;

(D) cosmetics are safe and properly labeled; and

(E) public health and safety are protected from electronic product radiation;

(3) participate through appropriate processes with representatives of other countries to reduce the burden of regulation, harmonize regulatory requirements, and achieve appropriate reciprocal arrangements; and

(4) as determined to be appropriate by the Secretary, carry out paragraphs (1) through (3) in consultation with experts in science, medicine, and public health, and in cooperation with consumers, users, manufacturers, importers, packers, distributors, and retailers of regulated products.

(c) INTERAGENCY COLLABORATION.—The Secretary shall implement programs and policies that will foster collaboration between the Administration, the National Institutes of Health, and other science-based Federal agencies, to enhance the scientific and technical expertise available to the Secretary in the conduct of the duties of the Secretary with respect to the development, clinical investigation, evaluation, and postmarket monitoring of emerging medical therapies, including complementary therapies, and advances in nutrition and food science.

(d) COMMISSIONER.—

(1) APPOINTMENT.—There shall be in the Administration a Commissioner of Food and Drugs (hereinafter in this section referred to as the "Commissioner") who shall be appointed by the President by and with the advice and consent of the Senate.

(2) GENERAL POWERS.—The Secretary, through the Commissioner, shall be responsible for executing this Act and for—

(A) providing overall direction to the Food and Drug Administration and establishing and implementing general policies respecting the management and operation of programs and activities of the Food and Drug Administration;

(B) coordinating and overseeing the operation of all administrative entities within the Administration;

(C) research relating to foods, drugs, cosmetics, devices, and tobacco products in carrying out this Act;

(D) conducting educational and public information programs relating to the responsibilities of the Food and Drug Administration; and

(E) performing such other functions as the Secretary may prescribe.

(e) TECHNICAL AND SCIENTIFIC REVIEW GROUPS.—The Secretary through the Commissioner of Food and Drugs may, without regard to the provisions of title 5, United States Code, governing appointments in the competitive service and without regard to the provisions of chapter 51 and subchapter III of chapter 53 of such title relating to classification and General Schedule pay rates, establish such technical and scientific review groups as are needed to carry out the functions of the Administration, including functions under the Federal Food, Drug, and Cosmetic Act, and appoint and pay the members of such groups, except that officers and employees of the United States shall not receive additional compensation for service as members of such groups.

(f) AGENCY PLAN FOR STATUTORY COMPLIANCE.—

(1) IN GENERAL.—Not later than 1 year after the date of enactment of the Food and Drug Administration Modernization Act of 1997, the Secretary, after consultation with appropriate scientific and academic experts, health care professionals, representatives of patient and consumer advocacy groups, and the regulated industry, shall develop and publish in the Federal Register a plan bringing the Secretary into compliance with each of the obligations of the Secretary under this Act. The Secretary shall review the plan biannually and shall revise the plan as necessary, in consultation with such persons.

(2) OBJECTIVES OF AGENCY PLAN.—The plan required by paragraph (1) shall establish objectives and mechanisms to achieve such objectives, including objectives related to—

(A) maximizing the availability and clarity of information about the process for review of applications and submissions (including petitions, notifications, and any other similar forms of request) made under this Act;

(B) maximizing the availability and clarity of information for consumers and patients concerning new products;

747

(C) implementing inspection and postmarket monitoring provisions of this Act;

(D) ensuring access to the scientific and technical expertise needed by the Secretary to meet obligations described in paragraph (1);

(E) establishing mechanisms, by July 1, 1999, for meeting the time periods specified in this Act for the review of all applications and submissions described in subparagraph (A) and submitted after the date of enactment of the Food and Drug Administration Modernization Act of 1997; and

(F) eliminating backlogs in the review of applications and submissions described in subparagraph (A), by January 1, 2000.

(g) ANNUAL REPORT.—The Secretary shall annually prepare and publish in the Federal Register and solicit public comment on a report that—

(1) provides detailed statistical information on the performance of the Secretary under the plan described in subsection (f);

(2) compares such performance of the Secretary with the objectives of the plan and with the statutory obligations of the Secretary; and

(3) identifies any regulatory policy that has a significant negative impact on compliance with any objective of the plan or any statutory obligation and sets forth any proposed revision to any such regulatory policy.

(h) ANNUAL REPORT REGARDING FOOD.—Not later than February 1 of each year, the Secretary shall submit to Congress a report, including efforts to coordinate and cooperate with other Federal agencies with responsibilities for food inspections, regarding—

(1) information about food facilities including—

(A) the appropriations used to inspect facilities registered pursuant to section 415 in the previous fiscal year;

(B) the average cost of both a non-high-risk food facility inspection and a high-risk food facility inspection, if such a difference exists, in the previous fiscal year;

(C) the number of domestic facilities and the number of foreign facilities registered pursuant to section 415 that the Secretary inspected in the previous fiscal year;

(D) the number of domestic facilities and the number of foreign facilities registered pursuant to section 415 that were scheduled for inspection in the previous fiscal year and which the Secretary did not inspect in such year;

(E) the number of high-risk facilities identified pursuant to section 421 that the Secretary inspected in the previous fiscal year; and

(F) the number of high-risk facilities identified pursuant to section 421 that were scheduled for inspection in the previous fiscal year and which the Secretary did not inspect in such year.

(2) information about food imports including—

(A) the number of lines of food imported into the United States that the Secretary physically inspected or sampled in the previous fiscal year;

(B) the number of lines of food imported into the United States that the Secretary did not physically inspect or sample in the previous fiscal year; and

(C) the average cost of physically inspecting or sampling a line of food subject to this Act that is imported or offered for import into the United States; and

(3) information on the foreign offices of the Food and Drug Administration including—

(A) the number of foreign offices established; and

(B) the number of personnel permanently stationed in each foreign office.

(i) PUBLIC AVAILABILITY OF ANNUAL FOOD REPORTS.—The Secretary shall make the reports required under subsection (h) available to the public on the Internet Web site of the Food and Drug Administration.

SEC. 1003a[89] [21 U.S.C. 393a]. OFFICE OF PEDIATRIC THERAPEUTIC

(a) ESTABLISHMENT.—The Secretary of Health and Human Services shall establish an Office of Pediatric Therapeutics within the Food and Drug Administration.

(b) DUTIES.—The Office of Pediatric Therapeutics shall be responsible for coordination and facilitation of all activities of the Food and Drug Administration that may have any effect on a pediatric population or the practice of pediatrics or may in any other way involve pediatric issues, including increasing pediatric access to medical devices.

(c) STAFF.—The staff of the Office of Pediatric Therapeutics shall coordinate with employees of the Department of Health and Human Services who exercise responsibilities relating to pediatric therapeutics and shall include—

(1) one or more additional individuals with expertise concerning ethical issues presented by the conduct of clinical research in the pediatric population; and

(2) one or more additional individuals with expertise in pediatrics as may be necessary to perform the activities described in subsection (b).

89. Not officially enacted as part of the Federal Food, Drug, and Cosmetic Act, but designated as section 1003a of the Act on the FDA website.

SEC. 1004 [21 U.S.C. 394]. SCIENTIFIC REVIEW GROUPS

Without regard to the provisions of title 5, United States Code, governing appointments in the competitive service and without regard to the provisions of chapter 51 and subchapter III of chapter 53 of such title relating to classification and General Schedule pay rates, the Commissioner of Food and Drugs may—

(1) establish such technical and scientific review groups as are needed to carry out the functions of the Food and Drug Administration (including functions prescribed under this Act); and

(2) appoint and pay the members of such groups, except that officers and employees of the United States shall not receive additional compensation for service as members of such groups.

SEC. 1005 [21 U.S.C. 395]. LOAN REPAYMENT PROGRAM

(a) IN GENERAL.—

(1) AUTHORITY FOR PROGRAM.—Subject to paragraph (2), the Secretary shall carry out a program of entering into contracts with appropriately qualified health professionals under which such health professionals agree to conduct research, as employees of the Food and Drug Administration, in consideration of the Federal Government agreeing to repay, for each year of such service, not more than $20,000 of the principal and interest of the educational loans of such health professionals.

(2) LIMITATION.—The Secretary may not enter into an agreement with a health professional pursuant to paragraph (1) unless such professional—

(A) has a substantial amount of educational loans relative to income; and

(B) agrees to serve as an employee of the Food and Drug Administration for purposes of paragraph (1) for a period of not less than 3 years.

(b) APPLICABILITY OF CERTAIN PROVISIONS.—With respect to the National Health Service Corps Loan Repayment Program established in subpart III of part D of title III of the Public Health Service Act, the provisions of such subpart shall, except as inconsistent with subsection (a) of this section, apply to the program established in such subsection in the same manner and to the same extent as such provisions apply to the National Health Service Corps Loan Repayment Program.

(c) AUTHORIZATION OF APPROPRIATIONS.—For the purpose of carrying out this section, there are authorized to be appropriated such sums as may be necessary for each of the fiscal years 1994 through 1996.

SEC. 1006 [21 U.S.C. 396]. PRACTICE OF MEDICINE

Nothing in this Act shall be construed to limit or interfere with the authority of a health care practitioner to prescribe or administer any legally marketed device to a patient for any condition or disease within a legitimate health care practitioner-patient relationship. This section shall not limit any existing authority of the Secretary to establish and enforce restrictions on the sale or distribution, or in the labeling, of a device that are part of a determination of substantial equivalence, established as a condition of approval, or promulgated through regulations. Further, this section shall not change any existing prohibition on the promotion of unapproved uses of legally marketed devices.

Sec. 1007 [21 U.S.C. 397]. CONTRACTS FOR EXPERT REVIEW

(a) In General.—

(1) Authority.—The Secretary may enter into a contract with any organization or any individual (who is not an employee of the Department) with relevant expertise, to review and evaluate, for the purpose of making recommendations to the Secretary on, part or all of any application or submission (including a petition, notification, and any other similar form of request) made under this Act for the approval or classification of an article or made under section 351(a) of the Public Health Service Act (42 U.S.C. 262(a)) with respect to a biological product. Any such contract shall be subject to the requirements of section 708 relating to the confidentiality of information.

(2) Increased efficiency and expertise through contracts.—The Secretary may use the authority granted in paragraph (1) whenever the Secretary determines that use of a contract described in paragraph (1) will improve the timeliness of the review of an application or submission described in paragraph (1), unless using such authority would reduce the quality, or unduly increase the cost, of such review. The Secretary may use such authority whenever the Secretary determines that use of such a contract will improve the quality of the review of an application or submission described in paragraph (1), unless using such authority would unduly increase the cost of such review. Such improvement in timeliness or quality may include providing the Secretary increased scientific or technical expertise that is necessary to review or evaluate new therapies and technologies.

(b) Review of Expert Review.—

(1) In general.—Subject to paragraph (2), the official of the Food and Drug Administration responsible for any matter for which expert review is used pursuant to subsection (a) shall review the recommendations of the organization or individual who conducted the expert review and shall make a final decision regarding the matter in a timely manner.

(2) Limitation.—A final decision by the Secretary on any such application or submission shall be made within the applicable prescribed time period for review of the matter as set forth in this Act or in the Public Health Service Act (42 U.S.C. 201 et seq.).

SEC. 1008 [21 U.S.C. 398]. NOTICES TO STATES REGARDING IMPORTED FOOD

(a) IN GENERAL.—If the Secretary has credible evidence or information indicating that a shipment of imported food or portion thereof presents a threat of serious adverse health consequences or death to humans or animals, the Secretary shall provide notice regarding such threat to the States in which the food is held or will be held, and to the States in which the manufacturer, packer, or distributor of the food is located, to the extent that the Secretary has knowledge of which States are so involved. in providing notice to a State, the Secretary shall request the State to take such action as the State considers appropriate, if any, to protect the public health regarding the food involved.

(b) RULE OF CONSTRUCTION.—Subsection (a) may not be construed as limiting the authority of the Secretary with respect to food under any other provision of this Act.

SEC. 1009 [21 U.S.C. 399]. GRANTS TO ENHANCE FOOD SAFETY

(a) IN GENERAL.—The Secretary is authorized to make grants to eligible entities to—

(1) undertake examinations, inspections, and investigations, and related food safety activities under section 702;

(2) train to the standards of the Secretary for the examination, inspection, and investigation of food manufacturing, processing, packing, holding, distribution, and importation, including as such examination, inspection, and investigation relate to retail food establishments;

(3) build the food safety capacity of the laboratories of such eligible entity, including the detection of zoonotic diseases;

(4) build the infrastructure and capacity of the food safety programs of such eligible entity to meet the standards as outlined in the grant application; and

(5) take appropriate action to protect the public health in response to—

(A) a notification under section 1008, including planning and otherwise preparing to take such action; or

(B) a recall of food under this Act.

(b) ELIGIBLE ENTITIES; APPLICATION.—

(1) IN GENERAL.—In this section, the term "eligible entity" means an entity—

(A) that is—

(i) a State;

(ii) a locality;

(iii) a territory;

(iv) an Indian tribe (as defined in section 4(e) of the Indian Self–Determination and Education Assistance Act); or

(v) a nonprofit food safety training entity that collaborates with 1 or more institutions of higher education; and

(B) that submits an application to the Secretary at such time, in such manner, and including such information as the Secretary may reasonably require.

(2) CONTENTS.—Each application submitted under paragraph (1) shall include—

(A) an assurance that the eligible entity has developed plans to engage in the types of activities described in subsection (a);

(B) a description of the types of activities to be funded by the grant;

(C) an itemization of how grant funds received under this section will be expended;

(D) a description of how grant activities will be monitored; and

(E) an agreement by the eligible entity to report information required by the Secretary to conduct evaluations under this section.

(c) LIMITATIONS.—The funds provided under subsection (a) shall be available to an eligible entity that receives a grant under this section only to the extent such entity funds the food safety programs of such entity independently of any grant under this section in each year of the grant at a level equal to the level of such funding in the previous year, increased by the Consumer Price Index. Such non-Federal matching funds may be provided directly or through donations from public or private entities and may be in cash or in-kind, fairly evaluated, including plant, equipment, or services.

(d) ADDITIONAL AUTHORITY.—The Secretary may—

(1) award a grant under this section in each subsequent fiscal year without reapplication for a period of not more than 3 years, provided the requirements of subsection (c) are met for the previous fiscal year; and

(2) award a grant under this section in a fiscal year for which the requirement of subsection (c) has not been met only if such requirement was not met because such funding was diverted for response to 1 or more natural disasters or in other extenuating circumstances that the Secretary may determine appropriate.

(e) DURATION OF AWARDS.—The Secretary may award grants to an individual grant recipient under this section for periods of not more than 3 years. In the event the Secretary conducts a program evaluation, funding in the second year or third year of the grant, where applicable, shall be contingent on a successful program evaluation by the Secretary after the first year.

(f) Progress and Evaluation.—

(1) In general.—The Secretary shall measure the status and success of each grant program authorized under the FDA Food Safety Modernization Act (and any amendment made by such Act), including the grant program under this section. A recipient of a grant described in the preceding sentence shall, at the end of each grant year, provide the Secretary with information on how grant funds were spent and the status of the efforts by such recipient to enhance food safety. To the extent practicable, the Secretary shall take the performance of such a grant recipient into account when determining whether to continue funding for such recipient.

(2) No duplication.—In carrying out paragraph (1), the Secretary shall not duplicate the efforts of the Secretary under other provisions of this Act or the FDA Food Safety Modernization Act that require measurement and review of the activities of grant recipients under either such Act.

(g) Supplement Not Supplant.—Grant funds received under this section shall be used to supplement, and not supplant, non-Federal funds and any other Federal funds available to carry out the activities described in this section.

(h) Authorization of Appropriations.—For the purpose of making grants under this section, there are authorized to be appropriated such sums as may be necessary for fiscal years 2011 through 2015.

Sec. 1010 [21 U.S.C. 399a]. Office of the Chief Scientist

(a) Establishment; Appointment.—The Secretary shall establish within the Office of the Commissioner an office to be known as the Office of the Chief Scientist. The Secretary shall appoint a Chief Scientist to lead such Office.

(b) Duties of the Office.—The Office of the Chief Scientist shall—

(1) oversee, coordinate, and ensure quality and regulatory focus of the intramural research programs of the Food and Drug Administration;

(2) track and, to the extent necessary, coordinate intramural research awards made by each center of the Administration or science-based office within the Office of the Commissioner, and ensure that there is no duplication of research efforts supported by the Reagan–Udall Foundation for the Food and Drug Administration;

(3) develop and advocate for a budget to support intramural research;

(4) develop a peer review process by which intramural research can be evaluated;

(5) identify and solicit intramural research proposals from across the Food and Drug Administration through an advisory board composed of employees of the Administration that shall include—

(A) representatives of each of the centers and the science-based offices within the Office of the Commissioner; and

(B) experts on trial design, epidemiology, demographics, pharmacovigilance, basic science, and public health; and

(6) develop postmarket safety performance measures that are as measurable and rigorous as the ones already developed for premarket review.

SEC. 1011 [21 U.S.C. 399b]. OFFICE OF WOMEN'S HEALTH

(a) ESTABLISHMENT.—There is established within the Office of the Commissioner, an office to be known as the Office of Women's Health (referred to in this section as the "Office"). The Office shall be headed by a director who shall be appointed by the Commissioner of Food and Drugs.

(b) PURPOSE.—The Director of the Office shall—

(1) report to the Commissioner of Food and Drugs on current Food and Drug Administration (referred to in this section as the "Administration") levels of activity regarding women's participation in clinical trials and the analysis of data by sex in the testing of drugs, medical devices, and biological products across, where appropriate, age, biological, and sociocultural contexts;

(2) establish short-range and long-range goals and objectives within the Administration for issues of particular concern to women's health within the jurisdiction of the Administration, including, where relevant and appropriate, adequate inclusion of women and analysis of data by sex in Administration protocols and policies;

(3) provide information to women and health care providers on those areas in which differences between men and women exist;

(4) consult with pharmaceutical, biologics, and device manufacturers, health professionals with expertise in women's issues, consumer organizations, and women's health professionals on Administration policy with regard to women;

(5) make annual estimates of funds needed to monitor clinical trials and analysis of data by sex in accordance with needs that are identified; and

(6) serve as a member of the Department of Health and Human Services Coordinating Committee on Women's Health (established under section 229(b)(4) of the Public Health Service Act).

(c) AUTHORIZATION OF APPROPRIATIONS.—For the purpose of carrying out this section, there are authorized to be appropriated such sums as may be necessary for each of the fiscal years 2010 through 2014.

SEC. 1011[90] [21 U.S.C. 399c]. IMPROVING THE TRAINING OF STATE, LOCAL, TERRITORIAL, AND TRIBAL FOOD SAFETY OFFICIALS

(a) TRAINING.—The Secretary shall set standards and administer training and education programs for the employees of State, local, territorial, and tribal food safety officials relating to the regulatory responsibilities and policies established by this Act, including programs for—

(1) scientific training;

(2) training to improve the skill of officers and employees authorized to conduct inspections under sections 702 and 704;

(3) training to achieve advanced product or process specialization in such inspections;

(4) training that addresses best practices;

(5) training in administrative process and procedure and integrity issues;

(6) training in appropriate sampling and laboratory analysis methodology; and

(7) training in building enforcement actions following inspections, examinations, testing, and investigations.

(b) PARTNERSHIPS WITH STATE AND LOCAL OFFICIALS.—

(1) IN GENERAL.—The Secretary, pursuant to a contract or memorandum of understanding between the Secretary and the head of a State, local, territorial, or tribal department or agency, is authorized and encouraged to conduct examinations, testing, and investigations for the purposes of determining compliance with the food safety provisions of this Act through the officers and employees of such State, local, territorial, or tribal department or agency.

(2) CONTENT.—A contract or memorandum described under paragraph (1) shall include provisions to ensure adequate training of such officers and employees to conduct such examinations, testing, and investigations. The contract or memorandum shall contain provisions regarding reimbursement. Such provisions may, at the sole discretion of the head of the other department or agency, require reimbursement, in whole or in part, from the Secretary for the examinations, testing, or investigations performed pursuant to this section by the officers or employees of the State, territorial, or tribal department or agency.

(3) EFFECT.—Nothing in this subsection shall be construed to limit the authority of the Secretary under section 702.

(c) EXTENSION SERVICE.—The Secretary shall ensure coordination with the extension activities of the National Institute of Food and Agriculture of the Department of Agriculture in advising producers and small processors transitioning into new prac-

90. As numbered by 111 Pub. L. No. 353 (Jan. 4, 2011). Probably is supposed to be "Sec. 1012."

tices required as a result of the enactment of the FDA Food Safety Modernization Act and assisting regulated industry with compliance with such Act.

(d) NATIONAL FOOD SAFETY TRAINING, EDUCATION, EXTENSION, OUTREACH AND TECH-NICAL ASSISTANCE PROGRAM.—

(1) IN GENERAL.—In order to improve food safety and reduce the incidence of foodborne illness, the Secretary shall, not later than 180 days after the date of enactment of the FDA Food Safety Modernization Act, enter into one or more memoranda of understanding, or enter into other cooperative agreements, with the Secretary of Agriculture to establish a competitive grant program within the National Institute for Food and Agriculture to provide food safety training, education, extension, outreach, and technical assistance to—

(A) owners and operators of farms;

(B) small food processors; and

(C) small fruit and vegetable merchant wholesalers.

(2) IMPLEMENTATION.—The competitive grant program established under paragraph (1) shall be carried out in accordance with section 405 of the Agricultural Research, Extension, and Education Reform Act of 1998.

(e) AUTHORIZATION OF APPROPRIATIONS.—There are authorized to be appropriated such sums as may be necessary to carry out this section for fiscal years 2011 through 2015.

SEC. 1012[91] [21 U.S.C. 399d]. EMPLOYEE PROTECTIONS

(a) IN GENERAL.—No entity engaged in the manufacture, processing, packing, transporting, distribution, reception, holding, or importation of food may discharge an employee or otherwise discriminate against an employee with respect to compensation, terms, conditions, or privileges of employment because the employee, whether at the employee's initiative or in the ordinary course of the employee's duties (or any person acting pursuant to a request of the employee)—

(1) provided, caused to be provided, or is about to provide or cause to be provided to the employer, the Federal Government, or the attorney general of a State information relating to any violation of, or any act or omission the employee reasonably believes to be a violation of any provision of this Act or any order, rule, regulation, standard, or ban under this Act, or any order, rule, regulation, standard, or ban under this Act;

(2) testified or is about to testify in a proceeding concerning such violation;

(3) assisted or participated or is about to assist or participate in such a proceeding; or

91. As numbered by 111 Pub. L. No. 353 (Jan. 4, 2011). Probably is supposed to be "Sec. 1013."

(4) objected to, or refused to participate in, any activity, policy, practice, or assigned task that the employee (or other such person) reasonably believed to be in violation of any provision of this Act, or any order, rule, regulation, standard, or ban under this Act.

(b) PROCESS.—

(1) IN GENERAL.—A person who believes that he or she has been discharged or otherwise discriminated against by any person in violation of subsection (a) may, not later than 180 days after the date on which such violation occurs, file (or have any person file on his or her behalf) a complaint with the Secretary of Labor (referred to in this section as the "Secretary") alleging such discharge or discrimination and identifying the person responsible for such act. Upon receipt of such a complaint, the Secretary shall notify, in writing, the person named in the complaint of the filing of the complaint, of the allegations contained in the complaint, of the substance of evidence supporting the complaint, and of the opportunities that will be afforded to such person under paragraph (2).

(2) INVESTIGATION.—

(A) IN GENERAL.—Not later than 60 days after the date of receipt of a complaint filed under paragraph (1) and after affording the complainant and the person named in the complaint an opportunity to submit to the Secretary a written response to the complaint and an opportunity to meet with a representative of the Secretary to present statements from witnesses, the Secretary shall initiate an investigation and determine whether there is reasonable cause to believe that the complaint has merit and notify, in writing, the complainant and the person alleged to have committed a violation of subsection (a) of the Secretary's findings.

(B) REASONABLE CAUSE FOUND; PRELIMINARY ORDER.—If the Secretary concludes that there is reasonable cause to believe that a violation of subsection (a) has occurred, the Secretary shall accompany the Secretary's findings with a preliminary order providing the relief prescribed by paragraph (3)(B). Not later than 30 days after the date of notification of findings under this paragraph, the person alleged to have committed the violation or the complainant may file objections to the findings or preliminary order, or both, and request a hearing on the record. The filing of such objections shall not operate to stay any reinstatement remedy contained in the preliminary order. Any such hearing shall be conducted expeditiously. If a hearing is not requested in such 30–day period, the preliminary order shall be deemed a final order that is not subject to judicial review.

(C) DISMISSAL OF COMPLAINT.—

(i) STANDARD FOR COMPLAINANT.—The Secretary shall dismiss a complaint filed under this subsection and shall not conduct an investigation otherwise required under subparagraph (A) unless the complainant makes a prima facie showing that any behavior described in paragraphs (1) through (4) of subsection (a) was a contributing factor in the unfavorable personnel action alleged in the complaint.

(ii) STANDARD FOR EMPLOYER.—Notwithstanding a finding by the Secretary that the complainant has made the showing required under clause (i), no investigation otherwise required under subparagraph (A) shall be conducted if the employer demonstrates, by clear and convincing evidence, that the employer would have taken the same unfavorable personnel action in the absence of that behavior.

(iii) VIOLATION STANDARD.—The Secretary may determine that a violation of subsection (a) has occurred only if the complainant demonstrates that any behavior described in paragraphs (1) through (4) of subsection (a) was a contributing factor in the unfavorable personnel action alleged in the complaint.

(iv) RELIEF STANDARD.—Relief may not be ordered under subparagraph (A) if the employer demonstrates by clear and convincing evidence that the employer would have taken the same unfavorable personnel action in the absence of that behavior.

(3) FINAL ORDER.—

(A) IN GENERAL.—Not later than 120 days after the date of conclusion of any hearing under paragraph (2), the Secretary shall issue a final order providing the relief prescribed by this paragraph or denying the complaint. At any time before issuance of a final order, a proceeding under this subsection may be terminated on the basis of a settlement agreement entered into by the Secretary, the complainant, and the person alleged to have committed the violation.

(B) CONTENT OF ORDER.—If, in response to a complaint filed under paragraph (1), the Secretary determines that a violation of subsection (a) has occurred, the Secretary shall order the person who committed such violation—

(i) to take affirmative action to abate the violation;

(ii) to reinstate the complainant to his or her former position together with compensation (including back pay) and restore the terms, conditions, and privileges associated with his or her employment; and

(iii) to provide compensatory damages to the complainant.

(C) PENALTY.—If such an order is issued under this paragraph, the Secretary, at the request of the complainant, shall assess against the person against whom the order is issued a sum equal to the aggregate amount of all costs and expenses (including attorneys' and expert witness fees) reasonably incurred, as determined by the Secretary, by the complainant for, or in connection with, the bringing of the complaint upon which the order was issued.

(D) Bad faith claim.—If the Secretary finds that a complaint under paragraph (1) is frivolous or has been brought in bad faith, the Secretary may award to the prevailing employer a reasonable attorneys' fee, not exceeding $1,000, to be paid by the complainant.

(4) Action in court.—

(A) In general.—If the Secretary has not issued a final decision within 210 days after the filing of the complaint, or within 90 days after receiving a written determination, the complainant may bring an action at law or equity for de novo review in the appropriate district court of the United States with jurisdiction, which shall have jurisdiction over such an action without regard to the amount in controversy, and which action shall, at the request of either party to such action, be tried by the court with a jury. The proceedings shall be governed by the same legal burdens of proof specified in paragraph (2)(C).

(B) Relief.—The court shall have jurisdiction to grant all relief necessary to make the employee whole, including injunctive relief and compensatory damages, including—

(i) reinstatement with the same seniority status that the employee would have had, but for the discharge or discrimination;

(ii) the amount of back pay, with interest; and

(iii) compensation for any special damages sustained as a result of the discharge or discrimination, including litigation costs, expert witness fees, and reasonable attorney's fees.

(5) Review.—

(A) In general.—Unless the complainant brings an action under paragraph (4), any person adversely affected or aggrieved by a final order issued under paragraph (3) may obtain review of the order in the United States Court of Appeals for the circuit in which the violation, with respect to which the order was issued, allegedly occurred or the circuit in which the complainant resided on the date of such violation. The petition for review must be filed not later than 60 days after the date of the issuance of the final order of the Secretary. Review shall conform to chapter 7 of title 5, United States Code. The commencement of proceedings under this subparagraph shall not, unless ordered by the court, operate as a stay of the order.

(B) No judicial review.—An order of the Secretary with respect to which review could have been obtained under subparagraph (A) shall not be subject to judicial review in any criminal or other civil proceeding.

(6) Failure to comply with order.—Whenever any person has failed to comply with an order issued under paragraph (3), the Secretary may file a civil action in the United States district court for the district in which the violation was found to occur, or in the United States district court for the District of Columbia, to

enforce such order. In actions brought under this paragraph, the district courts shall have jurisdiction to grant all appropriate relief including, but not limited to, injunctive relief and compensatory damages.

(7) CIVIL ACTION TO REQUIRE COMPLIANCE.—

(A) IN GENERAL.—A person on whose behalf an order was issued under paragraph (3) may commence a civil action against the person to whom such order was issued to require compliance with such order. The appropriate United States district court shall have jurisdiction, without regard to the amount in controversy or the citizenship of the parties, to enforce such order.

(B) AWARD.—The court, in issuing any final order under this paragraph, may award costs of litigation (including reasonable attorneys' and expert witness fees) to any party whenever the court determines such award is appropriate.

(c) EFFECT OF SECTION.—

(1) OTHER LAWS.—Nothing in this section preempts or diminishes any other safeguards against discrimination, demotion, discharge, suspension, threats, harassment, reprimand, retaliation, or any other manner of discrimination provided by Federal or State law.

(2) RIGHTS OF EMPLOYEES.—Nothing in this section shall be construed to diminish the rights, privileges, or remedies of any employee under any Federal or State law or under any collective bargaining agreement. The rights and remedies in this section may not be waived by any agreement, policy, form, or condition of employment.

(d) ENFORCEMENT.—Any nondiscretionary duty imposed by this section shall be enforceable in a mandamus proceeding brought under section 1361 of title 28, United States Code.

(e) LIMITATION.—Subsection (a) shall not apply with respect to an employee of an entity engaged in the manufacture, processing, packing, transporting, distribution, reception, holding, or importation of food who, acting without direction from such entity (or such entity's agent), deliberately causes a violation of any requirement relating to any violation or alleged violation of any order, rule, regulation, standard, or ban under this Act.

SEC. 1126 [21 U.S.C. 399e]. NANOTECHNOLOGY

(a) IN GENERAL.—The Secretary of Health and Human Services (referred to in this section as the "Secretary") shall intensify and expand activities related to enhancing scientific knowledge regarding nanomaterials included or intended for inclusion in products regulated under the Federal Food, Drug, and Cosmetic Act (21 U.S.C. 301 et seq.) or other statutes administered by the Food and Drug Administration, to address issues relevant to the regulation of those products, including the potential toxicology of such nanomaterials, the potential benefit of new therapies derived from nanotechnology, the effects of such nanomaterials on biological systems, and the interaction of such nanomaterials with biological systems.

(b) ACTIVITIES.—In conducting activities related to nanotechnology, the Secretary may—

(1) assess scientific literature and data on general nanomaterials interactions with biological systems and on specific nanomaterials of concern to the Food and Drug Administration;

(2) in cooperation with other Federal agencies, develop and organize information using databases and models that will facilitate the identification of generalized principles and characteristics regarding the behavior of classes of nanomaterials with biological systems;

(3) promote Food and Drug Administration programs and participate in collaborative efforts, to further the understanding of the science of novel properties of nanomaterials that might contribute to toxicity;

(4) promote and participate in collaborative efforts to further the understanding of measurement and detection methods for nanomaterials;

(5) collect, synthesize, interpret, and disseminate scientific information and data related to the interactions of nano-materials with biological systems;

(6) build scientific expertise on nanomaterials within the Food and Drug Administration, including field and laboratory expertise, for monitoring the production and presence of nano-materials in domestic and imported products regulated under this Act;

(7) ensure ongoing training, as well as dissemination of new information within the centers of the Food and Drug Administration, and more broadly across the Food and Drug Administration, to ensure timely, informed consideration of the most current science pertaining to nanomaterials;

(8) encourage the Food and Drug Administration to participate in international and national consensus standards activities pertaining to nanomaterials; and

(9) carry out other activities that the Secretary determines are necessary and consistent with the purposes described in paragraphs (1) through (8).

SEC. 1138 [21 U.S.C. 399f]. ENSURING ADEQUATE INFORMATION REGARDING PHARMACEUTICALS FOR ALL POPULATIONS, PARTICULARLY UNDERREPRESENTED SUBPOPULATIONS, INCLUDING RACIAL SUBGROUPS

(a) COMMUNICATION PLAN.—The Secretary of Health and Human Services (referred to in this section as the "Secretary"), acting through the Commissioner of Food and Drugs, shall review and modify, as necessary, the Food and Drug Administration's communication plan to inform and educate health care providers and patients on the benefits and risks of medical products, with particular focus on underrepresented subpopulations, including racial subgroups.

(b) CONTENT.—The communication plan described under subsection (a)—

(1) shall take into account—

(A) the goals and principles set forth in the Strategic Action Plan to Reduce Racial and Ethnic Health Disparities issued by the Department of Health and Human Services;

(B) the nature of the medical product; and

(C) health and disease information available from other agencies within such Department, as well as any new means of communicating health and safety benefits and risks related to medical products;

(2) taking into account the nature of the medical product, shall address the best strategy for communicating safety alerts, labeled indications for the medical products, changes to the label or labeling of medical products (including black-box warnings, health advisories, health and safety benefits and risks), particular actions to be taken by health care professionals and patients, any information identifying particular subpopulations, and any other relevant information as determined appropriate to enhance communication, including varied means of electronic communication; and

(3) shall include a process for implementation of any improvements or other modifications determined to be necessary.

(c) ISSUANCE AND POSTING OF COMMUNICATION PLAN.—

(1) COMMUNICATION PLAN.—Not later than 1 year after the date of enactment of this Act, the Secretary, acting through the Commissioner of Food and Drugs, shall issue the communication plan described under this section.

(2) POSTING OF COMMUNICATION PLAN ON THE OFFICE OF MINORITY HEALTH WEB SITE.—The Secretary, acting through the Commissioner of Food and Drugs, shall publicly post the communication plan on the Internet Web site of the Office of Minority Health of the Food and Drug Administration, and provide links to any other appropriate Internet Web site, and seek public comment on the communication plan.

FEDERAL FOOD AND DRUGS ACT OF 1906[1]

Pub. L. No. 59–384, 34 Stat. 768 (1906)

[The 1906 Act was repealed by Section 902(a) of the 1938 Act. The 1906 Act is reproduced in the form in which it was enacted, *with subsequent significant amendments indicated in italics*. The numbers in brackets refer to the corresponding sections in the U.S. Code, the first edition of which appeared in 1926.]

An Act for preventing the manufacture, sale, or transportation of adulterated or misbranded or poisonous or deleterious foods, drugs, medicines, and liquors, and for regulating traffic therein, and for other purposes.

Be it enacted by the Senate and House of Representatives of the United States of America in Congress assembled,

SEC. 1 [21 U.S.C. 1]. MANUFACTURE OF ADULTERATED FOODS OR DRUGS

That it shall be unlawful for any person to manufacture within any Territory or the District of Columbia any article of food or drug which is adulterated or misbranded, within the meaning of this Act; and any person who shall violate any of the provisions of this section shall be guilty of a misdemeanor, and for each offense shall, upon conviction thereof, be fined not to exceed five hundred dollars or shall be sentenced to one year's imprisonment, both such fine and imprisonment, in the discretion of the court, and for each subsequent offense and conviction thereof shall be fined not less than one thousand dollars or sentenced to one year's imprisonment, or both such fine and imprisonment, in the discretion of the court.

SEC. 2 [21 U.S.C. 2]. INTERSTATE COMMERCE OF ADULTERATED GOODS

That the introduction into any State or Territory or the District of Columbia from any other State or Territory or the District of Columbia, or from any foreign country, or shipment to any foreign country of any article of food or drugs which is adulterated or misbranded, within the meaning of this Act, is hereby prohibited; and any person who shall ship or deliver for shipment from any State or Territory or the District of Columbia to any other State or Territory or the District of Columbia, or to a foreign country, or who shall receive in any State or Territory or the District of Columbia from any other State or Territory or the District of Columbia, or foreign country, and having so received, shall deliver, in original unbroken packages, for pay or otherwise, or offer to deliver to any other person, any such article so adulterated or misbranded within the meaning of this Act, or any person who shall sell or offer for sale in the District of Columbia or the Territories of the United States any such adulterated or misbranded foods or drugs or export or offer to export the same to any foreign country, shall be guilty of a misdemeanor, and for such offense be

---

1. Also known as "The Pure Food and Drugs Act" and "The Wiley Act."

fined not exceeding two hundred dollars for the first offense and upon conviction for each subsequent offense not exceeding three hundred dollars or be imprisoned not exceeding one year, or both, in the discretion of the court: Provided, That no article shall be deemed misbranded or adulterated within the provisions of this Act when intended for export to any foreign country and prepared or packed according to the specifications or directions of the foreign purchaser when no substance is used in the preparation or packing thereof in conflict with the laws of the foreign county to which said article is intended to be shipped; but if said article shall be in fact sold or offered for sale for domestic use or consumption, then this proviso shall not exempt said article from the operation of any of the other provisions of this Act.

SEC. 3 [21 U.S.C. 3]. RULES AND REGULATIONS

That the Secretary of the Treasury, the Secretary of Agriculture, and the Secretary of Commerce and Labor shall make uniform rules and regulations for carrying out the provisions of this Act, including the collection and examination of specimens of foods and drugs manufactured or offered for sale in the District of Columbia or in any Territory of the United States, or which shall be offered for sale in unbroken packages in any State other than that in which they shall have been respectively manufactured or produced, or which shall be received from any foreign country, or intended for shipment to any foreign country, or which many be submitted for examination by the chief health, food, or drug officer of any State, Territory, or the District of Columbia, or at any domestic or foreign port through which such product is offered for interstate commerce, or for export or import between the United States and any foreign port or country.

SEC. 4 [21 U.S.C. 11]. CHEMICAL EXAMINATIONS

The examinations of specimens of foods and drugs shall be made in the Bureau of Chemistry of the Department of Agriculture, or under the direction and supervision of such Bureau, for the purpose of determining from such examinations whether such articles are adulterated or misbranded within the meaning of this Act; and if it shall appear from any such examination that any of such specimens is adulterated or misbranded within the meaning of this Act, the Secretary of Agriculture shall cause notice thereof to be given to the party from whom such sample was obtained. Any party notified shall be given an opportunity to be heard under such rules and regulations as may be prescribed as aforesaid, and if it appears that any of the provisions of this Act have been violated by such party, then the Secretary of Agriculture shall at once certify the facts to the proper United States district attorney, with a copy of the results of the analysis or the examination of such article duly authenticated by the analyst or officer making such examination, under the oath of such officer. After judgment of the court, notice shall be given by publication in such manner as may be prescribed by the rules and regulations aforesaid.

SEC. 5 [21 U.S.C. 12]. LEGAL PROCEEDINGS

That it shall be the duty of each district attorney to whom the Secretary of Agriculture shall report any violation of this Act, or to whom any health or food or drug officer or agent of any State, Territory, or the District of Columbia shall present satisfactory evidence of any such violation, to cause appropriate proceedings to be commenced and prosecuted in the proper courts of the United States, without delay, for the enforcement of the penalties as in such case herein provided.

SEC. 6 [21 U.S.C. 7]. DEFINITIONS

That the term "drug," as used in this Act, shall include all medicines and preparations recognized in the United States Pharmacopoeia or National Formulary for internal or external use, and any substance or mixture of substances intended to be used for the cure, mitigation, or prevention of disease of either man or other animals. The term "food," as used herein, shall include all articles used for food, drink, confectionery, or condiment by man or other animals, whether simple, mixed, or compound.

SEC. 7 [21 U.S.C. 8]. ADULTERATIONS

That for the purposes of this Act an article shall be deemed to be adulterated:

In case of drugs:

First. If, when a drug is sold under or by a name recognized in the United States Pharmacopoeia or National Formulary, it differs from the standard of strength, quality, or purity, as determined by the test laid down in the United States Pharmacopoeia or National Formulary official at the time of investigation: Provided, That no drug defined in the United States Pharmacopoeia or National Formulary shall be deemed to be adulterated under this provision if the standard of strength, quality, or purity be plainly stated upon the bottle, box, or other container thereof although the standard may differ from that determined by the test laid down in the United States Pharmacopoeia or National Formulary.

Second. If its strength or purity fall below the professed standard or quality under which it is sold.

In the case of confectionery:

If it contain terra alba, barytes talc, chrome yellow, or other mineral substance or poisonous color or flavor, or other ingredient deleterious or detrimental to health, or any vinous, malt or spirituous liquor or compound or narcotic drug.

In the case of food:

First. If any substance has been mixed and packed with it so as to reduce or lower or injuriously affect its quality or strength.

Second. If any substance has been substituted wholly or in part for the article.

Third. If any valuable constituent of the article has been wholly or in part abstracted.

Fourth. If it be mixed, colored, powdered, coated, or stained in a manner whereby damage or inferiority is concealed.

Fifth. If it contain any added poisonous or other added deleterious ingredient which may render such article injurious to health: Provided, That when in the preparation of food products for shipment they are preserved by any external application applied in such manner that the preservative is necessarily removed mechanically, or by maceration in water, or otherwise, and directions for the removal of said preservative shall be printed on the covering or the package, the provisions of this Act shall be construed as applying only when said products are ready for consumption.

Sixth. If it consists in whole or in part of a filthy, decomposed, or putrid animal or vegetable substance, or any portion of an animal unfit for food, whether manufactured or not, or if it is the product of a diseased animal, or one that has died otherwise than by slaughter.

SEC. 8 [21 U.S.C. 9 & 10]. MISBRANDING

That the term "misbranded," as used herein, shall apply to all drugs, or articles of food, or articles which enter into the composition of food, the package or label of which shall bear any statement, design, or device regarding such article, or the ingredients or substances contained therein which shall be false or misleading in any particular, and to any food or drug product which is falsely branded as to the State, Territory, or country in which it is manufactured or produced.

That for the purposes of this Act an article shall also be deemed to be misbranded:

In the case of drugs:

First. If it be an imitation of or offered for sale under the name of another article.

Second. If the contents of the package as originally put up shall have been removed, in whole or in part, and other contents shall have been placed in such package, or if the package fails to bear a statement on the label of the quantity or proportion of any alcohol, morphine, opium, cocaine, heroin, alpha or beta eucaine, chloroform, cannabis indica, chloral hydrate, or acetanilide, or any derivative or preparation of any such substances contained therein.

Third.[2] If its package or label shall bear or contain any statement, design, or device regarding the curative or therapeutic effect of such article or any of the ingredients or substances contained therein, which is false and fraudulent.

In the case of food:

First. If it be an imitation of or offered for sale under the distinctive name of another article.

Second. If it be labeled or branded as to deceive or mislead the purchaser, or purport to be a foreign product when not so, or if the contents of the package as

2. Added by 37 Stat. 416 (1912) (the Sherley Amendment).

originally put up shall have been removed in whole or in part and other contents shall have been placed in such package, or if it fail to bear a statement on the label of the quantity or proportion of any morphine, opium, cocaine, heroin, alpha or beta eucaine, chloroform, cannabis indica, chloral hydrate, or acetanilide, or any derivative or preparation of any of such substances contained therein.

Third. If in package form, and the contents are stated in terms of weight or measure, they are not plainly and correctly stated on the outside of the package. [*Third.*[3] *If in package form, the quantity of the contents be not plainly and conspicuously marked on the outside of the package in terms of weight, measure or numerical count: Provided, however, That reasonable variations shall be permitted, and tolerances and also exemptions as to small packages shall be established by rules and regulations made in accordance with the provisions of Section three of this Act.*]

Fourth. If the package containing it or its label shall bear any statement, design, or device regarding the ingredients or the substances contained therein, which statement, design, or device shall be false or misleading in any particular: Provided, That an article of food which does not contain any added poisonous or deleterious ingredients shall not be deemed to be adulterated or misbranded in the following cases:

First. In the case of mixtures or compounds which may be now or from time to time hereafter known as articles of food, under their own distinctive names, and not an imitation of or offered for sale under the distinctive name of another article, if the name be accompanied on the same label or brand with a statement of the place where said article has been manufactured or produced.

Second. In the case of articles labeled, branded, or tagged so as to plainly indicate that they are compounds, imitations, or blends, and the word "compound," "imitation," or "blend," as the case may be, is plainly stated on the package in which it is offered for sale: Provided, That the term blend as used herein shall be construed to mean a mixture of like substances, not excluding harmless coloring or flavoring ingredients used for the purpose of coloring and flavoring only: And provided further, That nothing in this Act shall be construed as requiring or compelling proprietors or manufacturers of foods which contain no unwholesome added ingredient to disclose their trade formulas, except in so far as the provisions of this Act may require to secure freedom from adulteration or misbranding.

Fifth.[4] *If it be canned food and falls below the standard of quality, condition, and/or fill of container, promulgated by the Secretary of Agriculture for such canned food and its package or label does not bear a plain and conspicuous statement prescribed by the Secretary of Agriculture indicating that such canned food falls below such standard. For the purposes of this paragraph the words canned food mean all food*

3. Amended by 37 Stat. 732 (1913) (the Gould Amendment). In 1919, Congress further amended this provision to provide, "The word 'package,' as used in this paragraph, shall include and shall be construed to include wrapped meats inclosed in papers or other materials as prepared by the manufacturers thereof for sale." 41 Stat. 271 (1919) (the Kenyon Amendment).

4. Added by 46 Stat. 1019 (1930) (the McNary–Mapes Amendment).

which is in hermetically sealed containers and is sterilized by heat, except meat and meat food products which are subject to the provisions of the Meat Inspection Act of March 4, 1907, as amended, and except canned milk; the word class means and is limited to a generic product for which a standard is to be established and does not mean a grade, variety, or species of a generic product. The Secretary of Agriculture is authorized to determine, establish, and promulgate, from time to time, a reasonable standard of quality, condition, and/or fill of container for each class of canned food as will, in his judgment, promote honesty and fair dealing in the interest of the consumer; and he is authorized to alter or modify such standard from time to time as, in his judgment, honesty and fair dealing in the interest of the consumer may require. The Secretary of Agriculture is further authorized to prescribe and promulgate from time to time the form of statement which must appear in a plain and conspicuous manner on each package or label of canned food which falls below the standard promulgated by him, and which will indicate that such canned food falls below such standard, and he is authorized to alter or modify such form of statement, from time to time, as in his judgment may be necessary. In promulgating such standards and forms of statements and any alteration or modification thereof, the Secretary of Agriculture shall specify the date or dates when such standards shall become effective, or after which such statements shall be used, and shall give public notice not less than ninety days in advance of the date or dates on which such standards shall become effective or such statements shall be used. Nothing in this paragraph shall be construed to authorize the manufacture, sale, shipment, or transportation of adulterated or misbranded foods.

SEC. 9 [21 U.S.C. 13]. GUARANTY FROM MANUFACTURER

That no dealer shall be prosecuted under the provisions of this Act when he can establish a guaranty signed by the wholesaler, jobber, manufacturer, or other party residing in the United States, from whom he purchases such articles, to the effect that the same is not adulterated or misbranded within the meaning of this Act, designating it. Said guaranty, to afford protection, shall contain the name and address of the party or parties making the sale of such articles to such dealer, and in such case said party or parties shall be amenable to the prosecutions, fines, and other penalties which would attach, in due course, to the dealer under the provisions of this Act.

SEC. 10 [21 U.S.C. 14]. SEIZURE OF ORIGINAL PACKAGES

That any article of food, drug, or liquor that is adulterated or misbranded within the meaning of this Act, and is being transported from one State, Territory, District, or insular possession to another for sale, or, having been transported, remains unloaded unsold or in original unbroken packages, or if it be sold or offered for sale in the District of Columbia or the Territories, or insular possessions of the United States, or if it be imported from a foreign country for sale, or if it is intended for export to a foreign country, shall be liable to be proceeded against in any district court of the United States within the district where the same is found, and seized for confiscation by a process of libel for condemnation. And if such article is condemned as being adulterated or misbranded, or of a poisonous or deleterious character, within the meaning of this Act, the same shall be disposed of by destruction or sale, as the said court may direct, and the proceeds thereof, if sold, less the legal costs and charges, shall be paid into the Treasury of the United States, but such goods shall not be sold in any jurisdiction contrary to the provisions of this Act or the laws of that jurisdiction: Provided, however, That upon the payment of the costs of such libel proceedings and the execution and delivery of a good and sufficient bond to the effect that such articles shall not be sold or otherwise disposed of contrary to the provisions of this Act, or the laws of any State, Territory, District, or insular possession, the court may by order direct that such articles be delivered to the owner thereof. The proceedings of such libel cases shall conform, as near as may be, to the proceedings in admiralty, except that either party may demand a trial by jury of any issue of fact joined in any such case, and all such proceedings shall be at the suit of and in the name of the United States.

SEC. 10A [21 U. S. C. 14a].[5] SEA FOOD SOLD IN INTERSTATE COMMERCE

The Secretary of Agriculture, upon application of any packer of any sea food sold in interstate commerce, may at his discretion designate supervisory inspectors to examine and inspect all premises, equipment, methods, materials, containers, and labels used by such applicants in the production of such food. If the food is found to conform to the requirements of this Act, the applicant shall be authorized, in accordance with regulations prescribed by the Secretary of Agriculture, to mark the food so as to indicate such conformity. Services to any applicant under this section shall be rendered only upon payment of fees to be fixed by regulations of the Secretary of Agriculture in such amount as to cover the cost of the supervisory inspection and examination, together with the reasonable costs of administration incurred by the Secretary of Agriculture in carrying out this section. Receipts from such fees shall be covered into the Treasury and shall be available to the Secretary of Agriculture for expenditures incurred in carrying out this section. Any person who forges, counterfeits, simulates, or falsely represents, or without proper authority uses any mark, stamp, tag, label, or other identification devices authorized by the provisions of this section or regulations thereunder, shall be guilty of a misdemeanor, and shall on conviction thereof be subject to imprisonment for not more than one year or a fine of not less than $1,000 nor more than $5,000, or both such imprisonment and fine.

SEC. 11 [21 U.S.C. 15]. EXAMINATION OF IMPORTED FOOD AND DRUGS

The Secretary of the Treasury shall deliver to the Secretary of Agriculture, upon his request from time to time, samples of foods and drugs which are being imported into the United States or offered for import, giving notice there to the owner or consignee, who may appear before the Secretary of Agriculture, and have the right

5. Added by 48 Stat. 1204 (1934).

introduce testimony, and if it appear from the examination of such samples that any article of food or drug offered to be imported into the United States is adulterated or misbranded within the meaning of this Act, or is otherwise dangerous to the health of the people of the United States, or is of a kind forbidden entry into, or forbidden to be sold or restricted in sale in the country in which it is made, or from which it is exported, or is otherwise falsely labeled in any respect, the said article shall be refused admission, and the Secretary of the Treasury shall refuse deliver to the consignee and shall cause the destruction of any goods refused delivery which shall not be exported by the consignee within three months, from the date of notice of such refusal under such regulations as the Secretary of the Treasury may prescribe: Provided, That the Secretary of the Treasury may deliver to the consignee such goods pending examination and decision in the matter on execution of a penal bond for the amount of the full invoice value of such goods, together with the duty thereon, and on refusal to return such goods for any cause to the custody of the Secretary of the Treasury, when demanded, for the purpose of excluding them from the country, or for any other purpose, said consignee shall forfeit the full amount of the bond: And provided further, that all charges for storage, cargo, and labor on goods which are refused admission or delivery shall be pad by the owner or consignee, and in default of such payment shall constitute a lien against any future importation made by such owner or consignee.

Sec. 12 [21 U.S.C. 5]. Definitions and Liabilities

That the term "Territory" as used in this Act shall include the insular possessions of the United States. The word "person" as used in this Act shall be construed to import both the plural and the singular, as the case demands, and shall include corporations, companies, societies and associations. When construing and enforcing the provisions of this Act, the act, omission, or failure of any officer, agent, or other person acting for or employed by any corporation, company, society, or association, within the scope of his employment or office, shall in every case be also deemed to be the act, omission, or failure of such corporation, company, society, or association as well as that of the person.

Sec. 13 Effective Date

That this Act shall be in force and effect from and after the first day of January, nineteen hundred and seven.

Approved, June 30, 1906.

PUBLIC HEALTH SERVICE ACT
(selected provisions)

42 U.S.C. §§ _____

SEC. 351 [42 U.S.C. 262]. REGULATION OF BIOLOGICAL PRODUCTS

(a) BIOLOGICS LICENSE.

(1) No person shall introduce or deliver for introduction into interstate commerce any biological product unless—

(A) a biologics license under this subsection or subsection (k) is in effect for the biological product; and

(B) each package of the biological product is plainly marked with—

(i) the proper name of the biological product contained in the package;

(ii) the name, address, and applicable license number of the manufacturer of the biological product; and

(iii) the expiration date of the biological product.

(2)(A) The Secretary shall establish, by regulation, requirements for the approval, suspension, and revocation of biologics licenses.

(B) PEDIATRIC STUDIES.—A person that submits an application for a license under this paragraph shall submit to the Secretary as part of the application any assessments required under section 505B of the Federal Food, Drug, and Cosmetic Act.

(C) The Secretary shall approve a biologics license application—

(i) on the basis of a demonstration that—

(I) the biological product that is the subject of the application is safe, pure, and potent; and

(II) the facility in which the biological product is manufactured, processed, packed, or held meets standards designed to assure that the biological product continues to be safe, pure, and potent; and

(ii) if the applicant (or other appropriate person) consents to the inspection of the facility that is the subject of the application, in accordance with subsection (c) of this section.

(D) POSTMARKET STUDIES AND CLINICAL TRIALS; LABELING; RISK EVALUATION AND MITIGATION STRATEGY.—A person that submits an application for a license under this paragraph is subject to sections 505(*o*), 505(p), and 505–1 of the Federal Food, Drug, and Cosmetic Act.

(3) The Secretary shall prescribe requirements under which a biological product undergoing investigation shall be exempt from the requirements of paragraph (1).

(b) Falsely labeling or marking package or container; altering label or mark

No person shall falsely label or mark any package or container of any biological product or alter any label or mark on the package or container of the biological product so as to falsify the label or mark.

(c) Inspection of establishment for propagation and preparation

Any officer, agent, or employee of the Department of Health and Human Services, authorized by the Secretary for the purpose, may during all reasonable hours enter and inspect any establishment for the propagation or manufacture and preparation of any biological product.

(d) Regulations governing licenses; recall of product presenting imminent hazard; violations

(1) Upon a determination that a batch, lot, or other quantity of a product licensed under this section presents an imminent or substantial hazard to the public health, the Secretary shall issue an order immediately ordering the recall of such batch, lot, or other quantity of such product. An order under this paragraph shall be issued in accordance with section 554 of Title 5.

(2) Any violation of paragraph (1) shall subject the violator to a civil penalty of up to $100,000 per day of violation. The amount of a civil penalty under this paragraph shall, effective December 1 of each year beginning 1 year after the effective date of this paragraph, be increased by the percent change in the Consumer Price Index for the base quarter of such year over the Consumer Price Index for the base quarter of the preceding year, adjusted to the nearest 1/10 of 1 percent. For purposes of this paragraph, the term "base quarter", as used with respect to a year, means the calendar quarter ending on September 30 of such year and the price index for a base quarter is the arithmetical mean of such index for the 3 months comprising such quarter.

(e) Interference with officers

No person shall interfere with any officer, agent, or employee of the Service in the performance of any duty imposed upon him by this section or by regulations made by authority thereof.

(f) Penalties for offenses

Any person who shall violate, or aid or abet in violating, any of the provisions of this section shall be punished upon conviction by a fine not exceeding $500 or by imprisonment not exceeding one year, or by both such fine and imprisonment, in the discretion of the court.

(g) Construction with other laws

Nothing contained in this chapter shall be construed as in any way affecting, modifying, repealing, or superseding the provisions of the Federal Food, Drug, and Cosmetic Act.

(h) Exportation of partially processed biological products

A partially processed biological product which—

(1) is not in a form applicable to the prevention, treatment, or cure of diseases or injuries of man;

(2) is not intended for sale in the United States; and

(3) is intended for further manufacture into final dosage form outside the United States,

shall be subject to no restriction on the export of the product under this chapter or the Federal Food, Drug, and Cosmetic Act if the product is manufactured, processed, packaged, and held in conformity with current good manufacturing practice requirements or meets international manufacturing standards as certified by an international standards organization recognized by the Secretary and meets the requirements of section 801(e)(1) of the Federal Food, Drug, and Cosmetic Act (21 U.S.C. 381(e)).

(i) Definition; application

In this section:

(1) the term "biological product" means a virus, therapeutic serum, toxin, antitoxin, vaccine, blood, blood component or derivative, allergenic product, protein (except any chemically synthesized polypeptide), or analogous product, or arsphenamine or derivative of arsphenamine (or any other trivalent organic arsenic compound), applicable to the prevention, treatment, or cure of a disease or condition of human beings.

(2) The term "biosimilar" or "biosimilarity", in reference to a biological product that is the subject of an application under subsection (k), means—

(A) that the biological product is highly similar to the reference product notwithstanding minor differences in clinically inactive components; and

(B) there are no clinically meaningful differences between the biological product and the reference product in terms of the safety, purity, and potency of the product.

(3) The term "interchangeable" or "interchangeability", in reference to a biological product that is shown to meet the standards described in subsection (k)(4), means that the biological product may be substituted for the reference product without the intervention of the health care provider who prescribed the reference product.

(4) The term "reference product" means the single biological product licensed under subsection (a) against which a biological product is evaluated in an application submitted under subsection (k).

(j) Application of Federal Food, Drug, and Cosmetic Act

The Federal Food, Drug, and Cosmetic Act, including the requirements under sections 505(*o*), 505(p), and 505–1 of such Act, applies to a biological product subject to regulation under this section, except that a product for which a license has been approved under subsection (a) shall not be required to have an approved application under section 505 of such Act.

(k) LICENSURE OF BIOLOGICAL PRODUCTS AS BIOSIMILAR OR INTERCHANGEABLE.—

(1) IN GENERAL.—Any person may submit an application for licensure of a biological product under this subsection.

(2) CONTENT.—

(A) IN GENERAL.—

(i) REQUIRED INFORMATION.—An application submitted under this subsection shall include information demonstrating that—

(I) the biological product is biosimilar to a reference product based upon data derived from—

(aa) analytical studies that demonstrate that the biological product is highly similar to the reference product notwithstanding minor differences in clinically inactive components;

(bb) animal studies (including the assessment of toxicity); and

(cc) a clinical study or studies (including the assessment of immunogenicity and pharmacokinetics or pharmacodynamics) that are sufficient to demonstrate safety, purity, and potency in 1 or more appropriate conditions of use for which the reference product is licensed and intended to be used and for which licensure is sought for the biological product;

(II) the biological product and reference product utilize the same mechanism or mechanisms of action for the condition or conditions of use prescribed, recommended, or suggested in the proposed labeling, but only to the extent the mechanism or mechanisms of action are known for the reference product;

(III) the condition or conditions of use prescribed, recommended, or suggested in the labeling proposed for the biological product have been previously approved for the reference product;

(IV) the route of administration, the dosage form, and the strength of the biological product are the same as those of the reference product; and

(V) the facility in which the biological product is manufactured, processed, packed, or held meets standards designed to assure that the biological product continues to be safe, pure, and potent.

(ii) DETERMINATION BY SECRETARY.—The Secretary may determine, in the Secretary's discretion, that an element described in clause (i)(I) is unnecessary in an application submitted under this subsection.

(iii) ADDITIONAL INFORMATION.—An application submitted under this subsection—

(I) shall include publicly-available information regarding the Secretary's previous determination that the reference product is safe, pure, and potent; and

(II) may include any additional information in support of the application, including publicly-available information with respect to the reference product or another biological product.

(B) INTERCHANGEABILITY.—An application (or a supplement to an application) submitted under this subsection may include information demonstrating that the biological product meets the standards described in paragraph (4).

(3) EVALUATION BY SECRETARY.—Upon review of an application (or a supplement to an application) submitted under this subsection, the Secretary shall license the biological product under this subsection if—

(A) the Secretary determines that the information submitted in the application (or the supplement) is sufficient to show that the biological product—

(i) is biosimilar to the reference product; or

(ii) meets the standards described in paragraph (4), and therefore is interchangeable with the reference product; and

(B) the applicant (or other appropriate person) consents to the inspection of the facility that is the subject of the application, in accordance with subsection (c).

(4) SAFETY STANDARDS FOR DETERMINING INTERCHANGEABILITY.—Upon review of an application submitted under this subsection or any supplement to such application, the Secretary shall determine the biological product to be interchangeable with the reference product if the Secretary determines that the information submitted in the application (or a supplement to such application) is sufficient to show that—

(A) the biological product—

(i) is biosimilar to the reference product; and

(ii) can be expected to produce the same clinical result as the reference product in any given patient; and

(B) for a biological product that is administered more than once to an individual, the risk in terms of safety or diminished efficacy of alternating or switching between use of the biological product and the reference product is not greater than the risk of using the reference product without such alternation or switch.

(5) GENERAL RULES.—

(A) ONE REFERENCE PRODUCT PER APPLICATION.—A biological product, in an application submitted under this subsection, may not be evaluated against more than 1 reference product.

(B) REVIEW.—An application submitted under this subsection shall be reviewed by the division within the Food and Drug Administration that is responsible for the review and approval of the application under which the reference product is licensed.

(C) RISK EVALUATION AND MITIGATION STRATEGIES.—The authority of the Secretary with respect to risk evaluation and mitigation strategies under the Federal Food, Drug, and Cosmetic Act shall apply to biological products licensed under this subsection in the same manner as such authority applies to biological products licensed under subsection (a).

(6) EXCLUSIVITY FOR FIRST INTERCHANGEABLE BIOLOGICAL PRODUCT.—Upon review of an application submitted under this subsection relying on the same reference product for which a prior biological product has received a determination of interchangeability for any condition of use, the Secretary shall not make a determination under paragraph (4) that the second or subsequent biological product is interchangeable for any condition of use until the earlier of—

(A) 1 year after the first commercial marketing of the first interchangeable biosimilar biological product to be approved as interchangeable for that reference product;

(B) 18 months after—

(i) a final court decision on all patents in suit in an action instituted under subsection (*l*)(6) against the applicant that submitted the application for the first approved interchangeable biosimilar biological product; or

(ii) the dismissal with or without prejudice of an action instituted under subsection (*l*)(6) against the applicant that submitted the application for the first approved interchangeable biosimilar biological product; or

(C)(i) 42 months after approval of the first interchangeable biosimilar biological product if the applicant that submitted such application has been sued under subsection (*l*)(6) and such litigation is still ongoing within such 42-month period; or

(ii) 18 months after approval of the first interchangeable biosimilar biological product if the applicant that submitted such application has not been sued under subsection (*l*)(6).

For purposes of this paragraph, the term "final court decision" means a final decision of a court from which no appeal (other than a petition to the United States Supreme Court for a writ of certiorari) has been or can be taken.

(7) EXCLUSIVITY FOR REFERENCE PRODUCT.—

(A) EFFECTIVE DATE OF BIOSIMILAR APPLICATION APPROVAL.—Approval of an application under this subsection may not be made effective by the Secretary until the date that is 12 years after the date on which the reference product was first licensed under subsection (a).

(B) FILING PERIOD.—An application under this subsection may not be submitted to the Secretary until the date that is 4 years after the date on which the reference product was first licensed under subsection (a).

(C) FIRST LICENSURE.—Subparagraphs (A) and (B) shall not apply to a license for or approval of—

(i) a supplement for the biological product that is the reference product; or

(ii) a subsequent application filed by the same sponsor or manufacturer of the biological product that is the reference product (or a licensor, predecessor in interest, or other related entity) for—

(I) a change (not including a modification to the structure of the biological product) that results in a new indication, route of administration, dosing schedule, dosage form, delivery system, delivery device, or strength; or

(II) a modification to the structure of the biological product that does not result in a change in safety, purity, or potency.

(8) GUIDANCE DOCUMENTS.—

(A) IN GENERAL.—The Secretary may, after opportunity for public comment, issue guidance in accordance, except as provided in subparagraph (B)(i), with section 701(h) of the Federal Food, Drug, and Cosmetic Act with respect to the licensure of a biological product under this subsection. Any such guidance may be general or specific.

(B) PUBLIC COMMENT.—

(i) IN GENERAL.—The Secretary shall provide the public an opportunity to comment on any proposed guidance issued under subparagraph (A) before issuing final guidance.

(ii) Input regarding most valuable guidance.—The Secretary shall establish a process through which the public may provide the Secretary with input regarding priorities for issuing guidance.

(C) No requirement for application consideration.—The issuance (or non-issuance) of guidance under subparagraph (A) shall not preclude the review of, or action on, an application submitted under this subsection.

(D) Requirement for product class-specific guidance.—If the Secretary issues product class-specific guidance under subparagraph (A), such guidance shall include a description of—

(i) the criteria that the Secretary will use to determine whether a biological product is highly similar to a reference product in such product class; and

(ii) the criteria, if available, that the Secretary will use to determine whether a biological product meets the standards described in paragraph (4).

(E) Certain product classes.—

(i) Guidance.—The Secretary may indicate in a guidance document that the science and experience, as of the date of such guidance, with respect to a product or product class (not including any recombinant protein) does not allow approval of an application for a license as provided under this subsection for such product or product class.

(ii) Modification or reversal.—The Secretary may issue a subsequent guidance document under subparagraph (A) to modify or reverse a guidance document under clause (i).

(iii) No effect on ability to deny license.—Clause (i) shall not be construed to require the Secretary to approve a product with respect to which the Secretary has not indicated in a guidance document that the science and experience, as described in clause (i), does not allow approval of such an application.

(*l*) Patents.—

(1) Confidential access to subsection (k) application.—

(A) Application of paragraph.—Unless otherwise agreed to by a person that submits an application under subsection (k) (referred to in this subsection as the "subsection (k) applicant") and the sponsor of the application for the reference product (referred to in this subsection as the "reference product sponsor"), the provisions of this paragraph shall apply to the exchange of information described in this subsection.

(B) In general.—

(i) PROVISION OF CONFIDENTIAL INFORMATION.—When a subsection (k) applicant submits an application under subsection (k), such applicant shall provide to the persons described in clause (ii), subject to the terms of this paragraph, confidential access to the information required to be produced pursuant to paragraph (2) and any other information that the subsection (k) applicant determines, in its sole discretion, to be appropriate (referred to in this subsection as the "confidential information").

(ii) RECIPIENTS OF INFORMATION.—The persons described in this clause are the following:

(I) OUTSIDE COUNSEL.—One or more attorneys designated by the reference product sponsor who are employees of an entity other than the reference product sponsor (referred to in this paragraph as the "outside counsel"), provided that such attorneys do not engage, formally or informally, in patent prosecution relevant or related to the reference product.

(II) IN-HOUSE COUNSEL.—One attorney that represents the reference product sponsor who is an employee of the reference product sponsor, provided that such attorney does not engage, formally or informally, in patent prosecution relevant or related to the reference product.

(iii) PATENT OWNER ACCESS.—A representative of the owner of a patent exclusively licensed to a reference product sponsor with respect to the reference product and who has retained a right to assert the patent or participate in litigation concerning the patent may be provided the confidential information, provided that the representative informs the reference product sponsor and the subsection (k) applicant of his or her agreement to be subject to the confidentiality provisions set forth in this paragraph, including those under clause (ii).

(C) LIMITATION ON DISCLOSURE.—No person that receives confidential information pursuant to subparagraph (B) shall disclose any confidential information to any other person or entity, including the reference product sponsor employees, outside scientific consultants, or other outside counsel retained by the reference product sponsor, without the prior written consent of the subsection (k) applicant, which shall not be unreasonably withheld.

(D) USE OF CONFIDENTIAL INFORMATION.—Confidential information shall be used for the sole and exclusive purpose of determining, with respect to each patent assigned to or exclusively licensed by the reference product sponsor, whether a claim of patent infringement could reasonably be asserted if the subsection (k) applicant engaged in the manufacture, use, offering for sale, sale, or importation into the United States of the biological product that is the subject of the application under subsection (k).

(E) OWNERSHIP OF CONFIDENTIAL INFORMATION.—The confidential information disclosed under this paragraph is, and shall remain, the property of the subsection (k) applicant. By providing the confidential information pursuant to this paragraph, the subsection (k) applicant does not provide the reference product sponsor or the outside counsel any interest in or license to use the confidential information, for purposes other than those specified in subparagraph (D).

(F) EFFECT OF INFRINGEMENT ACTION.—In the event that the reference product sponsor files a patent infringement suit, the use of confidential information shall continue to be governed by the terms of this paragraph until such time as a court enters a protective order regarding the information. Upon entry of such order, the subsection (k) applicant may redesignate confidential information in accordance with the terms of that order. No confidential information shall be included in any publicly-available complaint or other pleading. In the event that the reference product sponsor does not file an infringement action by the date specified in paragraph (6), the reference product sponsor shall return or destroy all confidential information received under this paragraph, provided that if the reference product sponsor opts to destroy such information, it will confirm destruction in writing to the subsection (k) applicant.

(G) RULE OF CONSTRUCTION.—Nothing in this paragraph shall be construed—

(i) as an admission by the subsection (k) applicant regarding the validity, enforceability, or infringement of any patent; or

(ii) as an agreement or admission by the subsection (k) applicant with respect to the competency, relevance, or materiality of any confidential information.

(H) EFFECT OF VIOLATION.—The disclosure of any confidential information in violation of this paragraph shall be deemed to cause the subsection (k) applicant to suffer irreparable harm for which there is no adequate legal remedy and the court shall consider immediate injunctive relief to be an appropriate and necessary remedy for any violation or threatened violation of this paragraph.

(2) SUBSECTION (k) APPLICATION INFORMATION.—Not later than 20 days after the Secretary notifies the subsection (k) applicant that the application has been accepted for review, the subsection (k) applicant—

(A) shall provide to the reference product sponsor a copy of the application submitted to the Secretary under subsection (k), and such other information that describes the process or processes used to manufacture the biological product that is the subject of such application; and

(B) may provide to the reference product sponsor additional information requested by or on behalf of the reference product sponsor.

(3) LIST AND DESCRIPTION OF PATENTS.—

(A) LIST BY REFERENCE PRODUCT SPONSOR.—Not later than 60 days after the receipt of the application and information under paragraph (2), the reference product sponsor shall provide to the subsection (k) applicant—

(i) a list of patents for which the reference product sponsor believes a claim of patent infringement could reasonably be asserted by the reference product sponsor, or by a patent owner that has granted an exclusive license to the reference product sponsor with respect to the reference product, if a person not licensed by the reference product sponsor engaged in the making, using, offering to sell, selling, or importing into the United States of the biological product that is the subject of the subsection (k) application; and

(ii) an identification of the patents on such list that the reference product sponsor would be prepared to license to the subsection (k) applicant.

(B) LIST AND DESCRIPTION BY SUBSECTION (k) APPLICANT.—Not later than 60 days after receipt of the list under subparagraph (A), the subsection (k) applicant—

(i) may provide to the reference product sponsor a list of patents to which the subsection (k) applicant believes a claim of patent infringement could reasonably be asserted by the reference product sponsor if a person not licensed by the reference product sponsor engaged in the making, using, offering to sell, selling, or importing into the United States of the biological product that is the subject of the subsection (k) application;

(ii) shall provide to the reference product sponsor, with respect to each patent listed by the reference product sponsor under subparagraph (A) or listed by the subsection (k) applicant under clause (i)—

(I) a detailed statement that describes, on a claim by claim basis, the factual and legal basis of the opinion of the subsection (k) applicant that such patent is invalid, unenforceable, or will not be infringed by the commercial marketing of the biological product that is the subject of the subsection (k) application; or

(II) a statement that the subsection (k) applicant does not intend to begin commercial marketing of the biological product before the date that such patent expires; and

(iii) shall provide to the reference product sponsor a response regarding each patent identified by the reference product sponsor under subparagraph (A)(ii).

(C) DESCRIPTION BY REFERENCE PRODUCT SPONSOR.—Not later than 60 days after receipt of the list and statement under subparagraph (B), the reference product sponsor shall provide to the subsection (k) applicant a detailed statement that describes, with respect to each patent described in subparagraph (B)(ii)(I), on a claim by claim basis, the factual and legal basis of the opinion of the reference product sponsor that such patent will be infringed by the commercial marketing of the biological product that is the subject of the subsection (k) application and a response to the statement concerning validity and enforceability provided under subparagraph (B)(ii)(I).

(4) PATENT RESOLUTION NEGOTIATIONS.—

(A) IN GENERAL.—After receipt by the subsection (k) applicant of the statement under paragraph (3)(C), the reference product sponsor and the subsection (k) applicant shall engage in good faith negotiations to agree on which, if any, patents listed under paragraph (3) by the subsection (k) applicant or the reference product sponsor shall be the subject of an action for patent infringement under paragraph (6).

(B) FAILURE TO REACH AGREEMENT.—If, within 15 days of beginning negotiations under subparagraph (A), the subsection (k) applicant and the reference product sponsor fail to agree on a final and complete list of which, if any, patents listed under paragraph (3) by the subsection (k) applicant or the reference product sponsor shall be the subject of an action for patent infringement under paragraph (6), the provisions of paragraph (5) shall apply to the parties.

(5) PATENT RESOLUTION IF NO AGREEMENT.—

(A) NUMBER OF PATENTS.—The subsection (k) applicant shall notify the reference product sponsor of the number of patents that such applicant will provide to the reference product sponsor under subparagraph (B)(i)(I).

(B) EXCHANGE OF PATENT LISTS.—

(i) IN GENERAL.—On a date agreed to by the subsection (k) applicant and the reference product sponsor, but in no case later than 5 days after the subsection (k) applicant notifies the reference product sponsor under subparagraph (A), the subsection (k) applicant and the reference product sponsor shall simultaneously exchange—

(I) the list of patents that the subsection (k) applicant believes should be the subject of an action for patent infringement under paragraph (6); and

(II) the list of patents, in accordance with clause (ii), that the reference product sponsor believes should be the subject of an action for patent infringement under paragraph (6).

(ii) NUMBER OF PATENTS LISTED BY REFERENCE PRODUCT SPONSOR.—

(I) IN GENERAL.—Subject to subclause (II), the number of patents listed by the reference product sponsor under clause (i)(II) may not exceed the number of patents listed by the subsection (k) applicant under clause (i)(I).

(II) EXCEPTION.—If a subsection (k) applicant does not list any patent under clause (i)(I), the reference product sponsor may list 1 patent under clause (i)(II).

(6) IMMEDIATE PATENT INFRINGEMENT ACTION.—

(A) ACTION IF AGREEMENT ON PATENT LIST.—If the subsection (k) applicant and the reference product sponsor agree on patents as described in paragraph (4), not later than 30 days after such agreement, the reference product sponsor shall bring an action for patent infringement with respect to each such patent.

(B) ACTION IF NO AGREEMENT ON PATENT LIST.—If the provisions of paragraph (5) apply to the parties as described in paragraph (4)(B), not later than 30 days after the exchange of lists under paragraph (5)(B), the reference product sponsor shall bring an action for patent infringement with respect to each patent that is included on such lists.

(C) NOTIFICATION AND PUBLICATION OF COMPLAINT.—

(i) NOTIFICATION TO SECRETARY.—Not later than 30 days after a complaint is served to a subsection (k) applicant in an action for patent infringement described under this paragraph, the subsection (k) applicant shall provide the Secretary with notice and a copy of such complaint.

(ii) PUBLICATION BY SECRETARY.—The Secretary shall publish in the Federal Register notice of a complaint received under clause (i).

(7) NEWLY ISSUED OR LICENSED PATENTS.—In the case of a patent that—

(A) is issued to, or exclusively licensed by, the reference product sponsor after the date that the reference product sponsor provided the list to the subsection (k) applicant under paragraph (3)(A); and

(B) the reference product sponsor reasonably believes that, due to the issuance of such patent, a claim of patent infringement could reasonably be asserted by the reference product sponsor if a person not licensed by the reference product sponsor engaged in the making, using, offering to sell, selling, or importing into the United States of the biological product that is the subject of the subsection (k) application,

not later than 30 days after such issuance or licensing, the reference product sponsor shall provide to the subsection (k) applicant a supplement to the list provided by the reference product sponsor under paragraph (3)(A) that includes such patent, not later than 30 days after such supplement is provided, the subsection (k) applicant shall provide a statement to the reference product sponsor in accordance with paragraph (3)(B), and such patent shall be subject to paragraph (8).

(8) NOTICE OF COMMERCIAL MARKETING AND PRELIMINARY INJUNCTION.—

(A) NOTICE OF COMMERCIAL MARKETING.—The subsection (k) applicant shall provide notice to the reference product sponsor not later than 180 days before the date of the first commercial marketing of the biological product licensed under subsection (k).

(B) PRELIMINARY INJUNCTION.—After receiving the notice under subparagraph (A) and before such date of the first commercial marketing of such biological product, the reference product sponsor may seek a preliminary injunction prohibiting the subsection (k) applicant from engaging in the commercial manufacture or sale of such biological product until the court decides the issue of patent validity, enforcement, and infringement with respect to any patent that is—

(i) included in the list provided by the reference product sponsor under paragraph (3)(A) or in the list provided by the subsection (k) applicant under paragraph (3)(B); and

(ii) not included, as applicable, on—

(I) the list of patents described in paragraph (4); or

(II) the lists of patents described in paragraph (5)(B).

(C) REASONABLE COOPERATION.—If the reference product sponsor has sought a preliminary injunction under subparagraph (B), the reference product sponsor and the subsection (k) applicant shall reasonably cooperate to expedite such further discovery as is needed in connection with the preliminary injunction motion.

(9) LIMITATION OF DECLARATORY JUDGMENT ACTION.—

(A) SUBSECTION (k) APPLICATION PROVIDED.—If a subsection (k) applicant provides the application and information required under paragraph (2)(A), neither the reference product sponsor nor the subsection (k) applicant may, prior to the date notice is received under paragraph (8)(A), bring any action under section 2201 of title 28, United States Code, for a declaration of infringement, validity, or enforceability of any patent that is described in clauses (i) and (ii) of paragraph (8)(B).

(B) SUBSEQUENT FAILURE TO ACT BY SUBSECTION (k) APPLICANT.—If a subsection (k) applicant fails to complete an action required of the subsection (k) applicant under paragraph (3)(B)(ii), paragraph (5), paragraph (6)(C)(i), paragraph (7), or paragraph (8)(A), the reference product sponsor, but not the subsection (k) applicant, may bring an action under section 2201 of title 28, United States Code, for a declaration of infringement, validity, or enforceability of any patent included in the list described in paragraph (3)(A), including as provided under paragraph (7).

(C) SUBSECTION (k) APPLICATION NOT PROVIDED.—If a subsection (k) applicant fails to provide the application and information required under paragraph (2)(A), the reference product sponsor, but not the subsection (k) applicant, may bring an action under section 2201 of title 28, United States Code, for a declaration of infringement, validity, or enforceability of any patent that claims the biological product or a use of the biological product ..

(m) Pediatric Studies.—

(1) Application of certain provisions.—The provisions of subsections (a), (d), (e), (f), (h), (i), (j), (k), (*l*), (n), and (p) of section 505A of the Federal Food, Drug, and Cosmetic Act shall apply with respect to the extension of a period under paragraphs (2) and (3) to the same extent and in the same manner as such provisions apply with respect to the extension of a period under subsection (b) or (c) of section 505A of the Federal Food, Drug, and Cosmetic Act.

(2) Market exclusivity for new biological products.—If, prior to approval of an application that is submitted under subsection (a), the Secretary determines that information relating to the use of a new biological product in the pediatric population may produce health benefits in that population, the Secretary makes a written request for pediatric studies (which shall include a timeframe for completing such studies), the applicant agrees to the request, such studies are completed using appropriate formulations for each age group for which the study is requested within any such timeframe, and the reports thereof are submitted and accepted in accordance with section 505A(d)(3) of the Federal Food, Drug, and Cosmetic Act—

(A) the periods for such biological product referred to in subsection (k)(7) are deemed to be 4 years and 6 months rather than 4 years and 12 years and 6 months rather than 12 years; and

(B) if the biological product is designated under section 526 for a rare disease or condition, the period for such biological product referred to in section 527(a) is deemed to be 7 years and 6 months rather than 7 years.

(3) Market exclusivity for already-marketed biological products.—If the Secretary determines that information relating to the use of a licensed biological product in the pediatric population may produce health benefits in that population and makes a written request to the holder of an approved application under subsection (a) for pediatric studies (which shall include a timeframe for completing such studies), the holder agrees to the request, such studies are completed using appropriate formulations for each age group for which the study is requested within any such timeframe, and the reports thereof are submitted and accepted in accordance with section 505A(d)(3) of the Federal Food, Drug, and Cosmetic Act—

(A) the periods for such biological product referred to in subsection (k)(7) are deemed to be 4 years and 6 months rather than 4 years and 12 years and 6 months rather than 12 years; and

(B) if the biological product is designated under section 526 for a rare disease or condition, the period for such biological product referred to in section 527(a) is deemed to be 7 years and 6 months rather than 7 years.

(4) EXCEPTION.—The Secretary shall not extend a period referred to in paragraph (2)(A), (2)(B), (3)(A), or (3)(B) if the determination under section 505A(d)(3) is made later than 9 months prior to the expiration of such period.

* * *

SEC. 361 [42 U.S.C. 264]. REGULATIONS TO CONTROL COMMUNICABLE DISEASES

(a) Promulgation and enforcement by Surgeon General

The Surgeon General, with the approval of the Secretary, is authorized to make and enforce such regulations as in his judgment are necessary to prevent the introduction, transmission, or spread of communicable diseases from foreign countries into the States or possessions, or from one State or possession into any other State or possession. For purposes of carrying out and enforcing such regulations, the Surgeon General may provide for such inspection, fumigation, disinfection, sanitation, pest extermination, destruction of animals or articles found to be so infected or contaminated as to be sources of dangerous infection to human beings, and other measures, as in his judgment may be necessary.

(b) Apprehension, detention, or conditional release of individuals

Regulations prescribed under this section shall not provide for the apprehension, detention, or conditional release of individuals except for the purpose of preventing the introduction, transmission, or spread of such communicable diseases as may be specified from time to time in Executive orders of the President upon the recommendation of the Secretary, in consultation with the Surgeon General[1].

(c) Application of regulations to persons entering from foreign countries

Except as provided in subsection (d) of this section, regulations prescribed under this section, insofar as they provide for the apprehension, detention, examination, or conditional release of individuals, shall be applicable only to individuals coming into a State or possession from a foreign country or a possession.

(d) Apprehension and examination of persons reasonably believed to be infected

(1) Regulations prescribed under this section may provide for the apprehension and examination of any individual reasonably believed to be infected with a communicable disease in a qualifying stage and (A) to be moving or about to move from a State to another State; or (B) to be a probable source of infection to individuals who, while infected with such disease in a qualifying stage, will be moving from a State to another State. Such regulations may provide that if upon examination any such individual is found to be infected, he may be detained for such time and in such manner as may be reasonably necessary. For purposes of

1. So in original. Comma probably should not appear.

this subsection, the term "State" includes, in addition to the several States, only the District of Columbia.

(2) For purposes of this subsection, the term "qualifying stage", with respect to a communicable disease, means that such disease—

(A) is in a communicable stage; or

(B) is in a precommunicable stage, if the disease would be likely to cause a public health emergency if transmitted to other individuals.

(e) Preemption. Nothing in this section or section 363 [Special Quarantine Powers in Time of War], or the regulations promulgated under such sections, may be construed as superseding any provision under State law (including regulations and including provisions established by political subdivisions of States), except to the extent that such a provision conflicts with an exercise of Federal authority under this section or section 363.

SEC. 362 [42 U.S.C. 265]. SUSPENSION OF ENTRIES AND IMPORTS FROM DESIGNATED PLACES TO PREVENT SPREAD OF COMMUNICABLE DISEASES

Whenever the Surgeon General determines that by reason of the existence of any communicable disease in a foreign country there is serious danger of the introduction of such disease into the United States, and that this danger is so increased by the introduction of persons or property from such country that a suspension of the right to introduce such persons and property is required in the interest of the public health, the Surgeon General, in accordance with regulations approved by the President, shall have the power to prohibit, in whole or in part, the introduction of persons and property from such countries or places as he shall designate in order to avert such danger, and for such period of time as he may deem necessary for such purpose.

* * *

SEC. 368 [42 U.S.C. 271]. PENALTIES FOR VIOLATION OF QUARANTINE LAWS

(a) Penalties for persons violating quarantine laws

Any person who violates any regulation prescribed under sections 264 to 266 of this title, or any provision of section 269 of this title or any regulation prescribed thereunder, or who enters or departs from the limits of any quarantine station, ground, or anchorage in disregard of quarantine rules and regulations or without permission of the quarantine officer in charge, shall be punished by a fine of not more than $1,000 or by imprisonment for not more than one year, or both.

(b) Penalties for vessels violating quarantine laws

Any vessel which violates section 269 of this title, or any regulations thereunder or under section 267 of this title, or which enters within or departs from the limits of any quarantine station, ground, or anchorage in disregard of the quarantine rules and regulations or without permission of the officer in charge, shall forfeit to the United States not more than $5,000, the amount to be determined by the court, which shall be a lien on such vessel, to be recovered by proceedings in the proper district court of the United States. In all such proceedings the United States attorney shall appear on behalf of the United States; and all such proceedings shall be conducted in accordance with the rules and laws governing cases of seizure of vessels for violation of the revenue laws of the United States.

* * *

SECTION 5 OF ORPHAN DRUG ACT

21 U.S.C. § 360ee

SEC. 5 [21 U.S.C. 360ee]. GRANTS AND CONTRACTS FOR DEVELOPMENT OF DRUGS FOR RARE DISEASES AND CONDITIONS

(a) The Secretary may make grants to and enter into contracts with public and private entities and individuals to assist in (1) defraying the costs of qualified testing expenses incurred in connection with the development of drugs for rare diseases and conditions, (2) defraying the costs of developing medical devices for rare diseases or conditions, and (3) defraying the costs of developing medical foods for rare diseases or conditions.

(b) For purposes of subsection (a):

(1) The term "qualified testing" means—

(A) human clinical testing—

(i) which is carried out under an exemption for a drug for a rare disease or condition under section 505(i) of the Federal Food, Drug, and Cosmetic Act (or regulations issued under such section); and

(ii) which occurs before the date on which an application with respect to such drug is submitted under section 505(b) of such Act or under section 351 of the Public Health Service Act; and

(B) preclinical testing involving a drug for a rare disease or condition which occurs after the date such drug is designated under section 526 of such Act and before the date on which an application with respect to such drug is submitted under section 505(b) of such Act or under section 351 of the Public Health Service Act.

(2) The term "rare disease or condition" means (1) in the case of a drug, any disease or condition which (A) affects less than 200,000 persons in the United States, or (B) affects more than 200,000 in the United States and for which there is no reasonable expectation that the cost of developing and making available in the United States a drug for such disease or condition will be recovered from sales in the United States of such drug, (2) in the case of a medical device, any disease or condition that occurs so infrequently in the United States that there is no reasonable expectation that a medical device for such disease or condition will be developed without assistance under subsection (a), and (3) in the case of a medical food, any disease or condition that occurs so infrequently in the United States that there is no reasonable expectation that a medical food for such disease or condition will be0 management of a disease or condition for which distinctive nutritional requirements, based on recognized scientific principles, are established by medical evaluation.

(c) For grants and contracts under subsection (a), there is authorized to be appropriated $30,000,000 for each of fiscal years 2013 through 2017.

MEDICARE PRESCRIPTION DRUG, IMPROVEMENT, AND MODERNIZATION ACT OF 2003

TITLE XI—ACCESS TO AFFORDABLE PHARMACEUTICALS

SUBTITLE B—FEDERAL TRADE COMMISSION REVIEW

Pub. L. No. 108–173, 117 Stat. 2066, 2461–64

SEC. 1111. DEFINITIONS

In this subtitle:

(1) ANDA.—The term "ANDA" means an abbreviated drug application, as defined under section 201(aa) of the Federal Food, Drug, and Cosmetic Act.

(2) ASSISTANT ATTORNEY GENERAL.—The term "Assistant Attorney General" means the Assistant Attorney General in charge of the Antitrust Division of the Department of Justice.

(3) BRAND NAME DRUG.—The term "brand name drug" means a drug for which an application is approved under section 505(c) of the Federal Food, Drug, and Cosmetic Act, including an application referred to in section 505(b)(2) of such Act.

(4) BRAND NAME DRUG COMPANY.—The term "brand name drug company" means the party that holds the approved application referred to in paragraph (3) for a brand name drug that is a listed drug in an ANDA, or a party that is the owner of a patent for which information is submitted for such drug under subsection (b) or (c) of section 505 of the Federal Food, Drug, and Cosmetic Act.

(5) COMMISSION.—The term "Commission" means the Federal Trade Commission.

(6) GENERIC DRUG.—The term "generic drug" means a drug for which an application under section 505(j) of the Federal Food, Drug, and Cosmetic Act is approved.

(7) GENERIC DRUG APPLICANT.—The term "generic drug applicant" means a person who has filed or received approval for an ANDA under section 505(j) of the Federal Food, Drug, and Cosmetic Act.

(8) LISTED DRUG.—The term "listed drug" means a brand name drug that is listed under section 505(j)(7) of the Federal Food, Drug, and Cosmetic Act.

SEC. 1112. NOTIFICATION OF AGREEMENTS

(a) AGREEMENT WITH BRAND NAME DRUG COMPANY.—

(1) REQUIREMENT.—A generic drug applicant that has submitted an ANDA containing a certification under section 505(j)(2)(A)(vii)(IV) of the Federal Food,

Drug, and Cosmetic Act and a brand name drug company that enter into an agreement described in paragraph (2) shall each file the agreement in accordance with subsection (c). The agreement shall be filed prior to the date of the first commercial marketing of the generic drug that is the subject of the ANDA.

(2) Subject matter of agreement.—An agreement described in this paragraph between a generic drug applicant and a brand name drug company is an agreement regarding—

> (A) the manufacture, marketing or sale of the brand name drug that is the listed drug in the ANDA involved;

> (B) the manufacture, marketing, or sale of the generic drug for which the ANDA was submitted; or

> (C) the 180–day period referred to in section 505(j)(5)(B)(iv) of the Federal Food, Drug, and Cosmetic Act as it applies to such ANDA or to any other ANDA based on the same brand name drug.

(b) Agreement with Another Generic Drug Applicant.—

(1) Requirement.—A generic drug applicant that has submitted an ANDA containing a certification under section 505(j)(2)(A)(vii)(IV) of the Federal Food, Drug, and Cosmetic Act with respect to a listed drug and another generic drug applicant that has submitted an ANDA containing such a certification for the same listed drug shall each file the agreement in accordance with subsection (c). The agreement shall be filed prior to the date of the first commercial marketing of either of the generic drugs for which such ANDAs were submitted.

(2) Subject matter of agreement.—An agreement described in this paragraph between two generic drug applicants is an agreement regarding the 180–day period referred to in section 505(j)(5)(B)(iv) of the Federal Food, Drug, and Cosmetic Act as it applies to the ANDAs with which the agreement is concerned.

(c) Filing.—

(1) Agreement.—The parties that are required in subsection (a) or (b) to file an agreement in accordance with this subsection shall file with the Assistant Attorney General and the Commission the text of any such agreement, except that such parties are not required to file an agreement that solely concerns—

> (A) purchase orders for raw material supplies;

> (B) equipment and facility contracts;

> (C) employment or consulting contracts; or

> (D) packaging and labeling contracts.

(2) Other agreements.—The parties that are required in subsection (a) or (b) to file an agreement in accordance with this subsection shall file with the Assistant Attorney General and the Commission the text of any agreements between the parties that are not described in such subsections and are contingent upon,

provide a contingent condition for, or are otherwise related to an agreement that is required in subsection (a) or (b) to be filed in accordance with this subsection.

(3) DESCRIPTION.—In the event that any agreement required in subsection (a) or (b) to be filed in accordance with this subsection has not been reduced to text, each of the parties involved shall file written descriptions of such agreement that are sufficient to disclose all the terms and conditions of the agreement.

SEC. 1113. FILING DEADLINES

Any filing required under section 1112 shall be filed with the Assistant Attorney General and the Commission not later than 10 business days after the date the agreements are executed.

SEC. 1114. DISCLOSURE EXEMPTION

Any information or documentary material filed with the Assistant Attorney General or the Commission pursuant to this subtitle shall be exempt from disclosure under section 552 of title 5, United States Code, and no such information or documentary material may be made public, except as may be relevant to any administrative or judicial action or proceeding. Nothing in this section is intended to prevent disclosure to either body of the Congress or to any duly authorized committee or subcommittee of the Congress.

SEC. 1115. ENFORCEMENT

(a) CIVIL PENALTY.—Any brand name drug company or generic drug applicant which fails to comply with any provision of this subtitle shall be liable for a civil penalty of not more than $11,000, for each day during which such entity is in violation of this subtitle. Such penalty may be recovered in a civil action brought by the United States, or brought by the Commission in accordance with the procedures established in section 16(a)(1) of the Federal Trade Commission Act (15 U.S.C. 56(a)).

(b) COMPLIANCE AND EQUITABLE RELIEF.—If any brand name drug company or generic drug applicant fails to comply with any provision of this subtitle, the United States district court may order compliance, and may grant such other equitable relief as the court in its discretion determines necessary or appropriate, upon application of the Assistant Attorney General or the Commission.

SEC. 1116. RULEMAKING

The Commission, with the concurrence of the Assistant Attorney General and by rule in accordance with section 553 of title 5, United States Code, consistent with the purposes of this subtitle—

(1) may define the terms used in this subtitle;

(2) may exempt classes of persons or agreements from the requirements of this subtitle; and

(3) may prescribe such other rules as may be necessary and appropriate to carry out the purposes of this subtitle.

SEC. 1117. SAVINGS CLAUSE

Any action taken by the Assistant Attorney General or the Commission, or any failure of the Assistant Attorney General or the Commission to take action, under this subtitle shall not at any time bar any proceeding or any action with respect to any agreement between a brand name drug company and a generic drug applicant, or any agreement between generic drug applicants, under any other provision of law, nor shall any filing under this subtitle constitute or create a presumption of any violation of any competition laws.

SEC. 1118. EFFECTIVE DATE

This subtitle shall—

(1) take effect 30 days after the date of the enactment of this Act; and

(2) shall apply to agreements described in section 1112 that are entered into 30 days after the date of the enactment of this Act.

FAIR PACKAGING AND LABELING ACT

15 U.S.C. §§ 1451–1461

15 U.S.C. § 1451. CONGRESSIONAL DECLARATION OF POLICY

Informed consumers are essential to the fair and efficient functioning of a free market economy. Packages and their labels should enable consumers to obtain accurate information as to the quantity of the contents and should facilitate value comparisons. Therefore, it is hereby declared to be the policy of the Congress to assist consumers and manufacturers in reaching these goals in the marketing of consumer goods.

15 U.S.C. § 1452. UNFAIR AND DECEPTIVE PACKAGING AND LABELING; SCOPE OF PROHIBITION

(a) Nonconforming labels

It shall be unlawful for any person engaged in the packaging or labeling of any consumer commodity (as defined in this chapter) for distribution in commerce, or for any person (other than a common carrier for hire, a contract carrier for hire, or a freight forwarder for hire) engaged in the distribution in commerce of any packaged or labeled consumer commodity, to distribute or to cause to be distributed in commerce any such commodity if such commodity is contained in a package, or if there is affixed to that commodity a label, which does not conform to the provisions of this chapter and of regulations promulgated under the authority of this chapter.

(b) Exemptions

The prohibition contained in subsection (a) of this section shall not apply to persons engaged in business as wholesale or retail distributors of consumer commodities except to the extent that such persons (1) are engaged in the packaging or labeling of such commodities, or (2) prescribe or specify by any means the manner in which such commodities are packaged or labeled.

15 U.S.C. § 1453. REQUIREMENTS OF LABELING; PLACEMENT, FORM, AND CONTENTS OF STATEMENT OF QUANTITY; SUPPLEMENTAL STATEMENT OF QUANTITY

(a) Contents of label

No person subject to the prohibition contained in section 1452 of this title shall distribute or cause to be distributed in commerce any packaged consumer commodity unless in conformity with regulations which shall be established by the promulgating authority pursuant to section 1455 of this title which shall provide that—

(1) The commodity shall bear a label specifying the identity of the commodity and the name and place of business of the manufacturer, packer, or distributor;

(2) The net quantity of contents (in terms of weight or mass, measure, or numerical count) shall be separately and accurately stated in a uniform location upon the principal display panel of that label, using the most appropriate units of both the customary inch/pound system of measure, as provided in paragraph (3) of this subsection, and, except as provided in paragraph (3)(A)(ii) or paragraph (6) of this subsection, the SI metric system;

(3) The separate label statement of net quantity of contents appearing upon or affixed to any package—

(A)(i) if on a package labeled in terms of weight, shall be expressed in pounds, with any remainder in terms of ounces or common or decimal fractions of the pound; or in the case of liquid measure, in the largest whole unit (quarts, quarts and pints, or pints, as appropriate) with any remainder in terms of fluid ounces or common or decimal fractions of the pint or quart;

(ii) if on a random package, may be expressed in terms of pounds and decimal fractions of the pound carried out to not more than three decimal places and is not required to, but may, include a statement in terms of the SI metric system carried out to not more than three decimal places;

(iii) if on a package labeled in terms of linear measure, shall be expressed in terms of the largest whole unit (yards, yards and feet, or feet, as appropriate) with any remainder in terms of inches or common or decimal fractions of the foot or yard;

(iv) if on a package labeled in terms of measure of area, shall be expressed in terms of the largest whole square unit (square yards, square yards and square feet, or square feet, as appropriate) with any remainder in terms of square inches or common or decimal fractions of the square foot or square yard;

(B) shall appear in conspicuous and easily legible type in distinct contrast (by topography, layout, color, embossing, or molding) with other matter on the package;

(C) shall contain letters or numerals in a type size which shall be (i) established in relationship to the area of the principal display panel of the package, and (ii) uniform for all packages of substantially the same size; and

(D) shall be so placed that the lines of printed matter included in that statement are generally parallel to the base on which the package rests as it is designed to be displayed; and

(4) The label of any package of a consumer commodity which bears a representation as to the number of servings of such commodity contained in such package shall bear a statement of the net quantity (in terms of weight or mass, measure, or numerical count) of each such serving.

(5) For purposes of paragraph (3)(A)(ii) of this subsection the term "random package" means a package which is one of a lot, shipment, or delivery of packages of the same consumer commodity with varying weights or masses, that is, packages with no fixed weight or mass pattern.

(6) The requirement of paragraph (2) that the statement of net quantity of contents include a statement in terms of the SI metric system shall not apply to foods that are packaged at the retail store level.

(b) Supplemental statements

No person subject to the prohibition contained in section 1452 of this title shall distribute or cause to be distributed in commerce any packaged consumer commodity if any qualifying words or phrases appear in conjunction with the separate statement of the net quantity of contents required by subsection (a) of this section, but nothing in this subsection or in paragraph (2) of subsection (a) of this section shall prohibit supplemental statements, at other places on the package, describing in nondeceptive terms the net quantity of contents: Provided, That such supplemental statements of net quantity of contents shall not include any term qualifying a unit of weight or mass, measure, or count that tends to exaggerate the amount of the commodity contained in the package.

15 U.S.C. § 1454. RULES AND REGULATIONS

(a) Promulgating authority

The authority to promulgate regulations under this chapter is vested in (A) the Secretary of Health and Human Services (referred to hereinafter as the "Secretary") with respect to any consumer commodity which is a food, drug, device, or cosmetic, as each such term is defined by section 321 of Title 21; and (B) the Federal Trade Commission (referred to hereinafter as the "Commission") with respect to any other consumer commodity.

(b) Exemption of commodities from regulations

If the promulgating authority specified in this section finds that, because of the nature, form, or quantity of a particular consumer commodity, or for other good and sufficient reasons, full compliance with all the requirements otherwise applicable under section 1453 of this title is impracticable or is not necessary for the adequate protection of consumers, the Secretary or the Commission (whichever the case may be) shall promulgate regulations exempting such commodity from those requirements to the extent and under such conditions as the promulgating authority determines to be consistent with section 1451 of this title.

(c) Scope of additional regulations

Whenever the promulgating authority determines that regulations containing prohibitions or requirements other than those prescribed by section 1453 of this title are necessary to prevent the deception of consumers or to facilitate value comparisons as to any consumer commodity, such authority shall promulgate with respect to that commodity regulations effective to—

(1) establish and define standards for characterization of the size of a package enclosing any consumer commodity, which may be used to supplement the label statement of net quantity of contents of packages containing such commodity, but this paragraph shall not be construed as authorizing any limitation on the size, shape, weight or mass, dimensions, or number of packages which may be used to enclose any commodity;

(2) regulate the placement upon any package containing any commodity, or upon any label affixed to such commodity, of any printed matter stating or representing by implication that such commodity is offered for retail sale at a price lower than the ordinary and customary retail sale price or that a retail sale price advantage is accorded to purchasers thereof by reason of the size of that package or the quantity of its contents;

(3) require that the label on each package of a consumer commodity (other than one which is a food within the meaning of section 321(f) of Title 21) bear (A) the common or usual name of such consumer commodity, if any, and (B) in case such consumer commodity consists of two or more ingredients, the common or usual name of each such ingredient listed in order of decreasing predominance, but nothing in this paragraph shall be deemed to require that any trade secret be divulged; or

(4) prevent the nonfunctional-slack-fill of packages containing consumer commodities.

For purposes of paragraph (4) of this subsection, a package shall be deemed to be nonfunctionally slack-filled if it is filled to substantially less than its capacity for reasons other than (A) protection of the contents of such package or (B) the requirements of machines used for enclosing the contents in such package.

(d) Development by manufacturers, packers, and distributors of voluntary product standards

Whenever the Secretary of Commerce determines that there is undue proliferation of the weights or masses, measures, or quantities in which any consumer commodity or reasonably comparable consumer commodities are being distributed in packages for sale at retail and such undue proliferation impairs the reasonable ability of consumers to make value comparisons with respect to such consumer commodity or commodities, he shall request manufacturers, packers, and distributors of the commodity or commodities to participate in the development of a voluntary product standard for such commodity or commodities under the procedures for the development of voluntary products standards established by the Secretary pursuant to section 272 of this title. Such procedures shall provide adequate manufacturer, packer, distributor, and consumer representation.

(e) Report and recommendations to Congress upon industry failure to develop or abide by voluntary product standards

If (1) after one year after the date on which the Secretary of Commerce first makes the request of manufacturers, packers, and distributors to participate in the development of a voluntary product standard as provided in subsection (d) of this section, he determines that such a standard will not be published pursuant to the provisions of such subsection (d), or (2) if such a standard is published and the Secretary of Commerce determines that it has not been observed, he shall promptly report such determination to the Congress with a statement of the efforts that have been made under the voluntary standards program and his recommendation as to whether Congress should enact legislation providing regulatory authority to deal with the situation in question.

15 U.S.C. § 1455. PROCEDURE FOR PROMULGATION OF REGULATIONS

(a) Hearings by Secretary of Health and Human Services

Regulations promulgated by the Secretary under section 1453 or 1454 of this title shall be promulgated, and shall be subject to judicial review, pursuant to the provisions of subsections (e), (f), and (g) of section 371 of Title 21. Hearings authorized or required for the promulgation of any such regulations by the Secretary shall be conducted by the Secretary or by such officer or employees of the Department of Health and Human Services as he may designate for that purpose.

(b) Judicial review; hearings by Federal Trade Commission

Regulations promulgated by the Commission under section 1453 or 1454 of this title shall be promulgated, and shall be subject to judicial review, by proceedings taken in conformity with the provisions of subsections (e), (f), and (g) of section 371 of Title 21 in the same manner, and with the same effect, as if such proceedings were taken by the Secretary pursuant to subsection (a) of this section. Hearings authorized or required for the promulgation of any such regulations by the Commission shall be conducted by the Commission or by such officer or employee of the Commission as the Commission may designate for that purpose.

(c) Cooperation with other departments and agencies

In carrying into effect the provisions of this chapter, the Secretary and the Commission are authorized to cooperate with any department or agency of the United States, with any State, Commonwealth, or possession of the United States, and with any department, agency, or political subdivision of any such State, Commonwealth, or possession.

(d) Returnable or reusable glass containers for beverages

No regulation adopted under this chapter shall preclude the continued use of returnable or reusable glass containers for beverages in inventory or with the trade as of the effective date of this Act, nor shall any regulation under this chapter preclude the orderly disposal of packages in inventory or with the trade as of the effective date of such regulation.

15 U.S.C. § 1456. ENFORCEMENT

(a) Misbranded consumer commodities

Any consumer commodity which is a food, drug, device, or cosmetic, as each such term is defined by section 201 of the Federal Food, Drug, and Cosmetic Act (21 U.S.C. 321), and which is introduced or delivered for introduction into commerce in violation of any of the provisions of this chapter, or the regulations issued pursuant to this chapter, shall be deemed to be misbranded within the meaning of chapter III of the Federal Food, Drug, and Cosmetic Act [21 U.S.C. 331 et seq.], but the provisions of section 303 of that Act (21 U.S.C. 333) shall have no application to any violation of section 1452 of this title.

(b) Unfair or deceptive acts or practices in commerce

Any violation of any of the provisions of this chapter, or the regulations issued pursuant to this chapter, with respect to any consumer commodity which is not a food, drug, device, or cosmetic, shall constitute an unfair or deceptive act or practice in commerce in violation of section 45(a) of this title and shall be subject to enforcement under section 45(b) of this title.

(c) Imports

In the case of any imports into the United States of any consumer commodity covered by this chapter, the provisions of sections 1453 and 1454 of this title shall be enforced by the Secretary of the Treasury pursuant to section 801(a) and (b) of the Federal Food, Drug, and Cosmetic Act (21 U.S.C. 381).

[15 U.S.C. § 1457 terminated effective May 15, 2000]

15 U.S.C. § 1458. COOPERATION WITH STATE AUTHORITIES; TRANSMITTAL OF REGULATIONS TO STATES; NONINTERFERENCE WITH EXISTING PROGRAMS

(a) A copy of each regulation promulgated under this chapter shall be transmitted promptly to the Secretary of Commerce, who shall (1) transmit copies thereof to all appropriate State officers and agencies, and (2) furnish to such State officers and agencies information and assistance to promote to the greatest practicable extent uniformity in State and Federal regulation of the labeling of consumer commodities.

(b) Nothing contained in this section shall be construed to impair or otherwise interfere with any program carried into effect by the Secretary of Health and Human Services under other provisions of law in cooperation with State governments or agencies, instrumentalities, or political subdivisions thereof.

15 U.S.C. § 1459. DEFINITIONS

For the purpose of this chapter—

(a) The term "consumer commodity", except as otherwise specifically provided by this subsection, means any food, drug, device, or cosmetic (as those terms are defined by the Federal Food, Drug, and Cosmetic Act [21 U.S.C. 301 et seq.]), and any other article, product, or commodity of any kind or class which is customarily produced or distributed for sale through retail sales agencies or instrumentalities for consumption by individuals, or use by individuals for purposes of personal care or in the performance of services ordinarily rendered within the household, and which usually is consumed or expended in the course of such consumption or use. Such term does not include—

(1) any meat or meat product, poultry or poultry product, or tobacco or tobacco product;

(2) any commodity subject to packaging or labeling requirements imposed by the Secretary of Agriculture pursuant to the Federal Insecticide, Fungicide, and Rodenticide Act [7 U.S.C. 136 et seq.], or the provisions of the eighth paragraph under the heading "Bureau of Animal Industry" of the Act of March 4, 1913 [21 U.S.C. 151 et seq.], commonly known as the Virus–Serum–Toxin Act;

(3) any drug subject to the provisions of section 503(b)(1) or 506 of the Federal Food, Drug, and Cosmetic Act (21 U.S.C. 353(b)(1) and 356);

(4) any beverage subject to or complying with packaging or labeling requirements imposed under the Federal Alcohol Administration Act (27 U.S.C. 201 et seq.); or

(5) any commodity subject to the provisions of the Federal Seed Act [7 U.S.C. 1551 et seq.].

(b) The term "package" means any container or wrapping in which any consumer commodity is enclosed for use in the delivery or display of that consumer commodity to retail purchasers, but does not include—

(1) shipping containers or wrappings used solely for the transportation of any consumer commodity in bulk or in quantity to manufacturers, packers, or processors, or to wholesale or retail distributors thereof;

(2) shipping containers or outer wrappings used by retailers to ship or deliver any commodity to retail customers if such containers and wrappings bear no printed matter pertaining to any particular commodity; or

(3) containers subject to the provisions of the Act of August 3, 1912 (37 Stat. 250, as amended; 15 U.S.C. 231–233), or the Act of March 4, 1915 (38 Stat. 1186, as amended; 15 U.S.C. 234–236).

(c) The term "label" means any written, printed, or graphic matter affixed to any consumer commodity or affixed to or appearing upon a package containing any consumer commodity.

(d) The term "person" includes any firm, corporation, or association.

(e) The term "commerce" means (1) commerce between any State, the District of Columbia, the Commonwealth of Puerto Rico, or any territory or possession of the United States, and any place outside thereof, and (2) commerce within the District of Columbia or within any territory or possession of the United States not organized with a legislative body, but shall not include exports to foreign countries.

(f) The term "principal display panel" means that part of a label that is most likely to be displayed, presented, shown, or examined under normal and customary conditions of display for retail sale.

15 U.S.C. § 1460. SAVINGS PROVISIONS

Nothing contained in this chapter shall be construed to repeal, invalidate, or supersede—

(a) the Federal Trade Commission Act or any statute defined therein as an antitrust Act;

(b) the Federal Food, Drug, and Cosmetic Act; or

(c) the Federal Hazardous Substances Labeling Act.

15 U.S.C. § 1461. EFFECT UPON STATE LAW

It is hereby declared that it is the express intent of Congress to supersede any and all laws of the States or political subdivisions thereof insofar as they may now or hereafter provide for the labeling of the net quantity of contents of the package of any consumer commodity covered by this chapter which are less stringent than or require information different from the requirements of section 1453 of this title or regulations promulgated pursuant thereto.

FEDERAL TRADE COMMISSION ACT
(selected provisions)

15 U.S.C. §§ _____

SEC. 5 [15 U.S.C. 45]. UNFAIR METHODS OF COMPETITION UNLAWFUL; PREVENTION BY COMMISSION

(a) Declaration of unlawfulness; power to prohibit unfair practices; inapplicability to foreign trade.

(1) Unfair methods of competition in or affecting commerce, and unfair or deceptive acts or practices in or affecting commerce, are hereby declared unlawful.

(2) The Commission is hereby empowered and directed to prevent persons, partnerships, or corporations, except banks, savings and loan institutions described in section 18(f)(3), Federal credit unions described in section 18(f)(4), common carriers subject to the Acts to regulate commerce, air carriers and foreign air carriers subject to the Federal Aviation Act of 1958, and persons, partnerships, or corporations insofar as they are subject to the Packers and Stockyards Act, 1921, as amended, except as provided in section 406(b) of said Act, from using unfair methods of competition in or affecting commerce and unfair or deceptive acts or practices in or affecting commerce.

* * *

SEC. 12 [15 U.S.C. 52]. DISSEMINATION OF FALSE ADVERTISEMENTS

(a) Unlawfulness

It shall be unlawful for any person, partnership, or corporation to disseminate, or cause to be disseminated, any false advertisement—

(1) By United States mails, or in or having an effect upon commerce, by any means, for the purpose of inducing, or which is likely to induce, directly or indirectly the purchase of food, drugs, devices, services, or cosmetics; or

(2) By any means, for the purpose of inducing, or which is likely to induce, directly or indirectly, the purchase in or having an effect upon commerce, of food, drugs, devices, services, or cosmetics.

(b) Unfair or deceptive act or practice

The dissemination or the causing to be disseminated of any false advertisement within the provisions of subsection (a) of this section shall be an unfair or deceptive act or practice in or affecting commerce within the meaning of section 45 of this title.

Sec. 13 [15 U.S.C. 53]. False Advertisements; Injunctions and Restraining Orders

(a) Power of Commission; jurisdiction of courts

Whenever the Commission has reason to believe—

(1) that any person, partnership, or corporation is engaged in, or is about to engage in, the dissemination or the causing of the dissemination of any advertisement in violation of section 52 of this title, and

(2) that the enjoining thereof pending the issuance of a complaint by the Commission under section 45 of this title, and until such complaint is dismissed by the Commission or set aside by the court on review, or the order of the Commission to cease and desist made thereon has become final within the meaning of section 45 of this title, would be to the interest of the public,

the Commission by any of its attorneys designated by it for such purpose may bring suit in a district court of the United States or in the United States court of any Territory, to enjoin the dissemination or the causing of the dissemination of such advertisement. Upon proper showing a temporary injunction or restraining order shall be granted without bond. Any suit may be brought where such person, partnership, or corporation resides or transacts business, or wherever venue is proper under section 1391 of Title 28. In addition, the court may, if the court determines that the interests of justice require that any other person, partnership, or corporation should be a party in such suit, cause such other person, partnership, or corporation to be added as a party without regard to whether venue is otherwise proper in the district in which the suit is brought. In any suit under this section, process may be served on any person, partnership, or corporation wherever it may be found.

(b) Temporary restraining orders; preliminary injunctions

Whenever the Commission has reason to believe—

(1) that any person, partnership, or corporation is violating, or is about to violate, any provision of law enforced by the Federal Trade Commission, and

(2) that the enjoining thereof pending the issuance of a complaint by the Commission and until such complaint is dismissed by the Commission or set aside by the court on review, or until the order of the Commission made thereon has become final, would be in the interest of the public—

the Commission by any of its attorneys designated by it for such purpose may bring suit in a district court of the United States to enjoin any such act or practice. Upon a proper showing that, weighing the equities and considering the Commission's likelihood of ultimate success, such action would be in the public interest, and after notice to the defendant, a temporary restraining order or a preliminary injunction may be granted without bond: Provided, however, That if a complaint is not filed within such period (not exceeding 20 days) as may be specified by the court after issuance of the temporary restraining order or preliminary injunction, the order or injunction shall be dissolved by the court and be of no further force and effect: Provided further, That in proper cases the Commission may seek, and after proper proof, the court may issue, a permanent injunction. Any suit may be brought where such person, partnership, or corporation resides or transacts business, or wherever venue is proper under section 1391 of Title 28. In addition, the court may, if the court determines that the interests of justice require that any other person, partnership, or corporation should be a party in such suit, cause such other person, partnership, or corporation to be added as a party without regard to whether venue is otherwise proper in the district in which the suit is brought. In any suit under this section, process may be served on any person, partnership, or corporation wherever it may be found.

* * *

SEC. 14 [15 U.S.C. 54]. FALSE ADVERTISEMENTS; PENALTIES

(a) Imposition of penalties

Any person, partnership, or corporation who violates any provision of section 52(a) of this title shall, if the use of the commodity advertised may be injurious to health because of results from such use under the conditions prescribed in the advertisement thereof, or under such conditions as are customary or usual, or if such violation is with intent to defraud or mislead, be guilty of a misdemeanor, and upon conviction shall be punished by a fine of not more than $5,000 or by imprisonment for not more than six months, or by both such fine and imprisonment; except that if the conviction is for a violation committed after a first conviction of such person, partnership, or corporation, for any violation of such section, punishment shall be by a fine of not more than $10,000 or by imprisonment for not more than one year, or by both such fine and imprisonment: Provided, That for the purposes of this section meats and meat food products duly inspected, marked, and labeled in accordance with rules and regulations issued under the Meat Inspection Act [21 U.S.C.A. § 601 et seq.] shall be conclusively presumed not injurious to health at the time the same leave official "establishments."

(b) Exception of advertising medium or agency

No publisher, radio-broadcast licensee, or agency or medium for the dissemination of advertising, except the manufacturer, packer, distributor, or seller of the commodity to which the false advertisement relates, shall be liable under this section by reason of the dissemination by him of any false advertisement, unless he has refused, on the request of the Commission, to furnish the Commission the name and post-office address of the manufacturer, packer, distributor, seller, or advertising agency, residing in the United States, who caused him to disseminate such advertisement. No advertising agency shall be liable under this section by reason of the causing by it of the dissemination of any false advertisement, unless it has refused, on the request of the Commission, to furnish the Commission the name and post-office address of the manufacturer, packer, distributor, or seller, residing in the United States, who caused it to cause the dissemination of such advertisement.

Sec. 15 [15 U.S.C. 55]. Additional Definitions

For the purposes of sections 52 to 54 of this title—

(a) False advertisement

(1) The term "false advertisement" means an advertisement, other than labeling, which is misleading in a material respect; and in determining whether any advertisement is misleading, there shall be taken into account (among other things) not only representations made or suggested by statement, word, design, device, sound, or any combination thereof, but also the extent to which the advertisement fails to reveal facts material in the light of such representations or material with respect to consequences which may result from the use of the commodity to which the advertisement relates under the conditions prescribed in said advertisement, or under such conditions as are customary or usual. No advertisement of a drug shall be deemed to be false if it is disseminated only to members of the medical profession, contains no false representation of a material fact, and includes, or is accompanied in each instance by truthful disclosure of, the formula showing quantitatively each ingredient of such drug.

(2) In the case of oleomargarine or margarine an advertisement shall be deemed misleading in a material respect if in such advertisement representations are made or suggested by statement, word, grade designation, design, device, symbol, sound, or any combination thereof, that such oleomargarine or margarine is a dairy product, except that nothing contained herein shall prevent a truthful, accurate, and full statement in any such advertisement of all the ingredients contained in such oleomargarine or margarine.

(b) Food

The term "food" means (1) articles used for food or drink for man or other animals, (2) chewing gum, and (3) articles used for components of any such article.

(c) Drug

The term "drug" means (1) articles recognized in the official United States Pharmacopoeia, official Homoeopathic Pharmacopoeia of the United States, or official National Formulary, or any supplement to any of them; and (2) articles intended for use in the diagnosis, cure, mitigation, treatment, or prevention of disease in man or other animals; and (3) articles (other than food) intended to affect the structure or any function of the body of man or other animals; and (4) articles intended for use as a component of any article specified in clause (1), (2), or (3); but does not include devices or their components, parts, or accessories.

(d) Device

The term "device" (except when used in subsection (a) of this section) means an instrument, apparatus, implement, machine, contrivance, implant, in vitro reagent, or other similar or related article, including any component, part, or accessory, which is—

(1) recognized in the official National Formulary, or the United States Pharmacopeia, or any supplement to them,

(2) intended for use in the diagnosis of disease or other conditions, or in the cure, mitigation, treatment, or prevention of disease, in man or other animals, or

(3) intended to affect the structure or any function of the body of man or other animals, and

which does not achieve any of its principal intended purposes through chemical action within or on the body of man or other animals and which is not dependent upon being metabolized for the achievement of any of its principal intended purposes.

(e) Cosmetic

The term "cosmetic" means (1) articles to be rubbed, poured, sprinkled, or sprayed on, introduced into, or otherwise applied to the human body or any part thereof intended for cleansing, beautifying, promoting attractiveness, or altering the appearance, and (2) articles intended for use as a component of any such article; except that such term shall not include soap.

(f) Oleomargarine or margarine

For the purposes of this section and section 347 of Title 21, the term "oleomargarine" or "margarine" includes—

(1) all substances, mixtures, and compounds known as oleomargarine or margarine;

(2) all substances, mixtures, and compounds which have a consistence similar to that of butter and which contain any edible oils or fats other than milk fat if made in imitation or semblance of butter.

* * *

FEDERAL MEAT INSPECTION ACT
(selected provisions)

21 U.S.C. §§ 601–695

SUBCHAPTER I—INSPECTION REQUIREMENTS, ADULTERA-TION AND MISBRANDING

21 U.S.C. § 601. DEFINITIONS

* * *

(j) The term "meat food product" means any product capable of use as human food which is made wholly or in part from any meat or other portion of the carcass of any cattle, sheep, swine, or goats, excepting products which contain meat or other portions of such carcasses only in a relatively small proportion or historically have not been considered by consumers as products of the meat food industry, and which are exempted from definition as a meat food product by the Secretary under such conditions as he may prescribe to assure that the meat or other portions of such carcasses contained in such product are not adulterated and that such products are not represented as meat food products. This term as applied to food products of equines shall have a meaning comparable to that provided in this paragraph with respect to cattle, sheep, swine, and goats.

* * *

(m) The term "adulterated" shall apply to any carcass, part thereof, meat or meat food product under one or more of the following circumstances:

(1) if it bears or contains any poisonous or deleterious substance which may render it injurious to health; but in case the substance is not an added substance, such article shall not be considered adulterated under this clause if the quantity of such substance in or on such article does not ordinarily render it injurious to health;

(2)(A) if it bears or contains (by reason of administration of any substance to the live animal or otherwise) any added poisonous or added deleterious substance (other than one which is (i) a pesticide chemical in or on a raw agricultural commodity; (ii) a food additive; or (iii) a color additive) which may, in the judgment of the Secretary, make such article unfit for human food;

(B) if it is, in whole or in part, a raw agricultural commodity and such commodity bears or contains a pesticide chemical which is unsafe within the meaning of section 346a of this title,

(C) if it bears or contains any food additive which is unsafe within the meaning of section 348 of this title,

(D) if it bears or contains any color additive which is unsafe within the meaning of section 379e of this title: *Provided*, That an article which is not adulterated under clause (B), (C), or (D) shall nevertheless be deemed adulterated if use of the pesticide chemical, food additive, or color additive in or on such article is prohibited by regulations of the Secretary in establishments at which inspection is maintained under this subchapter;

(3) if it consists in whole or in part of any filthy, putrid, or decomposed substance or is for any other reason unsound, unhealthful, unwholesome, or otherwise unfit for human food;

(4) if it has been prepared, packed, or held under insanitary conditions whereby it may have become contaminated with filth, or whereby it may have been rendered injurious to health;

(5) if it is, in whole or in part, the product of an animal which has died otherwise than by slaughter;

(6) if its container is composed, in whole or in part, of any poisonous or deleterious substance which may render the contents injurious to health;

(7) if it has been intentionally subjected to radiation, unless the use of the radiation was in conformity with a regulation or exemption in effect pursuant to section 348 of this title;

(8) if any valuable constituent has been in whole or in part omitted or abstracted therefrom; or if any substance has been substituted, wholly or in part therefor; or if damage or inferiority has been concealed in any manner; or if any substance has been added thereto or mixed or packed therewith so as to increase its bulk or weight, or reduce its quality or strength, or make it appear better or of greater value than it is; or

(9) if it is margarine containing animal fat and any of the raw material used therein consisted in whole or in part of any filthy, putrid, or decomposed substance.

(n) The term "misbranded" shall apply to any carcass, part thereof, meat or meat food product under one or more of the following circumstances:

(1) if its labeling is false or misleading in any particular;

(2) if it is offered for sale under the name of another food;

(3) if it is an imitation of another food, unless its label bears, in type of uniform size and prominence, the word "imitation" and immediately thereafter, the name of the food imitated;

(4) if its container is so made, formed, or filled as to be misleading;

(5) if in a package or other container unless it bears a label showing (A) the name and place of business of the manufacturer, packer, or distributor; and (B) an accurate statement of the quantity of the contents in terms of weight, measure, or

numerical count: *Provided*, That under clause (B) of this subparagraph (5), reasonable variations may be permitted, and exemptions as to small packages may be established, by regulations prescribed by the Secretary;

(6) if any word, statement, or other information required by or under authority of this chapter to appear on the label or other labeling is not prominently placed thereon with such conspicuousness (as compared with other words, statements, designs, or devices, in the labeling) and in such terms as to render it likely to be read and understood by the ordinary individual under customary conditions of purchase and use;

(7) if it purports to be or is represented as a food for which a definition and standard of identity or composition has been prescribed by regulations of the Secretary under section 607 of this title unless (A) it conforms to such definition and standard, and (B) its label bears the name of the food specified in the definition and standard and, insofar as may be required by such regulations, the common names of optional ingredients (other than spices, flavoring, and coloring) present in such food;

(8) if it purports to be or is represented as a food for which a standard or standards of fill of container have been prescribed by regulations of the Secretary under section 607 of this title, and it falls below the standard of fill of container applicable thereto, unless its label bears, in such manner and form as such regulations specify, a statement that it falls below such standard;

(9) if it is not subject to the provisions of subparagraph (7), unless its label bears (A) the common or usual name of the food, if any there be, and (B) in case it is fabricated from two or more ingredients, the common or usual name of each such ingredient; except that spices, flavorings, and colorings may, when authorized by the Secretary, be designated as spices, flavorings, and colorings without naming each: *Provided*, That to the extent that compliance with the requirements of clause (B) of this subparagraph (9) is impracticable, or results in deception or unfair competition, exemptions shall be established by regulations promulgated by the Secretary;

(10) If it purports to be or is represented for special dietary uses, unless its label bears such information concerning its vitamin, mineral, and other dietary properties as the Secretary, after consultation with the Secretary of Health and Human Services, determines to be, and by regulations prescribes as, necessary in order fully to inform purchasers as to its value for such uses;

(11) If it bears or contains any artificial flavoring, artificial coloring, or chemical preservative, unless it bears labeling stating that fact: *Provided*, That, to the extent that compliance with the requirements of this subparagraph (11) is impracticable, exemptions shall be established by regulations promulgated by the Secretary; or

(12) If it fails to bear, directly thereon or on its container, as the Secretary may by regulations prescribe, the inspection legend and, unrestricted by any of the foregoing, such other information as the Secretary may require in such regulations to assure that it will not have false or misleading labeling and that the public will be informed of the manner of handling required to maintain the article in a wholesome condition.

(*o*) The term "label" means a display of written, printed, or graphic matter upon the immediate container (not including package liners) of any article.

(p) The term "labeling" means all labels and other written, printed, or graphic matter

(1) upon any article or any of its containers or wrappers, or

(2) accompanying such article.

* * *

(w) The term "amenable species" means—

(1) those species subject to the provisions of this chapter on the day before November 10, 2005;

(2) catfish, as defined by the Secretary; and

(3) any additional species of livestock that the Secretary considers appropriate.

* * *

21 U.S.C. § 602. CONGRESSIONAL STATEMENT OF FINDINGS

Meat and meat food products are an important source of the Nation's total supply of food. They are consumed throughout the Nation and the major portion thereof moves in interstate or foreign commerce. It is essential in the public interest that the health and welfare of consumers be protected by assuring that meat and meat food products distributed to them are wholesome, not adulterated, and properly marked, labeled, and packaged. Unwholesome, adulterated, or misbranded meat or meat food products impair the effective regulation of meat and meat food products in interstate or foreign commerce, are injurious to the public welfare, destroy markets for wholesome, not adulterated, and properly labeled and packaged meat and meat food products, and result in sundry losses to livestock producers and processors of meat and meat food products, as well as injury to consumers. The unwholesome, adulterated, mislabeled, or deceptively packaged articles can be sold at lower prices and compete unfairly with the wholesome, not adulterated, and properly labeled and packaged articles, to the detriment of consumers and the public generally. It is hereby found that all articles and animals which are regulated under this chapter are either in interstate or foreign commerce or substantially affect such commerce, and that regulation by the Secretary and cooperation by the States and other jurisdictions as contemplated by this chapter are appropriate to prevent and eliminate burdens upon such commerce, to effectively regulate such commerce, and to protect the health and welfare of consumers.

21 U.S.C. § 603. EXAMINATION OF ANIMALS PRIOR TO SLAUGHTER; USE OF HUMANE METHODS

(a) Examination of animals before slaughtering; diseased animals slaughtered separately and carcasses examined

For the purpose of preventing the use in commerce of meat and meat food products which are adulterated, the Secretary shall cause to be made, by inspectors appointed for that purpose, an examination and inspection of all amenable species before they shall be allowed to enter into any slaughtering, packing, meat-canning, rendering, or similar establishment, in which they are to be slaughtered and the meat and meat food products thereof are to be used in commerce; and all amenable species found on such inspection to show symptoms of disease shall be set apart and slaughtered separately from all other amenable species, and when so slaughtered the carcasses of said amenable species shall be subject to a careful examination and inspection, all as provided by the rules and regulations to be prescribed by the Secretary, as provided for in this subchapter.

(b) Humane methods of slaughter

For the purpose of preventing the inhumane slaughtering of livestock, the Secretary shall cause to be made, by inspectors appointed for that purpose, an examination and inspection of the method by which amenable species are slaughtered and handled in connection with slaughter in the slaughtering establishments inspected under this chapter. The Secretary may refuse to provide inspection to a new slaughtering establishment or may cause inspection to be temporarily suspended at a slaughtering establishment if the Secretary finds that any amenable species have been slaughtered or handled in connection with slaughter at such establishment by any method not in accordance with the Act of August 27, 1958 (72 Stat. 862; 7 U.S.C. 1901–1906) until the establishment furnishes assurances satisfactory to the Secretary that all slaughtering and handling in connection with slaughter of livestock shall be in accordance with such a method.

21 U.S.C. § 604. POST MORTEM EXAMINATION OF CARCASSES AND MARKING OR LABELING; DESTRUCTION OF CARCASSES CONDEMNED; REINSPECTION

For the purposes hereinbefore set forth the Secretary shall cause to be made by inspectors appointed for that purpose a post mortem examination and inspection of the carcasses and parts thereof of all amenable species to be prepared at any slaughtering, meat-canning, salting, packing, rendering, or similar establishment in any State, Territory, or the District of Columbia as articles of commerce which are capable of use as human food; and the carcasses and parts thereof of all such animals found to be not adulterated shall be marked, stamped, tagged, or labeled as "Inspected and passed"; and said inspectors shall label, mark, stamp, or tag as "Inspected and condemned" all carcasses and parts thereof of animals found to be adulterated; and all carcasses and parts thereof thus inspected and condemned shall be destroyed for food purposes by the said establishment in the presence of an inspector, and the Secretary may remove inspectors from any such establishment which fails to so destroy any such condemned carcass or part thereof, and said inspectors, after said first inspection, shall, when they deem it necessary, reinspect said carcasses or parts thereof to determine whether since the first inspection the same have become adulterated, and if any carcass or any part thereof shall, upon examination and inspection subsequent to the first examination and inspection, be found to be adulterated, it shall be destroyed for food purposes by the said establishment in the presence of an inspector, and the Secretary may remove inspectors from any establishment which fails to so destroy any such condemned carcass or part thereof.

21 U.S.C. § 605. EXAMINATION OF CARCASSES BROUGHT INTO SLAUGHTERING OR PACKING ESTABLISHMENTS, AND OF MEAT FOOD PRODUCTS ISSUED FROM AND RETURNED THERETO; CONDITIONS FOR ENTRY

The foregoing provisions shall apply to all carcasses or parts of carcasses of amenable species or the meat or meat products thereof which may be brought into any slaughtering, meat-canning, salting, packing, rendering, or similar establishment, and such examination and inspection shall be had before the said carcasses or parts thereof shall be allowed to enter into any department wherein the same are to be treated and prepared for meat food products; and the foregoing provisions shall also apply to all such products, which, after having been issued from any slaughtering, meat-canning, salting, packing, rendering, or similar establishment, shall be returned to the same or to any similar establishment where such inspection is maintained. The Secretary may limit the entry of carcasses, parts of carcasses, meat and meat food products, and other materials into any establishment at which inspection under this subchapter is maintained, under such conditions as he may prescribe to assure that allowing the entry of such articles into such inspected establishments will be consistent with the purposes of this chapter.

21 U.S.C. § 606. INSPECTION AND LABELING OF MEAT FOOD PRODUCTS[1]

(a) IN GENERAL. For the purposes hereinbefore set forth the Secretary shall cause to be made, by inspectors appointed for that purpose, an examination and inspection of all meat food products prepared for commerce in any slaughtering, meat-canning, salting, packing, rendering, or similar establishment, and for the purposes of any examination and inspection and inspectors shall have access at all times, by day or night, whether the establishment be operated or not, to every part of said establish-

1. According to § 11016(b)(2) of Pub. L. No. 110–246 (June 18, 2008), this section is not applicable until the date on which the Secretary issues final regulations.

ment; and said inspectors shall mark, stamp, tag, or label as "Inspected and passed" all such products found to be not adulterated; and said inspectors shall label, mark, stamp, or tag as "Inspected and condemned" all such products found adulterated, and all such condemned meat food products shall be destroyed for food purposes, as hereinbefore provided, and the Secretary may remove inspectors from any establishment which fails to so destroy such condemned meat food products: *Provided,* That subject to the rules and regulations of the Secretary the provisions of this section in regard to preservatives shall not apply to meat food products for export to any foreign country and which are prepared or packed according to the specifications or directions of the foreign purchaser, when no substance is used in the preparation or packing thereof in conflict with the laws of the foreign country to which said article is to be exported; but if said article shall be in fact sold or offered for sale for domestic use or consumption then this proviso shall not exempt said article from the operation of all the other provisions of this chapter.

(b) Catfish. In the case of an examination and inspection under subsection (a) of a meat food product derived from catfish, the Secretary shall take into account the conditions under which the catfish is raised and transported to a processing establishment.

21 U.S.C. § 607. LABELING, MARKING, AND CONTAINER REQUIREMENTS

(a) Labeling receptacles or coverings of meat or meat food products inspected and passed; supervision by inspectors

When any meat or meat food product prepared for commerce which has been inspected as hereinbefore provided and marked "Inspected and passed" shall be placed or packed in any can, pot, tin, canvas, or other receptacle or covering in any establishment where inspection under the provisions of this chapter is maintained, the person, firm, or corporation preparing said product shall cause a label to be attached to said can, pot, tin, canvas, or other receptacle or covering, under the supervision of an inspector, which label shall state that the contents thereof have been "inspected and passed" under the provisions of this chapter; and no inspection and examination of meat or meat food products deposited or inclosed in cans, tins, pots, canvas, or other receptacle or covering in any establishment where inspection under the provisions of this chapter is maintained shall be deemed to be complete until such meat or meat food products have been sealed or inclosed in said can, tin, pot, canvas, or other receptacle or covering under the supervision of an inspector.

(b) Information on articles or containers; legible form

All carcasses, parts of carcasses, meat and meat food products inspected at any establishment under the authority of this subchapter and found to be not adulterated, shall at the time they leave the establishment bear, in distinctly legible form, directly thereon or on their containers, as the Secretary may require, the information required under paragraph (n) of section 601 of this title.

(c) Labeling: type styles and sizes; definitions and standards of identity or composition; standards of fill of container; consistency of Federal and Federal–State standards

The Secretary, whenever he determines such action is necessary for the protection of the public, may prescribe: (1) the styles and sizes of type to be used with respect to material required to be incorporated in labeling to avoid false or misleading labeling in marketing and labeling any articles or animals subject to this subchapter or subchapter II of this chapter; (2) definitions and standards of identity or composition for articles subject to this subchapter and standards of fill of container for such articles not inconsistent with any such standards established under the Federal Food, Drug, and Cosmetic Act, and there shall be consultation between the Secretary and the Secretary of Health and Human Services prior to the issuance of such standards under either Act relating to articles subject to this chapter to avoid inconsistency in such standards and possible impairment of the coordinated effective administration of these Acts. There shall also be consultation between the Secretary and an appropriate advisory committee provided for in section 661 of this title, prior to the issuance of such standards under this chapter, to avoid, insofar as feasible, inconsistency between Federal and State standards.

(d) Sales under false or misleading name, other marking or labeling or in containers of misleading form or size; trade names, and other marking, labeling, and containers approved by Secretary

No article subject to this subchapter shall be sold or offered for sale by any person, firm, or corporation, in commerce, under any name or other marking or labeling which is false or misleading, or in any container of a misleading form or size, but established trade names and other marking and labeling and containers which are not false or misleading and which are approved by the Secretary are permitted.

(e) Use withholding directive respecting false or misleading marking, labeling, or container; modification of false or misleading matter; hearing; withholding use pending proceedings; finality of Secretary's action; judicial review; application of section 194 of title 7

If the Secretary has reason to believe that any marking or labeling or the size or form of any container in use or proposed for use with respect to any article subject to this subchapter is false or misleading in any particular, he may direct that such use be withheld unless the marking, labeling, or container is modified in such manner as he may prescribe so that it will not be false or misleading. If the person, firm, or corporation using or proposing to use the marking, labeling or container does not accept the determination of the Secretary, such person, firm, or corporation may request a hearing, but the use of the marking, labeling, or container shall, if the Secretary so directs, be withheld pending hearing and final determination by the Secretary. Any such determination by the Secretary shall be conclusive unless, within thirty days after receipt of notice of such final determination, the person, firm, or corporation adversely affected thereby appeals to the United States court of appeals for the circuit in which such person, firm, or corporation has its principal place of business or to the United States Court of Appeals for the District of Columbia Circuit. The provisions of section 194 of Title 7 shall be applicable to appeals taken under this section.

(f) Lamb and mutton

The Secretary, consistent with United States international obligations, shall establish standards for the labeling of sheep carcasses, parts of sheep carcasses, sheepmeat, and sheepmeat food products.

21 U.S.C. § 608. SANITARY INSPECTION AND REGULATION OF SLAUGHTERING AND PACKING ESTABLISHMENTS; REJECTION OF ADULTERATED MEAT OR MEAT FOOD PRODUCTS

The Secretary shall cause to be made, by experts in sanitation or by other competent inspectors, such inspection of all slaughtering, meat canning, salting, packing, rendering, or similar establishments in which amenable species are slaughtered and the meat and meat food products thereof are prepared for commerce as may be necessary to inform himself concerning the sanitary conditions of the same, and to prescribe the rules and regulations of sanitation under which such establishments shall be maintained; and where the sanitary conditions of any such establishment are such that the meat or meat food products are rendered adulterated, he shall refuse to allow said meat or meat food products to be labeled, marked, stamped or tagged as "inspected and passed."

21 U.S.C. § 609. EXAMINATION OF ANIMALS AND FOOD PRODUCTS THEREOF, SLAUGHTERED AND PREPARED DURING NIGHTTIME

The Secretary shall cause an examination and inspection of all amenable species, and the food products thereof, slaughtered and prepared in the establishments hereinbefore described for the purposes of commerce to be made during the nighttime as well as during the daytime when the slaughtering of said amenable species, or the preparation of said food products is conducted during the nighttime.

21 U.S.C. § 610. PROHIBITED ACTS

No person, firm, or corporation shall, with respect to any cattle, sheep, swine, goats, horses, mules, or other equines, or any carcasses, parts of carcasses, meat or meat food products of any such animals—

(a) Slaughtering animals or preparation of articles capable of use as human food

slaughter any such animals or prepare any such articles which are capable of use as human food at any establishment preparing any such articles for commerce, except in compliance with the requirements of this chapter;

(b) Humane methods of slaughter

slaughter or handle in connection with slaughter any such animals in any manner not in accordance with the Act of August 27, 1958 (72 Stat. 862; 7 U.S.C. 1901–1906);

(c) Sales, transportation, and other transactions

sell, transport, offer for sale or transportation, or receive for transportation, in commerce, (1) any such articles which (A) are capable of use as human food and (B) are adulterated or misbranded at the time of such sale, transportation, offer for sale or transportation, or receipt for transportation; or (2) any articles required to be inspected under this subchapter unless they have been so inspected and passed;

(d) Adulteration or misbranding

do, with respect to any such articles which are capable of use as human food, any act while they are being transported in commerce or held for sale after such transportation, which is intended to cause or has the effect of causing such articles to be adulterated or misbranded.

21 U.S.C. § 611. DEVICES, MARKS, LABELS AND CERTIFICATES; SIMULATIONS

(a) Devices to be made under authorization of Secretary

No brand manufacturer, printer, or other person, firm, or corporation shall cast, print, lithograph, or otherwise make any device containing any official mark or simulation thereof, or any label bearing any such mark or simulation, or any form of official certificate or simulation thereof, except as authorized by the Secretary.

(b) Other misconduct

No person, firm, or corporation shall—

(1) forge any official device, mark, or certificate;

(2) without authorization from the Secretary use any official device, mark, or certificate, or simulation thereof, or alter, detach, deface, or destroy any official device, mark, or certificate;

(3) contrary to the regulations prescribed by the Secretary, fail to use, or to detach, deface, or destroy any official device, mark, or certificate;

(4) knowingly possess, without promptly notifying the Secretary or his representative, any official device or any counterfeit, simulated, forged, or improperly altered official certificate or any device or label or any carcass of any animal, or part or product thereof, bearing any counterfeit, simulated, forged, or improperly altered official mark;

(5) knowingly make any false statement in any shipper's certificate or other nonofficial or official certificate provided for in the regulations prescribed by the Secretary; or

(6) knowingly represent that any article has been inspected and passed, or exempted, under this chapter when, in fact, it has, respectively, not been so inspected and passed, or exempted.

21 U.S.C. § 612. NOTIFICATION

Any establishment subject to inspection under this Act that believes, or has reason to believe, that an adulterated or misbranded meat or meat food product received by or originating from the establishment has entered into commerce shall promptly notify the Secretary with regard to the type, amount, origin, and destination of the meat or meat food product.

21 U.S.C. § 613. PLANS AND REASSESSMENTS

The Secretary shall require that each establishment subject to inspection under this Act shall, at a minimum—

(1) prepare and maintain current procedures for the recall of all meat or meat food products produced and shipped by the establishment;

(2) document each reassessment of the process control plans of the establishment; and

(3) upon request, make the procedures and reassessed process control plans available to inspectors appointed by the Secretary for review and copying.

* * *

21 U.S.C. § 620. IMPORTS

(a) Adulteration or misbranding prohibition; compliance with inspection, building construction standards, and other provisions; humane methods of slaughter; treatment as domestic articles subject to this chapter and food, drug, and cosmetic provisions; marking and labeling; personal consumption exemption

No carcasses, parts of carcasses, meat or meat food products of amenable species which are capable of use as human food, shall be imported into the United States if such articles are adulterated or misbranded and unless they comply with all the inspection, building, construction standards, and all other provisions of this chapter and regulations issued thereunder applicable to such articles in commerce within the United States. No such carcasses, parts of carcasses, meat or meat food products shall be imported into the United States unless the livestock from which they were produced was slaughtered and handled in connection with slaughter in accordance with the Act of August 27, 1958 (72 Stat. 862; 7 U.S.C. 1901–1906). All such imported articles shall, upon entry into the United States, be deemed and treated as domestic articles subject to the other provisions of this chapter and the Federal Food, Drug, and Cosmetic Act: *Provided*, That they shall be marked and labeled as required by such regulations for imported articles: *Provided further*, That nothing in this section shall apply to any individual who purchases meat or meat products outside the

United States for his own consumption except that the total amount of such meat or meat products shall not exceed fifty pounds.

(b) Terms and conditions for destruction

The Secretary may prescribe the terms and conditions for the destruction of all such articles which are imported contrary to this section, unless (1) they are exported by the consignee within the time fixed therefor by the Secretary, or (2) in the case of articles which are not in compliance with the chapter solely because of misbranding, such articles are brought into compliance with the chapter under supervision of authorized representatives of the Secretary.

(c) Payment of storage, cartage, and labor charges by owner or consignee; liens

All charges for storage, cartage, and labor with respect to any article which is imported contrary to this section shall be paid by the owner or consignee, and in default of such payment shall constitute a lien against such article and any other article thereafter imported under this chapter by or for such owner or consignee.

(d) Prohibition

The knowing importation of any article contrary to this section is prohibited.

(e) [Omitted]

(f) Inspection and other standards; applicability, enforcement, etc.; certifications

Notwithstanding any other provision of law, all carcasses, parts of carcasses, meat, and meat food products of amenable species, capable of use as human food, offered for importation into the United States shall be subject to the inspection, sanitary, quality, species verification, and residue standards applied to products produced in the United States. Any such imported meat articles that do not meet such standards shall not be permitted entry into the United States. The Secretary shall enforce this provision through (1) the imposition of random inspections for such species verification and for residues, and (2) random sampling and testing of internal organs and fat of the carcasses for residues at the point of slaughter by the exporting country in accordance with methods approved by the Secretary. Each foreign country from which such meat articles are offered for importation into the United States shall obtain a certification issued by the Secretary stating that the country maintains a program using reliable analytical methods to ensure compliance with the United States standards for residues in such meat articles. No such meat article shall be permitted entry into the United States from a country for which the Secretary has not issued such certification. The Secretary shall periodically review such certifications and shall revoke any certification if the Secretary determines that the country involved is not maintaining a program that uses reliable analytical methods to ensure compliance with United States standards for residues in such meat articles. The consideration of any application for a certification under this subsection and the review of any such certification, by the Secretary, shall include the inspection of individual establishments to ensure that the inspection program of the foreign country involved is meeting such United States standards.

(g) Administration of animal drugs or antibiotics; terms and conditions; entry order violations

The Secretary may prescribe terms and conditions under which amenable species that have been administered an animal drug or antibiotic banned for use in the United States may be imported for slaughter and human consumption. No person shall enter amenable species into the United States in violation of any order issued under this subsection by the Secretary.

(h) Reciprocal meat inspection requirement

(1) As used in this subsection:

(A) The term "meat articles" means carcasses, meat and meat food products of amenable species, that are capable of use as human food.

(B) The term "standards" means inspection, building construction, sanitary, quality, species verification, residue, and other standards that are applicable to meat articles.

(2) On request of the Committee on Agriculture or the Committee on Ways and Means of the House of Representatives or the Committee on Agriculture, Nutrition, and Forestry or the Committee on Finance of the Senate, or at the initiative of the Secretary, the Secretary shall, as soon as practicable, determine whether a particular foreign country applies standards for the importation of meat articles from the United States that are not related to public health concerns about end-product quality that can be substantiated by reliable analytical methods.

(3) If the Secretary determines that a foreign country applies standards described in paragraph (2)—

(A) the Secretary shall consult with the United States Trade Representative; and

(B) within 30 days after the determination of the Secretary under paragraph (2), the Secretary and the United States Trade Representative shall recommend to the President whether action should be taken under paragraph (4).

(4) Within 30 days after receiving a recommendation for action under paragraph (3), the President shall, if and for such time as the President considers appropriate, prohibit imports into the United States of any meat articles produced in such foreign country unless it is determined that the meat articles produced in that country meet the standards applicable to meat articles in commerce within the United States.

(5) The action authorized under paragraph (4) may be used instead of, or in addition to, any other action taken under any other law.

21 U.S.C. § 621. INSPECTORS TO MAKE EXAMINATIONS PROVIDED FOR; APPOINTMENT; DUTIES; REGULATIONS

The Secretary shall appoint from time to time inspectors to make examination and inspection of all amenable species, inspection of which is hereby provided for, and of all carcasses and parts thereof, and of all meats and meat food products thereof, and of the sanitary conditions of all establishments in which such meat and meat food products hereinbefore described are prepared; and said inspectors shall refuse to stamp, mark, tag, or label any carcass or any part thereof, or meat food product therefrom, prepared in any establishment hereinbefore mentioned, until the same shall have actually been inspected and found to be not adulterated; and shall perform such other duties as are provided by this chapter and by the rules and regulations to be prescribed by said Secretary; and said Secretary shall, from time to time, make such rules and regulations as are necessary for the efficient execution of the provisions of this chapter, and all inspections and examinations made under this chapter, shall be such and made in such manner as described in the rules and regulations prescribed by said Secretary not inconsistent with provisions of this chapter.

21 U.S.C. § 622. BRIBERY OF OR GIFTS TO INSPECTORS OR OTHER OFFICERS AND ACCEPTANCE OF GIFTS

Any person, firm, or corporation, or any agent or employee of any person, firm, or corporation, who shall give, pay, or offer, directly or indirectly, to any inspector, deputy inspector, chief inspector, or any other officer or employee of the United States authorized to perform any of the duties prescribed by this chapter or by the rules and regulations of the Secretary any money or other thing of value, with intent to influence said inspector, deputy inspector, chief inspector, or other officer or employee of the United States in the discharge of any duty provided for in this chapter, shall be deemed guilty of a felony, and, upon conviction thereof, shall be punished by a fine not less than $5,000 nor more than $10,000 and by imprisonment not less than one year nor more than three years; and any inspector, deputy inspector, chief inspector, or other officer or employee of the United States authorized to perform any of the duties prescribed by this chapter who shall accept any money, gift, or other thing of value from any person, firm, or corporation, or officers, agents, or employees thereof, given with intent to influence his official action, or who shall receive or accept from any person, firm, or corporation engaged in commerce any gift, money, or other thing of value, given with any purpose or intent whatsoever, shall be deemed guilty of a felony and shall, upon conviction thereof, be summarily discharged from office and shall be punished by a fine not less than $1,000 nor more than $10,000 and by imprisonment not less than one year nor more than three years.

* * *

SUBCHAPTER II—MEAT PROCESSORS
AND RELATED INDUSTRIES

21 U.S.C. § 641. PROHIBITION OF SUBCHAPTER I INSPECTION OF ARTICLES NOT INTENDED FOR USE AS HUMAN FOOD; DENATURATION OR OTHER IDENTIFICATION PRIOR TO DISTRIBUTION IN COMMERCE; INEDIBLE ARTICLES

Inspection shall not be provided under subchapter I of this chapter at any establishment for the slaughter of cattle, sheep, swine, goats, horses, mules, or other equines, or the preparation of any carcasses or parts or products of such animals, which are not intended for use as human food, but such articles shall, prior to their offer for sale or transportation in commerce, unless naturally inedible by humans, be denatured or otherwise identified as prescribed by regulations of the Secretary to deter their use for human food. No person, firm, or corporation shall buy, sell, transport, or offer for sale or transportation, or receive for transportation, in commerce, or import, any carcasses, parts thereof, meat or meat food products of any such animals, which are not intended for use as human food unless they are denatured or otherwise identified as required by the regulations of the Secretary or are naturally inedible by humans.

21 U.S.C. § 642. RECORDKEEPING REQUIREMENTS

(a) Classes of persons bound; scope of disclosure; access to places of business; examination of records, facilities, and inventories; copies; samples

The following classes of persons, firms, and corporations shall keep such records as will fully and correctly disclose all transactions involved in their businesses; and all persons, firms, and corporations subject to such requirements shall, at all reasonable times upon notice by a duly authorized representative of the Secretary, afford such representative access to their places of business and opportunity to examine the facilities, inventory, and records thereof, to copy all such records, and to take reasonable samples of their inventory upon payment of the fair market value therefor—

(1) Any persons, firms, or corporations that engage, for commerce, in the business of slaughtering any cattle, sheep, swine, goats, horses, mules, or other equines, or preparing, freezing, packaging, or labeling any carcasses, or parts or products of carcasses, of any such animals, for use as human food or animal food;

(2) Any persons, firms, or corporations that engage in the business of buying or selling (as meat brokers, wholesalers or otherwise), or transporting in commerce, or storing in or for commerce, or importing, any carcasses, or parts or products of carcasses, of any such animals;

(3) Any persons, firms, or corporations that engage in business, in or for commerce, as renderers, or engage in the business of buying, selling, or transporting, in commerce, or importing, any dead, dying, disabled, or diseased cattle, sheep,

swine, goats, horses, mules, or other equines, or parts of the carcasses of any such animals that died otherwise than by slaughter.

(b) Period of maintenance

Any record required to be maintained by this section shall be maintained for such period of time as the Secretary may by regulations prescribe.

* * *

21 U.S.C. § 645. FEDERAL PROVISIONS APPLICABLE TO STATE OR TERRITORIAL BUSINESS TRANSACTIONS OF A LOCAL NATURE AND NOT SUBJECT TO LOCAL AUTHORITY

The authority conferred on the Secretary by section 642, 643, or 644 of this title with respect to persons, firms, and corporations engaged in the specified kinds of business in or for commerce may be exercised with respect to persons, firms, or corporations engaged, in any State or organized Territory, in such kinds of business but not in or for commerce, whenever the Secretary determines, after consultation with an appropriate advisory committee provided for in section 661 of this title, that the State or Territory does not have at least equal authority under its laws or such authority is not exercised in a manner to effectuate the purposes of this chapter including the State providing for the Secretary or his representative being afforded access to such places of business and the facilities, inventories, and records thereof, and the taking of reasonable samples, where he determines necessary in carrying out his responsibilities under this chapter; and in such case the provisions of section 642, 643, or 644 of this title, respectively, shall apply to such persons, firms, and corporations to the same extent and in the same manner as if they were engaged in such business in or for commerce and the transactions involved were in commerce.

SUBCHAPTER III—FEDERAL AND STATE COOPERATION

21 U.S.C. § 661. FEDERAL AND STATE COOPERATION

(a) Congressional statement of policy

It is the policy of the Congress to protect the consuming public from meat and meat food products that are adulterated or misbranded and to assist in efforts by State and other Government agencies to accomplish this objective. In furtherance of this policy—

(1) Development and administration of State meat inspection program equal to subchapter I ante and post mortem inspection, reinspection, and sanitation requirements

The Secretary is authorized, whenever he determines that it would effectuate the purposes of this chapter, to cooperate with the appropriate State agency in developing and administering a State meat inspection program in any State which has enacted a State meat inspection law that imposes mandatory ante mortem and post mortem inspection, reinspection and sanitation requirements that are at least equal to those under subchapter I of this chapter, with respect to all or certain classes of persons engaged in the State in slaughtering cattle, sheep, swine, goats, or equines, or preparing the carcasses, parts thereof, meat or meat food products, of any such animals for use as human food solely for distribution within such State.

(2) Development and administration of State program with authorities equal to subchapter II authorities; cooperation with Federal agencies

The Secretary is further authorized, whenever he determines that it would effectuate the purposes of this chapter, to cooperate with appropriate State agencies in developing and administering State programs under State laws containing authorities at least equal to those provided in subchapter II of this chapter; and to cooperate with other agencies of the United States in carrying out any provisions of this chapter.

(3) Scope of cooperation: advisory assistance, technical and laboratory assistance and training, and financial and other aid; limitation on amount; equitable allocation of Federal funds; adequacy of State program to obtain Federal cooperation and payments

Cooperation with State agencies under this section may include furnishing to the appropriate State agency (i) advisory assistance in planning and otherwise developing an adequate State program under the State law; and (ii) technical and laboratory assistance and training (including necessary curricular and instructional materials and equipment), and financial and other aid for administration of such a program. The amount to be contributed to any State by the Secretary under this section from Federal funds for any year shall not exceed 50 per centum of the estimated total cost of the cooperative program; and the Federal funds shall be allocated among the States desiring to cooperate on an equitable basis. Such cooperation and payment shall be contingent at all times upon the administration of the State program in a manner which the Secretary, in consultation with the appropriate advisory committee appointed under paragraph (4), deems adequate to effectuate the purposes of this section.

* * *

(d) "State" defined

As used in this section, the term "State" means any State (including the Commonwealth of Puerto Rico) or organized Territory.

SUBCHAPTER IV—AUXILIARY PROVISIONS

21 U.S.C. § 671. INSPECTION SERVICES; REFUSAL OR WITHDRAWAL; HEARING; BUSINESS UNFITNESS BASED UPON CERTAIN CONVICTIONS; OTHER PROVISIONS FOR WITHDRAWAL OF SERVICES UNAFFECTED; RESPONSIBLE CONNECTION WITH BUSINESS; FINALITY OF SECRETARY'S ACTIONS; JUDICIAL REVIEW; RECORD

The Secretary may (for such period, or indefinitely, as he deems necessary to effectuate the purposes of this Act refuse to provide, or withdraw, inspection service under title I of this Act with respect to any establishment if he determines, after opportunity for a hearing is accorded to the applicant for, or recipient of, such service, that such applicant or recipient is unfit to engage in any business requiring inspection under title I because the applicant or recipient, or anyone responsibly connected with the applicant or recipient, has been convicted, in any Federal or State court, of (1) any felony, or (2) more than one violation of any law, other than a felony, based upon the acquiring, handling, or distributing of unwholesome, mislabeled, or deceptively packaged food or upon fraud in connection with transactions in food. This section shall not affect in any way other provisions of this Act for withdrawal of inspection services under title I from establishments failing to maintain sanitary conditions or to destroy condemned carcasses, parts, meat or meat food products.

For the purpose of this section a person shall be deemed to be responsibly connected with the business if he was a partner, officer, director, holder, or owner of 10 per centum or more of its voting stock or employee in a managerial or executive capacity.

The determination and order of the Secretary with respect thereto under subsection (e) shall be final and conclusive unless the affected applicant for, or recipient of, inspection service files application for judicial review within thirty days after the effective date of such order in the appropriate court as provided in section 404. Judicial review of any such order shall be upon the record upon which the determination and order are based.

21 U.S.C. § 672. ADMINISTRATIVE DETENTION; DURATION; PENDING JUDICIAL PROCEEDINGS; NOTIFICATION OF GOVERNMENTAL AUTHORITIES; RELEASE

Whenever any carcass, part of a carcass, meat or meat food product of cattle, sheep, swine, goats, horses, mules, or other equines, or any product exempted from the definition of a meat food product, or any dead, dying, disabled, or diseased cattle, sheep, swine, goat, or equine is found by any authorized representative of the Secretary upon any premises where it is held for purposes of, or during or after distribution in, commerce or otherwise subject to subchapter I or II of this chapter, and there is reason to believe that any such article is adulterated or misbranded and is capable of use as human food, or that it has not been inspected, in violation of the provisions of subchapter I of this chapter or of any other Federal law or the laws of any State or Territory, or the District of Columbia, or that such article or animal has been or is intended to be, distributed in violation of any such provisions, it may be detained by such representative for a period not to exceed twenty days, pending action under section 673 of this title or notification of any Federal, State, or other governmental authorities having jurisdiction over such article or animal, and shall not be moved by any person, firm, or corporation from the place at which it is located when so detained, until released by such representative. All official marks may be required by such representative to be removed from such article or animal before it is released unless it appears to the satisfaction of the Secretary that the article or animal is eligible to retain such marks.

21 U.S.C. § 673. SEIZURE AND CONDEMNATION

(a) Proceedings in rem; libel of information; jurisdiction; disposal by destruction or sale; proceeds into the Treasury; sales restrictions; bond; court costs and fees, storage, and other expenses against claimants; proceedings in admiralty; jury trial; United States as plaintiff

(1) Any carcass, part of a carcass, meat or meat food product of cattle, sheep, swine, goats, horses, mules or other equines, or any dead, dying, disabled, or diseased cattle, sheep, swine, goat, or equine, that is being transported in commerce or otherwise subject to subchapter I or II of this chapter, or is held for sale in the United States after such transportation, and that (A) is or has been prepared, sold, transported, or otherwise distributed or offered or received for distribution in violation of this chapter, or (B) is capable of use as human food and is adulterated or misbranded, or (C) in any other way is in violation of this chapter, shall be liable to be proceeded against and seized and condemned, at any time, on a libel of information in any United States district court or other proper court as provided in section 674 of this title within the jurisdiction of which the article or animal is found.

(2) If the article or animal is condemned it shall, after entry of the decree, (A) be distributed in accordance with paragraph (5), or (B) be disposed of by destruction or sale as the court may direct and the proceeds, if sold, less the court costs and fees, and storage and other proper expenses, shall be paid into the Treasury of the United States, but the article or animal shall not be sold contrary to the provisions of this chapter, or the laws of the jurisdiction in which it is sold: *Provided*, That upon the execution and delivery of a good and sufficient bond conditioned that the article or animal shall not be sold or otherwise disposed of contrary to the provisions of this chapter, or the laws of the jurisdiction in which disposal is made, the court may direct that such article or animal be delivered to the owner thereof subject to such supervision by authorized representatives of the Secretary as is necessary to insure compliance with the applicable laws.

(3) When a decree of condemnation is entered against the article or animal and it is released under bond, or destroyed, court costs and fees, and storage and other proper expenses shall be awarded against the person, if any, intervening as claimant of the article or animal.

(4) The proceedings in such libel cases shall conform, as nearly as may be, to the proceedings in admiralty, except that either party may demand trial by jury of any issue of fact joined in any case, and all such proceedings shall be at the suit of and in the name of the United States.

(5)(A) An article that is condemned under paragraph (1) may as the court may direct, after entry of the decree, be distributed without charge to nonprofit, private entities or to Federal, State, or local government entities engaged in the distribution of food without charge to individuals, if such article—

(i) has been inspected under this chapter and found to be wholesome and not to be adulterated within the meaning of paragraphs (1) through (7) and (9) of section 601(m) of this title and a determination is made at the time of the entry of the decree that such article is wholesome and not so adulterated; and

(ii) is plainly marked "Not for Sale" on such article or its container.

(B) The United States may not be held legally responsible for any article that is distributed under subparagraph (A) to a nonprofit, private entity or to a Federal, State, or local government entity, if such article—

(i) was found after inspection under this chapter to be wholesome and not adulterated within the meaning of paragraphs (1) through (7) and (9) of section 601(m) of this title and a determination was made at the time of the entry of the decree that such article was wholesome and not so adulterated; and

(ii) was plainly marked "Not for Sale" on such article or its container.

(C) The person from whom such article was seized and condemned may not be held legally responsible for such article, if such article—

(i) was found after inspection under this chapter to be wholesome and not adulterated within the meaning of paragraphs (1) through (7) and (9) of section 601(m) of this title and a determination was made at the time of the entry of the decree that such article was wholesome and not so adulterated; and

(ii) was plainly marked "Not for Sale" on such article or its container.

(b) Condemnation or seizure under other provisions unaffected

The provisions of this section shall in no way derogate from authority for condemnation or seizure conferred by other provisions of this chapter, or other laws.

830

21 U.S.C. § 674. FEDERAL COURT JURISDICTION OF ENFORCEMENT AND INJUNCTION PROCEEDINGS AND OTHER KINDS OF CASES; LIMITATIONS OF SECTION 6079(E) OF THIS TITLE

The United States district courts, the District Court of Guam, the District Court of the Virgin Islands, the highest court of American Samoa, and the United States courts of the other Territories, are vested with jurisdiction specifically to enforce, and to prevent and restrain violations of, this chapter, and shall have jurisdiction in all other kinds of cases arising under this chapter, except as provided in section 607(e) of this title.

* * *

21 U.S.C. § 678. NON–FEDERAL JURISDICTION OF FEDERALLY REGULATED MATTERS; PROHIBITION OF ADDITIONAL OR DIFFERENT REQUIREMENTS FOR ESTABLISHMENTS WITH INSPECTION SERVICES AND AS TO MARKING, LABELING, PACKAGING, AND INGREDIENTS; RECORDKEEPING AND RELATED REQUIREMENTS; CONCURRENT JURISDICTION OVER DISTRIBUTION FOR HUMAN FOOD PURPOSES OF ADULTERATED OR MISBRANDED AND IMPORTED ARTICLES; OTHER MATTERS

Requirements within the scope of this Act with respect to premises, facilities and operations of any establishment at which inspection is provided under title I of this Act, which are in addition to, or different than those made under this Act may not be imposed by any State or Territory or the District of Columbia, except that any such jurisdiction may impose recordkeeping and other requirements within the scope of section 202 of this Act, if consistent therewith, with respect to any such establishment. Marking, labeling, packaging, or ingredient requirements in addition to, or different than, those made under this Act may not be imposed by any State or Territory or the District of Columbia with respect to articles prepared at any establishment under inspection in accordance with the requirements under title I of this Act, but any State or Territory or the District of Columbia may, consistent with the requirements under this Act, exercise concurrent jurisdiction with the Secretary over articles required to be inspected under said title, for the purpose of preventing the distribution for human food purposes of any such articles which are adulterated or misbranded and are outside of such an establishment, or, in the case of imported articles which are not at such an establishment, after their entry into the United States. This Act shall not preclude any State or Territory or the District of Columbia from making requirement[2] or taking other action, consistent with this Act, with respect to any other matters regulated under this Act.

21 U.S.C. § 679. APPLICATION OF FOOD, DRUG, AND COSMETIC ACT

(a) Authorities under food, drug, and cosmetic provisions unaffected

Notwithstanding any other provisions of law, including section 902(b) of the Federal Food, Drug, and Cosmetic Act (21 U.S.C. 392(a)), the provisions of this chapter shall not derogate from any authority conferred by the Federal Food, Drug, and Cosmetic Act prior to December 15, 1967.

(b) Enforcement proceedings; detainer authority of representatives of Secretary of Health and Human Services

The detainer authority conferred by section 672 of this title shall apply to any authorized representative of the Secretary of Health and Human Services for purposes of the enforcement of the Federal Food, Drug, and Cosmetic Act with respect to any carcass, part thereof, meat, or meat food product of cattle, sheep, swine, goats, or equines that is outside any premises at which inspection is being maintained under this chapter, and for such purposes the first reference to the Secretary in section 672 of this title shall be deemed to refer to the Secretary of Health and Human Services.

* * *

2. So in original. Probably should be "requirements".

CIGARETTE LABELING AND ADVERTISING ACT[1]
(selected provisions)

15 U.S.C. § 1333

SEC. 4 [15 U.S.C. 1333]. LABELING

(a) LABEL REQUIREMENTS—

(1) IN GENERAL.—It shall be unlawful for any person to manufacture, package, sell, offer to sell, distribute, or import for sale or distribution within the United States any cigarettes the package of which fails to bear, in accordance with the requirements of this section, one of the following labels:

WARNING: Cigarettes are addictive.

WARNING: Tobacco smoke can harm your children.

WARNING: Cigarettes cause fatal lung disease.

WARNING: Cigarettes cause cancer.

WARNING: Cigarettes cause strokes and heart disease.

WARNING: Smoking during pregnancy can harm your baby.

WARNING: Smoking can kill you.

WARNING: Tobacco smoke causes fatal lung disease in nonsmokers.

WARNING: Quitting smoking now greatly reduces serious risks to your health.

(2) PLACEMENT; TYPOGRAPHY; ETC.—Each label statement required by paragraph (1) shall be located in the upper portion of the front and rear panels of the package, directly on the package underneath the cellophane or other clear wrapping. Each label statement shall comprise the top 50 percent of the front and rear panels of the package. The word "WARNING" shall appear in capital letters and all text shall be in conspicuous and legible 17-point type, unless the text of the label statement would occupy more than 70 percent of such area, in which case the text may be in a smaller conspicuous and legible type size, provided that at least 60 percent of such area is occupied by required text. The text shall be black on a white background, or white on a black background, in a manner that contrasts, by typography, layout, or color, with all other printed material on the package, in an alternating fashion under the plan submitted under subsection (c).

---

1. As amended by Title II of the Family Smoking Prevention and Tobacco Control Act, 123 Stat. 1776, 1842-45 (2009). This Title similarly amended the Comprehensive Smokeless Tobacco Health Education Act, 15 U.S.C. § 4402. 123 Stat. at 1846-48. Title II contains additional provisions relevant to FDA regulation of tobacco product labeling and advertising that are not included in this Supplement.

(3) Does not apply to foreign distribution.—The provisions of this subsection do not apply to a tobacco product manufacturer or distributor of cigarettes which does not manufacture, package, or import cigarettes for sale or distribution within the United States.

(4) Applicability to retailers.—A retailer of cigarettes shall not be in violation of this subsection for packaging that—

(A) contains a warning label;

(B) is supplied to the retailer by a license- or permit-holding tobacco product manufacturer, importer, or distributor; and

(C) is not altered by the retailer in a way that is material to the requirements of this subsection.

(b) Advertising Requirements—

(1) In general.—It shall be unlawful for any tobacco product manufacturer, importer, distributor, or retailer of cigarettes to advertise or cause to be advertised within the United States any cigarette unless its advertising bears, in accordance with the requirements of this section, one of the labels specified in subsection (a).

(2) Typography, etc.—Each label statement required by subsection (a) in cigarette advertising shall comply with the standards set forth in this paragraph. For press and poster advertisements, each such statement and (where applicable) any required statement relating to tar, nicotine, or other constituent (including a smoke constituent) yield shall comprise at least 20 percent of the area of the advertisement and shall appear in a conspicuous and prominent format and location at the top of each advertisement within the trim area. The Secretary may revise the required type sizes in such area in such manner as the Secretary determines appropriate. The word "WARNING" shall appear in capital letters, and each label statement shall appear in conspicuous and legible type. The text of the label statement shall be black if the background is white and white if the background is black, under the plan submitted under subsection (c). The label statements shall be enclosed by a rectangular border that is the same color as the letters of the statements and that is the width of the first downstroke of the capital "W" of the word "WARNING" in the label statements. The text of such label statements shall be in a typeface pro rata to the following requirements: 45-point type for a whole-page broadsheet newspaper advertisement; 39-point type for a half-page broadsheet newspaper advertisement; 39-point type for a whole-page tabloid newspaper advertisement; 27-point type for a half-page tabloid newspaper advertisement; 31.5-point type for a double page spread magazine or whole-page magazine advertisement; 22.5-point type for a 28 centimeter by 3 column advertisement; and 15-point type for a 20 centimeter by 2 column advertisement. The label statements shall be in English, except that—

(A) in the case of an advertisement that appears in a newspaper, magazine, periodical, or other publication that is not in English, the statements shall appear in the predominant language of the publication; and

(B) in the case of any other advertisement that is not in English, the statements shall appear in the same language as that principally used in the advertisement.

(3) MATCHBOOKS. — Notwithstanding paragraph (2), for matchbooks (defined as containing not more than 20 matches) customarily given away with the purchase of tobacco products, each label statement required by subsection (a) may be printed on the inside cover of the matchbook.

(4) ADJUSTMENT BY SECRETARY. — The Secretary may, through a rulemaking under section 553 of title 5, adjust the format and type sizes for the label statements required by this section; the text, format, and type sizes of any required tar, nicotine yield, or other constituent (including smoke constituent) disclosures; or the text, format, and type sizes for any other disclosures required under the Federal Food, Drug, and Cosmetic Act [21 U.S.C. 301 et seq.]. The text of any such label statements or disclosures shall be required to appear only within the 20 percent area of cigarette advertisements provided by paragraph (2). The Secretary shall promulgate regulations which provide for adjustments in the format and type sizes of any text required to appear in such area to ensure that the total text required to appear by law will fit within such area.

(c) MARKETING REQUIREMENTS —

(1) RANDOM DISPLAY. — The label statements specified in subsection (a)(1) shall be randomly displayed in each 12-month period, in as equal a number of times as is possible on each brand of the product and be randomly distributed in all areas of the United States in which the product is marketed in accordance with a plan submitted by the tobacco product manufacturer, importer, distributor, or retailer and approved by the Secretary.

(2) ROTATION. — The label statements specified in subsection (a)(1) shall be rotated quarterly in alternating sequence in advertisements for each brand of cigarettes in accordance with a plan submitted by the tobacco product manufacturer, importer, distributor, or retailer to, and approved by, the Secretary.

(3) REVIEW. — The Secretary shall review each plan submitted under paragraph (2) and approve it if the plan —

(A) will provide for the equal distribution and display on packaging and the rotation required in advertising under this subsection; and

(B) assures that all of the labels required under this section will be displayed by the tobacco product manufacturer, importer, distributor, or retailer at the same time.

(4) APPLICABILITY TO RETAILERS.—This subsection and subsection (b) apply to a retailer only if that retailer is responsible for or directs the label statements required under this section except that this paragraph shall not relieve a retailer of liability if the retailer displays, in a location open to the public, an advertisement that does not contain a warning label or has been altered by the retailer in a way that is material to the requirements of this subsection and subsection (b).

(d) GRAPHIC LABEL STATEMENTS.—Not later than 24 months after the date of enactment of the Family Smoking Prevention and Tobacco Control Act[2], the Secretary shall issue regulations that require color graphics depicting the negative health consequences of smoking to accompany the label statements specified in subsection (a)(1). The Secretary may adjust the type size, text and format of the label statements specified in subsections (a)(2) and (b)(2) as the Secretary determines appropriate so that both the graphics and the accompanying label statements are clear, conspicuous, legible and appear within the specified area.[3]

2. Pub. L. No. 111–31, 123 Stat. 1776, 1842, which was enacted June 22, 2009.

3. According to Pub. L. No. 111–31, § 201(b), 123 Stat. 1845, "the amendment made by subsection (a) shall take effect 15 months after the issuance of the regulations required by subsection (a). Such effective date shall be with respect to the date of manufacture, provided that, in any case, beginning 30 days after such effective date, a manufacturer shall not introduce into the domestic commerce of the United States any product, irrespective of the date of manufacture, that is not in conformance with section 4 of the Federal Cigarette Labeling and Advertising Act (15 U.S.C. 1333), as amended by subsection (a)." FDA issued final regulations at 76 Fed. Reg. 36628 (June 22, 2011).

ADMINISTRATIVE PROCEDURE ACT AND RELATED STATUTES
(selected provisions)

CHAPTER 5, SUBCHAPTER II—ADMINISTRATIVE PROCEDURE

5 U.S.C. §§ 551 *et seq.*

5 U.S.C. § 551. DEFINITIONS

For the purpose of this subchapter—

(1) "agency" means each authority of the Government of the United States, whether or not it is within or subject to review by another agency, but does not include—

(A) the Congress;

(B) the courts of the United States;

(C) the governments of the territories or possessions of the United States;

(D) the government of the District of Columbia;

or except as to the requirements of section 552 of this title—

(E) agencies composed of representatives of the parties or of representatives of organizations of the parties to the disputes determined by them;

* * *

(4) "rule" means the whole or a part of an agency statement of general or particular applicability and future effect designed to implement, interpret, or prescribe law or policy or describing the organization, procedure, or practice requirements of an agency and includes the approval or prescription for the future of rates, wages, corporate or financial structures or reorganizations thereof, prices, facilities, appliances, services or allowances therefor or of valuations, costs, or accounting, or practices bearing on any of the foregoing;

(5) "rule making" means agency process for formulating, amending, or repealing a rule;

(6) "order" means the whole or a part of a final disposition, whether affirmative, negative, injunctive, or declaratory in form, of an agency in a matter other than rule making but including licensing;

(7) "adjudication" means agency process for the formulation of an order;

(8) "license" includes the whole or a part of an agency permit, certificate, approval, registration, charter, membership, statutory exemption or other form of permission;

(9) "licensing" includes agency process respecting the grant, renewal, denial, revocation, suspension, annulment, withdrawal, limitation, amendment, modification, or conditioning of a license;

(10) "sanction" includes the whole or a part of an agency—

(A) prohibition, requirement, limitation, or other condition affecting the freedom of a person;

(B) withholding of relief;

(C) imposition of penalty or fine;

(D) destruction, taking, seizure, or withholding of property;

(E) assessment of damages, reimbursement, restitution, compensation, costs, charges, or fees;

(F) requirement, revocation, or suspension of a license; or

(G) taking other compulsory or restrictive action;

(11) "relief" includes the whole or a part of an agency—

(A) grant of money, assistance, license, authority, exemption, exception, privilege, or remedy;

(B) recognition of a claim, right, immunity, privilege, exemption, or exception; or

(C) taking of other action on the application or petition of, and beneficial to, a person;

(12) "agency proceeding" means an agency process as defined by paragraphs (5), (7), and (9) of this section;

(13) "agency action" includes the whole or a part of an agency rule, order, license, sanction, relief, or the equivalent or denial thereof, or failure to act; and

(14) "ex parte communication" means an oral or written communication not on the public record with respect to which reasonable prior notice to all parties is not given, but it shall not include requests for status reports on any matter or proceeding covered by this subchapter.

5 U.S.C. § 552.[1] PUBLIC INFORMATION; AGENCY RULES, OPINIONS, ORDERS, RECORDS, AND PROCEEDINGS

(a) Each agency shall make available to the public information as follows:

(1) Each agency shall separately state and currently publish in the Federal Register for the guidance of the public—

---

1. Section 552 is commonly known as the FREEDOM OF INFORMATION ACT.

(A) descriptions of its central and field organization and the established places at which, the employees (and in the case of a uniformed service, the members) from whom, and the methods whereby, the public may obtain information, make submittals or requests, or obtain decisions;

(B) statements of the general course and method by which its functions are channeled and determined, including the nature and requirements of all formal and informal procedures available;

(C) rules of procedure, descriptions of forms available or the places at which forms may be obtained, and instructions as to the scope and contents of all papers, reports, or examinations;

(D) substantive rules of general applicability adopted as authorized by law, and statements of general policy or interpretations of general applicability formulated and adopted by the agency; and

(E) each amendment, revision, or repeal of the foregoing.

Except to the extent that a person has actual and timely notice of the terms thereof, a person may not in any manner be required to resort to, or be adversely affected by, a matter required to be published in the Federal Register and not so published. For the purpose of this paragraph, matter reasonably available to the class of persons affected thereby is deemed published in the Federal Register when incorporated by reference therein with the approval of the Director of the Federal Register.

(2) Each agency, in accordance with published rules, shall make available for public inspection and copying—

(A) final opinions, including concurring and dissenting opinions, as well as orders, made in the adjudication of cases;

(B) those statements of policy and interpretations which have been adopted by the agency and are not published in the Federal Register;

(C) administrative staff manuals and instructions to staff that affect a member of the public;

(D) copies of all records, regardless of form or format, which have been released to any person under paragraph (3) and which, because of the nature of their subject matter, the agency determines have become or are likely to become the subject of subsequent requests for substantially the same records; and

(E) a general index of the records referred to under subparagraph (D);

unless the materials are promptly published and copies offered for sale. For records created on or after November 1, 1996, within one year after such date, each agency shall make such records available, including by computer telecommunications or, if computer telecommunications means have not been established by the agency, by other electronic means. To the extent required to prevent a clearly unwarranted invasion of personal privacy, an agency may delete identifying details when it makes available or publishes an opinion, statement of policy, interpretation, staff manual, instruction, or copies of records referred to in subparagraph (D). However, in each case the justification for the deletion shall be explained fully in writing, and the extent of such deletion shall be indicated on the portion of the record which is made available or published, unless including that indication would harm an interest protected by the exemption in subsection (b) under which the deletion is made. If technically feasible, the extent of the deletion shall be indicated at the place in the record where the deletion was made. Each agency shall also maintain and make available for public inspection and copying current indexes providing identifying information for the public as to any matter issued, adopted, or promulgated after July 4, 1967, and required by this paragraph to be made available or published. Each agency shall promptly publish, quarterly or more frequently, and distribute (by sale or otherwise) copies of each index or supplements thereto unless it determines by order published in the Federal Register that the publication would be unnecessary and impracticable, in which case the agency shall nonetheless provide copies of such index on request at a cost not to exceed the direct cost of duplication. Each agency shall make the index referred to in subparagraph (E) available by computer telecommunications by December 31, 1999. A final order, opinion, statement of policy, interpretation, or staff manual or instruction thau affects a member of the public may be relied on, used, or cited as precedent by an agency against a party other than an agency only if—

   (i) it has been indexed and either made available or published as provided by this paragraph; or

   (ii) the party has actual and timely notice of the terms thereof.

(3)(A) Except with respect to the records made available under paragraphs (1) and (2) of this subsection, and except as provided in subparagraph (E), each agency, upon any request for records which (i) reasonably describes such records and (ii) is made in accordance with published rules stating the time, place, fees (if any), and procedures to be followed, shall make the records promptly available to any person.

(B) In making any record available to a person under this paragraph, an agency shall provide the record in any form or format requested by the person if the record is readily reproducible by the agency in that form or format. Each agency shall make reasonable efforts to maintain its records in forms or formats that are reproducible for purposes of this section.

* * *

(4)(A)(i) In order to carry out the provisions of this section, each agency shall promulgate regulations, pursuant to notice and receipt of public comment, specifying the schedule of fees applicable to the processing of requests under this section and establishing procedures and guidelines for determining when such fees should be waived or reduced. Such schedule shall conform to the guidelines which shall be promulgated, pursuant to notice and receipt of public comment, by the Director of the Office of Management and Budget and which shall provide for a uniform schedule of fees for all agencies.

(ii) Such agency regulations shall provide that—

(I) fees shall be limited to reasonable standard charges for document search, duplication, and review, when records are requested for commercial use;

(II) fees shall be limited to reasonable standard charges for document duplication when records are not sought for commercial use and the request is made by an educational or noncommercial scientific institution, whose purpose is scholarly or scientific research; or a representative of the news media; and

(III) for any request not described in (I) or (II), fees shall be limited to reasonable standard charges for document search and duplication.

In this clause, the term "a representative of the news media" means any person or entity that turn the raw materials into a distinct work, and distributes that work to an audience. In this clause, the term "news" means information that is about current events or that would be of current interest to the public. Examples of news-media entities are television or radio stations broadcasting to the public at large and publishers of periodicals (but only if such entities qualify as disseminators of "news") who make their products available for purchase by or subscription by or free distribution to the general public. These examples are not all-inclusive. Moreover, as methods of news delivery evolve (for example, the adoption of the electronic dissemination of newspapers through telecommunications services), such alternative media shall be considered to be news-media entities. A freelance journalist shall be regarded as working for a news-media entity if the journalist can demonstrate a solid basis for expecting publication through that entity, whether or not the journalist is actually employed by the entity. A publication contract would present a solid basis for such an expectation; the Government may also consider the past publication record of the requester in making such a determination.

(iii) Documents shall be furnished without any charge or at a charge reduced below the fees established under clause (ii) if disclosure of the information is in the public interest because it is likely to contribute significantly to public understanding of the operations or activities of the government and is not primarily in the commercial interest of the requester.

(iv) Fee schedules shall provide for the recovery of only the direct costs of search, duplication, or review. Review costs shall include only the direct costs incurred during the initial examination of a document for the purposes of determining whether the documents must be disclosed under this section and for the purposes of withholding any portions exempt from disclosure under this section. Review costs may not include any costs incurred in resolving issues of law or policy that may be raised in the course of processing a request under this section. No fee may be charged by any agency under this section—

(I) if the costs of routine collection and processing of the fee are likely to equal or exceed the amount of the fee; or

(II) for any request described in clause (ii)(II) or (III) of this subparagraph for the first two hours of search time or for the first one hundred pages of duplication.

(v) No agency may require advance payment of any fee unless the requester has previously failed to pay fees in a timely fashion, or the agency has determined that the fee will exceed $250.

(vi) Nothing in this subparagraph shall supersede fees chargeable under a statute specifically providing for setting the level of fees for particular types of records.

(vii) In any action by a requester regarding the waiver of fees under this section, the court shall determine the matter de novo: Provided, That the court's review of the matter shall be limited to the record before the agency.

(viii) An agency shall not assess search fees (or in the case of a requester described under clause (ii)(II), duplication fees) under this subparagraph if the agency fails to comply with any time limit under paragraph (6), if no unusual or exceptional circumstances (as those terms are defined for purposes of paragraphs (6)(B) and (C), respectively) apply to the processing of the request.

(B) On complaint, the district court of the United States in the district in which the complainant resides, or has his principal place of business, or in which the agency records are situated, or in the District of Columbia, has jurisdiction to enjoin the agency from withholding agency records and to order the production of any agency records improperly withheld from the complainant. In such a case the court shall determine the matter de novo, and may examine the contents of such agency records in camera to determine whether such records or any part thereof shall be withheld under any of the exemptions set forth in subsection (b) of this section, and the burden is on the agency to sustain its action. In addition to any other matters to which a court accords substantial weight, a court shall accord substantial weight to an affidavit of an agency concerning the agency's determination as to technical feasibility under paragraph (2)(C) and subsection (b) and reproducibility under paragraph (3)(B).

(C) Notwithstanding any other provision of law, the defendant shall serve an answer or otherwise plead to any complaint made under this subsection within thirty days after service upon the defendant of the pleading in which such complaint is made, unless the court otherwise directs for good cause shown.

* * *

(E)(i) The court may assess against the United States reasonable attorney fees and other litigation costs reasonably incurred in any case under this section in which the complainant has substantially prevailed.

(ii) For purposes of this subparagraph, a complainant has substantially prevailed if the complainant has obtained relief through either—

(I) a judicial order, or an enforceable written agreement or consent decree; or

(II) a voluntary or unilateral change in position by the agency, if the complainant's claim is not insubstantial.

(F)(i) Whenever the court orders the production of any agency records improperly withheld from the complainant and assesses against the United States reasonable attorney fees and other litigation costs, and the court additionally issues a written finding that the circumstances surrounding the withholding raise questions whether agency personnel acted arbitrarily or capriciously with respect to the withholding, the Special Counsel shall promptly initiate a proceeding to determine whether disciplinary action is warranted against the officer or employee who was primarily responsible for the withholding. The Special Counsel, after investigation and consideration of the evidence submitted, shall submit his findings and recommendations to the administrative authority of the agency concerned and shall send copies of the findings and recommendations to the officer or employee or his representative. The administrative authority shall take the corrective action that the Special Counsel recommends.

(ii) The Attorney General shall—

(I) notify the Special Counsel of each civil action described under the first sentence of clause (i); and

(II) annually submit a report to Congress on the number of such civil actions in the preceding year.

(iii) The Special Counsel shall annually submit a report to Congress on the actions taken by the Special Counsel under clause (i).

(G) In the event of noncompliance with the order of the court, the district court may punish for contempt the responsible employee, and in the case of a uniformed service, the responsible member.

(5) Each agency having more than one member shall maintain and make available for public inspection a record of the final votes of each member in every agency proceeding.

(6)(A) Each agency, upon any request for records made under paragraph (1), (2), or (3) of this subsection, shall—

(i) determine within 20 days (excepting Saturdays, Sundays, and legal public holidays) after the receipt of any such request whether to comply with such request and shall immediately notify the person making such request of such determination and the reasons therefor, and of the right of such person to appeal to the head of the agency any adverse determination; and

(ii) make a determination with respect to any appeal within twenty days (excepting Saturdays, Sundays, and legal public holidays) after the receipt of such appeal. If on appeal the denial of the request for records is in whole or in part upheld, the agency shall notify the person making such request of the provisions for judicial review of that determination under paragraph (4) of this subsection.

The 20–day period under clause (i) shall commence on the date on which the request is first received by the appropriate component of the agency, but in any event not later than ten days after the request is first received by any component of the agency that is designated in the agency's regulations under this section to receive requests under this section. The 20–day period shall not be tolled by the agency except—

(I) that the agency may make one request to the requester for information and toll the 20–day period while it is awaiting such information that it has reasonably requested from the requester under this section; or

(II) if necessary to clarify with the requester issues regarding fee assessment. In either case, the agency's receipt of the requester's response to the agency's request for information or clarification ends the tolling period.

(B)(i) In unusual circumstances as specified in this subparagraph, the time limits prescribed in either clause (i) or clause (ii) of subparagraph (A) may be extended by written notice to the person making such request setting forth the unusual circumstances for such extension and the date on which a determination is expected to be dispatched. No such notice shall specify a date that would result in an extension for more than ten working days, except as provided in clause (ii) of this subparagraph.

(ii) With respect to a request for which a written notice under clause (i) extends the time limits prescribed under clause (i) of subparagraph (A), the agency shall notify the person making the request if the request cannot be processed within the time limit specified in that clause and shall provide the person an opportunity to limit the scope of the request so that it may be processed within that time limit or an opportunity to arrange with the agency an alternative time frame for processing the request or a modified request. To aid the requester, each agency shall make available its FOIA Public Liaison, who shall assist in the resolution of any disputes between the requester and the agency. Refusal by the person to reasonably modify the request or arrange such an alternative time frame shall be considered as a factor in determining whether exceptional circumstances exist for purposes of subparagraph (C).

(iii) As used in this subparagraph, "unusual circumstances" means, but only to the extent reasonably necessary to the proper processing of the particular requests —

(I) the need to search for and collect the requested records from field facilities or other establishments that are separate from the office processing the request;

(II) the need to search for, collect, and appropriately examine a voluminous amount of separate and distinct records which are demanded in a single request; or

(III) the need for consultation, which shall be conducted with all practicable speed, with another agency having a substantial interest in the determination of the request or among two or more components of the agency having substantial subject-matter interest therein.

(iv) Each agency may promulgate regulations, pursuant to notice and receipt of public comment, providing for the aggregation of certain requests by the same requestor, or by a group of requestors acting in concert, if the agency reasonably believes that such requests actually constitute a single request, which would otherwise satisfy the unusual circumstances specified in this subparagraph, and the requests involve clearly related matters. Multiple requests involving unrelated matters shall not be aggregated.

(C)(i) Any person making a request to any agency for records under paragraph (1), (2), or (3) of this subsection shall be deemed to have exhausted his administrative remedies with respect to such request if the agency fails to comply with the applicable time limit provisions of this paragraph. If the Government can show exceptional circumstances exist and that the agency is exercising due diligence in responding to the request, the court may retain jurisdiction and allow the agency additional time to complete its review of the records. Upon any determination by an agency to comply with a request for records, the records shall be made promptly available to such person making such request. Any notification of denial of any request for records under this subsection shall set forth the names and titles or positions of each person responsible for the denial of such request.

(ii) For purposes of this subparagraph, the term "exceptional circumstances" does not include a delay that results from a predictable agency workload of requests under this section, unless the agency demonstrates reasonable progress in reducing its backlog of pending requests.

(iii) Refusal by a person to reasonably modify the scope of a request or arrange an alternative time frame for processing a request (or a modified request) under clause (ii) after being given an opportunity to do so by the agency to whom the person made the request shall be considered as a factor in determining whether exceptional circumstances exist for purposes of this subparagraph.

(D)(i) Each agency may promulgate regulations, pursuant to notice and receipt of public comment, providing for multitrack processing of requests for records based on the amount of work or time (or both) involved in processing requests.

(ii) Regulations under this subparagraph may provide a person making a request that does not qualify for the fastest multitrack processing an opportunity to limit the scope of the request in order to qualify for faster processing.

(iii) This subparagraph shall not be considered to affect the requirement under subparagraph (C) to exercise due diligence.

(E)(i) Each agency shall promulgate regulations, pursuant to notice and receipt of public comment, providing for expedited processing of requests for records—

(I) in cases in which the person requesting the records demonstrates a compelling need; and

(II) in other cases determined by the agency.

(ii) Notwithstanding clause (i), regulations under this subparagraph must ensure—

(I) that a determination of whether to provide expedited processing shall be made, and notice of the determination shall be provided to the person making the request, within 10 days after the date of the request; and

(II) expeditious consideration of administrative appeals of such determinations of whether to provide expedited processing.

(iii) An agency shall process as soon as practicable any request for records to which the agency has granted expedited processing under this subparagraph. Agency action to deny or affirm denial of a request for expedited processing pursuant to this subparagraph, and failure by an agency to respond in a timely manner to such a request shall be subject to judicial review under paragraph (4), except that the judicial review shall be based on the record before the agency at the time of the determination.

(iv) A district court of the United States shall not have jurisdiction to review an agency denial of expedited processing of a request for records after the agency has provided a complete response to the request.

(v) For purposes of this subparagraph, the term "compelling need" means—

(I) that a failure to obtain requested records on an expedited basis under this paragraph could reasonably be expected to pose an imminent threat to the life or physical safety of an individual; or

(II) with respect to a request made by a person primarily engaged in disseminating information, urgency to inform the public concerning actual or alleged Federal Government activity.

(vi) A demonstration of a compelling need by a person making a request for expedited processing shall be made by a statement certified by such person to be true and correct to the best of such person's knowledge and belief.

(F) In denying a request for records, in whole or in part, an agency shall make a reasonable effort to estimate the volume of any requested matter the provision of which is denied, and shall provide any such estimate to the person making the request, unless providing such estimate would harm an interest protected by the exemption in subsection (b) pursuant to which the denial is made.

(7) Each agency shall—

(A) establish a system to assign an individualized tracking number for each request received that will take longer than ten days to process and provide to each person making a request the tracking number assigned to the request; and

(B) establish a telephone line or Internet service that provides information about the status of a request to the person making the request using the assigned tracking number, including—

(i) the date on which the agency originally received the request; and

(ii) an estimated date on which the agency will complete action on the request.

(b) This section does not apply to matters that are—

(1)(A) specifically authorized under criteria established by an Executive order to be kept secret in the interest of national defense or foreign policy and (B) are in fact properly classified pursuant to such Executive order;

(2) related solely to the internal personnel rules and practices of an agency;

(3) specifically exempted from disclosure by statute (other than section 552b of this title), provided that such statute (A) requires that the matters be withheld from the public in such a manner as to leave no discretion on the issue, or (B) establishes particular criteria for withholding or refers to particular types of matters to be withheld;

(4) trade secrets and commercial or financial information obtained from a person and privileged or confidential;

(5) inter-agency or intra-agency memorandums or letters which would not be available by law to a party other than an agency in litigation with the agency;

(6) personnel and medical files and similar files the disclosure of which would constitute a clearly unwarranted invasion of personal privacy;

(7) records or information compiled for law enforcement purposes, but only to the extent that the production of such law enforcement records or information (A) could reasonably be expected to interfere with enforcement proceedings, (B) would deprive a person of a right to a fair trial or an impartial adjudication, (C) could reasonably be expected to constitute an unwarranted invasion of personal

§552(b)   *ADMINISTRATIVE PROCEDURE ACT*

privacy, (D) could reasonably be expected to disclose the identity of a confidential source, including a State, local, or foreign agency or authority or any private institution which furnished information on a confidential basis, and, in the case of a record or information compiled by criminal law enforcement authority in the course of a criminal investigation or by an agency conducting a lawful national security intelligence investigation, information furnished by a confidential source, (E) would disclose techniques and procedures for law enforcement investigations or prosecutions, or would disclose guidelines for law enforcement investigations or prosecutions if such disclosure could reasonably be expected to risk circumvention of the law, or (F) could reasonably be expected to endanger the life or physical safety of any individual;

(8) contained in or related to examination, operating, or condition reports prepared by, on behalf of, or for the use of an agency responsible for the regulation or supervision of financial institutions; or

(9) geological and geophysical information and data, including maps, concerning wells.

Any reasonably segregable portion of a record shall be provided to any person requesting such record after deletion of the portions which are exempt under this subsection. The amount of information deleted, and the exemption under which the deletion is made, shall be indicated on the released portion of the record, unless including that indication would harm an interest protected by the exemption in this subsection under which the deletion is made. If technically feasible, the amount of the information deleted, and the exemption under which the deletion is made, shall be indicated at the place in the record where such deletion is made.

(c)(1) Whenever a request is made which involves access to records described in subsection (b)(7)(A) and—

(A) the investigation or proceeding involves a possible violation of criminal law; and

(B) there is reason to believe that (i) the subject of the investigation or proceeding is not aware of its pendency, and (ii) disclosure of the existence of the records could reasonably be expected to interfere with enforcement proceedings, the agency may, during only such time as that circumstance continues, treat the records as not subject to the requirements of this section.

(2) Whenever informant records maintained by a criminal law enforcement agency under an informant's name or personal identifier are requested by a third party according to the informant's name or personal identifier, the agency may treat the records as not subject to the requirements of this section unless the informant's status as an informant has been officially confirmed.

(3) Whenever a request is made which involves access to records maintained by the Federal Bureau of Investigation pertaining to foreign intelligence or counterintelligence, or international terrorism, and the existence of the records is classified in-

848

formation as provided in subsection (b)(1), the Bureau may, as long as the existence of the records remains classified information, treat the records as not subject to the requirements of this section.

(d) This section does not authorize withholding of information or limit the availability of records to the public, except as specifically stated in this section. This section is not authority to withhold information from Congress.

(e)(1) On or before February 1 of each year, each agency shall submit to the Attorney General of the United States a report which shall cover the preceding fiscal year and which shall include—

(A) the number of determinations made by the agency not to comply with requests for records made to such agency under subsection (a) and the reasons for each such determination;

(B)(i) the number of appeals made by persons under subsection (a)(6), the result of such appeals, and the reason for the action upon each appeal that results in a denial of information; and

(ii) a complete list of all statutes that the agency relies upon to authorize the agency to withhold information under subsection (b)(3), the number of occasions on which each statute was relied upon, a description of whether a court has upheld the decision of the agency to withhold information under each such statute, and a concise description of the scope of any information withheld;

(C) the number of requests for records pending before the agency as of September 30 of the preceding year, and the median and average number of days that such requests had been pending before the agency as of that date;

(D) the number of requests for records received by the agency and the number of requests which the agency processed;

(E) the median number of days taken by the agency to process different types of requests, based on the date on which the requests were received by the agency;

(F) the average number of days for the agency to respond to a request beginning on the date on which the request was received by the agency, the median number of days for the agency to respond to such requests, and the range in number of days for the agency to respond to such requests;

(G) based on the number of business days that have elapsed since each request was originally received by the agency—

(i) the number of requests for records to which the agency has responded with a determination within a period up to and including 20 days, and in 20–day increments up to and including 200 days;

(ii) the number of requests for records to which the agency has responded with a determination within a period greater than 200 days and less than 301 days;

(iii) the number of requests for records to which the agency has responded with a determination within a period greater than 300 days and less than 401 days; and

(iv) the number of requests for records to which the agency has responded with a determination within a period greater than 400 days;

(H) the average number of days for the agency to provide the granted information beginning on the date on which the request was originally filed, the median number of days for the agency to provide the granted information, and the range in number of days for the agency to provide the granted information;

(I) the median and average number of days for the agency to respond to administrative appeals based on the date on which the appeals originally were received by the agency, the highest number of business days taken by the agency to respond to an administrative appeal, and the lowest number of business days taken by the agency to respond to an administrative appeal;

(J) data on the 10 active requests with the earliest filing dates pending at each agency, including the amount of time that has elapsed since each request was originally received by the agency;

(K) data on the 10 active administrative appeals with the earliest filing dates pending before the agency as of September 30 of the preceding year, including the number of business days that have elapsed since the requests were originally received by the agency;

(L) the number of expedited review requests that are granted and denied, the average and median number of days for adjudicating expedited review requests, and the number adjudicated within the required 10 days;

(M) the number of fee waiver requests that are granted and denied, and the average and median number of days for adjudicating fee waiver determinations;

(N) the total amount of fees collected by the agency for processing requests; and

(O) the number of full-time staff of the agency devoted to processing requests for records under this section, and the total amount expended by the agency for processing such requests.

(2) Information in each report submitted under paragraph (1) shall be expressed in terms of each principal component of the agency and for the agency overall.

(3) Each agency shall make each such report available to the public including by computer telecommunications, or if computer telecommunications means have not been established by the agency, by other electronic means. In addition, each agency shall make the raw statistical data used in its reports available electronically to the public upon request.

* * *

(f) For purposes of this section, the term—

(1) "agency" as defined in section 551 (1) of this title includes any executive department, military department, Government corporation, Government controlled corporation, or other establishment in the executive branch of the Government (including the Executive Office of the President), or any independent regulatory agency; and

(2) "record" and any other term used in this section in reference to information includes—

(A) any information that would be an agency record subject to the requirements of this section when maintained by an agency in any format, including an electronic format; and

(B) any information described under subparagraph (A) that is maintained for an agency by an entity under Government contract, for the purposes of records management.

(g) The head of each agency shall prepare and make publicly available upon request, reference material or a guide for requesting records or information from the agency, subject to the exemptions in subsection (b), including—

(1) an index of all major information systems of the agency;

(2) a description of major information and record locator systems maintained by the agency; and

(3) a handbook for obtaining various types and categories of public information from the agency pursuant to chapter 35 of title 44, and under this section.

* * *

(j) Each agency shall designate a Chief FOIA Officer who shall be a senior official of such agency (at the Assistant Secretary or equivalent level).

(k) The Chief FOIA Officer of each agency shall, subject to the authority of the head of the agency—

(1) have agency-wide responsibility for efficient and appropriate compliance with this section;

(2) monitor implementation of this section throughout the agency and keep the head of the agency, the chief legal officer of the agency, and the Attorney General appropriately informed of the agency's performance in implementing this section;

(3) recommend to the head of the agency such adjustments to agency practices, policies, personnel, and funding as may be necessary to improve its implementation of this section;

(4) review and report to the Attorney General, through the head of the agency, at such times and in such formats as the Attorney General may direct, on the agency's performance in implementing this section;

(5) facilitate public understanding of the purposes of the statutory exemptions of this section by including concise descriptions of the exemptions in both the agency's handbook issued under subsection (g), and the agency's annual report on this section, and by providing an overview, where appropriate, of certain general categories of agency records to which those exemptions apply; and

(6) designate one or more FOIA Public Liaisons.

(*l*) FOIA Public Liaisons shall report to the agency Chief FOIA Officer and shall serve as supervisory officials to whom a requester under this section can raise concerns about the service the requester has received from the FOIA Requester Center, following an initial response from the FOIA Requester Center Staff. FOIA Public Liaisons shall be responsible for assisting in reducing delays, increasing transparency and understanding of the status of requests, and assisting in the resolution of disputes.

5 U.S.C. § 552b.[2] OPEN MEETINGS

(a) For purposes of this section—

(1) the term "agency" means any agency, as defined in section 552(e) of this title, headed by a collegial body composed of two or more individual members, a majority of whom are appointed to such position by the President with the advice and consent of the Senate, and any subdivision thereof authorized to act on behalf of the agency;

(2) the term "meeting" means the deliberations of at least the number of individual agency members required to take action on behalf of the agency where such deliberations determine or result in the joint conduct or disposition of official agency business, but does not include deliberations required or permitted by subsection (d) or (e); and

(3) the term "member" means an individual who belongs to a collegial body heading an agency.

(b) Members shall not jointly conduct or dispose of agency business other than in accordance with this section. Except as provided in subsection (c), every portion of every meeting of an agency shall be open to public observation.

(c) Except in a case where the agency finds that the public interest requires otherwise, the second sentence of subsection (b) shall not apply to any portion of an agency meeting, and the requirements of subsections (d) and (e) shall not apply to any information pertaining to such meeting otherwise required by this section to be

---

2. Section 552b is commonly known as the GOVERNMENT IN THE SUNSHINE ACT.

disclosed to the public, where the agency properly determines that such portion or portions of its meeting or the disclosure of such information is likely to—

(1) disclose matters that are (A) specifically authorized under criteria established by an Executive order to be kept secret in the interests of national defense or foreign policy and (B) in fact properly classified pursuant to such Executive order;

(2) relate solely to the internal personnel rules and practices of an agency;

(3) disclose matters specifically exempted from disclosure by statute (other than section 552 of this title), provided that such statute (A) requires that the matters be withheld from the public in such a manner as to leave no discretion on the issue, or (B) establishes particular criteria for withholding or refers to particular types of matters to be withheld;

(4) disclose trade secrets and commercial or financial information obtained from a person and privileged or confidential;

(5) involve accusing any person of a crime, or formally censuring any person;

(6) disclose information of a personal nature where disclosure would constitute a clearly unwarranted invasion of personal privacy;

(7) disclose investigatory records compiled for law enforcement purposes, or information which if written would be contained in such records, but only to the extent that the production of such records or information would (A) interfere with enforcement proceedings, (B) deprive a person of a right to a fair trial or an impartial adjudication, (C) constitute an unwarranted invasion of personal privacy, (D) disclose the identity of a confidential source and, in the case of a record compiled by a criminal law enforcement authority in the course of a criminal investigation, or by an agency conducting a lawful national security intelligence investigation, confidential information furnished only by the confidential source, (E) disclose investigative techniques and procedures, or (F) endanger the life or physical safety of law enforcement personnel;

(8) disclose information contained in or related to examination, operating, or condition reports prepared by, on behalf of, or for the use of an agency responsible for the regulation or supervision of financial institutions;

(9) disclose information the premature disclosure of which would—

(A) in the case of an agency which regulates currencies, securities, commodities, or financial institutions, be likely to (i) lead to significant financial speculation in currencies, securities, or commodities, or (ii) significantly endanger the stability of any financial institution; or

(B) in the case of any agency, be likely to significantly frustrate implementation of a proposed agency action, except that subparagraph (B) shall not apply in any instance where the agency has already disclosed to the public the content or nature of its proposed action, or where the agency is required by law to make such disclosure on its own initiative prior to taking final agency action on such proposal; or

(10) specifically concern the agency's issuance of a subpena [sic], or the agency's participation in a civil action or proceeding, an action in a foreign court or international tribunal, or an arbitration, or the initiation, conduct, or disposition by the agency of a particular case of formal agency adjudication pursuant to the procedures in section 554 of this title or otherwise involving a determination on the record after opportunity for a hearing.

(d)(1) Action under subsection (c) shall be taken only when a majority of the entire membership of the agency (as defined in subsection (a)(1)) votes to take such action. A separate vote of the agency members shall be taken with respect to each agency meeting a portion or portions of which are proposed to be closed to the public pursuant to subsection (c), or with respect to any information which is proposed to be withheld under subsection (c). A single vote may be taken with respect to a series of meetings, a portion or portions of which are proposed to be closed to the public, or with respect to any information concerning such series of meetings, so long as each meeting in such series involves the same particular matters and is scheduled to be held no more than thirty days after the initial meeting in such series. The vote of each agency member participating in such vote shall be recorded and no proxies shall be allowed.

(2) Whenever any person whose interests may be directly affected by a portion of a meeting requests that the agency close such portion to the public for any of the reasons referred to in paragraph (5), (6), or (7) of subsection (c), the agency, upon request of any one of its members, shall vote by recorded vote whether to close such meeting.

(3) Within one day of any vote taken pursuant to paragraph (1) or (2), the agency shall make publicly available a written copy of such vote reflecting the vote of each member on the question. If a portion of a meeting is to be closed to the public, the agency shall, within one day of the vote taken pursuant to paragraph (1) or (2) of this subsection, make publicly available a full written explanation of its action closing the portion together with a list of all persons expected to attend the meeting and their affiliation.

(4) Any agency, a majority of whose meetings may properly be closed to the public pursuant to paragraph (4), (8), (9)(A), or (10) of subsection (c), or any combination thereof, may provide by regulation for the closing of such meetings or portions thereof in the event that a majority of the members of the agency votes by recorded vote at the beginning of such meeting, or portion thereof, to close the exempt portion or portions of the meeting, and a copy of such vote, reflecting the vote of each member on the question, is made available to the public. The provisions of paragraphs (1), (2), and (3) of this subsection and subsection (e) shall not apply to any portion of a

meeting to which such regulations apply: Provided, That the agency shall, except to the extent that such information is exempt from disclosure under the provisions of subsection (c), provide the public with public announcement of the time, place, and subject matter of the meeting and of each portion thereof at the earliest practicable time.

(e)(1) In the case of each meeting, the agency shall make public announcement, at least one week before the meeting, of the time, place, and subject matter of the meeting, whether it is to be open or closed to the public, and the name and phone number of the official designated by the agency to respond to requests for information about the meeting. Such announcement shall be made unless a majority of the members of the agency determines by a recorded vote that agency business requires that such meeting be called at an earlier date, in which case the agency shall make public announcement of the time, place, and subject matter of such meeting, and whether open or closed to the public, at the earliest practicable time.

(2) The time or place of a meeting may be changed following the public announcement required by paragraph (1) only if the agency publicly announces such change at the earliest practicable time. The subject matter of a meeting, or the determination of the agency to open or close a meeting, or portion of a meeting, to the public, may be changed following the public announcement required by this subsection only if (A) a majority of the entire membership of the agency determines by a recorded vote that agency business so requires and that no earlier announcement of the change was possible, and (B) the agency publicly announces such change and the vote of each member upon such change at the earliest practicable time.

(3) Immediately following each public announcement required by this subsection, notice of the time, place, and subject matter of a meeting, whether the meeting is open or closed, any change in one of the preceding, and the name and phone number of the official designated by the agency to respond to requests for information about the meeting, shall also be submitted for publication in the Federal Register.

(f)(1) For every meeting closed pursuant to paragraphs (1) through (10) of subsection (c), the General Counsel or chief legal officer of the agency shall publicly certify that, in his or her opinion, the meeting may be closed to the public and shall state each relevant exemptive provision. A copy of such certification, together with a statement from the presiding officer of the meeting setting forth the time and place of the meeting, and the persons present, shall be retained by the agency. The agency shall maintain a complete transcript or electronic recording adequate to record fully the proceedings of each meeting, or portion of a meeting, closed to the public, except that in the case of a meeting, or portion of a meeting, closed to the public pursuant to paragraph (8), (9)(A), or (10) of subsection (c), the agency shall maintain either such a transcript or recording, or a set of minutes. Such minutes shall fully and clearly describe all matters discussed and shall provide a full and accurate summary of any actions taken, and the reasons therefor, including a description of each of the views expressed on any item and the record of any rollcall vote (reflecting the vote of each member on the question). All documents considered in connection with any action shall be identified in such minutes.

(2) The agency shall make promptly available to the public, in a place easily accessible to the public, the transcript, electronic recording, or minutes (as required by paragraph (1)) of the discussion of any item on the agenda, or of any item of the testimony of any witness received at the meeting, except for such item or items of such discussion or testimony as the agency determines to contain information which may be withheld under subsection (c). Copies of such transcript, or minutes, or a transcription of such recording disclosing the identity of each speaker, shall be furnished to any person at the actual cost of duplication or transcription. The agency shall maintain a complete verbatim copy of the transcript, a complete copy of the minutes, or a complete electronic recording of each meeting, or portion of a meeting, closed to the public, for a period of at least two years after such meeting, or until one year after the conclusion of any agency proceeding with respect to which the meeting or portion was held, whichever occurs later.

(g) Each agency subject to the requirements of this section shall, within 180 days after the date of enactment of this section, following consultation with the Office of the Chairman of the Administrative Conference of the United States and published notice in the Federal Register of at least thirty days and opportunity for written comment by any person, promulgate regulations to implement the requirements of subsections (b) through (f) of this section. Any person may bring a proceeding in the United States District Court for the District of Columbia to require an agency to promulgate such regulations if such agency has not promulgated such regulations within the time period specified herein. Subject to any limitations of time provided by law, any person may bring a proceeding in the United States Court of Appeals for the District of Columbia to set aside agency regulations issued pursuant to this subsection that are not in accord with the requirements of subsections (b) through (f) of this section and to require the promulgation of regulations that are in accord with such subsections.

(h)(1) The district courts of the United States shall have jurisdiction to enforce the requirements of subsections (b) through (f) of this section by declaratory judgment, injunctive relief, or other relief as may be appropriate. Such actions may be brought by any person against an agency prior to, or within sixty days after, the meeting out of which the violation of this section arises, except that if public announcement of such meeting is not initially provided by the agency in accordance with the requirements of this section, such action may be instituted pursuant to this section at any time prior to sixty days after any public announcement of such meeting. Such actions may be brought in the district court of the United States for the district in which the agency meeting is held or in which the agency in question has its headquarters, or in the District Court for the District of Columbia. In such actions a defendant shall serve his answer within thirty days after the service of the complaint. The burden is on the defendant to sustain his action. In deciding such cases the court may examine in camera any portion of the transcript, electronic recording, or minutes of a meeting closed to the public, and may take such additional evidence as it deems necessary. The court, having due regard for orderly administration and the public interest, as well as the interests of the parties, may grant such equitable relief as it deems appropriate, including granting an injunction against future violations of this section or ordering the agency to make available to the public such portion of the transcript, recording, or minutes of a meeting as is not authorized to be withheld under subsection (c) of this section.

(2) Any Federal court otherwise authorized by law to review agency action may, at the application of any person properly participating in the proceeding pursuant to other applicable law, inquire into violations by the agency of the requirements of this section and afford such relief as it deems appropriate. Nothing in this section authorizes any Federal court having jurisdiction solely on the basis of paragraph (1) to set aside, enjoin, or invalidate any agency action (other than an action to close a meeting or to withhold information under this section) taken or discussed at any agency meeting out of which the violation of this section arose.

(i) The court may assess against any party reasonable attorney fees and other litigation costs reasonably incurred by any other party who substantially prevails in any action brought in accordance with the provisions of subsection (g) or (h) of this section, except that costs may be assessed against the plaintiff only where the court finds that the suit was initiated by the plaintiff primarily for frivolous or dilatory purposes. In the case of assessment of costs against an agency, the costs may be assessed by the court against the United States.

(j) Each agency subject to the requirements of this section shall annually report to the Congress regarding the following:

(1) The changes in the policies and procedures of the agency under this section that have occurred during the preceding 1–year period.

(2) A tabulation of the number of meetings held, the exemptions applied to close meetings, and the days of public notice provided to close meetings.

(3) A brief description of litigation or formal complaints concerning the implementation of this section by the agency.

(4) A brief explanation of any changes in law that have affected the responsibilities of the agency under this section.

(k) Nothing herein expands or limits the present rights of any person under section 552 of this title, except that the exemptions set forth in subsection (c) of this section shall govern in the case of any request made pursuant to section 552 to copy or inspect the transcripts, recordings, or minutes described in subsection (f) of this section. The requirements of chapter 33 of title 44, United States Code, shall not apply to the transcripts, recordings, and minutes described in subsection (f) of this section.

(*l*) This section does not constitute authority to withhold any information from Congress, and does not authorize the closing of any agency meeting or portion thereof required by any other provision of law to be open.

(m) Nothing in this section authorizes any agency to withhold from any individual any record, including transcripts, recordings, or minutes required by this section, which is otherwise accessible to such individual under section 552a of this title.

5 U.S.C. § 553. RULE MAKING

(a) This section applies, according to the provisions thereof, except to the extent that there is involved—

(1) a military or foreign affairs function of the United States; or

(2) a matter relating to agency management or personnel or to public property, loans, grants, benefits, or contracts.

(b) General notice of proposed rule making shall be published in the Federal Register, unless persons subject thereto are named and either personally served or otherwise have actual notice thereof in accordance with law. The notice shall include—

(1) a statement of the time, place, and nature of public rule making proceedings;

(2) reference to the legal authority under which the rule is proposed; and

(3) either the terms or substance of the proposed rule or a description of the subjects and issues involved.

Except when notice or hearing is required by statute, this subsection does not apply—

(A) to interpretative rules, general statements of policy, or rules of agency organization, procedure, or practice; or

(B) when the agency for good cause finds (and incorporates the finding and a brief statement of reasons therefor in the rules issued) that notice and public procedure thereon are impracticable, unnecessary, or contrary to the public interest.

(c) After notice required by this section, the agency shall give interested persons an opportunity to participate in the rule making through submission of written data, views, or arguments with or without opportunity for oral presentation. After consideration of the relevant matter presented, the agency shall incorporate in the rules adopted a concise general statement of their basis and purpose. When rules are required by statute to be made on the record after opportunity for an agency hearing, sections 556 and 557 of this title apply instead of this subsection.

(d) The required publication or service of a substantive rule shall be made not less than 30 days before its effective date, except—

(1) a substantive rule which grants or recognizes an exemption or relieves a restriction;

(2) interpretative rules and statements of policy; or

(3) as otherwise provided by the agency for good cause found and published with the rule.

(e) Each agency shall give an interested person the right to petition for the issuance, amendment, or repeal of a rule.

5 U.S.C. § 554. ADJUDICATIONS

(a) This section applies, according to the provisions thereof, in every case of adjudication required by statute to be determined on the record after opportunity for an agency hearing, except to the extent that there is involved—

(1) a matter subject to a subsequent trial of the law and the facts de novo in a court;

(2) the selection or tenure of an employee, except a administrative law judge appointed under section 3105 of this title;

(3) proceedings in which decisions rest solely on inspections, tests, or elections;

(4) the conduct of military or foreign affairs functions;

(5) cases in which an agency is acting as an agent for a court; or

(6) the certification of worker representatives.

(b) Persons entitled to notice of an agency hearing shall be timely informed of—

(1) the time, place, and nature of the hearing;

(2) the legal authority and jurisdiction under which the hearing is to be held; and

(3) the matters of fact and law asserted.

When private persons are the moving parties, other parties to the proceeding shall give prompt notice of issues controverted in fact or law; and in other instances agencies may by rule require responsive pleading. In fixing the time and place for hearings, due regard shall be had for the convenience and necessity of the parties or their representatives.

(c) The agency shall give all interested parties opportunity for—

(1) the submission and consideration of facts, arguments, offers of settlement, or proposals of adjustment when time, the nature of the proceeding, and the public interest permit; and

(2) to the extent that the parties are unable so to determine a controversy by consent, hearing and decision on notice and in accordance with sections 556 and 557 of this title.

(d) The employee who presides at the reception of evidence pursuant to section 556 of this title shall make the recommended decision or initial decision required by section 557 of this title, unless he becomes unavailable to the agency. Except to the extent required for the disposition of ex parte matters as authorized by law, such an employee may not—

(1) consult a person or party on a fact in issue, unless on notice and opportunity for all parties to participate; or

(2) be responsible to or subject to the supervision or direction of an employee or agent engaged in the performance of investigative or prosecuting functions for an agency.

An employee or agent engaged in the performance of investigative or prosecuting functions for an agency in a case may not, in that or a factually related case, participate or advise in the decision, recommended decision, or agency review pursuant to section 557 of this title, except as witness or counsel in public proceedings. This subsection does not apply—

(A) in determining applications for initial licenses;

(B) to proceedings involving the validity or application of rates, facilities, or practices of public utilities or carriers; or

(C) to the agency or a member or members of the body comprising the agency.

(e) The agency, with like effect as in the case of other orders, and in its sound discretion, may issue a declaratory order to terminate a controversy or remove uncertainty.

5 U.S.C. § 555. ANCILLARY MATTERS

(a) This section applies, according to the provisions thereof, except as otherwise provided by this subchapter.

(b) A person compelled to appear in person before an agency or representative thereof is entitled to be accompanied, represented, and advised by counsel or, if permitted by the agency, by other qualified representative. A party is entitled to appear in person or by or with counsel or other duly qualified representative in an agency proceeding. So far as the orderly conduct of public business permits, an interested person may appear before an agency or its responsible employees for the presentation, adjustment, or determination of an issue, request, or controversy in a proceeding, whether interlocutory, summary, or otherwise, or in connection with an agency function. With due regard for the convenience and necessity of the parties or their representatives and within a reasonable time, each agency shall proceed to conclude a matter presented to it. This subsection does not grant or deny a person who is not a lawyer the right to appear for or represent others before an agency or in an agency proceeding.

(c) Process, requirement of a report, inspection, or other investigative act or demand may not be issued, made, or enforced except as authorized by law. A person compelled to submit data or evidence is entitled to retain or, on payment of lawfully prescribed costs, procure a copy or transcript thereof, except that in a nonpublic investigatory proceeding the witness may for good cause be limited to inspection of the official transcript of his testimony.

(d) Agency subpenas [sic] authorized by law shall be issued to a party on request and, when required by rules of procedure, on a statement or showing of general relevance and reasonable scope of the evidence sought. On contest, the court shall sustain the subpena [sic] or similar process or demand to the extent that it is found to be in accordance with law. In a proceeding for enforcement, the court shall issue an order requiring the appearance of the witness or the production of the evidence or data within a reasonable time under penalty of punishment for contempt in case of contumacious failure to comply.

(e) Prompt notice shall be given of the denial in whole or in part of a written application, petition, or other request of an interested person made in connection with any agency proceeding. Except in affirming a prior denial or when the denial is self-explanatory, the notice shall be accompanied by a brief statement of the grounds for denial.

5 U.S.C. § 556. HEARINGS; PRESIDING EMPLOYEES; POWERS AND DUTIES; BURDEN OF PROOF; EVIDENCE, RECORD AS BASIS OF DECISION

(a) This section applies, according to the provisions thereof, to hearings required by section 553 or 554 of this title to be conducted in accordance with this section.

(b) There shall preside at the taking of evidence—

(1) the agency;

(2) one or more members of the body which comprises the agency; or

(3) one or more administrative law judges appointed under section 3105 of this title.

This subchapter does not supersede the conduct of specified classes of proceedings, in whole or in part, by or before boards or other employees specially provided for by or designated under statute. The functions of presiding employees and of employees participating in decisions in accordance with section 557 of this title shall be conducted in an impartial manner. A presiding or participating employee may at any time disqualify himself. On the filing in good faith of a timely and sufficient affidavit of personal bias or other disqualification of a presiding or participating employee, the agency shall determine the matter as a part of the record and decision in the case.

(c) Subject to published rules of the agency and within its powers, employees presiding at hearings may—

(1) administer oaths and affirmations;

(2) issue subpenas [sic] authorized by law;

(3) rule on offers of proof and receive relevant evidence;

(4) take depositions or have depositions taken when the ends of justice would be served;

(5) regulate the course of the hearing;

(6) hold conferences for the settlement or simplification of the issues by consent of the parties or by the use of alternative means of dispute resolution as provided in subchapter IV of this chapter;

(7) inform the parties as to the availability of one or more alternative means of dispute resolution, and encourage use of such methods;

(8) require the attendance at any conference held pursuant to paragraph (6) of at least one representative of each party who has authority to negotiate concerning resolution of issues in controversy;

(9) dispose of procedural requests or similar matters;

(10) make or recommend decisions in accordance with section 557 of this title; and

(11) take other action authorized by agency rule consistent with this subchapter.

(d) Except as otherwise provided by statute, the proponent of a rule or order has the burden of proof. Any oral or documentary evidence may be received, but the agency as a matter of policy shall provide for the exclusion of irrelevant, immaterial, or unduly repetitious evidence. A sanction may not be imposed or rule or order issued except on consideration of the whole record or those parts thereof cited by a party and supported by and in accordance with the reliable, probative, and substantial evidence. The agency may, to the extent consistent with the interests of justice and the policy of the underlying statutes administered by the agency, consider a violation of section 557(d) of this title sufficient grounds for a decision adverse to a party who has knowingly committed such violation or knowingly caused such violation to occur. A party is entitled to present his case or defense by oral or documentary evidence, to submit rebuttal evidence, and to conduct such cross-examination as may be required for a full and true disclosure of the facts. In rule making or determining claims for money or benefits or applications for initial licenses an agency may, when a party will not be prejudiced thereby, adopt procedures for the submission of all or part of the evidence in written form.

(e) The transcript of testimony and exhibits, together with all papers and requests filed in the proceeding, constitutes the exclusive record for decision in accordance with section 557 of this title and, on payment of lawfully prescribed costs, shall be made available to the parties. When an agency decision rests on official notice of a material fact not appearing in the evidence in the record, a party is entitled, on timely request, to an opportunity to show the contrary.

5 U.S.C. § 557. INITIAL DECISIONS; CONCLUSIVENESS; REVIEW BY AGENCY; SUBMISSIONS BY PARTIES; CONTENTS OF DECISIONS; RECORD

(a) This section applies, according to the provisions thereof, when a hearing is required to be conducted in accordance with section 556 of this title.

(b) When the agency did not preside at the reception of the evidence, the presiding employee or, in cases not subject to section 554(d) of this title, an employee qualified to preside at hearings pursuant to section 556 of this title, shall initially decide the case unless the agency requires, either in specific cases or by general rule, the entire record to be certified to it for decision. When the presiding employee makes an initial decision, that decision then becomes the decision of the agency without further proceedings unless there is an appeal to, or review on motion of, the agency within time provided by rule. On appeal from or review of the initial decision, the agency has all the powers which it would have in making the initial decision except as it may limit the issues on notice or by rule. When the agency makes the decision without having presided at the reception of the evidence, the presiding employee or an employee qualified to preside at hearings pursuant to section 556 of this title shall first recommend a decision, except that in rule making or determining applications for initial licenses —

(1) instead thereof the agency may issue a tentative decision or one of its responsible employees may recommend a decision; or

(2) this procedure may be omitted in a case in which the agency finds on the record that due and timely execution of its functions imperatively and unavoidably so requires.

(c) Before a recommended, initial, or tentative decision, or a decision on agency review of the decision of subordinate employees, the parties are entitled to a reasonable opportunity to submit for the consideration of the employees participating in the decisions —

(1) proposed findings and conclusions; or

(2) exceptions to the decisions or recommended decisions of subordinate employees or to tentative agency decisions; and

(3) supporting reasons for the exceptions or proposed findings or conclusions.

The record shall show the ruling on each finding, conclusion, or exception presented. All decisions, including initial, recommended, and tentative decisions, are a part of the record and shall include a statement of —

(A) findings and conclusions, and the reasons or basis therefor, on all the material issues of fact, law, or discretion presented on the record; and

(B) the appropriate rule, order, sanction, relief, or denial thereof.

(d)(1) In any agency proceeding which is subject to subsection (a) of this section, except to the extent required for the disposition of ex parte matters as authorized by law —

(A) no interested person outside the agency shall make or knowingly cause to be made to any member of the body comprising the agency, administrative law judge, or other employee who is or may reasonably be expected to be involved in the decisional process of the proceeding, an ex parte communication relevant to the merits of the proceeding;

(B) no member of the body comprising the agency, administrative law judge, or other employee who is or may reasonably be expected to be involved in the decisional process of the proceeding, shall make or knowingly cause to be made to any interested person outside the agency an ex parte communication relevant to the merits of the proceeding;

(C) a member of the body comprising the agency, administrative law judge, or other employee who is or may reasonably be expected to be involved in the decisional process of such proceeding who receives, or who makes or knowingly causes to be made, a communication prohibited by this subsection shall place on the public record of the proceeding:

(i) all such written communications;

(ii) memoranda stating the substance of all such oral communications; and

(iii) all written responses, and memoranda stating the substance of all oral responses, to the materials described in clauses (i) and (ii) of this subparagraph;

(D) upon receipt of a communication knowingly made or knowingly caused to be made by a party in violation of this subsection, the agency, administrative law judge, or other employee presiding at the hearing may, to the extent consistent with the interests of justice and the policy of the underlying statutes, require the party to show cause why his claim or interest in the proceeding should not be dismissed, denied, disregarded, or otherwise adversely affected on account of such violation; and

(E) the prohibitions of this subsection shall apply beginning at such time as the agency may designate, but in no case shall they begin to apply later than the time at which a proceeding is noticed for hearing unless the person responsible for the communication has knowledge that it will be noticed, in which case the prohibitions shall apply beginning at the time of his acquisition of such knowledge.

(2) This subsection does not constitute authority to withhold information from Congress.

5 U.S.C. § 558. IMPOSITION OF SANCTIONS; DETERMINATION OF APPLICATIONS FOR LICENSES; SUSPENSION, REVOCATION, AND EXPIRATION OF LICENSES

(a) This section applies, according to the provisions thereof, to the exercise of a power or authority.

(b) A sanction may not be imposed or a substantive rule or order issued except within jurisdiction delegated to the agency and as authorized by law.

(c) When application is made for a license required by law, the agency, with due regard for the rights and privileges of all the interested parties or adversely affected persons and within a reasonable time, shall set and complete proceedings required to be conducted in accordance with sections 556 and 557 of this title or other proceedings required by law and shall make its decision. Except in cases of willfulness or those in which public health, interest, or safety requires otherwise, the withdrawal, suspension, revocation, or annulment of a license is lawful only if, before the institution of agency proceedings therefor, the licensee has been given—

(1) notice by the agency in writing of the facts or conduct which may warrant the action; and

(2) opportunity to demonstrate or achieve compliance with all lawful requirements.

When the licensee has made timely and sufficient application for a renewal or a new license in accordance with agency rules, a license with reference to an activity of a continuing nature does not expire until the application has been finally determined by the agency.

5 U.S.C. § 559. EFFECT ON OTHER LAWS; EFFECT OF SUBSEQUENT STATUTE

This subchapter, chapter 7, and sections 1305, 3105, 3344, 4301(2)(E), 5372, and 7521 of this title, and the provisions of section 5335(a)(B) of this title that relate to administrative law judges, do not limit or repeal additional requirements imposed by statute or otherwise recognized by law. Except as otherwise required by law, requirements or privileges relating to evidence or procedure apply equally to agencies and persons. Each agency is granted the authority necessary to comply with the requirements of this subchapter through the issuance of rules or otherwise. Subsequent statute may not be held to supersede or modify this subchapter, chapter 7, sections 1305, 3105, 3344, 4301(2)(E), 5372, or 7521 of this title, or the provisions of section 5335(a)(B) of this title that relate to administrative law judges, except to the extent that it does so expressly.

CHAPTER 5, SUBCHAPTER III—NEGOTIATED RULEMAKING PROCEDURE ("NEGOTIATED RULEMAKING ACT")

5 U.S.C. § 561. PURPOSE

The purpose of this subchapter is to establish a framework for the conduct of negotiated rulemaking, consistent with section 553 of this title, to encourage agencies to use the process when it enhances the informal rulemaking process. Nothing in this subchapter should be construed as an attempt to limit innovation and experimentation with the negotiated rulemaking process or with other innovative rulemaking procedures otherwise authorized by law.

5 U.S.C. § 562. DEFINITIONS

For the purposes of this subchapter, the term—

(1) "agency" has the same meaning as in section 551(1) of this title;

(2) "consensus" means unanimous concurrence among the interests represented on a negotiated rulemaking committee established under this subchapter, unless such committee—

   (A) agrees to define such term to mean a general but not unanimous concurrence; or

   (B) agrees upon another specified definition;

(3) "convener" means a person who impartially assists an agency in determining whether establishment of a negotiated rulemaking committee is feasible and appropriate in a particular rulemaking;

(4) "facilitator" means a person who impartially aids in the discussions and negotiations among the members of a negotiated rulemaking committee to develop a proposed rule;

(5) "interest" means, with respect to an issue or matter, multiple parties which have a similar point of view or which are likely to be affected in a similar manner;

(6) "negotiated rulemaking" means rulemaking through the use of a negotiated rulemaking committee;

(7) "negotiated rulemaking committee" or "committee" means an advisory committee established by an agency in accordance with this subchapter and the Federal Advisory Committee Act to consider and discuss issues for the purpose of reaching a consensus in the development of a proposed rule;

(8) "party" has the same meaning as in section 551(3) of this title;

(9) "person" has the same meaning as in section 551(2) of this title;

(10) "rule" has the same meaning as in section 551(4) of this title; and

(11) "rulemaking" means "rule making" as that term is defined in section 551(5) of this title.

5 U.S.C. § 563. DETERMINATION OF NEED FOR NEGOTIATED RULEMAKING COMMITTEE

(a) Determination of need by the agency.—An agency may establish a negotiated rulemaking committee to negotiate and develop a proposed rule, if the head of the agency determines that the use of the negotiated rulemaking procedure is in the public interest. In making such a determination, the head of the agency shall consider whether—

(1) there is a need for a rule;

(2) there are a limited number of identifiable interests that will be significantly affected by the rule;

(3) there is a reasonable likelihood that a committee can be convened with a balanced representation of persons who—

(A) can adequately represent the interests identified under paragraph (2); and

(B) are willing to negotiate in good faith to reach a consensus on the proposed rule;

(4) there is a reasonable likelihood that a committee will reach a consensus on the proposed rule within a fixed period of time;

(5) the negotiated rulemaking procedure will not unreasonably delay the notice of proposed rulemaking and the issuance of the final rule;

(6) the agency has adequate resources and is willing to commit such resources, including technical assistance, to the committee; and

(7) the agency, to the maximum extent possible consistent with the legal obligations of the agency, will use the consensus of the committee with respect to the proposed rule as the basis for the rule proposed by the agency for notice and comment.

(b) Use of conveners.—

(1) Purposes of conveners.—An agency may use the services of a convener to assist the agency in—

(A) identifying persons who will be significantly affected by a proposed rule, including residents of rural areas; and

(B) conducting discussions with such persons to identify the issues of concern to such persons, and to ascertain whether the establishment of a negotiated rulemaking committee is feasible and appropriate in the particular rulemaking.

(2) Duties of conveners.—The convener shall report findings and may make recommendations to the agency. Upon request of the agency, the convener shall ascertain the names of persons who are willing and qualified to represent interests

that will be significantly affected by the proposed rule, including residents of rural areas. The report and any recommendations of the convener shall be made available to the public upon request.

5 U.S.C. § 564. PUBLICATION OF NOTICE; APPLICATIONS FOR MEMBERSHIP ON COMMITTEES

(a) Publication of notice.—If, after considering the report of a convener or conducting its own assessment, an agency decides to establish a negotiated rulemaking committee, the agency shall publish in the Federal Register and, as appropriate, in trade or other specialized publications, a notice which shall include—

(1) an announcement that the agency intends to establish a negotiated rulemaking committee to negotiate and develop a proposed rule;

(2) a description of the subject and scope of the rule to be developed, and the issues to be considered;

(3) a list of the interests which are likely to be significantly affected by the rule;

(4) a list of the persons proposed to represent such interests and the person or persons proposed to represent the agency;

(5) a proposed agenda and schedule for completing the work of the committee, including a target date for publication by the agency of a proposed rule for notice and comment;

(6) a description of administrative support for the committee to be provided by the agency, including technical assistance;

(7) a solicitation for comments on the proposal to establish the committee, and the proposed membership of the negotiated rulemaking committee; and

(8) an explanation of how a person may apply or nominate another person for membership on the committee, as provided under subsection (b).

(b) Applications for membership or committee.—Persons who will be significantly affected by a proposed rule and who believe that their interests will not be adequately represented by any person specified in a notice under subsection (a)(4) may apply for, or nominate another person for, membership on the negotiated rulemaking committee to represent such interests with respect to the proposed rule. Each application or nomination shall include—

(1) the name of the applicant or nominee and a description of the interests such person shall represent;

(2) evidence that the applicant or nominee is authorized to represent parties related to the interests the person proposes to represent;

(3) a written commitment that the applicant or nominee shall actively participate in good faith in the development of the rule under consideration; and

(4) the reasons that the persons specified in the notice under subsection (a)(4) do not adequately represent the interests of the person submitting the application or nomination.

(c) Period for submission of comments and applications.—The agency shall provide for a period of at least 30 calendar days for the submission of comments and applications under this section.

5 U.S.C. § 565. ESTABLISHMENT OF COMMITTEE

(a) Establishment.—

(1) Determination to establish committee.—If after considering comments and applications submitted under section 564, the agency determines that a negotiated rulemaking committee can adequately represent the interests that will be significantly affected by a proposed rule and that it is feasible and appropriate in the particular rulemaking, the agency may establish a negotiated rulemaking committee. In establishing and administering such a committee, the agency shall comply with the Federal Advisory Committee Act with respect to such committee, except as otherwise provided in this subchapter.

(2) Determination not to establish committee.—If after considering such comments and applications, the agency decides not to establish a negotiated rulemaking committee, the agency shall promptly publish notice of such decision and the reasons therefor in the Federal Register and, as appropriate, in trade or other specialized publications, a copy of which shall be sent to any person who applied for, or nominated another person for membership on the negotiating rulemaking committee to represent such interests with respect to the proposed rule.

(b) Membership.—The agency shall limit membership on a negotiated rulemaking committee to 25 members, unless the agency head determines that a greater number of members is necessary for the functioning of the committee or to achieve balanced membership. Each committee shall include at least one person representing the agency.

(c) Administrative support.—The agency shall provide appropriate administrative support to the negotiated rulemaking committee, including technical assistance.

5 U.S.C. § 566. CONDUCT OF COMMITTEE ACTIVITY

(a) Duties of committee.—Each negotiated rulemaking committee established under this subchapter shall consider the matter proposed by the agency for consideration and shall attempt to reach a consensus concerning a proposed rule with respect to such matter and any other matter the committee determines is relevant to the proposed rule.

(b) Representatives of agency on committee.—The person or persons representing the agency on a negotiated rulemaking committee shall participate in the deliberations and activities of the committee with the same rights and responsibilities as other members of the committee, and shall be authorized to fully represent the agency in the discussions and negotiations of the committee.

(c) Selecting facilitator.—Notwithstanding section 10(e) of the Federal Advisory Committee Act, an agency may nominate either a person from the Federal Government or a person from outside the Federal Government to serve as a facilitator for the negotiations of the committee, subject to the approval of the committee by consensus. If the committee does not approve the nominee of the agency for facilitator, the agency shall submit a substitute nomination. If a committee does not approve any nominee of the agency for facilitator, the committee shall select by consensus a person to serve as facilitator. A person designated to represent the agency in substantive issues may not serve as facilitator or otherwise chair the committee.

(d) Duties of facilitator.—A facilitator approved or selected by a negotiated rulemaking committee shall—

(1) chair the meetings of the committee in an impartial manner;

(2) impartially assist the members of the committee in conducting discussions and negotiations; and

(3) manage the keeping of minutes and records as required under section 10(b) and (c) of the Federal Advisory Committee Act, except that any personal notes and materials of the facilitator or of the members of a committee shall not be subject to section 552 of this title.

(e) Committee procedures.—A negotiated rulemaking committee established under this subchapter may adopt procedures for the operation of the committee. No provision of section 553 of this title shall apply to the procedures of a negotiated rulemaking committee.

(f) Report of committee.—If a committee reaches a consensus on a proposed rule, at the conclusion of negotiations the committee shall transmit to the agency that established the committee a report containing the proposed rule. If the committee does not reach a consensus on a proposed rule, the committee may transmit to the agency a report specifying any areas in which the committee reached a consensus. The committee may include in a report any other information, recommendations, or materials that the committee considers appropriate. Any committee member may include as an addendum to the report additional information, recommendations, or materials.

(g) Records of committee.—In addition to the report required by subsection (f), a committee shall submit to the agency the records required under section 10(b) and (c) of the Federal Advisory Committee Act.

5 U.S.C. § 567. TERMINATION OF COMMITTEE

A negotiated rulemaking committee shall terminate upon promulgation of the final rule under consideration, unless the committee's charter contains an earlier termination date or the agency, after consulting the committee, or the committee itself specifies an earlier termination date.

5 U.S.C. § 568. SERVICES, FACILITIES, AND PAYMENT OF COMMITTEE MEMBER EXPENSES

(a) Services of conveners and facilitators.—

(1) In general.—An agency may employ or enter into contracts for the services of an individual or organization to serve as a convener or facilitator for a negotiated rulemaking committee under this subchapter, or may use the services of a Government employee to act as a convener or a facilitator for such a committee.

(2) Determination of conflicting interests.—An agency shall determine whether a person under consideration to serve as convener or facilitator of a committee under paragraph (1) has any financial or other interest that would preclude such person from serving in an impartial and independent manner.

(b) Services and facilities of other entities.—For purposes of this subchapter, an agency may use the services and facilities of other Federal agencies and public and private agencies and instrumentalities with the consent of such agencies and instrumentalities, and with or without reimbursement to such agencies and instrumentalities, and may accept voluntary and uncompensated services without regard to the provisions of section 1342 of title 31. The Federal Mediation and Conciliation Service may provide services and facilities, with or without reimbursement, to assist agencies under this subchapter, including furnishing conveners, facilitators, and training in negotiated rulemaking.

(c) Expenses of committee members.—Members of a negotiated rulemaking committee shall be responsible for their own expenses of participation in such committee, except that an agency may, in accordance with section 7(d) of the Federal Advisory Committee Act, pay for a member's reasonable travel and per diem expenses, expenses to obtain technical assistance, and a reasonable rate of compensation, if—

(1) such member certifies a lack of adequate financial resources to participate in the committee; and

(2) the agency determines that such member's participation in the committee is necessary to assure an adequate representation of the member's interest.

(d) Status of member as federal employee.—A member's receipt of funds under this section or section 569 shall not conclusively determine for purposes of sections 202 through 209 of title 18 whether that member is an employee of the United States Government.

5 U.S.C. § 569. ENCOURAGING NEGOTIATED RULEMAKING

(a) The President shall designate an agency or designate or establish an interagency committee to facilitate and encourage agency use of negotiated rulemaking. An agency that is considering, planning, or conducting a negotiated rulemaking may consult with such agency or committee for information and assistance.

(b) To carry out the purposes of this subchapter, an agency planning or conducting a negotiated rulemaking may accept, hold, administer, and utilize gifts, devises, and bequests of property, both real and personal if that agency's acceptance and use of such gifts, devises, or bequests do not create a conflict of interest. Gifts and bequests of money and proceeds from sales of other property received as gifts, devises, or bequests shall be deposited in the Treasury and shall be disbursed upon the order of the head of such agency. Property accepted pursuant to this section, and the proceeds thereof, shall be used as nearly as possible in accordance with the terms of the gifts, devises, or bequests.

5 U.S.C. § 570. JUDICIAL REVIEW

Any agency action relating to establishing, assisting, or terminating a negotiated rulemaking committee under this subchapter shall not be subject to judicial review. Nothing in this section shall bar judicial review of a rule if such judicial review is otherwise provided by law. A rule which is the product of negotiated rulemaking and is subject to judicial review shall not be accorded any greater deference by a court than a rule which is the product of other rulemaking procedures.

CHAPTER 5, SUBCHAPTER IV—ALTERNATIVE MEANS OF DISPUTE RESOLUTION IN THE ADMINISTRATIVE PROCESS ("ALTERNATIVE DISPUTE RESOLUTION ACT")

5 U.S.C. § 571. DEFINITIONS

For the purposes of this subchapter, the term—

(1) "agency" has the same meaning as in section 551(1) of this title;

(2) "administrative program" includes a Federal function which involves protection of the public interest and the determination of rights, privileges, and obligations of private persons through rule making, adjudication, licensing, or investigation, as those terms are used in subchapter II of this chapter;

(3) "alternative means of dispute resolution" means any procedure that is used to resolve issues in controversy, including, but not limited to, conciliation, facilitation, mediation, factfinding, minitrials, arbitration, and use of ombuds, or any combination thereof;

(4) "award" means any decision by an arbitrator resolving the issues in controversy;

(5) "dispute resolution communication" means any oral or written communication prepared for the purposes of a dispute resolution proceeding, including any memoranda, notes or work product of the neutral, parties or nonparty participant; except that a written agreement to enter into a dispute resolution proceeding, or final written agreement or arbitral award reached as a result of a dispute resolution proceeding, is not a dispute resolution communication;

(6) "dispute resolution proceeding" means any process in which an alternative means of dispute resolution is used to resolve an issue in controversy in which a neutral is appointed and specified parties participate;

(7) "in confidence" means, with respect to information, that the information is provided—

(A) with the expressed intent of the source that it not be disclosed; or

(B) under circumstances that would create the reasonable expectation on behalf of the source that the information will not be disclosed;

(8) "issue in controversy" means an issue which is material to a decision concerning an administrative program of an agency, and with which there is disagreement—

(A) between an agency and persons who would be substantially affected by the decision; or

(B) between persons who would be substantially affected by the decision;

(9) "neutral" means an individual who, with respect to an issue in controversy, functions specifically to aid the parties in resolving the controversy;

(10) "party" means—

(A) for a proceeding with named parties, the same as in section 551(3) of this title; and

(B) for a proceeding without named parties, a person who will be significantly affected by the decision in the proceeding and who participates in the proceeding;

(11) "person" has the same meaning as in section 551(2) of this title; and

(12) "roster" means a list of persons qualified to provide services as neutrals.

5 U.S.C. § 572. GENERAL AUTHORITY

(a) An agency may use a dispute resolution proceeding for the resolution of an issue in controversy that relates to an administrative program, if the parties agree to such proceeding.

(b) An agency shall consider not using a dispute resolution proceeding if—

(1) a definitive or authoritative resolution of the matter is required for precedential value, and such a proceeding is not likely to be accepted generally as an authoritative precedent;

(2) the matter involves or may bear upon significant questions of Government policy that require additional procedures before a final resolution may be made, and such a proceeding would not likely serve to develop a recommended policy for the agency;

(3) maintaining established policies is of special importance, so that variations among individual decisions are not increased and such a proceeding would not likely reach consistent results among individual decisions;

(4) the matter significantly affects persons or organizations who are not parties to the proceeding;

(5) a full public record of the proceeding is important, and a dispute resolution proceeding cannot provide such a record; and

(6) the agency must maintain continuing jurisdiction over the matter with authority to alter the disposition of the matter in the light of changed circumstances, and a dispute resolution proceeding would interfere with the agency's fulfilling that requirement.

(c) Alternative means of dispute resolution authorized under this subchapter are voluntary procedures which supplement rather than limit other available agency dispute resolution techniques.

5 U.S.C. § 573. NEUTRALS

(a) A neutral may be a permanent or temporary officer or employee of the Federal Government or any other individual who is acceptable to the parties to a dispute resolution proceeding. A neutral shall have no official, financial, or personal conflict of interest with respect to the issues in controversy, unless such interest is fully disclosed in writing to all parties and all parties agree that the neutral may serve.

(b) A neutral who serves as a conciliator, facilitator, or mediator serves at the will of the parties.

(c) The President shall designate an agency or designate or establish an interagency committee to facilitate and encourage agency use of dispute resolution under this subchapter. Such agency or interagency committee, in consultation with other appropriate Federal agencies and professional organizations experienced in matters concerning dispute resolution, shall—

(1) encourage and facilitate agency use of alternative means of dispute resolution; and

(2) develop procedures that permit agencies to obtain the services of neutrals on an expedited basis.

(d) An agency may use the services of one or more employees of other agencies to serve as neutrals in dispute resolution proceedings. The agencies may enter into an interagency agreement that provides for the reimbursement by the user agency or the parties of the full or partial cost of the services of such an employee.

(e) Any agency may enter into a contract with any person for services as a neutral, or for training in connection with alternative means of dispute resolution. The parties in a dispute resolution proceeding shall agree on compensation for the neutral that is fair and reasonable to the Government.

5 U.S.C. § 574. CONFIDENTIALITY

(a) Except as provided in subsections (d) and (e), a neutral in a dispute resolution proceeding shall not voluntarily disclose or through discovery or compulsory process be required to disclose any dispute resolution communication or any communication provided in confidence to the neutral, unless—

(1) all parties to the dispute resolution proceeding and the neutral consent in writing, and, if the dispute resolution communication was provided by a nonparty participant, that participant also consents in writing;

(2) the dispute resolution communication has already been made public;

(3) the dispute resolution communication is required by statute to be made public, but a neutral should make such communication public only if no other person is reasonably available to disclose the communication; or

(4) a court determines that such testimony or disclosure is necessary to—

(A) prevent a manifest injustice;

(B) help establish a violation of law; or

(C) prevent harm to the public health or safety,

of sufficient magnitude in the particular case to outweigh the integrity of dispute resolution proceedings in general by reducing the confidence of parties in future cases that their communications will remain confidential.

(b) A party to a dispute resolution proceeding shall not voluntarily disclose or through discovery or compulsory process be required to disclose any dispute resolution communication, unless—

(1) the communication was prepared by the party seeking disclosure;

(2) all parties to the dispute resolution proceeding consent in writing;

(3) the dispute resolution communication has already been made public;

(4) the dispute resolution communication is required by statute to be made public;

(5) a court determines that such testimony or disclosure is necessary to—

(A) prevent a manifest injustice;

(B) help establish a violation of law; or

(C) prevent harm to the public health and safety,

of sufficient magnitude in the particular case to outweigh the integrity of dispute resolution proceedings in general by reducing the confidence of parties in future cases that their communications will remain confidential;

(6) the dispute resolution communication is relevant to determining the existence or meaning of an agreement or award that resulted from the dispute resolution proceeding or to the enforcement of such an agreement or award; or

(7) except for dispute resolution communications generated by the neutral, the dispute resolution communication was provided to or was available to all parties to the dispute resolution proceeding.

(c) Any dispute resolution communication that is disclosed in violation of subsection (a) or (b), shall not be admissible in any proceeding relating to the issues in controversy with respect to which the communication was made.

(d)(1) The parties may agree to alternative confidential procedures for disclosures by a neutral. Upon such agreement the parties shall inform the neutral before the commencement of the dispute resolution proceeding of any modifications to the provisions of subsection (a) that will govern the confidentiality of the dispute resolution proceeding. If the parties do not so inform the neutral, subsection (a) shall apply.

(2) To qualify for the exemption established under subsection (j), an alternative confidential procedure under this subsection may not provide for less disclosure than the confidential procedures otherwise provided under this section.

(e) If a demand for disclosure, by way of discovery request or other legal process, is made upon a neutral regarding a dispute resolution communication, the neutral shall make reasonable efforts to notify the parties and any affected nonparty participants of the demand. Any party or affected nonparty participant who receives such notice and within 15 calendar days does not offer to defend a refusal of the neutral to disclose the requested information shall have waived any objection to such disclosure.

(f) Nothing in this section shall prevent the discovery or admissibility of any evidence that is otherwise discoverable, merely because the evidence was presented in the course of a dispute resolution proceeding.

(g) Subsections (a) and (b) shall have no effect on the information and data that are necessary to document an agreement reached or order issued pursuant to a dispute resolution proceeding.

(h) Subsections (a) and (b) shall not prevent the gathering of information for research or educational purposes, in cooperation with other agencies, governmental entities, or dispute resolution programs, so long as the parties and the specific issues in controversy are not identifiable.

(i) Subsections (a) and (b) shall not prevent use of a dispute resolution communication to resolve a dispute between the neutral in a dispute resolution proceeding and a party to or participant in such proceeding, so long as such dispute resolution communication is disclosed only to the extent necessary to resolve such dispute.

(j) A dispute resolution communication which is between a neutral and a party and which may not be disclosed under this section shall also be exempt from disclosure under section 552(b)(3).

5 U.S.C. § 575. AUTHORIZATION OF ARBITRATION

(a)(1) Arbitration may be used as an alternative means of dispute resolution whenever all parties consent. Consent may be obtained either before or after an issue in controversy has arisen. A party may agree to—

(A) submit only certain issues in controversy to arbitration; or

(B) arbitration on the condition that the award must be within a range of possible outcomes.

(2) The arbitration agreement that sets forth the subject matter submitted to the arbitrator shall be in writing. Each such arbitration agreement shall specify a maximum award that may be issued by the arbitrator and may specify other conditions limiting the range of possible outcomes.

(3) An agency may not require any person to consent to arbitration as a condition of entering into a contract or obtaining a benefit.

(b) An officer or employee of an agency shall not offer to use arbitration for the resolution of issues in controversy unless such officer or employee—

(1) would otherwise have authority to enter into a settlement concerning the matter; or

(2) is otherwise specifically authorized by the agency to consent to the use of arbitration.

(c) Prior to using binding arbitration under this subchapter, the head of an agency, in consultation with the Attorney General and after taking into account the factors in section 572(b), shall issue guidance on the appropriate use of binding arbitration and when an officer or employee of the agency has authority to settle an issue in controversy through binding arbitration.

5 U.S.C. § 576. ENFORCEMENT OF ARBITRATION AGREEMENTS

An agreement to arbitrate a matter to which this subchapter applies is enforceable pursuant to section 4 of title 9, and no action brought to enforce such an agreement shall be dismissed nor shall relief therein be denied on the grounds that it is against the United States or that the United States is an indispensable party.

5 U.S.C. § 577. ARBITRATORS

(a) The parties to an arbitration proceeding shall be entitled to participate in the selection of the arbitrator.

(b) The arbitrator shall be a neutral who meets the criteria of section 573 of this title.

5 U.S.C. § 578. AUTHORITY OF THE ARBITRATOR

An arbitrator to whom a dispute is referred under this subchapter may—

(1) regulate the course of and conduct arbitral hearings;

(2) administer oaths and affirmations;

(3) compel the attendance of witnesses and production of evidence at the hearing under the provisions of section 7 of title 9 only to the extent the agency involved is otherwise authorized by law to do so; and

(4) make awards.

5 U.S.C. § 579. ARBITRATION PROCEEDINGS

(a) The arbitrator shall set a time and place for the hearing on the dispute and shall notify the parties not less than 5 days before the hearing.

(b) Any party wishing a record of the hearing shall—

(1) be responsible for the preparation of such record;

(2) notify the other parties and the arbitrator of the preparation of such record;

(3) furnish copies to all identified parties and the arbitrator; and

(4) pay all costs for such record, unless the parties agree otherwise or the arbitrator determines that the costs should be apportioned.

(c)(1) The parties to the arbitration are entitled to be heard, to present evidence material to the controversy, and to cross-examine witnesses appearing at the hearing.

(2) The arbitrator may, with the consent of the parties, conduct all or part of the hearing by telephone, television, computer, or other electronic means, if each party has an opportunity to participate.

(3) The hearing shall be conducted expeditiously and in an informal manner.

(4) The arbitrator may receive any oral or documentary evidence, except that irrelevant, immaterial, unduly repetitious, or privileged evidence may be excluded by the arbitrator.

(5) The arbitrator shall interpret and apply relevant statutory and regulatory requirements, legal precedents, and policy directives.

(d) No interested person shall make or knowingly cause to be made to the arbitrator an unauthorized ex parte communication relevant to the merits of the proceeding, unless the parties agree otherwise. If a communication is made in violation of this subsection, the arbitrator shall ensure that a memorandum of the communication is prepared and made a part of the record, and that an opportunity for rebuttal is allowed. Upon receipt of a communication made in violation of this subsection, the arbitrator may, to the extent consistent with the interests of justice and the policies underlying this subchapter, require the offending party to show cause why the claim of such party should not be resolved against such party as a result of the improper conduct.

(e) The arbitrator shall make the award within 30 days after the close of the hearing, or the date of the filing of any briefs authorized by the arbitrator, whichever date is later, unless—

(1) the parties agree to some other time limit; or

(2) the agency provides by rule for some other time limit.

5 U.S.C. § 580. ARBITRATION AWARDS

(a)(1) Unless the agency provides otherwise by rule, the award in an arbitration proceeding under this subchapter shall include a brief, informal discussion of the factual and legal basis for the award, but formal findings of fact or conclusions of law shall not be required.

(2) The prevailing parties shall file the award with all relevant agencies, along with proof of service on all parties.

(b) The award in an arbitration proceeding shall become final 30 days after it is served on all parties. Any agency that is a party to the proceeding may extend this 30–day period for an additional 30–day period by serving a notice of such extension on all other parties before the end of the first 30–day period.

(c) A final award is binding on the parties to the arbitration proceeding, and may be enforced pursuant to sections 9 through 13 of title 9. No action brought to enforce such an award shall be dismissed nor shall relief therein be denied on the grounds that it is against the United States or that the United States is an indispensable party.

(d) An award entered under this subchapter in an arbitration proceeding may not serve as an estoppel in any other proceeding for any issue that was resolved in the proceeding. Such an award also may not be used as precedent or otherwise be considered in any factually unrelated proceeding, whether conducted under this subchapter, by an agency, or in a court, or in any other arbitration proceeding.

5 U.S.C. § 581. JUDICIAL REVIEW

(a) Notwithstanding any other provision of law, any person adversely affected or aggrieved by an award made in an arbitration proceeding conducted under this subchapter may bring an action for review of such award only pursuant to the provisions of sections 9 through 13 of title 9.

(b) A decision by an agency to use or not to use a dispute resolution proceeding under this subchapter shall be committed to the discretion of the agency and shall not be subject to judicial review, except that arbitration shall be subject to judicial review under section 10(b) of title 9.

5 U.S.C. § 583. SUPPORT SERVICES

For the purposes of this subchapter, an agency may use (with or without reimbursement) the services and facilities of other Federal agencies, State, local, and tribal governments, public and private organizations and agencies, and individuals, with the consent of such agencies, organizations, and individuals. An agency may accept voluntary and uncompensated services for purposes of this subchapter without regard to the provisions of section 1342 of title 31.

CHAPTER 6—THE ANALYSIS OF
REGULATORY FUNCTIONS
("REGULATORY FLEXIBILITY ACT")

5 U.S.C. § 601. DEFINITIONS

For purposes of this chapter—

(1) the term "agency" means an agency as defined in section 551(1) of this title;

(2) the term "rule" means any rule for which the agency publishes a general notice of proposed rulemaking pursuant to section 553(b) of this title, or any other law, including any rule of general applicability governing Federal grants to State and local governments for which the agency provides an opportunity for notice and public comment, except that the term "rule" does not include a rule of particular applicability relating to rates, wages, corporate or financial structures or reorganizations thereof, prices, facilities, appliances, services, or allowances therefor or to valuations, costs or accounting, or practices relating to such rates, wages, structures, prices, appliances, services, or allowances;

(3) the term "small business" has the same meaning as the term "small business concern" under section 3 of the Small Business Act, unless an agency, after consultation with the Office of Advocacy of the Small Business Administration and after opportunity for public comment, establishes one or more definitions of such term which are appropriate to the activities of the agency and publishes such definition(s) in the Federal Register;

(4) the term "small organization" means any not-for-profit enterprise which is independently owned and operated and is not dominant in its field, unless an agency establishes, after opportunity for public comment, one or more definitions of such term which are appropriate to the activities of the agency and publishes such definition(s) in the Federal Register;

(5) the term "small governmental jurisdiction" means governments of cities, counties, towns, townships, villages, school districts, or special districts, with a population of less than fifty thousand, unless an agency establishes, after opportunity for public comment, one or more definitions of such term which are appropriate to the activities of the agency and which are based on such factors as location in rural or sparsely populated areas or limited revenues due to the population of such jurisdiction, and publishes such definition(s) in the Federal Register;

(6) the term "small entity" shall have the same meaning as the terms "small business", "small organization" and "small governmental jurisdiction" defined in paragraphs (3), (4) and (5) of this section; and

(7) the term "collection of information"—

(A) means the obtaining, causing to be obtained, soliciting, or requiring the disclosure to third parties or the public, of facts or opinions by or for an agency, regardless of form or format, calling for either—

(i) answers to identical questions posed to, or identical reporting or record-keeping requirements imposed on, 10 or more persons, other than agencies, instrumentalities, or employees of the United States; or

(ii) answers to questions posed to agencies, instrumentalities, or employees of the United States which are to be used for general statistical purposes; and

(B) shall not include a collection of information described under section 3518(c)(1) of title 44, United States Code.

(8) Recordkeeping requirement.—The term "recordkeeping requirement" means a requirement imposed by an agency on persons to maintain specified records.

5 U.S.C. § 602. REGULATORY AGENDA

(a) During the months of October and April of each year, each agency shall publish in the Federal Register a regulatory flexibility agenda which shall contain—

(1) a brief description of the subject area of any rule which the agency expects to propose or promulgate which is likely to have a significant economic impact on a substantial number of small entities;

(2) a summary of the nature of any such rule under consideration for each subject area listed in the agenda pursuant to paragraph (1), the objectives and legal basis for the issuance of the rule, and an approximate schedule for completing action on any rule for which the agency has issued a general notice of proposed rulemaking, and

(3) the name and telephone number of an agency official knowledgeable concerning the items listed in paragraph (1).

(b) Each regulatory flexibility agenda shall be transmitted to the Chief Counsel for Advocacy of the Small Business Administration for comment, if any.

(c) Each agency shall endeavor to provide notice of each regulatory flexibility agenda to small entities or their representatives through direct notification or publication of the agenda in publications likely to be obtained by such small entities and shall invite comments upon each subject area on the agenda.

(d) Nothing in this section precludes an agency from considering or acting on any matter not included in a regulatory flexibility agenda, or requires an agency to consider or act on any matter listed in such agenda.

5 U.S.C. § 603. INITIAL REGULATORY FLEXIBILITY ANALYSIS

(a) Whenever an agency is required by section 553 of this title, or any other law, to publish general notice of proposed rulemaking for any proposed rule, or publishes a notice of proposed rulemaking for an interpretative rule involving the internal revenue laws of the United States, the agency shall prepare and make available for public comment an initial regulatory flexibility analysis. Such analysis shall describe the impact of the proposed rule on small entities. The initial regulatory flexibility analysis or a summary shall be published in the Federal Register at the time of the publication of general notice of proposed rulemaking for the rule. The agency shall transmit a copy of the initial regulatory flexibility analysis to the Chief Counsel for Advocacy of the Small Business Administration. In the case of an interpretative rule involving the internal revenue laws of the United States, this chapter applies to interpretative rules published in the Federal Register for codification in the Code of Federal Regulations, but only to the extent that such interpretative rules impose on small entities a collection of information requirement.

(b) Each initial regulatory flexibility analysis required under this section shall contain—

(1) a description of the reasons why action by the agency is being considered;

(2) a succinct statement of the objectives of, and legal basis for, the proposed rule;

(3) a description of and, where feasible, an estimate of the number of small entities to which the proposed rule will apply;

(4) a description of the projected reporting, recordkeeping and other compliance requirements of the proposed rule, including an estimate of the classes of small entities which will be subject to the requirement and the type of professional skills necessary for preparation of the report or record;

(5) an identification, to the extent practicable, of all relevant Federal rules which may duplicate, overlap or conflict with the proposed rule.

(c) Each initial regulatory flexibility analysis shall also contain a description of any significant alternatives to the proposed rule which accomplish the stated objectives of applicable statutes and which minimize any significant economic impact of the proposed rule on small entities. Consistent with the stated objectives of applicable statutes, the analysis shall discuss significant alternatives such as—

(1) the establishment of differing compliance or reporting requirements or timetables that take into account the resources available to small entities;

(2) the clarification, consolidation, or simplification of compliance and reporting requirements under the rule for such small entities;

(3) the use of performance rather than design standards; and

(4) an exemption from coverage of the rule, or any part thereof, for such small entities.

5 U.S.C. § 604. FINAL REGULATORY FLEXIBILITY ANALYSIS

(a) When an agency promulgates a final rule under section 553 of this title, after being required by that section or any other law to publish a general notice of proposed rulemaking, or promulgates a final interpretative rule involving the internal revenue laws of the United States as described in section 603(a), the agency shall prepare a final regulatory flexibility analysis. Each final regulatory flexibility analysis shall contain—

(1) a succinct statement of the need for, and objectives of, the rule;

(2) a summary of the significant issues raised by the public comments in response to the initial regulatory flexibility analysis, a summary of the assessment of the agency of such issues, and a statement of any changes made in the proposed rule as a result of such comments;

(3) a description of and an estimate of the number of small entities to which the rule will apply or an explanation of why no such estimate is available;

(4) a description of the projected reporting, recordkeeping and other compliance requirements of the rule, including an estimate of the classes of small entities which will be subject to the requirement and the type of professional skills necessary for preparation of the report or record; and

(5) a description of the steps the agency has taken to minimize the significant economic impact on small entities consistent with the stated objectives of applicable statutes, including a statement of the factual, policy, and legal reasons for selecting the alternative adopted in the final rule and why each one of the other significant alternatives to the rule considered by the agency which affect the impact on small entities was rejected.

(b) The agency shall make copies of the final regulatory flexibility analysis available to members of the public and shall publish in the Federal Register such analysis or a summary thereof.

5 U.S.C. § 605. AVOIDANCE OF DUPLICATIVE OR UNNECESSARY ANALYSES

(a) Any Federal agency may perform the analyses required by sections 602, 603, and 604 of this title in conjunction with or as a part of any other agenda or analysis required by any other law if such other analysis satisfies the provisions of such sections.

(b) Sections 603 and 604 of this title shall not apply to any proposed or final rule if the head of the agency certifies that the rule will not, if promulgated, have a significant economic impact on a substantial number of small entities. If the head of the agency makes a certification under the preceding sentence, the agency shall publish such certification in the Federal Register at the time of publication of general notice of proposed rulemaking for the rule or at the time of publication of the final rule, along with a statement providing the factual basis for such certification. The agency shall provide such certification and statement to the Chief Counsel for Advocacy of the Small Business Administration.

(c) In order to avoid duplicative action, an agency may consider a series of closely related rules as one rule for the purposes of sections 602, 603, 604 and 610 of this title.

5 U.S.C. § 606. EFFECT ON OTHER LAW

The requirements of sections 603 and 604 of this title do not alter in any manner standards otherwise applicable by law to agency action.

5 U.S.C. § 607. PREPARATION OF ANALYSES

In complying with the provisions of sections 603 and 604 of this title, an agency may provide either a quantifiable or numerical description of the effects of a proposed rule or alternatives to the proposed rule, or more general descriptive statements if quantification is not practicable or reliable.

5 U.S.C. § 608. PROCEDURE FOR WAIVER OR DELAY OF COMPLETION

(a) An agency head may waive or delay the completion of some or all of the requirements of section 603 of this title by publishing in the Federal Register, not later than the date of publication of the final rule, a written finding, with reasons therefor, that the final rule is being promulgated in response to an emergency that makes compliance or timely compliance with the provisions of section 603 of this title impracticable.

(b) Except as provided in section 605(b), an agency head may not waive the requirements of section 604 of this title. An agency head may delay the completion of the requirements of section 604 of this title for a period of not more than one hundred and eighty days after the date of publication in the Federal Register of a final rule by publishing in the Federal Register, not later than such date of publication, a written finding, with reasons therefor, that the final rule is being promulgated in response to an emergency that makes timely compliance with the provisions of section 604 of this title impracticable. If the agency has not prepared a final regulatory analysis pursuant to section 604 of this title within one hundred and eighty days from the date of publication of the final rule, such rule shall lapse and have no effect. Such rule shall not be repromulgated until a final regulatory flexibility analysis has been completed by the agency.

5 U.S.C. § 609. PROCEDURES FOR GATHERING COMMENTS

(a) When any rule is promulgated which will have a significant economic impact on a substantial number of small entities, the head of the agency promulgating the rule or the official of the agency with statutory responsibility for the promulgation of the rule shall assure that small entities have been given an opportunity to participate in the rulemaking for the rule through the reasonable use of techniques such as—

(1) the inclusion in an advanced notice of proposed rulemaking, if issued, of a statement that the proposed rule may have a significant economic effect on a substantial number of small entities;

(2) the publication of general notice of proposed rulemaking in publications likely to be obtained by small entities;

(3) the direct notification of interested small entities;

(4) the conduct of open conferences or public hearings concerning the rule for small entities including soliciting and receiving comments over computer networks; and

(5) the adoption or modification of agency procedural rules to reduce the cost or complexity of participation in the rulemaking by small entities.

(b) Prior to publication of an initial regulatory flexibility analysis which a covered agency is required to conduct by this chapter—

(1) a covered agency shall notify the Chief Counsel for Advocacy of the Small Business Administration and provide the Chief Counsel with information on the potential impacts of the proposed rule on small entities and the type of small entities that might be affected;

(2) not later than 15 days after the date of receipt of the materials described in paragraph (1), the Chief Counsel shall identify individuals representative of affected small entities for the purpose of obtaining advice and recommendations from those individuals about the potential impacts of the proposed rule;

(3) the agency shall convene a review panel for such rule consisting wholly of full time Federal employees of the office within the agency responsible for carrying out the proposed rule, the Office of Information and Regulatory Affairs within the Office of Management and Budget, and the Chief Counsel;

(4) the panel shall review any material the agency has prepared in connection with this chapter, including any draft proposed rule, collect advice and recommendations of each individual small entity representative identified by the agency after consultation with the Chief Counsel, on issues related to subsections 603(b), paragraphs (3), (4) and (5) and 603(c);

(5) not later than 60 days after the date a covered agency convenes a review panel pursuant to paragraph (3), the review panel shall report on the comments of the small entity representatives and its findings as to issues related to subsections 603(b), paragraphs (3), (4) and (5) and 603(c), provided that such report shall be made public as part of the rulemaking record; and

(6) where appropriate, the agency shall modify the proposed rule, the initial regulatory flexibility analysis or the decision on whether an initial regulatory flexibility analysis is required.

(c) An agency may in its discretion apply subsection (b) to rules that the agency intends to certify under subsection 605(b), but the agency believes may have a greater than de minimis impact on a substantial number of small entities.

(d) For purposes of this section, the term "covered agency" means the Environmental Protection Agency and the Occupational Safety and Health Administration of the Department of Labor.

(e) The Chief Counsel for Advocacy, in consultation with the individuals identified in subsection (b)(2), and with the Administrator of the Office of Information and Regulatory Affairs within the Office of Management and Budget, may waive the requirements of subsections (b)(3), (b)(4), and (b)(5) by including in the rulemaking record a written finding, with reasons therefor, that those requirements would not advance the effective participation of small entities in the rulemaking process. For purposes of this subsection, the factors to be considered in making such a finding are as follows:

(1) In developing a proposed rule, the extent to which the covered agency consulted with individuals representative of affected small entities with respect to the potential impacts of the rule and took such concerns into consideration.

(2) Special circumstances requiring prompt issuance of the rule.

(3) Whether the requirements of subsection (b) would provide the individuals identified in subsection (b)(2) with a competitive advantage relative to other small entities.

5 U.S.C. § 610. PERIODIC REVIEW OF RULES

(a) Within one hundred and eighty days after the effective date of this chapter, each agency shall publish in the Federal Register a plan for the periodic review of the rules issued by the agency which have or will have a significant economic impact upon a substantial number of small entities. Such plan may be amended by the agency at any time by publishing the revision in the Federal Register. The purpose of the review shall be to determine whether such rules should be continued without change, or should be amended or rescinded, consistent with the stated objectives of applicable statutes, to minimize any significant economic impact of the rules upon a substantial number of such small entities. The plan shall provide for the review of all such agency rules existing on the effective date of this chapter within ten years of that date and for the review of such rules adopted after the effective date of this chapter within ten years of the publication of such rules as the final rule. If the head of the agency determines that completion of the review of existing rules is not feasible by the established date, he shall so certify in a statement published in the Federal Register and may extend the completion date by one year at a time for a total of not more than five years.

(b) In reviewing rules to minimize any significant economic impact of the rule on a substantial number of small entities in a manner consistent with the stated objectives of applicable statutes, the agency shall consider the following factors—

(1) the continued need for the rule;

(2) the nature of complaints or comments received concerning the rule from the public;

(3) the complexity of the rule;

(4) the extent to which the rule overlaps, duplicates or conflicts with other Federal rules, and, to the extent feasible, with State and local governmental rules; and

(5) the length of time since the rule has been evaluated or the degree to which technology, economic conditions, or other factors have changed in the area affected by the rule.

(c) Each year, each agency shall publish in the Federal Register a list of the rules which have a significant economic impact on a substantial number of small entities, which are to be reviewed pursuant to this section during the succeeding twelve months. The list shall include a brief description of each rule and the need for and legal basis of such rule and shall invite public comment upon the rule.

5 U.S.C. § 611. JUDICIAL REVIEW

(a)(1) For any rule subject to this chapter, a small entity that is adversely affected or aggrieved by final agency action is entitled to judicial review of agency compliance with the requirements of sections 601, 604, 605(b), 608(b), and 610 in accordance with chapter 7. Agency compliance with sections 607 and 609(a) shall be judicially reviewable in connection with judicial review of section 604.

(2) Each court having jurisdiction to review such rule for compliance with section 553, or under any other provision of law, shall have jurisdiction to review any claims of noncompliance with sections 601, 604, 605(b), 608(b), and 610 in accordance with chapter 7. Agency compliance with sections 607 and 609(a) shall be judicially reviewable in connection with judicial review of section 604.

(3)(A) A small entity may seek such review during the period beginning on the date of final agency action and ending one year later, except that where a provision of law requires that an action challenging a final agency action be commenced before the expiration of one year, such lesser period shall apply to an action for judicial review under this section.

(B) In the case where an agency delays the issuance of a final regulatory flexibility analysis pursuant to section 608(b) of this chapter, an action for judicial review under this section shall be filed not later than—

(i) one year after the date the analysis is made available to the public, or

(ii) where a provision of law requires that an action challenging a final agency regulation be commenced before the expiration of the 1–year period, the number of days specified in such provision of law that is after the date the analysis is made available to the public.

(4) In granting any relief in an action under this section, the court shall order the agency to take corrective action consistent with this chapter and chapter 7, including, but not limited to—

(A) remanding the rule to the agency, and

(B) deferring the enforcement of the rule against small entities unless the court finds that continued enforcement of the rule is in the public interest.

(5) Nothing in this subsection shall be construed to limit the authority of any court to stay the effective date of any rule or provision thereof under any other provision of law or to grant any other relief in addition to the requirements of this section.

(b) In an action for the judicial review of a rule, the regulatory flexibility analysis for such rule, including an analysis prepared or corrected pursuant to paragraph (a)(4), shall constitute part of the entire record of agency action in connection with such review.

(c) Compliance or noncompliance by an agency with the provisions of this chapter shall be subject to judicial review only in accordance with this section.

(d) Nothing in this section bars judicial review of any other impact statement or similar analysis required by any other law if judicial review of such statement or analysis is otherwise permitted by law.

5 U.S.C. § 612. REPORTS AND INTERVENTION RIGHTS

(a) The Chief Counsel for Advocacy of the Small Business Administration shall monitor agency compliance with this chapter and shall report at least annually thereon to the President and to the Committees on the Judiciary and Small Business of the Senate and House of Representatives.

(b) The Chief Counsel for Advocacy of the Small Business Administration is authorized to appear as amicus curiae in any action brought in a court of the United States to review a rule. In any such action, the Chief Counsel is authorized to present his or her views with respect to compliance with this chapter, the adequacy of the rulemaking record with respect to small entities and the effect of the rule on small entities.

(c) A court of the United States shall grant the application of the Chief Counsel for Advocacy of the Small Business Administration to appear in any such action for the purposes described in subsection (b).

CHAPTER 7—JUDICIAL REVIEW

5 U.S.C. § 701. APPLICATION; DEFINITIONS

(a) This chapter applies, according to the provisions thereof, except to the extent that—

(1) statutes preclude judicial review; or

(2) agency action is committed to agency discretion by law.

(b) For the purpose of this chapter—

(1) "agency" means each authority of the Government of the United States, whether or not it is within or subject to review by another agency, but does not include—

(A) the Congress;

(B) the courts of the United States;

(C) the governments of the territories or possessions of the United States;

(D) the government of the District of Columbia;

(E) agencies composed of representatives of the parties or of representatives of organizations of the parties to the disputes determined by them;

(F) courts martial and military commissions;

(G) military authority exercised in the field in time of war or in occupied territory; or

(H) functions conferred by sections 1738, 1739, 1743, and 1744 of title 12; chapter 2 of title 41; subchapter II of chapter 471 of title 49; or sections 1884, 1891–1902, and former section 1641(b)(2), of title 50, appendix; and

(2) "person", "rule", "order", "license", "sanction", "relief", and "agency action" have the meanings given them by section 551 of this title.

5 U.S.C. § 702. RIGHT OF REVIEW

A person suffering legal wrong because of agency action, or adversely affected or aggrieved by agency action within the meaning of a relevant statute, is entitled to judicial review thereof. An action in a court of the United States seeking relief other than money damages and stating a claim that an agency or an officer or employee thereof acted or failed to act in an official capacity or under color of legal authority shall not be dismissed nor relief therein be denied on the ground that it is against the United States or that the United States is an indispensable party. The United States may be named as a defendant in any such action, and a judgment or decree may be entered against the United States: Provided, That any mandatory or injunctive decree shall specify the Federal officer or officers (by name or by title), and their successors in office, personally responsible for compliance. Nothing herein (1) affects other limitations on judicial review or the power or duty of the court to dismiss any action or deny relief on any other appropriate legal or equitable ground; or (2) confers authority to grant relief if any other statute that grants consent to suit expressly or impliedly forbids the relief which is sought.

5 U.S.C. § 703. FORM AND VENUE OF PROCEEDING

The form of proceeding for judicial review is the special statutory review proceeding relevant to the subject matter in a court specified by statute or, in the absence or inadequacy thereof, any applicable form of legal action, including actions for declaratory judgments or writs of prohibitory or mandatory injunction or habeas corpus, in a court of competent jurisdiction. If no special statutory review proceeding is applicable, the action for judicial review may be brought against the United States, the agency by its official title, or the appropriate officer. Except to the extent that prior, adequate, and exclusive opportunity for judicial review is provided by law, agency action is subject to judicial review in civil or criminal proceedings for judicial enforcement.

5 U.S.C. § 704. ACTIONS REVIEWABLE

Agency action made reviewable by statute and final agency action for which there is no other adequate remedy in a court are subject to judicial review. A preliminary, procedural, or intermediate agency action or ruling not directly reviewable is subject to review on the review of the final agency action. Except as otherwise expressly required by statute, agency action otherwise final is final for the purposes of this section whether or not there has been presented or determined an application for a declaratory order, for any form of reconsideration, or, unless the agency otherwise requires by rule and provides that the action meanwhile is inoperative, for an appeal to superior agency authority.

5 U.S.C. § 705. RELIEF PENDING REVIEW

When an agency finds that justice so requires, it may postpone the effective date of action taken by it, pending judicial review. On such conditions as may be required and to the extent necessary to prevent irreparable injury, the reviewing court, including the court to which a case may be taken on appeal from or on application for certiorari or other writ to a reviewing court, may issue all necessary and appropriate process to postpone the effective date of an agency action or to preserve status or rights pending conclusion of the review proceedings.

5 U.S.C. § 706. SCOPE OF REVIEW

To the extent necessary to decision and when presented, the reviewing court shall decide all relevant questions of law, interpret constitutional and statutory provisions, and determine the meaning or applicability of the terms of an agency action. The reviewing court shall—

(1) compel agency action unlawfully withheld or unreasonably delayed; and

(2) hold unlawful and set aside agency action, findings, and conclusions found to be—

(A) arbitrary, capricious, an abuse of discretion, or otherwise not in accordance with law;

(B) contrary to constitutional right, power, privilege, or immunity;

(C) in excess of statutory jurisdiction, authority, or limitations, or short of statutory right;

(D) without observance of procedure required by law;

(E) unsupported by substantial evidence in a case subject to sections 556 and 557 of this title or otherwise reviewed on the record of an agency hearing provided by statute; or

(F) unwarranted by the facts to the extent that the facts are subject to trial de novo by the reviewing court.

In making the foregoing determinations, the court shall review the whole record or those parts of it cited by a party, and due account shall be taken of the rule of prejudicial error.